ELEMENTARY SCHOOL SCIENCE AND HOW TO TEACH IT

5TH EDITION

GLENN O. BLOUGH
University of Maryland

JULIUS SCHWARTZ
Formerly with the Bureau of Curriculum Development, Board of Education of the City of New York

Holt, Rinehart and Winston, Inc.

New York Chicago San Francisco Atlanta Dallas Montreal Toronto London Sydney

ACKNOWLEDGMENTS

To **William Ramsey,** co-author of *Modern Earth Science* and *Foundations of Physical Science,* for his review of the chapter on the earth and its resources. To **Michael Chriss,** Department of Astronomy, College of San Mateo, for his review of the chapters on astronomy. To **Jerome Spar,** Professor of Meteorology, New York University, for his review of the chapter on weather. To **Marvin Druger,** Professor of Biology and Science Education, Syracuse University, for his review of the chapters on living things. To **Eugene S. Gaffney,** Department of Vertebrate Paleontology, American Museum of Natural History, for his review of the chapter on the history of life. To **Martha Munzer,** author and environmental education consultant, for her review of the chapter on ecology. To **Theodore D. Benjamin,** Department of Education, Herbert H. Lehman College of the City University of New York, for his review of the chapters on matter and energy. To **Homer E. Newell,** National Aeronautics and Space Administration, for his review of the chapter on flight and space travel. And to those science teaching specialists who gave specific and helpful suggestions and criticisms for the methods sections, our sincere appreciation for their time and effort.

Library of Congress Catalog Card Number: 73-5202

ISBN: 0-03-091539-2

Printed in the United States of America
1 2 3 4 5 6 7 9 0 071 9 8 7 6 5 4

A NOTE ON THE AUTHORS

Glenn O. Blough, former president of the National Science Teachers Association (1957–1958), is also a former member of the staff of the United States Office of Education. He has taught in the elementary school for many years and is Professor of Education at the University of Maryland.

Julius Schwartz was Consultant in Science to the Bureau of Curriculum Development of the New York City Board of Education. He has taught science at every level from kindergarten through graduate school. Much of the material contained in this textbook has been tested in his classes for teachers in training and in service at the Bank Street College of Education in New York City.

PREFACE

Science discoveries add to our scientific knowledge. Classroom experimentation, research in child development, new insights into ways children learn, and the study of the problems of children growing up in an urban environment—all produce improved ways of teaching.

This fifth edition of *Elementary School Science and How to Teach It* includes both changes in science content and new and more effective methods of science teaching in elementary schools.

With the greater emphasis on science teaching in the elementary school there have been a number of innovations which help teachers at both preservice and in-service levels. The tendency to make our objectives more specific is being translated into classroom practice.

In the 1960's there emerged new and significant national projects, new curriculum materials, new textbooks and learning materials. These continue to go through processes of refinement. This new edition attempts to show how these new approaches and trends may be used to best advantage in the classroom. This text is designed to meet the needs of *all* teachers by providing:

Selected background knowledge in science, highlighting the concepts and principles essential for the teaching of science in the elementary school.

A variety of ways for helping children learn science, with special emphasis on the kind of inquiry that engages them in the processes of discovery.

A guide to the use of the environment—urban as well as suburban and rural—as a resource and as a laboratory for investigation.

Elementary School Science and How to Teach It continues to be a practical guide to teaching as well as a storehouse of science reference material. It retains its familiar organization. Part I presents a general statement on teaching elementary science that will bring the teacher up to date on methods of instruction. It discusses the objectives of teaching science in both general and specific aspects. Expected behaviors are described, as are the methods for achieving them. Both are closely linked to the specific subject matter and the processes involved. Case studies of classroom experiments and procedures illustrate these practices. Part I also offers an expanded section which helps the teacher make lesson and unit plans, and assists both teacher and administrator in organizing a science curriculum from kindergarten through the elementary grades. Several of the major projects are identified, described in detail, and compared. Many examples of the procedures are illustrated, and further references are footnoted. More stress is placed on criteria for selecting materials—textbooks, supplementary materials, and apparatus. New information on testing and evaluation has been added, as well as material on the use of television and of community resources. Particularly, Part I stresses the methods of instruction that will help pupils learn *how to discover*—by identifying problems, proposing solutions, making hypotheses, testing them, and, in short, utilizing the tools and methods of scientific investigation. The processes are specifically identified, and classroom procedures for their use are described with many examples.

The content and methodology for teaching science in early childhood has been considerably expanded. Activities appropriate for younger children are described in detail in each of the content-related chapters of the book.

Parts II, III, and IV are again divided into A and B chapters. Each A chapter presents a specific body of science content; the accompanying B chapter describes how to teach this content. The A chapters include science information that is important to the teacher both as a citizen in our scientific world and as a leader of children's science learning in the classroom.

The problems of ecology; advances in astronomy,

space science, earth science; history of life; and sex education are more inclusively dealt with by adding new material, deleting obsolete information, and relating people's concerns to developments in these fields.

Although the material remains nontechnical, in the sense that it is not loaded with unnecessary science vocabulary and formulas, it is nonetheless substantial, accurate science.

The B chapters present up-to-date methods for helping children learn how to learn. Experiments are suggested that challenge children to explore on their own and give teachers guidance in assisting the children. These experiments present a variety of approaches and possible solutions demonstrating methods of encouraging children to use their capacities to investigate. Specific aids to help pupils use and see the importance of using the processes of discovery—experimenting, observing, making hypotheses, describing and communicating these observations, constructions, and many other purposeful activities that will stimulate problem-solving discovery—are detailed. Mathematics plays an important role in many of the experiments and activities. Suggestions are included for introducing children to the nature and use of the Metric System. Assistance is also given in selecting, obtaining, and using both classroom-constructed and commercially purchased science apparatus.

Teachers, to be successful at helping children use the processes of investigation, must themselves become investigators who are at home in the use of learning processes. Several features are included in this book to help the teacher in this respect. Each A chapter concludes with the feature, "Resources to Investigate." Each B chapter contains a section called "Discovering for Yourself," and, new to this edition, a section called "Preparing to Teach." Taken together, these sections are intended to supplement the text in supplying resources and methods for the kind of discovery learning the teacher is urged to encourage in the classroom. These suggestions for discovery, investigation, and preparation may be used by teachers in courses and workshops in colleges and universities as assignments, and the results may be shared in class for the mutual benefit of all. The sections are also very practical for on-the-job use.

The fifth edition is illustrated with drawings and photographs that reflect advances in graphics, art, and design that have taken place in the past few years. The Bibliography has been updated in light of the virtual explosion of printed material for both teachers and children in methods and subject matter.

Great stress has been placed in making the book a permanent guide and reference work for the teacher-in-training, as well as for the teacher-in-service; it is written to be kept on the teacher's desk for ready reference and use over many years.

A companion volume to this book is *Making and Using Classroom Science Materials in the Elementary School* by Glenn O. Blough and Marjorie H. Campbell.* It contains further suggestions for teaching science in the elementary school, as well as detailed descriptions of how to make and use a wide variety of teaching aids.

Washington, D.C. —G.O.B.
New York, N.Y. —J.S.

*(New York: Holt, Rinehart and Winston, Inc., 1954.)

CONTENTS

(Courtesy of U.S. Department of the Interior.)

PART I

TEACHING ELEMENTARY SCIENCE

(Courtesy of U.S. Department of Agriculture.)

CHAPTER 1
SCIENCE IN THE ELEMENTARY SCHOOL

The results of science surround us. We hear the weather forecast, watch television, talk on the telephone, and fly through the air.

Some of the achievements of science are spectacular and almost unbelievable. Men walk on the moon, gather rocks, and come home. We know the composition of distant stars; in fact, the element helium was identified on the sun before we found it on earth. We photograph the surface of Mars and the back side of our satellite, the moon.

Some science achievements are near at hand. We take them for granted, but they have greatly changed our lives: We have learned to use the energy of burning fuels, falling water, and splitting atoms to provide electricity.

We have solved many of the mysteries of our own bodies, and used the information to make life easier. We have solved the riddle of what goes on in the tiny cells of green leaves, have learned that here all of the basic food for our existence is manufactured from a gas in the air plus water from the soil. Once man's knowledge did not include this understanding.

We could fill pages of this book with other examples of how our world has become a scientific one and how scientific discoveries influence, engulf, and enlighten and sometimes frighten us.

Throughout centuries men have wondered about their environment. Scientists have advanced the frontiers of knowledge and have formulated laws, principles, and generalizations that have changed our life styles. There is still more to learn, but no one can deny that science surrounds us and that those who have a speaking acquaintance with its findings can live a fuller and richer life.

We have long since moved from the innocent wonder of observing to the understanding of why and how things happen. The wonder continues for those who look about them. Teachers who retain this wonder and zeal to know and transmit it to children enrich both their own lives and those of the children they teach. Teachers who are curious about how scientists discover can help children to understand and use these methods; they contribute immeasurably to their own development and that of girls and boys in their classes.

"But there's so much to know," you may say. That's so. But no teacher can be an eight-hour answering service for boys and girls. She shouldn't be, even if she could. Nevertheless all teachers of children need to know *some* science. They can't teach it unless they know it any more than they can teach the new math without knowing how to add, subtract, multiply, and divide. And science, of the kind teachers need in order to teach children, is not all that difficult to learn. It has a helpful logic; it's immediately available for observation; it's fascinating, relevant, and exciting, as you will see as you become more intimately acquainted with it.

Teachers need some basic knowledge of what is to be taught, how this can be organized, and must know good classroom procedure. Helping teachers to cope with these necessities is the purpose of this book. We have avoided unnecessarily technical vocabulary, but have included the essential words for comprehending basic science concepts. There is enough information in various areas of science subject matter to supply the teacher with the information he needs to interpret the world he lives in, and help pupils to do the same. There is enough guidance for teaching so that teachers can help children explore their world in a scientific manner.

Chapter 1 through 5 provide in a practical way some general and specific suggestions for teaching science. They are based largely on the authors' experience and that of many of their teacher colleagues in helping children learn science, and on the findings of the modern projects and research. These first five chapters and the methods chapters (B chapters) describe and explain these tried-and-found-useful practices and procedures. The remaining chapters (A chapters) deal with the subject matter of various fields of science. The preface describes some of the important innovations and changes made in this revised edition.

But before we go further, let's consider the nature of science itself. There are many definitions. Before you read on, consider your own ideas. What does science mean to you?

The following quotations concern the nature of science as seen through the eyes of scientists, philosophers, educators, and others. As you read, and, we hope, enjoy these provocative statements, ask yourself: "What are the implications of these statements for me as a teacher of science and children?"

Collecting and examining material from a pond raises questions and problems that result in the use of methods of inquiry. (*Courtesy of Phyllis Marcuccio.*)

The progress of science from the beginning has been a conflict with old prejudices. *–T.H. Huxley*

Unexpected Vistas

Of one thing, however, we may be reasonably sure. If developed and applied in good faith, the methods called scientific are bound to lead to unexpected vistas and unpredictable solutions. *–René Dubos*

Most people probably imagine that science advances like a steam roller, cracking its problems one by one with even and inexorable force . . . Science (actually) advances as though by pulling out of a drawer which gives on one side only to jam on the other. *–C.D. Darlington*

Research is to see what everybody has seen and to think what nobody has thought. *–Albert Szent-Györgyi*

A Passion for Discovery

No man of science wants merely to know. He acquires knowledge to appease his passion for discovery.
–Alfred North Whitehead

Thus invention, scientific thinking, and aesthetic creation do have in common a facility for the rearranging of previously experienced elements into new configurations. When Sandburg says that "the fog creeps in on little cat feet", and a child calls eraser scraps "mistake dust", and a painter shows the four sides of a barn at once and a writer speaks of something as being as "relentless as a taximeter" and a man converts a runner into a wheel, and a Newton sees the analogy between apples and planets, there is manifest an activity of the mind that seems to be of the same weave despite the differences of coloration. *–H. Broudy*

. . . any particular scientific theory is a provisional tool with which we can carve knowledge of the material world . . . The scientific theory is, however, only true as long as it is useful. *–E.N. da C. Andrade*

There is no such thing as *the* scientific method.
–James B. Conant

Science is an interconnected series of concepts and conceptual schemes that have developed as a result of experimentation and observation and are fruitful of further experimentation and observations. In this definition the emphasis is on the word "fruitful."
–James B. Conant

Science is built up with facts, as a house is with stones. But a collection of facts is no more a science than a heap of stones is a house. *–Poincaré*

The Great Ocean of Truth

The white man drew a small circle in the sand and told the red man, "This is what the Indian knows," and drawing a big circle around the small one, "This is what the white man knows." The Indian took the stick and swept an immense ring around both circles: "This is where the white man and the red man know nothing." *–Carl Sandburg*

I do not know what I may appear to the world; but to myself I seem to have been only like a boy playing on the seashore, and diverting myself in now and then finding a smoother pebble or a prettier shell than ordinary, whilst the great ocean of truth lay all undiscovered before me.
–Isaac Newton

What can be distilled from these quotes that will be helpful in science teaching? In essence they say: Science is more than a collection of facts; it is a man-created structure of linked concepts. Imagination, even dreaming form a part of scientific research. Science grows, constantly building on the discoveries of many investigators, on past experience and often leads to unexpected discoveries. Yet it is a hard task master, for it always demands proof and verification for its theories. A scientific theory is a provisional tool for discovery; it is retained only as long as it produces new knowledge.

In contrast to these learned definitions, what do *children* say in response to the question, "What do you think science is?"

books about stuff you never heard of

looking and listing

It's space and stars

growing things

learning about where you live

listening and boring

something we don't have much of

doing experiments

finding out

Examine these responses. What's the message? While they are from one particular fourth grade there are reasons to think they may be typical. They reveal what these children think science is. From these reactions teachers may find ways of improving the science program and discover that what children are feeling and saying may be quite different from what the teacher feels and says or hopes for. We do well to pay attention to the feelings and thoughts of children. Which kind of response would probably come from children you know?

How important to a teacher is a definition of science? A well-known science authority has said: "An understanding of the nature of science is fundamental to good science teaching for if the teacher lacks this concept she will also fall short in her teaching." The impact of this statement will become more and more obvious as you read on.

WHAT IS SCIENCE EDUCATION IN THE ELEMENTARY SCHOOL?

There are some differences of opinion among scientists and prominent science educators about what the major emphases of science in the elementary school should be. For example, the American Association for the Advancement of Science labels its science program for children a *Process Approach*. The achievement of children is measured by observing their abilities to use skills such as observing and classifying, describing, recognizing and using numbers and number relations, recognizing and using time and space relations, measuring, inferring, and predicting. As we shall see, this approach produces an entirely different science content program for children than one based on the idea that science is essentially a structure of concepts and principles.

(*See* Chs. 2 and 4.)

Another project, at the University of Illinois, places emphasis on the content and structure of a large block of science subject matter (astronomy), although it, too, aims to introduce children to the methods of discovery. Other projects and examples of teaching illustrate that what we believe about the nature of science strongly influences our teaching procedures.

(*See* Ch. 4.)

As you proceed in your study of science you will come to regard science as double-barreled—methods of discovery *and* an organized body of the subject matter that is discovered. Science consists both of a *content* (the facts and generalizations) and of *methods* of discovery. In actual practice what is discovered (the content) is inseparably linked to the process of investigation. *To be consistent with this concept of science the school must provide children with experiences in both of these facets of science.* Our classrooms are laboratories where children, for example, not only learn how magnets behave under certain conditions but also where they learn to formulate problems, grow in ability to propose solutions, and design and carry out investigations. Children make mistakes; revise their methods; discover that there may be many answers, only tentative solutions, or no answers at all.

SCIENCE AND CHILDREN

But the science program in the elementary school also depends on the nature of children. They are natural investigators and have an unending stream of questions on their lips: "What makes it thunder?" "If the earth is round, why don't people in Australia fall off?" "What makes a satellite stay up?" "Why did the fish in our aquarium die?" Good teachers make use of this innate curiosity in children by using these questions as a launching pad for helping children inquire and discover.

Children find the answers to their science questions through the methods of inquiry—sensing the problem, hypothesizing, gathering data, drawing conclusions or not drawing them, and testing them. In this way they are learning how to learn. They are inquiring. They are using processes to discover.

For children, the study of science consists of exploring the world about them. It appears natural for children to try out things to see how they work, to experiment, to manipulate, to be curious, to ask questions, to seek answers. These tendencies, with which children seem to be naturally equipped, make science a natural part of their education and a necessary subject to include in their school experiences.

We all live with science, but that doesn't mean that we *think* scientifically, nor are we all scientifically literate. Throughout this book we will emphasize scientific thinking—observing clearly and objectively, asking questions, evaluating evidence and drawing tentative conclusions, withholding judgment and avoiding prejudice. These and other elements of scientific thinking are or should be a part of everyday living. It is through their use that we not only learn to solve science problems but the problems of: How shall I vote? How shall I make up my mind about what to believe? What car shall I buy? The study of science has special contributions to make to the lives of children as we shall see in the discussion of goals.

(*See* Ch. 2.)

But science is not a thing apart from the rest of the interests and activities in school life. It is closely interwoven with other interests, and its methods of study are much the same as those used in exploring any interest.

What is it? Wool socks contain various unidentified objects. Using the sense of touch, children attempt to describe, identify, and compare. With some leadership from the teacher this becomes more than a game. It emphasizes using the senses to collect information which results in discoveries. (*Courtesy of Phyllis Marcuccio.*)

THE TEACHER'S BACKGROUND

Science teaching is not widely different from the teaching of other subject areas in the elementary school. A skillful teacher of children is well on the way to becoming a good science teacher. In some respect teaching science is easier than teaching some of the other subjects because most children, given the opportunity, are enthusiastic about it. Many children are easily motivated, although there are some who need inspiration from their teachers and classmates. There is plenty of opportunity for using materials and for doing things. This gets children out from behind their desks.

Many teachers already teach more science than they realize. They keep an aquarium or a pet animal in the classroom; they help children keep a weather chart, raise house plants in their classrooms, help children plant gardens, or take them to the zoo and planetarium. These activities are high in science potential, but many teachers need a more scientific approach to help children get more science learning from these activities. For example, teachers and children build an aquarium but may often pay little attention to it. Water evaporates from it, snails lay eggs on the glass, plants reproduce, tadpoles grow legs unnoticed. The aquarium is full of What? Why? Where? and How? With more careful planning, happenings such as these can be utilized for the greater enrichment of children's science experiences.

If you are a teacher who says, "My children sometimes seem to know more science than I do," there are several sources of help. For example, acquaint yourself with the innovative projects that are described and incorporated in this book. Consult your state, county, or city bulletins on the teaching of science. Use the teachers' manuals that are issued with the textbooks used in school. They are good resources for evolving your own ways of approaching the teaching of science. Consult periodicals that feature articles on science teaching (*see* the Bibliography for a list of magazines).

Read science material that is written for children, as well as books (such as this text) written on your own level. Don't be ashamed of approaching a new science area through the use of a children's book. If it helps you, use it (*see* the Bibliography for a specially selected list of such books).

Join a science association where you can hear more about current practices in science teaching—the Council for Elementary Science International, for example. Talk to other science teachers, observe their teaching, listen to their ideas, and weigh them for your own use. Attend workshops or take an extension course designed especially for elementary teachers.

Apply the knowledge of science you gain through your hobbies to what you do in the classroom. Outdoor gardening, tropical fish raising, bird watching and feeding, star gazing, and camping all help to give you background experience in approaching science teaching.

Make use of local resource persons such as scientists, college and university personnel, and special science teachers. Don't forget especially talented and interested pupils. Children in general are more sophisticated in science now than they were formerly because of the increased emphasis on science beginning as early as the nursery school, and because of television and other vicarious experiences. Let's not underestimate their potential.

Work through some of the "Discovering for Yourself" and "Preparing to Teach" sections in later chapters of this book, and make use of the "Resources to Investigate." These may lead you to creative and useful ideas of your own invention. Do some of the experiments suggested for pupils. There is no substitute for first-hand experience for teachers as well as for pupils.

Remember that science is always subject to change, as are the ways of teaching it; so be open-minded. Examine some of the learning materials especially designed to promote inquiry which are described in this book.

Above all, allow yourself to experience the wonder and excitement of scientific knowledge in everyday life.

SOME TRENDS IN ELEMENTARY SCHOOL SCIENCE

Trends in teaching are hard to identify. Some are well established and flourishing; others are straws in the wind. Some of the most important ones are indicated below:

Content and Methods of Teaching

More stress is being placed on the *methods* of science; children are coming to understand these methods by first-hand involvement in situations which demand their use rather than by being told about "the scientific method."

The greater emphasis on *discovering for yourself* allows children to help determine what problems are to be solved and to propose methods for solution. There is more *doing* with a definite purpose and less *reading about* science. There is a more open-ended approach in which solutions lead to other problems and other courses of action.

Research dealing with how much and what kind of science children are capable of learning indicates that more science content and, in some cases, more complex subject matter can be included in the curriculum.

A greater connection between science and mathematics is tending to make science teaching more quantitative, and thus more scientific, and in many instances the teaching of mathematics is becoming more meaningful. Specific examples of this relationship will be found throughout this book. There are also examples of conversion to the metric system, a trend which is being urged by many and is becoming a part of our everyday living. The examples of its use are given where measurement is important and not as tables to be memorized. This gradual introduction to the system in the elementary school seems very desirable. Measuring the length of a table with a metric ruler, weighing an apple in grams, measuring a container of milk in liters are examples of helping children *think* in metric terms.

Classroom teachers are experimenting with a variety of approaches to the teaching of science. New ideas developed by national projects and state and local programs are being tested in the classroom.

Meeting Needs of Children and Society

Science teaching is being geared to the needs, interests, and abilities of the learners. There is increasing emphasis on individualized instruction. Children work in small groups or by themselves, progressing at their own rates without pressure from the teacher or their classmates. New teaching materials and equipment and new classroom designs make such instruction possible.

Emphasis is placed on recognizing and dealing with children on the basis of their individual growth and development. Children with special aptitudes and interests are challenged; children with learning difficulties are given special help. At the same time there is emphasis on providing a challenging and interesting program for *all* children. The Head Start project and other programs are being developed for the very young. Science in the kindergarten is receiving more and more attention.

There is greater emphasis on the human applications of science, on its use in solving such problems as the deterioration of the earth's environment, hunger and disease, ignorance and prejudice.

DEVELOPMENT OF SCIENCE CURRICULUM

Science in the most forward-looking elementary school systems is taught as a continuous development from kindergarten through twelfth grade. It is becoming a

Gathering data through firsthand experiences is learning how to learn. What kinds of material will a magnet attract? (*Courtesy of Phyllis Marcuccio.*)

definite part of the elementary curriculum. Scarcely any school system is now without some kind of science program.

Scientists, psychologists, curriculum specialists, science educators, and classroom teachers are experimenting, preparing materials, testing their hypotheses, and evaluating results to improve the curriculum and teaching. Some of these activities are national projects. Some are state and local programs.

USE OF RESOURCES

Using community resources to bring science to life is evident in the forward-looking schools. (*See* the "Resources to Investigate" sections in the B chapters.)

More scientific apparatus and equipment is being made available for use in elementary schools. In many cases this has resulted in providing material for each child's use.

Television as a teaching aid is increasing both in amount of time spent and effectiveness as teachers learn to schedule it in the same way that they use audiovisual aids, texts, and other learning aids (*see* Chapter 5).

Wider use is being made of science trade (supplementary) books to augment the ever-increasing number of basic texts.

Special science teachers, science supervisors, team-teaching arrangements, and teacher aids are being used in varying degrees to assist teachers in their science teaching.

These are some indications of how our science program in the elementary school is changing. Paying some attention to them will help new teachers to see the directions in which the science phase of their elementary curriculum may move, and will help experienced teachers to improve their science work. This book reflects these trends in its presentation of both subject matter and methods of teaching.

But our success in science teaching depends to a large degree on our answer to this basic question: *What are our goals?* Cupboards full of equipment, shelves of books, a first-class curriculum are only *helps* to excellence in teaching. The greatest asset to successful science teaching is a basic understanding of the goals. From this viewpoint the next chapter is the foundation for success.

(Courtesy of Phyllis Marcuccio.)

CHAPTER 2
THE GOALS IN ELEMENTARY SCHOOL SCIENCE

Sometimes there seems to be little connection between what we say our goals are and what happens in our classrooms. If our goals are really to be guides they must be carefully conceived, exact, and realistic. They must be blueprints for actions that will result in changes in behaviors. We must also consider them in terms of individual children. Not all children achieve them in the same way nor to the same degree at the same pace.

In considering the goals for any subject-matter area in the elementary school it is important to look first at the objectives for the total elementary-school program. The goals of the elementary school have been stated in many places in many ways. Without going into details and technicalities, we can sum up these objectives this way: The goal is to help children gain the ideals, understandings, and skills essential to becoming well-rounded, full-functioning adults. How is science an essential part of this development?

First, what is involved in reaching this broad general purpose of the elementary school? Certainly we must teach the skills of reading, writing, and arithmetic for they are essential equipment for enjoyment, for gaining information, and for communication. Add the ability to use one's hands to make them do what one wants them to do, and the skill of seeing things around you and seeing them accurately. Include the skill of listening intelligently and of speaking effectively, so that we can express our ideas coherently and accurately. And the skill of sensing problems and solving them in a scientific way, so that the results are dependable. This involves being open-minded, fair, careful in arriving at conclusions, accurate, and free of prejudice and superstition.

The National Science Teachers Association[1] has summarized the general goals of all education as: "learning how to learn, how to attack new problems, how to acquire new knowledge—using rational processes—building competence in basic skills—developing intellectual and vocational competence—exploring values in new experiences—understanding concepts and generalizations—learning to live harmoniously within the biosphere."

This leads us to add that attending school for six or eight years, from nine o'clock to three, is supposed to accomplish still more. Classroom experiences should provide many occasions to identify and understand social procedures and problems, to make hypotheses and have opportunities to carry them out through working together. Children need to check results, to say to each other: "How well did we do this?" "Was our plan good?" "What would have made it better?"

While they are working together, they should be developing social sensitivity to the needs of one another and of the group. They should be learning cooperation, democratic procedure, and group planning; they can learn these things only through using them every day and seeing how they operate.

The school environment should be a place conducive to developing the physical and mental health of children. Among other things, this means that the schoolroom should be a cheerful place, alive with purposeful industry, where children have successful experiences and develop good feelings about themselves. It should be a place

[1] N.S.T.A.: *Position Statement on School Science Education For the 70s. The Science Teacher* (November 1971).

of real achievement, where children learn to work diligently and to take pride in accomplishment. It should be a place where children are free to say: "I don't understand." "I think so and so." "I want to ask a question." A place where children feel secure and at home, where they belong, where they can live happily, a place from which pupils often go home tired at the end of the day, having engaged in hard work that has real purpose. It should be a place where pupils stretch their minds through challenging mental activities, just as they stretch their muscles at recess. The opinion of so many that "We are underestimating the capacity of many of our elementary school pupils" is not just idle musing.

Furthermore, the elementary school, if it is to achieve our purposes, ought also to be a place where children learn to develop wholesome interests for their leisure time. Because of school there ought to be less of "Mother, there's nothing to do!" on rainy Saturdays and summer days. There ought to be numerous interesting things children want to do at home because they have experienced pleasure and satisfaction in doing them at school.

The elementary school must be a place where children acquire useful knowledge. And we do not mind running the risk of repetition by saying: "Let's stop being slightly apologetic when we say we expect children to learn some meaningful knowledge that is important to them." We shall discuss this in more detail later on.

Science, or any other subject in school, is included in the curriculum because it can contribute something to the goals of the entire school experience. We have just listed some general goals for this total experience. Now let us see how science can be geared to them.

OUR INTENTIONS FOR ELEMENTARY SCHOOL SCIENCE[2]

Our goals should speak with a loud clear voice. They should be specific and exact. They should direct us and answer the questions why and how. They should indicate our expectations and describe, as far as possible, how these expectations are to be realized and how we can tell if they are reached.

It is helpful to think of our objectives in the light of what behaviors or performances may result. We may describe such objectives as behavioral or performance objectives, which may be classified according to what we expect from children as the result of achieving these objectives. There are those that are chiefly concerned with teaching and understanding concepts and generalizations in science—in other words

[2] R.J. Kibler, L.L. Barker, and O.T. Miles: *Behavioral Objectives and Instruction* (Boston: Allyn and Bacon, Inc., 1970) 196 pp. A.F. Eiss and M.B. Harbeck: *Behavioral Objectives in the Affective Domain* (Washington, D.C. National Science Teachers Association, 1969) 42 pp. A.S. Fishler et al.: *Objectives for Modern Elementary Science* (New York: Holt, Rinehart and Winston, Inc., 1971) 143 pp. J.M. Cook and H.H. Walbesser: *Constructing Behavioral Objectives* (College Park, Md.: Maryland Book Exchange, 1972) 57 pp. J.J. Koran et al.: *How to Use Behavioral Objectives in Science Instruction* (Washington, D.C.: National Science Teachers Association, 1970) 12 pp. J.M. Atkins: "Behavioral Objectives in Curriculum Design: A Cautionary Note" *The Science Teacher* (May 1968).

the knowledge and understandings which we hope that children will assimilate. But we also hope that they will develop certain attitudes, interests, appreciations, and values (see later discussion) and that they will develop manipulative and other skills as a result of their science learning experiences. We must then formulate goals involving all of these areas. It is quite obvious that some of these goals are easier to state in specific terms than others.

The objectives concerning subject matter have traditionally received the most attention. Since achievement here is more easily and exactly measured, they are more easily stated in exact terms. In contrast, objectives concerned with stimulating interest, developing appreciation and values, and developing process skills are harder to measure with any degree of objective accuracy. Since we consider them to be of such great importance we continue to focus our attention on them.

The use of "action" words is important in making our objectives more specific and in suggesting ways of achieving and evaluating this achievement. Since we are looking for behaviors, we can concentrate on: a result of participation in certain specifically indicated experiences (observations, experiments, experiences, manipulations, and so on); we expect children to be able to identify, demonstrate, use, state, analyze and compare, predict, list, define, state a rule, and so forth. Such action words (illustrations will follow throughout this chapter and others) indicate in a more precise manner what we expect to achieve. Such objectives accompany and direct our procedures for each science experience with children. Let us now examine some of the general and specific goals for teaching science in the elementary school.

Concepts and Generalizations

There is no question that the subject matter of science *is* important. We *do* need persons in our society who are well informed about the world in which they live. An informed person is likely to be an interesting one, we would probably agree. But let us not consider a person educated in science just because he can tell us how many legs a cricket has, that a certain pair of pliers is an example of a first-class lever, what a tufted titmouse looks like, or the definition of chemical change. Such items are important when children learn how to put them together into meaningful ideas.

We must teach ideas in context, in relation to broad concepts. The distance to the moon, for example, is meaningful when it helps us understand why a radar beam bounced on the moon from the earth takes about three seconds for the round trip. When we say that children should learn science subject matter we mean that they should be able to formulate concepts and generalizations useful in interpreting the world in which they live. And we keep in mind that *what* we learn is important, just as *how* we learn it is important. This leads us to a summary statement of one of the general objectives for teaching science: *To help children to learn and understand some generalizations or "big meanings" that they can use in solving problems in their environment.*

To make this goal more meaningful and useful to us we must break it into parts that are more precise, linked more closely to what we expect children to do about it and how, and, if possible, how much we expect from them.

Interest and appreciation are part of this experience with the wonder of life. There is no substitute for observing at firsthand, and the time and effort that goes into making the necessary arrangements are well spent. (*Courtesy of U.S. Department of Agriculture.*)

The following description of a classroom experience will help to make these ideas more concrete. We shall first describe the experience, and then examine it for its possibilities for developing behaviors and performances. While the experience obviously intends to do more than deal with the aspect of attaining science knowledge, we will concentrate chiefly on that phase of the lesson, leaving the other objectives until later where we discuss them in greater detail.

Children are working with a problem about what heating and cooling does to matter—solids, liquids, and gases. A question has arisen: Why does running hot water over the metal lid of a glass jar make it easier to unscrew? In investigating this problem (we will have more to say about methods of investigation in the next section) some children suggest that: "The hot water washes away some sticky food between the cover and the jar." (Incidentally, this *may* be a factor.) Other children suggest that: "The heat does something to the metal cap itself, makes it looser in some way." Children suggest other hypotheses to explain what happens.

They decide to use several clean empty jars (to test the sticky-food hypotheses) with the caps screwed on tight. They again find that a cap held in hot water turns more easily. Someone suggests: "Let's hold a lid in cold water." They find that in this jar the lid seems even tighter than before. Why? It is proposed that heating makes the metal lid get larger—expand—and pull away from the glass. Cooling does the opposite. Is it really true that heating a metal can make it larger? How about other
(*See* Ch. 16B.)
solids? How about liquids and gases? Children propose a series of experiments involving other predictions, hypotheses, tests, and observations, as well as some research reading. The children arrive at some generalizations: *Solids, liquids, and gases expand when they are heated and contract when they are cooled. Not all of them expand equally.* Such generalizations come as a result of many experiences; they are put together gradually; they are not memorized from printed material; they are not caught by slight exposure as children catch mumps.

Now what can the children do with this information? They examine a thermometer to see that it works by expansion and contraction of a liquid—mercury or alcohol—with changes in temperature. They observe how sidewalks and pavements and metal bridges are constructed to allow for expansion caused by an increase in temperature. They use their discoveries to interpret things they see.

Now let us examine these experiences from the standpoint of some of the specific objectives concerning both subject matter and performance. Our thinking goes along this path: As a result of investigating in different ways (experiences, experiments, environmental observations, discussions, and exploratory reading) the children should be able to *gather data* (information) from the experiences in which they have participated, *describe* what happens when hot and cold water are applied to various solids under different conditions, *demonstrate* these happenings when provided with the essential materials, and *construct* a generalized statement that describes the results of heating and cooling of certain solids under specified conditions. These are examples of the behaviors we expect and concentrate on.

Concepts and generalizations are an economical way of organizing vast amounts of information. Scientists use concepts in their research; teachers and children can use them to facilitate learning. To know that the fluid in a thermometer "rises" when the temperature is higher is useful but limited; to know that heating a substance makes it expand is to have the key for the understanding of many phenomena.

At the end of each of the "A" chapters and at the beginning of the "B" chapters you will find lists of science concepts which should be helpful to you and the children you teach. They focus our attention on the "big meanings" we seek.

Processes of Discovery

Another closely related major objective for the study of science is *to help pupils to grow in ability to use science processes*. This is a general statement of our objective. As we proceed we shall indicate behavioral aspects that make it more specific.

A science class should be a place to ask questions as well as to answer them. It is probably true, unfortunately, that we as teachers are in the habit of giving greater recognition to the pupils who know the answers than to those who ask thoughtful questions. The thinking child says: "If that is true, *why*. . . ?" Or "I understand that, but *why*. . . ?" Science is problem seeking as well as problem solving.

We begin then to give more and more attention to helping children formulate problems. These problems may arise because of children's experiences: "Miss Brown, last night I saw the moon come up. It was big and the color of oranges. How come?" Problems may result from children's reading: "Mr. Jacobs, it says here that sunlight is made of all different colors. How can that be?" Problems may arise on trips as a spillover from the investigations of other problems, from current events, and from many other sources. An important role for the teacher is to plan situations which provoke children to pose problems.

Problems and questions trigger the process of investigating and may result in discovery. In Chapter 3 and throughout the book you will find examples and more details of the use of processes, and of the behavioral outcomes we expect from this use. Here is a bird's-eye view of the processes of discovery and what they involve. Each of these is described in greater detail in the next chapter and they are all used extensively in the "B" chapters.

Observing A fundamental process which in a sense underlies many of the other processes. What does it involve? It is quite possible to look but not actually to see. We all do this. Real observation requires thoughtful looking. It is closely linked with being able to describe what is observed. "What can we discover by looking closely?" "Try to tell what you see." These are both approaches in stimulating children to use and sharpen their powers of observation. Observations should lead to exactness. How much? How many? How long? Children should come to understand that there is a difference between observing and inferring.

Communicating When we urge children to *tell* what they observe, we are stimulating the use of a skill that is fundamental to our everyday living. Children and adults are frequently heard to say: "I know what it is, but I can't tell it." Learning to communicate orally; in writing; through the use of diagrams, graphs, and in other ways is an integral part of processes that help discovery and understanding in science.[3]

Hypothesizing Having made careful observations and discussed the observations, we encourage children to formulate possible explanations. In the illustration of the experiences with heating materials children proposed various possible explanations about why the placing of the metal-capped can under hot water made it easier to open. Formulating hypotheses is one of the early steps in the process of discovery. An "educated guess," a possible prediction for our purposes is like an hypothesis.

Experimenting The term experimenting has often been used loosely to mean following directions from the text or showing something that is already known or playing with

[3] M.C. Petty: *Record and Use Data* (Washington, D.C.: National Science Teachers Association, 1967).

apparatus. When it is used as a process to discover something that is not known to the child, to test an hypothesis, to attempt to solve a real problem, it becomes a scientific endeavor. As in the other processes, there are many degrees of sophistication in experimenting. These and other aspects of experimenting are discussed in the next chapter.

Measuring Exactness is fundamental to many of the processes of discovering. How much, how many, how often, and so on are important. Learning to use the tools of measuring, to record the results in some graphic form, and thus to have available some quantitative basis for predictions or generalizations or hypothesis is an integral part of many science experiences and experiments.

Classifying Learning to group things in light of their characteristics is an important process of discovery. If you think about this you will realize that this process is often used in everyday life. For example, it is often a step in identifying. As a result of careful observation children identify likenesses and differences; they compare and contrast and from these data attempt to classify objects and living things.

For example, in an aquarium it is helpful to classify things according to living and nonliving. The living things may be further classified as plants and animals; the nonliving things into solids, liquids, and gases.

We see that classifying often gives meaning to things and situations. In its simplest form it may require using only one or a few characteristics; in the multistage classification several characteristics are used.

Generalizing As has been indicated earlier and is illustrated throughout the book, children and the rest of us find it difficult to remember thousands of facts. However, assembling these facts, realizing the relationships, grouping them into a meaningful whole constitutes an important aspect of the process of discovering. Refer again to the experiences children had with the heating and cooling of materials and it becomes obvious that the generalizations arrived at come as the result of these many experiences, observations, and experiments. How complex the generalizations are depends on the maturity of the children, the materials and experiences available, and on other factors which we will discuss and illustrate in detail in many places later on.

Predicting (*See* also hypothesizing.) To be able to make reasonable predictions on the basis of available data is an important process. When we examine the processes used by scientists we see that predictions, and the hypotheses relating to them, are of vast importance in the seeking of scientific knowledge. If our teaching is related to our stated objectives children will find many opportunities to predict possible outcomes. As they learn to observe, examine, contrast, compare, and use the other processes they also learn to react to such questions as: "What do you think will happen if. . . ?" "If we tried this again would the same thing happen?" "In the same way?"

There is no intended implication in the foregoing that the *order* in which these processes are presented is the order children must follow; that they *all* must be present in any investigation; nor that the processes of discovery are limited only to these.

It is implicit in our review of processes that children will express their understanding of them in terms of their behavior. Thus children will be able to: *formulate* some hypotheses for testing, *devise* experiments to gather information, and *communicate* their ideas.

Throughout this book you will find applications of these process elements as they apply to inquiry and problem-solving situations. Here, for example, is an actual experience from a sixth-grade class that illustrates how a teacher and children work when the goal is to combine the process with the subject matter, when the emphasis is on the processes of discovery as well as other objectives. It should be remembered that even though these examples are from actual classrooms, *all* children do not react the same and so in other situations the experiences may turn in many other directions.

New classrooms are being added to the school building and construction is going on just outside the window. Children watch at recess with their noses pressed to the glass. They see men with pulleys lift wheelbarrows full of bricks; steam shovels at work; construction elevators being built; and all sorts of machines cutting, digging, pulling, and pushing. It is the chief topic of conversation. The teacher watches, too. The children raise questions: "How can a man lift a big hunk of the cement sidewalk with an iron bar?" "How can a man lift a hundred bricks by pulling down on a pulley rope with one hand?" These and other problems are raised, stated carefully, and recorded. The teacher says: "I'd like to know how these machines work, too." And she adds some of her own problems to the list. As the study proceeds, other questions and problems are added.

Then, because she has an eye on the goals of improving ability to use science processes to discover she says: "Now these are good problems. How shall we solve them?" And the pupils after some discussion say: "We can experiment. We can look in science and library books. We can ask the workmen. We can ask other people who know. We might watch the machines more closely. We might find a motion picture that will help us." After these possibilities are considered, the pupils select the problem about the use of the iron bar and the piece of sidewalk.

Can a child give a teacher a lift? Many suggestions are offered, predictions are made, and trials are conducted to test these predictions. (*Courtesy of the Elementary Science Study of Education Development Center, Inc.*)

To help pupils see how experiences may be used as a process of discovery the teacher brings into the classroom some bricks and a board from the construction scene. She says to her class: "Can anyone in this class lift me?" After a quick survey everyone gives up and she says: "Can anyone in our class use these bricks and this board to lift me?"

Several suggestions are made. Pupils discuss the suggestions and make some hypotheses and predictions about them. One suggestion is to place a brick on the floor and lay the board across it at about a midpoint. Several pupils indicate the belief that this is the situation they had observed outdoors. One student stands on one end of the board and asks the teacher to stand on the other. This does not produce the desired results, so the pupils suggest other hypotheses for testing. "Use more bricks to give more height." "Don't put them in the middle; leave more length of board on one side of the bricks than the other." "What would happen if we moved the bricks closer to Miss Wright?" These possibilities are tested. Children begin to sense a relationship between the distance the push moves to the distance the weight lifts. They suggest measuring to see what the relationship is. The measuring results in further trials.

This brief description of the beginning experience serves to illustrate a problem that originated from the environment and resulted in meaningful investigations. Pupils suggested hypotheses. They were given an opportunity to predict outcomes. They tried out their hypotheses. They revised their plans. They measured. They gathered mathematical data. They began to see relationships. They were using some of the processes of discovery that may eventually lead to making some generalizations regarding the function of levers. They began to see the relevancy of these materials to their own lives.

But all discoveries cannot be made through direct experiences, experimentation, and observation. Other learning methods are also important. As the study proceeds, children gather reading materials to find out more about levers and how they work and are used. In so doing they use language-arts skills to locate materials by the use of an index, table of contents, or card catalogue. They plan an interview with the construction foreman to ask questions about machines and how they work. This calls for making an outline of their findings and for presenting a well-organized, clear oral report to the class. They locate pictures that can be arranged in sequence to show some of the ways in which machines are helpful. They find a motion picture that will help to clear up their ideas about how machines work. They devise other ways to gather information, test it, and apply it to their problems about machines. In all of these activities the children proceed on their own as far as possible. The teacher suggests possibilities when necessary and when children's experiences are limited.

(*See also* Ch. 3.)

These pupils are discovering more about how to state their problems carefully; they are learning how to collect appropriate materials to solve the problems. They test their findings and record them in brief sentences. Later, in discussing her work with the pupils, Miss Wright says: "The study of machines seemed very successful because the children wanted to solve the problems. They were interested in setting up ways to find out. It turned out to be an open-ended experience that grew and developed as we went along. They learned something about using the processes of discovery and so did I. I learned that sometimes simple materials are most useful, that near-at-hand problems raised by the children can be very important; and I came to know that the pupils liked solving problems that are their own."

As we examine the possible behavioral outcomes from such activities, experiments, and observations we intend that pupils will demonstrate growth in being able to: *identify* and *state* specific problems, *construct* some inferences from observations, *propose* and attempt to *test* hypotheses, *describe* their findings, and so on.

Learning how to use processes of discovery is one of our important goals. How does this fit into our general elementary-school plan for children? Certainly our success in living with one another is increased if we are skillful in solving our daily problems—knowing what is pertinent, reliable information; learning how to apply it; knowing how to check the validity of results. As you use this book you will find many other examples of using science processes to learn science, as well as examples that show how a teacher creates a learning environment in which significant problems will be found.

Pupils need help in seeing how the processes of discovery in science are like processes of discovery in other areas. They may never make this connection unless it is called to their attention. The teacher may frequently say: "You remember how we found some of the answers when we worked on the problems about machines? How can we use what we learned there to help us find the answers to this new problem in our social studies?" The new problem may be: "How can we organize a good safety patrol for our school?" Such problems as this help pupils to transfer lessons in using processes to their everyday living.

Scientific Attitudes

In general terms we say that *the experiences in science should help children develop and use scientific attitudes.* We have been saying this for years, but we need to *do* more about it. The development of scientific attitudes, like the development of processes of discovery, come about only through conscious effort. First, to achieve this important objective we must understand what it means and we must think of it in terms of the behaviors and performances we expect from children. Then, we must teach so that children cannot get along without using scientific ways of thinking. Here are some of the characteristics that a scientifically-minded person possesses:

He is open-minded, willing to change his mind in the face of reliable evidence; and he respects another's point of view.

He looks at a matter from many sides before he draws a conclusion. He does not jump to conclusions or decide on the basis of one observation; he deliberates and examines until he is as sure as he can be.

He goes to reliable sources for his evidence. He challenges sources to make sure that they *are* reliable.

He is not superstitious; he realizes that nothing happens without some cause.

He is curious. He is careful and accurate in his observations.

It is these characteristics that we are trying to help children develop through science experiences. But it is possible to work with science apparatus, read source books, respond in science classes, set up exhibits for science clubs, and do a lot of other things without making any use of scientific attitudes. This happens every day in some of our science classes, because teachers do not actually *try to see that scientific attitudes are emphasized* and set up their objectives in terms of expected performances (*see* specific examples in later illustrations of practices). Every time children attempt to experiment, whenever they use other processes of discovery, whenever they read, take a field trip, see a motion picture, communicate their findings to the class, identify a problem to solve, their scientific attitudes ought to be showing. It should become a real part of their thinking equipment. There should be much of "Hey, wait a minute!" "Let's try that again." "How do you know that's true?" "I've changed my mind since I read what scientists say." "Where did you find that answer?" "You may be right, but tell me more about where you found your information." "I think our hypothesis should be revised." These remarks and similar ones should often be heard in our science classes as well as in social studies, arithmetic classes, and other places where children are working together and using processes of discovery.

Now let us be specific. In a fourth-grade class the pupils have been studying plants and how they grow. They have experimented and found that plants need water. Someone asks: "What happens to the water?" The children set up some hypotheses about the course of the water through the plant. The teacher asks: "What can we do so that we can see where the water does go?" "Color the water so we can see it," is a logical suggestion. So pupils take a stalk of celery, cut off the bottom of the

(*See* p. 298.)

stem with a sharp knife, and set the stem in a jar of water colored with red ink. They predict possible results. Later they examine the stalk, cut it open to observe the channels, and note the colored veins in the leaves which show where the water went. Someone then remarks: "I've read that some of the water goes off from the leaf into the air." The teacher asks: "Could you suggest a way to find out whether this is true?" A student suggests that they put something over a plant to catch any water that might come from the leaf. Pupils invert a quart jar over a small geranium plant. They do this and the next day notice that there are tiny droplets of water collected on the inside of the jar. "What does this show?" the teacher asks. The children seem to concur that it shows the geranium leaves give off water. "But," the teacher asks, "could the water have come from somewhere else?" (unless one of the children happily asks this question first). The water might have come from the soil in which the plant was growing or from the air around the leaf; the pupils have not investigated all the possibilities.

(*See also* Ch. 3.)

They have not controlled all the variables.

The teacher invites them to reconsider because she believes in the importance of helping pupils to think more scientifically. As a result someone suggests: "Maybe some of the water is coming from the soil. We ought to cover the soil with plastic wrap, then maybe the water couldn't get out of the soil." "Let's try it and see." The experiment is reassembled in its improved form (testing a variable). Again the water condenses on the inside of the jar, and the pupils are about to be satisfied with the results when a student says: "Maybe the moisture is coming from the air in the jar. It could be, you know." Indeed, it could. The teacher comments favorably on this kind of thinking: "How can we find out?"

Interest developed from firsthand experiences. These children have collected material from a local pond. They are examining it with a magnifying glass and will take it to their classroom for further study. (*Courtesy of U.S. Department of Agriculture.*)

Someone suggests using two sets of equipment exactly alike except that only one jar is over a growing plant; the other contains soil covered with plastic wrap and air. "Then if the jar with the plant has water on it and the other one doesn't, we'll know that the water really came from the plant" (formulating hypotheses; controlling variables).

The group performs similar experiments and does additional "research" reading before the pupils finally decide that the leaves of plants give water off into the air. The teacher *intends* to see that the scientific attitude is kept in mind. She helps the children plan so that they can see the results of making and using careful observations and controls.

Does it take more time to experiment in this way? Yes, it does, but how better can you spend time than in helping children be more careful and accurate in their judgments? Frequently in experimenting the subject matter learned may be of less importance than the methods used and the attitudes acquired. These methods of observing, questioning, checking details, inferring, testing, and withholding judgment should be called into play whenever experimenting takes place, whether the experiments come from a basic textbook, a supplementary science book, or are originated by the children.

Whenever children read there is plenty of opportunity for the application of scientific thinking. When young children ask: "Is that really a true story?" there is opportunity for them to get acquainted with the differences between factual material and fiction and to learn that one is used for the purpose of finding answers or getting information and the other more usually for entertainment and enjoyment.

The pupils' discovery of mistakes (or what appear to be mistakes) in books or other printed material may be a landmark in the development of their scientific attitudes. To realize that a statement's appearance in print is no guarantee of its accuracy may be an eye opener to a child who is being introduced to reliability as a criterion for selecting material to read for gathering information. One book, for example, may state that the earth has only one satellite; another may say the earth has only one *natural* satellite, although it has many man-made ones. Here is an opportunity for communication and discussion. Children come to appreciate the importance of using up-to-date material for reference work. They come to know that such words as "known" and "natural" are extremely important, as are such phrases as "scientists think," "it is generally believed," "it may be true that," "some people say," and "evidence seems to indicate that." This same attitude should permeate our activities in social studies and other areas of learning in the elementary school.

The following letter written by an eight-year-old to an author is an illustration of challenging the accuracy of information:

> Dear ____________________
>
> You wrote a book called the *Pet Show*, didn't you? One of the stories in it is called the "Guinea Pigs at the Show." One sentence says, "They can run about when they are only a few days old."
>
> This is not true.
>
> They can run about the day they are born.
>
> Yours truly,
> Mary Lou ____________________
>
> P.S. I raise them.

Here, obviously, is a pupil who is learning to evaluate some of her reading and to relate it to her own experience. Some adult, either at home or at school, may have urged her to write to the author to find out why her experiences and the book did not seem to agree. Through such an experience the child learns something about how books are written, how limited experience may sometimes be misleading, how scientific observations may differ from a child's observations, and how different statements of fact may only *seem* to be in disagreement.

Children's reports of horsehairs turning to snakes and other superstitions should be subjected to investigation and checking to develop scientific attitudes. Statements such as the following are often made by children—and grown-ups too: "You can't believe the weatherman!" "Animals can tell if the winter is to be very cold." "You can tell your future by the stars." These remarks offer excellent opportunities for the use of scientific investigation and checking. They involve finding the answers to such questions as: "Who says so?" "How can we find out the facts?" "Why do some people say these things?"

We have given only a few examples of situations that can help children to develop scientific attitudes. Other ideas for accomplishing this important purpose will be presented as we go on. Watch for them in the B chapters.

Stating objectives in behavioral form makes them specific and helps us to come closer to being able to evaluate them. Attitudes are hard to assess, but they do regulate behavior. When we are more specific in saying: "As a result of these experiences and experiments children should *exhibit* an attitude of withholding judgment and *develop* a tendency to challenge information sources," our teaching focus becomes sharper.

Interest and Appreciation

In general terms learning in science is supposed *to create in children an interest in and an appreciation for the world in which they live.* The attitudes which we have just discussed are closely related to interest and appreciation. They, too, are difficult to achieve and hard to measure, Let us examine a background situation to clarify the idea.

Just now, as this is being written, the evening sky is flaming with a hundred hues. The clouds five miles away, made of countless droplets of water, are reflecting some of this light through the window. The window glass itself was made by heating sand to which chemicals have been added, and the result offers protection from the weather. Growing almost into the window, vine leaves glisten green in the light of late afternoon. In leaves such as these the food for the world is being made. The leaf is a wonderful manufacturing plant where water, lately fallen from the sky as rain, comes up from the roots in the ground and meets with carbon dioxide from the air. In the green leaf, in the presence of sunlight, food is manufactured from this water and carbon dioxide. All living things depend on this process. In the world about us there are, indeed, great things to wonder about: How can sunlight be changed to brilliant colors at sunset? How are clouds formed? How is glass made? How do plants manufacture food? How did the world itself come to be, and how has it changed through the ages? Some wise person has said: "He who can no longer pause to wonder is as good as dead."

Young children deserve to find in schools a nurturing influence for their natural curiosity about the world. They deserve also to have this curiosity extended to new fields about which they have never wondered because they did not know they exist. They deserve the opportunity to come to appreciate, through understanding, the wonders of the world—to be "at home" in the world. Exactly how this appreciation is to be developed, we still have much to learn. Experience seems to show that children do not gain it through listening to sentimental gushing from an adult. Perhaps it comes about when adults provide opportunities for children to discover *for themselves.* We can provide opportunities to observe firsthand, to feel, to see, to use the senses so that satisfying experiences will result. Perhaps through knowledge thus gained, through satisfying experiences, each child may develop for himself an appreciation that fits his person. Certainly there can be great thrills in discovery, great satisfaction through contact with natural objects and phenomena.

As these paragraphs were being written the colors disappeared from the west. Twilight is here and soon night will come. Our side of the earth is turning from the sun; darkness comes. Elsewhere the dark side of the earth is turning toward the sun and day is coming. In a few weeks the leaves will drop from the vine outside the window; the days will grow colder; autumn will be here, then winter, then spring, and summer. Here is the cycle of the seasons. There is also the cycle that water follows as it disappears from the surface of the earth and appears again, falling from the sky as rain; the cycle of seeds from tiny cells to adult plant and the production of seeds again. These and similar phenomena are what we have in mind when we think of providing opportunities to increase children's interest and develop their appreciations, which in turn will lead to growing comprehension and insight. As in the case of the other objectives discussed, this one is realized only if we intend it to be and plan learning experiences for children accordingly. We hope to bring about changes in behaviors and think of our results in terms of showing evidence of a broadening interest through *asking* more searching questions, *bringing* to class examples that show increased curiosity, *selecting* science books of a more diversified content.

Let's remember that children are individuals and differ in ability, background, interests, and many other characteristics; you cannot expect *all* of them to be equally interested in any *one* topic or subject. The best a teacher can do is to make it possible for children to explore their present interests, discover new ones, and derive satisfaction from pursuing them. Above all, let us try to keep interest alive, not kill it by forcing children to go further than their interests and abilities will carry them. It is just as important to know where and when to stop the study of a problem in science as when to start it.

Remember that children will in their later school experience have other opportunities to study science; consequently it is not necessary for them to exhaust the subject in the elementary school. Even if it were to be their last school contact with scientific material, there is still nothing to be gained by running it into the ground. The vast majority of pupils will find satisfaction in science as they do in their other school subjects, with interest spurts and lags, depending on the specific problems being considered. Some—we hope relatively few—will have but a passive interest in science, and during science classes their minds may be far away. It is when the minds of *most* of the pupils are elsewhere during science study that we should show real concern. It is then that we should examine critically the content and techniques of teaching.

Responsible, Intelligent Citizenship

Knowledge of science concepts; understanding of science processes; and the development of attitudes, interests, and appreciation are all of little avail if we produce adults who are unable or unwilling to use these in helping to solve the serious problems which face the world today. We are only beginning to realize how serious some of these problems are. The interest in ecology and the state of our environment came with an almost explosive suddenness revealing many urgent problems: general deterioration of the environment, the exhaustion of our natural resources, over-population, drug addiction, illiteracy, ignorance and prejudice, threat of nuclear war, poverty, urban decay, crisis in transportation.

While the production of responsible, intelligent citizens is a general goal for all education, it is obvious that science education has some very significant concepts and methods to contribute. The science experiences in the elementary school lay the ground work for these contributions when we involve children *now* in projects in their schools and communities. With these projects children have the satisfaction of knowing that *what they do makes a difference.* Problems such as the following may trigger worthwhile projects (further related material will be found in Chapters 14A and B).

What can we do about the lot next to our school which is filled with papers and rubbish?

Where does the soot on our playground come from? What can be done about this?

How can the environment of our school and community be improved?

While we cannot overestimate the importance of helping children to develop into responsible intelligent citizens, we accomplish little when we superimpose adult views on them. As with the other aims we have discussed, the interests, drives, capacities, and the developmental levels of children must be understood and respected. Nor should we be deceived by children's verbal performance in the use of ecological terms. We must continue to search for evidence that the *behaviors of students* have changed, that they have established certain desirable *values* as evidenced by their discussions and actions.

As in case of other objectives we come closer to achieving our goals if they are conceived as behaviors. For example, in connection with a study of environmental pollution: As a result of participating in activities planned to help produce responsible, intelligent citizens children will be able to: *observe* an environment and *describe* its conditions, *identify* some of the most pressing problems, *plan* specific courses of action to improve environmental situations, *demonstrate* by specific behaviors the ability to assume leadership and responsibility in helping bring about changes for the better in the immediate environment, and *originate* and *pursue* experiences and experiments that provide data about unsolved environmental problems.

Perhaps we have written too emphatically and too much about objectives. But they are important, for they guide our science teaching in every detail. We shall continue to refer to them and try to make them even more concrete throughout this text. Every day we teach, we should challenge the things we do with children by asking ourselves: "What behaviors do we expect on the part of children?" If the answer is questionable, then let us try hard to find a better way of teaching. If the answer is satisfactory, let us strive to increase the effectiveness of what we are already doing. Let us attempt to be more specific in our expectations and pattern our evaluations

(*See* Ch. 5.)

of these expectations. Above all, let us keep in mind that science deserves to be included in the elementary curriculum only to the extent that it contributes to the goals of the total program.

What we have said about keeping in mind the goals of learning in science are equally true for the teaching of every other subject in the elementary school. We point this out to emphasize our contention that good science teaching is very similar to good teaching in other subjects. Great strides could be made in our educational program if we applied the following criterion to the curriculum: Does the study of this problem, the use of this activity, this plan of work actually contribute to the attainment of our overall goals? If problems, activities, and plans that did not meet this standard were discarded and replaced our school program would be immeasurably revitalized.

It's what happens in the classroom that counts. The next chapter concentrates on specifics for improving what happens there.

(Courtesy of Phyllis Marcuccio.)

CHAPTER 3

HELPING CHILDREN LEARN SCIENCE

Whatever children do to learn science should be *purposeful.* It should move pupils toward the accomplishment of the goals of science teaching. It should be *challenging* and *appropriate* because it is on the intellectual and interest level of the learner. It should use the processes of inquiry that lead to some meaningful discoveries. Keeping these things in mind, experimenting is not done simply to provide activity; murals are not made because something is needed for the bulletin board; field trips are not taken because a school is near the zoo. Activities are designed to accomplish aims. They should seem purposeful to children here and now.

With the goals in mind, then, how can we help children achieve them? Many of the aims are achieved through using the processes of inquiry. By experimenting, observing, reading, taking field trips, talking with someone who knows, looking at pictures, and in many other ways children become informed and grow in ability to use the skills of inquiry. When children inquire they acquire appropriate attitudes, appreciations, skills, and knowledge if the teacher so intends and possesses the necessary teaching skills.

STUDYING CHILDREN

Before there can be success in helping children achieve goals, knowledge of their growth and development, how they think, and how their capacities change as they mature is necessary. The more carefully and intelligently teachers observe children in and out of the classroom, the more likely they are to be successful.

We have been aided in the study of children by those who have studied children and have organized, recorded, and interpreted their findings in terms of sound approaches to teaching. Among others, the work of the Swiss psychologist, Jean Piaget[1] is important. Although there is some disagreement about the interpretation and use of all of his findings, they are important because they focus attention on child development and the importance of designing our teaching to conform to such knowledge. Piaget's research has been directed toward determining how children think and reason as they grow and mature. He directs teachers to observe and attempt to interpret children's responses—how they typically do or do not perform under certain conditions.

Piaget's observations in essence indicate that the thinking of children develops in stages as they grow. The thinking of the youngest school-age children, approximately kindergarten through grade one, is characterized as *pre-operational.* It is concerned chiefly with objects and firsthand experiences. He contends that children usually do not connect to any great degree with logical operations and do not appear to make connections between events that happen. If we subscribe to this concept the science experiences at this early age should be involved with easily observable materials and firsthand experiences.

From this stage and roughly through grades five or six children are described as

[1] For further information: E.A. Crittenden: "Piaget and Elementary Science," *Science and Children* (December 1970); C.S. Lavatelli: *Piaget's Theory Applied to an Early Childhood Education Curriculum* (Boston, Mass.: A Center for Media Development, Inc., 1970); J. Piaget: *The Child's Conception of the World* (New York: Harcourt, Brace, 1929).

being in a *concrete observations stage.* Logical thinking begins to develop and children begin to reason on the basis not of the limited appearance of materials only but from experiences and observations which modify their thinking. The child begins to use some degree of logical thinking and observation, but for many children at these ages abstract thinking is not common. Formulating broad generalizations is somewhat difficult for many. It is important to remember that these stages are not watertight compartments, that *all* children are not alike in their development and will not reach the suggested stages at a uniform time.

A stage of *formal operations* follows in which children are able to do more abstract thinking, see relationships, plan experiences and experiments, and interpret their observations. They become more proficient at recognizing and dealing with variables in the experimental process and in proposing hypotheses and testing them.

Experiences with children indicate that there are many degrees of proficiency in the use of these processes and also great variations within any one group in ability to deal with them. Observations of children as they attempt to understand new ideas show that such understandings result from being able to recall what they have learned from previous experiences and to relate this understanding to new experiences. Children change their concepts as they add understandings developed from new experiences. Their needs are best met when some logical structure to the experiences is provided, and when these experiences are within their comprehension and are meaningful to them.

This brief survey of some of Piaget's ideas will be enhanced by examination of some of the conservation tasks he describes and their use with children reproduced here.[2] Some insights into how children think and how such knowledge may be used to work more intelligently with children in their science activities is developed by using Piaget's materials even on an informal basis.

Description of Conservation Tasks

1. Conservation of number.

Six black checkers in one row and six red checkers in another row were arranged for the child.

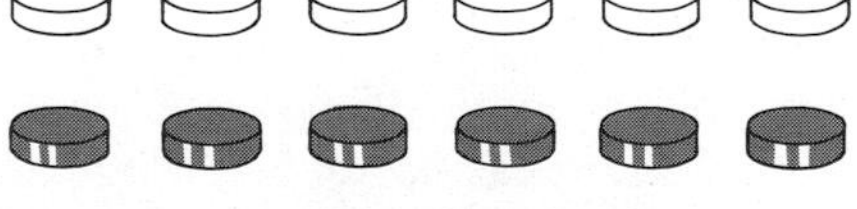

The child was asked if he agreed that there was the same number of red checkers as there were black checkers. After he agreed to this fact, the red checkers were stacked, one on top of the other, and the black checkers were left as they were:

[2] Reproduced by permission from John W. Renner et al.: "Piaget IS Practical," *Science and Children* (October 1971), copyright 1971 by the National Science Teachers Association: see also Rodger Bybee and Alan McCormack: "Applying Piaget's Theory," *Science and Children* (December 1970) and E. Duckworth: "Piaget Rediscovered," *Journal of Research in Science Teaching* (vol. 2, 3, 1964).

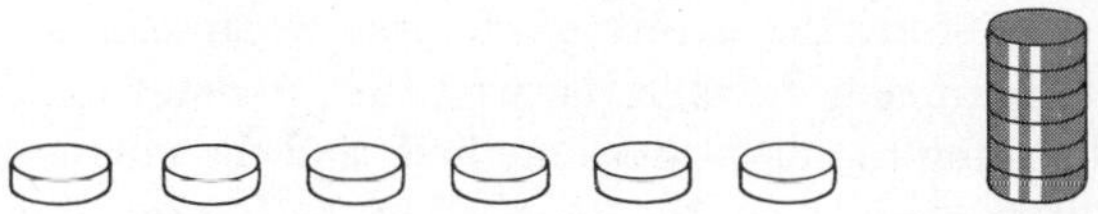

The child was then asked if there was still the same number of black checkers as there were red checkers and why.

2. *Conservation of solid amount.*
See Rodger Bybee and Alan McCormack, "Applying Piaget's Theory." *Science and Children* 8: 14–17; December 1970. Task 1, Conservation of Matter.[2]

3. *Conservation of liquid amount.*
See Bybee and McCormack,[2] Task 2, Conservation of Volume. There is a specific test designed by Piaget for the conservation of volume.

4. *Conservation of length.*
Place a rod 12 inches long and three other pieces each 4 inches long next to each other. These rods represent two roads. Next, place a toy car at the beginning of each road:

Ask the child if he agrees that both roads are the same length. After he agrees to this fact, pose the problem: "If the cars travel the same speed, which car, the red one or the black one, will reach the end of the road first? Or will they reach the end of the road at the same time? Record the child's answers. Then move one piece of the three-piece road ahead of the other two pieces, ask the same question, and why.

5. *Conservation of area.*
See Bybee and McCormack,[2] Task 7, Conservation of Area.

6. *Conservation of weight.*
Form two balls of clay equal in size and let the child experience that they weigh exactly the same:

Deform one of the balls of clay to make a pancake and do not let the child handle the clay.

Ask the child which would weigh more, the ball or the pancake, or would they both weigh the same and why,

We study the nature of children because in so doing we are guided in selecting and organizing the material we teach, in determining our methods of instruction, and in learning to adjust these methods and the curriculum to fit the needs, interests, and abilities of children. We know all of this but we may be somewhat like an unsuccessful farmer who was encouraged by his well-meaning neighbors to see the county agriculture agent for more "know-how" about farming. After a bit of reflection the farmer said: "I don't farm as well as I know how now." It is so with teaching. There is much that we know about children and learning that we do not use to best advantage. Some things we know about children from observing them and from our experience with them; research has indicated a few of these and some seem obvious when common sense prevails. Making use of the ideas in the following paragraphs can greatly increase the effectiveness of science teachers.

Knowledge of children and how they learn indicates that we help them most when we help them discover, help them see relationships in these discoveries, and organize what they discover into meaningful ideas instead of requiring them to learn by rote. Experience shows that they learn and remember better under such circumstances.

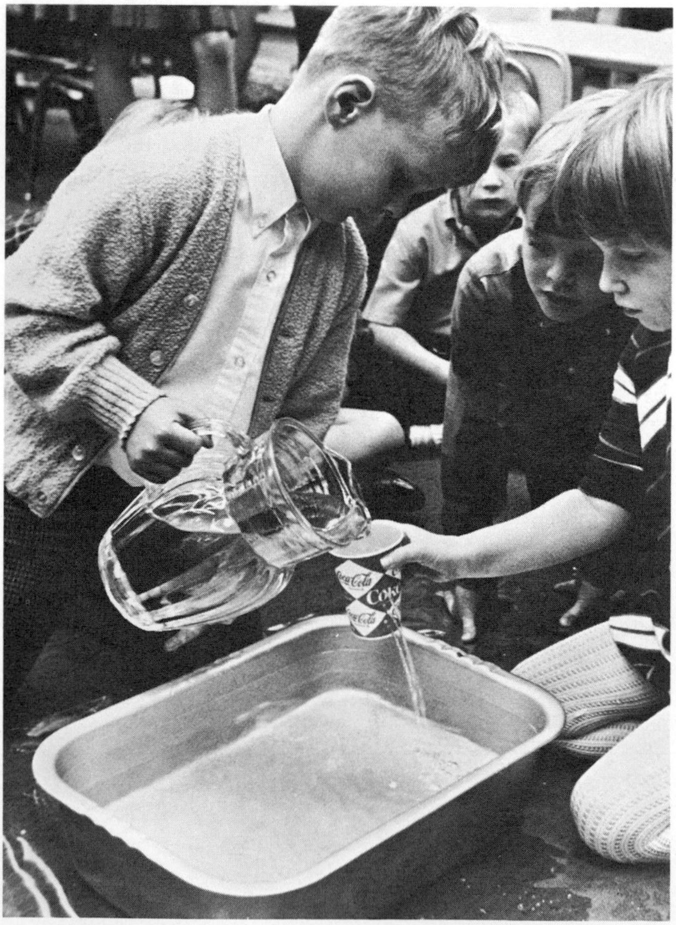

These young children are trying to see what happens to water under different conditions. Experiences such as these expose children to the idea of trying things, looking to see, telling what you see, and wondering and asking. More sophisticated use of materials and observations comes with later experiences. (*Courtesy of Mildred T. Ballou, Ball State University, Muncie Indiana.*)

Experience also shows that they learn how to learn better through experience rather than by being told, and that a variety of learning experiences is highly desirable.

Observation and experience also indicates that what the child learns depends in part on what he already knows and thus can bring to the new situation. This idea gives some clues about the importance of a developmental curriculum.

Anyone who has observed children knows that they are "natural-born" investigators. This indicates the importance of providing opportunity for them to manipulate, to try out, to see "what will happen if. . . ," and to take apart and put back together. By all means it is important to try to keep this tendency alive by providing opportunity for it to grow and develop, instead of holding it down so that it has completely disappeared by the time the child has passed through the elementary school. Sometimes the approach is so academic that children with this natural tendency to manipulate have to wait until Saturday before they can express it. Good teachers realize that this inclination of pupils to investigate is a valuable one, and that there must be more *purposeful doing* in science teaching.

Children are interested in, and react to, *all* aspects of their environment. Interest studies seem to show, as everyone who has worked thoughtfully with children knows, that children's questions concern all kinds of environmental objects and phenomena. Observations in an elementary school show that children are excited about astronomy, electricity, airplanes, spaceships, animals, and so on. Today's science must be broader than the study of ducks and dandelions of former years if it is to take into account what we know about children's interests.

Children like to plan and carry out their plans and as has been indicated earlier they become increasingly able to do this as they grow and develop. The examples of classroom procedures described in this book show how children may help to plan ways for solving their problems and to continue planning as they proceed in their experimenting, reading, observing, and other experiences. If more attention is paid to children's desire for participation—the importance of which is difficult to overestimate—we, as teachers, must make fewer of the planning decisions ourselves and place more and more responsibility on the children. This does not mean that the teacher is unimportant in the plans. Because he knows many things that should be considered in planning, he should not hesitate to use his knowledge when it is advisable.

As we have seen, not all children learn in the same way or at the same rate, nor can they all *assemble their learning* at the same speed and in the same way. There is no reason to expect *all* children to arrive at an understanding of a science concept at the same time, as we've said. Even though children may all be exposed to the same experiences they may each arrive at different concepts as a result of these experiences. Furthermore, these concepts may not be the ones the teacher had in mind; they may be quite different. Some of this variation may be due to the differences that exist between teacher objectives and those of children. We are often inclined to believe that the two are the same when in reality they may be quite different.

These circumstances indicate that we must evaluate, insofar as possible, on an individual basis and that the evaluations must be continuous. The fact that many different types of activities (experimenting, observing, reading, and so on) are involved

(*See* Ch. 5.)

in science investigating makes it possible for pupils of varying interests and aptitudes to participate.

It seems reasonable to assume that children who have a purpose to accomplish will work more profitably than those who do not. The more sense the purposes make to children, the better.

INVESTIGATING AND EXPERIMENTING TO FIND OUT

There is something fascinating to children about experimenting. "Wow, we're going to experiment today!" may be heard, when science material is brought out. This interest in "trying out" is an important one to capitalize on. We should not take away any of the fun of experimenting, but at the same time we should help children to realize that experimenting is an important way of discovering or attempting to discover answers.

Following printed directions and recording the results in blank spaces is not experimenting. Following the recipe is generally quite sufficient when baking a cake, but our goals for experimenting are quite different. There is a significant difference between an experiment and some of the experiences we sometimes call experiments. An experiment involves a problem to which pupils do not know a solution. Children are attempting to test a hypothesis, variables exist and controls are used. It is obvious from this description that some degree of maturity in ability to see relationships, formulate hypotheses, plan, and interpret are essential on the part of children. This may account in part for the fact that according to Piaget and others, true experiments in contrast to experiences are generally reserved for more mature pupils.

There are, however, many examples of even very young children experimenting. When children in the kindergarten try to find out how to dry wet mittens quickly and place one on a hot radiator and one on a pie plate they may be dealing with hypotheses, variables, and controls. When they are rolling balls down an incline and try to discover how to make them roll farther by proposing to make the incline steeper, and then try this out, they are also dealing with hypothesizing, using variables, measuring, and drawing conclusions. Teachers do well to keep this idea in mind as they work with groups of various age and attempt to draw their own conclusions about whether or not the youngest children actually can experiment.

In connection with experimenting in the true sense consider this illustration. Pupils have brought magnets to school, have used them informally, and have shown each other the things they have observed. One child hypothesizes that magnets will pick up metals. Some pupils agree with him; some do not. They make other hypotheses: "It will pick up only hard things." "It will pick up only iron and steel things." Some admit that they have no idea what materials magnets will attract. "How can we find out what a magnet picks up?" the teacher asks. "Try picking up many different things," the children say. "Let's do that!" The pupils through discussion decide to:

1. Write the purpose of the experiment on the board—"to find out what things a magnet will pick up." Someone suggests: "Let's find out if it's right to say that

it will pick up metals, too"; and the teacher adds: "to find out whether a magnet will pick up metals."

2. Devise plans for experimenting. These simple directions are worked out by the children:
   a. Gather metals and other things that we want to test, such as paper, cork, glass, an iron thumbtack, a steel needle, an iron nail, a steel penpoint, cloth, a nickel, a penny.
   b. Try to predict what may happen in each case.
   c. Use a strong magnet carefully to see whether it will pick these up.
   d. Make a pile of the things the magnet will pick up and one of the things it will not pick up.
   e. See if the experiment really answers our questions.

The plans are followed carefully, and pupils finally decide: "Some of our predictions were right. Our experiment seems to show that this magnet will pick up things made of iron and steel." They decide that they need to do some reading to be sure of their answers, because they cannot try out *all* materials. Their reading seems to confirm their original conclusion, except that nickel was listed as a metal that would be attracted by a magnet. This leads to additional reading and investigating.

(*See* Chs. 19A and B.)

Then someone again raises the question about the statement that magnets would attract metals. This question is settled by looking up a definition of metals: "Substances such as iron, gold, silver, copper, lead, tin, aluminum, steel, bronze, and brass." The definition and the results of the experiment help pupils to evaluate the statement made by one person that magnets will pick up metals.

What is good about this procedure? The experimenting was done in response to a perplexing problem; experimenting seemed the logical way to attempt to find answers. The design for the experiment and the plan for its use was made by pupils with some help from the teacher. The pupils made some observations and predictions and did not generalize from too little evidence. The experience contributed something toward accomplishing the overall objectives of science teaching.

Reexamine the discussion of behavioral objectives in Chapter 2. What behaviors can we expect as the result of many experiences such as the one described here? *After* you have attempted to answer this question read the concluding statements in this section.

(*See* p. 43.)

What is also significant is the *spirit*—the *atmosphere*—of the classroom. The teacher encouraged pupils to bring magnets to school. Opportunity was provided for them to engage in informal activity and free exchange to show each other what they had observed. They felt the classroom was the place to ask and investigate.

It is not always essential nor desirable to write the problem or the procedure on the board. Indeed this procedure "turns off" many children. It is, however, always important to urge pupils to state the problem exactly as they wish to solve it and to plan the procedure just as they wish to follow it. It may be, and frequently is, necessary to make changes in the plan as the experiments go on. The teacher will help where needed so that the most effective results may be achieved. How much the teacher helps depends on many factors that vary with groups, but the best teachers don't talk too much!

By some standards this experiment might be described as "quite cut and dried"; that is, there are not many opportunities for creative thinking on the part of individuals, and the activity probably ends with the discovery of answers leaving not many offshoots of other ideas for later pursuit. What can be done to make such an experience more "open-ended"; that is, more "on-going" and thought-provoking? Here are suggestions.

Let pupils try more materials before they read. Suggest (hopefully the children may suggest) that magnets of different strengths, shapes, and sizes are used to observe any differences in results, that different shapes and sizes of materials to be attracted are employed, that different parts of the magnet are used and the results noted, that different weights of metals are studied. This may help children to realize that "attract" is a better description of what happens between magnet and metal than "pick up." A magnet may attract a heavy piece of iron and still not pick it up. Provide more opportunity for the pupils to predict possible outcomes. These suggestions and others made by pupils will help introduce children to the methods used by scientists, who "leave no stone unturned" as they search for answers to problems and related information.

These are but a few examples of procedures that "open up" rather than "close

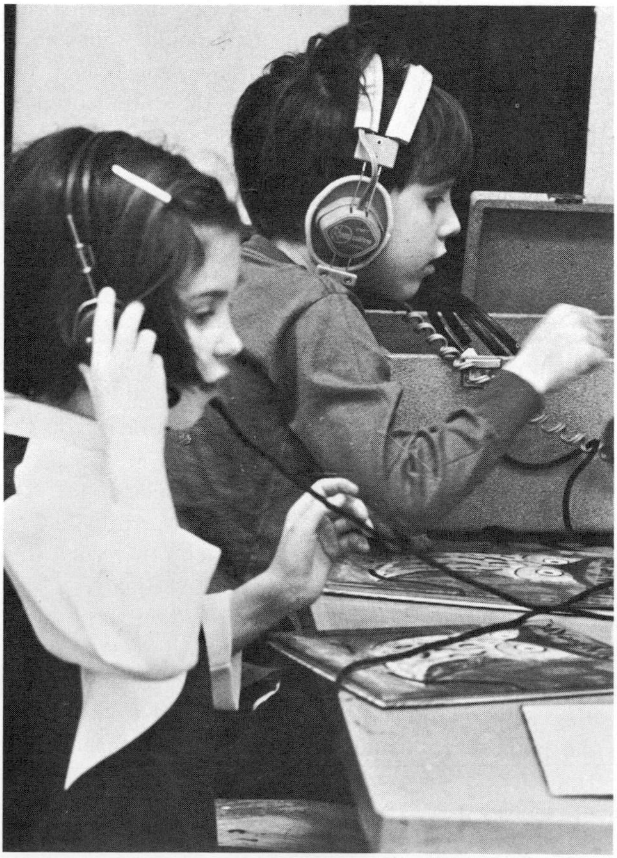

Today's learning centers involve the use of listening skills, as well as the more usual visual observations. Descriptions, directions, information come from some of the newer media, such as those used by these children. (*Courtesy of Phyllis Marcuccio.*)

up." Further "open-endedness" may be encouraged by questions beginning: "What would happen if. . . ?" "Where could you find. . . ?" "What other ways are there of. . . ?" "How could you prove that. . . ?" "How could you make a. . . ?" Other illustrations of such ideas will be found in the B chapters.

A further improvement in experimenting is, whenever possible, to make the results more scientific through the use of mathematics. Both science and mathematics are made more meaningful when they are related. This use of mathematical skills (recognizing number relations) runs all the way from counting the number of thumbtacks that different magnets can hold to measuring the lengths of shadows made by a stick at various times of the day and includes such projects as working out the relationships of the amount of effort needed to lift a weight, determining the length of the part of the lever on which force is being applied, figuring out the amount of air pressure on a rectangular tin can. More about recognizing number relations in various experiments and experiences will be pointed out in the B chapters.

In connection with the use of mathematics we should take into account the very real possibility that the United States will eventually convert to the metric system. Such a transition will involve much direct teaching in schools. When we measure distance, weight, and so on in science we have opportunities for practical and meaningful experiences with it.[3] The chart reproduced here from the U.S. Bureau of Standards illustrates many of the common measurements.

All You Will Need to Know about Metric[4] (for Your Everyday Life)

The metric is based on the decimal system. The metric system is simple to learn. For use in your everyday life you will need to know only ten units. You will also need to get used to a few new temperatures. There are other units which most persons will not need to learn. There are even some metric units with which you are already familiar: those for time and electricity are the same as you use now.

Basic Units

Meter: A little longer than a yard (about 1.1 yards).
Liter: A little larger than a quart (about 1.06 quarts).
Gram: About the weight of a paper clip

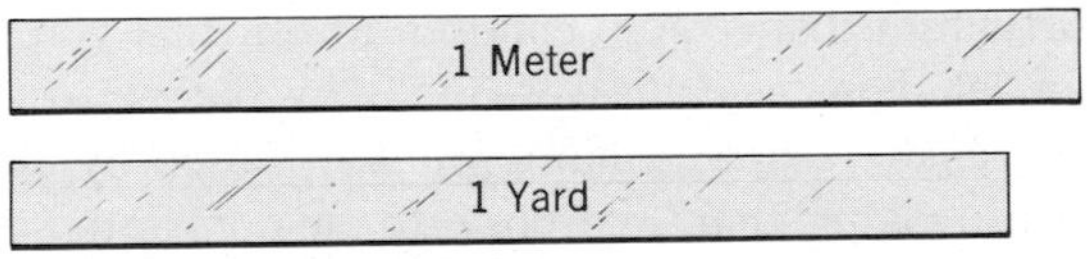

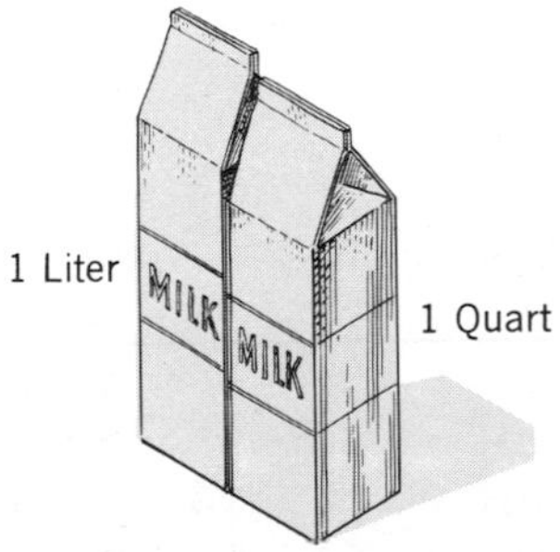

(comparative sizes are shown)

[3] L.M. Branscomb: "The U.S. Metric Study," *The Science Teacher* (November 1971) pp. 58–62; N.J. Holmes and J.J. Snoble: *How to Teach Measurements in Elementary School Science* (Washington, D.C.: National Science Teachers Association).

[4] For more information write to Metric Information Office, National Bureau of Standards, Washington, D.C. 20234.

Common Prefixes (to be used with basic units)
Milli: one-thousandth (0.001).
Centi: one-hundredth (0.01).
Kilo: one-thousand times (1000).

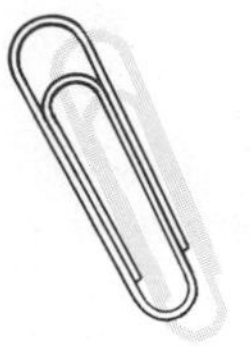

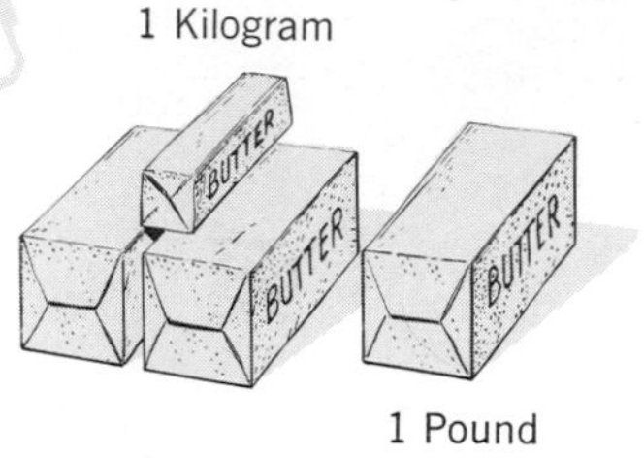

For example: 1000 millimeters = 1 meter
100 centimeters = 1 meter
1000 meters = 1 kilometer

Other Commonly Used Units
Millimeter: 0.001 meter (diameter of paper clip wire).
Centimeter: 0.01 meter (width of a paper clip—about 0.4 inch).
Kilometer: 1000 meters (somewhat further than ½ mile—about 0.6 mile).
Kilogram: 1000 grams (a little more than 2 pounds—about 2.2 pounds).
Milliliter: 0.0001 liter (five of them make a teaspoon).

Other Useful Units
Hectare: About 2½ acres.
Tonne: About 1 ton.

Temperature (degrees Celsius, formerly called centigrade) are used

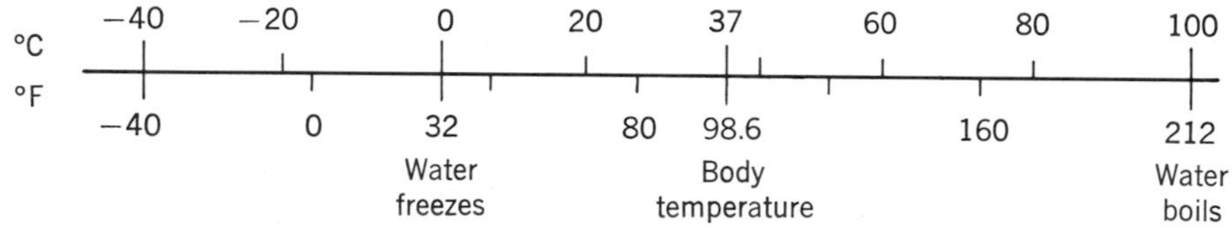

The following are specific suggestions to help make investigating and experimenting a more effective experience:

1. Keep the experiment simple or break a complicated experiment into simple parts. Whenever possible use simple, sometimes dependable homemade equipment. A caution is in order here: In addition to simple materials it is important for children to use more sophisticated apparatus and material for obvious reasons; the weather bureau does not use a pinwheel to determine wind speed!
2. Provide opportunities that require children to think. If you plan to *tell* children the answers or let them *read* the answers, why bother to experiment? Experimenting to find answers to a genuine problem raised by children is sure to be more thought-provoking than one done to demonstrate something that is already known by many of the pupils.
3. Let pupils do as much of the planning as they can. Then follow the plan. When it is necessary to make changes, pupils will have some basis for making them, because they themselves helped make the original plan.
4. Challenge pupils when they make sweeping generalizations from one experiment. "Magnets will pick up all nails." After a limited experience with a box

of nails the teacher may say: "Do all of you believe that we can say this?" The discussion will result in further experimentation.

5. Keep experiments simple and safe enough for pupils to do by themselves. If classes are large and there is sufficient material available, pupils may work in groups to give many of them opportunity for experimentation. It is often possible to leave the material available for individual use when part of the class is engaged in other activities. The teacher should remember that it is one thing to manipulate apparatus and quite another to watch while somebody else does it. The best situation exists when *every* child has an opportunity to experiment or engage in the activity.
6. Provide opportunities for children to react to: "Can anyone think of something we can try or some ways of experimenting that may help us solve this problem?" This procedure gives a chance for real thought, careful planning, organization, predicting, and interpreting. We reiterate: Do not expect all early-age pupils to be proficient with these in-depth skills.
7. Help pupils to apply the information gained by experimenting to the world about them. It is this application to "real-life" situations that is often missed.
8. Urge pupils to keep in mind the purposes of experimenting. It is often advisable to have on the chalkboard a simple statement of the problem to guide the thinking as the experimenting goes on and as the conclusions are drawn. Individual pupils with varying backgrounds and interests should be encouraged, as time and space allow, to follow their own paths. The examples of open-endedness throughout this book illustrate the point.
9. Examine the policy of requiring a complete record of all experiments performed in school. It is not always necessary or desirable. Sometimes it seems sensible to record in a sentence or two the important discoveries of an experiment, either for future reference or to be sure that the ideas are clearly understood. If the experiment is one that takes several days to complete, it may be helpful to record each day's observations by making drawings, writing a short paragraph, or by making a graph or chart of the findings. The guiding idea may well be: "Is there any good reason for writing, or communicating in some other way, anything about this experiment?" The B chapters contain many examples of such communicating.
10. Keep experiments as "scientific" as possible, stressing the importance of control of the variables. For example, if the importance of light to plants is being investigated, light should be the only variable. A number of plants should be kept in the dark, a number of similar plants in the light. But all other conditions should be the same for both groups.
11. Remember that when experiments do not follow the predicted path, real problems arise, and pupils, in attempting to discover why, think more, plan better, and learn more than would otherwise be the case. In a truly scientific sense every experiment "works," although it may not take the course anticipated.
12. Remember also that an experiment is an experiment in the true sense only if pupils do not already know the outcome. Such experiments will provide opportunity for thoughtful observing, predicting, communicating, and interpreting.

What about our behavioral objectives in relation to the kinds of activities we have been considering? Let us look at some examples. As a result of experimenting and investigating children should be able to:

construct some hypotheses as a result of observation.
devise some inferences on the bases of observations.
manipulate simple apparatus or material to insure valid observations.
identify some variables that should be taken into account.

Obviously these are but a few examples of possible behaviors to look for, and they do not result from one experience, but we hope they will from many.

This book cannot possibly provide an exhaustive list of experiments in the chapters that follow. However, many are included, and suggestions are made for helping pupils devise others. The 12 points just given are illustrated in the examples you will find throughout the B chapters. Science books are rich sources of experiments, and the books listed in the Bibliography supplement the experiments given in this text and those devised by children.

READING TO FIND OUT

Despite our emphasis on firsthand experiences, experimenting, direct observation, and doing, let's not neglect reading as a way to learn science. It is still legitimate to read. Children cannot learn everything by experimenting or by firsthand experiences. Neither can anyone else. We learn much from reading textbooks, supplementary books, bulletins, magazines, and newspapers, as well as from written records. Reading is sometimes condemned as a way to learn science because it is often used so much that the science course degenerates into a course of reading *about* science. This criticism is leveled not against reading as a way to learn but against the *way* in which we use reading and the *amount* of reading we do. We often hear school supervisors say: "Don't use your science books as readers!" How then? Let us see how to use a science book in a way that avoids this criticism.

Assume that the area of study has been decided upon: Children are going to study sound. One of the big problems is: "How are sounds made?" Suppose we begin by suggesting to the class that each pupil bring something that will make a sound. To heighten interest we may say: "Try to bring something that no one else will think of."

As preparation for attempting to solve this problem you, as the teacher, have read carefully the section in the pupils textbook about sound, and have also read Chapters 20A and 20B in this book; you have explored to see what other reading materials are available, have located in the school building and in the neighborhood examples of the use of the principles of sound, and have assembled some material you may need that the children probably cannot find themselves.

The next day, pupils come in with their sound makers. You suggest that as each child demonstrates his sound maker pupils observe carefully to: (1) see what makes the sound, and (2) tell how the sounds are different from each other. This precedure may promote interest, stimulate observations, and raise questions and problems.

The sound making begins. Ned has brought his violin, Charlie his trumpet; and they make sounds with them. Mary and Alice use rubber bands, plucking them when they are stretched; Paul stands up in front of everybody and shouts, "Hey!" There are several other examples of sound. After these demonstrations you suggest that everybody listen quietly to hear any sounds around them. They hear the clock tick. A car starts up outside, and the sound changes as the car gains speed. Across the street someone is hammering; perhaps driving a nail into a board. A bell rings somewhere in the school building.

After each sound is made, the pupils state what they think may be the answer to the two questions. They formulate hypotheses. It's made if something moves. You have to hit something. Some are made in some way, some in another. They are not at all sure what it is that makes the sounds, but they have classified them: Some are loud, some soft, some high, some low. There is discussion about how Paul made sound when he said, "Hey!"

"Let's feel our throats when we talk," the teacher suggests. "Something in there quivers," somebody volunteers. "That's what my violin string does when I draw the bow across it. It vibrates," Ned says. But what is it that makes the sound? The teacher suggests that pupils observe closely to see if something is vibrating in each case where sound is made. They see, and feel, and listen. The children agree on the basis of their experiences that when something is making sound it is vibrating. They set up further experiments to test this idea. But other questions have arisen, for example: "What has this to do with the sound I hear, and how does the sound get to my ears?"

Pupils are now faced with a problem they cannot solve through the use of experiences and experiments alone. This is a time for reading. The teacher has assembled a number of library books, and the pupils find the section on sound in their textbooks if they are available. They find pictures that show pupils making sounds. The pupils read to see whether they can discover answers to their question. They read about vibrations. They find experiences they can have with a tuning fork. The teacher produces tuning forks. "How can we use these to help us?" she asks. The pupils suggest ways. They feel the vibrations in the tuning forks. Mary and Alice are asked to demonstrate their rubber bands again, because the books mention vibration in connection with rubber bands of various sizes. After these experiences pupils return to their books and finish reading about vibrations, how they make sounds, and how sounds travel in waves from place to place.

As the study proceeds, the pupils read further, study pictures and diagrams in their books, search for supplementary books on the subject of sound, pursue some of the experiences described in the books, follow up some of their own experiments, and do other things to find information. An important skill for a teacher is that of getting into books when necessary and getting out of them when not. It is getting stuck in books that is bad. Bibliographies provide an extensive list of books of a supplementary nature. These books often supply the exact material needed, and should be relied on heavily for their contribution to the science program.

Contrast the foregoing procedure with: "Today we are going to study sound. Open your books to page eighteen. Read the first six pages and then tell me what you have read." It is this kind of class activity that makes people say: "Don't use you science books as readers. Don't do so much reading *about* science." It is also the kind of precedure that makes children dislike science.

There is much to be said in favor of building a library of science books in addition to the basic text or texts: (1) They meet the needs of *individual* children; (2) they provide in-depth information; (3) children develop the habit of using many sources; (4) they permit pupils to work independently; and (5) they may serve with special effectiveness those pupils who have reading difficulty.

Reading, then, is one of the important tools to use in learning science. We can step up the effectiveness of reading if we keep in mind the following things:

1. Read with specific purposes—to check conclusions, to answer a question or find information helpful in solving a problem, to find additional information, to learn how to experiment, or for other definite reasons. Helping children to *be selective in recording and reporting only the material that is appropriate to solving problems* may be one of the most important skills children learn as they read in science.
2. Reading is often more effective if it is done from several supplementary sources that provide more information and different points of view. Communicating the results then becomes a part of the science experience, because not everyone has read the same material.
3. In science, pupils may come to a clearer realization that there is a real difference between materials that are read for fun and those read for information. (See the discussion on scientific attitude.)
4. (*See* pp. 24-7.) Selecting the material to be read may be done by both the pupils and teacher. Tables of contents, indexes, and other reference tools are necessary. Pupils may take notes on their reading. This may be an essential part of the "research reading" done in science. Selecting material on varying levels of difficulty is essential if reading is to function as a tool for learning. In any grade it is unusual for all pupils to be ready to read the science book written for that grade.
5. Don't overdo reading. Use if *after* firsthand experiences, not as beginning activity. Encourage children to read on their own, but don't use it as the major activity.
6. Selecting books for use by children should be done with considerable care. For example: They should be up-to-date and accurate; the illustrations should be accurate and helpful; the writing should be clear and appropriate to the subject matter; the entire work should be directed toward helping children achieve the objectives we have set up for the science program.

Let's also remember that reading opens new doors to children, that an interest in science developed in the classroom will stimulate children to read for pleasure—about spaceships, stars, and dinosaurs, for example. The possibilities are endless.

Again, what about the behavioral objectives? Here are examples of performances we look for. As a result of satisfactory experiences with reading when it is appropriate, children will be able to or inclined to:

locate printed materials pertinent to the problem;
evaluate material for accuracy;
select science books for recreational reading;

Recording firsthand observations made on a school-ground field trip is part of real and important ecology study. What is happening to the buds, flowers, and leaves? Making many records of such observations provides data for problem solving. (*Courtesy of Ronald Glick.*)

investigate many printed sources and check them against each other;
use table of contents, index, and other helps in locating materials.

OBSERVING

When children bring unfamiliar science "things" to school the wise teacher may say "Let's examine it carefully to see what we can find out." The senses are used to gather information that may be used in making discoveries. What can you find out by looking, feeling, listening, and using your other senses? The observations are assembled. Questions are raised and now there is some information to use as pupils plan other means of gaining more information. Effective science experiences often begin with thoughtful observation.

We hope children will become more skillful in observing, more accurate in reporting what they see, and more scientific in their interpretations. Observing is not a skill divorced from experimenting, reading, and the other ways to learn. It is an essential part of all activities that pupils engage in. As we shall see in the following examples, observing is prerequisite to predicting and inferring, to comparing and contrasting, and interpreting. Children should grow in ability to differentiate between the process of observation and the inferring that they may do as a result of the observations. The senses are used in the former—what is observed may then be used in making the inferences. Pupils can learn to become more accurate observers as they progress in their study of science and to see that observing and *using* the results of their observations are two different processes.

As children report what they see, the teacher and children will often discover variations in what individual children report even though they have all been observing the same objects or processes. It is often worthwhile to investigate the reasons for such differences. For example, each first grader was given a pea pod and asked to report the number of peas in their pods. The variation reported ranged from 3 to 9 peas. Investigation of the reports showed the following: (1) The number of peas in the pod do vary. (2) Joe and Joan ate some of their peas. (3) Rosa lost some of hers when she popped open the pod. (4) There were some undeveloped peas in some of the pods; should these be counted or not?

We often characterize a good observer as one who has learned to use his senses—to feel, see, hear, smell, and touch—purposefully. In a study of sound children *feel* vibrations of a piano, *see* the vibrating strings, and *hear* the sound. Careful use of the senses makes learning more vivid. Pupils observe to see changes in seeds as they sprout, to see changes in frog eggs as they hatch, to see what happens in an experiment.

In climates in which there are distinct changes in the seasons teachers often take pupils for walks to observe these changes. There is great variety in what is accomplished on these walks. Some of them produce little of value; others are truly eye openers. Keep in mind that young children cannot observe as many different things at one time as older pupils can. Trips for young children should be short. Third-grade pupils, therefore, may take a walk to observe the things that happen only to plants as cold weather comes. On the other hand, sixth-grade pupils on a similar trip may make observations about both plants and animals, assemble the data they have gathered and use them to make comparisons, to see relationships and to make inferences to interpret and sometimes to generalize.

The effectiveness of a walk may be greatly enhanced if pupils go to gather information to help solve a problem. Thus a third-grade class may take a walk to find out how plants change as the seasons change. To note *change,* pupils will need to make several trips, to observe carefully and to record their observations for future reference. Suppose the first trip is taken in early autumn. In many parts of the United States pupils may infer from their observations that some plants are dying; some are making seeds; some are losing their leaves; some are keeping their brown leaves, and that some plants, such as the evergreens, do not seem to change very much.

Pupils may bring the following things into their classroom to observe more closely: several kinds of seed pods (to examine them, to count the seeds, and to try to grow the seeds); specimens to show the different ways in which plants spread their seeds; twigs from trees (to find out where the buds are formed and how they are protected in winter); grass plants to see which part dies and which stays alive (some of the grass may be planted indoors to see whether it will grow if it is watered and kept at room temperature); twigs from trees that still have their leaves (to see how the leaves join the twig); evergreen twigs (to see if some of the needles are new and green and others old). Children may use magnifying glasses to see buds and seeds closely. Many of these observations may well be considered "open-ended" experiences, for they and others like them will lead to further investigations, provide opportunity for the development of individual interests, creative thinking, and continuing exploration.

After careful observing pupils may together prepare a record, commonly called an "experience chart," to record their observations. This chart, together with the materials observed, will be kept for future reference. Pupils may include drawings and perhaps photographs to stimulate more detailed observations, as well as for esthetic reasons.

A month or so later the same trip is taken to observe the same plants to gather more data on how plants are changing as the seasons change. A second record is made and kept with the earlier record and collected materials.

During the school year five or six trips are taken, each for the same purpose. Records are made. In May the final chart is prepared and pupils examine all their previous records. Now they are prepared to give a more complete answer to their original problem. They are beginning to see the importance of observing over a sufficiently long period of time before drawing conclusions. They are learning to observe carefully to be certain their reports will be accurate. They also see the sense of keeping carefully made records. They begin to see the difference between observations and inferences.

Contrast this with the common practice of mounting leaves on a chart labeled "Our Leaves," or collecting seed-dispersal samples and calling them "World Travelers."

As we have said, we must help children to distinguish between an *observation* and an *interpretation*. For example, a jar of water is exposed for a number of weeks. The level of water is marked on the jar. Children *observe* that the level is 6 inches deep at the beginning, $5\frac{1}{2}$ inches deep 1 week later, $4\frac{1}{2}$ inches 2 weeks later, and so on. An *interpretation* of the data is that the water level in the container dropped consistently over a two week period. Moreover, the interpretation they have placed on the data provides a basis for *prediction:* "What do you think will happen in the weeks to come?" This may lead to *hypothesizing*. "What really happened to the water?" They may say: "It went into the air." Their hypothesis may then lead to *experimenting*. Although we are not suggesting that the steps always take place in this order, they are the processes used in learning, and these steps often begin with observation.

As a result of many experiences in observation we can begin to see that children are able to:

identify and *describe* properties using their senses;
apply their information in the making of discoveries;
compare the results of their observations and attempt to generalize;
classify the objects they have observed according to similar and different characteristics;
describe conditions and characteristics they observe.

FIELD TRIPS USEFUL IN PROBLEM SOLVING[5]

The previous description of a field trip embodies the essentials for making a good excursion. Trips to the zoo, the museum, a greenhouse, the water-purification plant, a new building under construction, the park, and similar places are important in making science more meaningful. But taking a field trip with a group of fourth-graders may be a headache to the teacher and useless boondoggling for the children unless some of the following points are observed:

1. There should be a real reason for making the trip and it should be obvious to all. The trip should be a part of an on-going study.
2. There should be planning for safety, transportation, a suitable guide, time schedule, note taking, and other details before the trip.
3. The teacher, with a committee of pupils, might well make a preliminary trip to determine the suitability of the place, brief the guide about the nature and needs of the group, and make other necessary arrangements. Certainly the teacher should if possible make such a preliminary trip.
4. There should be group discussion about conduct and courtesy on the trip. Public relations are at stake every time children leave the school to make a visit. The adults who help children on the trip are quite reasonable in expecting interested attention from them. Groups not accustomed to making trips need to set up standards to insure a profitable visit. This does not mean that the discipline has to be so rigid as to spoil the fun. It means reasonable conduct, often determined by the pupils themselves, but taken seriously. Parent participation has been very effective in helping to insure a good field-trip experience.
5. Individuals and small groups may be designated to watch or listen for certain things and report them to the class. Specific responsibility of this kind often produces very good results.
6. Do not hurry children too much or plan for them to see more than they are able to take in at one exposure. Sometimes in our zeal to keep the group together we forget that children are individuals and cannot all react with the same speed or be interested at the same time in the same things. A hurried trip to see too many things may be as unsatisfactory as not going.
7. The follow-up conversations and the recording of information is important. Accurate reporting of what was seen and observed is essential, but the child who said to his field-tripping friend: "Don't look or you'll have to write!" had a point. Do not overdo the writing. Application of information to the specific problems and questions is best done in the classroom on return.

Potentially, "going to see" is one of the most enjoyable and instructive ways to learn. When teachers, pupils, and the adults in the place to be visited work together in planning and carrying out the excursion, the results are most likely to be those we hope for. Specific suggestions for field trips for special purposes are described in the B chapters. (See also "Resources to Investigate" in the B chapters for suggestions.)

[5]P.D. Hurd, *Teach Science through Field Studies* (Washington, D.C.: National Science Teachers Association, 1965), 11 pp.; and M.J. Brennan, "The Conceptual Field Trip," *Science and Children* (March 1970).

AUDIOVISUAL AIDS

As we have said earlier children cannot learn everything by firsthand or direct experiences. The reasons for this are obvious. There are many approaches to learning and audiovisual aids have some unique contributions to make to the process. In the past few years many new and excellent audiovisual materials have been produced. It is quite possible that there have been greater strides made in producing them than we have made in improving how we use them. Our discussion will deal first with the use of visuals in books and proceed to other more complicated aids.

Pictures

We have all had the experience of asking someone to explain something to us and having him make a sketch that supplements his explanation so well that when he is finished we understand him perfectly. We have also had the experience of reading a book and finding ourselves lost in a wordy explanation, only to come upon a sketch or drawing or map that illuminates the idea so that we understand completely.

Good teachers make extensive use of the illustrations in books (diagrams, drawings, photographs, graphs along with the captions) in their teaching. The use of the overhead projector with such illustrations is a great assistance in enlarging them and in making them available for all pupils at the same time. The resulting discussion helps to clear up misconceptions, supply data, and provide a source for making hypotheses.

Pictures that tell a sequential story are being used to good advantage by many teachers. These may come from magazines and newspapers and may be filed for ready use. Children can help collect them. They may show the story of seasonal changes in plant and animal life or any other idea where sequence is important.

Copies of the *National Geographic Magazine*, old copies of *Life*, and other magazines are excellent for use in identification of insects, birds, other animals, and rocks and minerals. Many large color pictures on science topics are now available commercially. Pictures and diagrams are especially useful when science classes are considering such questions as: "What does a volcano look like? What is it like inside a spaceship? What kinds of machines are used to build a skyscraper?" Pictures are most useful if they are organized so that they will help to supply information to help solve some specific problems. A vertical filing system, with all pictures filed upright, is indispensable if pictures are to be easily accessible to teacher and pupil. Many schools keep a central file of pictures which have been assembled cooperatively by the teachers and children.

Chalkboard

The *chalkboard* is available to every teacher. But, as is the case with so many obvious, close-at-hand possibilities, it is sometimes overlooked. A large drawing that illustrates an idea—for example, how the parts of a seed are located in relation to each other—is a very effective teaching aid. Colored chalk helps to show the ideas more clearly. Large chalkboard drawings make it possible for all children in a group to center attention on the same place while they discuss a problem. The use of the board is not limited to teachers. Pupils should be encouraged to make more extensive use of the chalkboard to explain their ideas. In so doing, they often find that their ideas are not quite clear or are perhaps inaccurate; consequently, they discover the need for more observation, experimentation, or reading. Such procedures should be considered as additional learning experiences, should be encouraged, and not embarrassing to children.

Observation of current practice in the use of chalkboards would indicate that the following points are essential, although they may seem obvious to some readers:

1. Make all diagrams and other illustrative material large enough to be seen by all pupils, and make the labels and other writing neat and legible.
2. Seat pupils where they can all see the board; do not clutter the board with too much material.
3. Organize the presentation so that it can be followed easily.
4. Use colored chalk when it will add to the ease of comprehension.
5. Start with a clean board.
6. Use rulers and other aids to produce a clear, easily understood drawing or table.
7. Sit down in the back of the room occasionally and look at the chalkboard work from the pupils' view.

Motion Pictures

Motion pictures are widely used but are not always as effective as they might be, perhaps because we expect them to teach by themselves. They don't do this any more than books do. In the hands of skillful teachers a film has unique contributions to make toward achieving our objectives for science teaching. Take, for example, the time-lapse sequence of seeds sprouting or buds opening. Here, as in many similar instances, *motion* is important. The film provides something that even firsthand experiences do not do. Films take children on vicarious field trips to places not otherwise available. By animation they show processes and phenomena (the circulation of air, water vapor, and so on) that produce more complete understanding or raise further questions. Their comprehensive scope makes them ideal for use in summarizing and extending the knowledge gained through firsthand experiences. Following these suggestions will help improve their use:

1. Select the film as carefully as you would a book. Children cannot comprehend a film that is too difficult for them any better than they can a high-level book. Any film indicated as appropriate for both high school and elementary school is almost certain to be useless at one level or the other, unless it is on some relatively nontechnical subject as, for example, life in a beaver colony.
2. The film selected should bear directly on the problem or problems under consideration if it is to give the best service.
3. Films should be previewed before they are used. This is done by the teacher, sometimes with the assistance of a committee of pupils, to plan for its wise use. If there is no time to preview a film its effectiveness may be limited. Film guides often provide excellent suggestions for the use of the movie.

4. Pupils should be prepared for seeing the film by arranging problems and questions in sequence as they are dealt with in the film, acquainting children with any unfamiliar vocabulary used, calling attention to difficult spots that need advance discussion, and to new material in the film that the class has never considered, and in other ways paving the way for good listening and looking.
5. There should always be a real reason for using a film. Just because there is a film in the school building about the Great Wall of China, the teacher is probably not justified in calling off work on "How we can make our community a better place to live in." Films are shown in science classes because they are often the most effective way to move in the direction of attaining objectives.
6. It may be important to show a film more than once. If it is especially long or difficult it may bc shown in parts, with discussion at the stopping places. The attention span of children may be a clue to how much of a film may be shown at any one time.
7. The follow-up discussion of a motion picture, like the follow-up of a field trip, is often the most important part of the film's use. It will be based on the "things to look for" or other preparations that were made before the showing.
8. Showing a film *without* the sound, with pupils supplying their own commentary has been done with success. Later, after discussion, the film may be shown *with* the sound.
9. There are many commercially prepared films available, and many schools keep a classified list of these along with descriptions that help teachers decide about their usefulness. Films shown on television shouldn't be overlooked. Advance notice of the times for showing them are often available and some schools provide such information.

Slides and Filmstrips

Many of the suggestions made for the use of films apply also to the use of slides and filmstrips, which can easily be projected and studied by individuals or small groups. Children can sometimes produce their own slides.

(*See* Ch. 10B.)

A filmstrip is a series of pictures on a length of film. The pictures usually make a continuous sequence. Using a filmstrip has certain advantages as well as disadvantages over using a motion picture. A filmstrip projector is easy to operate. Filmstrips are inexpensive; it is even possible to make them yourself. The filmstrip presents the pictures in a fixed sequence; this may be a disadvantage if that sequence is not suitable.

There are many excellent filmstrips available. Many are with sound comments that make them more useful. More learning probably takes place when children produce their own commentary after they have viewed the filmstrip.

Charts

Commercially produced charts for use in elementary-school science classes are frequently expensive and often not worth the price, although recently there is improvement in the preparation of such charts especially for this level. Charts that children themselves make are often more appropriate. For example, charts that children prepare to show animal classification or a chart made to show changes in temperature by weeks as fall changes to winter or to record other data are good learning activities. A chart can play an important part in a current project or serve as a summary.

Models

Expensive models also may not be worth their cost. For example, in the elementary school we are not usually concerned with the detailed study of parts of a flower or of the human ear. Therefore, an expensive model of these may not be needed. Pupil-made models may often serve the purpose. For example, a model of the solar system constructed to show relative sizes and distances can involve careful reading, accurate measuring, use of arithmetic, and considerable meaningful class discussion before it (*See* Ch. 7B.) is satisfactorily finished. The making of a visual aid in this case is a purposeful activity, as long as it does not take an undue amount of time. The finished product is useful, but so is the method of production. There are many other examples of model-making and construction that constitute worthwhile activity in elementary-school science classes. (*See* the B chapters for examples.)

Television and Radio

Recent monitoring of school telecasts by the authors indicates that much depends on the teaching ability and background of the television teacher. This in itself is not surprising. The success of any teaching depends on the same factor, but when the television teacher reaches thousands of children, poor teaching is a double tragedy not only for the viewing children but for the many teachers who may be inclined to copy the poor methods and techniques.

The monitoring indicated that in many cases there was only a little provision for the involvement of the viewing children and instead of complementing, supplementing, and enriching the science program in the schools it *was* the program—the same subject matter, the same time, and the same amount for all children. This situation raises considerable doubt as to the value of such experiences.

On the positive side children were exposed to field trips and explorations which they themselves, for one reason or another, were unable to engage in. They saw close-ups of movements of animals and got acquainted with animals and plants which they would otherwise not have seen. Sometimes there were unanswered questions and open-ended experiences presented that resulted in individual activities by some of the interested children.

At present the research into the results of television experiences remains inconclusive. More investigation is needed to determine what a good telecast should look like, how the television teacher can relate more closely to the audience, how the involvement of children can be built into the lessons, how the entire television program can fit more snugly into the on-going school program, and how the television teacher and the classroom teacher can have closer communication.

Television presentations are useful if they:

1. are designed to supplement and enrich the curriculum the school is following.
2. concentrate on doing and showing things that cannot be done as well or better in the confines of a classroom.
3. are presented on the level of comprehension and interest of the children.
4. demonstrate awareness of the objectives of science teaching.
5. use good teaching techniques.
6. provide manuals that describe the programs in advance and give educationally sound suggestions for using the program.
7. stimulate inquiry on the part of viewers and lead them into open-ended experiences.

Classroom reception must be good; the time of the telecast must fit into the school day; and the physical setup for classroom reception must be satisfactory. It must be more than a "tell-and-show" program. If these conditions exist, the key to satisfactory results is in the hands of the classroom teacher. He must approach the use of television with an open mind, and share the responsibility for improving the programs by responding with helpful and constructive criticism and suggestions. Lines of communication between television producers and teachers and the classroom users must always be open.

There is no doubt that television is a valuable teaching tool. It is not intended to replace the classroom teacher any more than any other teaching aid. If the programs are good they can do much toward furthering the objectives of science teaching.

We have been discussing the education television programs designed for and beamed into schools. In addition to such programs a considerable number of after-school and weekend science programs, both from local stations and on national hook-ups, may be used to advantage. At the beginning of the school year teacher and pupils may make special efforts to obtain from local sources the time, date, and subject matter of such programs. Suggestions for watching the programs and reporting on them may be devised by pupils and teachers.

The foregoing discussion of telecasts applies also to the use of radio programs, which must meet these same criteria; and the classroom conditions must meet the standards described. The rest is up to the teacher.

As in the case of television, radio broadcasts designed for the general public often include programs of scientific interest that may be used in elementary schools. Advance notice of these broadcasts is usually available and is indeed necessary if full use is to be made of them in the science program.

Our treatment of audiovisual and other aids to teaching in science is admittedly brief. It is intended to focus attention on the basic principle that intelligent use of any teaching aid in science requires careful preparation and thorough integration with the on-going science program.

We have explored classroom procedures and stressed their importance; now let us examine the science program and its organization.

(Courtesy of U.S. Department of the Interior.)

CHAPTER 4

ORGANIZING THE SCIENCE PROGRAM

Jerome Bruner,[1] in his book *The Process of Education,* includes a statement that has produced much discussion and controversy: "We begin with the hypothesis that any subject can be taught effectively in some intellectually honest form to any child at any stage of development." We do not have space here to trace Dr. Bruner's development of this idea and refer the reader to his book. But we do wish to call attention to a significant and sometimes overlooked statement made later in the same chapter: "We might ask, as a criterion for any subject taught in primary school, whether, when fully developed, it is worth an adult's knowing, and whether having known it as a child makes a person a better adult." In other words, we must not only ask whether a subject or part of a subject *can* be taught; we must also ask whether it is *worthwhile to teach it.* We hope you will keep this idea in mind as the selection and organization of science material is described.

THE NEW PROGRAMS

What guides shall we use in designing a science curriculum for the elementary school? The answers are varied but they all agree that: The content—facts, concepts, principles—and the methods of study should result in attaining the goals that have been set. If learning to use the processes of inquiry is the major objective, the program will emphasize this; if processes and content are considered equally important, this influences the selection of content and the methods of learning.

Descriptions of some of the National Projects are included as examples of modern science curricula. The presentations are necessarily brief. The references given in the footnotes present more detailed information in each case. The real flavor of any program comes through when teaching it; and we observe the behaviors of children, discuss their feelings, and evaluate their reactions and accomplishments. It is then that we see the significance of a program that is described as "individualized," "action centered," "process oriented," and so forth.

The descriptions included here tend to emphasize what is intended to happen with children in classrooms rather than historical material and accounts of preparation of material and methods of operation.

The many examples of lessons, units, or activities incorporated, described, or referred to in the B chapters are included to give more specific meaning to the general descriptions given here.

In the section following "The New Programs" a part entitled "Striking a Balance" indicates specific criteria for the selection of content and methods in developing an elementary-science program. Observations in many school systems indicate that they often use parts of many of the National Programs, adapt them to the local situations,

[1] J.S. Bruner, *The Process of Education* (New York: Random House, Inc., 1960).

and include them with locally-planned program material. The criteria listed are designed to be used in a variety of such situations.

CONCEPTUALLY ORIENTED PROGRAM IN ELEMENTARY SCIENCE (COPES)[2]

Project Objectives

Overall project purpose: To develop a K-6 science curriculum based on the "great ideas" or conceptual major schemes in science.

The ultimate goal of the COPES program is to help develop scientific literacy by developing an understanding of the nature of matter in terms of a few basic conceptual schemes. Each scheme is presented in a K-6 structured learning sequence with the purpose of contributing to this understanding. The concepts are organized in a hierarchy which is both scientifically and pedagogically logical. The order of the sequence is in the form of a "spiral" development.

The five conceptual schemes selected to form the core of the COPES curriculum are:

1. The Structural Units of the Universe: the notion that the universe is made of such units as atoms, molecules, crystals, cells, organisms, and so on, and that the study of such units is central to the understanding of nature.
2. Interaction and Change: the idea that the universe at every level—stars, planets, rock formations, living things, and so on—is constantly changing, and that force is the agent of change.
3. Conservation of Energy: the idea that the total amount of matter and energy in the universe remains constant.
4. Degradation of Energy: the concept that changes occur in such a way as to bring the universe closer to a final state in which it will have lost the ability to do useful work.
5. The Statistical View of Nature: the view that natural events can be predicted only by observing large numbers and by arriving at an average, analogous to a game of chance, where the overall outcome can be reliably predicted, but not the result of a single event.

[2] The general description is quoted from the project directors' (Dr. Morris H. Shamos and Dr. J. Darrell Barnard) account in *The Eighth Report of the International Clearinghouse on Science and Mathematics Curricular Developments 1972*, J. David Lockard, ed., a joint project of the American Association for the Advancement of Science and the Science Teaching Center, University of Maryland; and J.D. Barnard "COPES, A New Elementary Science Program," *Science and Children* (November 1971).

All five schemes are developed concurrently through the grades.

The COPES curriculum is action-centered. Almost all activities require exploration of a nonreading nature to be carried out by individuals or small groups of students. It is also a fundamental principle of COPES that as the major and supporting science concepts are being developed within the structured sequences, basic skills, where appropriate to the teaching materials, must be concurrently developed and refined. The learning, understanding, and appreciation of science cannot proceed properly without these basic skills (or processes of science). Although the materials are designed to involve children in various methods of investigation the primary objective is an understanding of basic concepts.

It is expected that COPES will form the major portion (about 80 percent of an elementary science curriculum, the remainder being devoted to applications or projects of the individual school's or teacher's choosing. The philosophy of the COPES program can be found in its descriptive brochure (March 1971), COPES Project, New York University, 4 Washington Place, New York, New York 10003.

Characteristics of the Project

Each learning activity should get children intellectually involved in ways that lead them personally to arrive at the concept. Children *must repeatedly use* such skills as analyzing, classifying, communicating, experimenting, interpreting, mathematical reasoning, measuring, observing, and predicting. Skills and concepts become inextricably involved in learning science. For example, children *observe* a variety of objects in arriving at the notion that color, size, odor, texture, and the like are properties of objects that can be used in classifying them into groups. They analyze their observations of a single property as it is exhibited among a group of similar objects, and from this they infer the *notion* of variability of the property among objects of a single property (*see* Observing, Chapter 4 and Chapters 12B and 15B).

In later grades children record their observations in graphic and tabular form to *communicate* the data collected and to analyze it. Measurement involves quantifying properties such as width, length, and so on. *Experimenting* is used in investigating chance events such as coin tossing. These and other processes are focused on the understandings involved in the five conceptual schemes.

The processes and schemes of COPES are an integral part of many of the problems developed in the B chapters. "Water Mix Experiments" in Chapter 16B and "Interactions in the Electric Circuits" in Chapter 19B are two examples of specific materials.

Present Commercial Affiliations

Teacher's Guides are being published and distributed by The Center for Field Research and School Services, New York University, 51 Press Building, Washington Square, New York, New York 10003.

SCIENCE CURRICULUM IMPROVEMENT STUDY (SCIS)[3]

Project Objectives

SCIS usually capsulizes its purposes as the development of scientific literacy. But it is important to delineate exactly what is meant by that term:

1. Sufficient knowledge and understanding of the fundamental concepts of both the biological and physical sciences for effective participation in twentieth-century life.
2. The development of a free and inquisitive attitude and the use of rational procedures for decision-making.

Characteristics of the Project

Content, Process, and Attitude Educators frequently distinguish among content, process, and attitude when they describe an educational program or evaluate its outcomes. The SCIS program combines these factors. Children are introduced to knowledge of scientific content through their experiences with diverse physical and biological materials. And, in the course of their investigations, they engage in observation, measurement, interpretation, prediction, and other processes.

The SCIS program helps children form positive attitudes toward science as they explore phenomena according to their own preconceptions. They learn to cope confidently with new and unexpected findings by sifting evidence and forming conclusions.

Interaction Central to modern science, and therefore also to the SCIS program, is the view that changes take place because objects interact in reproducible ways under similar conditions. Changes do not occur because they are preordained or because a "spirit" or other power within objects influences them capriciously. By *interaction* we refer to the relationship among objects or organisms that do something to one another, thereby bringing about a change. For instance, when a magnet picks up a steel pin we say that the magnet and the pin interact. The observed change itself, the pin jumping toward the magnet, is evidence of interaction. Children can easily observe and use such evidence. As they advance from a dependence on concrete experiences to the ability to think abstractly, children identify the conditions under which interaction occurs and predict its outcome.

[3] The project objectives are quoted from the director's (Dr. Robert Karplus) account in *The Eighth Report of the International Clearinghouse on Science and Mathematics Curricular Developments 1972* (see footnote 2 for details). For further descriptions see also R. Karplus and H.D. Their: "Science Teaching Is Becoming Literate," *Education Age* (January–February 1966); and B.S. Thomson and A.M. Voelker: "Programs for Improving Science Instruction in the Elementary School, SCIS," *Science and Children* (May 1970) and *Science Curriculum Improvement Study*, a descriptive brochure (Rand McNally and Company).

Major Scientific Concepts The four major scientific concepts we use to elaborate the interaction viewpoint are matter, energy, organism, and ecosystem. Children's experiences and investigations in the physical-science sequence are based on the first two; the last two provide the framework of the life-science sequence.

Matter—perceived as the solid objects, liquids, and gases in the environment—is tangible. It interacts with human sense organs, and pieces of matter interact with each other. Material objects may be described and recognized by their color, shape, weight, texture, and other properties. As children investigate changes in objects during their work in the SCIS physical-science program they become aware of the diversity of interacting objects and of their properties.

The second major concept is *energy*, the inherent ability of an animal, a flashlight battery, or other system to bring about changes in the state of its surroundings or in itself. Some familiar sources of energy are the burning gas used to heat a kettle of water, the unwinding spring that operates a watch, and the discharging battery in a pocket radio. The counterpart of an energy source is an energy receiver; and a very important natural process is the interaction between source and receiver that results in energy transfer.

The third concept is that of a living *organism*. An organism is an entire living individual, plant or animal. It is composed of matter and can use the energy imparted by its food to build its body and be active. The organism concept therefore represents a fusion of the matter and energy concepts; but it is also broader than these, so we identify and describe it separately.

As children observe living plants and animals in the classroom or outdoors they become aware of the amazing diversity of organisms and their life cycles. They observe how plants and animals interact with one another and with the soil, atmosphere, and sun in the vast network of relations that constitute life. The focus of the SCIS life-science program is the organism-environment relationship.

The study of life focused on organism-environment interaction leads to the *ecosystem* concept. Thinking about a forest may help you understand the ecosystem. A forest is more than an assemblage of trees. Living in the shade of the trees are shrubs, vines, herbs, ferns, mosses, and toadstools. In addition, the forest swarms with insects, birds, mammals, reptiles, and amphibians. A forest is all of these plants and animals living together. The animals depend on the plants for food and living conditions. The plants use sunlight, carbon dioxide, water, and minerals to make food to sustain themselves and other organisms in the forest. The interrelated plants, animals, sun, air, water, and soil constitute an ecosystem.

Process-oriented Concepts In addition to the scientific concepts described above, four process-oriented concepts are also extremely important. They are *property, reference frame, system,* and *model.* These concepts, together with others that relate to specific units, are at the heart of the processes of observing, describing, comparing, classifying, measuring, interpreting evidence, and experimenting.

A *property* is any quality that enables you to compare objects. Properties also enable you to describe or compare concepts.

Every description and comparison of natural or social phenomena reflects the observer's point of view or *frame of reference.* For the young child, who relates objects to himself rather than to one another, the discovery of other frames of reference is a challenge.

The basic concept, as included in the SCIS program, is simple: The position and motion of objects can be perceived, described, and recognized only with reference to other objects. When you say: "The car is at the south end of the parking lot," you describe the location of the car relative to the parking lot.

The third process-oriented concept is that of a *system,* which SCIS defines as a group of related objects that make up a whole. It may include the battery and circuits that make up an operating pocket radio, or it may consist of a seed and the moist soil in which it is planted. The system concept stems from the realization that objects or organisms do not function in isolation but exist in a context while interacting with other objects or organisms.

The fourth process-oriented concept, the scientific *model,* may be illustrated by the example of an automatic vending machine that dispenses candy. You insert a coin into a slot, push one of several buttons, and out falls a particular candy bar. You could imagine that the coin unlocks the buttons and that a button pushes your candy off its shelf and down the chute. Such an imagined system would be a model. A scientific model is a mental image of a real system to which you assign certain parts or properties that you cannot see directly. The successful model provides a possible explanation of how the system functions, but it may not give an accurate description of what really happens in the system. Usually the model is simpler than the real system it represents.

Scientific models permit children to relate their present observations to their previous experiences with similar systems. Models satisfy the children's need for thinking in concrete terms. Models also lead to predictions and new discoveries about the system being investigated. You may, for instance, make predictions and test your candy-machine model by pushing a different button or by pushing two buttons at once.

Present Publishing Affiliations

Publisher of the final edition units of the SCIS program is Rand McNally & Company, P.O. Box 7600, Chicago, Illinois 60680.

ELEMENTARY SCIENCE STUDY (ESS)[4]

Project Objectives

ESS hopes to enrich every child's understanding, rather than to create scientific prodigies or direct all children toward scientific careers. Rather than beginning with

[4] The general description is quoted from the project director's (Christopher Hale) account in *The Eighth Report of the International Clearinghouse on Science and Mathematics Curricular Developments 1972* (see footnote 2 for details). *See also* R.E. Rogers and A.M. Voelker: "Programs for Improving Science Instruction in the Elementary School, ESS," *Science and Children* (January–February 1970).

a discussion of basic concepts of science, ESS puts physical materials into children's hands from the start and helps each child investigate through these materials the nature of the world around him. It incorporates both the spirit and the substance of science in such a way that the child's own rich world of exploration becomes more disciplined, more manageable, and more satisfying. Careful attention is given to all materials used so that all equipment looks like materials which are normally accessible to children in their own environment and not imposingly "scientific."

Characteristics of the Project and Materials

There is little or no sequence development in the ESS program. There is less emphasis on specific objectives and less attempt at formal evaluation than in many of the other programs. The emphasis is not on the teaching of a series of science concepts but rather on providing children with experiences such as tadpole development, the habits of mealworms, the ways of lighting bulbs with batteries, and so on (see examples indicated later).

The materials used with children are selected to motivate and to raise questions, and children are encouraged to use the materials themselves either in small groups or individually to find answers to their questions in their own ways. Through these procedures children are encouraged to discuss their observations and findings. The early experiences may be characterized as "messing about." Such, more or less, unstructured experiences permit children to learn different things at different rates, to enjoy the learning experiences, and to learn more "because they are doing what they want to do instead of what someone else wants them to do." As Philip Morrison, a member of the original ESS steering committee, has stated: "The particular key which opens a new door for a particular child is not predictable. Therefore our curriculum is not at all to be cut into separate disciplines, fenced off by frontiers of technique and history." The teacher's role under such circumstances is one of guide, consultant, and motivator.

Many units have been produced, the majority of which are for grades four, five, and six. There are some for earlier grades, a few for seventh and eighth grades. As you would expect from the foregoing description, the materials emphasize "active involvement, freedom to pursue one's interests, imagination, individuality." They are aimed at "developing self-directing, autonomous and self-actualizing individuals."

Reference to the content and methods of many of the units are made in the following B chapters: 6B "Rocks and Charts"; 7B "Where Is the Moon?"; 10B "Curious Gerbils," "Growing Seeds," "Eggs and Tadpoles," "Pond Water," "Small Things," "Behavior of Mealworms," "Earth Worms"; 11B "Mosquitos"; 15B "Mystery Powders"; 19B "Batteries and Bulbs"; 20B "Whistles and Strings"; 21B "Light and Shadows."

Present Commercial Affiliation

Webster Division, McGraw-Hill Book Company, Manchester Road, Manchester, Missouri 63011.

SCIENCE—A PROCESS APPROACH (SAPA)—

An Elementary-School Science Curriculum Program Developed by the Commission on Science Education of the American Association for the Advancement of Science[5]

Project Objectives

Science—A Process Approach is designed to present instruction which is intellectually stimulating and scientifically authentic. It is based on a belief that the scientific approach to gaining knowledge of man's world has a fundamental importance in the general education of every child.

There are a number of ways of conceiving of the meaning of "process" as exemplified in Science—A Process Approach. First, an emphasis on process implies a corresponding de-emphasis on specific science "content." The content is there—the children examine and make explorations of solid objects, liquids, gases, plants, animals, rocks, and even moon photographs. But, with some few notable exceptions, they are not asked to learn and remember particular facts or principles about these objects and phenomena. Rather, they are expected to learn such things as how to infer internal mechanisms in plants, how to make and verify hypotheses about animal behavior, and how to perform experiments on the actions of gases.

A second meaning of process centers on the idea that what is taught to children should resemble what scientists do—the "processes" that they carry out in their own scientific activities. Scientists do observe, and classify, and measure, and infer, and make hypotheses, and perform experiments. How have they come to be able to do these things? Presumably, they have learned to do them over a period of many years by practicing doing them. If scientists have learned to gain information in these ways, surely the elementary forms of what they do can begin to be learned in the early grades. This line of reasoning does not imply the purpose of making everyone a scientist. Instead, it puts forward the idea that understanding science depends on being able to look on and deal with the world in the ways that the scientist does.

The third and perhaps most widely important meaning of process introduces the consideration of human intellectual development. From this point of view processes are in a broad sense "ways of processing information." Such processing grows more complex as the individual develops from early childhood onward. There is a "progressive intellectual development within each process category. As this development proceeds it comes to be increasingly interrelated with corresponding development of other processes." The following is a description of the sequence of development:

Observing Beginning with identifying objects and object-properties, this sequence

[5]Quoted from the project director's (John R. Mayor) account in *The Eighth Report of the International Clearinghouse on Science and Mathematics Curricular Developments 1972* (see footnote 2 for details), and *Science—A Process Approach: Purposes, Accomplishments, Expectations,* AAAS Misc. Pub. No. 67-12 (September 1967). Copies are available from the association on request. *See also Science—A Process Approach,* Xerox Education Sciences, 1972.

proceeds to the identification of changes in various physical systems, the making of controlled observations, and the ordering of a series of observations.

Classifying Development begins with simple classifications of various physical and biological systems and progresses through multistage classifications, their coding and tabulation.

Using Numbers This sequence begins with identifying sets and their members, and progresses through ordering, counting, adding, multiplying, dividing, finding averages, using decimals, and powers of ten. Exercises in number-using are introduced before they are needed to support exercises in the other processes.

Measuring Beginning with the identification and ordering of lengths, development in this process proceeds with the demonstration of rules for measurement of length, area, volume, weight, temperature, force, speed, and a number of derived measures applicable to specific physical and biological systems.

Using Space-Time Relationships This sequence begins with the identification of shapes, movement, and direction. It continues with the learning of rules applicable to straight and curved paths, directions at an angle, changes in position, and determinations of linear and angular speeds.

Communicating Development in this category begins with bar graph descriptions of simple phenomena, and proceeds through describing a variety of physical objects and systems and the changes in them, to the construction of graphs and diagrams for observed results of experiments.

Predicting For this process, the developmental sequence progresses from interpolation to extrapolation in graphically presented data to the formulation of methods for testing predictions.

Inferring Initially, the idea is developed that inferences differ from observations. As development proceeds, inferences are constructed for observations of physical and biological phenomena, and situations are constructed to test inferences drawn from hypotheses.

Defining Operationally Beginning with the distinction between definitions which are operational and those which are not, this developmental sequence proceeds to the point where the child constructs operational definitions in problems that are new to him.

Formulating Hypotheses At the start of this sequence, the child distinguishes hypotheses from inferences, observations, and predictions. Development is continued to the stage of constructing hypotheses and demonstrating tests of hypotheses.

Interpreting Data This sequence begins with descriptions of graphic data and inferences based upon them, and progresses to constructing equations to represent data, relating data to statements of hypotheses, and making generalizations supported by experimental findings.

Controlling Variables The developmental sequence for this "integrated" process begins with identification of manipulated and responding (independent and dependent) variables in a description or demonstration of an experiment. Development proceeds to the level at which the student—being given a problem, inference, or hypothesis—actually conducts an experiment, identifying the variables, and describing how variables are controlled.

Experimenting This is the capstone of the "integrated" processes. It is developed through a continuation of the sequence for controlling variables, and includes the interpretation of accounts of scientific experiments, as well as the activities of stating problems, constructing hypotheses, and carrying out experimental procedures.

While these processes are emphasized and used throughout this text the specific examples from SAPA are referred to in Chapter 10B "Growth of Mold on Bread" and "Living Things Are Composed of Cells"; Chapter 15B "Solids, Liquids and Gases—States of Matter"; and Chapter 19B "Conductors and Nonconductors."

Characteristics of the Project

The identification and the acquisition of skills in the processes of science is the primary objective of the program, which is arranged sequentially as determined by a hierarchy of these processes (*see* description earlier). The science content used to achieve this overall goal is selected from various fields and includes mathematical content when needed. The objectives for the various exercises are stated in terms of the pupil behavior which can be observed as the result of participation in the activity. Pupil achievement and progress are a built-in part of the program.

In addition to the emphasis on process, two other characteristics distinguish SAPA from the other programs:

1. Each lesson is prescribed, with the teacher "stating the problem or by assisting the children in identifying a problem" . . . giving the children "directions and hints to guide them in finding solutions" . . . , followed at the end with a "group appraisal problem" which provides a "measure of how well the group has mastered the skills and concepts specified as the expected learning outcomes for the exercise."
2. Since the emphasis is on the acquiring of process skills, the science content may vary from lesson to lesson; from day to day there may be little or no subject-matter continuity. The fact that children might be classifying leaves one day would not mean that they would go on with their leaf study the next. There is a sequence and development, but primarily it is that of process skills.

Present Commercial Affiliation

Xerox Education Sciences, 555 Gotham Parkway, Carlstadt, New Jersey 07072.

COMMON FEATURES OF THE PROJECTS

While each of the projects has distinctive characteristics there are certain common features. These may be useful guides when we are considering programs and methods of instruction. The role of the teacher becomes that of a guide to learning rather than a fountain of knowledge for children.

Scientists have been actively involved in most of the projects in determining content, methods of instruction, and general development.

There is emphasis on involvement on the part of the learner. Children are involved in the planning. The emphasis is on direct experiences.

New subject matter not previously included in the elementary-school curriculum has been introduced.

In many cases there are specifically designed laboratory materials and equipment.

The emphasis in the projects is experimental. Methods are tried out and revised in the light of findings.

In many of the projects concepts of a more abstract nature are introduced earlier in the learning experiences of children.

There is less emphasis on subject matter as such and more emphasis on processes—on learning how to learn—on emphasizing discovery, creative and critical thinking.

The experiences are characterized as being "open-ended." That there may be several solutions and answers and the activities may lead into other related activities.

There is emphasis on exactness. Many projects stress a quantitative approach and emphasize the development of mathematics skills.

OTHER PROJECTS

The four national projects which we have selected to develop in detail are by no means all of the significant projects. The Minnesota Mathematics and Science Teaching Project (Minnemast),[6] the University of Illinois Elementary School Science Project,[7] the Intermediate Science Curriculum Study (ISCS),[8] and many other programs are significant but have not been included because of space limitations.

[6] R.B. Ahrens: "Minnemast—The Coordinated Science and Mathematics Program," *Science and Children* (February 1965).

[7] "Astronomy for Grades Five through Eight, University of Illinois Elementary School Science Project," *Science and Children* (February 1965).

[8] *See* "Newsletters," the Director, 507 South Woodward Avenue, Tallahassee, Florida 32304.

STRIKING A BALANCE

It is apparent that, as Philip Morrison of the Massachusetts Institute of Technology has stated: "Method is meaningless in the absence of subject matter, stuff to work on," and that "subject matter is sterile if it is not permeated with questions about how, and why we bother to find out." What then are the essential ingredients in designing an elementary-science program? Consider the following:

Is there consideration given to the complete scope of the science program, nursery school through grade 12?

The elementary-school curriculum should, in fact must, be decided partially on the basis of a nursery-school through high-school sequence. Changes in the junior and senior high-school program must be taken into consideration in formulating the program in the earlier years. We must keep in mind that school does not stop at the end of grade 6, even though we in the elementary school sometimes act as though it did. It does not start at grade 7 either, as some junior high-school teachers seem to suppose.

The best science programs are planned by groups representing all grade levels. Each year more school systems attempt such planning. When primary, intermediate (or middle school), and secondary school teachers work together in deciding content, in selecting books, and in determining ways to work a better program results. Under such circumstances there is less likely to be disturbing overlapping or duplication of subject matter. The attitude of all teachers concerned is almost sure to be better. As teachers at different levels learn more about the work of teachers at other levels, they grow in understanding of the problems of these teachers and in ability to fit their own work into the total sequence.

Are the purposes and content of other subject matter areas considered?

The subject-matter content of the other elementary-school subjects, notably social studies and mathematics, also influence the selection of the content of science. While these areas are distinctly different disciplines, in some instances they relate closely to science; in others they should exist independently (*see* "Organizing for Instruction" pages 71–75 for further discussion).

Is there individualization of instruction? Are there opportunities for children to work on their own, with adequate materials, and to proceed at their own pace without pressure?

While we nod agreeably when we are told of the differences that exist in children, we too often attempt to teach and treat them all alike. Various pressures, our haste to "cover" material, and so forth are probably responsible for this. Especially in science, where there is ample opportunity for working on individual investigations, we can use these opportunities more wisely. Increased emphasis on laboratory work is a step in this direction; more available material is also helpful.

Are there opportunities for children to use science in the investigation of problems that are of real concern to them?

The nearer we come to identifying problems the answers to which make a difference to children the more nearly we come to achieving our objectives. Relevance is indeed something to be taken into account. Whenever each of us examines and tries to evaluate his educational experience it becomes increasingly evident that the experiences that are meaningful are the ones we remember and feel good about.

Is the program flexible enough to permit "science excursions" into the unplanned, the unexpected, the unusual, the unknown (to the teacher and children alike) *for capturing "teachable moments"?*

Experienced teachers know that unplanned-for-times are often the most productive, and the curriculum that does not permit time for exploring such avenues cannot be as effective as it should be (*see* "Organizing for Instruction," pages 71–75 for further discussion).

Does the organization and selection of content and processes take into account what we know about how children learn?

If we subscribe to the teaching of Piaget, if we study children intelligently, if we apply our knowledge of how children grow and develop we are much less likely to select irrelevant material, and employ inappropriate methods of instruction (*see* also "Observing Children," pages 99–100).

Are there built-in procedures of evaluation to permit needed changes?

Accountability is not just a new word in educational jargon. More and more emphasis is being placed on evaluating on the basis of how well we are accomplishing our objectives. Our behavioral objectives indicate what we hope children will be able to do as a result of their experiences. Constant attempts to determine our successes (and failures) are essential and we must continue to make changes in light of our discoveries. Programs should always be considered tentative and thus subject to revision (*see* "Evaluating Our Teaching," pages 103–104).

Are there varied kinds of experiences to provide for individual needs, interests, and capacities of children?

It makes sense to consider interests and capacities of children if we are planning a curriculum for them. If science subject matter is interesting and challenging to children they will want to learn it; and if they want to learn it they will tackle the problems relating to it. Children need to have their curiosities and intellectual needs satisfied as they pursue their interests.

Interest is a tremendous motivating factor. It manifests itself through the books children choose, the things they discuss, their hobbies. School experiences should broaden and deepen these interests. It is often caught from others, especially from teachers who have curiosity. Interests differ widely among children in kind, quality, intensity, and longevity. It cannot therefore be our only criterion for subject matter selection.

Is the specific environment of children—supermarkets and factories, roadways and automobiles, earthworms and robins, lawns and sidewalks—used as a laboratory for learning science?

The environment of children supplies us with information on which to base content selection. The local environment is important. What are the local problems that must be solved in making the home, school, and community safe, healthy places in which to live? Are there problems of soil erosion, weather forecasting, air and water pollution? Are there special scientific activities going on in the community? Is the program sensitive to community needs and wishes? What is the relationship of the science program in helping solve inner-city problems?

Then, too, the world environment of children must be taken into account. The air age, the atomic age, the space age—the modern scientific world in general—must be understood if men and women are to become intelligent citizens of the world.

Does the curriculum include material from the many areas of science subject matter?

As we indicated earlier each year of the science sequential development may include problems from various areas of science—biology, chemistry, physics, astronomy—and/or the integrating ideas among them (*see also* the last item of this list).

Does the program recognize the talents and interests of the teachers who are involved?

None of the programs can be successful if we do not consider those who are to teach it. The best teachers continue to grow in interest in their scientific environment and expand their knowledge of it (*see* "Teachers Background," Chapter I).

Does the science program take into account the school organization?

An open school, a team-teaching situation, a school program designed around individualized instruction, a middle school, a departmentalized instruction program, a school dedicated to the self-contained classroom concept—each of these, and there are others, influence the selection of content, and methods of instruction and teaching cannot be effective if they are not considered.

Is provision made for the poor reader or nonreader, as well as the good reader?

As we have indicated elsewhere children cannot develop all the generalizations, skill in using processes, and other objectives through firsthand activities. Reading still must constitute a sensible part of their experiences, and reading material must be supplied that fits the many and varied needs of children. The desire to improve reading skills often stems from the desire to know more about the science world (*see* "Reading to Find Out," Chapter 3).

Are there themes and threads of subject matter areas evident in the curriculum?

Patterns, intending to acquaint pupils with subject-matter material as they progress year to year, consist of conceptual schemes or important basic principles such as the following:

1. Under ordinary conditions, matter can be changed but not annihilated or created.
2. Under ordinary conditions energy can be changed or exchanged, but not annihilated.
3. There is an interchange of materials and energy between living things and their environment.
4. The organism is a product of its heredity and environment.
5. The universe and its component bodies are constantly changing.
6. Living things have changed over the years.[9]

Other pervasive themes, such as space, time, change, adaptation, variety, inter-

[9] P.F. Brandwein: *The Teaching of Science: Elements in a Strategy for Teaching Science in the Elementary School* (Cambridge, Mass.: Harvard University Press, 1962), pp. 132–136.

relationships, and interaction of forces have been widely used as the bases for selecting material for the elementary-science curriculum.

These major schemes or areas may be broken down into teachable units, each building on another. Each year material from each of the major schemes is included. The development of skills in problem-solving or in the processes of science investigation in such programs as these comes as the pupils learn the subject matter.[10]

SUMMARY

These points indicate certain common features regarding science programs which are based on:

1. A combination of factors such as needs of children, their growth and development, their environments, the content of science, and the total school program.
2. The development of skills and processes essential to scientifically literate adults.
3. The broad themes of science.

Each of these represents an emphasis which influences curriculum makers, textbook writers, and by all means classroom teachers.

ORGANIZING FOR INSTRUCTION

We have given some attention to the criteria for selecting subject matter. How now shall this body of subject matter be organized for study? There are several factors to be considered, and again we examine the goals. If we are to bring about comprehension of broad conceptual schemes of science, help pupils grow in ability to use the processes of inquiry, and accomplish our other objectives we must make definite provision in the program to include sufficiently challenging and appropriate material. If we are to satisfy children's curiosity and broaden their interests and strengthen their attitudes, they themselves should have some voice in the how, when, and where of science experiences.

Can the material be built and organized entirely around the questions children ask, the things they bring in, or other incidental happenings? No. Such an incidental science program is likely to be inadequate and disorganized.

While some of our best teaching may result when incidental problems are raised because of some local happening, current reading, or because of science material that children bring in, a well-rounded program nevertheless cannot be achieved *only* through such incidental teaching. Nor can a good program be built if we *ignore* these incidental learning situations. How, then, can we allow for them and still have an organized program?

[10] *See also* the National Science Teachers Association position statement, "School Science Education for the 70's" in *The Science Teacher* (November 1971).

Many schools have solved this problem of organization, in part at least, through including two types of experiences in their programs and through operating within a flexible general framework. Incidental learning may, for example, include a brief consideration of sea shells, or it may center around a new type of airplane, or around a recent or anticipated eclipse. Sometimes, after the short initial discussion, an "investigation committee" studies the problem further and brings a report to the class, finds reading material for interested pupils, or arranges an exhibit of pictures on the bulletin board. If, on the other hand, the incidental experience turns out to be of more than passing interest, the schedule is flexible enough to permit a shift in plans. In many instances, with careful planning this experience may result in attaining many of the same objectives as a planned experience. Frequently the incidental experience can be geared into the planned experience.

Now let us be more specific about organizing an area of subject matter such as astronomy, which is commonly included in the science programs of the elementary school. We need to provide continuity of both subject matter and process throughout the elementary grades.

In the early grades (prekindergarten, kindergarten, and grades 1, 2, and 3) pupils will have many and varied experiences with measuring lengths of shadows, watching the changes of seasons and their effect on living things, observing the moon or the Big Dipper and reporting what they have seen, and taking note of the varying lengths of days and nights. An especially appropriate problem for prekindergarten to grade 3 might be: "How is the sun important to us?" In this connection pupils may come to know that: The sun is very hot. The sun is very large. It looks small because it is so far away. The sun keeps us warm. It helps plants to grow. It helps to make us healthy. The earth travels around the sun.[11]

Children will observe common phenomena such as the effect of light on the growth of plants. There will be opportunity to measure and record the temperatures at different times, predict and infer, and communicate findings on the basis of observations. (Detailed examples of such experiences, along with some typical problems to solve, will be found on the opening pages of Chapter 7B.)

In later grades (4, 5, and 6) pupils may spend some time studying about the sun's family—the solar system. They will add to their knowledge of the sun and other members of the solar system. Their experiences will build on those of the earlier grades. They will learn details about the planets, comets, meteoroids, meteors, meteorites, and the moon.[12] They will discuss causes of day and night and observe the seasons change and learn about eclipses. They will perform experiments with controlled variables, formulate hypotheses, and see examples of how scientists discover. They will delve into the methods used by astronomers to make their discoveries. (*See* Chapter 7B for descriptions of activities and possible problems).

In the more advanced grades the picture enlarges; and pupils study the relationship between the solar system and the universe; learn the cause of seasons and tides; study stars and their distances, size, and composition; study the Milky Way and other galaxies;

[11] G.O. Blough and I. DePencier: *How the Sun Helps Us* (New York: Harper & Row, Publishers, 1972).

[12] B.M. Parker: *The Sun and Its Family* (New York: Harper & Row, Publishers, 1970).

learn about novae, nebulae; and discuss the possibilities of whether or not there are other solar systems.[13] They will study in more detail how scientists make discoveries. Here again, these experiences enlarge on those developed in earlier grades and expand to include new material and more complicated processes of discovery. (*See* Chapter 8B.)

It is apparent that each time an area of science (in this case astronomy) is encountered, the new work builds on that previously experienced, adds to it, and increases in difficulty. The generalizations become more complex as the pupils progress; the processes of discovery become more involved. There is only enough repetition to make a connection, not enough to cause pupils to lose interest. The same overall objectives hold for all levels. On each level pupils should be left with the idea that there is still more interesting material to learn; indeed, that there are still many things that scientists themselves have not discovered. *And we hope that teaching proceeds in such a way that pupils will want to learn more.*

As has been pointed out earlier *all* pupils will not arrive at the same generalizations, nor will they all understand them in equal depths. The ideas given are for general guidance. Younger children need more concrete experiences. As they grow and develop, they can begin to deal with more abstract ideas.

We have indicated briefly a possible organization of subject matter (astronomy) to bring about an understanding of principles and generalizations and to develop processes of discovery. We have said little about organization to achieve the other objectives of science teaching. But we assume that if the teaching is good, no matter

[13] B.M. Parker: *Beyond the Solar System* (New York: Harper & Row, Publishers, 1970).

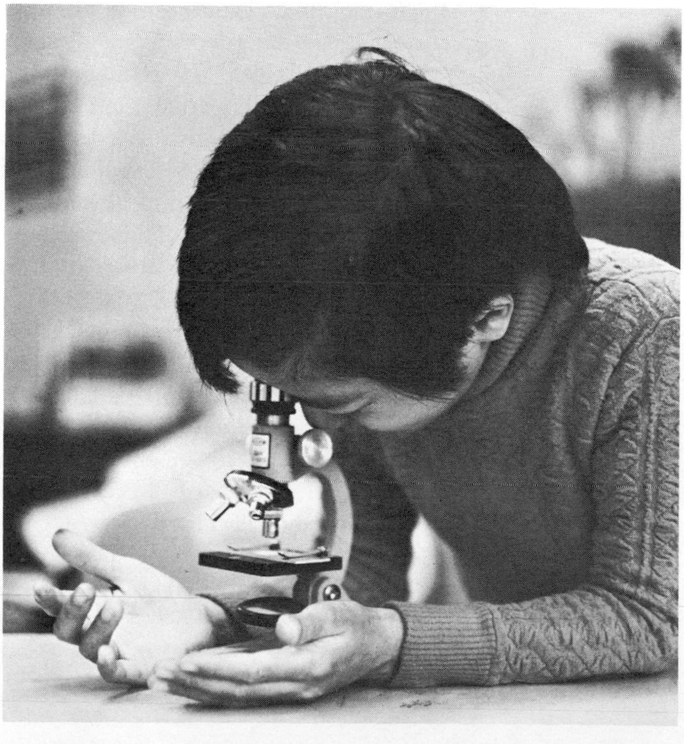

Learning to observe more closely helps to supply data. Examining mold, pond-water life, or an onion skin are examples of such observations. (*Courtesy of Phyllis Marcuccio.*)

what organization of subject matter is followed, there will be continuous emphasis on the processes indicated earlier, on the development of attitudes, and on interest and appreciation. We can assume this, however, only if we *intend* to provide experiences that will attain these objectives.

There is general agreement that science is an essential part of any effective elementary program and time must be allocated for it. Science often seems to fuse naturally with other learnings; usually, however, it stands more or less by itself. Let us examine briefly the implications involved in this statement.

If you review our original statement of goals you will recall that we discussed the relationship of science to the total school program and indicated that it contributes in many ways to the achievement of our overall goals. For this reason it is sometimes considered in relation to the other curriculum subjects, especially social studies.[14]

As we indicated earlier sometimes these subject-matter areas need each other. Sometimes they do not. How can we tell? One clue appears when we examine our overall objectives. If, in order to achieve them we need subject matter from both social studies and science, we put them together. Otherwise we do not. To do anything else may well distort the aims, pull in inappropriate subject matter from both areas, and result in a hodgepodge.

An example of sensible fusion of science with social studies occurs when pupils work on a problem like "What are the important ecological problems in our state and how can they be solved?" This overall problem may break down into others such as "Why did the rains last spring do so much damage in our community?" "Why must we conserve our water supply and how can we do it?" In attempting to solve these and related inquiries we consider soil, water, wild life, and mineral and human resources. We need a considerable amount of science information in order to understand the formation and composition of soils, the action of wind and water on soil and other materials, the interdependence of animal and plant life, and so on. But these cannot be fully comprehended without a study of modern man's relationship and responsibility to his world. Each learner must see the problem within his own frame of reference, and see how his actions relate to those of others. The scientific and social aspects of the problems of ecology are closely related. If we are to achieve the goals we need the information, skills, and attitudes offered by both subject-matter areas; it makes sense to combine them. There are other, similar situations.

There are also many situations in which these two subject areas do not fuse easily. In these cases we may not achieve the objectives of either if we insist on considering both areas together. For example, in a study of the westward expansion in social studies, the fact that the progress of peoples to the West in our early history was hampered by bad weather conditions is hardly a compelling reason for launching a study of weather. To do so gets off the track, and the small study of weather pulled in will be inadequate to answer children's real concerns about the current weather in their surroundings. Weather is a great influence in the children's lives. They are interested in how weather is caused, how it changes, and how these changes can be forecast.

[14] National Council for the Social Studies: "Science and Social Studies in Today's Elementary School," *Twenty-seventh Yearbook, Science and the Social Studies* (1956–1957), pp. 186–199.

The westward movement is an important part of the history of our country. But the two do not need each other to achieve the objectives set up for the study of either one. Forcing them together damages them both.

Astronomy, for example, needs little or no social studies to achieve its objectives. This science subject matter stands on its own, although a discussion of former beliefs and superstitions of people with respect to the sun, moon, and stars may be of value in enhancing our present understandings.

One important aspect of the fusion of science and social studies lies in the total objectives for both of them. In both areas we are concerned with learning how to use processes of discovery and how to foster social and scientific attitudes. We are concerned with producing responsible, intelligent citizens. Here there is a real relationship. Our processes of discovery in both areas are similar; they reinforce each other.

Health education and science may sometimes profit by being fused. For example, in health education, when the problems of diet and foods are being considered, the "horse sense" of eating certain foods in proper amounts will be more obvious if we treat some of the aspects of diet as more or less pure science. When pupils learn that their growing bones contain the chemical elements of calcium and phosphorus, they understand more readily the importance of drinking milk which also has both these elements.

Science provides the biological basis for teaching sex education. It is in such cases as these that science and other areas, if they are considered together, benefit each other and increase the contributions to children's learning.

In the processes of discovery in science it is often essential that pupils use the skills of the language arts in communication. There is a definite opportunity for fusion. If it seems necessary and desirable to read, we read. If writing and speaking are useful we use them. If it becomes necessary to use art skills we employ them, but we do not use any area merely to be able to say that we have "integration."

An easy way to kill interest in science is to require pupils to do unnecessary writing. The idea of writing up each experiment performed in detail is guaranteed to dampen enthusiasm. So, too, is adding technical science vocabulary to the spelling list. Some common science words may be learned through use and reading context, but at age eight or nine it is hardly important that children learn to spell photosynthesis. (Some of the activities in the B chapters give specific examples of integrating other study areas with science.)

BEGINNING TO TEACH

No matter how the science program is organized or what methods are employed, the teacher has an important leadership role. This does not mean that he makes all the decisions. He guides, plans beforehand, outlines general directions, and knows the possibilities. In this picture there are still opportunities for children to make decisions—of the kind they are capable of making—to proceed within the framework of the overall plan. (See details of lesson and unit planning in Chapter 5.)

There are certain first steps which the teacher will take in planning. Let us suppose that he wants to teach some concepts about evaporation and condensation of water in the third or fourth grade. There are several things the teacher may do to prepare himself. If he lacks information he should read subject matter on the grade level he will teach, as well as material on a more advanced level. If he is inexperienced, he may do some of the simple experiments suggested in the books and investigate some of the local resources available. In short, he should do some of the things suggested in Chapter 9B. He may investigate other possible sources of information—audiovisual aids, maps, bulletins. Then he may carefully write down some of the specific goals that this experience with the phenomena of evaporation and condensation might achieve in terms of behaviors. In so doing, the teacher will keep in mind the general and specific objectives of the total elementary-school program, as well as those for teaching science in the elementary school. He sees these ideas in a broad context of interrelation of subject matter. The teacher's intentions for this unit might be something like these:

1. To provide experiences that will help pupils formulate simple science principles and generalizations about the evaporation and condensation of water.
2. To help pupils apply these principles and generalizations in interpreting events that happen around them.
3. To provide opportunity for using skills in the process of discovery.
4. To broaden children's interests in the everyday phenomena in their environment.

In terms of behaviors expected, he might note that as a result of participating in the experiences, experiments, observations, and other activities pupils should be able to:

construct statements of observations in the area of evaporation and condensation.

ask questions about evaporation and condensation in their environment.

demonstrate by the use of materials and apparatus some of the principles and generalizations.

differentiate between observations and inferences.

describe illustrations involving evaporation and condensation from their environment that apply their findings.

devise some original experiences and experiments to test their hypotheses and describe the implications.

apply the generalizations arrived at to other phenomena.

Now the teacher has committed himself. He has pledged himself to use these aims as a guide from now on. Unless he takes his aims seriously he is wasting time.

Remembering that one of the overall objectives is to emphasize science principles rather than to accumulate isolated, unimportant facts, let us think through what such subject matter might include. The reading the teacher has done; the curriculum guide, if there is one; and the available textbooks may serve as a general outline of the possible scope of the unit. The teacher may make this list of important ideas as he reads to gain the necessary subject-matter background or he may find such a basic list in teacher's guides to textbooks. In the study of evaporation and condensation the following are examples of the subject matter ideas that might be used as an outline:

When water evaporates, it changes to water vapor.
Wind and heat make water evaporate more rapidly.
Water evaporates into the air from many places.
When water vapor changes back into water we say it condenses.
Water vapor often condenses on cold things.
Water vapor may condense to make dew.
Dew evaporates.
Water vapor may come out of the air as frost on freezing-cold surfaces.
Frost melts into water when warmed.
Rain comes from clouds.
Some clouds are made of many tiny drops of water; some are made of tiny crystals of ice.
Some of the rainwater evaporates; some of it goes into the ground.
There are many kinds of clouds.
Snowflakes are made of ice crystals.
Snow melts into water when warmed.

While these are the general ideas it is important to remember that *all* children will not develop an understanding of *all* of the ideas. They are to be considered as a general guide of the subject matter to be included.

Up to now the teacher is building his own background so that he will have more confidence, so that he will have a clearer direction for how the study might proceed. *This does not mean that he himself does all the planning in advance.* He is getting ready to do a more intelligent job of guiding the pupils as they work.

The following description of classroom procedure may give the impression of teacher domination. This is due to the fact that we intend to indicate the various kinds of activities the teacher may engage in, rather than to describe children's responses. In actual practice, children will be considerably more involved both in planning and carrying out the plans.

For purposes of illustration our subject matter has already been selected, and the teacher needs to think of ideas for launching the study—for making it interesting, real, concrete, vital, relevant, and enjoyable—of raising some perplexities that will result in problems and questions. The teacher creates a stimulating learning environment in which pupils may make observations that result in raising some significant problems. Where to begin?

Well, the water level in the schoolroom aquarium keeps getting lower, so that every week the water needs to be replenished. Water colors in paint boxes dry up as they are being used and more water must be added. Why? Wet clothes are hung near heat to help them dry. It rains; the sun comes out; the grass dries; pupils can then go out to play. These are everyday happenings involving evaporation. Children see them and are curious. If they have not noticed them, the teacher draws their attention to some and suggests that they observe others; these are all possible starters.

Suppose we use the aquarium as a starting point. Since pupils have noticed that the water is disappearing the question arises: "Where do you suppose the water goes?" Pupils offer hypotheses: "The aquarium leaks." Or "The water goes into the air." Or "The fish drink it." These are some of the possible responses. They may be explored briefly but the actual testing of the hypotheses comes after further discussion.

"Have you seen other places where water disappears like this?" the teacher asks. Pupils list a number of places. "Where do you think the water is going?" Pupils suggest places. "Sometimes water disappears quickly, sometimes slowly. Why do you suppose this happens?" Pupils offer possible explanations. Through such preliminary discussions, pupils raise problems, interest is aroused, and a readiness for the study is developing.

Such preliminary experiences are essential if we are to establish problems of any consequence that represent children's concerns. Questions that are worth answering are listed. Some of them may be: "What happens to the water when it disappears?" "Why can't we see it then?" "Why does it disappear?" "Could we keep it from disappearing?" "Can we get it back again?" "How can we make it disappear faster?"

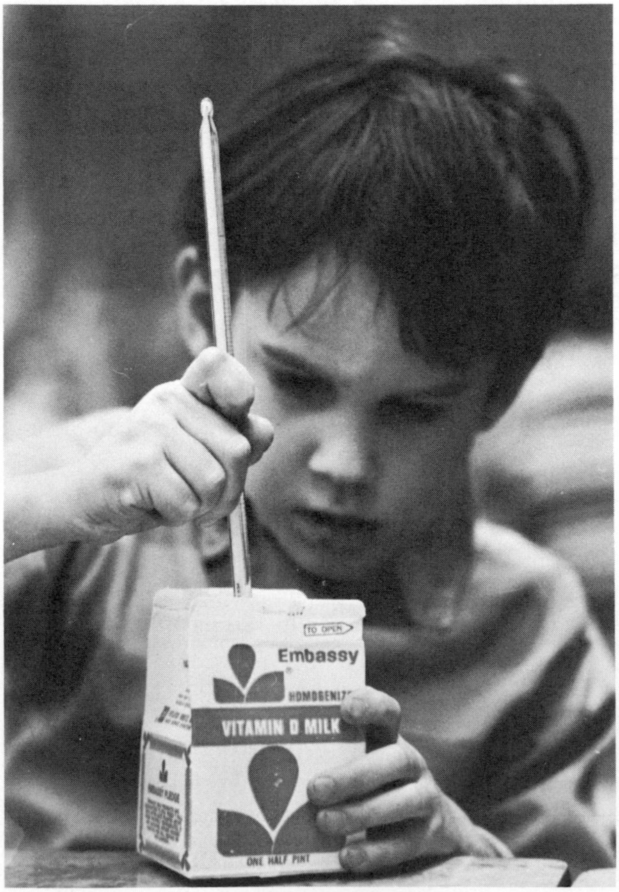

Using scientific instruments to gather accurate data constitutes an important activity, and there is no substitute for each child having an opportunity to use such instruments. Thermometers are examples of instruments that can supply data under many different circumstances. Here the temperature of crushed ice in water is being observed. (*Courtesy of Phyllis Marcuccio.*)

The teacher may add some other questions if the children's questions omit some of the important ideas. In this case no mention has been made of heat and wind. They are important, so questions are added concerning them. This, as has been previously pointed out, is important. Other questions and problems will be added as the study goes on.

"Now how can we find answers?" the teacher asks. Suggestions from the pupils are important here. We want them to suggest ways to investigate, and then to use some of these ways so that they will arrive at possible conclusions. The pupils suggest reading, experimenting, asking questions, observing, and other methods. These suggestions will vary. If the children have had previous science experiences their suggestions will be more sophisticated than otherwise.

"What shall we do first?" Pupils make suggestions. The questions may be arranged by the teacher and children in some order that seems logical for answering. They select a question and decide which way of finding the answer will be appropriate. The whole class may work on the same problem, or if it seems best (depending on the age of the children, their experience at group work, materials available, and so on), pupils may work in groups, each group concentrating on a different problem. Everyone assumes some responsibility for finding printed materials, finding or devising experiments, locating apparatus and other learning materials. A special library committee working with the teacher may search for books. These sources will suggest various experiments and activities. Suggestions have already been made for the use of reading material, for experimenting, and for observing. These suggestions are kept in mind as the study proceeds.

(*See* Ch. 3.)

In experimenting, as in all other activities, it is essential to keep experiments geared to the purposes of teaching. For example, we want to help pupils grow in the use of scientific attitudes. We say: "Don't let pupils jump to conclusions, and be sure to use a control whenever possible as children are experimenting." As we have previously indicated, the use of experimenting involves varying degrees of sophistication. Not all children will comprehend the importance of the use of a control. It is essential, however, that children be exposed to the idea, and begin to experience the meaning involved. Let us illustrate.

In this unit one of the problems may be: "Why do things seem to dry faster on a windy day?" Pupils will suggest hypotheses; to test these ideas, they experiment by putting a wet spot on the chalkboard and fanning it vigorously with a piece of cardboard. The spot will soon disappear.

Pupils may be inclined to conclude immediately that the wind made by fanning caused the water to evaporate faster. But they shouldn't. As an alert boy once said under such circumstances: "I don't know how fast a spot dries without fanning." So the question arises: "How can we arrange our experiment so that we can be sure that it is only the *wind* that is helping the water evaporate faster?" "Put two spots on the chalkboard, fan one, and don't fan the other," someone says. So two spots are made near each other and only one is fanned. Someone says: "Some of the fanning is getting on both spots." "What shall we do?" "Put the spots farther apart," a pupil suggests. This is done, but one of the spots is small, the other large. "There's still something wrong with the experiment." "What is it?" "The spots must be just alike or we can't decide that the wind is helping." The experiment is tried again, this time with two spots as nearly alike as possible put on at the same time and sufficiently far apart. The pupils are willing to decide that the experiment may help them to solve their problem. They make some predictions, then some observations. But before they can make reliable inferences they should repeat the experiment, try out variations of it, and make additional observations.

When we work with high-school and college students we urge them to use a *control* in performing an experiment to make the results more valid. In the case of the wet spots on the chalkboard the spot that was not fanned was the control. With some groups we may decide not to use the word control; instead we urge pupils to try to answer the question: "How can we be *sure* that fanning makes a difference?" In general, questions about "control" must be designed to have children see the need (1) to exclude influences *except* the one being tested, and (2) to be able to make fair comparisons.

Children will be urged to repeat experiments. Children will caution each other about nonscientific procedures in experimenting if they get in the habit of making accurate observations and of drawing reasonable inferences from the results obtained.

But, as we have said earlier, experiments help us to solve problems, and the applications of the conclusions drawn from the experiment help us to interpret situations in our environment. Consequently, after the experience with wind on the wet spots the teacher may say: "Now, have you ever seen other situations where wind helps evaporation?" The pupils suggest such examples as blowing on ink to make it dry faster, hanging clothes on a line, use of hair dryers, and the like; they compare these with what happened in the experiment.

As the study proceeds, textbook and other informational sources will be used as they are needed. Children may see a motion picture that explains the causes of evaporation and condensation.

It is essential that the teacher keep in mind the generalizations originally assembled if the children's experiences are to lead toward an understanding of them. The pupils will not immediately connect the disappearance and reappearance of water with the concept of what causes rain, snow, and other weather forms. This connection will come to them as their study progresses. As we pointed out earlier, the teacher sees these processes of evaporation and condensation as part of a larger conceptual framework and, wherever possible, provides opportunity for children to see connections with other weather concepts. The teacher is guided in this by the maturity of the children as well as other factors.

If there is sufficient interest in the study pupils may want to plan a culminating activity. This may be done in many ways. Again it is important for pupils to plan—with the guidance of the teacher. They may wish to show the results of their work to another grade, to their parents, or at a school assembly. For this purpose they can plan, perform, and explain a series of easy demonstrations; plan and draw a series of large pictures that show the important ideas they have learned; or write stories to illustrate the generalizations they have discovered. Here is an example of communicating—writing, speaking, and listening—as necessary activities in science. Here also is a great opportunity to waste time by getting bogged down with aimless activity, constructing things that are of no use to anyone. Keep both eyes on the objectives and do not get carried away with yards of brown paper, papier-mâché, and cardboard boxes, which may have nothing to do with purposeful review.

The foregoing is an illustration of long-range planning. Details of how lesson and unit plans may be made are given in Chapter 5.

The best science teaching is not necessarily done by persons who can answer all the questions that children ask, or, to speak more exactly, by teachers who have extensive backgrounds in science subject matter. The best teaching of science is often done by classroom teachers who understand children, know how to work with them, and are willing to increase their own science backgrounds through study and activity. These teachers must still sometimes say: "I don't know the answer to that, but I can help you find out." They know enough science to point the way, to lead into worthwhile areas of study, and to organize for learning. But the more science they know, the more confidence they have.

In the final chapter of Part I we look at some of the miscellaneous problems that bother teachers who are trying to improve their science teaching.

(Courtesy of Florida Department of Education.)

CHAPTER 5

PROBLEMS AND QUESTIONS ABOUT TEACHING

Some of the problems in this chapter deal with obtaining materials and resources, some with the identification of the various specimens that children constantly bring to school; others center about planning lessons and units and selecting instructional materials, and still others deal with evaluation. The problems have been raised again and again by students and by experienced teachers; the possible solutions are similar wherever they occur.

WHERE CAN I GET SCIENCE MATERIALS?

The increased emphasis on science in the elementary school has resulted in the purchase of much scientific apparatus. Some is needed; some is not. Science apparatus and material for elementary schools should be purchased on the basis of what is required to teach the course of study; we should not order materials and then decide how we can use them. It should be appropriate to the age, abilities, and interests of children. Some of it can be homemade, provided making it teaches children science; time spent making apparatus that can be easily purchased may be wasted. Children should become acquainted with scientific instruments as well as with improvised materials. Much science equipment is available from homes and elsewhere in the community. Teachers should keep all these criteria in mind when choosing equipment. So should superintendents and principals.

Safety

Anything unsafe to handle should not be used in the elementary school. Most people can do an excellent job of teaching science in the first six grades without concentrated acids, bunsen burners, and similar materials that may be safety hazards.

Ordering Materials

Ordering materials from scientific supply houses is hardly a job for the amateur because of the technical ways in which sizes and descriptions are commonly given in catalogues. Some supply houses provide special catalogues for use at the elementary-school level. When these are not available the teacher should seek assistance from qualified science teachers. Kits of essential material already selected and boxed ready for use are available. Some of these kits contain collections useful in carrying out any kind of program; others are chiefly useful in conjunction with a specific series of textbooks, projects, or programs. Some are designed to teach a specific topic, such as weather or magnetism. Teachers sometimes find these kits most convenient. Many of the programs described in Chapter 5 and used in the B chapters provide specific kits designed especially for use in teaching the lessons and units.

Many persons working together may assume responsibility for assembling appropriate materials for science teaching: the school administration, the teacher, teacher aids, parents, and pupils. Some equipment is purchased, some borrowed, some gathered.

Organizing Materials

Organizing and taking care of science material is a problem that involves both teachers, who use the materials, and principals, who must keep track of the inventory. To be useful, material must be near at hand and organized so that it is easy to locate. Frequently-used materials should be in the classroom if there is space available. Material that is used only infrequently and that is shared by the whole school should be kept in central storage with a convenient checkout system so that it can always be located. An elementary school teacher with some interest and background in science may assume responsibility along with the school principal for the initial organizing and assembling of the material. Then under the teacher's supervision a committee of pupils can be of considerable assistance in dispensing and checking material in and out. In some schools specially designed cabinets have been built or purchased and placed in rooms where no experimenting space is available.[1]

WHAT COMMUNITY RESOURCES ARE AVAILABLE?

There is much useful material in the immediate surroundings. But where is it? How can it be obtained? What is appropriate? It is amazing how many magnets, magnifying glasses, garden seeds, insect specimens, musical instruments, and similar materials children can contribute or lend if they are urged to do so. There are countless places to visit, people to enlist, and other resources to use if we begin to look for them and we challenge pupils to help provide them.

Children sometimes get the impression that what they are studying happens only in faraway places. A great many of the things children study in science can be observed within a mile or two of where they are. For example, our concern with environmental ecological problems directs us to study our surroundings in a very practical and useful way. Almost everything described in the B chapters of this book can be seen if you look around the room where you are sitting, go outside, walk a mile or so, and keep watching. In addition to the suggestions given here, there are many others in the "Discovering for Yourself" sections at the end of each A chapter and in the "Resources to Investigate" at the end of each B chapter.

The School

There is a wealth of useful scientific material in the school. Note the following examples:

[1] For further discussion of materials and equipment *see* G.O. Blough and M.H. Campbell: *Making and Using Classroom Science Materials in the Elementary School* (New York: Holt, Rinehart and Winston, Inc., 1954); A. Piltz: *Science Equipment and Material for Elementary Schools*, Office of Education Bulletin, no. 28 (1961); and *Science Equipment and Materials: Science Kits*, no. 332 (Washington, D.C.: U.S. Government Printing Office). *Also see Science for Children*, vol. 4, no. 5 (Washington, D.C.: National Science Teachers Association, 1967), an issue devoted to materials.

(See Ch. 16B.)

Pupils are learning how heat travels and how heating systems function. The book diagrams are helpful. Experiments and experiences are important. Reading is necessary, too. But heat is traveling into the schoolroom from somewhere—from a furnace in another building, from one in the basement of the building where the pupils are studying, or perhaps even from a stove in the classroom itself. Usually the school custodian will help children take a trip to the furnace room, look into the furnace, trace the water or steam pipes to the room, discover how and where air currents travel in the room. These and similar activities bring reality to science.

(See Ch. 19B.)

Pupils are studying electricity. They learn about fuses, lights, conductors, insulators, switches, and meters. If the school uses electricity all these things are available. Again, the school custodian knows where these things are available. Again, the school custodian knows where the fuse box is, can change a fuse, knows where the meter is, how the switches operate, and many other things. These help to get the phenomenon of electricity out of the book and into the realm of the child's experience.

(See Ch. 15B.)

Pupils are studying what things are made of. They observe the process of rusting and of burning (furnace), note the various products of chemical change (window glass, paper, and so on) in the schoolroom, examine the fire extinguisher to see how it operates by means of a chemical change, and observe how undesirable chemical changes are controlled and desirable ones encouraged. Do not overlook thermostats, electric bells, pulleys and other simple machines, light fixtures, pianos and other musical instruments, plants, pressure cookers in the school cafeteria, school radios, telephones, aquariums. The list of materials is nearly endless.

Around the School

Look out of the schoolroom window. The schoolyard is teeming with science material; much of it very useful. The class is studying the effects of erosion on land forms. A heavy rain falls. A trip to the edge of the schoolyard reveals a temporary stream, brown as coffee, carrying away the top soil of the playground. A tumblerful of the water held to the light reveals the cause of the color. Letting the glass stand for an hour will settle the soil at the bottom. The sidewalk next to the yard is covered with soil washed from the playground. Here is a real example of erosion. A small gully is beginning to form, and the experience of having observed it and of trying to stop erosion by using appropriate means is a beginning to understanding conservation practices. If the schoolyard is black-topped, nearby parks or similar areas will do as substitutes.

Children are studying problems related to environmental pollution. Unfortunately the schoolyard is usually rampant with examples. Starting with the near-at-hand cannot help but make the problems real and help to provide solutions.

The class is studying animals and how they live together. In the ground just outside the window ants are busy taking care of their young, guarding the queen, feeding her, getting food, and doing the many other things pupils have read about. Seeing ants under a magnifying glass, watching them carry food, seeing them make a tunnel are all activities that illustrate the science they are studying.

Many other things wait to be discovered in the schoolyard: birds, insects, and other animals; trees and other plants going through the annual cycle of growth and dormancy; swings and seesaws, which illustrate gravity and leverage; plants with special adaptations; flowers, rocks, seed pods; dew and other forms of precipitation; fungus growths; nodules on clover roots; and examples of different kinds of soils. Exploration of these helps to bring science ideas to life and to create appreciation of them. They are the sources of data for problem solving.

At Home

The homes of children contain many examples of science objects and phenomena. Children are studying machines and how they help to do work. Modern homes contain many of the things commonly used to illustrate the principles of doing work. In the kitchen there are egg beaters, can openers, knives, corkscrews, and many other tools. In the shop, tool box, or tool chest there are hammers, saws, and chisels. In the basement: washing machines and other appliances. Perhaps there are pumps, farm machinery, a windmill, pulleys for loading hay, inclined planes for loading livestock, balances for weighing, pulleys for hanging out clothes or storing hay. In a city environment: street-cleaning apparatus, trucks that grind up garbage and leaves, and others. These are all illustrations of the use of science principles.

Suppose children are learning how we use plants in daily living. They keep an account of the different kinds of plants that are growing in their home gardens or farms or in pots on windowsills. They search the kitchen cupboard for examples of spices and herbs. While learning how plants are adapted to the environment they dig up dandelions to examine the long root system, bring various kinds of leaves to school for examination, and bring plants to school that show special adaptations.

Other science resources of the home include heating and lighting systems, refrigerators, pets, farm animals, sources of pollution, methods of insect control, and fuels.

In the Community

Every community is rich in resources that are indispensable to good science teaching. They include not only places to visit but persons to consult. The use of an individual as a resource carries with it certain responsibilities for both pupils and teachers. Extending an invitation, planning for active audience participation, introducing the visitor to the group, and conducting questioning periods must all be planned for by the teacher and pupils. Careful planning is essential if pupils are to receive maximum benefits from resource persons. A list of questions may be prepared in advance to help give proper focus. There is no reason to assume that Mr. Jones, one of the parents, who built his own telescope and knows more about Mars than anybody in town, can talk helpfully to a fifth grade. He may not have seen so many children in one room since his own school days, and he may have little idea of their interests and capacities. The list of questions prepared by the class and teacher and a talk with the teacher prior to his appearance will be very helpful to him and advantageous to the pupils.

You can make a long list of places to visit in your community that would be fruitful in terms of science experience. Your list would probably include the water-purification plant, the airport, industrial plants, museums, weather bureaus, parks, radio stations, city departments, greenhouses, bird sanctuaries, and markets. Again, the value of such visits will be greatly enhanced by careful pupil-teacher planning to answer such questions as: "What arrangements must be made before taking the trip?" "How can we make best use of our time?" "What things do we want to find out?" "How can we best organize this information?" "What use shall we make of the findings after the trip?"

These examples of places to visit in the community are more likely to be accessible to schools in towns and cities. There are, however, many other places to visit in rural areas or in villages. Some of them are a gravel pit or stone quarry, where rocks and fossils may be gathered and where different layers of soil and rock may be observed; woods, where plants and their relationship to the environment may be observed, and where the study of ecology can become a very real experience; a burned-over area, where the destructive effects of fire can be observed; a field, where plants can be examined, insects collected, and erosion effects noted; a new building under construction, where machines are at work and insulation, heating equipment, electrical equipment, and other installations can be observed; a sawmill, where tools and trees can be studied and conservation practices or the lack of them can be observed; a farm, where there are problems of raising animals and plants and where many other scientific processes go on; a garden, where scientific principles of plant growth and insect control can be observed; an apiary, where the social life of insects can be observed; and a school camp, which is an ideal setting for the study of living things.

Special consideration of community pollution problems are developed in Chapter 14. We mention it here for the sake of emphasis. It is in the community itself that the problems are found and observations can result in some understanding of the problems as well as suggestions for solving them.

WHAT SHALL WE DO WHEN CHILDREN ASK "WHAT IS IT?"

We continually urge children to bring things to school to use in science learning. One of the first things they are likely to ask about a stone or an insect or some other "nature lore" is "What is it?" Answering this question is often difficult. If you have taught in the elementary school you can recognize yourself in the next paragraph. If you have not taught and are going to you will soon come to realize what Miss Cohen is up against.

"Miss Cohen, this morning I saw a strange bird sitting in a tree in our back yard. It was black and white and made the funniest sound. What was it?" "Miss Cohen, my brother says this rock is fool's gold. Is it?" In spring wilted specimens of flowers are brought to school. The children ask what they are, and chances are Miss Cohen does not know.

It is not possible for *any* teacher to know the name of *every* insect, flower, plant, or rock that is brought to school. When children ask "What is this?" we often honestly must say: "I don't know." But let us add: "Perhaps we can find out what it is." Then we can help children learn how to find out. Now let us go back to the naming.

In the first place naming the thing is not an end in itself. We need to have its name because we are going to learn about it. So we cannot go wrong when we say: "Let's look at it carefully. What can we learn by looking at it by touching it and using other senses?" Then: "Does anyone think that he knows what it is?" Trying to answer the question "What is it?" starts us on the road to careful observation; and as soon as we begin to observe we begin also to learn something besides the name. Such observations and discussions of what has been observed is often a springboard into ecological understanding when children and the teacher ask: "Where was it found?" "When was it found?" "What other living things were nearby?" "What was it doing?" "How would you describe the place where you found it?" (Temperature? Shade? Water? are examples)

It is part of being "scientific" for Billy to look carefully so that he will not say: "Miss Cohen, I saw a strange bird that made a funny sound. What was it?" As an example, here are some of the things pupils should learn to observe about a bird if they want to identify it: *its general appearance*—size, shape, and color markings; *its head*—color, crest, and shape of beak; *its feet*—webbing and size; *its habitat*—swamp, field, buildings, forest; *its food*—seeds, berries, worms, insects. What begins as simple identification can develop into better understanding of a living animal or plant and its ecology.

As you can see, "What is it?" may provide a "teachable moment" that leads into an investigation making use of process skills; that is, observing, classifying, measuring, communicating, inferring, formulating hypotheses, and even experimenting.

Perhaps you feel that you still could not identify many of the common birds even if you knew all of the information indicated in this paragraph. That is quite understandable, because there are so many. In the Bibliography we have listed a number of inexpensive books that will help you in identification of birds, insects, flowers, and other living things. Some of them are for sale in local stores. The color of specimens in these books is not always accurate (neither is it in some of the very expensive books), but the descriptions are clear. By carefully matching observations with these descriptions, you and the children ought to have fair success. Again, it is good scientific practice to say: "I think," or "from what we are able to tell" when you try to identify and you are not sure. Don't forget that often there are persons in the community—a parent, teacher, or someone else—who make a hobby of knowing everything in sight. These people are very useful. So is your local museum. What we have said about identifying birds is equally applicable to finding out about shells, insects, plants, rocks and other things that children find and like to share.[2]

[2] G.O. Blough et al.: "How Are Living Things Put in Groups?" in *Science Is Experimenting* (Glenview, Ill.: Scott, Foresman and Company, 1968).

Above all the early experiences of children in science should be meaningful, appropriate, and enjoyable. Collecting a soil sample; taking it back to your desk; looking at it with a hand lens; and showing, telling, and asking about it meet these criteria for many children. (*Courtesy of Phyllis Marcuccio.*)

It is fun and useful to know the names of things when you are studying about them. As you use the names they gradually begin to stick in your mind because you have used them again and again. But it is dull to sit down and learn the names of fifteen birds from pictures when you have no need to know them. If somebody likes to learn to identify things—some people do—he should not be discouraged, but let's not require everybody to do it just because it is suggested as an activity at the end of a chapter.

Let's not underestimate the good that comes when the teacher encourages children to bring materials to class. It helps them to look upon their environment as something to be studied and enjoyed. It says eloquently to children: "The study of science deals with real things, living and nonliving, and the real happenings around you."

The teacher who spends some time at an Audubon Camp,[3] joins a local bird-watching or geology club, participates in locally-sponsored field trips, and has other similar experiences is better able to help children with identification problems as well as with related learning, and at the same time derives much personal pleasure from such experiences.

[3]National Audubon Society, 950 Third Ave., New York, N.Y.

WHAT SCIENCE CAN BE TAUGHT IN NURSERY SCHOOL AND KINDERGARTEN?

Needs of the Young Child

In the early school years the study of science is so closely interwoven with the total educational experience of children that it is especially important to examine the general needs of the young child to assist us in identifying opportunities and setting limits to our science program.

What comes first to your mind when you consider the needs of young children? Proper food, adequate clothing and shelter? Security? Freedom from anxiety and pressures? Probably these and many other so-called basic needs. When you observe children in class situations and on the playground and in other informal situations they often reveal further needs, such as the need for attention, for belonging, for success and being accepted. These and others[4] provide guidance in designing the total school program. There are further needs, no less important, that give us more specific help in designing and carrying out the science program.

At an early age children demonstrate a tendency to explore by using their senses: to participate actively, to inquire, to use techniques of learning as befits their stages of development. A child's curiosity grows and develops as he engages in such firsthand experiences. The young child must have many concrete experiences before he can begin to work with abstract ideas. There is much more to say about needs of young children and how the study of science helps to meet them, but the important thing is that meeting the needs of children when they are young will continue to enhance their growth and development in later years.

This passage[5] summarizes the school's concern:

> The role of the school is to meet the needs of each child through a well-planned, dynamic program which prepares him for successful participation in the world in which he lives. The school gives the child the opportunity to inquire, discover, participate, and achieve in the company of his peers. The school helps the child find order and purpose in his environment by providing him with techniques for learning how to cope with the expanding horizons of his world. Meeting the child's needs at his present stage of development provides the basis for a purposeful and satisfying life. There is no doubt, too, that meeting his needs now will also help to shape his future.

Most children come to nursery school and kindergarten with television, travel, radio, and daily living experiences that have made them curious. These experiences vary with circumstances; in some cases there is much more to build on than in others.

[4] For further discussion *see Piaget's Theory Applied to an Early Childhood Curriculum* with an introduction by Celia Stendlar Lavatelli (Boston: A Center for Media Development Inc., 1970), 163 pp.; and *Prekindergarten and Kindergarten Curriculum Guide,* series no. 5 (Board of Education of the City of New York, 1969–1970).

[5] Reprinted from *Prekindergarten and Kindergarten Curriculum Guide 1969–70* series no. 5 by permission of the Board of Education of the City of New York (Brooklyn, N.Y.: Board of Education of the City of New York).

Science possibilities show up in the day-to-day living in the classroom if the teacher recognizes them and knows how to help children explore them.

Reread the long-range goals and statements of behavioral objectives for the elementary school and for science in Chapter 2. Whatever we do at the earliest level must gear into these. Above all, let us make the beginning experiences meaningful, appropriate to the age and development of children, and enjoyable. We must keep in mind that children's needs vary with the individual, as do their capacities to accomplish the goals. A good start is important.

The suggestions that follow are organized around the major goals for teaching science. There is some overlapping in these ideas and not *all* children will be ready to respond equally to the suggestions. Each B chapter contains additional ideas for science experiences for younger children.

Learning and Using Process Skills

1. Try to make as much use of natural curiosity as possible by following and expanding it. Inquisitive children will ask many science questions and not always at convenient times. No one can—or should—answer all of them. Teachers are only human and on some days and with some children it can be difficult even to *hear* them!
2. Go as far as you can to help children say exactly what they want to find out. The statement of the questions or problems is important in using inquiry skills. Do not keep at this, however, if the children are too immature to make sense out of it. Do not insist on verbalization if children are not ready.
3. Help children grow in ability to suggest and use process skills: asking, listening, observing with *all* their senses, investigating to see what happens, reporting by showing and telling, manipulating, measuring, and so on. They should be better at using such skills in June than they were in September.
4. Keep tying experiences together: "Remember what we did the other day to find out? Could we try it again? What else could we do?"
5. Label these experiences *science.* Children *and their parents* should know that they are having an early brush with science experiences.
6. Encourage girls to participate. If you believe that attitudes are established early then help girls as well as boys to be successful in science. Girls, too, live in the age of science.
7. Remember that the processes of inquiry are as important as what is discovered. This idea is illustrated over and over in the examples in this text.
8. Keep in mind that there are many instances at this level where problems are left unsolved. This is as it should be. We come back to such problems as the children mature.
9. Guide inquiry by helping children to identify new processes to use. The kinds of processes children can handle with success change as children grow and develop, just as the kinds of subject matter that they can deal with changes. Do not tell the answers. When you tell, discovery stops.
10. Remember that you cannot hurry inquiry or discovery.

Developing Attitudes

What can we do to help the very young take the beginning step in the direction of developing attitudes and expanding their interests and appreciations? This is a part of every unit, every lesson every day. Here are suggestions:

1. We can provide many opportunities for using the senses to discover and thus provide satisfying experiences.
2. We can help to provide an environment full of opportunities of interest, for exploring, for making things to express ideas.
3. We can use books, and when children ask: "Was that a *true* story?" we can make use of this circumstance to begin the evaluating of materials. Some children as they listen to reading may at a very early age begin to differentiate between just-for-fun stories and books that are sources of information. In such a discussion the teacher does not always provide answers or try to close the problem. She encourages children to express their thoughts and feelings. Remember that a story may appear to be true *emotionally* for a child, although it is in the *form* of fantasy. Young children grow slowly in understanding the distinction between reality and fantasy, and they do not all grow in this respect at the same rate.
4. We can make greater use of trying out things to discover. "Shall we try it *again* and see what happens?" Repeating experiences intended to show the same idea are important if we intend to help children withhold judgment and develop related scientific attitudes.
5. We can make more effective use of observation experiences to develop questioning attitudes. "Could we *look at more* pictures and books?" "Shall we each take a turn at looking to check if we all see the same thing?" (Observe carefully and often.) "What can we find out by looking?" "What can we do to be sure?"
6. We can urge children to show and discuss, to listen and to think, to manipulate and wonder. This may be slow at first. It grows as the children do. It will not develop unless we expect it to.
7. We can provide materials and problems that will develop interests children have not thought about. It is with a variety of materials that children learn to create, broaden their horizons, and work out ideas.
8. We must remember that we cannot help another develop interest in, or have some appreciation for, science unless we ourselves have some of each.

Learning Subject Matter

Can we expect these young children to begin to learn some science information? Yes. And since the methods of learning and content learned are so closely related, our suggestions overlap some of those made earlier when we discussed process skills.

1. Adapt the learning of information to the children's level, but *do not underestimate* children's abilities and interests. Experiences indicate that many are able to go

much further and faster in the pursuit of information than we have sometimes thought. Remember it is not only *can* they, but *should* they?

2. *Intend* and demonstrate that they can begin to learn some science ideas.
3. Help pupils put ideas together. Recall related information and help children go as far as they can in seeing relationships.
4. Construct a record of some of the science ideas children have learned. Many of them cannot read. They do not need to. They can listen; and they can reach and touch.
5. Demonstrate that even simple experiences with common materials open up such science areas as space, living things, sound, light, weather, motion and force, and the nature of materials. The method of organization of the material is based on natural themes which constitute an invitation to explore: "Getting Wet and Drying"; "Discovering with Our Senses"; "Seesaws and Balances"; "Seeds and Fruits"; "Uphill and Downhill"; "Blowing Soap Bubbles"; "Science in a Pan of Water"; "Science in a Sandbox"; "All Kinds of Pets"; "Science in Wheels"; and "Science in Block Building".[6] These are not necessarily in one neat, consecutive sequence; they may be picked up and dropped at various intervals.

HOW DO I MAKE LESSON AND UNIT PLANS?

There are many ways to make lesson and unit plans, just as there are many ways to teach. Sometimes a class period is spent in group work, individualized instruction, laboratory work, independent study, children using multimedia instructional aids, and so on. This being the case there must also be many forms for developing and recording plans. Some plans are formal and include details; some are very sketchy. No matter what the style of teaching there are legitimate reasons for planning. Good teachers feel that they need some sort of guide to follow. Certainly we are not likely to teach well without some preliminary planning. We need to think out possible ways to teach, to make some provision for materials that we may need, and to formulate carefully what we hope pupils will be able to do as a result of their experiences. But remember: *Making a lesson or unit plan does not mean that the teacher will do all the planning and leave none for the children.* The teacher's outline should allow plenty of opportunity for children to plan together or make whatever decisions they can and should make. Remember too: *When you begin to work with pupils, your plan may change entirely; it is almost certain to be modified.* What is the thinking that goes into planning a lesson? Let's examine the following illustration.

PLANNING A LESSON

Suppose that we are studying magnets in grade 4 or 5. Let us assume that pupils have thus far learned the kinds of materials magnets will attract, the substances

[6] *See Science: Grades K–2* and *Prekindergarten Curriculum* (Brooklyn, N.Y.: Board of Education of the City of New York).

magnetism will travel through, how to make a magnet by rubbing a needle on a magnet, and the law of magnets (opposite poles of a magnet attract each other; like poles repel). They have discovered these ideas through various experiences; and they have done some reading. Now they are interested in making a compass, which they have learned has something to do with magnetism. You suggest that before the next lesson pupils try to find out as much as they can about how to make one. This is not a formal assignment. It provides an opportunity for those who are interested to do some "research."

(*See* Chs. 19A and B.)

Assuming that the lesson will be one in which pupils will more or less work together in attempting to solve a problem, you may think something like this: "I want to build on what the pupils already know, use any investigating they may have done outside of class, help them to formulate some hypotheses, and test them and solve the problem of how to make a compass, help them to use their ideas in making compasses, and raise some new problems about compasses and their uses." (*See* the more organized statement of some of the behavioral objectives in the lesson plans that follow.)

You will probably begin your lesson by letting pupils tell or show what they discovered about compasses. Naturally, you will not know in advance what ideas they will have. You are prepared with materials which can be used by the pupils to make compasses: needles, dishes of water, magnets, and flat corks.

It is possible that someone will bring a small compass from home. You may have suggested this to the pupils in a previous discussion. If so, you let him show it to the class and tell what he thinks he knows about it. Some of this information may be correct; some wrong. You assume that pupils will challenge the accuracy of some of the statements, and part of your plan will be to help pupils find out whether the statements are true or not.

If no one has brought materials you show those you have assembled, and plan to say something like this: "Can anyone use these materials to try to make a compass?" Pupils will discuss their ideas and then organize into groups to try them out. Now pupils have some background for their theories and suggestions from their "research."

They attempt to make several compasses in order to compare them and give more pupils opportunity to learn by doing. When the compasses are made (the needle is magnetized by rubbing it—one way only—on the magnet and is floated on the cork in the dish of water), you expect someone to ask: "What makes the needle point north and south?" This problem and others will undoubtedly be left for your next lesson (*see* the plan that follows).

This, in general, is some of the *thinking* you may do before you sit down to plan (this is just *one* of the many ways of thinking about a plan; *your* way will be different, depending on your background and other factors). Look back at your intentions. Is this thinking pointed toward achieving them? Have you provided opportunities for children to plan and to think? Will they use ways of finding out for themselves? Will this kind of plan keep their interest alive? Is it a flexible plan? How much of the material you write down depends on you and your situation? You may need only a brief outline of how you hope to go ahead, but you should think out ways of proceeding—especially if you have not done much science teaching. (*See* the accompanying lesson plans.)

Several descriptions of teaching procedures in this section of the book are really examples of lesson-planning procedures—*see* Chapter 2 (Heat, p. 18; Plants, p. 25) and Chapter 3 (Magnets, p. 38; Sound, p. 44; Seasons, p. 48). Many of the B chapters contain material easily developed into plans.

LESSON PLAN FOR MIDDLE GRADES—SUBJECT: COMPASS

Objectives	As a result of the activities and discussions some, and hopefully many, of the children will be able to: *construct* predictions on the basis of thought and observations; *demonstrate* the experimental methods of arriving at some tentative conclusions; *plan, describe,* and *demonstrate* a method or methods of making a compass; *construct* hypotheses on the basis of their experiences; *identify* further problems resulting from their experiences. Note: *Depending on the length of the lesson and maturity of children, these objectives will need adjustment. These may be a large order for some children and some teachers. They are examples to be modified by individual teachers.*
Problem	To have children make a compass.
Materials	Flat corks, needles, glass or plastic dishes, magnets.
Strategy-Procedure (*This part of the plan contains motivation, questions to be asked by teacher or anticipated from pupils, activities, and science processes to be stressed.*)	Ask pupils what they have found out from their reading about how a compass can be made from the materials they have brought. Pupils offer hypotheses and perhaps make some predictions about what will happen if they try out their ideas. If pupils do not have materials ask them how they might use those you have on hand to make a compass. After suggestions are made, children formalize their plans and try (working in groups) to use the materials to make compasses. Children tell and show their results and compare the various compasses. If there are differences pupils propose hypotheses to account for them, and proceed to check them and attempt to predict what will happen when their plans are carried out.
Outcomes (*These are determined by your objectives. Some refer to science information and concepts, some to processes of inquiry.*)	*Concepts* 1. A steel needle can be made magnetic by stroking it in one direction on a magnet. 2. A free-floating magnetized needle points in a north-south direction. It is a compass. *Processes* 1. Observing and describing. (How do the

LESSON PLAN FOR MIDDLE GRADES (*Continued*)

Outcomes (*Continued*)

needles behave?) (What happens under various circumstances?)
2. Predicting. (What do you think will happen to a steel needle if it is rubbed on a magnet? What do you think will happen if you float the needle on the cork?)
3. Experimenting. (Finding out if an unmagnetized needle behaves in the same way as a magnetized one. Use both kinds when comparing results.)
4. Comparing or describing. (How do magnetized needles compare with each other? With commercial compass needles? With unmagnetized needles?)
5. Generalizing. (The magnetized needles pointed in a north-south direction.)
6. Communicating. (Describing what happens and discussing the possible causes and results.)

New Problems

What makes a compass point in a north-south direction? How can we tell which of the ends of the needles are pointing north? Can we magnetize just one end of a needle? Is the pointed end of the needle always the north end? Are there other ways to make a compass? (These point the way to further exploring in the next lessons.)

Teacher may suggest that pupils think of ways to solve these problems. They will be the essence of the lessons that follow.

LESSON PLAN FOR KINDERGARTEN—SUBJECT: MAGNETS

Objectives

As a result of the experiences and observation some and hopefully many of the children will be able to:
demonstrate that some magnets are stronger than others; *demonstrate* that magnets attract some materials and not others; *plan* experiences to gather data to help solve a problem; *describe* what happens when magnets are brought in contact with various materials.

See note (*p. 95*) *for lesson plan with middle grades.*

Problem

To find out what a magnet can do.

LESSON PLAN FOR KINDERGARTEN (*Continued*)

Materials	Various shapes, sizes, and strengths of magnets and materials to be tested. (Small objects: clips, fasteners, buttons, bottle caps, large nails, blocks, blunt scissors, and so on.) Also use other materials in the room.
Strategy-Procedure	Leave magnets and the objects on a table for a few days. (Children play freely with materials.) When children are ready they show what they have found out about the magnets. They use magnets to pick up things. They may show that some magnets are stronger than others; that magnets have different shapes, and that they pick up some things and not others.
Outcomes	*Concepts* 1. A magnet picks up some kinds of things but not others. 2. A magnet sticks to some kinds of things but not others. 3. Some kinds of things (little) jump up to a magnet. *Processes* 1. Observing. (To see which things are attracted and which are not.) 2. Classifying. (Children distinguish between the objects which are attracted and those which are not and compare magnets of different shapes and strengths.) 3. Experimenting. (Testing various materials to see the effects of magnets on them. Manipulating a variety of magnets and making some observations of the results.) Note: *While at this age children are not expected to deal with variables and controls they can use a modified form of manipulation to see that information may be gained by careful manipulating and observing.* 4. Communicating. (As far as seems reasonable children show and tell their observations.) *New Problems* What things around the room will a magnet attract? How can you tell which magnet is strongest? Note: *If possible, children should begin to see that it is the material (iron) that an object is made of and not the name of the object (nail) that is important.* However, if children are not ready for this distinction do not force it on them.

A UNIT PLAN[7]

As in the case of the lesson plan there are many ways to make a long-range plan and as many ways to record them. The reasons for making the plan are obvious. Among other things the teacher must decide on the general scope and sequence, find materials and books, decide on some of the major activities and problems, think through the objectives and possible ways to evaluate, and see this unit of subject matter as it relates to larger concepts. These, as is true of the lesson plan, will be altered as the teaching and learning goes on. The following specific suggestions will help you.

(*See* Ch. 2.)

Objectives The general goals and the more specific behavioral objectives described are the framework from which unit objectives are derived, and as has been emphasized earlier objectives stated in behavioral terms are direct, specific, and aimed at changes in behavior which we hope to accomplish. Such statements give better direction to the teaching and help in the evaluative process.

Initiating Experiences Nobody questions the importance of getting a good start. Children cannot discover problems, suggest solutions, or be interested in something they know little or nothing about. For example, before the unit on evaporation and condensation can begin children should make many observations that raised questions to be solved.

Possible Problems These will be tentative and subject to change as the unit proceeds. Some are identified at the beginning and will give direction to the content. Others arise as the study proceeds. The more problems children identify from their experiences the more likely the inquiries will be effective. The problems in the B chapters are examples.

Science Concepts These are general statements of subject matter. For an example see the list on page 259 (evaporation and condensation), and the generalizations at the beginning of each B chapter.

Possible Activities Activities help to solve the problems and achieve the objectives set up at the beginning of the unit. As the unit goes on some of these will be discarded or revised, and new ones will be added. They include observations, experiments, constructions, discussions, trips, and so forth. (The B chapters are full of suggestions for such activities.)

Materials and Bibliography The initial list will change as the unit proceeds and new apparatus, materials, and books are needed (*see* Bibliography).

Culminating Activity Do not always construct something! Whatever you do should give children the opportunity to organize what they have learned, clear up misun-

[7] S.S. Blank: "Planning a Teaching Unit for the Primary Grades," *Science and Children* (April 1972).

derstandings, review, and give opportunities for using materials to express ideas. There need not always be a "culminating activity," especially in the early grades. (The B chapters contain many suggestions.)

Evaluation Although various kinds of evaluations will go on as the unit does, there may be times when more formally-organized evaluations are necessary. Keys to evaluation are found when we examine behaviors we indicated in the objectives. *See* the suggestions for evaluation later in this chapter.

You will find this skeleton outline very useful as a guide to planning a unit of work adapted to fit your needs.

HOW CAN WE TELL HOW WELL WE ARE ACCOMPLISHING OUR INTENTIONS?

The problem of evaluation for some teachers is relatively simple because they base the total evaluation on whether or not a pupil makes a satisfactory grade on a test that covers the subject matter studied. But our objectives for science teaching in the elementary school are much broader. The importance of testing for the recall of facts is questionable. These facts in themselves may be of no great consequence. As we have previously said, we are really concerned with the understanding of concepts; with how much the children have learned about how to use methods of inquiry; and with the attitudes, interests, and appreciations that have developed. It is the changes in behaviors that concern us. This makes evaluation difficult.

Most of the paper-and pencil examinations that are given to children are designed to test their retention of facts. But suppose that the child can name ten trees in his neighborhood. What of it, if he goes out on Saturday and breaks the branches from a young sapling that has been planted along the street? A child gets a "hundred" on his subject-matter examination, but refuses to change his mind in the face of evidence, jumps to conclusions, is prejudiced, and in general is unscientific. Has he "passed"? What of his behavior? Have you as his teacher passed or failed?

We come again to a consideration of how the objectives are conceived and stated. If they have been written in terms of the behaviors we hope to accomplish we observe for these behaviors—to see if children on the bases of the experiences they have had are able to perform certain tasks; demonstrate specific skills; as well as in other ways, which we have emphasized elsewhere, show that they have changed in behavior. The *extent to which children are successful* still remains difficult to measure. Much research and experimentation must be done in the field of evaluation, and our progress depends considerably on our observations of children's actions.

OBSERVING CHILDREN

One way to evaluate the effectiveness of science teaching is to observe the behaviors of children—especially if we record these observations in and out of the classroom and accumulate them for the time when we are to formulate an opinion. When these observations are made in terms of our objectives we look for evidence that children can demonstrate ability to *do;* we look for incidents that show growth in ability to *use* processes—contributions made by individuals during class discussion of a problem, originality and resourcefulness that are demonstrated in doing "research" to find solutions through reading, and suggestions made in formulating hypotheses and setting up experiments and designing experiences to test them. Our observations would also include evidence of growth in scientific attitude—willingness to withhold judgment until sufficient evidence is available, questioning sources of information, willingness to change an opinion in the face of conclusive evidence, and a "wait-a-minute" attitude toward hastily-reached conclusions. There are many situations in which such attitudes are observable as children work together in science.

Observing and recording these anecdotes of behavior takes time, but the information they yield is important. Some teachers jot them down systematically. Here are a few anecdotes which one teacher recorded:

J.S. Selects and reads science books in his free time as well as in formal school situations.

J.D. Brings his chemistry set and similar materials to school to demonstrate. When questions were raised that he could not answer he acted as chairman of a group to find the answers. Exercises initiative and good leadership.

C.L. Demonstrates his scientific attitude when he discovers statements in a reference book that disagree with something an adult friend of his has said. He exhibits good attitude about changing his mind.

C.F. Exhibits progress in being able to get along in small groups as they experiment.

F.B. Has not improved leadership qualities even though she has been given many opportunities to do so.

J.T. Made beautiful sketches of stages of tadpole development.

F.A. Constructed a bird-feeding station at home and reported his observations to the group. As a result of class activity he invited the class to come to see it.

G.B. Has not shown evidence of improvement in general interest.

D.B. Told class about TV program she had watched on our vanishing wild life.

S.W. Has begun to ask very searching questions.

Such records as these help teachers to survey behaviors on which to base an evaluation. To be valid, records must be made over a comparatively long period of time. We must remember that in science, as elsewhere, we are trying to evaluate on an individual basis. What represents accomplishment for one child because of his potentialities may be much less important for another.

CHILDREN CAN HELP IN EVALUATING

Children themselves should, whenever possible, help to evaluate the work of their group as well as their own work. There are many situations in which this is possible and many reasons why it is desirable. Such evaluation may begin by letting children help to set up the standards of accomplishment whenever possible stated in the form of desirable behaviors. These may later be used as criteria for evaluation. For example, some fifth-grade pupils were studying electricity. Pupils raised problems and planned ways to solve them. These plans were carried out. At the end of the unit pupils decided to show and describe some experiments to the fourth grade. This involved making a summary of the broad concepts they had learned, planning demonstrations to illustrate them, obtaining the materials, and planning how to perform and explain experiments so that younger children could understand them. It also involved planning the details of the program and making arrangements about the time and place for it.

From time to time as the activity progressed, the teacher and pupils sat down together to answer the question: "How are we doing?" The first time this happened the pupils raised this question: "How can we know how well we are doing?" Together the group set up some ways to judge. Some of them were: "Is everyone getting an opportunity to help in the planning and working?" "Is our science correct?" "Do our demonstrations show what we want them to show?" "Is everyone getting his job done on time and in the best way he can?" "Are we enjoying ourselves?" These examples show some of the things the children thought were important.

Some of the comments made at the final evaluation period were interesting and revealing: "Some of us didn't speak loudly enough to be heard." "Some of us forgot to ask the fourth-graders if they had any questions." "Our explanations seemed to be clear to the fourth-graders." "Our program was too long; some of the children got tired." These examples illustrate how children can evaluate group activity and use their findings to improve.

It is important to help children learn to give and take constructive criticism from one another when such evaluating periods are held. Here is an opportunity to exercise scientific attitude—basing conclusions on reliable evidence and being open-minded and not prejudiced.

The evaluating activities described provide opportunity for the teacher to observe individuals and see how and if they are showing evidences of changes in behavior with respect to the behavioral objectives originally determined. There is opportunity to see which children seem to have a satisfactory grasp of the essential subject matter, which children have shown progress in ability to solve problems, which are improving in attitudes, and which appear to have developed an increasing interest and appreciation.

EVALUATION INSTRUMENTS[8]

As long as we give grades for accomplishment in science and as long as we conduct educational experiments to discover more about teaching and learning we shall need

[8] C.H. Nelson: *Improving Objective Tests in Science* (Washington, D.C.: National Science Teachers Association), 24 pp.; P.E. Blackwood and T.R. Porter: *Evaluating Science Learning in the Elementary School* (Washington, D.C.: National Science Teachers Association, 1968), 8 pp.

some kinds of measuring tests. Tests have their limitations, but their effectiveness is improved by observing these suggestions:

Tests must be designed to measure, insofar as possible, the attainment of all the goals and not merely the children's mastery of subject matter.

Test scores should be *only one* of the criteria for evaluating progress.

Tests should be used as a teaching device, as well as an evaluation instrument.

Tests evaluate the success of the teacher as well as the learner.

Tests should be so constructed that pupils will have to do the following kinds of things: recall information and apply it to new situations, see relationships between facts, analyze data and draw appropriate conclusions from them, make decisions on the basis of material read, demonstrate predetermined behaviors appropriate to their levels of growth and development, and demonstrate the ability to use specific process skills.

Tests should be simple, clear, and short and should contain a variety of types of questions.

The testing program must be designed and administered in such a way that children do not feel threatened, so that they do not get the idea that the whole learning experience was for the purpose of "passing the test," so that their own self-image is not undermined, so that the genuine satisfactions and delights and learnings which came with the original experiences are not debased.

A good test may require a child to attempt to *design* an experiment in order to solve some specific problem. It may present him with a faulty setup of an experiment and ask him to *react* to it. It may present a paragraph, a picture, a chart, or some other material and ask him to attempt to *draw conclusions* from it. The material may be selected to emphasize attitudes or methods of investigation or some other elements of science objectives. The pupil may be asked to *identify* relationships to show that he sees how facts can be added together to make generalizations. The pupil may be asked to *identify objects* in order to discuss them or to show what he knows about them. He may be asked to *classify* objects, to *estimate*, to *predict, measure, infer, demonstrate.*

It is not always essential that tests be in written form. Laboratory tests, in which children are asked to solve certain problems with materials, are often effective. (Given: wire, bulb, socket, switch, dry cell—hook them up to make the bulb light.) Oral response to a situation can be more effective for some children.

Above all, remember that all pupils cannot be expected to progress at the same rate toward any specific goals. Try to consider growth as a individual matter, and remember that children's goals may differ from those of the teacher, that they both change, and that evaluation is long-range and continuous.

Directing attention to what children *can do or should be able to do* as a result of their study of science, a New York City plan[9] asks: *Can children* set up experiments, state the problem, suggest ways to solve a problem, manipulate materials, record data,

[9] *Science: Grades 3–4* (Brooklyn, N.Y.: Board of Education of the City of New York, 1966).

interpret data, generalize from the results of an experiment, state new concepts, apply these concepts? It also asks *are children:* increasing their interest in science, increasing their awareness of their environment, reading science periodicals and books, engaging in science activities on their own, developing keener observation, seeking answers to their own questions, distinguishing fact from fancy, beginning to expect order and predictability in relation to natural phenomena?

EVALUATING OUR TEACHING

We wrap ourselves in curriculum construction, theories of teaching, selecting and judging materials, and similar educational matters, and forget that *everything depends on what happens when we work with children.* After all, no matter how well all the preliminary planning is done, science dies on the vine unless our work with children is good.

There are many ways of setting up criteria for judging our accomplishments. Sometimes the whole class acts together in planning or pursuing a common goal, but there are probably more instances where children work independently or in small groups, use various multimedia approaches to learning, or are involved in other more or less diverse activities. Whatever our teaching methods, here are general criteria to use as a nucleus. Individual teachers may add and modify them to fit their class situations. Teachers may ask such questions as these:

What student behaviors indicate the extent to which objectives are being achieved? If you are unable to answer this question with some degree of satisfaction the probability is that you have wasted some time.

Was there pupil interest? Did it grow? If many children are bored, the fault may lie with the methods used, with the subject-matter selection, or it may be due to other causes that can be determined only by careful evaluation.

Was there sufficient pupil participation? Participation is of many different kinds—asking or answering questions, making thoughtful suggestions, giving careful attention, pursuing individual or group activities and so on.

Did I give attention to the individual needs of pupils? Those who need special opportunities, those who have special talents and interests, those who need encouragement, and those who for many other reasons need individual attention should receive it when conditions make this possible.

Did pupils think, and did I give them time to think? If pupils can get along without thinking for themselves, the experience is not likely to be a success; if the procedure is so hurried that no one gets an opportunity to think, one of the main purposes is lost. Remember that you cannot hurry discovery.

Did the situation promote good attitudes and appreciations, interests and fun? Unless the situation is satisfying to pupils and teacher there is not likely to be much learning.

Was there opportunity for pupil planning? There are many opportunities for planning, and pupils cannot grow in ability to plan effectively unless they have chances to do so.

Was there good pupil-teacher relationship? This hardly has anything to do with always letting pupils do what they want. When decisions are made cooperatively pupils can contribute according to their varying abilities and experiences, and there is more likelihood that there will be mutual respect. The good teacher is able to identify situations in which children have the background for making decisions.

Was the material adapted to the ability of the group? Material that is too difficult is discouraging; material that does not challenge causes pupils to lose interest.

This is obviously not an exhaustive set of criteria. It serves to illustrate the kinds of questions useful in evaluating the results of day-to-day teaching. Obviously the set of standards used in judging one type of science experience may not be appropriate for evaluating another. The desired goals are the important factor to consider in any event. A comparison of the items in "Striking a Balance" will be helpful in seeing the relationship of these suggestions with those made for the science program.

(*See* Ch. 4.)

HOW CAN I HELP CREATIVE AND ESPECIALLY GIFTED CHILDREN?

While we are not trying primarily to make scientists of elementary pupils we *are trying* to identify pupils with special interests, aptitudes, and gifts, and to encourage them in their talents. Many famous scientists have begun at the elementary-school level. Unfortunately, too many of them have been successful in their careers in *spite* of their early school experience and not *because* of it. The most successful elementary-school teachers provide opportunities for especially talented pupils by evidencing interest in their accomplishments, providing resources (people, places, printed material, and so on) for them, using them as special science assistants, and encouraging them in other ways.

There are many sets of criteria for identifying especially talented and creative children.[10] These include such items as: shows continued interest in science problems, is able to do abstract reasoning, has a good scientific vocabulary, persists in attempting to solve problems, is skillful in manipulating apparatus and materials, and chooses to read scientific material generally above the level of his fellow students.

Having identified pupils who appear to be gifted and creative in science, it is important to remember that they have many of the same needs as all other children have, and these should be provided for. Although their talent should be encouraged, it should not be exploited to the point where overall development suffers.

A good science program is designed so that children with science aptitudes will naturally make themselves known because opportunities for individual expression are provided. Science talent expresses itself in different ways—one student may be gifted in designing apparatus, another in dealing with the mathematical aspects of science,

[10] A. Piltz and R. Sund: *Creative Teaching of Science in the Elementary School* (Boston: Allyn and Bacon Inc., 1968), pp. 60–71; and R.W. Bybee: "Creativity, Children and Elementary Science," *Science and Children* (March 1972).

Do children demonstrate abilities to observe, communicate their observations, gather data, draw possible conclusions? Teachers who are skillful at observing children and thus accumulating information make more adequate evaluations than those who rely only on pencil-and-paper questions. (*Courtesy of Phyllis Marcuccio.*)

a third in raising especially thoughtful problems. A teacher may encourage talent by allowing time for creative ventures, by giving approval for progress in independent learning, and by having available books, science kits, science magazines, and other aids that will permit individual students to work on their own.

In dealing with especially gifted children if you as the teacher cannot provide stimulus, guidance, and other assistance you must look elsewhere for it. Sometimes the best contribution a teacher can make to a child is to put him in touch with a scientist or a science teacher who is able and willing to provide the necessary help. Science clubs for gifted children have been very successful where they have good leadership.

HOW CAN I HELP SLOW LEARNERS?

Children who may generally be considered as "slow learners" have often been known to respond well in science experiences. This may be due to the fact that there can be much learning through doing; through observing with the senses; through experimenting, constructing, and so on. Coupled with this, evaluation in science can depend less on paper-and-pencil tests and more on the observation of behaviors. Underlying all of these factors is our approach to the slow learner. What are the possible reasons for the slowness? Are we making every conceivable effort to overcome the obstacles? Are we using motivating forces to the fullest? Are we taking potential accomplishment into account? How well have we analyzed the individual's difficulties? How reasonable are we in our expectations? These are the same questions we ask ourselves in any area of the curriculum where slow learning is a factor; the answers are the same for any area.

HOW CAN TEACHERS PREPARE TO HELP CHILDREN LEARN TO USE METHODS OF INQUIRY?

We have elsewhere gone into considerable detail about the nature and meaning of inquiry. We summarize by saying that inquiry methods are those in which students learn by investigating, by using science processes. Students originate problems and devise various ways of collecting information. The results may be in the form of discovery both in subject matter and in learning how to investigate. Teachers cannot help children use methods of inquiry if they themselves do not possess the skills.

At the end of each of the A chapters there is a section called "Discovering for Yourself." Some of the suggested investigations require only brief observation and some recording. Some involve reading from several sources. Some provide opportunity for organized inquiry of the type that teachers hope to inspire in their pupils. Some involve science subject matter; some are concerned with teaching methods. Teachers who themselves have engaged in systematic inquiry are most successful in helping others to do the same. With this end in view we suggest that teachers and prospective teachers engage in some investigations.[11]

Here are some specific suggestions:

Select a problem that interests you and to which you do not actually have a solution. State it carefully and delimit it in scope to make it reasonable. The problem may come from your immediate environment—growth or lack of growth of plants, behavior of an animal, a superstitious saying, a statement you have read which you wish to challenge, an account in a newspaper that causes you to wonder. A problem may come as the result of some discussion in which various points of view are expressed. Or it may arise through some experience in and about your home: cooking, gardening, repairing, or some other activity.

Make your hypotheses carefully, record them, and keep them in mind.

Plan your procedure step by step as carefully as you can, realizing that you will make many changes as your investigation proceeds.

Take notes as you work, including not only your observations, readings, and discoveries but also your frustrations, blind alleys, and unexpected problems. In this way you will appreciate more vividly the difficulties that your pupils will encounter on *their* paths of investigation.

Exercise caution in drawing conclusions—*see* Chapter 2 for a discussion of the use of scientific attitude.

[11] J.J. Koran, Jr.: "How Can Elementary Students and Teachers Be Models of Scientific Process?" *Science and Children* (April 1972).

Examine your activity and try to state in behavioral terms what has resulted. As a result of your work what actions are you now more capable of carrying out? (Demonstrating, constructing, describing, collecting, classifying, developing, and so on.)

Discovering for Yourself

1. Make a list of what you regard as the most important generalizations made in Part I. Explain how you might use them to guide you in your teaching.
2. Suppose the teacher in the schoolroom next to yours is apprehensive about teaching science. What encouragement and advice can you give her?
3. What are the trends in elementary-science teaching that will most influence your work in the classroom? How may they change your methods of teaching?
4. Observe a science activity in an elementary school and evaluate it on the basis of the criteria which you will devise on the basis of your study of Part I.
5. What would you say to a teacher who states: "We would be better off without science textbooks in our elementary science classes"?
6. Try to observe a single child during the whole school day to identify characteristics in him that make science a natural and necessary part of the curriculum.
7. Suppose you are a member of a textbook selection committee. What do you consider to be some of the most important criteria to consider?
8. Suppose the faculty of your school is concentrating on improving the science program. You have been asked to describe what the National Science Foundation-sponsored projects have to contribute. List the most important points you would make.
9. Your school is assembling a professional library. You have been asked to select the books needed by the faculty to help implement the science program. Make a list of fifteen or twenty items. Limit your budget to about $200. List the criteria you would use in selection.
10. List the similarities and differences you have discovered between teaching science and teaching other areas of learning in the elementary school.
11. How would you decide what science apparatus to order for use in teaching elementary science? Select a specific grade level to answer this question.
12. How would you describe a good elementary-science teacher?
13. Take a walk around the block where a school you are familiar with is located. What potential resources for the science program can you find? How would you use these resources?
14. Read the science news reported in a local newspaper for a period of one week. What specific areas of science were involved in these reports? What difficulties did you encounter in reading this material? What in your own science background helped you? What additional background would have been helpful?
15. Design a week's work in a specific science topic for a specific grade. What adaptations would you make for disadvantaged children? How would you know that your plan is working? What unique features of the science program do you think make it a valuable source in meeting the needs of the disadvantaged, of children for whom English is a second language?

(Courtesy of Wide World Photos.)

PART II

THE EARTH AND THE UNIVERSE

CHAPTER 6A
THE EARTH AND ITS SURFACE

On the sands of the sea's edge . . . there is a sense . . . of the unhurried deliberation of earth processes that move with infinite leisure. . . .

—Rachel Carson, The Edge of the Sea

(Courtesy of Monkmeyer, Ruth Block photographer.)

AT THE EDGE OF THE SEA

An ocean wave, born of a far-off wind, travels thousands of miles across open sea and breaks near a sandy shore. Impelled by the tumbling wave, a rush of water carries a load of sand particles up the face of the beach. Here the water spends the last bit of its windborn energy, dropping the sand as it slows down and stops. Now gravity takes over and pulls the sheet of water back into the ocean.

Meanwhile, a brisk on-shore wind lifts up some dry sand particles that were left on the upper beach by an earlier wave. As the wind hurdles the dune that slopes up from the beach, it is slowed down; gravity snatches part of the sand from it. And so the dune grows.

In this single instant on the beach the forces of wind and of gravity, working on water and sand, have altered a tiny portion of the earth's face. On the sea's edge we are constantly reminded that the earth and its surface are changing today, and that these changes are part of the processes that began in the past and will extend into the future.

TO THE CENTER OF THE EARTH

A journey to the center of the earth, fancifully described by the novelist, Jules Verne, would not be practicable for many reasons. One of these reasons is the rising temperatures encountered with descent. At a depth of only 3 miles the temperature is literally high enough to make the blood boil.

Actually, man has seen very little of the interior of the earth. Even the deepest oil wells are but pinpricks in the earth, penetrating a mere 5 miles into a sphere whose center is nearly four *thousand* miles from its surface. We have had to rely mainly on indirect evidence, such as the outpouring of volcanoes and seismograph records of earthquakes, for our knowledge of the earth's interior. We shall look at this evidence presently.

Studies by scientists have revealed that the earth is composed of a series of concentric shells, each made of different materials. The outermost shell is the *crust,* a relatively rigid zone that varies in thickness from 3 to 40 miles. Most familiar to us is the loose material on the surface

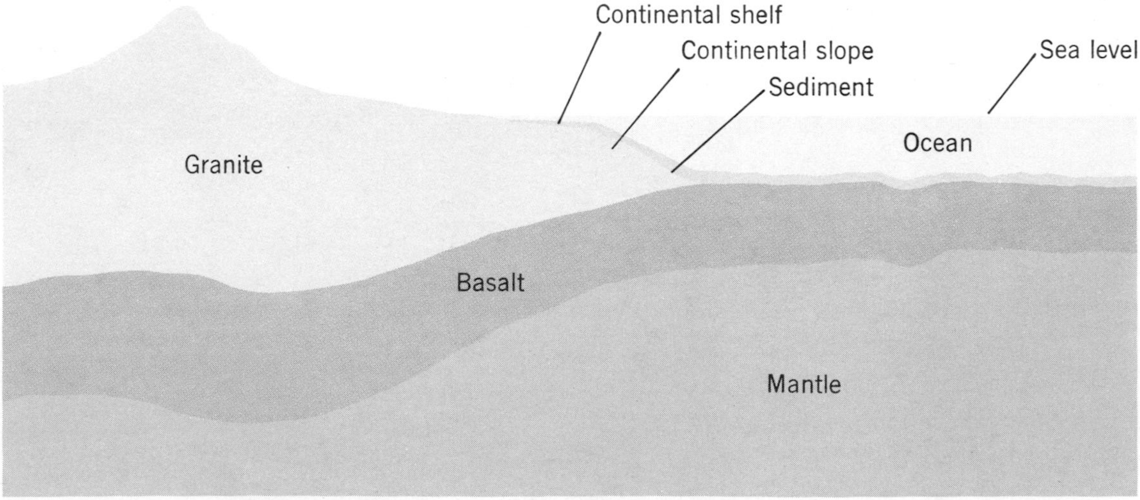

A basic difference between the continents and the ocean basins lies in the fact that they are made of different crustal material. The continents are underlaid by granite "floating" on heavier basalt. The oceans lie on basalt. The diagrammatic cross-section shows the difference at the edge of a continent.

of this shell: soil, sand, gravel, rock fragments, and boulders. We know that this loose material is only "skin" deep. If we dig a few feet, or at most a few hundred feet, we strike the solid bedrock in the earth's crust. In mountainous areas much of the bedrock lies exposed to man's view. In other areas, such as the plains, the bedrock is almost completely covered by soil. Here it is exposed only occasionally by the cutting action of rivers or the digging of man, or because an isolated mass of hard rock has not yet been leveled and broken down. The exposed bedrock is called an *outcrop.*

The covering of soil and other loose materials is discontinuous, varying in depth from zero to a few hundred feet, but the crustal rock forms a continuous layer, underlying the continents and extending under the beds of the oceans.

Before descending to the interior of the earth, let us spend a few moments more examining its face. Looking at the planet Earth from the moon, one would be impressed by the fact that most of it is covered with water. The Pacific Ocean alone covers about half of the globe; all the seas together cover about 70 percent of the area of the earth. The floors that underlie the oceans are not flat; soundings have shown that they are as rugged in profile as the continents. The world record for depth, 36,198 feet, is in the Marianas Trench of the Pacific Ocean. In comparison, Everest, highest of all our continental mountains, extends 29,028 feet above sea level.

These mountain heights and ocean depths of the earth's crust, enormous as they may appear to man, are insignificant in relation to the size of the earth. On the average classroom globe a true scale representation of these irregularities in the earth's surface would scarcely be visible to the eye.

Continents and oceans lie on the crust of the earth. The crust is not uniform in thickness, as is evident in the illustration of the earth's crust. It averages about 20 miles under the continents, but only 7 miles under the oceans. Over millions of years great forces under the earth have caused the crust to bend and buckle, forces that raise mountains and fracture the crustal rocks.

The crust is made largely of two kinds of rocks: basalt and granite. Basalt is found under continents and oceans. Granite lies over the basalt only on the continents; the crust under the oceans is entirely basalt. The crust is solid except for deep pockets of hot, liquid rock called *magma.* These pockets are the reservoirs for the volcanoes that occasionally burst through the upper crust.

Beneath the crust lies the *mantle,* a zone about 1,800 miles thick, composed of rock at

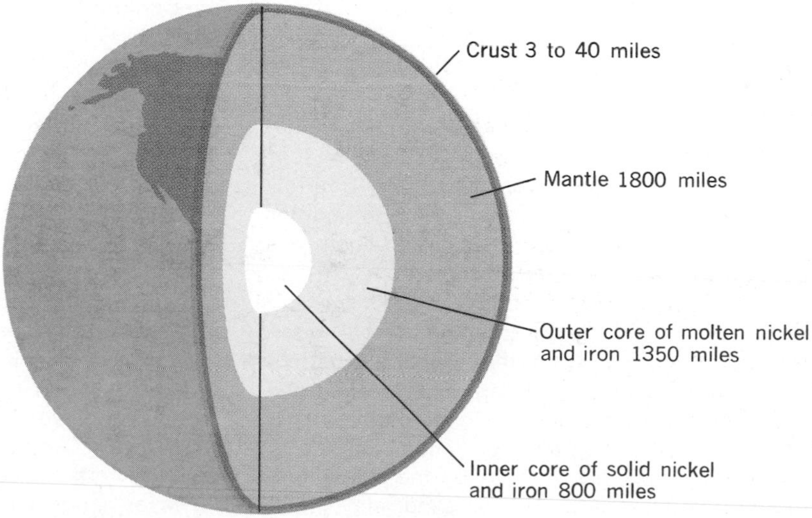

The inside of the earth according to present-day knowledge.

red- to white-hot temperatures, possibly as high as 4000° F. The rock in the upper region of the mantle is slightly plastic; although not melted, it can move or "creep" slowly. It may seem strange that rock can flow without melting, but this characteristic applies to many materials under constant stress, such as steel, glass, and ice. A familiar example of such creep is the behavior of the toy substance known as "silly putty" which bounces like hard rubber, but when left overnight collapses and flattens.

The rock of the mantle, which probably contains much iron, is believed to be heavier than the crustal rock but lighter than the material in the innermost zone, the *core.* The core is a sphere about 2,150 miles in radius, just about the size of the planet Mars. The core is hotter than the mantle; its temperature may be as high as 10,000° F. The outer part of the core is 1,350 miles thick, and is probably made of nickel and iron in a hot, plastic condition. The inner core apparently is also made of nickel and iron, but it appears to behave more like a true solid than does the outer core, having a consistency like that of hard rubber.

Thus, in this 4,000-mile trip to the center of the earth we have encountered from 3 to 40 miles of bedrock in the crust, about 1,800 miles of hot rock in the mantle, about 1,350 miles of molten metal in the outer core, and about 800 miles of solid metal in the inner core.

KINDS OF ROCK

On the huge granitic masses of the original continents there has formed over millions of years a relatively thin layer of rock. We can understand the many rock formations we encounter on the landscape better if we group them according to their methods of origin.

(See pp. 143–4.)

Some rocks have been formed from the cooling and hardening of hot molten material from deep within the earth's crust. These are called *igneous* rocks. An example is basalt, a characteristic rock in the lava that flows from volcanoes.

Some rocks are formed by the cementing together of materials such as sand, clay, mud, and pebbles. These are the *sedimentary* rocks. An example is sandstone, formed by the joining together of sand particles.

Some rocks are formed by the changing of existing rocks into new kinds. These are the *metamorphic* rocks. An example is marble, which is derived from limestone.

All rocks, then, may be classified as igneous, sedimentary, or metamorphic, depending on their methods of formation. Let us consider each of these groups more carefully.

Igneous Rock

The millions of tons of molten rock that pour out of volcanoes illustrate the method of origin of igneous rock. Pockets of hot liquid rock—*magma*—found deep in the earth sometimes erupt to the surface through fissures in the crust and spread over the earth. (When magma reaches the surface, it is called *lava.*) Such rocks as obsidian, pumice, and basalt are formed in this way.

Obsidian, sometimes called volcanic glass, results from the rapid cooling of surface lava; it is a dark, glassy rock. In thin slices it transmits light. A mass of this rock makes up Obsidian Cliff in Yellowstone National Park.

Pumice is so full of holes formed by escaping gas at the time of its origin that it is often light enough to float in water. Basalt is the dark-colored, heavy, dull rock common in lava flows such as the series making up the Columbia Plateau in the northwestern United States. This plateau—with its 150,000 square miles of hardened lava in places 1 mile thick—is one of the earth's greatest volcanic constructions.

Sometimes the liquid magma does not reach the surface of the crust in its upward movement. Instead it forces its way into or between masses of rock. Here it solidifies into coarse, granular rocks such as granite, which is the most common of all igneous rocks in the continental crust of the earth. Although granite is formed under the crust, it is often found exposed in some areas because the overlying rocks have been gradually worn away. Granite is a popular building stone in many parts of the world. In the United States, however, its greatest use is for monuments.

Granite is easily recognized because of its speckled appearance. Close examination reveals that the speckling is caused by the different kinds of materials in its makeup. Among these materials, called *minerals,* are quartz, a glasslike substance, and feldspar, which comes in a variety of colors. Mica, a sparkling mineral, is also often present in granite.

Masses of granite rock can be seen in the Rockies, the Adirondacks, the Black Hills of South Dakota, and the White Mountains of New Hampshire.

Sedimentary Rock

Sedimentary rocks are interesting because their method of formation permits them to preserve plant and animal remains in a chronological sequence, as we shall see in Chapter 13A. These rocks are built up under water by the depositing there of materials such as sand, clay, mud, pebbles, and gravel. These materials, called *sediments,* are brought to the shallow waters of lakes and oceans by the streams or rivers that flow into them. Wind and moving glaciers of ice are also transporting agents. Other sedimentary rocks are made from plant and animal remains, such as shells or ferns. Still others are derived from minerals such as rock salt or gypsum that were once dissolved in the water. The pressure of accumulating materials slowly forces the lower layers of sediment to stick together and to harden into rock. In this process some natural cementing materials such as lime and quartz found in ocean and lake waters may help join together coarser sediments, such as sand or gravel. The kind of rock produced depends on the kind of materials deposited. Cemented sands become sandstone; hardened clay and mud form shale; cemented pebbles form conglomerate; sea shells provide the material for limestone; plants provide materials for coal.

Sedimentary rocks are very common. Many are easy to identify. Sandstone is obviously made of grains of sand. Sometimes the grains are very loosely joined, and if two pieces are rubbed, grains of sand are dislodged. Shale when wet smells like mud from which it was actually formed.

Most sedimentary rock formations have a banded, "layer-cake" appearance owing to the different kinds of materials that are deposited, one on top of another, where the rock is forming. For example, if yellow clay is deposited over white clay, different layers of shale will form. Or if sand is deposited over clay, a layer of sandstone will form over a layer of shale. The kind of "layer-cake" rock that is made depends on the size, color, and texture of the particles that go into it.

Metamorphic Rock

Soft coal is found in western Pennsylvania, hard coal in eastern Pennsylvania. All this coal was formed in the same geological period. Why, then, are these two coals so different? A study of the coal beds reveals that those in the hard-coal region are buckled into tight folds, whereas those in the soft-coal area are nearly horizontal. We infer from this, and from much other evidence in other areas, that high pressure and high temperature associated with the crushing and folding of the beds changed the soft coal, which is classified as sedimentary rock, into hard coal, which is classified as metamorphic rock.

The change involved in the transformation of soft or bituminous coal into hard or anthracite coal is one example of *metamorphism.* In general, it may be said that when bedrock is subjected to greatly increased pressures or very high temperatures or both it may be changed in its chemical and physical properties to become metamorphic rock. The pressure may result from large movements of the earth's crust that crumple and fold the bedrock. The heat may come from the friction of moving layers or from the proximity of hot magma.

We list here some of the important metamorphic rocks and the rocks from which they are derived:

Metamorphic Rock	*Derived from*
Anthracite coal	Bituminous coal
Gneiss	Granite or shale
Marble	Limestone
Quartzite	Sandstone
Slate	Shale

Pegmatite, an igneous rock.

Sandstone, a sedimentary rock.

Slate, a metamorphic rock. (*Photos by John King.*)

THE MINERALS IN ROCKS

If a rock is thought of as a kind of fruit cake the minerals in it may be compared to the cake's nuts, raisins, cherries, citron, and other ingredients. Minerals are natural substances of definite chemical composition. More than 2,000 different minerals have been identified in the rocks of the earth's crust. Some—such as gold, diamond, and ruby—are found in relatively few rocks. Ten min-

Sedimentary limestone near Lake St. John, Quebec. The layers provide a clue to the method of origin of this kind of rock. (*Courtesy of Dr. Benjamin Shaub.*)

erals, including familiar quartz and mica, make up about 90 percent of the rocks.

Rocks, like cakes, vary in their ingredients. Limestone, for example, is commonly made only of the mineral calcite. Granite, as we have seen, always has feldspar, quartz, and at least one other mineral in it. It owes its speckled appearance to the separate crystals of these minerals. (*See* the figure on p. 118.)

THE AGE OF ROCKS

Evidence gathered by scientists shows that the earth is very old. Let us see how scientists determine the age of the earth's rocks.

When a rock formation is deposited on top of another formation by natural processes, such as sedimentation or volcanic eruption, the layer on top, if undisturbed, must be younger than the one underneath it. This relationship, known to geologists as the Law of Superposition, may now seem obvious, but the concept was not expressed until the end of the eighteenth century. The Law led early geologists to establish the first

(*See* p. 395.)

geologic time scale. This was rough, but it revealed the enormous extent of geologic time.

A more accurate determination of the *absolute age* of rocks had to wait, first for the discovery of natural radioactivity, the knowledge that some atoms change by themselves into other atoms at regular and constant rates, and second for the development of laboratory techniques for measuring the degree of change.

Uranium, for example, which is widely distributed in rocks, undergoes radioactive decay,

(*See* pp. 549–50.)

eventually ending up as lead. With the passage of time the amount of uranium in a rock decreases and the amount of lead increases. We know two things about uranium in rocks which enable us to use it as a "time clock":

1. Measurement shows that each year 1 ounce of uranium will yield 1/7,600,000,000 ounce of lead.
2. The rate of change of uranium to lead is constant under all conditions of temperature, pressure, and chemical surroundings.

Most of this radioactive uranium is found in igneous rock. We infer that it was incorporated as a mineral at the time the rock solidified from molten materials. From that point on the radioactive "clock" began ticking, with uranium breaking down into lead at the rate just given.

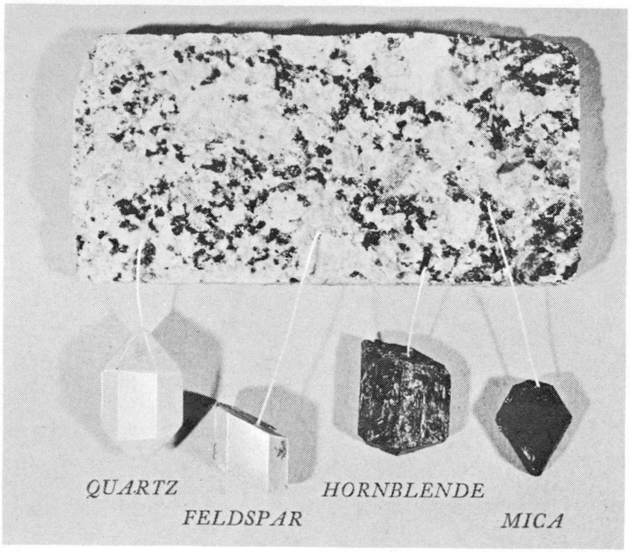

Granite rock is speckled with grains of the different minerals of which it is composed. Four typical minerals found in granite are shown here. (See text on pp. 116–7.) (*Courtesy of Dr. Benjamin Shaub.*)

It may be helpful in understanding the workings of the atomic clock to think of an old-fashioned hourglass which has just been inverted so that all the sand is at the top. The sand begins sifting through the narrow neck to the bottom. Think of the sand in the upper part as the original uranium and that in the lower as the lead resulting from its decay. The passage of time is marked by the relative amount of sand in the upper part (uranium) as compared to that in the lower (lead).

In addition to uranium other elements found in rocks have atoms (*isotopes*) which are radioactive, breaking down slowly to form other elements. Potassium and rubidium are useful in dating rock for this reason. Radioactive potassium breaks down into argon at a slow but constant known rate. To determine the age of a rock it is necessary to measure the ratio of argon to potassium. The higher the percentage of argon, the older the rock. Since potassium is found in metamorphic as well as igneous rock it has broader use than uranium as an atomic clock.

Natural radioactivity has provided a more exact measure of the age of rock than any other thus far. The oldest rock measured in this way is about $3\frac{1}{2}$ billion years old. We infer that the earth itself is about 5 billion years old.

FORCES THAT CHANGE THE EARTH

Men once thought mountains, plains, plateaus, and other large features of the earth had always existed. The science of geology reveals that two processes work continuously in sculpturing and altering the face of the earth: the forces of construction and those of destruction.

The constructive forces, as the geologist defines them, are those that lift up land masses to produce forms such as mountains. Earthquakes and volcanoes reflect the working of these constructive forces. The destructive forces are those which tend to level down the mountains and hills. The cutting action of running water and scouring by glaciers of ice are among the forces that erase the high places of the earth.

Both of these processes are at work today. Let us consider the first to see how the mountains of the earth were built.

KINDS OF MOUNTAINS

The birth of a mountain in our own time, Parícutin in Mexico, is described on pp. 126–7.

(*See* pp. 145–6.)

Parícutin is one of a type of *volcanic mountains* that has arisen as individual peaks. Mount Popocatepetl, also in Mexico, and Mount Etna, in Sicily, are of this type. Some volcanic mountains form chains, possibly because they have burst out of weak points in a line in the earth's crust, such as those in the Hawaiian and Aleutian islands.

Volcanic activity may force magma under previously existing layers of rock, as we have seen in our study of igneous rock. This may lift the overlying rocks sufficiently to form *domed mountains,* which are usually oval or circular in shape. The Black Hills of South Dakota, the Henry Mountains of Utah, and the Adirondack Mountains of New York are examples of domed mountains.

Folded mountains are formed when sedimentary or lava rock masses are subjected to tremendous earth pressures which crumple them into long, parallel ridges. Folding of the crust accounts, at least in part, for great mountain ranges such as the Alps, Andes, Appalachians, and Rockies.

It is difficult to believe that anything as hard as rock can be folded into waves. Rocks, contrary to popular belief, are quite elastic. Just as a long bar of something as hard as steel can be bent, so too can long sections of the rocky crust of the earth.

Sometimes, however, when the pressuring forces are sufficiently great, the crust may break. The fracturing of rock may be accompanied by slippage along the break; that is, the rocks on one side are pushed up higher than rocks on the other side of the break, resulting in the elevation of the rock on one side. This sudden slipping, followed sometimes by the tilting of raised rock, results in the formation of *block mountains.* The largest of the block mountains in the United States are the Sierra Nevadas, which are over 400 miles long and 50 to 80 miles wide, with the elevated side of the broken rock facing eastward to form one side of the Great Basin.

LIFE HISTORY OF MOUNTAINS

Mountains have their own kind of life history, passing from youth to maturity and then to old age. The life span of mountains covers hundreds of millions of years, but we are familiar with many stages of their development because there are mountains of different ages in existence today. The Laurentians, for example, are older than the Appalachians, which in turn are older than the Rockies.

In their early youth mountains are still grow-

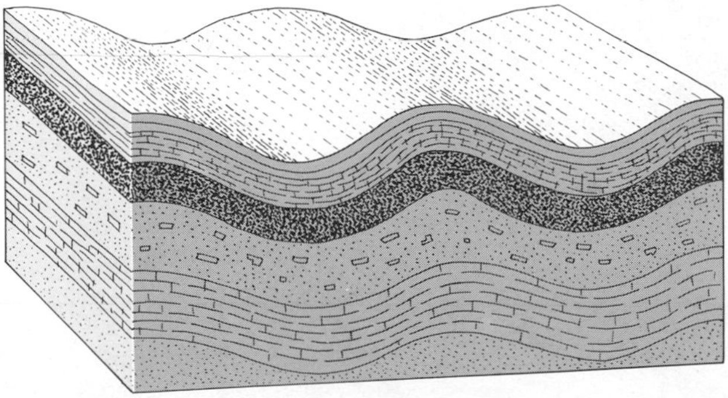

FOLDED MOUNTAINS

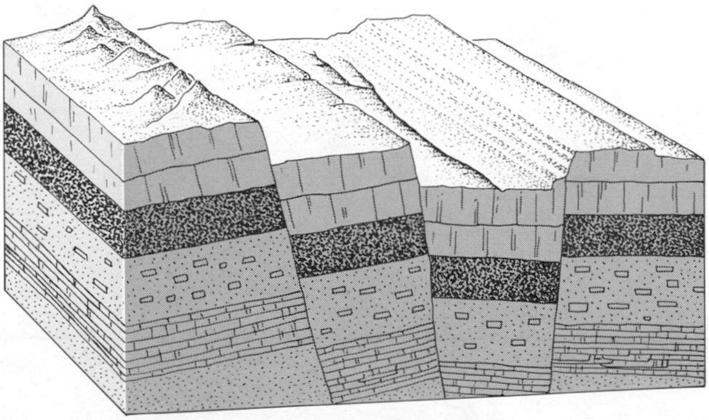

BLOCK MOUNTAINS

(*Left*) When the crust of the earth is subjected to pressure it may buckle up into long parallel ridges to form folded mountains. (*Right*) Block mountains are formed when large blocks of the earth's crusts are raised and tilted. Block mountains are usually rectangular in shape.

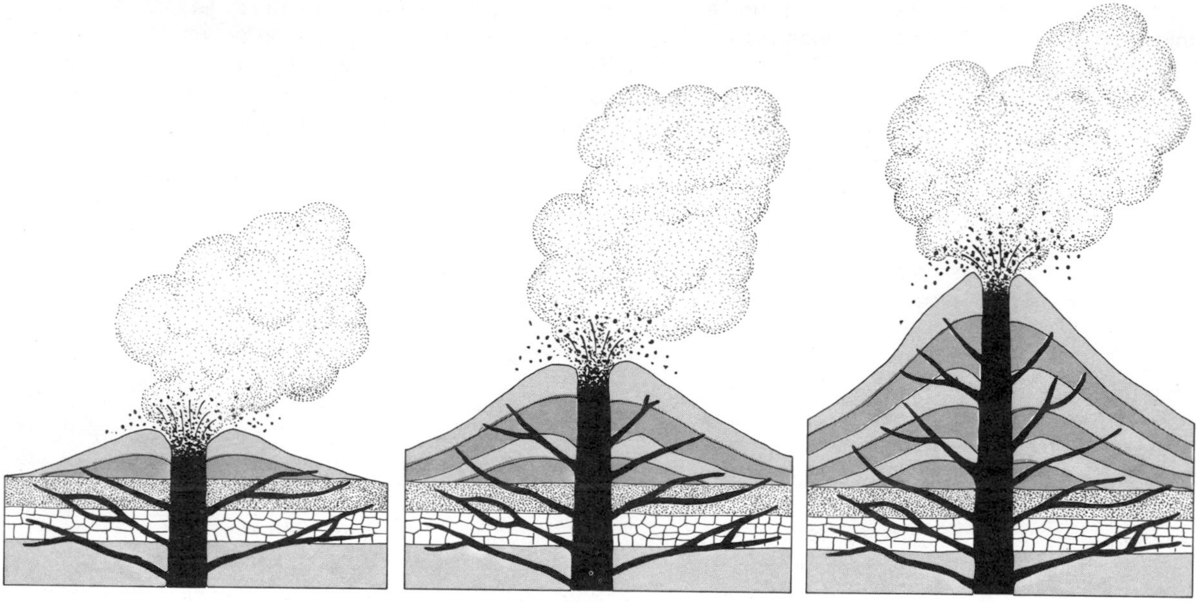

Hot liquid rock under pressure from the earth's interior is pushed up to the surface and gradually builds a volcanic mountain.

High jagged peaks, narrow valleys, and steep slopes are characteristic of young mountains—an aerial photograph of the peak of Grand Teton in Wyoming. (*Courtesy of the Union Pacific Railroad.*)

ing, evidencing this by volcanic eruptions, earthquakes, by the slow rising of rock layers, or by all of these. Young mountains are high and rugged, with sharp peaks, narrow valleys, and steep slopes. The Himalayas, Andes, Sierra Nevadas, and the Rockies are young mountains.

When mountains have stopped growing they are said to be mature. Weathering and erosion breaks rocks into fragments and carries them away. Peaks are lowered; slopes become gentler; valleys become wider. The Appalachians, White Mountains, Adirondacks, and Green Mountains of Vermont are mature mountains.

Continued erosion, principally by running water, brings mountains into their old age. This wearing down eventually erases the peaks and may produce a flattened area called a *peneplane,* whose level aspect is occasionally relieved by some rolling hills or by solitary rock masses, known as *monadnocks,* that have withstood the forces of destruction. Manhattan and the Bronx in New York City are located on a peneplane. Stone Mountain in Georgia is a monadnock on the Piedmont Upland, which is a raised peneplane.

Mountains seldom pass through all stages of this life cycle without interruption. Marked crustal uplift or submergence under the ocean, internal earth stresses, lava flows, and other events alter the rate and character of the aging process.

THE OCEANS

Interest in the oceans has increased markedly in recent years—for a number of reasons. We look to life in the oceans for a possible solution of the earth's food problems. We seek ways of extracting the untapped mineral wealth dissolved in its waters. We hope to harness the energy of ocean tides and wave movements to generate electricity. We are now conducting large-scale experiments to find more efficient ways of extracting fresh water from ocean water to relieve shortages and to open up desert areas for cultivation. We study the oceans to understand better the role they play in weather and climate patterns of the earth. We bring cores of the sediments that have accumulated for millions of years up from the ocean's bottom to find new clues to the earth's history. We look to the ocean depths as a new challenge for exploration and adventure.

In the past the study of the oceans was limited principally to the search for new trade routes. Today the relatively young science of oceanography uses the principles and techniques of biology, chemistry, physics, and geology for investigating the mysteries of the seas.

Some of the most significant discoveries in oceanography have been made on the floor of the ocean. For hundreds of years navigators have sailed the oceans without knowing the shape of its bottom, except in shallow coastal waters. It was generally assumed that the ocean bottom was shaped like a saucer or soup dish, deepest in the middle and rising smoothly to meet the surrounding continents. It came as quite a surprise, therefore, when it was found that the deepest parts of the ocean were relatively close to land masses.

A simple but effective tool for determining the depth of the ocean was the *sounding lead,* a weight lowered by a hemp line from a ship until it hit bottom. The length of the line gave the depth at any point. After World War I, sound waves were bounced from the ship to the bottom. The time needed for the sound to return was a gauge of depth (*see* Chapter 20A for a fuller explanation).

With these and other devices oceanographers found that the ocean bottom is far from being a smooth plain; its mountains and valleys rival anything found on the continents. Perhaps the most exciting discovery was that of the ocean ridges, a system of mountain ranges 40,000 miles long, which extend through all the ocean basins of the earth. The ocean ranges are regions of frequent earthquake and volcanic activity. The eruption of Surtsey, a submarine volcano off Iceland in 1963, and the resulting growth of an island there, are evidence of the crustal unrest in the ridge regions of the oceans.

Running along the Mid-Atlantic Ridge and dividing it into an east and west portion is a deep valley or rift. The significance of the Ridge and the rift will be discussed later in the chapter in "The Drifting Continents."

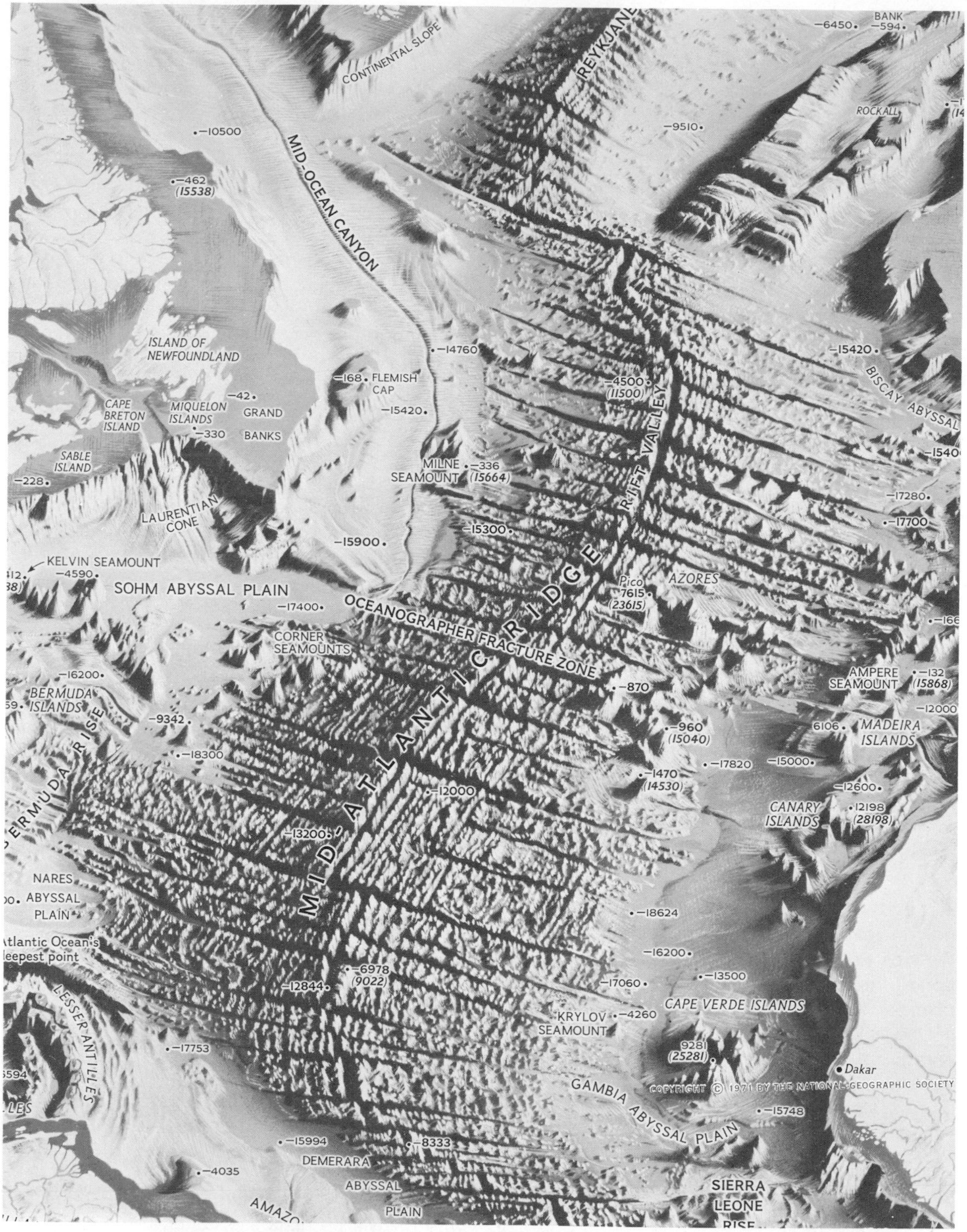

Part of the Atlantic Ocean floor.

The ocean bottoms have a geography that is as varied as that of the continents. They are characterized by high mountains, deep trenches, underwater volcanoes, and broad plains. The text explains why the mid-ocean ridge and the rift valley that lies along it are of particular significance in relation to the theory of drifting continents. (*Courtesy of the National Geographic Society.*)

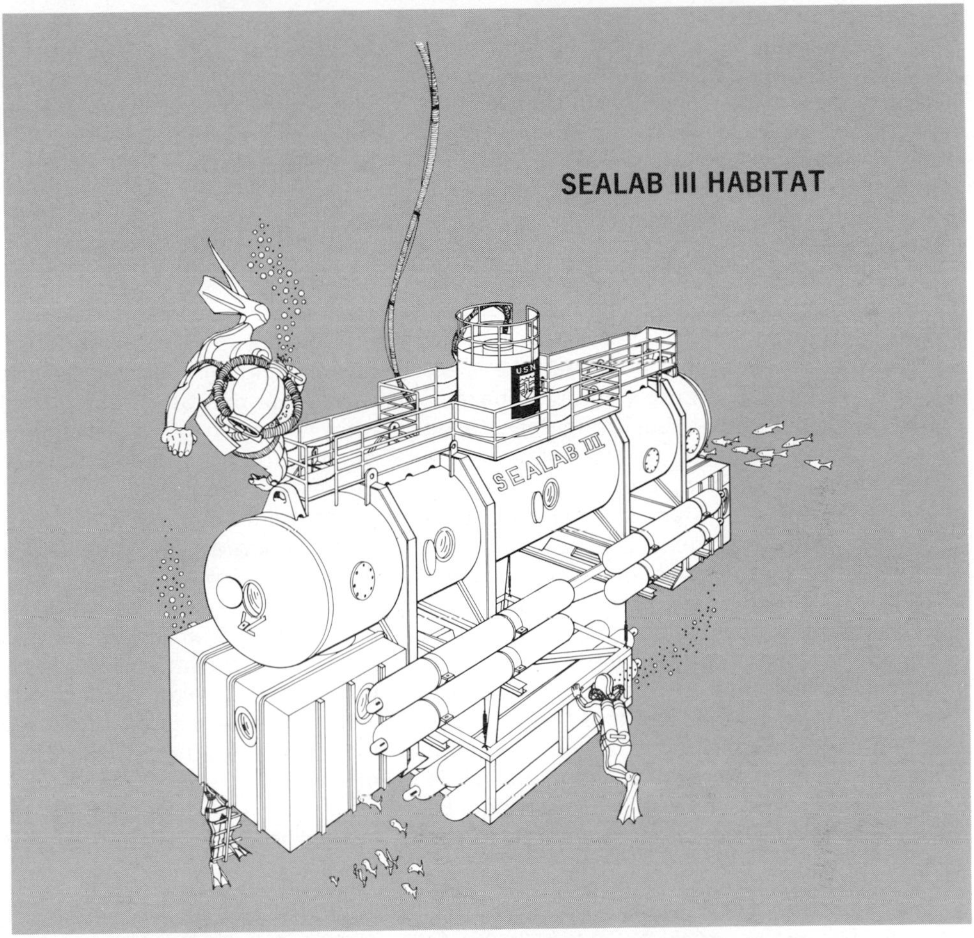

Sealab III is typical of the underwater laboratories where aquanauts can live for many weeks while they study the environment, the life, and the resources of the seas.

Almost as dramatic as the finding of the undersea mountain ranges was the discovery of the deep-sea trenches, which drop precipitously from the ocean floor. Some of the trenches of the Atlantic and Pacific have walls that are steeper than parts of the Grand Canyon.

In summary, we may say that the sea floor is characterized by mountain ranges, deep trenches, underwater volcanoes, and vast plains. Bordering all continents are shelves and slopes that are the submerged parts of the continents. The crust under the oceans is thinner than that of the continents. Both the continents and the ocean basins are fundamental parts of the crust of the earth.

EARTHQUAKES

The earth scientist, with his long-range point of view, regards earthquakes as constructive events because they are part of the process that pushes up and builds rock structures above the surface of the earth. To the common man, however, earthquakes are fearful happenings, resulting in widespread destruction of life and property in the areas where they occur. In 1923 an earthquake in Japan took a toll of 140,000 people killed or missing. The highest loss of life due to earthquakes on record is estimated at 830,000—the result of an earthquake in China in 1556.

Ninety-five percent of all earthquakes occur in two geographic belts, one ringing both sides of the Pacific Ocean and the other crossing the Mediterranean area. These belts also include most of the world's active volcanoes and young mountains. Indeed, earthquakes, volcanoes, and mountain building are all associated with turbulence in the earth, with great crustal pressures and tensions. We have seen, in our study of mountain formation, how the pressures within the crust may cause it to buckle up and fracture. An abrupt movement of large blocks of the earth's crust on each side of the fracture is essentially what happens during an earthquake.

Earthquakes often occur along lines called *fault lines* that represent an old wound in the earth's crust produced by a previous fracturing of the rock. The San Francisco earthquake of 1906 took place along such a line, called the San Andreas Fault, that extends for several hundred miles from northern to southern California. This line was known to geologists for many years prior to the quake. On both sides of the line pressures and tensions were built up in the adjoining rocks. The 1906 break released the tensions as rocks snapped, like the springing of a steel trap. Map studies of the location of roads and rivers before and after the break show that this earthquake resulted from a *horizontal* movement along the San Andreas Fault. Roads and fences that crossed the Fault were offset as much as 21 feet, moving northward on the west side of the fault and southward on the east side.

Some earthquakes result from a *vertical* movement of rock. In Yakutat Bay, Alaska, a section of seacoast was lifted as much as 47 feet during an earthquake in 1899. In the Alaska earthquake of March 1964 some 35 feet of vertical motion along the Hanning Bay Fault built Fault Cove in Montague Island.

The abrupt release of energy in the snapping and shifting of rocks starts strong destructive waves that can be detected thousands of miles away by delicate instruments called seismographs. The principle on which the seismograph operates is shown in the illustration. In this simplified model a heavy weight is suspended from a spring and a pen is attached to the weight. A drum, driven by a clock mechanism, turns slowly so that the pen writes on it. If an earthquake occurs, the drum shakes, because it is firmly attached to a platform whose base shakes with the earth. The weight remains stationary because very little of the force of the earth's tremor is transmitted to it through the spring, and because of its own inertia. As a result, a wavy line is inscribed on the turning drum. This is like writing by holding your pen firmly in your right hand and

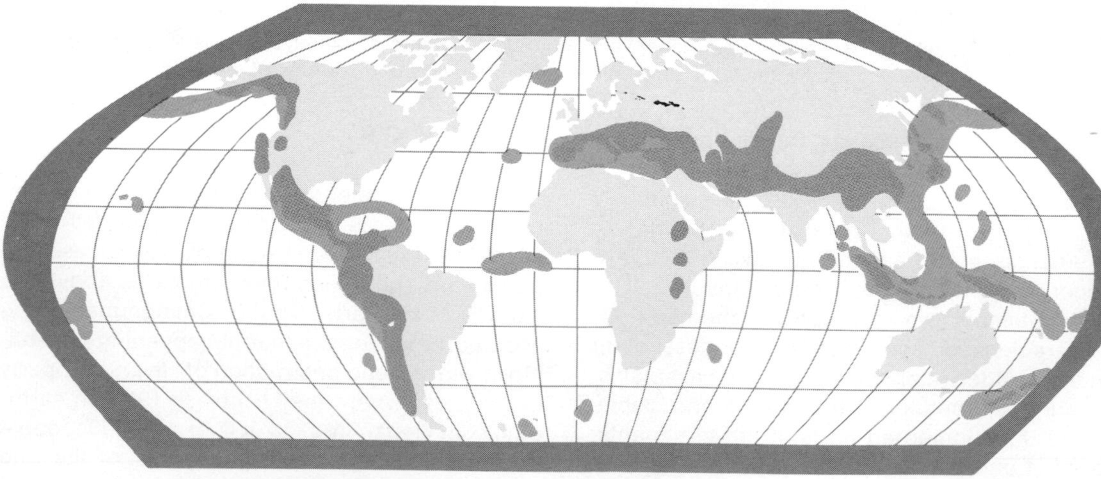

The principal earthquake belts of the earth. These coincide to a large extent with the regions of active volcanoes and growing mountains.

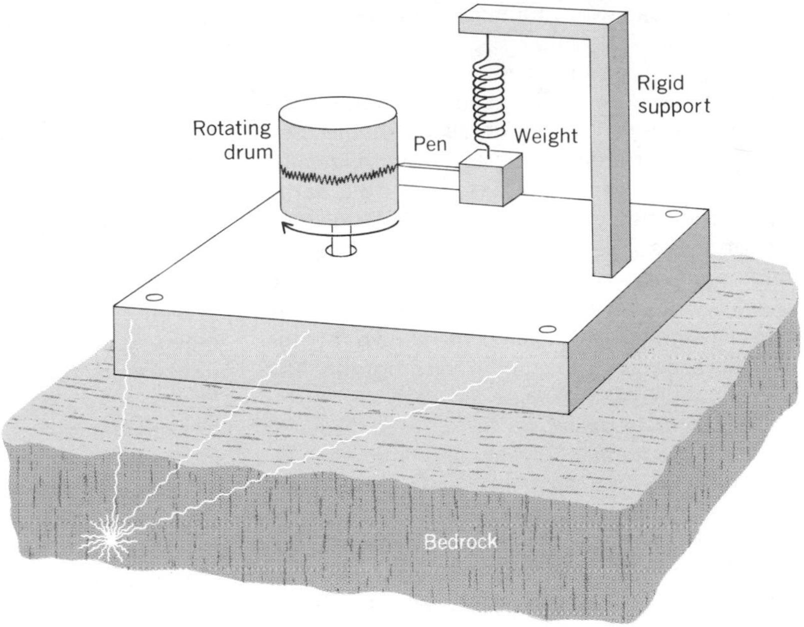

The principle of the seismograph (*see* text for explanation).

The distinct straight line from lower left to upper right is the trace of the San Andreas Fault west of Bakersfield, California. It was along this fault that the crust of the earth slipped in the 1906 earthquake. (*Courtesy of Monkmeyer.*)

by jiggling a pad with your left hand while moving the pad toward the left.

The *seismogram,* the name given to the lines written on the drum, is a record of earthquake vibrations written by the vibrations themselves. From this record the seismologist determines the duration, magnitude, and distance of the earthquake from the seismograph center. The *duration* of the quake is easily read because the minutes and hours are imprinted on the clock-driven cylinder. The magnitude of the quake, the amount of energy released, is shown by the height of the wavy lines on the seismograph. The determination of the *distance* from the earthquake center is based on the fact that several kinds of earthquake waves originate simultaneously at the point of the quake. The exact *location* of the center can be determined by the records of at least three widely separated stations within a few hours after the earthquake has started. Each of three observatories draws a circle using its distance from the earthquake as the radius. The site of the earthquake is the common point where the three circles intersect.

The study of seismograph records has revealed a great deal about the internal structure of the earth. As earthquake waves pass through the body of the earth their *speed* and their *path* are affected by different kinds and states of materials. One kind of earthquake wave, for example, will not pass through liquids at all; from this scientists hypothesized that the outer part of the earth's core—through which this wave does not pass—is in a liquid state. Earthquake waves, then, act like x-rays, enabling us to "see" through the earth.

(*See* p. 113.)

Many strong earthquakes originate in the crust under the Pacific Ocean. Here they may start ocean waves that travel as fast as 500 miles per hour and may break over coastal areas in waves as high as 60 feet. These are mistakenly called tidal waves, although they have nothing to do with tides. The scientific name is *tsunamis* (tsŏonä'mēz), a word of Japanese origin. In 1946 an earthquake originating off the Alaskan peninsula started great waves that traveled 2,000 miles to the Hawaiian Islands, causing widespread damage.

Shallow oceanic earthquakes have also been found to occur frequently in the region of the Mid-Atlantic Ridge, particularly in the deep rift valley that separates this long mountain range. This oceanic valley, directly above a belt of crustal unrest, is twice as wide, twice as deep, and, from a scenic standpoint much more impressive than the Grand Canyon.

(*See* p. 122.)

In comparing the total energy of different earthquakes seismologists use the *Richter Scale.* The energy is measured by a seismograph located at a standard distance from the earthquake's center. An increase of 1 unit on this scale expresses a 10-fold increase in the magnitude of the seismograph reading, but a 31-fold increase in earthquake energy at the source. Thus a 6 quake releases about 30 times more energy than a 5, and about 900 times more energy than a 4 quake. A quake of magnitude 2 is the smallest quake normally felt by humans. Earthquakes with a Richter value of 6 or more are considered major in magnitude. The California earthquake of 1906 had a value of 8.3; that of 1971 6.6.

The accurate forecasting of earthquakes is obviously of great importance. In recent years scientists have intensified their study of changes in earthquake-prone areas in an attempt to discover any symptoms that would warn of earthquakes. The following are among the phenomena under investigation: the little quakes that precede big ones and certain changes in the speeds of the waves they produce; the uplifting or tilting of the land; the accumulation of strains along faults; the frequency of earthquakes to determine whether they occur according to some time schedule.

VOLCANOES

On February 20, 1943, Dionisio Palido, a farmer in Parícutin, Mexico, went to plow his fields for the coming sowing of corn. He noticed with surprise that a small familiar hole in the ground had opened a little wider to become a crevice. At 4:00 o'clock he heard thunder and saw nearby trees trembling. In the hole the ground swelled and then raised itself 6 or 7 feet high. A fine ashy dust began to issue from part of the crack. Smoke arose with a loud continuous hissing and there was a smell of sulfur. Dionisio fled back to the village.

Later, red-hot stones, ashes, and sparks were thrown into the air from the opening. By midnight incandescent rocks were being hurled high into the sky from this roaring hole in the earth.

Thus was a volcano born in a Mexican cornfield in our own century. In all written human history we have records of the beginnings of no more than 11 volcanoes, and information about all before Parícutin is meager. Parícutin provided scientists with a "case study" they could investigate firsthand. From the third day of its birth skilled observers with many instruments at their disposal recorded all the significant events in the birth and growth of this volcano.

And grow it did. On February 21, the second day of its life, it grew from 30 to 150 feet in height. Lava—molten rock—began to pour out, advancing slowly over the cornfield at the rate of 15 feet per hour.

Seven weeks after its birth this lusty infant was almost 500 feet high. Heavy ash flying out of the volcano covered the countryside for miles, raining on the fields and eventually destroying the village of Parícutin.

At the age of 7 months the Parícutin volcano had become a mountain 1,500 feet high and about 1 mile in diameter. By 1952, at the age of 9 years, the volcano had become relatively quiescent.

Parícutin is a dramatic reminder that the earth and its surface are changing today, and that these changes are a part of a process that began in the past and will extend into the future.

Not all volcanoes are explosive; some pour lava out of craters or from breaks in their sides. Mauna Loa and Kilauea on the island of Hawaii are famous volcanoes of this type.

Some volcanoes grow rapidly—Parícutin, as we have seen, was 1,500 feet high at the end of 7 months; Monte Nuovo, born in 1538 at the edge of the Bay of Naples, rose to a height of 440 feet in *1 day.*

Some volcanoes continue to erupt for centuries; others cease very quickly. Many are dormant at present; they may become active or they may never erupt again.

We have noted that volcanoes are symptomatic of internal disturbances in the earth. They are concentrated in regions of the world where earthquakes and young mountain belts are located. Just why this is so will be discussed in the next section.

Recently we have developed techniques for forecasting eruptions. Seismograph records are helpful because volcanic activity is accompanied by earth vibrations. For 20 days before the birth of the Parícutin volcano numerous earth tremors were felt in the nearby countryside. Other clues include the tilting of the ground around volcanoes and local changes in the earth's electrical currents and magnetism.

THE DRIFTING CONTINENTS

How were the earth's continents and ocean basins formed? Have these global features remained fixed in shape and in position since their formation? How did the major mountain belts originate? Why are mountains, volcanoes and earthquakes found in distinct and usually narrow zones? Why are they not randomly distributed over the earth's surface? Why do the continents seem to fit together like a giant jigsaw puzzle?

Questions of this nature have puzzled geologists for many centuries, but it is only in the last decade that an explanation, known as *plate tectonics,* has provided an answer supported by a wealth of evidence. According to this theory the outer shell of the earth is divided into a mosaic of rigid plates that move slowly around the sphere. As the plates move apart, slide past each other, or converge new crust is created, continents drift, and mountains are formed.

The name *lithosphere* has been given to the rigid shell of the earth; it includes the crust and upper layers of the mantle. Evidence suggests that the lithosphere is 50 to 100 miles thick, and that it "floats" on a molten weaker layer called the *asthenosphere.*

(*See* p. 128.) The lithosphere is divided into six major plates and a number of smaller ones.

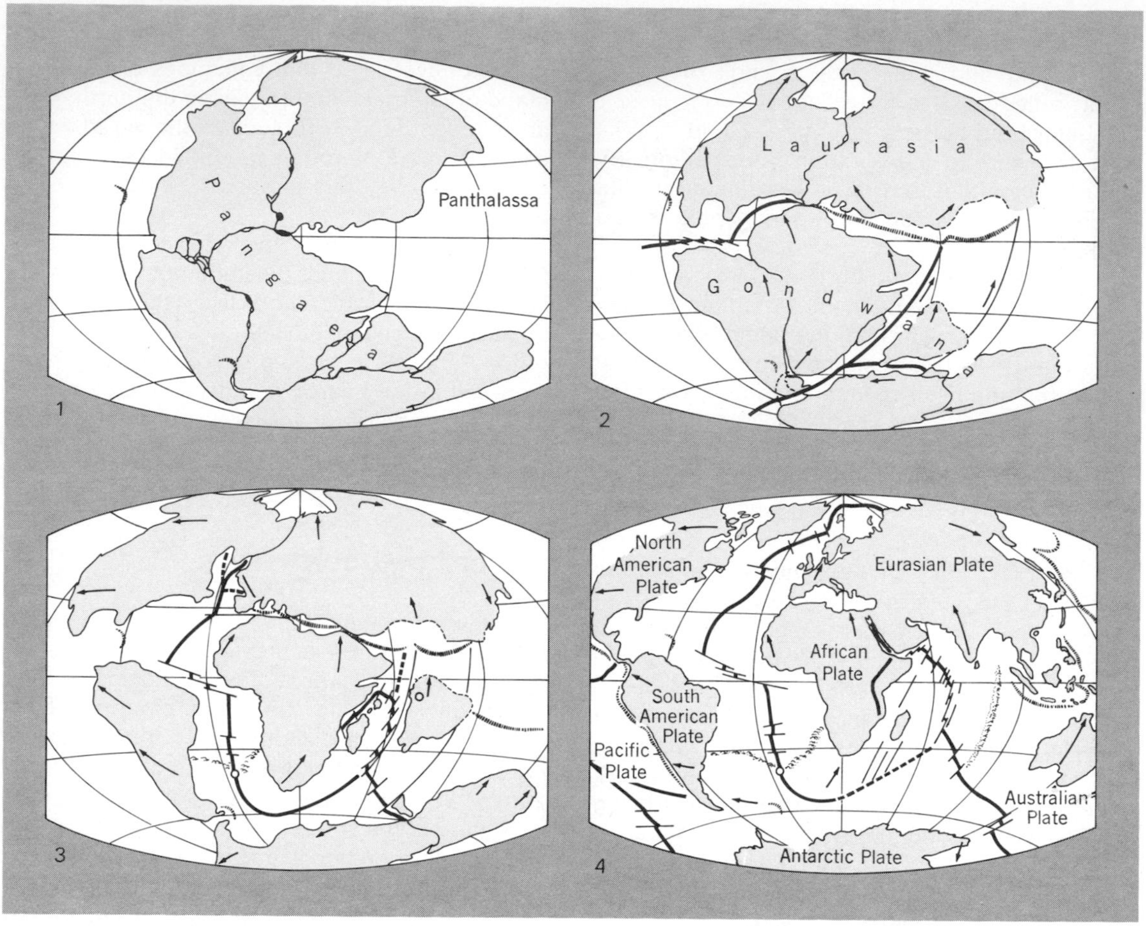

The breakup of the universal land mass of Pangaea into the many continents of today. *(Copyright © 1970 by Scientific American, Inc. All rights reserved.)*

Pangaea

According to plate tectonics the continents and ocean basins have been (and are now being) rafted along by the same underlying crustal conveyor belt—the moving plates. How has this system changed the earth?

Present evidence indicates that some 200 million years ago all the continents were joined in one land mass which geologists call Pangaea ("all lands"). The remainder of the earth was ocean, or rather the ancestral Pacific Ocean, called Panthalassa. Pangaea broke up and the continents were rafted to their present positions. New ocean basins were formed between the continents as they separated.

(*See* figure this page.)

Does this seem incredible? Then look at the

east coast of South America and the west coast of Africa. Can you see how they might have fitted together?

The original concept of Pangaea was proposed by Alfred Wegener in the 1920s. He puzzled over the matching coasts of Africa and South America, and was struck by a report of similarities in certain fossil bones found in the two places and in living species on these ocean-separated coasts. He postulated that it was not the animals, but the continents that had moved. To add more weight to his theory of drifting continents Wegener studied the world's mountain ranges. He noticed that if he joined the old and new world, mountain ranges on opposite continents formed a single continuous belt. For example, the Sierras of Argentina linked up perfectly with the Cape Mountains in South Africa. (*See* pp. 117–8.) Moreover, geological dating showed that the separated ranges were formed at about the same time.

Wegener's theory was not accepted for a number of reasons; it was not until the early fifties that his old ideas were revived.[1] In probing the oceans depths, as we noted previously, scientists discovered an ocean ridge system some 40,000 miles long, winding through all the basins of all the oceans. It was also discovered that a depression or valley divided the ridge into two sides. It was conjectured that this valley marked the location of an underlying *rift* in the earth's shell, where new molten rock was pouring up from the asthenosphere.

The discovery of the ridge and its valley supported the theory of continental drift, since it provided "visible" evidence of the sites of the original splits in Pangaea.

A spreading rift, according to the theory of plate tectonics, develops under a continent that (*See* pp. 549–50.) is resting on a crustal plate. Molten basalt from the asthenosphere spills out of the rift and hardens into rock, pushing in opposite directions to form ocean crust. In this way Africa and South America were split apart and pushed farther away from each other as the new ocean floor of the Atlantic was created. The Mid-Atlantic ridge with its rift is thought to be the scar or seam left by the splitting and parting land masses.

If new plate material is constructed, how do the plates fit together without buckling? Evidently the crustal conveyor belt system (like that in an escalator) connects zones of surface creation to zones of surface destruction. The latter are found near deep oceanic trenches, the kind that ring the Pacific. Here the edge of one advancing plate dives down under the leading edge of another and is consumed in the underlying mantle.

The *Glomar Challenger*

For a decisive test of the theories of sea-floor spreading and continental drift a research project was initiated to collect data from widely scattered parts of the ocean floor. For this purpose the ocean-exploring ship, *Glomar Challenger,* capable of drilling into the ocean floor and equipped with six laboratories for studying deep-sea cores, began its voyages in 1968.

The investigations of the *Glomar Challenger,* known as the Deep Sea Drilling Project, are financed by the National Science Foundation and managed by the Scripps Institution of Oceanography at La Jolla, California. After four years of sea drilling in 220 locations in the ocean floor the *Challenger* has produced a vast treasury of data on the history of the earth. The cores of sediment and rock extracted from the sea floor reveal many details about the formation of its crustal plates and their movements; about the age and origin of ocean basins, climates, and currents millions of years ago; the origin of submarine mountains and the pattern of past reversals in the earth's magnetic field.

The sea-floor drillings in many locations uncovered convincing physical evidence for sea-floor spreading and continental drift. The sediments that were brought up in the cores were older and thicker as the ship drilled farther away from the ocean ridges. The rate of spreading equalled or surpassed predictions: "During the lifetime of a man, the sea-floor can move a distance easily the length of his body. . . ," according to Dr. Melvin N.A. Peterson of Scripps.

[1] *See* Frederic Golden: *The Moving Continents* (New York: Charles Scribner's Sons, 1972) for a most readable account of Wegener and the concept of drifting continents.

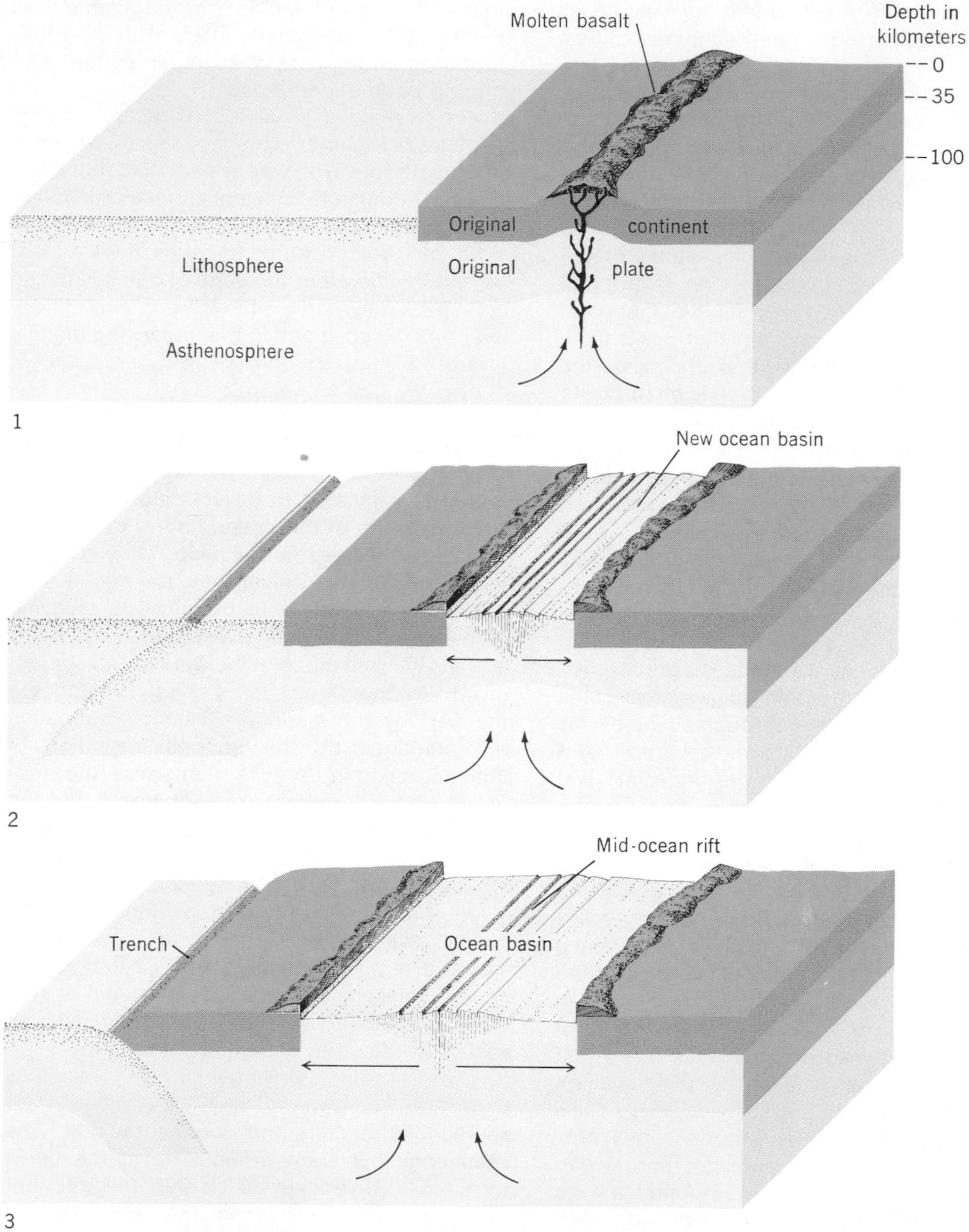

The splitting and drifting of continents according to the theory of plate tectonics: (1.) A continent (shown darker) resting on a single crustal plate begins to split as molten basalt wells up from under the plate. (2.) A new ocean basin is created between the two newly-separated continents. The spreading crustal plates carry the two continents farther away from each other. (3) The ocean basin widens. A mid-ocean ridge remains.

Other Plate Products: Mountains, Volcanoes, and Earthquakes

We have seen how plate tectonics accounts for the drifting of continents and the building of ocean bottoms. The concept of rigid plates moving around the earth and interacting at their boundaries has been remarkably successful in explaining other phenomena.

Sometimes plates slide past each other in opposite directions, as do the North Pacific and North American plates under California's San Andreas Fault. If the plates are stuck for a while stresses build up. When the build-up is sufficient the plates lurch forward and rocks in the earth's crust rupture, causing tremors or earthquakes.

A collision of continents may occur when a plate carrying one continent dives under an opposing plate carrying another. Since the continental crust is too light and too buoyant to be carried down into the asthenosphere the plunging continent pushes up the opposing one, forming a mountain range. Evidently the Himalayas were formed when a plate carrying India collided with the ancient Asian plate some 40 million years ago.

Another kind of collision may occur when a plate that has only an ocean above it descends into a trench. This may occur at the margin of a continent or of a major arc of islands. As the oceanic plate descends, it initiates pressure and heat changes which result in the thrusting up of a mountain belt. A good example of this is the western coast of South America, where a huge oceanic plate is plunging into a deep trench off the South American plate. As the ocean plate dives beneath the continental plate it pushes up the Andes Mountains and initiates deep earthquakes. The western North American mountains—the Sierra Nevadas, the Coast Range, and the Rocky Mountains—also resulted from similar interactions of oceanic and continental plates.

Some mountains, such as the Appalachians of North America, were formed 250 million years ago—before the final break-up of Pangaea—by the opening and closing of a prototype Atlantic Ocean.

Most earthquakes occur in narrow zones (*See* p. 128.) associated with the boundaries of plates. The earthquake network is seen to be associated with a variety of characteristic features such as rift valleys, volcanic chains, and deep ocean trenches. The areas within the plates are largely free of earthquakes. Geologically speaking, the action is where the plates end.

Before Pangaea

The earth is some 5 billion years old. Pangaea split up only 200 million years ago. What happened before Pangaea? Evidence from some ancient mountains indicates that plate tectonics operated in pre-Pangaean times, shifting and altering the continents and the ocean basins. And, from what we can see happening today, we know that the moving plates will make a changed earth in the future.

WEARING DOWN OF THE LAND

We have seen how forces working from the interior of the earth have thrust up the large features of our planet. Let us turn our attention to the forces that have modeled these features into the present face of the earth. First we shall consider *weathering,* the process by which rocks crumble and disintegrate. Then we shall look at *erosion,* the process which not only breaks rocks but also carries the fragments away.

WEATHERING

Frost Action

(*See* pp. 147–8.) Water, entering the pores or crevices of rocks, may contribute to their disintegration. If the temperature drops sufficiently the water changes into ice. In freezing, water increases about 9 percent in volume. The ice in the crevice acts as a wedge, forcing the rock apart and splitting off chunks from it.

Chemical Action

The chemicals found in nature act on rocks, changing them into new materials and breaking them down. The oxygen of the atmosphere unites with the iron that is present in many rocks, making it rust and decay. Water combines with some of the substances in rock—mica, for example—to form new materials that eventually crumble. The carbon dioxide of the air dissolves in rain water to form a weak acid known as carbonic acid. This acid works on various minerals. Feldspar, a mineral found in granite, is decomposed by carbonic acid into clay.

Living Things

Plants affect rocks mechanically and chemically. The roots of trees and shrubs sometimes grow into the crevices of rocks and may exert enough pressure to split them apart. Some kinds of lichens live on rocks and produce chemicals that attack and dissolve the surface of the rock, thus making it possible for these plants to absorb necessary minerals.

(*See* pp. 146–7.

When plants and animals die and decay, acids are formed that react chemically with rock and help to weather it away.

EROSION

Weathering *breaks* rocks into fragments of various shapes and sizes—boulders, pebbles, all the way down to the molecules of the minerals of which they are composed. Erosion breaks rock and also *moves* broken rock, including that formed by weathering. The agents of erosion are running water, ocean waves, moving ice, wind, and gravity.

(*See* pp. 142, 146–8.)

Running Water

The Grand Canyon of the Colorado River is the work of running water. Long ago the Colorado River flowed on high level land over the layers of sedimentary rock that had been laid down in previous eras. As time went on the running water, aided by fragments of rock that it carried, cut deeper and deeper into the rock. Weathering, discussed earlier, gravity, and rain helped the river attack the walls of the valley and widen the narrow cut into its present V shape.

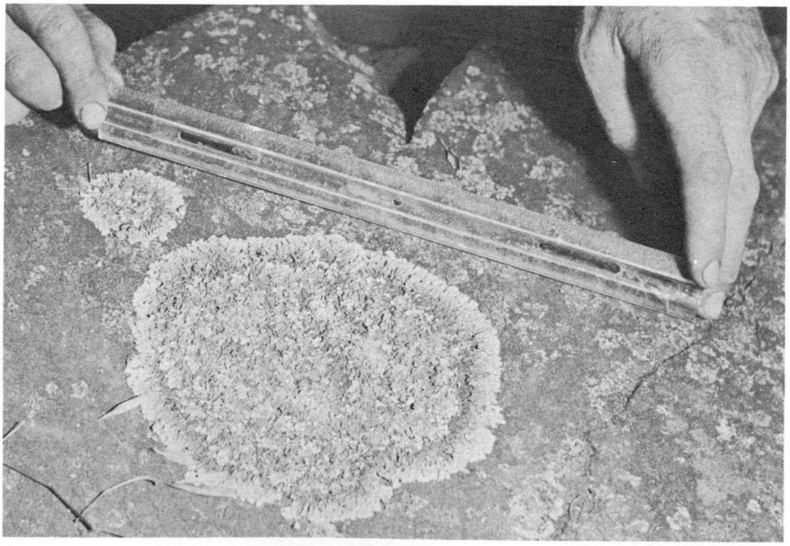

The rock-dissolving acids produced by lichens make tiny pits in the rock's surface. (*Courtesy of Monkmeyer.*)

The Grand Canyon and the Colorado River which carved it are seen in this view from Toroweap Point. (*Courtesy of the Union Pacific Railroad.*)

A river, then, carves a valley as it flows downhill on its way to the sea. At first the valley is narrow and V-shaped. The young river, using rock fragments as tools, rushes rapidly through the valley—filing, scraping, and sanding out a deeper and deeper bed. As the river's bed deepens, its banks cave in and the valley is widened. The river begins to slow down. Its ability to rush over large boulders and other obstructions is lost. The river is more easily deflected sideways into a meandering course.

Running water is the most important tool of nature in wearing down the surface of the earth. Not only does it cut and dislodge, it transports the materials that it and other forces have pried loose. The rivers of the United States carry about 1 billion tons of materials to the oceans each year. This represents an average leveling down of the entire surface at the rate of 1 foot in 8,000 years. What is most significant to us now is that much of this transported material is the valuable topsoil that is essential to our existence. This is a conservation problem created in part by man, and one that can and must be solved by man. (We shall discuss this more fully in Chapter 14A.)

Running water is responsible, at least in part, for many land forms that we do not have space to discuss here: gullies, badlands, potholes, rapids, waterfalls, flood plains, oxbow lakes, and deltas.

Ocean Waves

Ocean waters also affect the surface of the earth. Ocean waves smash our rocky seacoasts with a force that may rise to thousands of pounds in each square foot, splitting and moving rocks and scouring away bedrock by the grinding action of sand and pebbles. Boulders dislodged from rock cliffs are slowly pounded into pebbles and sands.

Ice

In the last million years great ice sheets have moved down from the Arctic regions, covering Canada, the northern United States, and northern Europe. During this Great Ice Age the ice sheets advanced and retreated many times, the last advance reaching its maximum about 20,000 years ago and the last retreat ending as recently as 6,000 years ago. At one time almost a third of the present land surface of the earth was covered with glaciers; today only a tenth is under glacial ice. Four-fifths of this is on the Antarctic Continent.

What is now New York City was once under a solid mass of ice half a mile high. A trip to Central Park in Manhattan will reveal many evidences of this glacial visit. The outcrops, or exposed bedrock, in this city oasis are scratched, grooved, and polished in a way that is characteristic of rock over which a glacier of ice has passed. Here and there, perched on the outcrop, are large boulders made of rock entirely different from the underlying bedrock, which in Central Park is mica schist. Evidently these boulders were plucked out of some mass of rock by the glacier some miles to the north of New York City and then dropped in their present position when the ice melted.

New York City and Long Island mark the southernmost advance of the Atlantic end of the last glacier. This front is revealed to us by a mass of loose earth—including sand, gravel, and boulders—that was deposited when the tip of the glacier melted. This material, forming what is known as a *terminal moraine,* extends 140 miles from Brooklyn across the northern half of Long Island to its eastern tip.

We are able to study glaciers at firsthand because some exist today. Glaciers begin as great snow fields that are slowly compacted into ice by the accumulation of more snow on top. Glaciers form in those regions where snow accumulates more rapidly than it melts. This happens in two places: near the tops of high mountains and in the frigid zones of the earth.

Valley glaciers originate in mountains and, as they grow, fill the valleys leading down, as a river might. The western United States has valley glaciers in the Sierra Nevadas, the Rockies, and the Cascade Mountains. The glaciers in Glacier National Park in Montana and Mount Rainier National Park in Washington attract thousands of tourists every year.

Continental glaciers originate over large cold land masses in the frigid zones, where they cover the land with ice sheets thousands of feet thick. When the ice becomes thick enough it moves out in all directions toward the seacoasts. Greenland and Antarctica are almost entirely covered by glaciers of this type.

Glaciers, like rivers, move downhill from the upper snow fields where they are formed. Glaciers in the Alps move at average speeds of 1 to 3 feet per day; those in Alaska and Greenland may move as much as 40 feet or more per day. These masses of ice always move forward, but their fronts may advance, remain stationary, or retreat. The front advances over the land as long as the mass of ice moves faster than it melts. When the rates of moving and melting are equal the front is stationary. In Greenland the glaciers advance faster than they melt, even at sea level. In Greenland and other places when glaciers reach the seacoast they break off to become *icebergs.*

Valley glaciers are great movers of materials on the earth's surface. They gouge out huge depressions and carry the material along to be deposited elsewhere as the glaciers melt. Passing through V-shaped valleys these glaciers change them into U-shaped ones. Continental

The southernmost advance of the glaciers in the last ice age. There are many evidences of the glacier's visit—rock deposits, lakes, grooves and scratches in rock, moraines, outwash plains, and others—in the regions formerly covered by ice.

glaciers also carry along huge boulders and soil and deposit them elsewhere. The soil of much of the northern part of the United States has been materially changed by continental glaciers that visited this area during the last million years.

Lakes and ponds are often the result of glaciation. Valleys become blocked with the soil and rocks of moraine deposits, which act as dams to hold back water. In some cases glaciers have gouged out or deepened basins that now hold water. The Great Lakes occupy ancient river valleys that were deepened and dammed by glaciers.

The glacial periods, or ice ages, of the past were presumably caused by fluctuation in the earth's temperature, when a drop of several degrees allowed a vast accumulation of ice to occur. It is thought that in the glacial periods the

A valley glacier, such as this one in the Chugach Mountains, Alaska, is a river of ice. Its origin is in high mountain snowfields, where snow is compressed into ice. As the glacier moves down the valley it grinds away at its walls, slowly transforming the original V-shape into a U-shape. (*Courtesy of Laurence Lowry, Rapho-Guillmette.*)

sea level may have been as much as 300 feet lower than it is now, because much of the oceans' water was locked up in glaciers.

It is conjectured by scientists that we are now in a warm, or *interglacial,* period. Measurements taken in recent years suggest that the sea is now rising at the rate of $2\frac{1}{2}$ inches per 100 years. Perhaps this rise is due to the rapid melting of the world's glaciers. It is estimated that if the existing glaciers melted completely, the sea level might rise by more than 150 feet.

Wind

We have seen how running water and moving glaciers carry soil and other materials across the earth's surface. Wind also is a carrier of soil. This has been dramatically and tragically demonstrated in the dust storms that have plagued some areas of our country.

There are other results of wind erosion that we see occasionally when wind piles up sand into dunes. There are huge hills of sand in many parts of the United States. They are alike in appearance, and they are all created in essentially the same way.

(*See* p. 137.)

We all know that a strong wind can carry sand. Some of the sand carried by the wind is dropped when the wind slows down because of an obstacle or for some other reason. The pile of sand thus deposited gradually forms a hill called a dune. The windward slope of a dune is gentle; the lee side drops more sharply. The transfer of sand from the windward to the lee side results in the slow movement of the entire dune in the direction of the wind. Dunes may march as much as 100 feet in 1 year.

The formation of sand dunes requires a great deal of dry sand to be moved and stretches of flat surfaces over which the wind can sweep. The migration of dunes sometimes buries towns, farms, and forests. On the eastern shores of Lake Michigan westerly winds have built dunes that are migrating inland over Indiana, slowly burying a forest area known as Dune Park. The migration of dunes can sometimes be halted by the planting of grasses and shrubs in the sand.

Gravity

When weathering separates a rock fragment from a large mass gravity eventually takes it down to the lowest part of the surrounding area. An accumulation of broken rocks at the foot of a cliff, called *talus,* is a product of gravity.

Gravity is also responsible for the less obvious *soil creep,* causing the soil covering to move very slowly downhill over a period of time. A more dramatic and often disastrous movement of soil results in a landslide. Landslides are sometimes set off by earthquakes, sometimes by heavy rains.

Gravity is also the force responsible for the movement of running waters in rivers and waterfalls and of valley glaciers, which, as we have seen, are prime agents of erosion.

SOIL FORMATION

Pour a handful of ordinary garden soil into a jar of water and shake it vigorously. When it settles, skim off some of the material floating on top. Much of this will be bits of leaves, stems, and roots of

(*See* pp. 142, 150.)

Sand dunes, such as these in Fremont County, Idaho, are formed whenever there are strong winds blowing from one direction and a sufficient quantity of loose sand. Note the contrast between the gently rising slope on the windward side (on the left) and the shorter, steeper leeward side. The sand ripples duplicate in miniature the windward and leeward slopes of the larger dune. (*Courtesy of U.S. Department of Agriculture, Soil Conservation Service.*)

plants, partially decomposed. Examine the material that has settled to the bottom carefully to find grains of sand and small pebbles, both of which are broken rock.

Soil has its origin in the decay of plants and animals and the weathering of rock. Soil is a final product in the destruction of rock. It is our greatest natural resource.

THE EARTH'S CHANGING SURFACE

Twenty-five hundred years ago the Greek philosopher Heraclitus said: "There is nothing permanent in the world except change." The earth itself is always changing; so, too, are the theories that men have held about the causes and the nature of these changes. Scientists and explorers are uncovering a new portrait of the planet Earth.

Two chapters in this book are related to this one and may profitably be read in connection with it: 13A, "The History of Life," and 14A, "Ecology and Survival."

In this brief picture of the earth and its changing surface, we have emphasized certain ideas; the chief ones follow (generalizations such as these will be found at the end of each of the A chapters; their purpose is to emphasize the essential meanings of the subject matter of the chapter):

The earth is very old and has undergone great changes in its lifetime.

Scientists study rocks to learn about the history of the earth.

The earth is believed to be composed of concentric parts of different materials: The outermost is a hard rocky crust; next is a zone of heavier red-hot rock; the outer part of the core is composed largely of molten metal, the inner core largely of solid metal.

Seventy percent of the surface of the earth is covered by seas.

The study of the oceans has taken on increased importance.

The landscape of the ocean floor is as varied as that of the continents.

An ocean mountain range or ridge 40,000 miles long runs along the ocean bottoms of the earth.

Rocks originate in three ways: from the cooling of molten materials, the cementing of small fragments, and the changing of existing rocks into new forms.

Rocks are made of one or more kinds of minerals.

Minerals are natural inorganic substances of definite chemical composition.

The co-architects of the earth's surface are the forces of construction and destruction—the forces that build mountains and those that level them down.

Mountains are formed from volcanic activities or from the buckling of the earth's crust.

Mountains have their own kind of life history, passing from youth to maturity and then to old age.

According to the theory of plate tectonics, the earth's outer shell is divided into a mosaic of rigid plates that move slowly around the sphere.

As the plates move apart, slide past each other, or converge new crust is created, continents drift, and mountains are formed.

The boundaries of the plates are marked by chains of volcanoes, mountain-building, and earthquake activity.

General acceptance is accorded the theory that a single land mass split and separated forming the present continents of the earth.

Temperature changes, chemical action, and living things are important in the splitting and breaking down of rocks.

The large forces responsible for the leveling down of the land are running water, ocean waves, moving glaciers, wind, and gravity.

Soil, our greatest natural resource, is a product of the destruction of rock.

Discovering for Yourself[2]

1. Make, or obtain if available, a rough map of the county in which you live. Indicate location of streams and bodies of water, unusual land forms, and other geological features. Then from observation, reading, and other sources describe how you think the surface of the area may have changed during (a.) the last 5,000 years, and (b.) the last 50,000 years.
2. Make a tour of the surrounding counties to observe erosion effects, land changes made by rivers, and other landscape changes.
3. Follow a stream to see (a.) how the stream has changed the earth around it, (b.) the load being carried, (c.) the swiftness of the stream, and (d.) the deposits of the stream. Examine a sample of the water.
4. Observe a local area after a heavy rainstorm to determine (a.) where erosion is taking place, (b.) why it is taking place, (c.) the materials that are being carried away, (d.) where materials are being deposited, (e.) the effects of deposits, and (f.) the effects on the area covered by the rain.
5. Make a rock collection using as many sources as you can for identification, and write an informative label for each specimen telling its origin, use, and composition.
6. Find out what the most pressing problems of soil erosion are in your state and what is being done about them.
7. Keep newspaper clippings dealing with earthquakes, floods, volcano eruptions, and other major "earth-changing" events for a period of two months. How did each of these events alter the surface of the earth?
8. Plan an imaginary summer vacation trip in the United States to see important and dramatic geological formations. What is your itinerary? What would you look for in each place? What important principles of geology would be illustrated?
9. Investigate, through printed sources, the San Andreas Fault in California. What is a fault? Can earthquakes be predicted? Should new houses be constructed on the fault site? What is the use of a seismograph?
10. Try to find out about the work of oceanographers. What tools, materials, and apparatus do they use? What are some of the important discoveries they have made during recent years, and how may their findings affect us in the future?

[2]Here, as in each subsequent A chapter, will be found activities designed to help you learn more about the science subject matter, as well as how to teach it more effectively. They are for use by preservice as well as in-service teachers. How many of them will be useful for a specific locality and school system will depend on local conditions. They have all been found helpful in many situations.

(Courtesy of U.S. Department of the Interior.)

CHAPTER 6B

TEACHING "THE EARTH AND ITS SURFACE"

To help children find out about the earth on which they live and to observe its changes more intelligently they need to observe the things that happen around them every day. Some of the changes in the earth's surface are easy to see in any environment, city or country. The hills, valleys, rocks, excavations, and soil in the neighborhood are sources to investigate. The school yard, "empty" lot, and park—exposed as they are to sun, wind, and rain—are excellent places to observe the forces of nature at work. The street becomes a "rainshed" area and the gutter a "riverbed" whenever it rains. The school building, with its natural and man-made stone, shows how we use some of nature's resources.

In investigating the surface of the land children compare natural and man-induced changes. A valley cut through rock by a river requires millions of years, whereas a man-made roadcut is the work of days. In connection with man-made changes children may attempt to make value judgments: "Should this road be built?" "Should this swamp be filled in?" "Should this mountain be strip-mined?"

(*See* pp. 19–23.)

This chapter like the other "B" Chapters provides many opportunities for engaging children in the processes of science and for achieving some of the behavioral and other objectives that we are striving toward. In particular the content of this chapter offers opportunities for *inferring* from observed facts: A pebble found in a stream is smooth and round, but a bit of stone found at the base of a rocky cliff is rough and jagged. Why? Since children are engaged in collecting rocks and examining soil content there are opportunities for them to invent their own *classification* systems for organizing these materials.

Related to the content of this chapter, and helpful to the teacher in planning broad units, are Chapters 13A and B and 14A and B.

SOME BROAD CONCEPTS: "The Earth and Its Surface"

The earth is covered with rocks, soil, and water.
There are many different kinds of rocks.
The earth's surface is constantly changing.
Water and wind help change the earth's surface.
Rocks were made in different ways.
Soil is made from the breaking down of rocks and plant and animal remains.
Man depends on soil, water, and rocks for his existence.

FOR YOUNGER CHILDREN

Although the following activities may be used at any grade level depending on circumstances, they have been found especially appropriate for younger children. They will need to be adapted to fit specific situations to meet the interests and maturity of children, materials available, and other factors. In many cases the processes and behaviors expected have been identified.

What Kinds of Rocks Can We Find in Our Neighborhood?

Collect different kinds of rocks on a class field trip to a nearby park, vacant lot, excavation, building under construction, and add specimens brought by individual children and the teacher. Undoubtedly the collection will include some man-made rock (don't reject them) such as fragments of brick and concrete. Where did the rocks come from? Examine them: feel them, lift them, look at them carefully, smell them, scratch them with a metal nail, scratch a smooth stone with them. Describe what you observe. How are the rocks alike? How are they different from each other? Color, shape, size, and other characteristics? After rocks have been examined carefully put some of them in a bag and break them with a hammer. Look closely at the broken rocks. Compare the inside surface with the outside. Describe how they are alike and how different.

Ask the children to suggest ways of arranging their rock collection to make an interesting display. Some children may wish to classify their rocks according to size, some according to color, some according to the place where they were found, and other ways. Have them carry out one of their proposals to make a rock display.

What Is Soil?

Collect a pail of soil from a forest. Dig under the leaves to get a good sample. Use magnifying glasses and examine the soil carefully. What can we discover by looking, feeling, smelling. Try to identify the various materials. Discuss whether or not there is anything in the soil that can grow. Can the tiny sticks? Pebbles? Dry leaves? Put the soil in a shallow plant jar, keep it moist, and observe. Did anything grow? (Seeds in the soil will probably sprout, although children may not have identified any seeds in their examination.) Did any of the other materials grow? Urge the children to discuss why. Will anything grow from the other samples examined? How can we find out? What is the soil made of?

What Did the Rain Do?

Walk in the school yard or nearby street immediately after a rain. What is happening to the water that fell? Dig into the soil if possible. How deeply has the water soaked into the soil? Look for puddles. Look for tiny streams. Look at the water that is running in the streams. Where is the water going? Does the water carry away any of the soil? How can we tell? Catch a glassful of water and let it settle. Is there any soil (mud) at the bottom? What has the water done to the soil around trees, on lawns, on grassy hillsides? As a result of these firsthand experiences children may state that rain water either flows along on the surface of the ground, forms puddles, or sinks into the soil. Depending on the nature of their experiences, other conclusions are possible and desirable.

Is the Earth's Surface the Same Everywhere?

Look at pictures (collected from the *National Geographic* magazine, travel folders, textbooks, and so on) of different places on the earth—seashore, mountains, deserts, farmland, tropical forest, polar regions, and other areas depending on the pictures available. Ask children to describe the places: Rocky? Dry? Wet? Hot? Cold? Smooth? Rough? Living things? Select two pictures and ask the children to try to compare them. Ask them to tell how these places on the earth are alike or different from the place where the children live. This will help children understand that the earth's surface varies greatly in different parts of the earth.

Along with the picture study suggest that children recall their own experiences on trips to distant places; try to discover human resources—a parent, teacher, member of the community—who have slides or pictures of trips that show the earth's surface. Discuss with children living conditions in the various environments (science and social studies combination); encourage children to *infer* the real shape of features shown, since the picture is only a flat representation of the real thing.

How Can We Make Rock?

Make a "man-made" rock such as concrete by mixing $\frac{1}{2}$ cup of cement powder and 1 cup of clean dry sand in a large tin can. Children should participate in the measuring. Add enough water to make a thick creamy mixture. Pour into a milk carton and allow to harden for several days. Ask children to *predict* what they think will happen. Remove the carton and let the children *examine* and *describe* the result. Ask children to look for places where man-made rock such as this is used. *Compare* their rock with the sidewalk or concrete floor. Where is concrete used in your neighborhood?

OTHER PROBLEMS FOR YOUNGER CHILDREN

1. How is the earth's surface near us different at different times of the year?
2. What do ice and snow do to the earth's surface near us?
3. What useful things do we get from the earth?
4. How does water in streams and rivers get dirty?
5. How can we clean muddy water?
6. How can we separate sand from pebbles?

FOR OLDER CHILDREN

How Can We Make a Rock Collection?[1]

Making a collection of rocks and related activities can result in children being able to *classify* the rock specimens either by doing single-stage classifying using one

[1] *See also Teacher's Guide* Elementary Science Study (ESS): *Rocks and Charts* (Manchester, Mo.: Webster Division, McGraw-Hill Book Co.). Children are given rocks and make charts using their own standards to compare and classify, exchange charts to see if they can understand each others, *Teacher's Guide,* Science Curriculum Improvement Study (SCIS): "Observing Rocks," "Sorting Rocks," and *"Material Objects"* (Chicago: Rand McNally). Stresses describing the properties of rock specimens and sorting them.

characteristic and then another—that is, color, hardness, formation, and so on—or, for some children, by using more than one characteristic. *Arrange* rocks according to their characteristics; *invent* methods of classification; *observe* characteristics through the use of the senses; *identify* some of the common rocks and *describe* what has been learned by making an exhibit or record. The most valuable rock collection is one that children participated in making on class trips or on trips with their families or friends.

A strong magnifying glass will be of great help to children as they study rocks. Begin with: "What can you find out by looking? How are the rocks alike? How are they different from each other?"

Break rocks apart with a hammer to look inside. A rounded rock looks different on the inside from the outside. Children may first *observe* and *describe* the rocks before they are broken and try to account for the appearance (shape, size, texture). After the rocks have been broken, children again examine and describe and attempt to *predict* what would happen if the pieces were put into a swift-moving stream and left there for years.

Many kinds of rocks are difficult to identify. Here are some identification sources: the local museum's rock and mineral collection, a small rock or mineral collection purchased from a supply house, pictures from books (*see* the Bibliography), a local high-school science teacher.

Children, even with your help, may not be able to identify all the rocks they collect. Perhaps you can put those together in a box with a sign: "We do not know what kinds of rocks these are." An important thing for children to learn is that there will be problems which they cannot solve immediately. There are problems, many of them, for which even scientists do not know the answers.

Encourage pupils to devise their own methods of classifying the collections using such titles as: "Rocks Used in Our Community," "Hardest Rocks," "Softest Rocks," "Unusual Rocks," "Rocks Formed under Water," "Rocks from Volcanoes." They may use other classifying ideas.

Pupils can use their reading resources to discover how the rocks were formed and how they came to be in their present shape. A written account of the discoveries placed with the collection in the school corridor will create interest.

Pupils will discover that rocks are made of a variety of minerals. These differ in luster, size, shape, hardness, and so on. Many minerals—quartz, mica, agate, flint, and graphite (the "lead" of lead pencils)—are already known to children. They can test rocks to see which are hardest, and put them in groups. The softest rocks can be scratched with a fingernail. The hardest will scratch glass. Some especially interested and talented pupils may be able to classify rocks according to their origins—igneous, sedimentary, and metamorphic.

How Are Rocks Used in Our Neighborhood?

An interesting rock-hunting trip[2] may be organized to help children observe the uses of rocks. Pupils and teacher, as a result of study and observation, can prepare

[2] Adapted from *Science: Grades K–2* (Brooklyn, N.Y.: Board of Education of the City of New York, 1966).

a guide with "stops" in sequential order. The first trip may be in and around the school itself. A later trip may include places and buildings in the neighborhood. Examples of the "stops": (1.) the classroom: blackboards (slate); (2.) the corridor: wall behind drinking fountain (marble); (3.) the corridor: stairs (bluestone steps); (4.) the basement: drinking fountain (soapstone); (5.) main lobby: steps (marble, terrazzo); (6.) entrance (limestone); (7.) front steps (granite); (8.) sidewalk (concrete); and (9.) curbstone (concrete, bluestone, or granite). In writing the guide pupils tell the origin, color, use, and other special information about each of the rocks.

Urge pupils to observe churches, banks, libraries, and other buildings to see examples of different kinds of rocks. Suggest that they find out where these rocks came from. If some of the rocks came from a quarry in the community perhaps visits may be made there to observe the layers of rocks and to learn how rock is cut and transported. If there is a monument works nearby, pupils may be able to obtain samples of granite and marble for examination.

What Is Sandstone Made of?

Suggest to children that they examine some pieces of sandstone with a magnifying glass. What can be observed? Grind two pieces of the sandstone together over a piece of paper. Examine the resulting grains of sand through the magnifying glass. What do you see? Where did the grains come from? What is the sandstone made of?

On a piece of white paper give each child some sand from a beach. Describe what you see. What shape are the grains? What colors are they? Are they all the same size? Touch a magnet to the grains.

The lighter colored or colorless grains are probably quartz. Reddish-brown ones are often garnet. Black ones may possibly be magnetite, an iron compound, which children can identify by using a magnet. These are but a few of the approximately 2,000 minerals found in rocks.

Compare the sand from the sandstone with the sand from the beach. Are they alike? In what ways are they different from each other?

From this experience children can conclude that sand may be formed by the grinding together of rocks and that rocks may be formed if grains become pressed together and cemented.

How Are Mountains Formed?

Sometimes making a small model serves to clarify ideas. For example, a model may illustrate the effects of pressure of layers of rocks that cause them to become curved and tilted in the formation of mountains.

Place layers of different colored plasticene in a cardboard box. Sprinkle talcum powder between the layers so that they will not stick together. After the layers are packed, cut out the ends of the cardboard box, but leave the layers in place; then slowly push the ends toward the middle. This forces the layers into a position resembling folded mountains. With a sharp knife cut down through the middle of the layers

Sand and sandstone. What are they made of? Rubbing one piece of sandstone with another and examining the results helps to solve this problem. Using a magnifying glass before and after grinding and comparing samples of sand with the "handmade" sand are both helpful ideas. (*Courtesy of Phyllis Marcuccio.*)

and lift the two parts away from each other to expose the layers which were folded into mountains. A baking pan may be used to hold the model. What does the model show? Why did we use different colors of plasticene? What caused the curves and the tilting? Have you ever seen where something like this has really happened on the earth's surface? Where?
(**Note:** folding is only *one* way in which mountains are formed.)

How Is the Earth Near Us Changing?

Field trips to some nearby locations reveal some of the changes in the earth's surface caused by various forces. Some of these changes may be observed on school ground, others on longer field trips. The trips should be taken to gather information for solving such problems as: "What forces are changing the earth's surface? How are they changing it?" The children might go to observe a river or creek to see how it is wearing away its banks, observe the speed of the flow, examine stones from the creek bed, and note that sometimes the bed is covered with stones (the lighter material has been carried away by water). They can observe trees and other plants growing out of rock formations, observe how the rocks have split and examine small plants growing in rocky surfaces. If they try to lift one of the plants from its growing place they will see how the tiny roots are growing into crevices in the rock itself.

A trip to a so-called "empty" lot may help pupils to see the results of forces that change the earth. They try to answer, through careful observation, such questions as: (1.) How have people changed the surface of the lot (for example, people make shortcut paths across the lot producing a bare area)? What effect does this have on the surface? (2.) What signs of erosion can be seen (soil that has been moved, gullies, exposed rocks, roots of trees, and other plants, effects of wind)? (3.) What are the rocks like? How do you think they have changed through the years? How do you think they got there?

A trip to an excavation near your school is a good place to see what the earth is like under the surface. Pupils may note the darker topsoil and compare it with the subsoil. They may also note different rock and soil layers.

An extended trip to look for different land and rock forms will provide information. *Observe land forms:* hills, bluffs, plains, beaches and *rock forms:* outcrops, boulders, layered rocks, faults; *effects of glaciers:* lakes, terminal moraines, and so on. What pupils are able to observe depends on the location.

The same forces that change the land in a country environment are also at work in the city. Survey of a city block reveals trees disturbing sidewalks, plants growing in cracks in the pavement, water washing, crumbling buildings, smooth and sharp-edged stones, and so forth.[3] What happens when a water hydrant is open and the water flows out? How are pieces of brick changed by the weather? What changes lawns, pavements, and sidewalks?

Pictures may have to be substituted for some of the experiences just described. Magazines, travel folders, geography books, and other sources supply pictures of topographic features that may be arranged to illustrate the story of earth changes. Pictures taken by the children themselves are for obvious reasons preferable. If they are successful they may be shown to other classes in the school accompanied by explanations by the children who took them. Pictures taken in a city environment and compared to rural photographs yield interesting ideas.

How Can Water Break Rocks?

The experiences and experiments described here are focused on understanding of how water changes the earth's surface. It is often difficult for children to observe

[3] *Operation New York.* Using the Natural Environment of the City as a Curriculum Resource. (Brooklyn, N.Y.: Board of Education of the City of New York, 1960); E.H. Wilson: "Urban Education, The Relevant Approach," *Science and Children* (January–February 1971); *and* S.K. Shugrue et al.: "No Space for Soil," *Science and Children* (January–February 1972). *See also* Chapters 14A and 14B, and R.B. Bartholomew: *How to Tell What's Underground*, leaflet (Washington, D.C.: National Science Teachers Association, 1972).

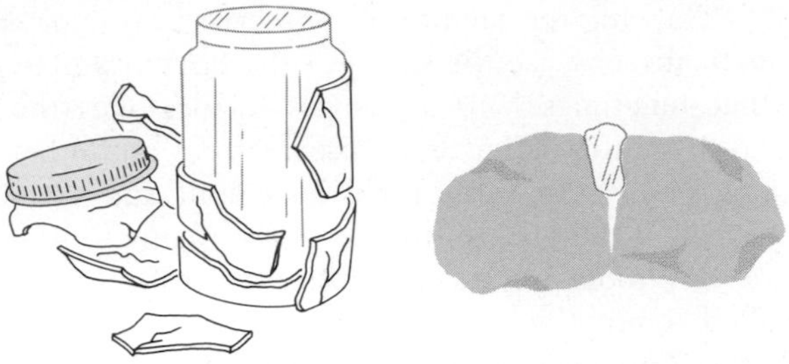

Freezing water has broken the jar in the refrigerator, much as water breaks rocks when it seeps into cracks and expands as it freezes.

the effects of freezing water in their earth's surface environment. They can, however, plan an experience that will demonstrate the effects of water expansion when it freezes. Ask them to try to do so. If they need it help them by filling a glass jar with water to the top and screwing the cover on. Now what can we do? Freeze the water. What do you think will happen? Place the jar in a clear plastic bag so that the results can more easily be examined and set it in the freezing compartment of the refrigerator to let it freeze. What happens? Would an *empty* jar with a screwed-on lid also break if it were placed in a similar situation? Try it. What caused the jar full of water to crack? Would it crack if it had not been filled to the top? Try it.

The jar cracks because the water expands when it changes to ice. Where else have you ever seen this happen? Plumbers or garage mechanics sometimes can supply metal pipes or parts that have been cracked by freezing water. Seeing these will help pupils realize that as water freezes, it exerts a great force that can break things. If there are rock formations nearby pouring water on them may help pupils to see how it sinks down into the cracks.

Children are impressed with the "push" that freezing water can give. They may be interested in attempting to find out how much "bigger" water gets (increase in volume) when it freezes. Ask children to *estimate* how much by filling a clean empty food can about three-fourths of the way with water. Mark or scratch a line to show the height of the water. Then ask children to try to estimate how much the water will expand when it freezes. Mark some of their estimates on the can. Place in the freezer and note the height after freezing. Repeat the experiment with different shapes and sizes of containers. A rigid *plastic* (not glass) container, such as a toothbrush case, can also be used by individual children at home to report their findings to the class. Ask: Did it expand by $\frac{1}{2}$? $\frac{1}{4}$? Was the expansion the same with different containers? Here is an opportunity to use careful measurements both in inches and millimeters. Keep records of the measurements made under various circumstances and help children describe what the data seem to show. (The expansion will be about 9 or 10 percent.)

How Much of Ocean Water Is Salt?

In connection with their study of oceans children will be interested in finding out about salty water. If possible get a sample of sea water; if not aquarium or pet shops may have materials for making artificial sea water. Follow the directions. (For

Digging into the soil for a sample to examine. What does it look like? Collect some, look at it carefully. What is it made of? (*Courtesy of Phyllis Marcuccio.*)

the purpose of this study it is also satisfactory to stir $1\frac{1}{2}$ teaspoons of salt into a glassful of water.) If the water is clean let the children taste it to see that it is salty. If possible *weigh* the water before boiling and then weigh the remaining salt. For example, begin with 100 grams of sea water; after boiling there should be about $3\frac{1}{2}$ grams of salt. Sea water is about $96\frac{1}{2}$ percent water and $3\frac{1}{2}$ percent salt. (Only one of the salts in sea water is table salt; there is also calcium carbonate and others.)

Boil the water until almost all of it has evaporated. Pour the remaining water into a clean, shallow pan and let it evaporate. What is left? Let the children taste the substance to see that it is salty. What happened to the water? What happened to the salt? Boil some salty water and let the cloud of steam condense on a plate. Taste the condensed drops. Are they salty? What does this tell you?

How Can We Separate Different Parts of the Soil?

Obtain a bucket of soil from forest, field, park, or other natural site. Spread the soil out on a large sheet of paper and sort out the pebbles, decaying or skeletonized bits of plant and animal matter, humus, and so on into separate piles. Use a screen or a coarse strainer to separate the larger particles from the smaller ones. The teacher may suggest placing some of the soil in a large jar, adding an equal volume of water, shaking vigorously, and then allowing the mixture to settle for some time, perhaps a day or so. Before it settles, ask children to predict what will happen. Characteristically the pebbles will settle on the bottom; then sand, silt, clay, and humus above in that order. Bits of plant and animal material may float on top of the water.

Ask students to suggest uses for this "jar-shake" technique. Some may suggest using it to compare the contents of different kinds of soil.

As a result of these experiences and experiments (and others) children should begin to be able to *construct* statements of observations in quantitative manner, *predict* possible outcomes based on observations and experiences, *devise* a test of a hypothesis, *describe* and *communicate* observations made under specific circumstances. These behaviors do not result for *all* children nor from only *one or a few* experiences. (*See* discussion of goals in Chapter 2.)

OTHER PROBLEMS FOR OLDER CHILDREN

1. What expeditions are scientists now conducting to study the earth?
2. What does the force of gravity have to do with changing the surface of the earth?
3. How does man change the surface of the earth?
4. How deep is the soil in different places around your school?
5. How do the Earth satellites help us learn more about the earth's surface?

Resources to Investigate with Children[4]

1. Local public buildings to see the uses of rocks and minerals.
2. Local landscape to observe land forms and changes in them—rivers, streambeds, banks, pits, shores of bodies of water, valleys, and other forms. In the city: parks, the streets and sidewalks, vacant lots, excavations, and similar places.
3. A well-driller to furnish samples of different soils and rock formations from underground and for information about local conditions under the earth's surface.

[4]Here, and in each of the subsequent chapters, will be found a list of people, places, things, and special kinds of resources helpful in teaching the material of the chapter and developing the goals indicated for the various experiences. How many of these resources will be useful for a specific locality depends on local conditions. They have all been found helpful in many situations. Whenever the suggestions to write for information are made, the teacher should assume the communicating responsibility with such help from children as seems appropriate.

A section called *"Preparing to Teach"* is also included at the end of each chapter. As the name indicates, these are practical suggestions to help teachers and prospective teachers get ready to teach the subject matter under consideration more effectively.

4. Samples of different kinds of soil to discover how they are alike and how different, as well as what they are made of.
5. State roads commission for information about land formations where roads are being constructed.
6. Soil conservation department and geologists for information on erosion problems of local area and on conservation practices in action.
7. Pictures from books and magazines that show the earth's surface at many places on the earth, to compare and contrast and discover what changes may have occurred in these places.
8. National Park Service, Washington, D.C. 20242, for information about national parks. Examine texts and pictures for information about park geology.
9. The American Geological Institute, Earth Science Education Project, P.O. Box 1559, Boulder, Colorado 80302. Material for teachers.

Preparing to Teach[5]

1. Assemble an exhibit of teaching materials you would use in helping children learn about changes in the earth's surface, and describe briefly how you would use the materials.
2. Prepare a paper-and-pencil examination that you think will help to evaluate what pupils in one of the grades 4, 5 or 6 should learn about the subject matter of one problem in this chapter. (*See* section on evaluation in Chapter 5.)
3. Write the behavioral objectives you think may be observed as the results of the study of one of the problems in this chapter. Be as specific as possible and relate the objectives to the subject matter at hand. For example: Children should be able to identify the different kinds of rocks found in their school buildings. Remember that you are trying to determine the changes in actions, values, and beliefs that you hope will result. Try to devise some ways of determining the extent to which these objectives have been attained (*see* discussion of behavioral objectives in Chapter 2).
4. Make a list of the materials and apparatus you would try to obtain if you were teaching the material in this chapter.
5. List the experiences, experiments, and demonstrations you would try to provide for children of a particular grade as they study this material. Books in the Bibliography will help you.
6. Plan some experiences useful in providing opportunities for children to employ their senses to make inquiries into the material of this chapter.
7. Prepare a list of possible out-of-school experiences that will give children an opportunity to use skills of inquiry and make discoveries. Suggest ways children might report their findings.
8. Write for *Geology,* a free price list, no. 15, from the Superintendent of Documents, U.S. Government Printing office; Washington, D.C. 20402, for list of materials available for teaching the contents of this chapter.

[5] Teachers may wish to read these sections early in order to order materials suggested and have them on hand when needed.

CHAPTER 7A

THE SUN AND THE PLANETS

(Courtesy of NASA.)

THE EARTH IN SPACE

(See p. 194.) We are no longer earthbound beings. We are able to share with astronauts, at least vicariously, the thrill of orbiting the earth and of seeing its nighttime and daytime sides; of "walking" in space; of walking, riding, and flying around the moon. We look at our own planet Earth from the moon with the help of on-the-spot television cameras. We move from a distance of $35\frac{1}{2}$ million miles from Mars (when Earth is closest to Mars) to less than 900 miles, thanks to the cameras on the Mariner spacecraft, and discover for the first time that its surface has an astonishing variety of features: many moonlike craters, deep winding channels that may have once been fast-flowing streams, giant volcanic mountains, enormous chains of canyons. With the launching of the unmanned spacecraft, Pioneer X, in 1972 to Jupiter and beyond we wait for reports of new findings about the members of our solar system. We look forward confidently to the deep penetration of space by men to whom the earth will appear but a tiny speck in a vast universe.

THE SUN'S FAMILY

The sun is the center of a family of heavenly bodies known as the *solar system.* The head of (See pp. 184–6.) the family is the sun, and the principal members are the 9 planets that revolve around it, each in a near-circular orbit. In order of increasing distance from the sun the planets are Mercury, Venus, Earth, Mars, Jupiter, Saturn, Uranus, Neptune, and Pluto. They all move in the same direction around the sun; their orbits lie in nearly the same plane, with Pluto the exception. Somewhat less familiar are the 2,000 known small asteroids (also called planetoids) and the many thousands of smaller ones that revolve around the sun in the space between the orbits of Mars and Jupiter.

Six of the planets have close "relations"—the satellites that revolve around them. Thirty-two satellites in all have been observed, 1 for Earth (which we call "moon"), 2 for Mars, 12 for Jupiter, 10 for Saturn (its tenth satellite was discovered as recently as 1966), 5 for Uranus, and 2 for Neptune. The other three planets are moonless so far as is known.

Also included in the sun's family are the numerous comets, with eccentric orbits that bring some of them close to the sun and then out into the far reaches of the solar system. Billions of meteoroids, varying in size from a grain of sand to a huge boulder, also move around the sun and are counted as members of its family.

The solar system is a vast race track with planets and their attendant satellites, comets, asteroids, and meteoroids streaking around their celestial center—the sun.

GRAVITY AND THE SOLAR SYSTEM

Why do members of the solar system not fly away from the sun as they hurtle through space at thousands of miles an hour? What keeps them in their orbits? Sir Isaac Newton provided an answer in the seventeenth century with his law of gravitation. In its simplest form the law states: (See pp. 194–5.) *All bodies, from the largest star in the universe to the smallest particle of matter, attract each other with what is called a gravitational force.*

The strength of the gravitational force between two bodies depends on (1.) *their masses* (the amount of material in them), and (2.) *the distance between them.* The greater the distance, the weaker the force. (More exactly, the attraction varies inversely as the square of the distance between the two bodies. If the distance between two bodies is doubled, the gravitational attraction is only one quarter as great. If the distance is halved, the attraction is four times as great.)

The planets and other bodies in the solar system do not streak off into space because of mutual gravitational attraction between these bodies and the sun.

But if all bodies attract each other, why don't they rush toward each other and smash? For example, why don't the earth and sun move together and merge?

Newton helps us again at this point with one

of his laws of motion which states that a body in motion will move forever in a straight line with unchanging speed unless a force changes its motion. The body in motion in this instance is the earth. The *tendency* of the earth to maintain its motion at the same speed (of about $18\frac{1}{2}$ miles per second) and in a straight line prevents it from falling into the sun. But, as we have seen, there is also a force that acts to change the earth's motion: the gravitational force between the earth and the sun. The net result—the compromise—of both motion *and* gravity is the almost circular orbit of the earth around the sun.

The laws of motion and of gravitation also account for the paths of other planets around the sun and the orbits of the moons around the planets. These laws have also enabled scientists to plan and carry out the launching of many artificial satellites that now orbit the earth.

THE SUN

Space travelers journeying to the outer edges of the solar system, to Pluto and beyond, would find the sun appearing smaller and smaller in the sky until it looked just like a star—which is exactly what it is. Our sun is but one of the billions of stars in the universe, and only a moderate-sized one at that. It looks larger and brighter than the other stars because it is so much closer to us. The sun is about 93 million miles from the earth. This figure means more if we translate it into other terms. Assume that a spaceship travels at an *average* rate of 17,500 miles per hour (fast enough to circle the earth in $1\frac{1}{2}$ hours). At this speed it would require about 7 months to reach the sun.

(*See* pp. 182–3, 186–7.)

The Structure of the Sun

(*See* pp. 186–7.)

The familiar bright disc of the sun has a diameter of 864,000 miles, about 109 times that of the earth. All that we can observe directly of the sun is in its outer layers, collectively known as the sun's *photosphere.* Above the photosphere is the solar atmosphere, made up of the *chromosphere* and the *corona.* The bulk of the sun is in its hidden interior.

Ordinarily we see only the photosphere, a layer that is only a few hundred miles deep. Its name, which means "light sphere," indicates that it is the layer from which light escapes from the interior. The brightness of the photosphere prevents us from seeing the outer layers of the sun's atmosphere. During a total eclipse of the sun, however, when the photosphere is hidden by the moon, these other layers are prominently displayed.

Just outside the bright photosphere is the chromosphere (color sphere), a transparent, gaseous layer about 5,000 miles thick, colored red with glowing hydrogen.

Enveloping the sun is the transparent corona, which reaches out many millions of miles. Indeed, astronomers now believe that the corona may extend as far as the outer regions of the solar system. This means that the earth and the other planets are *within* the sun's atmosphere. From time to time eruptions hundreds of thousands of miles high stream out of the photosphere to form colorful *prominences.*

Photographs taken through a telescope show that the sun's disc (photosphere) is not uniform; here and there are darker areas called *sunspots.* Sunspots have been studied carefully by scientists. They are believed to be associated with magnetic disturbances in the sun. Sunspots grow large and then disappear, but it may take several weeks or months for this to happen. Sunspots appear dark because the temperature in these areas is somewhat less than elsewhere on the surface of the sun.

Sunspots range from about 500 miles in diameter, barely detectable through a telescope, to 50,000 miles or more. If a particular sunspot is watched day after day it appears to move from west to east. This apparent movement is due to the turning of the sun on its axis. As the sun rotates, it carries the sunspots around with it. However, the sun is gaseous; it does not rotate as a solid. As a consequence all parts of the sun do not move together: Its equator takes 25 days and the region at the poles takes about 45 days for a complete rotation.

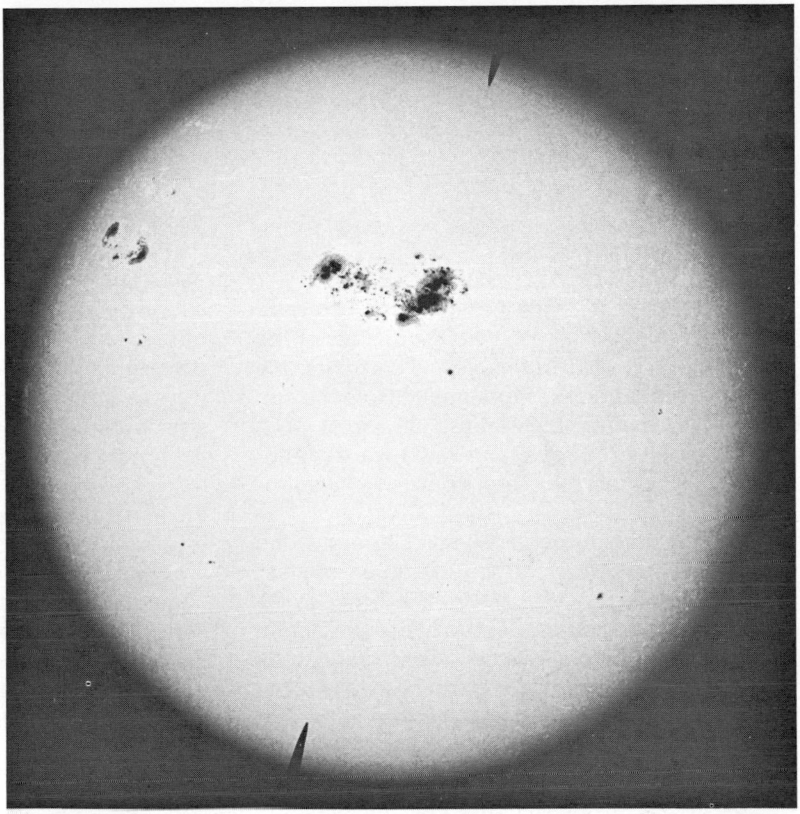

These sunspots were observed on April 7, 1967. The number rises to a maximum on the average of once every 11 years; 1947 was a peak year. (*Courtesy of Mount Wilson and Palomar Observatories.*)

The Solar Wind

In addition to light and heat and other radiations the sun emits out of the sunspot regions electrically charged *atomic particles,* mostly protons and electrons. Moving at a velocity of millions of miles an hour these particles escape from the sun's corona and sweep through the solar system, constituting what has been called the "solar wind." Orbiting earth satellites and spaceships have detected these particles.

The earth is constantly in the solar wind, but we are more aware of it when there is a solar "gale"; that is, when there is a sudden intensification of the particle bombardment. The particles strike the earth's ionosphere, an electrically charged layer of the earth's upper atmosphere. Ordinarily, the ionosphere bounces shortwave radio waves back to earth, making long-range radio communication between distant stations on earth possible. When, however, the ionosphere layers are disturbed by a solar "gale," the reflection of radio waves back to the ground is disrupted; this results in radio distortion and fadeouts.

(*See* p. 221.)

Another effect of this barrage from the sun on our atmosphere is to produce the beautiful display called the *auroras,* the northern and southern lights.

The constant bombardment of the atoms in the earth's atmosphere, even when "gentle," causes the atoms to emit light in the form of the *air glow,* also called night-sky glow. Air glow is the main source of illumination of the moonless night sky in places away from large cities.

Both the solar wind and radiations from the sun (*see* the next paragraph) constitute a hazard for space travelers, but one that space scientists believe can be met by appropriate shielding of the spacecraft and by avoiding space travel at times of severe solar bombardment. Orbiting Solar Observatories (OSO) and Pioneer satellites watch the sun, giving warnings of hazardous eruptions.

The Sun's Energy

For billions of years the sun has been radiating energy into the vast reaches of space. The visible light rays that illuminate the earth are one form of this energy. Also emanating from the sun are invisible x-rays, ultraviolet rays, infrared rays, and radio waves. Altogether they are known as *electromagnetic radiations.*

(*See* p. 661.)

What is the source of the sun's energy? The sun is now thought of as a gargantuan nuclear reactor, deriving its energy from a process resembling that of the hydrogen bomb. The sun's energy is *not* produced by burning. It has been calculated that if the sun were made of coal there would be a sufficient supply for burning to last only 80,000 years.

(*See* pp. 550–1.)

By means of instruments that measure the temperature of distant objects through an analysis of their light scientists have calculated that the temperature on the surface of the sun is about 10,000° F. This fiercely hot temperature, however, would not be sufficient to sustain the hydrogen-bomb type of activity going on inside the sun. Scientists calculate that the temperature there is somewhere near 25,000,000° F.

The sun shines in all directions all the time. The earth is not the only object to receive its rays. The small part of the sun's radiant energy that does reach the earth heats its surface comfortably, supplies green plants with the light essential for the manufacture of food, and thereby makes plant and animal life possible.

(*See* pp. 182–3, 186–7.)

THE PLANETS

Planet means "wandering star," a word used by the ancients to describe those heavenly bodies that changed their position in relation to the "fixed stars" of the constellations. They found, for example, that the individual stars making up the Big Dipper were always in the same spot in this constellation, whereas the planets Venus and Mars were seen in different places at different times, appearing to wander among the stars.

(*See* pp. 184–6.)

Today we know that the planets are not stars. Planets shine by light reflected from the sun, whereas stars (like our sun) shine by virtue of their own internal nuclear activities. The nine planets are much smaller than most of the stars we see in the sky. Their *apparent* brillance and size is caused by their closeness to the earth.

The "wandering" of planets is related to their movement in a solar "race track" in which the earth is also moving. If we think for a moment of a real race track with nine horses galloping around it at different speeds, a jockey on a horse named Earth would see the other horses and their riders in different *relationships* as lap after lap was completed, both with respect to each other and when viewed against fixed objects in the distant landscape, such as buildings and trees.

Let us look at the planets from another vantage point, that of an observer on the North Star (which is seen overhead from the earth's North Pole). He would see that all the planets move in the same counterclockwise direction, and that their paths, or orbits, except for that of Pluto, are almost circular. If he used Earth time as his standard he would find that Mercury on the inside track completed its circuit in 88 days, Earth in $365\frac{1}{4}$ days, outermost Pluto in almost 250 *years.*

A space observer would note that while the planets were moving around the sun they were also spinning like tops. The word *revolution* is used to designate the circuit around the sun; the word *rotation* designates the spinning. Revolution relates to a planet's orbit, to its "year." Rotation relates to its spinning, to its night and day.

It is difficult to visualize the vast distances, the empty voids in the solar system, without recourse to man-sized models. Picture the sun reduced to the size of a 50-foot balloon. On this scale Mercury would be a handball, $2\frac{1}{4}$ inches in diameter, about 2,000 feet away from the balloon. Venus would be a small melon, $5\frac{1}{2}$ inches in diameter, about $\frac{3}{4}$ mile from the sun. Earth, slightly larger than Venus, would be located 1 mile from the sun. Mars, the size of a ball 3 inches in diameter, would take its place $1\frac{1}{2}$ miles from the sun.

Now we come to the "big four" in the planet world. In our scale they have the following sizes and distances from the sun: Jupiter, 5 feet and 2 inches, $5\frac{1}{4}$ miles; Saturn, 4 feet and 5 inches, $9\frac{1}{2}$ miles; Uranus, 22 inches, 19 miles; Neptune, 21 inches, 30 miles.

Pluto, a small planet, would be a ball about 3 inches in diameter, 39 miles average distance from the sun.

Mercury

Mercury is so close to the sun and is so enveloped by its brightness that most city dwellers rarely get a chance to see it. We must look for this planet on the western horizon just after sunset or on the eastern horizon just before sunrise. Added to our difficulty is the fact that Mercury is quite small; its diameter is less than the width of the Atlantic Ocean.

Mercury completes its trip around the sun in 88 days. In 1965, however, it was found with the help of radar and radio-telescope that Mercury rotates about once every 59 days. Measurements taken by a device called a thermocouple through Mount Wilson's 100-inch reflecting telescope show that the surface temperature on the sunny side is about 770° F., hot enough to melt lead.

(*See* pp. 209–10.)

The sharp outline of the silhouette of Mercury when it passes in front of the bright face of the sun (this is called a *transit*) suggests that it lacks an atmosphere. If Mercury had a visible atmosphere, a luminous ring should appear around the planet while it is in transit. Mercury is not expected to have an atmosphere because of its high temperature and the low velocity of escape; none has been observed to date.

(*See* p. 685.)

Venus

Venus has been called the mysterious planet, because even with our best optical tele-

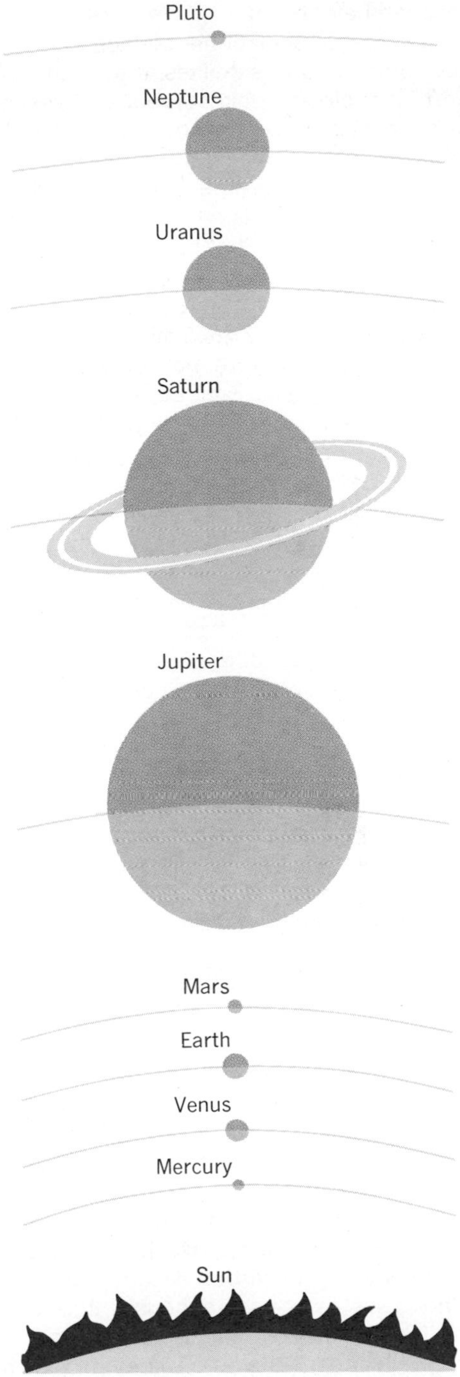

The planets are drawn to scale in this diagram, but not the distances between their orbits. The table on page 167 gives additional data on the planets.

scopes we have not been able to penetrate the thick clouds that blanket her surface at all times. Space probes and satellites are giving us a clearer and closer look at Venus. Telescopes have been hoisted on balloons to an altitude of 80,000 feet, above almost all of the earth's air. Clearer views are possible at high altitudes because the telescope is above the turbulence, dust, and water vapor that blurs celestial objects when viewed from the surface of the earth.

On December 14, 1962, the Mariner II spacecraft flew within 21,645 miles of Venus after a 109-day voyage of more than 180 million miles. Mariner's instruments radioed 65 million separate bits of information back to Earth. On October 18, 1967, the Soviet capsule Venus IV landed on Venus. The next day the American Mariner V swept within 2,500 miles of the planet. The Soviet capsules, Venus VII in 1970 and Venus VIII in 1972, parachuted through the Venusian atmosphere and sent back data from its torrid surface. In summary, data from all of these probes (substantiated partly by direct earth observations) indicates the following:

1. The surface temperature of Venus is very high, apparently approaching 880° F. in spots. However, its polar and perhaps some of its mountainous regions may be cooler. The space probes confirm the previous finding by radio telescopes that the surface temperature of Venus is very high.

(*See* pp. 209–10.)

2. The pressure of the atmosphere on the surface of Venus is about 90 times that of the surface pressure on Earth. (This is equal roughly to the pressure of water one would encounter almost a half-mile under the surface of the sea.)
3. The atmosphere of Venus is composed of almost pure carbon dioxide with only traces of water vapor. This may account for the high temperature within the Venus atmosphere, since the carbon dioxide acts like the glass in a greenhouse roof. Sunlight may pass through, building up heat beneath the carbon dioxide "roof." But, like the glass in the greenhouse, it does not permit the reradiated heat to escape back into space. (The three findings just presented about the Venusian atmosphere should be compared with the earth's atmosphere described in Chapter 9A.)

(*See* pp. 518–9.)

4. Venus has either a weak magnetic field or none.
5. The surface material of Venus at the point sampled resembles granite rocks of the kind found on earth.

All in all the Mariner and Venus spacecraft observations, when combined with radar and telescopic studies made from Earth, have discouraged the romantic conception that may have persisted of Venus as a place with earthlike qualities.

Venus moves in an orbit between that of Mercury and the Earth, taking about 225 days for a trip around the sun. Venus is almost the same size as the Earth, being only 300 miles less in diameter. Named for the ancient goddess of love, Venus is, with the exception of the sun and the moon, the brightest object in the sky.

The problem of how long the day on Venus is has long been a mystery to scientists. Recent observations indicate that it takes Venus 244 (Earth) days to turn just *once* on its axis. We have noted that it takes Venus only 225 (Earth) days to make one revolution around the sun. This means that a full day on Venus is longer than its year! Note that Venus rotates from east to west in the reverse direction from that of its revolution.

Seen through a telescope Venus and Mercury appear to change in shape over a period of time. These are *phases,* similar to the moon's phases, discussed later in this chapter.

Earth

It is interesting to compare the answers that children of different generations give to the question: "How do we know the earth is round?" A half-century ago the stock answer would have been based on the story of Columbus watching ships sail over the horizon with the mast disappearing from view last. In the last few decades a typical and more spontaneous answer has been: "Because we can fly around it." Today's children can say with accuracy: "Because we have taken pictures of the earth from rocket ships that show its roundness," or "Because astronauts orbited around it and saw that it was round." Perhaps for tomorrow's space-traveling children the question will be an academic one: they will be able to see the earth as a planet in space.

If we measure the planet Earth we find that it is not quite a perfect sphere: Its diameter of 7,900 miles from pole to pole is 27 miles less than its equatorial diameter.

Earth, the third planet from the sun, hurtles along in its orbit at the rate of about 66,000 miles per hour to complete its yearly tour of approximately 600 million miles. This path is not a perfect circle; it is slightly elliptical, with the sun not quite in the center. As a result the earth is closest to the sun on about January 3, when it is 91½ million miles away, and farthest away on July 3, when it is 94½ million miles away. On about April 1 and October 1 the distance is between these extremes, about 93 million miles. These statistics may be surprising to those who have assumed that the seasons are determined by the distance of the earth from the sun. We shall consider the cause of seasons presently.

While the earth is executing its yearly orbit or revolution around the sun it is spinning on its axis, performing this rotation almost exactly 365¼ times in this period. Places at the equator turn with the spinning planet at the rate of about 1,000 miles per hour; Salt Lake City, which is about halfway between the equator and the North Pole, turns at the rate of about 800 miles per hour. Spin a classroom globe of the earth and you will see why this difference occurs.

Day and Night

Because the earth is an opaque ball and receives light from one principal source, only one side of it can be lighted at one time. The half receiving light is in daylight while the other half is having night. Because the earth rotates on its axis, day and night alternate in regular fashion.

(*See* pp. 187–8.)

The apparent daily motion of the sun across the sky from east to west is due to the actual turning of the earth from west to east.

The Seasons

Put in simplest terms the different seasons in the place where you live are determined by the differences in the amount of heat received from the sun at different times of the year. Consider for a moment just 1 square foot of any open field in your locality. Disregarding local weather conditions, the amount of heat received daily by this designated square will depend on two factors: (1.) the number of hours of sunlight and (2.) the strength of the sunlight.

(*See* pp. 188–9, 190.)

Point 1 is determined by the fact that in summer the days are longer, which means that there are more hours of sunlight to heat soil, rocks, and water.

Point 2 refers to the fact that in our summer, when the sun rides high in the sky, the strength of the sunlight received is greater because its rays strike our part of the earth almost vertically. In winter, when the sun is lower in the sky, the rays of sunlight come to us at more of a slant. These slanting rays are spread over more of the earth's surface than rays that strike vertically; they therefore give less heat. Furthermore, slanting rays travel a greater distance through our atmosphere than those that strike vertically. The more air they go through, the more of their energy is absorbed along the way and the less is left to heat the surface of the earth.

(*See* p. 189.)

But we have not yet explained why days vary in length, or why the sun's rays are more nearly vertical at some times than others. To understand this we must leave our little square foot in the field and adjust our vision for a space view of the earth in relation to the sun.

Let us be guided by three important space facts:

1. The earth moves, as we have found, in an orbit around the sun.
2. The earth's axis is not upright with reference to the plane of this orbit; it leans over, like the Tower of Pisa.
3. The earth's axis always points in the same direction in space—toward the North Star (except

for some wobbling, called precession, like that of a spinning top).

Because of these three factors the northern and southern hemispheres are alternately slanted toward the sun and away from it.

For simplicity, we shall refer mainly to the Northern Hemisphere in discussing the following sequence of seasons.

At position *A* in the diagram (June 22) the Northern Hemisphere is tipped toward the sun. The part around the North Pole has continuous daylight, despite the daily rotation of the earth. There is no night in the "land of the midnight sun" at this time of the year. As we go farther south the number of daylight hours varies from 24 at the North Pole to 12 at the equator. The Southern Hemisphere is in winter at this time and the South Pole region is in the midst of its 6 months of night.

Thus the tilted position of the earth makes for longer days in the Northern Hemisphere at this time. It also exposes the earth there to the strong, more vertical rays of the sun, which contribute to the heating up of that part of the earth. To sum up, long days and strong rays make summer.

Let us bypass position *B* for a moment and go to *C* (December 22). Compared to *A*, everything is reversed. The Northern Hemisphere is tilted away from the sun. The North Pole is in continuous night. Generally, the Northern Hemisphere has short days and long nights. The rays of the sun strike at a greater slant. Short days and slanting rays make winter.

At *B* (September 23) and *D* (March 21) the beginning of the fall and spring seasons, respectively, the axis of the earth points neither toward nor away from the sun. Days and nights are equal in length all over the earth. Neither the Northern nor Southern Hemisphere receives stronger rays of sunlight.

Even though the moon is the earth's satellite we shall pass over it until later, to maintain continuity in the story of the planets.

Mars

More than any other planet Mars has excited the imagination of man. Novelists and philosophers as well as scientists have speculated and theorized about the possibility of life on this planet.

Those defending such a possibility point to the similarity of Mars to Earth: A Martian day is

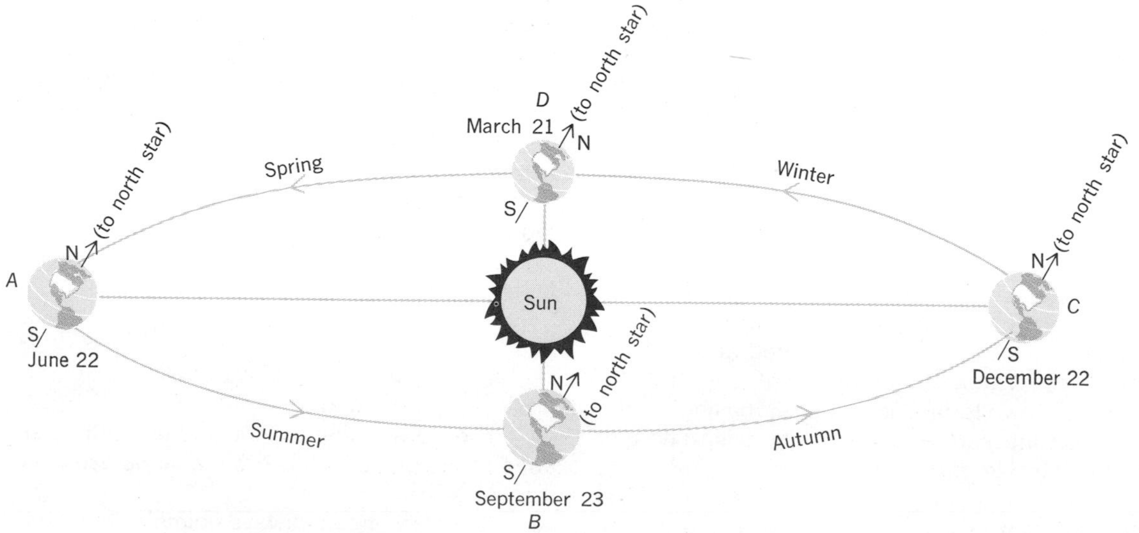

The causes of the seasons. For a detailed description *see* pages 159–160.

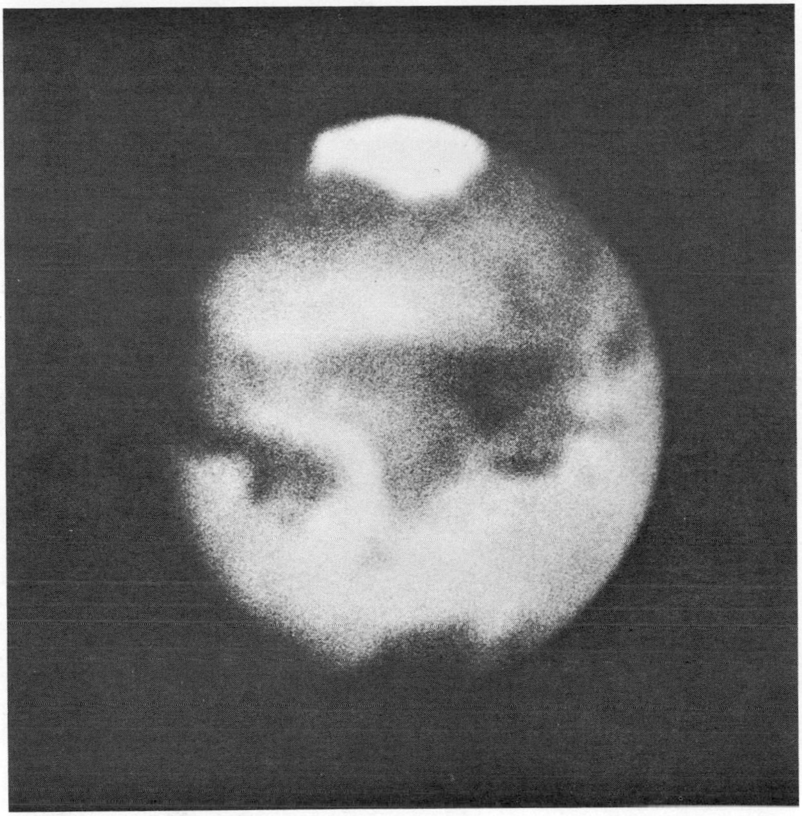

Mars during a close approach in 1956 when it was only 35½ million miles from the earth. The south polar cap shown here (*top*) changes size with the seasons. Its nature is in dispute; it may be composed of frozen carbon dioxide gas. (*Courtesy of Mount Wilson and Palomar Observatories.*)

almost identical with ours, 24 hours and 37 minutes; Mars has an atmosphere with clouds in it; its axis is tilted at about the same angle as that of Earth, thus producing similar seasonal changes. Temperatures, although not as high as those on Earth, reach 70 to 80° F. near its equator. The changing colors observed during the different seasons might be attributed to changes in plant life.

Those who argue against the possibility of life on Mars point to the fact that its atmosphere, which is less than 1 percent as dense as that of Earth, is largely carbon dioxide, there being no detectable trace of oxygen or nitrogen and practically no water vapor; and that the average temperature for the planet is 20 to 30° *below* 0° F. (Earth's average is 60° F. *above*). They point to the evidence indicating that the white caps that spread from the poles in winter are at best thin layers of solid carbon dioxide—dry ice—and that most of the planet is a dry, barren desert.

On July 14, 1965, the National Aeronautics and Space Administration's Mariner 4 spacecraft flew as close as 6,000 miles to Mars, giving new and more accurate information on this planet's size, gravity, its magnetic field, and its path around the sun. Mariner 4 snapped 21 historic photographs which revealed for the first time that the surface of Mars was densely pitted with craters, like those of the moon. It was the kind of landscape that looked to geologists as if it had not been changed for billions of years.

The initial conclusion from Mariner 4, and from 6 and 7 which followed later, was that Mars must be a dead world, geologically speaking—much like the moon. A surprising turnabout came as a result of the reports of Mariner 9, launched in May 1971, which began orbiting

An unexpected feature of the Martian surface is this sinuous valley photographed by Mariner 9 in February 1972 from a distance of about 1,000 miles. The valley is some 250 miles long and resembles a giant version of an earth "arroyo," a kind of watercut gully found in the mountainous southwestern United States. It also resembles the sinuous rills on earth's moon, believed to be associated with lava flows. Whether made by water or by lava, the valley is one of the new discoveries of space astronomy. (*Courtesy of NASA, JPL.*)

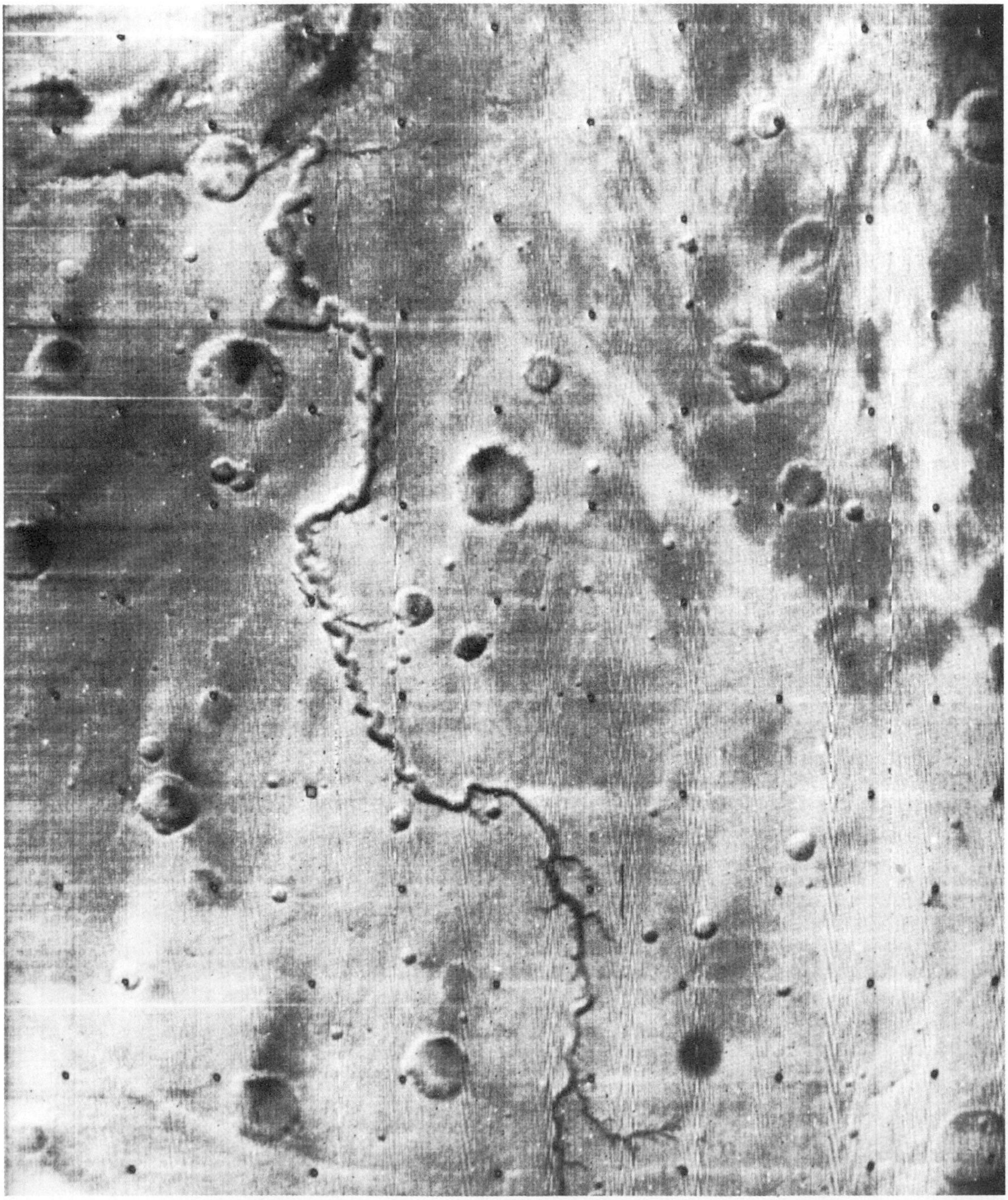

Mars in November of that year. From the photographs and data transmitted to Earth a new portrait of Mars emerged, that of a dynamic and varied planet, with towering volcanoes, deep chasms, glacial terraces, meandering channels, and moonlike craters. Its "weather" included high winds, clouds of water vapor and dust, and great temperature extremes.

Most significant of all was the evidence that water seems to have played an active role in the evolution of the planet's surface, some of this apparently having occurred in the last 50,000 years as seen from its "geological" features. Other findings of Mariner 9 include the following:

The temperature varies from 200° F. below 0 at the North Pole to 80° F. above at the equator.

Ozone has been detected over the polar regions, but the amount is less than $\frac{1}{100}$ that of Earth's atmosphere. (For the significance of ozone to life *see* pp. 221 and 679.)

The south polar icecap recedes from 2,000 miles in diameter in the winter to 200 miles in the spring.

No sign of life has been detected, but nothing seen would exclude some simple form of microscopic life.

Two prime sites on Mars have been selected as potential landing areas for two unmanned Viking spacecraft in the summer of 1976. The primary objective will be to determine if Mars has life of any kind. Other experiments will report on the winds, earthquake activity, and surface chemistry of the planet.

Two tiny moons circle the planet Mars. Photographs of the two moons sent to Earth by Mariner 9 showed both to be irregular chunks rather than spherical bodies. The inner, larger moon, Phobos, is about 10 by 14 miles in size. It races around Mars in 8 hours. Phobos looks like a huge rock, gouged and chipped, presumably as a result of collisions with other large rocks. This may be a common occurrence, since Mars is in the neighborhood of the belt of the minor planets (*see* next section). Deimos, the outer satellite, is only about $5\frac{1}{2}$ by 7 miles in size, and takes about 30 hours for its circuit around Mars.

Phobos means "fear" and Deimos means "panic"—appropriate companions of the god of war, Mars. Both of these satellites were discovered in 1877 by the American astronomer Asaph Hall.

At intervals of about 15 years the paths of Mars and Earth bring them very close to each other, so that only 35 million miles separate the two planets. At these times astronomers direct their instruments toward the ruddy planet to see if they can find answers to many unsolved problems about Mars. September 1956 provided such an opportunity; so, too, did August 1971. Mars is studied at other times too, by Earth-based instruments, and as we have seen, by orbiting satellites.

The Minor Planets

In a broad zone between the orbits of Mars and Jupiter are a swarm of smaller bodies, the minor planets, sometimes called asteroids. Seventeen hundred of these, ranging in size from 1 to 500 miles, have been registered and named by astronomers. The first and largest to be discovered was Ceres, which is about 480 miles in diameter. Although most of the asteroids move in an orbit between those of Mars and Jupiter, some occasionally come quite close to Earth: Icarus, Hermes, Eros, and Geographos, for example.

One explanation for the asteroids is that there originally were only a few larger minor planets which later were fragmented by collisions into the present swarm of smaller bodies.

Jupiter

The next four planets we shall consider are the giants of the solar system. They differ from the inner planets not only in size but in the speed of their rotation, taking only 10 to 15 hours to complete their daily spin. All have such deep atmospheres that we do not know where the solid part of the planet begins. Except for Neptune they have numerous moons.

The leader among the giants, with a diameter

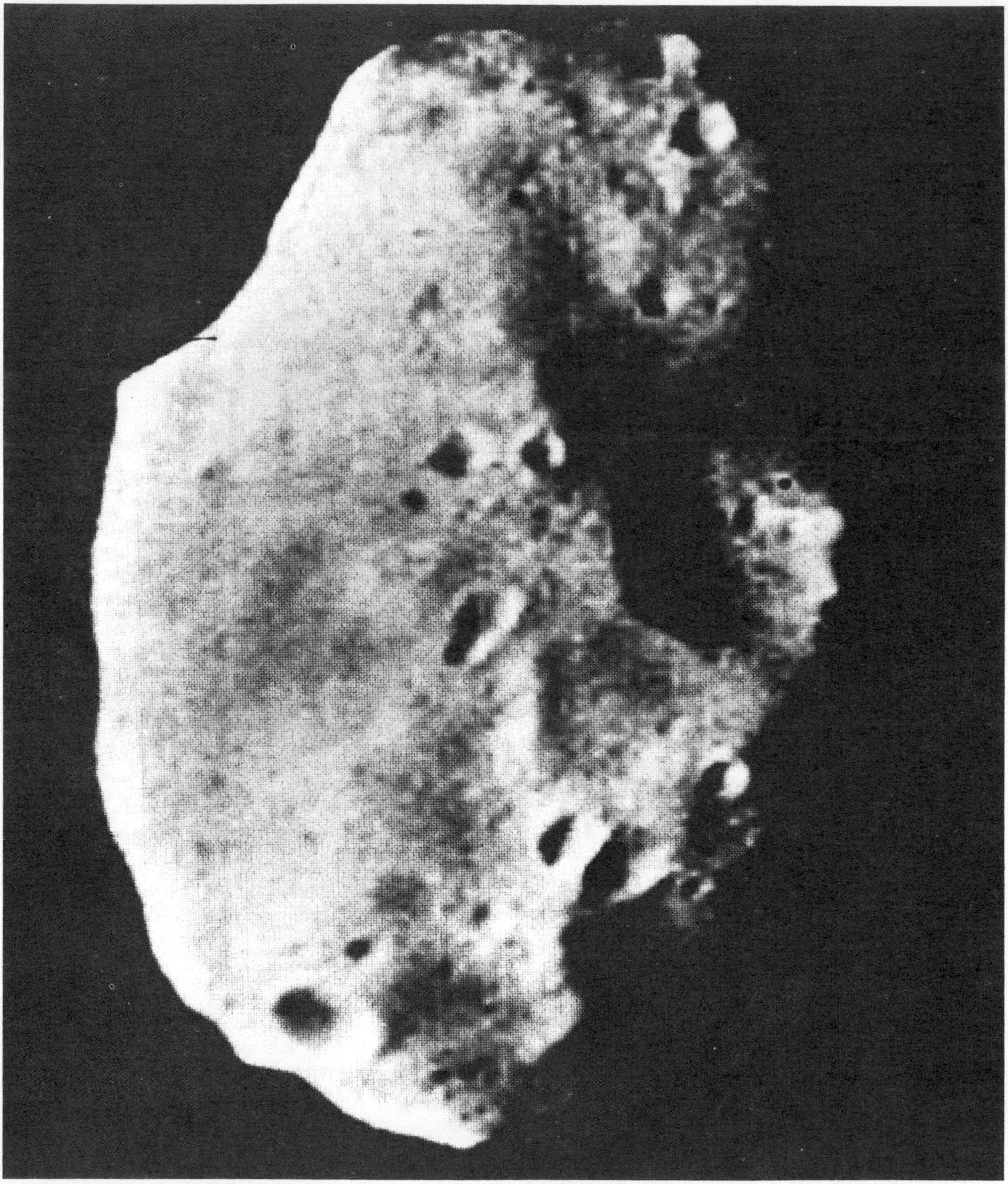

Phobos, the larger inner moon of Mars, as photographed by Mariner 9. The profusion of craters suggests that Phobos is very old. (*Courtesy of NASA, JPL.*)

11 times that of Earth, is Jupiter, named after the most powerful of the Greek gods, Zeus. To the naked eye Jupiter is often the brightest object in the night sky except for the moon, and may be confused with Venus. But through the telescope, Jupiter, unlike Venus, is encircled by yellow, red, sometimes blue bands, alternating with darker stripes, all more or less parallel to its equator. Close inspection by astronomers has shown that these banded markings are not on the solid part of Jupiter; they seem to be floating in the deep atmospheric ocean that surrounds the planet. Outside this atmospheric ocean there are 12 moons revolving around Jupiter. Four of these were discovered by Galileo. Recent evidence indicates that one of these, Io, possesses an atmosphere.

On March 7, 1972, the spaceship Pioneer 10 began a 22 month journey to Jupiter. It was the first craft to navigate through the belt of the minor planets, to a rendezvous with Jupiter on December 2, 1973. It will cross the orbit of Uranus in 1980, and at some point beyond the orbit of Pluto will leave the solar system headed in the general direction of the star, Aldebaron. To reach this star Pioneer 10 will have to travel for $1\frac{7}{10}$ million years.

Jupiter's size has led some astronomers to wonder whether this giant body is a dead or almost dead star that the sun captured into orbit. Jupiter's composition tends to support this idea, since the two most prominent constituents of its mass are hydrogen and helium. These elements are abundant in stars, but almost absent in the planets Mercury, Venus, Earth, and Mars, which were certainly not originally stars.

Moreover, Jupiter emits into space almost three times as much energy as it receives from the sun. This suggests that under the outer layers of frozen hydrogen and helium is the core of a dying star that is still producing surplus energy by the thermonuclear process characteristic of stars.

(*See* Ch. 17A.)

Other constituents of Jupiter include the gases ammonia, methane, and water vapor. Perhaps Pioneer 10 will give a clearer picture of the chemical makeup and the origin of this mysterious giant planet.

Saturn, the "showpiece of the solar system," with its ring system, photographed with a 100-inch telescope. Saturn's rings were first seen by Galileo in 1610. (*Courtesy of Mount Wilson and Palomar Observatories.*)

Saturn

Seen through a telescope Saturn is an unforgettable sight. This showpiece of the solar system has three broad, thin rings that wheel around its equator. The rings are not solid; they are made of chunks of frozen ammonia and carbon dioxide possibly around a rocky core.

Saturn, one of the giant planets, has 10 moons. One of them, Titan, is larger than our moon and is notable for the fact that it shares with Jupiter's Io the distinction of being the only satellite among the 32 in the solar system on which we have detected an atmosphere. The 10th moon, Janus, was discovered as recently as 1966 by the French astronomer Audouin Dollfus.

Uranus

All the planets described thus far are bright, naked-eye objects, and were known to the ancients. The next three—Uranus, Neptune, and Pluto—revolving in the bleak outer regions of the solar system, were discovered by later astronomers equipped with telescopes. Uranus is 20 times as far from the sun as Earth is, Neptune 30 times, and Pluto 40 times. From Pluto the sun looks so small that it appears starlike, except for its greater brightness.

Uranus was discovered in 1781 by the astronomer William Herschel, who, while making a systematic survey of stars, noticed one that refused to stay in place. Barely visible to the unaided eye, Uranus under powerful telescopes appears as a tiny green object with faint parallel bands. Unlike all the other planets, which spin like tops on the imaginary platforms of their orbits, Uranus spins like a top that is tilted severely, so that its axis lies almost in the plane of its orbit. Uranus' 5 satellites revolve in the plane of this planet's equator.

Neptune

If the discovery of Uranus might be termed an "accident," that of Neptune certainly could not. This planet was discovered when astronomers noticed that Uranus was not following the orbit expected by astronomers; instead it seemed to deviate slightly in its path as if it were being attracted by another planet. In 1846 two astronomers, Adams and Leverrier, working independently, determined the position where that unknown planet should be. When telescopes were focused on that position at the time indicated, the planet Neptune was discovered.

Neptune has 2 moons. The larger one, Triton, is slightly larger than our moon.

Pluto

Pluto, the outermost of the planets yet discovered, takes nearly 250 years to make its journey around the sun. Since its discovery in 1930 by Clyde Tombaugh, we have been able to observe only a small part of Pluto's orbit.

How can a distant planet be found among billions of stars? Astronomers make use of the fact that planets move in relation to the stars in the sky. Many photographs are taken by aiming the telescope at a portion of the sky that calculation has shown is a place where such a planet may be detected. These are compared with photographs of corresponding portions taken at a later date. Compare the two photographs shown here, taken at a six-day interval. One object has changed position with respect to the stars; this is the planet Pluto.

Beyond Pluto, are there other planets in our solar system? A search of the skies by Tombaugh and other astronomers, reaching out into space 5 times the distance of Pluto, has found no other planets. But every now and then there are suggestions that our solar system might have a tenth planet.[1]

Are there planets outside our solar system? Scientists speculate that, because stars are suns,

[1]In April 1972 a hypothetical tenth planet was announced, called "Bradley's Planet" after its predictor. The prediction was based on observed deviations of Halley's Comet from its orbit. This tenth planet is not yet accepted as definite (and may never be), but it is considered as a real possibility. There have been no visual sightings of this hypothetical planet to date.

SOME APPROXIMATE PLANETARY DATA

Name of Planet	*Diameter (thousands of miles)*	*Average Distance from Sun (millions of miles)*	*Length of Year (revolution around sun)*	*Average Speed in Orbit (miles per second)*	*Length of Day (time for 1 rotation)*	*Number of Moons*	*Surface Gravity (Earth = 1)*
Mercury	3	36	88.0 days	30	59 days	0	.38
Venus	8	67	224.7 days	22	244 days	0	.9
Earth	8	93	365.26 days	18.5	1 day	1	1.00
Mars	4	140	687.0 days	15	1 day	2	.38
Jupiter	89	480	11.86 years	8	10 hours	12	2.64
Saturn	75	890	29.46 years	6	10 hours	10	1.13
Uranus	31	1800	84.01 years	4	11 hours	5	1.07
Neptune	33	2800	164.8 years	3.4	16 hours	2	1.08
Pluto	4 (?)	3700	248.4 years	3	6 days	0	0.3 (?)

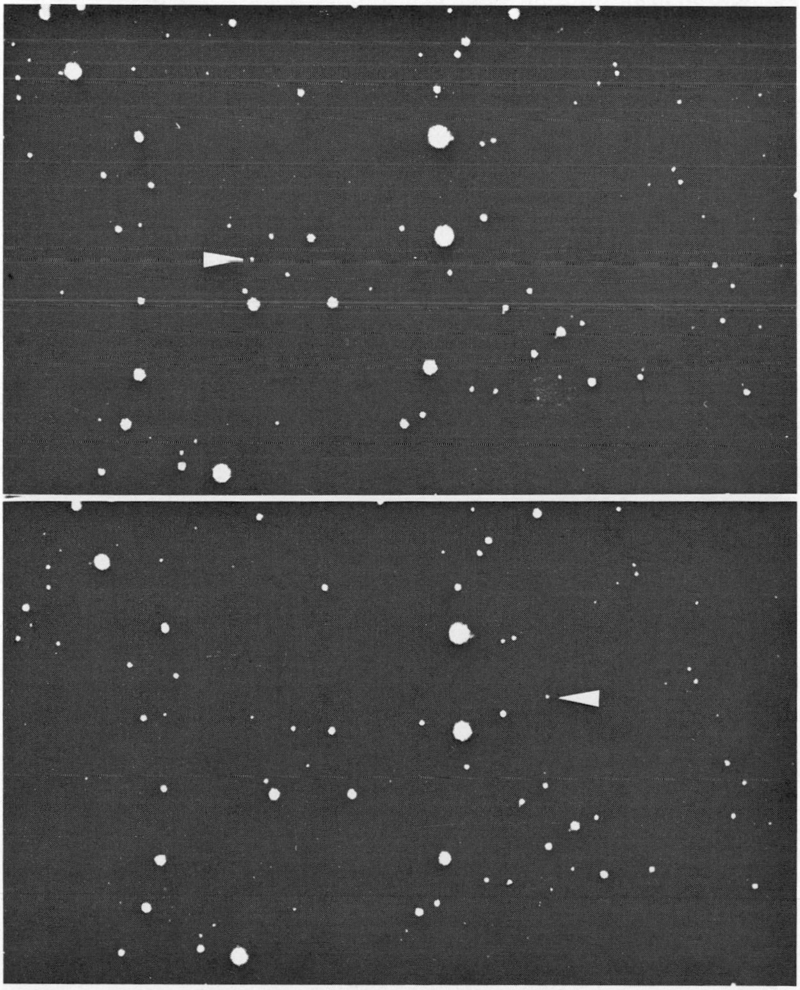

These are copies of small sections of the Pluto discovery plates showing images (those marked) of Pluto. This planet was found by C.W. Tombaugh in 1930, while he was engaged in the search program and examination of these plates. The upper plate was made on January 23, 1930, the lower on January 29, 1930. (*Courtesy of Lowell Observatory.*)

it is possible that many of them, too, may have families of planets around them. Our present instruments would be inadequate, however, to see planets as large as Jupiter, even on the nearest star.

Beyond the solar system 3 of the first 12 stars nearest the sun have unseen companions, found by the observation of gravitation-induced "wobbles" in the motions of these stars. Whether or not these are planets is still unknown, but we know of no other explanation for them at present.

(*See* p. 198.)

Barnard's star is a case in point. It moves slowly with respect to the background of more distant stars, but shows a wave in its motion. The slight wave suggests that it and an unseen companion, too small to be detected from Earth, revolve around a common center. Calculations indicate that the unseen body has a mass only 50 percent greater than that of the planet Jupiter, and must therefore be a planet itself.

Comets

Halley's comet, named after the English astronomer Edmond Halley, is the most famous of all the comets. Halley was the first to show that comets are true members of the solar system, not interlopers from outer space.

Comets differ from planets in a number of important respects. They generally have extremely elongated elliptical orbits, which may bring them close to the sun at one end of their swing in space. It is when comets come near the sun that we can observe them. Unlike planets, comets circle the sun in every direction and in every plane.

"Many experts estimate that a typical comet may have only a trillionth of the mass of Earth. Thus, despite the large sizes of comets, they are mostly 'empty space.' A comet has been described as the nearest thing to nothing that anything can be and still be something."[2]

The comets that attract the most attention are those consisting of a head and a long tail. Although the head is the more permanent part, it has little substance; it is thought to be made of small fragments of rock and metal and of gases. When a comet is far from the sun it shines, like planets, by reflecting sunlight. When it is close to the sun it shines almost entirely by the process of fluorescence, as its chemicals are

[2]George Abell: *Exploration of the Universe* (Holt, Rinehart and Winston, Inc., 1969).

This photograph of Halley's comet was taken through a telescope on May 29, 1909. (The white streaks are the tracks of stars produced on the film by the turning of the earth in this time-exposure photograph.) (*Courtesy of the American Museum of Natural History.*)

set aglow by ultraviolet radiation from the sun. (*See* pp. 155–6.) The solar wind exerts increasing pressure on the minute particles in the head as the comet approaches the sun. Some of the particles are thus pushed away from the head, forming a tail that may become truly spectacular as the comet nears the sun. Tails many millions of miles long have developed in some comets. The tail points generally away from the sun; as the comet approaches the sun the tail is behind the head; as it speeds away from the sun the tail precedes it. The tail, like the head, glows by fluorescence.

Comets, like all orbiting bodies in the solar system, travel at varying speeds, fastest nearer the sun, slower farther from the sun. Nevertheless, they do not streak across the sky like a rocket, as some people think. They may be watched for days, weeks, or even months in their paths around the sun. Most comets are small objects in the sky and require a telescope, because they are so faint, to distinguish them from stars.

Some comets, such as Encke's comet, return frequently. This particular one has a nearly circular path and revolves around the sun every $3\frac{1}{3}$ years. On the other hand, Halley's comet, which appeared last in 1910, pursues an elongated course that brings it back, on average, once every 76 years. It has a date with you in 1986!

Meteoroids

(*See* p. 194.) If there are any "visitors from outer space" they are the meteoroids that fly into the atmosphere of the earth. On a clear night, especially at certain times of the year, these "visitors" streak across the sky, causing people to exclaim: "Look at the shooting star!" These streaks are not from stars but from meteoroids, fragments of material varying in size from a grain of sand to a boulder of many tons. The glowing streak we see is not far off in starry space but just 60 miles or so up in our own atmosphere.

As the meteoroids are heated by friction with the air their surfaces boil off to form brilliantly glowing gases. The *meteor* is the region of glowing gas; it may be anywhere from a few feet to several hundred yards in diameter. The heat is sufficient to cause most of the millions of meteoroids that enter the earth's atmosphere each day to vaporize or burn so that only their fine dust ever reaches the earth's surface. Those that do land in a solid chunk are called *meteorites.* The largest meteorite found so far is called Hoba West and lies where it fell near Grootfontein, South West Africa. It weighs more than 50 tons. The largest meteorite on display is in New York City's Hayden Planetarium and weighs about 34 tons.

Larger meteorites were probably responsible for the well-known Barringer Meteorite Crater in Arizona, which is $\frac{3}{4}$ of a mile in diameter and 600 (*See* p. 171.) feet deep, and for the Chubb Crater in Canada, about 2 miles across. Other impact craters are found in Tennessee, Australia, Germany, and elsewhere. (The South African circular mountain range may be a 50-mile-diameter meteor impact.)

There are three kinds of meteorites: *irons,* about 90 percent iron and the rest nickel; *stony irons,* part iron and part stone; *stones,* made entirely of stony materials.

This is a good place to clarify the difference between meteoroids, meteors, and meteorites. When the particle is in *space* it is called a meteoroid; when it enters the earth's *atmosphere* and glows it is called a meteor; if it survives and lands on the *ground* it is called a meteorite.

Billions of meteoroids are scattered throughout the solar system. Some travel alone; others travel in meteoroid swarms. It is thought that the swarms have resulted from the breakup of a comet. When the earth passes through the path of one of these meteoroid swarms we have a *meteor shower.* Records made during meteor showers show that the streaks or trails made by the meteors appear to radiate from a point in the sky called the *radiant.* Swarms are named for the constellation or group of stars where the radiant *appears* to be located. Thus, the Leonids are named after the constellation Leo.

No telescope is needed for watching a meteor shower. The best show that can be depended on is the Perseid shower, radiating from the constellation Perseus from August 10 to 14, with best viewing about August 11th. As many as 40 to 60 meteors per hour may be observed then, preferably after midnight and in the absence of bright moonlight. The Orionids appear around October 18 to 23. The Leonid shower occurs between November 14 to 18, and is best seen after midnight. The Geminid radiant passes overhead at 2:00 A.M. on December 14 for locations in the Southern United States, and almost overhead for other locations in this country.

The Moon

The U.S. Ranger, Orbiter, and Surveyor, and the early Apollo series of lunar probes, with their television cameras and chemical analyzers, have given us a first-row view of the moon's surface. The later Apollo landings have placed us, via television, right on the moon and sent us hopping and skipping on its dusty soil, and scooting over its rolling surface in a Rover vehicle. Yet the excitement of the first classes of students and

Dr. Harrison H. Schmitt, geological scientist of the Apollo 17 team, examines a huge split boulder on the moon, from which samples were chipped for study on earth. The surrounding Taurus-Littrow landing site, named after the nearby Taurus Mountains and Littrow Crater, is a small lunar valley near the southeastern rim of *Mare Serenetatis* (the "Sea of Serenity"). (*Courtesy of NASA.*)

science professors spending a semester studying the moon *on the moon* will be high. One can imagine their diaries reading, in part, something like this:

Meteorology Study Group Precipitation: none; clouds: none; check reports that water vapor may escape from cracks in the surface; wind: none; temperature of surface: very hot during the lunar day, reaching over 250° F., higher than the boiling point of water, very cold during night, lower than 250° below 0° F.; drill holes and insert thermocouples in different locations to determine heat at increasing depth in order to measure the rate of heat loss from the interior of the moon; barometric pressure: always zero; general appearance of sky: always black because there is no appreciable atmosphere to scatter the sunlight; stars always out; forecast: always the same except when Earth eclipses the sun; unofficial reaction: a good place to visit, but not to live.

Physics Study Group Weight of 180-pound man on spring scale: 30 pounds, only $\frac{1}{6}$ as heavy as on Earth; confirmed Apollo finding that a feather and a rock dropped at the same time land together; atmosphere: practically none, pull of gravity not strong enough to prevent the escape of gases to space; transmission of sound: by radio only, no air to carry sound waves; radiation of sun: intense, strong ultraviolet and x-rays; magnetism: moon's rocks are magnetized, but many show reverse polarity, in some areas upward and in others downward. Did the moon, like the earth, reverse its polarity, or were the rocks flipped over? Where did the moon's original magnetism come from? Equipment needed: air tanks; pressurized, insulated suits; dark glasses; walkie-talkie, TV cameras. Distance back to earth: 222,000 to 253,000 miles; velocity needed to escape from moon and return to earth: $1\frac{1}{2}$ miles per second (on Earth escape velocity is 7 miles per second). Fun to leap around on.

Geology Study Group Rocks: age, by radioactive dating, between 3 and 4 billion years old; examine rocks in highlands to determine whether they're older than those in the lowlands. Kind: in highlands, anorthosite, a rock that is rare on earth; in plains and basins, basalt (on earth a common material of volcanic origin); soil: dusty, safe to walk on. Main types of land formations: marias ("seas"), mountain ranges, craters, rills, rays. Marias: large, gray, smooth areas, darker than rest of the moon—not seas, no water; naked-eye view of "man in the moon" from earth due to these darker areas compared with lighter highland surfaces. Investigate theory that the marias are hardened fields of lava formed as a result of a very large fall of meteorites or a comet that heated and melted the surface of the moon into a flowing mass of lava. Mountain ranges: average height, 5,000 to 12,000 feet; some 26,000 to 33,000 (Earth's Mount Everest is 29,000 feet); most mountains rugged, steep-walled, some rounded; most impressive mountain range: Leibnitz Mountains, near south pole of moon (shown at *top* of old lunar charts and photographs). Craters: most impressive crater, Copernicus, surrounded by a ring wall 12,000 feet high at highest point, diameter 56 miles, floor of crater depressed below level of surrounding territories; investigate to determine whether it was gouged out 850 to 950 million years ago; most craters have large central peaks. Investigate to determine whether craters are caused by impact of meteoroids on surface of moon, like Barringer Meteorite Crater in Arizona, or whether they are caused by volcanic activity—or whether both of these influences have produced different kinds of craters. Rills: cracks or crevasses in the moon's surface, some broad and flat, some narrow and deep, like Grand Canyon. Is the layering seen by astronauts in rills from many lava flows? Rays: brilliant white streaks on surface of the moon, up to 2,000 miles long; always emanate from some crater. Other geological investigations: look for volcanoes and possible volcanic activity; how mountains were formed; check rocks to see if any water is trapped in them; dig for possible valuable minerals in moon's crust; investigate evidence that the moon has a crust 225 miles thick. (Earth's crust varies from about 3 to 40 miles.) Moonquakes: very weak and infrequent. No objection to this.

Astronomy Study Group Viewing conditions: excellent, good chance to study planets and

The Eratosthenes Crater, photographed from the Command/Service Module of Apollo 17 as it circled the moon. Named after the Greek astronomer, who in about 200 B.C. first measured the circumference of the earth, this crater is a pit surrounded by a circular steep wall with a mountain peak in the center. Nearby (*left*) is one of the Apennine Mountains. Below Eratosthenes is *Mare Imbrium* (the "Sea of Showers"), one of the lunar "seas," and several small craters. On the right horizon the rim of Copernicus may be seen. (*Courtesy of NASA.*)

stars without distortion or interference from an atmosphere; length of day and night about 2 weeks each. Opportunity to observe Earth: Earth always visible from one side of moon, never visible on other side. General appearance of Earth: looks like a big, blue-white moon, diameter about 4 times that of moon; most of the time only clouds are seen; hardly any geographical details; in moon's night, Earthshine bright enough to read by; Earth has phases: full-Earth, quarter-Earth, crescent-Earth, and so on. Appearance of sun: bright disc against pitch-black sky. Corona visible, as is also the *zodiacal light,* a faint glow extending from the sun into space. Does the difference in their mineral content and in their density rule out the possibility that Earth and the moon were ever one? How was the moon formed? Was it hot or cold at the beginning?

Biology Study Group No immediate evidence of large plant or animal life, except ours. No traces of biologically-formed chemicals in lunar soil. No microorganisms appear in our culture media of lunar soil. No fossils. Expect to turn in short report, but will continue search.

Lunarnaut Study Group Flying conditions around moon smooth, but only by rocketship; no

A crescent earth with the far side of the moon in the foreground, photographed from Apollo 17 prior to its transearth journey. (*Courtesy of NASA.*)

atmosphere to support wings of airplane or supply oxygen for combustion. Care needed not to rocket off moon because gravitational pull only $\frac{1}{6}$ that of Earth.

Phases of the Moon

Everyone who has ever watched the moon from night to night knows that it seems to change shape. If the moon is observed for a month it may be seen *waning* from a full moon to a quarter to a thin crescent, then to the new moon ("no" moon) and then *waxing* to crescent, quarter, and full. These changes are known as the *phases* of the moon.

(*See* pp. 183, 191–3.)

To understand the cause of the moon's phases it is essential to keep in mind the role played by the sun, earth, and moon in this celestial spectacle:

1. The sun throws a light on the moon.
2. The earth provides a vantage point from which we view the show in this "theater in the round."
3. The moon, the performer, circles the earth once a month. Half of the moon is always illuminated, but we are not in a position to see the lighted half all the time.

When we do see the whole lighted half we call it a full moon. When only half of the lighted part is visible we see a quarter moon. When all of the lighted part faces away from the earth we have "no" moon or a new moon. The suggested demonstration will help in an understanding of the phases of the moon.

(*See* pp. 191–3.)

To correct a common error it must be emphasized that the phases of the moon are *not* caused by "a shadow thrown on the moon by the earth." The dark portion of the moon is dark simply because it is turned away from the sun.

Why is it that we see approximately the same face of the moon—the same "man in the moon" to the naked eye, the same craters, marias, and mountains with the help of the telescope? One more space fact must be added to the three just given to understand this.

4. As the moon circles the earth it turns on its axis in such a way that it presents approximately the same face to the earth. The moon rotates once as it revolves once.

The demonstration suggested on pages 192–3 will be helpful in understanding this.

Tides

The everlasting succession of low and high tide makes the edge of the sea a constantly changing boundary. The range of tides varies widely in different localities, depending on the nature of the shoreline and the ocean floor. Thus, in the open ocean the tidal range may be 2 or 3 feet. In Cape Cod Bay the range may be as much as 10 or 11 feet, and in the narrowing Bay of Fundy of Nova Scotia the range may be as much as 60 feet.

For about 6 hours the incoming *flood tide* rises higher and higher, covering more and more sloping beaches and climbing up on rocky shores. Then for 6 hours the falling *ebb tide* recedes.

Two factors are responsible for the rhythm of the tides: the gravitational pull of the moon

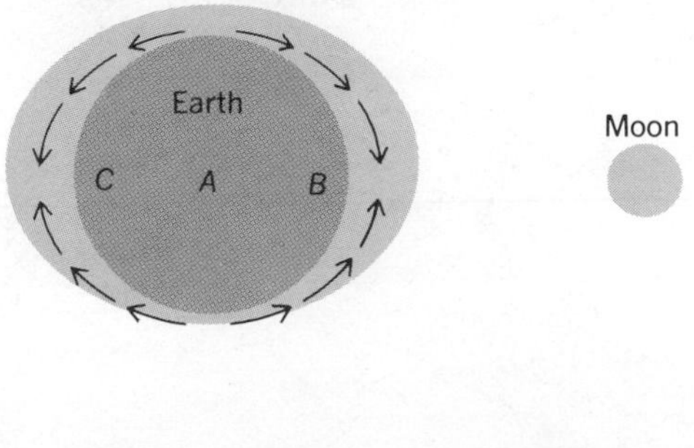

Tidal bulges in the oceans. In this diagram the earth and moon are viewed from a position in space "above" the North Pole (*see* text for explanation).

(and to a lesser extent the sun) and the rotation of the earth. Let us consider gravitation first.

The law of gravitation states in part, as we have seen, that every body attracts every other body in the universe. Thus the earth attracts the moon, and the moon attracts the earth. The pull of the moon is relatively weak, but is strong enough to have an effect on all parts of the earth—on the atmosphere and oceans as well as on the solid part. But the law of gravitation also states that the strength of the pull depends in part on the distance between the two bodies, being greater for closer objects. This has an interesting effect on the earth.

Referring now to the diagram of the cross-section of the earth it will be noted that different parts of the earth are at different distances from the moon. Thus point *B* on the earth's surface is 4,000 miles closer to the moon than point *A* in the center of the earth. Point *A* in turn is 4,000 miles closer to the moon than point *C*. Consequently, *the strength of the moon's pull is different on different parts of the earth.*

Consider first the effect of the varying pulls on the half of the earth facing the moon. Under the influence of the moon's gravity a flow of water occurs toward the region of the ocean nearest the moon. The water piles up there to produce a tidal bulge—a *high tide* at *B*.

At the same time there is another bulge in the ocean on the side of the earth away from the moon. This is more difficult to understand until we realize that the earth *as a whole,* with its mass centered at *A*, is pulled harder (because it is closer to the moon) than the part of the ocean away from the moon. Consequently, water piles up into a tidal bulge, another high tide at *C*.

The water drawn into the two bulges must come from somewhere. It comes from the ocean areas between them, causing a depression there. Thus, at any one time, we have two bulges, or *high tides,* as shown in the diagram, and two depressions, or *low tides,* in the earth's oceans.

As the earth completes a rotation every 24 hours it turns one place after another toward the moon's direct pull. As a result, the high and low tides sweep around the earth to produce the tidal rhythm, high, low, high, low approximately every 24 hours.

We say "approximately" because the moon, too, is shifting its position as it moves in its orbit around the earth. As a result, the time between one high tide and the next is not 12 hours, but an average of 12 hours and 26 minutes.

The U.S. Government provides tables and charts for mariners, showing times when high and low tides occur at many places along coasts. There are signs on many beaches for the benefit of swimmers, indicating the day-to-day schedule of tides. Ships' arrivals and departures are timed according to the tides, to make certain that channels are deep enough for incoming ships and to prevent ships from having to push their way out to sea against an incoming tide.

The pull of the sun also affects tides. Although the sun's gravitational force is much greater than that of the moon, its tide-raising force is less than half that of the moon. This paradox is explained by the principle that was discussed in relation to the moon: *Tides are due to a difference in the gravitational force on different parts of the earth.* Look again at *A*, *B*, and *C*, but substitute the sun for the moon. We shall have to push the sun far off the page—about 100 feet away—to make the distances proportional. Even though the sun's gravitational force at that distance is 167 times as great as the moon's, its tide-generating force is less because the difference of a mere 4,000 miles between *B* and *A*, or *A* and *C*, is less significant *in relation to the great distance of the sun from all these locations.*

The sun's gravitational force may work with or against the moon's pull, depending on the relative position of the sun, moon, and earth. When the sun is in line with the moon, as it is

TYPICAL SCHEDULE OF HIGH TIDES

	A.M.	*P.M.*	*Time between High Tides*
Tues., July 31	1:03	1:38	12 hr. 35 min.
Wed., Aug. 1	2:08	2:44	12 hr. 36 min.
Thurs., Aug. 2	3:21	3:54	12 hr. 33 min.
Fri., Aug. 3	4:31	4:58	12 hr. 27 min.
Sat., Aug. 4	5:33	5:56	12 hr. 23 min.
Sun., Aug. 5	6:28	6:48	12 hr. 20 min.
Mon., Aug. 6	7:19	7:38	12 hr. 19 min.

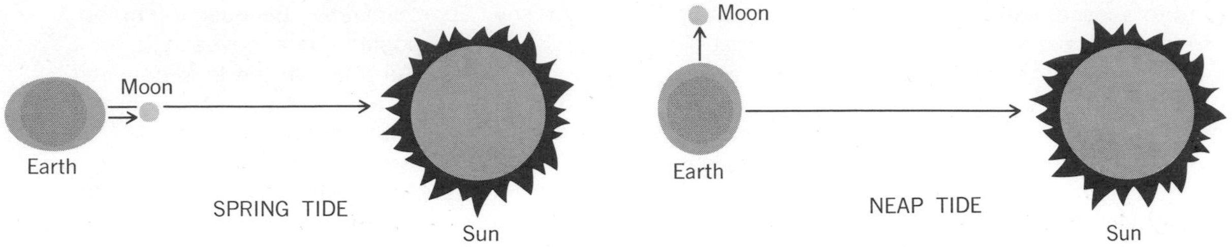

(*Left*) How the sun and moon work together to make strong spring tides. (*Right*) The sun and moon are shown working against each other to cause weak neap tides.

during periods of full moon and new moon, it *adds* its pull, thereby causing high high tides and low low tides. This tide is called a *spring tide,* although it has nothing to do with the spring of the year. Spring tides occur twice a month. They should be thought of as tides that "spring up" high.

When the sun pulls at right angles with respect to the pull of the moon on the earth, as it does when the moon is in its first and last quarter, it hinders the moon's efforts, producing tides that neither rise very high nor fall very low. These are the *neap tides,* which also occur twice a month.

ECLIPSES

Eclipses occur when the sun, earth, and moon are on a straight line in space. There are two kinds of eclipses, solar and lunar.

Solar eclipses occur when the moon passes directly in front of the sun, obscuring it from our vision. If you shut one eye and look at an electric bulb across the room, you can hide its light with a penny held at the right distance from you. The penny (the moon) has eclipsed the bulb (the sun). Note that although the penny is smaller it can eclipse the larger bulb because it is closer to you.

(*See* p. 193.)

A friend observing you at this time would see the shadow of the penny on your open eye. Similarly, an astronaut in space would observe that the shadow of the moon falls on the earth during a solar eclipse. The moon is smaller than the earth and close to it, so its shadow falls on only a small portion of the earth's surface, and is never more than 167 miles wide in regions near the equator, somewhat wider at far northern or southern latitudes. However, the moon is moving around the earth, so the path of its eastward-moving shadow may form a band thousands of miles long. (To return to the penny-bulb demonstration: If you moved the penny to the left its shadow would sweep across your head.) This narrow track is called the eclipse path. (Also the rotation of the earth in the same direction as the moon's orbital motion slows down the shadow path on the earth and makes an eclipse of the sun last as long as $7\frac{1}{2}$ minutes at a maximum. How would you demonstrate this effect to your friend?)

During a total eclipse of the sun, a small, dark nick is first seen in its edge. The dark area grows larger and larger. Just before totality, the sky is darkened considerably, and there is a strange hush of nature's sounds. When the sun disappears completely a pearly halo—the corona—appears around the blackened disc of the sun. A few stars appear. This period of total eclipse never lasts more than $7\frac{1}{2}$ minutes. Astronomers, many of whom have traveled halfway around the world to see the eclipse, are in a frenzy of activity at this time—observing, photographing, and recording the event in their effort to learn more about the corona and the prominences of the sun. Then the moon slips off, and the edge of the sun appears again and grows. The eclipse is over.

(**Note:** Do not look at a solar eclipse directly. None of the so-called protective devices, such as sunglasses, stained or smoked glass, and old film negatives can give absolute protec-

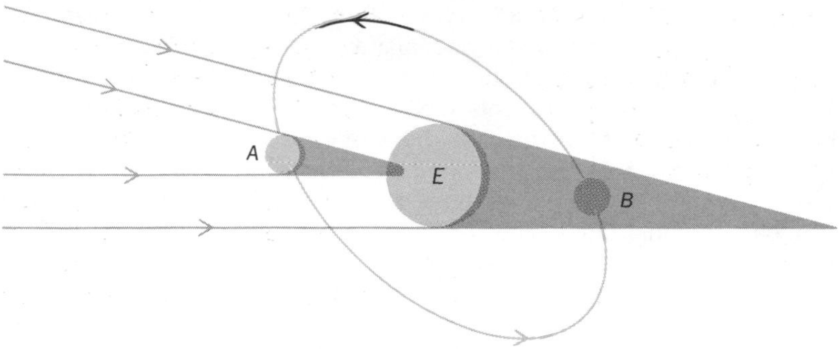

When the moon is at position B it is in the shadow of the earth. We then have an eclipse of the moon. When it is in position A the moon casts a shadow on part of the earth and hides the sun from view there. We then have an eclipse of the sun. (The arrows on the left show the direction of the sun's rays.)

tion against the solar rays that burn the retina of the eye. The only safe way to view the eclipse is indirectly—for example, by projecting the sun's image through a pinhole in a piece of cardboard or through binoculars onto a white surface.)

In any year 2 to 5 eclipses of the sun will occur, but no more than 3 of these can be total. In a partial eclipse only part of the sun is hidden by the moon. Since solar eclipses follow narrow paths across the earth they are rare for a particular locality. In New York City, for example, a total eclipse of the sun occurred on January 24, 1925. This was the first eclipse of this kind there since the fifteenth century! The next total eclipse will occur there on October 26, 2144. The following are the dates and places of the total eclipses visible in North America recently and during the rest of the twentieth century:

1970 March 7	Florida, South Carolina, Georgia, North Carolina.
1972 July 10	Northern North America.
1979 February 26	Idaho, Washington, Montana.

Lunar eclipses occur when the earth is between the sun and the moon, thereby blocking off the moon's source of light and darkening it. As we observe an eclipse of the moon, therefore, we are watching the shadow of the earth pass across the moon's face. An eclipse of the moon can be observed by all the people on that half of the earth that can see the moon at the time. Therefore all of us have many opportunities to observe lunar eclipses in our lifetime. Lunar eclipses occur 2 or 3 times a year.

Eclipses of the sun occur only during the period of the new moon, for it is only then that a sun–moon–earth lineup, in that order, is possible. Eclipses of the moon occur only during the full moon, when a sun–earth–moon lineup may occur. Then why is there not an eclipse of the sun and an eclipse of the moon every month? The answer lies in the peculiar track that the moon follows around the earth. Picture the earth and the sun sitting on an imaginary table in space. As the earth moves around the sun its orbit remains on this table, similar to toy railroad tracks.

The moon's track around the earth, however, cuts through the table at an angle. Sometimes the moon is above the table and sometimes below it. It is only when there is a coincidence of the moon being on the table (in the plane of the earth's orbit) at the time of a new or full moon that an eclipse occurs.

HOW THE SOLAR SYSTEM WAS FORMED

The question of the origin of our solar system has intrigued astronomers for the past 200 years and has resulted in a number of theories. All the theories fall into one of two camps: Some authorities envision a gradual evolution of the solar system, others a violent revolution. We shall consider both.

The classic *nebular hypothesis* of the French astronomer, Marquis Pierre Simon de Laplace, proposed in 1796, is evolutionary in nature. This theory suggests that the sun and planets were derived from a huge gaseous cloud or nebula slowly rotating in space. This cloud extended beyond the limits of the known planets. Because of the gravitational attraction among its particles, the cloud contracted and, as it did, spun faster. You can demonstrate such an increase in speed by spinning yourself on a piano stool with your arms outstretched and holding some books and then suddenly pulling your arms and the books to your side. You will find that this "contraction" of yourself makes you go faster. Similarly, the figure skater on ice can increase his spin rate by bringing his arms close to his sides. As the nebula spun faster, rings of gaseous matter were separated from the central mass, one at a time, revolving in the same plane as the nebula and in the same direction. The material in the rings collected, cooled, and condensed in the plane of the material into planets. In this way the outer planets were formed first. With additional shrinking of the central cloud more rings were formed, one after another, accounting for all the planets. According to this theory satellites of the planets are thought to have been formed in a similar way from the planets when they were still in a gaseous state. Thus the planets revolved around the central mass, which became the sun, and the satellites revolved around the planets.

Another famous theory, violent in nature, is the *planetesimal hypothesis* proposed by the geologist T.C. Chamberlin and the astronomer F.R. Moulton of the University of Chicago in 1905. This theory postulates that a star came very close to our sun, exerting a powerful pull on it. Just as the moon causes tides on the earth, so the passing star caused great tides to form on the sun. Great quantities of material were torn away by this tidal attraction. These then condensed into the separate planets.

Dissatisfaction with both of these theories, arising from increased knowledge, has resulted in a number of new hypotheses being proposed by scientists in this century. One of these is the *dust cloud hypothesis,* advanced by Fred L. Whipple of Harvard Observatory. This theory, evolutionary rather than revolutionary in nature, resembles the nebular hypothesis in some respects. In brief, it suggests that planets and stars were formed from immense collections of tiny particles floating in space. In such a cloud the mutual gravitational attraction of its particles caused it to condense or contract. Within the huge cloud minor turbulent motions caused streams of dust, or subclouds, to form. These minor clouds contracted further to become the various planets, while the major cloud condensed into the sun. The tremendous heat generated by the compression of material to form the sun made it white hot and promoted nuclear reactions, mentioned earlier in this chapter, which permitted it to shine as a star. The planets, however, cooled off because they were too small for thermonuclear reactions to commence.

Although there is a good deal of speculation in these and other theories, they are not wild dreams. Each theory is tested against these criteria:

1. Is it in accordance with known physical principles—with our knowledge of gravitation, heat, light, behavior of atoms?
2. Is the process within the realm of probability?
3. Does it account for our present solar system—its size, motions, members?

This survey of the solar system contains a great many facts and concepts which may be grouped together into some larger statements. Here are some of the important generalizations:

The sun is the center of a huge system of heavenly bodies that revolve around it. Included in the sun's family are planets, minor planets, satellites, comets, and meteoroids.

The mutual gravitational attraction between the planets and the sun prevents the planets from flying out of their orbits.

The sun is a nearby star; stars are distant suns.

The sun shines by virtue of its own nuclear reactions; the planets shine by reflecting sunlight.

Life on earth would be impossible if it were not for the sun.

Physical conditions on the different members of the solar system vary. Thus far we have no conclusive evidence of life on any other planet than Earth.

The planets move in the same direction in nearly circular orbits around the sun.

The earth is the third planet from the sun. It is one of the smaller planets in the solar system.

Day and night are caused by the rotation of the earth on its axis.

The earth's rotation causes the apparent motion of the sun, moon, and stars across the sky.

It takes the earth one year to complete one revolution around the sun.

Seasons are caused by the tilt in the earth's axis and the revolution of the earth around the sun.

The moon's changing appearance—its phases—results from its revolution around the earth.

Tides are caused by differences in the gravitational force on different parts of the earth. The tide-raising influence of the moon is greater than that of the sun.

Eclipses occur when the earth, sun, and moon are on a straight line in space.

Scientists differ in their views about the origin of the solar system.

(**Note:** See the "Discovering for Yourself" section at the end of Ch. 8A).

(Photo by John King.)

CHAPTER 7B

TEACHING "THE SUN AND THE PLANETS"

Space exploration is continually providing motivation for the study of planets. In this era of explorations of the moon, Venus, Mars, and other planets children are exposed to our exploits in space through reading and seeing television. In the future some of today's children may be space travelers.

Beginning to understand the concepts of distance, direction, length, weight, and motion can be developed by experiences in the immediate environment; in the smaller space of a street, for example, by comparing the length of a city block to a footstep; the distance to a smoke stack, to clouds, and other objects in the daytime sky. Observing a cloud moving in front of the sun provides an opportunity to discover that clouds are closer to us than the sun. Pupils may *estimate* distances and, when possible, *measure* to see if they are accurate. They can *construct inferences* from their observations. There are many opportunities for *interpreting data.*

Arithmetic conceptions are often necessary to the understanding of science concepts. For example, if pupils read that the earth is about four times as far across as the moon, it is important that we attempt to bring meaning to this concept. Here models are helpful: a ball to represent the moon, a globe four times the diameter of the ball to represent the earth. Space distances are better understood if they are compared to some distance with which pupils are familiar—for example, the number of miles to a distant city to which many of the pupils may have traveled. The concept of years of time may also be developed if pupils associate their own ages, or some other time span in their experience, with the unfamiliar and much longer time figure's associated with outer space concepts.

The use of models is natural for the material in this chapter to clarify concepts of size, distance, time, motion, and relative position in space. In using models it is important to have children participate, physically and mentally, in their construction and use. Models will be helpful in the transition from an earth viewpoint ("the sun moves across the sky") to a space viewpoint ("the earth turns").

SOME BROAD CONCEPTS: "The Sun and the Planets"

The solar system is made up of the sun and the bodies that revolve around it.

The sun's energy is the source of life on the earth.

Day and night are caused by the earth's rotation on its axis.

The tilt of the earth's axis and its revolution around the sun cause the seasons.

The moon's phases result from its revolution around the earth.

Eclipses result when the earth, moon, and sun are in a straight line in space.

The moon and the planets shine by reflected sunlight.

The turning of the earth makes the sun, moon, and stars appear to move across the sky.

Gravitational attraction between the planets and the sun prevents the planets from flying out of their orbits.

The entire solar system moves through space.

FOR YOUNGER CHILDREN

Following are examples of experiences that have been used with younger children to develop an understanding of some of the concepts in this chapter. In cases where elementary-school pupils have had little experience with science these may be used with older children as well.

How Does the Sun Help Plants?

Select several plants (house plants, seedlings of beans, or others) as similar as possible. Ask children to *observe* the plants carefully and *compare* them and point out similarities (same kind of plant, same size, and so on). Ask: "How do you think we can find out if these plants need light?" Put some in the dark, keep others in the light. Observe the differences. "How long should we leave the plants in the dark?" "What dark place would you suggest?" Look for possible places (dark closet, cloakroom, and so on). "How do you think the plants will change?" "How shall we take care of both groups of plants?" Help children to see that there must be only one variable—light. All other conditions must be the same—amount and time of watering, air available, soil conditions as similar as possible, same kinds of plants; use *several* plants in each situation since changes could be due to an unhealthy plant. (See Part I for discussion of the concept of the variables and the maturity of children.)

Ask children to try to *predict* what will happen. How soon? When the children examine the plants from time to time ask them to observe any differences and try to account for them. Were their predictions correct? Ask pupils to continue to observe effects of light or lack of it on plants. Some pupils may know about the use of artificial light on plant growth. If possible, some pupils may try to grow plants under artificial light.

What Makes a Shadow? How Do Shadows Change?[1]

On a sunny morning take the children for a walk to observe shadows. What shadows can be seen? What things make shadows? How are the shadows like the things that make them? How can we measure the length of a shadow? Choose a child to stand at one end of a long piece of paper so that his shadow falls on the paper. Draw an outline of the shadow. Measure the length with a yard or meter stick. Record the length and the time of day. Look for the sun. Where is it in the sky? Low? High? Keep the record. At noon outline and measure the same child's shadow. Record the length and time of day. Look for the sun in the sky. Is it high or low? If possible, take another measurement near the close of school. Record the data. Again look for the sun's location in the sky. Use the three records and ask children to compare them. Help them to try to account for the differences in appearance of the three shadows.

[1] *See also* "Sunlight and Shadows," *Science: Grades K–2* (Brooklyn, N.Y.: Board of Education).

Urge them to observe shadows at home at different times of the day and report their observations. Some children will not be able to *infer* a relationship between the height of the sun and the length of shadows. Provide further experiences for them at future times during the year.

Some children will need further experiences with shadow observations before they can demonstrate and state the idea that objects make shadows when light cannot pass through them. Use a gooseneck lamp and try to make a shadow with a book, a toy, a clear piece of glass. Turn off the light. Now can you see a shadow when the room is dark? Go outdoors on a cloudy day. Can you find shadows? Why?

Observe specific places where sunlight comes into the classroom or other parts of the school building at different times of the day. Ask children to try to account for the change.

In case of very young children the two problems "What makes a shadow?" and "How do shadows change?" being considered here should be dealt with separately.

What Makes the Earth Warm?

At noon on a sunny day take the children outside and ask them to *describe* the day (sunny, warm, and so on). Ask them to try to find warm things by feeling them (grass, the sidewalk, soil, rocks, the pavement, windowsills). Ask them to feel of some of these same things in the shade. How do they feel? Why?

Place a thermometer in a sunny window. Watch what happens. Set the thermometer in the shade. Watch what happens. Why? Use two saucers with two ice cubes on each. Set one in a sunny window and keep the other out of the sun. Observe the difference. Why? On a partly cloudy day take the children outside to experience the effect when clouds cover the sun and when the sky is clear. Help children plan other experiences to note the effects of the sun.

How Does the Moon Change?[2]

Even very young children are aware of the moon. They have heard about moon flights and have observed the moon at night. Some calendars show outlines of moon phases on different days of the month. Some children are able to observe the moon at different times and can match the moon's actual appearance with these phases. With help at home and drawings from school some children are able to make observations and infer that (1.) the moon does not always have the same appearance, (2.) sometimes more of it can be seen than at others, (3.) it is not always in the same place every evening.

[2] *See also* Elementary Science Study (ESS): *Where Is the Moon, Teacher's Guide* (Manchester, Mo.: Webster Division, McGraw-Hill Book Co.), a booklet for children called *Where Was the Moon* and notes called *"Reminders,"* which help children identify objects in the sky over a period of time.

How Much Does the Temperature Change in a Day?

Discuss with children their experiences with temperature changes during a day. When is it warmest? Coolest? How much do you think the temperature changes? How can we find out?

This can introduce children to using a measuring instrument to provide accurate data from which to draw conclusions. Lead them to the idea of thermometer and changes in temperatures by using the Pyrex flask thermometer described in Chapter 16B and use the concepts developed in the previous activity, "What Makes the Earth Warm?"

Record their estimates of the warmest and coldest times and their ideas of differences in temperatures. *List* the temperatures taken with a thermometer at different times of the day (on several days). *Compare* these temperatures with the children's estimates.

Other Problems for Younger children

1. How do living things change as the seasons change?
2. Which way is the center of the earth?
3. What kinds of things do not make shadows?
4. Where is the sun in the sky?
5. How can you make your shadow change?
6. How can shadows help us tell time?
7. What do mirrors do to sunlight?
8. What can we see in the sky at night?

FOR OLDER CHILDREN

What Are the Planets Like?

One good look at the stars, or an observation of the moon with field glasses, is more valuable than looking at dozens of diagrams or star charts. If pupils studying planets can actually see one their enthusiasm will repay any effort a teacher makes to bring about such an experience. In the community amateur astronomers with telescopes are often more than willing to let pupils look through their telescopes and, if properly briefed beforehand, will be very helpful to pupils.

Science News and other magazines[3] indicate periodically which planets are visible at any given time and where to locate them. It is helpful to go outdoors with children during the day at school and point to the section of the sky where they may expect to see the planets at night. It may help them to learn where the planet will be on

[3] *Science News* (Washington, D.C.: Science Service). One issue each month contains a star map with interpretation. *Science and Children* (Washington, D.C.). Frequent star maps. *Sky and Telescope* (Cambridge, Mass.: Sky Publishing Corp.). Similar information.

a particular night in relation to the moon (if there is one visible in the early evening) or to some easily identified star groups.

Have children investigate the problem "Does a planet move?" by observing one planet for a number of weeks. They will observe that during one evening the planet appears to move across the sky from east to west. Venus, for example, may be seen to disappear over the western horizon an hour or two after sundown. Ask the children to try to interpret this motion. Some may suggest that the turning of the earth causes this apparent motion in the same way as it does for the sun. Ask the children, during this period of observation, to locate the observed planet in relation to nearby stars and to make a sketch of what they see. Continue this for a number of weeks. Children will discover that the planet changes position in relation to the stars and constellations. What causes this? The answer may be deferred (while children speculate and offer ideas) until the next problem, where a model of the solar system is developed.

How Can We Make Models of the Solar System?

Making a clay or paper-cutout model of the solar system is particularly useful in the fifth and sixth grades, when pupils know enough arithmetic to get approximately correct proportions of the sizes of various planets as well as their relative distances from one another and from the sun. From various sources pupils will get figures that (*See* Ch. 7A.) tell distances and diameters of the various planets. Then they will have to decide on a scale that they can use in order to get all the members of the solar system into the classroom and to have the sun (the largest body) as well as Mercury (the smallest

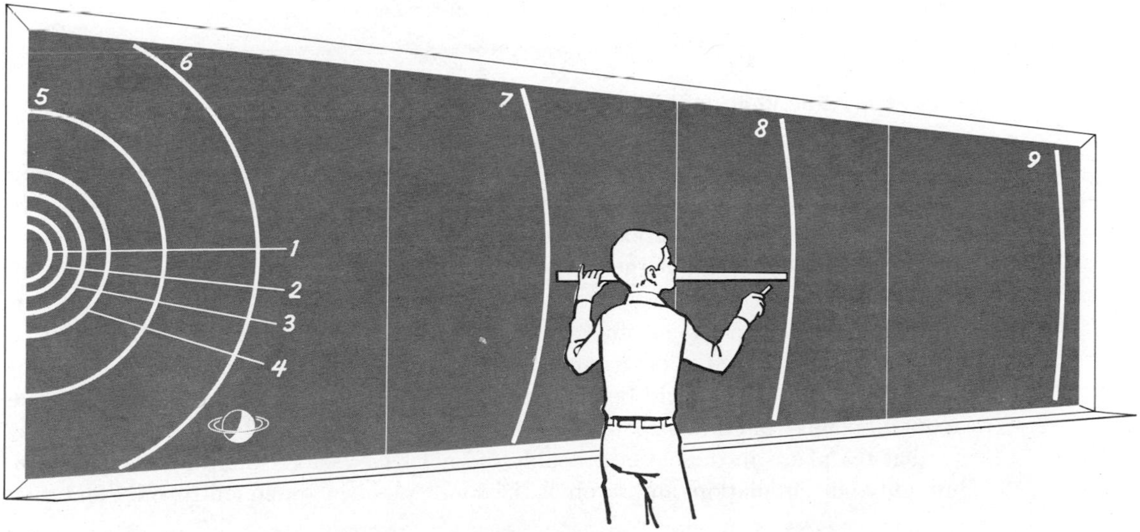

Such an activity as this affords an excellent opportunity for the meaningful use of mathematics. Better concepts of the vastness of space, relationships between heavenly bodies, and the place of the earth in the solar system can result when pupils solve the problems related to making this graphic representation.

FACTS FOR A "CHALKBOARD PLANETARIUM"

Number and Name of Planet	*Distance from Sun in Millions of Miles*	*Distance to be Measured from Left Side of Chalkboard (Scale: 1 inch = 20 million miles)*
1. Mercury	36	$1\frac{3}{4}$ inches
2. Venus	67	$3\frac{1}{4}$ inches
3. Earth	93	$4\frac{3}{4}$ inches
4. Mars	140	7 inches
5. Jupiter	480	2 feet
6. Saturn	890	3 feet 8 inches
7. Uranus	1,800	7 feet 6 inches
8. Neptune	2,800	11 feet 8 inches
9. Pluto	3,700	15 feet 5 inches

body) included. They may in fact need to use a larger area than the classroom, depending on the scale they select. Such a project might be started by asking pupils: "What figures will we have to know to make the model solar system? How can we adjust the figures to a scale?" Pupils should be urged to make their own plan and then carry it out. Here is an excellent opportunity to let them try out their ideas and remedy any mistakes they make. It is important to note that distances in space are so great that it is practically impossible to use the same scales for the size of the planets and the distances between them. An outdoors model[4] where there is more space is an interesting possibility.

(*See* above.)

A "chalkboard planetarium"[5] uses the facts on the chart to give pupils a better concept of space relationships in the solar system.

How Is the Sun Important to Us?

(*See* p. 182.)

Refer to "How Does the Sun Help Plants?" for some of the details of an experiment concerning the sun and plants. Older children are able to give greater attention to the control idea. They will also have more experiences from which to make predictions and may know more about the use of artificial light for plant growth.

It is one thing to read or hear that the sun is necessary for plant growth; it is quite another to experiment and see the results. As far as possible there should be only one difference in the environment of the plants—the presence of sunlight. After two weeks the plants should be compared. Remember that pupils cannot generalize about *all* plants from their experience here. Moreover, some pupils may say, and rightly so, that the plants in the closet probably did not have exactly the same temperature, humidity, air circulation, and so on as the sunlit plants. Consequently, only tentative

[4] M. Swan: "Outdoor Model of the Solar System," *Science and Children* (September 1970). (Washington, D.C.), gives data to use in constructing model using only one scale for size and distance.
[5] Adapted from *Science: Grade* 5 Brooklyn, N.Y.: Board of Education of the City of New York, 1968).

conclusions can be drawn from the experiment. Pupils may observe examples outdoors, where plants do not grow well because of lack of sunlight.

In addition to plants' dependence on the sun other relationships are important: The sun heats the earth and affects our weather; it gives us light; it affects our ocean tides and keeps the earth in the solar system.

What Causes Day and Night?

Before proceeding with the demonstration described here urge pupils to try to devise their own methods of using a light and a globe to demonstrate the cause of day and night. This may help them to recall the information they need in order to illustrate the causes.

Because many science and geography books suggest how to demonstrate the cause of day and night our description is brief. As a source of light use either a flashlight, floor lamp with a shade, or any lamp with a good reflector. Use a globe for the earth. Remind pupils to imagine that they are living on the globe. A chalk mark on the spot where they live will help. Darken the room, shine the light on the globe, watch the chalk mark, and begin to turn the globe from west to east (counterclockwise) slowly. Turn the globe around once on its axis so that pupils can observe what happens during one complete rotation. Then begin with the position of the chalk mark at sunrise, and let a pupil tell what he would be doing at different stages of the rotation—for example: "Now I am having breakfast"; "Now I am on my way to school." If the class is large, let small groups take turns standing close so they can observe easily. Pupils should remember the following things in order to understand the causes of day and night:

The earth is round, like a ball; consequently, only half of it can be lighted at once.

The earth gets its light from the sun. The lighted half has day; the unlighted half has night.

The earth makes one rotation every 24 hours. Nighttime follows daytime.

Pupils may make a chart indicating the number of hours of daylight and darkness during each of the months of the year, 12 rows across the chart—1 row for each month.

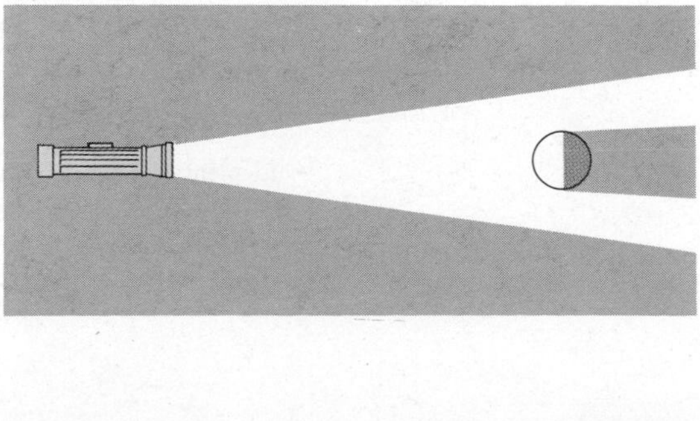

The flashlight illuminating the ball shows how only half of the earth (a ball-shaped object) can be lighted at one time.

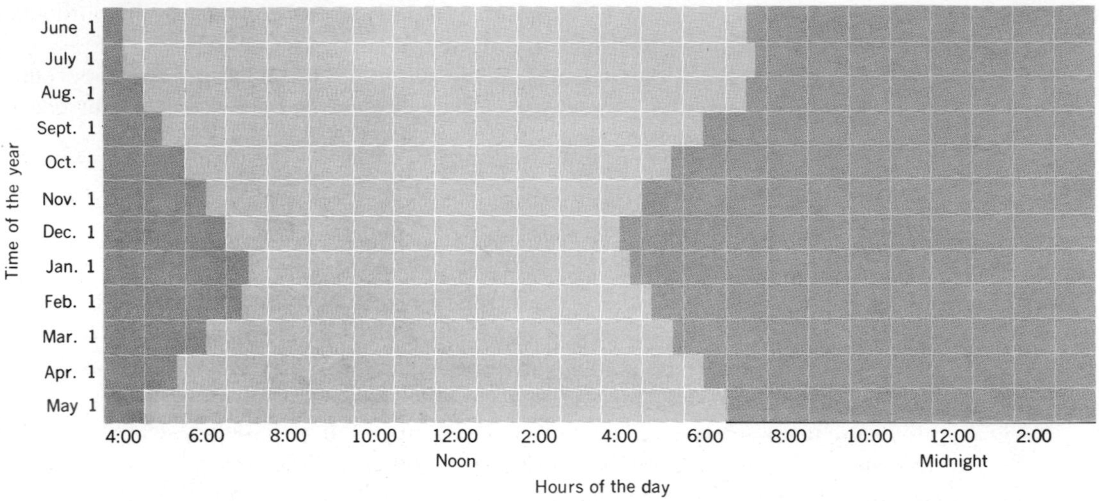

Making a record of hours of daylight and darkness requires careful research and accurate recording of data. (Each of the hour numbers on the chart refers to the line above the left end of the number.) Newspapers, almanacs, radio broadcasts, and similar references may be used as sources of information. Pupils can devise other methods of making such a record.

From this chart pupils can answer such question as: "When do we have the most hours of daylight?" "When do we have the fewest hours of daylight?" "Is there much or little daylight on your birthday?" "When are the hours of daylight and darkness about the same?" The data for such a chart may be obtained from an almanac or from daily newspapers and calendars.

What Causes the Seasons?[6]

Help pupils understand that for any particular part of the earth, such as the United States: (1.) In summer there are more hours of sunlight, and therefore more heating of the earth, than in winter when there are fewer hours of sunlight; and (2.) in summer the sun is more directly overhead; it heats the earth more than it does in winter when it is lower in the sky and its rays strike the earth more obliquely. Both these phenomena are observable.

Children can understand these phenomena much better by actual experience with heat.[7] To demonstrate the influence of the direction of the sun's rays use two pieces of black paper placed on pieces of corrugated cardboard (because of its insulating properties). Place one to receive the sun's rays directly (90° angle), the other flat on

[6] *See also* Elementary Science Study (ESS): *Daytime Astronomy, Teacher's Guide* (Manchester, Mo.: Webster Division, McGraw-Hill Book Co.), ways to help children organize their observations of changes in the sky throughout the year.

[7] Adapted from *Science: Grades 3–4* (Brooklyn, N.Y.: Board of Education of the City of New York, 1966).

the surface. On a sunny day place each in sunlight in the schoolroom. Let children feel and compare the warmth on both pieces after 2, 4, 6, 8, and 10 minutes, and record their findings. There may be some disagreement among children about feeling the difference. How can we be more accurate and certain of the results? Place thermometers under each piece of black paper and read them after the same intervals.

The difference in length of days may be emphasized by asking pupils to recall the difference in light when they get up at 7 A.M. in September as compared with the same time in December. The chart or graph of daylight and darkness hours will also help pupils to understand seasons. Here again, arithmetic serves as a tool for science, and the activity is another example of helping children to see the importance of collecting data over a long period of time before drawing conclusions.

Both of these experiences, one with the changes in length of day the other with changes in the strength of the sunlight, help children understand the cause of seasons.
(*See* p. 180.)
Along with these experiences a model planetarium may help pupils gain a space view of the cause of the seasons. Working individually, or in small groups, let them manipulate the model and come up with hypotheses about the cause of the seasons. Two questions may help: "Does the model show how the length of daylight might change as the earth travels around the sun?" "Does the model show how the angle at which the sun strikes the earth might change during the yearly orbit?" Use the questions only as a last resort; let the children grope for solutions until you discover what assistance they need.

These demonstrations should be supplemented by several outdoor trips to observe the position of the sun during different times of the day and at different times of the

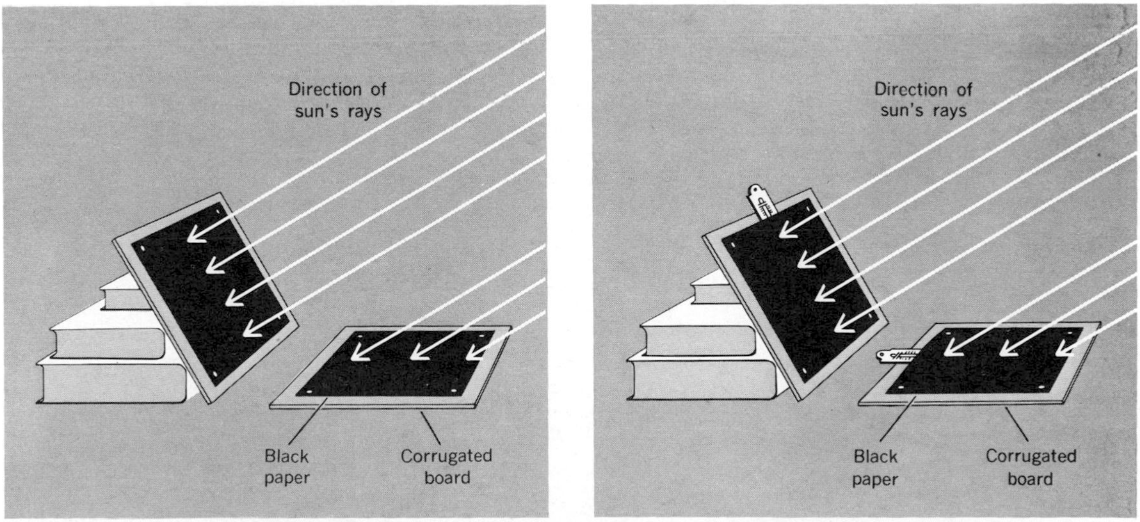

The angle makes a difference. It is one thing to read or hear about the principle illustrated here, and quite another to plan and carry out an experience such as this to show it. Experimenting without and then with a thermometer helps pupils to see the importance of accurate measurements.

year. This illustrates the point we have made before: that *demonstrations are done to help pupils understand a phenomenon, but not as ends in themselves. It is how well the pupils see the relationship of the demonstration to the problem or phenomena that determines its value.*
(**Note:** Demonstrations should not be confused with experiments. They are done for different reasons.)

What Is the Moon Like?[8]

In this era of "Man *on* the Moon" children will supply much information about the moon's surface, about gravity on the moon, moon rocks, and so on. Inventory their ideas first and then proceed as follows:

What can you discover by looking at the moon using a pair of binoculars? What changes in appearance can you see from night to night? What kind of a path does it seem to make across the sky? When does it rise and set? Is its path like the sun's path?

Begin by urging children to *observe* for themselves, *record* their observations, to *predict* what will happen from night to night and to try to *demonstrate* their observations.

If possible, arrange for children to look at the moon through a telescope and *describe* their observations. There is no substitute for this experience.

Many calendars indicate the dates of the new moon and the other phases. Urge pupils to observe these phases and draw pictures of the shape of the moon on different dates. Have them indicate under their drawings the date, the time, and the part of

[8] *See also* M. Zimmerman: "The Inconstant Moon," *Science and Children* (April 1970), a detailed account of a moon study in a sixth grade; G. McGlathery: "How Is Your Moon Geography?," *Science and Children* (April 1971); and *Apollo 15 at Hadley Base* and *On the Moon with Apollo 15* (Washington, D.C.: Superintendent of Documents, Government Printing Office). Other materials from this source available (*see* Bibliography).

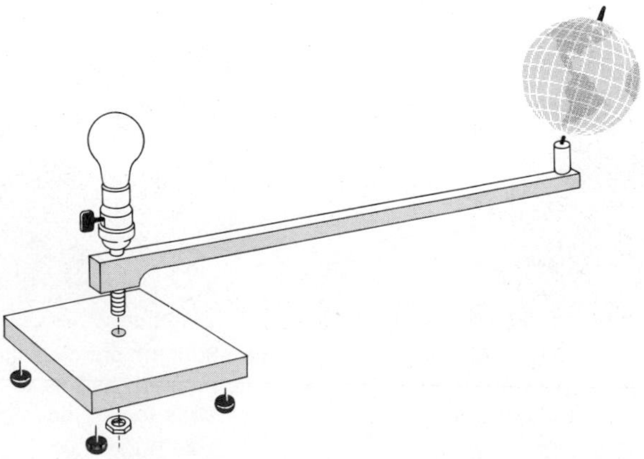

The details and construction of a planetarium. In using this apparatus it is important to remember to keep the earth's axis always pointing to the north. Commercially-made models use a chain arrangement to rotate the earth and to keep it tipped in the proper direction. Pupils in the photograph that opens this chapter are using a planetarium like this.

the sky the moon was in (east, west, and so on). They may also note in newspapers, calendars, or almanacs the time of moonrise and moonset.

If pupils examine almanacs they are almost sure to run across information about planting seeds in accordance with the phases of the moon. Despite the fact that we live in an age of scientific knowledge there are still people who plant certain vegetables during certain phases of the moon. A discussion of what plants need in order to grow and some reading about superstitions will help pupils to form an opinion of such practices.

Why Does the Moon Seem to Change Shape?

Use the results of observations made in the previous problem. Suggest that children draw on the chalkboard the various shapes of the moon they have observed. Suggest also that they try to arrange them in the order that they would occur during the month. Then let them attempt to *construct hypotheses* that might explain these apparent changes. As the demonstration goes on (*see* following) and they begin to develop some ideas urge them to distinguish between ideas that support their hypotheses and those that do not. They may be able to revise their ideas as they attempt to test their hypotheses.

Many pupils in the elementary school find it difficult to understand what makes the moon seem to change its shape as it travels around the earth. Even the following commonly-used demonstration is not always effective with all pupils. It is difficult for them to transpose what they see in the demonstration to what they observe in the sky.

To represent the moon use a basketball or a ball of similar size. To represent the sun use a lamp such as was suggested for the demonstration of the cause of day and night. Darken the room and turn on the lamp. Stand in the light of the lamp and hold the ball at arm's length, a little higher than the lamp (teacher demonstrates). Your head represents the position of the earth. Remind pupils that to understand how the shape of the moon seems to change we must remember three things: (1.) the moon's light comes from the sun, (2.) the moon is ballshaped and can be lighted on only one side, and (3.) the moon revolves around the earth once every month (approximately once every 27½ days). Pupils should be reminded also that they can see the moon only from the position of the earth—that is, the teacher's head. (In this demonstration it is especially important that each pupil be given an opportunity to participate, because only the demonstrator is in a position to actually see the changes.)

Begin by holding the ball in a position between the sun and the earth, a little higher than the head. This represents the position at new moon, when scarcely any of it is visible to us on the earth, because the light from the sun cannot strike the side of the moon we see. As you turn slowly toward the left, still holding the ball a little over your head, more of the moon will gradually become lighted. Stop a quarter of the way around and you are in the position of first quarter. Draw a chalk mark on the ball to outline the lighted part so that the shape becomes apparent. Keep turning in the same direction another quarter of the way around. Now you are in the position

The girl is demonstrating the phases of the moon. The ball represents the moon. The light from the window represents sunlight. She is a viewer on earth, standing in one spot and turning in order to move the "moon" in its orbit. The pictures show what she sees.

of full moon (remember to keep the ball a little higher than your head). Approximately two weeks have passed since new moon. Keep turning and observe the lighted part of the ball. It is now growing smaller. Turn another quarter of the way around and you are in the position of third quarter. Approximately three weeks of the month have gone. Keep turning in the same direction to the original position. A month has passed. The moon has changed from new moon to first quarter, to full moon, to third quarter, and back again to new moon.

Using a lamp to light up a basketball is a way of helping pupils understand what happens in the night sky, but pupils' right answers to the questions we ask about the ball and light do not necessarily mean that they fully understand the cause of the moon's phases. It is quite a mental jump from the schoolroom demonstration out into space where the phenomenon is taking place.

There has been much emphasis on the fact that we see only one side of the moon and children are curious to know why. Let children suggest their hypotheses. List them on the chalkboard. Suggest that pupils attempt to demonstrate their ideas. Then do the following demonstration for them and ask them to observe carefully. Use a chair or any other object for the earth. Face it and remind children that if at any time in your journey around the earth your face is turned in the opposite direction you will have rotated. Now make a revolution around the object, always keeping your face toward it. Children will see that the moon rotates once as it revolves once, and thus the same side of the moon is always toward the earth. Children may recall that some recent space probes have photographed the side of the moon we cannot see from the earth.

What Makes an Eclipse?

Ideally the best time to study an eclipse is when it is occurring. Naturally this is difficult to arrange (*see* Chapter 7A for future time table of eclipses). The entire school can be involved in the observations since, like any other of nature's spectacles, it has meaning at every level.

(**Note:** See the caution against looking directly at the sun in Chapter 7A.)

Before using the demonstration that is described here urge children to try to illustrate their ideas on the chalkboard or by using the materials in various ways. Give them help only when they run out of steam themselves.

The demonstration used to show moon phases may also be used to show eclipses. Use an electric lamp, a ball, and the same positions as were used to show moon phases. The question may arise: "Why don't we have an eclipse every month as the moon travels around the earth?" It should be made clear that the earth, sun, and moon are not often in line and in the same plane. A child will see that when his head (the earth) is between the light (the sun) and the ball (moon), and all three are in line, the shadow of his head falls on the ball and eclipses it (an eclipse of the moon). If the ball is now moved to a position between the head and light they will see that the ball has cut off the light of the lamp (the sun). The shadow of the ball now falls on the child's face (an eclipse of the sun), but this cannot occur unless these heavenly bodies are in the same plane.

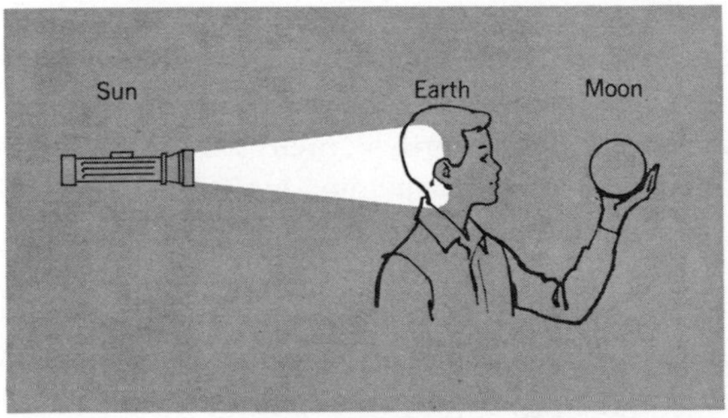

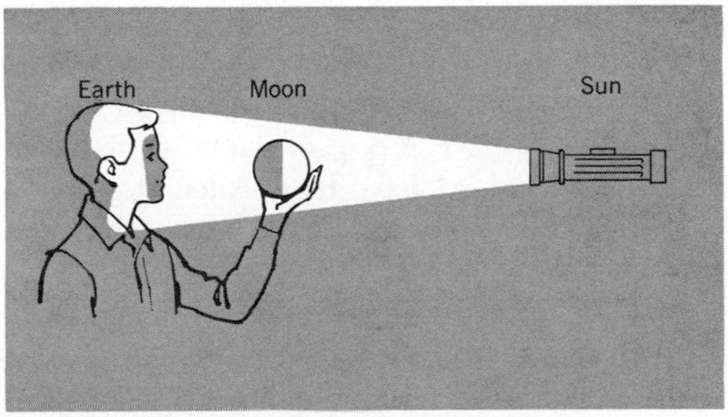

It is important to remember that while demonstrations such as this are indeed helpful in understanding science principles pupils need help in translating what they see into an understanding of what actually happens in the sky. (*Left*) A pupil demonstrates an eclipse of the moon; (*right*) an eclipse of the sun.

What Are "Shooting Stars"?

Pupils may be encouraged to watch the evening sky to see meteors, especially on the dates suggested in Chapter 7A. If they do observe any, they should be urged to describe what they saw, including the date, time, and sky location. It is sometimes possible to borrow a meteorite from a local, state, or college museum. Pupils are greatly interested in an object that has come from outer space. To hold in your hand a piece of material that has actually fallen from the sky is exciting. If they actually have one to feel and lift pupils will be much more enthusiastic in doing some reading "research" about meteoroids, meteors, and meteorites. They will want to know whether it was found locally and what kind of materials it is made of. A museum may be able to supply this information.

How Can We Plan a Space Trip?[9]

Some children like to write stories, and a group may like to write an imaginary story about a space trip. They can plan to allocate various responsibilities to specific scientists such as astronomers, navigators, commissary men, and geologists—each gathering material from reading and elsewhere that would need to be taken into account in planning the trip. This involves reading, selecting appropriate science facts, listing unsolved problems, judging validity, organizing materials, and so on. (**Note:** For more material on space *see* Chapter 22.)

What Does Gravity Do?

Pupils have had many experiences with gravity, but may not have thought much about them. Suggest that they do the following, observe what happens, and then put their ideas together. Three problems related to gravity and the solar system are: (1.) What is meant by weight? (2.) Why doesn't the earth fly out of the solar system? (3.) Why doesn't the sun's gravity pull the earth into it?

1. How much would you weigh on the moon? The purpose of this question is to start pupils thinking about gravity. Ask the children to write their weights on pieces of paper. (This represents the pull of the earth's gravity on them.) Then have them calculate their weights on the moon by dividing by 6. Why is there such a difference? (The moon, a smaller body, has a smaller pull than the earth.) What would happen if a boy weighed himself on a spring scale on top of a very high mountain on the earth? (He would weigh less because he is farther from the center of the earth.) If the earth is turning why don't we all fly off? (Because gravity pulls us toward the center of the earth.) Suggest that pupils think of other ways to show that the earth's gravity pulls things toward it.

[9] *See also Man in Space* (Superintendent of Documents, Government Printing Office, Washington, D.C.).

2. Why doesn't the earth fly out of the solar system? Attach a weight to a string and swing it in a vertical plane. (Arrange for many children to have this experience.) Ask them to observe what happens and describe it. How is this like the earth's path around the sun? How is it different? Why doesn't the weight fly away? What does the string do? What would happen if it were cut? (In *part* the string *represents* the pull of gravity that the sun exerts on the earth.)
3. Why doesn't the sun's gravity pull the earth to it? Again swing the weight on the string. What happens when you stop swinging? (The weight falls.) The earth and all the planets move just at the right speed so that they do not fly off into space *or* fall into the sun.

OTHER PROBLEMS FOR OLDER CHILDREN

1. Why is it very cold at the North and South Poles?
2. Why are the seasons on the Southern Hemisphere different from those on the Northern Hemisphere?
3. How would conditions on the earth be different if its axis were not tilted?
4. How do we know that the sun turns?
5. What are comets like?
6. How can we locate planets at different times of the year?
7. How can we make and use a sundial?
8. How is our earth related to the solar system?
9. What are the other planets like?
10. What are sunspots?
11. How does the earth appear from space?

(**Note:** "Resources to Investigate with Children" to learn more about the sun and the planets will be found at the end of Chapter 8B.)

CHAPTER 8A

THE STARS AND THE UNIVERSE

(Courtesy Mount Wilson and Palomar Observatories.)

TO MEASURE THE STARS

How shall we measure the universe? What kind of a yardstick shall we use for the immense spaces between the stars? Our imagination, already staggered by the millions and billions of miles within the solar system, searches for a new unit to apply to the vast reaches of the space beyond—for some measure that speaks in small familiar numbers.

We might try to use *time* to measure distance. The American Indians did that when they said that a certain place was 2 moons away. They meant that the distance was such that it would require 2 months of journeying to reach it with their limited means of travel. We can use time to make distances in the solar system comprehensible. We can figure how much time a spaceship, moving at an average rate of 17,500 miles per hour (fast enough to circle the earth in $1\frac{1}{2}$ hours), would take to reach the various points of interest in our planetary system. These figures have had meaning to us ever since February 20, 1962, when John H. Glenn, Jr., made three orbits around the earth, covering each orbit in about $1\frac{1}{2}$ hours, traveling at the speed of 17,500 miles per hour. That day changed the concept of distance for every person who watched breathlessly this historic flight from liftoff to touchdown. From that day on we could think: At that (average) speed Glenn could reach the moon in 11 hours, the sun in 7 months.

These statistics are manageable units for measuring distances within the solar system. But as we leave the solar system for deeper space we get into difficulties if we use "spaceship time" to measure distances. The numbers get big again! We look for something that can zip through space at a faster rate, and we find it in a ray of light. Light takes time to travel from one point to another; we are not aware of this because it moves at the incredible speed of about 186,000 miles per *second.* Such a rate would send it seven times around our earth in 1 second.

Let us apply this speed-of-light scale to the distances of the moon and the sun from the earth. Light from the moon reaches the earth after a brief journey of $1\frac{1}{3}$ *seconds;* from the sun about 8 *minutes* is required. From distant Pluto, near the outermost bounds of our known solar system, $5\frac{1}{3}$ *hours* are required. With this new scale we may now say that the moon is $1\frac{1}{3}$ seconds away from the earth, the sun 8 minutes, Pluto $5\frac{1}{3}$ hours.

Look at the stars some clear night. These, as we learned in Chapter 7A, are distant suns outside our solar system, so distant that they appear as points of light in the blackness of space. The nearest star (and the brightest) that can be seen with the naked eye in the Northern Hemisphere is Sirius in the constellation Canis Major (Big Dog). Light from Sirius takes about 8 *years* to reach our eyes.

Astronomers use the speed of light as a convenient method for measuring the universe, with the *light year* as the basic unit. A light year is a measure of *distance,* not of time; it is the distance that light, traveling at the speed of about 186,000 miles per second, traverses in 1 year (approximately 6,000,000,000,000, or 6 trillion, miles). The star Sirius, then, is 8 light years away from us. Arcturus, another bright star, is 36 light years distant. Polaris, the North Star, is about 650 light years away.

This use of time as a cosmic yardstick suggests a fascinating idea. When you look at the North Star you are seeing the light that left it approximately 650 years ago. By now, Polaris may have moved to another place (even the so-called "fixed" stars of the ancients are not really stationary); or it may have exploded and become cold and dark. Our descendants 650 years hence will know the whereabouts and the condition of the present Polaris.

So, when you look at the sky tonight, you are peering not only into the vastness of space but also into events of the past. You are looking not only far into distance but also far back into time.

THE STARS

Distance, Size, Color

Ask a young child how many stars he sees on a clear night and he will answer "thousands" or "millions." Actually, only about 2,500 to 3,000 stars can be seen with the unaided eye from any spot on the earth at any time[1]; some 9,000 stars can be seen throughout the year from the whole earth. With the use of telescopes and cameras millions of stars can be detected.

Another assumption of viewers is that the observed brightness of stars is indicative of their real brilliance. This illusion occurs because we have no perspective into the depth of space; all the stars appear to be at the same distance. Actually, Sirius appears bright because it is close; Rigel in the constellation of Orion appears dimmer than Sirius because it is about 100 times as far away. However, if all the stars were moved to the same distance from the earth Rigel would shine 700 times as brightly as Sirius.

The *apparent* brightness of a star depends on three factors: its distance from the earth, its size, and its temperature. The nearest star (except the sun) to the earth is Alpha Centauri. Visible south of the United States, this star is $4\frac{1}{3}$ light years away. The most distant single star visible to our unaided eyes is about 3,500 light years away. The most distant star that the powerful 200-inch Palamar Mountain telescope can isolate as an individual body is 50 to 75 million light years away, except for supernova, seen very much farther. The most distant astronomical objects, called *quasars,* picked out by this telescope are estimated to range somewhere between 4 and 8 billion light years away!

(*See* p. 200.)

Stars vary considerably in size. Small ones, known as *white dwarfs,* may be only 10,000 miles or less in diameter, about the size of the earth. A *giant,* such as Antares, has a diameter 450 times that of our sun. In the range of stars from dwarf to giant our sun is considered an average-sized star.

If you look carefully at the stars in the sky you will see that they are not all the same color. Some are reddish, some yellowish, some white, some bluish-white. The difference in color is due to differences in the temperature of the stars. If a piece of metal is heated, it first turns red, then orange, then yellow, then white. Blacksmiths used to get a rough idea of the temperature of the iron that they were heating by watching its color. This holds true for stars also. The coolest ones are reddish, hotter ones yellowish, still hotter ones white, hottest ones blue-white. Betelgeuse, in the constellation of Orion, with a temperature of about 4000° F., is a red star. Our sun, with a temperature of about 10,000° F., and Capella are yellow stars. Sirius is a white star. Rigel, a blue-white star, has a temperature of about 50,000° F. All these are the measurable *surface* temperatures; the interiors of stars are much hotter, running into millions of degrees.

The high temperature of the sun, as we found in Chapter 7A, is not the result of burning but of nuclear reactions in which hydrogen atoms combine to form helium atoms, as in a hydrogen bomb. This is also true of the other stars of the universe.

[1]But this is on a clear night away from the lights and smog of urban areas. In fact, astronomers are finding that even far from cities smog diminishes the number of stars they see; this is a very clear and sensitive check on what we are doing to our atmosphere here on earth!

Magnitude

We have seen how the apparent brightness of a star is determined by distance, size, and temperature. For convenience in viewing and identifying stars astronomers classify them according to their *magnitude.* In speaking of stars magnitude does *not* mean size, but apparent brightness. The smaller the number given, the brighter the star. Thus the *first-magnitude* stars are the brightest. These are $2\frac{1}{2}$ times as bright, on the average, as a second-magnitude star. A second-magnitude star is $2\frac{1}{2}$ times as bright as a third-magnitude star, and so on. The faintest star that we can ordinarily see with the unaided eye is of the sixth magnitude, but on a very dark night we can see even fainter stars. Stars a good deal fainter than the sixth magnitude can be seen only with the telescope. At present we can photograph stars of the twenty-third magnitude with the Palomar Mountain telescope. These stars are about 1 five-millionth as bright as first-magnitude stars.

There are 20 stars of the first magnitude or brighter. Some of the more commonly known are Sirius, Vega, Capella, Arcturus, Rigel, Procyon, Altair, Betelgeuse, Aldebaran, Pollux, Spica, Antares, Formalhaut, Deneb, and Regulus. Sirius, brightest of the first-magnitude stars, is not as bright as three planets in our solar system—Venus, Mars, and Jupiter.

The original brightness scale was devised about 250 B.C. by Hipparchus, a Greek astronomer. Using a scale from 1 to 6, he catalogued about 1,000 stars, using 1 for the brightest and 6 for the faintest stars. Later astronomers refined the scale and extended it to higher numbers (7, 8, and so on) to accommodate the *fainter* stars discovered with telescopes. In order to include objects *brighter* than magnitude "1" astronomers assigned negative values to them: minus 1, minus 2, and so on (zero is also used, between 1 and minus 1). Thus very bright Sirius has a magnitude of minus 1.4. The moon when full has a magnitude of minus 12.6 and the sun minus 26.7. There is nothing really "negative" about such brilliant objects. We have been forced to assign negative values to them because we have adhered to the method instituted by Hipparchus.

Double Stars and Star Clusters

Stars are frequently found in groups or clusters. They are often grouped in pairs, one revolving around the other. To be more accurate we should say that both revolve around their common *center of gravity,* which is a point between the two. Several thousands of these double stars, or *binary stars,* have been found. Most binary stars cannot be detected except with the aid of a telescope or spectroscope. Bright Sirius is a double star; it circles around its invisible (to the eye) partner once every 50 years.

There are also larger groups of stars, *star clusters,* held together by gravitational attraction, which move together through space. The Pleiades is such a group. You can see 6 of its members with the naked eye; with a telescope we find some 250 members. Star clusters should not be confused with *constellations,* which are configurations of stars named by the ancients for a particular object, person, or animal.

(*See* pp. 200–3.)

Variable Stars

Some individual stars change in brightness and hence are called *variable stars.* Some vary in brightness in regular intervals. The cycle from bright to dim to bright again may take from a few

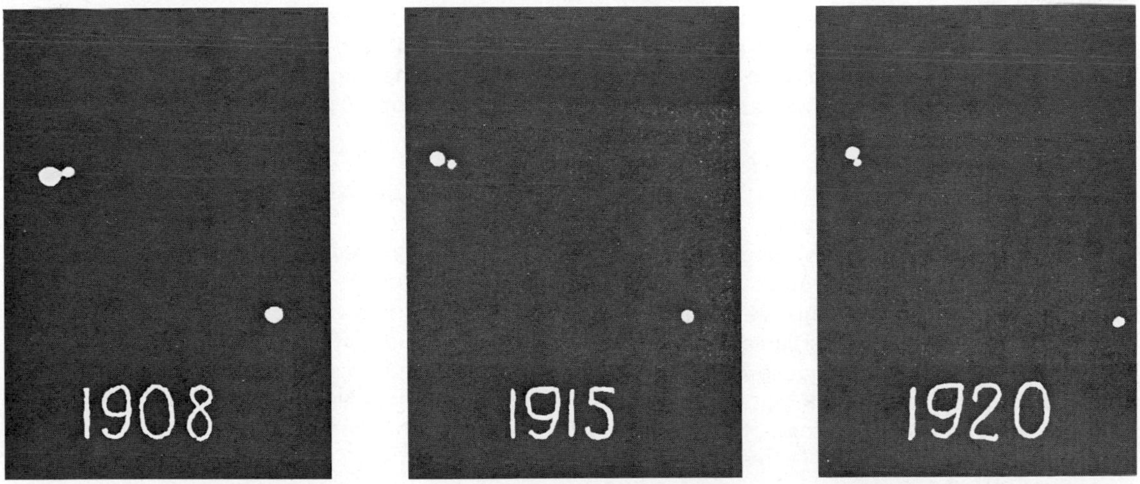

Three photographs of Kruger 60, a double star—a system of two stars that revolve around each other under the influence of their mutual gravitational attraction. The discovery of the motion of double stars was the first observational evidence that gravitation existed outside the solar system. Double stars are not exceptional; they may be the rule for the stars we see in the sky. (*Courtesy of Yerkes Observatory.*)

hours to hundreds of days, depending on the star. One type of variable star is known as a *cepheid,* named for a notable fluctuating star in the constellation of Cepheus. Stars of this type brighten up and fade again like clockwork. The star Delta Cephei, for example, takes 5 days and 9 hours to pass from its brightest phase down to its faintest and then back to its brightest. Also there are *irregular variables* that vary in brightness in an unpredictable manner.

"New" stars or *novae* are stars that have previously been inconspicuous and then suddenly flare up and become as much as 70,000 or 80,000 times as bright. The name "nova" is inaccurate, because there is no evidence that these are new stars. We do not know what causes these stars to flare up, but it is probably a result of natural aging in a star's lifetime.

The appearance of a *supernova,* an extraordinarily bright nova, is a rare event. A Danish astronomer, Tycho Brahe, described a "new star" that appeared on a November evening in 1572, when a previously unseen star flared up brighter than Sirius. The following night it was brighter than the planet Venus. It was so bright in the days that followed that it could be seen even in the daytime. In December of that year its brightness began to diminish. By March of the following year ". . . the new star," says Tycho, "disappeared without leaving a trace visible to the naked eye. . . ." Tycho's star remained undetected until 1958 when the radio telescope (to be described presently) enabled astronomers to rediscover it.

We know more about supernovae than novae, even though they are rarer, because they leave traces that we can study. For example, Chinese records mention a blazing star that appeared in the year 1054. We have reason to believe that the explosion of this star produced a cloud of starry material observable today as the Crab Nebula, so named because of its crablike appearance. The flaring of a star into a supernova up to hundreds of millions of times its former brightness is believed to represent an explosion on a celestial scale.

In recent years astronomers have gathered evidence which leads them to believe that the stars in the sky are of widely varying ages. According to the current theory of stellar evolution a star comes into being through the contraction of a mass of gas and dust, a *protostar.* This stage, which may be thought of as the star's childhood, is comparatively short. Then for most of its life the star is full grown (adulthood) and more or less stable. Most of the stars we see are, therefore, in this state. These mature stars range from blue-white (very hot) to red (coolest) in color.

Motion

Alas for those who are looking for a firm, immovable rock in this giddy universe! Even the "fixed" stars are not fixed but are moving rapidly through space in various directions. Some are moving toward and some away from our solar system, most of them at speeds of many miles per second. Despite this speed, the chances that stars might collide are very small because space is so vast and the distances between stars very great. If the sun were the size of an orange, the earth would be a grain of sand 30 feet away and the nearest star would be another orange 2,000 feet away.[2]

The speeds and the directions of hundreds of stars are known to astronomers. This drifting over periods of thousands of years causes even the shape of the star patterns—the *constellations*—to change. The Big Dipper will become an open scoop 100,000 years from now!

THE CONSTELLATIONS

When night falls, the glittering sky beckons to us to join in the ancient hobby of stargazing.

(*See* pp. 215–6.)

Primitive people long ago traced pictures of familiar objects, animals, and humans in the pattern of stars. The American Indians painted them on buffalo skins. The ancient Greeks and Romans filled the heavens with their gods and heroes.

The resemblance of groups of stars, or con-

[2] Robert Jastrow: *Red Giants and White Dwarfs* (Harper and Row, 1970).

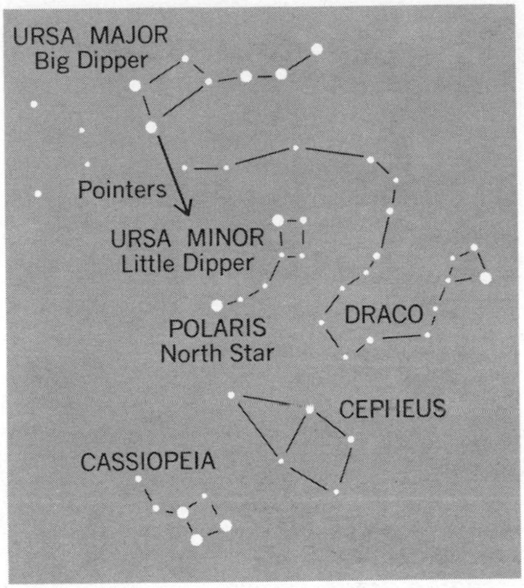

The constellations near the North Star are easy to find, and they provide a guide to other star groups.

stellations, to these imaginary figures may be difficult for us to follow. We may prefer to think of the stars that make up Pegasus, for example, as a baseball diamond with stars at home plate, first, second, and third base and along the right- and left-field foul lines, rather than as a white-winged horse. Whether we group stars on the basis of their mythology or in a more modern way, knowing the constellations is fun and also serves as a convenient guide for locating individual stars and other heavenly bodies.

The part of the heavens that we can see on any night is limited by the fact that we live in the Northern Hemisphere of an opaque globe. People living in the Southern Hemisphere look out on a different portion of the sky.

Our view of the heavens is also influenced by the seasons, because the earth is in different positions in its orbit around the sun in the course of a year. Some constellations can be seen only in summer and some only in winter. Fortunately, there are some star groups that are always visible—the constellations around the Pole Star (North Star). Among these are the Big Bear, the Little Bear, Draco, Cassiopeia (kăs′ĭ-ō-pē′ya), Perseus, and Cepheus. A good way to begin your acquaintance with the stars is to find the Big Dipper, which is part of the constellation of the Big Bear, in the northern sky. Two stars that form the part of the dipper opposite the handle are known as the "pointers." A line drawn through these pointers and extending about five times the distance between them will lead you to the Pole Star, known also as Polaris.

Polaris is also at the tip end of the handle of the Little Dipper, which is part of the constellation of the Little Bear. Polaris, although not a very bright star, is the brightest in the Little Dipper. The two dippers are so placed that when one is upright the other is upside down, with their handles extending in opposite directions.

If you trace a line from the pointers to the Pole Star and then extend it an equal distance across the sky you will come close to Cassiopeia. Five of the stars of this constellation make up a big W or M in the sky. Near Cassiopeia, the mythological Queen of Ethiopia, is her husband Cepheus. Cepheus forms a pattern not unlike a triangle mounted on a square. One of the most famous of the variable stars, Delta Cephei, is located in this constellation.

Come back to the Big Dipper and follow its *handle* this time to find the bright star Arcturus (ark-tū′rŭs), one of the few stars mentioned in the Bible. Arcturus, which means "Bear Driver," is located in the tail of a kite-shaped constellation, Bootes (boō′tēz), the Herdsman.

Pegasus, mentioned earlier, is one of the outstanding constellations in the autumn sky. Its three brightest stars, together with the brightest

An active imagination will help you make a bear out of this constellation of stars. Interestingly, this constellation was known as "The Bear" to such widely separated groups as the ancient Greeks, the Scandinavians, and the American Indians. Find the Big Dipper in the tail and haunch of the bear.

star in adjacent Andromeda, form the four-cornered figure known as the Square of Pegasus. In Andromeda, which extends away from the Square, is a hazy patch of light. This filmy wisp in the sky is in reality a galaxy and is actually made of 100 billion stars! We shall have more to say of such collections presently. This one is notable because it is one of the very few visible to the naked eye.

A line of bright stars from Pegasus through Andromeda points the way to Perseus. One of the stars in this group is variable Algol, which has a 3-day cycle of brightness and dimness. Perseus is also distinguished, as indicated in Chapter 7A, because it marks the location of brilliant meteoric showers that occur in August.

Draco, the Dragon, may be difficult to find because it does not have any first-magnitude stars in it and its hard-to-describe outline wriggles between the two dippers, curves toward Cepheus, and then toward Hercules.

Hercules, like Draco, has no bright stars. The ancients pictured Hercules as a kneeling figure with an upraised club ready to crush the head of Draco. A brilliant globular cluster of stars in Hercules may be seen with the naked eye under only the best sky conditions.

One of the brightest constellations and the most spectacular of the winter season is Orion, the mighty hunter. The three stars that make up the belt of this figure, equally spaced in a straight row, are seen even by city dwellers who glance up at the sky. The belt is in the center of a nearly rectangular figure, which makes up the body of Orion. The giant star Betelgeuse marks one corner of the rectangle, the right shoulder of the warrior. Blazing Rigel, diagonally across, marks his left leg.

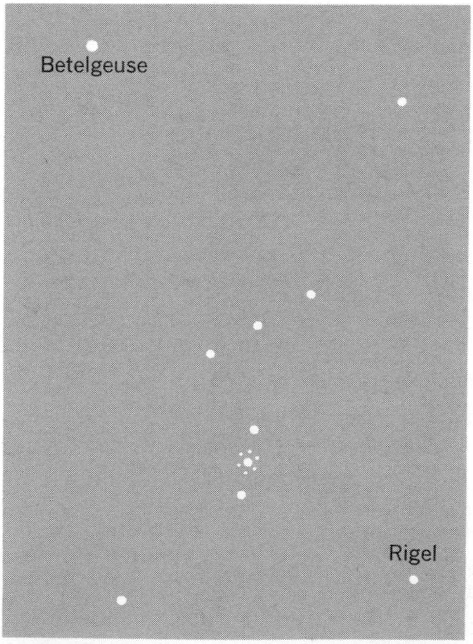

Considered by many sky watchers the most magnificent of all constellations, Orion dominates the winter sky with more bright stars and telescopic marvels than are present in any other group of stars. Knowing the old legends about this constellation and the others makes them more interesting to observe. Interest deepens as modern star knowledge is added as, for example, the fact that Rigel is 21,000 times as bright as the sun.

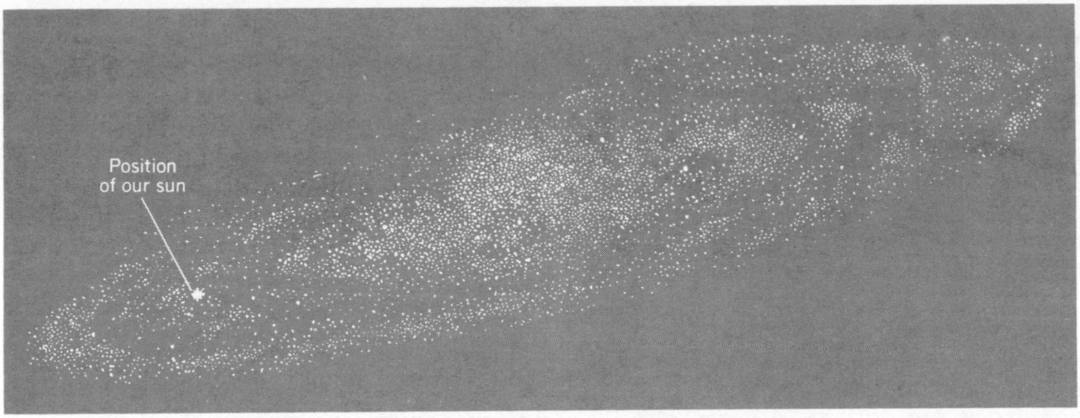

The sun is one of the billions of stars in our Milky Way galaxy.

Trace along Orion's belt to the brightest star in all the sky, Sirius, in the constellation of the Great Dog. Sirius is the nearest star visible to the naked eye for viewers in the United States. You will recall that light reaches us from the sun in 8 *minutes* and from Sirius in 8 *years.*

As we watch the sky on a pleasant summer night the constellations appear to wheel slowly across the heavens. This apparent motion is due to the turning of the earth on its axis. One star, however, appears fixed in the sky throughout the night. This is Polaris, which lies over the North Pole of the earth, over one end of the axis on which the earth turns. All the stars seem to revolve around the North Star. Constellations close to it, such as the Dippers, appear to circle the Pole Star during the night. Stars more distant from Polaris trace bigger circles in the sky; those most distant appear to rise in the east and set in the west.

THE MILKY WAY

What is our address in the universe? What is the place of our solar system—the earth, the other planets, and the sun—in the starry sky? What, in short, is the structure of the universe, and where are we located in that structure?

If we turn to the constellations for an answer we do not get much help. For the most part these sky patterns are composed of stars that happen to lie approximately in the same direction from the earth. When we look outward our eyes cannot discern the *depth* of space. No wonder the ancients thought that the sky was a round dome studded with twinkling lights. Careful observations and calculations by astronomers have revealed that although all the stars *seem* to be equally far away, some of them are at great distances beyond others.

The constellations in themselves do not reveal the three-dimensional structure of space. Then how are the stars arranged? If we look up at the heavens on a clear night, away from the city lights, we see stretching across the sky a broad luminous band—the Milky Way. Examination even with a pair of binoculars or a small telescope reveals that the Milky Way consists of billions of stars, so concentrated in depth in the direction in which we are looking that they make a "milky" band in the sky. The sky on either side of the milky band has many fewer stars; the farther from the Milky Way, the fewer the stars. What does all of this reveal about the organization of stars?

Astronomers puzzling over this have concluded that we are in the midst of a huge disc or pinwheel-shaped collection of stars. They call this Milky Way system our *galaxy* (a word derived from the Greek *gala,* which means milk). Because we are *within* this disc of stars our vision is somewhat obscured. It might help in our understanding if we could view our galaxy from the *outside.* We would then see it as a giant pinwheel made of billions of stars, one of these our sun, rotating slowly around a compact, brilliant center. Now adopt the viewpoint of an observer *inside* the pinwheel. Look toward the *edge* of the wheel. A thick conglomeration of stars in the form of a band is seen; looking toward the *sides* of the wheel fewer stars are seen.

Our Milky Way, then, is a view from inside the great galaxy of stars in which we are situated. All the stars that can be seen with the naked eye and most of those observed with telescopes are a part of the Milky Way system, which contains about 100 billion stars. However, there is ample space within our galaxy—enough to hold billions of times as many stars as it does!

How big is our galaxy? To measure it we again use the speed of light as our yardstick. We calculated previously that, if we traveled at the speed of light, it would take us a little over 1 second to reach the moon, 8 minutes to reach the sun, and $4\frac{1}{3}$ years to reach the nearest star. Traveling at this speed—about 186,000 miles per second—it would take us about 100,000 years to go from one edge of the galaxy to the other, and about 10,000 years to go across its greatest thickness. Our galaxy, then, is a wheel about 100,000 light years across and 10,000 light years thick.

Just where is the solar system in this wheel? Astronomers say that we are roughly 30,000 light
(*See* p. 203.)
years away from the center out toward the rim of the wheel and in the central *plane* of the wheel.

The whole galaxy is turning like a pinwheel. All the stars are revolving in the same direction around the center, but at different speeds. Despite the fact that our sun and its solar system are moving at 140 miles per second in a roughly circular orbit, it takes 200 million years to complete a revolution around the center. Our solar system is also taking a trip all its own; it is heading in the general direction of the constellation Hercules at the rate of about 12 miles per second.

Perhaps a better understanding of our galaxy can be gotten by looking at another one, at a galaxy *outside* our Milky Way system. The best known of these is the Great Spiral in Andromeda, which is revealed by telescopes as a collection of 100 billion stars with spiral arms like those of a Fourth of July pinwheel. Pictured at the opening of this chapter is the famous spiral nebula in the constellation Ursa Major (Big Dipper), with distinct spiral arms. This, like the Andromeda Spiral, has been likened to our galaxy in shape and in its starry population.

Our Milky Way is one of a cluster of nineteen known local galaxies, called the *local group,* that cover a region about 3 million light years in diameter. The three largest members are all spiral galaxies—our Milky Way galaxy, the Andromeda galaxy, and the Spiral Galaxy in Triangulum. Beyond the local group we find other groups of galaxies. As far as we can see in all directions we find galaxies and clusters of galaxies.

It has been estimated that there are at least 10 billion galaxies in the universe.

BETWEEN THE STARS

How empty is "empty space"? By earthly standards *interstellar space* (space between stars) *is* empty, because we have not been able to obtain a vacuum in our laboratories that is as devoid of matter as is the space between the stars. Astronomers have found, however, that there are vast clouds of dust and gas in the almost complete vacuum of space. The term *nebula* (plural nebulae) refers to such clouds, some of which are located in our Milky Way and some outside in other galaxies.

Relatively dense opaque clouds of dust produce the *dark nebulae.* They are thick enough to obscure a considerable portion of the starlight passing through them. They appear as dark curtains, dimming or hiding the stars behind them. The head of the "horse" in the Horsehead Nebula in Orion is part of a dark nebula.

In other nebulae the starlight is scattered or reflected by the interstellar dust so that the dust itself becomes illuminated by the starlight. These are called *reflection nebulae,* an example of which is to be found around each of the brightest stars in the Pleiades cluster.

In some nebulae, known as *emission nebulae,* the *gas* near hot stars glows by a process of fluorescence in which light of one wavelength is absorbed and re-emitted at another wavelength. (An example of fluorescence is the conversion of invisible ultraviolet into visible light in a household fluorescent lamp.) Easily seen with binoculars is such a nebula in the middle of the hunter's sword in the constellation of Orion.

The gas of interstellar space is mostly hydrogen, but it also includes helium, oxygen, and other elements. Hydrogen also makes up most of the gas that is found in stars. It is theorized that all the chemical elements of the stars were manufactured out of hydrogen by nuclear processes, and that this process is still going on.

(*See* pp. 550–1.)

The clouds of dust and gas in space are of special interest to astronomers, for it is thought that out of a compression of such stuff that stars are born. And as stars age, cool, and die, they return to space by nova and supernova explosions a great deal of the gas and dust out of which they were originally formed. Then new stars are made again from these clouds.

Thus, as older stars come to the end of their cycle they provide the material for the birth of new stars. It is thought that our sun is a "second-generation" star, having been formed about 5 billion years ago from material part or most of which was ejected from older stars.

THE UNIVERSE

Again we ask, what is our place in the universe? Just as a child becomes aware of larger and larger units—home, neighborhood, city, and so on—so have astronomers discovered a hierarchy in the heavens. Our galaxy, 100,000 light years in diameter, is only one of the billions of galaxies that make up the universe.

To come back to our original question about our address in the universe, the best answer we can give at this time is:

Planet: Earth
  Star: Our Sun
    Galaxy: Milky Way
      Cluster of Galaxies: Local Group
        Universe

One more thought about our "address in space." If you were to return to your hometown after an absence of several years you would be astonished if you found that the distances between all the houses had increased so that your next-door neighbor was now 1 mile away, and the whole town was spread out over an area 10,000 times its original size. If for each house you substitute a galaxy you are now prepared to understand what astronomers call an "expanding universe." The study of distant galaxies with the spectroscope, an instrument to be described shortly, indicates that the galaxies are fleeing from each other at a terrific rate, some at a speed of 75,000 miles per second, or about two-fifths the speed of light! Astronomers have also found that the farther away galaxies are from us, the faster they are moving. It should be made clear that the expansion in the "expanding universe" refers to the increase in the space between galaxies and not to the size of the galaxies themselves. Thus, our lonely address in the vastness of space becomes lonelier as our neighbors become more and more distant.

HOW THE STARS ARE STUDIED

The basic equipment that man possesses for the exploration of the heavens are his eyes, intelligence, and imagination. To aid his senses man has invented devices such as the telescope, the camera, spectroscope, and radio telescope. With all these, and many more man has measured the distances and sizes of stars, estimated their temperatures, analyzed their composition, charted their motions, and described their evolution. Let us take a brief look at some astronomical instruments.

Telescope

In 1928 George Ellery Hale, an American astronomer, made a plea for the construction of a new telescope. Hale based his plea on three unsolved problems of astronomy: the evolution of stars, the structure of the universe, and the composition of matter. The Rockefeller International Education Board responded by making a grant of $6,000,000 that made the construction of a

200-inch telescope possible and led to the establishment of an observatory on Palomar Mountain, California, in 1948. Thus, a new instrument, then the most powerful of all telescopes, named the Hale telescope after its originator, was added to man's devices for his study of the stars.

The Hale telescope, like all others, gives man a bigger "eye" because it can gather more light than the human eye and because it can magnify the view. The Hale telescope is an example of a *reflecting telescope,* using a large circular mirror 200 inches across (almost 17 feet!) to collect and focus the light of stars. The *refracting telescope,* on the other hand, uses a lens to gather and focus light. Galileo used a refracting telescope when he explored the heavens and discovered the plains, mountains, and craters of our moon and the satellites revolving around the planet Jupiter. In both kinds of telescopes—reflector and refractor—the image is magnified by a lens in the eyepiece through which one looks.

The Yerkes refracting telescope—the largest of its kind in the world—has a light-gathering lens 40 inches in diameter. The telescope is 60 feet long and is located at Williams Bay, Lake Geneva, Wisconsin. The second largest refractor is the 36-inch telescope at the Lick Observatory of the University of California on Mount Hamilton, California.

The Hale telescope, with its 200-inch $14\frac{1}{2}$-ton mirror, has the light-gathering power of a million eyes. It has already taken thousands of photographs of distant stars and galaxies. With it astronomers have detected objects billions of light years away. Using the 200-inch reflector, it was found that our estimates of all distances to other galaxies were wrong by a factor of 2. So in 1952 we doubled our measurements and the scale of the universe. Thus, Andromeda is not 1 but 2 million light years away. Another major discovery made with this huge light-gathering instrument was that of *quasars,* the most brilliant energy-laden heavenly objects known. Other contributions include studies relating to galaxies, pulsars (rapidly pulsating sources detected by radioastronomy), and the evolution of stars.

(*See* pp. 209–10.)

Other reflecting telescopes include the 120-inch one at the Lick Observatory on Mount Hamilton, California; the 107-inch at the McDonald Observatory in Fort Davis, Texas; the 104-inch at the Crimean Astrophysical Laboratory at Nauchny in the U.S.S.R., and the 100-inch

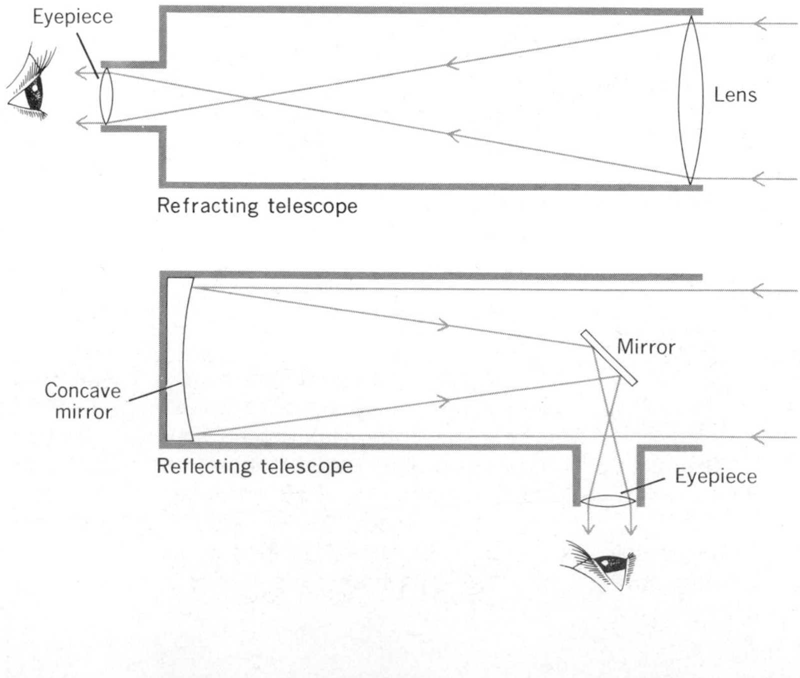

In a refracting telescope light from distant objects is gathered and focused by a lens. In a reflecting telescope light is gathered and focused by a concave mirror.

on Mount Wilson near Pasadena, California. Under construction in the U.S.S.R. is a 236-inch reflecting telescope.

Telescopes are usually placed near mountain tops because the air there is generally freer of dust and haze, and because the location is usually distant from the lights of cities. They are protected from the weather by domes that open to the sky. Motors turn the telescope so that it moves westward to compensate for the eastward rotation of the earth. Thus, the heavenly bodies "stand still" for prolonged observation.

In the vast architecture of a large modern observatory the astronomer, although only a tiny figure, controls the operation of the massive machinery, instructing his engineers by telephone how to keep the telescope steadily fixed on a particular point in the sky.

Camera

No longer does the astronomer spend much time looking through a telescope. Instead, he replaces its eyepiece and his own eye with a photographic plate or film and devotes himself to keeping the "picture" in view. Thus, the telescope becomes a camera. The human eye, even when aided by a telescope, has limitations. It tires after awhile. It is not sensitive to color in dim light. It cannot retain images very long, hence it cannot build up weak images into strong ones. The camera overcomes these limitations. It does not tire. Film can be made that is very sensitive to light and to different colors. Film can retain and build up weak images into strong ones, even if it takes several nights of exposure for the same picture. As a consequence we can photograph and detect stars through a telescope which are too faint to be seen with the eye through the same telescope.

A recently invented device, the electronic camera, does its work by intensifying starlight by electronic means. The new and brighter image is then photographed by conventional methods.

Other devices include infrared, x-ray and gamma-ray detectors, which go beyond the range of visible light.

All large astronomical telescopes are used almost exclusively as cameras, equipped with electronic gear, rather than instruments for direct viewing. It is through the use of photography that scientists all over the world are working together, charting each section of the heavens to obtain a more detailed picture of the universe and a better understanding of its evolution.

Spectroscope

How can we know the chemical composition of the stars? The answer lies in the fact that the light emitted by heavenly bodies, when analyzed, furnishes scientists with evidence of the types of atoms that are present there. Let us see how scientists analyze starlight.

When sunlight passes through one side of a glass prism a rainbow of colors, called a spectrum, emerges from the other side. The white light of the sun is a mixture of different colors. The prism bends each of these colors at a slightly different angle and fans out the white light into its component colors.

A special instrument called a spectroscope combines the simple prism with a viewing lens. If sunlight is examined with a spectroscope the colors are segregated further into a long band ranging in color from red through orange, yellow, green, and blue, to violet. With a good spectroscope and keen eyes it can be seen that the sun's spectrum is not really continuous, but that it is crossed by narrow, vertical dark lines.

Scientists have found that each of the known chemical elements, if heated to glowing, produces a different and characteristic "keyboard" of colors when viewed through a spectroscope. Thus, the element sodium produces two separate bright yellow "keys" in a definite place on the "keyboard." No other element does this. If an astronomer finds evidence of these lines in the spectrum of a star, he knows that the star contains sodium. (*See* illustration on page 208.)

In practice astronomers combine the spectroscope and the telescope so that light gathered by the telescope from distant bodies is passed through a spectroscope for analysis. A photographic plate is combined with the spectroscope to make a permanent record of the spectrum.

When used in this way the instrument is called a *spectrograph.*

Astronomers knowing the color "chord" of each element are able to determine the chemical makeup of a particular star by examining its light with the spectrograph. Some of the astronomical findings that have resulted from this technique are:

1. The sun is composed of many chemical elements; its main constituent is hydrogen.
2. Most stars have a chemical composition similar to that of the sun.
3. The chemical elements glowing in the sun and the stars are the same as those found on earth. Incidentally, the element helium was first discovered in a spectroscopic view of the sun and later found on the earth!

In addition to determining the chemical makeup of celestial bodies the spectrograph tells us whether a star or a galaxy is approaching us or receding from us. To understand how this is possible it is necessary to understand the *Doppler effect.* Perhaps you have noticed that when a train which is sounding its whistle passes you and speeds away its pitch drops. The apparent change of pitch in *sound* has its parallel in the world of *light.* Motion (with respect to the listener) can change the frequency and therefore the pitch of a sound wave. Motion (with respect to an observer) can also change the frequency and therefore the color of a light wave. As a source of light moves away from you its color spectrum shifts toward the red end as viewed in the spectroscope. The amount the spectrum lines shift from their normal position gives us a measure of the speed of recession. It was this technique that enabled Hubble in 1929 to discover that all galaxies are rushing away from each other.

The spectrograph is a valuable astronomical instrument for other reasons:

1. The spectrograph reveals the temperature of individual stars.
2. It may tell whether the body emitting the light rays is solid or gaseous.
3. It reveals the presence of invisible gases between the visible source and us.
4. It may tell whether a body is rotating.
5. It may tell us about the magnetic field of a star.
6. It tells us about the ingredients of the atmospheres of other planets.

And much more!

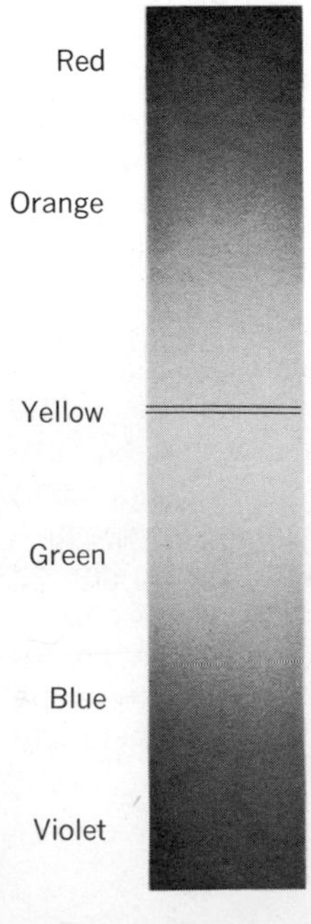

The spectroscope, when used with a telescope, provides information about the chemical composition of stars. Each chemical element has its own "fingerprint." In the illustration two dark lines in the yellow part of the spectrum indicate the presence of sodium in the outer gaseous region of the star under observation.

The radio telescope detects and measures radiation from the stars and from matter between the stars which was not previously detectable. Astronomers of the National Radio Astronomy Observatory scan the sky with this 300-foot dish at Green Bank, West Virginia, in their search for new information about the universe. (*Courtesy of National Radio Astronomy Observatory.*)

Radio Telescope

All of us have had the experience of picking up static on our radios. Static is caused by a jumble of radio waves of different wavelengths. Your radio converts this jumble into "noise" or static, just as it converts regular broadcasts that are beamed over a single wavelength into the sounds of music or speech. Static may originate from man-made electrical disturbances, such as that caused by a nearby power line. Static is also nature-made, occurring during lightning storms and, as we learned in Chapter 7A, during periods of great solar activity.

In 1931 Karl G. Jansky, an electrical engineer at the Bell Telephone Laboratories, was experimenting with large antennas for long-range radio communication when he encountered interference in the form of radio "static" coming from an unknown source. He concluded from his investigations that the radio disturbance was coming from outer space.

This theory was tested and confirmed by Grote Reber, a radio engineer, who in 1936 built an aerial shaped like an upside-down umbrella, 30 feet in diameter, to scan the skies for radio waves. With this aerial and a sensitive radio Reber plotted the first radio map of the sky. Reber's maps showed that the signals were strongest in the Milky Way region.

Using improved *radio telescopes,* as these sensitive radios are called, astronomers were able to focus on particular points in space where the signals were strong. These points were called "radio sources." Strangely enough, at first only a small fraction of the radio sources that were located corresponded to objects seen with conventional telescopes. Hundreds of these sources were noted and plotted on new radio maps of the skies.

The radio telescope, then, enabled us to detect heavenly objects and celestial events that optical devices had failed to reveal. Here was a new instrument for penetrating space, one that operates day and night. Radio telescopes are not affected by atmospheric conditions, except for man-made radio interference. As interest mounted, new posts were set up all over the world to tune in on these radio waves and to discover more of these radio sources. (It should be understood that it is *not* sound waves but radio waves that are "broadcast" from the sources.)

Radio astronomy has made it possible to

explore certain dark areas in the sky in which interstellar dust has blocked the light from our conventional telescopes. With the radio telescope we have found that galaxies are larger than we thought they were. The arms of our own spiral Milky Way have thus been traced out into what seemed to be "empty" space. We have also found that what we have called "empty" space between the stars is not really empty—it contains hydrogen and other gases.

Radio telescopes are an extremely important tool in astronomy. They are penetrating deeper into space than optical telescopes and are providing us with significant clues about the structure of the universe and about its past and future. A new era in astronomy has opened.

Space Probes

Hundreds of space probes have been launched since 1957. Chapter 7A told of some of the remarkable findings resulting from the space flights to Mars, Venus, and the moon (*see also* Chapter 22A for a discussion of space vehicles). In addition, credit is given to the space probes for the discovery of the Van Allen radiation belts, the mapping of the earth's magnetic field, and other significant findings. Mounted on the Orbiting Astronomical Observatory, a platform in space, man's telescopes and other instruments may reveal hitherto unavailable information about stars and galaxies and about the nature of interstellar space. Some day they may announce the existence of other solar systems in space and of other planets which resemble Earth.

From this survey of the universe a number of fundamental concepts emerge. Some of the essential ones are listed below in the generalizations.

Distance in the universe is so great that astronomers measure it in light years.

Constellations are sky patterns of stars that happen to lie approximately in the same direction from the earth.

The apparent nightly motion of the stars is due to the turning of the earth.

The apparent brightness of a star depends on its distance from the earth, its size, and its temperature.

When we view the stars and galaxies we are not only looking far out into distance but also far back into time.

The Milky Way is our inside view of the great disc-shaped galaxy of stars in which our solar system is located.

Our sun is one of 100 billion stars in our Milky Way galaxy.

The stars in the Milky Way are revolving around its center.

Other galaxies resembling ours exist.

In the nearly perfect vacuum in the space between stars there are vast clouds of dust and gas.

The astronomical hierarchy in which we live, according to the most recent knowledge, is planet, solar system, galaxy, local group of galaxies, universe.

Everything in the universe is in motion.

We live in an expanding universe, with galaxies racing from each other at terrific speeds.

The most important instruments for exploring the universe have been the telescope, camera, spectrograph, and radio telescope.

In recent years such instruments as image intensifiers, infrared detectors, x-ray and gamma ray detectors, and many more have been added to the tools of the astronomer.

Space probes and space stations carry astronomical instruments to positions where more information may be gathered.

Each year our knowledge of the universe increases.

Discovering for Yourself[3]

1. Read several issues of *Science News* (*see* Bibliography: Magazines) to learn about new astronomical discoveries. How do these discoveries modify or add to the knowledge reported in Chapters 7A and 8A?
2. Locate as many first-magnitude stars as you can.
3. Observe a planet. Tell at what hour in what sky location you saw it. Describe it and tell how it differs from any other object in the sky. Observe its position at the same hour for a period of one week or more.
4. Observe the moon through a pair of field glasses. Record your observations.
5. Do further reading about sunspots. Be prepared to discuss your findings from the standpoint of importance.
6. Find out when the next partial or total eclipses of the moon and sun will take place. Explain your procedure in obtaining the information.
7. Obtain and discuss the latest information about possible life on the planet Mars.
8. Try to observe meteorites in a local museum and find out their histories. Watch a meteor shower on one of the dates given in Chapter 7A. From what directions do the meteors appear to come? How many meteors do you see in an hour?
9. Observe the moon for a two-week period. Record the time of observation and location in the sky. Keep a record (by making line drawings) of its appearance.
10. Find the North Star and make a drawing of the constellations near it that you can see on a clear night.
11. Make four observations of the Big Dipper at intervals on the same night. Make a drawing of your observations.
12. Look at stars, planets, and the moon through a telescope and describe your experience.

[3]This section gives suggestions for both of the astronomy chapters.

(Courtesy of Borg-Warner Corp.)

CHAPTER 8B

TEACHING "THE STARS AND THE UNIVERSE"

With the increase of space explorations the universe becomes more and more a part of the children's world. With each new space conquest children themselves are propelled into space—in thought, in imagination, in feeling.

There is no adequate substitute for actual observations of the night sky. While the vastness of space is indeed difficult to comprehend, some knowledge of the distances and some observations of stars and star groups will increase the interest and appreciation of children for the vast universe in which our solar system and the earth are but tiny specks.

We can help children know the stars and star groups by suggesting that they look for the easy-to-find ones first. Suggest that they look for just *one* star or *one* constellation on any evening. In this way they can begin to recognize some of the prominent features of the night sky. Give them specific instructions about the hours, direction, and how far up in the sky to look for each observation. Following this, the children can describe what they have seen and make additional studies from charts and books. Many of the general suggestions given for Chapter 7A are also appropriate to use here.

SOME BROAD CONCEPTS: "The Stars and the Universe"

Distances in the universe are measured in light years.

The apparent brightness of a star depends on its distance from the earth, its size, and its temperature.

The use of instruments has been very important in the study of astronomy.

The apparent motion of stars each night is due to the turning of the earth.

Everything in the universe is in motion.

Constellations are patterns of stars.

Our solar system is a tiny speck in the vast Milky Way.

The Milky Way is one of thousands of galaxies that form the universe.

FOR YOUNGER CHILDREN

Obviously the investigations of many of the following problems must be done at night and in many situations a night meeting with younger children is impractical. It is helpful to find a knowledgeable adult who can help younger children make some easy observations of the night sky. Under most circumstances we must rely on parents or other adults to help children at home with night observations. In a city environment sky observations are difficult to make because of the lights and buildings.

What Can We Discover by Looking at the Sky at Night?

Urge pupils to report their night-sky observations. Suggest that they try to watch a particular part of the sky after sunset to see what happens as it gets dark. Many will report: Stars do not all look the same. Some are brighter than others. They are

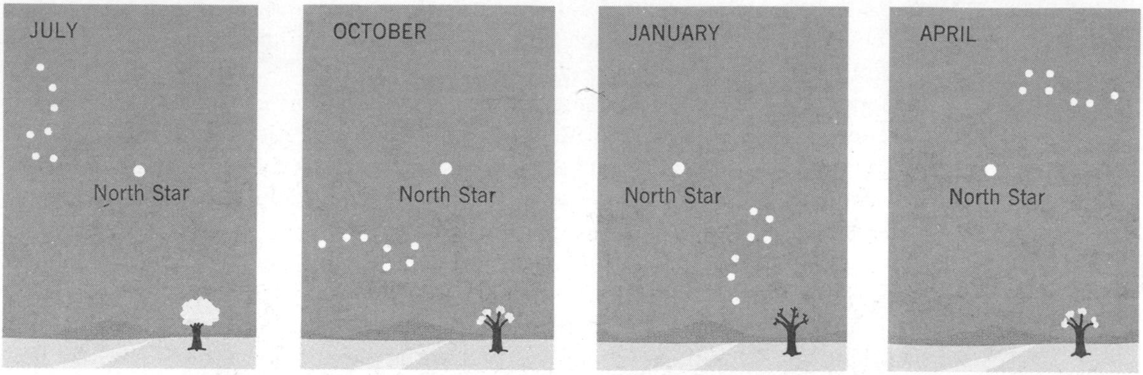

The Big Dipper is one of the easiest star groups to locate; since it may be used to locate the North Star, it is one of the most important in orienting a star gazer. Observing it at different times of the night helps pupils to understand the effect of the earth's rotation on what we see in the night sky. Observing it at the same time of night during different seasons, as shown in the illustration, leads to an understanding of the changing view of the stars as the earth orbits the sun.

not all the same color. They twinkle. Some stars are in groups. They do not all appear at the same time in the evening. These are some of the ideas younger children may discover by themselves.

Help pupils by making sketches of the most easily found star groups, such as the Big and Little Dipper, Orion, Cassiopeia, and so on. Use this opportunity to help children tell the directions by suggesting in which areas certain star groups can be found. Urge children to take the drawings of star groups home to use in their observations. Let them try to make their own drawings and show them to the class. Suggest that they attempt to count the stars to give them an idea of the vast number.

If possible, suggest that they observe the Big Dipper at different times of the evening to see how it changes.

Use pictures of the night sky to supplement or substitute for the observations. For city children who cannot easily make night observations a visit to a planetarium is especially helpful, as are photographs and diagrams of the night sky.

Why Does the Sun Look Smaller than the Earth even though It Is Larger?

Show pictures of the sun and the earth that illustrate their relative sizes. There are many experiences that children may have to help them understand the relationship of distance and size—an airplane on the ground and the same airplane high in the sky, for instance. Why does the plane look smaller in the sky? Other illustrations include: Two children the same size and height standing together. One walks to the far end of the playground. Why do they now appear to be different sizes? Two flashlights that are about equal in brightness. One is carried some distance away from observers; the other is near at hand. Now are they the same brightness? Why?

OTHER PROBLEMS FOR YOUNGER CHILDREN

1. How do telescopes help astronomers?
2. How is the light from the moon different from light from the sun?
3. How are stars different from each other?
4. Why are some stars brighter than others?

FOR OLDER CHILDREN

How Can We Find the Constellations?

A first look at the sky on a clear night is a thrilling and awesome sight. It's also confusing if you are trying for the first time to learn your way around. Use some of the suggestions for observing the sky given for use with younger children. Discuss the observations children make. Suggest that pupils try to locate some of the most easily identified star groups, one or a few at a time. Start with the Big Dipper, part of the constellation Ursa Major. If the teacher draws the constellation on the board, relating its position to the school or other landmark, pupils can more easily find it.

The North Star is easy to locate from the Big Dipper (*see* the star map, page 201 and the diagram on this page). The two stars opposite the handle are the pointers. A line drawn through these stars away from the Dipper's bottom for a length of about 5 times the distance between the pointers will locate the North Star. A simple map that the children have sketched will help them to locate the North Star at night. Pupils can be urged to use a compass in determining the section of the sky where the North Star is located. If they find north, then look up to the sky about halfway from the horizon to straight overhead, they will see the star. There are several constellations in the area of the sky surrounding the North Star (*see* star map, page 201).

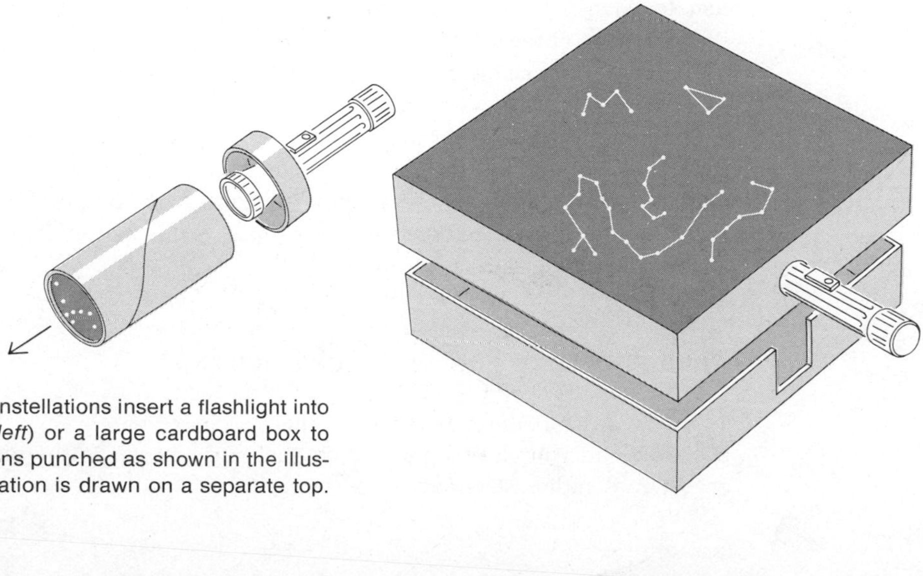

While studying the constellations insert a flashlight into either a cereal box (*left*) or a large cardboard box to illuminate constellations punched as shown in the illustration. Each constellation is drawn on a separate top.

The constellation Orion is another interesting group easily found. This is in the southern sky in the winter months. Three bright stars mark Orion's belt. With the use of the star map the rest of the constellation can be located.

A device for showing star groups is made from a cardboard box. Leave the cover on and remove one end of the box. Cut several pieces of paper the size of the end of the box, and on each piece make one constellation by punching holes to represent the stars. Use a flashlight to illuminate the inside of the box. When the constellation cards are held over the open end of the box the light shines through the holes and the constellation shows up very well, especially if the room is darkened. The details about the kind of paper to use, the brightness of the light, the shape of the box, and so forth can be worked out by pupils.

Another easily-made device is constructed from a cylindrical cereal box, as shown. The constellations are made by punching holes in the bottom. Pupils will think of ways to remove the circular bottom piece and insert similar pieces, each with a different constellation.

Constellations may also be represented on pieces of large paper placed against a bright window, with holes to represent individual stars. Remember that one successful identification night trip outdoors is worth more than any number of these paper representations.

How Can We Study the Stars?

As pupils continue to look at the sky on clear nights and report what they see, they wonder about many of the observations they make. This wondering is a great motivation for "research" reading. Why do some stars appear brighter than others? Why do they appear different in color? How can you tell the difference between stars and planets? What is the Milky Way? Which objects are part of the solar system? How are they different from other objects? How do constellations around the North Star seem to change during the night? Why do we see different constellations during different times of the year? Why do stars seem to twinkle? Answering these questions will combine observing, reading, and communicating their findings (*see* Part I for suggestions on the use of reading material).

Help pupils study a star map to discover which first-magnitude stars are currently visible and suggest that they try to locate them at night.

(**Note:** Some variations of the activities suggested in Chapter 7B are appropriate for use in helping pupils understand more clearly the material on constellations and galaxies.)

OTHER PROBLEMS FOR OLDER CHILDREN

1. How do stars differ from each other?
2. How can you classify the objects that can be seen in the night sky?
3. Why is radio astronomy important?

4. What constellations near it can you locate from Ursa Major?
5. Why are stars different colors?
6. How are telescopes made?

RESOURCES TO INVESTIGATE WITH CHILDREN[1]

1. A telescope in a local observatory or a smaller telescope owned by an amateur astronomer for viewing the moon and other objects in the night sky.
2. The evening sky to observe visible planets and to see the moon through binoculars.
3. The daytime and night sky to observe the moon—its shape and location in relation to the sun.
4. Meteorites in a local museum collection.
5. Magazine and newspaper accounts of current astronomical discoveries.
6. A local amateur astronomer to answer questions about astronomy.
7. Leaders of Scouts and 4-H Clubs to conduct evening trips to study the heavens.
8. Aeronautic and marine personnel in the community for information about the uses of the heavenly bodies in navigating and about constellations seen in other parts of the world.
9. Various persons in the community for field glasses to use in observing the moon.
10. Local planetarium, if there is one in your vicinity.

Preparing to Teach[2]

1. Plan ways to make a model of the solar system that could be used in the classroom or out of doors (*see* footnote in Chapter 7B). Describe how you would help children make such a model and develop some of the behavioral objectives you would expect as a result.
2. Assemble up-to-date bulletin-board material and plan how it may be displayed and used to help children learn some of the concepts in these chapters. (Magazines, newspapers, science organizations, and so on are good sources.)
3. Find out how to make a sundial and prepare a plan that you can utilize in teaching children how to make and use it.
4. Prepare a large-sized star map showing how to locate a dozen of the easiest-to-locate constellations. Work out plans for using the map with children to help them plan and draw one for their own use.
5. Devise a demonstration that will help pupils understand how a much smaller body, the moon, can blot out a much larger body, the sun, during an eclipse. Plan how you would use the demonstration.

[1] This section suggests resources to investigate for both astronomy chapters.
[2] This section suggests ideas for preparing to teach for both of the astronomy chapters.

CHAPTER 9A

THE AIR AND THE WEATHER

We who inherit the Earth dwell like frogs at the bottom of a pool. Only if man could rise above the summit of the air could he behold the true Earth, the world we live in.[1]

—*Socrates,* 400 B.C.

[1] Plato, *Phaedo.*

(*Courtesy of NASA.*)

THE OCEAN OF AIR

In the Space Age man has risen from the bottom of the ocean of air to gain a new viewpoint of the earth and its enveloping atmosphere. With the television eyes of satellites permanently circling in space around the earth we now look *down* at the weather map which nature draws in the sky with clouds. Observations made by the satellites provide warnings of hurricanes and other catastrophic weather, enabling people to strengthen levees, take shelter, and make other provisions to minimize loss. Increased knowledge attained by satellite study may eventually enable man to modify weather to his advantage.

THE ATMOSPHERE

Hurricanes, thunderstorms, snowstorms, balmy breezes, hot spells, cold snaps, dense fogs, and rainbows are symptomatic of the ever-changing conditions within the earth's atmosphere. To understand weather it is essential to gather information about the air—its composition, temperature, humidity, pressure, movements, and other characteristics—and to combine this information into a comprehensive picture. Weathermen, or meteorologists as they are called, gather measurements in many places around the earth and at many altitudes, from the surface of the earth up to the top of the atmosphere. They make observations hour after hour, day after day, and thus are able to write a continuous story about the weather.

We shall see later just what kind of instruments are used for making measurements. First let us take a look at the atmosphere. Covering the entire earth and extending upward for hundreds of miles, the atmosphere acts as a protective blanket, moderating the temperature and shielding us from harmful rays and particles from outer space that bombard our planet.

(*See* figure on p. 220.)

Distribution of Air

The air in our atmospheric ocean is not uniform in density: It becomes thinner and thinner at higher levels. Mountain climbers are painfully aware of this at high altitudes. At 18,000 feet, or $3\frac{1}{2}$ miles, there is only half as much oxygen (and other air constituents) in each lungful of air as at sea level. Half of the total weight of the air in the atmosphere lies below the $3\frac{1}{2}$-mile mark and half above it. Ninety-nine percent of the air is under the 20-mile level, leaving only 1 percent thinly scattered in the hundreds of miles above.

Scientists have divided the atmosphere into a series of layers, one on top of the other, to portray differences in temperature, chemical composition, pressure, and other properties at varying altitudes. If you consult different sources you will find somewhat different atmosphere diagrams, or *profiles.* Recent studies of the atmosphere with rockets and satellites are yielding new secrets of the earth's upper atmosphere and causing scientists to modify earlier profiles. We present a simplified profile in which the atmosphere is divided into five layers: the *troposphere, stratosphere, mesosphere, thermosphere,* and *exosphere.*

The Troposphere

The layer in which we live is the troposphere. This word means "turbulent sphere," and is appropriate, because all storms great and small and, indeed, almost all weather phenomena appear to occur in this layer. Another characteristic of the troposphere is the steady drop in temperature with increased altitude: The temperature drops about $3\frac{1}{2}°$ F. for each 1,000 feet of ascent. In the troposphere the sky appears blue because the air and dust particles in it scatter the white light of the sun in such a way that its blue rays are bent into our line of vision. The blue skies we see are not far off in space; they are a phenomenon produced in the nearby troposphere, as, too, are the clouds. In the upper part of the troposphere are high-speed winds known as the jet stream. These are discussed more fully on page 238.

(*See* p. 654.)

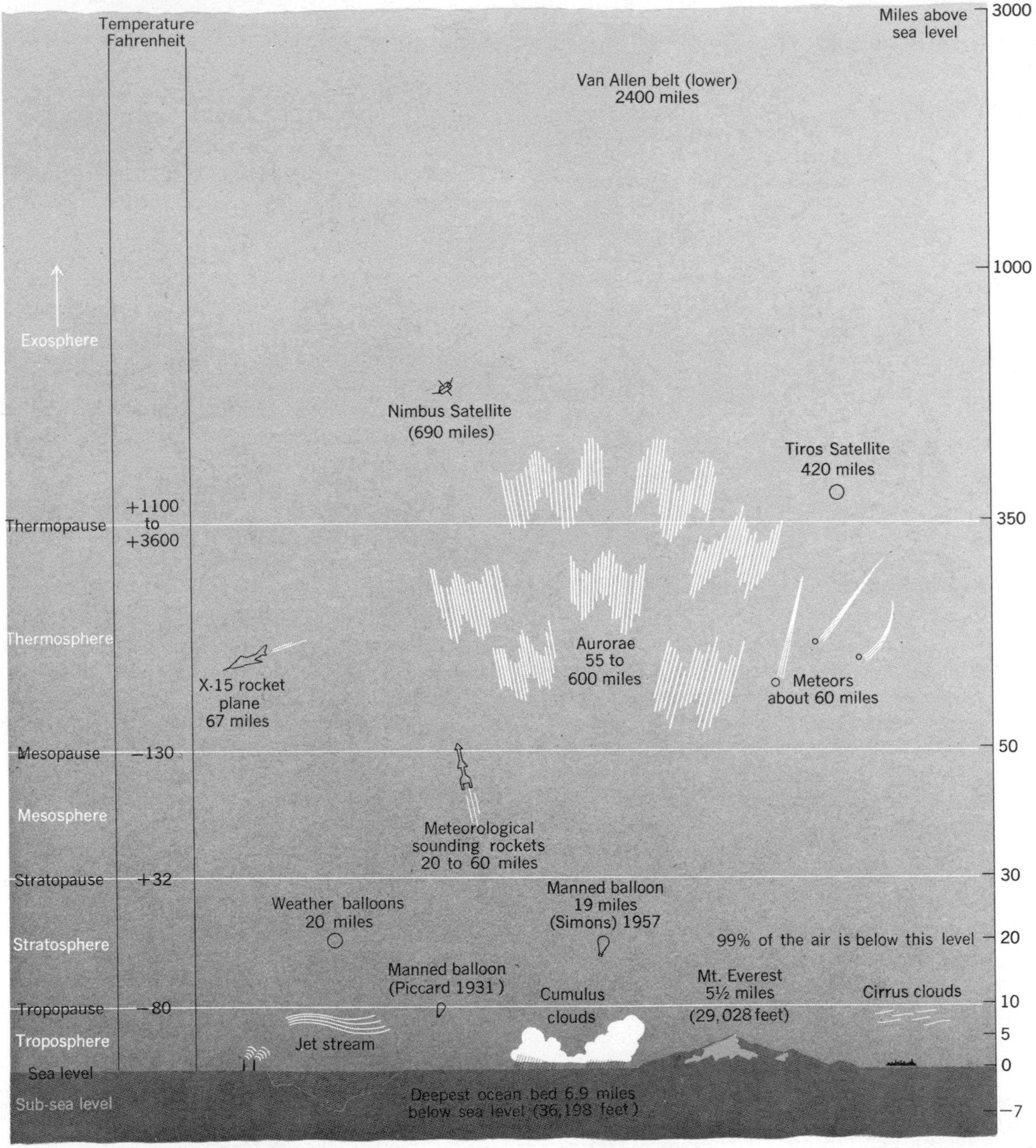

The earth's atmosphere.

The troposphere varies in height from 10 miles at the equator to about 5 miles at the poles. It is about 7 miles high in the middle latitudes. The height of this layer is also influenced somewhat by the seasons and by general weather conditions. At the upper boundary of the troposphere the temperature, which is about 80° F. below zero remains constant with increasing altitude. This is where the stratosphere begins.

The Stratosphere

This layer extends from the top of the troposphere to a height of 30 miles above sea level. The air in the stratosphere is almost moistureless and cloudless. The temperature of the stratosphere remains at minus 80° F. until about 14 miles above the earth and then begins to rise, reaching about plus 32° F. at 30 miles. This surface of maximum temperature marks the top of the stratosphere. Winds in the stratosphere decrease with increasing altitude; there are no up or down air currents, no storms. Men have penetrated the lower stratosphere in balloons and planes. In 1957 G. Simons, an Air Force balloonist, soared 19 miles above the earth, higher than anyone had ever reached in a balloon.

A concentration of a special form of oxygen called *ozone* is produced in the upper stratosphere and in the layer above it. (The oxygen in the air we breathe is composed of two atoms of oxygen—O_2—whereas ozone has three atoms—O_3—in each of its molecules. See Chapter 15A for a discussion of atoms and molecules.) Ozone absorbs most of the powerful ultraviolet radiation from the sun. In this way it protects living things on earth from rays that in full strength would prove deadly. The ultraviolet rays that do penetrate to the earth's surface tan our skins, prevent rickets, and kill bacteria.

The Mesosphere

In the mesosphere (middle sphere), which extends from the top of the stratosphere to 50 miles above the earth, the temperature falls steadily with increasing altitude, reaching a very cold minus 130° F. at its upper boundary.

In 1961 pilots flying X-15 rocket planes penetrated deep into the mesosphere, reaching heights over 40 miles above the earth. Later flights penetrated its "roof," climbing to a height of 67 miles.

The Thermosphere

Above the mesosphere is the thermosphere (heat sphere). In it the temperature increases rapidly with height up to about 125 miles above sea level. Above this level the temperature varies widely according to the degree of solar activity from about 1100° F., when the sun is quiet, to possibly 3600° F., during periods when solar activity is at its maximum.

(*See* p. 154.)

The thermosphere contains part of an atmosphere layer known as the *ionosphere* (electrically charged sphere), which moves up and down because of the influence of the sun. In the ionosphere x-rays and ultraviolet rays from the sun are absorbed by the scattered atoms and molecules of the extremely thin air. As a result many of these are electrically charged, and become *ions,* from which the name ionosphere is derived.

The fascinating auroral displays, the Northern and Southern Lights, originate in the ionosphere. Electrically charged particles streak down from the sun, and, guided by the earth's magnetic field, strike atoms and molecules in the ionosphere and cause them to glow, thus producing the display of lights.

In the thermosphere, which extends from 50 to 350 miles above sea level, the air is incredibly thin, being 10 million times rarer than the air at sea level. Thin as it is, the air in the thermosphere offers enough frictional resistance to most of the meteoroids that flash through it to cause them to become white-hot and to be reduced to dust. The thermosphere (and to some extent the mesosphere) serves, therefore, as a screen protecting the earth from the millions of meteoroids that bombard it daily.

The Exosphere

The exosphere begins at the upper limit of the thermosphere and extends outward thousands of miles. In the exosphere, the air is so thin that molecules of it can travel vast distances without hitting each other.

One of the major achievements of the exploration of the atmosphere by satellite was the discovery of the existence of two belts of high radiation, known as the Van Allen belts after their discoverer. These doughnut-shaped belts, one inside the other, consist of fast-moving electrons

(*See* pp. 485–6.)

and protons which spiral in the lines of force in the earth's magnetic field. The center of one belt is 2,400 miles and the other 10,000 miles from the earth.

COMPOSITION OF THE AIR

The air that enters your lungs with each breath is not one but many substances. The two most abundant parts of air are nitrogen, which accounts for nearly four-fifths of the air, and oxygen, which makes up about one-fifth.

Nitrogen, the chief constituent of air (78 percent), is also an essential element in proteins, which are basic in the makeup of all living things. As we shall see in Chapter 14A some atmospheric nitrogen is made available to plants by the action of certain bacteria in the soil.

Oxygen, a chemically active component of the air (21 percent), is essential for respiration in plants and animals and for the combustion of fuels.

Carbon dioxide, making up only $\frac{3}{100}$ of 1 percent of the air, is extremely important to life. Green plants absorb carbon dioxide from the air and combined it with the hydrogen in water molecules to produce the food essential for their life and eventually for that of all animals as well. This important process will be discussed in Chapter 10A.

Water vapor, found in amounts varying from 0 to 3 or 4 percent of the air, exerts a profound influence on the distribution of life on this planet, because a region's capacity for supporting life is determined principally by the amount of water, in the form of rain or snow, that is available. Most of the water vapor is found in the lower 4 miles of the atmosphere. As we shall see, water vapor plays an important part in the changing weather picture.

We have thus far accounted for about 99 percent of the air (excluding the variable water vapor content). The remaining 1 percent consists primarily of the gases argon, neon, helium, krypton, and xenon, Sprinkled in the air also is a varying amount of dust.

SUN, AIR, AND WATER

The drama of weather is better understood if we follow closely the roles played by the sun, air, and water. The sun is the leading figure in the spectacle, providing the heat energy that keeps the whole show moving. The air is the vehicle that circulates and transports all kinds and conditions of weather around the earth. Water appears in many forms—dew, sleet, fog, clouds, rain, and snow; it disappears from view as water vapor.

Sun

From a distance of about 93 million miles the sun warms the earth. If all parts of the earth were heated equally there would not be much weather to talk about. But the sun's heat is not distributed equally. Let us see why:

1. For one thing the sun's rays reach only half of the earth at any one time, the side in daylight. We live on a turning earth, so there is a daily cycle of heating and cooling accompanying day and night.
2. Sunshine is not equally strong all over the earth. The fact that the earth is round means that different parts of its surface receive sunlight at different angles. Thus areas near the equator face the sun directly and receive more radiation than the belts farther away from the equator that receive more slanting rays. As a result the equatorial regions receive more heat than the temperate, and the temperate more than the polar (*see* Chapter 7B for a demonstration of the principle involved).
3. We saw in Chapter 7A how the tilted axis of the earth and the yearly revolution of the earth around the sun cause variations in the amount of heat received at different times of the year, thereby causing the seasons.
4. The amount of heat absorbed by any area of the earth depends in part on the kind of surface that is being heated. Water heats up much more slowly than land. Hence the air temperatures influenced by these underlying surfaces are

different: It is cooler in summer at the seacoast than inland at the same latitude.

5. Even without the first four factors operating the atmosphere of the earth, considered vertically, would exhibit variation in temperature. As we learned previously, temperatures drop off in the troposphere at the average rate of $3\frac{1}{2}°$ F. for every 1,000 feet of elevation. It may seem unusual that temperatures should drop as one gets nearer the sun until one considers that the few thousand feet involved are a very tiny percentage of the 93 million miles to the sun. Far overshadowing relative distance from the sun are two other factors:

a. The atmosphere is heated from below by the earth itself. The sun's radiant energy is first absorbed by the rocks, soil, and water of the earth, and changed into heat. These warmed substances, in turn, heat the layer of air closest to the surface of the earth through infrared radiation (radiant heat).

b. The air at the bottom of the atmosphere, being denser, dustier, and more moist, is able to absorb more of the sun's radiation than air in the upper layers (as well as more of the important infrared radiation from the earth). This absorbed radiation is converted into heat, thus warming the air.

It is apparent, then, that the amount of solar energy received and absorbed varies considerably from place to place and from time to time. This results in an uneven heating of the earth and has a profound effect on the weather.

Air

Weather, as we indicated at the beginning of this chapter, is a condition of the atmosphere and hence of the air that makes up the atmosphere. In Chapter 7A we saw how the peculiar "weather" of the moon, or rather the absence of weather, is due to the fact that it has no atmosphere. The earth's air acts as a huge insulator, holding in the heat absorbed from the sun's rays by the earth's surface. As an insulator it moderates the temperature of the earth so that we do not freeze at night or broil by day.

The uneven heating of the earth results in an uneven heating of the air above it, so that all around the earth there are parcels of air, big and small, with different temperatures. *Because cold air is heavier than an equal volume of warm air, cold air sinks and pushes up the lighter warm air.* On a small scale this happens in a room heated by a radiator. If the circulation of the air in a room is traced by means of smoke or streamers of tissue paper, it will be noted that the warm air above the radiator rises to the ceiling and then moves away, while the colder air near the floor moves toward the radiator to be heated in turn.

(*See* pp. 260–1.)

Thus, in a radiator-heated room we see that the difference in temperature in the air causes up-and-down movements, or air currents, and lateral movements across the room, a kind of homemade "breeze."

The same principle that explains the movement of air in a heated room applies, on a larger scale, to a summer seacoast. The sun beating down on the coastal land heats it, and consequently the air over it, more than it heats the ocean and its overlaying air. Because of this the land behaves like the room radiator, and circulation is started in which a "sea breeze" of cool air sweeps in from the ocean, pushing up the air warmed by the land, which then rises and streams out aloft toward the ocean. At night, however, the land loses its heat more rapidly than the water. The air above it is chilled, while the ocean air is relatively warm. The colder air now sweeps from the land to the water, producing the "land breeze", as shown on p. 224.

On a global scale the hot equatorial regions may be thought of as the earth's "radiator." Air heated in the tropics accumulates and forms a warm mass of air. In the polar regions the air is chilled to form a cold mass. Circulation is set up in the troposphere in which warm air rises over the equator and streams toward the poles, while cold air from the poles slips down toward the equator. This circulation is complicated by many factors, but it is clear that it provides a mechanism whereby the heat of the earth can be distributed, a mechanism that brings to us in the temperate zones air that has been chilled at the poles and air that has been heated at the equator.

Water

Although we talk of water "shortages" the amount of water on the earth is fairly constant, but it is not always available when and where we want it. The endless cycle of evaporation and condensation depicted in the diagram (on p. 225) keeps the water of the earth in constant circulation. Water evaporates from the soil, from leaves of plants, from the lungs and skin of animals, and from puddles, ponds, lakes, and seas. In the process of evaporation molecules of water bounce out of their liquid surroundings to mix with other components of the air. This highly scattered, invisible form of water is known as *water vapor.* The heat provided by the sun and the fanning by the winds hasten evaporation, as anyone who has hung wet clothes on a line to dry knows.

(*See* pp. 255–60.)

Aloft, a chilling of air containing water vapor causes the water molecules to come together in tiny droplets to form a cloud. We see cloud formation on a small scale when we breathe out on a cold day and "see" our breath. The droplets in a cloud may merge to form larger, heavier drops that fall as rain and return to the soil, streams, lakes, and oceans (*see* pages 236, 248–9 for a fuller explanation of cloud droplet formation and precipitation). Water vapor may also return in other forms—as snow, dew, and frost. We shall consider these and other forms of precipitation presently.

The water cycle, also known as the *hydrologic cycle,* provides a means of circulating water from oceans, lakes, and seas to the land areas.

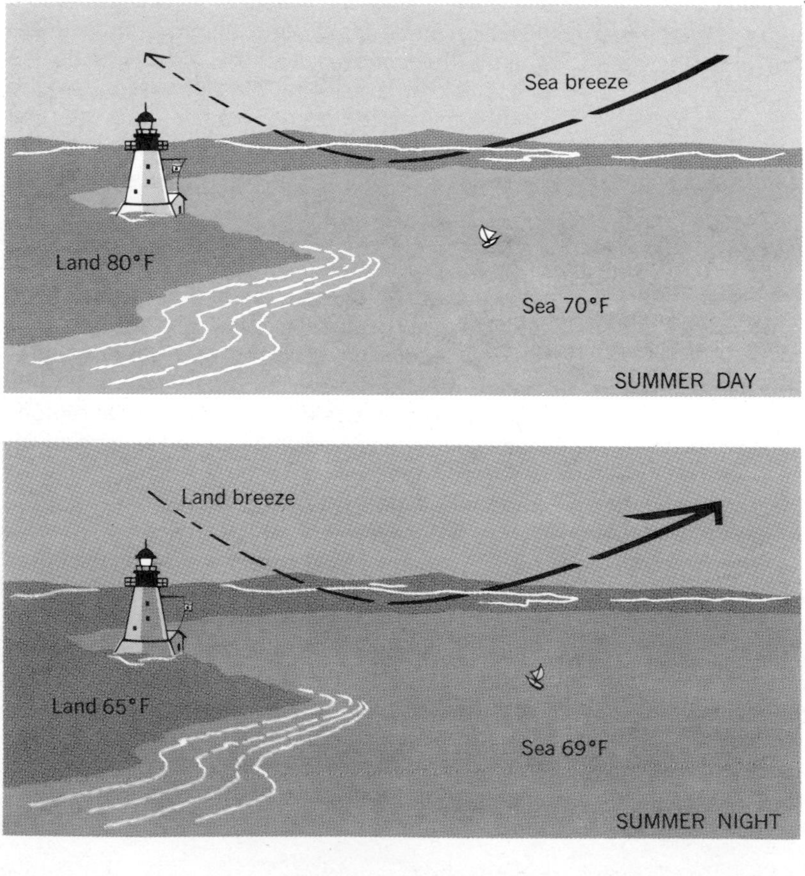

During the daytime the air over the sea is cooler than the air over land. A cool sea breeze blows. At night, when conditions are reversed, a land breeze blows.

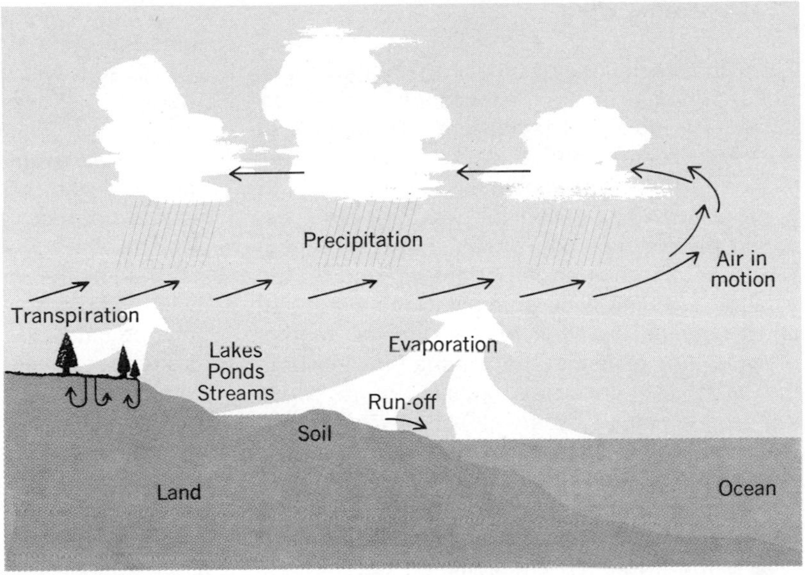

The endless cycle of evaporation and condensation keeps the water of the earth in constant circulation.

The water cycle also serves as nature's water-purification system, because minerals, mud, and debris are left behind when water evaporates into the air. The water that comes down is relatively pure and clean.

MEASURING THE WEATHER

To describe present weather conditions accurately and to forecast weather successfully it is necessary to use weather instruments. Measurements of rainfall and snowfall, of wind direction and wind velocity, of the temperature, humidity, and pressure of the air must be recorded. The meteorologist collects such information from many points on the earth and as high into the atmosphere as possible. He keeps records and makes charts day after day, using these to forecast the weather.

Measuring Rain and Snow

Probably the oldest weather instrument was a rain gauge. Any straight-walled vessel, such as a jar, served as a measure of the amount of rain in any rainfall. A standard rain gauge catches the rain in a funnel whose mouth area is exactly ten times as big as the opening of the cylinder into which it empties. Thus the amount of rainfall is "magnified" ten times. If 4 inches of rain accumulate in the collecting cylinder, the actual rainfall is $\frac{4}{10}$ inch.

(*See* pp. 254–6.)

Snowfall is measured directly by plunging a stick into the snow at an average open location. Snow varies in its yield of water. The rainwater equivalent of the snowfall is determined by melting a given portion of snow. Light, fluffy snow with a good deal of air in it may give only 1 inch of water for 15 inches of snow; a dense, packed snowfall may yield 1 inch of water from only 6 inches of snow. The average is about 1 inch of water for 10 inches of snow.

The National Weather Service also uses a type of gauge that *weighs* the amount of precipitation (rain or snow) falling into the gauge. The weight is "translated" automatically on a chart into depth of water in inches. If, for example, 13 ounces of rain were caught in the gauge a recording pen would indicate that 0.45 inch of rain had fallen.

Measuring Wind

Wind, as defined by the meteorologist, refers to *horizontal* air motion, as distinct from vertical motion. To measure the wind is to determine its direction and speed. The wind vane measures direction. (It is more popularly called the weather vane, because people have known for a long time that wind direction has an important bearing on the weather.) A wind vane points into the wind, that is, toward the direction from which the wind is blowing. For example, if a wind is blowing from the west, the arrowhead points to the west. Winds are named by the direction *from* which they come. A wind blowing from west to east is designated a west wind.

(*See* pp. 252, 263–4.)

The speed of the wind is measured by an instrument called an *anemometer.* A common type is the three-cup anemometer. Each cup is a hollow hemisphere. The three cups are attached by spokes to a central pivot. The wind spins the cups around, as it would a pinwheel, at a speed that is proportional to the wind speed. The speed is transmitted electrically to an indicator.

The *aerovane* is a combined anemometer and wind vane. This instrument, which is now standard at most weather stations, looks like an airplane without wings. A three-bladed propeller is turned by the wind at a rate that is proportional to the wind's speed. The streamlined vane not only indicates the wind direction but also acts as a rudder to keep the propeller facing the wind. Both speed and direction are conveyed to recording instruments in the station.

The direction and speed of winds at different levels of the atmosphere are determined with the aid of balloons. These balloons, containing hydrogen or helium, are released into the air. They are equipped with a radio transmitter that is tracked by equipment on the ground.

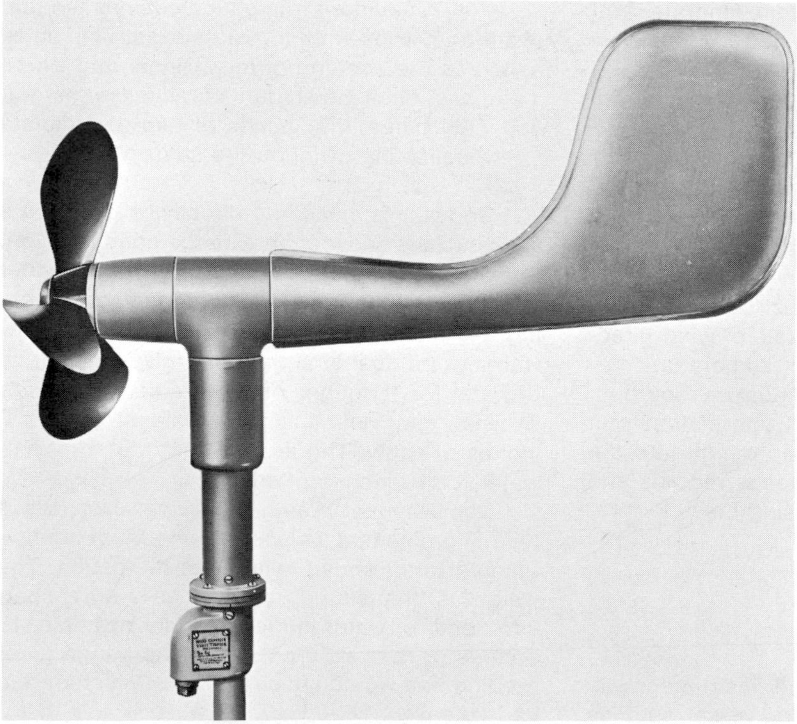

The direction and speed of the wind may be read indoors from dials connected to this aerovane. (*Courtesy of Bendix Environmental Science Division.*)

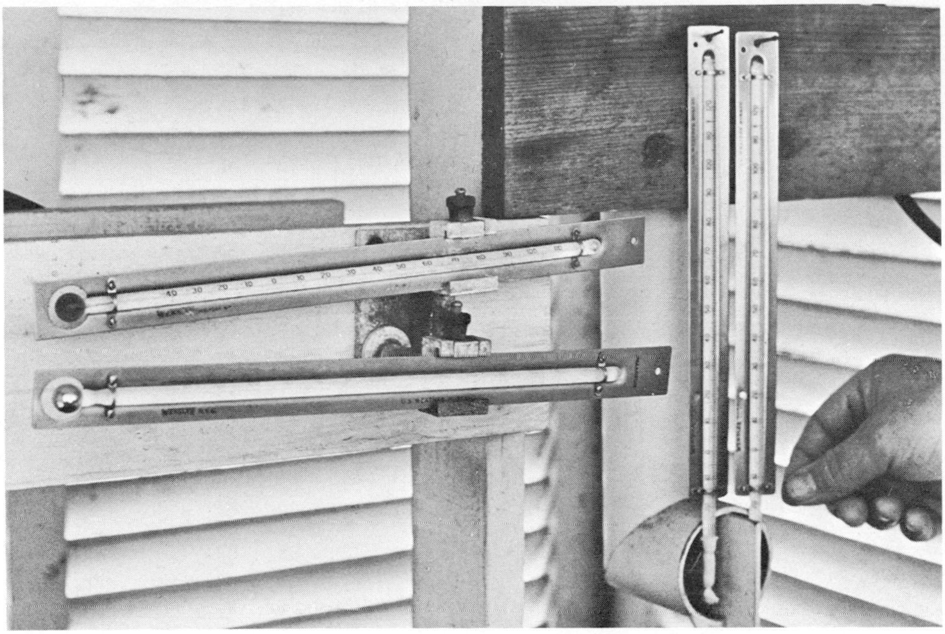

Some of the instruments housed in a weather instrument shelter. The two thermometers (*left*) show the maximum and minimum temperatures, respectively, for the recording period. The other pair (*right*), wet- and dry-bulb thermometers, provide data for determining the relative humidity. The instruments are shielded from the sun, but not from the air, which circulates freely through the shelter. (*Courtesy of ESSA.*)

Measuring Temperature

The weatherman uses his thermometer to tell the temperature of the air. All significant readings are made in an enclosure open to the air, *but shaded from the sun.* (Reading a thermometer with the sun beating on it will merely show how effectively the thermometer is absorbing the sun's rays. It will not give any significant figure, nor will it agree with another thermometer of different size or shape held in the same location. It is not intended to be used in sunlight. A full discussion of the thermometer is to be found in Chapter 16A.)

It is extremely important for the meteorologist to know the temperature at different elevations above the earth. We shall see shortly how he takes the temperature of the air aloft.

Measuring Humidity

(*See* p. 259.) As we have seen, water vapor is the most variable of the gases of the atmosphere, ranging from 0 to about 4 percent. The hygrometer is an instrument for measuring the water-vapor content of the atmosphere. One kind of hygrometer is the *wet- and dry-bulb thermometer,* also called a *psychrometer.* You can understand the principle of this instrument if you recall two common experiences: First, you may have noticed how slowly wet clothing dries on a humid day, how rapidly on a dry day. Second, you may recall the coolness you feel on the skin of your hands or face as water evaporates from them.

The wet-bulb thermometer shown is one that has a moist cloth wrapped around its bulb. As water evaporates from the cloth into the air, the thermometer drops markedly. If the air is humid evaporation is slow and the temperature falls little.

In short, we calculate the moisture content of the air from the rate of evaporation of a moist cloth. By comparing the temperature of the wet-bulb thermometer with that of an ordinary dry-bulb one, and by using the chart on page 228 the humidity of the air can be determined. The humidity referred to is *relative humidity* and is expressed as a percentage.

RELATIVE HUMIDITY IN PERCENTAGES

Readings of Dry-bulb Thermometer	*Difference in Degrees Fahrenheit between Wet- and Dry-bulb Thermometers*															
	0	1	2	3	4	5	6	7	8	9	10	11	12	13	14	15
60°	100%	94%	89%	84%	78%	73%	68%	63%	58%	53%	49%	44%	40%	35%	31%	27%
61°	100	94	89	84	79	74	68	64	59	54	50	45	40	36	32	28
62°	100	94	89	84	79	74	69	64	60	55	50	46	41	37	33	29
63°	100	95	90	84	79	74	70	65	60	56	51	47	42	38	34	30
64°	100	95	90	85	79	75	70	66	61	56	52	48	43	39	35	31
65°	100	95	90	85	80	75	70	66	62	57	53	48	44	40	36	32
66°	100	95	90	85	80	76	71	66	62	58	53	49	45	41	37	33
67°	100	95	90	85	80	76	71	67	62	58	54	50	46	42	38	34
68°	100	95	90	85	81	76	72	67	63	59	55	51	47	43	39	35
69°	100	95	90	86	81	77	72	68	64	59	55	51	47	44	40	36
70°	100	95	90	86	81	77	72	68	64	60	56	52	48	44	40	37
71°	100	95	90	86	82	77	73	69	64	60	56	53	49	45	41	38
72°	100	95	91	86	82	78	73	69	65	61	57	53	49	46	42	39
73°	100	95	91	86	82	78	73	69	65	61	58	54	50	46	43	40
74°	100	95	91	86	82	78	74	70	66	62	58	54	51	47	44	40
75°	100	96	91	87	82	78	74	70	66	63	59	55	51	48	44	41
76°	100	96	91	87	83	78	74	70	67	63	59	55	52	48	45	42
77°	100	96	91	87	83	79	75	71	67	63	60	56	52	49	46	42
78°	100	96	91	87	83	79	75	71	67	64	60	57	53	50	46	43
79°	100	96	91	87	83	79	75	71	68	64	60	57	54	50	47	44
80°	100	96	91	87	83	79	76	72	68	64	61	57	54	51	47	44

Just what is meant by relative humidity? If, for example, we say that the relative humidity is 100 percent, we mean that the air is as full of water vapor as it can be; if more water vapor were added, it would fall out of the air as mist or rain. Fifty percent relative humidity means that the air is holding only half the amount of water vapor that it could.

A glance at the chart shows that the percentages given are true for a particular temperature. In other words, the capacity of air to hold water varies with its temperature: warm air can hold more water vapor than cold air. This is important in weather phenomena, for it means that if a given portion of air is chilled, its water-holding capacity decreases. Without any change in its actual water *content* the relative humidity of such a portion of air increases, and, if it exceeds 100 percent, water will be condensed out of it. This is just what happens on a warm summer day when warm, moist air rises in the morning to cooler regions to form the thunderclouds of the afternoon.

How to Calculate Relative Humidity Look at the relative-humidity chart. If the air temperature given by the dry-bulb thermometer is 70° and the wet-bulb thermometer falls to 64° the difference is 6°. Look along the 70° line until you come under the number 6. The relative humidity is 72 percent.

Another instrument for measuring relative humidity is the *hair hygrometer,* which makes use of the fact that human hair shortens when the atmosphere is dry and lengthens when it is moist. Blond hair seems to work best. It is first treated to remove oils, and then a few strands of it are fastened into a device in such a way that the hair moves a pointer over a scale of humidity percentages. Readings are made directly, without having to consult a chart, but this instrument is not quite as accurate as the wet- and dry-bulb thermometers.

The *dew point* is another way of describing the humidity of the air. We just discussed the fact that when air is chilled it can hold less water vapor, and that if it is chilled sufficiently water will condense out of it. At what temperature will this happen for a given mass of air (without any change in the amount of water vapor or in the air pressure)? This temperature is called the dew point. For example, at what temperature will the air in your room right now reach its dew point? One way of finding out is to chill it. Don't open your windows or turn on your air conditioner, because that would change the amount of water vapor in the air. Just place a thermometer in a thin-walled metal cup (silver is best) and add water and a little ice. Stir constantly. When enough ice has been added to cool the cup of water sufficiently (and the air immediately next to the cup), the outer surface of the container will be clouded with beads of water. This water came from the air. Read your thermometer at this moment to find the dew point of your particular mass of air. The instrument that you have just constructed and used is called a *dew-point hygrometer.*

The dew point is important to a meteorologist because it helps him forecast the formation of fog or clouds.

Measuring Air Pressure

It is most important for the meteorologist to know the air pressure because it is a "symptom" of existing conditions in the atmosphere and consequently is essential in making a "prognosis" of weather conditions to come. For example, differences in air pressure from one region to another serve as a force to move air masses and the weather that attends them.

When we say that air has pressure we mean very simply that air pushes or presses against things. We are not referring to breezes or hurricane winds but to quiet, untroubled air. We are not aware of this pressure because we live our lives in it and because it pushes in on us equally from all directions. Moreover, the air in our body cavities and the blood in our veins and arteries push our body structures outward with equal pressure. Let us change our elevation, however, as we do when we descend or rise rapidly in an elevator or in an automobile on a mountain and our eardrums tell us quickly of the changing pressure.

What gives air its push, its pressure? To answer in one word it is its *weight.* We live at the bottom of an air ocean that rests its weight on the earth. Let us think of just a small portion of the earth's surface, just 1 square inch of it. Let us assume that we were able to ascend slowly in a balloon from the surface of the earth to the top of the atmosphere, collecting all the air *directly over this square inch* into an empty (empty even of air) steel cylinder. On returning to earth we would find that the cylinder weighs 15 pounds more than it did at the outset. There are approximately 15 pounds of air weighing down on every square inch of the surface of the earth (at sea level). Or, to put it in other words, the *pressure* of the air at sea level is about 15 pounds per square inch, as shown on p. 230.

Air pressure, then, is due to the weight of air above us. Obviously it should be less on a mountain top, and it is; it is greater in a mine below sea level.

In 1643 Torricelli invented an instrument for measuring air pressure, the mercury barometer. To make a mercury barometer a glass tube about 36 inches long, closed at one end, is filled with mercury. It is then inverted into an open jar containing more mercury. If this experiment is performed at sea level the mercury will fall a few inches, but it will then stop. Approximately 30 inches will remain in the tube, as shown in the diagram on p. 230. The space above the mercury is empty; it is a vacuum.

Why does the mercury not flow out of the tube? Torricelli's first thought was that this might be an example of Aristotle's theory that "nature

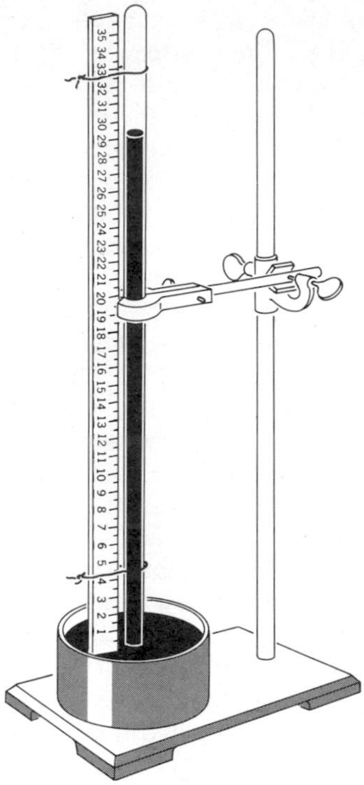

A simple mercury barometer. Air pressure on the mercury in the dish supports the column of mercury in the tube. Increasing atmospheric pressure causes the mercury to rise; decreasing pressure allows it to fall.

abhors a vacuum.'' According to this line of reasoning, if all the mercury flowed out it would leave a long vacuum in the tube, giving nature a great deal to abhor. But Torricelli noticed something that was to be of great significance in meteorology: *The height of the mercury column varied from day to day.* He reasoned from this that ''nature would not, as a flirtatious girl, have a different horror of a vacuum on different days,'' and he looked elsewhere for an explana-

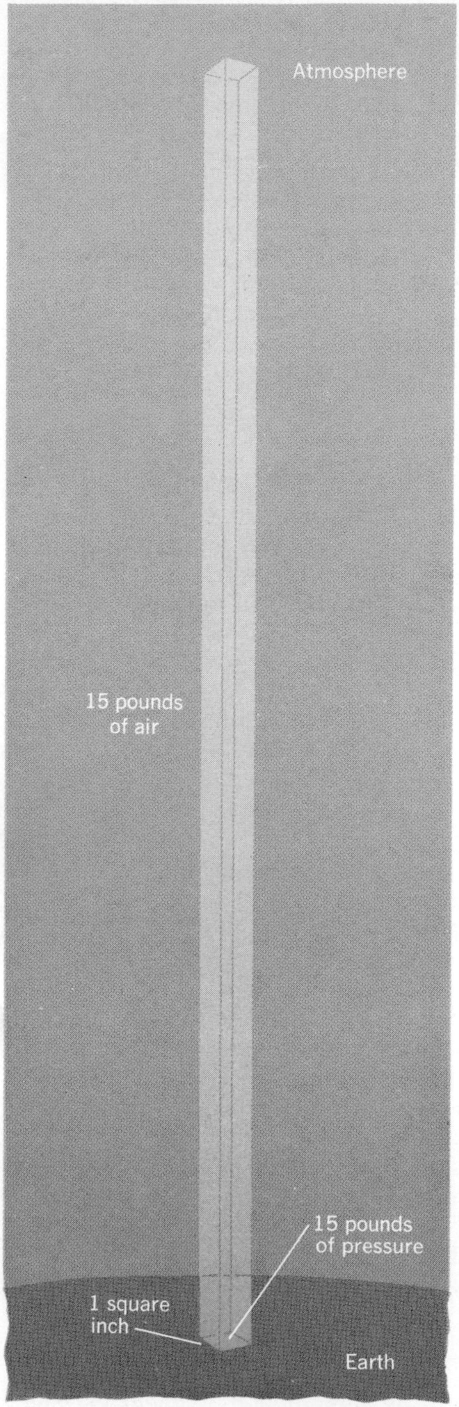

A column of air over 1 square inch of the earth's surface, extending to the top of the atmosphere, weighs 15 pounds. Another way of saying this is: The atmosphere exerts a pressure of 15 pounds on every square inch of the surface of the earth.

tion. This brought him to the conclusion that we hold currently: The mercury in the tube is supported by the pressure of the air on the surface of the mercury in the jar. You might think of the mercury barometer as a kind of balance, in which the weight of the atmosphere on the mercury is counterbalanced exactly by the weight of the mercury in the tube.

Mercury is used in barometers because it is the heaviest common fluid available. If water were used, the barometer tube would have to be about 40 feet high! In meteorology the pressure of the air is expressed in inches of mercury, which may seem to be a curious way of measuring pressure unless you think of the construction of a mercury barometer. The 30 inches represent the *equivalent* of a pressure of approximately 15 pounds per square inch. Professional meteorologists prefer to express pressure in a unit known as the *millibar* (based on the metric system). The atmospheric pressure at sea level is equal to approximately 1,000 millibars.

Within a few years after the discovery of the mercury barometer it was found that high air pressure was often associated with fair weather and low pressure with unsettled or rainy weather. Much later it was found that air will tend to flow from a region of high pressure to one of low pressure. Knowing these high and low areas enables the weather man to forecast the circulation of air. We shall discuss the relationship of air pressure to the general weather pattern in more detail presently.

Mercury barometers are awkward to carry from place to place. A much more convenient type is the *aneroid* barometer shown here. The word "aneroid" means "without liquid." Instead of a liquid, the aneroid barometer contains a flexible disc-shaped metal box from which much of the air has been removed (*see* "partial vacuum" in lower diagram). As air pressure increases, it squeezes the top and bottom of the box together slightly; as air pressure decreases, they spring apart. This slight movement is conveyed by levers to a pointer that sweeps over a scale calibrated to correspond with the mercury barometer. Aneroid barometers are used in homes, on ships, and in airplanes.

The dark pointer on the aneroid barometer indicates air pressure. The other pointer is set by hand so that a change for any period of time can be noted easily. The numbers correspond to inches of mercury. Evidently, the barometer shown here fell a bit more than half an inch since it was last set. The delicate mechanism inside the aneroid barometer (*see* diagram below) consists essentially of a disclike box from which air has been exhausted, and a connecting system of levers that operates the pointer to indicate the change in pressure. (*Courtesy Taylor Instrument Company.*)

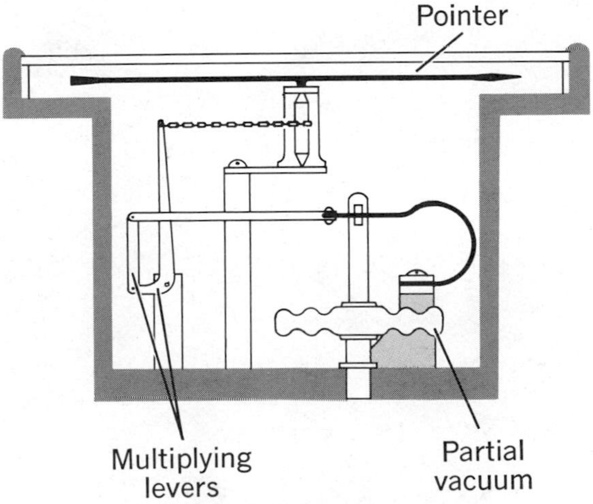

The Four "Rs" and One "S"

As long as the measurement of wind, moisture, temperature, and pressure was confined to the surface of the earth our knowledge of weather was severely restricted. We had to know the characteristics of the air at various levels above us if we were to have the full picture of the weather at work. The modern four Rs that we employ for this upper-air study are *radiosonde, reconnaissance, radar,* and *rockets.* To the four Rs we have now added an S—*satellites.*

The radiosonde is a balloon-borne package of instruments that measures temperature, humidity, and pressure at regular intervals as the gas-filled, unmanned balloon ascends to heights of approximately 20 miles. The measurements are converted into radio signals that are broadcast back to earth. Eventually the balloon bursts in the rarefied air of the upper atmosphere and the instruments are parachuted back to earth.

The use of airplanes equipped with weather instruments for reconnaissance into the atmosphere, including flights into dangerous hurricanes, has given us vital information that could not be obtained in any other way.

Radar, originally used as an important instrument of navigation by ships and planes, was found to be useful as a weather detector. Radar screens are sensitive to raindrops, snowflakes, and layers of air of contrasting temperature or moisture content. Radar has been used suc-

A radiosonde is about to be released at sea. It will carry aloft a package of instruments that measure and radio back the temperature, humidity, and pressure at different levels of altitude to the ship. Unlike the land-launched radiosonde the instruments are not retrieved. (*Courtesy of ESSA.*)

cessfully as a rain and storm detection and tracking instrument, showing the presence of atmospheric disturbances hundreds of miles away. We shall see later how it has been used by the National Weather Service for this purpose.

Meteorological rockets are now used to extend our observations of the atmosphere above the current limits of balloons, which carry instruments only up to a height of 20 miles.

The four Rs have extended the "vision" of meteorologists over a greater area of the earth's surface and up into different levels of the earth's atmosphere. Such coverage is essential because *the whole atmosphere is a single closely interacting mass of air.* Disturbances arising in one part may affect distant regions. Worldwide data are needed for long-range forecasts, even for a local region. But the majority of the conventional weather stations, even those employing the four Rs, are located in the temperate-zone land areas of North America, Europe, and Eastern Asia. Meteorological, or weather satellites, on the other hand, fly in orbits that provide coverage of the entire globe.

On April 1, 1960, TIROS I, a meteorological satellite bearing two television cameras, was launched into orbit (TIROS = Television and Infrared Observational Satellite). By June of the same year its cameras had taken and broadcast to stations on earth about 20,000 pictures of entire cloud systems in great detail. TIROS II and TIROS III, which followed, had notable careers. One of the historic achievements of TIROS III was the spotting of Hurricane Esther on September 10, 1961, *before it was detected by any other means.*

Through the beginning of 1967 ten of the TIROS satellites had been sent up; at that time TIROS IV was still in active operation, having sent back almost a half-million photographs. A second generation of weather satellites, named Nimbus, with more sensitive instruments, was added to the array of weather stations in the sky.

The National Weather Service, now a division of the National Oceanic and Atmospheric Administration, has developed its own series of weather satellites, using cameras and other instruments which were tested and developed in the TIROS program. ESSA I, launched on February 2, 1966, was the first in this series. ESSA (Environmental Survey Satellite) travels in an orbit that passes over both the north and south polar regions. As the satellite moves along in its orbit the earth rotates below it; in one day ESSA photographs the entire earth and sends its pictures to stations on its surface.

A satellite photograph of Hurricane Ginger off the coast of the Carolines. In an attempt to disperse the storm's energy research planes of Project Stormfury dropped silver iodide into the hurricane. The results were not conclusive. (*Courtesy of NASA.*)

It is now possible to determine the vertical temperature profile in the atmosphere below by using meteorological satellites to measure the infrared radiation (heat waves) emitted by the earth into the atmosphere. By means of such radiometric soundings meteorologists are now able to monitor continuously the three-dimensional structure of the atmosphere over almost the entire globe.

WATER IN MANY FORMS

Fog, clouds, dew, rain, frost, snow, sleet, and hail are the visible forms that water assumes. Water disappears from view when its molecules scatter into the air to become water vapor. When we "see" our breath on a cold day we are viewing the result of the transformation of invisible water vapor in the air from our lungs into a visible form: the molecules of water vapor in the exhaled air cluster together and condense into a small visible cloud. This example also reminds us that for water vapor to condense the air containing it must be cooled sufficiently.

Dew and Frost

Eyeglass wearers sometimes have the experience of entering a warm room after being outside on a cool day and having a film of moisture form on their lenses. This occurs because the chilled surface of the glasses cools the surrounding air below its dewpoint; consequently the vapor in the air condenses on the glasses. Dew forms in a similar way outdoors. Dew is caused when objects at or near the earth's surface become cooler than the surrounding air. Grass, leaves, automobiles, and outdoor furniture, for example, lose their heat more rapidly at night than does the air around them. If the air contains considerable moisture, these objects may cool the air to its dew point, causing the water vapor to condense on them. A clear night favors dew formation because then the earth rapidly radiates its day-stored heat into the atmosphere. (Clouds act as blankets at night to prevent the loss of heat.) A night with little or no wind also helps dew formation, because winds stir up the atmosphere so that no one part of it is cooled sufficiently to permit condensation of water vapor by cold surfaces.

(*See* p. 229.)

Frost is formed in the same manner as dew except that the temperature of the objects upon which condensation occurs is below the freezing point, that is, below 32° F. The water vapor changes *directly* into feathery ice crystals. Frost is *not* frozen dew.

Fog

Almost everyone has walked in a fog. Fogs are clouds touching the ground. It is composed of small droplets of water, about $\frac{1}{1000}$ inch in diameter, which have condensed from water vapor, but which because of their small size remain suspended in the air (*see* the material on clouds which follows for method of droplet formation).

Ground fogs are caused by rapid cooling of the air near the earth's surface at night when the sun goes down. The conditions essential for this kind of fog are similar to those for dew formation, except that light winds, instead of a dead calm, help in mixing the cold air near the ground with air a short distance above. Ground fogs are often found in valleys, where cold, heavy air accumulates at night and in the early morning. When the sun warms the air the fog disappears. This occurs because warm air can hold more moisture, and the fog droplets evaporate into it.

Advection fogs result when the warm, moist air from one region moves horizontally over a cool surface. Fogs like this are formed off Newfoundland, where the warm moist air over the Gulf Stream blows over the cold Labrador Current. Summer fogs occur off California, when warm ocean air flows over cold coastal waters.

There are many other kinds of fog which we will not consider here, including frontal, orographic, and evaporation fogs.

Clouds

The clouds aloft, like the fog near the ground, are formed by condensation. We have to add only that each of the tiny droplets in a

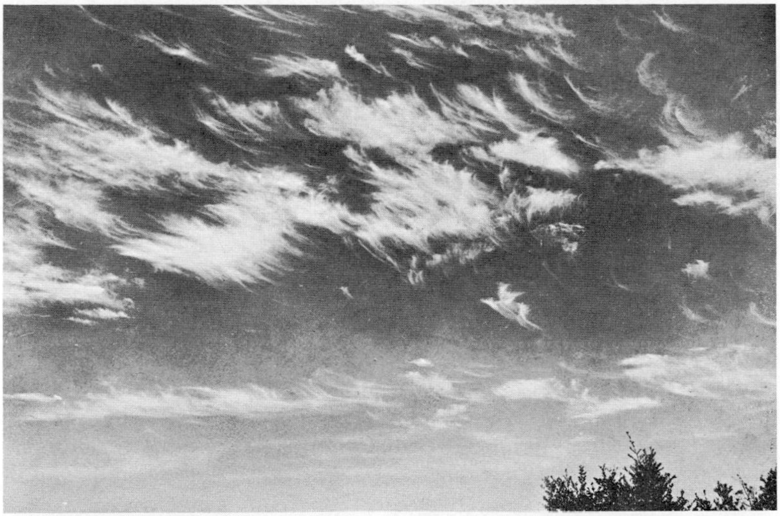

Cirrus clouds are high clouds, usually more than five miles above the earth. They are composed of ice crystals. (*Courtesy of U.S. Weather Bureau, F. Ellerman.*)

Cumulus clouds of this kind usually come with fair weather. (*Courtesy of U.S. Weather Bureau, T. Floreen.*)

Stratus clouds are generally thin uniform clouds that give the whole sky a gray tone. (*Courtesy of Standard Oil of New Jersey.*)

cloud forms around a very small particle (so, too, do fog droplets). Such particles must be *hygroscopic,* that is, able to absorb moisture. Salt spray from the ocean is one source of these particles, known as *condensation nuclei.* Microscopic particles from the smoke of fires, from explosive volcanoes, and from meteoroids also supply large numbers of condensation nuclei to the atmosphere.

Since ancient times many systems have been devised for identifying cloud types. Today, in accordance with an international meteorological agreement, all clouds are classified according to two factors: form and height. Let us consider form first. Three basic cloud forms are recognized—*cirrus, cumulus,* and *stratus.* These are shown in the photographs on p. 235.

Cirrus, meaning "curl," are the most delicate. These clouds, sometimes called "mare's tails," are white, feathery, and filmy. They do not obscure the sun very much. Cirrus clouds are the highest of all clouds, averaging 6 miles in altitude. They are composed of ice crystals.

Cumulus, meaning "heap," are dense clouds that build up to huge heaps. They have flat bases, are white and billowy above, and cast shadows on the earth. Cumulus clouds are formed in rising currents of air and are the characteristic clouds seen on fair days.

Stratus, meaning "layer," refer to clouds that cover the whole sky, obscuring the sun. They give us smooth gray skies, and are composed of water droplets in summer and ice crystals in winter. A fog is a stratus cloud on the ground.

The word "nimbus" when attached to a cloud name refers to precipitation. Thus nimbostratus clouds are usually accompanied by rain or snow; cumulonimbus are towering cumulus clouds, called thunderhead clouds, which frequently are associated with thunderstorms.

These basic cloud *forms*—cirrus, cumulus, and stratus—are further subdivided by a classification system that takes *altitude* into account. This system includes high, middle, and low clouds, and those with vertical development.

Rain

The droplets of moisture that make up most clouds are so small (only a few $\frac{10}{1000}$ of an inch) that they remain suspended in the air, kept up by updrafts within the cloud. They are also prevented from falling because of the resistance that the millions of air molecules offer them. (Note how slowly feathers fall.) And, even if these small cloud drops did fall, they would evaporate into water vapor before reaching the ground.

Then how do raindrops form? Meteorologists believe that two processes account for the growth of cloud drops to raindrop size: *coalescence* and an *ice-crystal process.* First consider coalescence. Some of the larger droplets in a cloud bump into smaller ones as they fall through a cloud. The larger drops are called *collectors,* because as they fall they capture smaller ones. The collectors may become so large that they break up. Some of the broken drops fall as rain. Some of them act as collectors, which again grow and produce more raindrops.

But how do the original large droplets form? Some scientists believe that the collector droplets are formed by the condensation of water vapor on *large* condensation nuclei—on large salt particles, for example. When cloud droplets grow in size and become heavy enough, they fall through the atmosphere as rain.

The second process occurs when ice crystals appear in a cloud composed of supercooled liquid water (liquid water at a temperature below 32° F.). In this case the water vapor in the cloud condenses more rapidly on the ice than on the liquid droplets, and the ice crystals grow into snowflakes. If the snowflakes fall through air which is above the freezing point they may melt into raindrops.

Snow

It is often possible for the lower portion of a single cloud to consist of water droplets and the upper portion of snowflakes. In the snowflake portion the temperature is below freezing, so that the water vapor there condenses directly into ice crystals. As more water vapor is deposited on the ice crystals they grow sufficiently large to fall as snow. (Snow is *not* frozen rain.) When snow falls, its beautiful six-sided crystals may come down separately or they may coalesce into large fleecy clots.

Sleet

Sleet is rain that freezes as it falls. If raindrops that were formed in a relatively warm layer of air pass through a layer with freezing temperatures they freeze into small, hard ice pellets.

Glaze

Glaze is formed when rain falls on trees, streets, and other objects that are below freezing temperatures. The rain freezes into a coating of ice that sometimes becomes so heavy on tree branches and telephone and telegraph wires that it causes them to break.

Hail

Hail sometimes occurs during thunderstorms and can be produced only if there are strong currents of rising air. Hail begins as a kernel of ice or packed snow which is carried aloft by vertical air currents through a part of a thundercloud containing supercooled water. The supercooled cloud water freezes onto the hail kernel, and the hailstone begins to grow. The hailstone may fall and be swept up again. More water freezes on the hailstone, and it therefore grows larger. This process may be repeated a number of times, so that it is possible for hailstones to be as large as hen's eggs. They consist of a number of concentric layers that can easily be distinguished if the stones are cut in two. When they are so large that they can no longer be lifted by air currents they fall to earth.

The largest hailstone recorded in the United States weighed $1\frac{2}{3}$ pounds. The annual damage to crops and property from hail in the United States is $300 million.

WIND

The basic cause of winds, as we have seen, is the unequal heating of the earth by the sun. Differences in heat create differences in pressure; it is pressure differences that make winds blow.

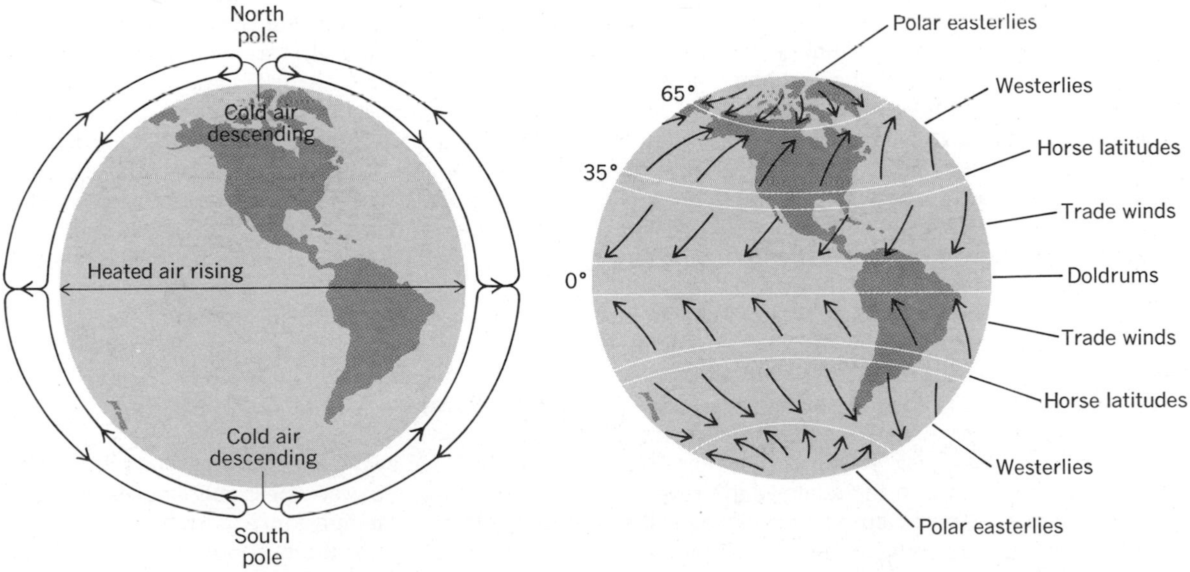

The diagram (*left*) shows how air would circulate over the surface of the earth if the earth did not spin on its axis. The earth's rotation deflects winds to produce the wind systems shown in the diagram (*right*). The added influence of land and water masses is not shown.

Because the earth is hottest at the equator and coolest at the poles a global wind circulation is set up, with cold air moving on the surface toward the equator and warm air moving aloft toward the poles, as shown on the left of the diagram.

Wind Belts

But the wind picture is not quite as simple as this. If it were, we would have, in the Northern Hemisphere, surface winds sweeping from the north to the south and winds aloft moving in the opposite direction. In the Southern Hemisphere the reverse would be true. Thus all winds would be either north or south winds. The large-scale, sun-powered wind system just described is steered in different directions by the rotation of the earth. Without describing the complex mechanism involved, we can say that the result of the earth's rotation is to deflect winds to the east and the west and to produce the wind belts shown in the diagram on p. 237.

Land, Water, and Wind

Thus far we have seen that global or planetary winds arise from the unequal heating of the earth and are then steered into belts. This wind picture could apply to any planet that is heated at the equator, rotates like the earth, and has an atmosphere. Earth's complete wind picture is determined by its special geography—by its land masses and bodies of water. Land and water affect wind because they do not heat up or cool off at the same rate. On pp. 223–4 we saw how land and sea breezes are produced by the differences in heating and cooling of day and night. Winds are also generated by seasonal variations. In the winter continents are colder than nearby oceans. Cold, heavy air sweeps from the continent over the ocean. In the summer the reverse is true, with ocean-cooled air blowing over the continent. Such seasonal tendencies change the prevailing winds to produce what is termed a *monsoon* circulation.

Mountain and valley winds are another example of how geography produces minor terrestrial winds. During the day the exposed slopes of the mountains absorb the sun's energy faster than the valleys do. Warmed air blows up the slopes to make a gentle *valley breeze.* At night the slopes cool off more rapidly than the valleys. The heavy cooled air drains down from the cold slopes to the valleys, causing a *mountain breeze.*

The Jet Streams

For many years we have known of belts of high-speed winds in the upper troposphere, but only in recent years have meteorologists paid attention to them. During World War II American pilots flying above 20,000 feet encountered unbelievably strong west headwinds, sometimes over 200 miles per hour. As airplane flight reached these altitudes and wind observations at higher levels were improved, the existence of these high-speed winds became more and more apparent. These winds became known as the *jet stream.*

The jet stream has been likened to a narrow current flowing around the earth. Two jet streams have been found in the Northern Hemisphere, one near the pole and one over the middle latitudes; apparently there are two similar ones below the equator. The jet streams change their shape to form *waves* that encircle the earth. Eventually the waves break loose from the main stream, forming pockets of cold air in the south and warm air in the north. The exact relation of jet streams and their waves to world weather patterns and to long-range forecasting is still under investigation. The charting of jet streams is of vital concern to airlines.

AIR MASSES

If you have ever gone into a cool, dank cellar on a hot day you were probably impressed by the contrast in temperature and humidity between the cellar and the outdoor air. In entering the cellar you moved from one weather to another, from one kind of air to another.

The air in the cellar had acquired its odor,

dampness, and temperature because it had stagnated there and taken on the qualities imposed by its surroundings. Something like this happens on a global scale.

When a large portion of the atmosphere comes to rest or moves slowly over land or sea areas the air will tend to become similar in temperature and moisture to the underlying surface. If the surface is warm the air above it will be warmed. If the surface is cold the air above it will be cooled. If the surface is moist the air above it will become moist; if the surface is dry the air will lose moisture. A large body of air that takes its character from the surface beneath it is called an *air mass.* An air mass may cover hundreds of thousands of square miles and be miles high, but the temperature and humidity at any particular level is fairly uniform.

The place where an air mass originates is called a *source region.* There are two general source regions—the tropics and the snow- or ice-covered polar areas—for it is in these regions that huge masses of air stagnate long enough to acquire their identifying characteristics. After remaining for some time over the area where they form, air masses eventually begin to move, the cold ones drifting toward the equator and the warm ones toward the poles.

Air masses retain their identity and characteristics even when they move far from their source regions. Only slowly and gradually are air masses modified by the new surface conditions that they encounter.

The analysis of air masses has been made possible by the extensive use of radiosonde and by the establishment of weather-observation stations over wide areas of the earth, even over the frozen arctic. Thus the meteorologist's view has expanded vertically and horizontally.

Fronts

If the air masses are regarded as armies then their battleground is the United States and other areas located in the temperate zones of the world. For it is in these zones that there is a meeting of warm and cold air masses; it is here that one air mass advances over the earth, pushing the other back; it is here that the *fronts,* a word borrowed by the meteorologists from the military, extend for hundreds and sometimes thousands of miles and mark the violent clashes of opposing air masses. Almost anywhere in the United States you are in territory occupied by a warm or cool mass of air. The chances are that the present temperature will not last very long. Soon the advancing opposing army of air will make itself known by clouds, thunder, lightning, and other special effects. When the front passes, you are again in occupied territory—occupied by the new "victorious" air mass. In the heat of the "battle" some mixing of opposing masses does occur; the front lines that originally may have been straight may be thrown into waves, reflecting local advances of warm air here and cold air elsewhere. But what is most remarkable during the clash is that, by and large, each air mass retains its own identity, its own distinguishing banners of temperature and humidity.

The diagrams on pp. 240–1 depict some of the events occurring along a *warm front* and *cold front,* respectively. Each shows a vertical section of the atmosphere measuring 600 miles, from St. Louis to Pittsburgh, and extending 5 or 6 miles upward from the surface of the earth.

Let us examine the warm front first. Warm air is on the march, pushing against the cold air. Because it is lighter, it rides up the cold air mass. You might think of the boundary as a kind of hill, not as steep as depicted in the picture, but one up which the warm air is traveling. As the warm air moves upward it is cooled; the moisture in it condenses, resulting in cloud formation and the precipitation of rain. The first part of the diagram will be better understood if one keeps *two* kinds of motion in mind: (1) *Warm air is moving up the slope,* and (2) *the whole picture is sliding eastward over the map.*

Consider a viewer in Pittsburgh. Within the next 24 to 48 hours he may expect the weather picture to slide over him, because St. Louis's weather today is Pittsburgh's tomorrow. At present, he sees high, wispy, cirrus clouds, and because he is weatherwise he knows that this often is the harbinger of a warm front with its attendant weather. As the hours go by the eastward-moving cirrus clouds are replaced by lower and lower clouds of the stratus type. When the heavy, low nimbostratus clouds pass overhead rain falls steadily. Finally, the front that was originally near St. Louis passes Pittsburgh. A new mass of air is now over the city, with higher temperature and higher humidity. The sky clears slowly; the army of warm air is "occupying" the city.

The part of the diagram on p. 241 shows the same area as before, but with a cold front in evidence. This time it is the cold air that is advancing toward Pittsburgh. The cold front differs in several respects from a warm front. The slope of the hill or front is steeper. The front moves more rapidly. The weather phenomena over a cold front are more dramatic, more sudden, more violent. The warm air is lifted above the advancing cold air to form towering *cumulonimbus* clouds, or thunderclouds. Thunderstorms occur along the front.

(*See* pp. 244–5.)

A weather observer in Pittsburgh would not be given as much advance notice by the clouds as he would in the case of a warm front. High cumulus clouds appear on the horizon in the direction of Columbus, Ohio. As the front nears, rain falls with increasing intensity. As the front passes, there is often a fairly rapid clearing with a falling of temperature and humidity. A cold air mass now occupies Pittsburgh.

It is apparent that air-mass and air-front analysis, developed after World War I, are essential to an understanding of weather. *Highs* and *lows,* however, have been well known for many years as an important ingredient of the weather picture.

HIGHS AND LOWS

In the daily weather report on radio and television, and in weather maps printed in newspapers, prominence is given to the highs and lows across the country. Just what is their significance?

A high refers to an area of high air pressure and a low to an area of low air pressure. In general, a high-pressure area is characterized by clear, dry weather, whereas a low brings with it a host of weather changes, mostly bad.

Low-pressure areas, or lows, and also called *cyclones* by meteorologists. Cyclones should not be confused with tornadoes, which will be described later. A low may cover an area hundreds or thousands of miles in diameter. In a low the lowest pressure is in the center, with pressure increasing away from the center. Winds blow in a counterclockwise motion around a low in the Northern Hemisphere and veer toward the center.

(*Left*) This is a vertical section through a warm front and the air masses associated with it, which are described in the text. A viewer in Pittsburgh would first be made aware of the approaching warm front by high cirrus clouds, followed by lower and lower clouds as the weather "picture"

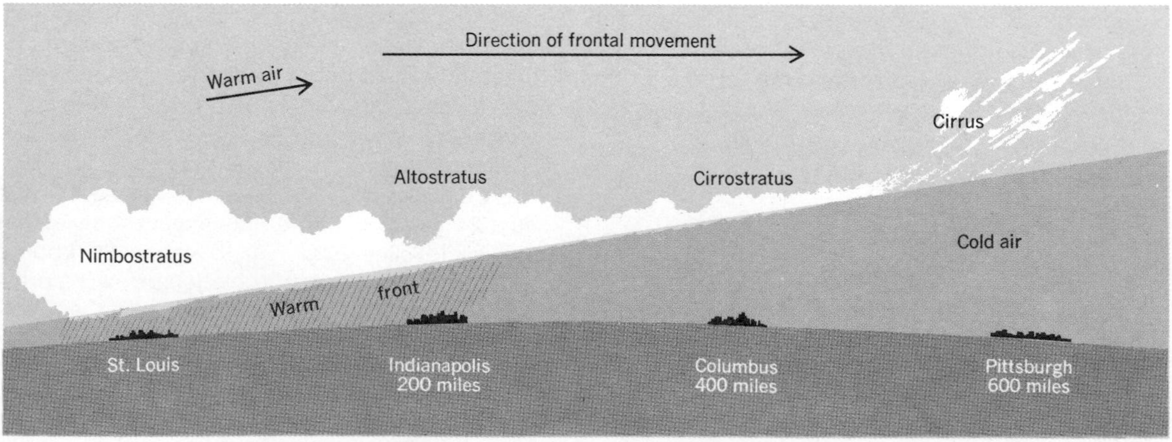

In high-pressure areas, called *anticyclones,* the opposite conditions obtain: Highest pressures are at the center, and winds blow clockwise and outward from the center in the Northern Hemisphere. (In the Southern Hemisphere the winds blow in the opposite direction: clockwise around lows, counterclockwise around highs.)

Cyclones, or lows, generally move southeastward and northeastward across the country with the rest of the weather picture. They usually end their visit in the United States somewhere in New England, and then blow out to sea. Lows move at the rate of about 500 miles per day in summer and 700 miles per day in winter.

The origin of many cyclones in temperate zones has been determined to be related to a development on the front between warm and cold air masses. Such lows occur at those places along the front where a kink or wave appears, as we shall see later when we study weather maps.

Lows, being notorious for their stormy weather, attract most of the attention of the public, while highs are neglected. Highs generally bring good weather. One reason for this is that the air in highs is usually descending, which means that it is being warmed. Because warm air can hold more moisture than cold air (without showing it), this is a factor in making the air in highs dry and clear. Highs are often associated with heavy, cold, continental air masses. Such highs bring intense cold waves to the United States. Bad weather may occur at the cold fronts of these high-pressure areas, but good weather is soon to follow as the cold, high-pressure air mass takes hold. Anticyclones move eastward and southeastward across the country.

HURRICANES

A cyclone arising in the tropics may develop into a full-fledged *hurricane,* the most dangerous and the most destructive of all storms. Like its less harmful cousin, the cyclone or low, a hurricane is a low-pressure area, but its pressure is much lower. The winds spiral counterclockwise toward the center, in the Northern Hemisphere, at furious velocities often exceeding 100 miles per hour. Rain falls at a heavy rate. The area covered by a hurricane averages only 200 to 400 miles in diameter, as contrasted with the 1,000-mile diameter of a typical cyclonic low. In addition, hurricanes have a special feature of their own: a calm, clear, central "eye" about 15 miles in diameter.

The destructiveness of most hurricanes is due principally to the mountainous waves

moves eastward. Finally the front passes, and Pittsburgh is in a warm air mass. (*Right*) Cold fronts are steeper than warm fronts and move faster. The characteristic towering cumulonimbus clouds arrive rather suddenly. The weather changes abruptly when the cold front arrives.

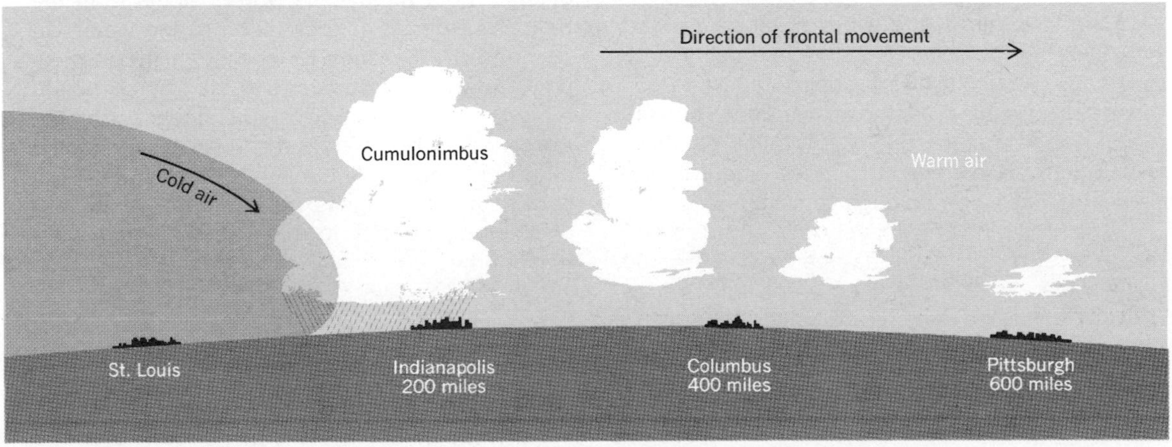

1962 hurricane damage on Fire Island off Long Island, New York, when the angry Atlantic undermined these homes. (*Courtesy of National Oceanic and Atmospheric Administration.*)

whipped up by these tropical storms, sinking and grounding ships, causing high seas that inundate low coastal areas, wiping out farms and towns.

The strength of the winds must be at least 74 miles per hour for a storm to qualify as a hurricane. Maximum wind speeds of 75 to 150 miles per hour are common in hurricanes striking a coast, and speeds up to 200 miles per hour have occurred in some hurricanes, according to estimates based on damage to structures.

The area of the most destructive winds along the path of a hurricane may be from 30 to 100 miles wide. As the storm develops and moves forward it may traverse a path several thousand miles long from its birthplace in the Caribbean or tropical Atlantic until it blows itself out over the continent or in the North Atlantic. (In the western Pacific, where they are more frequent and often larger and more violent, these intense tropical storms are called *typhoons.*)

While the winds of the hurricane are blowing at great speed around the center the entire storm system may move forward very slowly, and sometimes even remain stationary for a short time. In the tropics the forward speed of the entire hurricane is about 15 miles per hour; as it moves away from the tropics the speed may reach 50 miles per hour.

Hurricane Power

The power of a hurricane has been estimated to be the equivalent of several thousand atomic bombs per second! How does it develop this power? The answer lies in the three fundamental weather factors that we stressed earlier in the chapter: heat, water, and air.

Heat poured down by the sun, day after day, warming tropical waters and the air above them, is the basic source of the power. The resulting evaporation of water from the oceans into the atmosphere is a process that traps and stores much of this heat. It takes a great deal of heat to change water into water vapor. This energy is not lost but is carried off by the water vapor in a latent or hidden form. The energy is released as heat again when the water vapor condenses into clouds. The enormous heat liberated stirs up the characteristic fierce winds of hurricanes.

A hurricane, then, may be thought of as a gigantic heat engine. Its power stems from the heat released by condensation of the water vapor, and it unleashes its energy in the form of powerful winds. Conditions in the tropics, where the strong sun beats over the ocean, promote the growth of hurricanes. The whole story of how a hurricane forms under these conditions is not known; meteorologists have offered a number of different theories to explain this violent phenomenon.

Warning Service

One of the important functions of the National Weather Service is the Hurricane Warning

The principle of radar as it pertains to weather surveillance is shown here. Radio waves (large arrows) are emitted from the rotating radar antenna (1). A portion of this radio energy is reflected back (small arrows) from rain, snow, or hail particles in the storm (2). The waves are received by the antenna and sent to a radarscope (3). The storm areas appear as bright spots on a dark background, and their direction and distance from the station can be read on the radarscope (4).

Service, which was set up in 1935. In recent years notable improvements in tracking and forecasting the movements of hurricanes have resulted from the use of radar observations at coastal stations, from the receipt of additional weather reports from reconnaissance aircraft, from the more complete data obtained by radiosonde from heights up to 20 miles above the earth's surface, and from the "eyes" of weather satellites in space.

In 1956 the Weather Service set up a radar network that will eventually blanket the United States, detecting and tracking not only hurricanes but also tornadoes and other severe storms. Radio signals sent out by radar bounce off raindrops and are reflected back to the sets, where they are electronically converted to the picture seen on the radar screen. The eye of hurricane Carla (September 1961) first appeared on the Weather Service's radarscope at Galveston, Texas, when it was located over the Gulf of Mexico, 250 miles away. Carla was then tracked by radar for the next 46 hours.

TORNADOES

A tornado is a violent local storm with upward-spiraling winds of tremendous speed. Tornadoes are often mistakenly called cyclones; the word cyclone, however, refers to any center of low pressure, whereas a tornado is the most violent storm known to man. Tornadoes are much smaller in area than hurricanes, averaging only about 1,200 feet, or $\frac{1}{5}$ mile, in diameter. The average distance traveled by a tornado is about 16 miles.

A tornado is recognized by its rotating, funnel-shaped cloud, extending toward the earth from the base of a thundercloud and colored from gray to black with the dust and debris that have been forced into it. All tornadoes have a common characteristic: the rapidly rotating winds that cause them to spin like a top. When it is near, a tornado usually sounds like the roaring of hundreds of airplanes.

The destructiveness of tornadoes is due in part to their violent winds, which have been estimated to exceed 250 miles per hour. The maximum speeds of the internal winds of a tornado have never been measured directly, because no anemometer has yet survived the test. Dry straws have been driven through telephone poles from the impact of tornado winds.

The devastation caused by a tornado is also due to the extremely low pressure of the whirling column of air, which makes it behave like a giant vacuum cleaner suspended from the sky, "sucking" in trees, houses, cars, animals, and people! Pressure as low as $25\frac{1}{2}$ inches has been recorded (about 30 inches is normal). The low pressure that suddenly develops outside buildings may cause them to explode from the normal pressure inside.

Tornadoes move in erratic paths at speeds averaging 25 to 40 miles per hour. Most move from the southwest to the northeast. Tornadoes, however, have been known to come from any direction, even stopping their forward movements, turning, and looping their paths.

We are not sure exactly how tornadoes develop, but we do know some of the accompanying circumstances. Ordinarily, cold air, being relatively heavy, moves under warm air, as we saw in the description of fronts. Under special conditions, however, a layer of dry, cold air may be thrust over a mass of moist, warm air. Warm air forces its way up through the cold cap in corkscrew fashion. Cold and warm air mix, aided by strong winds aloft. A vortex is formed around a low-pressure center and thus becomes a tornado.

It is not possible to predict the exact spot where a tornado will develop, but the National Weather Service is able to prepare a forecast that alerts people to the possibility of tornado activity in an area. The principal tornado forecasts are made in the Weather Service's Severe Local Storm Forecast Center at Kansas City, Missouri.

When a tornado passes over a body of water, a *waterspout* may result. The lower portion of the funnel cloud is made of spray, instead of the dust and debris found in a tornado over land. Actually there is very little water in a typical "spout." Most of it is fine mist or spray, with perhaps a few feet of water at its base.

THUNDERSTORMS

Thunderstorms are weather "factories." Pilots flying into them can expect to see a great many weather "products," including lightning and thunder, updrafts and downdrafts, heavy rain, snow, and hail, as well as ice formation on the wings of the plane. It is obvious that for pilots thunderstorms represent a severe and dangerous form of atmospheric activity.

Thunderstorms have their beginning in the rising of a large mass of warm, moist air to higher levels where it becomes cooler. As it cools, the water vapor in it condenses to form towering thunderclouds. This hoisting up of air may occur, as we have seen on page 241, when an advancing cold front wedges itself under a warm, moist mass of air. An almost continuous line of thunderstorms may form along the front, which becomes known as a *squall line.*

A second cause of thunderstorm formation arises from the topography of the land. Moist air blowing up the slopes of hills and mountains helps form cumulus and cumulonimbus clouds as it is chilled at higher levels.

Third, the local heating of the ground and the moist air above it on a warm, sunny day gives rise to the typical summer thunderstorm.

Lightning and Thunder

When Benjamin Franklin sent a kite sailing in a thunderstorm he demonstrated for the first time that lightning was electricity. The flash that ran down the string of the kite in this dangerous experiment behaved like man-made electricity. We shall consider this particular type of electricity, called static electricity, in Chapter 19A. For the moment it will do to recall some of our common experiences with static electricity. When we scuff our feet on a carpet and touch a metallic object, such as a doorknob, a spark jumps from our finger to the object. This is an electric spark, small but effective enough for us to feel it. When we comb our hair we hear a crackling sound as electric sparks jump. When we tear a piece of adhesive tape apart in the dark we can see sparks. In each case a charge of electricity has been built up on a surface by rubbing or tearing; the electricity is then discharged in the form of a spark that jumps through the air.

The production of high electric charges in thunderstorms is a complex process, not fully understood, in which water droplets in a cloud become electrically charged. Eventually, the thundercloud builds up enough electricity to cause a discharge. We see this as a flash of lightning. This discharge may take place within the cloud, between one cloud and another, or between the cloud and the earth.

As the lightning leaps through the air it heats it and causes it to expand suddenly. This starts a tremendous sound wave, which reaches our ears as thunder. Why do we hear thunder after we see lightning? Light travels so rapidly, about 186,000 miles per second, that we see the flash practically as it occurs. Sound, on the other hand, travels relatively slowly, moving 1 mile in 5 seconds. It is possible to estimate the distance between yourself and a lightning bolt by counting the number of seconds between the flash and the thunder. Dividing this by 5 gives the answer in miles. For example, if you count 10 seconds between the flash and the rumble of thunder, the distance of that particular bolt is 2 miles.

A building of steel and concrete is practically lightning-proof, because the electricity follows the steel down into the ground. The Empire State Building in New York City has been struck hundreds of times without harm to anyone.

There is very little danger of being struck by lightning if one observes the following:

Inside a house stay away from the chimney, because it is the tallest part of a house and the most likely to be struck. Stay clear of attics, doors, and windows. Keep out of a bathtub or shower. There is little chance of being hurt by lightning in large buildings or modern homes.

Outdoors avoid high ground. Lie down; stay away from trees, poles, and other tall objects. If you must stand under a tree choose a short one and one that is in a group of trees rather than a high or isolated tree. Caves and holes are relatively safe. Stay away from metal fences, pipes, and wires.

Keep off golf courses and open beaches. Avoid, if possible, being in or on the water. If you are inside a car, bus, or train stay there.

So-called "sheet" lightning, or "heat" lightning, consists simply of flashes from distant thunderclouds. Sheet lightning occurs when the electrical discharge is from cloud to cloud. The flashes are hidden, and only a large lighted area is seen. "Heat" lightning is the flash of ordinary lightning so far away that thunder is not heard.

THE WEATHER MAP

As interest in weather conditions grows, more newspapers and telecasts are using a map as a means of picturing the weather. On page 246 is a typical newspaper weather map, depicting conditions prevailing at 7:00 P.M. Eastern Standard Time on March 20, 1973.

Before the invention of the telegraph such a map would have been impossible, for it is based on *simultaneous reports* from around the country. Indeed, the telegraph played an important role in the beginning of a weather service. After the first telegraph lines were set up in 1844 the operators, on opening their lines in the morning, sent messages describing the weather in their parts of the country. This practice showed that it would be practical to gather reports of developing storms and to warn of their approach. In 1870 Congress set up a national weather service to issue storm warnings and to keep records of the climate. As time went on the Weather Bureau, as it became known in 1890 (now the National Weather Service), expanded its services to include flood warnings and to provide various kinds of weather information for farmers, fruit growers, ranchers, and foresters. With the development of aviation, demands for detailed weather data increased, and improved services were made available.

(*See* pp. 261–2.)

How is a typical weather map made? Weather observations of the temperature, air pressure, wind, and other conditions are received every six hours by the National Weather Service's National Meteorological Center at Suitland, Maryland, from thousands of weather stations all over the world, including ships at sea among which are several stationary "weather ships" in the Atlantic and Pacific oceans. Surface observations are made every hour at many stations, and upper air observations every twelve hours. These reports are supplemented by observations from the military and other agencies of the government, as well as from aviation services and merchant vessels of all nations. All the national weather services of the world, including our Weather Service, freely exchange information through standard message forms agreed on by the World Meteorological Orga-

This map, prepared by the National Weather Service, presents a comprehensive picture of weather all over the country. It is discussed in detail in the text. (©*1973 by The New York Times Company. Reprinted by permission.*)

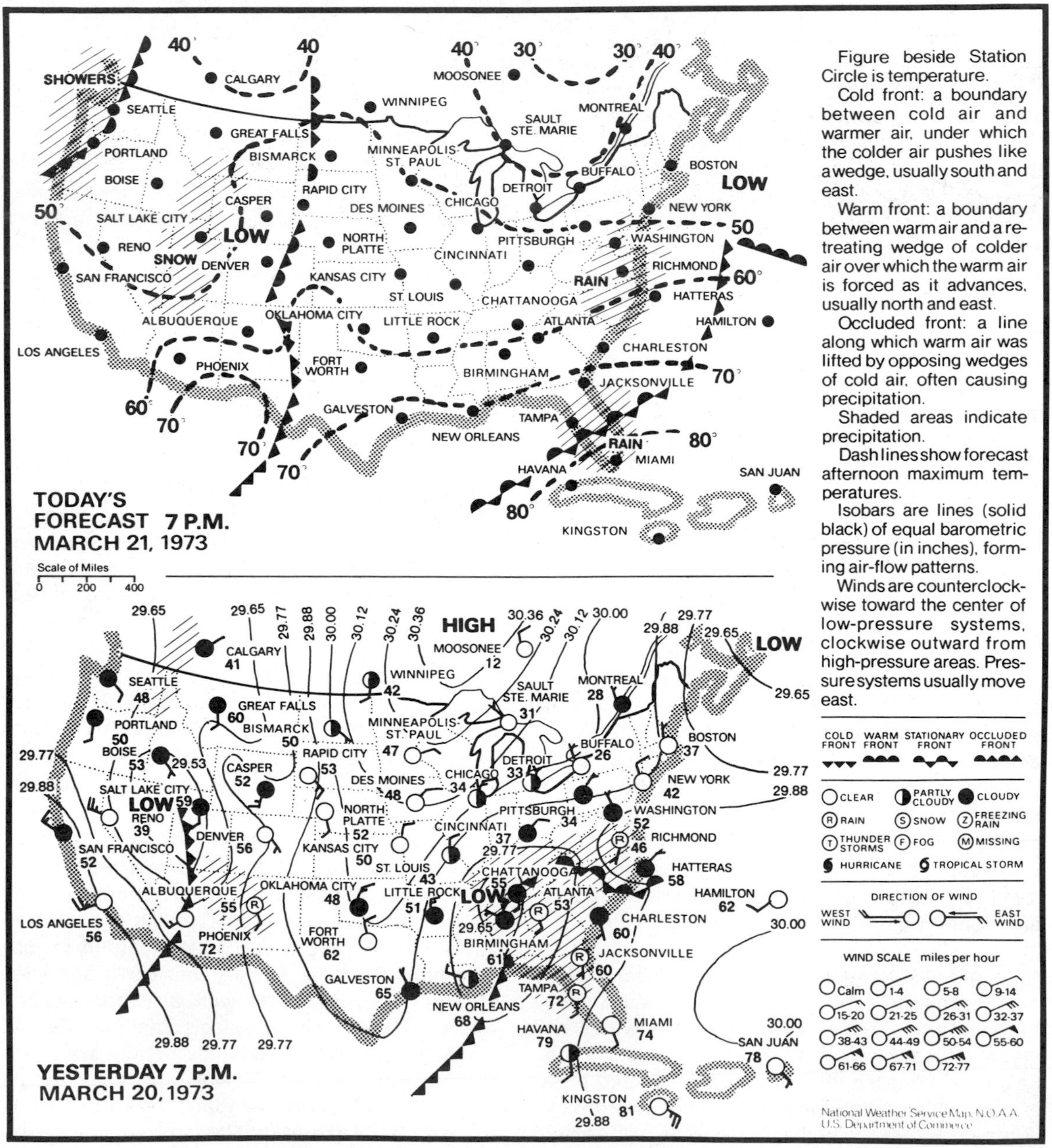

nization, a specialized agency of the United Nations.

At the Weather Service's Center a complete weather map is drawn up, which is then transmitted by a facsimile machine to all the forecast centers in the country, in much the same way that wirephoto pictures are sent by newspapers.

To enable the forecaster to make his analysis and predictions, information is needed about weather conditions in the atmosphere to a height of several miles above the earth's surface. We have discussed how radar, airplane reconnaissance, and radiosondes carried up by balloons help gather upper-air data. From these data upper-level weather maps are prepared.

The weather map shown here is a simplified version of the map drawn by the Weather Service. Examine it carefully to see what it tells about general weather conditions, wind, temperature, precipitation, pressure, and fronts across the country. The following questions may be helpful when using the map. With respect to the city closest to you: What was the general weather condition at 7:00 P.M. on March 20, 1973? What was the direction of the wind? What was the strength of the wind? What was the temperature? What was the air pressure? What is the *forecast* for the maximum afternoon temperature for March 21, 1973? With respect to the United States: What weather, if any, appears to be associated with any high-pressure areas? Low-pressure areas? Cold fronts? Warm fronts? What is the direction of winds around lows? Around highs? Comparing today's forecast with yesterday's weather: In what direction does the weather "picture" seem to move? What do *you* forecast for tomorrow?

FORECASTING WEATHER

"Probability of precipitation 10 percent today, 50 percent tonight, and 20 percent tomorrow."

This kind of statement has been a part of Weather Service forecasts since 1966. The probability forecast represents an honest expression of the forecaster's fallibility. In the past the Service had to make a categorical forecast—rain or no rain—even though there were doubts in the forecaster's mind about the chances of precipitation actually occurring. With the probability forecast, decision-making about taking or not taking a raincoat rests with the public.

(*See* pp. 261–4.)

Throughout this chapter we have indicated some of the ways in which the weather may be predicted. In general, the weatherman looks backward to study the tendencies of weather of past days and hours and then tries to project into the future. Weather maps are an important aid in summarizing this information, and may be compared to the "chart" of a patient's progess that the doctor studies.

The Weather Service is aided in making forecasts by the knowledge that the weather pattern shown on the map moves eastward across the country at the rate of about 500 miles per day in summer and 700 miles per day in winter. Hence the saying "Chicago's weather today is New York's tomorrow." The Weather Service is also aided by its knowledge of the special tracks that low-pressure areas or cyclones take as they swing across the United States. Lows, starting from the northwest, southwest, and southeast sweep across the country toward New England, bringing with them rain, drizzle, snow, and associated conditions.

THE REVOLUTION IN METEOROLOGY

A revolution in meteorology that is affecting weather forecasting is now in progress. Some of the elements in this revolution may be summarized as follows:

1. The development and refinement of a wide range of measuring and transmitting tools have increased the amount of significant information and the speed at which such information is obtained.
2. Air masses, fronts, highs, and lows, although still important as a part of the fundamental pattern of weather, are being subordinated to data collected on a global basis and at many levels of the atmosphere. These data are treated mathematically in complex computers

which are programed to take into account the many factors that contribute to the determination of the weather.

3. Meteorology is being linked more closely with specialized studies such as those of the oceans, the sun, the Arctic, all the way to atmospheres of other planets and the influence of radiations from outer space.

4. Meteorology is becoming a truly international affair. In the United Nations the cooperative efforts of all nations are demonstrated best in this area. This is natural, because weather flows from land to land without recourse to passports. Weather is part of our global environment, and consequently no true understanding and benefit can come from meteorology without the mutual support and complete cooperation of the nations of the world.

MAN-MADE WEATHER

One of the puzzling questions in meteorology has been: "How does rain form in clouds?" or, to state it more precisely: "Just how do the tiny droplets that make up a cloud join together to form raindrops and snowflakes?" On page 236 we presented the "collector drop" theory and the "ice crystal" theory. The latter theory, originally proposed as far back as 1911, was the basis for an investigation initiated by Nobel Prize-winning Irving Langmuir and Vincent Schaefer, then his assistant, in the General Electric Research Laboratory in 1946. The two scientists were puzzled by the fact that even in clouds with temperatures below freezing snow crystals often did not form. They decided to conduct experiments with such clouds, called supercooled clouds. Schaefer found that if he breathed into a home-freezer compartment he could produce a low-temperature cloud like those found in nature. To his delight he discovered that when he dropped a very cold substance such as dry ice (solid carbon dioxide) into the freezer the vapor cloud changed into millions of shimmering snow crystals. Other substances, provided they were 38° below 0° F. or colder, also caused a fall of snow.

At about the same time Bernard Vonnegut was investigating another technique for making supercooled clouds turn into snow. He found that silver iodide particles could induce the formation of ice crystals in clouds.

Why did dry ice and silver iodide change waterdrop clouds into ice clouds? Previous theory had suggested that when ice crystals form in a supercooled cloud the crystals can grow large enough to fall as snow or rain. Was it possible that supercooled clouds do not always have ice crystals in them? This might be the reason that some clouds pass by without giving any rain. Perhaps ice crystals dropped into such clouds, like seeds, would start the growth of snowflakes or raindrops. Such seeds might grow by collecting water in the cloud into large snowflakes or raindrops, as they did in the laboratory.

In 1946 Schaefer went up in an airplane and scattered crushed dry ice into a cloud. The dry ice formed a line of ice crystals that broadened into a wide channel in the clouds. The same result was obtained later with silver iodide: The part of the supercooled cloud that was seeded had been changed into ice crystals. As a result of all these experiments projects were initiated to test the value of cloud-seeding operations in causing snow and rain and in dissipating unwanted fogs. These studies indicated that precipitation could be increased in local areas by as much as 10 percent where specific favorable conditions prevailed, but that large-scale changes of weather or climate by cloud seeding was still something for the future.

In evaluating rain-making efforts long-range experiments are needed to answer the question: "Would it have rained just as much if we had not seeded the clouds?"

At present various agencies of the federal government are active on a number of fronts of weather modification. These include studies and tests designed to develop the capability to blunt and weaken the thrust of hurricanes, tornadoes, and other severe storms; to increase, lessen, or redistribute precipitation; to suppress hail in crop areas; to cope with lightning discharges in forest areas; and to dissipate both warm and supercooled fog.

Project Stormfury, a cooperative program of the United States Departments of Commerce and

Navy, seeks to modify and diminish the force of hurricanes by seeding them with silver iodide crystals. In tests on two hurricanes some significant lessening of wind force was noted, but more trials are needed to confirm the effectiveness of hurricane seeding.

WEATHER AND CLIMATE

The difference between weather and climate is chiefly one of *time*. Weather is the state of the atmosphere—its temperature, humidity, wind, pressure, cloudiness, and so on—at any particular hour or day. Climate is the history of these characteristics over a long period of time.

Climate may be defined briefly as "average weather." But an average may be misleading. For example, St. Louis, Missouri, has an average yearly rainfall of about 40 inches, while Bombay, India, has 74 inches. In St. Louis, however, the rainfall is evenly distributed, so that no one month has less than 3 inches of rain. In Bombay, on the other hand, the rain falls in torrential cloudbursts during four summer months; the rest of the year is almost rainless.

The climate of a region is customarily described in terms of its year-round temperature and rainfall. Climate in any region is controlled by a number of factors:

1. Latitude: distance from the equator.
2. Altitude: height above sea level.
3. The presence of land and sea masses.
4. The prevailing winds: the winds that blow steadily across an area.
5. The topography: mountains and plains.
6. Ocean currents, such as the Gulf Stream.

Space does not permit a discussion of how these factors influence climate, although some references to them are scattered through this chapter. For a full treatment of climate the reader may refer to the Bibliography for texts on climatology, meteorology, and earth science.

From our discussion of the air and the weather certain fundamental concepts emerge. Some of these are:

Man lives at the bottom of an ocean of air.

Half of the air in the atmosphere is in the atmosphere's lowest $3\frac{1}{2}$ miles.

Scientists divide the atmosphere into five layers: the troposphere, stratosphere, mesosphere, thermosphere (which includes most of the ionosphere), and exosphere.

In the troposphere temperature falls about $3\frac{1}{2}°$ F. for every 1,000 feet of altitude.

Weather happens in the troposphere.

Air is a mixture of nitrogen and oxygen, water vapor, carbon dioxide, other gases and dust.

Air is essential for life.

Changes in the atmosphere determine the weather.

The sun, air, and water play leading roles in weather.

The sun is the prime source of energy for the weather "machine."

The unequal distribution of the sun's heat on the earth has a profound effect on weather.

Air serves to distribute heat and water around the earth.

The water cycle involves the circulation of water from oceans and lakes to the air, thence to the land, and then back to oceans and lakes again.

Because weather is a three-dimensional phenomenon, knowledge of the characteristics of the air at various levels is essential for a full understanding of weather.

Wind movements are initiated by the unequal heating of the earth by the sun.

Large masses of cold and warm air influence the weather of the world.

Weather in the United States and in other temperate zones of the earth is influenced by the interaction of cold and warm air masses.

More research is needed to determine to what extent man can control weather.

Discovering For Yourself

1. Discover as much as you can about the use of weather satellites.
2. Clip weather maps and reports from a daily paper. Interpret them by telling (a) the different things about air that are shown, (b) how the forecast is made from the data given, and (c) how conditions on the map have changed since the previous day.
3. Observe cloud formations on several successive days to discover how the clouds change from time to time. See what relationship they have to the weather, and identify them.
4. Look out of a window and see what you can tell about the temperature and movement of air by observing birds, smoke, trees, people, and any other things that will provide clues.
5. Explain what makes the various air currents in your house—in the kitchen, near open windows, near air ducts, and elsewhere.
6. Try to find a toy or gimcrack that operates by the use of air pressure or air currents, and explain its operation.
7. Look for places in your indoor environment where water evaporates and condenses. Explain the conditions that are responsible. Explain how these conditions are similar to those outdoors that cause precipitation. How could you use this activity with children?
8. Observe different kinds of thermometers that are in use in your home environment. Tell how they differ from each other and how they are similar.
9. Keep a record of the accuracy of local weather forecasts for a two-week period. Observe the elements of the scientific attitude discussed in Part I. Write a paragraph setting forth your conclusions.
10. Visit a weather station to observe the instruments used and the records kept, and find out as much as you can about how the data are utilized to forecast weather. Find out how computers help make such forecasts.
11. Select some weather "sayings" and try to test their accuracy by observation. Write a paragraph setting forth your conclusions.
12. Learn to read a hygrometer, a barometer, and other weather instruments.

(Courtesy of Phyllis Marcuccio.)

CHAPTER 9B
TEACHING "THE AIR AND THE WEATHER"

Weather phenomena relate to many other areas of science. The cause of seasons (Chapter 7B); molecules, atoms, and chemical change (Chapter 15B); observing the effects of running water (Chapter 14B)—all relate to an understanding of the content of this chapter.

Many examples of the processes of discovering in science are important in the study of weather and are included in the activities described: *observing, using numbers, measuring, predicting, inferring,* and so on. Pupils should understand that weather is the condition of the atmosphere, and that various weather phenomena which they experience are caused by changes in the air around them. Children deepen their understanding of weather as they observe at firsthand, as they measure weather conditions with various instruments and record the results, and as they experiment.

SOME BROAD CONCEPTS: "The Air and Weather"

Weather refers to the conditions of the air—temperature, amount of moisture, and wind.

Changes in the condition of the air determine the weather.

Wind is air in motion and is caused by unequal heating of the earth by the sun.

Air is a mixture of different gases—chiefly nitrogen, oxygen, carbon dioxide.

The water cycle involves evaporation of water to form water vapor and the condensation of the water vapor into water.

There is a constant cycle of water from oceans to air to oceans.

Weather is influenced by the actions of cold and warm air masses.

The sun, the air, and water play an important role in weather.

There are many different kinds of weather.

We live at the bottom of an ocean of air.

Climate is the average weather for a place over a long period of time.

FOR YOUNGER CHILDREN

How Does the Wind Change?

Begin by suggesting that children *observe* things around them (smoke, flags, leaves on trees, papers, and leaves on the ground). Let them *report* what they see and tell how they think the wind changes from day to day. Help them *record* their findings. Let them try to draw some conclusions from their observations. What can we do to learn more about the changes in speed and direction of the wind? Construct something that can show us when and how much these changes occur. Suggest that children make pinwheels and take them outside. Let them try to *predict* what they think will happen when the wheels are held up in the wind at different times in a day and on several days. What can children *infer* from their experiences? Suggest that children continue to *observe* other things that are moved by the wind. What inferences can they make from these observations?

Wind also changes directions. Children can observe this as they see flags moved by the wind. They may make a simple wind vane. Some young children may need help with learning directions, and the use of this instrument will motivate them. Remember that winds are named for the direction from which they come and that arrows in weather vanes point in the direction from which wind comes. Urge children to keep a record of wind direction for several days, examine the record, and make a statement of their discoveries.

How Do Clouds Change?

Children like to watch clouds and think about the cloud shapes they see. On several cloudy days take children outside and urge them to observe the clouds. What do they look like? What can you discover about them? How are they alike and how do they differ from each other (size, shape, color, movement)? What is happening to them? What do you think makes them move? Are they higher than the flagpole? A high building? Than birds? Than airplanes? Are they as far away as the sun? Can you tell what kind of weather is coming by watching the clouds? Draw pictures of the clouds you see and tell about your pictures.

What Kinds of Weather Are There?

Urge children to observe weather conditions for several days—at school and on the way to and from school. Help them find words that describe the weather—cloudy, warm, cold, windy, sunny. Make a list of the words and urge children to use them as they observe and describe the weather.

Make a weather clock by cutting a large circular disc from stiff cardboard. Divide the clock face into sections and let children select words from their list to place in the various sections. Fashion two clock hands and attach them with brass fasteners. Urge children to suggest how the weather clock might be used. If we set our clock in the morning when we come to school will it be correct all day? Why do we need two clock hands? Some children may wish to make their own small weather clocks using paper plates, and change them as the weather changes.

Suggest that children find pictures of different kinds of weather and describe the weather shown. What can you tell about the weather by looking at the picture? Is the wind blowing? Can you tell if it is hot or cold? What else can you discover?

How do people and animals change their activities when the weather changes? For learning how temperature changes during the day see the suggestions on page 184 of Chapter 7B.

What Happens to Puddles of Water?[1]

Ask the children for their ideas. One child may say: "The cat drinks it." She may be right! Another may volunteer: "It sinks into the ground." He may be right. How

[1] For further information *see* G.O. Blough: *Water Appears and Disappears* (New York: Harper and Row. 1972).

can we find out? Investigate the puddle. Observe and measure it for a few days. Leave on open dish of water in the classroom. What happens to it? Adapt the material about evaporation and condensation for older children, emphasizing the observations children can make of the two processes, measuring and applying what they have learned to their immediate environment (*see also* "What Does Heat Do to Water" in Chapter 16B).

What Do Storms Do?

After a heavy rain, snow, or strong wind take the children outside to observe what effects the storm has had. Look at the plants. Observe the ground to see what changes the water has made. What is happening to the water? Children can make a list of effects of the storm.

How Can We Measure Rainfall?

A straight-sided coffee can serves to measure the amount of rainfall, when placed in the open. After the rain has stopped bring the can inside and measure the depth of the water with a ruler that measures in millimeters as well as inches. Let the children help to measure. Do this on several different occasions and keep a record of the results. After measuring, let the water stay in the can and have children predict what they think will happen to it. How long will evaporation take? Can we measure the amount of snowfall? How?

What Happens When Snow and Ice Melt?

What are snow and ice made of? If the weather is cold collect snow and ice in a container and urge children to observe what happens when it is brought indoors; otherwise use ice from a refrigerator and observe the change. What made the ice melt? How can we make it melt faster? How can we change the water into ice? Children may use a thermometer to try to find out how cold the snow and ice are.

SOME BEHAVIORAL OBJECTIVES

As a result of the experiences described here, and others, children should be able to: *describe* different kinds of weather; *read* a simple thermometer and *record* the temperatures; *observe* various kinds of weather and *record* their observations; *use* with accuracy the words that describe different kinds of weather; *demonstrate* the processes of evaporation and condensation; *construct* some simple hypotheses on the basis of observations; *describe* the information shown in pictorial material.

OTHER PROBLEMS FOR YOUNGER CHILDREN

1. How do weather reports help us?
2. What makes rain and snow?
3. What are snowflakes like?
4. How should we dress for different kinds of weather?
5. What weather signs show that weather changes are coming?
6. How does wind help and harm us?
7. What happens to clouds?
8. How can we find out what the weather will be?

FOR OLDER CHILDREN

What Is the Weather Like Today?

Too often the study of weather is confined to the classroom, while weather goes on outside. Begin a study of weather with a field trip to answer the questions: "What is the weather like today?" "What can you tell about the air by using your senses?" "What are the clouds like?" The observations and discussions may raise several other questions and problems about weather, for pupils are almost certain not to agree on all of their observations. By using their senses they should report something about the air's temperature, that air is going from one place to another ("wind's blowing"), perhaps that the air "feels damp," and that they can feel the warmth of the sun. Their cloud description may indicate that the clouds are moving, that some are getting larger, some are disappearing, some are darker than others, and so on. Pupils may learn to recognize some of the cloud formations pictured in Chapter 9A. A record of a week's weather changes is bound to raise many problems like those in the following examples.

How Can the Amount of Rainfall be Measured?

How much rain fell last night in the downpour? An inch? Two inches? Pupils may estimate and then, for future use, make a simple rain gauge to measure the rainfall.[2] The illustration shows the completed gauge, which can be made from an ordinary coffee can set in Plaster of Paris. Because of evaporation, amounts of rainfall should be measured immediately after the rain.

Another type of rain gauge is made by inserting a cork and a funnel into the top of an olive jar. Making such a gauge is an excellent opportunity to have children plan and design an instrument to try to solve a particular problem. It is difficult to read rainfall of less than $\frac{1}{4}$ inch with the simple tin-can gauge. Discuss why this is so, and ask the children how they might make an instrument to measure small amounts

[2] G.O. Blough and M.H. Campbell: *Making and Using Classroom Science Materials in the Elementary School* (New York: Holt, Rinehart and Winston, Inc., 1954), p. 114.

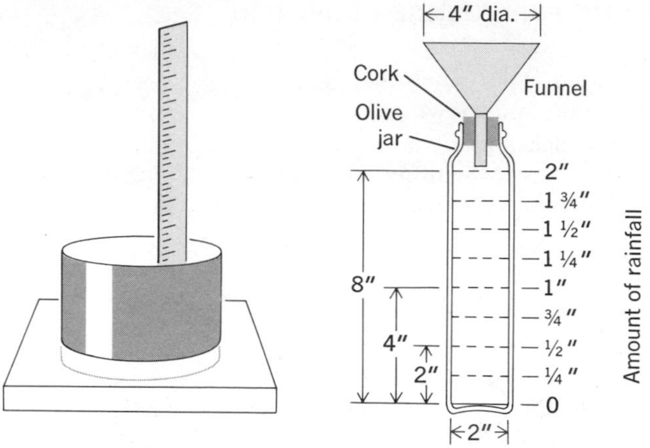

A rain gauge can be made of a tin can set in plaster of Paris. A somewhat more elaborate gauge consists of an olive bottle with a funnel, using the dimensions and markings shown here.

of rain. The use of a funnel, as shown in the illustration, increases the area for catching rain. This increase in area must be compensated for in the making of a scale. Thus, 4 inches of water in the collecting bottle represents 1 inch of rainfall. (**Note:** In this instance, the *diameter* of the wide end of the funnel is 4 inches, whereas that of the reservoir—the olive jar—is only 2 inches. The *area* of the funnel opening, however, is four times that of the jar. Consequently, the height of the rain collecting in the jar must be divided by 4 to give the correct reading.)

(*See* pp. 41–2.)

The use of the metric system is to be encouraged in measurements such as this.

Children may use the rain gauge to compare readings at the school with those of the National Weather Service. A discrepancy does not mean that either one is necessarily incorrect, because rainfall is not always exactly the same in the various localities covered by the weather report. National Weather Service records are more accurate because of the equipment used.

Older children can find out what the average rainfall (obtained from the records) is for each month of the year in their locality. They can summarize this information in a chart or graph and compare averages for their locality with others in the state or in the country as a whole. In this way, they begin to understand that climate is "average weather" for a locality.

What Makes Water Evaporate?

It may be necessary for children to have some experiences with evaporation as a process before they begin to experiment with the influence of such factors as temperature, wind, and surface on the rate of evaporation. These experiences may grow out of questions they ask about their environment such as: "Why must we add water to our aquarium?" Pupils hypothesize. In response to: "Probably the fish drink it," the teacher asks: "Can you plan an experiment to find out if this is the reason?"

Pupils put water in a jar without fish and compare it with that in a jar with fish. They mark the level; record the date; observe, and keep recording the change. They may make a graph or some other record. How long did evaporation take? Where did the water go? What is the answer to our problem about fish? There are many other similar experiences with evaporation (*see* books in the Bibliography).

How water changes to vapor and gets into the air and how it gets out are important concepts. The effects of temperature, wind, and amount of surface exposed on the rate of evaporation can be determined by experimenting (*see* the following examples).

About Temperature Build on the experiences that children can recall about evaporation and temperature. What ideas have they? Use their ideas as a basis for testing, and urge them to attempt to plan experiences and experiments that will test.

Put the same amounts of water into two identical containers. Heat one over a hot plate or a hot radiator and leave the other at room temperature. Use a thermometer for exactness. Or put the same amount of water in similar trays and set one in the sun and the other in the shade. Ask children to try to *predict* the outcome. Compare the results by pouring the contents of both into measuring cups. Pupils should be encouraged to summarize their observations and attempt to make some *inferences* from

"Making it rain" helps children understand the relationship of temperature to the processes of evaporation and condensation. Exploring to find other places in the environment where this happens, and describing the conditions present in each case, helps children to understand the ideas better. (*Photo by John King.*)

these observations. The use of mathematics is important here. After 6 hours the water in the tray in the shade has gone down from 10 to 9 ounces, while the water in the sun has gone down from 10 to 8 ounces. Or, in the shade 1 ounce of water evaporated, while in the sun 2 ounces of water evaporated. Or, water evaporated twice as quickly in the sun as in the shade. Again, the use of the metric system is to be encouraged.

Wet two identical pieces of cloth. Place one in a warm location and leave the other at room temperature. Pupils will think of situations in which they have seen that higher temperatures speed the process of evaporation: Clothes dry faster if placed in a warm place; the sun evaporates water from grass and pavements; the water on sidewalks in the sun evaporates faster than it does from sidewalks in the shade. We stress the importance of using a control. The only difference between two situations must be that one is kept warmer than the other. The warm place should be no windier than the other, and the cloths should be hung or placed in similar positions so that equal amounts of surface are exposed. We should stress also the importance of not drawing sweeping conclusions from *one* experiment. Comparison of the evaporation from the two wet cloths can be made by feeling the cloths or, more accurately, by weighing them at intervals. The latter is a good example of how *measurement* is a useful process of science. (Pupils must understand that the cloth weighs less as water evaporates from it.)

About Wind Again make use of children's experiences and give them opportunities to devise experiments that will provide data for constructing inferences, hypotheses, and general ideas.

(*See* pp. 79–80.)

Observing what happens to a wet spot on the chalkboard is a useful experience. From this children will get ideas for experiments with other materials that show the effects of wind on wet surfaces. Examples of application are: Blowing on wet ink to dry it; the wind drying wet pavements; hair dryers. Children will think of other applications and will arrange to control the variables and interpret their observations.

About Amount of Surface Exposed Wet two similar handkerchiefs. Leave one crumpled up and one spread out. Ask children to *predict* from which cloth the water will evaporate first. Urge them to suggest other experiences that will show the effects of surface exposure.

Put the same amounts of water in a tall olive bottle and in a saucer. Pupils may *hypothesize* about what the results may be. Compare the results mathematically as described in the experiments on temperature. Make graphs to show the amounts of water remaining in each container after equal intervals of time. Applications: Wet bathing suits and towels should be spread out to dry; water spilled on the floor evaporates faster if spread out.

What Makes Water Condense?

Pupils may *observe* condensation (changing from a gas to a liquid) taking place on cold-water pipes and faucets, on pitchers of cold liquid, on a cold window or a cold mirror, and in the air on a cold day when they "see" their own breath. Discuss: Where does the moisture come from? What causes it to form?

Place some ice in a metal cup, stir for a few moments, and note the result. Let pupils formulate predictions as to where the droplets come from. If they think that the droplets "leaked" through from the inside help them to devise some way to *test* their idea. They might add coloring to the ice water and see if the droplets are also colored. Suggest putting hot water in another tin cup to observe the results. What does this show? After they have decided that the air is the only possible place from which the drops could have come, they must answer the question: "What was done to make the water come out of the air?" Pupils may hypothesize that the cup cooled the air in contact with it. They experiment on several different days to see if there are differences. If necessary, suggest that they keep records of the relative humidity as shown by a hygrometer or the weather report to see what relationship, if any, exists. They may record their findings and try to interpret them.

After pupils have experimented with evaporation and condensation suggest that they go to the window and tell how many different kinds of places they can see from which water is evaporating. Do the same for condensation. Then name places in the school building where these two processes take place. The experiment described on pp. 25–6 suggests a way of showing that plants give water off into the air.

Ordinarily pupils at the elementary school level do not concern themselves about how relative humidity is calculated. Pupils can, however, read a hair hygrometer, which gives a direct reading of the relative humidity, and understand the meaning of the term "relative humidity" even though they do not go into *how* the percentage is determined. Those who wish to make a simple hygrometer may consult the book *Making and Using Classroom Science Materials.*[3]

As these experiments and observations go on it may be advisable to keep a record of the important science concepts that pupils have learned so that they can later be put together and used to understand weather phenomena. The breadth of these concepts will depend on the experience, interest, and intellectual maturity of pupils. Here are examples of important ideas pupils should have encountered from the experiments and observations in evaporation and condensations:

Water evaporates into the air from many places.
Heat makes water evaporate more quickly.
Wind makes water evaporate more quickly.
Cooling of the air may cause water to condense.
Water condenses on many cool surfaces.
Water evaporates more quickly when it is spread out more.

How Is Water Recycled?

Now pupils can begin to put together what they have learned about evaporation and condensation in order to understand some of the causes of rain and other forms of precipitation.

The covered terrarium in the schoolroom is an excellent place to observe the water

[3]G.O. Blough and M.H. Campbell, *ibid.*, pp. 114–115.

cycle. Suggest that children watch the glass surface of a terrarium for several days, report their findings, and try to interpret their observations. The water evaporates from all of the wet things in the terrarium. When the moist air cools, the water vapor condenses on the glass. Discuss: "Where does the water come from?" "Why did it form on the glass?" "Why does it then sometimes disappear?" Show the same idea by using a clean, dry glass jar. Place an inch or so of water in the bottom. Screw the lid on. Set the jar so that part of it is in sunlight. In a short time the vapor that evaporates will condense in droplets on the cool glass.

The children can easily demonstrate "rain" by holding a cold plate or pie tin over the spout of a tea kettle of boiling water. They can observe the condensation. If the water is collected and left standing they can observe that it soon evaporates.

In using the materials described in the previous paragraphs it is important that pupils see the relationship between what happens to these materials and what happens outdoors. Thus, in the kettle demonstration the heating device represents the sun, the white cloud comes from the kettle, the cold plate represents cold temperatures aloft, and the drops are rain. In the terrarium the cooler sides of the terrarium represent the cold temperatures experienced aloft. When the air is warmed, the water evaporates. Urge children to look for and report other examples of water cycles. Suggest that children draw a diagram of the water cycle on the chalkboard and show that they understand the ideas.

What Makes the Wind?

A convection box may be used to help pupils see how winds are caused. First let pupils examine the box. Ask: "Can you figure out how to make a wind in the box?" "If you can, then you can understand what makes the wind blow outdoors." The box has two openings in the top, each covered by a glass chimney. The front is covered by glass. Under one of the holes is a candle which heats the air around and over it. The surrounding cooler, heavier air pushes in and forces the warmed, lighter air up the chimney. This circulation of air is a small-scale wind. You cannot see the wind, but if you hold a smoking splinter of wood or piece of damp paper above the cooler chimney you will see smoke being carried *down* that chimney, across the box, and *up* the other chimney. (The word "tracer" is useful to describe the role of the smoke in this demonstration.) Caution should be exercised in the use of this apparatus because it involves lighting matches. Pupils should not strike matches unless an adult is present.

To carry the principle of this demonstration to the cause of winds on the earth develop the idea that the air around the burning candle represents our equatorial regions. The large winds start blowing as the heated air in this region is pushed up and starts flowing toward the poles. Cold air from the poles flows toward the equatorial regions.

After children have observed the currents in the convection box they are ready to apply what they have seen to the schoolroom. Why is the ceiling the hottest place in the room? With the door closed, open a window at the top and bottom and hold a stick with tissue-paper streamers tied to it at each of these openings. Why is the wind coming *in* at the bottom and going *out* at the top?

This convection box, which may be made at school or purchased from a supply house, is used to show how wind is caused by the unequal heating of air.

Demonstrate the difference in the heating and cooling of land and water (which causes land and sea breezes) with these materials: two baking dishes, two thermometers, soil, and water. Put soil in one dish and an equal amount of water in the other. Place a thermometer in each. Let both stand until the temperatures are the same. Place both in sun light for about 15 minutes in such a way that the *bulbs* of the thermometers are shielded from the direct rays. Note the temperature. Place both in the shade for about 15 minutes. Note the temperatures again.

To study upper wind directions release helium-filled balloons into the air. Attach a plastic bag enclosing a self-addressed postal card and a note to the finder asking for the return of the card giving the date and location. This activity has produced some exciting results.

After these experiences the children are ready to try to explain what is making the wind blow today. They can answer such questions as: "What heats the earth?" "Is it heated to the same temperature everywhere? If not, why not?" "Would the wind blow toward the warmer place or toward the cooler?"

At this point, pupils may add to the lists of concepts about air such statements as:

Wind is moving air.
Winds blow because of unequal heating of the air.
Warm air is pushed up by colder air.

What Do Weather Maps Show?

(*See* p. 246.)

Many newspapers carry weather maps which may be posted on the bulletin board along with forecasts. As pupils study the maps they will discover how the measurements of temperature, air pressure, wind direction, wind speed, and precipitation are indicated, and become familiar with the symbols used.

Pupils may try to determine how forecasts were made from the maps. Excellent aids in learning about weather maps, as well as other weather materials, are available from the Government Printing Office.[4]

Keeping track of the accuracy of local weather reports over a period of time is interesting for children. Reports may be taken from the radio, newspapers, or by telephone. A committee may be appointed to obtain the report each day and decide whether or not it has been accurate. Stress the importance of making accurate observations, withholding judgment, and other elements of scientific attitudes discussed in Part I. For example, if the forecast is for rain in the *vicinity* of the school and it does not rain *at the school itself* additional investigation is necessary before a decision can be reached.

In addition to maps reports from radar and satellites are used in forecasts. Pupils should be urged to watch for such reports as they appear in magazines and newspapers.

SETTING UP A WEATHER STATION[5]

In many localities a visit to a weather station is taken when upper elementary-school classes study weather. Specifically, pupils go to learn more than they already know about weather forecasting, to increase their interest in scientific procedures, to satisfy their curiosity about some of the materials they have experienced, and to increase their appreciation for the work of scientists.

Here are some specific questions pupils might ask at a weather station: "What do scientists learn from the instruments?" "How are these facts put together?" "How do the instruments work?" "How is the weather map made?" "Who uses the weather reports?" "Who pays for maintaining the weather station?" "What help are computers at a weather station?"

While a visit to the weather station is interesting, a station which children themselves set up is perhaps a better learning situation. They can gather data on wind direction, air pressure, temperature, and so on. Weather instruments can be assembled, and pupils can use them to try to make their own forecasts. These may not—probably will not—be accurate. Pupils do not possess sufficient experience and knowledge, nor accurate instruments, and their observations are only local. But a greater understanding and appreciation of the work of the National Weather Service can be gained through this activity. The illustrations show some of the weather instruments that can be made. The rain gauge has been described earlier.

[4] Address Superintendent of Documents, U.S. Government Printing Office, Washington, D.C. 20402 asking for the latest free price list No. 48, *Weather* (pamphlets and other materials on many aspects of weather).

[5] G.W. Donaldson and R.E. Roth: "Building a Teaching Weather Station," *Science and Children* (April 1970).

Barometers

(*See* p. 231.)

Aneroid barometers are now often found as standard equipment in an elementary school or as home weather instruments. Pupils should learn to read the barometer scale in inches to the first decimal place. The printed words on the dial—RAIN, CHANGE, FAIR—have only limited significance. (Some students might keep records to judge the reliability of these designations.) The barometer measures only one thing: air pressure. A movement toward high pressure *usually* indicates the approach of clear dry weather. A movement toward low pressure *usually* indicates the approach of unsettled weather.

To learn more about how the barometer works children might observe to see if a difference in reading can be detected if the barometer is carried to the top floor of the school or to a nearby hill; keep a daily record of the reading over a period of a month and compare it with general weather conditions; make a graph to show observations (what connection is there between barometric pressure and weather conditions?); observe to see if there is a difference in the reading indoors and outdoors. As they progress with their study of air and weather pupils may want to keep track of barometer readings given in the newspaper and on the radio.

Pupils might also keep records and compare their readings with those of the National Weather Service. They should learn that a barometer is a delicate scientific instrument and not a toy; that it is for the purpose of supplying information and must be handled carefully.

Anemometer

The wind gauge in the illustration is made from two hollow rubber balls cut in half and nailed to the ends of crossed sticks. The anemometer may be fastened to a post or a part of a building where the wind is unobstructed. An electric fan can be used to test ease of operation before it is installed outside.

Again we have an instrument in which pupils make use of mathematics. If one of the half-balls is painted red it will be easier to count the number of turns per minute.

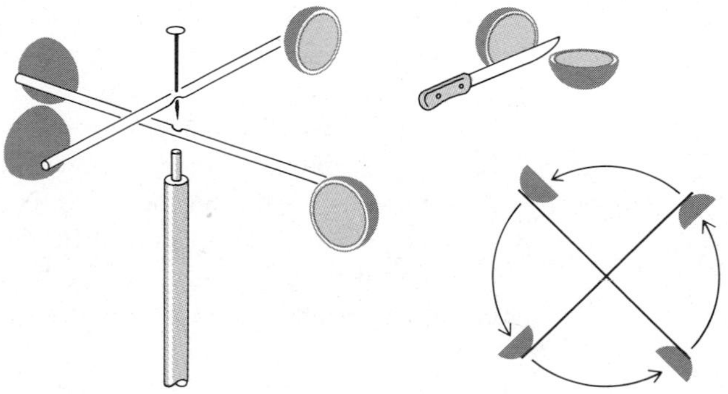

A four-cup wind-speed wind gauge. Pupils may like to experiment with materials other than those suggested here. (*See* books listed in Bibliography for other ideas of how to make and use weather instruments.)

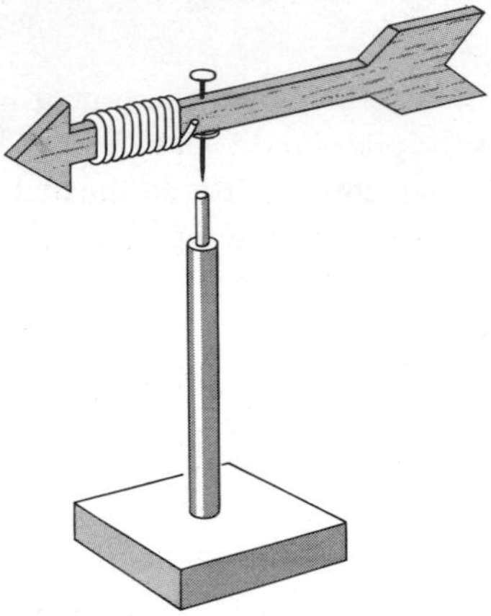

A wind vane. Wire wrapped around the arrow as needed will help to balance the instrument so that it can swing freely. Pupils will need to experiment with this construction in order to produce an effective instrument.

Knowing this, pupils will be able to see the comparative wind speeds on different days in a relative sense. Thus, 90 turns per minute on one day compared with 45 turns the next means that the wind speed on the first day was twice that of the second.

Wind Vane

The wind vane illustrated consists of an arrow made of light wood and placed on a pivot. It is important that the arrow be carefully balanced and that the pivot hole be large enough to permit the arrow to swing freely but not large enough to permit the arrow to tilt. A washer between the wooden arrow and its support will allow the arrow to move more freely. A compass should be used to determine wind direction.

OTHER PROBLEMS FOR OLDER CHILDREN

1. How has man learned to control the weather?
2. How does air pressure affect weather?
3. What information do weather satellites supply?
4. What causes lightning and thunder?
5. What is the difference between weather and climate?
6. Why is the weather different at different times of the year?
7. What causes the temperature to change from time to time?
8. What is the relationship of the jet stream to weather forecasting?
9. How does radar help meteorologists? How does it work?
10. What is a temperature inversion? How does it keep smog hanging over a city for days?
11. What is a Celsius thermometer? How do we change Fahrenheit degrees into Centigrade and vice-versa?

12. What records are kept by the National Weather Service?
13. How are computers used by the National Weather Service?

Resources to Investigate with Children

1. Local newspapers for weather maps and weather forecasts.
2. Local or nearby weather station to observe weather instruments and to learn how data are used in forecasting.
3. Local farmers, nurserymen, and fruit growers to learn how the Weather Service helps them, and how they protect their crops in extreme or unusual weather.
4. Truck drivers and sailors for information on how they learn about sudden weather changes and what the Weather Service does for them.
5. Airports to observe weather instruments and to learn how information is gathered and disseminated.
6. Newspaper accounts of unusual weather conditions such as tornadoes, hurricanes, and heavy frosts for explanations of causes and results and other information.
7. National Weather Service and its branches for samples of available information.
8. Local small-craft owners for information about how they use the barometer and other weather instruments, and for accounts of how they get weather warnings and other weather information.
9. Newspaper accounts of recent advances in meteorology, such as the use of satellites.

Preparing to Teach[6]

1. Plan an introductory activity for the study of weather that you can use to create interest and provoke thoughtful questions from children.
2. Select from various reference books a series of experiments that will help pupils learn about air pressure, evaporation, condensation, temperature, and weather instruments.
3. Construct some of the weather instruments described in the text or elsewhere. Make a weather clock that can be used with young children.
4. Plan a lesson that can be used to introduce the thermometer and its uses to a third grade.
5. Assemble pictures that can be used to acquaint young children with different kinds of weather. Plan questions to go with the pictures.
6. Construct a multiple-choice examination that will help to check understandings developed about weather in one specific grade.

[6] An excellent survey of weather is contained in *The Science Teacher* (December 1971).

(Courtesy of Jack Dermid, from National Audubon Society.)

PART III

LIVING THINGS

CHAPTER 10A
THE NATURE AND VARIETY OF LIFE

(Courtesy of Monkmeyer.)

A POND NEAR HOME

Life is found almost everywhere on earth—on frozen tundras, on dry deserts, and in hot springs. Life exists in the ocean deeps, on wave-battered shores, in sunless caves, on windswept mountain peaks, and high in the earth's atmosphere.

A pond near your home is populated with an astonishing variety and number of plants and animals. A floating water lily leaf exposes its green surface to sunlight and air. Its wet lower surface is home to many tiny animal forms. A frog with turreted eyes sees above water while most of its body is submerged. Whirligig beetles gyrate in crowds on the surface, capturing small insects there. A female dragonfly skims over the water, laying her eggs as she dips the tip of her abdomen beneath the surface. Any drop of the pond's water is a little world teeming with microscopic plants and animals. Flatworms, water fleas, leeches, snails, crayfish, turtles, salamanders, water snakes—the directory of pond residents becomes longer and longer as we search more and more.

WHAT IT MEANS TO BE ALIVE

The forms of life are many and varied. What makes these different forms alike—and alive?

All reproduce their kind; all are adapted to the environment they inhabit; all respond to stimuli; all secure food and obtain energy from it, or transform it into living material for growth; most can secure oxygen; all dispose of their wastes. Let us consider some of these characteristics of living things.

Reproduction

The bread mold scatters its spores so successfully that a piece of bread exposed to the air almost anywhere on the earth will be invaded by these reproductive bodies, which, if conditions are favorable, will develop into new cottony molds. Bacteria multiply so rapidly that within a day one becomes millions. An oak tree produces thousands of acorns, each capable of becoming a new tree. The female oyster produces as many as 60 million eggs each season. The female housefly lays up to 600 eggs at a time. One female fly in April could have $5\frac{1}{2}$ trillion descendants by September if all survived. Mammals—such as deer, elephants, and squirrels—have smaller numbers of offspring. What they lack in numbers they make up in parental care, in intelligence and in other characteristics that insure their survival.

Sensitivity

A living thing is sensitive. It responds to outside forces, or *stimuli,* generally in such a way that it improves its chances for survival. The leaves of the geranium plant growing in its pot on the windowsill respond to the rays of the sun by turning toward the light. The roots of a plant respond to gravity by growing down, just as the stems respond in the opposite fashion by growing up. The chilling of a pond to temperatures close to freezing is the stimulus for a series of responses in a frog: It dives down to the bottom, covers its eyes with the transparent "third" eyelids, expels air from its lungs, digs into the mud, and hibernates.

Adaptation

The kangaroo rat is well adapted to life in the desert. Its sole supply of water is in the food that it eats and the water produced by its own cellular respiration. Cacti have fleshy, succulent stems in which large quantities of water may be stored. Such plants are able to survive for long periods without an external source of water. The beaver is adapted for life in the water, possessing webbed hind feet for swimming and sharp teeth for cutting trees in its dam-building activities.

The term "adaptation" includes all the characteristics—structural and functional—which enable an organism to survive and reproduce in a particular environment. Adaptation is the result of evolutionary processes operating over millions of years.

(*See* pp. 392–3.)

Using Food for Energy

Plants and animals secure food in such different ways that it will be more profitable to consider this later. All living things use food for energy. In a series of complex chemical changes the energy stored in food molecules is slowly released (*see* Chapter 15A for a discussion of chemical changes). This process enables the roots of a plant to break through the soil, or a beaver to gnaw down trees and build a dam. In brain cells the energy derived from food helps an engineer design a rocket ship.

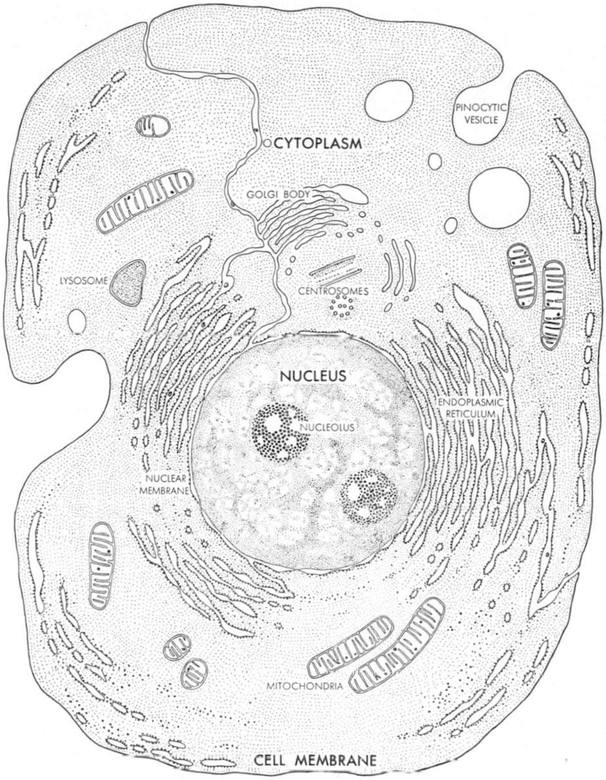

This modern diagram of a typical cell is based on what is seen through the electron microscope which magnifies 100,000 times and more. Aided by such magnifications and by the revelations of chemistry, the biologist now envisions the cell as much more than a drop of protoplasm; he sees it as a highly organized molecule factory.

Growth

One of the characteristics of living things is growth. A human baby that weighs about 7 pounds at birth matures into a grownup weighing 140 pounds or more. Where does this increase come from? Part of the food taken in is converted into living substance called *protoplasm.* Growth, then, means an increase in this complex chemical material of life. Within a plant or animal the protoplasm is characteristically found in separate building blocks, or *cells.* As a living thing grows and builds more protoplasm out of the food it consumes, it also increases the number of cells of which it is composed.

Securing Oxygen

Deprived of oxygen almost all living things, plant or animal, die. Oxygen is required for the release of energy from food, which is necessary for all life activity. Not all living things, however, obtain their oxygen directly from the atmosphere. Some—such as fish, lobsters, clams, and other forms of aquatic life—extract the oxygen from the air that is dissolved in the water in which they live. You can see this air as bubbles on the sides of a glass of tap water which is allowed to stand in a warm room for a few hours. The animals just mentioned are equipped with special devices, such as gills, to extract the dissolved oxygen from the water. Warm-blooded animals—the birds and mammals—require the most oxygen, be-

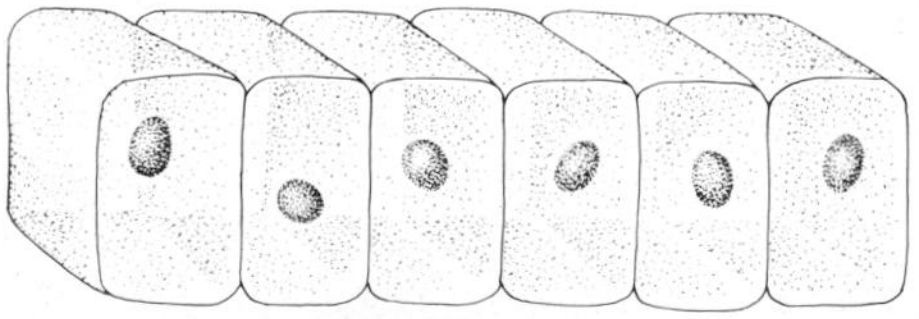

The cell, the building block of life, is made of living protoplasm. The typical cell contains a nucleus surrounded by streaming cytoplasm, and is covered by a thin cell membrane. In addition plant cells have a protective cell wall outside the membrane. Cells multiply by splitting in two. Each then grows to the size of the original cell by converting food into protoplasm.

cause they must produce heat constantly to maintain their normal body temperatures. Oxygen consumption is very high in smaller birds, such as the hummingbird, whose body temperature is normally 130° F.

Certain kinds of microbes do not require oxygen for the release of energy from food. Yeasts, which are tiny plants, may secure energy by fermenting sugar; that is, by splitting sugar into alcohol and carbon dioxide. Certain bacteria also are able to obtain energy from foods in the absence of oxygen.

Waste Disposal

The wastes of the living organism generally are poisonous to it. To live, the organism must continually rid itself of these wastes. Simple animals, such as the one-celled protozoans that live in the water, simply expel liquid wastes into the water through their covering membranes. In complex animals the kidneys, skin, and lungs (or gills) assume the vital job of getting rid of such liquid and gaseous wastes as water, salts, urea, and carbon dioxide. Solid wastes are discharged from an opening at the end of the food tube.

CENSUS OF THE LIVING

The *taxonomists* (scientists who study the family tree of living things) list some $1\frac{1}{2}$ million *species,* or kinds, of living organisms. Most of these are small organisms seldom noticed by the average person. The insect group includes, by far, the major number of species, 700,000 having been described and named to date. New kinds of insects are being discovered at the rate of nearly 2,000 each year!

The two broad groups of living things are the plant and animal *kingdoms.* (Some scientists use a third kingdom, Protista, "the first ones," which includes the simple animals and plants.) The kingdoms are subdivided into groups. In the animal kingdom the major groups are called *phyla.* Classification in the plant kingdom has been undergoing revision in recent years, with the result that the term "division" is now replacing the category "phylum." We shall not go into the complex problems of modern plant taxonomy but will identify the characteristic kinds of plant life. It would be helpful to read Chapter 13A, which deals with the evolution of various forms of life, in connection with the brief survey of plants and animals that follows.

THE PLANT KINGDOM

Most people know what a plant is and have no trouble in differentiating a maple tree from a bear. Yet all of us run into difficulties when we try to describe the distinguishing characteristics of *all* plants. We may call attention to the presence of chlorophyll and the ability of plants to use this green pigment in the manufacture of food. But mushrooms do not have this pigment and cannot synthesize food. And, some one-celled animals *do* have chlorophyll. We might call attention to the fact that plants do not move. Yet some of the microscopic aquatic plants move about freely. Furthermore, certain animals, such as corals, are anchored to one spot.

(*See* pp. 316–8.)

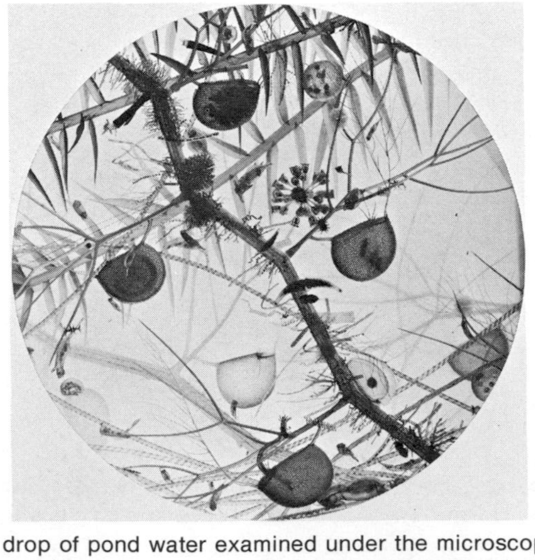

A drop of pond water examined under the microscope reveals a world of tiny plants and animals. These have been skillfully depicted in this exhibit of glass models at the Museum of Natural History in New York City. (*Courtesy of American Museum of Natural History.*)

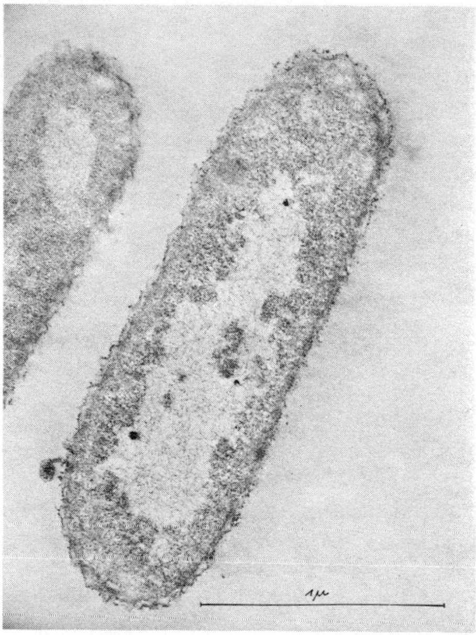

A single bacterium, magnified 30,000 times by the electron microscope, is infected by a much smaller organism, a virus. The virus has attached itself to the bacterium (*see* projection on lower left side) and is preparing to inject its contents into the cell. A virus that infects a bacterium is known as a bacteriophage. (*Courtesy of Carl Zeiss, Inc.*)

Our inability to distinguish all plants from all animals should not disturb us. The blurring of such distinctions occurs principally in the primitive and simpler plants and animals. It supports the belief of biologists that the two kingdoms began their independent courses of evolution from similar types of organisms.

The Simplest Plants

Algae are generally aquatic, simple plants that lack true stems, leaves, and flowers. All algae contain chlorophyll. Algae vary in size from microscopic, single-celled forms to the 200-foot-long, many-celled giant seaweeds, or kelps, which live attached to rocks at the edge of the sea.

Algae for microscopic study may be obtained by scraping the green film that is sometimes seen on the walls of an aquarium. Pond water is a rich source of many algae. The green, silky threads found near the edge of a pond may be those of the beautiful Spirogyra.

Algae play an important part in ocean life. Certain algae, particularly *diatoms,* are the principal food makers in the assortment of tiny plants and animals called *plankton.* In turn, plankton, which is found at or near the surface of the sea, serves directly or indirectly as the basic food supply for all marine life, from the smallest fish to the great whales. It is for this reason that the plankton layer has been called "the pastures of the sea," and the diatoms "the grasses of the sea."

Bacteria are tiny one-celled plants that reproduce typically by splitting in two. Most bacteria do not have chlorophyll and consequently cannot manufacture their own food. They obtain food from other living things or from dead plants and animals. Some bacteria, for example, live parasitically on plants or animals, causing disease. Bacteria are also of great benefit to living things. Every plant and animal is a storehouse of valuable chemicals. If these chemicals remained locked up within the organisms after death, there would soon be a scarcity of them for the living. Bacteria cause the rotting or decay of dead plants and animals, thus restoring their essential chemicals to the soil or to the water in lakes and oceans. These chemicals—nitrates, for example—then become available again for use by green plants and eventually by animals. It is probably true that without bacteria, most life on the planet Earth would disappear.

The *fungi* include a variety of groups of plants lacking chlorophyll: yeasts, molds, and mushrooms. Fungi play a similar role to that of bacteria; they are typically organisms that promote the decay of plant and animal materials. Somewhere in the life cycle of fungi *spores* for reproduction are formed.

Yeasts, like bacteria, are microscopic, one-celled plants. Some yeasts produce a chemical change in sugar, causing it to break down into alcohol and carbon dioxide gas. Man has put this to practical advantage. Yeasts ferment the sugar in crushed grapes into alcohol, making wine. In bread-making the carbon dioxide produced by the action of living yeast plants "raises" the dough and so helps make a light, tasty bread.

Molds are commonly seen growing on fruit, bread, and in other places where they are not wanted. Some molds are useful in the aging of cheeses. Molds have taken on added importance because extracts from them have been found useful in fighting bacteria harmful to man. Penicillin, streptomycin, and neomycin are but a few of the growing list of *antibiotics,* as these substances are called.

The *mushroom* is known best by its stalk and cap, which is actually the reproductive part of this fungus plant. There is no simple rule for telling edible from poisonous mushrooms. The only way to be sure is to *know* the particular mushroom you pick to eat by *all* its characteristics.

A *lichen* is a strange plant because it is really two plants growing together: an alga and a fungus. Lichens are found commonly as greenish-gray patches on rocks and soil.

The Mosses

All the members of this division of the plant kingdom possess chlorophyll. Mosses have no true roots, stems, or leaves such as are found in the more complex flowering plants. The size of these plants is severely limited because they lack a good conducting system of tubes for the distribution of food, water, and minerals. These tubes, found in the higher plants, are needed to carry vital supplies long distances from the soil. Hence, a moss plant more than a foot high would be a rarity.

The Ferns and Their Relatives

The ferns are the first plants—in the gamut of simple to complex—equipped with well-developed roots, stems, and leaves and an efficient conducting system of tubes. This enables them to grow to great size. The heyday of the ferns in the early days of life on earth is described in Chapter 13A. In the carboniferous period ferns were the most highly developed plants on the earth, comparable in size to our present forest trees. Horsetails and club mosses, small relatives of ferns, also had their heyday in this period, reaching heights of 75 and 100 feet.

If you turn over a fern leaf you will frequently find brown spots. These contain the spore cases, within which are numerous minute spores. When these spores are scattered, they start the growth of new ferns.

The Seed Plants

The seed plants are the most complex of all plants. They include all the common herbs, shrubs, and trees. Differences in the method of seed production determine the separation of the seed plants into two major groups. In one group there are no flowers, and the seeds are generally produced in open cones, as in the pine tree. This group, known as the *gymnosperms* ("naked seed"), includes the yew, hemlock, spruce, fir, cypress, sequoia, and redwood. It was once thought that the giant redwood qualified for the distinction of being the oldest and largest land plant now on the earth. Today we believe that the Big Tree of Tule in Mexico has this honor. It is at least 5,000 years old, and its trunk diameter is 50 feet.

The flowering plants, called the *angiosperms,* bear their seeds inside closed seed cases. Angiosperms generally have thin, sheetlike leaves, in contrast to the needlelike or scalelike leaves of the gymnosperms.

There are over 250,000 kinds of flowering plants. They are found as small herbaceous plants and as vines, shrubs, and trees. It was from this group of plants that people long ago selected those with useful qualities for cultivation. A large part of our food is derived from seeds, particularly the grains. From grain comes the flour that makes the "staff of life"—bread. Our clothing is woven from such plant fibers as cotton and linen. When we become ill we often heal ourselves with plant products. Although modern chemists can synthesize many drugs we still depend on plants for such vital extracts as digitalis for regulating heart action, opium and its derivatives for relief of pain, and cocaine and its derivatives for anesthesia. Modern chemical industry uses cellulose, which the plant makes as a covering around its cells, as the raw material for such products as rayon and the cellulose-based plastics.

We should not overlook the esthetic appeal of flowering plants, which bring a rainbow of colors and many exotic odors to the planet Earth.

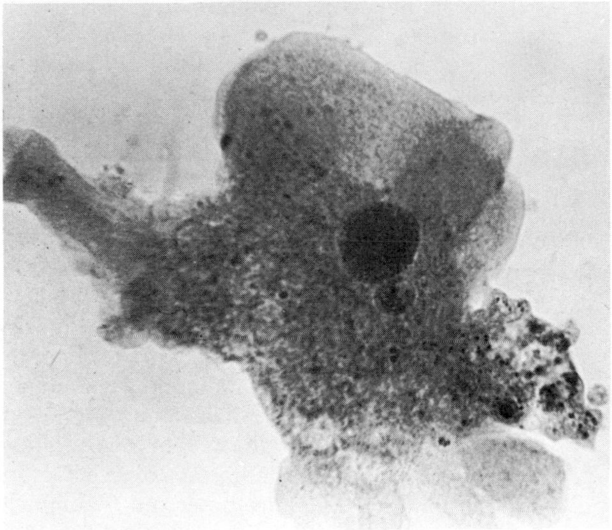

An actual photograph of a living ameba taken through a microscope. This one-celled animal changes its shape as it streams along, and feeds by wrapping itself around its food. (*Courtesy of Pfizer, Inc.*)

THE ANIMAL KINGDOM

What in common speech is called an "animal" is usually one of the four-footed, fur-bearing mammals, such as a sheep, dog, horse, or cow. These are simply the most familiar animals. There are many markedly different forms–worms, starfish, birds, for example–equally entitled to be called animals. Initially, we note that animals fall readily into one of two types. Some have a backbone, and some do not. Animals without a backbone are called *invertebrates;* those with a backbone are the *vertebrates.* The vertebrates come first to our minds because they are familiar and are generally large. However, of all the different kinds of animals only 5 percent are vertebrates, the rest are invertebrates.

(*See* pp. 316–8.)

Protozoans

The simplest of the invertebrates are the one-celled animals. These are called *protozoans,* a name that means "first animals." They are too small to be seen with the unaided eye, so it is not surprising that they were not discovered until the microscope was invented. Antony van Leeuwenhoek, the Dutch lens grinder of the seventeenth century, using a single-lens microscope of his own making, was the first person to see protozoa. He called them *animalculae* (small animals), which they literally are. Among the thousands of protozoans that have been described since that time, there is an amazing diversity. Some are without a fixed shape and possess few parts, such as the ameba, widely studied today in biology classes. Others have intricate internal structures and skeletons of beautiful designs. Most live as independent animals, but some are parasites.

Most protozoans are one-celled animals. They reproduce characteristically by splitting in two, or, as one biologist remarked, they multiply by dividing.

Sponges

The sponges are the first phylum of many-celled animals with cellular *specialization:* Certain cells take food out of sea water, digest it, and pass it along to others that specialize in protection, mechanical support, and reproduction. The saclike bodies of sponges are living waterways. Currents of water sweep in through microscopic pores that cover the entire surface. Minute food particles are removed from the water, which is then swept out through a large opening at one end of the animal. The *natural* sponge used occasionally in homes and in industry is the dried and cleaned skeleton of sponge animals.

Corals and Their Relatives

Extending partway around the continent of Australia is the famed Great Barrier Reef. This is essentially a huge growth of coral, a member of the *coelenterate* (se-lĕn'tĕr-at) phylum of animals. The reef is built mainly of the skeletons of thousands of generations of coral animals. The corals and their relatives—the sea anemones, the jellyfish, and the Portuguese man-of-war—are alike in having a body that is essentially a hollow sac, with a single opening surrounded by movable tentacles. The tentacles are used for capturing tiny animals and bringing them into the sac, where they are digested. There is more division of labor in the coelenterates than in the sponges: muscle cells move the tentacles, or in times of danger contract the entire body into a compact cylinder; elongated nerve cells coordinate the contractions; and specialized sensory cells respond to external stimuli such as gravity, light, or direct contact. The saclike body of the corals and jellyfish with its hundreds of specialized cells is the forerunner of the more complex body form of higher animals with organs and systems.

Worms

We include here three different phyla of animals—flatworms, roundworms, and segmented worms. A free-living flatworm, Planaria, is commonly found in ponds, where it feeds on small organisms. A planarian worm exhibits *bilateral symmetry:* Its right half is approximately a mirror image of its left. Associated with such symmetry is an anterior (head) and a posterior (tail) end, and an upper and under surface. With a head goes a concentration of nerves and sense organs. These characteristics (and others that we shall not describe here) distinguish the flatworms, and the round and the segmented worms as well, from the corals and jellyfish. Bilateral symmetry is the rule in the animals that are most familiar to you.

Free-living flatworms are exceptional; most, such as the tapeworm and flukes, live parasitically at the expense of other animals.

The roundworms are widespread over the earth. A spadeful of garden soil teems with millions of them. Some roundworms are parasitic on other animals. The one of chief importance in the United States is the hookworm. The scientific name of this worm is indicative of its role. It is *Necator americanus,* which means "the American killer." Hookworms were once the scourge of the Southern states. They enter the body from the soil by burrowing through the soles of the feet. They make their way to the small intestine where they hook on, feed, and reproduce. The eggs pass out with the feces and develop into worms.

Another parasitic roundworm is the trichina worm, which is taken into the body by eating insufficiently cooked pork.

The segmented worms are typified by the common earthworm. This burrower makes its way through the soil by swallowing it and digesting the plant and animal matter in it. In doing this it performs a useful function in agriculture. Tunneling up, it brings the lower layers of soil with rich mineral content into the upper part, making the minerals available for plant growth. Also, the progress of the worm through the soil makes the soil porous, so that water and air, which are essential to plant life, can percolate through and reach the roots of plants. One of the first scientists to point out the significant contribution of the earthworm was Charles Darwin, who estimated that earthworms brought 18 tons of soil to the surface of 1 acre each year.

Mollusks

The mollusks are the second largest phylum of invertebrates, numbering about 100,000 species. Their tasty, soft, fleshy bodies have made them an important source of food to man. The mollusks with a one-piece shell include snails, conches, and whelks. Many people collect the colorful and decorative shells of these animals. Some are used in making jewelry and ornaments. The mollusks with two shells are represented by oysters, clams, and scallops. Oysters are the makers of the treasured pearl. When a foreign particle gets into its body, the irritated mollusk secretes a pearly material around the particle.

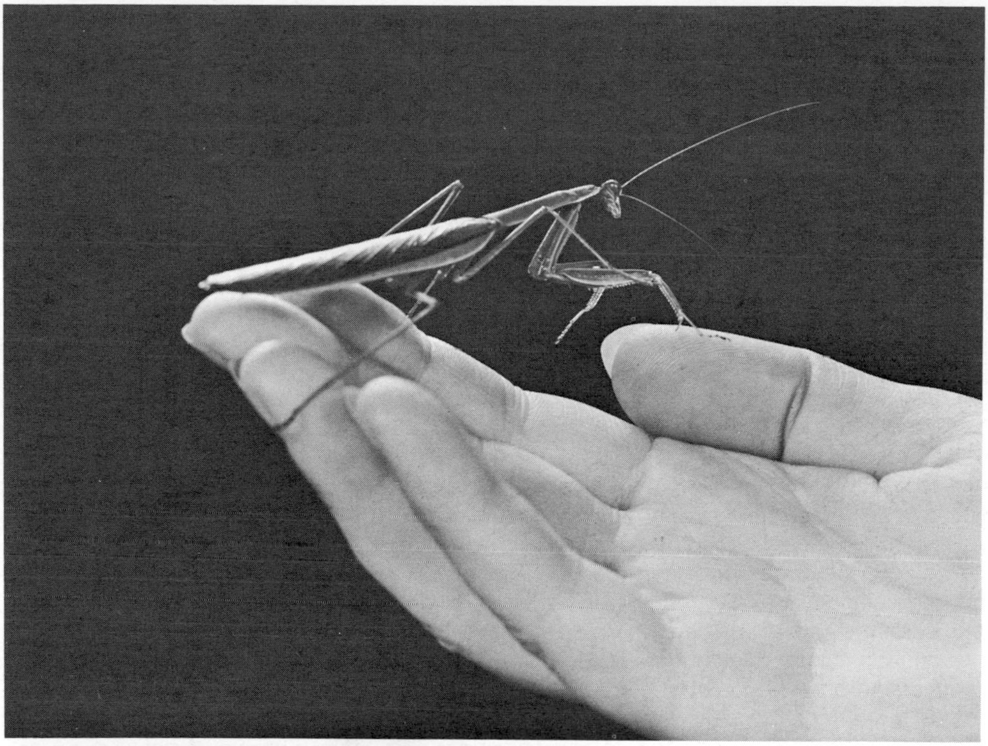

The praying mantis typifies insect characteristics: 3 pairs of legs and division of the body into 3 parts—head, thorax, and abdomen. (*Courtesy of American Museum of Natural History.*)

Man takes advantage of this reaction and induces oysters to make pearls. A particle of sand or other substance is put under the shell, and the oyster proceeds to build a pearl around it. A third group of mollusks includes the nautilus, the squid, and the octopus. The squid is a jet-propelled animal. It usually moves by taking in water and ejecting it forcefully to the back through a narrow tube or funnel. This pushes it rapidly in the opposite direction from the squirted water. It can steer itself by turning the funnel in different directions.

The giant squid is the largest known living invertebrate; it may grow up to 50 feet in length and weigh as much as 2 tons. It is probably one of the animals responsible for the age-old legends of "sea monsters."

The Jointed-legged Invertebrates

Of all the major phyla in the animal kingdom this one, the *arthropods,* contains by far the largest number of different species of animals. All the arthropods have an external skeleton made of a tough material, called chitin, and jointed legs. There are five main classes in this tremendous group.

The *crustaceans* (krŭs-tā'shănz) include crayfish, lobsters, shrimps, and crabs. With a few exceptions these animals breathe with gills, and most of them live in the sea. They range in size from microscopic water fleas and barnacles an inch wide to the 35-pound American lobster and the Japanese spider crab, with a span of 20 feet between the tips of its first pair of legs. This group is an important source of food for human beings.

Centipedes and *millipedes* have many legs, not hundreds and thousands, as their names imply, but several dozen. Centipedes have one pair of legs attached to each body segment, whereas the millipedes have two pairs on each segment.

Spiders and their allies have four pairs of walking legs and are generally air breathers. Included in this class, called the *arachnids* (ȧ-răk′nĭdz), are not only the spiders but also scorpions, ticks, and mites. The king or horseshoe crab is also an arachnid, a relative of the extinct trilobites discussed in Chapter 13A. A larval stage of the horseshoe crab bears a striking resemblance to a trilobite.

The *insects* have three pair of legs and their bodies are divided into three parts: head, thorax, and abdomen. They are the largest group in the animal kingdom, represented, as indicated previously, by 700,000 separate known species. There are 112,000 known kinds of butterflies and moths alone! The insects have penetrated almost every niche of the earth, adapting themselves to an amazing variety of environmental conditions. Insects live in frigid and in tropical zones, in desert and in rain forest, on prairie and on mountain top.

Some insects are harmful to man. The corn borer destroys man's food while it is growing in the fields. The clothes moth destroys his clothing, and the termite his wooden home. The anopheles mosquito carries the protozoan that causes malaria.

But there are some insects that are helpful to man. Bees, wasps, and butterflies help in the pollination of flowers of many plants that we depend on for food. The products of the honeybee and silkworm are used directly. Some insects help to keep harmful insects under control. An example is the dragonfly, which devours flies and mosquitoes.

Spiny-skinned Animals

The *echinoderms,* or spiny-skinned animals, are typified by the starfish. All the starfish and their relatives live in salt water. Despite their name the starfish are no more kin to fish than are the shellfish, such as oysters and crabs. In addition to their spiny skins starfish are noted for their system of water tubes. Water is drawn into an opening in the body and then forced under pressure into thousands of small cylinders called *tube feet* that protrude from its arms. These feet have suckers at their ends. The starfish moves itself from place to place by applying and then releasing its tube feet on the surface on which it is moving. The pull of the tube feet also helps starfish open the clams, oysters, scallops, and mussels that serve as its food.

In addition to the starfish the echinoderms include animals with such self-describing names as brittle stars, basket stars, sea urchins, sand dollars, sea cucumbers, and sea lilies.

Animals with Backbones

The most highly developed group of animals is the backboned animals, the vertebrates. These are characterized by an internal bony skeleton. There are five main classes of backboned animals: fish, amphibians, reptiles, birds, and mammals. We shall consider them briefly here because they will be referred to frequently in the latter part of this chapter and in the next three chapters.

Fish have scaly skins and two-chambered hearts, breathe by means of gills, lay eggs without a shell, and are cold-blooded.

A cold-blooded animal is one that does not maintain a constant body temperature; its temperature varies with the temperature of its environment. Fish, amphibians, and reptiles are cold-blooded. Cold-blooded animals become sluggish and frequently hibernate when the temperature drops. Birds and mammals are warm-blooded, maintaining approximately the same temperature at all times. The ability to do this makes these animals relatively independent of outside conditions, so that they can remain active in very cold weather. (Some birds apparently conserve energy by having their body temperature drop sharply at night, when they are unable to feed.)

Amphibians include frogs, toads, newts, and salamanders. They have three-chambered hearts and moist skins, lay eggs, and are cold-blooded. In most cases the amphibians spend part of their life in water and part of it on land. Some, such as the mud puppies and hellbenders, never leave the water; some, such as most frogs and newts, divide their time between water and land; some, such as toads, some frogs, and some salamanders, spend most of their adult life on land.

Almost all amphibians mate in the water and lay their eggs there. The young, or tadpoles, breathe through gills, but the adult uses its lungs and moist skin for respiration. A few of the amphibians are used by man for food; many are helpful because they feed on harmful insects.

Reptiles breathe through lungs, have three- or four-chambered hearts and scaly skins, lay eggs covered by a tough shell, and are cold-blooded. Typical reptiles are snakes, lizards, alligators, crocodiles, and turtles. Some of these are used for food by man; others are prized for their skin or shell. Some of the reptiles, notably certain snakes, make venom with which to poison their prey. The poisonous snakes in the United States are the coral, copperhead, water moccasin, and rattlesnake. Despite their deadly venom rattlesnakes kill few people in this country. Given a chance a rattlesnake will silently glide away rather than join in battle with man.

Birds have achieved mastery of the air. They have feathers and four-chambered hearts, breathe through lungs, lay eggs covered with a hard shell, and are warm-blooded. If you have ever held a live chick in your hand you are well aware of how warm birds are. They are the warmest of all animals, with average temperatures of 100 to 110° F. This need to keep warm makes birds large eaters. Many of the smaller birds, such as the warblers, will eat their own weight of food in a day. Birds are of great value to man in helping to keep insect pests under control. The birds of prey, such as hawks and owls, are now recognized as important aids in helping to keep down the numbers of four-footed vermin, such as mice and rats. Birds are also an important source of food to man.

The *mammals* are warm-blooded animals that possess hair and sweat glands and nurse their young on milk from mammary glands. They are the only vertebrates possessing a *diaphragm* that separates the abdomen from the chest cavity. They are distinguished by the complexity of their brains, which is greatest in man.

Within the mammal group there is a wide variety in structure and in ways of living. Some mammals, such as the bat, whose forelimbs are fitted for flight, have taken to the air. Other mammals, such as the whale, live in the ocean but must rise to the top to breathe in air with their lungs. Some mammals—such as the hoofed camel, deer—and horse, are vegetarians. Others—such as the lion, tiger, and wolf—are flesh eaters. The animals with the greatest development of the brain are the monkeys, apes, and man. Mammals vary widely in size from the tiniest rodents to the sulphur-bottom whale, the largest animal that ever lived, past or present.

In this brief survey of the plant and animal kingdoms we have stressed the economic importance of the various forms of life to man. In so doing we do not wish to leave the impression that the different plants and animals have evolved for the particular purpose of serving man or that they should be considered solely in this light. Each is a living thing, from bacteria to man. Man is but one of the multitude of living things on this planet.

THE METHOD OF CLASSIFICATION

(*See* pp. 316–8.)

Biologists classify living things according to this scheme:

Kingdom
  Phylum
    Class
      Order
        Family
          Genus
            Species

To understand this system, let us see how it is used to classify a human being—literally, to put him in his place:

Kingdom: *Animal.* We are one of the $1\frac{1}{4}$ million of them.

Phylum: *Chordates.* Most of the animals in this group are better known as vertebrates, animals with backbones, which include fish, amphibia, reptiles, birds, and mammals.

Class: *Mammals.* Man is one of 6,000 kinds in this hairy, warm-blooded group that feeds milk to its young.

Order: *Primates.* Man is a distinguished member of this order, which also includes monkeys, lemurs, and apes.

Family: *Hominidae.* This group includes not only present-day man but also ancient prehuman forms such as Kenyapithecus, fossils of which were found in Africa. This form is believed to (*See* p. 407.) have lived 20 million years ago. (The word "family," when used in classification, has nothing to do with our everyday use of this word.)

Genus: *Homo.* A smaller group that includes Peking man and present-day man.

Species: *sapiens.* This group is limited to human beings only. It includes all men living on earth today, but has recently been expanded by some taxonomists to include Neanderthal and Cro-Magnon man.

An examination of this method of classification reveals that as one proceeds from kingdom to species there are fewer and fewer kinds in each group and the kinds of living things in each group are more and more alike. This method of classification also provides a scientific way of naming an organism. The name consists of the genus and species designation. Thus, man's scientific name is *Homo sapiens.* This "two-name" system of naming plants and animals was invented by Linnaeus, a Swedish botanist, and described in his book, *Systema Naturae,* published in 1735. The method provides a name for every organism, a name internationally accepted and recognized. At the same time the name fits the living thing into its natural place in its kingdom. For example, the common house cat has the name, *Felis domestica;* the lion is *Felis leo;* the tiger, *Felis tigris.* The system of naming reveals that these three animals belong to the same genus, that they are all closely related.

What criteria have been used by taxonomists for determining the place of an organism in the classification scheme? A review of the plant and animal groups just described would indicate that *structure*—both internal and external—is of paramount importance. Six legs separate the insects from the eight-legged spiders. Within the insect class the kind of mouth parts, number and type of wings, and the nature of the metamorphosis (changes from egg to adult) determine the *order* of an insect, such as beetle, true bug, butterfly, or moth. More recently, taxonomists have employed such characteristics as chromosome number and type, and subtle chemical differences and similarities.

THE FLOWERING PLANT

The landscapes of the earth are bedecked with over 200,000 varieties of flowering plants. The diversity of form, size, and color of the herbs, shrubs, and trees create the varied fields and forests of our planet. Yet all these plants show basic similarities in their internal structure and in the functioning of their roots, stems, leaves, and flowers.

The Leaf: Food Factory

(*See* pp. 296–9.) Climb to the top of a hill and look out over the countryside. The dominant color of the meadows, valleys, and hillsides is green. This is no accident, for green is the color of chlorophyll, the stuff that makes life on earth possible. It is this green pigment that enables every plant possessing it to combine atoms from two of the commonest substances on our planet, water and carbon dioxide, to form sugar. In plants we take this process for granted. But if you were looking at a glass of carbonated water (which is nothing but water and bubbles of carbon dioxide gas) and suddenly the water and bubbles disappeared and just as suddenly a lump of sugar appeared in the bottom you would say, "magic!" Yet green plants perform this chemical "magic" every day (chemical changes will be discussed more fully in Chapter 15A).

The main food factory of common plants is located in the leaves. A leaf is well adapted for its job. Leaves are constructed to present a broad surface to the sunlight, the source of energy for the food-making process. Yet because they are thin no cell is far removed from the surface. Immediately below the upper epidermis, as the layer of cells comprising the leaf surface is called, is a closely packed group of cells of the *palisade* layer, which are conspicuous for the large number of chlorophyll bodies within them. Beneath the palisade layer is the *spongy* layer, composed of irregularly shaped cells which have fewer chlorophyll bodies. It is in the palisade and spongy layers that food manufacturing occurs.

The sun's rays coming through the semi-transparent epidermis reach the chlorophyll bodies in the palisade and spongy cells. The raw materials for food making come to these cells from two sources, the air and the soil. On the surface of the leaf are found numbers of microscopic openings, each between two *guard cells.* These openings are the *stomata* of the leaf. Changes in the shape of the guard cells cause the stomata to open or close. Air passes freely through the stomata into air spaces inside the leaf. The gas carbon dioxide is then taken out of the air by the food-making layer of cells. Meanwhile, water is absorbed from the soil by the millions of minute cells, the *root hairs,* projecting from the plant's roots. From the root hair cells water moves to tubes inside the roots which transport it up through the stem into the veins of the leaf. At last the water reaches the food-making cells. Here the green chlorophyll has trapped some of the energy of sunlight. The energy is used (in a series of steps) to make sugar from atoms supplied by molecules of water and carbon dioxide. A valuable by-product, oxygen, also results from the chemical process (*see* the chemical equation for this process on page 484). The oxygen is released by the leaf through the stomata to the air. In this way the atmosphere of the earth is freshened with some 400 billion tons of oxygen each year, replacing the oxygen used up by living things.

(The knowledge that green plants take in carbon dioxide and release oxygen during sugar manufacture should not make us forget that *in the process of respiration plants, like animals, take in oxygen and give off carbon dioxide.* It is *untrue* to say that "plants breathe in the opposite way that animals do.")

The scientific name for the process of sugar-making is constructed of two words that emphasize the key aspect of the action: photo, which means "light," and synthesis, which means "putting together." *Photosynthesis,* "putting together by means of light," is exactly what happens in the process.

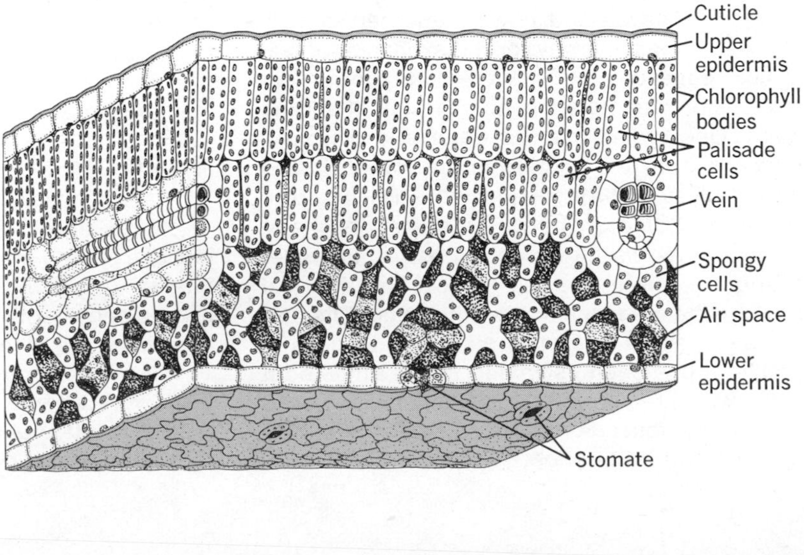

The food factory of the plant—a block diagram of a section of a leaf.

Much has been added to our knowledge of photosynthesis in the last 50 years. It is now known that light energy, water, carbon dioxide, nitrates, and sulfates are combined in the chlorophyll bodies of leaves to produce many organic compounds. Amino acids, the building blocks of proteins, are synthesized there. These are essential for cell growth. Carbohydrates—sugars and starches—are synthesized to meet the energy requirements of cells.

The remarkable process of photosynthesis not only produces the basic materials essential for the existence of green plants, but eventually supplies all living things on our planet with the chemical compounds needed for the substance of their structures and for the energy to carry on life processes. Moreover, as we have seen, photosynthesis returns to the atmosphere the oxygen that is taken out of it by living organisms.

In recent years scientists have succeeded in duplicating part of this process in test tubes. Perhaps someday they will be able to manufacture food in large quantity from abundant chemicals. Until that day we shall have to continue to depend for our food upon the living cells of plants, using chlorophyll to trap energy from sunlight, and carbon dioxide and water as the basic raw materials.

The Stem: Transporter and Supporter

(*See* pp. 298–9.)

The stem of a plant supports the leaves and flowers and serves as a passageway for the exchange of materials between the leaves and roots. Two streams of vital materials flow through the living plant. One stream carries water and dissolved minerals from the roots through the stem and into the leaves through a pipelike tissue known as *xylem.* Some of the water is used in photosynthesis, as we have seen. Most of the water evaporates from the air spaces of the leaf through the stomates to the outside air. The loss of water, known as *transpiration,* can be considerable. It has been estimated that a single corn plant, which requires 100 days to grow from seed to maturity, loses 50 gallons of water to the atmosphere in that period.

The other stream in plants transports manufactured food, principally sugar, from the leaf down through the stem and then to other plant structures, such as flowers and roots. The tissue responsible for the distribution of food is known as *phloem.*

In the stems of herbaceous plants, such as the soft stems of low-growing plants, the xylem and phloem tissues are contained within *vascular bundles.* The "strings" in a plant structure, such as a celery stalk, are a familiar example of these bundles. Branches of the vascular bundles run into the leaves, where they become the veins. In

(*See* figure p. 283.)

a tree the water-carrying xylem tissue makes up the sapwood, generally the outer part of the solid central cylinder of the tree. The sugar-carrying phloem lines the inner bark. Between the xylem and phloem lies the *cambium,* a thin sheet of dividing cells that contributes to the growth of the stem by adding new xylem and phloem cells.

Girdling a tree—that is, removing a complete ring of bark and cambium from it—kills the tree, for it severs the pipelines that carry food and destroys the layer of cells responsible for the continued life and growth of the plant.

The cambium grows new layers each year, adding to the girth of the tree. It grows more actively in the spring, so there is a marked difference between the spring growth and that of the rest of the year. This results in *annual rings,* which can be seen when a tree is cut across. Counting these rings gives an estimate of the age of the tree.

The Root: Anchor and Absorber

(*See* pp. 297–9.)

The root is both an anchoring and an absorbing device. The outer layer of the root contains cells with long projections called root hairs. These microscopic "hairs" reach out into the soil to a surprising degree and absorb water and dissolved minerals. In a single rye plant it was found that there were 14 billion root hairs. If the surfaces of all these hairs were spread out flat, they would cover an area of 4,300 square feet. This means that these root hairs are in contact with 4,300 square feet

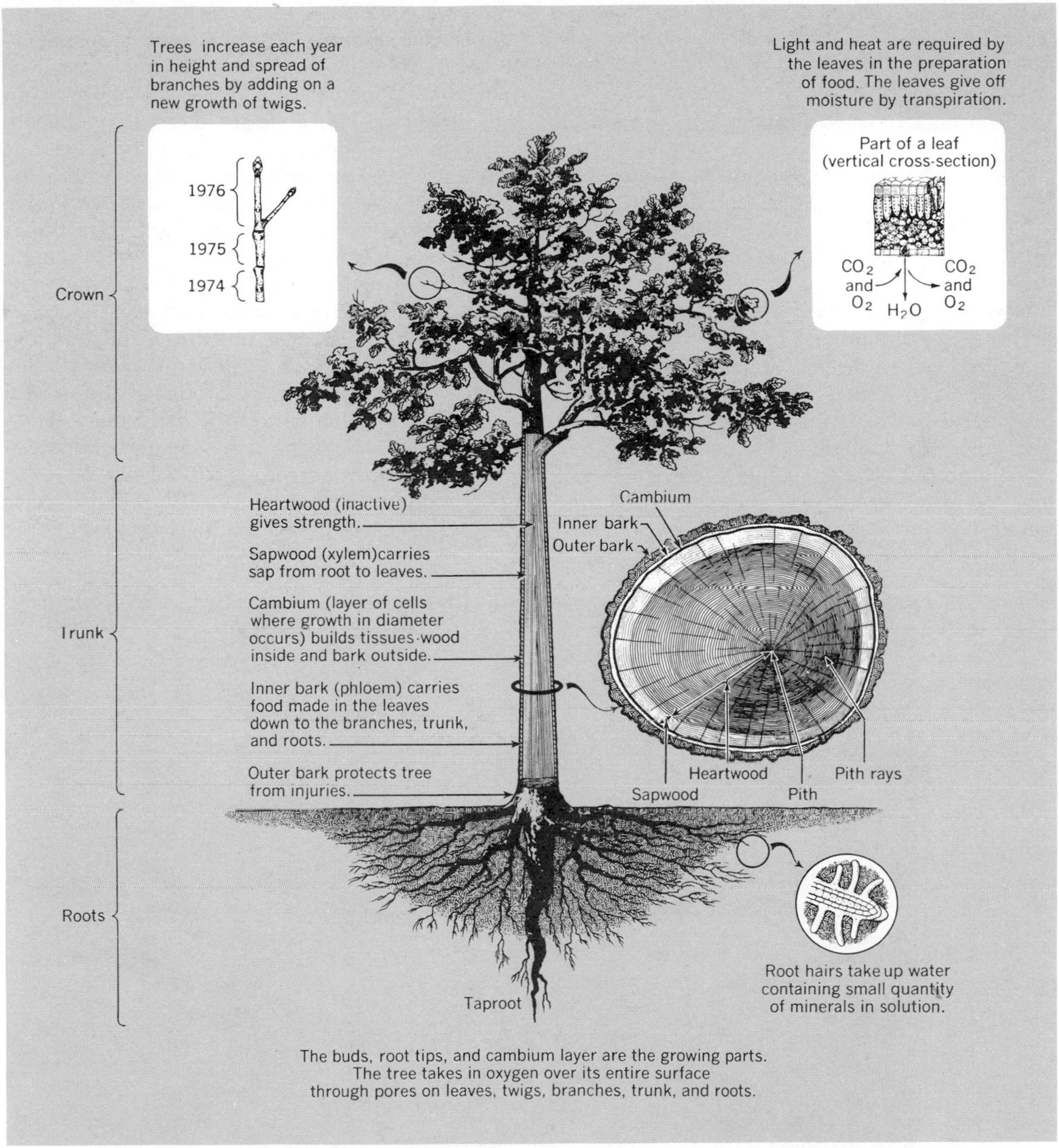
Trees increase each year in height and spread of branches by adding on a new growth of twigs.
1976
1975
1974
Crown
Light and heat are required by the leaves in the preparation of food. The leaves give off moisture by transpiration.
Part of a leaf (vertical cross-section)
CO_2 and O_2
H_2O
CO_2 and O_2
Trunk
Heartwood (inactive) gives strength.
Sapwood (xylem)carries sap from root to leaves.
Cambium (layer of cells where growth in diameter occurs) builds tissues-wood inside and bark outside.
Inner bark (phloem) carries food made in the leaves down to the branches, trunk, and roots.
Outer bark protects tree from injuries.
Cambium
Inner bark
Outer bark
Heartwood
Sapwood
Pith
Pith rays
Roots
Taproot
Root hairs take up water containing small quantity of minerals in solution.
The buds, root tips, and cambium layer are the growing parts. The tree takes in oxygen over its entire surface through pores on leaves, twigs, branches, trunk, and roots.

of soil, from which they can absorb valuable minerals and water. The materials absorbed by the root hairs are passed through other cells into the xylem and thence to the stem and leaves of the plant.

The larger roots have tough fibers that give them the great strength needed to hold the plant in the ground. This, added to the gripping effect of the enormous root system, with each root hair firmly embedded in soil particles, enables even large trees to withstand the buffeting of strong winds.

The Flower: Seed Producer

(*See* pp. 309–10.)

The flower contains the organs of the plant devoted to reproduction, which involves the union of two cell nuclei to form a new individual. The flower makes these nuclei—sperm and egg—and also provides for their coming together and uniting. A typical flower has a number of brightly colored petals that often have a distinctive odor. The color and odor serve to attract insects needed for *cross pollination,* which is the transfer of pollen from one flower to another of the same kind. Some flowers do not require insects to carry their pollen; the wind serves this purpose. Wind-pollinated flowers make huge amounts of pollen, which compensates for the pollen wasted by this hit-or-miss method. Some flowers are *self-pollinated,* the transfer of pollen taking place from the male to the female parts of the same flower.

The part of the flower engaged in pollen-making is the *stamen.* The top of the stamen is an enlarged sac, called the *anther,* where the pollen is formed. Supporting the anther is a long, thin stalk, the *filament.* The pollen grain is a microscopic structure containing the male reproductive nucleus, the sperm. To succeed in its function the pollen must be carried to the *pistil* of a flower of the same kind. The pistil generally consists of three parts. The large lower portion is the *ovary.* Within it are produced the *ovules.* Inside each ovule is an egg, the female reproductive cell. Above the ovary is the slender stem-like *style.* The top of the style is the *stigma,* which is equipped with hairs and a sticky secretion to hold any pollen grains that may land on it. The

The organs of reproduction of the lily: six stamens and a single pistil. (*Courtesy of Rapho-Guillumette, E.A. Heiniger.*)

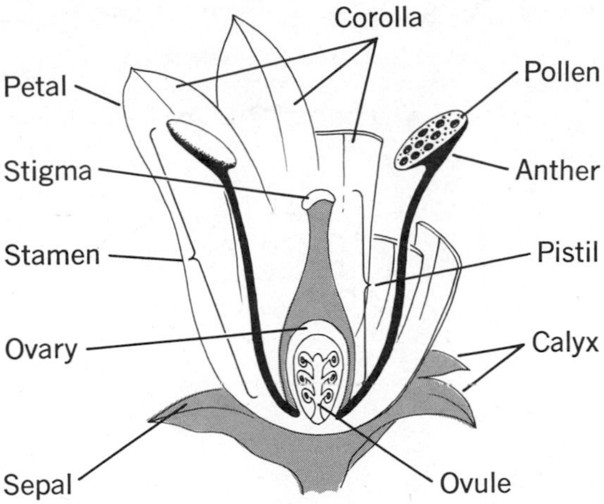

The flower contains the reproductive organs of the plant. Shown here are the characteristic structures found in most flowers.

pollen grain grows a tube that extends down through the style and into the ovary. Finally it reaches a special opening in the ovule. The sperm of the pollen grain passes into the ovule through the channel thus made and unites with the egg. This union of the sperm and the egg is called *fertilization.* The fertilized egg resulting from this union will develop into an *embryo,* a baby plant.

After fertilization the flower seems to wither. Parts no longer needed, such as petals, stamens, and parts of the pistil, wither or fall off, but the remaining parts of the flower grow to many times their original size. The fertilized egg develops into an embryo. The ovule develops into a seed. The ovary develops into a fruit. A fruit, then, is a ripened ovary containing seeds. That is why the tomato is really a fruit, even though people customarily call it a vegetable.

There are many different kinds of fruits. They include edible varieties such as apples, string beans, green peppers, and cucumbers, as well as inedible varieties such as milkweed pods, rose "apples," winged maple keys, and sycamore "buttonballs."

A seed is made up of the young plant, a food supply, and a protective coat. The embryo has two parts, one of which becomes the roots and the other the stem and leaves. As the seed dries, its food supply is concentrated or "dehydrated." This makes seeds a prime food for human beings. The most important plant foods are seeds, such as corn, wheat, rice, barley, oats, and beans. In addition to their food value plant seeds furnish such valuable substances as oil—for example, linseed oil—and drugs, such as opium from the poppy seed.

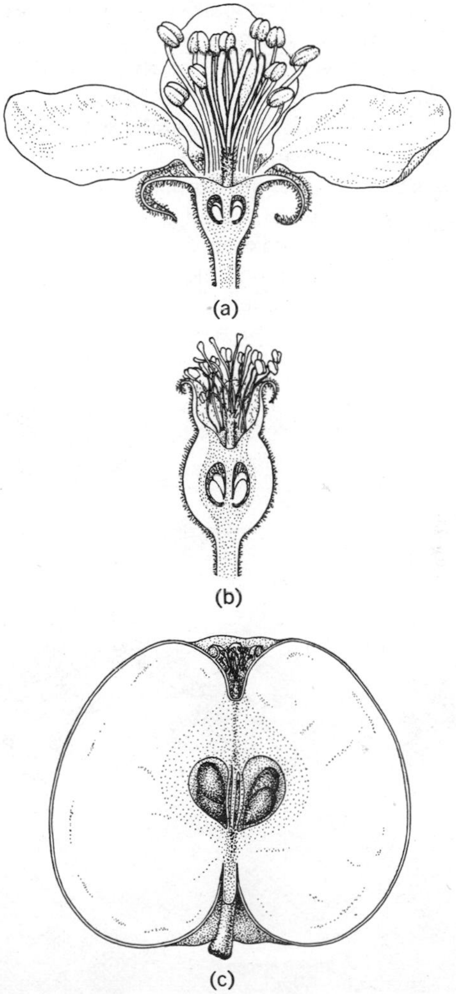

The apple blossom produces the apple. Note how some of the floral parts become less conspicuous or drop off as the ovary ripens to become the core of the seed-carrying fruit. (a.) Flower of apple; (b.) older flower after petals have fallen off; (c.) section of the mature fruit.

The Seed: Plant Producer

Germination—the development of a seed into a plant with roots, stem, and leaves—depends on (See pp. 302–5.) the availability of food, oxygen, suitable temperature, and water. The food supply is contained within the seed. There is enough food there to last until the roots are established in the ground and the first green leaves exposed to the sun are ready to carry on photosynthesis. Oxygen is essential for the oxidation of food and the resulting release of energy. The soil in which plants grow must be porous to allow air to circulate down to the roots. The warmth needed for germination is supplied by the sun, which warms the ground. Water is essential for the germination of the seed. Water softens the hard seed coat and penetrates the seed. The cells take in water, become active, and reproduce. All chemical processes in the cell, such as the digestion of stored starch into sugar, require water as a medium. Water is also

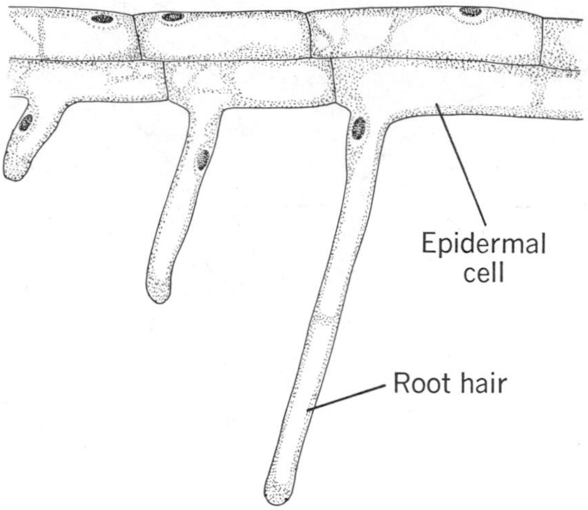

The stages of development of root hairs from a root of timothy. Each root hair is an extension of a cell.

needed as a vital component of the new protoplasm, the living material, forming in the cells of the rapidly growing plant.

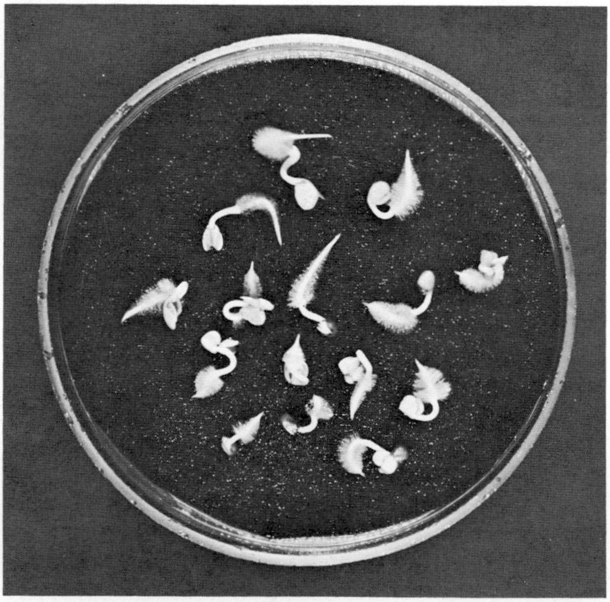

A magnifying glass shows that the fine fuzz of these radish seedlings is made of thousands of delicate root hairs. (From *Botany* by Carl E. Wilson; copyright 1952 by Holt, Rinehart and Winston, Inc. Reprinted by permission of Holt, Rinehart and Winston, Inc.)

With the softening and swelling of the seed coat the part of the embryo that will form the roots breaks out. Roots serve to obtain water (See figure p. 287.) and to anchor the plant in the soil. In seeds such as the bean the root-making part forms an arch. This arch soon breaks through the soil. Thereupon the arch straightens out and the two food storage halves of the seed, the *cotyledons,* are thus pulled out of the ground. Protectively sandwiched between the cotyledons are the first leaves and the embryo stem. Once above ground the cotyledons separate. The food stored in the cotyledons is slowly digested and transported to other parts of the seedling. The stem elongates and the leaves grow, turn green, and start making food.

In seeds that have only one cotyledon, such (See figure p. 287.) as corn, development is a bit different. The roots develop first, but then a spearlike sheath emerges that encloses the first leaves. Its spear shape permits it to push through the soil readily while protecting the tender leaves within. Soon this spear point shows above ground, and the leaves unfold, turn green, and start making food. In these plants the main bulk of the seed, containing the food for the embryo, remains below ground. The food is soon used up, and the seed remnants shrivel as the seedling grows.

The water, minerals, and carbon dioxide that the plant takes in are used in food manufacture and in building protoplasm in its cells. The plant enlarges as millions of the building bricks, cells, are added. The stem reaches higher and higher, and more and more leaves are formed. The plant is now on its own.

LIFE CYCLE OF SOME VERTEBRATES

Samuel Butler once said "the hen is the egg's way of making more eggs." We may not accept this definition, but we can see in it an emphasis on the continuity of life: egg to adult to egg and so on.

The life of most animals begins when an egg and sperm join. The fertilized egg resulting from the union of these two sex cells begins to divide into many cells and to form an embryo. The embryo continues to develop, ultimately becoming an adult, either male or female. Sperm produced by the male and eggs by the female unite, and the cycle is repeated. Let us examine the life history of some typical vertebrate animals.

Fish

The spawning season for fish in temperate zones is in the spring. The return of the salmon to the Columbia River for spawning is well known. Salmon live in the ocean, but travel far up rivers to breed. The 10,000 or more eggs produced in the ovaries of each female fish are released into the waters of a quiet pool. Millions of sperm, made in the testes of the male, are deposited on the eggs, fertilizing them. After spawning the exhausted adults usually die. The fertilized eggs develop into young salmon, which eventually swim to the ocean. When mature, these salmon will find their way back to the same stream where they were spawned and continue the cycle of reproduction.

Some fish, such as many of the tropical fish with which people stock their home aquaria,

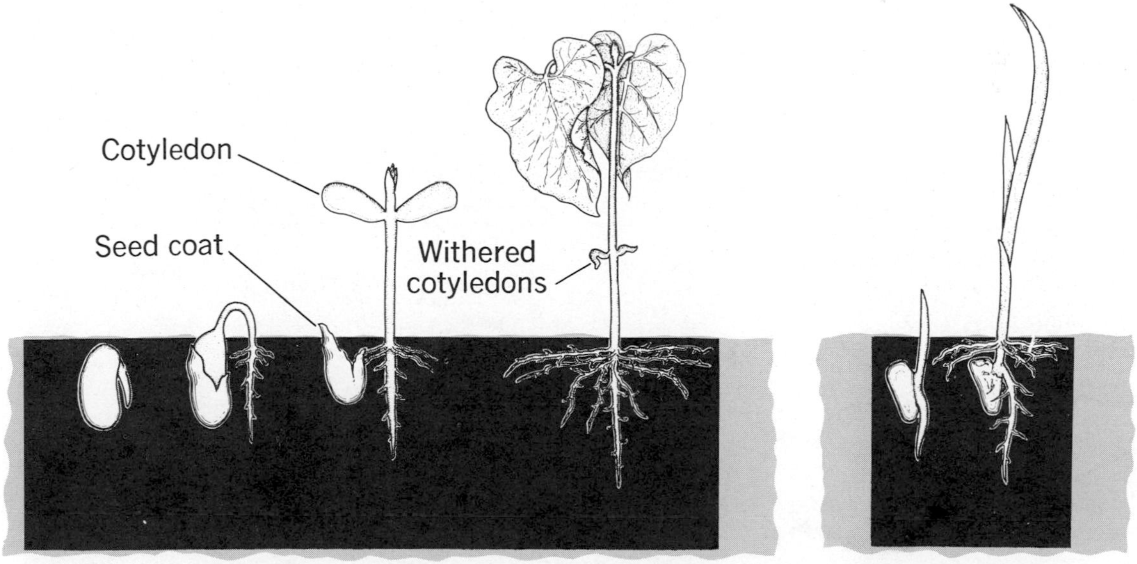

(*Left*) Stages in the germination of the garden bean. The two cotyledons provide food until the plant is able to make its own. (*Right*) Germination of the corn seed. The single cotyledon of the corn seed remains underground as the seedling grows.

seem to bear their young alive. This is only apparent, because the fish actually lay eggs, but these eggs after fertilization are retained within the body of the female to complete their early growth. These "live bearers" are not live bearers in the sense that mammals are, because there is no direct connection of the tissues of the growing embryo with those of the female. Hence neither food nor oxygen can be supplied from the bloodstream of the mother, as is the case in mammals.

Frogs

Frogs mate in the spring, the male typically clasping the female until the eggs are expelled. The male then fertilizes the eggs in the water by discharging sperm over them. Mating thus increases the chances of sperm meeting eggs. After mating the pair separate, having no interest in their offspring. What the eggs lack in safety they make up in number, anywhere from several hundred to several thousand eggs being laid by

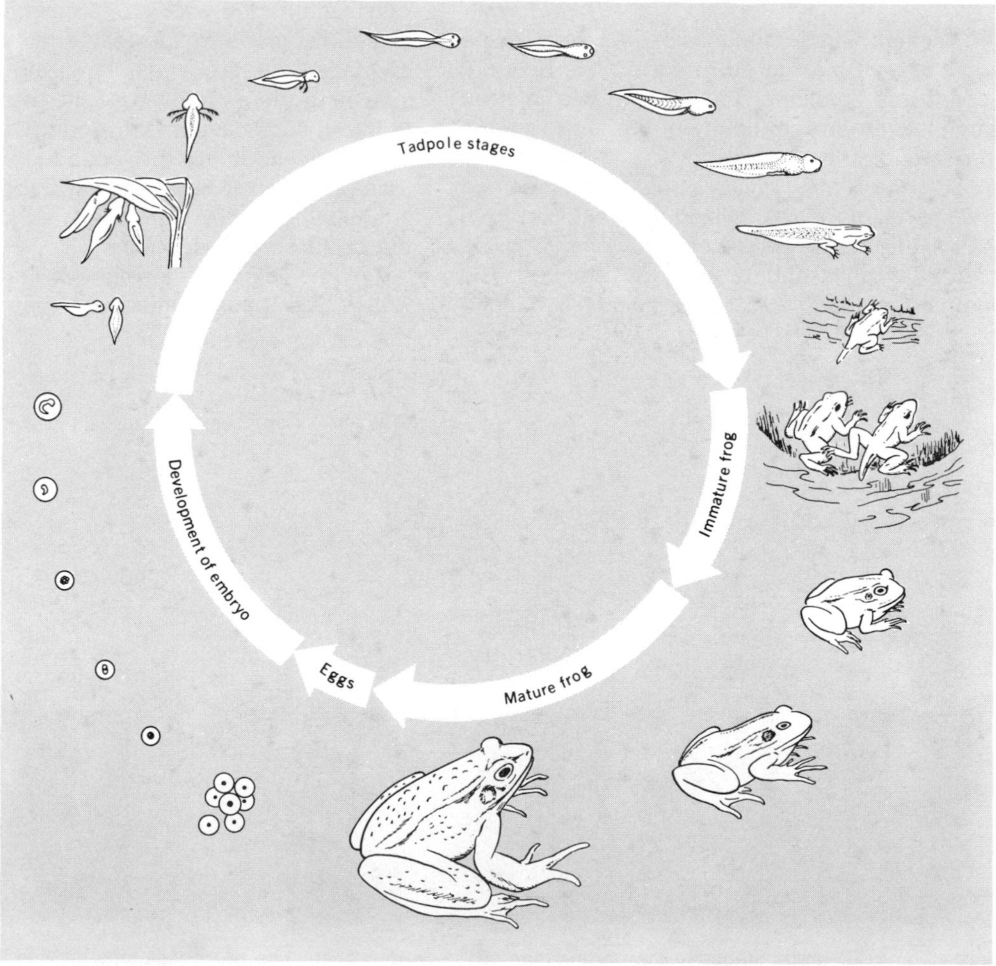

The gradual metamorphosis of the frog illustrates how completely some animals change as they develop. The frog's fishlike ancestry is revealed in its early stages of development.

one female, the number depending on the species of the frog. Moreover, each egg is amply stocked with yolk, which supplies the developing embryo with food until well after hatching has occurred.

Each egg is embedded in a clear jellylike sphere. All the eggs laid by the frog stick together in a mass; this provides some degree of protection against fish and other pond enemies. The development of the egg from its very first stages to adult frog is interesting and may be watched easily if some of the eggs are placed in a jar or aquarium with some pond water. While still inside the jelly the egg changes into a tiny embryo that wriggles occasionally. After about 10 days to 2 weeks the tadpole wriggles out of the jelly, which by now has started to disintegrate.

The tadpole breathes through gills, which are flaps of tissue with thin outer membranes and a rich supply of blood. As the pond water streams over the gills oxygen dissolved in the water passes through the thin membrane into the bloodstream. At the same time the excess carbon dioxide waste in the blood is discharged through the gills into the water.

The tadpole grows, eating bits of plant material that are in the pond. Its tail grows into a fin capable of moving the tadpole rapidly through the water. At this stage the developing frog is indeed very much like a fish. This is no accident, for the frog, like all higher vertebrates, reveals in its early development traces of its fishlike ancestry. (More precisely, in their early development higher animals exhibit similarities to the *embryonic stages* of lower forms. The tadpole resembles the *embryo* fish.) After some time hind legs and then front legs develop; the material of the tail is broken down and absorbed by the frog to build other parts of its body. The gills are replaced by lungs; other internal changes occur. The frog changes its diet, eating only living worms and insects.

The common leopard frog completes this change or *metamorphosis,* as it is called, in a few months. The bullfrog, on the other hand, remains a tadpole for 2 years, only then changing into an adult frog.

The frog is a cold-blooded animal. In the colder parts of the country, with the approach of winter, it slows down and hibernates in the mud at the bottom of its pond. In this torpid state all body functions are reduced to a minimum. Living on food stored during the lush days, it is able to survive until warm days arrive again. The moist skin of the frog is thin enough to permit the passage of oxygen from the pond water into its blood and the exit of carbon dioxide.

Reptiles

In land animals fertilization is internal; that is, the sperm reaches the egg while it is inside the body of the female. This is essential, because the sperm and eggs require a moist environment to survive. Consequently reptiles, birds, and mammals must have internal fertilization.

Most reptiles lay eggs covered with a soft, leathery shell. Some, like the turtle, deposit the eggs in sand and then depart, providing no care for the young. The sun warms the sand and incubates the eggs. The newborn turtle is ready to fend for itself and soon starts off in search of food. In some snakes, like the common garter snake, the eggs after fertilization are retained in the body of the female. The young snakes hatch from the eggs inside the mother and then leave the body of the female.

Birds

Birds reproduce in essentially the same way as reptiles. Fertilization is internal; development, however, is always external. Nest construction follows mating, which takes place at different times for different birds. Owls and hawks mate early. Their offspring can be fed on the young of such animals as rabbits, rats, and field mice, which are abundant in early spring. Birds that feed their young on insects mate later. When the young are born, there is a sufficient supply of insects to feed them.

Most birds' eggs hatch after about 3 weeks of incubation. During the period of incubation the mother bird is confined to the nest to keep the eggs warm; she leaves only for a few moments to get water and to exercise. In many species of birds the mother is fed during incubation by the father, who is kept busy bringing food to the nest. The eggs are carefully drawn up into the feathers of the mother bird for greater warmth. The shell is porous, permitting oxygen to pass through it from the air to the developing embryo. The bulk of the bird's egg furnishes a complete "diet" for the embryo. Many birds hatch out in a helpless state and depend on their parents for food for some time.

Mammals

In mammals the minute egg (barely visible to the unaided eye) is fertilized within the body of the female; it then attaches itself to the mother. Here it remains for the period of development. The mother and the embryo develop a special membrane, the *placenta,* through which food and oxygen are supplied to the developing embryo. The wastes of the embryo also pass through this membrane into the bloodstream of the mother. There are, however, two mammals that lay external eggs: the remarkable duck-billed platypus and the spiny anteater. Both, however, exhibit the mammalian characteristic of feeding their young with milk from mammary glands.

Most mammals take care of the young after they are born. They supply food and protect their young. In man, this period of care is longer than in any other animal. A detailed summary of reproduction in man will be found in Chapter 12A.

Some of the important generalizations of this chapter are:

Life exists almost everywhere on earth.

Living things use food for energy and growth, dispose of their wastes, are sensitive and are adapted to their environment, and can make others like themselves.

Living things are built of basic units called cells.

Within the cell there is an architecture of many special structures that carry on the activities of life.

There are more than $1\frac{1}{2}$ million different kinds of plants and animals on the earth.

The modern system of classifying living things is based on their structure.

Living things need food, water, and oxygen to stay alive and to grow.

Plants with chlorophyll manufacture the food essential to the existence of all living things on the earth.

Living things reproduce their kind in a variety of ways.

Some living things, such as protozoa and bacteria, reproduce simply by splitting in two.

Most plants and animals reproduce by producing sperm and egg cells that unite to form new organisms.

Living things go through a series of stages in their development from fertilized egg to adult.

Discovering for Yourself

1. Incubate some chickens' eggs; examine them as they develop.
2. Visit a greenhouse to find out how plants are supplied with what they need for growth, and investigate any experiments with plant growth that are taking place.
3. Visit a garden-supply shop to check out new types of fertilizer and new methods and types of pest control.
4. Collect and examine current seed and nursery catalogues to discover new varie-

ties of fruits, vegetables, and flowers. Learn as much as you can about the processes by which these were produced.

5. Make a collection of seed-dispersal adaptations showing the seeds, as well as their covering.
6. Make a collection of plants to show protective adaptations, and explain how the adaptations help the plant in its environment.
7. Make a collection of flowers to show adaptations for cross-pollination. Explain how the structures of the flowers function with reference to insects and wind and any other agents of cross-pollination.
8. Visit an orchard or a nursery to find out how plants are cared for (pruned, protected against weather changes, kept free from damaging insects, and so forth).
9. Sprout five different kinds of seeds. Plant an exhibit to show likenesses and differences in the ways in which these seeds change as they germinate and how the seedlings begin to grow.
10. Dig up five different common weeds or other plants. Wash the root systems and examine them. Explain what you have discovered about adaptation to environment and the functions of the various plants' roots.
11. Collect six different kinds of insects to discover how they are alike, how they are adapted to different environments, how they get food, how they protect themselves, and how they reproduce.
12. Observe a mammal, a reptile, a bird, a fish, and an amphibian to see how each gets food, is adapted to a specific environment, protects itself, and changes as it grows.
13. Collect frogs' and toads' eggs and watch the young develop.
14. Investigate at firsthand the plant and animal life associated with any of the following: pond, vacant lot, swamp, lawn, woodland, stream, beach, field. Find out as much as you can about adaptation to environment in each case.
15. Study one square foot of lawn, swamp, or forest floor. List all the plants and animals you can discover there. Observe over a period of time for changes.
16. Make a collection of living things and classify them into groups indicating the characteristics that put them into these specific groups.
17. Visit a local zoo and make a plan for using it to find material on "how are animals adapted to different environments" or some other broad problem.
18. Devise an experiment to show differences in kinds of house-plant fertilizers.
19. Order silkworm eggs, hatch them, feed the larvae, and observe the cycle.
20. Dig into an ant colony. Use a magnifying glass to observe the insects.
21. Make an exhibit demonstrating various ways plants reproduce.

(Courtesy of U.S. Department of Agriculture.)

CHAPTER 10B TEACHING "THE NATURE AND VARIETY OF LIFE"

The study of living things offers many opportunities for field trips, observations by individuals and small groups, and for group activities that involve planning and working together.

These can take place in an urban environment as well as in the country or elsewhere. A tree and a strip of grass by the sidewalk, a windowbox, a small garden, school gardens, classroom plants and animals, parks, botanical gardens, zoos, and so forth—all supply materials for observations and learning.

The information gained through experiences with living things should be related and organized into important generalizations. We are interested not so much in teaching isolated facts about birds, trees, and butterflies as in developing important understandings useful in interpreting living things in relation to the environment. We are interested in interrelationships; for example, how insect-eating birds affect plant life, how the trees in a particular area play a vital role in providing a home for animals, how trees are essential in protecting the soil from erosion, how living things reproduce. We are concerned with man's relationship to these living things and in helping pupils learn to enjoy the outdoors and develop a desire to explore and protect it. The ecology phase of this study is of utmost importance. The chapter has a very close relationship with Chapter 14, "Ecology and Survival."

The material considered in Part III lends itself to the development of many behavioral objectives. As a result of the activities pupils will be able to *observe* properties and characteristics of living things and *construct classification* schemes, *predict* certain events and possibilities on the basis of observations of living things in their environment, *distinguish between observations and inferences* in association with the living things in their environment, *identify* and *control variables* when experimenting with conditions of living things, *describe* structures and conditions observed, and *communicate* possible interpretations of these observations.

SOME BROAD CONCEPTS "The Nature and Variety of Life"

Life exists almost everywhere on the earth.

Living things can move; grow; take in food, air, and water; dispose of wastes; and reproduce.

Living things are made of many different kinds of cells.

Living things reproduce in many different ways.

Green plants manufacture their own food; animals depend on plants.

Living things need food, air, water, and proper temperatures.

Living things change as they grow.

FOR YOUNGER CHILDREN

What Plants Live in Our Neighborhood?

A first step in learning about living things is to explore the immediate environment of the school ground and the areas near school. With younger children observations of plants may be made at one time and animals at another.

Our objectives are to help pupils become aware of their surroundings, to *observe* carefully, to *make comparisons,* to *identify* characteristics, to *report* what they see. Prepare for the trip by asking: "Where shall we look?" "What do you think we may see?" "What can we bring back to study?" The following are examples of observations to make: (1.) *A tree.* "What can you discover by looking at it?" (Its branches; the leaves are green and flat; there are many leaves; and so on.) "What do you think this tree needs to grow? How old do you think it is? Trees that are surrounded by pavement and sidewalk often die. Why?" If possible, let each child examine *a leaf* carefully and report observations. A few leaves may be taken for more careful examination later. (2.) *A shrub.* "How is it like the tree?" "How is it different from it? (3.) *Grass.* "Where did it come from?" "How is it like the other plants we have seen?" "How different?" "What happens if a path is made over it? Why?" Dig up a few plants and take them for further observation. (4.) *Small plants* growing in the grass—dandelion, clover, plantain, and others. "What can we discover?" "How are they different from grass?" Dig up a plant with its root system for further study.

If possible, observe vegetable and flower gardens using a similar procedure. What plant parts can we discover (stem, leaf, root, flower, seed)? Pictures from books and other references may be used to supplement the environmental experiences in making discoveries about plants in other environments.

As a follow-up to the trip examine the leaf specimens with a magnifying glass. Grow some grass seeds; examine the grass plants and the plants that were growing in it. Report the observations.

What Do Plants Need to Live and Grow?

Use the observations made on the field trip to the neighborhood as a beginning. "What do you think these plants need so they can stay alive and grow?" List the

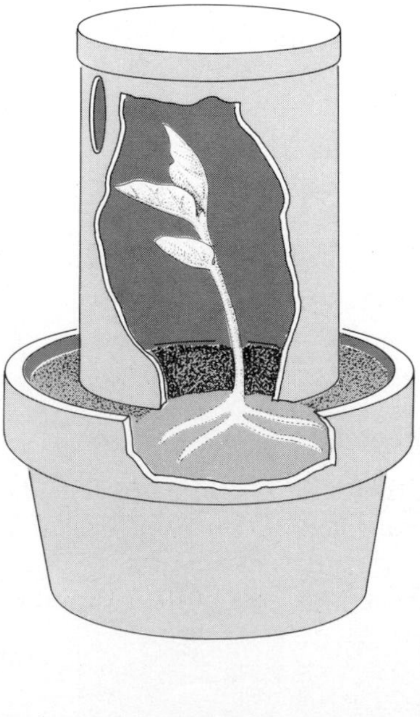

This simple experiment or variations of it may be used to show that plants grow toward light. Similar plants should be grown uncovered to indicate the difference in growth.

children's suggestions. Then assist them in setting up experiments to test the importance of water, light, soil, temperature, air, and other factors. *See* page 182 in Chapter 7B as an example of using experiments to discover the relationship of plants and light. Follow this general procedure with other plant needs. If possible, each child should plant a few seeds, care for the plants as they grow, observe them, record changes, and report the findings. Children also may select a specific plant outdoors and observe: buds, seeds, leaves, flowers, and other parts, and use the data in a similar way. If possible, plant a garden (*see* details later in this chapter) so that children can see the results when plants have, or fail to have, the proper conditions for growth.

What Animals Live in Our Neighborhood?

Again a trip to the immediate environment is a good beginning. Urge the children to stop, look, and listen, and before the trip discuss where they may look to find animal life: in trees, in grass, in the ground, in the air, on the ground, and other places. It is desirable to make more than one trip to solve this problem. Urge children to observe their home environments, as well as their surroundings on the way to and from school. Concentrate on some of the following: identifying the animals; looking for likenesses and differences; observing the methods of moving, the structure, and activities; comparing the places where the animals live. Children, depending on the location, will probably see bees, ants and other insects, birds, squirrels, domestic animals, and many others. After the trips help children to list the animals they saw and discuss some of the observations. This will in all probability raise problems. In a city environment a vacant lot,[1] trees along the sidewalk, cracks in the sidewalk, windowboxes, small parks, and others are worth exploring. A comparison of such an environment with a large park presents an interesting problem of why there are more animals living in the park than in some other city environments.

What Do Animals Need to Live and Grow?

If the problem of the needs of plants has been used in previous work, children may begin by discussing whether or not animals have the same needs. Caring for an animal at home or at school is one of the best ways to discover what they need. Keeping caterpillars and other insects, a few fish in an aquarium, a caged bird, or other easily-kept animals will be helpful. From this children may expand their experiences by observing other animals to determine what common needs all animals have. Observations may also include how animals obtain the things they need and what things different kinds of animals eat. How do they eat? Where do they find food? How do they protect themselves? are just a few of the questions to be asked. For further suggestions see similar activities for older children.

[1] *See Vacant Lot Studies: An Environmental Investigation* (Washington, D.C.: National Wildlife Federation), 1972; for "Visitors to the Vacant Lot," "Plants in the Vacant Lot," "Community and the Vacant Lot."

How Do We Use Plants and Animals?[2]

Suggest that children observe their home, school, and community environments to find examples of ways plants and animals are used (food, clothing, shelter, fun, and so on). Under each category list examples. Children may like to work in groups, each group exploring one place (a grocery store, the school, the street, at home, for example). One group may try to assemble pictures of plant and animal uses from magazines and other sources, and classify them according to the categories they make up. Depending on the group and the interest pupils may discuss such problems as: "How can we help to make a better place for the animals and plants to live?" "What kinds of farm crops are raised in our neighborhood?" "What birds live in our neighborhood?" "Why are they important?" For other suggestions *see* Chapter 14B on "Ecology and Survival."

OTHER PROBLEMS FOR YOUNGER CHILDREN

1. What do the different parts of a plant do?
2. How do animals build homes?
3. How do plants reproduce?
4. How do plants change as they grow?
5. How do animals change as they grow?

FOR OLDER CHILDREN

What Do Plants Need?

When pupils are considering the problem of what plants need in order to grow they may list things they think are needed and then consider the question: "How can we set up experiments to find out if plants need water, sunlight, good soil, and a proper temperature?" Pupils can plan the experiments themselves, make a summary of the plan on the chalkboard, and then follow the plan, change it if necessary, and note the results. Here is an example of such a procedure as a fifth-grade class planned it.

Purpose of the Experiment To find out whether plants need sunlight.

Our Plan

Bring four small geranium plants that are alike. (George will bring them.)

Be sure that all plants are healthy and that they are all growing in the same kind of soil.

Set two plants on the window ledge where they will be in sunlight part of the day and set the others in a dark closet.

Water all plants with the same amount of water. (Perry and Albert will do this.)

[2] *See also* G.O. Blough: *Useful Plants and Animals.* (New York: Harper and Row Publishers), 1972.

Put labels on the plants so that no one will move them and spoil our experiment. (Alice will make the label which is to say: "Please do not touch.")

Every week bring the plants together and compare them for growth, for color, and for anything else that we can see.

This plan evolved only after lengthy discussion and with some help from the teacher in designing the experiment in such a way that it would be possible to draw some valid conclusions from it. The pupils understood the reasons for including plants that were not subject to the experimental condition (darkness). They saw that this control served as a basis of comparison. As they put it later: "If we didn't have the plants in the *light* we wouldn't know whether darkness or something else made the differences in the plants." In drawing conclusions pupils were urged not to decide from the one experiment that *all* plants need sunlight. Several pupils volunteered to perform a similar experiment at home.

After the experiment was finished and pupils had reported on their home experiments the class took a trip around the schoolyard to see places where plants did not grow well—*perhaps* because of the lack of light. They observed places where plants were growing toward the light. In a shaded place they found plants that had grown much taller and more spindly than the same kinds of plants growing in direct sunlight. It is also important for children to understand that some plants require less direct sunlight than others.

When the pupils returned from this trip one of them found an experiment in a book that was designed to find out whether plants grow toward the light. They planted radish seeds in the soil in two 4-inch flower pots. After the seeds sprouted, the pupils cut a round cereal box in half to make a cardboard cylinder that fitted over the growing seeds in one of the flower pots and excluded light. Then they cut a round hole in one side of the box near the top. This was the only source of light. The young plants covered with the box grew toward the hole where the light came in. The other pot was left uncovered. The pupils frequently compared the two. They observed that the plants in the uncovered pot grew toward the windows. They also noted that the plants growing in their schoolroom turned toward the light.

Pupils can themselves design experiments to discover that plants need light. The experiments with the geranium and with the radish seeds show two ways of approaching the experimental idea with pupils; in one the pupils themselves devised an experiment; in the other they found an experiment in a book that served their purpose. In both cases it is important to remember that the method used in experimenting is just as valuable as the knowledge gained from it. In both cases the setting up of "controls" as a basis for comparison was a critical and essential part of the experiment. It is also important for children to *apply the results* of experiments to everyday observations in the world of living things.

We have illustrated some methods used in experimenting to see that plants need light. Their need for the other essentials (water, good soil, air, and proper temperature) may be demonstrated in similar ways. (*See* the Bibliography for books that give more details about plant experiments.)

Plants and water may be studied in the following ways: Sprout some radish seeds on moist blotting paper and look at the rootlets through a magnifying glass. The "fuzz" on the rootlets is made up of root hairs through which water enters the plant. Discuss the advantages of a plant's having thousands of root hairs instead of a single root.

Plant about a dozen lima bean seeds. After the shoots have come above the ground and the first leaves have appeared, try the following experiment to see what happens when the root hairs are injured. Pull two or three of the plants out of the soil. Replant them in other soil. Lift two or three of the other plants out of the soil with a trowel, being careful not to disturb the roots. Replant them also. Do not disturb the remaining plants. Suggest that pupils try to predict what will happen to each group. Children should grow in ability to see the difference between a *prediction* (made on the basis of some knowledge and considerable observation) and a *guess* (made on less background). They may also grow in *ability to evaluate* their predictions in terms of their confidence in them. Which prediction do we really have the most ideas to support?

Observe all three groups of plants. The plants pulled up by the roots will probably wilt, since many of their root hairs were torn off. New ones must be formed before the plant can get water. The plants that were lifted gently will not wilt. The remaining

The nature of the transportation system of the plant is more easily understood through observation of this experiment. Pupils may use other plant stems, including those of flowers, in order to trace the path of liquids as they are carried within the stem.

plants are left as a control so that pupils can see what happens if plants are not disturbed at all. Now return to the predictions made earlier and relate the observations.

When water once gets inside the plant it must be carried to the leaves, for it is there that the manufacturing of food takes place. By the use of stalks of celery and some red ink pupils can observe how water goes to the leaves. Try to have the children *propose* the use of ink by first showing just the celery stalks and a glass of water and then asking them how they might detect the rise of water in the stalk. Use celery stalks with yellow leaves, if possible. With a sharp knife, cut the bottoms from the stalks of celery. Put just enough red ink in a glass of water to color the water a bright red. Place the celery stems in the water and set them in the light. Observe the leaves from time to time. After 2 or 3 hours, cut one of the stalks and look for the tubes that are carrying the colored water to the leaves. Let the children describe what they see and try to interpret their observations. Look closely at the leaves and you will see the red liquid in the veins. The red color makes it easy to see the parts in which water is moving. It is useful to introduce the word "tracer" here: The colored ink makes it possible to trace the course of the water. (This is similar in principle to the use of radioactive atoms to trace the flow of materials in living things.) An interesting variation of this experiment is shown in the drawing. The celery stalk has been split part way so that the difference can be noted.

How Can We Keep Animal Pets?[3]

There are many reasons for keeping a pet rabbit, guinea pig, hamster,[4] or gerbil in the classroom. (Mongolian gerbils[5] have begun to be used as classroom pets relatively recently. Many pet shops stock them.) Pupils can observe what one kind of animal needs in order to live and grow.[6]

Here are some things to keep in mind, whatever the purpose of keeping a pet animal: (1.) It should never be kept in a schoolroom unless it can be made comfortable; (2.) unless an animal is accustomed to captive life it should never be kept for a long

[3] G.O. Blough and M.H. Campbell: *Making and Using Classroom Science Materials in the Elementary School* (New York: Holt, Rinehart and Winston, Inc., 1954), pp. 62–67. Gives details, including food chart, about feeding and caring for animals, and describes how to make cages for different kinds of animals.

[4] These animals are rodents and are popular for use in laboratory experiments and as pets in school. Hamsters may be purchased at local pet shops. *See also Hamster Raising,* Leaflet no. 25 and *Selection and Care of Common Household Pets* (Washington, D.C.: U.S. Government Printing Office).

[5] S. Simon *Discovering What Gerbils Do* (New York: McGraw Hill, 1971). Help for gerbil raisers; and Elementary Science Study Booklet (ESS): *The Curious Gerbils* (Manchester, Mo.:) Webster Division of McGraw-Hill Book Company), 1966. Describes care and observation with experimental questions. P. Dawson: "Reptiles in Your Classroom," *Science and Children* (Washington, D.C. April 1972); and "An Open Letter to Science Teachers on the Uses of Live Animals in Science Teaching," *Science and Children* October 1970). Questions and answers about the National Science Teacher's Association point of view about keeping animals in the classroom—important.

[6] G.K. Pratt: *Care of Living Things in the Classroom* (Washington, D.C.: National Science Teachers Association).

time; (3.) children should plan in advance for the needs of the animal and share responsibility for its care; and (4.) children should exercise care in handling the animal, and animals should not be handled too much.

Each animal should have:

1. Enough space to move around and be comfortable.
2. An environment as nearly like its natural habitat as possible.
3. A place to hide from sight.
4. Proper food, clean water, and good ventilation.
5. A cage that can be kept clean and free of odor.
6. Adequate food, heat, and water over weekends.

Taking care of animal pets should not become a chore and responsibility of the teacher. These duties are real, and it makes a difference if they are not carried out correctly—one of the important prerequisites for helping pupils learn to assume responsibility. As pupils observe the animal they may make a list of the things the animal needs in order to grow.

As children keep a pet animal there may be an opportunity for purposeful use of mathematics. The children might weigh the pet periodically and, if feasible, measure its dimensions. The making of tables and graphs clarifies and defines more exactly the growth of the animal. The children can express their observations mathematically with such statements as: "Our pet gained 4 ounces (grams?) last week." Or "Our pet gained 2 pounds (kilograms?) during its first month in the classroom, but only 1 pound during the second month." Or "The graph shows that our pet gained slowly when it was first brought to school, but then its weight shot up rapidly. Now it is slowing down again."

(*See* pp. 41–2.)

Although they probably cannot be classified as pets, a most exciting activity is to keep a swarm of bees and observe their ways. The interest and enjoyment of the children is reward enough for the trouble. A narrow house with glass sides so that pupils can observe the bees at work can be purchased with a stock of bees. Or almost anyone who keeps bees will be interested in helping a school obtain some for observation. The beekeeper will often be a useful source of information and may let pupils come to see the bees at his apiary. One end of the hive extends outdoors under the window so that the bees can come and go just as they would from any other hive. If the exit from the hive is on the first floor of the building it should not open directly onto the playground; if it does, there is danger of pupils getting stung by the bees.

The feeding of animals in the classroom and outdoors sometimes presents problems. Here are specific suggestions for kinds of animal food as well as some advice based on classroom experience in coaxing animals to eat various things.

Ants	Dead spiders or insects, bread crumbs, small food scraps, cracked rice, sugar and water, crumbled nut meats, honey or molasses, and water. Place on top of soil where ants live, either on the soil or in a small dish.
Birds, Tame	Prepared bird foods, cuttlefish bone, lettuce, watercress or chickweed, carrot, apple, pieces of bread, hard-boiled egg, grit of some sort. Special food is needed during moulting season (consult pet store). Fresh water.

Birds, Wild	Wild-bird seed, small flower seeds, peanut butter, grains, bread broken into small pieces, suet, apple, unsalted nuts, raisins, grit, cranberries, sunflower seeds, and fresh water. A very satisfactory food for outdoor birds in winter is known as bird pudding. It is made of suet, wild-bird seeds, and other kinds of seeds, raisins, and unsalted nuts. Heat the suet until it liquefies. Let it cool and then stir into it the ingredients listed. As it begins to thicken, pour the pudding mixture into paper cups, pine cones, or other feeding devices. Be sure the mixture is packed under the scales of the cones. The cones may be tied to branches of trees where birds will find them. The cups may be put into feeding trays and fastened so that the wind will not blow them away.
Butterflies	Fresh, thick sugar-and-water solution. Will sometimes take nectar from flowers.
Caterpillars	The leaves upon which the animals were found feeding. Give fresh leaves daily. Experiment with various kinds of leaves. (*See also* moth larvae.)
Chameleons	Any small moving insect. When hungry, they will eat bits of hamburger on a string moved before their eyes. Chameleons do not drink as many animals do. Dewdrops are their source of water. Green branches with their stems in water should be kept in the case and frequently sprinkled with water.
Chickens and Ducks	Commercial chicken feed, vegetables, meat scraps, grit, water.
Crayfish	Chopped meat, water, plants.
Crickets	Pulpy fruits, lettuce, bread, peanut butter, crushed seeds.
Earthworms	Obtain their food from the soil.
Frogs and Toads	Earthworms, meal worms, caterpillars, nearly any living insects, soft grubs. Small bits of ground meat if it is moved in front of the animal on a toothpick or thread. (*See also* tadpoles.)
Goldfish	Commercially prepared fish food, ant eggs, ground-up dog biscuit, a small pinch of oatmeal or cornmeal. Do not overfeed. Do not give more food than they will eat immediately.
Grasshopper	The leaves they were eating when found. Celery, ripe bananas. Experiment with different kinds of foliage.
Guinea Pigs or Cavies	About the same foods as rabbits eat. Do not feed potato parings. Clean drinking water.
Guppies	Food commercially prepared, same as other tropical fish.
Hamsters	Dog biscuit, plus a small supply of fresh vegetables such as carrots, cabbage, and lettuce; bits of fresh fruit; sometimes a little meat. Nuts, corn, oats, wheat, and other grains. Peas can be used to vary the diet. Water is necessary, but if enough green food is given, use less water. The animals must have dog biscuits, pellets, or grain frequently to keep their teeth sharp.
Horned Toads	Ants, meal worms.
Lizards	Flies, crickets, meal worms.

Moth Larvae	*Cecropia:* leaves of willow, maple, apple, and many other trees. *Polyphemus:* leaves of willow, oak, apple, plum, birch, basswood, and other trees. *Promethia:* leaves of wild cherry, ash, lilac, tulip, and sassafras trees. *Luna:* leaves of hickory, walnut, sweet gum, and several other trees. *Cynthia:* lilac, sycamore, cherry, and others.
Mongolian Gerbils	Seeds, roots, grass, lettuce, carrots, kibbled dog food.
Newts	Parts of dead insects, ant eggs, finely ground beef.
Praying Mantis	Living insects.
Rabbits	Commercial pellets. If the pellets cannot be obtained from a pet or feed store, feed wheat or buckwheat mixed with soybeans or peanuts. Rabbits eat various kinds of green vegetables—not wet—a little chopped clover, some greens, a little dry bread now and then. Wild rabbits get water from dew-covered grass; tame rabbits must be given water. Feed twice a day. Do not overfeed.
Rats (White) and Mice	Small grain, bread crusts, vegetables, egg yolks, meat scraps, breakfast foods, water.
Salamanders	Insects, small bits of ground meat moved before their eyes on a toothpick or thread, earthworms, meal worms.
Snails, Land	Lettuce, celery tops, spinach or any soft vegetables, grapes, apple.
Snails, Water	Fish food, lettuce, aquarium plants, spinach, shredded shrimp.
Snakes	Earthworms, many kinds of insects, small pieces of meat wriggled in front of their noses, eggs. They need not eat every day. Some will not eat in captivity; some do not eat for weeks at a time. Do not keep them if they will not eat. Let them escape into a suitable environment.
Tadpoles	Water plants or green pond scum. Much food is obtained from the water. Cooked oatmeal, cooked spinach, cornmeal, lettuce or spinach leaves, and bits of hamburger put into water in small quantities.
Turtles	Commercially prepared foods, nearly all kinds of insects, bits of hard-boiled eggs, lettuce, berries, meal worms, earthworms. Place the food for turtles on the water. Many of them eat only under the surface of the water. Do not overfeed.

(**Note:** There are conflicting reports on the advisability of keeping turtles in the classroom because some are contaminated with salmonella bacteria. Check with the Public Health Service.)

What Does a Seed Need in Order to Sprout?

What can we learn about seeds by examining them? Collect many kinds of seeds (beans, pea, bird seeds, grains, and others). Compare the seeds. How are they alike? How different? What are their shapes? Find the scar? What is it? Soak the seeds and then examine and compare them. Sprouting seeds can show many things about how plants grow.

Large seeds are best, because their germination and the growth of the plants may

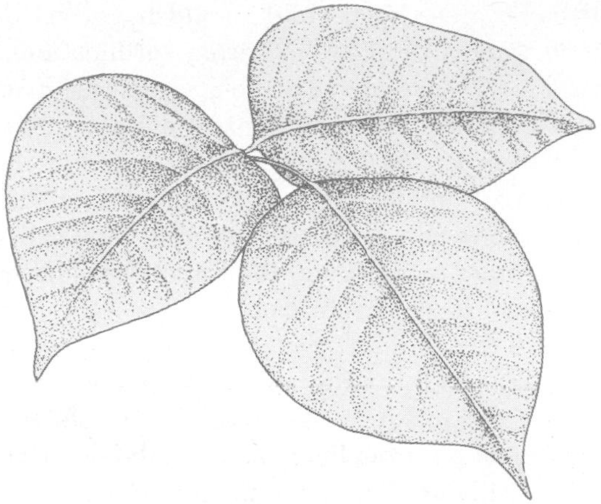

"Leaflets three, let them be!" There is considerable variation in the appearance of the poison ivy plant; the drawing shows the typical shiny leaflets arranged in groups of three. It is obviously important for everyone to recognize poisonous plants, a number of which are found in the United States.[7]

be observed easily. In some communities beans, corn, and other seeds can be brought from home by the children. In others seeds can be purchased. Some of the experiments with growing seeds can be done as class projects, but it is desirable for each child to have seedlings of his own to watch each day and to compare with those of other pupils. Often pupils enjoy doing some of the experiments at home and bringing the results to school. In one class each pupil brought a different kind of seed, watched it sprout, and compared results: "How are the seeds and plants alike?" "How are they different from each other?" "Why did some grow better than others?"

Seeds may be sprouted in a number of different ways: on moist blotting paper or cotton in a covered flat plate or dish; next to the glass in a drinking glass so that pupils can watch the roots grow down and the stem grow up; or directly in soil.[8] It is quite easy to make a diary record that tells what happens as the seeds sprout. The record may be illustrated by simple drawings to show how growth takes place, or pupils may find drawings in books and other sources and compare their sprouting seeds with the drawings.

Urge pupils to examine seeds to see their structure. Lima beans are good because

[7] *See Poison Ivy,* Health Information Series, no. 65 (Washington, D.C.: Superintendent of Documents, U.S. Government Printing Office).

[8] For further information *see* Blough and Campbell, *ibid.,* pp. 74–80, and Elementary Science Study (ESS): *Growing Seeds, Teacher's Guide* (Manchester Mo.: Webster Division, McGraw-Hill Book Co., Inc.). Activities that inspire children to "Let's try it. Let's plant it. Let's grow it." Contains specific help for teachers and children, but leaves plenty of opportunity for creativity. Provides list of easily-obtained materials. Part I deals with "What are seeds?" What do they do?" Part 2 suggests experiences and experiments about how fast seedlings grow. Class kit and film loops available.

the parts are large and easily seen. Each child should have one or more seeds to examine. Soak the seeds in water overnight (to hasten germination). Leave them on moist blotting paper for 1 or 2 days or until the germinating parts can easily be distinguished. Use toothpicks to take the seeds apart. Look for the three parts of the seed (coat, tiny plant, stored food). After children have identified the parts they can discuss the function of each part and make predictions about what happens to these parts as the plant grows. As they observe seeds sprouting they can verify their predictions. They may examine other seeds to find the three parts and try to make some generalizations about seeds and their germination.

Children may experiment to determine the effects of varying *one* of the external conditions: temperature, light, moisture, soil, air. They may also devise experiments to find out whether a bean seed could grow into a plant if the stored food were taken away from it. (Lift the tiny plant out from between the halves of a soaked bean, plant it, and see what happens.) It will die because the first food for the plant is that stored in the seed. The children may try to determine what happens if half of the food material is removed, leaving the tiny plant attached to the other half. They may also set up

What are the brown spots? Children examine fern fronds in their study of how plants reproduce. (*Courtesy of U.S. Department of Agriculture.*)

an experiment to discover which part (the stem or the root) comes out of the seed first as it germinates. This open-ended approach lends itself to many other experiences with seeds and plants.

If pupils want to test seeds to see whether they will germinate before planting them in their school garden they can try to sprout some of the seeds on moist blotting paper, and perhaps calculate what percentage or fraction of the seeds sprouted—an excellent occasion to make use of mathematics.

Collecting seed pods and fruits that show methods of seed dispersal is a standard activity in autumn. Get more mileage from this by examining the materials to see how the structure insures dispersal (use a magnifying glass), find the seeds, try to count them, try to sprout them, and open them to see the inside structure.

Pupils can devise experiments to try to determine: What happens when seeds are planted at different depths? What difference does soaking seeds before they are planted make? Will seeds germinate and grow if they are kept *under* water? What difference does temperature make in the germination of seeds?

How Can We Plant a Garden?

Through the experience of planting and caring for a school garden pupils can learn much about how plants grow; but in order to produce a truly valuable science experience much planning must be done. Weeks before the time for planting there should be discussion of such questions as: "Why shall we have a garden?" (for pleasure, to give flowers and vegetables to other people, to learn about growing plants, to grow vegetables to eat, to make our schoolyard more attractive, and so on). Pupils can use these aims to evaluate their progress and results. They also discuss: "What shall we plant in the garden?" "What must we do to the soil in the garden before it is ready for seeds?" "What kinds of tools do we need and where shall we get them?" "Where and how can we get the seeds for planting?" The school garden should provide a real opportunity for problem-solving—children decide on the problems, make and carry out their plans, and then evaluate their work. Insofar as possible, all children in the school should be involved.

The following resources are helpful in planning and planting a successful school garden:

1. The county agriculture agent, a high-school agriculture or biology teacher, or a greenhouse owner can help test the soil so that pupils can decide whether it needs fertilizer and whether the drainage is proper.

2. Seed catalogues can help children decide what to plant by the illustrations and the descriptions, which tell how long the plants take to mature, what kinds of soil they need, and so on.

3. Seed packages contain directions for depth and time of seed planting.

4. Interested parents who are experienced gardeners may be willing to give assistance and advice.

A school garden provides opportunities for cooperation, learning about plants and their needs, careful observation, planning and assuming responsibility. This is long-term activity that provides opportunity for firsthand experiences that are meaningful and pleasurable. (*Courtesy of Phyllis Marcuccio.*)

5. Inexpensive government publications and other published materials about gardening and insect-pest control will be helpful.[9]

6. Many people save flower and vegetable seeds from the previous year's harvest; parents may supply such seeds for planting in the school garden.

In school gardening it is important to remember that: (1.) there is considerable mathematics involved in gardening—number of rows, distances apart, number of plants that will fit into a given space, amount of space for each pupil, and so on; (2.) there is opportunity to help children learn cooperation and thoughtfulness in sharing tools, seeds, and plants; and (3.) a garden is an ideal place to evaluate a plan. If the rows are straight and even, if the plants are not crowded, and so forth the plan has had

[9] Write to Superintendent of Documents, U.S. Government Printing Office, Washington, D.C. for pamphlets and other low-cost material, for free *price list no. 41 Insects,* and free *price list no. 44 Plants. Also see* the Bibliography for some good books on gardening for use by children.

some degree of success. Evaluation should be made on the basis of all of the reasons for making the garden, not merely in terms of its yield.

The gardening experience provides a practical application of what has been learned through observing, reading, and experimenting.[10] Specifically, it shows what plants need to grow, how they change as they grow, how long it takes various plants to mature, how plants grow under different conditions, what happens when plants are too crowded, how plants of different kinds reproduce, and how plants change as the seasons change.

How Can We Raise Plants Indoors?

If the schoolroom is sunny or if there is some other suitable room growing plants indoors for later outdoor planting is a good learning activity. Cabbages, tomatoes, peppers, zinnias, and marigolds are best planted in flats (shallow boxes) filled with good soil. The flats may be purchased or they may be built by pupils from wooden boxes. The soil should be fine and the seeds planted and cared for according to the directions on the packages.

Sow seeds thinly and cover them lightly with fine soil. Water them frequently enough to keep the soil damp but not wet. A piece of glass placed over the seed container will retain the moisture and aid in the growing. Seedlings raised indoors do better if they are fed once a week or so with a solution of plant fertilizer in water. Garden supply stores, florists, hardware stores, and many other sources sell different kinds of plant fertilizer. Follow the directions on the container.

As soon as seeds germinate and the seedlings are growing well, water them only in the mornings and only if the soil is dry. When the plants are about 2 inches high, if they are growing too thickly they should be thinned by transplanting some of them into another flat. Before the plants are set outside they need to be prepared for this change. Give less water and set the flats outside for a few hours each day. Keep them out for a longer time each day for a week or two. If conditions warrant, children should be encouraged to take some of the plants home to plant outdoors, in window-boxes and elsewhere.

The plants that are commonly grown in schoolrooms are good for plant study. Their possibilities are often overlooked. Geraniums, coleus, ferns, ivy, begonias, bulbs of different kinds, cacti, and other plants may be observed to discover the answers to such questions as: "Where do the new leaves grow?" "Which plants grow fastest?" "How are they all alike in their growth?" "Are seeds formed on any of them?" "Are there spores on the ferns?" "Do they all need the same amount of light and water?" Particularly helpful references on indoor plants are listed in the Bibliography.

Since most schoolrooms contain plants the following specific suggestions may be helpful to teachers and pupils:[11]

[10] *See* Blough and Campbell, *ibid.*, for further details about gardening.

[11] *Science: Grades 3–4* (Brooklyn, N.Y.: Board of Education of the City of New York, 1966).

Sufficient Water Plants should be watered only when the soil feels dry. However, when adding water be sure to give the soil a thorough soaking, not just a sprinkling.

Good Drainage The pot or box should have holes in the bottom to allow excess water to escape. (The roots of a plant require air. Water that remains may prevent air from entering the soil.)

Suitable Temperature Plants should not be placed on hot radiators or in hot or cold drafts. Protect plants over cold weekends.

Proper Light Conditions Experience is the best teacher here. A geranium, for example, needs a good deal of sunlight. Cactus also thrives in sunlight. Begonias and some ferns, on the other hand, should not be kept in direct sunlight for many hours at a time. Many plants will grow well with only a few hours of sunlight. No green plant will do well in a dark area.

Good Soil Although each plant has its own soil requirements any good garden or potting soil will usually be satisfactory. The addition of sand will make the soil more porous. If the soil dries too quickly peat moss or humus can be added. Commercial fertilizer may be used according to the directions on the package.

Other Care Leaves should be showered or washed with a sponge from time to time. Insect pests can be removed by washing or by the use of specific insecticides.

How Do Plants Reproduce?

Seeds are but one of the several ways by which plants reproduce. In some plants a part such as a root, stem, or leaf may be separated from the plant to start a new one. Pupils can plan experiences to discover some of the other ways. Some plants reproduce by bulbs. If a bulb is cut open a series of fleshy layers may be seen, as well as the flattened stem. Narcissus and other plant bulbs can be grown in the schoolroom if the simple directions that accompany them are followed.

New geranium plants can be started from cuttings (slips) from older plants. Take off most of the large leaves and put the cutting in moist sand until roots develop. New ivy plants can be started in this way or by putting the cuttings in water until roots appear. Pussy willows brought to school and placed in water often start roots and can be planted to grow into willow trees if there is a suitably damp place.[12]

Children will be interested in the use of a plant hormone (Rootone) to stimulate rooting. They can try to devise experiments with and without its use to compare them. Directions are included with the purchase.

Children can watch underground stems of the potato grow into a plant by putting

[12] *Plant Propagation in the Classroom; Outdoor-Indoor Adventures with Wild Plants,* Audubon Nature Bulletins (New York: National Audubon Society), practical help in growing plants.

a potato in some good soil. If several are planted, pupils may dig them up now and then to see where the roots develop and where the stems come from, and to note that the potato itself is shriveling up, partly because it is supplying food to the growing shoots. If the potatoes are left growing, pupils can watch the shoots come above ground and see the leaves develop. If a potato is left in a closed container on the table without being planted, pupils can see the sprouts begin to grow and note how differently the potato develops if it has no soil.

A strawberry plant, either wild or cultivated, growing in rich soil in a large flowerpot will send out runners. New plants grow out from these runners.

Some nongreen plants like molds reproduce by spores.[13]

How Do Flowers Make Seeds?

Children can examine flowers to discover "Where do seeds come from?" "What must a plant have in order to produce seeds?" "Where in the flower is the seed formed?" "What must happen in a flower in order to produce the seed?" The following suggestions will be helpful in solving some of these problems.

Perhaps the best way for children to discover the seed-making role of flowers is to watch one kind, *alive*, day after day on a small plant, bush, or tree. A magnifying glass is most useful in revealing the minute structures and the beauty within a flower. If they can begin with a flower bud they will see it swell and open. They will observe the flower to see the anthers grow, split open, and expose their load of dusty pollen. Children will observe the sticky tip of the pistil ready to receive the pollen. As the flower matures, they observe the base of the pistil (the ovary) swell with its developing seeds. As other parts of the flower shrivel and drop off the ovary grows larger into a full-sized fruit, laden with seeds.

Even a cut flower standing in water will reveal some stages in its development toward seed production. *The advantage of beginning with living flowers is that it permits children to make their own discoveries and record changes as they observe them. This is in marked contrast to the method of presenting children with a flower and having them identify its parts, and then trying to have them understand the complexities of its structure and its functions.*

The process of discovery comes as children are able to observe living things engaged in the processes of living. Later they may consult books, charts, and other references to deepen and extend their understandings. They will then have some basis for trying to answer such questions as: "What does the pollen do?" "How do bees

[13]Elementary Science Study (ESS): *Microgardening. Teacher's Guide* (Manchester, Mo.: Webster Division, McGraw-Hill Book Co. Inc.). Five areas of investigation into microgardening with molds: What are molds like? What influences the growth of molds? Where do molds come from? What influences the rate of mold growth? What can molds do? Directions for growing mold cultures, sources from which to obtain materials, suggestions for study and experimentation, as well as appropriate background subject matter, are a part of the booklet. Film loops, basic kits, and advanced kits are available. *See also Growth of Mold on Bread. Science A Process Approach,* AAAS Xerox Edition (Coldstadt, N.J. Xerox Education Sciences). Stresses controlling variables.

help some flowers in seed making?" "Where is the part that becomes the seed?" "How does the pollen get to the seed-forming part?"

Flowers from a garden and from house plants may be examined as soon as they begin to fade. Pupils should be urged to bring from gardens some examples of flower specimens that show seeds forming. After the seeds have been formed, the seed container can be opened to show the seeds inside. Pumpkins, squash, melons, peas, beans, morning glories, and marigolds are interesting to examine. Vacant lots in the city provide wild seeds as well as the flowers that produce them. On some of these dead parts of the blossom can still be seen hanging from the seed-bearing part.

How Can We Raise Silkworms?

When children are learning how animals change as they grow, silkworm raising is an interesting experience. They can watch the eggs hatch, see the young larvae eat, watch the larvae grow and change their skins, see them make cocoons, watch the moths emerge and mate, and see the eggs being laid to start the cycle over again. All of this can happen in a schoolroom in about 2 months. Leaves of mulberry trees are essential food for silkworms.

Silkworm eggs may be purchased from biological supply houses.[14] These are accompanied by directions for raising them. If the eggs arrive before mulberry leaves have developed, they may be kept in a cool place (refrigerator) until the food is ready. Eggs hatch in 7 to 10 days after they are taken from the cool place. The silkworm larvae eat for about 1 month and then form cocoons. In about 2 weeks the moths emerge. They mate almost immediately, and the females lay eggs; then the adults die. A few moths will lay enough eggs to supply the whole neighborhood, and pupils often like to take them home and raise silkworms during the summer. Eggs may be kept in a cool place for extended periods.

The following general plan for raising silkworms, used in a fifth-grade class, is one way to proceed:

1. Box of eggs was opened and children looked at them with magnifying glasses. Several questions were asked about them. These were recorded for future answering.
2. Teacher asked: "What things do we have to plan for if we are to raise silkworms?" (Food, place to keep them, schedule of feeding, and so on.)
3. Good reader from the class read (aloud) the leaflet that came with the eggs, while pupils listened for suggestions useful in carrying out the plans they have made.
4. Class discussed leaflet material and made plans by volunteering for various jobs—bringing food (mulberry leaves), preparing food, and so on.
5. Class listed sources of information they needed that would help them answer such questions as: "How do the silkworms change as they grow?" "How is the silkworm like other animals in the way it grows and how is it different?"

[14] *Rearing the Silkworm Moth,* Turtox Service Leaflet no. 13; *The Care of Living Insects, no. 34; Moth Cocoons,* no. 38 (Chicago, Ill. 60620: General Biological Supply House, 8200 South Hoyne Ave.).

Many of these procedures can be used in studying any caterpillars pupils bring in. Pupils should be encouraged to bring some of the leaves they find the caterpillars on and to try out different kinds of leaves if they are not sure of the food of the caterpillar. The caterpillars may grow, shed their skins, and spin cocoons; or, in the case of butterfly larvae, produce chrysalids. These may be kept until, with good luck, the adult insects emerge.

How Can We Raise Tadpoles?

Wherever frogs and toads croak in the spring there are eggs for the taking. Hatching them in the schoolroom is not difficult and is very helpful in showing children how some animals go through their development from egg to adult.[15]

Frogs' eggs are laid in clumps, toads' eggs in long strings. Both may be scooped up from ponds or quiet waters in the park or elsewhere in spring and brought to school for observation. Bring only a few eggs. Toads and frogs are useful animals and this is a specific occasion to teach conservation. If they are kept in glass jars (gallon pickle or jelly jars are good) they can be observed easily, or if there are no fish or turtles in the aquarium the eggs and tadpoles can be kept there. Bring some water plants with the water from the pond. The young tadpoles will eat algae or decaying bits of plants and animal material. As they grow, they will also eat tiny bits of hard-boiled egg, but the pond water will probably contain the the necessary plant food for them.

The length of time for hatching and the rate at which tadpoles develop depends in part on the kind. Some kinds of frogs mature faster than others. The rate of hatching and developing also depends on the temperature. This provides an excellent opportunity for setting up a carefully controlled experiment. Children can make some predictions and after the experiments make some inferences.

Divide a batch of eggs into three equal parts. Place one batch in a jar of water in a cool place. Place another batch in a similar jar in a warm place. A third may be kept at room temperature. Except for temperature, all conditions are kept the same (controlled variables). Thus, if it is necessary to place the cool batch in a dark cellar, the other two batches should also be in darkness. Day-by-day records of changes in size and appearance should be kept.

Here is a general plan used by a group of pupils as they observed eggs and tadpoles:

1. Pupils observed the eggs to see how they changed as they hatched. They made large drawings to show these changes.
2. They observed the tadpoles to see how they moved, how the legs formed, what happened to the gills, and what happened to the tails. They kept a record of the dates of these changes.

(*See* pp. 288–9.)

3. They compared their observations with the information they had read, and made

[15] Elementary Science Study (ESS): *Eggs and Tadpoles. Teacher's Guide* (Manchester, Mo.: Webster Division, McGraw-Hill Book Co. Inc.). Collecting, caring for eggs and tadpoles, observing and experimenting with these living things are all carefully described. Subject matter background is included. Very helpfully illustrated. Class kit, film loops, and film available.

an outline of the most obvious and important changes that the animals underwent.

4. A library committee assembled reading material from books and encyclopedias about frogs and toads and their development.

A record of the development of frogs or toads can be made by children on a series of slides and used in a projector. The drawings may be made on cellophane or similar materials or, if slides of a more permanent nature are desired, clear or ground glass can be used. Cut the material to the size that will fit the projector and use ink or colored pencils for the drawing. Children should be encouraged to make preliminary sketches. When their attempts have been evaluated, they can be transferred to the slides and arranged in sequence for showing. The cellophane must be made stiff enough to fit into the projector either by fastening with tape to a piece of glass or by framing it with stiff cardboard. Many other subject matter areas lend themselves to slide illustration.

How Do Animals Care for Their Young?

To guide observations the class may prepare a series of questions such as: "How are the young fed?" "How are they protected?" "How long will they stay with their parents?" "Do both parents help to take care of the young?"

It is surprising how many kinds of animals with young are available for observation. Pupils can make a list of animals that are known to live in the community and then do as much firsthand observing as possible, reporting their findings.

Pupils may visit—as a class, in small groups, or individually—the zoo; a pet shop; a kennel where dogs are bred; a city aquarium; a place where canaries are raised; a fur farm; a dairy farm; and the schoolyard or park to see birds, squirrels, and other animals. They can find out how fish, reptiles, insects, and amphibians, as well as the mammals we have suggested, care (or do not care) for their young.

A good beginning in sex education has been made when children observe the birth of puppies and kittens, watch the mother care for them, and frankly discuss with their parents and teachers what they have seen. Intelligently answering the questions children ask, helps to satisfy their curiosity in a normal fashion and provides opportunity for parents and teachers to enter naturally into a discussion of sex matters (*see* Chapter 12A).

How Do Animals Eat?

There are also many opportunities for pupils to observe how animals get their food. Pupils can list the animals that they might possibly watch, plan for observing them, and report their findings. Here is a list of animals studied by a third grade: snails, earthworms, fish, silkworms, canaries, chickens, dogs, cats, frogs, horses, cows, sheep, and squirrels. Each animal was observed to find out what kind of food it eats, what parts of its body helps it to eat, and any other interesting things about the way the animal eats.

At the zoo pupils can observe how different kinds of animals eat, and how they are adapted for food getting. The zoo also provides examples of various ways in which animals protect themselves, and live in various environments.[16]

How Can We Set Up an Aquarium?

An aquarium set up by the teacher before school begins in the autumn is never as much fun for the children or as useful to them as one they plan and make themselves. Children often volunteer to bring fish to school from an outdoor pool, and this motivates the making of the aquarium.

The planning may begin by letting the pupils discuss such questions as: "What kind of place shall we make for the fish?" "What materials shall we need?" "Where can we get them?" "How shall we use them?" There will be opportunity to share, to contribute to the group, to work together, and to assume responsibility.

You will need: a container, some sand, some small stones, a few water plants, a few snails, and the fish. The container may be of almost any size or shape, but one that is rectangular and holds 3 gallons or so is preferable. It can be purchased locally or ordered from a supply house. Many supply houses furnish detailed directions for stocking and caring for an aquarium. Begin by scrubbing the aquarium thoroughly. The sand may come from a variety of sources: the beach, a sand bar of a river, a builders' supply yard, or a pet shop. Wash it by running water through it until the water is clear. Water plants are usually most satisfactory when purchased from local ten-cent stores, pet shops, or biological supply houses, although it is possible to get them from ponds[17] or lakes or from an outdoor pool. Buying water plants at a pet shop may be an interesting experience for a young child or for a committee. While they are there they can also buy some snails. Only a few are needed; there will soon be more.

Having assembled the materials, plan with the children how they are to be put together.[18] If you are using city water pour it back and forth from one container to another to let chlorine from the water escape into the air, or let it stand for a day in a container before placing plants and animals in it. After putting the sand in the bottom of the aquarium set a saucer or plate on it so that when you pour the water in it will not disturb the sand. Half fill the aquarium with water, put stones around the base of the water plants to help hold them down, and finish filling the aquarium. Put in the fish and snails. Later you may wish to add tadpoles or other suitable water animals. The aquarium may be covered with a piece of glass to prevent the water from evaporating.

[16]G.O. Blough and M.H. Campbell: *When You Go to the Zoo* (New York: Whittlesey House, McGraw-Hill, Inc., 1955.) Details of animal adaptation for food getting.

[17]Elementary Science Study (ESS): *Pond Water. Teacher's Guide* (Manchester Mo., Webster Division, McGraw-Hill Book Co. Inc.). A trip to a pond to collect, examine, observe, and investigate the material collected. Develops methods for investigating and suggests additional problems.

[18]G.O. Blough: *An Aquarium* (New York: Harper & Row, Publishers, 1972). A book to consult in making and using an aquarium in the elementary school. Easy reading.

Although goldfish are commonly used in aquaria, other kinds of fish are also available. Tropical fish, however, need considerable attention; the water temperature must be kept nearly constant; and, for other reasons, they are not easily reared in the usual schoolroom aquarium unless the teacher or some pupil has made a hobby of raising such fish.

After the aquarium is set up, if the proportion of plants and animals is balanced, it needs little attention. The plants in their food-manufacturing process give off oxygen to the water and use carbon dioxide. The animals use this oxygen in their breathing and give off carbon dioxide. It is often necessary to experiment to discover the proper proportions of plant and animal life. Overfeeding is one of the chief causes of the death of fish. Further information about aquaria is contained in *The Fresh Water Aquarium.*[19]

An aquarium is useful in helping to solve many of the problems that arise in the study of plants and animals. Children may observe animal life to see how the animals are adapted for life in the water, and watch both plants and animals to see how they grow and how they change as they grow.[20] An aquarium is also useful in stimulating children to ask questions such as: "What are the bubbles coming out of the plant?" "Where did all the new snails come from?" "Why does the fish open and close its mouth?" "Why do the fish sometimes come to the top of the water?" When aquaria are utilized as a source of information they are excellent teaching tools.

In connection with a study of oceanography you may wish to try your hand at making a salt-water aquarium. It involves some expense and "know-how."[21] The reference gives addresses for the purchase of marine life, and directions for making and using salt-water aquaria.

How Can We Make a Terrarium?[22]

A terrarium is a replica of a land habitat made with suitable soil, water, and plant and animal life characteristic of the kind of environment it represents. It provides a home for plants and animals brought in by children: small toads, frogs, small snakes, turtles, and salamanders. The general procedure suggested for use with children in initiating an aquarium project is also appropriate in making a terrarium.

The container may be of almost any general shape or size, from a one-gallon glass jar to a large aquarium tank. An aquarium tank that leaks may be adequate for use as a terrarium.

A trip to a wood lot to gather material is an opportunity for careful observation of the ecology of an area and for learning conservation practices. Take only a little

[19] *Good Teaching Aids* (New York: National Audubon Society). Illustrated material about making and maintaining an aquarium and terrarium; also many classroom and ourdoor activities.

[20] Blough and Campbell, *ibid.*, for further details about aquarium-making.

[21] *Science and Children*, "The Saltwater Aquarium" (Washington, D.C., May 1966). Gives directions and references for a salt-water aquarium.

[22] J. Hoke: *Terrariums* (New York: Watts, 1972). An excellent source book.

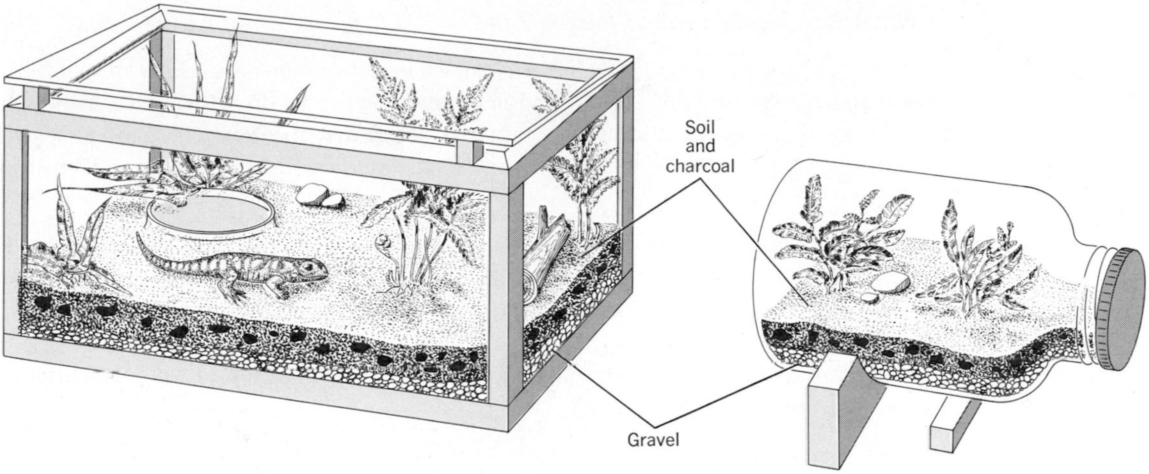

A terrarium may be planted in almost any shape or size of container. The gallon jar (*right*) is set in a round groove in a wooden block. The original jar cover may be used to cover the opening, or some transparent paper can be placed over the opening and held by a rubber band.

moss of different kinds, a few varieties of wood plants, some rich soil, and anything else that you think will give the terrarium a "woodsy" touch. Do not collect rare plants. Some pieces of charcoal placed in the bottom of the terrarium will absorb gases and help to keep the soil from becoming sour.

Cover the bottom of the terrarium container with coarse gravel or sand, bury several pieces of charcoal in it, and then add rich soil from the woods. Plant the small plants in this and cover the remaining soil with the moss. Brightly colored stones placed here and there, where the different pieces of moss meet, add interest. Sink a small dish to hold water into the soil, and cover the terrarium container with a piece of glass, which the school custodian can cut to the size of the container. When you have finished planting the materials sprinkle the plants with water, put water in the dish, and the habitat is ready for a small animal. It will probably not be necessary to add water.

Observing the terrarium is the reason for constructing it. Suggest that pupils observe the terrarium independently for a few days and then give them an opportunity to report their observations and try to explain them. Water will evaporate and condense as the temperature changes, so that it seems to "rain" in the terrarium. Observing this is very useful in studying air and weather.

Changes will occur in the plants. If it is too wet mold may appear. If it is too dry some plants will wither. If there are animals (earthworms, small toads, salamanders, and so on) their behaviors will be interesting and they must be fed and cared for. There are many variations of this procedure in making terraria which may be used to reproduce different kinds of habitats in miniature.

What Can We See with a Microscope?[23]

Many elementary schools are now in possession of one or more shiny new microscopes, and many teachers and supervisors wonder what to do with them. Although it is not good policy to permit apparatus to determine the curriculum it is worth considering the potential of the microscope in the studying of living things. Here are one or two general rules:

1. The younger the child the lower the power of microscope that should be used.
2. Move step by step from the visible world to the microscopic world (naked eye—5-power magnifying glass—10-power magnifying glass—25-50-100-power microscope).
3. The microscope should serve as a tool in the understanding of some large ideas —and not as an end in itself.

Now a few suggestions for things to see:[24]

1. A drop of water from a stagnant pond to see tiny plants and animals there.
2. A thin strip of tissue from an onion to see cells.
3. Pollen from a flower to see the thousands of grains in a small bit of pollen.
4. A bit of yeast in water to see thousands of living yeast plants (high power).
5. A thin strip of material taken from the outside of a leaf to see the many openings (stoma) in it.
6. A bird's feather to see the way in which it is "hooked" together.
7. Some snail eggs to see evidence of their development.
8. Green film scraped from the side of an aquarium to see algae (and possibly protozoans).
9. Bread mold to see growing threads, reproductive spores cases, and spores.
10. Tail of tadpole or small goldfish (whose body has been wrapped in moist cotton) to see capillaries, blood cells, and circulation of blood.
11. Water fleas (Daphnia) obtained from pet shops to see their heart beat, digestive tract, and reproduction.
12. Parts of insects to see the compound eyes, pads at ends of legs (flies), and so on.

How Can We Classify Living Things?

As we have indicated earlier there are degrees of classification. Younger children group things often in their own systems, often on the basis of one characteristic—color,

[23] Elementary Science Study (ESS): *Small Things. Teacher's Guide* (Manchester, Mo.: Webster Division, McGraw-Hill Book Co. Inc.). Introduces children to the microscope and how to use it. Describes and illustrates how to prepare a slide, using stains to study various kinds of cells. Describes how to help children discover for themselves the small things that live in pond water (with accompanying drawings of paramecium, amoeba, and others). Kits, work sheets, film, and film loops available. *See also* "Living Things Are Composed of Cells." *Science a Process Approach*, AAAS Xerox Edition (Coldstadt, N.J. Xerox Education Sciences). A complete unit including methods and content.

[24] G.O. Blough: *The Microscope in the Elementary Science Program* (Bronxville, N..Y.: Educational Materials and Equipment Co.). Free with inquiry regarding microscope outfit and the E.M.E. Cyclops Wide Field Microscope.

Bees go in and out of the glass hive through a passageway under the window. An adult is pointing to the queen. Children can observe the many activities, record their observations, and discuss their findings. Honey is stored in the upper section. (*Courtesy of U.S. Department of Agriculture.*)

size, shape, and so on. Older children may develop the skill of using multicharacteristics. The skill of classification rests on the ability to observe and identify characteristics and to compare and contrast.

To make classification meaningful to children it must serve a useful purpose. For example, in studying the inhabitants in and near a pond children may notice the variety of insects. They begin to observe insects, collect them, and perhaps raise them. They note similarities and differences in their size, parts, habits, and developments. They begin to see, with the aid of references, that insects all have certain common structural characteristics. *All* children will not arrive at this conclusion at the same time nor will they all recognize which characteristics are significant.

As they continue to observe and have other experiences with insects they begin to see that certain insects have characteristics in common and can therefore be placed in a group by themselves. They begin to get some insights into the *orders* of insects.

Children can assemble many different kinds of plants or animals or both and observe them carefully to find classifying characteristics. "How can the living things be put into groups?" is the problem. They may at first separate plants from animals, then separate the vertebrate animals from the invertebrates, then try to classify vertebrate animals into five groups. Encourage children to go as far as they can without consulting books. After they have established the distinguishing characteristics with the live or preserved animals available they can use pictures that are detailed enough to show structure. They begin by originating their own scheme of classifying them. As they improve in the skill of identifying significant likenesses and differences they will probably change their original schemes.

How Can We Study Ants and Spiders?

A convenient observation house in which to watch life in an ant colony can be made from a clear-glass, 1-quart jar that has a screw top. A block of wood placed in the center of the jar will keep the ants from tunneling too far down to be seen.

Wrap black paper around the outside of the glass jar to make it dark inside, and remove the paper when you want to see the ants. Feed them bread crumbs, sugar, and various other things, experimenting to find out what they like. Give them a little water in a small dish on top of the soil, and not too much food. The story of "What We Saw the Ants Do" is an interesting one for children to write and illustrate.

Illustrations of two other more elaborate ant houses are shown. The plasticine

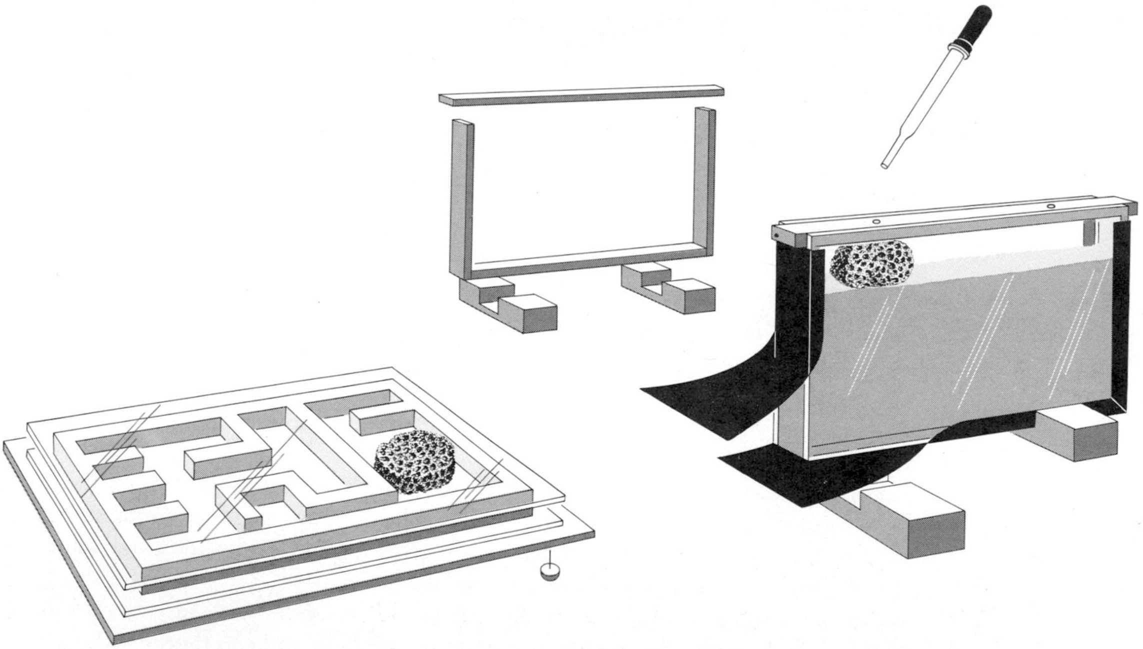

Begin the study of ants by suggesting that pupils observe carefully to discover what is happening inside the house. Reading and further observations may be used to check their original ideas. Use black paper to cover these ant colonies when they are not being observed. Ants will tunnel nearer the glass if they are kept in the dark (*see* text description).

walls are about $\frac{3}{4}$ inch high and 1 inch wide. One piece of glass fits under the walls, the other above them. This one is lifted off to feed the ants. The entire structure is set in a shallow pan of water to keep the ants from escaping. The other house is made of a frame of two pieces of glass (12 by 10 inches), cloth tape, four sticks about $\frac{1}{2}$ by $\frac{1}{4}$ inch, and two blocks to hold the frame upright. A fourth piece of wood forms the top of the ant house. Remove the top to feed the ants. Use a magnifying glass for observation.[25] Stock the ant house by digging into an anthill. Be sure to get plenty of ants.

Spiders are fascinating creatures to watch, and web-making is an awe-inspiring operation. Pupils may be encouraged to search for spider webs that are in the process of construction to observe the operation, and then to observe how the web functions in the capture of food for the spider.

Can Animals Learn?[26]

The question "Can animals learn?" will provoke a flood of answers from pupils, who will be only too happy to relate how their pet dog, cat, turtle, fish, or other animal "learned" how to do something. An experiment that can be easily conducted is to see if fish in an aquarium can learn to respond to tapping by coming to the surface. Each time fish are fed (and this should not be more than once every 2 days) the feeding is preceded by tapping the aquarium glass with a coin. After some days (or weeks) the fish may respond to the tapping by coming to the top. As a control the fish in a similar aquarium should be fed without the tapping, and then compared with the others to see if they respond to the tapping.

Experiments like this and observations of animal behavior will open up many other questions. Children will begin to understand that much of animal behavior is unlearned or inherited, whereas other behavior is learned.

The *behavior of mealworms* has been developed by the Elementary Science Study.[27] Pupils asked and investigated such questions as: "How do meal worms explore a box?" "How does a meal worm sense the presence of a wall so that he can follow it?" "How does the meal worm find bran?" Pupils can, through careful observations, formulate some interesting hypotheses and attempt to evaluate them.

The Elementary Science Study has also developed material on the common earthworm[28] that gives many useful ideas about how to observe animal behaviors.

[25] J. Schwartz: *Through the Magnifying Glass* (New York: McGraw-Hill, Inc., 1954).

[26] B. Ford: *Can Invertebrates Learn?* (New York: Julian Messner, 1972).

[27] Elementary Science Study (ESS): *Behavior of Mealworms, Teacher's Guide* (Manchester, Mo.: Webster Division, McGraw-Hill Book Co. Inc.), "Mealworms are a convenient classroom animal". Contains directions for obtaining and caring for meal worms and suggests many possibilities for observing their behaviors, experimenting with them to attempt to find answers to questions and record observations. Photos and students books available.

[28] Elementary Science Study (ESS): *Earthworms, Teacher's Guide* (Manchester, Mo.: Webster Division, McGraw-Hill Book Co. Inc.). Suggestions for collecting, caring for, observing, and experimenting with earthworms are contained in this unit of study. Since earthworms are easily obtained and observed, this makes an excellent beginning to the study of animal behavior.

OTHER PROBLEMS FOR OLDER CHILDREN

1. How do animals and plants move from place to place?
2. How do living things depend on green plants?
3. What are one-celled plants and animals like?
4. How do animals reproduce?
5. What are the life cycles of some common plants and animals?

Resources to Investigate with Children

1. Garden clubs for information and for a possible person to assist with school gardening.
2. County agriculture agent for help in answering questions and as general resource persons.
3. Florists, nurserymen, and gardeners for soil and other supplies, and for information about growing things in the classroom and in outdoor gardens.
4. Pet shops and dealers for information about care of animals and for supplies.
5. Animal hospitals for information about care of animals and for other assistance.
6. Successful farmers for information about local crops and how they are planted and cared for.
7. Forester to learn about how tree seeds are gathered and planted and how the young trees are cared for.
8. State agricultural college and experiment stations for information about plant-growing experiments and similar information.
9. Museums and botanic gardens for a better understanding of the orderly classification of plants and animals.
10. Local resources for the study of living plants and animals in their environment: parks, ponds, lakes, streams, swamps, fields, woodlands, vacant lots, lawns, home gardens, trees on streets, seashores, rivers.
11. Local beekeeper for information about habits and care of bees.
12. Exterminators for samples of dead termites and other insects and for information about their habits.

Preparing to Teach

1. Make a terrarium and aquarium as described in this chapter so that you will be better able to assist children in similar activity. List problems that would be appropriate for children to try to solve as they observe these teaching tools.
2. Write for some of the material suggested in the footnotes so as to have it on hand when you need it.
3. Collect teaching pictures of plant and animal life and classify them according to the problems given in the chapter. These will be a nucleus collection and children can be encouraged to add to it.

4. Try to obtain a soil-testing kit and get acquainted with its use.
5. Try starting house plants from cuttings, seeds, and so on, and raise them.
6. Make a list of other experiments not described here that may be used in solving some of the problems listed in the chapter.
7. Find larvae on different outdoor plants, feed and observe them. Keep track of your difficulties and successes to help you when you use such activities with children.
8. Prepare a list of experiences especially useful for children with special interests and abilities in the area of plant and animal study. Add a bibliography of books especially rewarding to them.
9. Make a unit plan to follow in helping pupils of a specific grade do one of the following; (1.) Make a garden; (2.) keep a pet in the classroom; (3.) raise plants indoors.

CHAPTER 11A

LIVING THINGS AND THE SEASONS

(Gordon S. Smith from National Audubon Society.)

THE TIDES OF LIFE

The tides of life ebb and flow with the seasons. Changes in life parallel changes in the sun's position. In the spring the sun warms up the earth. Moisture is released from the bondage of frost and is absorbed by the roots of plants. The energy of the sun's rays is trapped by green leaves to help in the manufacture of food. The animal world begins to stir out of its winter sleep as the earth warms up.

In the temperate zone the most marked seasonal changes come in the spring and fall. During the winter cold, life seems to be at a standstill. In reality it is not. There are slow changes in both plant and animal life, but these are hidden from casual view. As the sun moves higher in the sky with the advance of spring these processes accelerate and one day make their presence known. The first spring flowers seem to appear overnight. The first robin is welcomed by winter-weary human beings. While the snow is still on the ground, sap begins to run in the maples.

Summer is the season of full growth. The trees and other plants are in lush foliage. The rearing of young is the main concern of many animals. Food is stored by both plants and animals against the coming cold season.

Fall finds the migrating birds on their way back to warmer climes. The broad-leaved trees shed their vernal dress after one brave splurge of color. The hibernators find dens they will use for their long winter snooze. Those animals that remain active may change their fur to fit the temperature and sometimes the color of their surroundings. With winter, activity slows to its lowest ebb. Only a few hardy animals are seen about, and the plant world is dormant in the frozen soil.

The turning of the seasons brings changes—in temperature, light, water, and food—that affect profoundly the activities of plants and animals. This chapter is devoted to the annual cycle of life in those areas of the temperate zone which are characterized by the four familiar seasons. Some of the happenings described here apply only in part to areas having other seasonal patterns.

ANIMALS IN SPRING

Spring is the time of renewal. The animal world comes out of its winter lethargy. Among the first of the new animals to be seen in our northern spring are the migrating birds. Weeks before, they have begun their northward flight, and, by the first days of March the earliest arrivals are with us. The proverbial robin and, soon after, the song sparrow, purple grackle, and red-winged blackbird lead the van. By May the migration is at its peak. The numerous species of warblers, the thrushes, and various sparrows are in full force, heading for their nesting grounds. At this time one is amply rewarded by getting up before the sun and out to the countryside or city park to hear the early morning symphony of the birds. Male birds parade their fine feathers and engage in the acrobatics of court-

Caterpillars are ravenous eaters. As they grow, they shed their skins; this permits another period of eating and growing. (*Courtesy of American Museum of Natural History.*)

ship. Then starts the earnest business of building the nest, laying the eggs, and caring for the young. This will occupy many birds until well into the summer.

The urge to mate is strong in most animals at this season. Fish and frogs spawn, and soon the waters teem with the new generation. Our spring peeper is one of the first of the frogs to lay its eggs. It heralds its mating time by its clear sweet piping in March.

Insects emerge from their overwintering states and begin anew the cycle of life. Some insects have survived the winter in adult form. Among the butterflies a mourning cloak may be seen sailing over snow banks in the earliest spring days. This is an adult of last fall that has hibernated, something very unusual among butterflies. Ordinarily the adults die in the fall, leaving behind only the eggs that they laid or immature forms, caterpillars or pupa, which develop from the eggs. With the warming of the air, the eggs hatch out and the larvae start foraging for food.

PLANTS IN SPRING

The tulips, lilies, crocuses, and other flowers of Easter are to city dwellers the welcome affirmation that spring has come. Country people, or even city folk who have a park close by, see floral heralds of spring much earlier. Among the very first to flower is the plant that has taken its name from the skunk, the skunk cabbage. While the snow is still on the ground this hardy green flower pushes its spike up through the mud where it thrives, the hooded flowers appearing before the cabbage-like leaves uncurl. The odor, from which it derives its name, may not attract human beings but it does attract flies and other insects which are necessary for its pollination. The spring beauty rises from the leaf litter on the forest floor, and later Solomon's seal, yellow bellwort, and the wild geranium make their appearance.

(*See* pp. 337, 342.)

The buds on the trees become visibly swollen in early spring. Shortly after, the leaves will seem to burst forth overnight. However, this is not merely an overnight growth. In most woody plants all the leaves that are to develop on a branchlet in one season are laid down in the bud the previous summer. If you open a leaf bud in the winter you will find there tiny but complete leaflets. In the spring the rush of newly obtained water fills the leaflets' cells, causing them to swell and to multiply rapidly. The bud coverings are forced open and new leaves emerge into the sunlight. In many trees, as in the red maple, the flower buds open before the leaf buds, bedecking the bare branches with colorful flowers before the green and yellow leaves appear.

As water is made available in the soil, sap begins to run in the sugar maples. Spring is the time of maple sugaring in our northeastern states—particularly New York, Vermont, and New Hampshire. A hole is bored through the bark of the sugar maple tree. The sap oozes out through a hollow tube inserted in the hole into buckets attached to the tree. The sap is collected and then boiled down in huge evaporators to make maple syrup. Some of the syrup is boiled again until most of the water is gone, and solid maple sugar results. The richly sweet taste of the first chunk of maple sugar is a memorable childhood delight for those fortunate enough to have lived in sugar-maple country.

ANIMALS IN SUMMER

Summer is the lush time. Food is plentiful; the earth is warm; and the days are long. The cares of raising a family occupy many of the higher animals, notably the birds and mammals, during the summer. Among the birds the young must be fed and they must learn to fly. There are some birds that are able to take care of themselves as soon as they hatch out of the eggs. The common chicken is a good example of this. So is the killdeer. Most of our song birds, however, are born helpless. The parents spend the daylight hours endlessly hunting food, much of which is given to the young. In some species the food is predigested by the parent birds and then regurgitated into the open mouths of fledglings. Some birds shirk the duties of parenthood. The cowbird deposits its eggs in the nests of other birds, frequently of small birds such as warblers.

When the eggs hatch out the much larger cowbird crowds the rightful family and pirates the food that should go to the offspring of its foster parents.

The cold-blooded vertebrates show little care for their young. Most lay their eggs and then depart. The young must face the hazards of the world alone as soon as they hatch from the egg. Young tadpoles emerging from their jelly capsules feed on plant fragments in ponds and grow fat, later developing hind and then front legs and becoming tiny frogs. As frogs they change their diet, eating insects and worms.

The mammals devote considerable care to their offspring. The opossum, a primitive mammal, gives birth to young that are only partially developed, each being smaller than a honeybee at first. They must then be transferred to a pouch on the underside of the mother to finish their development. Long afterward they may be seen clinging closely to the mother as she journeys about in search of food. The opossum is the only American pouched mammal, or *marsupial.* Other marsupials are found mainly in Australia, examples being the kangaroo and the wallaby.

The more common mammals—deer, foxes, rabbits, and domestic animals, such as sheep, cows, and horses—keep their young close by during infancy. The young are fed and protected until such time as they are independent. Summer is the family time.

PLANTS IN SUMMER

With the coming of summer the sounds of spring are hushed in the forest. The fullness of foliage casts dark green shadows over the forest floor. The burst of blossoms is over, except for a late show put on by a few plants such as the touch-me-not and the pokeweed.

Inside the cells of green leaves atoms are juggled to form molecules of sugar and other products essential to plant life. Roots push deeper into the soil, and stems extend their growing ends. Under the bark of trees new layers of cells are being added to the growth initiated in the spring, which will result in the formation of a new annual ring.

As the summer wears on the foods manufactured by leaves are stored in twigs, trunks, and roots. This stored food will provide the energy required for the plant's growth in the spring to come. At the same time food is also being sent through the ducts of the plant into fruit and seeds, providing the material needed to start new generations of plants.

Deep in the soil microscopic agents of decay, molds and bacteria, are busy in the never-ending process of decomposition of dead plant and animal material. These nongreen plants complete the mechanism of decay started by the feeding processes of termites, earthworms, ants, snails, and other soil creatures, thereby replenishing the soil with the minerals essential for the green plant world above. The materials of life are recycled endlessly . . .

ANIMALS IN AUTUMN

Fall in the temperate zone is a time of "getting ready" for winter. The change of seasons is gradual, one blending imperceptibly into the next. Similarly, the "preparations" for the next season by living things are gradual.

It is not altogether accurate to say that living things "prepare" for the coming of winter. To "prepare" generally means a conscious action that anticipates a future condition. The "preparations" referred to in this chapter are built-in, automatic behavior patterns with no conscious planning implied. In the animal kingdom this means storing away food to be used during cold winter days when food is scarce. Some animals, such as the squirrels and chipmunks, store nuts and other food in caches where they may find them in midwinter. Other mammals who spend the winter in a long sleep must store food, too, but they store it within their own bodies. The black bear gorges himself during the summer and early fall and stores up fat to be used during hibernation.

The birds that will migrate south in the fall also busy themselves storing some extra nourishment within their bodies, although many of them will feed on the way as they migrate. However, some birds cross large bodies of water, such as the Gulf of Mexico, and they need the added food to sustain them during this flight.

Bird Migration: When and Where?

(*See* pp. 339–41, 343–4.)

Among the birds the earliest migrants begin to journey south in July. These include some of the shore birds. Generally, the last to arrive in the spring are the first to leave in the fall. The southward movement occurs in waves. If the weather should suddenly turn cold there will be a heavy exodus of birds. If the weather remains balmy and summerlike the migrants leave in small groups. By the turn of October the warblers and thrushes are in full flight to their southern winter havens. In mid-October the geese and ducks and other water fowl stream along the flyways (*see* illustration) to warmer climates.

When November arrives, the migration is about over. Those birds that go south have gone. Those birds that will winter over are busily hunting for food. It is not strange that few of the winter residents are insect eaters, because most of the insects have by this time succumbed to the cold, and only next year's eggs remain. The chief exceptions are those birds that feed on insects and insect larvae living in the bark of trees. The nuthatches, chickadees, and occasional brown creepers busy themselves searching tree bark for insects hidden there. These insects are harmful to our trees, so these birds do a large service to us in protecting against this damage. The sparrows and other seed eaters comprise much of the rest of the bird population at this time. Sometimes a robin who can change its diet of insects to one of seeds, which are more readily found at this season, lingers on.

Bird Migration: Why and How?

The migrations of birds are fascinating and puzzling. When the birds that have frequented our backyards, parks, and woods leave in the fall it is natural to ask: "Where do they go?" "How are they guided in their flight?" "Will the same individuals return?"

Although there is still much mystery associated with migration there are some obvious advantages that are derived from this annual roundtrip between breeding grounds and winter quarters. The migratory habit enables a bird to enjoy northern summers while avoiding the severity of northern winters. In flying south the birds escape the depletion of the food supply caused by the disappearance or hibernation of insects or the covering of seeds or other ground foods by a mantle of snow and ice. Another unfavorable condition in northern climes is the shortened day, with fewer hours of light by which to obtain food at a time when the birds need more food to maintain body heat against the cold.

In the spring the northward flight to regions that are uninhabitable earlier in the year gives the migrants more space and food for themselves and their offspring.

We know the advantages of migration, but that does not explain the mechanism that starts a bird on its long trip. A recent view takes as its major premise the fact that the quantity of light and the length of day have a direct stimulating effect on birds. The proponents of this theory point out that birds, such as swallows and shore birds, start their southward movements when the food supply in the north is *most* abundant. Similarly northbound robins and bluebirds leave an abundant food supply in the south in the spring.

The calendar regularity of arrival and departure leads defenders of this theory, called *photoperiodism* (light period), to conclude that the increasing light in the spring and the decreasing light in the fall are the stimuli that trigger the migratory response in birds.

Experiments have been performed in which birds are confined in outdoor cages from which light may be excluded for varying periods each day. These experiments indicate that the *timing* of the yearly cycle of sexual maturity may be altered by changes in the length of day and night. Thus photoperiodism in nature may serve to synchronize the reproductive cycle with the migratory cycle: The birds reach favorable breeding grounds at the time when their sex organs are active.

The photoperiodism theory, however, has

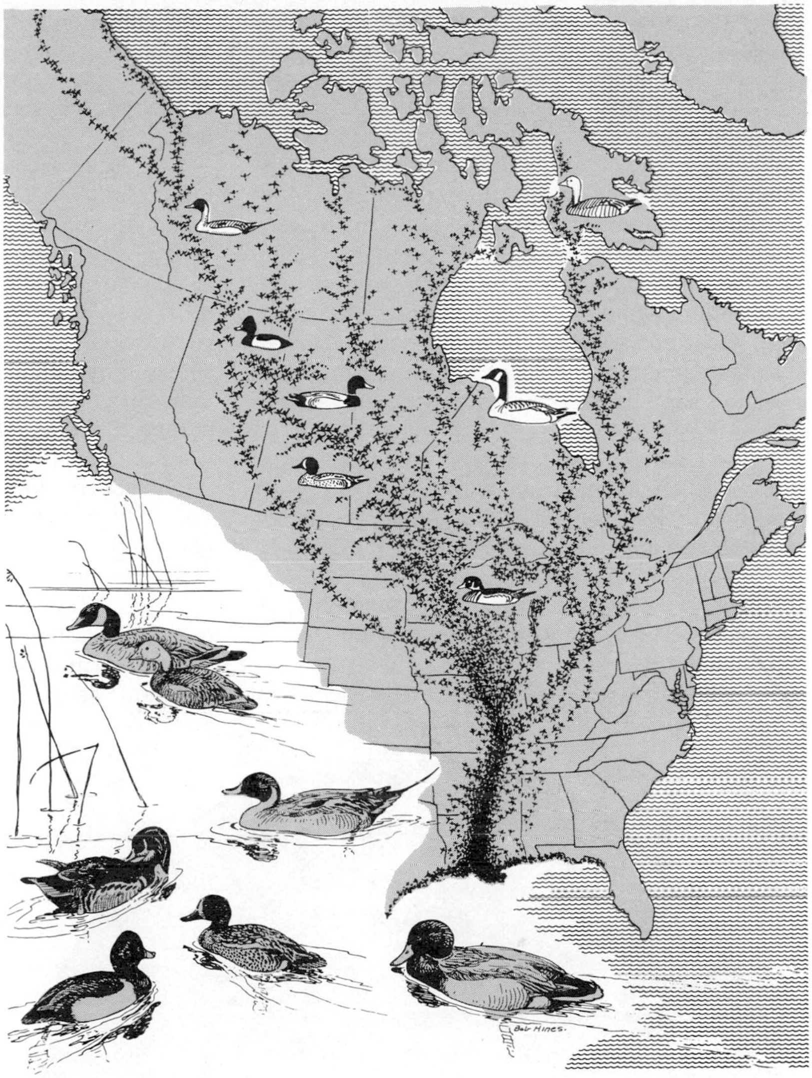

The Mississippi flyway is one of the four great flyways for birds, which cover practically the entire width of the North American Continent and extend from the Arctic Coast to South America.

some limitations and does not explain migration in some species.

Many other questions about migration remain unanswered. Why do the same species always follow the same route north and south? Why should the arctic tern, the champion "globe-trotter," start out from beyond the Arctic Circle and fly south until it passes beyond the tip of South America to Tierra del Fuego, only to turn around in the spring and fly back again to the polar north? How does a young bird, newly hatched out during the spring, "know" the flyway by which its species always travels, even though it does not migrate with the older birds? It is easy enough to say "instinct" and feel that we have answered the questions. But scientists are not satisfied with such glib answers, which merely substitute a word for an explanation. These and other mysteries of bird migration are being studied at the present time.

Bird-migration routes have been traced by means of birdbanding. Birds are trapped in one place and small aluminum identification rings are fixed to their legs. The birds are then released. Banding does not harm the bird in any way. A record is kept of the banding, and if the bird is later trapped elsewhere the information can be tabulated and analyzed and the routes accurately mapped. Birdbanding has revealed that in some species an individual bird frequently returns and nests in the same tree, bush, or box that it used in the previous season. These records also show that the same individuals migrate year after year over the same route, making the same stops on the way.

The unerring accuracy in the flight of birds has long challenged our curiosity. The great shearwater, for example, which ranges the entire Atlantic Ocean, returns each fall to the islands of Tristan da Cunha, which are mere specks in the sea. What is the "sense of direction" that enables the birds to do this? How do birds find their way?

Elaborate cage experiments have shown that starlings, which fly by day, use the sun as a compass. Homing experiments have revealed that rivers and mountains also serve as guides, especially when the day fliers near their destination.

But how do night-flying birds find their way? Franz Sauer, a German scientist, made the astonishing discovery that Old World warblers, which he studied under experimental conditions in a planetarium, navigate by means of star patterns (*see* illustration).

Navigation by the sun and the stars is not simply a matter of aiming at a target. We recall that both the sun and stars appear to move across the sky. The birds under investigation were able to adjust their courses to the change in position of these heavenly bodies during the day or night. This means that they have a kind of built-in time clock that enables them to change their course hour by hour.

It appears, then, that most suggested means of bird navigation parallel those used by humans: landmarks, the sun, and the stars. In 1972 two German researchers, Wolfgang and Roswitha

This amazing experiment conducted in a planetarium indicates that night-flying birds navigate by the stars. The experiment is performed under a 20-foot dome. The dome and bird cage are shown in cross-section. A felt cloth from the bottom of the cage to the floor cuts out light from below. The sector of the artificial sky visible to the bird is indicated by solid lines. The sector visible from the opposite side of the perch is shown with broken lines. "Flight direction" means the direction in which the bird faces.

Wiltschko, presented evidence that the mechanism of navigation of the European robin was a magnetic compass! The researchers subjected caged birds ready for the spring migration of 1971 to artificial magnetic fields of the same intensity as the earth's, but in varying directions. They found that the robins responded to these artificial fields just as they would to the earth's.

We do not know just where this astoundingly accurate orientation system is located inside a bird, nor have we proved that all birds navigate in this way. But experiments such as those described with birds (and with many other animals) should make us pause before we say that animals guide themselves "just by instinct." To brush off all intelligent-looking but unlearned behavior simply as an "instinct" tends to obscure the mechanisms operating in such behavior. A more rewarding approach to the understanding of animal behavior is to try to discover the kinds of stimuli that animals respond to and to search for the mechanisms working inside animals that make such responses possible.

In 1935 Frederick C. Lincoln, as a result of his studies of birdbanding data, discovered the existence of four great flyway systems over North America: the Atlantic flyway, the Mississippi flyway, the Central, and the Pacific. The terms "flyway" and "migration route" have been used interchangeably in the past, but the modern definition of a flyway is a vast geographic region with extensive breeding grounds and wintering grounds connected with each other by a more or less complicated system of migration routes. Each flyway has its own population of birds.

PLANTS IN AUTUMN

With the waning sun of autumn the plant kingdom begins to fade from the scene. Late-flowering plants have been pollinated and have formed their seeds for the next generation. The annuals, those plants that survive for one year only, turn brown and shrivel. The low-growing, soft-stemmed perennials, which live from year to year, lose much of their aboveground structure, leaving only roots or underground stems.

(*See* p. 337.)

The Scattering of Seeds

Many of the seeds and fruits are a colorful part of the autumn scene. Formation of the fruit with its seeds is only the first step in the propagation of plants. To germinate next year the seed must reach a suitable place. If the seeds of a plant simply fell beneath it they would have to compete with each other and with the parent plant for room, soil minerals, water, and light. The conflict is diminished by the scattering of seeds. Examination of the varied devices and agencies of seed dispersal is an excellent study in adaptation. We shall consider how seeds are adapted for dispersal by wind, animals, water, and by mechanical means.

For many seeds, the wind is the distributing agent. Some wind-dispersed seeds and fruits are equipped with fine, feathery plumes or tufts of hair that act much as a parachute does. The seed is sustained in the air long enough for the wind to blow it some distance. Familiar examples of plants whose seeds are so equipped are the cattail, milkweed, aster, dandelion, goldenrod, and the sycamore tree. Children are familiar with the ethereal, gray sphere of dandelion seeds, each equipped with a delicate parachute. They take delight in seeing how few puffs it takes to dislodge all the seeds. Other seeds are adapted for wind journeys by having wings. The familiar "polly nose" of the maple tree is an example of this type. Other common winged seeds are those of the ash, elm, tulip, pine, and Ailanthus trees. Wind dispersal is sometimes accomplished by the movement of the entire aboveground part of the plant, which, when mature, rolls along the ground and drops its seeds. This happens in tumbleweeds, which include amaranth pigweeds, Russian thistle, and some grasses. One pigweed plant may scatter as many as 10 million seeds in this way!

Seeds that are adapted for dispersal by animals may have an edible fruit with seeds whose coats are indigestible. In this case, as in the apple, the fleshy, edible part of the fruit is eaten by an animal, such as a deer, together with the seeds. The indigestible seed coat prevents destruction of the seed in the juices of the animal's digestive system. Ultimately, the seeds are elimi-

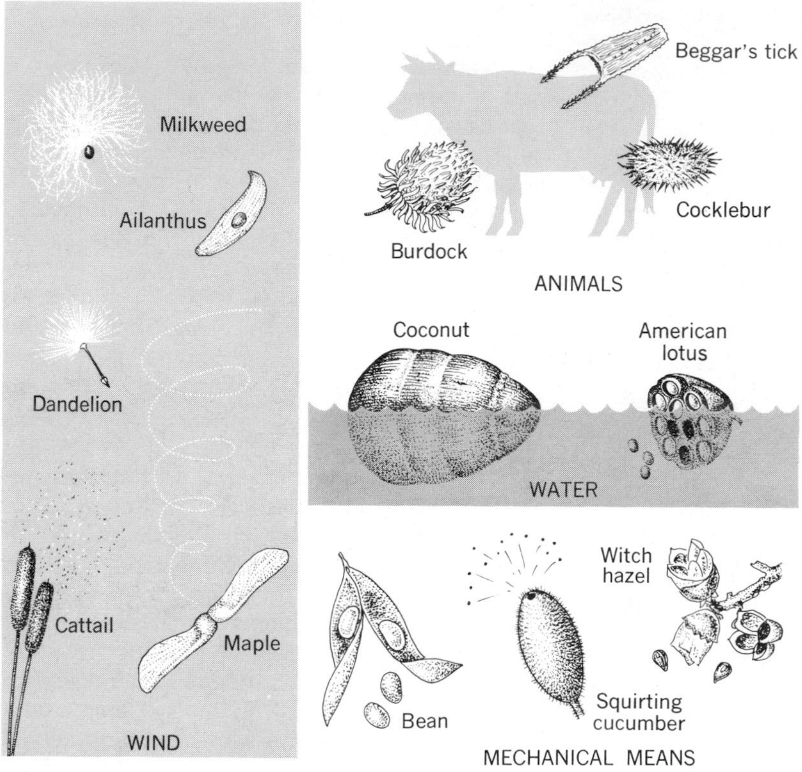

Examples of seeds dispersed by wind, animals, water, and mechanical devices.

nated with the other food wastes. By this time the animal will probably be distant from the site where the fruit originally grew, and so the plant is spread. The scattering of edible nuts—such as walnuts, acorns, and hickory nuts—depends on a slight variation of this process. If the animal eats the nut the seed is destroyed. But many animals—squirrels, chipmunks and field mice—bury such nuts in the ground for future feeding. Those nuts that the animals do not dig up may germinate in the following spring and further colonize their species.

Animals help scatter seeds in another way. Some seeds have hooks that catch on the fur of an animal as it brushes past the plant. Later on the seed is brushed off, but by this time the animal may have carried the seed a long way from the mother plant. The common cockleburs, burdocks, "sticktights" of the burr marigold, and "beggar's ticks" are examples of seeds that hitchhike on the fur of animals or the clothes of humans.

Water is an agent in the scattering of seeds. Seeds and fruits are often transported over short distances by the washing of rain along the ground or over long distances by streams. The classic example of a water-dispersed seed is the coconut. As it comes from the tree it is a massive fruit whose outer part, or husk, is made of myriads of interwoven fibers in which air is trapped. (This outer part is removed before the coconut reaches the market.) This is buoyant enough to support the heavy inner nut that contains the embryo. The covering of the coconut is waterproof, another necessity of a water-borne seed. How effective this device is may be seen from the fact that the coconut palm is one of the first plants to appear on newly created coral islands or atolls in the south Pacific. There is no doubt that some of these coconuts float for thousands of miles on the ocean surface.

Some seeds are scattered by being propelled from the plant. An example of this is found in the witch hazel tree, which blooms in the fall when the nutlike fruits formed from flowers of the previous fall are also evident. These have an interesting seed-scattering device. As the fruit dries, the cover suddenly breaks open and the small black seeds are shot out some distance in a way similar to the shooting of an orange seed from between the fingers.

Leaf Fall

The color spectacle of fall is provided by the deciduous trees, the broad-leaved trees that shed all their leaves in the fall. Many of these assume colors that vie with the rainbow. The change in color is accomplished partially by the addition of new pigments and partially by the unmasking of colors that were always there. Some of the colors, such as the reds and scarlets of oaks and maples, illustrate the former and are due to chemical changes in the leaf. Other colors, especially the yellows and browns—displayed by birches, poplars, elms, and most garden plants—illustrate the latter and are the result of loss of chlorophyll, which colors most leaves green during the spring and summer months. With the green gone, the hidden pigments become visible.

Leaf fall is an adaptation for conserving water. The broad leaf gives off large quantities of water to the air when it is active. This water must be replaced from the soil, or the tree suffers severe damage and may die. In the winter, soil water is unavailable in the frozen ground. The detaching of the leaves prevents a water loss that would be fatal. Toward the end of the summer a separation layer of special, corklike cells begins to form across the base of the leaf stalk, or *petiole.* This layer gradually grows, cutting off circulation of sap to the leaf. Eventually the loosened leaves separate from the twig and flutter to the forest floor. It is said of this happening that trees are remarkable surgeons: They tie off their veins *before* performing an operation.

Some trees, such as certain oaks and beeches, form an incomplete layer of cells between the leaf stalk and the twig. As a consequence the leaves remain on the branches all winter. It is not until buds begin to swell in the spring that the old leaves fall off. Such leaves are dead, however, and have ceased to make food.

Such evergreen trees as the conifers—pines, hemlocks, firs, and spruces—retain most of their leaves during the winter. These trees *do* shed their leaves, but not all at one time. Usually, one-third of the leaves are shed each year. The trees have special adaptations to prevent excessive water loss, even though leaves remain on the trees all winter.

Buds

When fallen leaves have left the tree branches bare it is easy to see the leaf or flower buds that were made during the summer. The leaves, or flowers, as the case may be, are encased within bud scales. The scales are tough and waterproof and so can protect the delicate structures within during the severe months of winter. Some buds, such as those of the willow tree, also have a cover of fuzzy hairs to avoid excessive loss of water. Buds of some poplars are coated with a sticky wax for the same purpose.

Buds containing flowers are particularly susceptible to cold. They are in no great danger when in the dormant condition, however. Danger arises when a premature warm spell causes the buds to develop rapidly, so that the flowers are in blossom when a freeze occurs. With the blossoms open their delicate structures are no longer covered by protective scales. Below-freezing temperatures are fatal to the flowers of almost all fruit trees. Cherry, apple, pear, and peach crops have been ruined by low temperatures that kill the flowers.

ANIMALS IN WINTER

Winter in the temperate zones is the quiet time. It is a time that tests the vitality of plants and animals. Now survival hangs by a delicate thread. Not only is food scarce but all living conditions become precarious. The greatest danger of all is cold.

(*See* p. 343.)

Hibernation

The animals that do not migrate either hibernate or are equipped to withstand the cold of this season. Most of the cold-blooded animals hibernate, because their rate of living is regulated by the temperature. During the late autumn frogs and other amphibians bury themselves in the mud at the bottom of their ponds and go into a state of suspended animation. Tadpoles, much like the fish that they resemble, frequently remain active and swim about during the fall and winter.

Insects winter as eggs, larvae, pupae, or adults in their many habitats—under the bark of trees, in the mud of ponds, in the soil. Moth larvae or pupae are wrapped in silken cocoons. The thousands of eggs of the praying mantis, packed together in a straw-colored egg case, wait for the warm days of May and June to hatch into tiny mantids.

The reptile world becomes torpid with the cold and goes into hibernation. Some turtles, such as the mud turtle, dig into the mud of ponds and remain there during the winter. Snakes seek out a hole in a tree or a crevice in rocks and there diminish their rate of living, or *metabolism,* to the point where they can exist without requiring food. At times, if the weather becomes unseasonably warm, snakes may emerge to bask in the sun's warm rays. Fish have remarkable abilities to withstand the cold. It is not unusual to find fish swimming about actively in the water beneath the ice, and one can fish in winter by chopping a hole in the ice and dropping a line into the water.

Some of the furry host, the mammals, hibernate even though they have protection against the cold. It is not enough to have a fur coat to keep warm. It is also necessary to obtain sufficient food. Those mammals that can subsist on the meager plant food available can remain active during the cold months. The deer foraging through the snow for acorns and other food is an example of this. The common black bear, as we have said, has gorged himself during the summer and early fall and stored up much fat. Late in the fall the bear holes up in a protected nook and sleeps a good part of the winter away. If the weather becomes warm the black bear may come out for a short time. Invariably it returns to hibernate until the first warmth of spring. It is interesting to note that the bear's cubs are born during the hibernating period. By the time spring arrives, the cubs are quite large and frisky. They will remain with their mother, however, until at least fall.

Active Animals

The few mammals that are abroad in midwinter must forage unceasingly for food. When the snow covers the ground the plant eaters may find it hard to reach roots which is their customary food and may turn to eating the bark of trees. This in turn may kill the trees, if the animal succeeds in girdling the trunk; that is, gnawing a circle completely around the tree. Deer are frequently hard hit by cold winters. In many northern states game wardens set out special food to keep these animals alive during the winter. When the snow drifts to great heights it is sometimes necessary to resort to airlifts to supply food to stranded animals. The same must sometimes be done to save herds of range cattle cut off by huge snow drifts.

Even the predators find lean pickings at this time. Wolves, foxes, and coyotes are limited in food resources because many of their usual prey are in hibernation or are sticking close to their burrows and dens. The extra fat gained during the lush days of summer may help to tide such animals over until food becomes available in the spring. In particularly hard seasons predators may be emboldened by hunger to invade built-up areas and prey upon man's domestic animals.

Winter birds eat voraciously to keep their bodies warm. A piece of suet nailed to a tree or a tray of seeds and bread crumbs placed outdoors is appreciated by the hungry birds, particularly when snow covers the ground.

PLANTS IN WINTER

With their leaves shed and the severed tubes sealed, the broad-leaved trees are able to con-

(*See* p. 342.) serve what water they have through the winter. Evergreens can retain their needlelike leaves because these have a thick waxy coat of *cutin,* which reduces the loss of water. Even though the sun shines weakly during the winter evergreens are able to make some food by photosynthesis and thus supplement what was made during the warmer months. One winter condition that puts a severe strain on trees is freezing rain. Under certain conditions rain that falls may freeze on the branches to such an extent that the sheer weight of the ice breaks the boughs. Snow piled on the branches may do the same thing. Although these two phenomena can produce picturesque scenes they are a menace to the trees unless their fibers are elastic enough to bend under the weight without breaking.

Everything appears to be in a deathlike sleep. As winter wears on restless human beings venture outdoors to look for signs of life. If they dig up some frozen soil and place it in a jar indoors they will be amazed at the changes that occur as the soil warms up. Seeds begin to sprout and insects emerge. A few twigs cut from forsythia or from some other woody plants and placed in a jar of water indoors will burst their buds weeks before their time, putting on a premature spring show for winter-weary eyes.

Some of the important generalizations from this chapter are:

The income of energy from the sun influences the activities of living things.

Green plants require sunlight for food manufacture.

Living things are able to adapt themselves to changes in temperature, light, and availability of food and water.

Animal behavior is based on heredity, but is modified by environment.

In the temperate zone some animals, mainly birds, migrate in spring and fall.

Spring is the reproductive season for most animals.

Many hibernating animals store summer food for winter use.

Seeds are adapted in various ways for dispersal by wind, animals, and water.

Some plants store food in roots, stems, or leaves.

Most broad-leaved trees shed their leaves in the fall, thus conserving water.

Animals active in winter are adapted for securing food and protecting themselves against cold.

During hibernation animals reduce their rate of living, or metabolism.

Discovering for Yourself

1. Observe a specific tree branch carefully over as long a period as possible to determine how it changes with the seasons. Do the same with other specific plants and note the changes. Keep records, including photographs if possible, that may be used later to draw conclusions. Write a plan for carrying out this activity with children.
2. Observe an animal, such as a squirrel or a bird, at various times over a long period and try to decide which actions can be attributed to changes in seasons. List your findings. Spring or fall in temperate climates are the best for such observations.
3. Observe birds in your vicinity during spring or fall months to determine how the kinds and numbers seem to vary with the seasons. Try to find out about the migratory habits of birds.
4. Construct a winter feeding station for birds. Keep a list of the birds that are

attracted to it. Keep a log of the times various birds appear, and try to determine what kinds of foods attract various birds.

5. Provide different kinds of food for a wild animal such as a squirrel. Observe what happens to the food and try to decide whether or not this action is in any way related to seasonal behavior.
6. Gather twigs (during the dormant period) from various trees or shrubs. Bring them indoors, place the stems in water, and observe the results. Examine the buds with a magnifying glass on successive days and try to draw some conclusions from the observation.
7. Collect various kinds of caterpillars, feed them, and observe any changes that take place.
8. Collect various kinds of seed cases. Examine them to determine methods of seed dispersal; observe the arrangement of contents; examine with a magnifying glass.
9. Visit a pond or any other natural setting at different times to determine changes in plant and animal life associated with changes in the season. Keep a record which includes date, temperature, appearance and disappearance, changes in habits, and variety of structure of specific plants and animals.
10. In winter dig up a square foot of soil to a depth of 4 or 5 inches. Bring it indoors and place it in a box, empty aquarium, or any other available container which can be covered. Observe the emergence of life—insects, worms, sprouting seeds, and so on.

(Courtesy of U.S. Department of the Interior.)

CHAPTER 11B

TEACHING "LIVING THINGS AND THE SEASONS"

Changes in seasons in some parts of the United States are not as dramatic and marked as they are in temperate climates, but they do occur. The best time to study seasonal changes is when they are occurring, consequently the problems suggested in this chapter may stretch through the whole school year.

Very young children find it somewhat difficult to encompass a whole season in their thinking; they are affected more by what happens on a single day, or here and now, than by the complete picture of the seasons. The effect of a snowfall on trees, of a strong wind, of a heavy rain are the kinds of things they will want to investigate; here they can see cause-and-effect relationships. As children mature, they are able to observe events over a longer period of time and to discover significant trends in a series of happenings.

This chapter is closely related to Chapter 7, where the cause of seasons is explained; to Chapter 9, "Weather and Climate," to life cycles in Chapter 10; and to Chapter 14, "Ecology and Survival."

SOME BROAD CONCEPTS: "Living Things and the Seasons"

Living things adapt themselves to changes in temperature, light, and availability of food and water.

Many animals, chiefly birds, migrate in autumn and spring.

Some animals hibernate; others store food and make other changes with the coming of winter.

Plants store food in seeds, roots, stems, and leaves.

Plants are adapted in various ways for dispersal of their seeds.

FOR YOUNGER CHILDREN

What Are Our Seasons Like?

Using the observations children can make, the experiences they have during the various seasons, and pictures of the four seasons children can construct some ideas that describe conditions of the seasons where they live. As we indicated in the introduction the best time to study a season is when it is occurring. This means that records might be kept so that comparisons can be made between autumn and winter, spring and summer. Observations will include temperature changes, height of the sun in the sky, hours of day and night, and so on. It is important that children come to realize that the seasons are not the same over all of the earth, and especially in different parts of the United States. If children have traveled, lived in different climates, or have relatives and friends who have had such experiences use this to help children understand the idea that seasons everywhere are not alike.

(*See* Ch. 7A.)

What Happens to Plants as the Seasons Change?

Make short trips to observe plants at different times of the year. Marking a specific tree branch, plot of grass, flowering plant, vegetable, and so on is helpful in directing the observation. Look for specific changes in buds, leaves, blossoms, seeds, bark, and other parts. In autumn collect seeds and seed cases, examine them carefully to see how the seeds are scattered. Try to count the seeds in a seed case; try to sprout some of them. In spring bring in small twigs from various trees and bushes; put the stems in water and observe changes. Try to open some of the buds. What is inside? Observe to see how the buds open. Are they leaf buds? Flower buds? Or both? Try to identify the twigs; which kind seem to open and develop first? What is happening to twigs outside? What will this branch look like at different seasons? Visit a vegetable stand or food market in autumn to look for plant parts where food is stored. Which are roots, stems, fruits, seeds, leaves? Where was this food made? Why is it important to you? A collection of pictures and photographs can be assembled and classified according to seasons to tell the seasonal story of plant changes.

What Happens to Animals as the Seasons Change?

An inventory of animals that live in the school ground and neighborhood might be made first. List the kinds of animals: birds, earthworms, insects, frogs, turtles, squirrels, and so on. Observe to gather information about these animals in autumn, winter, spring, and summer. The information will be gathered as the seasons pass and children may attempt to make some generalized statements as a result.

The life cycles of common insects may be observed as the seasons change; activities include: collecting various kinds of caterpillars, feeding and observing them, collecting cocoons to watch the adults emerge, observing the activities of bees and ants, looking for insect eggs in the barks of trees.

A feeding station in winter (*see* later detailed discussion) yields information about winter and permanent bird residents, their food, their beak structure, adaptations for eating different kinds of foods, and so on. Animal tracks in the snow sometimes tell the story of animals in winter. Observations of the appearance and activities of animal pets also yield information.

Pictures or actual photographs of the seasonal activities of animals and reading material will supplement observations.

OTHER PROBLEMS FOR YOUNGER CHILDREN

1. How do animals change their homes as the seasons change?
2. At which season of the year do plants grow fastest?
3. How do evergreen trees change as the seasons change?
4. What happens to seeds when they are planted?
5. What happens to leaves after they fall from the trees?

FOR OLDER CHILDREN

How Can We Observe Seasonal Changes?

The environment in which children live will in some measure determine the methods by which they attempt to solve this problem. Changes in seasons means changes in temperature, food, light, and water. To some degree changes in these environmental factors occur no matter if the environment is city or country or what section of the country. In warmer climates the changes are less pronounced.

The following are important to keep in mind: firsthand observations are necessary; measurements of conditions (such as temperature) are essential; repeated observations many times of the year must be made; observing small specific areas may be more productive than observing larger areas (a specific tree, a marked section of the school yard); observing to collect data on a specific problem may give focus to the activity; record-keeping is important in order to supply data from which to draw conclusions.

Select a specific area: the school yard, the park, a pond area, the neighborhood, or 100 square feet of yard, a field, or a woods. In early autumn make such observations as: "What is the temperature?" "What are the plants like?" "What are the animals like?" "What is the height of the sun in the sky?" "What food are the animals finding?" Keep a record of the observations. The record may be in the form of notes, photographs, charts, and exhibits.

As the school year progresses, revisit the specific area making records of similar observations.

Pupils in the early grades may make one series of trips to observe only plants and another to observe animals, or perhaps they will observe only one living thing. Older children may observe both plants and animals on the same trip. Pupils will need to call up past experiences and observe many times before they can draw any conclusions. They may look at some of these plants: grass, trees, shrubs, flowers, weeds, and vegetables. They may watch such animals as insects, birds, squirrels, and frogs. Here are some of the kinds of things that pupils may infer about plants on their autumn trips in temperate climates: Many plants are storing food. Some are making seeds. Some plants die. Some lose their leaves. Some make buds. About animals they may infer: Some animals are getting heavier fur. Some are building homes. Some are migrating. Some are storing food. It will probably take several trips to see all these things.[1] Older children might keep a diary of school-year-long observations.

A record of observations during each of the visits and as complete as possible will help refresh pupils' memories as successive trips are taken. There is, in this case, a real reason for making a record. The records made over this long period of time will supply data useful in answering the question: "How do animals and plants change as the seasons change?" The final record will be made up of sentences such as: "Some trees lose their leaves in autumn. They grow buds. The buds open in the spring. Some are leaf buds. Some are flower buds."

[1] *Audubon Plant Study Program* (New York: National Audubon Society); and V.A. Stehney: "Looking for Animal Homes in the Woods," *Science and Children* (May 1972). Excellent suggestions for exploring at different seasons.

As more observations are made, the children can discuss: "What important things have we found out about living things and the seasons?" This is another occasion for stressing that animals and plants do not actually *prepare* for winter in the same sense that we ourselves get ready for the cold by putting up storm windows and getting our warm clothes out of moth balls. We *know* that winter is coming. Our experience tells us that we shall need certain things because of the changes. We can *plan ahead.* Animals and plants do not.[2]

What Can We Learn by Feeding a Wild Animal?

Begin by asking children if they have ever observed wild animals eating. "What did the animals eat?" "Where were they?" "Did they carry any of the food away?" "What else did you observe?"

One way to learn about the food animals eat and where they store it is to feed them and find out what they do with the food. If squirrels or chipmunks live near the school, children can bring nuts, corn, and other seeds, feed them, and observe the results. A real interest in observing animals may result from such activity. Children are amazed to see how many trips to a hollow tree or to a hole in the ground an animal will make. They are also surprised to see how much food animals will take. This may be a time to stress evidence which indicates that animals cannot anticipate weather conditions and that often the amount of food stored by an animal depends on how much is available. Chipmunks, for example, will carry away quarts and quarts of shelled corn whether they need it or not.

In a city park, along a sidewalk area, in a vacant lot, and similar places squirrels, pigeons, and other birds may be fed and observed. Often such animals are accustomed to people and can be more easily observed than in other circumstances.

How Can We Maintain a Bird-Feeding Station?

Which birds stay with us all winter? How can we find out?

Maintaining a bird-feeding station may prove a very enjoyable experience if it is done carefully and planned well. On the other hand, if the feeding station is not well placed or is not stocked with proper food the experience may be disappointing. Books that describe bird-feeding stations often mislead children, for they depict cardinals, bluejays, woodpeckers, chickadees, and other winter residents all clamoring for food. Such a rushing business is usually not done by a school bird feeder—certainly not the day after it is installed.

There are many kinds of bird feeders that pupils can make.[3] Some are trays

[2] *Bulletins on Animals and How They Live* (New York: National Audubon Society); and G.O. Blough: *Soon after September* (New York: McGraw-Hill, Inc., 1959).

[3] *Homes for Birds,* Conservation Bulletin no. 14 (Washington, D.C.: U.S. Government Printing Office, 1969). Additional information may be obtained from the National Audubon Society, 950 Third Ave., New York, N.Y. 10022. *See also* G. O. Blough: *Bird Watchers and Bird Feeders* (New York: McGraw-Hill, Inc., 1963).

Everyone in school is interested in this bird feeder that was made by older children. Here the youngest children are adding food. Observing, keeping records, trying out different kinds of foods, and identifying birds are part of this all-school project. (*Courtesy of Phyllis Marcuccio.*)

fastened to a window; some may be hung from pulleys and pulled away from the window on a line; some can be fastened to trees or posts.

Here are some hints about making and maintaining a feeding station: The school custodian, parents, a boy from an upper grade, or in many classes the pupils themselves can make the feeding station. Be sure that the station is out of the reach of cats. Water, especially in dry and freezing weather, helps attract birds. Various grains, bird seeds, sunflower seeds, bread crumbs, raisins, suet, apples and other fruit are satisfactory foods. Be sure that the wind does not blow the food away; keep the station well stocked; and remove any uneaten food if it is spoiled. The feeder should be in a sheltered place, but, if possible, in view of the schoolroom window. In a city environment it should be placed as near trees as possible. Birds usually will not use the feeder if it is in the midst of playing children. Suet attracts birds in a city environment.

Discovering what kinds of foods different birds eat is an activity that presents opportunity for the use of scientific attitudes. Pupils should not generalize from one instance, should not decide without careful observation, and should withhold conclusions until there is sufficient evidence from observation and reading to justify them. For example, the fact that birds have not eaten sunflower seeds on the feeder for several days is no reason for deciding that birds do not like sunflower seeds.[4]

How Do Insects Change with the Seasons?

Insects make changes as the seasons change and fortunately many of these can be observed. Discuss with children the stages of the life cycle—egg, larva, pupa, and adult. Urge them to search for some of these stages at different times of the year and report their findings.

If there is a woods, park, a vacant lot or a backyard where there are dead trees and logs pupils may be able to find hibernating insects under the bark or in the cracks. They may be able to find bunches of insect eggs and small cocoons there also.[5] They may see the shiny band of the tent caterpillar eggs on wild cherry and apple trees. If the ground is not frozen they may dig down into an ant hole to see whether they can discover any ants.

Children often bring cocoons to school and like to keep them and see the moths emerge. This can be a very exciting and instructive experience. If cocoons are scarce in your neighborhood they may be purchased from a biological supply company, accompanied by directions for their care. Cocoons are best kept in a wire cage of some kind so that they can be easily observed when the moths emerge. A satisfactory cage can be made by using a plant pot and some window screen. Make a wire-screen cylinder about 1 foot long and a little narrower than the diameter of the plant pot. Fill the pot with soil. Stand the wire cylinder up on the soil and push it down into the soil, so that it will stand erect. Cover the top of the cylinder with a thin piece

[4] Blough and Campbell, *ibid.*, pp. 67–72. Gives many examples of ways to feed birds in winter and illustrates many different kinds of bird-feeding stations.

[5] G.O. Blough: *Discovering Insects* (New York: McGraw-Hill, Inc., 1967); and *Bulletins on Insects and Spiders* (New York: National Audubon Society).

of wood. If the cocoons are fastened to twigs, as they often are, you can stand them up; otherwise, you can fasten them to the inside of the screen or lay them on the soil. A terrarium is also a good place to keep cocoons. They should be moistened occasionally to simulate conditions of rain or snow they would encounter outdoors.

If male and female moths of the same kind emerge at the same time they may mate. The female will lay fertile eggs, and the larvae can be raised to spin cocoons if they are fed the right kind of leaves and are properly cared for (*see* discussion of silkworm raising, Chapter 10).

Insects can be collected by spreading an open newspaper (or a piece of cloth) under a bush. Shake the branches. Gather up the paper and funnel the contents into a wide-mouth jar. Empty the jar into a terrarium or screen-covered empty aquarium. Compare the number and kinds of insects found at different times of the year.

Mosquitoes are also exciting insects to observe in studying life cycles.[6]

How Do Trees Change during the Year?

Observing an individual tree over a long period of time will yield considerable information about how it changes. Groups of children can select different trees and compare observations. Observe buds and their development, new growth, blossoms, fruit, seeds, and so on.

The structure of a bud and the changes that take place as it opens often go unnoticed by most children and adults. Small twigs of trees and shrubs can be brought to school and examined to answer such questions as: "What covers the outside of the bud?" "What is on the inside?" "How are all the buds alike?" "How do they differ from one another?" Some of the buds may be cut open with a sharp knife. In early spring each child can bring two or three twigs, put them in water in a sunny window, and observe them each day to note the changes. Here is another activity for which a magnifying glass comes in handy. Toothpicks can be used in taking buds apart to study their structure. Pupils may be surprised to discover that maples, oaks, and other trees have flowers that are very beautiful. Twigs of apple trees are interesting to keep indoors. The buds are large, and the flower buds open as the leaves develop.[7]

Observe a tree in a schoolyard periodically for the whole school year to see how the leaves change during the year; what birds, insects, and other living things inhabit it; what seeds and fruits are produced, and what happens to them; what characteristics help to identify it; and how it changes as the seasons change.

Studying the annual rings of a tree that has been cut down is an interesting experience for children. Difference in spacing of rings may be very revealing. Closely

[6] Elementary Science Study, (ESS): *Mosquitoes, Teacher's Guide* (Manchester, Mo.: Webster Division, McGraw Hill Book Co., Inc.). Investigating the changes in the life cycle of the mosquito with special emphasis on collecting eggs, raising larvae, and learning how to learn by experimenting to solve certain problems about how far mosquitoes can fly, when they fly, how they find you, and what they prefer to bite. Also contains the essential subject matter.

[7] *Audubon Tree Study Program, Audubon Plant Study Program,* and *Bulletin on Plant Identification* (New York: National Audubon Society).

spaced rings can indicate a long dry spell; wide spaces a wet one. Counting the rings gives an indication of the age of the tree. If a tree in the neighborhood is cut or blown down in a storm children can observe the rings, damaged branches, hollow sections, birds' nests, and so on.

What Happens to Frogs in the Winter?

Frogs and toads, like other animals, change as the seasons change. Eggs are laid in the spring; they hatch into tadpoles and develop into adults. In winter they hibernate. They bury themselves in the mud in ponds. All their bodily activities are slowed down. The heart beats very slowly; breathing takes place only through the moist skin. The frog draws on the food stored in its tissues to maintain life.

Children can actually see indications of hibernation by placing some frogs in water that has been chilled to near the freezing point. Stir some ice cubes into a jar of cold water. (As a control, put others in water at room temperature.) Ask children to observe carefully and try to explain their observations. In a short time the frogs in the cold water will dive down, expelling air from their lungs to reduce their buoyancy. Transparent third eyelids slip over their eyes. They will stay at the bottom as long as the water is icy. Frogs can be induced to hibernate at any time of the year. If the hibernating frogs are removed from the cold water and placed in warm water they will soon become active.

This demonstration is always an exciting one for children, and it has a number of values. It indicates that hibernation is not a result of planning or preparation; rather it is an automatic response to a particular environmental influence. It reveals how we can understand "nature" better—by controlled experiments in which we test one factor at a time.

What Can We Discover about Bird Migration?

In many localities it is possible to observe flocks of birds gathering before they migrate. Migrating ducks and geese can often be observed, and children should be encouraged to watch for them.[8] A group of pupils who want to find out about migrating birds and birdbanding may make a report that will stimulate a discussion of "Where and How Birds Migrate and How Scientists Are Learning More and More about Migration." (The Bibliography suggests books that give extensive information about bird migration.)

Together with information about bird migration pupils often find maps that show routes. They are interested to learn in what places birds of their locality spend the winter, how far the birds must fly to reach these places, and whether there are

[8] Audubon Bird Study Program (New York: National Audubon Society); and U.S. Department of the Interior (Washington, D.C.: Publication Unit of the Bureau of Sport Fisheries and Wild Life); bulletins and other materials.

mountains or bodies of water that the birds must cross. These questions stimulate map study and may make use of information gained in geography and social studies.

There may be an authorized birdbander in your neighborhood who will have a great deal of interesting information for the class. A high-school biology teacher nearby may know one of the thousands of birdbanders scattered around the country. A trip can be made to see how the birds are caught, to learn how they are banded and how the records are kept, and to hear about data that the birdbander may have discovered. The biology teacher himself may have had interesting experiences with birdbanding and migrating. As we have stated before, there is much to be said in favor of making such contact with secondary-school teachers.

OTHER PROBLEMS FOR OLDER CHILDREN

1. What can we find out by examining animal tracks?
2. How can we investigate animal superstitions?
3. Why do leaves change colors in autumn?
4. How does the color of animals help to protect them?

Resources to Investigate with Children

1. The surrounding environment to note seasonal changes in individual animals and plants.
2. Pets to see how they change with the seasons.
3. Local bird enthusiasts and Audubon Club members for information about bird migration, birdbanding, and similar activities.
4. Individual trees on the schoolground or nearby to be observed for seasonal changes.
5. Ponds and streams to observe water animals during the seasons.
6. State conservation departments for information about birdbanding, bird refuges, wildlife preservation, game laws and how they vary with the seasons, and similar information.
7. Florists, nurserymen, and gardeners for information about seasonal changes in plants and about pruning, root and bulb storage, and so on.
8. National Audubon Society, 950 Third Ave., New York, N.Y. 10022, for pictures, bulletins, and other helpful material. Write for a catalogue of material.
9. Vegetable market to observe examples of food storage in plants used by man.
10. A farm to observe and learn about the care and feeding of farm animals at different seasons, and to learn of the relationship between farm crops and the seasons.
11. Zoo for information on the care and feeding of young animals, care of injured animals, seasonal changes, and other matters.

Preparing to Teach

1. Attempt to become an observer or a participant in the Christmas Audubon Bird Count. These counting activities are held in many parts of the United States. Make contact with the local Audubon Club. Keep a record which will supplement your work with children.
2. Plan experiences that will help children understand how pollination of flowers takes place.
3. Visit a park, pond, or other area that will be useful in helping children make discoveries about changes of seasons. Keep a record of your observations that will help children engage in similar activity.
4. Collect insects, mount them, and have them ready to exhibit in order to show interested children how to make an insect collection.
5. Plan how you would introduce a study of living things and seasons with children. Assemble visual materials you can use for this introduction.
6. Examine recent printed materials on environmental education and plan how you would incorporate the material in your work.
7. Conduct a survey of a schoolground area and plan how you would use the area in solving the problems of this chapter. Include trees, shrubs, fence corners, and other places in the immediate neighborhood.

CHAPTER 12A
THE HUMAN BODY AND HOW IT WORKS

(Courtesy of Zimbel from Monkmeyer.)

WONDER OF WONDERS

Man wonders over the restless sea
The flowing water and the sight of the sky
And forgets that of all wonders
Man himself is the most wonderful.

Since St. Augustine wrote these words in the fourth century A.D., man's knowledge of himself has increased enormously, but so too has his wonder. This wondering has led him to scrutinize himself intently, to examine the minute details of his body structure, and to unravel many mysteries of the body's functioning.

HOW MAN STUDIES HIMSELF

Man views his body in many ways. The older view was concerned mainly with the body's gross structures—its systems and organs, its bones, muscles, and blood vessels. Today we study the body alive. We record the fluctuations of the heartbeat electrically on a graph. We observe the rhythmic waves of the food tube through a fluoroscope. We inject a radioactive substance into the bloodstream and follow its progress through the body with a Geiger counter. We use a television camera to view the inside of the human body in color.

We place bits of the body's tissues under the microscope, and the magnified view thus obtained reveals the billions of building blocks of the body—the cells. With the electron microscope, which magnifies up to 200,000 times, biologists have penetrated the innermost parts of the cell and revealed unimagined structures there. We use the most refined techniques of chemistry to detect the molecules of living material inside each cell and to discover how the activities of these molecules in cell "laboratories" make life possible. We use the tools and techniques of the biologist, chemist, and physicist to unravel the many mysteries of life hidden in the minute structures within the cell.

With these tools and techniques we have made great progress in the many fields of research that have contributed to man's health. In the last 100 years we have detected the microscopic organisms that are responsible for many of man's diseases—bacteria, protozoans, and viruses. We have found how to combat these diseases with serums, vaccines, drugs, and antibiotics. We have discovered the role of the hormones, important chemicals released into the bloodstream, in regulating the development and functioning of the body. We have discovered the vitamins, essential components in the foods we eat.

We study the heredity and environment of man to see how each of these influence his development. We see in his heredity, not without some difficulty and uncertainty, the contribution of his parents, grandparents, and more distant ancestors. We investigate the impact on him of his surroundings, which include not only climate, food, shelter but also the social forces in human society. Finally, we see man as a part of the continuing story of life that started some 3 billion years ago.

CELLS

The human body, like all living things plant or animal, is built of structural units called cells. (See p. 381.) Each cell, as we saw in Chapter 10A, is a tiny glob of living protoplasm. The cell typically contains a nucleus surrounded by cytoplasm and is covered by a thin cell membrane. Cells of the body come in many shapes and sizes. They are fitted to do many jobs—to protect and cover the body's surfaces, to receive and transmit nerve impulses, to contract and relax, to manufacture special chemicals, to store foods, and to perform dozens of other surfaces. A body cell, unlike an ameba (a one-celled animal), is not independent. It is affected by its relation with other cells and by the behavior of the whole cellular community, the body, of which it is a part.

BLUEPRINT OF THE BODY

Let us take a close look at the body to see how it is built and how it works. The body is made up of a number of obvious large parts—the limbs,

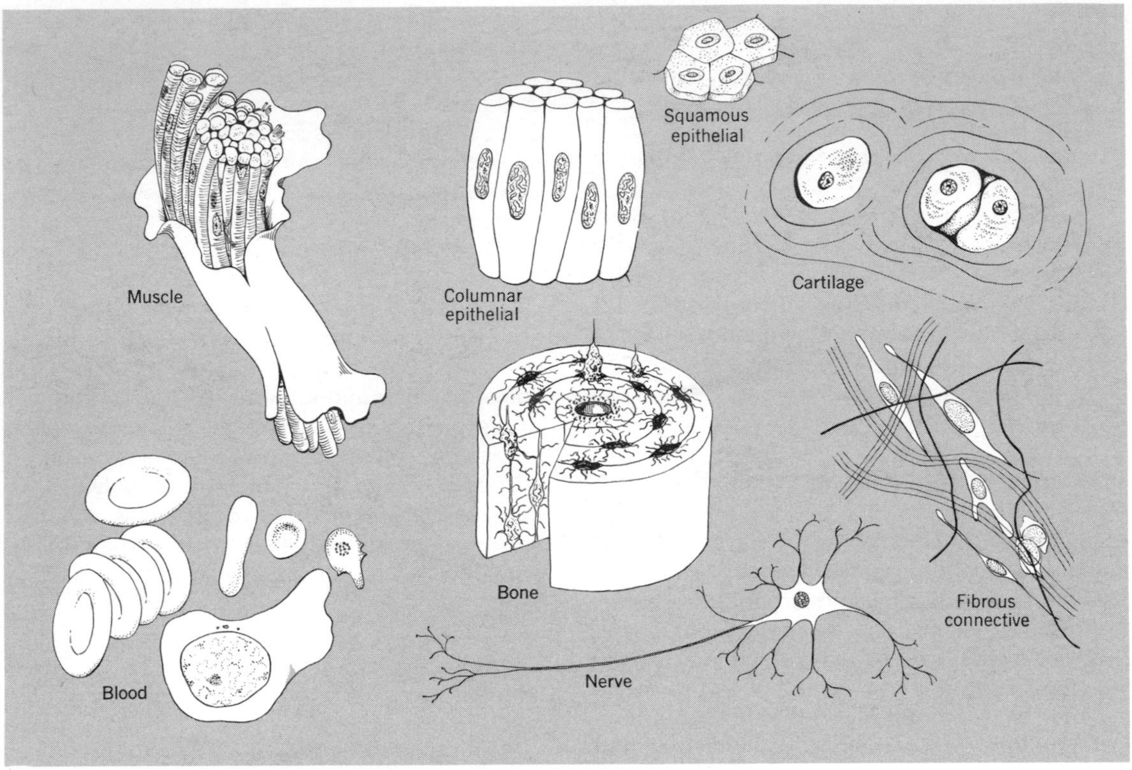

Each tissue cell is uniquely fitted for its job: the long, thin fibers of muscle cells that can contract quickly; the bricklike cells of epithelium, functioning as a protective wall; the freely moving cells of blood tissue; the long, complex cells of nerve tissue with their specialized receiving and sending parts; and the scattered cells of bone and cartilage, with their tough intercellular material.

eyes, ears, and internal parts, such as the stomach and liver. Such large parts of the body, called organs, have a special job to perform. The legs are used to carry us from place to place. The eyes respond to light, enabling us to see. The arms and hands are used for doing all sorts of jobs, including grasping, lifting, and turning. The heart pumps the blood around the body. The stomach is active in a special phase of digestion. Each organ performs an essential task.

Select a convenient organ, such as the forearm, and examine its structure. On the outside is skin. Within the arm you can feel the hard, supporting framework, the bones. If you wiggle your fingers while clasping the forearm with the other hand you can feel the muscles that activate the fingers. When the skin is cut, even by the merest scratch, blood flows out. You have undoubtedly struck your elbow (the "funny bone") sometimes in just the special way to get a tingling sensation. You have unwittingly stimulated the nerve that is near the surface at that point. The various parts of the arm—skin, bones, muscles, nerves, blood vessels—are held together by connective bands.

Organs are composed of different kinds of tissues. Thus, in the arm there is blood tissue, muscle tissue, epithelial tissue, and supporting tissues: cartilage, bone, and fibrous connective tissue. As in any good organization the tissues must cooperate with each other to perform the work of the organ. Another way of saying this is that an organ is a group of tissues working together to perform a major function in the body. Let us examine the tissues more closely to see how they are constructed and how they work.

Epithelial Tissue

An example of the covering type of tissue is found in the outer layers of the skin, called *epithelium.* Here the cells are packed closely like bricks, thereby serving as an effective wall to keep body fluids in and foreign bodies out. The epithelium of the skin is only paper thin, but we are painfully aware of its importance when a bit of salt gets into a cut. The outermost cells of the skin's epithelium are dead and are shed continuously. What is commonly called dandruff is bits of epithelium flaking off from the scalp, a perfectly normal process if it does not occur excessively. As dead cells are lost from the outside, new ones are continuously forming underneath.

The lining of the kidney tubules, of the digestive tract, of the lungs and other organs is composed of epithelial tissue. Every organ of the body has its own epithelium covering. Around the heart, for instance, Is the epithelium called the *pericardium.* In addition to lining and covering body parts epithelium is a primary chemical factory of the body. Many glands contain epithelial tissue, which manufactures and secretes the useful products of the gland—enzymes and hormones, for example.

Muscle Tissue

To understand better how a muscle performs, shred a bit of uncooked meat (muscle tissue) and view it under a microscope. You will see that it is made of many long fibers. (These individual fibers, unlike most cells, contain a *number* of nuclei.) Millions of muscle cells shortening at the same time cause the whole muscle to do its job—to shorten and pull. That is why the bulge appears on your arm when you bend your elbow. All the voluntary muscles of our body—that is, those that we can move at will—are composed of such cells. Examples are the muscles of the arms and legs.

The heart is essentially a hollow muscle, although its cells differ somewhat from those found in the muscles of the arm. Heart, or cardiac, muscle tissue contracts automatically and rhythmically. This may be observed in the heart muscle of an embryo chick, where the muscle contractions begin long before there are any nerve connections. A third type of muscle tissue is found in parts of the digestive tube, such as the stomach and small intestine, and in the arteries and veins.

Supporting Tissue: Bone and Cartilage

The supporting tissues of the body are bone, cartilage, and fibrous connective tissue. Bone is hard because of the deposit of minerals, mainly calcium phosphate, in the spaces between the bone cells. At birth our bones are not hard. The soft supporting tissue in them, except in the skull bones, is cartilage. (The human skull is made of 22 bones that form a box to hold and protect the brain, plus 6 tiny ear bones. At the time of birth some of these bones are separated by soft membraneous regions, which make it possible for the head of the child to pass through the birth canal without injuring the mother or child.) The original cartilage is later replaced by bone, but in some parts of the body the cartilage is permanent. The outer ear, for example, and the tip of the nose, as well as the ends of all long bones, are made of cartilage. This is useful in places where strength must be combined with flexibility. Cartilage (you may know it as "gristle") is also found in the windpipe, where rings of cartilage serve to keep the passageway open. In cartilage tissue, as in bone, the material deposited *between* the cells carries on the supportive or protective function of the tissue.

Bone is formed continuously in childhood. Milk is an excellent source of the bone-building minerals—calcium and phosphorus. That is why milk has such an important role in children's diets. The bone minerals are constantly being torn down and rebuilt, even in adults. Most of the calcium of the body is in the bones, but calcium must also be available in the bloodstream for the contraction of muscles and for the clotting of blood. When the amount of calcium in the blood falls below a certain level the blood "borrows" some from the bones. This automatic calcium-transfer system is one of many "feed-back" processes that occur in the body.

Supporting Tissue: Fibrous Connective Tissue

Connective tissue does what its name implies: It connects the tissues of the body and holds them together. This binding type of tissue is found everywhere in the body. (The white strands seen in roast beef and ham are connective tissue.) Among the special types of connective tissue are tendons and ligaments. Tendons are the cords that connect muscles to bones. When the muscle contracts, it pulls on the tendon and in this way moves the bone to which the tendon is attached. If you place the fingers of your left hand on the inside of the right elbow and then flex the right forearm you will feel the tendons moving back and forth at the joint. The cords you see on the back of the hand when you straighten your fingers are also tendons. They connect the finger bones to the muscles in the forearm. The most famous tendon in the body is the Achilles' tendon. You can feel this tough tendon in the back of the ankle. The calf muscle lifts the heel by its tendon of Achilles.

Ligaments are usually broad, flat bands of tough, elastic tissue that connect bone to bone, holding the bones in place at the joint. Ligaments can stretch and then return to their original size. If a ligament is torn, the joint may become dislocated; that is, one of the bones may be displaced from its normal position.

Blood

Blood tissue is unique in that its cells can move freely in a liquid. This is an asset for a material that must be readily transported to every minute part of the body. The liquid part of the blood is *plasma.* This is mainly water in which is dissolved many important substances, as we shall see later in our study of blood circulation. Immersed in the plasma are the red cells, the white cells, and the platelets. The red cells' job is to carry oxygen around the body. One of the primary jobs of the white cells is to fight off invasion by harmful organisms, such as bacteria. Platelets help in the clotting of blood.

Nerve Tissue

Nerve tissue contains the longest cells in the body. Some of these may be as much as 3 feet long, such as the cells from the skin of the foot that carry sensory messages to the spinal cord. However, these cells are so thin that a bundle 1 inch thick might contain 25,000 of them. Nerve cells come in a variety of sizes and shapes, but are all designed to carry messages called *nerve impulses.*

Some nerve cells provide incoming paths for messages from sense organs and thus provide us with information. Others carry the outgoing messages from the brain and stimulate body activity in muscles and glands. The headquarters of all nerves is the spinal cord and the brain. The brain is made up of an astounding number of nerve cells, an estimated 30 trillion.

Tissues, Organs, and Systems

All the tissues we have examined are made of cells and their products. We may say that a tissue is a group of similar cells working together for a specific job. Different kinds of tissues work together for a larger purpose. Thus, as we have seen, the arm contains muscle, nerve, bone, blood, and other tissues working together to make possible the functioning of the arm. The same is true for all the organs of the body, such as the heart, stomach, liver and kidneys.

Efficient operation of the body requires division of work into different departments, just as in a city government or a large industrial plant. The departments of the body are called systems. All the organs concerned with preparing food for the use of the body are part of the digestive system. The circulatory system handles transportation of materials throughout the body.

The respiratory system is made up of the organs that supply oxygen and get rid of certain wastes. The excretory system is the sanitation department of the body, ridding the body of its wastes. The nervous system has as its primary job controlling the body.

NUTRITION

It's a very odd thing—
As odd as can be—
That whatever Miss T eats
Turns into Miss T.
—*Walter de la Mare*[1]

The body has the remarkable ability to select needed chemical substances from the beans, beef, milk, and lettuce you consume, and to convert them into just the kind of substances needed to make the body's own flesh and bones. When you have ceased growing, food is essential for the repair and replacement of worn-out tissue. Food also fills the energy needs of the body.

(*See* pp. 377–8, 380–1.)

Food Essentials

A trip to the supermarket provides convincing evidence of the tremendous number of food products that are available for human consumption. This variety, however, is only on the surface: There are only a few kinds of essential substances in all these foods—the carbohydrates, fats, proteins, minerals, vitamins, and water.

(*See* pp. 377–8, 380–1.)

The common carbohydrates are sugar and starch. They are similar chemically, and both are changed into the same substance—glucose—by digestion. Carbohydrates constitute the prime fuels of the body. Fats and oils are the other large class of fuel nutrients. Pound for pound, fats produce about twice as much energy when oxidized in the body as do the carbohydrates. In cold climates, such as the polar regions, people rely heavily on fat intake to supply the heat needed to maintain normal body temperature. Eskimos, for example, eat large amounts of blubber, the fat of the whale.

Water, minerals, and proteins are essential for the structure and the workings of the body. Water is taken in directly in the form of drinking water or as part of food, because foods have a great deal of water in them. Minerals are required in small amounts. These are provided by the food we eat if our diet is a good one. The role of calcium and phosphorus in building bones has been mentioned previously. Other minerals serve other vital functions. Iron, for instance, is an essential constituent of hemoglobin, the oxygen-carrying pigment in red blood cells. Liver is an excellent source of this element. Iodine is required for proper functioning of the thyroid gland. Fluorine has been included in the list of needed minerals (and now is added to drinking water in some localities), because it seems to be a factor in preventing tooth decay. Common salt (sodium chloride) is also an essential ingredient of the diet.

Proteins, the most complex of the food substances, are abundant in meat (muscle), eggs, cheese, and beans, and are essential in building protoplasm, enzymes and hormones, and other essential body materials.

Not all proteins are identical in their chemical makeup. The dissimilarity among proteins arises from the nature of the protein molecules: Each is made of an assortment of one or more of 22 kinds of smaller units called *amino acids.* Proteins might be compared to words, each of which is made of one or more of the 26 letters of the alphabet. In the process of digestion proteins are broken down into their amino acids, which then pass into the bloodstream. The body cells select from this assortment of amino acid "building blocks" those which are needed for their particular structure and their particular function. A variety of proteins from different sources is essential in a good diet. As might be expected, those proteins of *animal* origin—for instance, the proteins of milk, eggs, and meat—

[1]From *Poems for Children* by Walter de la Mare. Courtesy of The Literary Trustees of Walter de la Mare, and The Society of Authors as their representative. Copyright 1930 by Henry Holt and Company, Inc.; reprinted by permission of Holt, Rinehart and Winston, Inc.

have the highest nutritional value for man, because the assortment of amino acids in animal proteins most closely resembles that of the body's proteins. However, it does not matter whether the essential amino acids come from a cow, pig, fish, soybean, or any other source; they always end up in distinctly human protein.

Vitamins are found in foods in minute amounts. Unlike most of the other food essentials vitamins are not used directly as fuels or growth materials. Instead, they act as regulators of chemical activity and of growth in the body. At first the chemical nature of the vitamins was not known and so they were designated by the letters of the alphabet, for example, vitamin A. With increased understanding of the chemical structure of these substances their specific chemical names are gradually replacing the less exact earlier terminology. Thus, vitamin C is called ascorbic acid. Vitamin B has turned out to be an entire group of vitamins, with more than a dozen thus far separated and identified out of this complex group.

The proper place to obtain the vitamins that the body needs is from food. A good diet will supply all the nutritive needs of the body. Vitamins in concentrated form should be taken only on the advice and under the supervision of a physician.

Diet

Diet is one of the most popular subjects of ordinary conversation. Oddly enough, people generally mean a special diet, such as a reducing diet, when they mention the word. In reality *diet* means the foods that a person customarily eats. The primary rules of diet are: (1.) Sufficient food must be eaten to supply the body's energy needs, and (2.) a properly varied diet is needed to supply the materials for the growth and functioning of the body.

The word "Calorie" is frequently misunderstood. A Calorie is not a substance in food. It is simply a measure of heat. A Calorie is the amount of heat needed to raise the temperature of 1 liter (a bit more than 1 quart) of water 1° centigrade. In other words, to speak of the Calories that a portion of food contains is merely to indicate how much heat will be produced when that food is burned. A few examples of the approximate daily Calorie requirements of human beings are: a workman doing heavy manual labor—4,000 Calories; a housewife—1,800 to 2,300 Calories; an active teenage school boy—2,500 to 3,800 Calories. If a person eats much more of the fuel foods than his body requires daily the extra material may be changed into fat tissue. This is ordinarily undesirable, because the added fat serves no useful purpose and is a burden for the body to carry around. Insurance statistics show that people who are 10 percent or more overweight for their particular build shorten their lives measurably. Because most cases of overweight are the result of overeating, the prevention and remedy are obvious.

(*See* pp. 510–11.)

CONSTANCY OF THE INTERNAL ENVIRONMENT

As you climb a mountain the character of the environment changes: There is a drop in temperature and air pressure; the wind, light, and moisture may vary. But the internal environment of the body, its temperature and chemical state, remain relatively constant.

The term *homeostasis* is used to describe the body's mechanisms for correcting the disturbing effects of environmental forces. Thus, when camping out on the mountain top a drop in temperature triggers nerve impulses that stimulate the muscles and the walls of the smaller arteries to relax. The blood supply to body tissues is increased, and, with it, more sugar and oxygen for energy to warm the body.

About 100 years ago Claude Bernard, a French physician, first described the interior of an animal as a separate, isolated environment. He emphasized that an essential part of the activities of an animal consisted of regulating that environment. In this way the cells of an animal are provided with constant conditions, regardless of any changes in the external environment. Essential in maintaining a stable internal environment is the transport system of the body—the bloodstream and the body fluids. Excess heat is removed from tissues by the blood and brought to the skin, where it is released during the evaporation of sweat. Excess urea is removed from the blood by the kidneys and excreted in the urine.

The lungs, kidneys, skin, large intestine, and ductless glands, which will be discussed presently, are the chief organs involved in maintaining the constancy of the body's internal environment.

DIGESTION—PREPARING FOOD FOR THE USE OF THE BODY

We would starve, despite all the food that we eat, if it were not for the digestion of food. Most of what we eat is not in proper form to pass into the blood or to be used by the cells of the body. The digestive system is composed essentially of a long tube together with the digestive glands that secrete chemicals which act on food in the tube. The entire tube is known as the alimentary canal. It is surprisingly long—about 30 feet in adults. Most of this length is made up of the coiled small intestine, which is about 22 feet long.

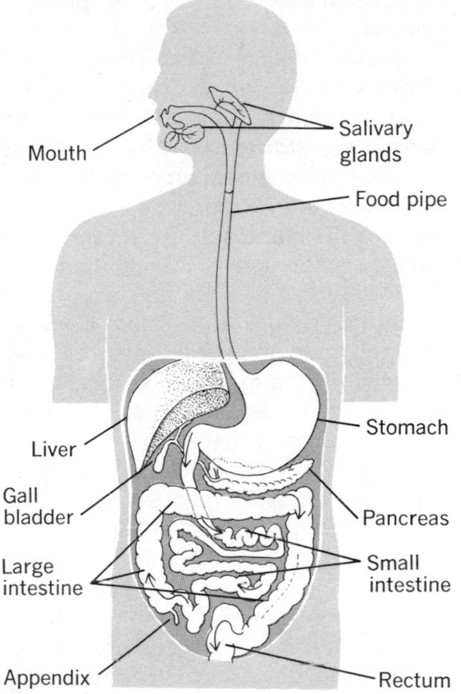

The general appearance and location of the main digestive organs are shown here. Various glands secrete chemicals that change food as it moves through the alimentary canal.

Inside the Food Canal

Before we consider the changes in food as it travels through the alimentary canal let us preview what is going to happen. The food mass is going to be chopped, ground, and finally reduced to a kind of liquid mush. At the same time the molecules of the proteins, carbohydrates, and fats in the food are going to be split into smaller molecules. This molecule-splitting will be accomplished by the action of enzymes of the various digestive fluids. It will serve two purposes. First, it will permit the molecules to pass through the membranes of the small intestine into the bloodstream and thus become available to the entire body. Second, it will transform the complex molecules into a form in which they can be used by the cells of the body for building new protoplasm or for the production of energy.

The food enters the body via the mouth. (*See* figure above.) Solid food is operated on by 32 specialized tools, the teeth. The 8 front teeth are the *incisors* that cut and slice like a knife and chisel. The 4 sharply pointed *canines* grip the food like pliers, ripping it as it is pulled away. The 20 cusped *molars* do the grinding and mashing job of a mortar and pestle. Breaking up the food into small particles exposes it to the chemical action of digestive juices. While the food is being chewed, the muscular tongue mixes the food with saliva and kneads it against the mouth's bony roof. Saliva is made in three pairs of salivary glands whose secretion is brought into the mouth by tubes or ducts. Enzymes in saliva start the digestion of cooked starches, splitting the large molecules into the smaller ones of sugar. After a few moments in the mouth, the food is swallowed and passes through the food pipe, or *esophagus,* into the stomach.

Food may remain in the stomach up to 4 hours, depending upon the kind of food. While there it is churned about and mixed with gastric juice from the gastric glands. This juice contains, among other substances, an enzyme that helps to digest proteins. Surprisingly, some of the stomach glands manufacture hydrochloric acid. The minute amount of this acid that is made helps the enzymes to work and also helps dissolve minerals in the food. After it leaves the stomach the food is pushed into the small intestine, which is the main center for digestion in the body. And, as we shall see, it is the place where digested food leaves the food tube and enters the blood. Into the small intestine pour the juices of three digestive glands—intestinal juices given off by the glands in the walls of the small intestine itself, bile from the liver, and pancreatic juice from the pancreas. The enzymes in the juices of the intestinal glands and the pancreas, as well as certain salts in bile, complete the process of breaking down carbohydrates, proteins, and fats into simpler substances.

Out of the Canal

Digested food is able to pass through the thin membranes of the small intestine into the blood. This process is known as absorption. The small intestine is admirably fitted for the job of absorption. Its 22-foot length; thin walls abundantly supplied with capillaries; millions of microscopic, fingerlike projections called *villi*—all serve to make it an effective "blotter" for carrying out the function of absorbing digested foods and then transferring them to the circulatory system.

Waste Disposal

The indigestible part of food goes into the large intestine. This is large in diameter as compared to the small intestine, but it is much shorter in length, being only about 5 feet long. The material in the large intestine is mainly composed of cellulose from plant foods and bacteria. Water is removed from this mass as it moves along. The waste products form semisolid feces that are eliminated from the body through the rectum.

RESPIRATION—HOW THE BODY BREATHES

A person may be able to survive without food for a week or more. Without oxygen, however, the human being cannot live for more than a few minutes. Oxygen is required by every cell for the oxidation of food to produce energy. It is the job of the respiratory system to supply oxygen vital for life and also to rid the body of the carbon-dioxide wastes resulting from cellular oxidation.

(*See* pp. 271–2.)

Mechanics of Breathing

The lungs and the structures connected to it form a continuous open system with the outside. The lungs are enclosed in an airtight chest cavity whose size is increased and decreased during breathing. If you place your hand on your chest you will notice that it rises and falls as you breathe. Not so readily noticed is the movement of the diaphragm, an arched muscular partition between the chest and the abdomen. Air is not "sucked" into the lungs, but is forced in by atmospheric pressure through the action of the diaphragm and of the chest muscles. During inhalation the diaphragm contracts and is thus pulled downward. At the same time the muscles of the ribs contract and pull them up and out. These movements enlarge the chest cavity and reduce its pressure on the lungs. The outside air, with its greater pressure, is thus pushed into the lungs.

(*See* figure p. 355.)

(*See* pp. 378–9.)

During exhalation the diaphragm moves up and the ribs move down and in. These movements decrease the size of the chest cavity, increasing its pressure and squeezing the air out of the lungs. When the person is at ease this cycle takes place about 12 to 15 times per minute. During exercise, or other strenuous activity, we breathe more rapidly and more deeply. This

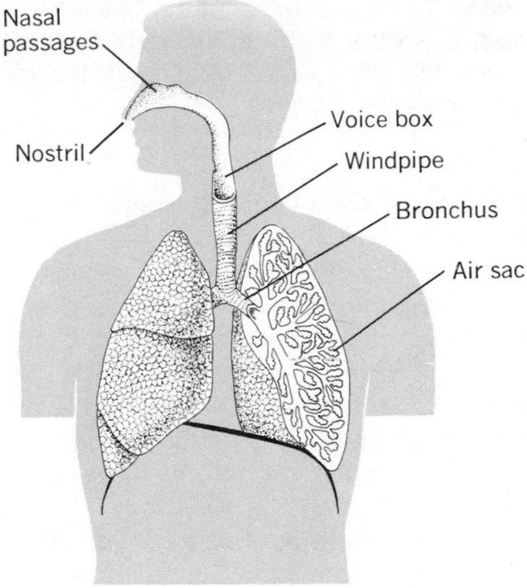

The pathway of air from the nostrils to the air sacs is shown in this diagram.

supplies added oxygen necessary for the increased energy required by such activity. When a person sleeps, the breathing rate lessens.

Pathway for Air

Inhaled air passes through the nostrils, where small hairs strain out large dust particles. It then traverses the nasal passages. The labyrinthine arrangement of the bones in the nasal passages enormously increases the area of mucous membrane over which the air must pass. This is desirable because the mucous membrane moistens, cleans, and warms the air to body temperature. If these actions did not take place the air entering the lungs might damage the lung membranes and thus not only cause irritation but also provide an entry for harmful microorganisms. This is the reason it is more healthful to breathe through the nose than through the mouth.

The air now enters the throat cavity and then passes the trapdoor guarding the entrance to the windpipe. This trapdoor, the *epiglottis,* closes when we swallow food to prevent food particles from entering the windpipe. The windpipe branches into two pipes, the *bronchi.* These lead the air by means of smaller and smaller tubes ultimately into the air sacs of the lungs.

Exchanges in the Air Sacs

The air sacs are microscopic chambers in the lung tissue. The lungs have nearly 1 billion of these balloonlike structures. This provides an enormous area for the absorption of oxygen from the air. The air sacs have very thin walls, richly supplied with capillaries. The oxygen passes through the thin walls of the air sacs and capillaries and into the blood and eventually is carried to every cell in the body. Moving in the opposite direction, carbon dioxide and water vapor leave the blood capillaries and pass into the air sacs. When we breathe out these gases pass out of the body as part of the exhaled air.

Cigarette Smoking and the Respiratory System

Cigarette smoking has come to the forefront as a cause of respiratory-system damage, notably cancer of the lungs. In 1962 the American Cancer Society reported: "The fact that cigarette smoking is the major cause of lung cancer has been proved beyond a reasonable doubt."

In 1967 a report issued by the U.S. Public Health Service renewed and strengthened the earlier warning that cigarette smoking caused lung cancer. This report, based on more than 2,000 studies which involved more than 1 million humans, backed up its earlier conclusions and also described cigarette smoking as "the principal" cause of lung cancer and as the most important cause of death and disability from chronic bronchitis. It also describes cigarette smoking as a possible cause of death from coronary heart disease.

In a typical study, one of 300,000 veterans, it was found that persons age 55 to 64 who smoked two packs a day were 34 times more likely to die from lung cancer than were nonsmokers. With respect to heart disease the report found that between the ages of 45 and 54 male smokers of ten or more cigarettes a day are three times more likely to die and female smokers twice as likely as persons who never smoked.

The report also concluded that cessation of smoking could delay or avert a substantial portion of deaths from lung cancer and early deaths from chronic bronchiopulmonary disease and heart disease.

It is probably true that if cigarette smoking were not a national habit the overwhelming evidence of the hazard it presents to health would have resulted in legislation barring the manufacture and sale of cigarettes. At this time the most urgent question for parents and teachers is: "How can we prevent this habit from establishing itself in youth?" In this effort they must have the backing of legislation that not only regulates cigarette advertising but also makes use of the mass media to promote a desirable image of the nonsmoker in the eyes of young people.

Periodic chest x-rays are one of the most valuable health measures for early detection of tuberculosis and of lung cancer. In most communities x-rays are provided without cost.

CIRCULATION—HOW MATERIAL IS TRANSPORTED AROUND THE BODY

The Heart

More than 300 years ago William Harvey demonstrated that blood flows in a continuous, closed circuit through the body. This was the first time in history that an accurate concept of circulation was formed. Even now, when knowledge of circulation is widespread, we are awed at the marvels of the heart mechanism. Here is a living pump that pushes blood through 70,000 miles of blood vessels, and beats 100,000 times per day every day of our lives.

(*See* p. 379.)

The heart is a muscular pump about the size of a fist, weighing less than 1 pound. It is made of four compartments. The upper two are known as *auricles,* the lower two as *ventricles.* The left ventricle is the largest chamber, making up three-quarters of the whole heart in size. Its muscle wall is three times as thick as that of the right ventricle. This difference is related to the job performed by each of these parts: The left ventricle must push the blood completely around the body, but the right ventricle pushes the blood only to the nearby lungs.

Around the Circulatory System

With the help of the illustration let us join the blood entering the right auricle and journey with it throughout the body until it makes a complete circuit. But before we do, take a quick look at our itinerary. Blood enters the right side of the heart from all parts of the body, goes to the lungs, returns to the left side of the heart, and then goes to all parts of the body. It is then returned to the right side of the heart and the trip starts all over again. Stated more briefly, blood travels from the body to the right heart to the lungs to the left heart to the body. Notice that to make a complete round trip blood has to go through the heart twice. Now for the details:

Blood is brought to the right auricle by two veins, the *venae cavae.* This blood has come from every part of the body except the lungs. When the right auricle is filled with blood the trapdoor or *valve,* as it is called, between it and the right ventricle opens, and the blood flows into the ventricle. The valve closes as the right ventricle contracts and sends the blood through *arteries* (blood vessels that carry blood away from the heart) to the lungs. In the *capillaries* that envelop the air sacs of the lungs the blood picks up oxygen and gets rid of carbon dioxide and some water. The blood now goes back to the left side of the heart by means of *veins* (blood vessels that return blood to the heart).

The oxygenated blood from the lungs enters the left auricle. When this chamber fills, the valve between it and the ventricle opens and the blood flows into the left ventricle. The valve then closes, which prevents a backflow of the blood as the large muscles of the left ventricle contract. This sends the blood coursing throughout the body by way of the *aorta,* the largest blood vessel in the body. In the adult it is slightly thicker than a man's thumb. The aorta sends branches into the head and arms, and the main line continues down through the chest and abdomen and sends

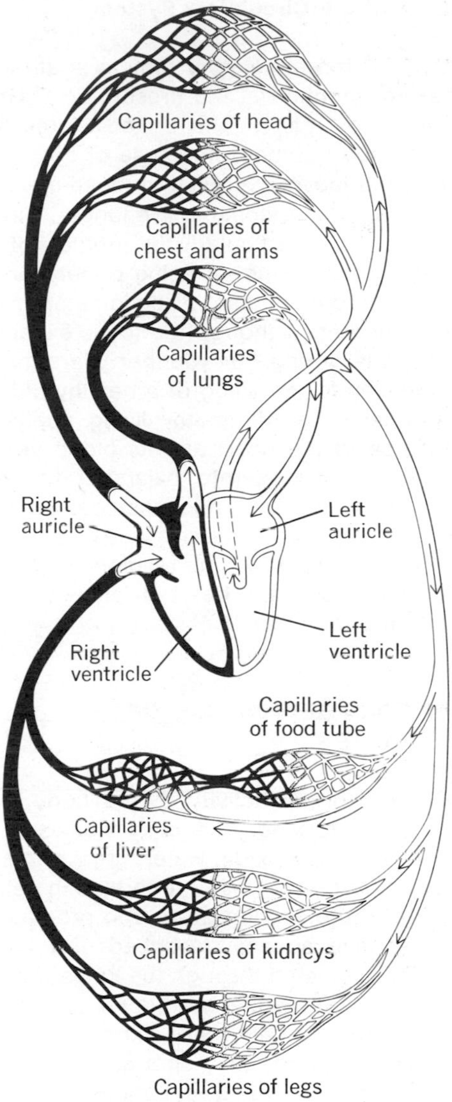

Blood moves around the body in a continuous closed circuit of arteries, veins, and capillaries, with the heart serving as a pump.

off a number of branches. It finally divides into two arteries that supply the legs.

The blood from the arteries is widely dispersed through a branching network that divides first into *arterioles,* and then into millions of thin-walled capillaries to reach all the cells of the body. Here oxygen, food, and other needed substances are transferred from the blood to the cells. In turn, the tissues give up their waste products to the blood. The capillary network reunites to form the veins, which then return the blood to the heart again by way of the venae cavae, the largest veins in the body. The cycle then starts over again. It has been estimated that it takes about 15 seconds for the blood to make one complete circuit of the body.

Of the 4,000 gallons of blood that are pumped through the heart daily none is absorbed through the walls of the chambers. The muscles of the heart receive blood containing oxygen and food in the same way as all other tissues. For this purpose a special set of arteries branch off from the aorta and go immediately to the heart structure. These are the coronary arteries. The coronary veins bring the blood back from the heart tissues to rejoin the main circulation. Blockage of the coronary blood vessels leads to heart attacks.

Blood

The bloodstream is the distribution system of the body. This surging fluid carries food and oxygen to all the cells of the body. It receives and delivers many chemical products, such as the hormones. It collects wastes and brings them to the organs that remove them from the body. The blood also contains chemicals and cells that protect the body from disease. In addition, the blood has its own built-in system for plugging leaks in any of its pipes.

Blood is composed of red and white blood cells, platelets, and a liquid in which they are immersed. The liquid is the plasma.

The red cells (also known as red corpuscles), as we noted previously in our study of tissues, are the oxygen carriers. These cells contain hemoglobin, which is made of an iron compound combined with protein. Hemoglobin, which is responsible for the red color of blood, is the substance that enables the red cells to carry oxygen. In the lungs the hemoglobin combines with oxygen. When the blood reaches the tissues of the body the oxygen is released. Lack of iron in the diet may lead to one type of *anemia,* a blood condition in which there is an insufficiency of hemoglobin.

There are about 25 trillion red cells in the body. Each cell lives only about 4 months. New red cells are manufactured in the red marrow of bone at the rate of about 2 million per second.

The white corpuscles may be regarded as the standing army of the body. One of their primary jobs is to fight off invading bacteria and other harmful microorganisms. This they do by engulfing the harmful organisms, digesting them, and thus destroying them. White corpuscles are able to squeeze through tiny openings in the capillary walls and leave the bloodstream. They move, much like an ameba, to any part of the body where danger threatens. This has earned them the name of "wandering cells." Normally, there are about 6,000 to 10,000 white corpuscles in every cubic millimeter—a tiny drop—of blood. In this same drop there will be about 5 million red corpuscles.

The plasma is about 90 percent water, in which many substances are dissolved. These include fats, sugars, proteins, antibodies (protective substances against disease), hormones, enzymes, minerals, and wastes. The adult human has about 5 quarts of blood. The donation of 1 pint of this precious fluid to the Red Cross, for building up the nation's stockpile of plasma for emergencies, will not harm a healthy adult. The body replaces such losses quickly.

Clotting is a self-protecting mechanism of the blood. Everyone has had the experience of cutting himself. Small cuts or scratches bleed for a few minutes and then, without any outside assistance, stop, and a hard clot forms. This prevents excessive loss of blood. In clotting, a plasma protein called *fibrinogen* coagulates into threadlike fibers that slow the outflow of blood, entrap the corpuscles, and thus form a clot.

The circulatory system is a *closed* system of arteries, veins, and capillaries. The capillaries, however, are thin-walled enough for some of the liquid part of the blood to pass through them and to bathe the tissues of the body. This escaped liquid, together with the white blood cells that have forced their way out of the capillaries, make up the fluid called *lymph*.

Care of the Circulatory System

Care of the circulatory system is attracting increasing attention at the present time. Health statistics show that in the United States heart disease is the number one cause of death. Part of this is the inevitable result of those measures that have enabled people to live longer. Circulatory ailments are particularly the problem of middle and old age, so in an aging population it is to be expected that these will become prominent health concerns. Although the toll is exacted in later life it is during our younger years that we pave the way for an ailing or a healthy old age. The normal rules of healthy living apply with equal force to the heart and its blood vessels. These include a moderate, balanced diet, exercise in the fresh air and sunshine, sufficient sleep, freedom from excessive worry, and a periodic medical checkup. The relation of cigarette smoking to coronary heart disease was discussed on pages 355–366.

EXCRETION—GETTING RID OF BODY WASTES

During normal activity of the body waste products are formed. The chief wastes of the body are carbon dioxide, water, urea, and salts. Water and carbon dioxide are formed in cells as a result of the oxidation of food to produce energy. We have already described how carbon dioxide is eliminated through the lungs. Water is disposed of in three places—the lungs, the skin, and the kidneys. The water exhaled from the lungs can be seen readily on a cold winter day. Sweat coming from the sweat glands of the skin is mostly water together with some salt. This is brought to the sweat glands by the blood circulating in the skin. Evaporation of the sweat not only rids the body of excess water but is an important way of cooling the body.

Urea is a product resulting from the breakdown of protein foods and of protoplasm. It is excreted chiefly by the kidneys. Each of the two kidneys has about 1 million microscopic filters. The blood flows through these filters, and the urea, salts, and water are removed. These flow into the bladder as urine, which is eliminated from the body periodically. The kidneys also perform the essential job of controlling the concentration of practically every chemical in the blood. They eliminate excess substances and retain valuable ones. As a result, the fluids that eventually leave the blood capillaries to bathe the cells of the body provide the cells with a uniformly favorable environment.

Urine gives valuable clues to body health. Among the substances for which urine is analyzed are sugar and albumen. Sugar in the urine may be indicative of diabetes. Albumen may signify that the kidneys are not functioning properly.

GROWTH

Food supplies the primary building material of the body. Proteins and water, together with other food substances, are changed by the body cells into new living protoplasm. This change of food to protoplasm is called *assimilation.* As more protoplasm is formed, cells become larger and then divide to form additional cells. This increase in the number of cells takes place by a process called *mitosis,* in which the hereditary units in the nucleus, the *genes,* are doubled and then equally divided between the two new cells. The *cytoplasm* (the protoplasm outside the nucleus) also divides, and thus two new cells are formed that are identical to the original cell. In this way an epithelial cell in the skin, splitting by mitosis, produces two new identical epithelial cells.

Some of the vitamins play an important part in regulating growth. Vitamin D, for instance, is needed for proper growth of the bones. Some of the hormones, the secretions of the endocrine glands, also have a role in growth regulation. We discuss these in another section of this chapter.

THE BODY FRAMEWORK AND HOW IT IS MOVED

The human body is built on the same plan as a modern skyscraper. There is a rigid internal

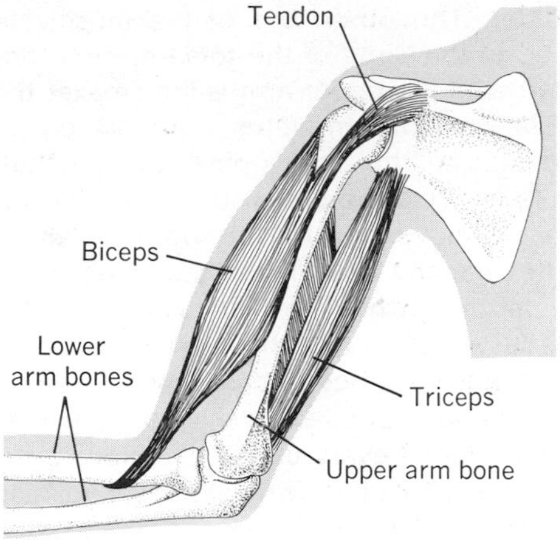

One muscle bends the arm and another muscle straightens it.

(*See* pp. 377–80.)

arrangement of beams and girders, the skeleton, to which the rest of the structure is attached. The human framework has the added feature of flexibility: Its parts can be moved. The long bones are designed as levers that are moved by the muscles attached to the bone framework. All in all, the bones and muscles are a wonderful mechanism of struts, arches, levers, and pulleys for supporting and moving the body. A typical long bone, such as the upper arm bone, is not solid. It is a cylinder, with the space within occupied by marrow. This hollow formation gives great strength combined with lightness. The bone tissue itself, as we have seen, is composed of scattered bone cells around which have been deposited mineral salts, chiefly calcium phosphate. The minerals give the hard quality to bone.

Muscles move bones by pulling, never by thrusting or twisting. The pulling results from the shortening or contraction of a muscle. Therefore, when you move any part of your body in one direction you are using a different muscle from the one you use to move the same part in the opposite direction. A convenient place to see how this operates is in the arm. *(As you read the following, consult the illustration here.)* On the upper surface of the upper arm is the bulging biceps muscle. This is attached firmly at the shoulder. The other end of the muscle is attached to the bone of the forearm by a tendon. Underneath the upper arm is the smaller triceps muscle, similarly connected. If you place your left hand around the right upper arm so that the fingers encircle the arm you will be able to discover the movements of the two muscles. When you flex the arm you will feel the biceps contract and harden while the triceps relaxes and loosens. When the forearm is lowered, the biceps relaxes and the triceps contracts. Through co-operating pairs of muscles man can move all his limbs in almost every useful direction. Complex motions, such as handwriting, may involve many pairs of muscles.

BODY CONTROL

The human body is under the dual control of the nervous system and the endocrine glands. The primary control is exerted through the nervous system, whose branching nerves penetrate the entire body. Chemical control is effected by the endocrine glands, through the hormones they secrete into the bloodstream. Let us look first at the nervous system.

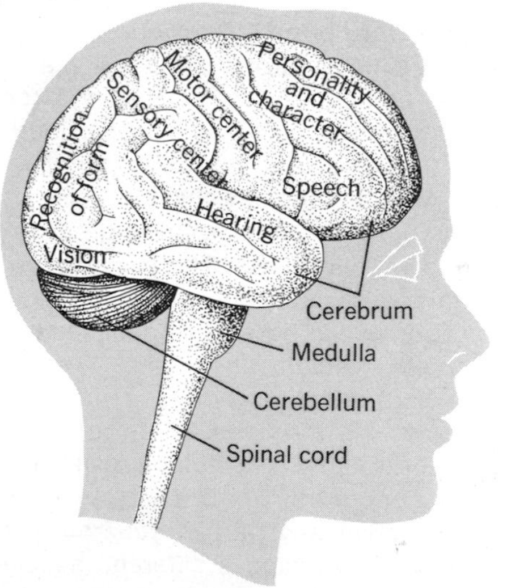

The three parts of the brain control different levels of activity. The cerebrum is the center for voluntary movement, for the reception of sensations, for reasoning and memory. The cerebellum controls balance and coordination of muscles, as in walking. The medulla controls such automatic functions as breathing, digestion, and heartbeat.

The Nervous System

The headquarters of the nervous system is the brain. Nerve pathways for most parts of the body enter and leave the brain by way of the main trunk line, the spinal cord. An exception to this are the important cranial nerves, which connect directly from the brain to various organs, principally in the head, without passing through the spinal cord. The exact nature of a nerve message is not known, but a combination of electrical and chemical changes pass along the nerve cells when a nerve impulse is transmitted. The eyes, ears, and sense organs in the skin, tongue, and nose are specialized for receiving sensations (*see* Chapter 20A for a description of the ears, and Chapter 21A for a description of the eyes). The unit of structure and function of the nervous system is the nerve cell, or neuron.

The brain's main parts are the cerebrum, the cerebellum, and the medulla, as shown. The *cerebrum* is the part of the brain where the centers that control consciousness, intelligence, reasoning, memory, imagination, and learning are located. Also in the cerebrum are centers that receive and interpret sensations, such as sight, hearing, smell, taste, pain, pressure, and others. Here also are the centers for initiating and directing voluntary activities. Lift your arm. The impulse for this action originates in the cerebrum, speeds from there down a nerve pathway in the spinal cord, and then along a nerve to muscles in your arm, causing them to contract.

The *cerebellum* is a coordinating center for muscular movements. Any action, such as walking, requires the coordinated functioning of many muscles. The precise timing of muscular contraction and relaxation is insured by the cerebellum. Another job of the cerebellum is the control of balance. In the mastoid bone of the skull, which also contains the inner ear mechanism, are three canals oriented at right angles

(*See* pp. 636–8.)

to each other in the three planes of space. As a fluid moves in the canals the position of the body in space is communicated to the cerebellum by the effect of this fluid on the sensitive nerve tissue lining the canals. The cerebellum automatically interprets these messages and sends impulses to the proper muscles to maintain the body in balance.

The *medulla* controls what might be termed the housekeeping functions of the body. Heart rate, breathing, and body temperature are some of the activities regulated by the medulla. It is obvious that this is a vital center. Any damage to the medulla may cause instant death. The medulla is just within the skull at the base of the brain. Nerve pathways in it continue downward without interruption into the spinal cord.

The *spinal cord* is the main pathway between the brain and the rest of the body. Through the spinal cord go many of the nerves that bring impulses to the brain from the body receptors, the sense organs. In the opposite direction impulses from the brain to many parts of the body pass through nerves in the spinal cord. In addition, the spinal cord is the center for many reflex actions.

A reflex action is the simplest type of action in the nervous system. If, unthinkingly, you touch a hot object with your finger, you pull your hand away before you are aware that it is hot. Awareness comes later. The action starts with stimulation of receptors in the finger by the hot object. The nerve impulse generated in the heat and pain receptors of the skin is carried along by sensory nerve cells to the spinal cord. Connections are made to motor nerve cells, which carry a message out to the muscle. The muscle contracts, pulling the arm away. All of this takes but a few thousandths of a second. Meantime, a second series of connections are made in the spinal cord, and a message starts up to the brain to "advise" the brain that the object was hot. This message, however, does not arrive in the brain until some thousandths of a second after the hand has been pulled away. We can appreciate the protective advantage of reflex actions when we realize that hundreds of these inborn, automatic actions are built into the workings of the human body.

Chemical Control

The endocrine glands constitute the other controlling system of the body. The action of these organs was first discovered in the middle of the nineteenth century. Scientists found that certain glands poured chemicals into the bloodstream that affected various parts of the body. Such chemical messengers were named *hormones,* which is a Greek word meaning "I excite." Minute amounts of hormones produce large effects. They enter the blood directly from the gland where they are made and are then quickly carried to all parts of the body. This explains the rapid action of some hormones. The main endocrine glands of the body are the pituitary, thyroid, islands of Langerhans, adrenals, thymus, and gonads.

The *pituitary* gland is attached to the base of the brain. It produces a number of different

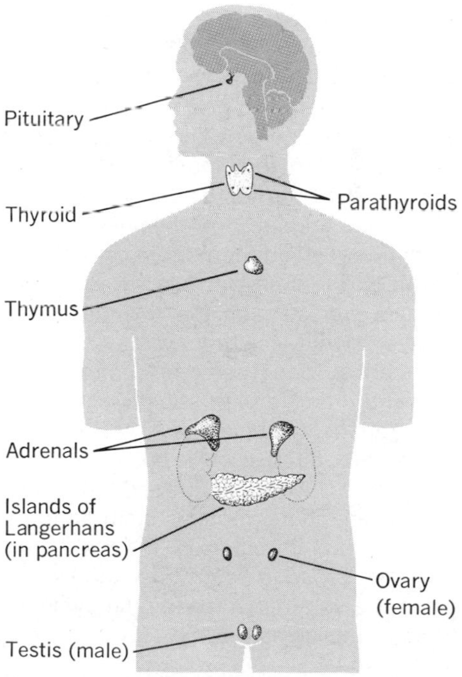

Chemical control of the body is exercised by the endocrine glands, whose secretions are carried by the blood to all parts of the body.

hormones. One of these regulates bone and body growth. Excessive secretion during childhood may produce a giant. Undersecretion, on the other hand, may make an individual a dwarf. Other hormones of the pituitary gland regulate blood pressure and many phases of the reproductive cycle. The pituitary gland is often called the "master gland," because it produces hormones that control many other ductless glands.

The *thyroid* gland is in the neck in front of the voice box. Its secretion, *thyroxin,* regulates the rate at which the body works, or body metabolism, and body development.

The *islands of Langerhans,* located in the pancreas, secrete *insulin* needed by the cells for the oxidation of sugar. Insulin extract, first used in January 1922 for the treatment of diabetes, has saved the lives of thousands of persons.

The *adrenal* glands lie on top of the kidney. One of their secretions, *adrenin,* is important in regulating blood pressure. It causes the heart to beat faster and more strongly and has been used as a lifesaving drug when the heart falters. Other secretions of the adrenal glands are involved in regulating cellular oxidation. One of these, *cortisone,* mentioned frequently in newspaper and magazine articles, has been used in the treatment of arthritis and certain skin conditions.

The *thymus* gland, located just below the neck and behind the top of the breastbone, has long been an enigma. The thymus increases in size until puberty and then begins shrinking until it is reduced to its size at birth. Recent studies on animals indicate that the thymus stimulates antibody and white-cell production and therefore is significant in body defense against bacteria, viruses, and other foreign substances.

The *gonads,* the testes and ovaries, not only make the reproductive cells but also manufacture hormones. These influence the so-called secondary sex characteristics such as the deep voice and broad shoulders of the male, and the breasts and broad hips of the female. In the female they also are involved in the cycle of egg production and menstruation.

HEREDITY

The passing of traits from parents to children has engaged human interest for many centuries. But it was not until 1865, when Gregor Mendel, an Austrian monk, reported on his classic experiments on thousands of pea plants, that the science of heredity, genetics, was founded. Mendel's work was ignored until 1900 when it was rediscovered simultaneously by three geneticists working independently. Thus genetics is a twentieth-century science.

Heredity has its basis in reproduction. The sperm contributed by the male and the egg by the female contain all the hereditary material that the new individual is going to receive from his parents. This hereditary material is concentrated in the nucleus of each of these cells. There it is organized into structures called *chromosomes,* which are visible under the microscope.

Every cell in the human body contains 23 pairs of chromosomes, or 46 chromosomes—with one exception. The exception is the sperm or egg cell that the mature individual produces. These contain only 23 chromosomes, one from each of the pairs. When the sperm and egg unite to form the fertilized egg this new cell contains 46 chromosomes, or 23 pairs of chromosomes. Therefore, the new individual arising from the fertilized egg has the same number of chromosomes as each of his parents, having received half from each.

Sex Determination

A careful study of the photographs of the 23 pairs of chromosomes in human body cell suggests how sex is determined. (Try to work it out for yourself before reading the following.) Note that the shapes of the chromosomes in male and female are almost identical—with, again, one exception. The male has a pair of chromosomes identified as XY, and the female a corresponding pair XX. These are known as the sex chromosomes. When a female produces eggs the chro-

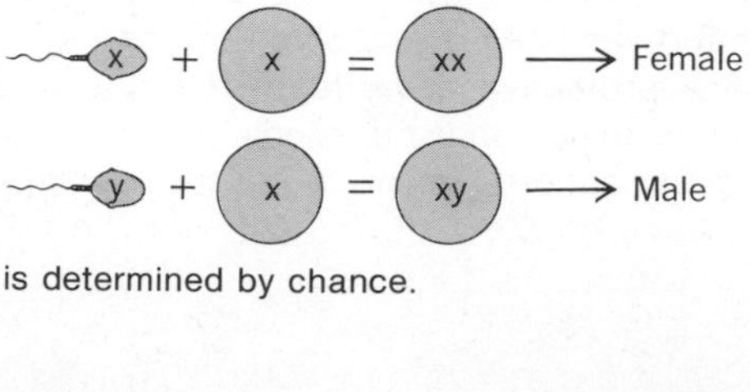

Sex is determined by chance.

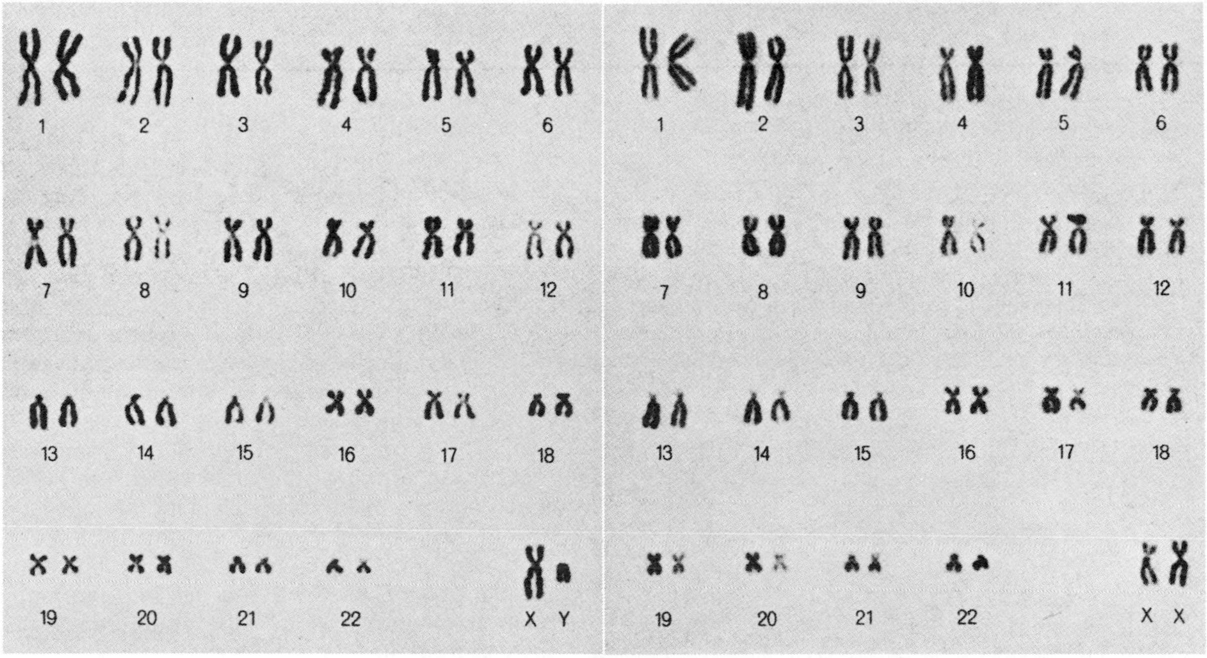

Each human body cell contains 46 chromosomes. The chromosomes shown here are those of human white blood cells, enlarged 1,400 diameters. Those on the left are from a male, those on the right from a female. (The symmetrical appearance of each chromosome is caused by the duplication of each of the 46 in preparation for cell division.) (*Courtesy of Scientific American.*)

mosome pairs separate; only one from each pair will be included in one egg. Each egg cell will therefore have a single X chromosome. In the male, however, half of the sperm cells will have an X chromosome and the other half a Y chromosome. Sex is determined at the moment of fertilization. If an X sperm enters the egg the combination XX will result in a female. If a Y sperm enters, the resulting XY combination produces a male. There are an equal number of X and Y sperm, so the chances of either fertilizing the egg are equal. This explains why approximately half the individuals born are male, half female.

Genes and DNA

Within the chromosomes are thousands of the basic determiners of the body's traits, the *genes.* It is beyond the scope of this book to go into the ways in which genes operate or to discuss in detail the principles of heredity. However, we cannot overlook the spectacular discoveries of the last decade that have led us close to the unraveling of the chemical nature of gene activity. It appears that the gene material is a complex molecule known as DNA, which is a convenient way of referring to deoxyribonucleic acid. The DNA molecule may be considered a kind of code, or form, which sets patterns for the making of the vital substances, particularly proteins, within a cell. From the viewpoint of the entire body DNA may be compared with the architect whose plans eventually result in the construction of a building from a heap of steel, concrete, and wood. The particular kind of DNA an individual has determines his characteristics. In reproduction the basic "information" encoded in the parental DNA is meticulously reproduced (replicated) and passed on to the offspring via the sperm and eggs.

A new phrase has come into being to characterize the discovery of these molecules of life—*molecular biology.* It is hoped that further research in molecular biology will lead to many medical triumphs, including the solution of the mystery of cancer.

Model of a DNA (deoxyribonucleic acid) molecule. Called "the code of life," DNA is the chemical found in the nucleus of a cell which stores, codes, and sends chemical "information" to the rest of the cell. Watson, an American, and Crick, a Briton, theorized from chemical and x-ray information that the parts of the DNA molecule were arranged in a double spiral fashion, as shown in the model. (*Courtesy of American Cancer Society.*)

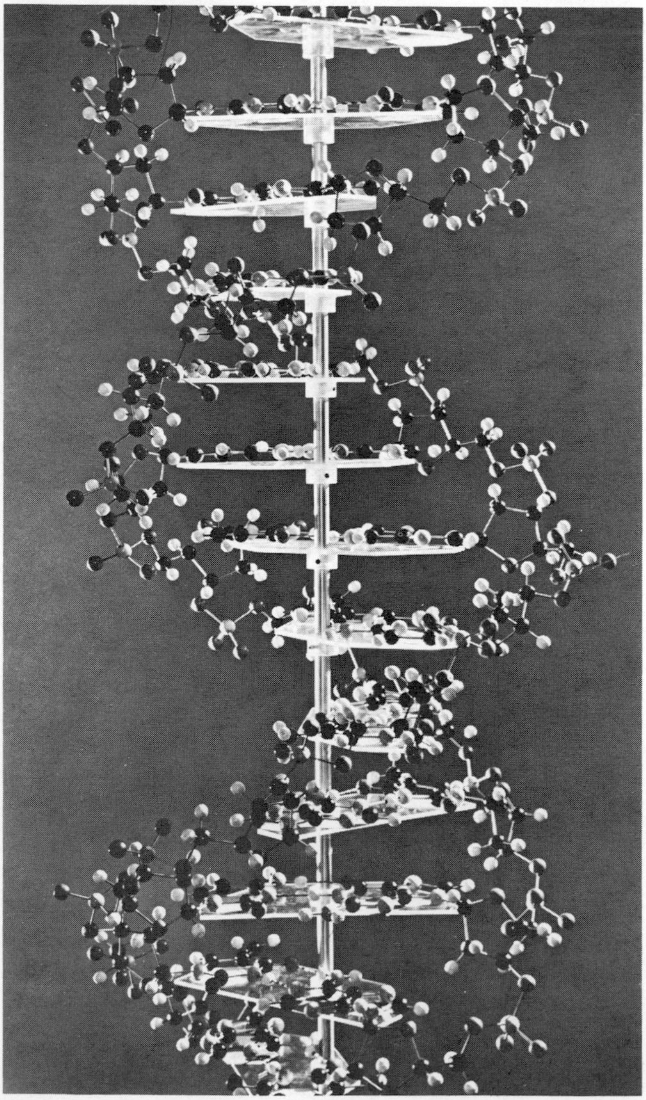

Before leaving this discussion of heredity we should understand that the characteristics of an individual are determined both by the particular package of genes he has inherited from his parents *and* by the environment in which he grows up. Heredity and environment work together to produce the individual.

REPRODUCTION

The basic design of sexual reproduction in all animals is a simple one. Life for the individual begins when a sperm meets and unites with an egg. Each sperm is a special kind of cell split off from other cells in an organ of the male called the testis. Each egg is similarly a special kind of cell made in the ovary of the female. The union of sperm and egg—fertilization—is followed by the rapid dividing of the fertilized egg cell into the many cells that eventually form the structures of the new individual.

(*See* pp. 382–3.)

In the animal kingdom there are many variations in the place where fertilization and development of the embryo occur. In some animals, as in frogs and many fish, fertilization occurs outside the body in the waters of ponds, streams, lakes, or seas. In land animals the meeting of sperm and egg, and the protection against the drying up of the sex cells, is insured by having fertilization occur within the female's body. This is true in insects and birds, for example. In fewer animals the resulting fertilized egg also develops internally. But only in mammals are special structures established for the nourishment of the developing embryo inside the female before birth, and for the production of milk for feeding after birth.

The following description of reproduction in human beings will be understood more clearly by reference to the accompanying illustrations.

The Male

At birth the human male has a complete reproductive system; not until the age of 13 to 15, however, does it begin to function. At this

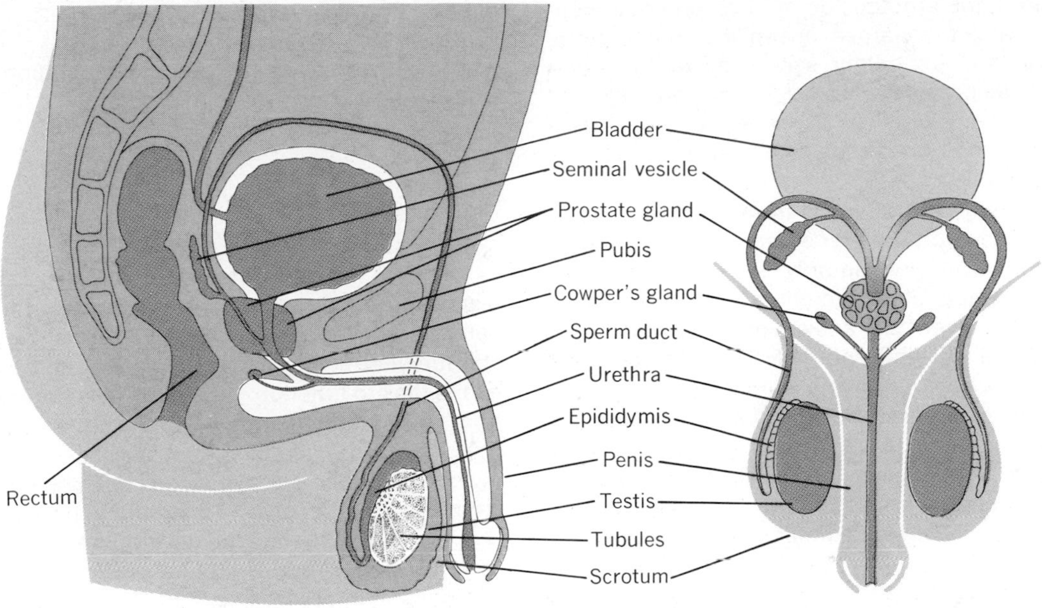

(*Left*) The male reproductive system, side view. (*Right*) The male reproductive system, front view.

time the pituitary gland produces hormones that stimulate the testes to engage in their dual roles: that of producing sperm and of secreting hormones. The sex hormone manufactured by the testes, known as *testosterone,* triggers the full development of sexuality in the male: the growth of the sex organs, the appearance of pubic hair, the deepening of the voice, the growth of the beard and of the Adam's apple, and the broadening of the shoulders. Accompanying these structural changes are also the profound changes in behavior characteristic of this period known as *puberty.*

The male sex structures consist essentially of a pair of testes and a tube from each which leads into the *penis.* The testes are external and are contained within a sac, the *scrotum,* suspended from the abdomen. Each testis has hundreds of tiny *tubules* in which sperm are formed. (Between the tubules are the tissues that manufacture the male sex hormone.) The sperm-making tubules in each testis lead to a common many-coiled tube, the *epididymis,* that half encircles the testis. Sperm then passes into the *sperm duct,* which extends from the scrotum into the abdomen. Near its end the duct flares out into a sperm reservoir (not shown in the diagram). When sperm are discharged they pass from this storage space into the *urethra,* a channel through the penis to the outside. In human beings, as well as in other mammals, the urethra is used as a passageway both for sperm and for urine, although not at the same time.

Secretions of other glands—the *seminal vesicles* and the *prostate*—are added to the sperm on their way out of the body. The secretions provide a fluid media for launching the free-swimming sperm and for protecting them after they are deposited in the female. The combined fluid, sperm plus secretions, is known as *semen.*

The penis is made of three columns of spongy tissue, permeated with blood sinuses, wide blood spaces. During sexual excitement the blood vessels draining these sinuses are constricted by reflex action. The blood coming into the penis piles up in the spongy tissues making the penis hard and erect.

When a climax of sexual excitement is

reached, the storage sac of the sperm duct contracts and discharges sperm into the urethra, where it is joined by secretions of the other glands as previously noted. The semen is ejected from the urethra with considerable force as a result of the contraction of a muscle at the base of the penis.

In the life of a typical male the discharge of semen may occur under different circumstances. It may occur involuntarily during sleep, often accompanied by a dream of a sexual nature. Such occurrences, known as *nocturnal emissions,* are perfectly normal. The stimulation of one's sex organs for the purpose of sexual excitement, *masturbation,* is almost universal among males, particularly in youth, and also leads to the discharge of semen. No harm is known to result from this practice. (Masturbation in females is likewise common, but does not lead to a discharge as in males.) From the viewpoint of the biological survival of the species the fruitful method of semen discharge occurs during *coitus,* or sexual intercourse, in which semen is propelled into the upper part of the vagina, the female structure adapted for receiving the penis. However, as we shall see shortly, coitus may or may not lead to fertilization, depending on whether or not an egg is available.

The Female

At birth the human female possesses a complete reproductive system, but it is not until puberty, about the age of 12 or 13 years (usually about a year earlier than in males), that the system begins to function. Here again it is hormones from the pituitary glands that awaken sexual development. One pituitary hormone stimulates the ovary to produce eggs. It also stimulates certain structures in the ovary to produce hormones, which in turn influence the development of sexuality: the deposition of fat that rounds the body contours, the development of the breasts, the broadening of the pelvis (which makes normal childbirth possible), the growth of pubic hair, and the enlargement of the sex organs. Psychologi-

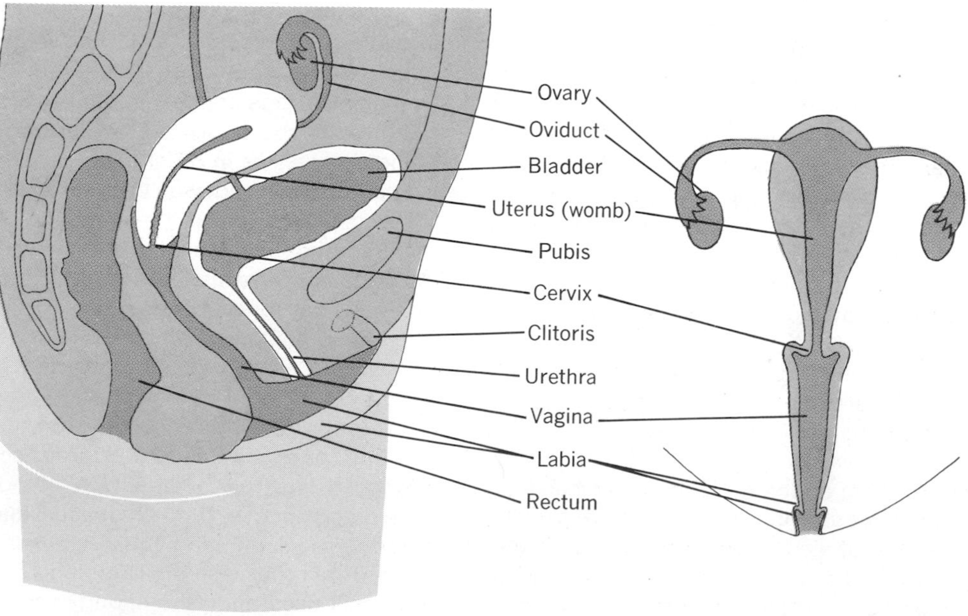

(*Left*) The female reproductive system, side view. (*Right*) The female reproductive system, front view.

cal changes also result from the influence of the sex hormones.

The female sex organs consist essentially of a pair of *ovaries,* two *egg tubes* leading from the ovaries to the *uterus,* followed by the *vagina,* which opens to the outside of the body.

The ovaries, located in the lower abdomen, are approximately the size and shape of an unshelled almond. Near the ovaries, but not directly connected to them, are the opening of the egg tubes, also known as the Fallopian tubes. The two egg tubes empty into the single uterus, also known as the *womb* in humans, a pear-shaped muscular organ that lies in the middle of the lower part of the body just behind the urinary bladder. The smaller, narrower end of the uterus, the *cervix,* is directed downward, and opens into the upper end of the vagina. The vagina, a narrow, sheathlike canal of muscle, lined with mucous membrane, has three functions: to receive the penis during coitus, to permit the discharge of menstrual fluids to the outside, and to serve as a birth canal for the passage of the emerging infant into the outside world.

In virgin females the external opening of the vagina is partially closed by the *hymen,* a thin membrane. The hymen usually remains intact until the first coitus, but is sometimes broken through vigorous activity before then.

Externally two double folds of skin (the *labia*) surround the opening of the urethra and the vagina. (In females, in contrast to the male, the passageways for the excretion of urine and for reproductive functions are entirely separate.) Also found in this region is the *clitoris,* a small structure located at the anterior (forward) juncture of the inner folds of the skin of the labia. The clitoris is sensitive and possesses erectile tissue, similar to that found in the penis, capable of enlargement during sexual excitement.

Egg Production

The onset of puberty in females is characterized by the activity of the ovaries. Inside the ovary are thousands of immature egg sacs, or *Graafian follicles.* During the 30 or more years following the beginning of puberty—except during pregnancy—one of these follicles will enlarge every 28 days. Within each sac one cell will ripen into an egg. As the follicle grows, it fills with fluid. Finally it ruptures right through the ovary wall and the egg is discharged out of the ovary. The discharge of the egg is called *ovulation.* The mature egg is only 0.14 millimeter in diameter, just visible as a speck to the unaided eye. (About 200 eggs could be lined up in 1 inch.)

The opening of the egg tube is lined with cells equipped with threadlike cilia. The beating of the cilia creates a current that draws the egg into it. For the next 3 to 6 days the egg will move down the egg tube on its way to the uterus. The life of an unfertilized egg is only about 1 day, so it follows that the egg is usually fertilized in the upper part of the egg tube.

Fertilization

The sperm cells are deposited in the upper part of the vagina and must travel 7,000 times their own length to reach the egg. (A man 6 feet tall swimming across a body of water would have to traverse about 8 miles to cover a comparable distance.) The number of sperm produced in one discharge is between 200 and 500 million. The fertilizing power of sperm in the female's body lasts from about 48 to 72 hours. If we take the higher figure for sperm survival, 3 days, it follows that coitus can lead to fertilization for only a maximum of about 4 days in each 28-day cycle: the 3 days before and the 1 day after ovulation. Incidentally, it is not necessary for the female to experience pleasure or reach a climax (orgasm) for fertilization to occur.

The sperm is much smaller than the egg: 75,000 sperm weigh only as much as one egg. The head of the sperm contains the nucleus; its long tail propels it through the liquid medium in which it travels. Although only one sperm will fertilize the egg a large number are required at the outset to insure the completion by at least that one of the long and arduous journey to the egg. Many of the sperm simply do not make it. Once the egg is penetrated by the successful sperm, changes occur that make the fertilized egg entryproof to all other sperm.

Development of the Embryo

If the egg is not fertilized it disintegrates. (Other changes associated with nonfertilization will be discussed presently.) If the egg is fertilized, it starts development immediately in the egg tube. For the next 6 to 12 days the egg divides many times to form a hollow ball of cells. In the meantime the uterus wall, stimulated by certain hormones, thickens and becomes enriched with many blood capillaries. The "soil," so to speak, is ready for the reception, the *implantation,* of the embryo. After implantation the uterine lining surrounds the embryo, which will live there for the next 9 months during the period of *gestation.*

As development proceeds, a new organ, the *placenta,* is formed jointly by the embryo and the uterus of the mother. The placenta, a disc of spongy tissue richly supplied with blood, functions, as we shall see shortly, as a place of exchange between the mother and the embryo. As development continues a membrane, the *amnion,* completely surrounds the embryo and encloses it in fluid. The liquid environment of the embryo cushions it against blows it might sustain from the normal movements of the mother or from accidental injury.

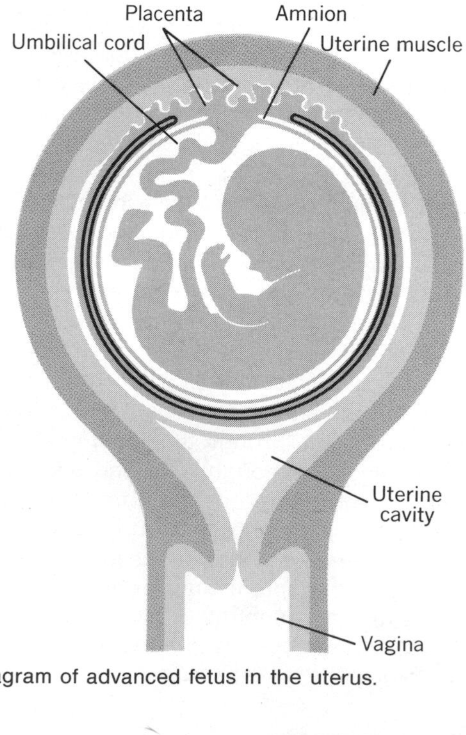

Diagram of advanced fetus in the uterus.

A stalk grows out from the embryo, later becoming the *umbilical cord,* which connects the embryo to the placenta. It has arteries and veins in it that conduct blood pumped by the embryo's heart to the placenta and then back to the embryo. It is important to note that there are no nerve connections between the mother and the embryo. So-called "maternal impressions" on children have no physical basis in nerve pathways. There is also no direct blood connection between mother and embryo. All exchanges take place by diffusion across the membranes of the placenta. Molecules of digested nutrients and oxygen pass out of the maternal blood across the membrane to the embryo; carbon dioxide and other wastes filter from the bloodstream of the embryo across the same membrane into the maternal blood.

The embryo, which is a small microscopic mass of cells on implantation, grows to about $\frac{2}{3}$ inch in 6 weeks. By then the embryo is distinctly human in appearance with all major features, such as fingers, toes, lips, ears, and nose. From the eighth week on it is called a *fetus.* At 5 months it is 12 inches long from head to foot. At this time the mother begins to feel "life"—the stretching and kicking of the fetus in its aquatic gymnasium.

Childbirth is heralded by contractions of the uterine wall causing "labor pains," which last for 12 to 24 hours before birth occurs, but may be of much shorter duration in subsequent childbirths. As the contractions become stronger the membranes around the fetus are broken and the fluid flows out. The contractions push the head of the baby downward against the opening of the uterus. The opening and the vagina itself are greatly enlarged at this time. The connections between the pubic bones become loosened somewhat so that they can spread apart. Finally, powerful uterine contractions force the baby into the vagina and out of the body. In its new environment of air the baby begins to breathe with its lungs, or may be induced to do so by a smack on its buttocks.

The umbilical cord is still attached to the newborn infant. The doctor ties it off near the child and then cuts it on the side near the mother. The tied region will heal and later form the navel. Further contractions of the uterus wall will force out the rest of the cord and the placenta, the *afterbirth.*

The Menstrual Cycle

The building up of the uterine walls and the ripening of the egg in the Graafian follicle are preparations for pregnancy. If the egg is not fertilized, it disintegrates as we have noted. Sometime later, about 2 weeks after ovulation, the uterine wall, with its extra supply of blood, also disintegrates. For a period of 3 to 5 days menstruation occurs. The sloughed-off uterine lining together with blood passes out of the vagina. (Menstruation is *not* the discharge of the unfertilized egg.) Menstruation and ovulation occur about every 28 days for a period of 30 or more years from puberty until *menopause* ("change of life"), except during pregnancy. The menstrual (after *mensis,* Latin for month) cycle of menstruation and ovulation will be understood by reference to the accompanying diagram. Menstruation occurs from day 1 through day 4. For the next 10 days the egg sac ripens. At about the same time the uterus wall builds up in preparation for pregnancy. At about the fourteenth day after the onset of the previous menstruation, ovulation occurs. After the twenty-eighth day, assuming that the egg is not fertilized, menstruation begins again.

It is important to note that there is considerable variation among females in the length of the menstrual cycle and in the timing of events in that cycle. Cycles may be as short as 21 or as long as 35 days in different individuals. They may be irregular in the same individual. It follows that contraceptive procedures based on a so-called "safe period" in the menstrual cycle must be worked out with the help of a specialist in such matters and cannot be considered entirely "safe" even then.

Pregnancy is suspected when the menstrual periods cease, but a menstrual period may be skipped for other reasons.

Multiple Births

It sometimes happens that shortly after fertilization the developing embryo will divide into two separate embryos. If they complete their development *identical twins* will be born. They are identical, or nearly so, because both originate from the same fertilized egg and consequently from the same set of chromosomes with their complement of the trait-determining genes. It follows from this and from the earlier discussion of sex determination that identical twins are always of the same sex.

Further splitting of early embryos may theo-

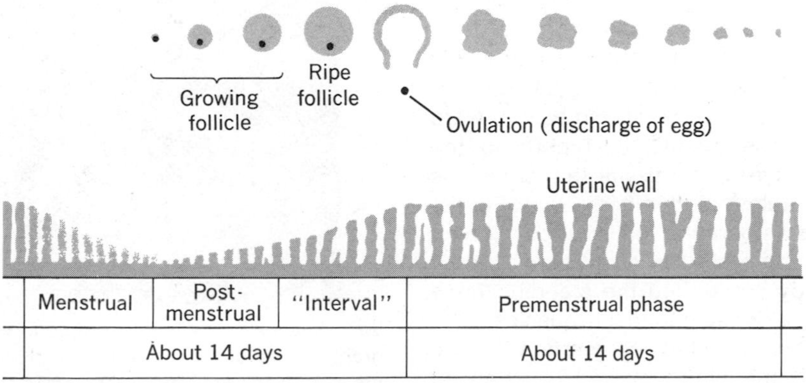

The cycle of menstruation and ovulation.

retically result in identical quadruplets, octuplets, and so on, although the chance of survival of high multiples is very slight. The few famous quintuplets probably represent the survival of five of eight early embryos.

Fraternal twins are produced in a different way. As we have seen, one egg is produced at a time about every 28 days. It sometimes happens that two eggs, or more, ripen at the same time. If each of these eggs is fertilized, fraternal twins may result. Fraternal twins are not identical because they come from different fertilized eggs, consequently from different sets of chromosomes and genes. They are no more alike than any siblings from the same parents would be; they just happen to be born at the same time. Fraternal twins may be of the same or different sex, because sex is determined for each separately by the kind of sperm, X or Y, that enters each egg.

HEALTH AND DISEASE

Many people think of health only when they do not have it—when they are ill. They regard health as the absence of illness. On the contrary, health is a positive phenomenon. It is the normal condition of the body with all of its parts working efficiently together. The old Greek concept of "a sound mind in a sound body" is still a good definition of health.

(*See* pp. 381–2.)

The body has natural lines of defense that ordinarily keep it safe from infectious diseases. The skin that surrounds the entire body is the first line against invasion. As long as the skin remains intact it serves as a strong wall to ward off harmful disease agents. Just beneath the outer skin is a layer of fat tissue that serves as an insulator to help maintain body heat. Fat tissue also serves as padding material, cushioning our bodies from the shocks of a "hard world." We have already mentioned the standing army of the body, the white blood corpuscles. The blood also carries the chemical warfare service of the body. In the blood plasma a variety of chemical substances, called *antibodies,* help to overcome microbes and their poisonous products.

Illness may result from various causes. Some diseases develop from nutritional lacks. These are the deficiency diseases, such as scurvy and rickets. Some diseases result from a breakdown of one of the body organs. An example of this is diabetes, a disease caused by a breakdown of cells of the islands of Langerhans in the pancreas. When they stop secreting sufficient insulin the body cannot effectively oxidize the sugar taken in with food.

Diseases Caused by Germs

Probably the most widespread diseases are those caused by other living things invading the body. The chief of these are certain disease-causing *microbes*—microscopic organisms often called *germs.* Both plant and animal microbes

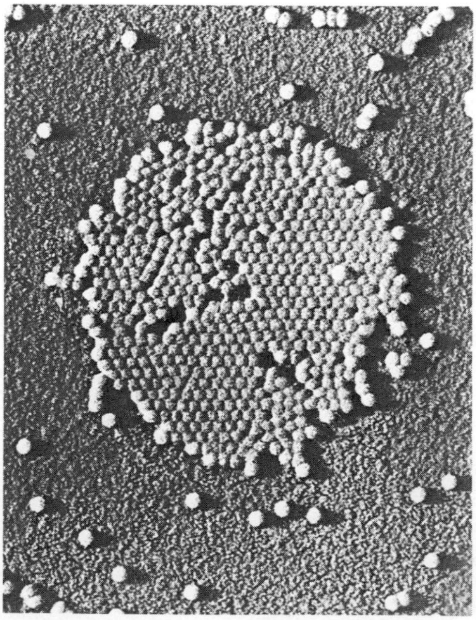

Each tiny sphere is that of the polio virus. This photograph was taken by an electron microscope, the viruses are magnified about 100,000 times! (*Courtesy of National Medical Audiovisual Center.*)

can cause disease. The chief plant offenders are the microscopic *bacteria.* Tuberculosis, diphtheria, scarlet fever, meningitis, typhoid fever, and one type of pneumonia are examples of diseases caused by bacteria. Some one-celled animals, *protozoans,* are disease producers. Probably the most widespread disease in the world is malaria, caused by a protozoan. The parasite is injected into the blood by an Anopheles mosquito carrying the organism. Another protozoan disease is amebic dysentery, common in tropical regions. A third group of microbes are the *viruses,* which are extremely minute particles having characteristics of both living and nonliving material. Smallpox, measles, poliomyelitis (infantile paralysis), yellow fever, and influenza are some of the virus-caused diseases.

How Germs Invade

Prevention of diseases caused by germs requires that we know how the microbes are spread. Some enter the body with the air breathed in, usually near an infected person. Measles, diphtheria, scarlet fever, whooping cough, the common cold, and smallpox are examples of diseases spread in this way. Some microbes, such as those causing typhoid fever and amebic dysentery, enter the body with food or water. Some microorganisms enter the body through breaks in the skin. Boils and skin infections may be caused by microorganisms that come in through this channel. In other cases the infective organism must be introduced by the bite of a carrier, as is the case with malaria. Yellow fever is likewise transmitted through the bite of a mosquito carrying the yellow fever virus. Rabies is acquired through the bite of a dog sick with rabies. The saliva of the rabid animal contains the rabies virus.

Vaccines

Protective substances that enable the body to resist disease have been a goal of medicine since earliest times. Only within the last century and a half has this aim been partially realized. In 1790 Edward Jenner, an English country doctor, discovered that individuals infected with cowpox, a mild disease resembling smallpox, acquired immunity against smallpox, a dangerous disease. Today, vaccination is recognized in all civilized communities as a preventive against the dread scourge. After Jenner's work almost a century passed before another immunizing agent for human beings was discovered. This was the *vaccine* against rabies produced by Pasteur.

A vaccine is a preparation of killed or weakened germs. When a vaccine is injected or placed on a scrape in the skin it causes the blood in the human to start chemical warfare against the particular type of germ in that vaccine. The blood produces antibodies to combat the weakened or killed germ in this simulated "invasion." These antibodies remain in the bloodstream for many years, and will be effective against a real invasion by the active, living germs of the specific disease. Vaccines are used against typhoid fever, smallpox, rabies, whooping cough, and yellow fever.

A great victory in medicine were the vaccines developed by Jonas Salk and Albert Sabin against infantile paralysis. The Salk polio vaccine consists of dead viruses, whereas the newer Sabin oral polio vaccine consists of live, but altered, viruses. Each vaccine has the ability to stimulate the body to produce antibodies that are active against virulent forms of polio virus. They have markedly reduced the incidence of polio, with its toll of paralysis and death.

Several kinds of measles vaccines are now licensed for use. The U.S. Public Health Service has recommended immunization for all children over 9 months old without a history of measles. In state after state measles vaccination has been required for school children. We look forward to the same victory against measles as was won against polio.

A vaccine may be made from poisonous substances, called *toxins,* produced by some disease-causing microorganisms. The toxins are first changed chemically into *toxoids,* which are used in developing immunity to such diseases as diphtheria, lockjaw, and whooping cough. The toxoid causes the body to produce its own antibodies.

Serums

Sometimes we use the antibodies produced in an animal to treat a human disease. We "borrow" the antibodies from an animal, such as a horse, which has been inoculated with weakened germs or toxins of the particular disease that is being combated. Blood extracted from such animals and prepared for injection constitutes a *serum.* Serum injections are used for diphtheria and lockjaw. The type of immunity acquired in this way is temporary and is frequently used as a cure rather than as a preventive measure.

Drugs against Disease

For thousands of years man has searched for drugs to fight disease. We are indebted to primitive man for quinine, from the bark of the cinchona tree, so effective against malaria. Many other valuable drugs have been extracted from plants. It was not until 1932, however, that a drug that would destroy many kinds of bacteria in the body was discovered. This was sulfanilamide. Since then a chemical family of *sulfa drugs* has been synthesized by scientists to fight different bacteria effectively. Between 1936 and 1940 the number of deaths from pneumonia decreased by 50 percent as a result of the use of sulfa drugs.

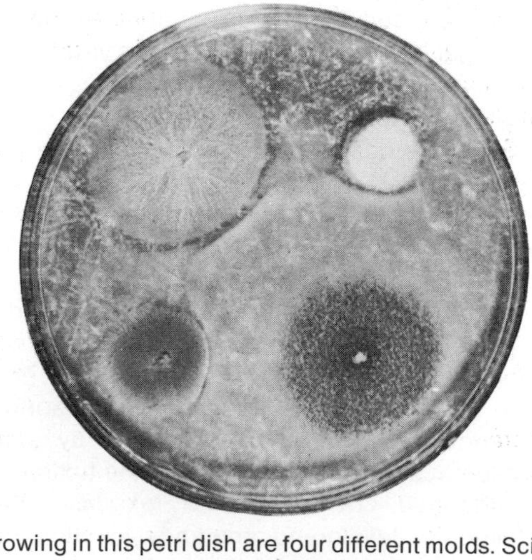

Growing in this petri dish are four different molds. Scientists grow thousands of cultures in hopes of finding new molds that can serve as the sources of new antibiotics. (*Courtesy of Charles Pfizer & Company, Inc.*)

Antibiotics

In 1927 Alexander Fleming, an English scientist, noted the peculiar behavior of some bacteria cultures that he had left untouched for some time. They had been contaminated with some mold growth and, oddly enough, where the mold was growing the bacterial colonies seemed to dissolve. This was the beginning of the golden age of antibiotics in modern medicine. An *antibiotic* is a substance produced by a living organism that can kill microbes or stop their growth. The bacteria in Fleming's culture had been destroyed by an antibiotic produced by the mold. It was named *penicillin,* after the mold Penicillium. The availability of penicillin in World War II undoubtedly reduced the number of deaths. Fleming was awarded the Nobel Prize for his work. Since the finding of penicillin, many other antibiotics, derived from other species of mold, have been used successfully against various diseases.

Cancer

Cancer has been known from ancient times, but it has only become a paramount health problem in this country in this century. It is now the second largest cause of death in the United States. This has come about, in part, because we are now living long enough to be stricken by cancer, which is mainly a disease of middle and old age. A *cancer* is an abnormal growth of cells. For reasons yet obscure the cells seem to become outlaw. They multiply out of control of the normal body limits. They invade neighboring tissue, crowd it, rob it of its nourishment, and destroy it. The greatest danger occurs when cells break away from the original growth and move through the body to colonize elsewhere. The aim of cancer fighting is to detect and remove the cancerous growth before colonization occurs. Most cancers, if detected early enough, are curable. One method of achieving this is to see a doctor if you detect any of the following signs of *possible* cancer, described by the American Cancer Society:

1. A sore that does not heal.
2. A lump or thickening in the breast or elsewhere.
3. Unusual bleeding or discharge.
4. Change in a wart or mole.
5. Persistent indigestion or difficulty in swallowing.
6. Persistent hoarseness or cough.
7. Persistent change in bowel or bladder habits.

In addition, periodic medical examinations are recommended for the detection of early signs of cancer.

How can cancer be fought when it is detected? At present, the best known methods are surgery and radiation. Surgery is still the primary treatment. The entire growth must be removed without leaving one cell behind. The second method involves destruction by means of x-rays, radium, and other radioactive substances including radioactive isotopes. It is fortunate that cancerous cells are more easily killed by these radiations than are normal cells.

(*See* pp. 541, 547–9.)

Chemotherapy, the use of specific chemicals, is a more recent approach to fighting cancer. Leukemias, breast cancers, prostate cancer, and lymphomas have been known to respond to chemotherapy, although conclusive results remain to be obtained. Science holds out the hope that one day we may find the specific cause or causes of cancer and learn how to prevent this disease.

Health and Society

Over the years society has found that some health problems can be helped by legal methods. Today every state has laws relating to health. Some of these are compulsory vaccination as a prerequisite to entrance into school, quarantine in cases of certain contagious diseases, medical licensing, sanitary and health codes, and many others. We also rely on education to improve the health of each individual.

Some of the important generalizations developed in this chapter are:

Man studies his body in many ways.

The unit of structure and work of the body is the cell.

Similar cells are organized into tissues for efficient performance of their job.

Groups of different tissues cooperate in organs that perform the major work of the body.

We require food for energy, for growth and repair, and for proper functioning of our bodies.

Food is prepared for the use of the body by the process of digestion.

A continuous supply of oxygen is needed to obtain energy from food.

The body has a number of automatic mechanisms that maintain a constantly favorable internal environment.

The respiratory system supplies oxygen to the body and gets rid of carbon dioxide.

Materials are transported around the body by the circulatory system.

Blood flows in a closed system of tubes around the body, pumped by the heart.

The skin, the kidneys, and the lungs rid the body of liquid and gaseous wastes.

Growth is the result of cell multiplication.

Movement in the body is powered by the contraction of muscles.

The bony skeleton serves as a framework for the body.

The body is under the dual control of the nervous system and the endocrine glands.

The genes in the nucleus of the cell carry the hereditary traits.

The gene material is a complex molecule known as DNA.

The DNA molecule may be regarded as a kind of code that sets patterns for the making of vital cell substances.

Heredity and environment work together to produce the individual.

The life of the new individual starts with fertilization, the joining of sperm and egg into a single cell.

Sex is determined at the moment of fertilization by the kind of sperm that enters the egg.

Identical twins originate from the same fertilized egg, nonidentical or fraternal twins from separately fertilized eggs.

Development of the embryo follows from the splitting of the fertilized egg cell into billions of cells.

The developing embryo is nourished by the diffusion of nutrients across a membrane shared by mother and embryo.

Wastes are removed by diffusion across the same membrane from embryo to mother.

Sexual maturity is guided and stimulated by hormones, chemical secretions, of the pituitary and the sex glands.

Reasonable adherence to the rules of hygiene will go far toward keeping the body in good health.

Application of medical discoveries has greatly prolonged life.

Man has developed powerful weapons in fighting disease.

Education is of prime importance in keeping our nation in good health.

Discovering for Yourself

1. Acquaint yourself with the latest research findings concerning the relationship of lung cancer and smoking.
2. Use the *Red Cross Handbook* or some other similar source and learn how to give artificial respiration and to attend to simple injuries.
3. Examine bones, muscles, tendons, and other body parts of animals from a meat market to learn about structure and function.
4. Look through a microscope at slides of body tissues, blood cells, bacteria, or other slide material related to the human body to see details.
5. Conduct, with the assistance of your local Board of Health, a study of the communicable diseases that have been prevalent in your community during the past two years. Find out how they are spread and what the public health service does about control.
6. Visit a research laboratory where experiments in nutrition or other related areas are being carried out. Learn as much as you can about the methods employed.
7. Take your body temperature and pulse and your rate of breathing. Exercise and note the change in pulse and respiration.
8. Try to find out more about molecular biology and DNA.
9. Find out how the electron microscope has contributed to new knowledge of cells.

(Courtesy of Xerox Corporation, George Platteter, obtained through AAAS.)

CHAPTER 12B

TEACHING "THE HUMAN BODY AND HOW IT WORKS"

Children are naturally curious about their bodies and how they work. Probably we have not capitalized sufficiently on this natural curiosity to teach about the general structure, function, and care of the human body. It is expected that study about their bodies will develop these attitudes: that the human body is a wonderful machine, that its development is natural, that with reasonable care the body can remain healthy.

The child's body, because it is alive, eats, breathes, grows, and responds to stimuli; should be observed and used as a firsthand source for developing concepts of how it is built, how it works, what it needs, and how it keeps well. Through this, children add to their understanding of all living things. The increased emphasis on sex education in the schools puts an even greater emphasis on helping teachers and children understand the human body.

Later chapters (20A, 20B, 21A, and 21B) give further information, as well as suggestions for teaching, about the eye and ear in connection with the material on light and sound.

SOME BROAD CONCEPTS: "The Human Body"

The parts of the body work together to carry on body functions.

Our bodies need proper food to supply energy for their activities.

The body is composed of different kinds of cells that perform various functions.

The body is composed of systems of organs that cooperate to carry on its many functions.

The body does some things automatically.

The skeletal system holds the body up, protects parts of it, and gives it shape.

Muscles are fastened to bones and make them move.

The food we eat must be digested before it can be used by the body.

FOR YOUNGER CHILDREN

How Can We Use Our Senses?[1]

Using our senses to discover is one of the most important elements in the process of learning. Resourceful teachers will devise different ways of helping children see how important the senses are. One interesting idea is to give each child a paper bag with the following or similar items: a small rubber ball, a marble, a rock, a toy, a piece of cloth, a nail, a bell, an onion. Suggest that pupils reach inside the bags (but not look) and see what they can discover by *touching*, then by *smelling*, then by *listening*, and last by *looking* at the items.

Prepare several "smell" jars—onion, orange, cucumber, cheese, and so on. Cover

[1] Adapted from *Science Grades K–2:* "Discovering with Our Senses" (Brooklyn, N.Y.: Board of Education of the City of New York, 1966); and J. Bendick: *The Human Senses* (New York: Franklin Watts, 1968).

the jars with foil so that children cannot see inside. What can you discover by using the sense of smell?

Assemble various objects of different textures—fur, sandpaper, wood, smooth and rough rocks, and such. Put them in a box or bag. What can you discover by using your sense of touch? Tell how the various materials feel.

Behind a screen make various sounds with a bell, crumpling paper, tapping a table, and other things. What can you discover by using your sense of hearing? Similar experiences with tasting can also be used. Children might list discoveries they made with the use of each sense.

The activity described is not just a one-time experience. Especially with young children, the use of the senses to find out is an important activity that leads to discovery. Children should be encouraged to gather information by the use of the senses, and then try to apply this information to make discoveries.

How Do We Use the Parts of Our Bodies?

It is important that children develop an appreciation for the wonder of their bodies—how the body is built and how it operates and functions. They might begin by making a list of the things their bodies have done during the past hours—eating, breathing, walking, running, reading, and so forth. What parts of the body were used in these activities? They may compare their bodies with some specific machine like an automobile. How are they alike? How different?

Suggest that children observe specific actions of other children to discover what body parts are used to perform certain tasks: lift a book, walk across the room, reach on a shelf, eat an apple, wash the chalkboard.

Suggest that they explore the different ways they can move their bodies by attempting to answer these questions: "What parts of your body can you move?" "How many ways can you move your head?" "How high can you reach?"

How Fast Are We Growing?

A favorite activity in many schools is to exhibit pictures of the children when they were babies or were very young. In what ways have you changed since your picture was taken? How much do you change in weight and height over a period of a year? Children might estimate the figures and perhaps compare their record with other class members. Again the use of metric measures is suggested.

(*See* pp. 41–2)

Where Does Our Food Come From?

First let pupils call upon their experiences of a visit to the grocer, to a farm, to the cafeteria, and other places, and try to list and classify the sources of the food they eat. They may devise various ways to classify the sources, such as animals, plants, gardens, fields, stores and others. Let them attempt to make their own classification by first making a list of the foods they have eaten recently—meat, cereal, fish, apples, potatoes, lettuce. There are many ways to group these foods—"Meats We Eat," "Vegetables We Eat," "Fruits We Eat" are some ways. The purpose of the activity is to help children see (1.) the great diversity and (2.) the many sources.

Related to this problem children may consider: "How are these foods kept from spoiling?" "What do we do to them before we eat them?" "Where did the foods grow?"

OTHER PROBLEMS FOR YOUNGER CHILDREN

1. Why should you know about your body?
2. How is your body like a machine? How is it different from a machine?
3. Why should you take care of your body?
4. What happens to the food you eat?
5. What are some of the most important parts of the body? What does each of these parts do?
6. How have your senses helped you today to find out about the world you live in?

FOR OLDER CHILDREN

How Much Air Do We Breathe?

Before recess or outdoor activity period ask the children to count the number of times they breathe in and out in a minute (about 18 to 20 times), while sitting quietly. Make a record of the findings. After the outdoor activity have the children

How much air can you breathe out of your lungs? A graphic experience such as this serves to make the scientific principles real and understandable. Arithmetical computations also add to the comprehension.

make another count. They will find a significant difference. Discussion should bring out the idea that the body requires air for its activities, and that the more active the body is, the more air is needed.

A simple way of *seeing* the amount of air breathed out is to breathe into a tube connected to a jug of water, as shown. As the air goes in water is pushed out of the jug. Using this device (which is called a *spirometer*) pupils may compare quiet and rapid breathing by seeing how many exhalations are necessary to empty the jug in each case.

By *dividing* 1 gallon by the number of exhalations needed to empty the jug pupils can estimate the amount of air in *one* breath. By *multiplying* the amount of air in one breath by the number of breaths in 1 minute pupils can estimate the amount of air breathed in 1 minute. Here again, pupils will see mathematics used meaningfully, and the use of the metric system by converting gallons into liters is suggested.

How Fast Does Your Heart Beat?

One way of measuring heartbeat is to measure the pulse, which is caused by the surge of blood through an artery. Two fingers (not the thumb) of one hand should be placed on the wrist of the other hand. A pencil or drinking straw balanced carefully over the pulse will also show the pulse beat. Suggest that each pupil determine his heartbeat while sitting quietly. Record it. Now suggest that they walk briskly in the schoolyard and again record the heartbeat. Now do the same after running. "What effect has exercise on the number of heartbeats per minute?" The pupils should understand that the increased rate of heartbeat brings blood, containing food and oxygen, more rapidly to all parts of the body.

How Does the Body Move?

Children can develop some general ideas of how muscles and bones move the body by observing their own motions. Ask them: "What parts of your body move back and forth like a hinge?" (Knee, elbow, and finger joints.) "Which parts move in circles?" (Ball and socket joints in shoulders and hips.) "What happens to your ribs when you breathe?" "How is the forearm moved?" Ask pupils to allow one arm to hang loosely with the palm forward. Have them feel the muscle in front that goes from the shoulder almost down to the elbow. A tendon connects this muscle, called the *biceps,* to the forearm bone. If they lift the forearm by bending the arm at the elbow they will feel the biceps muscle becoming shorter and thicker. The shortening of the biceps actually pulls on the forearm bones, causing the arm to rise. You may be able to get skeleton parts of animals that will show various kinds of joints.

How is the arm straightened out? Have pupils make a fist and with the other hand feel the muscles along the back of the arm that tighten as they straighten the arm. This muscle pulls the arm straight. With these simple observations on their own bodies children begin to understand that movement of large body parts is accomplished by the shortening of muscles, which work in pairs and pull on the bones.

They can also look for muscles, tendons, and bones in a chicken leg or in a shank of lamb (meat is usually muscle). They can list the ways in which their own muscles are used in the course of a day.

What Kinds of Foods Should We Eat?

Because it is easy to find out information about kinds of foods this assignment is appropriate: "Bring to class a list of all the sources we can use to find out information about kinds of foods and how they help us. Think of places, books, magazines, newspapers, and people." This activity of locating material will not only supply much useful informational material but will give pupils an opportunity to use their originality and resourcefulness in finding it.

If there is a school cafeteria it is a practical place to learn about foods. The manager or someone else on the staff can be asked to explain how the menu is decided and show how it provides a balanced diet.

The teacher will, with some planning, accumulate much material about foods that pupils can use. She may help to point out to pupils the importance of seeing that material that is commercially prepared is honest in presentation. There is much good material published by various manufacturers, but this should be evaluated for accuracy before it is used by pupils.

It is important to remember that no one factor is completely responsible for good health. The U.S. Department of Agriculture publishes information for teachers on school lunches and on nutrition.

In connection with the study of foods radio and television advertising may be considered. For example, the fantastic claims that are made about some kinds of bread can be discussed. The fact that you eat a certain kind of bread is no assurance at all that you will be healthy. Bread is only one of the important foods. The fact that your favorite radio personality advertises a certain brand of breakfast food is not sufficient reason for using it to the exclusion of others. It may be interesting for pupils to copy down some of these advertising claims and analyze them. A scientific approach is essential in trying to interpret advertising, and certainly a science class is an appropriate place to be introduced to this approach. Obviously young pupils cannot scientifically test these foods, but once they can see, for example, that every kind of bread cannot be the best they may become more alert in interpreting advertising. This same attitude holds true for patent-medicine advertising.

A very practical application of the principles learned about foods and a balanced diet can be made if children plan refreshments for a party: plan, prepare, and serve a meal at school; plan the menu for a picnic. The selection and preparation of foods involve many of the ideas that pupils have learned. Children can investigate diets in other countries to see how they compare with their own. (In connection with the study of food and how it supplies the needs of the body the practice of selling candy and soft drinks in school should be evaluated and made to conform to what are considered good health practices.)

The sources of foods are sometimes surprising to children, especially those who live in large cities. It may be interesting to list the foods served in the school lunchroom or at home on one typical day and let each pupil choose one kind of food and report as much as he can discover about its source. The following are typical: sugar, cereal, bread, milk, fruit juice, honey, vinegar, spices, butter, and cooking oils. Labels on packages help supply information.

What Are Cells Like?

Cells are the units of life. There are many kinds, and living things are composed of them. You might begin by asking: "What do you know about cells?" "Have you seen cells?" "How can we get some cells to examine?"

Children will suggest using a microsocope to see cells. If they are inexperienced with the use of a microscope this will be a natural instance for helping them use one. (*See also* Chapter 10, "What Can We See with a Microscope?")

The thin skin from an onion has long been the standard source for obtaining cells for examination. Place a bit of tissue, thin onion skin, on a moist glass slide. You may have to stain it a little in order to see it better by adding a small drop of diluted iodine or diluted ink. Now put on a cover slip. Before the children examine the specimen ask them to estimate how many cells they may be able to see, and perhaps ask them to describe what they think they may see. Help them to identify the nucleus and the wall around the cell. Does this give you an idea of how many cells there are in the whole onion?

Cells from the moist lining of the cheek is another easy source of cells. Use a tongue depressor or a toothpick to rub the inside area gently. Put a drop of water on a microscope slide and touch the tongue depressor to the water. You may have to do this several times, and it may be necessary to stain the material as you did the onion skin. You will see groups of cells that are probably dead cells. They are outside the cells that form the protective lining of the inside of the mouth. Ask the children: "Can you see the nucleus? The cell membrane?" "How do these cells compare with the onion cells with respect to size, shape, and parts?" "What do you think you would find if you looked at other parts of the human body or the onion plant?"

Other cell studies can include: blood, one-celled animals (paramecium), plant cells from an aquarium plant (elodea), and so on.

How Can We Keep Healthy?

As pupils learn more about the human body and what is needed to keep it well they begin to find out what good health practices are and how their own practices and habits can be improved. The following activity may be carried out as children work in three groups. The groups make a survey of health practices in their homes, in the school, and in the community, respectively.

To begin, the teacher can ask pupils to make plans for the activity. The groups list questions and the places they want to investigate. For example, *at home* they may find out how food is kept and prepared to avoid the effects of harmful bacteria, how dishes are washed, how milk and water are made safe, how the house is kept clean, and what safety measures are observed. *In the school* pupils can investigate how the drinking fountains are kept in a sanitary condition, how the building is kept clean, and what the health authorities do to prevent the spread of diseases in school. *In the community* they can study the work of the health department to see what health practices are required in restaurants, food stores, and public buildings, and how garbage and sewage disposal and water purification are carried on. Rat control has become very important in many areas. Children can investigate why it is necessary to rid areas of rats and other harmful animals. This committee can arrange for a member of the health department to come to school to answer questions and explain the work of the department, another example of the overlapping of science and social studies. That pupils learn about health, develop good health habits, and grow in ability to find and organize information is obviously important.

Pupils should become acquainted with the purpose and methods of inoculation against smallpox, diphtheria, polio, measles, and other diseases—often carried out in school. When tuberculosis tests or similar medical tests are being made in school there are opportunities for "incidental" learning. A visit to a dairy or a local food-processing plant or cannery may yield considerable practical information about sanitary practices in preserving and handling foods.

What Can We Learn about Sex Education?

The science program can make certain unique contributions to sex education because it can (1.) place reproduction in the setting of all living things—plant and animal life; (2.) affirm the natural and necessary character of reproduction; (3.) teach some of the vocabulary and describe the structures of reproduction; (4.) provide a basis for an objective discussion of reproduction; and (5.) provide a wealth of living material for the firsthand study of reproduction in other forms of life.[2]

The practice of teaching sex education in elementary schools ranges all the way from virtually ignoring the subject to including a carefully designed program built around the five points just enumerated. The following guidelines have been helpful to teachers and others interested in the problem.

Parents, teachers, school administrators, and community leaders should plan together the content, approach, and methods of the program. There is much to be said for continuing planning sessions in which all concerned can listen to each other, explore the possibilities, and become acquainted with the programs and plans that have been tried and found successful. Much depends on the ability of teachers and others to create a climate in which children and adults can communicate and face up to the problems related to sex education. While the ultimate success of the program depends on the ability of the teacher to communicate sensibly and openly with children it is obvious that the continued interaction of parents, school personnel, and community

[2] *Sex—Who Should Tell Your Child? The Instructor* (Danville, N.Y.: F.A. Owen Company, 1967); and *A Story about You* (Chicago: American Medical Association, 1967). For grades 4, 5, and 6.

leaders is also essential. Fortunately there are now several excellent books for children (*see* Bibliography) and audiovisual aids that are proving to be very helpful in sex education. One of the responsibilities of parents and administrators may be to assist in reviewing these aids and preparing a list of useful ones.

Following are examples of science concepts that are essential in developing an understanding of sex in elementary-school children.[3]

Early Grades

Learning that baby animals and human babies grow from eggs.

Understanding that living things produce other living things of the same kind.

Appreciating the fact that an egg from the mother and a sperm from the father are needed to produce a baby.

Later Grades

Understanding that animals vary in the length of time during which they care for their young.

Understanding the process of human fertilization, how the unborn baby grows, and how the baby is born.

Understanding the influence of environment as a factor that affects growth.

How Can We Practice Safety?

A great deal of useful material has been prepared to help in the teaching of safety.[4] The activities of school safety patrols are important and useful to the general study of safety.

Science classes may study pupils' use of bicycles and, with the help of the safety patrol, devise some regulations to insure safe practices in and around school. With the school custodian pupils can make up a similar set of suggestions for safety within the school building. Pupils can investigate places in and around school and at home that are possible hazards, and make suggestions about avoiding or correcting these hazards. There are many instances of excellent results from such work by pupils.

Safety education should be a part of many school activities and of the curriculum. The study should not be academic; it should be practical, sensible, and understandable. It should begin with very young children and continue throughout the school experience.

The *"Check List for Child Safety"* is reproduced by permission of the American Red Cross.

[3]From *Family Living, Including Sex Education* (Brooklyn, N.Y.: Board of Education of the City of New York, 1967).

[4]Write for information about current publications from the National Safety Council, 425 N. Michigan Ave., Chicago, Ill. 60611; and National Headquarters, American Automobile Association, Traffic Engineering and Safety Department, 8111 Gatehouse Road, Fairfax, Virginia or your local branch. Write for information about first-aid material from the American National Red Cross, Washington, D.C. 20006, or your local Red Cross chapter.

Its Smart to Be Safe—to Stay Safe You Have to Stay Smart

ALL DAY LONG—FROM THE MOMENT YOU START OUT TO SCHOOL

YES	NO	IF YOU'RE WALKING DO YOU
☐	☐	Cross streets at CORNERS?
☐	☐	Wait for GREEN LIGHT?
☐	☐	LOOK—ʞOO˥ both ways?
☐	☐	W-A-L-K, not RUN?
☐	☐	OBEY the safety patrol?

YES	NO	IF YOU'RE BICYCLING DO YOU
☐	☐	Drive CLOSE to CURB?
☐	☐	OBEY TRAFFIC RULES?
☐	☐	REFUSE HANDLEBAR rides?
☐	☐	Keep from HITCHING to AUTOS, BUSES, STREETCARS?

YES	NO	IF YOU'RE SKATING DO YOU
☐	☐	Tie on skates FIRMLY?
☐	☐	Skate ONLY on SIDEWALKS?

SKATING is only WALKING ON WHEELS SO
COVER the walking rules with your hand and see if you're SMART enough to SKATE to school SAFELY.

YES	NO	IF YOU'RE RIDING IN A BUS DO YOU
☐	☐	Quietly TAKE your SEAT?
☐	☐	KEEP FROM sticking your ARMS and HEAD out the window?
☐	☐	KEEP FROM talking to the driver?
☐	☐	LOOK—ʞOO˥ both ways when getting off?

YES	NO	DURING SCHOOL DO YOU
☐	☐	W-A-L-K, not RUN in HALLS?
☐	☐	W-A-L-K, not run on STAIRS?
☐	☐	WAIT your turn, not PUSH?
☐	☐	Know your FIRE DRILL?
☐	☐	Know the NEAREST EXIT?
☐	☐	Keep PENCILS, CRAYONS OUR OF MOUTH?

YES	NO	WHEN CLASS IS DISMISSED DO YOU
☐	☐	GO HOME RIGHT AWAY?
☐	☐	Know the SMART and SAFE way to WALK, SKATE, BICYCLE, or RIDE a BUS home?
☐	☐	COVER these RULES with your HAND and see if you are SMART enough to get home SAFELY.

YES	NO	WHEN YOU PLAY DO YOU
☐	☐	PLAY on SIDEWALK or PLAY AREA?
☐	☐	WAIT your turn, not PUSH?
☐	☐	SWIM in a SUPERVISED place?
☐	☐	KEEP FROM playing with fire?
☐	☐	Know ALL the WALKING, BICYCLING, and SKATING rules?

YES	NO	ANIMALS ARE NOT AS SMART AS YOU ARE SO DO YOU
☐	☐	KEEP FROM TEASING them?
☐	☐	AVOID strange animals?

YES	NO	AND WHEN YOU GET HOME DO YOU
☐	☐	Put your SKATES on a nail or hook?
☐	☐	Put your BICYCLE on the porch or in the garage or cellar—OFF THE SIDEWALK?
☐	☐	W-A-L-K, not RUN on STAIRS?
☐	☐	KEEP FROM playing with matches?
☐	☐	Put all TOYS in BOX or on SHELF?
☐	☐	Put MATCHES in METAL BOX?
☐	☐	KEEP FROM playing with FIREARMS?
☐	☐	KEEP FROM reaching for handles of pots on STOVE?
☐	☐	KEEP FROM touching ELECTRICAL FIXTURES with WET HANDS?
☐	☐	PICK UP PINS from FLOOR?

OTHER PROBLEMS FOR OLDER CHILDREN

1. What happens to your body as it grows?
2. What functions are performed by the various body systems?
3. How does your body protect itself from germs?
4. Why should you learn about your body?
5. How do we use our senses to find out about the environment?

Resources to Investigate with Children

1. Local doctors, dentists, and nurses for information about the human body and health.
2. Life-insurance companies for bulletins, charts, and other information.
3. Meat markets for bones and other animal-body parts to examine.
4. Local Red Cross for printed information about health and safety matters.
5. National Dairy Council, 111 N. Canal St., Chicago, Ill. 60606; Wheat Flour Institute, 14 E. Jackson Blvd., Chicago, Ill. 60604; Cereal Institute, Inc., 135 S. LaSalle St., Chicago, Ill. 60603; for catalogues of teaching material.

6. High-school biology teacher to show blood sample under microscope and for other aids.
7. Local health and sanitation officers to discuss health practices and rules and to obtain information about symptoms of child diseases.
8. Local museums containing displays of models of the human body.

Preparing to Teach

1. Prepare a list of the most essential problems that might be encountered in initiating a sex education program and plan how you would try to solve these problems.
2. Perform some of the exercises suggested for discovering by the use of the senses and make a record of the results to use in your teaching.
3. Learn as much as you can about drugs and youth.[5] Unfortunately this problem is often encountered in the elementary school.

[5] *Resource Book for Drug Abuse Education* (National Association for Drug Abuse Education, National Institute of Mental Health publication, available from Superintendent of Documents, U.S. Government Printing Office, Washington, D.C. 20402, 1971). Other materials available on request. State nature of your needs to insure proper response. *See also* Staff of the Child Study Association of America; *You, Your Child and Drugs* (New York: 9 East 89th St., 10028, 1971); and John S. Marr, M.D.: *The Good Drug and the Bad Drug,* an educator's guide for drug education in the elementary school (Philadelphia: J. B. Lippincott & Co., 1972).

CHAPTER 13A
THE HISTORY OF LIFE

All is change; only change is changeless.
—*Heraclitus,* 5th century B.C.

(*Courtesy of Field Museum of Natural History, Chicago, Charles R. Knight.*)

THE CHANGING EARTH

One of the most important achievements of science has been the discovery of *change,* the discovery that everything in the universe, from the scenery outside our window to the stars in the sky, has always been changing.

Hills are worn down into plains; rocks crumble into soil. New mountains rise from the earth; sea bottoms become dry land. The face of the earth changes and with it the kinds of animals and plants that live on it.

So slowly do these changes occur that man's memory, even when aided by written records, can scarcely be expected to encompass them. The few thousand years of civilization are but a fleeting moment in the giant calendar of earth events. Indeed, only in the last century have we understood the meaning of the evidence that lies around us, evidence that says: The earth is very old; the earth is ever-changing.

Animals and plants of the past have recorded their own history in a number of different ways. Let us consider some of these.

RECORDS OF PAST LIFE

Actual Remains

The remains of the woolly mammoth, an elephant with long thick hair that became extinct thousands of years ago, have been found in the ice and frozen soil of Alaska and Siberia. Arctic explorers reported that the animals were in an excellent stage of preservation; their sled dogs even enjoyed eating the flesh. Ancient man must have known living mammoths, for he made paintings and carvings of these creatures on the walls of his caves.

Natural asphalt is also an excellent preserver of animals. At the La Brea tar pits in Los Angeles, California, there is an ancient pool of hardened asphalt from which the bones and teeth of thousands of animals have been dug. Among these are the remains of birds, wolves, horses, and bison that lived about 15,000 years ago. Many animals were probably trapped while attempting to prey on creatures struggling in the sticky mass. The tar sealed the bones of these creatures and preserved them perfectly from decay. Best known of the entombed animals is the extinct sabertooth, a member of the cat family.

The teeth of sharks and the shells of shellfish are other examples of original materials that are sometimes preserved intact.

The remains of the woolly mammoth, the saber-toothed cat, and ancient shellfish are examples of *fossils,* which may be defined simply as records of ancient life. When most organisms die, they are not preserved. They usually decompose into chemicals that enrich the soil and waters of the earth. Only under special conditions do animals and plants leave some kind of permanent record of themselves.

We have seen how ice and asphalt provide a means for preserving the remains of animals. These, however, are unusual ways of fossil formation. Much more common are those in which plants and animals are submerged in water and covered with sand and mud. Let us see how.

Replaced Remains

In the Petrified Forest in Arizona are the stony relics of great conifers, the cone-bearing trees, that once grew there. At some time in the past, about 220 million years ago, these trees were submerged in water that flooded the ancient forests. How were these trunks changed into stone? The first stage in this transformation was the filling of the cavities inside the empty wood cells with minerals carried in solution in the water. Silica was the common mineral deposited in the cells by the waters percolating through the trees. Later the silica hardened into rocky quartz. During the process the woody cell walls became surrounded almost in their original state by the mineral matter.

This method of fossil formation, called *petrifaction,* is unique in that it preserves the finest details of organisms. Thus we can still see in the stony trees at the Petrified Forest and in Yellowstone Park the annual growth rings, knots, and even the microscopic cellular structure of these ancient plants. The bones of animals, being porous, may also be petrified by the infiltration of minerals such as silica or, in some cases, lime.

Prints in Stone

(*See* pp. 410–1, 413.)

We have all seen footprints of children or dogs in concrete sidewalks. These, obviously, were made while the concrete was moist and soft. Many plants and animals of the past have made records of themselves in a similar way.

Certain types of rocks, notably the *sedimentary* rocks, were once soft muds and sands and therefore impressionable, like the soft concrete just referred to. Most sedimentary rocks are formed by the gradual settling of materials to the bottoms of bodies of water. (These rocks are discussed more fully in Chapter 6A.) Plants and animals that happened to be buried in this soft material, called sediment, left an impression that became permanent when the sediments hardened into stone. The shell of a clam, for instance, may have fallen into the soft mud and sand at the bottom of a lake. Later the mud and sand slowly hardened into rock. The shell disintegrated and disappeared, but a permanent impression was left in the surrounding rock.

The impression of the shell is called a *mold,* which shows only the shape of the original organism. Sometimes the mold is filled with new mineral material, which then forms a *cast* of the original fossil. Shellfish commonly produce molds and casts. Ferns and fish leave mold fossils in many rocks.

In some cases the actual organic remains are found next to the imprint. Flattened fossils, such as those of leaves, are called *compressions* or *incrustations.*

The impressions of moving animals may be preserved as fossils in the form of footprints and trails. Dinosaurs wandering in the Connecticut valley about 220 million years ago left their footprints in the sand of that time, which later hardened into red sandstone rock. In traveling over sand and mud bottoms such forms as worms, shellfish, and arthropods left trails that were preserved.

These large holes were recognized as dinosaur footprints by paleontologist Roland T. Bird. Brontosaurus, or Thunder Lizard, left these prints in mud flats in a region now called Texas 135 million years ago. (*Courtesy of American Museum of Natural History.*)

Finding Fossils

Fossils are not rare, as some people think they are. In many localities in the United States

(*See* pp. 411–3.)

fossil hunts are practicable for amateurs. Local geological societies, museums, and state geological surveys will often be glad to furnish fossil prospectors with essential information. You may not find dinosaurs, but you may be able to discover fossils of seashells, fish, and leaves. Amateurs should cooperate with organizations just named to avoid indiscriminate collecting and possible destruction of valuable specimens.

Fossils may occur in any region where there are layers of sedimentary rock. Fortunately for fossil hunters these underlie most of the United States. Rocks exposed in cliffs, along the sides of ravines, in stream beds, in quarries, and in excavations along railroads and highways may yield fossils. In many cases good specimens are to be found in loose fragments of rock in these places. Sometimes the fossil must be broken from the rock. For this a hammer and stone chisel or a mason's hammer are useful. Permission of property owners should be sought before entering private areas and prospecting for fossils.

Importance of Fossils

Fossils tell us many things. Some, like those of the dinosaur and the saber-toothed cat, tell us of strange animals of the past that are now extinct. Some fossils, like those of ferns (plants that usually live in warm places) found in the Arctic regions, suggest that the climate there has changed. Fossil seashells found high in the Catskill Mountains and fossil coral reefs in Chicago indicate that these areas were once covered by seas. But most important of all, fossils, when studied in relation to the rock formations in which they are found, reveal the *sequence* of life down through the ages.

Ancient life has left us a monumental library inscribed in stone, in which the rocky books are stacked one on top of the other. The oldest volumes in this picture-book library are on the bottom of the pile and the most recent acquisitions are on top.

The library of stacked volumes is the layers of sedimentary rocks that have accumulated down through the ages. We recall from our previous consideration of "Prints in Stone" that these rocks and the fossils in them were formed underwater after the soft bed of mud and sand had hardened into stone. Layer upon layer of rock was built in this way. In a later period the whole mass may have been elevated by a great earth movement or the sea may have receded, making the rock a part of man's landscape.

The Grand Canyon of Colorado furnishes us with such a sample of ancient history. There, layers of rock a mile high have been exposed to man's view by the slow but relentless cutting action of the Colorado River and by weathering. A climb up the walls of the Canyon is a trip through time, for the building of its rocks required hundreds of millions of years. At the lowest or oldest rock formations we search in vain for fossils. As we proceed upward we find our first evidence of life, the remains of simple water plants, the algae. Climbing higher, we find fossils of simple animals without backbones. The trilobites, which we shall describe later, are a notable and characteristic example of these. Seaweeds are also represented here. A few hundred feet higher we detect the first evidence of vertebrate life in the fossilized remains of fish scales, along

The three lobes of the trilobite are clearly visible. The trilobites pictured here were found near Lockport, New York. Over 3,000 species of trilobites have been identified; they were the dominant form of animal life in early Paleozoic times. (*Courtesy of American Museum of Natural History.*)

A climb up the Grand Canyon is a trip through time, for the building of these layers of rock from bottom to top required a billion years. (*Courtesy of Union Pacific Railroad.*)

with contemporaneous relics of shells and corals. Much farther up the Canyon walls we discover the first evidence of land plants and animals. Primitive "evergreens" and fernlike plants are seen here; insect fossils are in evidence for the first time; tracks of crawling amphibians and reptiles are found in the sandstones. We notice also that some invertebrates, such as the trilobites, are no longer seen.

The Grand Canyon is but one of the thousands of places where the earth has written its own history. From a study of these, and from other evidence, scientists have come to the following conclusions:

1. Life has existed on the earth for at least 3 billion years.
2. The kinds of living things on the earth have been different in different periods.
3. Some types of life have become extinct.
4. Simple forms of life appeared first; more complex forms appeared later.
5. The more complex forms arose originally as modified descendants of simpler forms.

HOW LIFE CHANGES

The conclusion that life changed over millions of years of earth history is as solid as the rocks which furnish evidence of such change. Much more complex is the problem of *how* such changes occurred. What mechanism changes one species into another?

Consider an observable change that occurred in recent times. A certain British moth, *Biston betularia,* commonly known as the peppered moth, rests on tree trunks in the forests where it is found. The trees there were originally covered by light-colored lichens. The speckled moths were camouflaged on this background, making it difficult for predatory birds to detect them. In the population of speckled moths there were some rare dark gray moths of the same species.

Industrialization in certain parts of Britain, beginning about 1850, polluted the woods in some areas with soot, killing the lichens and darkening the tree trunks. As the trees darkened, the speckled moths became more conspicuous and apparently were easily detected and eaten by predatory birds. Now the dark gray moths' color matched that of the tree trunks.

Between 1848 and 1898 the percentage of dark gray moths of this species increased from 1 to 99 percent of the population! Now the speckled forms were rare.

The British peppered moth story is a case

There are light and dark moths in *both* of these photographs. Which can be seen most easily in each? How might camouflage play a role in evolution? Read the text for a discussion of natural selection.

Biston betularia, the Peppered Moth, and its black form, *carbonaria,* at rest on a lichened tree trunk in the unpolluted countryside. (*Courtesy of Dr. H.B.D. Kettlewell, University of Oxford.*)

Biston betularia, the Peppered Moth, and its black form, *carbonaria,* at rest on a soot-covered oak trunk near Birmingham, England. (*Courtesy of Dr. H.B.D. Kettlewell, University of Oxford.*)

study of *natural selection* in action. The principle of natural selection was originally proposed in the nineteenth century by Charles Darwin, the British naturalist, to explain the "Origin of Species." Let us examine this principle, modernized to accommodate findings since Darwin, to see how it would operate in the case of the peppered moths.

Variation Individuals of a species vary in color, shape, size, structure, and thousands of minute characters, many undetectable except under special circumstances. A good example of this are many breeds of dog with which we are familiar.

Only those characters resulting from heredity, such as blue eyes in the human or the dark gray color of the moth *Biston betularia,* are of potential significance in evolution, for it is only these that can be transmitted to future generations.

New characters constantly appear in individuals in the course of heredity because of *mutations*—sudden changes in the genes which govern traits—or because of recombinations of existing genes during the process of reproduction. In the fruit fly of the genus Drosophila, a favorite for the study of genetics since the early part of this century, hundreds of mutations have appeared.

Selection If industrialization had *not* occurred in Britain, if the trees had *not* darkened, the change in the moth population from 1 percent dark gray to 99 percent dark gray probably would not have occurred. (In addition to *Biston betularia* about 70 other species of British moth have been observed to exhibit a darkening trend in industrialized areas.) The presumption then is that a changing environment—in this case the darkening of the tree trunks—*favored the survival* of the dark gray moth and operated against the survival of speckled moths. This is an example of natural selection at work.

Note that it is the *population* that evolves, not the individual organism. The new environment did not change any individual moths from speckled to dark gray; the soot did not soil their wings. Rather, the environment had a selective influence, determining which moths would survive and reproduce.

Time and Place It is true that the dark gray moth cannot be regarded as a different species from the speckled moth. (The dark gray moth will mate successfully with the speckled one. This is one test of a species.) But picture what could happen in hundreds, thousands, or millions of years with the two factors just discussed in operation: the tendency for living things to vary and for the environment to change. Change could be added to change until a new species was formed.

Place affects evolution. When the members of a species in some area are separated by a river, mountain range, or ocean each new population will change in its own way, partly because of the new environment that each population may encounter and partly because of chance.

(*See* Ch. 6A.)

The influence of continental drift and plate tectonics on the evolution and dispersal of species over the earth remains to be evaluated. The drift of continents through different latitudes would have affected the climate that prevailed on that continent and therefore the evolution of plants and animals there.

Over long periods of time not only do new species arise but also the major groups, phyla, classes, and so on of plants and animals. Thus small subtle changes lead not only to new species but also to all evolutionary change.

THE ERAS OF THE EARTH

Current estimates of the age of the earth vary, but all agree in counting it in billions of years. Recent studies indicate that the earth is about 5 billion years old. The evidence for this and the methods of dating rock layers were discussed in Chapter 6A.

Geologists, the scientists who study the changing earth, divide the history of our planet into long time intervals called eras. Generally each era is separated from the next one by some great disturbance in the crust of the earth and by some marked changes in living things. The chart on p. 395 identifies the four eras of earth history and gives some of their outstanding characteristics.

In thinking about the vast span of geological time it is helpful to remember that:

1. For about two-fifths of its long history the earth was apparently barren of life.
2. Man is a newcomer. If all earth time were compressed into 1 year man would come on the scene on December 31 just a few hours before midnight.

The four eras, in order, are Cryptozoic ("obscure life"), Paleozoic ("ancient life"), Mesozoic ("middle life"), and Cenozoic ("recent life").

EARLY LIFE

The Cryptozoic (Obscure Life) Era

The way in which the earth, its sister planets, and the sun were formed is still an open question. (*See* Chapter 7A for a discussion of various theories of the origin of the solar system.) According to a currently popular theory the earth began as a cloud of cold dust and gas, which in time contracted to form the body of the earth. The primeval earth heated up slowly, taking perhaps 1 billion years to reach a molten state. It may be imagined that during the early Cryptozoic era the entire earth was a huge chemical laboratory in which the future materials of this planet were put together. In this liquid stage the heaviest substances sank to the center of the earth, the lighter floated to the surface, and others found their place in between. Huge bubbles of various gases, including water vapor, erupted from the molten mass to form the first atmosphere.

A thin crust of cooled rock formed on the surface of the earth. The churning molten mass underneath constantly burst through weak points in this skimpy covering, bringing outpourings of lava (molten rock) accompanied by smoke and flame. Wave upon wave of lava spread across the original crust and congealed into rock. There was no water in liquid form at that time and hence there were no rivers, lakes, or seas—only hot rock everywhere.

As the rocks hardened, more water vapor and other gases were released and rose into the atmosphere. The earth gradually became wrapped in an atmosphere so dense and cloudy that the sun could not penetrate it. Still it did not rain, because the earth was so hot that the moisture could not cool sufficiently.

After a long period of cooling, water in the upper part of the cloud blanket was able to condense, and rain began to fall, only to be changed back into steaming clouds before it could reach the sizzling surface of the earth. Eventually the first raindrops splashed on the warm rocks, only to be boiled away again. Cooling now took place more rapidly, however, so that at last rain began to trickle down the slopes and collect in little pools.

Then the rains increased. For thousands of years it rained incessantly. Rivulets became torrents, raging across the rocky land, filling the valleys and the basins of the earth. Thus were the oceans born.

As more and more water poured down the clouds thinned and the sun finally broke through, illuminating a landscape of rocky land masses and shallow seas. But upon the whole earth there was no living thing.

Life Begins

The origin of life is the mystery of mysteries. Down through the ages philosophers and scientists have sought an answer to the question: How did life begin?

In those early Cryptozoic times when the seas and the atmosphere seethed with chemical turbulence, it is possible that molecules joined together to form specks of living protoplasm, the starting points of all life. How did this happen?

In 1953 Stanley L. Miller, then a graduate student at the University of Chicago, performed a now-classic experiment on the origin of life. Miller constructed an airtight apparatus for circulating steam through a mixture of ammonia, methane, and hydrogen. (Ammonia is a gas used

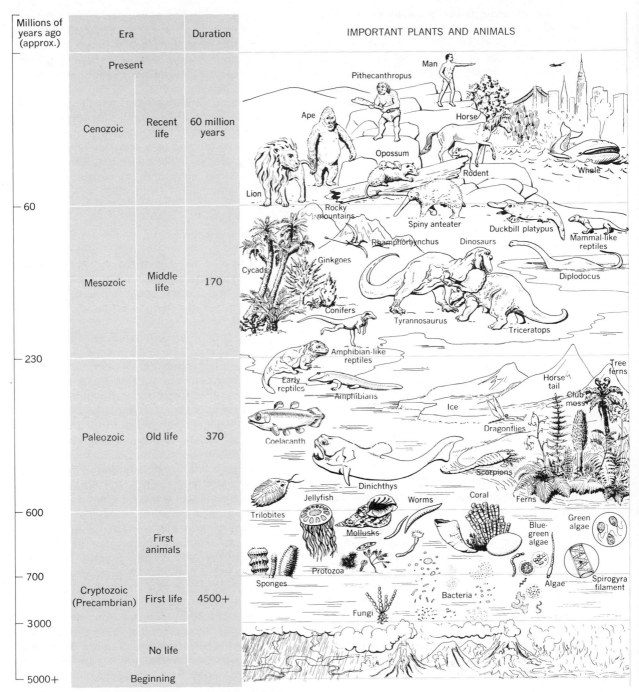

Millions of years ago (approx.)	Era		Duration
	Present		
	Cenozoic	Recent life	60 million years
60			
	Mesozoic	Middle life	170
230			
	Paleozoic	Old life	370
600			
	Cryptozoic (Precambrian)	First animals	4500+
700		First life	
3000		No life	
5000+	Beginning		

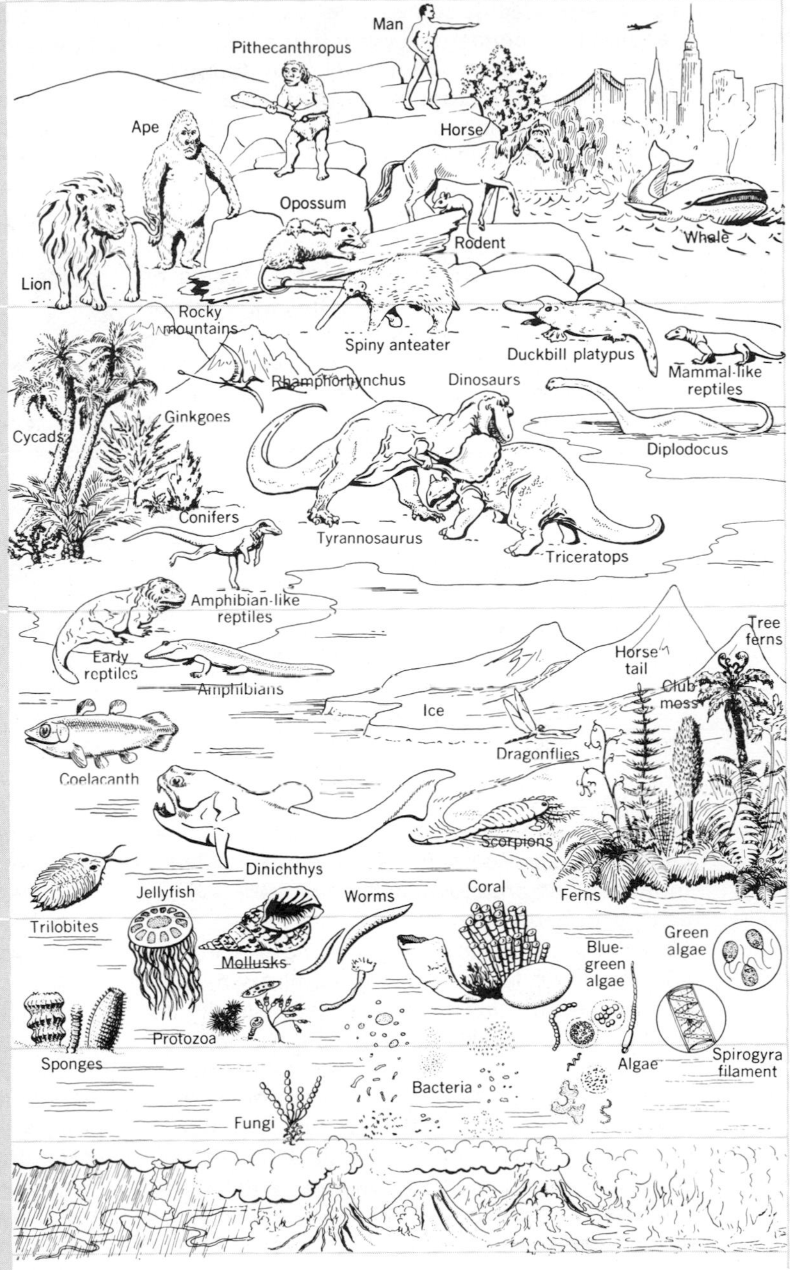

Progress of life through the eras.

in many cleaning fluids; methane is part of the natural gas used in home cooking and heating.) The mixture of steam and gas was subjected to high-energy electric sparks. After a week of such treatment the condensed water in the apparatus became deep red and turbid. And on analysis it was discovered that the water contained a mixture of amino acids.

To appreciate the significance of this experiment, consider the following:

1. There is evidence that suggests that the primitive atmosphere of the earth consisted of ammonia, methane, hydrogen, and water vapor in contrast to the present atmosphere of nitrogen, oxygen, carbon dioxide, and water vapor. (Methane is found today in the atmospheres of the planets Uranus and Neptune; methane and ammonia gases are found in the atmospheres of Jupiter and Saturn.)
2. Ammonia (NH_3), methane (CH_4), hydrogen (H_2), water vapor (H_2O) contain four of the essential elements—carbon, oxygen, hydrogen, nitrogen—for the complex amino acids essential for life. Electrical discharges such as lightning in an early atmosphere of ammonia, methane, and hydrogen, and radiation from the sun may have provided the energy needed to juggle the atoms in these chemicals, causing them to recombine into amino acids. Over millions of years the amino acids may have combined to form larger and more complex molecules—proteins. Other essential compounds that may have been formed in this pre-biological period were nucleic acids and carbohydrates.
3. These new compounds may have accumulated in ponds, lakes, and seas, forming what has been called a "thin organic soup." Slowly the earliest forms of life evolved from no life. Precells formed from clusters of organic compounds, which were able to grow and replenish themselves from materials originally formed by nonbiological reactions. The first organisms were able to obtain energy by a fermentationlike process in which no oxygen was required.

Since Miller's original experiment others have been performed, using other energy sources, such as ultraviolet radiation and different combinations of gases likely to be present in the primitive atmosphere of the earth. Other compounds essential for life were produced. Most biologists now believe that life originated by a process of slow development from nonliving chemical systems.

These ideas concerning the interrelationship of the evolution of the earth's atmosphere and the evolution of life are so new that they have yet to be tested and fully accepted by scientists, but they are the most consistent and plausible proposals yet advanced to explain the origin of life.

Life Develops

According to current theory life developed in two directions from the original bits of living material. One branch became one-celled organisms that lacked a definite nucleus. These were the ancestors of bacteria.

The main branch started as cells with a definite nucleus. The original organisms in this branch would probably have been hard to classify as either plants or animals. Some possessed whiplike tails for locomotion and mouths for the ingestion of food, but also contained chlorophyll for the chemical synthesis of food. These organisms, part animal and part plant, are thought by some biologists to have been the true ancestors of the animal and plant kingdoms. As time went on modified descendants of these first organisms developed in two different directions to form the basis for the plant and animal kingdoms.

The first true plants were the algae. You probably are familiar with algae as a green growth on the side of fish aquaria. Under the microscope this growth is revealed as a multitude of simple green plants without roots, stems, or leaves. The appearance of algae marked an important step in evolution, for now, with the aid of the green chlorophyll that these simple plants possessed, it was possible to utilize the energy of sunlight to synthesize foods quickly. At the same time, as a result of photosynthesis, great quantities of free oxygen were added to the atmosphere. Living organisms began to use this oxygen for the burning of food. Thus an ample supply of building materials and energy was made available. Now animal life flourished, since animals require free oxygen either in the air or dissolved in water.

(*See* pp. 273, 275.) Simple, one-celled animals, the protozoans, appeared on the scene.

Perhaps the best way to get a picture of early life is to examine a drop of stagnant pond water under the microscope and to discover there the teeming lilliputian world of bacteria, algae, protozoans, and other tiny organisms.

During the closing stages of the Cryptozoic a few groups of animals without backbones (the invertebrates) made their appearance in the sea. These included the protozoans, the sponges, jellyfish and their relatives, the sea pens, and various types of wormlike animals. Others were so unlike animals living today that they are hard to classify. Even the most advanced of the invertebrates, the arthropods—jointed-foot animals that were later to include crustaceans, spiders, and insects—had their beginnings in Cryptozoic times.

On the other hand, plants had not progressed very far by the close of this era. Those that had made their appearance included bacteria, blue-green algae, green algae, and mold plants.

The Cryptozoic era did not leave many fossil remains. After years of search in the rocks of this era we have only a few specimens of the simplest plants—algae and fungi—and low forms of marine invertebrates.

One indirect evidence of ancient plant life is represented in the "lead" of your pencil. This is not the metal lead, but a carbon material known as graphite. We have good reason to believe that some graphite is derived in large part from primitive seaweeds and simple animals. Graphite has been found in Cryptozoic rock, furnishing strong but indirect evidence that life was present some 2 billion years ago. Some forms of coal, which is of plant origin, have been found in Cryptozoic formations.

More direct evidence of earlier life was found in 1954 by the scientists Tyler and Barghoorn. Turning their microscope on rock determined to be 2 billion years old, these scientists discovered fossils of filaments and threads of fungi (moldlike plants) and algae. This find was made in Ontario, on the north shore of Lake Superior. Later discoveries by Dr. Barghoorn in Africa pushed life's origin back another billion years. He found fossils of bacteria 3 billion years old by making very thin slices of rock, treating them with weak acid to remove the mineral content, and examining the remaining material under the electron microscope.

ANCIENT LIFE

The Paleozoic (Ancient Life) Era

The next 370 million years of earth history, which began about 600 million years ago, were filled with important events. Plant and animal forms emerged from the seas and tenanted the land. Invertebrate animals multiplied and were

Much of North America was submerged beneath marine waters in Ordovician times (Paleozoic era). Creatures such as these are found as fossils in many parts of the country. (*Courtesy of Buffalo Museum of Science, wall painting by James Doherty.*)

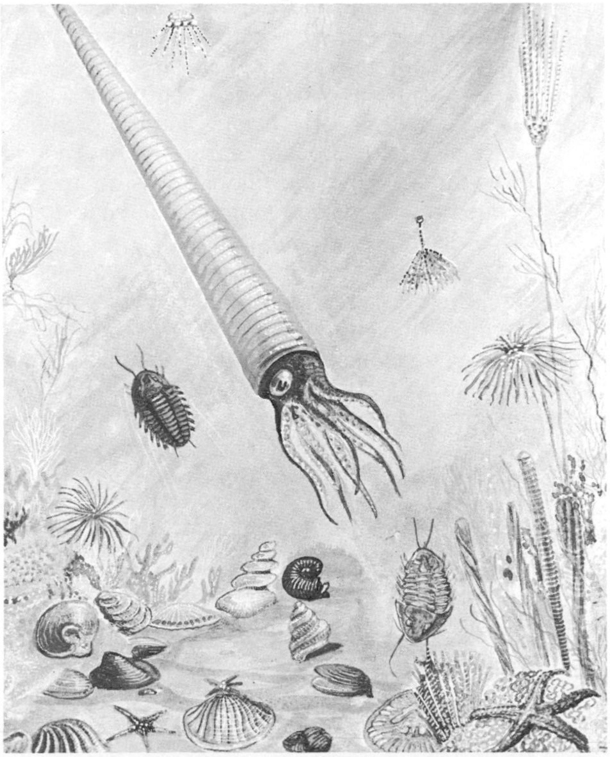

kings of the earth, only to be dethroned by the first-evolving vertebrates, the fish and amphibia. Reptiles had their beginnings.

The plant world flourished, clothing the barren land with green. The first forests appeared, including those that gave rise to most of the world's present supply of coal. Many of the major groups of plants were established before the end of the Paleozoic.

The physical events of this era were marked by widespread changes. Seas covered wide areas of the earth—at one time more than three-fifths of North America. Huge mountain ranges, the Appalachian and the Ural, were thrust up by gargantuan folds in the crust of the earth.

The Rise and Fall of the Trilobites

In early Paleozoic times life was confined to the water. In the shallow seas covering large parts of the continents and in the surface water of the deeper oceans lived protozoans, sponges, corals, worms, snails, starfish, crabs, and shrimps. Except for fish, which had not yet appeared, these are the types of animals we find in the sea today. But most of these ancient forms would look strange to our eyes, because they were quite unlike their modern descendants. And these ancient seas would appear strange also because of the trilobites who lived there. These ancient relatives of lobsters and crabs have since disappeared from the earth. Trilobite means "three-lobed," and the trilobite was so named because it was divided longitudinally into three clearly distinguishable parts.

Predominant on the earth for 100 million years, the trilobites averaged only 2 or 3 inches in length. These former kings of the earth dined on decaying plants and animals and microscopic organisms. Later the trilobites fell to a position of insignificance, possibly because of the rise of fish. By the close of the Paleozoic the trilobites became extinct. We know them today only as stony fossils.

Fish Come to the Earth

The animals living in the early Paleozoic era did not have backbones. Whatever supporting structures they possessed were external, consisting of shells or plates. The emergence of fish from these lower forms was a most significant event, marking the origin of animals with backbones, the vertebrates, a group that includes the fish, amphibia, the reptiles, the birds, and the mammals, including man himself.

Fish, then, were the first animals with backbones. The earliest forms, however, were quite different from the fish we know today. One of these was the 20-foot-long *Dinichthys,* the "terrible fish" of the Paleozoic era. Remains of this animal have been found in black shale rock near Cleveland, Ohio.

Dinichthys was well protected by hinged armor plates over the head, neck, and the front of the trunk. It was unique in being the only animal that used its jawbones for eating, because its teethlike structures were nothing but sharp projections of its upper and lower jaws. These fearful jaws were capable of slicing in two any of its contemporaries.

Before the close of the Paleozoic era sharks appeared, and then the fish with hard bones, which are the ancestors of today's forms.

Plants Invade the Land

The scorpions and insects apparently were the first animals to emerge from the waters of lakes and seas, but this event did not occur until late Paleozoic time; they had been preceded by the plants in the invasion of the land. For 2 billion years the plant kingdom had been confined to water and had not advanced beyond a simple seaweed level of development. Then, in a relatively short period, plants overran the land, carpeting it with green mosses, ferns, and seed plants.

Naturally, the transition from water to land was made at the edges of seas and lakes. On the seashore any of the new water plants that could withstand partial exposure to air might survive on the moist beach when ocean tides retreated. Similarly, lake plants that could withstand seasonal receding of lake waters in dry seasons might survive.

Having established a foothold on the rocky land, plants advanced steadily. Soil formed for the first time from the organic matter furnished by the decay of many generations of the first plant invaders and from the crumbling rock underneath.

The mosses may have been the first land plants to evolve from aquatic plants. Their conquest of the land was limited because they lacked the internal "tubes" that were needed to carry watery sap any great distance from roots through stems to leaves. As a result the representatives of this group were small and were confined to moist areas.

The ferns, however, did evolve the tubes through which water could be elevated many feet above the ground. Plants were now able to extend their invasion of the ground to the conquest of the air above it. Ferns towered over the Paleozoic landscape.

The Coal Forests

Most of the world's present supply of coal had its origin in Paleozoic forests. For a period of about 50 million years the prevailing moist climate and swampy terrain provided conditions favorable for the luxurious growth of a group of flowerless plants, many of which were destined for conversion into coal. Included in this group were the club mosses, horsetails and scouring rushes, and the true ferns.

Horsetails, which today are small plants

Giant ferns, club-moss trees (lycopods), and horsetail rushes are some of the plants shown in this restoration of an ancient landscape. Swamp forests of Pennsylvanian times, such as this one, provided the material for the formation of coal. In the foreground are two kinds of amphibians and a giant dragonfly. (*Courtesy of American Museum of Natural History.*)

characterized by hollow, jointed stems, were then trees 75 feet tall and 3 feet in diameter.

Club mosses, which today include the small, inconspicuous plants used as Christmas decorations, were the real giants of the coal forests. One of these, *Lepidodendron* (lĕp′ĭ-dō-dĕn′drŏn), had large, needlelike leaves and a branched, expanded crown. A fossil trunk of this plant found in an English coal mine was 114 feet long.

There were also many kinds of true ferns, some of which reached heights of 50 feet.

The conversion of the wood of these swamp plants into coal is not difficult to understand from a chemical point of view. Wood is essentially a chemical compound of carbon, hydrogen, and oxygen. Coal is essentially carbon. To change wood into coal it was only necessary to drive off the hydrogen and oxygen and subject the remaining black carbon to pressure.

Two peculiar conditions in the Paleozoic swamp forests favored the formation of coal. First, as generation after generation of trees died, they were protected against rapid rotting by their immersion in the waters of the swamp. Thus bacterial action, instead of decomposing the whole mass of wood, worked slowly on it, removing the hydrogen and oxygen and leaving a substance that had a high percentage of carbon in it.

The second condition responsible for coal formation was the sinking of the land. The resulting floods from nearby seas and rivers dumped thick layers of mud and sand over the accumulated vegetation. The coal forest's existence was thus terminated. In time the pressure of the mud and sand, and possibly some earth-heating, changed the buried vegetation into coal. The mud and sand eventually changed into rock.

The process just described would account for one layer or *seam* of coal. Later, as the flood waters receded and the land rose again the entire cycle was repeated, on top of the previous formation. Each swamp forest provided another layer of coal. In parts of present-day Illinois 50 such cycles have resulted in the deposition of 50 seams of coal.

The plant origin of coal is apparent because fossil impressions of fern fronds are frequently found in coal beds, as well as whole tree trunks that have been transformed into coal.

Animals Go Ashore

The luxuriant plant cover of Paleozoic times provided a home and a supply of food for the animals that were emerging from the crowded seas. Air-breathing scorpions and spiders, descendants of the sea scorpions, made their appearance. These eight-legged creatures were followed by the six-legged insects. Notable among these for a time were 800 different kinds of cockroaches, some of them 4 or 5 inches long. No wonder this period is sometimes called the Age of Cockroaches.

Primitive dragonflies with a wingspread of $2\frac{1}{2}$ feet flitted around the giant horsetails and club mosses in ancient coal forests. Evidence of these largest insects of all times was found in certain coal fields in Belgium. The richest occurrence of Paleozoic insect fossils yet discovered is in rock a few miles south of Abilene, Kansas, where more than 12,000 specimens have been collected.

The development of the insect group from Paleozoic times on is a fantastic success story, having its climax in the more than 700,000 different kinds of insects inhabiting the world today.

Land Vertebrates

In 1938 a curious fish was dredged up by fishermen working along the coast opposite East London, South Africa. This strange fish was well known to scientists—but only as a fossil! In fact, hundreds of fossil species of these ancient fish, called Coelacanths (seal′a-canths), had been found during the excavation for a new library at Princeton University, New Jersey. The scientific world bubbled with excitement as this "living fossil" was studied and compared with its fossil counterpart. Coelacanths are of particular interest because they are descendants of the primitive lobe-finned fish, which are believed to have given rise to land vertebrates. We shall find out more about the lobe fins presently.

The successful emergence of the vertebrate animals from their aquatic environment depended on the acquisition of two important organs—lungs and legs. The breathing structures of fish are gills. These are essentially flaps of tissue, richly supplied with blood vessels. In the water, which must constantly flow over the gills, there is dissolved air containing oxygen. Some of the oxygen passes through the thin gill membranes into the circulating blood. In air-breathing vertebrates, on the other hand, oxygen passes from the *air sacs* of the lungs through moist membranes into the blood stream.

How did lungs arise? Clues are provided by a close look at modern fish. Most fish have sac-like air bladders, a kind of "float" that helps them maintain a stationary position at different depths in the water without muscular effort.

In the curious lungfish that live today in Africa, South America, and Australia the sac takes on another function during the dry seasons these fish experience. The African lungfish, instead of trying to follow the receding waters into the river, burrows into the mud and forms a hardened mud capsule around itself. The capsule has a tube that permits air from the outside to pass into the mouth of the fish and thence to its air bladders, which function as lungs. The fish lives in the mud capsule for nearly half of the year, breathing with its lungs and living on the fat that it stores up during the wet season.

There is evidence that seasonal dryness, with the receding and even drying up of large areas, occurred during some periods of the Paleozoic. Thus the environmental conditions were favorable for the emergence of air-breathing animals. Those fish whose air bladders could serve as lungs, even to a small degree, would have an enormous advantage over others. These parttime air breathers may have provided the link between water and land vertebrates.

Legs were also essential for the liberation of the vertebrates from an aquatic existence. In fish the principal locomotor structure is the muscular tail. The paired fins are used for changing direction, for staying in one place, or for moving slowly. But the ancient lobe-finned fish were different. They had paired fins with a basic bone pattern remarkably like that of four-legged animals. It is probable that the forerunner of land animals were lobe-finned fish who were able to crawl out of the water and move about to some extent on land.

Descendants of walking lobe fins spent more and more time on land. From these were probably evolved the amphibians, which today are represented by frogs, toads, and salamanders.

The life history of modern frogs provides a good parallel to the evolution of life from water to land. Frogs begin life as fishlike tadpoles, propelling themselves through the water with their tails and breathing through gills. Before our eyes they transform themselves into land creatures, growing first hind and then front legs, losing their fishy tails, and developing air-breathing lungs. However, their exodus from the aquatic environment is only partial, because most species must return to the water to mate and to lay their gelatinous masses of eggs.

Complete liberation from the water was achieved by the reptiles, who made their appearance in the late Paleozoic era, probably as descendants of primitive amphibia. These reptiles had developed an egg with a tough covering that protected the embryo from drying up on land and yet was porous enough to permit it to breathe.

It must not be thought that *all* animals became terrestrial. Corals, clams, snails, fish, and many other forms continued to live and flourish in the sea.

End of the Paleozoic

The distance between Altoona and Philadelphia, both in Pennsylvania, was once 100 miles greater than it is today! Such is the estimate of the State Geological Survey of Pennsylvania. How is this possible?

Geologists tell us that the closing period of the Paleozoic was marked by revolutionary earth changes. Terrific pressures on the rocks of the earth's crust caused them to buckle up, just as a rug might if it were pushed together. As a result, mountain ranges, including the Appalachian, were thrust up, reaching majestic heights of 20,000 to 30,000 feet. Hence a shortening of lateral distances between places occurred.

This period of mountain building, which also produced the Alps in Europe, was followed by the receding of inland waters and the advance of sheets of ice across what is now Brazil, South Africa, and peninsular India. Great extremes of climate marked these late Paleozoic times.

Naturally these revolutionary upheavals

caused great destruction of life. Many marine invertebrates were hard hit by the draining of their homes at the edge of the sea. The warmth-loving, swamp-living plants of the coal forests were replaced by hardy, seed-bearing plants such as the conifers and cycads.

MIDDLE LIFE

The Mesozoic (Middle Life) Era

The Mesozoic is truly the age of reptiles. During these times reptilian dinosaurs ruled the land, reptilian "sea serpents" invaded and conquered the ocean, and reptilian "flying dragons" dominated the air. For over 100 million years the reptiles—modestly represented today by turtles, crocodiles, alligators, lizards, chameleons, and snakes—were the masters of all the habitats of the earth. Our museums are filled with the massive bones left by this mighty group in their Mesozoic graveyards.

The Dinosaurs

The stars of the ancient reptilian world were the dinosaurs. King of them all was *Tyranno-*

The skeleton of a man emphasizes the huge size of Brontosaurus. (*Courtesy of American Museum of Natural History.*)

This restoration of Brontosaurus is based on a careful study of its bone structure. Compare it with the skeleton shown above.

(See p. 414.) *saurus rex* (tĭ-răn′ô-sô′rŭs), 50 feet long from nose to tail and 18 feet tall when it stood erect on its hind legs. The head of this meat-devouring creature was 4 feet long and was armed with sharp teeth projecting 5 or 6 inches from the jaw. Tyrannosaurus's huge mouth, probably the most savage one of all time, provided this animal with a mighty weapon against less powerful dinosaurs.

(See p. 387.) *Stegosaurus* (stĕg′ô-sô′rŭs) perhaps the queerest-looking of all the dinosaurs, was equipped with a double row of long triangular plates carried erect along its body and extending from its relatively tiny skull along the whole length of its back, almost to the end of its tail. Near the end of its short tail were two pairs of heavy spikes, each 2 feet long, which must have been an effective weapon against the meat-eating dinosaurs. Despite this, Stegosaurus was vulnerable to a flank attack from an enemy.

Triceratops (trī-sĕr′ȧ-tŏps), with its curious bony shield extending backward from its 7-foot head, was protected by three formidable horns.

Brontosaurus (brŏn′tô-sô′rŭs), the "thunder lizard," another huge dinosaur, was 60 to 70 feet long and weighed about 30 tons. In contrast to Tyrannosaurus this creature walked on all fours and had a long slim neck ending in a small head adapted for its vegetarian habits. *Diplodocus* (dĭ-plŏd′-ô-kŭs), a close relative of Brontosaurus, was the longest creature ever to walk the earth. The best skeleton of this animal, now in the Carnegie Museum in Pittsburgh, is 87 feet long.

Reptiles Return to the Sea

The reptiles were the first vertebrates to achieve complete liberation from the water; they were also the first to return. The marine reptiles became the largest and most powerful creatures of the Mesozoic seas while their dinosaur cousins ruled the land. The aquatic *Ichthyosaurus* (ĭk′thĭ-o-sô′rŭs), for example, reached lengths up to 60 feet. Instead of legs, it had relatively small paddlelike limbs; a well-developed fishlike tail was its main organ of locomotion. Instead of going back to shore to lay eggs it gave birth to its young alive. The ichthyosaurs retained, however, the reptilian characteristics of breathing with lungs.

Another group of marine reptiles were the *mosasaurs* (mō′sȧ-sôrs), slender creatures some 50 feet long, looking very much like the legendary "sea serpents" supposedly "seen" now every few years by impressionable mariners.

An even dozen of dinosaur eggs—cracked. Fossil dinosaur eggs were first discovered in the Gobi Desert in Mongolia in 1923. Distinct bones of embryo dinosaurs were found in some of the eggs. The batch shown above was discovered in the third Asiatic expedition of the American Museum of Natural History in 1925. (*Courtesy of American Museum of Natural History.*)

Reptiles Invade the Air

The insects, as we have seen, were the first creatures to extend their domain to the regions of the air. The first *vertebrates* to leave the ground and the trees were the reptiles, represented by a group called the *pterodactyls* (tĕr′ô-dăk′tĭls). These pioneer gliders derived their flight power from a wing membrane made of skin which stretched from the greatly elongated joints of the fourth finger of the forelimb to the body as far back as the hip. The first three fingers were of ordinary length, each terminating in a claw that was probably useful for climbing and for clinging to branches of trees.

Some of the pterodactyls were no larger than a sparrow; others had a wing spread of 20 to 25 feet. *Pteranodon* (te-răn′ô-dŏn), one of the largest of the flying reptiles must have been a common sight in the Mesozoic air over what is now western Kansas, gliding with its 25-foot wing span over the ancient seas that once covered this area, and catching fish with its sharp bill. Despite this large wing span Pteranodon did not weigh much more than 20 or 30 pounds because its body was small and its bones were hollow.

The First Birds

Another branch of the reptiles took to the air at the same time as the pterodactyls. In the group was the first known true bird called *Archaeopteryx* (är′kê-ŏp′tĕr-ĭks). This creature was about the size of a domestic pigeon, but was only partially covered with feathers. The short rounded wings were probably not powerful enough for real flight, the animal being more of a glider that a flier.

Archaeopteryx had three fingers at the end of each wing, which were equipped with claws used for grasping and tearing. These early birds had strong jaws without bills; they had teeth—something no modern bird has. Also unique was their long bony tail. Thus the only strictly birdlike characteristic of Archaeopteryx was its feathers.

In the next era, from Archaeopteryx and its

Pterodactyl, a flying reptile, was a flesh eater with sharp teeth and long wings. Note fingers extending from the wing bones. (*Courtesy of American Museum of Natural History.*)

relatives there developed birds without teeth and claws, similar to the birds we know today. Modern birds, however, still reveal their reptilian ancestry in the scales that cover their legs.

Mammals Get Their Start

During much of Mesozoic time the dominant land vertebrates were the *mammal-like reptiles.* Later in the Mesozoic, the dinosaurs, which we have already described, flourished and became masters of the land. Only recently have paleontologists emphasized the abundance of the mammal-like reptiles that preceded the dinosaurs and dominated the land for almost as long. One of these mammal-like reptiles gave rise to the true mammals.

During most of the Mesozoic era small inconspicuous animals, most of them no larger than rats, were scurrying around, preserving their lives by their quickness of foot and agility in dodging dinosaurs. This was a new class of animals, which in the next era would become the rulers of the earth—the mammals, warm-blooded creatures that were covered with hair and suckled their young by means of mammary glands.

The mammals, themselves descendants of reptiles, played second fiddle to the dinosaurs and their cousins throughout the Mesozoic.

Other Mesozoic Events

The rise of reptiles, birds, and mammals in the Mesozoic era should not obscure the fact that changes were taking place in the other and older major groups of animals. In the invertebrate world of protozoa, mollusks, starfishes, lobsters, and insects, and also in the fish world, significant changes were occurring.

Notable advances were also being made in the plant kingdom. The cycads, palmlike seed plants without true flowers, were so abundant that the early Mesozoic is sometimes referred to as the Age of Cycads. Conifers—such as the spruces, pines, junipers, cypresses, and cedars—were abundant. Some of these probably reached a height of 200 feet, judging from the logs in the Petrified Forest of Arizona, described earlier. A third group that flourished during the Mesozoic was the ginkgoes, now represented by only one species, the ginkgo tree. This species was probably protected from extinction by cultivation in China and is now common as an imported tree all over the world.

The cycads, conifers, and ginkgoes are part of a group of seed-bearing yet flowerless plants. Another group, the plants with true flowers, also got its start in the Mesozoic, expanding rapidly near the end of this era to become the dominant plant form. The flowering plants include those which are best known and most valuable to man—hardwood trees such as oaks, maples, and elms, and the grasses and grains.

Plant evolution affected animal evolution. We find that bees and butterflies put in their appearance with the advent of flowering plants. Hardwood trees furnished shelter, and the cereal grains furnished food for many of the evolving mammals.

By the end of the Mesozoic and the beginning of the next era, all the common types of familiar plants had made their appearance. The animal kingdom, on the other hand, was still to expand enormously, admitting many new members to its ranks.

End of Mesozoic

The 170 million years of the Mesozoic ended in the Rocky Mountain Revolution. This was a period marked by the general raising of the land and by mountain-building activities. Tremendous stresses in the crust of the earth folded rocks into the great system of the Rocky Mountains, extending 3,000 miles from Alaska to Mexico.

With the raising of land masses, marshes dried up and inland seas retreated. The continental masses grew bigger. The earlier mild climate, which had permitted palms and fig trees to grow in western Greenland, gave way to colder temperatures. Climatic zones became more marked.

The closing of the Mesozoic brought the curtain down on the dinosaurs. Of the different kinds of reptiles, only lizards, snakes, crocodiles, and turtles survived into the next era—the Cenozoic.

Rulers of the earth for 100 million years, about 100 times as long as man's time on earth thus far, the dinosaurs disappeared completely, giving way at the close of the Mesozoic to those successful latecomers, the mammals.

RECENT LIFE

The Cenozoic (Recent Life) Era

The Rocky Mountain Revolution terminated the reign of reptiles and opened the Cenozoic era, the Age of Mammals. This most recent era, the one in which we live today, goes back about 60 million years. During these years the earth's surface was given the form familiar to us. Rivers in the western United States cut deep channels in rock to form magnificent gorges, such as that of the Grand Canyon. During the last million years of the Cenozoic glaciers advanced and retreated over the continents, putting their finishing touches to the face of the land.

Ranging from the surface waters of the seas to the highest mountain peaks, from dense forests to open plains, from the torrid tropics to the freezing arctic, mammals made the whole earth their home. Showing remarkable adaptations in their teeth, limbs, and their sense organs, mammals found food and safety in an amazing variety of habitats, including even the air, as demonstrated by the bats.

The Parade of Mammals

The diversity of mammalian life is reflected in the many groups that are familiar to us today. These had their origin in basic types that appeared early in the Cenozoic. An early stage in mammalian development is represented by two animals of Australia that are still with us, the duckbill and the spiny anteater. Both of these creatures have fur and nurse their young. But both retain the ancient reptilian characteristic of laying eggs! These egg layers, however, are not considered to be the ancestors of today's mammals. Rather, they are thought of as a unique side branch of mammals that descended directly from the early mammal-like reptiles, without giving rise to any more advanced groups.

More truly ancestral were the primitive mammals of the Mesozoic, mentioned previously, which were on the average no bigger than a rat or mouse. Two lines of evolution developed from these early forms. One led to the marsupials, the pouched mammals, of which the American opossum of today is an example. The tiny young of this species are raised in a kind of incubator or pouch where they find shelter and warmth, and where nourishment is provided by the inclosed teats. Marsupials are found almost exclusively in Australia. There all the native mammals are pouched.

Another line of evolution led to the placentals, those animals that nourish their developing young internally through a common membrane, the placenta. In the placenta food and oxygen are passed from the bloodstream of the mother to the separate but adjacent bloodstream of the embryo. The placentals include the carnivores, the rodents, hoofed mammals, whales, primates, and some other groups.

The carnivores or flesh-eating mammals have claws and sharp teeth that fit them for their way of life. Included in this group are the popular animals of the zoo: cats (including the lions, tigers, leopards, lynxes, and jaguars), dogs, wolves, foxes, weasels, badgers, minks, ermines, ferrets, skunks, and otters.

One group of mammals returned to the seas. This group includes the whales, porpoises, and dolphins, whose forelimbs have been modified to become finlike paddles. The hindlimbs are absent, and the tail is fishlike. The young are born alive and are nourished by milk from mammary glands, like other mammals. The sulphur-bottom whale is distinguished by being the largest animal known, living or extinct, reaching a length of nearly 100 feet and a weight of 150 tons.

The rodents are gnawing animals with two long chisel-like front teeth in each jaw. This group includes mice, rats, chipmunks, squirrels, woodchucks, muskrats, beavers, and porcupines.

The hoofed mammals include pigs, hippopotamuses, camels, sheep, goats, cattle, bison, giraffes, deer, and horses. They are vegetarians.

The Horse Gets Big

The horse is worthy of special mention in this chapter about ancient life because many splendid fossils of this animal have been found in North America. *Eohippus,* dawn horse, appeared early in the Cenozoic. No higher than a fox terrier, this diminutive horse had slender legs and a long slender face. It had four toes on its front feet and three on the hind feet. *Eohippus* browsed on shrubs, rather than on grass, as modern horses do. The subsequent evolution of the horse saw an increase in the size of its body and the development of specialized teeth for cropping and grinding grain. The toes were reduced in size, except for the middle one, which was enlarged to form the hoof.

Buried in the flesh of the legs of modern horses are two inconspicuous bones. These are the vestiges of the second and fourth toes, evidence of the kinship of today's horses to their many-toed forebears.

Although horses originated and developed in North America they became extinct on this continent, surviving only in Europe and Asia. They were reintroduced to their ancient home here by the early settlers.

Man Appears

The primates, which include monkeys, apes, and human beings, are distinguished by having a large brain. Our knowledge of human evolution is inadequate because relatively few fossils of man's forerunners have been unearthed, and most of these are only fragments of skulls and limb bones. However, our knowledge is constantly increasing. This we do know: that modern man appears to have been present on earth 40,000 years ago, manlike creatures some $2\frac{1}{2}$ million years ago, and his prehuman ancestors perhaps 20 million years ago; that today only one species of man, *Homo sapiens,* exists.

In the last two decades finds of great significance were made in Africa. Outstanding in making these discoveries was Louis S.B. Leakey, who with others uncovered evidence which indicates that Africa was a place of major importance for human evolution. Addressing a conference at the National Museum in Nairobi, Kenya, in 1967 Leakey summed up the paleontological findings gathered in Kenya which led to the belief that the family of man is close to 20,000,000 years old. He stated: "In terms of evolutionary history, man's separation from his closest cousins—the apes—is now carried back more than a million generations."

Leakey is known for his earlier discovery in 1962 of *Homo habilis* (man able to do things), a creature capable of making and using stone tools, in Olduvai Gorge, Tanzania.

The ancestry of man has been subject to some misunderstanding. No *living* member of the apes is the ancestor of man. Apes (as well as other primates) and man had common ancestors, but the two lines, as Leakey has stated, separated at least 20 million years ago.

Change Goes On

From our knowledge of the past there is every reason to believe that change will go on. The geologic forces that have been shaping the earth for billions of years will continue their activities. New forms of life will emerge.

With the coming of man to the earth a new force has been added—man's intelligence. With this intelligence he has the power to change the earth in many ways. For the first time a species exists that can deliberately and consciously influence its own future evolution—or its own extinction.

In looking back over the development of living things on the earth, certain ideas stand out that help us grasp the meaning of change through the ages. Some of the important ideas are:

The development of living things upon the earth has been from the very simple organisms to complex ones. Modern life developed from ancient life.

The changes have been extremely slow.

Great changes have taken place in the physical appearance and conditions of the earth during its long history.

These physical changes have influenced the evolution of plant and animal forms.

Natural selection provides a mechanism for evolutionary change. It accounts for the adaptation of plants and animals to the environment.

Many plants and animals that once lived on the earth have entirely disappeared.

Fossils tell us many things about ancient animals and plants and about conditions on the earth in past ages. Fossils in rock formations reveal the sequence of life through the ages.

There were living things in the seas long before they existed on the land.

The earth is very old—perhaps more than 5 billion years old.

For more than two-fifths of its long history the earth was barren of life.

Most biologists now believe that life originated on earth by a process of slow development from chemicals present in the primitive earth's atmosphere, first to non-living chemical systems, then to simple life forms.

Man is a newcomer; modern man appeared only about 40,000 years ago.

Man's intelligence is a new factor in evolution today.

Scientists continue their investigations to unravel the many mysteries of the earth's past.

Discovering for Yourself

1. Make a "time line" chart and arrange in order the important changes that occurred on the earth and to life on it through the ages.
2. Visit a museum, select three or four fossils, and try to determine what kind of environment the animal or plant may have lived in, how it may have become fossilized, and what present living thing it may be related to. The museum description will be helpful.
3. Watch newspapers for accounts of fossil discoveries. Read the accounts and apply the principles you have learned in this chapter to understanding the various implications of the brief newspaper account.
4. Make a cast of an animal track.
5. Find out what fossil animals and plants have been found in your state. What do these fossils tell you about changes that have taken place in your state through the ages?
6. Investigate the theories which try to explain how evolution is caused.
7. Investigate theories which try to account for the beginning of life on earth.
8. Make a survey of and write a report on recent discoveries about the evolution of primates, including man.

(Courtesy of Rapho-Guillumette, Hella Hammid.)

CHAPTER 13B

TEACHING "THE HISTORY OF LIFE"

Dinosaurs fire the imaginations of children. A museum trip to see fossils will provoke discussion and raise searching questions. Children often bring petrified wood and fossils to school from gravel pits, quarries, and rock ledges; they bring pictures of fossils from magazines, newspapers, and advertisements. Frequently, local newspapers tell about fossils that have been accidentally discovered.

Although in the study of fossils there are not so many opportunities to experiment with materials as, for example, in the study of sound or electricity, there are many occasions to stress the types of problems that scientists tackle. For example: "Why did dinosaurs become extinct?" "How do we know that the climate has changed and how the oceans were made?" "How can a plant or animal leave a print in hard rock?" "How did life start?"

There are also many opportunities to promote the use of scientific attitudes. For example, why must scientists use such words or phrases as "it seems evident that," "many people believe," "evidence seems to show," "it may be," or "it is generally believed" in telling about the earth's past? There are scores of opportunities to stress the importance of holding conclusions tentatively, of searching for reliable evidence, of not jumping to conclusions. There are many opportunities for reading and reporting.

SOME BROAD CONCEPTS: "The History of Life"

Changes in the kinds of living things on the earth have been from the simple organisms to complex ones.

Changes have been very slow.

Physical conditions on the earth have changed greatly through the ages.

Many animals and plants that once lived on the earth have become extinct.

Fossils tell us many things about past life and conditions on the earth.

The earth is very old.

FOR YOUNGER CHILDREN

Unlike material about living things the study of ancient animals and plants presents some unique problems for younger children. Time sequence and slow change are difficult for very young children to understand. Here, however, are some suggestions that have been tried successfully in early grades. They can also be used at any level.

What Is a Fossil?

If possible, make available for examination by children some small fossils—leaf prints, shell prints, and so on. Ask them to examine these carefully to see what they can discover by using their senses. Feel them. Lift them. Try to scratch them. Look carefully at them. Tell what you think these are. "How did the prints get there?" "How could a print get into something hard like this?" Children share their ideas.

"Could we make prints like this (*see* later suggestions in chapter)?" "Where do you think these came from?" "Can we find fossils near our school?"

What Were the Dinosaurs Like that Lived Long Ago?

The most exciting fossils for children are the dinosaurs. Many museums, even small local ones, have examples or collections of dinosaurs. Give children time to examine the giant fossils and later an opportunity to tell about what they saw and to ask questions. Help them read the labels and explanations.

If a trip is not possible, or to supplement it, use pictures and models of dinosaurs (*see* Bibliography). Children may listen as descriptions of the giant animals are read, and discuss their ideas. Supplement the visit and the examination of pictures and models by a discussion of what "long ago" means. Start with children's ages, adult ages, how old their town is, and other ages that may be a basis on which to build the concept of "long ago." This, like distances in space, is most difficult for children (and teachers!) to comprehend.

OTHER PROBLEMS FOR YOUNGER CHILDREN

1. What can we tell by looking at a dinosaur skeleton?
2. What do fossils tell us?
3. What were the dinosaurs like?
4. How do we know about dinosaurs?
5. What happened to the dinosaurs?

FOR OLDER CHILDREN

What Fossils Can We Find?

Finding fossils may be a first step in developing interest and arousing curiosity in children. Some fossils will be found in a "natural" state in many localities. Many are to be found in large and small museums, and some are found in the limestone of buildings in the community.

Children are interested in such questions as: "What kinds of fossils are found in our surroundings?" "How old are they?" "How were they formed?" "Are they like any plants or animals living today?" "What were our surroundings like when these animals lived?"

A nearby stone quarry, gravel pit, or ocean shore may be a good place to find fossils in their "natural" state. Try to find a person who knows something about the place and ask him to accompany you and the class if you plan a trip. Let pupils formulate questions to answer and list things they might find. If it does not seem advisable for all pupils to go, certain interested pupils may wish to take the trip and

The study of a real fossil obtained from a local source begins with observing and recording. The collector supplies additional information if possible. An authentic specimen is a great motivator. (*Courtesy of Phyllis Marcuccio.*)

report to the class. (For other suggestions for field trips refer to Chapter 3.)

The museum trip also needs preplanning. If possible, obtain the services of a person at the museum to accompany the class. The guide can help you find any published material about fossils and early geology in your state. If pupils have collected fossils they may take them along to the museum for examination. The resource person can explain how he can identify the specimens and will answer other questions. The museum or your local library may have a file of newspaper clippings that describe local or state fossil discoveries. Frequently the museum's curator is willing to give the school some common fossils or duplicates of his collection. These may be the beginning of a school fossil collection.

Limestone is formed underwater from materials derived from the shells of marine animals. Sometimes their fossil remains are left in the rock. When it is used in buildings these small fossils can sometimes be observed.

How Are Casts and Prints Made?

Making a cast of a sea shell may help pupils to better understand how fossils are formed. Place a layer of modeling clay in the bottom of a cardboard box. Press a clam shell into the clay to make a deep print. Carefully lift the shell out so that a clear print is left. Make a thick paste of plaster of Paris, add a little salt or vinegar to keep it from hardening too quickly, and pour the mixture into the shell print. When the paste hardens, you have a cast of the shell. Children should understand that a real fossil cast was made when the animal or plant made a print of itself in mud or other soft material and then decayed. The space was subsequently filled with material that later hardened somewhat as the plaster of Paris did. Pupils can make a cast of the footprint of a pet dog or cat.

Making a print of a sea shell will also help to develop the idea of how some fossils were formed. Make a thick paste of plaster of Paris. A milk carton can be used to hold the plaster. Cover some shells with a thin film of Vaseline to keep them from sticking, and cover them with the plaster. Let the plaster harden, then break it open to see the prints of the shells. It is important to compare this method of print-making with the way in which real fossil prints were made. Unless this is done, such activities are mostly busy work.

How Are Layers of Rock Formed in the Earth?

"What would happen if we put some soil, sand, pebbles, and smaller stones in a jar of water?" "What will happen if we shake this mixture?" "What will happen if we let it stand?" After children have made some predictions let them try the activity and observe what happens, and explain their observations.

The settling *resembles* the sedimentation that occurs in lakes and oceans. In some cases the weight of materials piling up over centuries (plus other factors) causes the material to harden into rock.

Pupils can observe the layers of rock and of soil in a cut in a road nearby and tell which layers they think might be the oldest and why they think so. If there are fossils in these layers where would the older ones be? Near the top or bottom? Can pupils explain why. In addition to seeing such layers they may be able to find—in geography books, in the *National Geographic Magazine*, in travel folders, and elsewhere—pictures of mountains and canyons that will help them to get an understanding of what the earth under their feet is like. Children may recall having seen rock layers in mountains when they traveled.

How Can We Make Models of Dinosaurs?

Dinosaurs are wonderful subjects for modeling, and pupils seem to like to model them in clay or in papier-mâché. If the models are to be successful from a science point of view they should be as nearly accurate as possible in structure and proportion details. If dinosaurs are to be placed in the natural habitat in which they were found, further study of text and pictures is necessary to insure an accurate result. This is a sensible situation in which art and science may well make use of each other.

If various models are made to the same scale (including one of modern man) children will be able to compare their sizes more easily. The dimensions of some ancient animals seem either unbelievable or incomprehensible to children. Many children have no very clear idea of how high, for example, 30 feet is. Try measuring some of these proportions and try to decide whether the animal could fit into the schoolroom, see over the school building, stretch the length of the corridor, or fit into the principal's office.[1] Estimating distances, sizes, and other measurements in the metric system is one way to get acquainted with the system.

In addition to model-making, pupils may enjoy drawing large pictures of ancient birds, amphibians, mammals, and plants, and organizing the pictures to show important ideas.

OTHER PROBLEMS FOR OLDER CHILDREN

1. How can we tell the age of a fossil?
2. What were the earliest animals and plants like?
3. How have living things changed through the ages?
4. Why is the work of paleontologists important?
5. Where are the large deposits of fossils in the United States?
6. What changes would a water-living plant or animal need to make in order to live on land?
7. How did life begin on the earth?
8. For what are the LaBrea tar pits in California famous?

Resources to Investigate with Children

1. The local, state, college, or university museums to look at fossils collected nearby. Sometimes such institutions lend collections to schools.

[1]G.O. Blough, *Discovering Dinosaurs* (New York, McGraw-Hill, Inc., 1960).

2. Newspapers and magazines for pictures and accounts of recent fossil discoveries.
3. A place where the highway cuts through a hill to observe layers of soil and various rock formations.
4. The state geologist and publications from his office and from local geological societies to learn about local land forms, rocks, fossils, and mineral deposits.
5. A local individual who makes a hobby of rock or fossil collecting.
6. Gravel pits, beaches, and other places that often yield fossils of different kinds.
7. Local environment to find club mosses and horsetails, which are examples of present-day plants that are very small but were once of huge proportions.

Preparing to Teach

1. Make a "teaching collection" of pictures that can be used in solving the problems in this chapter, and make brief plans about how to use them.
2. Select one of the "Other Problems" listed for younger or older children in the chapter and make a long-range plan for developing it with children (*see* Part I for suggestions).
3. Try to make a small collection of fossils that you can use in teaching.
4. Write to the Superintendent of Documents, Government Printing Office, Washington, D.C. 20402, for *Geology* price list no. 15 to obtain material useful in teaching the material in this chapter.
5. Find out how your state or community feels about teaching the concepts of evolution. At the elementary-school level children need not deal with a possible "conflict" between the teachings of science and those of religion, for they probably do not yet have the background to discuss the issues. But it is important for teachers to inform themselves regarding the various interpretations involved in the questions now being raised by concerned members of the community so that they can react intelligently if and when the need arises.

CHAPTER 14A

ECOLOGY AND SURVIVAL

We travel together, passengers on a little spaceship, dependent on its vulnerable reserves of air and soil; all committed for our safety to its security and peace; preserved from annihilation only by the care, and the work, and, I will say, the love we give our fragile craft.

—*Adlai Stevenson*, 1965

(*Courtesy of Union Pacific Railroad.*)

The concept of *Earth as a spaceship* is perhaps one of the most significant achievements of the Space Age. From the moon we view our planet whole, a tiny blue-white sphere in space. A closer view reveals that life on this sphere is confined to a very thin layer, only 13 miles thick, of air, water, and soil. We call this sun-bathed zone the *biosphere* or *ecosphere.*

The manned vehicles that we launch into space are equipped with life-supporting systems to provide food, water, air, and suitable temperatures. Provision is made for the removal of waste. On extended trips of the future these wastes would not be ejected as they are now, they would have to be recycled for reuse. The number of passengers that could be carried would be limited to the resources available for them.

Until comparatively recently we have regarded the Earth and its bounties as *limitless.* The earth spaceship concept compels us to recognize that the air, water, soil, and space for living are *limited and perishable.*

The spaceship concept says more than that. A spaceship is a closely interrelated and interacting system. If any one part breaks down the entire ship is threatened. If the oxygen supply falls (as it did on the Apollo XIII flight in 1970) not only is the passengers' vital air supply in danger but the oxygen-requiring fuel cells which produce electricity for all the other subsystems also are endangered. Anything that happens on the spaceship affects everything, from the moisture in the exhaled breath of the passengers to their individual behavior on the journey.

Spaceship Earth is a system with many interconnected transactions of materials and energy. The wastes of animals are food for soil bacteria; the excretions of the bacteria provide minerals for green plants; plants are food for animals. What happens in forests, fields, and lakes eventually affects the environment of the entire earth, its atmosphere, its soils and its waters, and consequently all living things. Our planet is a closed system in which indefinite expansion or exploitation of its resources would be disastrous to all life, including that of man.

As Norman Cousins has stated so precisely:

"The real meaning of the human expedition to the moon, if it is written correctly, is that the conditions required to sustain human life are so rare in the universe as to constitute the greatest achievement of creation. Yet the prime beneficiaries of this bounty are now engaged in converting their habitat into a wasteland, not less uncongenial to life than the surface of the moon. The biggest challenge of all, therefore, is to prove that intelligent life can exist on Earth.[1]

It is the responsibility of all engaged in teaching, at all levels, of all subjects, in school and out of school, to meet this challenge with planned programs of environmental education.

INCIDENT AT DONORA

On the morning of October 26, 1948, at Donora, Pa., the skies delivered a deadly warning that man had poisoned them beyond endurance.

As workers trudged to their jobs, a heavy fog blanketed the bleak and grimy town. It hung suspended in the stagnant air while local businesses—steel mills, a wire factory, zinc and coke plants—continued to spew waste gases, zinc fumes, coal smoke and fly ash into the lowering darkness. The atmosphere thickened. Grime began to fall out of the smog, covering homes, sidewalks and streets with a black coating in which pedestrians and automobiles left distinct footprints and tire tracks. Within forty-eight hours, visibility had become so bad that residents had difficulty finding their way home.

Donora's doctors were soon besieged by coughing, wheezing patients, complaining of shortness of breath, running noses, smarting eyes, sore throats and nausea. During the next four days, before a heavy rain washed away the menacing shroud, five thousand nine hundred and ten of the town's fourteen thousand residents became ill. Twenty persons—and an assortment of dogs, cats and canaries—died.

Time, January 27, 1967

The death rate in Donora leaped from an average of two for this period to twenty.

The Donora incident is but one of a number of mass tragedies that are shocking us into the realization that a pollutant-producing society can so diminish the quality of its environment that life itself is endangered.

Perhaps it is fortunate that none can escape

[1]"The Search for Intelligent Life," *Saturday Review,* August 9, 1969.

llution, for the universality of this evil is g us more and more aware that we cannot ... the environment for granted. With smarting eyes, clogged sinuses, and irritated lungs and throats city dwellers are asking each other:

What is wrong?
How did it get that way?
What should be done?
What can I do?
What will it cost?

These are the questions we must ask about all the resources that make Earth the planet with life on it.

THE ENVIRONMENTAL CRISIS

> . . . Only within the moment of time represented by the present century has one species—man—acquired significant power to alter the nature of his world. During the past quarter century this power has not only increased to one of disturbing magnitude, but it has changed in character. The most alarming of man's assaults upon the environment is the contamination of air, earth, rivers and sea with dangerous and even lethal materials.
>
> —Rachel Carson

The crisis which faces us today is deeper than the threatened depletion of a particular resource, the loss of some areas of unspoiled nature, or even the serious question of feeding ourselves adequately. What is the nature of the environmental crisis?

1. The advance of technology, which has brought us high-powered automobiles, chemical fertilizers, plastics, synthetic fibers, and electric power has reached a level where its processes and products threaten the earth's environment. "We are in an environmental crisis because the means by which we use the ecosphere to produce wealth are destructive of the ecosphere itself."[2] More prosaically, we are killing the goose that lays the golden eggs.
2. The environmental crisis is global in nature. The oceans and atmosphere have no boundaries as they distribute life-destroying pollutants to people everywhere. The whole earth is everybody's environment. We can no longer escape an undesirable environment by packing up and moving on.
3. We are in a crisis because time for taking the necessary corrective measures for survival seems to be running out. How many years or decades do we have to effect a reversal or slowing of the current downhill slide to avert disaster? How much contamination can the oceans accept before they die—as did Lake Erie? And if the oceans die, and with them the oxygen-producing algae, how long can life exist anywhere?
4. We are in a crisis today because economists, legislators, manufacturers, and farmers do not fully understand the nature of man's relation to his total environment. Because our schools, in the decades when the crisis has been growing, have not engaged in vital, imaginative programs of environmental education. Because the concept of "conquering nature" still prevails. Because the ethic that we are the custodians rather than the owners of the earth's resources and that each generation has the obligation to pass this inheritance on to the future is not part of our code. Because many still believe that unlimited growth is a good thing. Because we have not yet earnestly gotten into the business of planetary planning.

[2]B. Commoner: *The Closing Circle* (New York: Alfred A. Knopf, 1972).

ECOLOGY: KEY TO CONSERVATION

> From Nature's chain, whatever link you strike
> Tenth, or ten-thousandth, breaks the chain alike.
>
> —Alexander Pope, *Essay on Man*

The understanding of *ecology,* the study of the interrelationships of living things with each other and of living things with their physical environment, is the key to sound environmental practices.

Barry Commoner defines ecology in an informal set of "laws":

1. *Everything is connected to everything else.*
2. *Everything must go somewhere.*
3. *Nature knows best.*
4. *There is no such thing as a free lunch.*

As you read the remainder of this chapter, look for illustrations of these laws.

The diet of an Eskimo in his natural surroundings consists largely of seal meat, fish, and birds. All these food sources are ultimately dependent on tiny plants that live in the sea. Let us see how. The seals and birds feed on fish. The fish feed on smaller fish. Little fish feed on copepods, tiny relatives of the shrimp. Copepods feed on microscopic one-celled plants, called diatoms, which live near the surface of the sea. Diatoms are green plants that are able to make their own food by the process of photosynthesis. Hence, the diet of an Eskimo depends on diatoms.

(See pp. 280–2.)

This is a long chain, a chain of "who-eats-whom." Ecologists call it a *food chain.* The elimination of any link in it would mean the elimination of the Eskimo. If, for example, some act of man, such as the pouring of a quantity of radioactive waste into the sea, were to destroy the diatoms, it would inevitably mean the elimination of the Eskimo in his natural environment.

Consider another food chain, one closer to home. In a field green plants are eaten by meadow mice, which in turn are preyed upon by hawks. The green plants are the *producers:* They manufacture the food. The meadow mouse is a *consumer;* it feeds directly on the plants, so it is a *first-order consumer.* The hawk in this food chain is a *second-order consumer.*

(See pp. 465–6.)

A food chain: who—eats—whom.

The concept of producer and consumer in the world of nature is a helpful one, because it reminds us that food is not manufactured in canneries or frozen-food factories. When we say that a green plant is a producer, we mean that it takes simple nonliving material—water, carbon dioxide, and minerals—from its environment and juggles the atoms in these substances to put together the organic molecules of food needed for its own nutrition. (It is a mistake to call the minerals we use to enrich soil "plant food"; minerals are essentially raw materials that a plant incorporates in the food it makes.)

The food-making process that sustains the chain of life is dependent on the nonliving environment—the physical environment—of carbon dioxide in the air, and water and minerals in the soil. To these materials must be added *energy,* the energy of the sun which is incorporated into every food molecule that is put together in the green leaf "factory." Other features of the physical environment—temperature, space, gravity, wind, oxygen, together with those previously named—are important influences in the total living of all the organisms in the chain.

Eventually death overtakes the plants and meadow mice that survive the who-eats-whom process; even the predatory hawk succumbs. The return of the tissues of these organisms to the soil is the work of the microscopic bacteria and fungi of decay. They, too, are consumers, but because of their unique role in the economy of nature, it is helpful to call them *decomposers.*

Thus the food chain is an endless one: producer → consumer → decomposer → producer, and so on. Food is the medium through which the materials needed for the construction of body tissues and the energy for life processes are passed along the chain.

Food Webs

We have elected so far to construct an artificially simple chain. In the field we started with, the green plants are also eaten by rabbits and insects, which join the mice as first-order con-

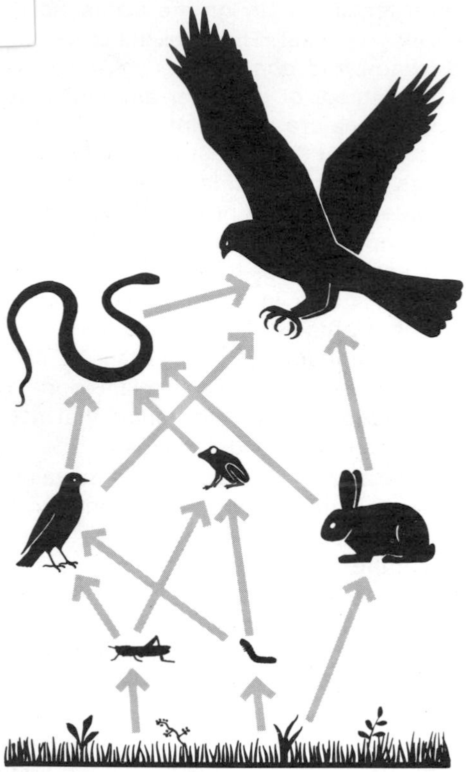

A simple food web suggests the complex interrelationships of living things.

sumers. The insects may be eaten by toads, the toads by snakes, the snakes by hawks. The rabbit, too, may be preyed upon by hawks. And the field mouse may be eaten by a snake. The simple food chain begins to branch to become a *food web,* which is much closer to the true pattern of nature.

Implicit in food chains and webs is a natural system of checks and balances. If for some reason the field mice multiply rapidly their numbers will be diminished by predation by hawks. Man can disturb the balance. The killing of hawks by farmers may result in an increase in meadow mice (and other rodents) harmful to his crops.

Pyramid of Numbers

The food chain tells us "who eats whom," but it does not tell us enough. We must also know "how much." Apply this question to the simple plant-meadow mouse-hawk chain but disregard the many other strands of the food web in a field. There must be more plants in the field than will be consumed by the meadow mice, or all green life there will be destroyed. There must be more mice than will be eaten by hawks; otherwise the hawks will finish the mice in one last meal.

If we express the quantity of living matter in this field in pounds we might find that 1,000 pounds of grass supports 50 pounds of mice, which in turn supports 10 pounds of hawks. (In each step we are also assuming that enough individuals survive to reproduce a new genera-

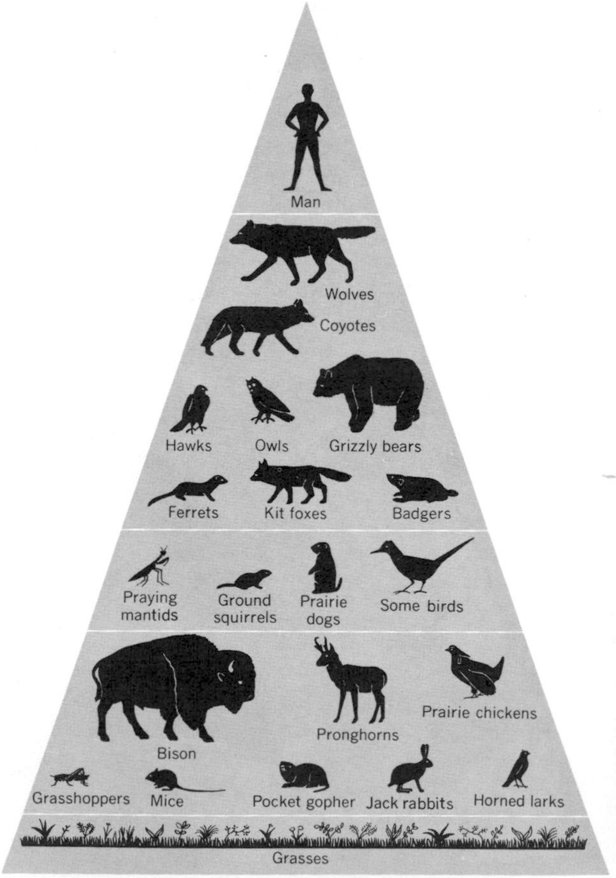

The pyramid of life on a prairie. Each level depends on the broader one under it for a supply of food. (*Based on a diagram in* Pyramid of Life *by Edith Raskin, McGraw-Hill, 1967.*)

tion.) A pyramid of numbers with a broad base of vegetation at the bottom and hawks at the apex summarizes the quantitative interrelationships in this small community.

Ecologists have constructed pyramids for large regions called *biomes,* which are communities of living things associated with a particular kind of vegetation typical of the area. The tundra of the arctic, the tropical rainforest, and the grassland are examples of biomes. A grassland or prairie pyramid is shown.

NATURE'S RECYCLING SYSTEMS

On Spaceship Earth we enjoy the advantages of an automatic self-renewing natural environment of water, air, and soil. Evolving over billions of years of Earth's history, the environment is in tune with the plants and animals that inhabit it. It can keep itself going indefinitely, barring a man-made ecological disaster.

The Water Cycle

The water cycle is one of Nature's great recycling systems. Water evaporates into the atmosphere from the surface of the ocean and other bodies of water, from soil, and the leaves of plants. In the atmosphere it is held as invisible water vapor, which under certain conditions forms clouds. The water in clouds falls back to the surface of the earth as rain or snow, eventually working its way back to lakes, seas, and oceans and thus completing the cycle. The process continues without end.

(*See* p. 466.)

The water cycle, then, circulates water from oceans, seas, and lakes to land areas. It also serves as a water-purification system, because when water evaporates to become water vapor it leaves behind minerals, mud, and debris. The water that falls from the clouds is relatively pure and clean.

The Carbon Dioxide-Oxygen Cycle

The carbon dioxide-oxygen cycle is driven by the complementary life processes of green plants and animals. In the process of food-making green plants take in carbon dioxide from the atmosphere and, with energy derived from sunlight, use it in the manufacture of starches, sugars, and other foods. The food-manufacturing process also results in the release of oxygen by plants. Animals consume plants, or part of them, and breathe in oxygen. The "burning" of food by animals (and to a lesser extent by plants) results in the release of carbon dioxide, thereby

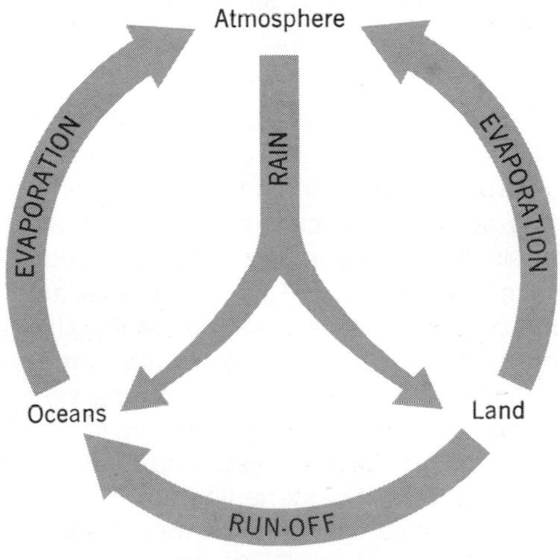

The Water Cycle.

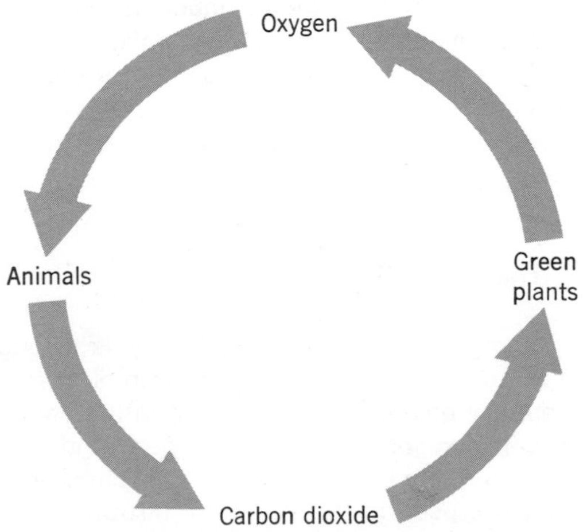

The Oxygen-Carbon Dioxide Cycle.

making it available again for the food-making process in green plants.

A similar exchange between plants and animals takes place in ponds, lakes, and in the oceans, but the oxygen and carbon dioxide there are dissolved in the water.

Bacteria also participate in the carbon dioxide-oxygen cycle. When plants and animals die, bacteria of decay break down their tissues, using them as food. In releasing energy from the food, bacteria take in oxygen and release carbon dioxide.

In Chapter 9A we noted that a special form of oxygen, known as ozone (O_3) in the upper atmosphere absorbs much of the ultraviolet light from the sun and is therefore protective of life in the biosphere below. Should the ozone content of the biosphere be diminished, life would be threatened by an increase in ultraviolet radiation. Some ecologists contend that the exhaust products of supersonic transport planes may affect the protective layer of ozone. Further discussion of the atmosphere appears later in this chapter. A camera stationed on the moon by the Apollo 16 mission and aimed at the earth has furnished data which supports the idea that photosynthesis by green plants may not be the only source of atmospheric oxygen. Initial findings suggest that solar radiation acting on water vapor (H_2O) in the upper atmosphere may provide a primary supply of oxygen.

There is evidence that the oxygen in the atmosphere was originally put there by early plant life. The free oxygen made possible the evolution of higher plants and animals. Today the supply of oxygen in the atmosphere is continually replenished by the process of photosynthesis, which as we have seen, also removes carbon dioxide from the air.

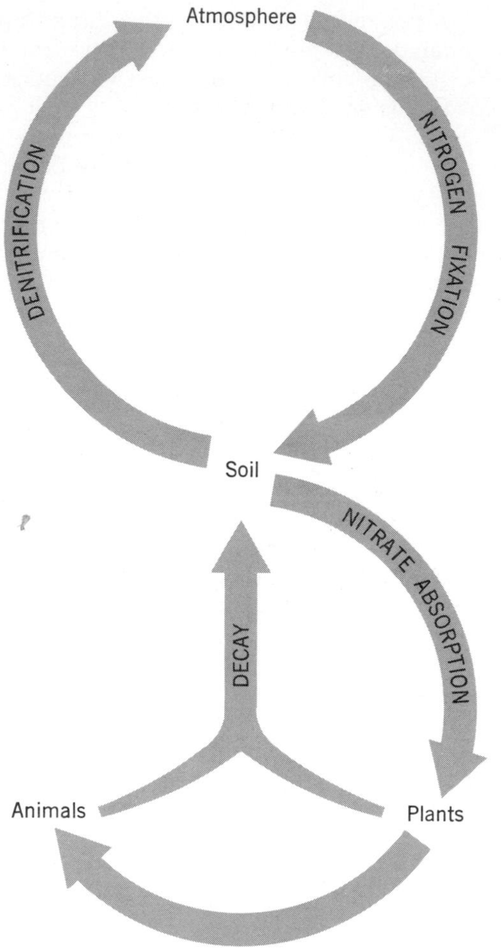

The Nitrogen Cycle.

The Nitrogen Cycle

Nitrogen moves in a complex cycle through the atmosphere, soil, and living things. It is an essential element for life, entering into combination with oxygen, carbon, hydrogen, and other elements in the construction of the amino acids, which are used in thousands of structures and vital processes in plants and animals. Proteins, nucleic acids, vitamins, enzymes, and hormones are all made of nitrogen-containing molecules.

Nitrogen is plentiful in the atmosphere, comprising about 79 percent of it, but it cannot be taken in by plants in this free gaseous form. Atmospheric nitrogen becomes available to plants only when it is combined with other elements to form soluble nitrogen compounds, notably nitrates. This process, *nitrogen-fixation,* is the work of certain bacteria which live on the roots of clover, beans, peas, and alfalfa and in the soil. Other soil bacteria liberate nitrates from plant and animal remains as they break down their tissues.

Plants absorb nitrates from the soil through their roots, and build the nitrogen in them into amino acids, which form the basis for the protein compounds necessary for their growth and functioning. Animals eat the plants and use the amino acids in them to make the kind of protein that they need. In nature, animal wastes and decomposed animal remains return nitrogen compounds to the soil and thus make them available again for the plant world. Some of the soil bacteria break down nitrates and release nitrogen to the air. So the cycle is complete.

Eutrophication

The web of life in a body of fresh water is self-sustaining. Algae provide food and oxygen for small organisms, which are eaten by frogs, fish, and other larger forms. The animals return carbon dioxide to the water; algae use carbon dioxide in photosynthesis to make more food. Bacteria of decay break down animal waste and return inorganic nitrates and phosphates for the growth of fresh algae.

The growth of algae in a pond or lake is controlled by three chief plant nutrients: carbon dioxide, nitrates, and phosphates. An excess of any of these may trigger an algal "bloom," a large, dense growth of algae. As the thickness of the layers of algae increases, less light reaches the lower parts of the growth. Any additional growth dies quickly. The decay bacteria that feed and multiply on the dead algae use up available oxygen for their own respiration, reducing the oxygen supply of the pond. Then the bacteria die, since they too need and cannot get oxygen. Fish and other organisms die. The fresh water ecological cycle collapses. This process is called *eutrophication.*

During recent years the volume of algae in many lakes has increased greatly for two reasons: (1.) farmers are using increased millions of tons of commercially manufactured nitrate fertilizer to restore soil fertility and increase agricultural productivity. The widespread use of nitrates on farmland sometimes results in an excessive runoff of these nitrogen compounds into streams and lakes. (2.) the increased use of phosphates, both in fertilizers in agriculture and in home and industrial use in detergents, increases the amount of this substance in rivers and lakes.

Thus it is as easy to disrupt a community by promoting growth as it is by reducing it. Eutrophication is followed by many unpleasant and dangerous consequences: making formerly clear water smelly, muddy, undrinkable; the gradual replacement of desirable fish with less edible ones; massive dieoffs resulting in beaches littered with foul-smelling algae and dead fish.

Cycles and the Environment

The water cycle, carbon dioxide-oxygen cycle, and the nitrogen cycle are but three of the many cycles which make our planet habitable. To quote from an article by Barry Commoner: "Altogether this vast web of biological interactions generates the very physical system in which we live: the soil and the air. It maintains the purity of surface waters and, by governing the movement of water in the soil and its evaporation into the air, regulates the weather. This is the environment. It is a place created by living things, maintained by living things, and through the marvelous reciprocities of biological evolution is essential to the support of living things."[3]

THE ENDURANCE OF RESOURCES

Inexhaustible Resources

The resources of the earth are of four kinds: inexhaustible, renewable, nonrenewable, and new and to-be-developed.

Some resources we shall have always. These are air, sunlight, and water. They are unique in that much as man may use them they continue in abundance. Water is such a resource. As long as the oceans cover the earth we shall have water. Lifted (with the help of the sun's warming rays) from the ocean as vapor that eventually falls as rain it is available for agriculture, industry, and for our personal needs. Dropping from falls water can be used as a source of power. Limit-

[3] *Damaged Global Fabric,* in *Our World in Peril: An Environment Review,* Sheldon Novick and Dorothy Cottrell, eds. (Greenwich, Conn.: Fawcett Publications, Inc.).

less though it is, water presents some of our most pressing problems of conservation. These are mainly problems of its quality, distribution, and use, as we shall see later in this chapter.

Although we include air and water as inexhaustible resources we are not excluding the grim possibility that we may diminish the quality of these resources beyond the point of no return. *Breathable* air and *drinkable* water are not necessarily inexhaustible.

Sunlight is the source of all our energy, except for nuclear energy from radioactive atoms on earth. Water power results, as we have just seen, from lifting of water with the help of the sun's energy; fossil fuels, such as coal and oil, are the products of the sun's radiant energy stored by plants in past times. Solar energy is used directly in solar cells which convert sunlight directly into electricity in solar furnaces and in homes heated by sunlight. Astronomers assure us that the sun will continue to be our powerhouse for at least a few billion years more.

Renewable Resources

Renewable resources are our soils, vegetation, animal life, and freshwater supplies. These are the resources that may be maintained indefinitely under wise management. It is to these resources that the past efforts of conservation have been mainly directed.

The renewable resources are dependent one on the other. Crops will not grow in soil without water. Animals play an important role in the life cycle of many plants and vice-versa. We need mention here only the pollinating work of the bee. Forests and grasslands store water and also prevent harmful rain runoff. Plant cover provides essential protection of the soil against erosion by water and wind. Weaken one link and the whole life-supporting chain is imperiled.

(*See* pp. 457–8, 468–70.)

Man is in a key position to keep this chain in working balance. The fields can continue to produce healthy crops each year if he maintains and improves the fertility of the soil. Forests can be managed to assure a perpetual yield of wood, a steady flow of water, and a constant source of pleasure. Game and other animal life can be helped to renew itself and to continue its role in the web of life.

Nonrenewable Resources

The nonrenewable resources are those that can be used up. Such materials as coal, oil, natural gas, metals, and most minerals are of this nature. When copper is mined, new copper will not "grow" in its place. When a lump of coal is burned, it is gone forever as a burnable material. All of our conventional fuels, except wood, fall into the category of resources that become unavailable once they are used.

Land as open space may be regarded as a nonrenewable resource. Once covered with concrete and steel it is "gone" as land for growing things. Wilderness once destroyed is a nonrenewable resource. The 2 million acres of the magnificent primeval redwoods of California have been reduced to $\frac{1}{4}$ million acres. The continued existence of this remnant of wilderness in a meaningful redwood national park is still in the balance at this writing.

Government and industry are tackling the problem of the conservation of our mineral and fuel resources in a number of ways: by finding new sources of material, by seeking new materials, by minimizing waste, and by learning how to use materials more effectively. Geologists are prospecting in every corner of the globe for new supplies. When deposits near the surface of the earth are depleted, men dig deeper into the earth. Wells have been drilled under the ocean to tap the petroleum and sulfur found there. Chemists have found how to extract magnesium and bromine from ocean waters in commercial quantity and at a marketable price. Scientists are learning how to utilize low-grade ores (such as taconite, with its relatively small percentage of iron) as higher grades become scarcer. New ways are being discovered of preventing rusting and corrosion, thus extending the life of the finished products.

Further discussion of nonrenewable resources will be found in the next section, "The Limits to Growth."

New and To-Be-Developed Resources

Less than a century ago crude oil was considered a useless substance. Less than 50 years ago some scientists were saying that the atom could never be split. Yet what enormous sources of energy we have been able to release from the molecules of gasoline and from the nuclei of atoms! New resources will be added as the skill and creativity of scientists and engineers discover uses for materials that may be of little or of no value today, or may presently be inaccessible. Perhaps, also, we shall be able to add to our resources those of the moon, or of Earth's sister planets.

To evaluate the new resources fairly it is essential to recognize that some, such as plastics, present serious problems of waste disposal and environmental pollution in contrast to the biodegradable products (those that decompose and enter into nature's recycling systems), such as paper and wood.

THE LIMITS TO GROWTH

How long can the world's population and industrialization continue to grow? This is the question that a team of researchers of the Club of Rome have addressed themselves to. The Club of Rome grew out of a 1968 meeting of 30 individuals from 10 countries—scientists, educators, economists, industrialists, and others. By 1972 it had a membership of approximately 70 persons of 25 nationalities. A research team of the Club investigated five major trends of global concern: accelerating industrialization, rapid population growth, widespread malnutrition, depletion of nonrenewable resources, and the deteriorating environment. The team fed information based on past and present trends into a computer in order to forecast the future.

These were the conclusions of the study:

1. If the present growth trends in world population, industrialization, pollution, food production, and resource depletion continue unchanged, the limits to growth on this planet will be reached some time within the next 100 years. The most probable results will be a rather sudden and uncontrollable decline in both population and industrial capacity.
2. It is possible to alter these growth trends and to establish a condition of ecological and economic stability that is sustainable far into the future. The state of global equilibrium could be designed so that the basic material needs of each person on earth are satisfied and each person has an equal opportunity to realize his individual human potential.
3. If the world's people decide to strive for the second outcome rather than the first the sooner they begin working to attain it, the greater will be their chances of success.[4]

Let us consider some of the areas of the Report's concern. (The following does not constitute a summary of the Report, nor does it necessarily reflect its viewpoint. The reader is referred to the Report itself for a complete statement.)

Population

In 1650 the earth's population was about $\frac{1}{2}$ billion; at that time it was growing at a rate which would result in a doubling every 250 years. In 1970 the population was 3.6 billion and it is now growing at a rate which will double the population every 33 years. By the year 2000 a population of about 7 billion is anticipated. If we continue to succeed in lowering mortality without lowering fertility, in 60 years there will be 4 people in the world for every 1 person living today.

In evaluating the impact of population growth one must recognize not only that there are more humans but that the world consumption of resources *per person* is steadily increasing. The question then is: How many population-doubling periods can the earth sustain?

The Commission of Population Growth and the American Future, established by the President and Congress in July 1969 released one part of its Report in March 1972, which concludes:

[4]Donella H. Meadows, Dennis L. Meadows, Jorgen Randers, William W. Behrnes III: *The Limits to Growth: A Report for the Club of Rome's Project on the Predicament of Mankind* (New York: Universe Books, 1972).

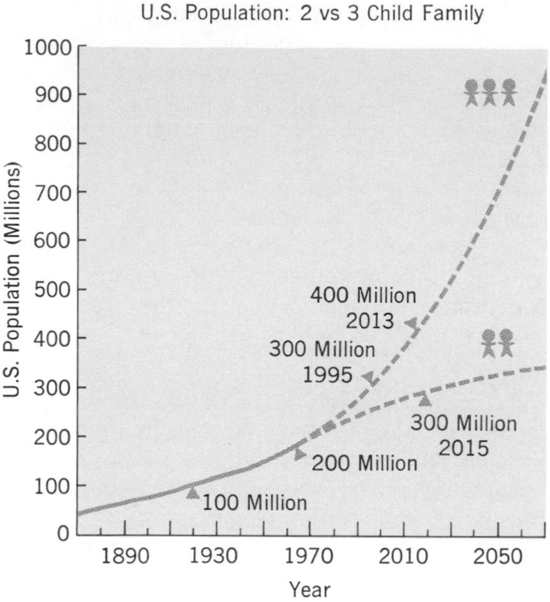

What the future population of the United States will be, based on a 2 versus 3-child family.

> In the long run, no substantial benefits will result from the further growth of the nation's population. Rather, it is our view that population growth of the current magnitude has aggravated many of the nation's problems and made their solution more difficult. . . The time has come for the United States to adopt a deliberate population policy.

When the average number of children per family is kept at 2 a state of zero population will be reached, which, according to the Commission, would benefit society at every level.

Food

The primary resource for producing food is land. The richest half of that land, and the most accessible, is under cultivation today. The remaining arable land will require large capital expenditures to reach, clear, irrigate, and fertilize before it is ready to produce food. But the land factor is not constant; arable land is withdrawn from food production for housing, roads, waste disposal, power lines, and other uses. The potato farms of Long Island are now suburban residential developments. Land is also lost by erosion. At the present rate of population growth and of land requirements there will be a serious land shortage before the year 2000. Even if the total world supply of arable land remained constant and its productivity were doubled or quadrupled the year of land crisis would only be delayed, not averted.

Nonrenewable Resources

Nonrenewable resources include those minerals and fuels which are vital raw materials for industry. The following is the Club of Rome's estimate of the number of years remaining before the supply of each of the resources will be exhausted. The estimate is based on (1.) present and projected use of the resource; (2.) knowledge of known reserves multiplied by 5 to allow for future discoveries. (*See* table below.)

According to the Club even if recycling and better product design were instituted: "as long as . . . population and industrial growth continue to generate more people and a higher resource demand per capita, the system is being pushed toward its limits—the depletion of the earth's non-renewable resources."

Nonrenewable Resources	*Years before Exhaustion*
Aluminum	55
Chromium	154
Coal	150
Copper	48
Iron	173
Lead	64
Natural Gas	49
Nickel	96
Petroleum	50
Silver	42
Tin	61
Zinc	50

Pollution

Pollution is discussed in a number of places in this chapter. The Club of Rome stresses the following:

1. Virtually every pollutant that has been measured appears to be increasing *exponentially.* Exponential growth may be represented by a series such as 1, 2, 4, 8, 16, . . . , in contrast to linear growth, as in the series 1, 2, 3, 4, 5, . . . The rates of increase of different pollutants vary, but most are growing faster than the population. Carbon dioxide, thermal energy (heat), and radioactive waste are just three of the disturbances. These are discussed in the section called "Energy in the Biosphere." The amounts of lead and mercury released into waterways and into the atmosphere from automobiles, incinerators, industrial processes, and agricultural pesticides are growing exponentially.

(*See* pp. 428–31, 458–65.)

2. In the case of land for agricultural purposes and nonrenewable resources growth reaches an upper limit—the total amount of arable land and of nonrenewable resources in our planet. There are, however, no upper bounds for pollution: "It is not known how much carbon dioxide or thermal pollution can be released without causing irreversible changes in the earth's climate, or how much radioactivity, lead, mercury, or pesticides can be absorbed by plants, fish or human beings before the vital processes are severely interrupted."

DDT pollution has attracted a great deal of attention, particularly since the publication of Rachel Carson's *Silent Spring.* DDT is a man-made organic chemical used to control insects by spraying. It can evaporate into the air and eventually fall back on the land, or into rivers and streams, eventually ending up in the ocean. Here the DDT is absorbed by plankton, the microscopic plants and animals living near the surface, which are eaten by small fish; small fish by larger fish; some of the fish are eaten by man. There is a tendency for DDT to become more and more concentrated in the tissues of living organisms as one progresses along food chains.

Even if world use of DDT (now banned in the United States for almost all purposes) were reduced gradually, beginning in 1970, and reaching zero by the year 2000, the DDT level in fish would rise for the next 10 years and not come back to the 1970 level until 1995—more than 20 years after the decision was made to reduce DDT application.

DDT in concentration is dangerous to life. It has increased in the body fat of humans in every part of the earth. Since it will continue to increase after we reduce its use we cannot afford to wait until the harm done is irreversible.

Conclusions

In conclusion the "Limits to Growth" proposes a transition from growth to *global equilibrium* by deliberate constraints on the growth of population, on industrial output, on pollution, and on the use of resources. The population and the stocks of capital—industrial, agricultural, and service—would remain constant.

A *Blueprint for Survival,*[5] issued in 1972 by 33 British scientists and philosophers, raised similar questions to those just discussed. The *Blueprint* calls for a move toward a "stable society," with limits on population and the use of resources, instead of industrialization and growth. Only in this way will we avoid ecological catastrophe in our children's lifetime, if not in our own.

A World-Wide Debate

The Limits to Growth and *Blueprint for Survival* have precipitated a world debate that will go on for a long time. Adverse criticism of these reports from various sources is presented here without comment:

1. The reports underestimate the capacity of the world to adjust to problems of scarcity.
2. To stop growth now would mean freezing the poor and the underdeveloped nations at their present level.

[5]Potomac Associates, Washington, D.C.

3. The regulations needed to enforce the national and world-wide measures envisioned in the reports might destroy our liberties and freedom.
4. The reports underestimate the role of the free market in controlling the production and use of materials. If, for example, we begin to run out of a resource, such as aluminum, the price will go up and reduce its use. Manufacturers will be encouraged to use something else; research and development will be stimulated to produce substitutes.
5. What technology has done to the earth technology can cure.
6. We need more electric power, not less, to carry out ecological measures such as the recycling of wastes, mass transportation, the clean-up of rivers and lakes, and the ending of poverty.

The ongoing debate about the Club of Rome report should, as the New York *Times* suggests (March 2, 1972), alert decision-makers of all ideologies to the urgency of the situation. It is hoped that the debate will have wide repercussions, opening up a new phase of *awareness, inquiry,* and *political action.*

ENERGY IN THE BIOSPHERE

For the past several summers and winters Americans have been confronted with the threat of electrical blackouts and brownouts caused by the extraseasonal drain on electrical energy. But this is more than a seasonal shortage—it is part of a national energy crisis.

Each year we are demanding more and more energy: more petroleum to move cars, trucks, buses, airplanes, and ships; more oil, natural gas, and coal to burn in the furnaces of electricity-producing utilities; more fuel and electricity for homes and industry.

In 1971, 98 percent of the total energy in the United States came from gas, oil, and petroleum, the *fossil fuels.* What is the future of these fuels?

According to the authors of *The Limits to Growth,* if the world's demand for these fuels continues to grow at the present rate then the potential reserves of coal will last 150 years, petroleum 50 years, and natural gas 49 years. (These figures are based on presently known *world* reserves multiplied by five.)

> Our appetite for energy seems to be infinite, but our supply of natural resources is all too finite.[6]

But the increased demand for energy is happening at a time when there is a mounting demand for an environment free from the desolation and pollution left by ugly strip-mining of mountains for coal, free from oil-tanker spills and leaking offshore wells, free from giant power lines cutting bare corridors through the countryside, free from the sulphur oxides and fly ash from the burning of coal, free from the potential perils of radioactivity from nuclear power plants, free from the encroachment on the land and the heat pollution of our waters by giant electric-power generators.

A particular concern arises from the fact that the burning of fossil fuels always produces carbon dioxide. This gas, a normal component of our atmosphere and essential for the food-making processes in green plants, has increased in concentration from 290 parts per million to 320 within the past century. By the year 2000 it will climb to between 375 and 400 parts per million. Scientists fear, for one thing, that the increased carbon dioxide may add to the "hothouse effect" (*see* pp. 518–9) reducing the normal loss of heat from the earth to space, and thereby raising the temperature of the atmosphere. What will this do to our ecology?

In summary, the energy problems of the earth are:

1. How long will our energy resources last?
2. Can new sources of energy be developed?
3. Can energy consumption continue to grow without an accompanying deterioration of the air, water, and land of the biosphere?

Let's turn our attention first to the original source of energy, the sun.

[6]R. E. Lapp: *We're Running Out of Gas* (New York *Times,* March 19, 1972).

The Sun

The sun is the ultimate source of almost all the energy now used in the earth's biosphere. Radiant energy of the sun is captured by chlorophyll in plants and stored in food molecules which are manufactured there in the process of photosynthesis. Later the stored energy is released by plants and by animals which eat the plants as required in their life processes. When you pedal your bicycle along a country road your muscles are releasing sun energy, trapped by photosynthetic plants perhaps only weeks or months ago and incorporated into the breakfast you ate this morning: the starch recently made in a corn or wheat plant, the milk from the cow which ate grass a few days before.

When primitive people learned to use fire to keep themselves warm they took the first step toward making use of an energy resource—wood—outside their own bodies. Wood, a product of plant life, is also a sun-energized resource.

Later in history the windmill and waterwheel were invented to supply extra power. Here, too, the source of energy was the sun, the driver of the "weather machine" which keeps air and water in motion.

Only in the last 125 years have we made important use of the fossil fuels—coal, oil, and natural gas. These had their origin in ancient plant and animal remains, whose molecules were first put together with the help of the sun's radiation.

In 1850 the dominant energy source was fuel wood; by 1910 75 percent of the total energy consumed came from coal, while fuel wood declined to only 10 percent. Between 1910 and 1960 natural gas and oil overtook coal.

(*See* Ch. 17A.)

Today a new source of energy, independent of the sun, is being used: This is atomic, or more properly nuclear, energy.

Nuclear Energy

It would seem that nuclear energy should be an answer to the power crisis. Nuclear reactors now produce 1.4 percent of the nation's electricity. By 1980 the figure is expected to be 25 percent. And by the year 2000 about 50 percent.

The present nuclear reactors obtain heat energy from the splitting of an extremely scarce form of uranium: U-235. There is danger of its depletion before the end of the century. Plans are now advanced for the construction of a "breeder reactor" which will "create" its own nuclear fuel producing 14 atoms of fissionable plutonium for every 10 atoms consumed. Both the conventional reactor and the breeder reactor, however, produce radioactivity and radioactive wastes, which constitute a potential threat to life. For the future a new kind of plant is projected, using atomic *fusion.* Fusion will produce few troublesome wastes. Is nuclear energy, then, the answer to the energy problem?

(*See* pp. 543–4.)
(*See* pp. 550–1.)

No, because the problem of heat or thermal pollution would still be with us. Let us examine this problem. The surface of the earth is heated by the sun. Ultimately the heat received is radiated back into space, thus maintaining a balance in the heat flow. Industrialization, with its rapid consumption of fuels, has increased the rate at which heat is released. Electric power plants, using nuclear or fossil fuels discharge their waste heat into nearby rivers, lakes, or oceans. Approximately two-thirds of the total energy output from a nuclear power plant is in the form of waste heat, usually discharged into nearby water. Thermal additions affect the aquatic environment adversely in a number of ways of which the following are only a few: Organisms may be killed by sudden exposure to heat; eggs and larvae of many animals are most susceptible. In marine situations commercially important shellfish and kelp beds may be severely damaged. A rise in temperature raises the rate at which fish and other aquatic organisms use oxygen, but at the same time lowers the water's oxygen-carrying capacity. Bacterial decomposition is accelerated, which also reduces the oxygen reserve. There is interference with spawning and other critical stages in the life cycle.

The concentrated generation and consumption of energy in densely populated urban areas may produce enough heat to affect local climate and ecological systems. In the long run thermal pollution may affect the atmosphere of the entire earth, with unforeseen climatic consequences.

In essence this means that even if the supply of fuel for energy is limitless—as it will be if nuclear fusion proves practical—the thermal impact on the environment of converting fuel to electricity and electricity ultimately to heat may be destructive to our environment. According to one projection[7] the rate of heat release in the United States 100 years from now will be almost equal to that which is received by direct radiation from the sun!

What we face, evidently, is the choice of slowing down and stopping our growth in terms of consumed energy, or the use of an energy source that does not add to the earth's heat load.

Here the solar-energy collector is in a stationary orbit. Two solar cell panels convert sunlight into electrical energy which is beamed to a receiving station on earth. (*Courtesy of Arthur D. Little, Inc., Grumman Aerospace Corp., Raytheon Co. and Textron Inc.*)

Other Energy Sources

New methods for harnessing the energy of the wind have been proposed. The daily rise and fall of ocean tides is a source of energy which may be converted into electricity. (A plant which does this is now in operation on the Rance Estuary on the Channel Island coast of France.) Solar cells which convert sunlight directly into electrical energy are already operating on satellites. One proposal for harnessing solar energy on a large scale argues that if the sunlight in 14 percent of the western desert regions of the United States were collected by special solar cells it would provide the amount of additional energy needed between now and 1990. All of the sources—wind, tides, solar energy—have the virtue of not adding to the earth's heat load.

Also proposed is a solar heat collector in a satellite in stationary orbit at a height of 22,300 miles from the earth, where it will rotate at the same rate as the earth itself and thus maintain itself over a fixed point on the earth. Solar cells in a 5 × 5-mile panel would intercept solar energy 24 hours a day and convert it into electricity. Electricity would then be converted into microwaves and beamed at a receiving station on the

[7] Claude M. Summers: *The Conversion of Energy, Scientific American* (September 1971).

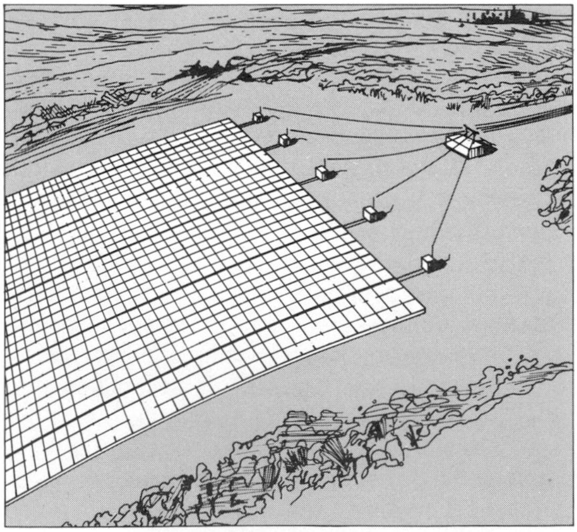

In this proposed design of a solar-energy "farm" the energy of sunlight is converted directly into electricity by solar cells. Shown here is a square-mile array of photovoltaic ("light/voltage") collectors. (*Courtesy of Goddard Space Flight Center, NASA, W.R. Cherry.*)

earth. Here it would be reconverted into electricity. Such a panel, it is calculated, would produce enough electric power to supply New York City.

Although this satellite collector would add to the earth's heat load (it would pick up radiation that would ordinarily miss the earth) it would introduce a smaller waste-heat load into the environment than fossil fuel or nuclear plants. Moreover, such an energy source would be free of other pollutants.

Tapping the heat from molten rocks, magma, under the earth's surface has been proposed (and in several places is now used) as a source of energy. When underground water comes in contact with magma, hot water and steam are produced. Where this occurs within a few miles of the surface and in sufficient quantity the hot water and steam can be trapped and used to turn turbines which power electric generators. In some areas cold water could be piped down, heated, and pumped to the surface. It is probable that tapping the earth's heat, known as *geothermal energy,* would be most successful along the (*See* Ch. 6A.) margins of major crustal plates in regions of volcanic activity, earthquake faults, and mountain building.

In summary, we are faced with the twin problems of quantity of energy and quality of our environment.

> What characterizes the industrial societies is their enormous consumption of energy and the fact that this consumption is primarily at the expense of "capital" rather than of "income," that is, at the expense of solar energy stored in coal, oil and natural gas rather than of solar radiation, water, wind and muscle power.[8]

And, as we have seen, nuclear power as we use it at present, is also based on a capital source, uranium 235.

In the process of consuming capital we are also adding toxic substances to the environment even in those "islands" of relative isolation from industrial pollutants. A study prepared by the Environmental Protection Agency of the United States in 1972 warned that the once high air quality of the southwest "will be increasingly and significantly degraded" by projected electric power plants in a four-state area (Utah, Colorado, Arizona, New Mexico).

It is evident from this discussion that there must be a reconciliation of human needs and desires for energy with the finiteness of Spaceship Earth. Such a reconciliation must engage all of the institutions of society.

THE RECYCLING OF REFUSE

In 1968 the average American threw away almost 300 cans, 150 bottles, and about 300 pounds of paper. Our no-return throw-away style of living is burying us under a mountain of garbage. About 85 percent of the refuse collected in the United States, at a cost of $4\frac{1}{2}$ billion annually, is simply dumped in open areas, where it reduces the entire neighborhood to an ecological slum. Moreover, we are running out of open areas for dumping. What should be done?

As we have seen, nature's way of dealing with wastes is to recycle them again and again. (*See* pp. 421–3.) Carbon dioxide is used as a raw material for food manufacture by green plants. The nitrogen in plant and animal waste is reclaimed in the soil and used by plants in protein manufacture.

We can learn from nature. Take, for example, the aluminum beverage can which piles up at camp sites, parks, and lakes, as well as in garbage dumps. Unlike the old tin-coated steel can, which eventually rusts away and disappears into the environment, the aluminum can is practically indestructible. Why don't we reuse the aluminum in them? One aluminum-producing company found that it can reduce 100 used cans into enough metal to manufacture 91 new ones. There is a saving not only of aluminum but of electric power, since it takes 10 kilowatt hours of electricity to separate a pound of aluminum from its ore, but only about 2 kilowatt hours to melt the same amount of used aluminum. The 8 kilowatts saved means that less fuel will be consumed to generate electricity, and consequently less thermal and chemical pollution of the environment will result.

Apparently, the reclamation of a single resource, such as aluminum, initiates a chain of

[8]Earl Cook: *The Flow of Energy in an Industrial Society, Scientific American* (September 1971).

environmental benefits. How can we encourage and enforce an aluminum-reclamation program? Perhaps by imposing a large deposit on each can, plus an educational drive, with incentives, in every community. Or perhaps we should consider returning to the old tin-steel can, or the old refillable bottles, which eventually could be ground up and used as land fill or could be remelted and used again.

Turn to another common material—paper. Sixty million tons of paper and paper products are manufactured each year in this country. Recycling paper would save the cutting down of billions of oxygen-producing, soil-and-wildlife-protecting trees. At the present time we recycle about 20 percent of our paper; about three times that amount could probably be recycled. To do this would require setting up a system of paper collection in which all of us would have to participate. The Fort Worth, Texas, City Council initiated a curbside collection of old newspapers in 1972. Fort Worth residents "consume" 2000 tons of newspapers a month. For every ton of newsprint that is recycled, 17 pine trees are saved. This would mean 34,000 pine trees each month!

It is estimated that 20 million cars fill our junkyards, disfiguring the nation as they slowly rust away. Some slow inroads are being made into the mountain of discarded autos by the operation of metal scrap "shredders" that can consume as many as 1,000 junk autos a day as they reduce them to small pieces of metal. After processing in the shredder the steel is returned to steel mills to be melted, machined, and reused. In California the state legislature recently passed a law under which all owners will pay an extra $1.00 registration fee to finance a $14.4 million one-time clean up of abandoned cars, for disposal in shredding machines.

The dumping of solid waste is a growing problem, particularly in urban areas. It is estimated, for example, that by 1975 New York City will have exhausted its dump space. One proposed solution is to compact all the garbage, made unobjectionable in terms of odor, insects, vermin, or flammability and transport it by train to places where there are relatively few people and much land. There it could be used for beautification as land fills, reclaiming land for parks and recreation sites. Such measures would involve the federal government, presumably by the action of its Environmental Protection Agency.

This is, however, only a stopgap measure, since population and garbage have been increasing while land-fill areas are decreasing. A long-range program requires that we reduce solid waste pollution by recycling and by using manufacturing processes which minimize the quantity of wastes produced.

The argument is advanced that the reclamation of resources is too costly, that it is cheaper to continue to tap fresh raw-material resources. Ecologists answer:

1. The aluminum can manufactured from new ore, the paper produced by felling trees is costly *to society* in terms of the resulting diminished quality of the environment. In a fair system of accounting the price of a product should include the cost of repairing environmental damage done by that product.
2. Recycling will slow down the consumption of our ever-diminishing nonrenewable resources, which include such materials as aluminum, chromium, copper, nickel, tin, and zinc. "Given present consumption rates and the projected increase in these rates, the great majority of the currently important non-renewable resources will be extremely costly one hundred years from now."[9]

Recycling alone will not prevent this increase in cost, but it will help delay it. We cannot afford not to recycle.

To make recycling economically feasible we must devise ways of separating trash materials mechanically to bring down the cost; industrial demand must be created for salvaged products; tax laws and freight charges must be revised to stimulate recycling and make it profitable. One company has a method which spins out metals and glass and other heavy materials and makes the paper waste remaining into pellets of cellulose fiber, ready to be remade into cardboard roofing shingles and other products.

Other methods under consideration, or being utilized, include: the use of electric fur-

[9] *The Limits to Growth* (New York: Universe Books, 1972).

naces that can be charged entirely with steel scrap, the use of "ecology bottles" made entirely of recycled glass, development of biodegradable plastics that will succumb to bacterial decay, the banning by legislation of nonreturnable cans and bottles.

CONSERVATION OF SOIL

The Problem

Productive soil is the basis of our existence. Almost all of our food and fiber, except that derived from the sea, comes from the soil. Soil also is the source of almost all the food required by domestic and wild animal life. History records what happened to Greece, Italy, and Spain with the loss of much of their productive soil. Yet many people today in America feel that "it can't happen here." They point to the huge yields of our farms and to the improvements in technology. Our main problem seems to be to dispose of our surplus. The federal government, to support the economy, has bought up billions of dollars worth of such crops.

Indeed, we have increased the productivity of our land markedly. The average acre in 1970 yielded approximately twice the crops than that of 60 years before because of a combination of factors. New plant strains have been developed with increased food yield, with greater ability to withstand drought, disease, insects, wind damage, and unfavorable climatic conditions. In addition, the use of farm machinery, the placing of more acres under irrigation, and the use of fertilizers have played a role in increasing productivity.

What then is the problem? We must measure the future in terms of our new needs created by an increased population. By the year 2000, less than three decades from now, it is expected that the population of the United States will advance from 200 million (1967) to between 250 and 300 million. The average of these two estimates, 275 million, represents an increase of almost 40 percent.

(*See* p. 426.)

While the population increases, the amount of available crop land will decrease in the United States and in the world. There will be increased land requirements for reservoirs, transportation, recreation, forests to meet commercial demands for lumber, for wildlife refuges and recreation. Cities and suburbs will merge into a huge megalopolis. All of these will mean less acreage for meeting the heightened demand for crops of food, feed, and fibers.

Against this background of exploding population and diminishing land availability, the protection of valuable topsoil from erosion by wind and water and from depletion of its minerals by unwise farming methods takes on new significance.

(*See* pp. 467–8.)

In the United States erosion has destroyed an estimated more than 50 million acres of farmland since colonial times. (This is an area larger than Nebraska.) Erosion has partially destroyed another 50 million and threatens another 100 million acres. The damage is primarily due to man and his farming, grazing, and lumbering practices.

Prevention of Erosion

Nine inches of topsoil lie between us and extinction. This is the upper layer of soil in productive farmland. In that top 9 inches are the vital materials necessary for plant growth. Remove them, and we come to soil that can barely support vegetation.

One of the ways of preventing excessive erosion on hilly farmland is *contour farming,* (*see* illustration p. 434) in which the land is plowed around the contours of the hill instead of up and down. This prevents water from running downhill. Another way of preventing wasteful erosion is *strip farming,* in which alternate strips of grass or similar cover crop are left to check the downhill runoff of water. Water that begins to run downhill in the cultivated strip is stopped when it reaches the cover crop. Still another method—perhaps a better one—is not to plow steep hillsides at all but to leave them for pasture, orchard, or forest.

Terraces can also be used to prevent erosion. On ground that has been terraced, water has time to soak into the soil during and after a rain instead of running directly down the hillside. Older nations have terraced their hilly land

Contour farming and strip farming, both used to trap water and hold the soil on a Minnesota farm (*see* p. 433 for details). (*Courtesy of U. S. Department of Agriculture, Soil Conservation Service.*)

for centuries, but in the United States we have never had to follow such a practice to any extent because of our abundance of good land.

Forests are of great assistance in preventing erosion. If you have ever been in the woods during a rain you have seen that the drops of water do not hit the ground with great force. They strike leaves and branches and gradually drop to the ground or run down a tree trunk. The ground under the trees is covered with leaves. It is soft and spongy and full of roots of trees and other plants. The roots bind the soil together and hold it in place. The humus on the surface serves as a sort of sponge to hold some of the water that falls during a period of rainfall. This water then drains very gradually into the soil during dry periods.

Soil erosion is a natural process. Ordinarily it takes place slowly, so that new soil constantly being created balances the loss. Man, however, by his unwise practices, can speed up erosion to the point where land becomes unproductive in one generation. We have realized why erosion is becoming a problem, and we have learned how to slow it down. The job that remains to be done is to convince people of the importance of action and to help them see how best to work at conservation.

Maintaining Soil Fertility

If soil is to be satisfactory for plant growth it must contain the essential mineral compounds.

(*See* p. 468.)

The most important—compounds of nitrogen, phosphorus, and potassium—seem to be the most easily removed from the soil by plants. Let us consider nitrogen first.

The nitrogen cycle was discussed on pages 422–3 under "Nature's Recycling Systems." When man harvests crops, he is in a sense, mining the soil of nitrogen. His crops will become poorer and poorer, unless he replaces the lost nitrogen by adding animal manure or commercial fertilizer to the soil. He can also help replenish the soil with nitrates by growing a crop of plants such as clover and then plowing it back into the soil.

The use of excessive quantities of nitrate fertilizer may have negative ecological consequences, since the part not used by plants may leach out into nearby streams, lakes, and rivers, encouraging the growth of algae. The subsequent decay of algae overburdens aquatic ecosystems with organic matter. Excess nitrate in drinking water sources is also potentially dangerous, especially for infants.

(*See* p. 423.)

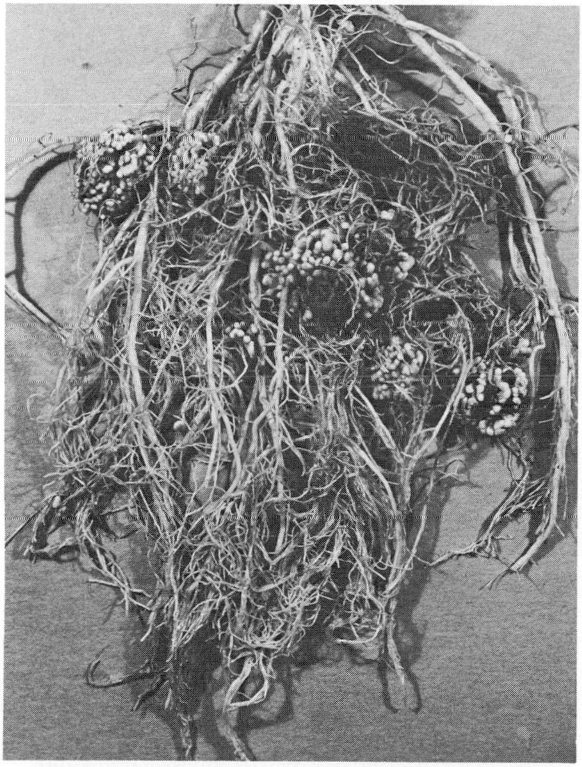

The root system of a single Austrian winter pea plant grown on a Texas farm. Note the many round nodules which contain nitrogen-fixing bacteria. Twelve hundred acres of these peas were planted on this farm in October 1956 for the purpose of enriching the soil. In the spring of 1957 they were plowed into the soil, adding needed nitrogen and organic matter. (*Courtesy of U.S. Department of Agriculture.*)

Phosphorus and potassium are essential for soil fertility too. Lack of phosphorus not only slows growing, it also results in crops that are deficient in this substance. People depending on such crops for the phosphorus required in their diet may have their health endangered by its lack. Farm animals suffer similarly from lack of this element. Potassium compounds are needed for sturdy plant growth. Calcium, sulfur, and magnesium are also essential to plant life, as are minute amounts of other elements.

CONSERVATION OF FORESTS

> If only people would catch a vision of our fabulous forests, their ancient heritage, their beauty and beneficence, their meaning for our lives today . . . before it is too late.
>
> —Rutherford Platt[10]

Forests not only provide wood products but they also assist greatly in preventing floods, reducing soil erosion, and in conserving water as we have seen. Forests provide a home for birds and other wild animals and recreation for millions of people.

More than three-fourths of the original forests of the United States have been cut down. Wasteful practices in the past have been responsible for much timber loss. No attempt at reforestation was made. When an area had been denuded of all marketable trees the lumberman moved on to a new area.

Fire

In the decade 1956–1965 fires consumed 43 million acres of forest land. In the single year 1970 there were over 116,000 forest fires in protected areas in the United States, an average of about 310 per day! Lightning accounted for only 11 percent of the fires; the rest were man-made: camp fires 3 percent, smoking 12 percent, debris burning 24 percent, incendiary (arson) 27 percent, equipment use 3 percent, and miscellaneous 20 percent.

[10]Rutherford Platt: *The Great American Forests* (Englewood Cliffs, N.J.: Prentice-Hall, Inc., 1965).

To control fires some of the larger forests have lookout stations and airplane patrols to locate the fires in their initial stages. Fire fighters are alerted and reach the scene before the fire has spread out of control. In addition, helicopters are used in some areas to bring "smoke jumpers" and their equipment to areas inaccessible by other means. Permanent fire lanes are cut through forests to halt the spread of fire and to facilitate the work of fire fighting.

Insects and Disease

The chief enemies of the forest are insects and disease. They destroy nearly seven times the amount of timber that fire does. Some of the insect enemies of the forest are leaf eaters; some, like certain beetles, are wood borers. The tree diseases are caused by such organisms as bacteria, fungi, and viruses; some of these disease parasites are conveyed from tree to tree by insects.

An example of the inroads of disease on trees is the case of the chestnut blight. This is a fungus disease of the American chestnut tree. It first received serious attention in 1904. Thirty years later the blight had killed off almost all the native chestnut trees in the northeast. Resistant strains of this valuable tree are now being developed, but it will be many decades before it is restored to its former abundance, if it ever is.

Another current concern is the destruction of the graceful elm tree by Dutch elm disease. Since its introduction into the United States in 1930 Dutch elm disease has wiped out nearly 50 million elm trees. The disease, found mainly east of the Mississippi River, is creeping farther westward. Only three states appear totally free of it—Florida, Montana, and Arizona.

The damage is caused by a fungus organism, but the fungus is spread only by tiny bark beetles. The disease can be checked by getting rid of the beetles. Communities that have carried out consistent control programs have proved that the elms can be saved. Scientists have also been seeking a kind of elm that is resistant to the disease.

Many insects that are harmful to trees and plants come here from other countries. Their immigration is accidental, occurring in shipments of fruits or vegetables from other shores. Airplanes can be a source of entry. Because of this, planes arriving from other lands are sprayed with insecticides as soon as they land at American airports. Quarantine and inspection are ways of stopping the entrance of some harmful insects, but even with the most stringent care the problem will continue to exist.

The Japanese beetle is a well-known example of an insect that came from abroad and wreaked havoc on our crops and trees. The prime reason foreign insects sometimes become a problem is that they leave their natural enemies behind them when they are brought to new territory. In combating such insects we often study them in their native habitat to find their natural enemies there. Such was the case with the Japanese beetle. It was found that a particular Japanese wasp was the chief enemy. This wasp was imported and raised in quantity and then released in areas where the beetle was out of control. The wasp lays its egg in the beetle larva. When the wasp young hatches out, it feeds on the larva and destroys it. Using a natural enemy to combat a harmful species is called *biological control.* In spite of this and other measures we have not conquered Japanese beetles. They do an immense amount of damage each year. Importation of natural enemies of insect pests must be preceded by careful study, for it is possible that the insect brought in to control one pest may itself prove to be a nuisance.

Insects can frequently be controlled on a small scale, such as on a small vegetable farm, by spraying plants with chemicals that kill the insects but do not harm plants. It is obvious that the cost and difficulty of application on large areas would be prohibitive. Therefore, to protect our forests against harmful insects by chemical spraying is out of the question. Moreover, widespread spraying might destroy insects and other forms of life that are essential in the chain of interrelationships described earlier in this chapter, and could lead to incalculable damage. That is why there must be unremitting study to discover natural enemies of insects.

An example of biological control is the method used to combat the gypsy moth, which has been a major killer of trees in the northeast.

In the spring of 1972 a biological "weapon" called Bacillus thuringiensis, or B.T. for short, was used by the Connecticut Department of Environmental Protection. Unlike chemical insecticides, such as DDT or Sevin, the bacillus is selective in what it kills. DDT, which was long used for gypsy moth control, kills a wide variety of animals and persists in active form in the environment as we have seen. Sevin destroys the bees needed to pollinate orchards and the wasps that prey on the leaf-eating larvae of the gypsy moth. B.T., on the other hand, strikes specifically at moth and butterfly larvae, killing them a few days after it is consumed on a leaf. The bacillus does not affect natural enemies of gypsy moths, as grackles, white-footed mice, short-tailed shrews, and ground beetles.

Another method of controlling the gypsy moth is based on the discovery that the female attracts the male with a scent. Recently, chemists have succeeded in synthesizing quantities of the female moth's sex attractant in a new product called Disparlure. Traps containing Disparlure attract the males; then they are sterilized (made infertile) or destroyed. Sterilized males, turned loose, displace normal males and mate with females, which then produce only infertile eggs.

Saving the Forests

The early settlers in America never dreamed that we might be short of timber. The concept that timber should be cultivated and harvested as a crop, instead of being "mined" out of the soil like ore, is a comparatively recent one. Theodore Roosevelt created a Bureau of Forestry in the early years of this century to protect our rapidly shrinking forest reserves. Gifford Pinchot, the Bureau's first chief, had the task of changing the prevailing attitude toward forests. According to Pinchot, people believed that forests were "inexhaustible and in the way." Corrective measures were initiated, including setting aside forest reserves and national parks. Forest owners slowly came to treat them as a crop instead of as a mineral to be mined. As a result of these and other measures the forest situation has improved markedly in many respects. However, the nation's future forest requirements are still not assured.

With increasing demand for wood, economists foresee that in less than 50 years the projected demand for forest products will exceed the capacity of forests to meet this demand by normal growth. This means that we shall have to consume more and more of our capital of trees. Some possible solutions have already been suggested: measures against fire, insects, and disease. These will not be enough. General improvements in forest management, increased imports, intensified exploration of tropical forests, further promotion of economies in the use of wood, and the utilization of wastes will help; but there are limitations in these methods. Possibilities for the substitution of other materials for forest products may include the increasing use of such construction materials as brick and concrete, aluminum, plastics, and fiberglass; the use of nonwood vegetable fibers such as sugar cane bagasse for making paper; aluminum foil and plastics instead of paper for packing. Some of these materials, such as plastics, may introduce problems of solid waste disposal, discussed on pages 431–3.

The federal government has set aside 187 million acres of public lands for the national forests. Supervised by the Forest Service of the United States Department of Agriculture the National Forest System is dedicated to "multiple use"; the forests, by law, are supposed to fulfill six functions: recreation, watershed maintenance, wildlife preservation, timber production, grazing, and mining.

In recent years the administration of our national forests has been criticized on a number of grounds: bulldozers are destroying some of the nation's last remains of pristine wilderness; instead of selective cutting the Forest Service has engaged in the "clear-cutting" of timber—stripping forest tracts bare, leaving unsightly bald patches; archaic laws and regulations are allowing choice tracts of forest land to be gouged and scarred by mining operations; nearly half of the national forage areas have been overgrazed.

Conservationists have charged that there has been overemphasis on the commercial functions of the forests at the expense and the long-term impairment of noncommercial functions. Various proposals are under consideration to improve the administration of the national forests and to provide for stricter governmental regulations and enforcement to protect the environmental values of our great forests.

Although not very important in supplying our national wood-products needs, school forests are doing a great deal to show children the need for conservation and how it may be carried out. Under this plan schools acquire rundown land by purchase or gift. Young trees are planted and cared for as far as possible by the children themselves. School forests are valuable for recreation and for the teaching of science, and they also afford an opportunity for firsthand study of conservation practices. The study in this case includes not only forest conservation but also conservation of birds, other wild animal life, and soil.

CONSERVATION OF WILDLIFE

> Everyone knows that the autumn landscape in the northwoods is the land, plus a red maple, plus a ruffed grouse. In terms of conventional physics, the grouse represents only a millionth of either the mass or the energy of the acre. Yet subtract the grouse and the whole thing is dead.
>
> Aldo Leopold, *A Sand County Almanac*

Early explorers told stories of animal abundance that gave them reputations as spinners of tall tales. But the tales were true. The number of animals in colonial days was prodigious. At one time 100 million bison roamed the western prairies. These animals were slaughtered for their hides and fur. Birds were exterminated for their decorative feathers. Enormous numbers of game and wild fowl were killed for sale as food. What saved part of our wildlife was the birth of a conservation movement in the final quarter of the nineteenth century. For some animals this came too late. The passenger pigeon was one of those that never recovered. The last-known passenger pigeon died in captivity in 1914. Gone, too, is the great auk, the Plains grizzly, the Labrador duck, the Arizona wapiti, the Bad Lands big horn—and many others.

It was inevitable that the number of wild animals should diminish as the United States became more thickly settled. Wild animals find it difficult to live in a land from which many of the forests have been eliminated. Animals also find it difficult to live where they are hunted ruthlessly. Many of them have been killed even though they had little value as food or for skins.

Animals whose skins were valuable were hit the hardest in the early days—animals such as the beaver, otter, mink, fisher, seal, lynx, wolf, bear, skunk, and muskrat had value in the markets of Europe. As a result of the ruthless exploitation of animals whose skins were valuable the United States was largely denuded of its fur bearers. This is particularly true of bison and seals. Had we not protected the seals by law they would have vanished entirely. Beaver, mink, and other fur bearers have had to be protected by closed or limited seasons, by limitations on numbers allowed to be taken, and other means.

In 1970 Congress passed an Endangered Species Conservation Act providing federal protection for certain animals whose extinction was threatened. One of these was the American alligator. Although the Act has provided a degree of protection for this beleaguered reptile, enforcement against poachers is difficult, despite the efforts of the understaffed Division of Management and Enforcement of the Bureau of Sport Fisheries and Wildlife. In addition to the appointment of more agents to apprehend poachers the shipping and marketing of alligator hides must be eliminated. In New York, South Carolina, and California it is against the law to sell any alligator products, no matter where they originate. Some of the "wild" furs now being sold represent endangered species. Here is an instance where consumer resistance could protect wildlife.

Other animals named in the Act are the wild horse, crocodile, polar bear, leopard, ocelot, tiger, cheetah, jaguar, red wolf, timber wolf, vicuna, giraffe, lion, and Spanish lynx.

Why Conserve Animals?

The economic value of wildlife is tremendous. Fisheries, for example, supply important food worth many millions of dollars annually. However, the value of wildlife cannot be counted only in dollars and cents. Our national parks, with their fearless animal populations, are a source of pleasure to many people.

Certainly we should expect some animals to retreat from the haunts of man. Such animals as the deer, elk, wolf, bear, and lynx cannot live well in cleared sections. Muskrats, beavers, otters, minks, and other water dwellers cannot remain when swamps and lakes are drained and when streams and rivers are used for water supply and irrigation.

We should not, however, drive these animals into extinction. We should protect them in the natural habitats that remain for them. And we should also be intelligent enough to leave desirable space for them. There is ample land that should not be cleared for agricultural or industrial purposes. In such spots the animals can live—if they are protected.

Why protect wild animals? In their natural habitat they are a pleasure to watch. They are as much a part of forests, lakes, ponds, streams, and meadows as the trees and flowers.

Each wild animal, as we have seen, is part of a life chain. This chain may lead directly to man. The destruction of coyotes in certain areas permitted a ruinous increase in the number of rodents. The killing off of Swainson's hawk in the west was followed by grasshopper plagues that destroyed millions of dollars worth of crops.

There is much that we do not know about interrelationships in nature. Even the simplest creature may be important in our existence. Let us remember this when someone asks: "What good is this animal?"

The person who asks such a question often implies also that unless the creature serves man's immediate needs its continued existence is unimportant. Besides being shortsighted, from man's selfish viewpoint, this attitude may also be challenged on an ethical or philosophical basis. Man is a fellow creature—not the master of creation.

Bird Conservation

Without birds we would certainly suffer more damage from insects to farm crops, trees, and shrubs than we do now. Many birds feed on insects and thus help to control the large numbers of them. Some of the harmful insects that birds eat are potato bugs, cutworms, chinch bugs, leaf beetles, and boll weevils.

The stomachs of many kinds of birds have been examined in an attempt to determine just how helpful they are. Examination of the stomachs of ruby-crowned kinglets, for example, revealed that 94 percent of their food was animal matter consisting of plant lice, mealy bugs, scale insects, caterpillars, and other insects. The stomach of one flicker contained 5,000 ants. A nighthawk's stomach contained 500 mosquitoes. A young red-eyed vireo is known to have eaten 100 grasshoppers a day in addition to many harmful insects. The diet of meadow larks is 99 percent insects—nearly all of them harmful to crops.

Sometimes birds are accused of doing harm to man. Hawks are often alleged to be harmful because they kill chickens, but they also kill mice, which dig out freshly planted corn and are destructive to other seeds and to crops. Many kinds of hawks live mainly on mice rather than on chickens. There is little doubt that they do more good than harm as far as man is concerned.

The widespread use of the now discredited DDT to combat insects injurious to vegetation boomeranged because it also killed or injured many of the birds that devour these insects. DDT affects the reproduction of birds, making the egg shells too thin for successful broods. Predatory birds are particularly vulnerable to a persistent pesticide such as DDT because they are at the top of a food chain, feeding on birds that have fed in turn on insects and plants which contain DDT. Hence, the birds of prey accumulate a higher dose of DDT and are more likely to suffer toxic effects than other birds.

Effective December 31, 1972, the Environmental Protection Agency banned almost all uses of DDT. This order represented a major victory for environmental groups and in particular for the late Rachel Carson, who in her now-classic book, *Silent Spring,* raised the cry against DDT.

Wildlife Sanctuaries

The need for wildlife management and protection has been recognized for a long time. As far back as the beginning of the eighteenth century practically all of the original colonies had established closed seasons on deer. But it was not until after the Civil War that protective legislation was established on a wide scale. The need for wildlife sanctuaries has been recognized, and many state and national areas have been set aside where wild animals can live and breed without interference. Scientific study of wildlife problems has increased. We know more about the interrelationships of living things than we did 50 years ago, but there are still vast unexplored realms that need investigation.

Nature preserves or sanctuaries, where all wild plants and animals are protected with as little disturbance by man as possible, are valuable as outdoor schoolrooms and scientific laboratories. Here the interrelationships discussed in this chapter can be studied. This is the purpose of the "nature centers" now being established in many communities with the guidance of the National Audubon Society and other conservation groups.

CONSERVATION OF WATER

(*See* pp. 468–70.)

Water, one of our most precious resources, is also our commonest and cheapest. Unlike copper or coal, water is indestructible; it will not wear out. Its supply is inexhaustible. The sea covers three-quarters of the earth and holds 300 million cubic miles of water. Locked in glaciers, ice caps, and ice sheets are 11 million more.

In the course of the water cycle, as we have seen, water circulates from ocean to air to land to ocean. The supply of water on our planet is ample; the problem is to obtain the right amount of fresh water in the right place at the right time. Water is a resource that moves; conserving it for use means controlling its movement.

Water Shortages

The basic cause of water shortages in big cities in recent years is the increased consumption of water. The U.S. Geological Survey found that in 1969 the water use for agricultural, industry, and domestic purposes came to 1,600 gallons for every person in the United States—every day! The same agency estimated that the total water use in the United States for 1970 would increase about 15 percent over 1965. It is expected that our demand for water will continue to increase, because of the expected increase in the population and in the ways in which we use water.

The supply of available water has not kept pace with the demand. Cities have not enlarged their water resources sufficiently to meet the new requirements of individuals and industries. Therefore, a dry winter and spring may bring a shortage because the reservoir system supporting the city does not have enough capacity to carry it over this dry spell.

The water shortage in cities has had at least one good effect: It has made city dwellers aware of their dependence on the land. It has made them realize, as one Washington official put it, that "water doesn't grow in faucets." The city dwellers leaıned a new word, "watershed," an area that acts as a basin to catch rainfall and to let it flow and seep slowly into the streams that feed rivers, lakes, and reservoirs.

Watersheds

As stated previously the problem of water conservation is one of having sufficient fresh water when and where it is needed. The watershed is of key importance in solving this problem. Let us look at watersheds more carefully.

(*See* pp. 467–70.)

Sooner or later much of the water from rain or snow appears as streams. Small at first, these upland water courses become wider and deeper as they approach valleys, where they combine to form larger streams and rivers. The area that produces the water that appears as a stream or river is a *watershed,* which are of many shapes and sizes. Some cover millions of acres, like the Columbia and Missouri river drainages.

Under natural conditions the soil, the plants in the soil (the "cover"), and the moisture of a watershed tend to be in balance. When man ignorantly or carelessly upsets the balance by destroying much of the plant cover the soil is exposed and washes away, often resulting in dust bowls, spreading deserts and ruined valleys, water shortages, polluted rivers, mud slides, and ravaging floods.

Forest land has enormous value as a regulator of water flow. Not only do forest soils retain and store water they also control water movement on and beneath the surface. This control spells the difference between clear, steady streams and erratic flows of muddy water, rising rapidly after rains and shrinking as rapidly, leaving only dry riverbeds.

An old Chinese proverb says: "To rule the mountain is to rule the river." A healthy forest cover on the slopes of hills and mountains restrains floods and provides a steady flow of clear water. When the cover is removed by fire or overcultivation, an imbalance is set up that permits less and less water to be taken in and stored in the soil to the detriment of farms, towns, and cities.

Water Table

We depend not only on the surface water that we can see and measure in streams, lakes, rivers, and reservoirs but on underground water; that is, water that is some distance below the ground level. Underground water begins as rain that sinks into the ground and then soaks into porous rock. As rain continues, the bottom rock layers become filled or saturated with water. The upper level of this underground water is called the *water table.* Above this, rock particles may be coated with a film of water, but air fills most of the pore space.

The underground rocks of the United States hold more water than all its surface reservoirs. The depth of the water table below the surface depends on many factors. In desert regions, for example, there may be so little rainfall that a water table never forms. Whenever the water table is high enough to reach the surface we may have a spring or swamp, or we may dig a well

Mud and wreckage are piled in front of stores along the desolate Main Street of North Topeka, Kansas, after the Kaw River waters receded. This is one small part of the ruin following the flood that swept across Kansas in 1951, leaving 41 dead, 165,000 persons homeless, 2 million acres of farmland under water, and property losses of over $1 billion. (*Courtesy of* Life *Magazine* ©, Time, *Inc., Francis Miller.*)

to tap this source. Such springs and wells are a direct source of water for millions of people in the United States, in farm areas and in many urban areas as well. A great concern in recent years has been the falling water table in many areas, caused in part by the increasing amount of water being pumped out of the ground and in part by drought. In some areas when the water table drops, salt water from nearby sources flows into the lowered water supply and makes it unfit for drinking.

The Quality of Water

A sampling of recent news events presents the problems of water quality only too vividly:

Scientists have isolated viruses from drinking water, apparently for the first time in the United States. They suspect that viruses seeped from the sewage systems through the ground to contaminate the water supply in a 100-foot-deep well.

The bacterial count in the waters of New York Harbor has increased several hundred percent in recent years.

A hepatitis outbreak in the Northeast was traced in part to infected clams dug up in Long Island Sound.

Toxic levels of mercury were reported in the livers of Alaskan fur seals; the first time that mercury pollution has been found in large aquatic mammals.

The heavy use of insecticides in Asian rice paddies killed off fish, a major source of protein food.

Residents of McFarland, California, received a warning letter from the local water company that the public water supply was no longer considered safe for infants to drink, since it contained an excessive amount of nitrates. (The source of nitrate here and elsewhere appears to originate from the use of nitrate fertilizer on irrigated cropland.)

The dumping of sewage sludge in the New York Bight, an area in the ocean 12 miles off Sandy Hook, for the last 40 years has killed off marine life in a 500-square-mile area, to the point where scientists have termed this a "dead sea."

Nearly all the beaches of Lake Erie have been closed by pollution; mounds of decaying fish and algae pile up each summer; its once sparkling water is dense with muck.

Egypt's Aswan Dam is causing serious damage to that country's sardine fishing and is creating a stable body of water which forms an excellent habitat for the snails which are host to a parasitic disease of humans, schistosomiasis.

Thermal pollution from electric power plants located on bodies of water used for cooling is causing sudden death to plants and animals in the heated waters.

In 1969 the oily chocolate-brown Cuyahoga River in Cleveland burst into flames, nearly destroying two railroad bridges.

A research ship from Woods Hole, Massachusetts, that towed a net to collect marine life in the Sargasso Sea, reported that after 24 hours of towing the mesh became so encrusted with oil that it was necessary to clean the nets with solvents. It was estimated that there was three times as much tarlike material as Sargasso weed in the nets.

In 1970 an estimated $1\frac{1}{2}$ billion gallons of crude oil or petroleum products were spilled into the waters of the world, either deliberately or accidentally.

The new supertankers carrying oil are being built larger and larger. The loss of one 300,000-ton tanker, several of which are under construction now, would equal the tonnage of all tankers lost at sea 10 years ago.

Normally, nature has a remarkable ability to clean up its own water by the process of filtering it through soils and sands, by aerating it as it tosses it over falls, by settling the debris in it in quieter waters, and, most important of all, by the process of recycling wastes through plant and animal food chains. But now the load of pollution is becoming too heavy. Rivers and lakes can no longer purify themselves. With nearly all our waterways befouled by sewage, silt, industrial wastes, and pesticides we are just beginning to apply solutions to the water-pollution problem. With continued urbanization and industrialization, with an exploding population the demands

Before a dam is built, the question must be asked: "What effect will building this dam have on the soil, the water, the plant and animal life, the people?" Answers must be gotten not only from the engineer but also from the communities affected and from the biologist, the chemist, the economist, the sociologist, the anthropologist, and others. Pictured here is Fontana dam, towering 480 feet, the highest dam east of the Rockies. Built by the Tennessee Valley Authority, Fontana is on the Little Tennessee River in North Carolina. The electric power installation generates 202,500 killowatts. (*Courtesy of Tennessee Valley Authority.*)

on a supply of clean fresh water will continue to increase and the problems of pollution become more acute.

Solutions to the Water Problem

What is the answer to water shortages and floods? Most important is the protection and extension of watershed areas. Concurrently, storage facilities—dams and reservoirs—must be constructed so that billions of gallons of water do not flow unused into the sea or cause destructive floods. Industry can help by reusing water, and home dwellers by eliminating the waste caused by dripping faucets and leaking pipes.

Another series of measures to alleviate water shortages is based on nature's water cycle, also known as the *hydrologic cycle.* In this cycle, described on page 421 and in Chapter 9A, pure water vapor is evaporated into the air from the oceans and is later precipitated as rain or snow. Falling on land, it eventually runs back into the oceans. In our cloud-seeding projects we are attempting to alter the cycle by making rain fall where it is most

(*See* pp. 248–9.)

needed. Thus far we have had only limited—perhaps questionable—success in this effort. A second method is *desalination.* In this instance we are supplementing nature's hydrologic cycle by getting fresh water from salt water by direct means. The government has sponsored experimentation to produce a cheap method of removing salt from water. A demonstration plant in Freeport, Texas, began operation in 1961 and was the first to supply the water needs of a United States municipality—1 million gallons of desalted water per day. Since then a number of other plants have been built to test the efficiency of different processes in producing fresh water from salt. On July 20, 1967, the largest United States desalination plant opened in Key West, Florida, a plant that will provide up to $2\frac{1}{2}$ million gallons of fresh water daily. Seven hundred and fifty desalting plants are now providing some 300,000,000 gallons of fresh water daily for cities and industries around the world.

A third method of altering the water cycle attempts to reduce the evaporation of water from reservoirs by building underground storage places for water, or by spreading a chemical film on the surface of reservoir waters.

What is being done about the water pollution problem? On January 1, 1966, the federal government strengthened earlier measures for combating water pollution by establishing a Water Pollution Control Administration. Later that year Congress enacted far-reaching legislation to speed the fight against water pollution. The legislation authorized increased appropriations for federal grants to construct municipal waste-treatment facilities, established a "clean rivers restoration" program, financed stepped-up research, and increased support for state and interstate agencies. This legislation strengthened the 1965 Federal Water Quality Act, which empowered the Secretary of Interior to start federal enforcement actions against pollution when the pollution is on an interstate body of water and its effects are felt in a state other than the one in which the discharges originate and the effects are damaging to health and welfare.

In 1972 a strengthened Federal Water Pollution Bill won Congressional approval. The new legislation sets a national goal of eliminating all pollution of water by 1985. All industries discharging into the nation's lakes and rivers will be required to use the "best practicable" technology to control pollution by 1977 and the best "available" technology by 1981. The bill also increases the appropriation for federal assistance to municipalities for sewage treatment and places stricter constraints on existing industrial pollution.

In general, measures to prevent and cure the ills of water pollution, some of which are under way in some areas, include:

The treatment of industrial waste to remove toxic materials, detergents, algae-promoting nitrates and phosphates.

The refining and recycling of useful waste materials of industry.

Search for methods of discharging heat from electric power plants without disturbing life in adjacent waters.

The correction of those agricultural practices which result in the washing of insecticides, herbicides, and fertilizers into waterways.

The proper handling of wastes in animal feedlots to avoid their discharge into adjacent waters; their processing to be recycled in the soil as fertilizer.

Phasing out of the dumping of sludge sewage into ocean waters.

The strict regulation of ships to prevent the deliberate dumping of waste tars and oils into the ocean and of offshore wells and oil tankers to prevent the accidental spillage of petroleum.

The setting up of standards of water purity and the enforcement of these standards by municipal, state, and federal governments, to include streams, lakes, rivers, and coastal waters.

CONSERVATION OF AIR

Air, like water, is an inexhaustible resource, but pure air—air fit to breathe, air that does not irritate our eyes, air that does not damage plant life, air that does not soil and corrode the materials that we use—is becoming scarcer. The seriousness of this problem is recognized in reports

(See p. 461.) of the U.S. Department of Health, Education and Welfare,[11] from which all of the extracts that follow in this section are taken.

Air—Pure and Polluted

Unpolluted air is a mixture of nitrogen, oxygen, water vapor, carbon dioxide, a few rare (See pp. 458, 463–4.) gases, a small scattering of dust particles from soil, pollen, and salt crystals whipped aloft by the wind from ocean spray. Normally winds and air currents distribute and dilute man-made contaminants into the ocean of air that surrounds the earth. Gradually the contaminants are eliminated by natural processes, including the cleansing action of rain. Generally these natural processes proceed at a slow rate. Wherever man's activities discharge pollutants into the air faster than nature's forces are able to distribute or destroy them, a buildup in pollution concentration occurs that may be destructive to materials, to plant and animal life, and to man's health. An acutely dangerous condition, such as the Donora tragedy discussed early in this chapter, (See pp. 417–8, 464–5.) may arise during a *temperature inversion,* an atmospheric phenomenon that prevents normal circulation of air. Ordinarily, warm air rises from the earth to colder layers above it, carrying much of man's pollution with it. Occasionally a layer of warm air forms above cooler air near the ground; the inversion acts as a lid, preventing the pollutants from rising and dispersing. Inversions are a major factor in the production of *smog*—a combination of smoke and fog.

> At the beginning of December 1952 the city of London went through a four day period of still air during which pollution accumulated in a pea soup fog. Months later a review of mortality statistics revealed that 4000 excess deaths had occurred in the city during a seven day period that began with the first day of the fog. The illness rate during the period, especially the cardio-respiratory illness rate, increased to more than twice the normal rate for that time of year, and did not return to normal until two to three weeks later. London went through a similar episode in 1962, and the city of New York went through much the same kind of disaster in 1953 and again in 1962 and 1966.

[11] *National Goals in Air Pollution Research,* 1960; *The Effects of Air Pollution,* 1966; *Air Pollution—A National Sample,* 1966.

Smog over a city. (*Courtesy of Monkmeyer.*)

But much more alarming than the smog disasters is the often unnoticed day-by-day erosion of the health of millions by polluted air. Among the diseases attributed in part to air pollution are the common cold, emphysema (a progressive breakdown of air sacs in the lungs), and bronchial asthma.

The Pollutants

> At levels frequently found in heavy traffic, *carbon monoxide* produces headache, loss of visual acuity, and decreased muscular coordination. . . . Although the burning of any carbon material produces carbon monoxide to some extent, our primary concern is the

burning of gasoline in the automobile, and the discharge low to the ground of carbon monoxide from the automobile exhaust.

Sulfur oxides, found wherever coal and oil are the common fuels, corrode metal and stone, and at concentrations frequently found in our larger cities reduce visibility, injure vegetation, and contribute to the incidence of respiratory disease and to premature death.

Beside their contribution to photochemical smog, described below, *nitrogen oxides* are responsible for the whisky brown haze that not only destroys the view in some of our cities, but endangers the takeoff and landing of planes. At concentrations higher than those usually experienced, these oxides can interfere with respiratory function and, it is suspected, contribute to respiratory disease. They are formed in the combustion of all types of fuels.

Hydrocarbons are a very large class of chemicals some of which, in particle form, have produced cancer in laboratory animals, and others of which, discharged chiefly by the automobile, play a major role in the formation of photochemical smog.

Photochemical smog is a complex mixture of gases and particles manufactured by sunlight out of the raw materials—nitrogen oxides and hydrocarbons—discharged to the atmosphere chiefly by the automobile. Smog, whose effects have been observed in every region of the United States, can severely damage crops and trees, deteriorate rubber and other materials, reduce visibility, cause the eyes to smart and the throat to sting, and, it is thought, reduce resistance to respiratory disease.

Particulate matter not only soils our clothes, shows up on our window sills, and scatters light to blur the image of what we see, it acts as a catalyst in the formation of other pollutants, it contributes to the corrosion of metals, and in proper particle size can carry into our lungs irritant gases which might otherwise have been harmlessly dissipated in the upper respiratory tract. Some particulates contain poisons whose effects on man are gradual, often the result of the accumulation of years.

To these air pollutants there must be added the radioactive debris produced by nuclear-bomb testing. This pollution is global in its distribution and in its fallout range. It still continues its threat to health when it is washed out of the atmosphere by rain, which may carry it into drinking water or crop-producing soil.

The Attack on Air Pollution

Air pollution must be dealt with on two fronts: legislation and education. Suitable laws need to be enacted and enforced on local, state, and federal levels. The general public needs to be informed. This means not only fuel dealers, building managers, installers of combustion equipment, architects, engineers, but all of us.

Some measures for controlling air pollution include:

Installation of devices that remove particles and poisonous gases resulting from industrial processes.

Changing where possible the techniques employed in industrial processes to eliminate or neutralize the production of poisonous materials.

Removal of sulfur from fuels or substitution of low-sulfur fuels for high-sulfur fuels.

City-region planning for the best location of industries with respect to homes, open areas, recreation areas.

Reduction of evaporation of gasoline from storage tanks, tank trucks, and carburetors of motor vehicles.

Production of electric power by methods other than burning fuel: atomic energy, solar energy, tidal energy, and natural steam and hot water sources from earth.

(**Note:** In using atomic energy for the generation of electricity we must guard against the contamination of our environment by the careless disposal of atomic wastes.)

Installation of auto exhaust-pipe and blow-by devices; redesigning of auto engines to minimize production of pollutants; use of lead-free gas.

Substitution of electric and other nonpolluting automobiles for gasoline-driven automobiles.

Far greater use of mass-transportation facilities. A busload of fifty people produces fewer pollutants than fifty automobiles. A trainload of 1,000 people pollutes less than twenty buses or 1,000 autos.

Prohibition of burning of leaves, trash, and garbage by individuals or municipalities.

In 1972 the Environmental Protection Agency of the federal government took legal action to curb air pollution by an electric-power company in Delaware that was, as the government stated, discharging 74,000 tons of sulfur dioxide into the air each year. The cause of the pollution was clear: The company was burning a high-sulphur coke. The action was taken under the Federal Clean Air Act of 1970, which strengthened the previous clean-air legislation. The Agency announced that the action was the first in a national crackdown on air pollution.

Under the Act of 1970 the EPA set minimum standards of air purity to curb pollution by sulphur dioxide and other pollutants, and required states to submit to the Agency their own plans for enforcing the standards. Each state must have an acceptable plan in force by 1975. The EPA is also empowered by the Act to enforce immediate action in case of an emergency; such an action occurred in 1971 when the EPA closed 23 industries in Birmingham, Alabama, when a temperature inversion caused a smog that imperiled health there.

The automobile is a major contributor to air pollution. Autos are responsible for 64.7 percent of carbon monoxide, 45.7 percent of hydrocarbons, and 36.6 percent of nitrogen oxide pollution of our nation's air. But in many cities the auto accounts for a much higher percentage of each of these pollutants.

A federal law required that 1968 and later-models cars sold in the United States be equipped with emission control devices. Under amendments to the Clean Air Act automobile companies are required to achieve at least a 90 percent reduction in hydrocarbons and carbon monoxide in their 1975 models, compared with the levels in 1970 models, and a similar reduction in nitrogen oxide emission in 1976 models.

The cost of air pollution is high. The loss in efficiency from the improper burning of fuels; the reduction of visibility; the agricultural losses—including damage to livestock and crops—the deterioration of materials, structures, and machines—including the cost of replacing or protecting precision instruments—and the damage to the health of human beings is estimated by the FEPA to be $16 billion a year. To control air pollution government and industry must spend billions. When we consider the priceless benefits of clean air to our health alone surely the adequate control of air pollution is a bargain.

CONSERVATION OF WILDERNESS

> History will think it strange that America could afford the moon . . . while a patch of primeval redwoods—not too big for a man to walk through in a day—was considered beyond its means.
>
> —Sierra Club

The fight for the redwoods is but one chapter in the long struggle to save the remaining wilderness of America. Only $2\frac{1}{2}$ percent of our land is preserved as wilderness—in national parks and monuments, national forests, and wildlife refuges.

Wilderness was once thought of as something to be subdued and conquered, something to be fought and destroyed. There is growing recognition today that wilderness itself is a most precious heritage.

The Wilderness Act, setting up the National Wilderness Preservation System, passed by Congress in 1964, was a clear declaration that wilderness no longer has to be fought or conquered. The act states: "a wilderness, in contrast with those areas where man and his own works dominate the landscape, is . . . recognized as an area where the earth and its community of life are untrammeled by man, where man himself is a visitor who does not remain." The Act gave much-needed recognition and protection to wilderness areas in the national parks, national forests, and national wildlife refuges. Congress must approve any change in established wilderness areas and must also approve creation of new wilderness areas.

But the concept of wilderness conservation is not one of exclusive isolation for the few. Rather, as the late Howard Zahniser of the Wilderness Society (the prime mover of the Wilderness Act) put it: "We work for wilderness preservation not primarily for the right of a minority to have the kind of fun it prefers, but rather to insure for everyone the perpetuation of areas

"In wildness is the preservation of the world."—Henry David Thoreau. Weber Grove in (proposed) Redwood National Park, California. (*Courtesy of U.S. Department of the Interior, Fred E. Mang for the National Park Service.*)

where human enjoyment and the apprehension of the interrelations of the whole community of life are possible, and to preserve for all the freedom of choosing to know the primeval if they so wish."

The City and the Wilderness

(*See* pp. 460–3.)

Most people now live in cities. It is estimated that in the next 20 years about 90 percent of the people in the United States will live on 10 percent of the land. Not all can travel easily to the large wilderness areas—to Yellowstone, the Grand Canyon, Yosemite. Yet people long for an accessible outdoors. We must now utilize, restore, and create areas close to large cities. Many natural wild or semiwild areas are still available: marshlands, desert lands, grasslands, ocean environments, geological formations, and wildlife communities. Some of these are within the boundaries of cities, many nearby. They need the same kind of protection and development for educational purposes as the large national parks.

The proximity of natural areas to urban centers makes them valuable as outdoor schoolrooms where the lessons of nature can be learned *in* nature. Municipal and state parks will also serve to relieve the pressure on national parks.

To meet the needs of the millions living in urban centers coordination in planning and in action is required of federal, state, and local authorities, as well as of conservation groups and individual citizens. Often this will require the purchase of land, or condemnation by a government agency—acquisition at a fair value without the owner's consent. This may be done if it is in the public interest. The U.S. Supreme Court, in an opinion written by Justice William O. Douglas in 1954, stated: ". . . the concept of the public welfare is broad and inclusive. The values it represents are spiritual as well as physical, aesthetic as well as monetary. It is within the power of the legislature to determine that the community should be beautiful as well as healthy, spacious as well as clean, well balanced as well as carefully patrolled."

To provide relief from intensive urbanization it is necessary to use or create areas within the city itself, *where people are.* Cities are beginning to develop greenbelts, parks, and vest-pocket parks within their confines.

Acquisition of natural areas is not a goal for governments only; many civic groups, including watershed associations, park foundations, and wildlife and nature conservation organizations, have had marked success in preserving open space. Two thousand acres of the Great Swamp in Morris County, New Jersey, were purchased by a committee of the North American Wildlife Federation, supported by civic organizations, when it was proposed that the swamp be drained and made into a jetport for the New York Port Authority. Later the land was turned over to the federal government. Now, as the Great Swamp National Refuge, it has an observation shelter and trail for visitors who wish to study and photograph wildlife in a natural setting. The unique Sunken Forest on Fire Island, with its primeval

A New York oasis: pint-sized Paley Park, which is nestled between business buildings on East 53rd Street. The park has 17 locust trees and a waterfall; chairs and tables for resting, contemplation, and al-fresco lunching—a calm spot in the mid-Manhattan bustle. (*Courtesy of Wide World.*)

stand of holly trees, was purchased by the Sunken Forest Preserve, Inc., to save it from a real-estate developer's bulldozer. Later, when Fire Island became a national seashore, the Sunken Forest was turned over to the Department of Interior for administration on behalf of the public. Each summer thousands of visitors under the expert guidance of park rangers explore the shaded trails of this unique forest.

The proximity of natural areas to urban centers makes them invaluable as outdoor schoolrooms where the lessons of nature can be learned in nature. Here a ranger of the National Park Service on Fire Island demonstrates the planting of dune grass, a measure calculated to stabilize and build the dunes which protect the island from the ravages of wind and waves. Later, the entire class of these New York City children, who spent a week of their school year in a pristine seashore environment, participated in a grass-planting project. (*National Park Service, Cecil W. Stoughton.*)

Fundamental to our use of land is our attitude toward it. Aldo Leopold in *A Sand County Almanac* states: "We abuse land because we regard it as a commodity belonging to us. When we see it as a community to which we belong, we may begin to use it with love and respect."

This attitude has come to be known as the *land ethic.*

CONSERVATION OF THE URBAN ENVIRONMENT

The rebuilding and renewing of our cities, where most of us now live, is one of the very most important of our conservation jobs. The building of new towns and communities, too, should help provide better habitats for man. A dozen new communities, through federal aid, are now being started, some still on the drawing boards, others under construction.

It is to be hoped that the new habitats of man will, in the words of the 1969 report of the National Committee on Urban Growth Policy, bring "man, buildings and nature once again into proper balance."

THE ENVIRONMENTAL AWAKENING

> . . . the most important business on earth, quite literally, the business of planetary planning.
>
> —Norman Cousins

In 1968, a Senate document of great potential significance stated:

> It is the intent of the Congress that the policies, programs, and public laws of the United States be interpreted and administered in a manner protective of the total needs of man in the environment. To this end, the Congress proposes that arrangements be established to make effective the following objectives of national policy for the environment.
>
> 1. To arrest the deterioration of the environment.
> 2. To restore and revitalize damaged areas of our nation so that they may once again be productive of economic wealth and spiritual satisfaction.
> 3. To find alternatives and procedures which will minimize and prevent future hazards in the use of environment-shaping technologies, old and new.

4. To provide direction and, if necessary, new institutions and new technologies designed to optimize man-environment relationship and to minimize future costs in the management of the environment.

The essence of this document was incorporated into the National Environmental Policy Act of 1969. The Act set up a three-man council on environmental quality to assist and advise the president; it requires the president to submit to Congress annual reports on the status of the nation's environmental programs. An Environmental Protection Agency was set up to implement and enforce environmental programs.

These actions by the national government culminated a 10-year effort to confirm the responsibility of the American government for the management of man's impact on his environment. The concepts and goals as stated in the formal language of the Act were actually the product of many decades of struggle and education by lone individuals and by conservation organizations.

But the 1969 Act is only a beginning. It will be tested as we cope with the difficult environmental problems of the United States, from urban parks to agricultural pesticides, from wetlands to the disposal of industrial wastes, from automobile exhaust products to thermal pollution.

> The new environmental challenge to man is obviously not mastery of the environment (a task that has required most of his efforts since the Stone Age), but mastery of his desires and his judgment with respect to the use of the environment.[12]

[12] Linton Keith Caldwell: *Environment* (New York: Doubleday and Company, 1971).

THE STOCKHOLM CONFERENCE

A United Nations Conference on Human Environment was convened in Stockholm in July 1972. Almost a complete cross-section of the world's 3.5 billion people was represented by delegates from 114 nations. Although there were differences, the most remarkable thing was that such a conference was actually held; that it acknowledged that a world-wide environmental emergency existed, and that nations despite their sovereignty had mutual responsibilities for such common property as the atmosphere and the oceans. Approval was given to an "action program" with 200 recommendations, ranging from monitoring climatic change and oceanic pollution to the preservation of the world's vanishing plant and animal species. And an administrative machinery was recommended to coordinate the world-wide environmental efforts of governments and agencies.

Margaret Mead, the noted anthropologist, summed up the thoughts of the many nongovernmental conservation groups who watched from the sidelines. In an address to the conference on behalf of these groups she said:

> This is a revolution in thought, fully comparable to the Copernican revolution by which, four centuries ago, men were compelled to revise their whole sense of the earth's place in the cosmos. Today we are challenged to recognize as great a change in our concept of man's place in the biosphere. Our survival in a world that continues to be worth inhabiting depends upon translating this new perception into relevant principles and concrete actions.

Some of the important generalizations from the material on ecology and survival are:

In the long run, man's welfare depends on the natural world around him. His well-being depends on other living things, on water, on air, on soil, on mineral resources, on open space.

Our planet is a closed system in which indefinite expansion or exploitation of its resources would be disastrous to all life, including that of man.

Life is limited to a 13-mile thick layer of our planet called the ecosphere or biosphere.

In the biosphere man enjoys the benefits of a self-renewing natural environment.

Two reasons for concern about the world's resources are:

1. The world's human population is increasing at an explosive rate.
2. Industrialization has resulted in an enormous increase in the consumption of resources and in the pollution of the environment.

A major goal of education is the recognition by man of his interdependence with his environment and with life everywhere, and the development of a culture that maintains that relationship through policies and practices necessary to secure the future of an environment fit for life and fit for living.

The understanding of interrelationships of living things with each other and with their physical environment—the science of ecology—is the key to sound environmental practice.

Food chains and food webs are pathways along which materials and energy are passed along in the world of living things.

The organisms that are part of a food chain or food web act as producers (usually green plants), consumers (usually animals), or decomposers (usually bacteria and fungi).

The number of living organisms necessary to support a food chain may be represented by a pyramid with a broad base of food producers, green plants, at the bottom, with plant-eating animals on the next steps, and with carnivorous animals up to the apex.

All living things are dependent on the interwoven cycles of water, carbon dioxide, oxygen, and nitrogen.

The consequences of disturbing the web of life are often unforeseen and often unfortunate.

Pesticide chemicals and others introduced into the environment by man must be used with caution because they may end up in plants and animals other than those for which they were intended, and because they may disturb a chain of interrelationships in such a way as to harm other forms of life.

Some resources—such as air, sunlight, and water—are inexhaustible. Air and water, however, can become unfit for living things.

Some resources—such as soil, vegetation, animal life, and fresh water—are renewable.

Some resources—such as coal, oil, natural gas, and metals, land as open space, and certain kinds of wilderness—are nonrenewable. Their supply cannot be replenished.

As we use up conventional energy sources, such as the fossil fuels, we are turning more to the fission of atoms. In both, however, there are serious pollution problems.

New resources to replace some of those in short supply may be discovered and developed in the future by scientists and engineers. New resources, however, sometimes present new environmental problems; there is need for research into these effects.

We must conserve resources as far as possible by recycling them.

All plant and animal life, including man's, is dependent directly or indirectly on the soil.

One-third of the valuable topsoil in the United States has been lost since the coming of the colonists, largely because of man's unwise practices.

The erosion of soil can be checked by contour plowing, strip farming, and terracing.

Forests are very important in preventing soil erosion and floods.

To maintain soil fertility it is necessary to return to the soil what the crops remove.

Rotation of crops, the planting of legumes, and the addition of fertilizers help maintain soil fertility. The potential harm to the environment that may be caused by chemical fertilizers, such as nitrates and phosphates, must be evaluated in regulating their use.

Fire, insects, disease, and wind are responsible for much forest destruction.

Forest conservation measures include combating fire, harmful insects, and tree diseases; practicing careful lumbering methods; reforestation; and the establishing of national and state forests.

The problem of water conservation is that of having the right amount of fresh water of good quality in the right place at the right time.

The basic cause of water shortages in cities in recent years is the increased consumption of water.

A matter of concern in recent years has been the falling water table in many areas.

Water conservation involves the protection and extension of watershed areas, construction of dams and reservoirs, improved industrial practices in relation to water usage—including the reuse of water—and elimination of waste.

The desalting of sea water may provide a possible solution of the fresh-water problem.

With growing urbanization and industrialization the seriousness of the air-pollution problem increases.

Air pollution is damaging to our health, particularly because of its effects on our respiratory systems.

Automobile exhausts and smokestacks produce most of the dangerous air pollutants.

Wildlife should be protected because of its economic value—both immediate and long range—its recreational value, and its right to exist.

Wilderness is a precious heritage.

Conservation includes the improvement of the urban environment. This includes better housing, more neighborhood facilities, reduction of air and noise pollution, and better planning.

The preservation of open areas in and near urban centers serves many vital purposes.

Conservation requires long-range planning.

Man is a part and a partner of nature.

The new environmental challenge is not mastery by man of his environment but mastery of his desires and judgment with respect to the use of his environment.

Discovering for Yourself

1. Investigate the source of your water supply and find out about the problems of its purification, pollution, adequacy, and so on.
2. Investigate the status of nuclear reactors in your area. Are they in operation? Planned? What are the effects?
3. Find out about the Clean Air Act of 1970 and the National Environmental Policy Act of 1969. What differences have the passage of these acts made in your environment? Does your state have "Clean-Air" plans that comply with the standards set up by the federal government?
4. Find out about the work of the Environmental Protection Agency (EPA). Write for the booklet, *Toward a New Environmental Ethic,* that describes EPA's work. Address the Superintendent of Documents, U.S. Government Printing Office, Washington, D.C. 20402.
5. Investigate examples of biological control used in your community or state—Japanese beetle, for instance. How successful is the attempt? What hazards are involved?

6. Investigate some of the newer sources of energy that are considered as possibilities in your area—the sun, wind, tides. What progress is being made? What are the difficulties? Why are these investigations important?
7. Find out about the Endangered Species Conservation Act. What difference has it made in the ecology of your state?
8. Investigate the effects of the use of DDT in your area and try to discover how laws banning its use have affected the ecology.
9. Investigate the latest information about the use of phosphate-containing detergents.
10. Examine carefully a wood lot or other area that has been burned. Find out what has happened to animal and plant life. Observe the area over a period of a month or as long as possible to see what happens.
11. Observe various hillsides after a heavy rain. Describe them and compare the results of the rain on the surface of each. Explain what happened.
12. Keep a record of the things that come from the earth that you use in one day. Indicate those that are in danger of becoming depleted, those that are being replaced in sufficient quantity, and those that appear to be in plentiful supply.
13. Find out about air pollution in your state. Is smog a problem? What is being done about it?
14. Interview a county agriculture agent or some other individual who is concerned with soil, water, and wildlife conservation in your area. Find out what the most pressing conservation problems are, why they have become critical, what is being done about them.
15. Visit an experimental farm or station and find out how research is being carried out to solve environmental problems.
16. Plan and carry out an experiment that will show the results of using or not using a commercial fertilizer in soil.
17. Get copies of the game laws of your state for the past five or ten years. Examine the laws. What changes have been made? Why have they been made?
18. Find out what the problems of forest conservation in your state are. Locate tree nurseries; visit one and report your findings. Gather seeds of various kinds of forest trees and try to germinate them. Talk with a forest ranger, forest lookout observer, or other individual who has firsthand information about forest conservation.
19. Find out where the Christmas trees in your community come from and how they are grown and transported. Cut a small section from the trunks of several Christmas trees and also measure the height of each tree. What can you tell about the tree by looking at the sections with a magnifying glass? Is there any relationship between the height of the tree and the rings in the section?
20. Read *Silent Spring* by Rachel Carson and *Since Silent Spring* by Frank Graham Jr. (*See* Bibliography.) What pesticides are in common use in the area where you live? What are the results?
21. Investigate noise pollution in your community. Why is it a problem? What is being done about it? Do *you* contribute to it?
22. Investigate the "let burn" policy that is being discussed by foresters and others. Is it true that some forest fires are actually desirable? In what ways? Do you agree with this point of view?

(Courtesy of Phyllis Marcuccio.)

CHAPTER 14B

TEACHING "ECOLOGY AND SURVIVAL"

The underlying principles of ecology and survival cannot be learned by sermons, except for the sermons that nature itself preaches. Environmental education should be based on *things to do*, here and now, so that children will start moving in the right direction with their muscles as well as their brains. It should be based on enjoyment of the outdoors. We should make every effort to heighten that enjoyment so that our children, now and later as adult citizens, will be motivated to save and protect that which gave them pleasure, peace, and beauty.

Ecology is a study of living things in relation to each other and their environment.[1] We do not need to define survival. This chapter ranks at the top in its importance and urgency. It is impossible to overestimate its content. Here we are indeed intending to influence behavior. With children it is important to maintain an attitude that is both realistic and at the same time optimistic. Certainly these are grave problems. There are also answers, but they involve all of us—every individual. Teacher leadership is necessary to develop the attitudes and concerns of the beginning citizen and to provide the children with information from which to act. Leadership from teachers comes about through being *informed, concerned,* and *active*—convinced that how individuals behave is important.

The study of ecology is urban as well as rural. It is based on an understanding of the interrelationships of man with his natural and physical environment. It is sound practice to study ecology *in* the environment. Any neighborhood, city, or county can serve as a laboratory for the study of these interrelationships. The problems of air, water, soil, and noise pollution that go with population increase are almost everywhere. The school grounds are constantly changing under the influence of the sun, rain, and wind. The trees on the street provide shade and beauty for human beings, protection for birds, food for insects. Parks, fields, streams, and rivers provide further opportunities for discovering interrelationships in nature. Bulldozers that uproot trees to provide building sites also give children an opportunity to study how man is changing the environment. The study of land use concerns us all, as do the food chains and environmental cycles on which we depend.

Each school can make an inventory of the environment and survey changes and needs. Recycling of paper, metals, and so forth are common and should be included in the survey. Children, teachers, parents, and other interested individuals may cooperate in making such an inventory and engage in the activities necessary to improve conditions that exist. The outcome of this survey may be a campaign to clear up an area, or any other project that involves children in constructive community activity. When children see that what they do makes a difference they have learned one of the prime concepts of ecology and survival.[2]

[1] *See Teacher's Guide to Ecology* and *Book A.: Nature and Needs, Book B.: Habits and Habitats, Book C.: Problems and Progress*, and *Our Polluted World*, American Education Publications, "Ecology Program" (Education Center, Columbus, Ohio, 1972).

[2] *Environmental Education in the Elementary School* (Washington, D.C.: National Science Teachers Association): B. Schultz: *"Ecology: The Definition," "Ecology for the Child,"* and *"Your Town: A Biotic Community with People"*; W.E. Steidle: *"The Environmental Education Act"; See also The New Environmental Education Program of the U.S. Office of Education* (Washington, D.C.: U.S. Government Printing Office, 1971).

We hope that when children become adults they will participate in and support the endeavors of local and national groups to further the improvement of our environment, that they will be able to distinguish between selfish interests of small pressure groups and the large interests of all people, that they will not be beguiled into sacrificing our precious inheritance for momentary gains.

In Chapter 14A we emphasized that ecology is concerned with *environment, living things, interrelationships,* and *resources* and their wise use and preservation. Other chapters are related to these concerns: "The Earth and Its Surface," "The Sun and the Planets," "The Air and Weather."

SOME BROAD CONCEPTS: "Ecology and Survival"

We depend for our existence on living things, water, air, soil, and mineral resources.

The world's population increase multiplies the problems of the care and use of its resources.

All living things are related to each other and to their environment.

Food chains are the paths followed by materials and energy in the world of living things.

Pesticides and other chemicals used by man may disturb the chain of interrelationships and must be used with caution.

Some of our resources are renewable; others are not.

When air, water, and soil become polluted they cannot serve their functions in the cycles of nature. Such pollution must be avoided.

We must conserve resources by recycling when possible.

All living things depend directly or indirectly on the soil.

Conservation involves the wise use of our resources in both city and rural environments.

FOR YOUNGER CHILDREN

There are many experiences for young children that will help prepare them for better understanding of ecology and its problems. Some of these activities—for example, keeping an animal pet, raising a garden, observing the places where animals live, seeing how animals take care of their young—have been described in other chapters.

Here we suggest additional activities focused on the development of understandings leading to attitudes and actions essential in ecology and survival.

Where Do the Things We Use Come From?[3]

As pupils explore their environment to see how they use plants and animals they consider where these and other things they use come from. They may begin by using

[3] J. Schwartz: *It's Fun to Know Why: Experiments with Things Around Us,* (New York: McGraw-Hill, 1973).

the list of plants and animals they make and expanding it to include additional materials, such as iron and other metals, bricks, glass, gasoline, and so on. Pictures from magazines and other sources that show things we use will be helpful. They may then examine the list and attempt to devise a classification: from under the ground, grow in soil, that come from animals, and others. Give children an opportunity to try out different classifications that seem to make sense to them.

(*See* pp. 424–5.)

Having made a grouping, suggest that children now try to reclassify the items according to: those that we use up, those we can replace, those we can use over again, or some other classification that will help children realize that some of the materials are plentiful, some are renewable, some nonrenewable, some inexhaustible.

This discussion can lead to consideration of how we need to conserve some of the materials, how this is being done, and how children can help. Recycling may be mentioned. It may be possible for children to visit a plant where some kind of recycling is taking place. The practices of paper collecting for recycling, using returnable bottles, and so on are important to consider.

What Makes the Air Polluted?

(*See* p. 461.)

This problem is developed in detail for older children but because of its importance it is also suggested here. Examine the "Air Pollution" section in the checklist that follows in the projects for older children and select items that seem appropriate for consideration by younger children. Begin by suggesting that they observe air conditions on several different days and see if they can notice any differences. Suggest that they observe sources of air pollution on their way to and from school (smokestacks, cars and busses, airplanes, and others) and report them. Keep a list of these sources. Help the children to discover what is being done to stop pollution. Discuss why our polluted air is not healthy to breathe.

In our zeal to develop interest, attitudes, and observing skills in young children we are sometimes inclined to go into greater detail than suits their interests and abilities. This should be avoided. It may be overcome by returning to the problem at many different times during the school year, instead of trying to force in-depth study at one time.

Why Is Soil so Important to Us?

The background for the solution of this problem is suggested in Chapter 6 and in the previous problems. Chapter 10 describes experiences and experiments intended to help children understand what plants need in order to live and grow.

If children have not had these experiences plan for them to:

1. Examine soil to find out what it is made of.
2. Plant seeds in different kinds of soil (good and poor), and observe the effects on plant growth.

Studying soil samples and using local sources to test them is an important part of learning about the ecology of an area. Here pupils are examining subsoil as well as a sod surface. (*Courtesy of U.S. Department of Agriculture, Soil Conservation Service.*)

3. Use fertilizer on some plants and not on others, and note the differences.
4. Explore the schoolyard to observe plants growing in different soil, noting the difference.
5. Examine vacant lots to see what plants are growing there.
6. List the things they use in one day that come directly and indirectly from the soil.

OTHER PROBLEMS FOR YOUNGER CHILDREN

(*See* Ch. 10B.)

1. How do we use plants and animals?
2. Where does our water supply come from?

3. How is water made safe for drinking?
4. What pollutes our drinking water?
5. How can we improve the appearance of our schoolyard?
6. Where do animals and plants live in our neighborhood?[4]
7. Why is the water cycle important to us?
8. What can we learn about the life of a tree?
9. What do water and wind do to soil?

FOR OLDER CHILDREN

How Can We Study a City Environment?

What is your environment like? Investigating this problem in the city and in the country involves important investigating skills and produces data that are essential in *identifying the problems* that exist as we live together in these environments, *emphasizing their importance,* and leading to *suggestions for attempting to solve them.* This is another of the many examples of how important it is to involve children in activities that are urgent in every respect.

The following checklist,[5] designed to assist pupils in surveying a city environment, was used as part of an "Earth Day" observance. Such a list helps attain the aims indicated in the previous paragraph. The list can be altered to fit other environments. Use of the list involves several important processes, including *observing, collecting* and *recording* data, and *interpreting* the data. The follow-up attempts to explain causes and plan action are very important.

AN ENVIRONMENTAL CHECKLIST

EARTHDAY, as April 22 is known, is the beginning of a long on-going effort to improve the environment. After collecting and interpreting the data, your class may want to consider the most effective ways in which it can participate in follow-up activities.

Name ____

PS ________________ Borough ________________ Address ________________

[4] *See Science Grade 5* for "Little Environments": "In the Schoolyard," "On and Under a Tree," "On the Lawn," "In the Soil," "In the Water" (Brooklyn, N.Y.: Board of Education of the City of New York, 1968; may be adapted for younger children. Contains many suggestions for observation.

[5] *See* J. Rosner: *An Environmental Checklist,* in *Newsletter* of the Elementary School Science Association, vol. 9, no. 2 (New York, N.Y.: Spring 1970). *See also Air Pollution, Water Pollution, Noise Pollution,* Teachers Editions (Reading, Mass.: Addison-Wesley Publishing Co., Inc., 1972). Suggestions for teaching; subject matter; illustrations; and D.C. Cox: *How to Investigate the Environment in the City:* Air and Water, leaflet (Washington, D.C.: National Science Teachers Association, 1972).

Was the walk in AM? ______________________ PM? ______________________

How long did the walk last? ______________________

Hours ______________________ Mins. ______________________

Walk around the square block on which your school is located. Look, listen, smell, touch. Check the things you find.

Air Pollution

1. How does the sky look? ______ clear ______ hazy ______ darker in some parts than in others.
2. Do your eyes tear or smart? ______ yes ______ no
3. Do you smell anything in the air? ______ yes ______ no
4. Do you like what you smell? ______ yes ______ no ______ some things
5. Check any of these things you smell ______ food ______ gasoline ______ car exhaust ______ garbage others ______________________
6. If possible, watch a bus leave a stop. Can you see the exhaust? ______ yes ______ no
7. Do you see exhaust coming from automobiles or trucks? ______ yes ______ no
   If yes, from how many autos or trucks ______________________
8. Do you see any airplanes? ______ yes ______ no
   If yes (a) how many ______
   (b) how many are leaving a trail of dark exhaust ______
9. Do you see dark smoke coming out of chimneys? ______ yes ______ no
   If yes, are these chimneys on ______ apartment houses ______ private house ______ factories ______ power plants ______ city-owned buildings
   others ______________________
10. Rub a tissue against the wall of a building, a fence, a lamp post or a mailbox. Does the tissue get dirty? ______ yes ______ no

Litter and Destruction

1. How many litter baskets do you see on the walk? ______
2. How many are ______ empty ______ partly filled ______ full ______ overflowing
3. Is there litter? ______ along the curb ______ on the sidewalks ______ near the buildings.
4. How many covered garbage cans do you see? ______
5. How many uncovered garbage cans do you see? ______
6. How many soda or beer can flip-tops do you see? ______
8. How many of the soda or beer cans are made of iron? ______ (use a magnet)
9. Is there broken glass along the curb? ______ yes ______ no
   on the sidewalk? ______ yes ______ no

10. How many times do you see evidence that people did not curb their dogs? ______
11. How many candy, gum or ice-cream wrappers do you find on the sidewalk or along the curb? ______
12. Are there any pieces of furniture or other household articles lying on the sidewalk or in the street? ______ yes ______ no.
    If yes, how many? ______
13. Are there any abandoned cars in the street? ______ yes ______ no
    If yes, how many? ______
14. Are newspapers lying on the sidewalk or flying around? ______ yes ______ no
15. How many vacant lots or strips of land do you see? ______
    How many are tidy and pretty? ______ How many ugly? ______
16. How many broken windows do you see? ______
17. In how many places do you see writing on the walls, billboards, public signs, or on sidewalks? ______

Noise Pollution

1. Stand still for two minutes and listen. Check all the sounds you hear. Add others not on the list. ______ fire engine ______ train ______ horn ______ ambulance ______ police siren ______ airplane ______ bus engine ______ truck engine ______ screeching brakes ______ fog horn ______ autos or trucks moving along the street ______ shouting ______ riveting ______ cement mixer ______ bulldozer.
2. How would you rate the general noise level?
   ______ very noisy ______ noisy ______ moderate ______ quiet

Trees and Plants

1. How many trees do you see? ______
2. How many of these trees
   (a) are growing straight ______ bend ______
   (b) have some soil around them ______ have no soil ______
   (c) have broken branches ______
   (d) have pictures or words carved on them ______
   (e) look healthy ______ look sickly ______
3. How many of the dead or sickly trees are near bus stops? ______
4. How many places do you see where trees have been removed? ______
5. How many of the following do you see?
   (a) windowboxes ______
   (b) small gardens ______
   (c) vest-pocket parks ______
6. Is there a park or a large green area within sight? ______ yes ______ no

Operation New York[6] is an example of a project designed to explore the use of a city outdoor environment for enriching teaching. The report suggests ways in which rocks, water, soil, plants, and animals may be used to provide meaningful and enjoyable experiences for girls and boys. It is a guide to the study of many interesting earth forms: hills, plains, rock outcrops, lakes, rivers, harbors, and beaches. Use is made of the locale of the school—the schoolyard, nearby buildings, excavations, sidewalks, and curbs—for an understanding of man's use of earth resources. Attention is directed to the forces of nature at work: erosion of soil in a vacant lot or nearby park, formation of "flood areas: following a storm, the wearing away of stone, the decay of leaves into soil. The interrelationships of living things—including man—with their physical surroundings are understood as boys and girls explore the many "little environments" that are found within the city. A study of this report will provide many suggestions to other city groups for using their environments more effectively.

Children may survey a city to find out how provisions are made for water, food, and other essentials. This investigation may be followed by a survey of waste disposal, air and water pollution, and other conditions.

The scientific and social aspects of the problems of conservation are related. This is one of the places where two areas of the curriculum (science and social studies) should certainly be considered together. These relationships will be obvious in many of the activities in this chapter.

What Causes Air Pollution?

The section on "Air Pollution" in the checklist points up observations children can make regarding the conditions of air as well as the causes of the pollution that exist. Understanding the urgency of the air pollution problem begins with observation.

It should be obvious that every citizen needs to be informed about the causes of pollution and possible cures of this national problem, and must be prepared to do his part.[7] The importance of helping children become conscious of the problems cannot be too great. The following problems may be investigated by small groups: "What are some of the chief causes of air pollution?" "What is the meaning of thermal inversions?" "What are some of the harmful effects of air pollution?" "What is being done to stop pollution?" "What are units of the government doing?" "Why must all states cooperate?" "How do scientists study this problem?"

Children can make some relatively simple tests for air pollution[8] using filter paper exposed to the air in different places and examining various materials that collect after

[6] *Operation New York: Using the Natural Environment of the City as a Curriculum Resource* (Brooklyn, N.Y.: Board of Education of the City of New York, 1960).

[7] Write for list of material from the Division of Air Pollution, Public Health Service, Department of Health, Education and Welfare, Washington, D.C. 20201; and for *Today and Tomorrow in Air Pollution*, Public Health Service Publication no. 1555 (Washington, D.C.: U.S. Government Printing Office, 1967); *Air Pollution Publications—A Selected Bibliography*, Public Health Service Publication, no. 979 (Washington, D.C.: U.S. Government Printing Office, 1967).

[8] *See Testing for Air Pollution, Science Study Aid* available from Educational Service Branch, U.S. Agricultural Research Center, Beltsville, Md. 20705.

several days of exposure with a magnifying glass. The papers can be weighed before and after exposure (*see* next section).

Examining air filters from furnaces and air conditioners; taking samples for examination also yields interesting data about pollution.

Sections of microscope slides may be covered with vaseline or similar substances and suspended by one end in various locations. The slides can then be examined under a microscope and compared. White handkerchiefs can also be spread on the ground in various locations.

The Newsletter[9] suggests the following procedure to use in collecting dust from the air, as well as information about it.

What Kind of Dust Is in the Air?

Use scotch tape (sticky side up) or a greased piece of paper (make a grease spot with oil or butter on white paper). Put the collecting materials in various places. Make sure to use a control for each site where the collection will be made. (Place one piece of the collecting material in an envelope. Keep the other in the open.) Make sure to write the date and location of each piece of collecting material.

After the dust has been collected, examine it with a magnifying glass, microscope, or microprojector. Note the differences in the kinds of dust collected; in the amount collected over periods of time, that is, one day, three days, six days. Keep records.

Date	*Place*	*Kind of Dust Collected*	*Where Do You Think It Came From?*

Try to find what kind of dust you have collected (particles of soil, carbon, lint, hair, feathers, pollen grains).

What Is Thermal Inversion?

The phenomenon of thermal inversion is increasingly evident in many areas and the principle can be easily demonstrated:[10]

Use 4 milk bottles or 16 ounce laboratory bottles. Place two in the refrigerator or outdoors on a cold day. Place the other two on a radiator, stove, or in a pan of hot water.

Hold a piece of paper with tongs. Light the paper with a match and let it burn in the bottle containing warm air. When the bottle is filled with smoke invert the cold bottle over it. The smoke will rise from the warm air to the cold.

[9] *Ibid., The Newsletter,* "What Kind of Dust Is in the Air?"

[10] *See Demonstration of Thermal Inversion.* J. Schwartz in *Newsletter* of the Elementary School Science Association. New York City, Vol. 10, No. 1 Fall 1970.

Repeat, placing smoke in the other cold bottle. Invert the second warn over it. Smoke remains in the cold air.

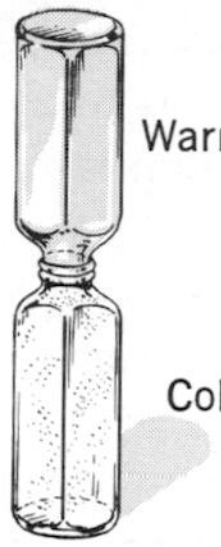

Concepts and Interpretations

1. An irregularity in the normal convection pattern is a "temperature" or thermal inversion.
2. In a thermal inversion the position of the cold and warm air layers are reversed. The cold air is close to the ground; the warmer air lies above it.
3. The cold air, being heavy, cannot rise through the layer of warm air, which serves as a lid and traps the colder air under it.

What Are Food Chains?

Children comprehend the meaning of ecology and develop concern for problems in the environment as they learn more about interrelationships of the living things around them.

(*See* p. 419.)

The interdependence of living things with their physical environment is best understood by studying it in small samples called food chains. A food chain might be defined simply as: "Who eats whom?" A school lawn is a good place to look for food chains. Grass, spiders, insects, slugs, earthworms, robins, starlings, Japanese beetles, aphids, ants, caterpillars, honeybees, squirrels, are involved in a number of food chains. Pupils will enjoy the detective work involved in tracking down some of these chains. For example, pupils find that robins eat earthworms, which eat soil. Leaves decay to form soil. The leaves of some plants are sucked of their juices by aphids, which in turn are "milked" by ants. There are countless numbers of such chains to be discovered through careful observation and reading to verify.

The relationships between living organisms and their environment is referred to as ecology, and there are many other examples of these relationships in addition to those we have described in our discussions of food chains. The habitat of a forest floor, the aquarium, a terrarium, a dead tree, the area around the base of a tree, and many other environments are excellent for study. There are four considerations: (1.) the characteristics of the environment (temperature, moisture, physical and chemical make up, food, light), (2.) the structure and characteristics of living things that inhabit the environment, (3.) the relationships of living things to each other and to the environment, and (4.) changes that occur when man interferes with the relationships. What, for example, happens to the plants and animals living on a forest floor when trees are cut, to the life in a pond when it is drained?

Pupils may demonstrate these ideas in their classrooms by setting a well-established aquarium or terrarium in a dark room or adding more animal life to an aquarium, and so on. Learning here involves careful gathering of data, making predictions, and attempting interpretations.

What Are Cycles?[11]

(*See* pp. 309–10.)

Chapter 9B describes evaporation and condensation and emphasizes the recycling of water. These experiences and experiments may be used to introduce the concept of cycles. The material in Chapter 10B includes material on the cycle plants make from seed to seed and describes the oxygen-carbon dioxide cycle as it happens in a balanced aquarium. These experiences and experiments may be added to those with the nitrogen cycle described in the preceding chapter. Children can examine soil from a woods and note the decaying bits of leaves and twigs. "What are they made of?" "Where did these materials come from?" "What will eventually happen to them?" "How does this decay take place?" "Then what happens to the materials?" Cycles take place in any environment, urban or rural, but most children are unaware of their importance.

What Is Biodegradable?

Closely associated by contrast with cycles and food chains is the concept that many materials *do not* decay or otherwise change and produce reuseable materials. As an introduction to this concept children may collect a bag or so of the usual trash that accumulates along the streets and roadsides: paper, wood, twigs, pieces of plastic, food scraps, aluminum foil, pieces of iron, cotton, leaves, wool, nylon and other synthetic materials, and so on.

"How can we find out what will happen to this material after a period of several weeks or months?" "What do you think will happen to some of the material?" "Will it all decay?" "Will some of it?" Suppose we make a list of the material, bury it in the ground where the rain will keep the soil moist, and see what happens. At intervals of three or four weeks dig up the material and examine it. Rebury it. Reexamine it. Use the list to record what appears to be happening to the various materials. What inferences can you draw from this experience? An indoor box of soil may be used instead of the outdoors if this is easier. Water the soil frequently.

[11] Science Curriculum Improvement Study (SCIS): *Life Cycles* (Chicago, Rand McNally and Co.). Investigation of ecosystems. Suggests experiences, methods of discovery, and illustrates subject matter. And G.O. Blough: *Cycles* (New York: McGraw-Hill, 1973).

What Does Rain Do to Soil?

Several of the concepts about soil and its uses may be learned from simple experiments. Pupils can demonstrate that soil is composed of materials of different kinds and characteristics. Refer to the experience described in "How Can We Separate Different Parts of the Soil?" in Chapter 6B. Much of the lightest material that floats or is in the top layers contains important nourishment for plants. It is carried away by water as it runs over land that is not protected by a cover of vegetation.

(See p. 150.)

Experimenting to solve a problem that involves setting up careful controls, collecting and recording data, and drawing conclusions is an important science learning experience. The charts indicate the date, amount of water poured, the amount that runs off, and the amount of soil washed off in each case (*see* text description).

After a heavy rainfall pupils can take samples of the water from a nearby stream and examine it to see what makes it look muddy. They can see particles of soil in the water. If the water is left standing for several hours the soil will settle to the bottom, and the water can be poured off and sediment examined so that pupils can see that it really is soil. The banks of the stream from which the water is taken should be examined to see the small gullies that the running water has worn away. If sections of the bank are sodded or covered with plants these may be compared with barren parts of the bank to see how plants keep the soil from being washed away.

After a heavy rain, pupils can explore the school grounds or other nearby places to see effects of the rain. They may notice places where soil has been washed over the sidewalks and find gullies from which the soil has been removed. They can look for similar places on their way to and from school. In many schools, pupils have planned ways to stop such runoff erosion and have successfully carried out their plans.

The drawing shows an experiment planned to compare the effect of water running over bare soil with that of water running over soil covered with grass. The arrangement was built of boards from packing boxes. Both slanting surfaces are covered with the same kind of garden soil; one surface is left bare, the other is covered with grass sod. Children can substitute grass seed, barley, or rye for the sod.

A measured amount of water is poured over each surface and caught again after it has run through the soil. The amounts and color of the two runoffs are then compared to see that the soil covered with sod takes up more water than the bare soil. They can use these findings in their outdoor observations. In a city environment this is evident on the playground, on sidewalks, in parks, vacant lots, and similar places.

In What Kind of Soil Do Plants Grow Best?

Get samples of several different kinds of soil from a fertile flower or truck garden, from the woods, from a place in the schoolyard where nothing seems to grow very well, and from a place where a cellar for a house is being dug. Place identical amounts of each soil into identical flowerpots with identical drainage, and plant several bean or corn seeds in the pots. Identify the various pots with appropriate labels. Observe the difference in the growth of the plants. Measure the growth and compare. Be sure to remember to have only *one* variable, in this case the kind of soil. Children will probably think of other experiences to demonstrate the effects of good and poor soil in growing plants.

Where Does Our Water Supply Come From?

(*See* pp. 440–4.)

The problem of an adequate water supply has become acute in many cities as well as rural areas. No matter in what regions pupils live, they can investigate to find the answers to such problems as: "Where does our water supply come from?" "How is it made pure?" "Is there any danger that the supply may be depleted?" "Should anything be done to increase it?" "Is it being polluted? By what?" "What steps are being taken to stop this pollution?"

If pupils live where water comes from deep wells they may be able to find a place where a well is being driven, talk to the well drillers, get samples of the soil and rock that is brought up in the drilling, and learn something about the nature of the layers through which drilling is being done.

In cities where water comes from lakes, rivers, or similar sources pupils can visit the water works to learn what the source of the water is, whether or not it is adequate, whether there are plans for enlarging the supply, and what sources of pollution exist. While they are on the visit they will want also to see how the water supply is purified. They can see the filter beds and learn about other methods used for purifying water.

Children may not realize that rain falling directly into a reservoir produces only a small part of the supply of water. Most of the water in a reservoir flows into it from the sloping land surrounding it. This land, called a watershed, receives the water originally as rain. Brooks and streams from the watershed feed the reservoir.

(*See* diagram below.)

To demonstrate how a watershed area collects water crumple a large piece of aluminum foil, then open it, and crease it lengthwise. Place it as shown and sprinkle water on it from a sprinkling can. Children will see how the water runs together from

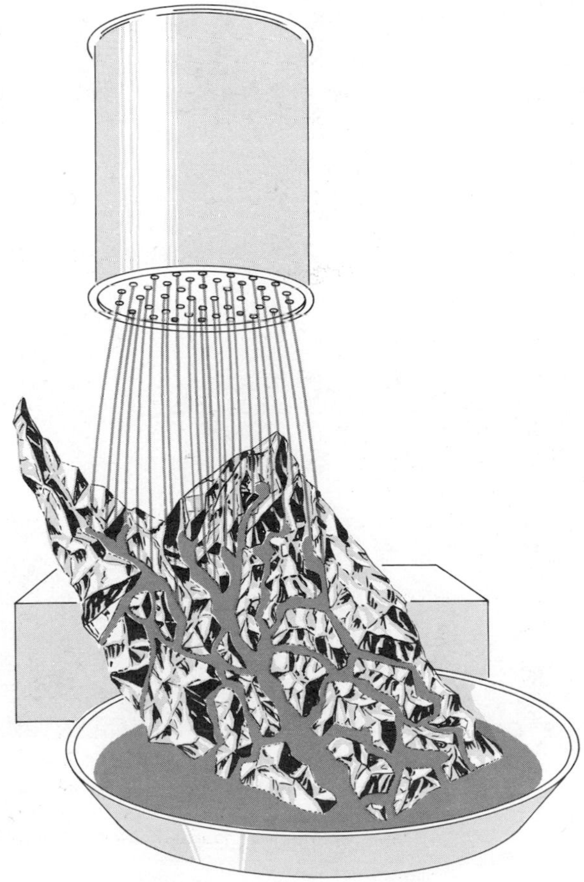

This demonstration helps make the idea of the watershed more meaningful (*see* text description). Children may be asked to compare what is illustrated here with a real watershed.

the wide area into the collecting "reservoir." Examples of such miniature "watersheds" in a city environment are rain falling on the schoolyard and running into a drain or puddle; rain falling on sidewalks and streets and washing into gutters.

(*See* p. 444.)

Detergents in our water supply are a continued source of pollution. Children may select several detergents, mixing them with equal amounts of water, and note how long it takes foam or bubbles to disappear. They can try to compare the results with an equal amount of pure soap plus water. Children can read accounts of contamination by various brands of detergents and help to promote the use of less polluting kinds.

This dramatic demonstration shows the importance of ground cover. A variation is described in the accompanying text. Almost any school yard or neighborhood furnish examples of erosion or lack of it, and a field trip increases the relevance of such demonstrations. (*Courtesy of U.S. Department of Agriculture.*)

How Can We Study a Rural Environment?

During the study of "Ecology and Survival" pupils in rural areas can take field trips to observe some environmental factors, in contrast to the urban survey suggested earlier. Such trips will identify problems, point up their importance, and suggest solutions. These trips are important enough to deserve some attention from the county agricultural agent or from some of his assistants, who are often more than willing to help plan the trip by suggesting places and persons to visit.

If extensive trips are not possible many things can be observed by individuals and reported to the group, and some can be seen on short field trips near the school. Class discussions to interpret the observations are important.

Here are suggestions for a one-day trip. Not all the things mentioned can be seen in any one place, and certainly not all can be studied on any one-day trip, but they have all been observed at various times by elementary pupils on conservation-oriented trips:

1. Observe how the highway department has taken steps to stop erosion of the roadside, especially where there are steep grades (planting, seeding, terracing, covering with straw and brush, and so on).
2. Observe fields that are idle and try to decide why the land is not being used (county agricultural agent will help). Observe what happens to unused hilly fields if they are not covered with grass or other plants.
3. Observe the trash and debris along the roadside. How did it get there? What will happen to it? How could this accumulation be stopped?
4. Observe the difference in erosion between pasture fields and bare fields.
5. Observe how streams cut through the land; look at the banks of streams; examine the water to see whether it is muddy or clear. Is the water polluted? From what source? What can be done to avoid this pollution?
6. Go into the woods and dig down to see how the floor of the woods can absorb water more readily than hard ground can. Notice how the roots hold soil together and how the leaves decay to make soil. Bring back a sample of the soil to examine more closely in the classroom. What cycle is illustrated here? Why is it important? Notice how the trees in the woods are different from those in an open field, and see why they are better for lumber. Try to find out how many acres of land the woods covers and, if possible, find out the value of the timber.
7. Look for a place—either a forest or a roadside—that has recently been burned over. Walk over the burned area and see what has happened to plants and animals and what damage has been done. Compare it with a nearby place that has not been burned over.
8. Observe the effects of insects on the leaves of trees and on other vegetation. Try to find out whether the damage is serious and whether anything can be done to stop it. Have pesticides been used? Can you find out what kinds?
9. Visit a farm where conservation practices are in operation. Try to find out how much the conservation activities cost, how they were accomplished, and why the farmer decided to invest in them. Find out whether the government gave financial assistance to the project. Ask how deep the well is, whether or not there

are springs on the farm, and how the farmer supplies water for his livestock. Try to determine whether there is pollution of the supply and if measures to prevent it are taking place.

10. Make and put out a campfire. If pupils take their lunch on the trip they may choose a location in which to build a fire, learn how to build one outdoors, and take special care in extinguishing it, using sand and water. One committee may be appointed beforehand to be responsible for making the fire, another to extinguish it. After the latter committee has done its work the group can evaluate the job by deciding whether the fire has actually been extinguished. Ashes should be spread out to make sure. The discussion should be held "on the spot" to make the idea real. Before leaving, pupils can observe the surroundings to answer the question: "What harm could this campfire have done if it had not been properly extinguished?"
11. Look for places that provide good shelter for birds, and see whether there are birds present. Try to observe the birds closely enough to see what they are eating.
12. Find places where young trees are coming up and try to decide how they came to grow there. Were they planted? Did they perhaps grow from the seeds of other trees nearby? Are they on highway property or on privately owned land? Why are they important?
13. Look for "No Hunting" and "No Fishing" signs, and try to decide why they were put up in these places.
14. Look for hawks or other preying birds and try to decide whether they are helpful or harmful. Discuss what facts should be known before a decision is made. Are they part of a food chain? Try to describe it.
15. Take two samples of soil from a cut in the highway—one from just under the sod, the other from farther down. Measure the depth of the layer of dark soil at the top and note how far the roots of different kinds of plants go into this soil. Take the two samples of topsoil and of subsoil back to the schoolroom for further examination and for use in experimenting.
16. Visit a sawmill to watch trees being sawed and see how trees are selected, cut, and trimmed for use. One group visited a sawmill and listened to an explanation of the conservation practices that were involved. Pupils were asked to estimate the value of one of the large trees that was about to be cut. After the pupils had given their estimates the mill owner told them his estimate. When the class had returned to school and was discussing the trip each pupil was asked what things he could buy with the money that the tree represented. This helped pupils to see the value of trees and to realize more clearly what happens when trees burn in a forest fire.
17. Select items from the checklist for urban areas and use appropriate ones for observation.

OTHER PROBLEMS FOR OLDER CHILDREN

1. Can we start a school forest? How?
2. What plant quarantines are in effect in our area? Why?

3. What plant diseases or insect pests are dangerous in our area?
4. What living things are in danger of extinction in our environment?
5. How can we help with conservation practices in our school and home environments?
6. What is being done about the use of dangerous insect sprays in our environment?
7. How can we beautify our school and community area?
8. Who makes and enforces the laws to prevent pollution of the environment?

Resources to Investigate with Children

1. Local air-pollution and water-pollution agencies to find out about present practices, problems, and possible solutions.
2. Leaders in a 4-H Club for information about what the young people of the state are doing to prevent pollution and clean up the environment.
3. State soil conservation department for information on erosion problems of local area and conservation practices in action.
4. State conservation department for printed matter, films, and other resources useful in teaching conservation.
5. National Parks Service for regulations regarding the collection and disposal of waste materials in national forests and for similar information.
6. For information about membership and printed material available to teachers write: Environmental Action, Room 731, 1346 Connecticut Ave., N.W., Washington, D.C. 20036; Friends of the Earth, 529 Commercial St., San Francisco, California 94111; Sierra Club, 1050 Mills Tower, 220 Bush St., San Francisco, California 94104; Keep America Beautiful, Inc., 99 Park Ave., New York, New York 10016; The Wilderness Society, 729 Fifteenth St., N.W., Washington, D.C. 20005; National Wildlife Federation, Servicing Division, 1412 Sixteenth St., N.W., Washington, D.C. 20036; The Conservation Foundation, 1717 Massachusetts Ave., N.W., Washington, D.C. 20036; National Audubon Society, 950 Third Ave., New York, New York 10022; The Environmental Protection Agency, Superintendent of Documents, U.S. Government Printing Office, Washington, D.C. 20402.
7. Surrounding farm and forest area, the schoolyards, vacant lots, streets and parks to observe good and poor conservation practices.
8. County agriculture agent, high-school biology teachers for materials, suggestions, and information on local and state conservation problems.
9. State geologist for information about mineral deposits and other similar resources.
10. The local water-purification and sewage-disposal plants to observe sources of water, and to discover what pollution problems exist and find out what can be done about them.
11. Game warden for information about hunting and fishing regulations.
12. Local agencies to find out what the pollution laws are, and to determine what action schools can take to assist in preventing pollution of air and water. Check the telephone number to use in reporting smoke and other kinds of pollution.

Preparing to Teach

1. Prepare a large chart that diagrams the elements in a food chain and plan how you would use it in teaching some phases of ecology.
2. Make a list of practical activities you would use with children (of a particular grade) to make the material in this chapter more meaningful. Make one for use in a rural area and another for use in an urban area. Compare the lists. What does this comparison show?
3. Collect ecology-pollution newspaper items from your local newspaper and classify them to use as examples in encouraging children to make similar collections of their own (water pollution, forest fire, recycling, and so on).
4. Conduct a land-use survey in your community to determine how the area is being utilized—how much for roads, for buildings, for food production, and so on. Prepare a chart or other record that can serve as a sample to encourage children to prepare their own. Try to determine how land use has changed during the past dozen years or so. How has the population changed?
5. Prepare a poster, chart, or bulletin board to illustrate some ecological statement, such as: "America's Most Destructive Natural Enemy is the Forest Fire." "We Cannot Afford Not to Recycle." "People Start Pollution: People Can Stop It." Keep a record of how the project was done and use it to help children do a similar one.
6. Visit a recycling plant and prepare a plan that will help a group of children get the most out of such a visit (*see* field trip discussion in Part I).
7. Prepare a large chart that shows an important cycle that may be used to help children understand the meaning of the ideas involved. Plan ways to use the chart to help pupils prepare similar cycle charts.

(*See* Ch. 14A.)

8. Write for *Programs in Environmental Education*, National Science Teachers Association, 1201 Sixteenth St., N.W., Washington, D.C. 20036. Study the bulletin and use the information to devise a plan of action in your school.
9. Plan a "New Town" from the beginning, taking into account the natural environment, housing, recreation, public buildings, industry, business, open space, transportation, and so on. How would you develop such a unit with your pupils?
10. Write to the Superintendent of Documents, U.S. Government Printing Office, Washington, D.C. 20402 for free *Ecology* price list no. 88 for many sources of inexpensive pamphlets and other information.

(Courtesy NASA.)

PART IV

MATTER AND ENERGY

CHAPTER 15A

MOLECULES, ATOMS, AND CHEMICAL CHANGE

. . . the little things are infinitely the most important.
—Sherlock Holmes

Nature, therefore works by unseen bodies.
—Lucretius, 57 B.C.

(Courtesy of Dr. Martin J. Buerger, Massachusetts Institute of Technology.)

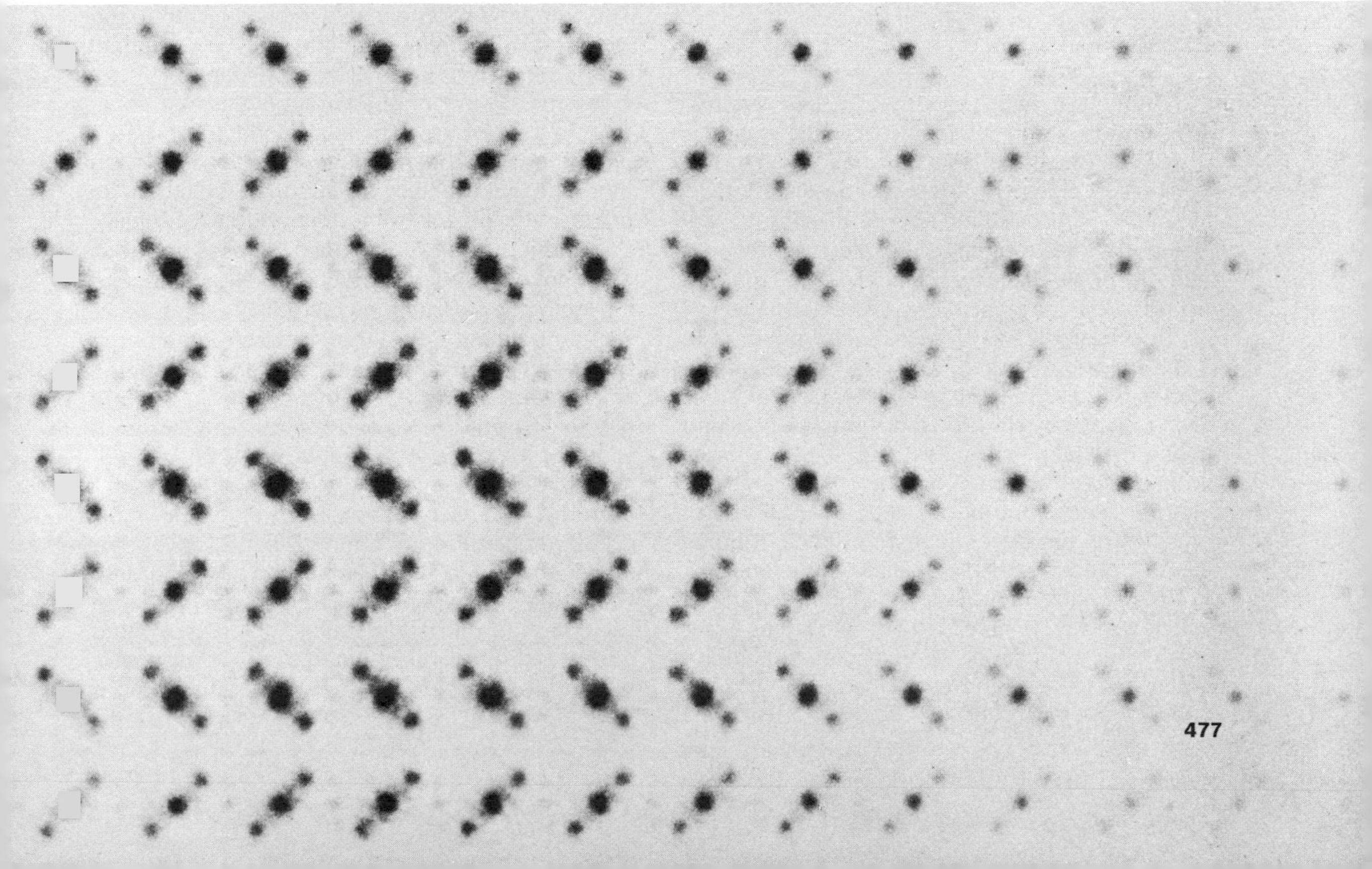

THE INVISIBLE BODIES

One of the most fundamental generalizations of science is that large-scale events have their causes in the behavior of minute particles. We have seen how the functioning of plants and animals is dependent on the activities of their component cells. The operations in a single cell depend on the genes within its nucleus. Let us probe more deeply for the more fundamental particles whose actions account for happenings in living and nonliving things—from the turning of a plant toward the light to the formation of a universe.

Consider a small amount of a common substance—a glassful of water. What do we know about the minute makeup of the water in this glass?

If we pour out half of it we still have the same substance left—water. Pour out half of the remainder and keep repeating this process. Would we ever reach a speck so small that to split it again would be to produce something other than water? Or is there no limit?

MOLECULES

There is a limit, and that limit is reached when only a single *molecule* of water is left in the glass. We can split such molecules (with the aid of an electric current or other source of energy), but if we do, we no longer have water; what we do have we shall discuss presently. The smallest particle of water, then, is a molecule of water.

(See pp. 498–9.)

To our sight, touch, taste, water appears to be a *continuous* substance; it is hard for us to imagine that it is made of separate, distinct particles. In a glass of water there are billions and billions of water molecules with a lot of empty space between them.

The theory that all substances are made of molecules is fundamental in all science. It holds true for liquids, gases, or solids. A gas such as air, for example, is made of molecules separated by wide spaces. Even an object as solid as a bar of iron is made of separate molecules, with much emptiness between the molecules.

Molecules differ from each other in a number of ways, as we shall see, but they have one thing in common: They are in constant motion at high speeds, striking other molecules and then bouncing off in new directions. Sometimes molecules "escape" from their surroundings. A street puddle "dries up" because its water molecules have bounced into the air and disappeared from view, adding to the water-vapor content of the atmosphere. If the air containing these molecules is chilled somewhat, as it might be as it rises to higher altitudes, the molecules of water lose some of their energy and merge to form the small droplets that make up a cloud.

When a lump of sugar dissolves in a cup of coffee the molecules of sugar fly away from the lump and move in among the molecules of liquid. Soon, if you taste the coffee, you taste the sugar.

A question that may arise when we consider the molecular nature of things is this: If all matter is composed of separate particles (which means that all matter is full of holes) what holds things together? What makes an iron bar so tough, so solid, so impenetrable? The answer lies in the attractive force that exists between molecules. This attractive force holds molecules together without any material coupling, just as a magnet exerts a force on a nail from a distance.

Thus, to our picture of molecules as separate, ever-moving entities we add one more characteristic: their mutual attraction for each other. In a solid this attraction is sufficient to prevent the object from changing shape easily. The motion of the molecules is restricted to a small space. In a liquid, such as water, molecular movement is not quite as restricted as in a solid. Although the attractive forces are strong enough to keep the molecules together, and at about the same average distance from each other, they are not strong enough to keep each molecule in a specific location. The water molecules occasionally escape from their particular neighborhood and wander through the liquid. This greater molecular freedom makes it possible for liquids to assume the shape of the container into which they have been placed. In a gas the more rapid motion of the molecules, combined with a molecular attraction reduced to practically zero, permits their rapid and free scattering. Open a bottle of ammonia in one corner of a room in which there are no drafts of air. Gradually the odor of ammonia will permeate every corner of the room as the ammonia molecules, escaping from the bottle, fly freely through the great spaces between the other molecules that comprise the air.

One more point should be stressed. The molecules of ammonia are different from the molecules of water and both of these are different from the molecules of other substances. But any water molecule is identical with any other water molecule, any ammonia molecule is identical with any other ammonia molecule, and so on.

To sum up, the molecular theory of matter makes four basic assumptions:

1. Matter is composed of exceedingly small separate particles called molecules.
2. Each different kind of matter is made up of its own particular kind of molecules.
3. Molecules are in rapid and ceaseless motion.
4. Molecules attract each other.

What proofs do scientists offer to back the molecular theory of matter? There are many; to describe them all would involve too detailed a presentation for this chapter. Let us mention just two:

1. Stir some dry, fine, oil pigment (carmine red will do) in a little water. Place a drop of this on a microscope slide and cover with a cover slip. Observe at a magnification of 440 power or higher. Observe the pigment carefully and you will see that individual specks of it move short distances in a zigzag fashion, never stopping. What causes this jiggling in a nonliving substance? We believe that it is due to the bombardment of these pigment particles by the smaller invisible molecules of water in which they are immersed. This is indirect evidence.
2. With the electron microscope, which magnifies up to 100,000 times, we have recently been able actually to photograph the individual molecules of many substances, such as the very large molecules of polio virus.

ATOMS

(*See* pp. 498–502.)

All matter, then, is made of separate, ever-moving molecules. Let us return now to the glass of water to see what would happen if we were to split its molecules.

In a common experiment performed in high-school science classes, an electric current is passed through some water. In this process, known as the electrolysis of water, two gases are produced, which on testing prove to be hydrogen and oxygen. Careful measurements would show that the weight of water that is lost is matched exactly by the combined weight of the two new gases that have been evolved. If this experiment were continued (with appropriate apparatus) to its very end all the water would disappear and in its place there would be hydrogen and oxygen gas.

If all the oxygen and hydrogen gas that is collected is now placed into a sturdy container and ignited with a flame there would be a powerful explosion—all the gases would disappear and all the original water would reappear.

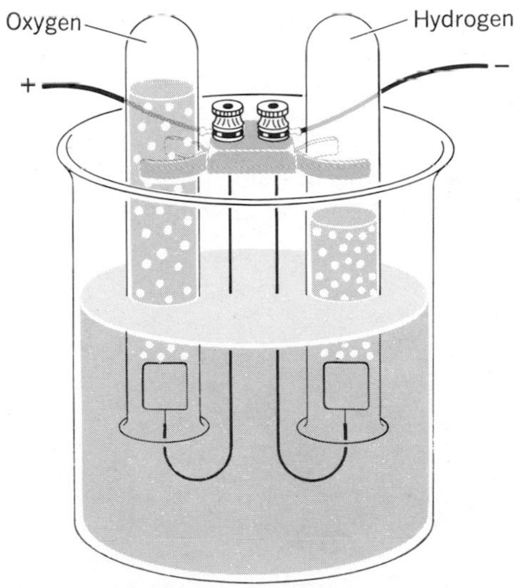

An electric current splits water into oxygen and hydrogen gases. This is possible because water molecules are composed of oxygen and hydrogen atoms.

Evidently, water can be "taken apart" to form two new substances and these two substances can be joined again to form water. This is possible because each molecule of water is made of two kinds of smaller particles—*atoms*. Specifically, each molecule of water is made of two atoms of hydrogen and one atom of oxygen, and nothing else. The word "splitting" used in reference to molecules is somewhat misleading; it conjures up a picture of breaking open a sphere and finding some new things inside. The water molecule is *nothing more* than a close partnership of two hydrogen atoms and one oxygen atom. The chemist's formula H_2O gives an exact name to this partnership (the subscript 2 means that there are two atoms of hydrogen).

We note also that the new substances produced bear little relationship in their properties to the original substance of which they were a part. Hydrogen is a highly burnable gas; oxygen is a gas that supports burning. The water from which they were obtained is a liquid (at room temperature) that does not burn. In other words, when hydrogen and oxygen atoms are linked in a water molecule the properties they display as unattached atoms are not in evidence. Their union results not in a compromise or a blending but in an entirely different substance. Indeed, the very essence of chemistry is to be found in such mysterious unions. Thus, an atom of a silver-colored, waxy, poisonous metal combined with an atom of a green, poisonous gas forms a molecule of ordinary table salt. The chemist would say here that an atom of sodium (Na) plus an atom of chlorine (Cl) forms a molecule of sodium chloride (NaCl).

Unions between atoms can be broken. The salt molecule, for example, can be separated into its component sodium and chlorine atoms. These atoms, moreover, show no effects from their former association. They are pure sodium and chlorine atoms again.

Molecules are generally made of linked atoms. In some cases, as in the helium found in the atmosphere, only one atom may comprise the molecule, in which case the molecule and the atom are identical. In other substances, as in a protein, thousands of atoms may be linked together to form a giant molecule.

Let us look at some molecules to become acquainted with their atomic makeup. Molecules of carbon dioxide, the gas that makes soda water bubbly, are made of one carbon and two oxygen atoms and have the formula CO_2. The free oxygen in the air we breathe is made of molecules having two atoms in them, both of them oxygen atoms. Its formula is O_2. The kind of alcohol found in some beverages is made of molecules containing carbon, hydrogen, and oxygen atoms, with the formula C_2H_6O. The sugar in grape juice has the formula $C_6H_{12}O_6$. Thus we see that different molecules may contain the same kinds of atoms but in different quantities. This is one reason (but not the only one) for the different nature of sugar and alcohol.

THE ELEMENTS

Man has long been curious about the basic composition of matter. The Greek philosopher

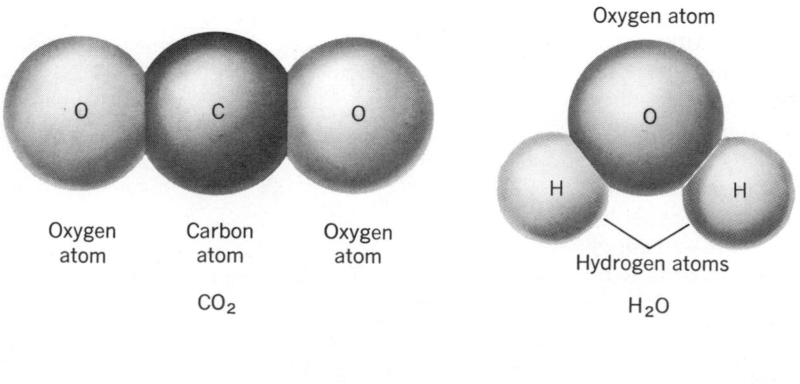

The carbon-dioxide molecule (*left*) is composed of one carbon atom and two oxygen atoms. The water molecule (*right*) is composed of two hydrogen atoms and one oxygen atom.

(*See* p. 498.) Aristotle said that all matter was made of four fundamental "elements": earth, air, fire, and water. By mixing these in various proportions, according to Aristotle, all kinds of substances could be formed. Bones, for example, were made of two parts of fire and one part each of earth and water; flesh consisted of equal parts of the four "elements."

Although we know today that not one of these four are truly basic elements, that indeed there are about 100 different ones, we are indebted to Aristotle and other Greek philosophers for their spirit of inquiry that led them to ask: "What are the fundamental particles of matter?" We are still searching for the answer to that question.

In the various substances named thus far we have come across five different kinds of atoms. These are carbon, hydrogen, chlorine, oxygen, and sodium. An investigation of all substances found in nature has revealed 88 different kinds of atoms up to now. In addition 17 atoms have been made by scientists, making 105 in all. (We will modify this number when we consider isotopes in Chapter 17A.) These basic materials are called *elements* by the chemists. There are 105 different kinds of atoms, so there are 105 different elements. Some familiar elements include the following:

aluminum	hydrogen	nickel	silver
argon	iodine	nitrogen	sodium
carbon	iron	oxygen	sulfur
chlorine	lead	phosphorus	tungsten
copper	mercury	platinum	uranium
gold	neon	radium	zinc
helium			

These elementary substances—unlike water, salt, and sugar—cannot be broken down into other simpler substances by ordinary chemical means. The metal silver is made up only of silver atoms; the gas helium is made only of helium atoms. Water, sugar, and salt, all made of molecules built of more than one kind of atom, are examples of what the chemist designates as *compounds*. The known compounds identified thus far number more than 4 *million,* but all of these are composed of various combinations of less than 1 *hundred* elements. The elements may be compared to the 26 letters of the alphabet; the compounds to the hundreds of thousands of words constructed from the alphabet.

Different elements are not equally abundant in nature. The most abundant element on the earth's surface is oxygen; the next is silicon. The two most abundant elements in the entire universe are hydrogen and helium. The ten most common elements make up 99 percent of the earth, as is shown in this chart:

PERCENTAGE OF ELEMENTS IN THE EARTH (CRUST, OCEANS, AND ATMOSPHERE) BY WEIGHT

Element	*Percent*
Oxygen	49.5
Silicon	25.8
Aluminum	7.5
Iron	4.7
Calcium	3.4
Sodium	2.6
Potassium	2.4
Magnesium	1.9
Hydrogen	0.9
Titanium	0.6
All others	0.7
	100.0

CHEMICAL SHORTHAND

For hundreds of years the alchemists, men who devoted their lives to the futile attempt to turn lead and other common metals into gold, used a kind of picture shorthand to represent the chemical elements which they knew. The circle, for example, was a symbol of perfection, so they used it for gold, the most perfect of all metals. Iron was represented by the lance and shield of Mars, the god of war. The looking glass of Venus was the symbol for copper, because legend had it that Venus had risen from the sea foam near Cyprus, famous for its copper mines. This colorful but cumbersome way of depicting the elements was confused by the fact that not all alchemists agreed on the choice of symbols.

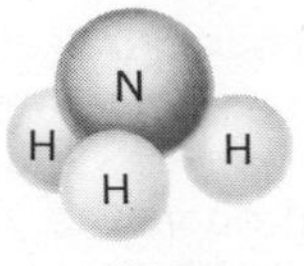

NH_3
Ammonia gas

This model of an ammonia gas molecule shows the three-dimensional relationships of its atoms.

In 1814 Berzelius, a Swedish chemist, initiated the system we use today. The symbol is usually the initial letter of the name of the chemical element. C represents carbon, O, oxygen, and so on. Those elements known to the ancients received their abbreviation from the Latin. The system was later broadened to include non-Latin names as well. If the first letter is common to two or more elements the initial letter and the first letter that they do not have in common is used. Thus copper is Cu (Latin cuprum), cobalt is Co, calcium is Ca. Elements discovered after 1800 end with the letters "ium."

To represent a compound Berzelius simply joined together the symbols of the atoms comprising the compound. This is its *chemical formula*. ZnS is the formula of zinc sulfide.

A symbol as used by a chemist not only stands for an element but for *one atom* of that element. A formula stands for a *molecule*. We have already noted that the numbered subscripts refer to the element immediately preceding it. Thus the H_2S (hydrogen sulfide) molecule contains two atoms of hydrogen and one of sulfur.

THE ARCHITECTURE OF MOLECULES

The molecular formula tells us only *what kinds* of atoms there are in a molecule and the *number* of each kind. It does not tell how the atoms are arranged within the molecule. For this important purpose a *structural formula* is needed—one that reveals the architecture of the molecule. For example, the chemical formula for ammonia gas is NH_3. Its structural formula:

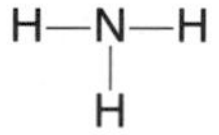

shows how the three hydrogen atoms are arranged in relation to the nitrogen atom. The *molecular model* shown helps visualize this relationship even more clearly.

The properties of a molecule are determined not only by the atoms that comprise it but also by the arrangement of its atoms. Consider the formula C_2H_6O. We said earlier that this is the formula for the kind of alcohol found in alcoholic beverages—ethyl alcohol. But it is also the formula for a chemical known as dimethyl ether, a different substance. The structural formula uncovers the difference. Ethyl alcohol's structural formula is:

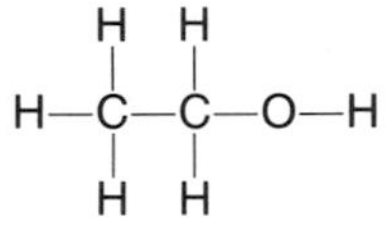

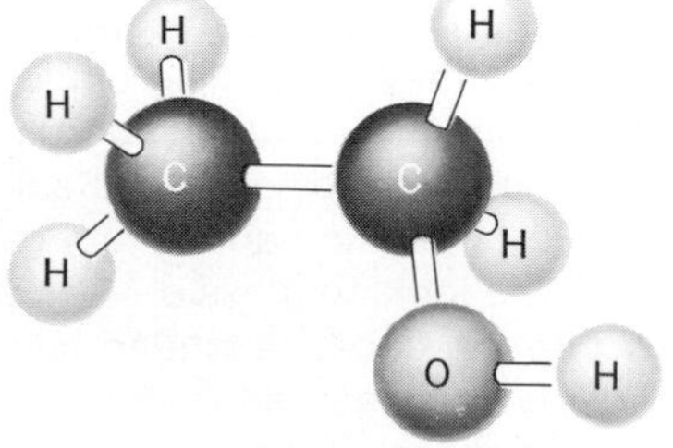
CH_3CH_2OH
Ethyl alcohol

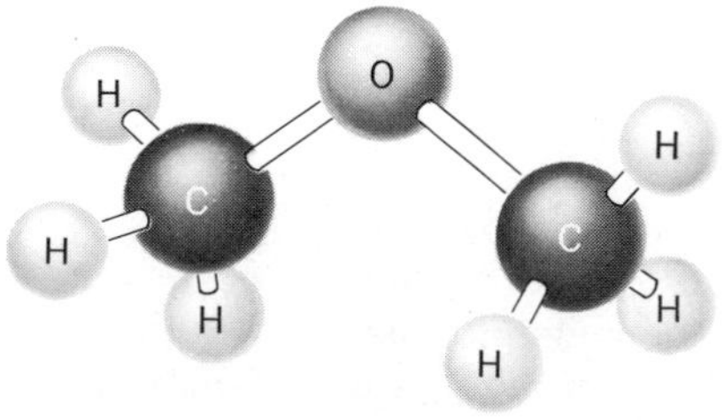
CH_3OCH_3
Dimethyl ether

Each of these molecules has the same kinds of atoms and the same number of each of these kinds, yet each are quite different chemically. The stickball model illustrates their structural difference. Try matching these models with the structural formulae given in the text.

Dimethyl ether's structural formula is:

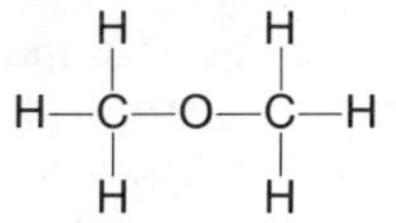

The structural formula is a two-dimensional view. The three-dimensional models shown are better representations because molecules are three-dimensional.

Molecules containing exactly the same set of atoms but differing in the way the atoms are arranged are called *isomers*.

CHANGES IN MOLECULES

Let us see what happens to molecules which are involved in some of the changes that take place around us. When water evaporates from a puddle into the air no new substance is made. Water vapor is still made of water; that is, it is still made of molecules containing two hydrogen atoms and one oxygen atom. It is still H_2O. The same is true when water freezes into ice. Such a change is referred to as a *physical* change. The changes described in the chapters to come on heat, machines, magnetism and electricity, sound, and light are concerned with physical changes.

Many changes, however, result in the formation of new substances that have characteristics very different from those of the original materials. The splitting of water into hydrogen and oxygen gases, previously described, is an example of this kind of change. Changes in which new substances are formed are called *chemical changes*.

Common Chemical Changes

We drop a nail outside and forget about it for a few weeks. When we pick it up we find that it has changed markedly. Instead of a smooth, shiny, hard exterior, it has a crumbly red coating. The iron in the nail has undergone a chemical change. We call the new substance produced *rust*. The chemist calls it *iron oxide*. Iron atoms in the nail have joined with oxygen atoms in the air to form molecules of iron oxide or rust.

(*See* pp. 499–502.)

Another everyday event that involves the joining of atoms is the tarnishing of silver. If a silver spoon is used for eating an egg a black layer of tarnish forms on the spoon. The silver combines with sulfur (always present in an egg) to make the black material, which is silver sulfide. The chemist describes this event in the following equation:

$$2Ag + S \rightarrow Ag_2S.$$

In words he says: two atoms of silver (2Ag) combine with one atom of sulftr (S) to form (→) one molecule of silver sulfide (Ag_2S). The arrow in the equation indicates the direction in which the chemical change is proceeding; the ingredients are on the left side of the arrow and the products are on the right. This is a properly balanced equation because it has the same kind and the same number of each kind of atom on each side of the equation. *In a chemical change atoms are conserved—they are neither created nor destroyed.*

Chemical changes occur during the burning of fuels. The atoms of the fuel combine with oxygen to produce a new substance. In this process energy is released in the form of heat and light. When coal burns, for example, the carbon in it combines with oxygen to form the gas, carbon dioxide:

$$C + O_2 \rightarrow CO_2.$$

The common candle has two kinds of atoms in its chemical makeup, carbon and hydrogen. When a candle burns, the carbon atoms of the candle combine with oxygen atoms of the air to form carbon dioxide, while the hydrogen atoms of the candle combine with oxygen atoms to form water:

$$C + O_2 \rightarrow CO_2 \quad \text{and}$$

$$2H + O \rightarrow H_2O.$$

However, because free oxygen molecules in the air contain two atoms (O_2), the second equation must be written:

$$2H_2 + O_2 \rightarrow 2H_2O.$$

Both the carbon dioxide and the water escape invisibly into the air. The soot that is formed on the bottom of any object heated by a candle is composed of *unburned* carbon atoms; that is, carbon atoms that have not combined with oxygen atoms.

The fact that the candle is finally "used up" might lead one to conclude that in burning there is destruction of matter. This is not so. *Every atom is accounted for.* Every carbon and hydrogen atom of the candle is now part of a new substance—in a different state—but not one atom has been destroyed.

The process of digestion, as we saw in Chapter 12A, involves chemical changes. The large starch molecules with their many atoms, for example, are broken into sugar molecules, which are smaller. The sugar molecules are small enough to pass through the intestinal membranes into the bloodstream.

In making of bread chemical changes play an important role. Yeast (one-celled plants) acts on the sugar in the dough to produce carbon dioxide gas and alcohol:

$$\underset{\text{dextrose sugar}}{C_6H_{12}O_6} \rightarrow \underset{\text{ethyl alcohol}}{2C_2H_6O} + \underset{\text{carbon dioxide}}{2CO_2}$$

One molecule of sugar is converted into two molecules of alcohol and two molecules of carbon dioxide. The carbon dioxide helps "blow up" the dough. This makes the bread light and spongy. The small amount of alcohol produced evaporates in the baking.

A similar change occurs in the process of wine making, except that in this case the carbon dioxide escapes while the alcohol is retained in the final product. In both bread and wine making, the yeast cells cause a chemical change in sugar called *fermentation*. (The yeast cells also profit from this transaction: The splitting of sugar molecules liberates energy essential for their life processes.)

A chemical change that makes life possible on earth has been referred to in a number of different places in this book. It is the process of photosynthesis, in which green plants combine atoms from carbon dioxide and water to form sugar and oxygen. (*See* pp. 280–2.) The following equation represents a summary of what is actually a series of complex steps in a living plant cell:

$$6CO_2 + 12H_2O \rightarrow C_6H_{12}O_6 + 6H_2O + 6O_2.$$

Changing these symbols to words a chemist says: 6 molecules of carbon dioxide plus 12 molecules of water yield 1 molecule of sugar plus 6 molecules of water plus 6 molecules of oxygen. In accordance with the principle of the conservation of atoms the number and kind of atoms on the right and left sides of this equation are equal. Count them and see. The chemical process of photosynthesis provides food and oxygen for the use of the plant and animal kingdoms and removes carbon dioxide from the earth's atmosphere.

We have seen how chemical changes are involved in rusting, tarnishing, burning, photosynthesis, digestion, and fermentation. Chemical changes are found in thousands of other everyday phenomena: the souring of milk, the spoiling of meat, repairing and building of tissues of living things, manufacture of soap and plastics. The understanding of these chemical changes becomes increasingly important each year in agriculture, industry, and medicine.

DALTON AND THE ATOMIC THEORY

It is evident from the examples we have considered that atoms are involved in all chemical changes. The true character of atoms was first conceived in 1808 by John Dalton, an English schoolmaster. In modern form the fundamental ideas of Dalton's atomic theory might be stated as follows:

1. All matter is composed of a limited number

of kinds of fundamental particles called atoms.

2. All atoms of any one kind are identical, indivisible, and unalterable (we shall modify this statement in Chapter 17A to bring it in line with modern atomic theory).

3. Molecules consist of definite combinations of atoms. The atomic construction of all the molecules of one kind is identical.

4. Chemical changes involve the making of new combinations of atoms to produce new molecules and hence new substances.

There is much evidence for the concept that molecules consist of definite combinations of atoms and that the atomic construction of all molecules of one kind is identical. One of the most direct forms of evidence is illustrated on page 477. Martin Buerger of the Massachusetts Institute of Technology used x-rays to record the positions of the atoms in a crystal of pyrites or "fool's gold," so-called because prospectors mistook this bright, shiny substance for real gold. Pyrites is a combination of iron and sulfur atoms, known as iron disulfide or FeS_2. Each pyrites molecule contains one iron atom and two sulfur atoms. The x-ray photograph does not show what an atom looks like, but it does show the *position* of the atoms in the crystal. The larger dot is the x-ray image of an iron atom; the two smaller ones flanking it are images of the two sulfur atoms.

INSIDE THE ATOM

Earlier in this book we looked into the vastness of space—at planets, stars, galaxies, and supergalaxies—trying to find some order in the universe. In this chapter we have focused thus far on the minute molecules and atoms that make up the matter of the universe. Let us now increase our magnification to "see" the architecture *within* the atom, to find there the smallest specks yet discovered.

The word *atom,* first used by the Greeks about 400 B.C. to identify what they considered to be the smallest particles of matter, means *indivisible*. But the investigations of the twentieth century have taught us that atoms are *divisible,* and that they are made of smaller, more fundamental particles.

Model of an Atom

To learn more about these particles let us look at some atoms closely. Sir Ernest Rutherford, the father of modern atomic physics, was the first to construct a model of the interior of the atom. According to this model, constructed in 1911, a single atom is a kind of miniature solar system. In the center, corresponding to the sun, is a structure called the *nucleus*. Whirling around the nucleus, like planets, are particles called *electrons*.

In 1913 Niels Bohr, a Danish chemist working in Rutherford's laboratory, proposed that the electrons of an atom revolve around the nucleus in definite circular orbits, with each orbit at a different distance from the nucleus. Later discoveries identified two particles within the atom's nucleus, *protons* and *neutrons*.

Consider a specific atom, that of the element hydrogen. The hydrogen atom is the lightest and simplest of all atoms. Its nucleus consists of a single particle, a proton. Around this proton a single electron whirls round and round, as depicted in the diagram on page 486.

Electrons are extremely light atomic particles possessing a quantity of electricity that has been designated a *negative charge*. The electron revolves at terrific speeds around the nucleus and at a relatively great distance from it. It is held in its orbit by the nucleus, just as the earth is kept from flying off into space by the attraction of the sun. In the case of the atom, however, the attraction is due to the equal but opposite *positive charge* of electricity of the proton in the nucleus. (Opposite electrical charges attract each other.) Although the electrical charges of the electron and proton are equal though opposite, their weights are markedly different, the proton being about 1,840 times as heavy as the electron.

A hydrogen atom, then, consists of one electron and one proton. Let us turn now to the heavier atoms. After hydrogen the next heavier atom is helium. What is the architecture of a helium atom? Revolving around the nucleus are

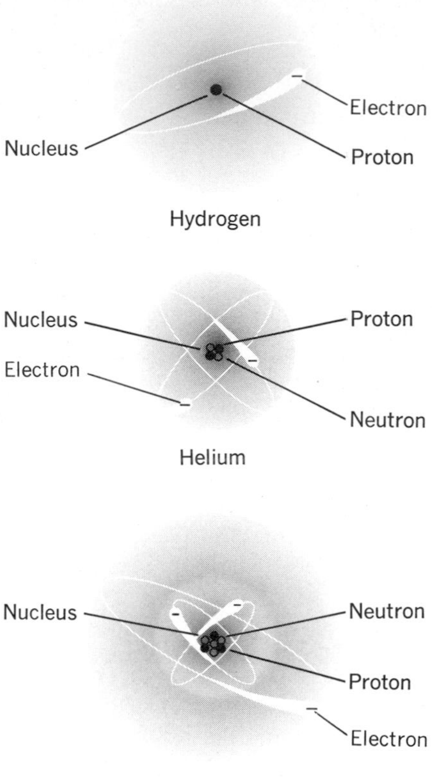

The hydrogen atom (*top*) has 1 electron whirling around a nucleus consisting of 1 proton. The helium atom (*middle*) has 2 electrons revolving around a nucleus made of 2 protons and 2 neutrons. The lithium atom (*bottom*), next in the atom ladder, has 3 electrons orbiting around a nucleus made of 3 protons and 4 neutrons.

two electrons. As you might expect these are prevented from flying off into space by *two* protons in the nucleus. But helium (and every other kind of atom except hydrogen) has a third kind of fundamental particle in its nucleus: the *neutron*. Helium has two neutrons. The neutron weighs about the same as a proton, but, as its name implies, it is electrically neutral—it has no electric charge.

Electrons, protons, neutrons—these seem to be the fundamental particles of atoms. (Atomic scientists have discovered others, but we shall limit our consideration to these three.) As we examine atoms of the heavier elements we find that they contain more protons and neutrons in the nucleus and more electrons outside the nucleus. In each case the number of protons exactly equals the number of electrons. Thus, carbon has 6 protons and 6 electrons, oxygen 8 protons and 8 electrons, and radium 88 protons and 88 electrons.

Just as it was hard to visualize the immense dimensions in the astronomical universe so it is equally difficult to picture the tiny dimensions on the atomic scale.

Rule a 1-inch line on a piece of paper. If you could line up hydrogen atoms along this 1-inch line there would be room for 250 million of them. Yet an electron is only 1/100,000 the size of one of these hydrogen atoms!

We stated before that an atom is a sort of miniature solar system. Most of the *real* solar system, as we learned earlier, consists of empty space. The proportion of empty space in an atom, however, is 10,000 times as great as in the solar system. Assume that we want to make a giant model of an oxygen atom. If we make the nucleus of this atom 1,500 feet across (the length of five football fields) and place it in the center of the United States, then its outer electrons would move in an orbit that would touch New York and San Francisco.

Indeed, all matter is filled with empty space. It has been estimated that if a giant hand could squeeze all the empty space out of the earth, until the nuclei of all its atoms touched each other, then our planet could be compressed to the size of a ball only $\frac{1}{2}$ mile in diameter.

The picture of an atom as a miniature solar system is useful, but some corrections are necessary to give a truer understanding of the atom.

1. The planets in the solar system move essentially in one plane—in a two-dimensional system. Electrons, on the other hand, travel in all three dimensions around the nucleus.
2. The planets are definite, discrete, round bodies. Electrons travel so rapidly that it is assumed they create a cloud of negative electricity around the nucleus.

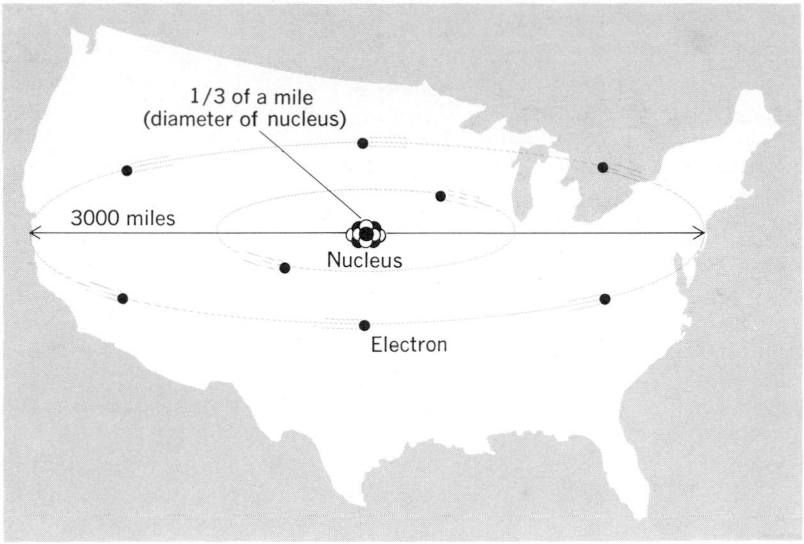

The space within the atom is vast compared to the size of its particles. This diagram gives some notion of where the 8 electrons of an oxygen atom would be if the nucleus of the atom were enlarged so that its diameter was one third of a mile.

UP THE LADDER OF ATOMS

(*See* p. 488.)

There is a wonderful ladder in nature, a ladder of atoms. Begin at the first rung with one electron and one proton and you have hydrogen. Climb to the second rung to where there are two electrons and two protons and you have helium. On the next rung three electrons and three protons give you lithium. Rung by rung, adding one electron and one proton each time, without a break you climb, passing atom after atom, as shown in the table, until you reach the highest rung. This has 105 electrons and 105 protons, the heaviest of atoms made *thus far* by atomic scientists. The number of neutral particles, or neutrons, increases, too, but not in this simple arithmetic way.

"The Ladder of Atoms" on page 488 includes some of the familiar atoms.

It is apparent that the essential difference between a substance such as lead and one such as gold lies in the *number* of electrons, protons, and neutrons that the atoms of these substances contain; the *kinds* of particles in each is the same. Thus, the medieval alchemists' dream of transmuting one element into another was not so farfetched after all, because all atoms are made of the same stuff. As we shall see in Chapter 17A, moreover, the changing of atoms into other kinds of atoms occurs in nature as well as in the laboratories of atomic scientists.

Electrons in Orbit

The arrangement of the electrons in an atom reveals a beautiful order and symmetry in nature. The electron pattern is also the key to the chemical properties of the atom (*see* pp. 488–9).

Let us climb up the atomic ladder again. We observe this time that the electrons are not scattered helter-skelter; they move in orbits called *shells* at different distances from the nucleus of the atom. In hydrogen there is but one electron revolving in its shell around the nucleus. Helium has two electrons in this first shell. Two electrons seems to be the limit for this shell in the atomic ballroom. Lithium, atom number 3, has two electrons in the innermost shell and one electron in a second shell. In the next seven elements, each with one more electron, the second shell fills up, but there is a maximum of eight electrons. Consequently, in neon (the familiar gas in neon tubes), atom number 10, the first shell has its

THE LADDER OF ATOMS

Name of Element	*Symbol*	*Number of Electrons* *Number of Protons* *Atomic Number*
Hydrogen	H	1
Helium	He	2
Lithium	Li	3
Carbon	C	6
Nitrogen	N	7
Oxygen	O	8
Fluorine	F	9
Neon	Ne	10
Sodium	Na	11
Magnesium	Mg	12
Aluminum	Al	13
Silicon	Si	14
Phosphorus	P	15
Sulfur	S	16
Chlorine	Cl	17
Argon	Ar	18
Potassium	K	19
Calcium	Ca	20
Chromium	Cr	24
Iron	Fe	26
Nickel	Ni	28
Copper	Cu	29
Silver	Ag	47
Tin	Sn	50
Iodine	I	53
Platinum	Pt	78
Gold	Au	79
Mercury	Hg	80
Lead	Pb	82
Radium	Ra	88
Uranium	U	92
Neptunium	Np	93
Plutonium	Pu	94
Lawrencium	Lw	103
Rutherfordium	Rf	104
Hahnium	Ha	105

maximum of two and the second shell a maximum of eight electrons.

(**Note:** We are oversimplifying the picture somewhat. We recall from the previous section that all the orbits are three-dimensional, with electrons traveling around the surface of an imaginary sphere and with much more fuzzy paths than the diagrams imply.)

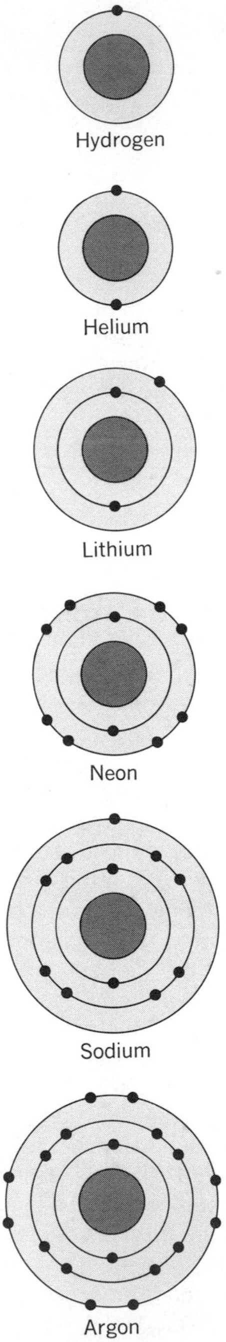

Electrons are arranged in orbits around the nucleus of the atom. This diagram does not show the three-dimensional nature of the atom.

Continuing, sodium, atom number 11 in our ladder, has ten of its electrons arranged like neon, but the eleventh one starts the third shell. The chart shows the distribution of electrons in shells of the first twenty elements.

ELECTRON SHELLS IN ATOMS

			Shells			
Atomic Number	*Name*	*Symbol*	*K or 1*	*L or 2*	*M or 3*	*N or 4*
1	Hydrogen	H	1			
2	Helium	He	2			
3	Lithium	Li	2	1		
4	Beryllium	Be	2	2		
5	Boron	B	2	3		
6	Carbon	C	2	4		
7	Nitrogen	N	2	5		
8	Oxygen	O	2	6		
9	Fluorine	F	2	7		
10	Neon	Ne	2	8		
11	Sodium	Na	2	8	1	
12	Magnesium	Mg	2	8	2	
13	Aluminum	Al	2	8	3	
14	Silicon	Si	2	8	4	
15	Phosphorus	P	2	8	5	
16	Sulfur	S	2	8	6	
17	Chlorine	Cl	2	8	7	
18	Argon	Ar	2	8	8	
19	Potassium	K	2	8	8	1
20	Calcium	Ca	2	8	8	2

What happens to the electron arrangements in the other atoms found in nature as we go up the ladder? We may summarize it in this way:

1. Seven shells or orbits in all are possible.
2. The maximum number of electrons in the different shells varies from 2 to 32.

We should not leave this consideration of atomic architecture without adding that (1.) the chemical properties of an element depends on the number of its electrons and the way the electrons are arranged in the limited number of possible shells; and (2.) each of the shells represents energy levels: the energy of electrons in different shells increases with increasing distance from the nucleus.

Readers who wish to pursue this further are referred to recent high-school and college texts in chemistry.

FIRE: A CHEMICAL HAPPENING

Chemical changes involve not only the forming of new substances but the transfer of energy also. When a green plant makes sugar (*see* the equation on page 484) it packs sun energy into each sugar molecule. When the sugar is "burned" in a living organism the energy is liberated. Similarly, when a candle burns, energy in the form of heat and light is released.

Fire is one of the most dramatic of all energy-releasing chemical changes. Fire is both useful and potentially dangerous to man, and so merits special discussion here.

Essentials for Burning

(*See* pp. 503–4.)

Three conditions are essential for any fire. First there must be something to burn, a fuel of some kind; then this fuel must be made hot enough to burn; and last there must be a continuous supply of oxygen to support the burning. Let us see how each of these three factors contributes to the making of a fire.

Reduced to its simplest terms burning is the process in which a fuel unites chemically with the oxygen of the air, a process that the chemist calls *oxidation*. Carbon and hydrogen are the common atoms in the fuels we use. To emphasize the importance of the release of energy we might rewrite the equations given on pages 483–484 in this way:

$C + O_2 \rightarrow CO_2 + e$, or carbon plus oxygen yields carbon dioxide plus energy

$2H_2 + O_2 \rightarrow H_2O + e$, or hydrogen plus oxygen yields water plus energy.

The carbon dioxide and water pass off invisibly in the smoke so we are not usually aware of these new products of burning. When we watch a campfire we do see the smoke because it contains unburned carbon particles. We also see the ash that remains, but this is the mineral content of the wood which does not burn. We see light and feel the heat. These represent forms of energy that are released as a result of chemical union of the atoms.

We should not say that oxygen burns. Rather, it *supports* the burning of fuels. A spark applied to a bottle of oxygen will *not* set it afire; oxygen is not a fuel and it cannot burn.

Hotter Fires

The intensity of fire can be increased, up to a point, by supplying more oxygen to it. When we fan a campfire we are bringing a greater quantity of oxygen to the burning fuel. In the coal furnace the rate of burning is controlled by regulating the amount of air that comes in contact with the coal. This is done by adjusting the furnace doors and turning the damper, which is a kind of door in the chimney. You may have seen men cutting through steel beams with sparkling torches. These are oxyacetylene torches, and they are fed by a tank of the fuel acetylene and a tank of oxygen. The intense heat produced is over 5000° F.

Oxidation is also hastened by reducing the fuel to small particles. When we break a piece of wood into small pieces we expose more of its surface to the air and consequently make more oxygen available. Similarly, in a kerosene lamp or a candle the fuels are dispersed through the wick in such a way as to help them evaporate easily. The evaporated fuels around the wick are exposed to more of the oxygen of the air and hence burn more rapidly. Again, when the carburetor of an automobile sprays a mixture of gasoline and air into the cylinders of the motor it breaks the liquid gasoline into a fine vapor so that each of its molecules is surrounded by oxygen atoms. The gasoline burns so rapidly that an explosion is produced, pushing with a force of thousands of pounds against each piston.

Kindling Temperature

The lowest temperature at which a substance will catch fire is called its *kindling temperature,* which is different for different substances. Phosphorus is used in the tips of strike-anywhere matches because it has a very low kindling temperature; the small amount of heat produced by rubbing is sufficient to ignite it. Carbon disulfide (a chemical used in some insecticides) will catch fire if it is poured on a hot steam radiator. As we have seen from the previous discussion of oxygen, the ease with which a substance catches fire depends not only on the nature of the substance but on other conditions, such as the size of its particles and the supply of oxygen.

The kindling temperature of wood is over 500° F. That of kerosene is somewhat lower; because of this it is often poured on wood (a dangerous practice) to ignite it. Gasoline also has a low kindling temperature. It is more dangerous than kerosene because it gives off vapors more rapidly. These vapors catch fire so easily that gasoline must never be used in starting fires, nor should it be stored in a place where its vapors can accumulate. Every year people are severely burned by using gasoline to start fires. Frequently they use it in stoves designed to burn kerosene.

Home dry cleaning with gasoline is very dangerous; gasoline fumes have been known to travel 15 or 20 feet across a kitchen and then to be ignited by the pilot light of a gas stove. Even when no flame is nearby rubbing may produce a tiny spark sufficient to ignite the gasoline vapor. Ether is another dangerous fluid. Like gasoline, it vaporizes easily, and its fumes are easily ignited.

Extinguishing Fire

(*See* pp. 503–4.)

The extinguishing (also the prevention) of fires is based on the elimination of one or more of the three factors essential for burning. Thus, to put out a fire we cut off the supply of oxygen, remove the fuel, and lower the temperature of the burning material below its kindling point. The exclusion of oxygen and the lowering of the temperature are the most widely used methods of extinguishing fires. The removal of flammable material is effective for small fires, such as those in coal bins, wood piles, or waste baskets. Fire lanes in forests, where all trees and brush are removed, also serve to stop the spread of fire.

Among the readily available ways of excluding oxygen are covering the fire with dirt or other material that will not burn, or throwing a heavy blanket or coat over the fire. The latter is particularly effective in putting out fire on a person's clothing. If a blanket or coat is not available the flames on a person's clothing can sometimes be smothered by rolling the person on the ground. Fire extinguishers achieve their effect by cooling the fuel and by smothering, which actually means keeping the oxygen away from the fire.

This brief exploration of molecules and atoms has emphasized certain basic generalizations. Some of these are:

All matter is made up of exceedingly small separate particles, called molecules, which are in ceaseless motion.

Molecules attract each other. In solids the attraction is greatest, in liquids less, in gases least.

Molecules are made of atoms linked together in definite combinations.

There are about 100 different kinds of atoms with different chemical properties, called elements.

Chemists have identified more than 4 million kinds of compounds.

In a physical change the composition of molecules is not changed.

In chemical changes the composition of molecules is altered. New materials are formed by assembling new combinations of atoms.

Compounds differ markedly in their properties from the elements of which they are composed.

The chemical properties of a molecule are determined not only by the kinds and numbers of the atoms that comprise it but also by the arrangement of these atoms.

In a chemical change atoms are conserved—they are neither created nor destroyed.

Atoms are composed of smaller particles, principally electrons, protons, and neutrons.

Protons and neutrons are found in the nucleus of the atom; the electrons are arranged in orbits around the nucleus.

The essential differences between the atoms of different elements lie in the number of protons, neutrons, and electrons that make up the atoms.

The chemical properties of an element depend on the number and arrangement of the electrons.

Three factors essential for burning are:

1. a supply of oxygen
2. a supply of fuel
3. enough heat to raise the fuel to its kindling point.

The intensity of burning can be increased by exposing more surface of the fuel to the oxygen in the air or by increasing the supply of oxygen.

Oxygen supports burning, but it does not burn.

The prevention and fighting of fires is based on the elimination of one or more of the three factors essential for burning.

Chemical changes involve a transfer of energy.

Chemical changes play an important part in our lives.

Discovering for Yourself

1. Make a list of destructive chemical changes that you observe, and indicate what is done to try to prevent each of the changes.
2. Use litmus paper to test the liquids and fruits in a kitchen to see if they are acids or bases.
3. Make drawings showing the changes in behavior and spacing of molecules as physical changes take place in matter.
4. Choose some chemical change that is important to you and learn as much as you can about it (what raw materials are used, what energy is involved, what waste products are there, how the characteristics of the finished product differ from those of the raw materials used).
5. Demonstrate the difference between a chemical and physical change by using some common materials.
6. Find out about some of the newest elements listed in Chapter 15A. Find out where they were discovered, by whom, when, and any other information you can. Keep a list of the sources you used, and describe your method of discovery.
7. List as many as you can of the elements (in a free state, that is, not chemically combined with any other element) in your house (copper in wire and in a penny, oxygen in the air, tin on the cover of cans, and so on).
8. List some of the simple chemical compounds you encounter during a day and give their atomic makeup: Water H_2O—hydrogen and oxygen; sugar $C_6H_{12}O_6$—carbon, hydrogen, and oxygen; table salt NaCl—sodium and chlorine; bubbles in carbonated water CO_2—carbon and oxygen; and others.
9. Make drawings of the electron arrangements in ten elements.
10. Investigate the "Periodic Table" of the elements. How has the Table enabled chemists to predict the properties of undiscovered elements? In what sense is the Periodic Table like the calendar of a month?
11. Learn how to use the fire extinguisher in your home, school, and automobile.
12. Use the Self-Inspection Blank and the Fire Safety Check List, which is available from American Insurance Association, 85 John Street, New York, N.Y. 10038.
13. Find out the latest methods for fighting forest fires.
14. Find the fire-alarm box nearest to your house, the number of your fire department, and learn how to report a fire.

(Courtesy of Dr. Mildred T. Ballou, Ball State University, Muncie, Indiana.)

CHAPTER 15B

TEACHING "MOLECULES, ATOMS, AND CHEMICAL CHANGE"

Children introduce themselves to the world of materials through many and varied experiences as they explore their environment. For example, as we have indicated in other chapters they test the qualities and characteristics of things through tasting, feeling, lifting, listening, smelling, scratching, breaking, twisting, wetting, crushing, biting, pushing, spilling, and so on. These are, in a way, tests that they themselves devise. We help this process by providing them with experiences that raise problems in their minds, and then by giving them opportunity for inquiry. In the early grades we do this when we encourage them to work with clay, sand, water, soil, and similar materials, and show what they can do by changing the materials. Their understanding of chemical and physical change may be deepened by firsthand experiences in the preparation, cooking, and preserving of foods; that is, observing the changes in color, shape, and texture that accompany processes such as the making of applesauce, cranberry sauce, popcorn, candles, butter, and gelatin desserts.

In all these experiences the wise teacher emphasizes the changes as they occur. "How did it change?" "Why do you think it changed?" "Could we change it back again?" are some typical questions to give more meaning to the experiences. In later elementary-school grades the phenomena of contraction and expansion of materials, burning, food manufacture in plants, and other changes are studied to see how changes in matter occur and why they are important.

Let us not be too concerned at the early level with the lack of scientific terminology. Science is a method of discovery. When questions about what happened are being answered through observation and discussion the study of science is beginning. As the study proceeds, more complicated examples will involve more technical terms.

SOME BROAD CONCEPTS: "Molecules, Atoms, and Chemical Change"

All matter is composed of molecules that are made up of atoms.

Matter exists as solids, liquids, and gases.

Matter can be changed from one state to another.

There are about 100 different kinds of atoms (elements), each with different properties.

Atoms combine to make compounds. There are millions of kinds of compounds.

In a physical change the make up of the molecules is not changed. No new material is made.

In a chemical change the make up of the molecules is changed. New material is made.

FOR YOUNGER CHILDREN

The following activities for early grades will contribute to an understanding of what things are made of and how they change. Stress *describing* and *comparing* when these are appropriate.

Refer to Piaget's experiments, Chapter 3, with conservation of matter for some methods of working, development of concepts, and descriptions of tasks for younger children.

What Materials Will Mix with Water?

Have on hand a lemon, some salt, sugar, commercial powder used for making cold drinks, and some sand. Ask children to *predict* what will happen in each case when the material is added to water. How can we tell what will happen? Children test their predictions. They may suggest making lemonade with the lemon, sugar, and water. Squeeze the lemon in water. Children observe and describe what they see (bits of the lemon float, seeds settle, the water changes appearance). "What has happened?" Use the term *dissolve* in helping children describe. Let children taste the material. "How do you know the lemon juice has mixed with the water?" "How could we try to make the mixture taste sweet?" Add sugar. Taste. "Will sugar dissolve in water? Can you see it?" "How do you know that it's in the water?" "Will salt and the other materials dissolve?" Children may wish to try further materials to see if they will dissolve. The sand does not dissolve.

Does stirring help material dissolve faster? Urge children to think of a way to find out by experiment. They should remember their previous experiences with the use of a control (for those who manage the idea). Put together equal amounts of water, equal amounts of sugar (a lump of sugar or whatever material is to be tested). Stir one; do not stir the other. Observe and describe the results. Several children should experiment so that they can compare results. Does heating the liquid make material dissolve faster? Would shaking? Try it.[1]

How Can We Change Water?

In order to help pupils understand that some materials may be in different forms—as a liquid, a solid, and a gas—suggest that they observe and attempt to describe what water is like (*see* also Material for Older Children). Use words that describe—wet, clear, liquid, and so on. "How can we change the water so that it will appear different?" Freeze it. Place the water in the freezing compartment of a refrigerator. "What do you think will happen?" "Will it still be water?" Examine the ice. Try to describe what it is like.

Let water stand in a warm room. Mark the height of the water in the glass. "What happens to it?" Let it stand for several days. "What happens?" Now try to describe it. "Can you get the water out of the air?" (*See* Chapter 9 for evaporation and condensation experiences.) "How are the liquid, the solid, and the gas different from each other? How are they alike?" "Did this change make a new material?"

[1] *Science K–2* (Brooklyn, N.Y.: Board of Education, City of New York, 1966). Describes in detail these and additional activities and experiments.

Where Can We Find Air?

As children study materials they make a list of places where air, a common material, is found. They may try to classify their lists: (1.) Things we put air into (tires, balloons); (2.) big places (the room, outdoors); (3.) little places (in an "empty" glass). "Is there air in water?" Let a glass of cool water stand for a few hours. "What do you think the bubbles are?" "Is there air in soil?" Drop some lumps of soil into a glass of water. "What do you think the bubbles are?" "Is air a material?" "How can you tell?"

How Does Mold Change Things?

Recall the material from Chapter 10B, "Elementary Science Study *Microgardening*" that describes molds and mold culture. In the present context we are emphasizing how mold changes the material it grows on. Children may observe the inside of a jack-o-lantern pumpkin as mold develops or bread that has molded. How does the mold change the pumpkin and the bread? How would you describe the changes in the properties of the material? How is this change different from the changes that water made when it was frozen or evaporated?

How Can We Describe Objects?

In Chapter 12B we described how children may be encouraged to use their senses to discover. We have suggested there, and elsewhere, that this is an on-going activity, since the use of the senses is an ever-present avenue to discovery. The Science Curriculum Improvement Study (SCIS) has developed a very careful study entitled *Material Objects*[2] that "introduces the child to fundamental concept of objects and their properties." The child "manipulates, describes, compares and changes the form of various materials" in his own environment. The study stresses the differentiation between *objects* and *nonobjects* and between describing the *properties* of objects in contrast to the *functions* of the objects.

(*See* Ch. 12.)

Referring to the use of senses to describe and discover we again suggest that the teacher may assemble in paper bags a variety of materials as is described in "Material Objects." Children select objects from the bag using their senses to discover and then to describe various properties of the material—size, texture, color, and so on. Children attempt to classify the materials in various ways according to their properties. Objects from the schoolroom, from a collecting trip, or from various other sources can be used in a similar way.

[2] The Science Curriculum Improvement Study (SCIS): *Material Objects. Teacher's Guide.* (Chicago: Rand McNally and Company). Guide includes activities related to "Objects and their Properties," the "Concept of Material," "Comparisons of Objects," "Experimenting with Objects." Equipment Kit is also available. For all grades.

OTHER PROBLEMS FOR YOUNGER CHILDREN

1. Why are changes in materials important?
2. Where do changes in water take place outdoors?
3. How can you separate salt from salt water?
4. How can you take the mud out of muddy water?
5. What happens if you put drops of vinegar on baking soda?
6. (*See* Ch. 6B.) What is soil made of?
7. How does heat change food?
8. (*See* Ch. 15.) What happens to things when they are heated and cooled?

FOR OLDER CHILDREN

How Can Matter Be Changed from One Form to Another?[3]

If children have had the earlier-described experience with melting ice and evaporating water they are ready to go farther with experiences of changing materials from one form to another. To see what is meant by changing matter from one form to another, pupils may perform simple experiments showing how this happens.

Supply each child or small group of children with an ice cube (uniform in size taken from an ice tray) and a plastic bag. Suggest that children use whatever methods they choose to melt the cube. Who can melt the cube fastest? Measure the amount of water in the bag to determine the degree of melting (solid to liquid). How would you describe what happens? Now heat the water until it evaporates (liquid to gas). Describe what happens. Then place water in an ice-cube tray and freeze (liquid to solid). "How have the characteristics changed?" "What are the distinguishing characteristics of a gas? A solid? A liquid?" "How are they alike? How different?" Note that in these examples no new material is produced. The substance has merely changed

[3] For additional suggestions *see* AAAS Xerox Edition: "The Solid, Liquid, and Gaseous States of Matter." *Science a Process Approach* (Carlstadt, N.J.: Xerox Education Sciences).

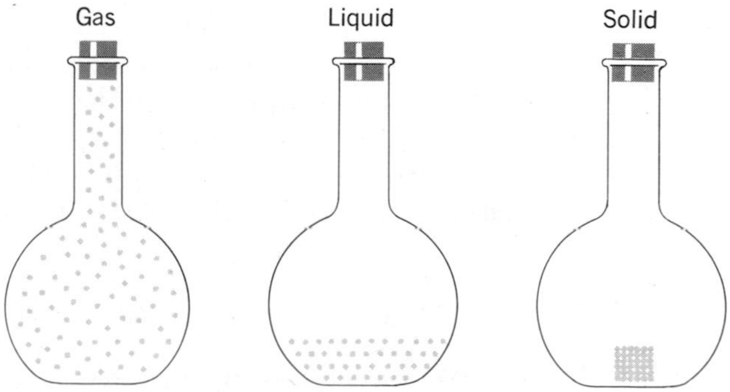

Visualization of the molecules in a gas, a liquid, and a solid. The concepts related to molecules and atoms, their structures and behavior, are indeed difficult for children to grasp; any representation that illustrates the ideas is helpful.

its form. Pupils can look for other changes from one form to another—especially in the kitchen where the refrigerator and stove are. They can read about important changes in the form of matter—for example, iron and other metals from liquid to solid, glass from liquid to solid. They can make a picture collection to show how everyday things are made by changing the form of matter (glass, metal objects, and so on).

Where Can We Find Examples of Elements?

One especially important aspect of this activity, as well as others in this unit, is experience in describing—in stating characteristics and comparing one with another. This is first done through careful observations, using the senses to discover. Later reading to check and to add to the discoveries is important.

Once pupils know what an element is, they can find many examples. Elements in addition to those indicated in Chapter 15A are listed in many books (*see* the Bibliography). Pupils can find common objects containing such elements as iron (nails), copper (electric wiring, pennies), mercury (in thermometers), tin (covering of cans), zinc (in galvanized iron), silver (jewelry), and many others, and display them on a table. They can find out more about some of these elements by reading in encyclopedias and elsewhere, and report their findings to the class. Before they begin reading they may make a list of questions they wish to answer about each element, such as: "Where is it found?" "For what is it used?" "Is it scarce?" The teacher can add: "What are its characteristics?" "How does it compare with other elements?" If pupils have questions such as these to guide their reading, they are not so likely to copy from sources and tell uninteresting things that neither they nor their classmates understand.

Chlorine, iodine, mercury, neon, sulfur, lead, nickel, oxygen, phosphorus, silver, platinum, silicon, and chromium have especially interesting uses. Each pupil may keep track of how he went about finding information—people he asked, books and other sources he consulted, places he went to observe. If we believe that learning how to locate information is often as important as the information itself we ought to make the most of activities such as this. Pupils can go to drugstores, garages, paint shops, factories, hardware stores, and similar places. To find information they can look through books and encyclopedias and talk to dentists, jewelers, merchants, and many other persons.

An important part of this activity is learning to discover through reading. Discuss why water, sugar, and salt are compounds. Pupils can make an exhibit of such compounds and report on some of the sources and uses of common ones. This may be tied up with discovering how local industries make use of various elements and compounds in their manufacturing process. An interesting and instructive experience in geography can result when pupils attempt to discover where these elements and compounds come from and how they are transported.

What Are Atoms and Molecules Like?

We can attempt, through some experiences, to help children understand that all materials are made of tiny particles and to learn something about their nature and behavior, even though we cannot explain this idea with the same kinds of information that cause scientists to believe this. Let children crush a sugar cube into fine bits. They may use any methods they can think of to break the sugar into tiny pieces. Let them use a magnifying glass to see that the bits they produced are still tiny bits of sugar. Ask children what they think they could do to make these tiny bits disappear. If they are dissolved in water they cannot be seen. Ask children how they could find out if the sugar is still there. If the water is tasted, they know that the sugar is there. The sugar has broken up into its smallest particles—molecules. Let children use the magnifying glass to examine the water. A powerful microscope could not reveal the tiny molecules of sugar. This is an example of the kind of experience that helps give clues to the idea that materials are composed of molecules.

If a bit of perfume is sprayed in the air, the odor can be detected at a distance. Why? Because the tiny molecules of the perfume have moved through the air. There are many other similar experiences that, while they do not present the proof that convinces scientists, are examples that can be explained by the theory. The difference between a chemical change (when the atoms *unite* or separate to make a new substance) and a physical change (when they do not unite or separate to form anything new) is more easily understood when pupils get an idea of the nature of molecules and atoms (*see* other activities in the chapter). The size of molecules is difficult for children to comprehend.

The idea of what atoms and molecules are and how they behave is an example of science information that pupils can talk about quite glibly, yet understand only vaguely. One way to help them understand more clearly some of the things they learn about atoms and molecules and how they behave is to aid them in illustrating what they have read. In addition to the textbooks and encyclopedias that pupils are using, several of the books in the Bibliography will supply ideas.[4] Pupils can make some of the following, either on the chalkboard or on a large sheet of white paper: a drawing of molecules in a solid, in a liquid, and in a gas; a drawing to show what happens to molecules of water when the water is boiling; a drawing of a molecule of hydrogen to show the number of atoms in it; a drawing to show what happens to molecules in a piece of iron when it is heated. They will think of other ideas to illustrate.

For older children a chart of all the elements is very interesting. They may borrow one from the high school. The chart will show the elements in order of their increasing weights and will show the symbols. Do not expect children to memorize anything on the chart. Leave it up for several weeks for the most interested ones to refer to. A few will want to learn some of the symbols. Put formulas of common compounds (salt, sugar, water) on the chalkboard and ask children to use the chart to help them tell what elements are in the compounds.

How Can We Produce Some Chemical Changes?

Chemical changes function continually in the lives of children, producing many of the things they use and the changes they see every day. There are many simple

[4] B.M. Parker: *Matter and Molecules and Atoms* (New York: Harper & Row, Publishers, 1957), 36 pp.; *The Everyday Atom* (New York: Harper & Row, Publishers, 1959), 36 pp.

experiments that show chemical changes. Textbooks and supplementary books give many more. Remember that the important idea for pupils to understand is that as a result of chemical changes new materials are made that may have characteristics entirely different from those of the elements or compounds that went into the process. Children will be interested in the symbols for elements, the formulas of compounds, and the chemical equations that describe chemical changes. Introduce them to the simple ones, some of which are illustrated in the following examples:

The formation of rust is a common chemical change and, while children frequently observe it happening, they are unaware that it is an example of a chemical change.

Get two identical large iron nails, and paint one with any kind of house paint or nail polish that is at hand. Do not paint the other one. Place both nails on moist blotting paper in a plastic container and put a cover on the container. Let pupils predict what they think will happen and tell why they think so. Observe what happens. "Why has the unpainted nail rusted?" Children may plan other similar experiences with different kinds of iron objects under different conditions to see the results. (Oxygen from the air has united with the iron in the unpainted nail to make the rust. Rust is a compound formed from the combining of iron and oxygen). Scrape off some of the rust and you will see that it no longer looks like the iron. It is a brown, crumbly material. The painted nail did not rust because the paint formed a protective layer that kept oxygen from uniting with the iron. Ask children to describe the nail before it rusted by telling its characteristics. Then ask them to describe rust in the same way. This will help them to understand what has happened. Ask children to find examples in their environment of objects that are rusting and some that are not. Ask them to try to explain why. Try the experiment with nails made of copper or other metals. Children will think of other variations.[5]

Another easily observed and demonstrated change is shown by placing some sugar in a spoon and heating it. Urge children to observe carefully and attempt to explain what change is taking place. Ask them to describe the sugar before it is heated and the material in the spoon after heating. Compare the two materials. After the white sugar has turned black let it cool and taste it. It will no longer taste sweet. Why? A chemical change has taken place and a new material has been formed. When sugar is heated, its molecules break down into water and carbon. The water bubbles off leaving the black carbon in the spoon.

Still another easily demonstrated chemical change is done with baking soda. Place one tablespoon of the soda in a drinking glass and slowly pour vinegar on it. Children observe and try to explain what is happening. The bubbles that are formed are carbon dioxide. A burning match held over the bubbles will be extinguished. In this instance one kind of chemical change (production of carbon dioxide) is stopping another (burning). Again ask children to compare the materials before and after the change. "Will a match held over vinegar go out?" "Will a match held over soda go out?" "Why did it go out when these two were put together?"

Put some cooked egg yolk on a polished silver spoon and leave it for an hour

[5] J. Schwartz: *It's Fun to Know Why: Experiments with Things around Us* (New York: McGraw-Hill, Co., 1973). Gives many experiments that children can perform with iron, coal, glass, bread, paper, cement, and other materials.

or so. Ask pupils to observe the change in the spoon and try to explain what happened. There is silver in the spoon, sulfur in the egg yolk. The black material on the spoon is made when these two elements unite. It is a compound called silver sulfide. Again compare the characteristics before and after.

Let children thoroughly chew soda crackers before swallowing them, being especially careful to note changes in taste. The sweet taste is due to a chemical action (enzyme-caused) which changes starch to sugar.

What Chemical Changes Go on Around Us?

The foregoing experiments are examples of what happens when a chemical change takes place. Such changes are going on all around pupils and even inside them. Suggest that on the basis of their experiences and observations children attempt to make a list of chemical changes they have seen going on around them. On the basis of discussion of this list pupils may be able to supply some answers to questions such as: "What

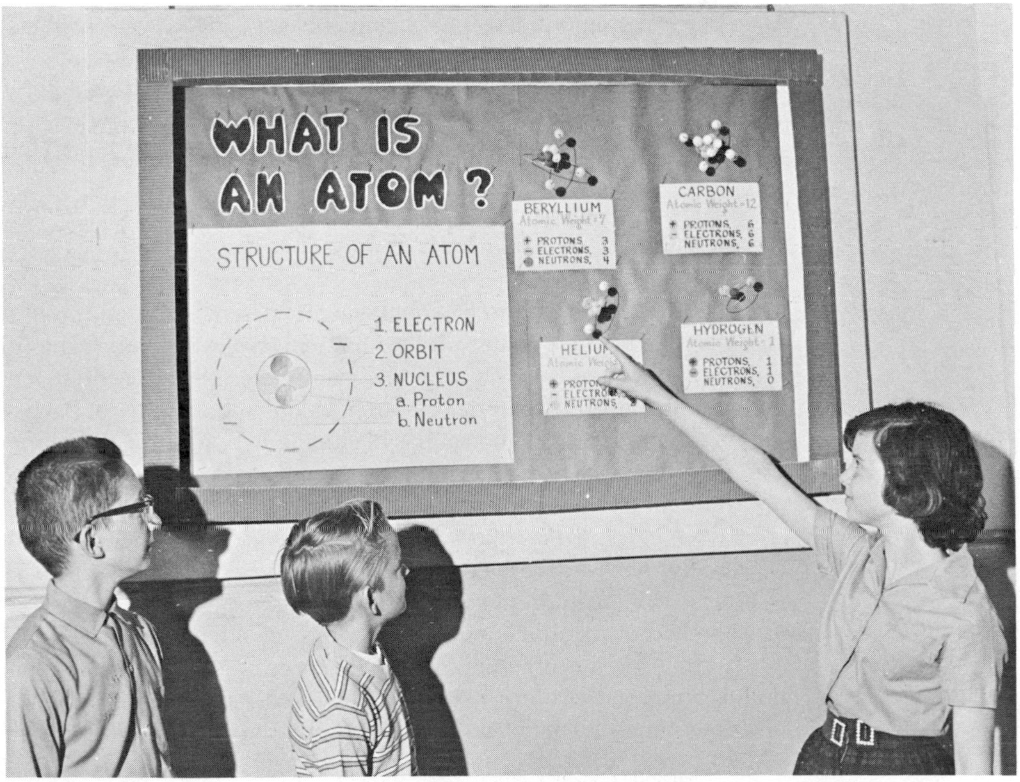

After reading from many sources these pupils illustrate the knowledge they have gained in a display; making such displays helps clarify pupils' understanding of difficult concepts. *(Courtesy of Bureau of Visual Education, Cleveland Public Schools, Cleveland, Ohio.)*

happens to a bridge when it rusts, and why is it frequently repainted?" "Why do we coat cans with tin?" "What happens when a fire burns?" "What happens to milk if it is left in a warm place for a few days?" "What happens when the soda-and-acid fire extinguisher is turned upside down?" "Why is baking powder used in cake making?"

Suggest that pupils do some reading and observing to find out about other important chemical changes such as: "How is window glass made?" "What happens when silver tarnishes?" "How can sodium (an element that would burn your tongue) and chlorine (a poisonous gas) be part of the common salt that is used every day?" "What must happen to oxygen and hydrogen to make them combine to form water?" "What
(*See* Ch. 10.) happens in green leaves that helps to feed us?" "What must happen to the food we
(*See* Ch. 12.) eat before it becomes a part of us?" "How are chemical changes used in making
(*See* Ch. 21.) photographs?" "Why are chemical changes important?" Life depends on some common chemical changes: oxidation of food in the body, making of starch and sugar in plants, and many others. Others change our way of living: making glass, making cement and paper, baking bread, and so forth.

Obviously not all chemical changes are desirable. We go to great pains and expense to stop or retard some. Let each pupil try to discover for himself and report to the class one example of a harmful chemical change and a way to stop it. The following suggestion to pupils will help to make such an investigation more interesting: "Try to find an example that no one else will find, and tell us where you found the example and how you happened to find it." Pupils will discover such things as painting, refrigeration, the use of dark or airtight containers, and keeping certain things dry.

How Can We Test Materials?

It is often important to find out what an unknown substance is or what a substance is made of. There are many ways to find out. Some are very complicated; others are quite easy. *Mystery Powders*[6] provides many concrete and useful suggestions for testing and identifying white materials—starch, baking soda, plaster of Paris, granulated sugar and salt—by the use of indicators. Beginning activities involve the use of the senses. Later, more sophisticated analysis with indicators and other laboratory techniques are used.

Investigating Physical and Chemical Changes[7] is based on *Mystery Powders* and shows how such a unit may be adapted for use in a public-school situation.
(**Note:** A caution here is in order: The sense of taste should be discouraged as a method of identification in most cases for obvious reasons.)

Testing for the presence of starch serves to illustrate how identifying tests are useful. Suppose there are two jars of material. One has some starch in it; the other one does not. You cannot tell which one has starch just by looking at them, so a test

[6] Elementary Science Study (ESS): *Mystery Powders. Teacher's Guide* for Grades 3–4 (Manchester, Mo.: Webster Division, McGraw-Hill Book Co.).

[7] *Investigating Physical and Chemical Changes.* Towson, Md.: Baltimore County Board of Education, 1971.

is in order. Remove a sample from each jar and put a few drops of iodine on each. What happens? Whenever a substance has starch in it it turns dark blue if it is tested with iodine. Children may test a potato, some bread, and other substances for the presence of starch by removing a small amount of it and testing it on a plate. Suppose you want to find out if there is more carbon dioxide present in the air that is exhaled from the lungs than in the air you inhale. Limewater is used to test for the presence of carbon dioxide. Use a straw to blow air from your lungs into the limewater. What happens? Carbon dioxide makes limewater turn milky. Pump some air (use an empty rubber-bulb type of plant sprayer) into another glass of limewater. Compare the results. What does the test show?

Suppose you wanted to find out if there is acid in something. Acids are sour. What sour things could you use? Litmus paper is used to test if things are acids or alkaline. The paper turns red in an acid medium and blue in an alkaline medium. Try vinegar, lemon juice, and other sour things. Try ammonia.

These examples (there are many others suggested in the books in the Bibliography and in *Mystery Powders*) introduce children to the idea that it is possible to find out what a material contains if you know how to test it.

How Can Fires Be Prevented and Extinguished?

Burning is an example of chemical change. The study of fire is of a very practical nature, for it is directly related to the safety of the home, the school, and the community. In the experiences suggested here it is essential to exercise the utmost caution. Fire safety should be practiced whenever matches or other fire is used. The activities should conform to school regulations if there are such. In some cases, with younger children, the experiments are best performed by the teacher to demonstrate safety precautions. As an outcome of this study children should not only understand the chemical nature of burning but also develop skills and attitudes essential for coping with fire and its prevention.

Use the material illustrated in the drawing on page 533. Suggest that children plan how this might be used to show that the chemical change of burning needs a supply of air. First they light the candle and set the lamp chimney over it on a smooth surface so that air cannot enter at the bottom. Observe what happens. Now they set the chimney on two flat-sided pencils to permit air to enter at the bottom. Again observe what happens. Cover the top of the chimney with a piece of glass. Now what happens? Remove the glass cover from the chimney and light the candle again. If a smoking splinter is held near the bottom of the chimney the smoke enters the chimney and moves up past the flame, showing which way the air is moving. The pupils will suggest that air must *enter* and *leave* if the candle flame is to continue to burn. The convection box used in Chapter 9B illustrated the same principle. The Hallowe'en candle in a pumpkin is another excellent opportunity for children to see the importance of providing fire with a supply of oxygen if chemical change is to continue.

After the experience with the lamp chimney pupils may be asked to tell where they have seen this same thing happen (draft through a stove or furnace, draft toward an outdoor campfire, draft toward a burning building). Discuss the importance of keeping windows and doors closed when part of a house is on fire. Review with children the three essentials for burning: (1.) fuel, (2.) enough heat to ignite fuel, and (3.) a supply of fresh air.

Having discovered what a fire needs to burn, pupils will be ready to discover how we keep these essentials away from a flame. There are several simple ways of showing some of the means by which we keep air away from fire in order to extinguish it. These experiments should be performed on an asbestos pad as a safety measure. Set a short candle in a bowl or a wide-mouthed jar. Light the candle and then cover the container with a piece of asbestos cloth. Observe what happens. "Why?" "Why does the candle go out?" Light the candle again. This time pour sand into the container to cover the candle. Try the same thing with water. This puts out the fire by reducing the temperature of the fuel. These simple demonstrations show why we suggest wrapping persons whose clothes are afire in a blanket; why we cover a campfire with earth; and why we use water to put out fires.

Another method of putting out fires is by removing the fuel. Put several pieces of crumpled paper on a pie plate. Light one. We can prevent the spread of fire to the other pieces by removing them. Use a tongs to remove them. These experiments with fire should be performed by the teacher or under the supervision of the teacher.

Other activities that children may engage in include the following: (1.) With the help of the school custodian check the fire safety measures observed in the school (*see* reference in "Discovering for Yourself," page 492); (2.) check the home for fire safety; (3.) visit the local fire station; (4.) investigate and report on community measures for fire safety.

OTHER PROBLEMS FOR OLDER CHILDREN

1. What are the differences between chemical and physical changes?
2. What chemical changes take place in commonly-used fire extinguishers?
3. What does the Periodic Table show about elements?
4. How do elements form other materials?
5. What happens when wood burns?
6. What is spontaneous combustion?
7. What is the difference between the rusting of a nail and the burning of a match? How are the two changes alike?
8. What does kindling temperature mean?

Resources to Investigate with Children

1. A professional or amateur photographer to illustrate how chemical changes are useful in picture making.
2. A chemistry set to illustrate chemical change.

3. A high-school chemistry teacher for materials and an exchange of ideas about teaching the material in this unit.
4. Local industries (soap factory, rubber factory, bakery) to see and learn about the use of elements and compounds as raw materials, chemical changes, and other phases of chemistry involved in industry.
5. The school building, pupils' homes, and public buildings to see how places are fireproofed and how caution should be exercised to prevent fires.
6. The school custodian to show and demonstrate a school fire extinguisher.

Preparing to Teach

1. Examine the activities in the various B chapters in this book to find those that lend themselves to the use of the senses to describe, compare, and classify. Plan how you might combine these into a total experience for children.
2. List the behavioral objectives you consider underlie the purposes of this chapter. State the objectives in terms which relate each one to the specific concepts of the chapter. How do they reinforce those objectives that are considered important for the total elementary-school program?
3. Devise models that will be useful in helping children learn more about the actions of molecules and atoms. For suggestions *see* Trieger, Seymour: *Atoms and Molecules* (Darien, Conn.: Teachers Publishing Co., 1964).
4. Make a chart to use with children that shows what happens in several examples of common chemical and physical changes. Describe how you would use the chart with children and how you would help them make similar charts of their own.
5. Clip accounts of destructive fires from the local newspaper for a month. Devise a plan for helping children analyse and classify them into: the causes, what might have prevented the fire, the extent of the damage, as well as other information children will think important in helping to understand the cause and prevention of fires.

CHAPTER 16A

HEAT AND HOW WE USE IT

(Courtesy of Bruce Roberts, Rapho-Guillumette.)

SOURCES OF HEAT

Heat consists in a minute vibratory motion of the particles of bodies.

—*Isaac Newton,* 1704

(*See* pp. 525–6.)

We rub our hands on a cold day, and they feel warmer. We burn gas under a kettle of water, the kettle gets hot, and the water boils. Electricity runs through the coils of wire in a toaster, and they get red hot. In the glare of the summer sun a sandy beach heats up.

Thus, heat is produced in a number of different ways. The mechanical work done in the process of rubbing our hands, the chemical energy released in burning, the electrical energy flowing through the wire, and the radiant energy winging 93 million miles from the sun—all these forms of energy made something warmer. How is it possible for different forms of energy to produce the same result—heat?

Before discussing the nature of heat further, we should understand the meaning of the word "energy" as the physicist uses it.

ENERGY

We live in a universe of matter and energy. We use such words as *stuff, material,* and *substance* to convey the meaning of matter. We may give countless examples of matter: steel, glass, water, sand, and air. Or we may think of the fundamental particles of which all matter is composed—molecules. Matter is all around us. So, too, is energy. Energy is defined as the ability to do work. The energy of the wind supplies the force that pushes a sailboat across the water. The energy in a stream of water exerts a force that turns a water wheel. The energy stored in the molecules of gasoline, when released in the cylinders of an automobile, pushes the pistons which makes the auto go.

Energy can be converted from one form to another. A light bulb is designed to convert electrical energy into light energy. A gong is a device for changing the energy of motion (mechanical energy) of a hammer into sound energy. Caruso is reputed to have shattered a glass with his great tenor voice—an example of a conversion of sound into mechanical energy. The radiant energy of sunlight striking the solar cells of a transistor radio is converted into electrical energy which in turn is converted into sound energy. Apparently all forms of energy are interchangeable.

The energy that a moving object possesses because of its motion, such as that of a moving stream of water, is known as *kinetic energy.* Some objects possess energy because of their position. The water behind a dam may not be in motion, but it has the potentiality of moving and doing work when it falls. Energy in this form is called *potential energy.* A jack-in-the-box has potential energy stored in its squeezed spring. When the lid is opened, the energy is passed from the spring to Jack, who then has kinetic energy as he jumps up. From the two examples just given it is apparent that potential energy may result from an object's position (water held by a dam) or condition (a squeezed spring).

THE NATURE OF HEAT

What is heat? What actually happens when something gets warmer? At one time some scientists believed that heat was a real *substance,* a fluid. They thought that when something got warmer, more of this fluid, which was named "caloric," flowed into it. Losing some of this caloric it became colder.

At the beginning of the nineteenth century Count Rumford of Bavaria challenged the caloric theory. He became interested in this subject when he observed the vast quantities of heat produced by working against friction during the boring of a hole through a cylinder of iron in the making of a cannon. He found it hard to believe that the apparently inexhaustible heat produced during the boring could be a material substance. He proposed the idea that nothing was "capable of being excited and communicated in the manner heat was excited and communicated in these experiments, except it be *motion.*" According to this theory heat, the result of mechanical energy being expended, *was energy itself,* not a substance; it was the energy of motion, not a fluid.

But how can "motion" be contained in a substance? When we finish with the rubbing of our hands visible motion has ceased. What has happened to the energy that has been expended? The molecular theory furnishes the answer. As we learned in Chapter 15A all matter is composed of exceedingly small separate particles called molecules. These molecules are in ceaseless motion. We have experimental evidence that when a substance is heated its molecules move with more speed or with more energy. Evidently the heat in a substance is the energy of the motion of its molecules. When you rub your hands you bump the molecules in the outermost layer of your skin and cause them to move faster. These in turn bump against those just beneath them, and so on. In this way the entire thickness of your skin is heated.

In all the materials cited before—the metal of the kettle and the water in it, the wire in the toaster, the sand on the beach—molecules have been activated into faster motion. This, then, is the meaning of heat: it is energy, the energy of moving molecules.

We now have an answer to the earlier question: How is it possible for different forms of energy to produce the same result—heat? It is possible because all these forms can *make molecules move*. In the rubbing of hands, as we have seen, motion is transferred directly to the molecules of the skin. In the kettle on the stove the chemical energy released by burning produces hot gases with highly excited molecules. These make the aluminum molecules of the pot dance more vigorously, which in turn make the molecules of water move rapidly. The case of the kettle is particularly interesting because the agitation of the molecules is transferred from a gas to a solid to a liquid. In the toaster the activity of electrons of the electric current causes the molecules of the nichrome coils to jiggle more rapidly. On the beach, energy from the sun comes in the form of waves. One of these waves is infrared rays. When the infrared waves strike the sand on a beach they make its molecules vibrate.

(*See* Ch. 21A.)

When we recognize heat as moving molecules, "cold" has a new meaning. It is simply a subjective way we have of characterizing less heat, less molecular activity.

An important effect of the increased molecular activity that results from heating should be mentioned here. As the molecules of almost all substances bounce more vigorously and more freely the substance they comprise expands. The metal in the kettle, the water, the coil, the sand all increase in size as they get warmer. Conversely, they contract as they cool. We shall discuss this more fully later and call attention to a very important exception to the rule.

TEMPERATURE

The common thermometer used to measure temperature is essentially a sealed glass tube containing a liquid such as mercury or colored alcohol. The principle involved in the functioning of a thermometer is that fluids generally expand when heated and contract when cooled. (Solids expand and contract, too, but the glass in a thermometer does not expand enough to affect the reading materially.) The hollow inside the thermometer, the *bore,* is very narrow; in some thermometers it is finer than a human hair. Thus, a small change in temperature causes enough expansion or contraction in the liquid to force it a noticeable distance up or down the bore. The tube is calibrated—that is, marked in degrees—so the expansion or contraction of the fluid can be measured in exact units.

Scales

There are two common temperature scales in use, the Fahrenheit and the centigrade scale. The Fahrenheit thermometer is so calibrated that it registers 32 degrees when the temperature is at the melting point of ice and 212 degrees at the boiling point of water. These are written 32° F. and 212° F., respectively. Thus there are 180° between the melting point of ice and the boiling point of water. The scale may be extended below and above these points.

(*See* pp. 524–8.)

Incidentally, the zero of the Fahrenheit thermometer does not mean "no degrees." This zero point was somewhat arbitrarily selected by its originator, Fahrenheit, who, on mixing some salt and ice, achieved a low temperature that he decided to call zero. In the making of a scale two points are needed to determine the calibration, so a second point of 100 was selected, which Fahrenheit believed was the temperature of the human body. It is said that this error (body temperature is actually 98.6° on this scale) was made because Fahrenheit based his figure on the temperature of a cow rather than a human.

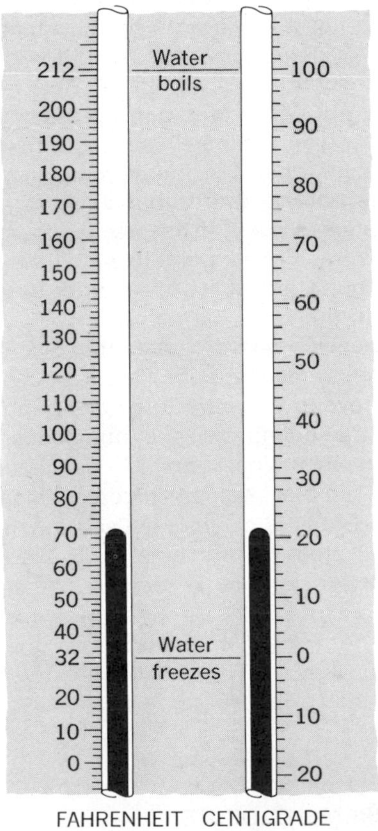

The Fahrenheit and centigrade scales. To convert from centigrade to Fahrenheit, multiply by 9/5 and add 32. To convert from Fahrenheit to centigrade, subtract 32 then multiply by 5/9. Or, simply place a straight edge across the two scales—and read!

The Fahrenheit scale is still in use in many English-speaking countries. The people there are accustomed to this scale and have resisted attempts to change it. The rest of the world, and scientists everywhere, use the centigrade scale.

On the centigrade scale zero marks the melting point of ice and 100 the boiling point of water. These are written 0° C. and 100° C., respectively. (Recently, the centigrade scale has been replaced by the Celsius scale, named after Anders Celsius, 1701–1744, who first devised the former scale. Although the two scales match numerically, the way in which the zero point is determined is somewhat different; for scientists doing extremely precise work the Celsius scale is more accurate under laboratory conditions. For some time to come, however, we may expect to see either of the terms—centigrade or Celsius—used interchangeably on thermometers and in publications.)

Absolute zero, −460° F. or −273° C., represents the lowest point that matter can theoretically reach. Scientists have produced temperatures only 1 millionth of a degree above absolute zero. In terms of molecular theory absolute zero represents the point at which molecules have the lowest possible energy, when they are very nearly at rest. A third scale, one sometimes useful to scientists, is the Kelvin scale, which begins with absolute zero as its zero but uses degrees that have the same size as the centigrade degrees. Here are some comparisons between the Kelvin scale and others.

	Fahrenheit (°*F.*)	*Centigrade* (°*C.*)	*Kelvin* (°*K.*)
Absolute zero	−460	−273	0
Freezing point of water	32	0	273
Boiling point of water	212	100	373

To convert from centigrade to Kelvin add 273° to the centigrade reading.

Some interesting temperatures (approximate) are shown in the following table:

	Degrees Fahrenheit	*Degrees Centigrade*
Surface of the sun	10,000	5,500
Electric arc light	7,232	4,000
Tungsten arc light	4,500	2,482
Kitchen-range flame	3,092	1,700
Iron melts	2,795	1,535
Mercury boils	675	357
Lead melts	620	327
Water boils	212	100
Ethyl alcohol boils	172	78
Highest official temperature record (Al'Aziziyah, Libya, Sept. 13, 1922)	136	58
Paraffin melts	128	52
Songbird's temperature	113	45
Body temperature	98.6	37
"Room temperature"	70	21
Ice melts	32	0
Freon boils	−2	−19
Mercury freezes	−40	−40
Lowest official temperature record (Vostock, Antarctica, 1960)	−127	−88.3
Ethyl alcohol freezes	−202	−130
Air boils (changes from liquid to gas)	−310	−190
Absolute zero	−460	−273

Thermometer Fluids

To be useful, a thermometer fluid must remain a liquid at the temperatures which the thermometer is intended to measure. If the fluid freezes solid it cannot flow; if it boils it will break the thermometer. The boiling point of mercury, 675° F., is high enough to permit its use in thermometers at moderately high temperatures. Its freezing point, −40° F. (that is, 40° below zero, F.), is low enough for its use in an average winter in temperate climates. Moreover, mercury expands uniformly throughout a wide temperature range, another essential in a thermometer fluid.

Alcohol boils at a much lower point (172° F.) than water; consequently, it cannot be used in thermometers that are to be exposed to high temperatures. Its low freezing point (−202° F.), however, makes it useful in polar and arctic regions. Alcohol is used also because it is cheaper than mercury and because it expands six times as much for a given rise in temperature and is therefore more sensitive to temperature variations. Alcohol is colored with a red or blue dye for visibility.

Thermometers for Different Purposes

Thermometers come in different shapes and sizes for different purposes. The clinical thermometer has a very narrow bore, so that a difference of $\frac{1}{10}$ degree is easily read. It is calibrated to read only from 92° to 110° F. Heat forces the mercury out of the bulb and up the bore, but a constriction in the bore keeps the mercury up in the stem when the thermometer is removed from the patient, even though the surrounding temperature is lower. In this way the thermometer registers the highest point to which the mercury goes. A quick jerk of the wrist forces the mercury back into the bulb.

Expansion and contraction is also the principle behind metal thermometers, such as those used in ovens, but here it is a solid rather than a liquid that changes size. In one common metal thermometer the basic unit is a coil made of two strips of metal welded together along their lengths. Brass is commonly used for the inside strip and steel for the outside. Brass expands more for a given rise in temperature than steel does. As a result the expansion or contraction due to heating or cooling causes the coil to loosen or tighten. This motion is conveyed to a pointer that sweeps over a scale calibrated in degrees.

MEASUREMENT OF HEAT

Which has more heat in it, a cupful of water at 212° F. (its boiling point) or a potful of water at 212° F.? Both have the same temperature, which, as we learned, means that the *degree of*

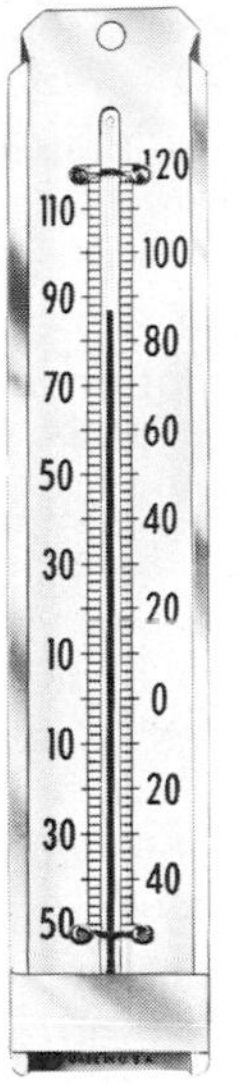

a

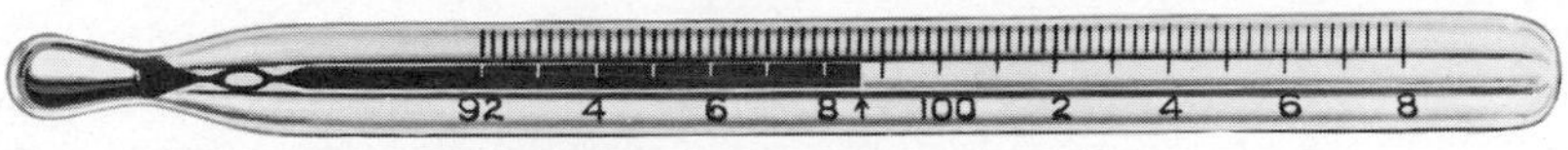

b

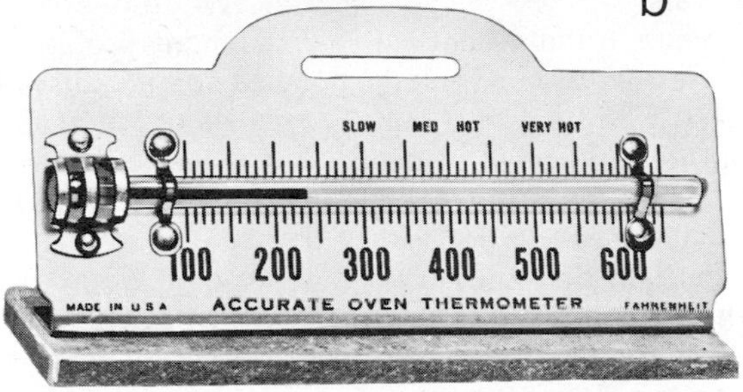

c

a. Outdoor wall thermometer.
b. Clinical thermometer.
c. Oven thermometer.
(a.) Courtesy of Taylor Instruments Companies; (b.) and (c.) Courtesy of Weksler Instruments Corporation.

activity of the molecules in each is the same. But the potful of water has *more* of these active molecules, hence we say that it has more heat in it. It takes much more burning of gas to produce a potful of boiling water than a cupful; in turn, the pot has more heat to give up to something else. That is why you can take the chill off a bottle holding baby's milk formula more quickly by putting it into a potful of hot water than into a cupful, other things being equal.

The unit used in measuring the *quantity* of heat is the calorie. The caloric is defined as the amount of heat necessary to raise 1 gram of pure water (about half a thimbleful) 1 degree centigrade. (This calorie is known as the small calorie; the large Calorie you use to "count the calories" in foods is equal to 1,000 of these small calories and is spelled with a capital "C.") Heat, then, is measured in units called calories; temperature is measured in units called degrees.

EFFECTS OF HEATING

The expansion and contraction of substances that is occasioned by their heating and cooling is important in everyday life. Railroad rails are laid with a small space between each section, because summer temperatures cause them to expand considerably. One mile of railroad track may be 4 feet longer on the hottest day of summer than on the coldest day of winter. The space between the sections of rail allows for expansion of steel; otherwise the expanding rails would buckle. Long metal bridges often have their sections mounted on rollers. Joints between each section allow for expansion on the hottest days. Sidewalks must be laid in sections with expansion joints between them for the same reason. Otherwise the sidewalk would buckle up and break.

(See pp. 525–6, 528–32.)

The steel tires on wagon wheels are put on hot so that they will contract and hold fast around the wooden wheels when they cool. Hot liquid poured into a cold glass sometimes causes it to crack because the heated inside surface expands suddenly, straining the unheated outside surface to the breaking point. Pyrex glass is useful because it contains substances that reduce the amount of contraction and expansion that can be induced by the loss or addition of heat.

Liquids as well as solids, as we have found

in our study of thermometers, expand when they are heated and contract when they are cooled. For this reason we do not fill automobile radiators to the top with cool water.

Water, however, is unique in that at certain temperatures it reverses the rule of contracting with cooling and expanding with heating. From 39° F. to 32° F., its usual freezing point, water expands slightly as it is cooled. As a result ice is lighter than water and floats on it. This peculiar behavior of water has important consequences for life on this planet. When ice forms on a lake or pond its lower density (it is only $\frac{9}{10}$ as heavy as liquid water) keeps it on top. There it acts as an insulating blanket, preventing the rapid loss of heat from the water below it. This is why ponds and lakes do not freeze solid to the bottom but have a liquid zone under the ice for the survival of aquatic life.

The fact that water expands as it changes into ice accounts for the bursting of uninsulated water pipes in the winter. Similarly, if water is allowed to freeze in an automobile it may break the metal block of the engine. Consequently, in cold weather we add antifreeze, a substance that has a low freezing point, to the water in our automobile cooling system. Water that freezes in bottles frequently breaks them. In Chapter 6A we saw how the freezing of water is one of the forces responsible for the splitting of rocks.

Why does water behave in this unusual manner? Why does water expand as it freezes? As in so many problems in science we turn to molecules for an answer. When water freezes into crystals of ice its molecules arrange themselves in the way shown in the illustration. In the ice crystals the spaces between the molecules are large. They cannot fit together as closely as they do in cold water.

We have seen how solids and liquids change in volume with temperature. Gases expand and contract even more. Air expands when heated and becomes lighter than an equal volume of cooler air. In Chapter 9A we saw how the unequal heating of the air is one of the driving forces in the weather "machine" of our planet. We make use of this principle in the heating systems and in the ventilation of our homes.

CHANGE OF STATE

(*See* p. 497.) Matter can exist in a solid, liquid, or gaseous state. These states may be described in terms of shape and size.

A solid substance, such as a cube of ice, has

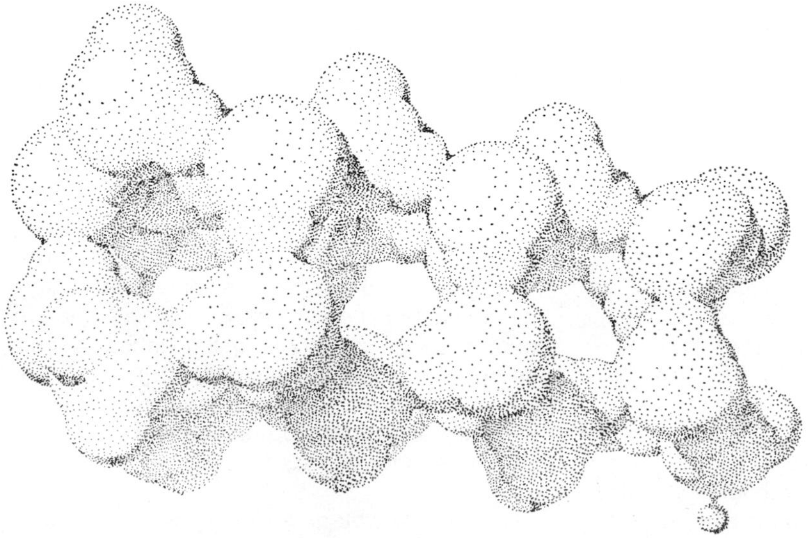

The molecular arrangement of water molecules in a small part of a crystal of ice. The large spheres represent oxygen atoms, the small ones hydrogen atoms. This drawing, based on x-ray studies, reveals that there is a good deal of space between the molecules, which explains why ice is less dense than liquid water and why it floats on it. When the ice melts, the breakdown of its structure allows molecules to fill some of the open spaces. (*Courtesy of W.H. Freeman and Company,* College Chemistry *by Linus Pauling, 3rd edition, Copyright © 1964.*)

a shape and a size (volume) of its own.

(See p. 531.) A liquid substance, such as water in a pitcher, takes the shape of its container but has a size of its own.

A gaseous substance, such as water vapor in a pressure cooker, takes both the shape and the size of its container.

The three states of matter can also be imagined in terms of molecules. The description that follows makes two assumptions:

1. The ceaseless movement of molecules tends to make them separate from each other and move in all directions.
2. An attractive force, *adhesion,* pulls them closer together.

In the solid state of a body, such as a bar of steel, the molecules move most slowly. The attractive forces between the molecules are strong enough to keep them vibrating in a fixed position. As a consequence the body keeps a definite and unchanging shape.

In the liquid state of a body, such as molten iron, the molecules vibrate more vigorously than they did when the body was in the solid state. The attraction between the molecules is not strong enough to keep them in a specific location, yet it is strong enough to make the entire body hold together. This is why a liquid can flow and take the shape of its container.

In the gaseous state the molecules of a body move more rapidly than in the liquid or solid forms of that body. The molecules are so far apart that the attractive force is very small. This explains why gases have no definite shape or size and why they spread to all parts of their container. The molecules in a drop of perfume pervade a room in a few seconds.

The description of these states in terms of molecules of matter also suggests why the volume or size changes when a body changes its state. In a solid the molecules are packed closely together; in a liquid they are farther apart (we noted one important exception in the preceding section); in a gas they are most scattered.

We can cause a change of state of any substance by adding or subtracting heat. Butter taken out of the refrigerator on a hot day gains heat and melts into a liquid. Water placed in the ice-cube compartment solidifies as it loses heat. Gaseous water vapor in the air condenses into a liquid as it loses heat.

When we say that a substance is a solid, liquid, or gas we really mean that it is commonly found in one of these three states at ordinary temperatures found on our planet. Thus mercury is usually regarded as a liquid, but it will solidify into a solid at $-40°$ F. or boil off as a gas at 675° F. Iron, copper, and other metals change from solids to liquids if they are heated sufficiently. Air is always thought of as gaseous; yet, with sufficient chilling, air can be converted into a liquid, known as *liquid air*. Sufficient chilling of one of the gases of the air, carbon dioxide, changes it into a solid; we know it as *dry ice* and use it when we wish to keep food at very low temperatures.

The temperature at which a substance changes from solid to liquid is known as its *melting point*. We make use of the fact that different substances have different melting points. Tungsten, the metal used for the filaments in electric lamps, can withstand temperatures of thousands of degrees without melting. On the other hand, an alloy of metals with a low melting point is useful in electric fuses, because a rise of temperature caused by a short circuit or an overloading of the electric line will cause it to melt and break

(See pp. 597–8.) the circuit. Automatic sprinkling systems also use such metals for plugs; the heat produced in a fire causes the plugs to melt, thereby releasing water from the pipes.

We also make use of the fact that different substances have different *freezing points*. Alcohol, for example, freezes only when it has been chilled to $-202°$ F., but water freezes at 32° F. For this reason alcohol (or some other antifreeze) is mixed with the water in the radiator of automobiles to prevent freezing as we have seen. The alcohol-water mixture has a lower freezing point than the water alone. Salt-water mixtures freeze only at temperatures lower than the freezing point of water. The practice of scattering salt on icy sidewalks results in a mixture that has a freezing point lower than the temperature of the air; hence, the ice melts.

HEAT MOVES

An iron poker is left in a camp fire. In a few minutes its handle gets hot. In a tree branch 40 feet above the fire a bird feels the fire's warmth. Campers sitting around the fire feel a warm glow on their faces.

In each of these instances heat was transferred—from the fire to the poker, bird, and campers, respectively. But the principal *method* of heat transfer involved in each was different. Let us consider each of these ways—called *conduction, convection,* and *radiation*—to see how objects gain or lose heat.

(*See* pp. 532–4.)

Conduction

Heat traveled from the end of the poker in the fire to the handle by conduction. It is simple to understand conduction when we recall that the poker, like all other substances, is made of molecules, in this case mostly iron molecules, and that the heat in the poker is due to the vibration of its molecules. The molecules in the end of the poker in the fire vibrate more rapidly. These, in turn, strike adjacent molecules in the cooler part, just outside of the flames, and cause them to vibrate more rapidly. This continues inch after inch up the poker until the handle becomes hot.

Conduction, then, is a method of heat movement in which energy is transferred from molecule to molecule by collision or bombardment. You burn your fingers on the handle of a hot skillet because the heat from the flame has started molecular activity that reaches your skin by conduction. Even the molecules in your skin vibrate vigorously as they are heated. Sense organs in your skin detect this vibration and send a special nerve message (*not* by heat conduction) to your brain. You thus become aware of the heat.

Not all objects conduct heat equally well. Because wood is a poor conductor of heat we use it for the handles of pots and pans. In general, metals are better conductors than nonmetals. Liquids, gases, and nonmetallic solids, all poor conductors of heat, are designated as heat *insulators* and are used to shield our bodies or objects from heat or to prevent the loss of heat. When we use a potholder to pick up hot pans and kettles we are making use of the insulating qualities of both the material and the air that is trapped in it to protect our hands from the heat.

Convection

How was the bird high in the tree warmed by the campfire? A layer of air directly over the fire was heated. The heat caused it to expand and thus made it lighter than the surrounding colder air. The heavier, colder air around the base of the fire swept into the fire and pushed the warmer, lighter air up to the bird. We saw in Chapter 9A how convection currents like these, caused by the unequal heating of the earth, were responsible for the large-scale movement of air and therefore of weather around the earth.

Convection currents are responsible for the heating of a room by a radiator. (A better name for this type of heater would be "convector.") Warm air heated by the radiator is pushed up and sweeps across to cooler parts of the room. Cold air falls and moves toward the radiator, where it is heated. Fireplaces are poor room heaters because most of the heat is convected up the chimney rather than out into the room.

Radiation

In conduction heat is transferred as molecules kick adjacent molecules. In convection a whole volume of heated material—gaseous or liquid—circulates. The transfer of heat by radiation is quite different from both of these. The transfer of heat from campfire to face is effected not by vibrating molecules or circulating air but by an energy wave called *infrared radiation*.

(*See* p. 661.)

This is a most important method, because it accounts for the heating of the earth by the sun. Obviously, conduction and convection could not carry heat from the sun to the earth, because most of the 93 million miles between them is empty space, almost devoid of molecules.

Infrared rays themselves should not be thought of as heat. The space between the sun and the earth is not heated by these waves, because there is practically nothing there to be heated. The rays might be compared to television waves emanating from a broadcasting station. These waves must be picked up by your TV set and converted into light for you to see a picture. Similarly, the infrared rays broadcast by the sun produce heat only when they strike and excite the molecules of substances.

Infrared rays are invisible to the human eye, lying just beyond the visible red rays in the spectrum of the sun's colors. All substances give off infrared radiation. If you hold your hand under an electric iron (to avoid heat by air convection) it is heated by radiation. You can detect the radiations of your own body by holding your open hand very close to the side of your face without touching it.

(*See* p. 661.)

EVAPORATION COOLS

Dip your finger into water that is at about body temperature and hold it up to the air. It feels cool as the water evaporates. Evaporation is a cooling process, or to put it in other words, a heat-removing process. Why? The molecular theory comes to our help again. We have found that the heat of a substance is due to the energy of all its moving molecules. But not all the molecules have the same speed. Some of the faster-moving (higher-temperature) molecules escape from the surface of the water on your skin, leaving the slower-moving (lower-temperature) ones behind. Consequently, the moment that evaporation begins, heat leaves the water that remains momentarily on your finger. The water, on being chilled, removes heat from your skin making it feel cool. We hasten cooling of a feverish patient by sponging him with alcohol, which evaporates quickly and thus cools more effectively than water.

The evaporation of perspiration from our skin serves to regulate body temperature. Our bodies are heat machines; the skin serves as a cooling system; perspiration is the cooling fluid, its evaporation providing the means by which excess heat is disposed of.

You may recall that in Chapter 9A we saw how the cooling effect of evaporation could be used to measure the humidity of the air, because evaporation and hence cooling take place more rapidly in dry air than in moist air.

INSULATION

Stated simply the purpose of insulation is to prevent heat from going where we do not want it to go. This is true whether we are considering our bodies or our homes. In all instances the flow of heat is regulated by controlling conduction, convection, and radiation, because these are the three methods by which heat travels.

Clothing

The purpose of clothing is to keep the wearer comfortable in the particular environment in which he happens to be. As stated previously our bodies are heat machines, maintaining a temperature of 98.6° F. In cold weather clothing prevents the rapid loss of heat from the body. It does this by providing layers of air pockets; that is, still air trapped in the fine meshes of the fabric. Trapped in this way air cannot transmit heat by convection; it prevents your body from losing heat. Birds protect themselves from cold by fluffing their feathers, thereby trapping more air. Woolen clothing is generally warmer than other materials because it can hold more spaces of trapped air. Thicker fabrics are generally warmer than thinner ones because they hold more of this "dead air."

In designing clothing for warmth, provision must also be made for the evaporation of perspiration. If the moisture is permitted to accumulate in the inner layers of the cloth it will fill some of the tiny air spaces that would otherwise provide insulation. Thus heat would be conducted away from the body more rapidly. To provide for the evaporation of perspiration several layers of fabric are generally better than a single layer.

Wind is also a source of danger and discomfort in cold weather, because the currents of air carry heat away from the clothing. That is why it is wise to have tightly woven cloth in the outermost layer of clothing to serve as a windbreaker.

In warm weather the problem is still insulation—insulation against the blistering heat of the sun. Clothing must be thick enough to prevent the sun's rays from penetrating and yet porous enough to permit evaporation, which as we recall, is the body's natural cooling process.

Dark-colored materials absorb more radiant heat than light-colored materials. Place a piece of dark fabric and a piece of light-colored fabric of the same size and material in the sunlight. Feel each after a few minutes and you will find that the dark cloth is much warmer. For this reason light-colored clothing is cooler than dark clothing of similar material when worn in sunlight and is recommended for summer wear.

(*See* pp. 531–2.)

Homes

The prevention of heat loss from homes makes them healthier and more comfortable to live in and serves to lower fuel bills at the same time. The principles involved are similar to those employed in clothing. Buildings are insulated in a number of ways. One method is to fill the spaces between the inner and outer walls with poor conductors, such as asbestos or spun glass. Insulation is thus improved, because these materials prevent air currents from convecting heat away; they also provide a way of trapping air, which, as we know, is a poor heat conductor.

(*See* figure below.)

Wood, brick, cement, and cinder block are

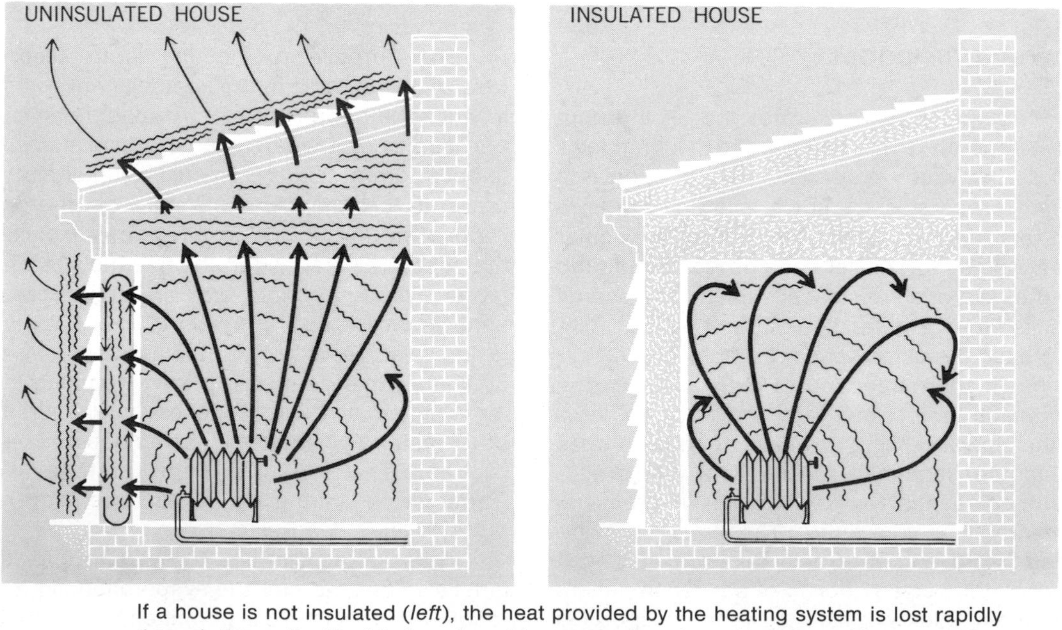

If a house is not insulated (*left*), the heat provided by the heating system is lost rapidly through the walls. Heat is transferred by conduction through walls and by convection currents in the air spaces between walls. In the insulated house (*right*) the heat is retained within the living space. Because insulation material is a poor conductor heat is lost slowly by conduction; and because insulation fills the air spaces it prevents convection currents from being set up.

used in building construction partially because they, too, are poor conductors of heat and hence will retard the flow of heat out of the building. Inside the building, hot-air pipes and steam pipes are often covered with asbestos, spun glass, or other material to prevent loss of heat from the pipes in the cellar or in other parts of the building where warmth is not needed. Refrigerators have a thick fibrous packing between the inner and outer walls to prevent the heat of the room from getting inside them. Weather stripping around windows and storm doors prevents considerable loss of warm air through these openings.

HEATING OF HOMES

At one time fireplaces were the only means of heating homes. But the fireplace was never a very effective heating device. Pioneers often had to spend winter evenings in bed to keep warm. Even if they came close to a roaring fire

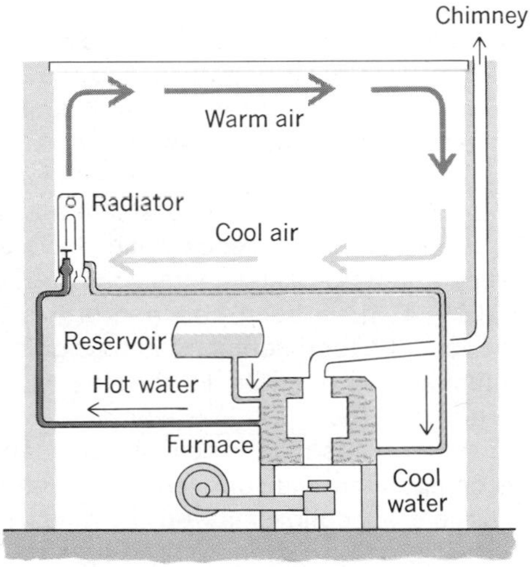

This oil-burning hot-water heating system illustrates the ways in which heat is transferred from one place to another. The flame from the oil burner heats the water by conduction through the walls of the boiler. The hot water flows upward by convection, being pushed up by the cool water returning from the radiator for reheating. The radiator warms the air of the room partly by radiation, but mostly by the convection currents of air indicated by arrows.

to receive heat by radiation, cold air chilled their backs. Commonly our ancestors heated a soapstone on the fire and then hurried off with it to warm an icy bed. No wonder they used feather beds and thick comforters!

In today's homes the fire has been moved into the basement or a special utility room. Its heat is conveyed to the rest of the house by means of circulating air or water.

REFRIGERATION

A discussion of refrigeration belongs in a chapter on heat because to cool something means to subtract heat from it. A refrigerator is a heat subtractor, at least as far as the food stored in it is concerned.

Mechanical (iceless) refrigerators have revolutionized the care of food. Such refrigeration is not confined to homes. Refrigerated railroad cars, trucks, and planes bring fruit, dairy products, fresh vegetables, meat, and fish hundreds and thousands of miles to our tables. We are able to keep food from one year to the next in deep-freeze units. They make out-of-season foods become in-season any time we choose. Let us see how refrigerators work.

Basically refrigeration depends on the principle that evaporation is a cooling or heat-removing process. Dab some alcohol on your wrist. It feels cool as the alcohol evaporates. The evaporating alcohol carries heat away from your hand; the alcohol vapor then disperses in the air of your room. If you had a way of collecting the alcohol vapor and could compress it back into a liquid you could repeat the original operation and thus keep your wrist cool. This kind of a cycle is possible in a refrigerator (*see* p. 518).

Instead of alcohol, *refrigerants* such as ammonia, methyl chloride, or Freon are used as evaporating fluids. The refrigerant travels through pipes in a closed system, as shown. As the refrigerant (in a liquid state) passes through the coils around the freezing compartment it evaporates into a gas, thereby removing heat from the interior of the refrigerator. (Recall that evaporation is a cooling or heat-removing process.) The gas then moves to the electricity-driven

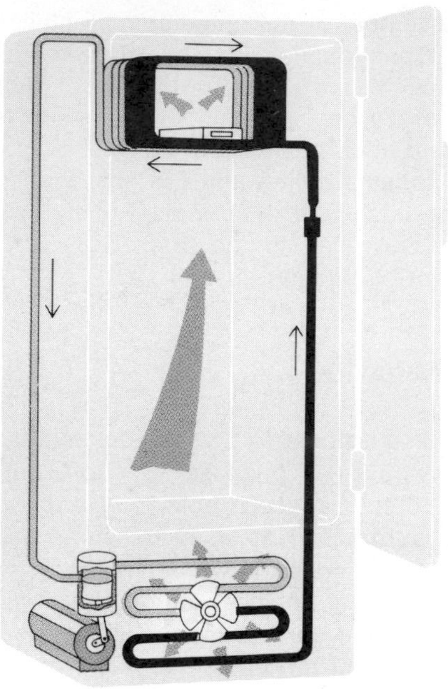

Refrigerant as a vapor
Refrigerant as a liquid
Heat flow

The mechanical refrigerator keeps its contents cold by transferring heat from the cooling compartment to the outside air.

pump and is forced into a condenser. Here it loses heat through the walls of this coiled-tube structure to the air of the room and is liquefied again. The cycle is repeated as long as cooling is required in the refrigerator. In this way the heat of the foods, the air, and surfaces inside the refrigerator is conveyed to the air of the room. Thus refrigeration transfers heat from where it is undesirable to where it is unobjectionable.

SOLAR ENERGY

All heat on the earth, save that obtained from (*See* Ch. 17A.) the nuclei of atoms comes, in the last analysis, from the sun. Not only does the sun warm the earth, but energy from sunlight makes it possible for plants to synthesize the food that provides fuel for their own needs and for the animals that eat them. The heat of the sun causes water to be evaporated from oceans into clouds. Falling as rain on the mountains the water from the clouds rushes down to the sea in streams and rivers. In the path of the falling water engineers place turbines hitched to generators which convert its wild energy into useful electricity. The common fuels we use—whether gas, oil, coal, or wood—are the remains of products of organisms that derived their original energy from the sun.

Coal, natural gas, and oil, the so-called "fossil fuels," are limited in their supply. In the (*See* Ch. 17A.) long run these fuels will be exhausted; natural gas first, then oil, and finally coal.

That is why all over the world there is an intense search for new sources of heat energy. Perhaps the solution to the problem is staring us in the face when we look up at the sky—in the sun itself, which for millions of years has poured its essentially perpetual energy on us. The energy the United States receives from the sun in about 2 hours is equivalent to the energy produced by our present fuel consumption in a whole year.

Why don't we use some of this vast supply? Various attempts have been made to utilize the heat of the sun directly. So-called sun machines, by concentrating the sun's rays on a small area by means of a number of mirrors or lenses, have been able to change water into steam and thus furnish power. Some of these devices have been used experimentally to melt metals; temperatures up to 7000° F. have been obtained in this way. A great deal of experimentation is now going on in a number of countries to develop efficient solar engines. Thus far, however, the cost of solar machines has made their use uneconomical in competition with conventional methods. One possible exception may be the small solar cooker that is being tested in torrid areas where fuel is scarce, such as in parts of India.

The sun's rays have been used in another way, in subtropical and even temperate climates, to furnish part of the heat needed in homes. You may be familiar with the fact that the inside of an automobile becomes quite warm, even in cool weather, if the sun is shining in and if the windows are closed. Glass admits much of the radiant energy from the sun. This is changed to heat energy when it strikes the upholstery in the interior of the car. The heat accumulates and the car warms up.

The principle underlying this is often called the "hothouse effect," because it accounts for the warmth that builds up in a gardener's hothouse in the winter. Here, again, the large expanse of glass permits the sun's rays to penetrate and to warm the soil and other materials in the hothouse. These heated substances also broadcast heat waves, but these are different from the original solar waves, so that instead of passing out through the glass roofs and walls they bounce back. Ordinary window glass, then, has the unique property of being transparent to 90 percent of the *sun's* radiant heat energy but opaque to the heat waves reradiated by objects under the glass. A hothouse is thus an energy trap.

This principle has been used in "solar houses," which have been developed by engineers (*see* p. 520). In these houses much of the walls consists of glass. Such houses require little artificial heat even on winter days in as cold a climate as that of Chicago—provided the sun is shining. Fuel bills have been materially reduced as a result. Overhanging eaves prevent the summer sun's rays from entering the house.

The sun's radiation may be used to heat water. Solar water heaters have been used for many years in California and Florida. One type has blackened coils of pipe under a glass cover that is placed on the roofs of houses and tilted in a southerly direction to receive as much radiation as possible. When the sun is shining the water becomes warm and circulates to radiators, or it may be used for washing.

Some experimental homes are now heated all year round by solar heat. The sun's heat is absorbed by water in a heat trap exposed to the sun. The warmed water is stored in an insulated tank, and heat from it is transferred to the various rooms as needed. This system works for extended periods when the sun is obscured by clouds.

Solar energy is now being converted directly into electrical energy by *solar batteries*. In such a battery sunlight provides the energy to dislodge electrons and to produce a current in a circuit. (*See* Chapter 19A for a fuller discussion of electric circuits.) The principle is not new; the photoelectric meter used in photography and the "seeing eye" for opening doors converts light

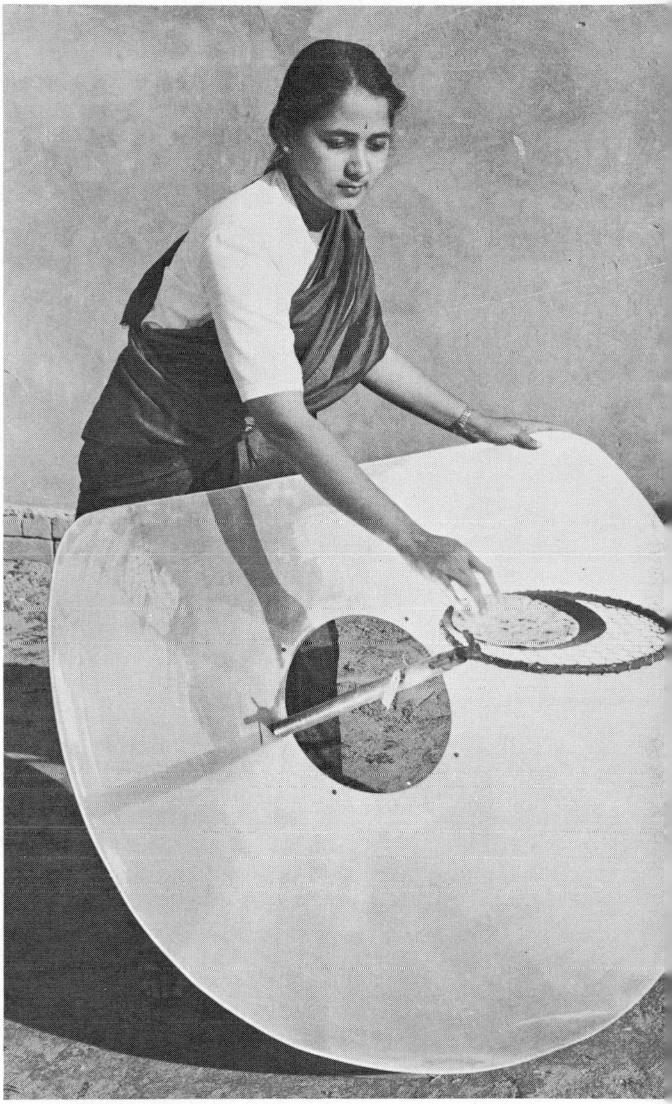

This solar oven uses a reflecting surface that concentrates the sun's rays on the centrally placed plate. India is among the countries experimenting with devices such as this to develop new sources of energy. (*Courtesy of the United Nations.*)

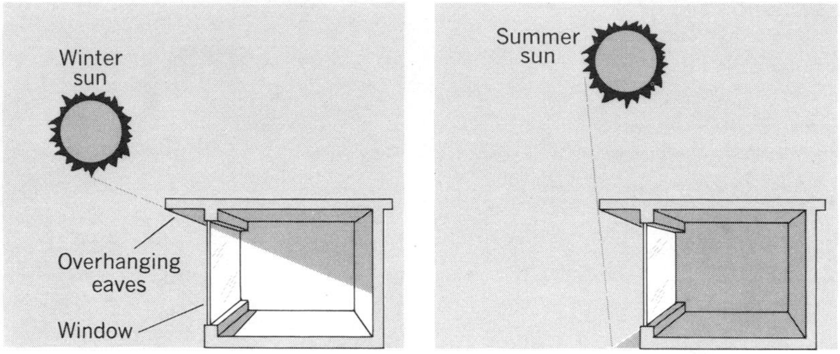

This schematic diagram shows how a solar house is warmed by the sun in winter and yet not overheated during the summer. Remember that the sun is much lower in the sky in winter than it is in summer.

into electricity. These, however, are not very efficient; only $\frac{1}{2}$ of 1 percent of the sun's light energy is changed into electricity. The solar battery is about 20 times as efficient. However, it is still not economically feasible to produce electricity on a large scale in this way. Solar batteries are used to supply electrical energy for equipment in many of the artificial satellites, such as the spacecraft Skylab. The many cells on its wings convert sunlight into the electrical energy needed by this space station. (*See* Chapter 14A for a discussion of solar cells as a source of heat on the earth and Chapter 22A for more details about Skylab.)

(*See* Ch. 19A.)

HEAT AND SPACE

Astronauts must cope with extremes in temperature in order to survive in space. Above the protective layer of the insulating atmosphere the side of a space vehicle facing the sun is very hot, whereas the side in the shade is very cold. To equalize the difference in temperature some kind of an air-conditioning system inside the spaceship is required.

On long trips it might be practicable to regulate the internal temperature by having the ship rotate so that all sides have equal exposure to the sun's radiation. As Apollo 8, with its crew of three astronauts, made its historic round-trip flight to the moon in December 1968, it rolled slowly, turning about six times each hour. (The rolling maneuver is appropriately called "barbecuing.") If the spaceship did not spin the side in darkness would be subject to a temperature of 250° below 0° F., whereas the sunlit side would be baked by a scorching +250° F.

Another way of moderating the temperature could be achieved by painting the space vehicle in a zebralike pattern of black stripes to absorb radiation, and silvery, polished stripes to reflect radiation.

In 1973 Skylab 1 suffered a damaged heat shield shortly after launching which resulted in soaring on-board temperatures. The astronauts were able to cool the space station by hoisting an improvised parasol against the intense sunlight.

The Apollo astronauts who landed on the moon were prepared for the unique heat problems they experienced there. The temperature of the surface on which they walked was over 250° F., well above the boiling point of water. A pair of thick, well-insulated shoes took care of the heat conducted directly from the ground. However, radiation from the sun, together with the reradiated energy from the moon's surface impinging on the astronauts' space suits, required heat protection built into the suits. Underneath each space suit was a special undergarment interwoven with a fine network of water-circulating tubes to carry away body heat. Covering the entire space suit was a "thermal garment" or white coverall with a hood to protect the astronaut from the blistering sunshine on the airless moon. An important unit of the Apollo space-suit system was the strap-on back pack which included a heat-dumping radiator.

If an astronaut moved into the shadow of a lunar boulder, he would experience a sudden drop in temperature, because there is no air on the moon to conduct and convect surface heat into sunless places. He might have to turn off his cooling equipment and turn on his heating system!

When spaceships leave or enter the earth's atmosphere they, like meteoroids, experience great heating because of the frictional resistance of the air. High temperatures may develop, ranging from 5000° to 18,000° F., which can be damaging to the vehicle and lethal for its occupants. Spaceships are designed to minimize this danger. They are shaped to minimize air friction and the resulting building up of heat. In addition, special materials are used that can withstand high temperatures. In spaceships, such as the Apollo, special heat shields absorb most of the heat and protect the part that houses the astronaut. The shield for the Apollo reentry capsule is made of honeycomb stainless steel covered with a layer of plastic material nearly 3 inches thick on the front end, where the heat is greatest. The plastic material melts and chars; some of it evaporates off the shield and in the process (called *ablation*) "throws away" the heat before it can penetrate the capsule.

Spaceships entering or leaving the moon have no frictional heat problems, because, as we have seen, the moon has no atmosphere. For each of the planets we wish to explore we must plan to meet the special heat problems related to landing, living, and leaving.

Some of the important generalizations in the foregoing material are:

A body has energy if it can do work.

Heat is a form of energy—the energy of moving molecules.

Energy can be converted from one form into another.

Energy of a body may be due to its motion (kinetic energy) or its position or condition (potential energy).

As a substance gets warmer its molecules move more rapidly; as it cools, less rapidly.

Cooling is the removal of heat.

Substances generally expand when heated and contract when cooled.

Water is unique in that it expands just before it freezes; this explains why ice is lighter than water.

The temperature or heat intensity of a body is measured in degrees; the total quantity of heat in a body is measured in calories.

Substances exist in three states—solid, liquid, and gaseous.

A solid has a shape and size of its own.

A liquid takes the shape of its container, but has a size of its own.

A gas takes the shape of its container and spreads to all parts of it.

The addition or removal of heat from a substance may cause it to change from one state into another.

Heat is transferred by conduction, convection, and radiation.

Different materials vary in their ability to conduct heat; those that conduct heat slowly are called insulators.

Clothing keeps us warm because it prevents the body from losing its heat too rapidly.

Clothing, blankets, and some home-insulating materials are effective in preventing the loss of heat because they contain trapped air, which is a poor heat conductor.

Dark-colored materials absorb more radiant heat than light-colored materials.

Heating systems make use of all three methods of heat transfer.

Modern refrigerators utilize the cooling effects of evaporation in their operation.

Scientists and engineers are trying to trap some of the abundant energy of the sun for man's use.

To explore space successfully it is necessary to cope with extremes of temperature.

Discovering for Yourself

1. Find out as much as you can about the heat problems that must be solved in space travel.
2. Locate as many different kinds of thermometers in your environment as you can. Compare their construction, purpose, and operation.
3. Make a list of the many ways in which heat is controlled in a kitchen.
4. Observe as many as possible of the sources of heat in your environment. List these sources.
5. Observe examples of heat causing materials (solids, liquids, gases) to expand. Record them.
6. Find examples of heat traveling by conduction, convection, and radiation.
7. Find examples of the use of insulation (against conduction, convection, and radiation) in your home and school.
8. Examine a refrigerator and a furnace to see how they use the principles of conduction, radiation, and convection.
9. Locate, observe, and describe different types of heating plants used in houses to find the differences between them, and the advantages of each.
10. Find out how man has experimented with the use of sunlight to heat water and to help heat houses.

(Courtesy of Phyllis Marcuccio.)

CHAPTER 16B
TEACHING "HEAT AND HOW WE USE IT"

Concepts about heat and heating have many applications in pupils' lives. Experimenting may lead to understandings that function in the room where they are learning, as well as at home and elsewhere. Their experiences will lead them to discover how we use what we know about heat in making our homes and other buildings more comfortable to live in.

Some of the concepts about heat may be learned as part of a weather unit or studied in connection with a unit on molecules, electricity, space, atomic energy, and needs of living things. Heat is a form of energy as is light, sound, electricity, and others, and is associated with many everyday phenomena. All of them can be converted into other forms of energy: light, motion, electricity, and so on. The study of heat provides another opportunity for helping children move from subjective feelings (I feel cold. I feel warm. It feels hot today.) to objective measurements. The temperature is 70° today. The water is 38°. The thermometer shows that today is warmer than yesterday.

SOME BROAD CONCEPTS: "Heat and How We Use It"

Heating and cooling change the size of substances.
Substances exist in three forms—solids, liquids, and gases.
Substances may be heated by conduction, convection, and radiation.
Heating systems make use of all three methods of heat transfer.
Heat is a form of energy, the energy of moving particles.
Energy may be converted from one form to another.
Materials that conduct heat slowly are called insulators.
Dark-colored materials absorb more radiant heat than light-colored materials.

FOR YOUNGER CHILDREN

What's Hot? What's Cold?

In discussing these two questions suggest to children that they express their ideas about what is hot and cold without the use of a thermometer. Ask such questions as: "Is it hot or cold today?" "Is the water in this cup hot or cold?" And so on. Then, "How can we be more exact about what is hot or cold?"

Even young children have had experiences with thermometers and will make suggestions about their use. The use of this measuring instrument is one way to introduce children to objective measurement. If they have never examined a thermometer give them an opportunity to do so, reporting what they can discover through *observation*—let them *describe* what they see and then try to *explain* how a thermometer can show temperature. Record their ideas. Discuss what they have discovered about the markings. "What do you observe about the numbers?" "What is the red (or silver) line?" "Can you make it change? How? Let's try it." Children may suggest: Put it in the sun; put it in cold water, in hot water; put your fingers around the bulb, breathe on it, and so on. Suggest that pupils select one or more of these ideas and try them, keeping a record of before and after temperatures. They may classify their ideas about the temperature line: "Gets longer," "gets shorter," "stays the same." Pupils can then examine their records and try to decide: "What makes the line on the thermometer change?" "How does it change if something is warmed? Cooled?" Pupils can explore problems such as: "How are thermometers used?" "What things change temperature around us?" They can be urged to keep a chart of temperature changes from day to day and to look for places where thermometers are used and try to decide why it is important to know the temperatures in those places.

The Conceptually Oriented Program in Elementary Science (COPES)[1] has developed "Conservation of Energy" activities which lead children to develop new concepts in order to explain things they observe. The fifteen experiences given intend to stress both concepts and skills in learning about heat energy. Examples: "Using Heat Energy to Melt Ice Cubes," "Measuring Temperature with a Calibrated Thermometer." While the material is suggested in the grade 3 sequence it is also useful for older children.

Where Does Heat Come From?

Refer to "What Makes the Earth Warm?" and "How Much Does the Temperature Change in a Day?" in Chapter 7B. These activities emphasize the idea that heat comes from the sun. "Where can you feel the heat of the sun?" On the sidewalk, grass, windowsill, and so on. Put a pan of water in the sun and a similar one in the shade. Measure the temperatures. "What does this show?" Suggest that children attempt to find out by observation what other sources of heat are common—in the kitchen? At the school? Elsewhere? "What can we find out about these sources?"

How Do We Use Heat?

Suggest that children observe at home, at school, and elsewhere different uses of heat. Many activities involve the use of heat—children keep track of such examples as: boiling water, making popcorn, baking cookies, drying wet things, melting butter, and so forth. Children can collect a list of such activities, along with those they observe elsewhere, and prepare a record of their findings (drawings, magazine pictures, sentences).

What Does Heat Do to Water?

Refer to "How Does Water Evaporate and Condense?" "What Makes Water Evaporate?," and "About Temperature" in Chapter 9B. Some of the material and procedures from these references may be used to solve this problem. Children can

[1]Conceptually Oriented Program in Elementary Science (COPES): *Teacher's Guide Water-Mix Experiments* (New York: New York University, 1972.)

place pans containing the same amounts of water in places of different temperatures to see what heat does to water—in the sun, on the stove, in the shade, and others. Measure the amount of water before and after and keep a record of the time involved, of, for example, the drying times for wet handkerchiefs of the same kind and size under warm and cool conditions. Keep a record of the temperatures and times involved.

OTHER PROBLEMS FOR YOUNGER CHILDREN

1. How does heat change things?
2. Do some things heat faster than others?
3. How can we keep things warm?
4. How can we keep things cool?
5. How does the temperature change at night?

FOR OLDER CHILDREN

Where Does Heat Come From?

Pupils can make a list of many different sources of heat—for example: friction, electricity, fires, atomic energy—and tell some of the uses for heat from each source. Then they can try to trace each of the sources back to the sun. This activity may raise several questions about heat, and is therefore useful in introducing the study of how we use heat. The questions can also form the beginning of a list of problems to solve, to which more will be added both by pupils and teacher as the study continues.

How Does a Thermometer Work?

Children will already have some hypotheses about how thermometers work. These may be listed, discussed, and defended. Individuals may suggest various methods for testing their ideas.

Depending on the responses and background of the children the teacher can, if necessary, provide some assistance by assembling the apparatus pictured on page 527.

Use a Pyrex flask, a one-holed rubber stopper to fit, and a $1\frac{1}{2}$-foot piece of glass tubing that will fit into the hole of the stopper. Fill the flask with water that has been colored with a few drops of red ink or vegetable coloring to make it easier to watch. Fit the glass tubing into the stopper so that a little of the tubing extends through the stopper. In inserting glass tubing into a stopper certain precautions are necessary to avoid breaking the tube and cutting oneself: (1.) Make sure that the hole is large enough to admit the tubing, (2.) wet the tube and the stopper, (3.) hold the part of the tube *near* the stopper and twist the stopper around the tube. Fit the stopper into the flask firmly. A little of the water should extend up into the tube. Tie a piece of thread around the tube at the level of the water. When the apparatus is assembled,

This flask filled with colored water can be used to show how heat causes a liquid to expand. A string may be tied around the tube to mark the level of water before it has been heated. (*Courtesy of Barlow Mountain Elementary School, Ridgefield, Connecticut.*)

the teacher may ask: "Can we use this material to test some of the hypotheses that were made?" "How is it like a real thermometer?" Children may suggest putting it in hot and cold places and using the thread as a marker.

The flask can be placed on an electric hot plate or into a container of hot water. Urge the children to watch the water level in the tube. (It rises as heat expands the water.) Hopefully they will suggest marking the new level with another piece of thread. Now cool the water by setting the flask in a pan of ice cubes. Watch the level of the water fall. (Cooling contracts the water.) Ask the children to try to explain what they have seen: "How hot was the water? How cold?" Obviously the children cannot tell because there are no degree markings. How could we improve on this apparatus to make it function more nearly like a thermometer? An adaptation of the following ideas may be worked out with the children.

Fasten an index card to the tube with Scotch tape. Place the flask up to its neck in a jar of hot water. Let it stand until the water stops rising in the tube. Then with a thermometer take the temperature of the water in the jar. Mark the card at the level of the water in the tube and next to it write the temperature just read. Now place the flask in a jar of cold water and let it stay there until the water stops falling in the tube. Again take the water temperature and mark it on the card.

With these two points you have a basis for making a *scale* of degrees. Mark off the degrees between the two points and then below and above them.

To use this crude thermometer over a period of time it will be necessary to place a drop of oil on top of the water in the tube to prevent evaporation. Also, if it is to be used outdoors in cold weather it will have to be remade, using about $\frac{3}{4}$ water and $\frac{1}{4}$ alcohol to prevent freezing.

The foregoing procedure presents the children with a partially completed instrument; they propose methods of testing it, offer hypotheses to explain how it works. They have invented a method of making it into a measuring device. This is an example of how a piece of apparatus can be used creatively with children. How much pupil participation takes place depends on the teacher's intentions and on the background and experiences of the children.

What Does Heat Do to Materials?

There are many ways to help pupils discover through inquiry that heating makes solids, liquids, and gases expand, and that cooling makes these materials contract. There are opportunities to *predict,* to *observe,* to *infer* from observation, and to *generalize* from observations and formulate concepts.

A complete experience with heat, its effects and measurement is contained in *Temperature, a Science Unit for Upper Grades.*[2] The approach is experimentation and

[2]Science Curriculum Improvement Study (SCIS-T): *Temperature. A Science Unit for the Upper Grades. Teacher's Manual* (Chicago: Rand McNally and Company).

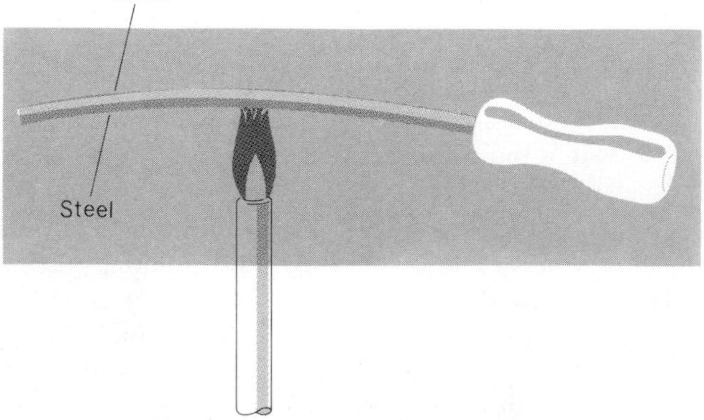

A piece of standard apparatus is sometimes useful for inviting inquiry. This bimetallic bar is made of a strip of brass welded to a strip of steel. At room temperature it is straight. When heated, the bar curves. Why? What do you think will happen if the bar is chilled below room temperature? Why? Bimetallic bars are a basic part of the thermostats that control room temperature. How do they do this?

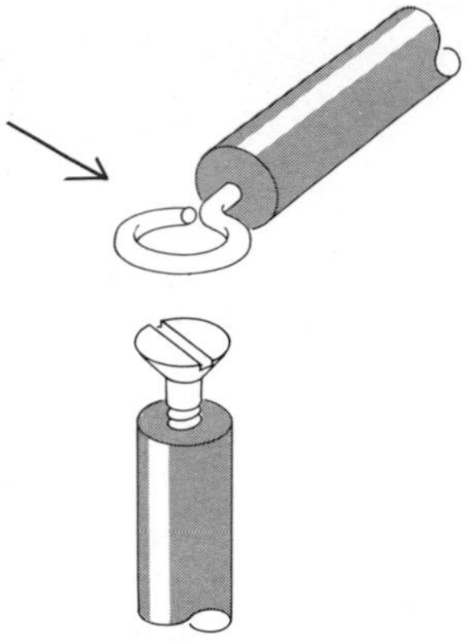

This screw and screw eye may be used to show that a solid expands when heated and contracts when cooled.

observation in the classroom and includes material on "Warming Behavior," "Thermometers and Temperature," "Expansion and Contraction," "Thermal Equilibrium," and "Interactions Causing Temperature Changes." The activities begin in a relatively unstructured approach. The section on thermometers, for example, is introduced without any specific instructions. The concept emphasis is on temperature and thermal equilibrium.

What Does Heating Do to Some Solids?

Begin by using the experiences children have had and ask them if they can formulate a general statement that they believe will be an answer to the problem.

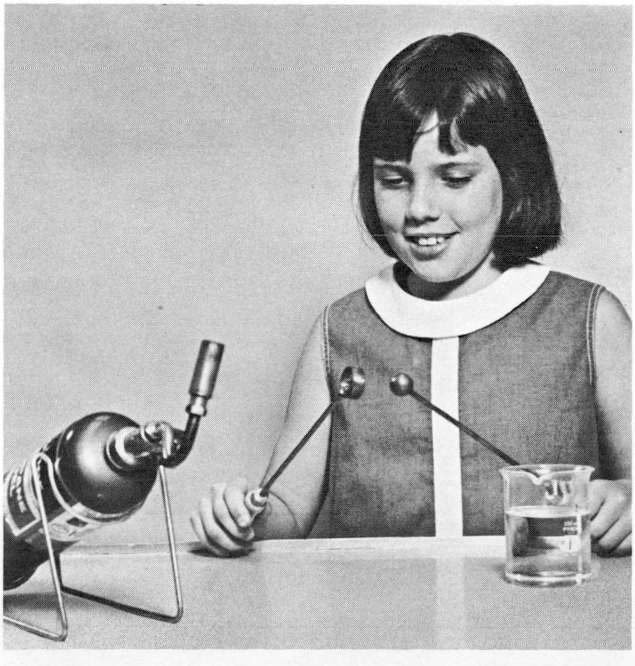

Experiences with heating and cooling the ball and the ring provide some similar basic generalizations useful in understanding everyday phenomena (*see* Ch. 2). An electric hot plate will supply the source of heat if gas is not available and may be safer to use. (*Courtesy of John King.*)

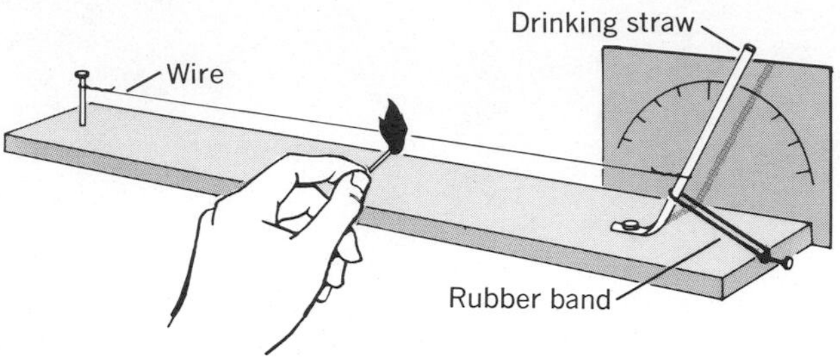

This improvised scale helps experimenters see how much expansion takes place as the wire is heated. Use a candle as the source of heat, if the heat from a match is not sufficient.

Ask them if they can demonstrate or suggest observations that bear out their statements.

The screw and screw eye pictured is a substitute for the commercially available ball and ring (also shown) often used to show that solids expand when they are heated and contract when they are cooled. The handles are made of $1\frac{1}{2}$-inch dowel about 1 foot long. With a nail make a hole in one end of each stick. The large screw eye is screwed into the end of one stick and the large screw head (just a little too large to go into the eye) is screwed into the other. When the screw eye is heated, it expands so that the screw head will go through it.

The home-made apparatus and the commercially manufactured ball and ring and bimetallic bar may also be used to observe the effects of heat on metals.

These experiments do not show that *all* solids expand when they are heated and contract when they are cooled, so pupils should experiment with other materials. They will find suggestions in books and elsewhere, and devise some themselves. They may also need to read to substantiate their ideas. Pupils should be urged to find other solids in their environment which are expanded by heat and contracted by cold. Examples are telephone and telegraph wires suspended from poles, pavements, sections of railroad tracks, and iron bridges. In some cases pupils can also observe how allowance is made for this expansion and contraction—for example, leaving spaces between sections of concrete sidewalks.

What Does Heating Do to Water?

Use the same apparatus and approach as that which demonstrated the principle of the thermometer. Applications of the principle that heat expands water are evident in automobile radiators, in our hot-water heaters, and other places where liquids are heated. (The unusual behavior of water between 39 and 32° F., discussed in Chapter 16A, is not characteristic of other liquids.) The thermometer itself is an example of the principle that heat causes liquids to expand; in thermometers the liquid is either alcohol or mercury.

What Does Heating Do to Air?

Using the approach suggested for previous work by drawing on the experiences and suggestions of the children the following, with adaptations, can be utilized:

Fasten a toy rubber balloon over the opening of a flask or test tube. (A Pyrex baby bottle may also be used.) Set the glass container into hot water or heat it gently over a flame. The balloon begins to fill up as the gas expands. The idea of air expanding on being heated has been used in the study of the cause of winds.

The flask, stopper, and tube used previously to show the expansion and contraction of liquids may also be used to show the expansion of air. Empty the flask and replace the stopper and the tube. Invert it so that the end of the tube is in a glass of water. Warming the flask, even by holding both hands around it, will be sufficient to cause air bubbles to escape from the tube into the water. When the air cools, it contracts, and water will be forced up the tube into the flask by outside air pressure.

How Does Heating and Cooling Change the Form of Matter?

To show that temperature changes affect the form of matter use variations of the experiments performed to show this principle in connection with the study of molecules and atoms (*see* Ch. 15B).

How Does Sunlight Affect Dark and Light Objects?[3]

Children may recall having had experiences with heat and light and dark objects and materials. Build on such experiences and then give children pieces of black and white paper and ask them how they might use these to find out more about the affects of heat on them. (Place them both in bright sunlight.) They might try putting the papers over thermometers to try to measure the differences and compare results.

There are many other ways to show that dark objects absorb heat more readily than light ones. The tin cans shown in the drawing have lids that fit tightly. One is

[3]G.O. Blough and M.H. Campbell: *Making and Using Classroom Science Materials in the Elementary School* (New York: Holt, Rinehart and Winston, Inc., 1954), p. 171.

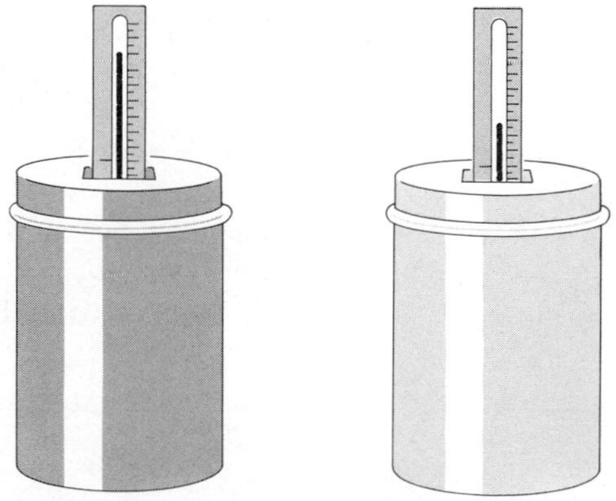

The two cans, one darkened by soot from a candle or black paint, the other painted white, may be set in bright sunlight to show its effect on light and dark objects. The two thermometers fit through slits made in the can covers.

painted black, or it may be darkened by holding it over a lighted candle so that carbon will form on it; the other is painted white, or it may be left with its tin surface unpainted. Each can top has a hole in it just a little larger than the thermometer that extends through to the inside. Ask children how they might use these cans to find out more about the affects of sunlight on temperatures under these conditions. Urge them to predict what will happen when their suggestions are followed.

The two cans can be set in bright sunlight and children can keep a record of the thermometer readings. After this experience urge children to apply their observations to their environmental experiences. They should be able to apply the findings to explain why dark and light clothing is worn at different seasons or in different parts of the world.

Light and dark pieces of cloth spread on the snow show similar results when the sun shines. The snow under the dark piece of cloth melts more rapidly. One application of the principle involved here is in the design of spaceships, where dark outside surfaces may be utilized to absorb energy from the sun's rays and white surfaces may reflect the energy. By the proper use of such surfaces satisfactory temperatures for human beings can be maintained within the ships.

Again testing a few materials to see how they respond to heat will not produce sufficient evidence on which to base sweeping generalizations. The observations must be supplemented by additional experiences and by reading.

A solar energy machine can be made by especially interested pupils.[4]

What Does Evaporation Do to Heat?

Let children wet one hand and fan it briskly. Compare this with the hand that has not been so treated. What difference is noted? "How do you account for this?" It is important for pupils to realize that when heat is taken away from anything it becomes cool. Heat is absorbed in the evaporation of water. (As pupils will remember from earlier experiments heat helps evaporation.) The heat to evaporate the water comes from the surface of the skin; consequently, the pupil's hand becomes cool.

An easy way to tell the direction of the wind is to go outdoors, wet the index finger, and hold it up as high as possible. The side of the finger that faces the wind feels cool. Pupils may recall having been sponged with alcohol when ill. Alcohol evaporates rapidly, and the cooling is rapid.

How Does Heat Travel?

An understanding of how heat is transferred from one place to another is important if pupils are to understand how their homes are heated and how temperature is controlled in other ways. It is not very important for them to be able to define the

[4] J. Schwartz and M. Green: "A Summer Project Comes to School," *Science and Children* (April 1964).

terms convection, radiation, and conduction, but they will be able to use these terms as they understand the processes. They must understand that heat travels in different ways, then come to the realization of how we make use of this knowledge. Some examples of experiences are given here; others will be found in textbooks and supplementary books.

How Does Air Carry Heat? Use a lamp chimney and a candle. Refer to "What Makes Wind" in Chapter 9B. Light the candle and set the chimney over it on two blocks to raise it above the table surface. Ask children to observe what happens when they hold a smoking paste stick at the bottom of the chimney. (The smoke will show that air is moving into the bottom of the chimney and is traveling up past the flame to the top of the chimney.) Feel the warmth at the top of the chimney. It is this moving air that carries the heat. Hold a thermometer 1 foot above the top of the chimney and note changes as the air is warmed. Hot-air heating systems operate on the principle of cold air pushing the warm air into rooms that are heated by the furnace.

Convection currents are continually at work all around us. If a thermometer is held near a register or radiator it will show that air is being warmed there. Hold the thermometer up near the ceiling either by standing on a stepladder or by attaching the thermometer to a window pole and lifting it near the ceiling. Pupils will see that

As the flame heats the air inside the chimney the air becomes lighter; cooler, heavier air entering the chimney at the bottom forces it up. Outdoors, such unequal heating produces wind. Indoors, convection currents from heating sources (radiators, registers, and so on) distribute heat to all parts of the room.

warm air has reached the ceiling. When they study the ways in which their homes are heated, they will apply what they have learned about convection as a method of heat transfer.

How Does Water Carry Heat? Fill a flask or Pyrex baby bottle or a beaker nearly full of water and heat it at the bottom. Hold a thermometer in the water at the top. Ask a child to read the thermometer when it is first inserted and again at intervals. "What does the temperature show?" "How did the heat get to the top of the water?" The water at the bottom is traveling to the top carrying heat with it. The heat is carried by convection currents. Some grains of sand or pieces of sawdust placed in the water will show how the currents are traveling. In hot-water heating systems heat is carried to the rooms by circulating water. The unequal heating of the water causes the movement.

How Is Heat Carried by Radiation? There are many common examples of heat being carried by radiation. Light a candle and suggest that children read a thermometer held about 8 inches above it. The higher temperature *above* the candle is caused by convection currents. Remove the thermometer from the candle and wait until it returns to room temperature. Now hold the thermometer at the *side* of the burning candle. The heat is caused by radiation. Read the thermometer before and after holding it at the side of the burning candle.

How Do Solids Carry Heat? Place the bottom of a metal spoon in a glass of hot water or other hot liquid. Let a child feel the handle from time to time to note what is happening. How do you think the handle gets warm? The heat has traveled along the spoon by conduction. Hot pans on the kitchen stove and fireplace tools conduct heat in this way. Ask: "Will all kinds of spoons carry heat equally well?" Try a wooden one. A plastic one? "Which one carries heat best?" Try other materials.

After these experiences pupils should be asked to look for places in their environment where heat travels from one place to another—at home, at school, in restaurants, and elsewhere. Kitchens, fireplaces, furnaces, and so on all depend on heat transfer. This investigating will probably lead to questions about other phases of the problem of heat control—insulation and home heating.

OTHER PROBLEMS FOR OLDER CHILDREN

1. What are heat insulators and how are they used?
2. How do we heat our houses and other buildings?
3. How are different things in our homes heated?
4. How are the different methods of heat transfer alike? Different?

5. How are automobiles heated?
6. How does a hot-water heater operate?
7. How is solar heat used?

Resources to Investigate with Children

1. Local builders to see how homes are equipped for good heating and how they are insulated. Children's homes to see how they are heated and insulated.
2. The kitchen at home (or at school) to see how heat is controlled in utensils, stoves, refrigerators, and other equipment.
3. A bakery to find out about sources and control of heat and about utensils that are used.
4. Home-economics departments for literature concerning cooking utensils and preservation of foods.
5. State university extension service for materials describing the heating of farm buildings, greenhouses, hotbeds, and other places.
6. The school building and the school custodian to learn how the school heating plant works and what science principles are involved in its operation.
7. Buildings or homes equipped with air conditioning.

Preparing to Teach

1. Plan some original experiments to show the advantages of wearing light-colored clothing in warm weather and dark clothes in cold weather. Plan how you would use the experiments to help children understand this concept.
2. Prepare large charts that show examples of energy transfer in the environment. Use drawings or pictures along with captions. Plan how to use the charts to help pupils construct other, similar charts that will help them comprehend the idea of energy transfer.

CHAPTER 17A

NUCLEAR ENERGY AND ITS USES

(Courtesy of Babcock & Wilcox)

THE ATOMIC AGE OPENS

Mankind's successful transition to a new age, the Atomic Age, was ushered in July 16, 1945, before the eyes of a tense group of renowned scientists and military men gathered in the desertlands of New Mexico to witness the first end-results of their $2,000,000,000 effort. Here in a remote section of the Alamogordo Air Base 120 miles southeast of Albuquerque the first man-made atomic explosion . . . was achieved at 5:30 A.M. of that day.

Mounted on a steel tower . . . a small amount of matter, the product of a chain of huge specially constructed industrial plants, was made to release the energy of the universe locked up within the atom from the beginning of time.

At the appointed time there was a blinding flash lighting up the whole area brighter than the brightest daylight. A mountain range three miles from the observation point stood out in bold relief. Then came a tremendous sustained roar and a heavy pressure wave which knocked down two men outside the control center. Immediately thereafter, a huge multicolored surging cloud boiled to an altitude of over 40,000 feet. Clouds in its path disappeared. Soon the shifting substratosphere winds dispersed the now grey mass.

The test was over, the project a success.

The steel tower had been entirely vaporized. Where the tower had stood, there was a huge sloping crater.

—War Department Report, 1945

The Atomic Age had opened for good and for evil. Three weeks after the test, on August 6, 1945, an atomic bomb was dropped on Hiroshima in Japan, and three days later one was dropped on Nagasaki, both with terrifying and devastating effects.

Let us retrace the events in science history leading up to this awesome happening.

ATOMIC ENERGY

In Chapter 15A we examined the interior of the atom and found there a cloud of electrons whirling around a nucleus made of protons and neutrons. We noted that the arrangement and the number of the electrons determines the chemical behavior of the atom: the way in which it combines or refuses to combine with other atoms. We found also that in the process of chemical change there is an exchange of energy. In photosynthesis, for example, energy from the sun is packed into a sugar molecule; when the sugar is burned, energy is released.

(*See* pp. 555–6.)

We shall now probe more deeply into the atom—into its nucleus—to discover a source of energy far, far greater than that which is released in such everyday chemical changes as in the burning of a candle or even the explosion of TNT.

Return to the year 1898, when the internal atomic architecture just described was unknown, when atoms were still thought of as hard, unbreakable, indivisible structures. In that year the Frenchman Henri Becquerel made a surprising discovery. Experimenting with a uranium compound (derived from the natural mineral pitchblende) he found that when it was placed near a photographic film *in total darkness* the uranium made an impression that showed up when the film was developed. This happened even when a piece of black paper separated the film from the uranium. To understand Becquerel's astonishment imagine yours if you were to accidentally snap the shutter of a camera in a totally dark room and find, on developing the film, an image of a necklace of pearls wrapped in a dark silken scarf that happened to be lying on the table.

Evidently the uranium compound was emitting a radiation that could pass through a sheet of paper and affect a photographic film without any outside stimulus. This was no ordinary chemical reaction, one that would soon come to an end. The uranium continued to radiate indefinitely. If this was not a chemical reaction where did the energy come from?

The French scientists, the Curies, became interested in Becquerel's discoveries. In the process of preparing uranium compounds they discovered a new kind of atom, radium, which was much more active than uranium. They found that a purified sample of radium remained warmer than its surroundings and continued to radiate without dimming. In a few days the radium emitted more energy than could be obtained from the explosion of an equal weight of TNT. But the explosion of TNT is a chemical change, in which the chemical energy is released instantaneously in a flash of light and heat. The energy of the radium, however, was steadily maintained, day after day, month after month, year after year. In 1,622 years the radium sample would still retain half of its energy.

In tracking down the source of this tremendous quantity of energy scientists devised various tools to study the nature of radiations emanating from the radium. With these tools three distinct varieties of radiation were found: *alpha particles, beta particles,* and *gamma rays.* As you read the following keep in mind that scientists did not know, at the beginning of this century, that electrons, protons, and neutrons are basic parts of the atom.

Alpha particles, flying from the radium atoms at the speed of 20,000 miles per second, are specks of matter with a positive electrical charge. These were later identified as particles containing 2 protons and 2 neutrons, which, you may recall from Chapter 15A, is exactly what the nucleus of a helium atom is made of.

Beta particles, coming from uranium atoms at the speed of 160,000 miles per second, are negatively charged. These are high-speed electrons.

Gamma rays, with much greater power to penetrate than the alpha or beta particles, are similar to light and x-rays in that they are energy in wave form.

Out of radium atoms came particles and energy. Thus began scientists' understanding of the architecture of atoms—of their component protons and electrons—and of the vast reservoir of energy stored in them.

Some Atoms Split Naturally

What was the source of uranium's penetrating rays? What was the source of radium's radiations, including the high-speed particles that flew out of it? Scientists found that some of the atoms of these substances were *splitting,* without man's intervention, to form new kinds of atoms, releasing radiations at the same time. Radium and uranium are but two of a group of atoms that are naturally radioactive. You can see evidence of splitting atoms if you look at the luminescent dial of a watch or clock with a magnifying glass in a darkened room. After your eyes have become accommodated to the darkness you will see many flashes, each one representing the splitting of a single radioactive atom.

(See pp. 555–7.)

Nuclear Artillery

The discovery of natural radioactivity not only gave scientists clues to atomic architecture and atomic energy it also provided them with ammunition for splitting *other* atoms. One of the bullets used was the high-speed alpha particle, which could penetrate the usually impenetrable nucleus of an atom. Using alpha particles Rutherford was able to achieve the first laboratory-controlled transmutation of an element in 1919, the first artificial changing of one atom into another. With an alpha particle as his bullet and a nitrogen atom as his target he was able to drive an extra proton into the nucleus of the nitrogen atom. If you consult the chart on page 556 you will see that nitrogen normally has 7 protons. Add one proton and you have oxygen with 8 protons in its nucleus! Rutherford had transmuted nitrogen into oxygen!

As these discoveries became known, scientists were electrified with the new ideas implicit in them:

Atoms were no longer the basic units of the universe.

Atoms were composed of more elementary parts.

Atoms were divisible.

Atoms of one element could be transmuted into entirely new atoms.

Atoms had a vast potential of energy locked in them, far exceeding anything previously known.

$E = mc^2$

This algebraic expression may well become the most significant equation in all history. To understand it we must go back to about 1900, to the then prevailing theories of the conservation of matter and the conservation of energy. Let us talk of matter first. We learned in

Chapter 15A that in chemical and physical changes matter may be altered in form or shape, but it is never lost, never destroyed. This principle is called the conservation of matter. Our reference to energy in relation to heat in Chapter 16A suggested that energy, too, was not lost but was merely changed into such other forms as heat, motion, light, and sound. The principle of the conservation of energy states that energy cannot be created or destroyed but can only be changed into other forms.

Until 1905 these two principles reigned. Then Einstein came along and tied them together. According to Einstein matter could be converted into energy and energy into matter. Matter *could* be destroyed, but it would reappear as energy. Energy *could* be destroyed, but matter would be created. There was now but one conservation law: the law of *the conservation of matter-energy.* This law might be stated: *The sum total of all the matter and all the energy in the universe is constant, and one may be changed into the other.* The interchangeability of matter and energy was expressed in the now-famous formula:

$$E = mc^2.$$

E represents energy, m is mass (the amount of matter), and c is the speed of light (about 186,000 miles per second). Energy equals mass times the speed of light times the speed of light.

Notice that energy is one side of the equation and mass (matter) is on the other. If the proper values were substituted in this equation it would reveal that an extremely small amount of material could be transformed into an enormous amount of energy, because the speed of light is 186,000 miles per second. c^2 in the equation is equal to 34,596,000,000. If, for example, we were able to destroy completely all the atoms in a pail of sand we would produce enough energy to supply the electric power requirements of the United States for a number of years.

All this was theory scribbled on pieces of paper until scientists began to tinker with atoms. The proof then came from a careful study of the weight of material that went into a nuclear reaction and the weight of material and the amount of energy that came out.

If you smash a piece of old furniture into kindling all the pieces (including the dust) when put together weigh as much as the original. When a heavy atom is split, however, the sum of its pieces—new atoms and particles—is *less* than the original atom. What happens to the missing mass?

Scientists found that the loss of matter was accounted for by the gain in free energy, just as Einstein had predicted. Some of the energy appears as the high-speed motion of the fragments, some as wave energy.

NEUTRON BULLETS FOR CHAIN REACTIONS

All of this added up to the fact that an exceedingly small amount of matter could be trans-

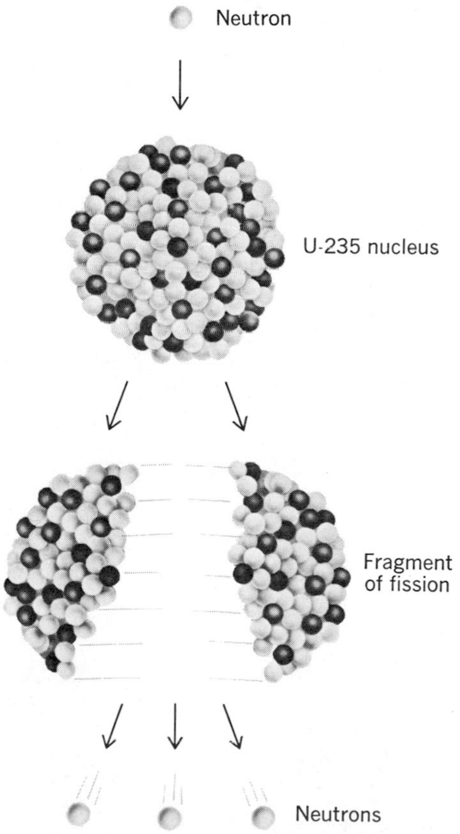

When the nucleus of a uranium-235 atom is split by a neutron a vast amount of energy is released, as well as neutron "bullets" to split more U-235 atoms.

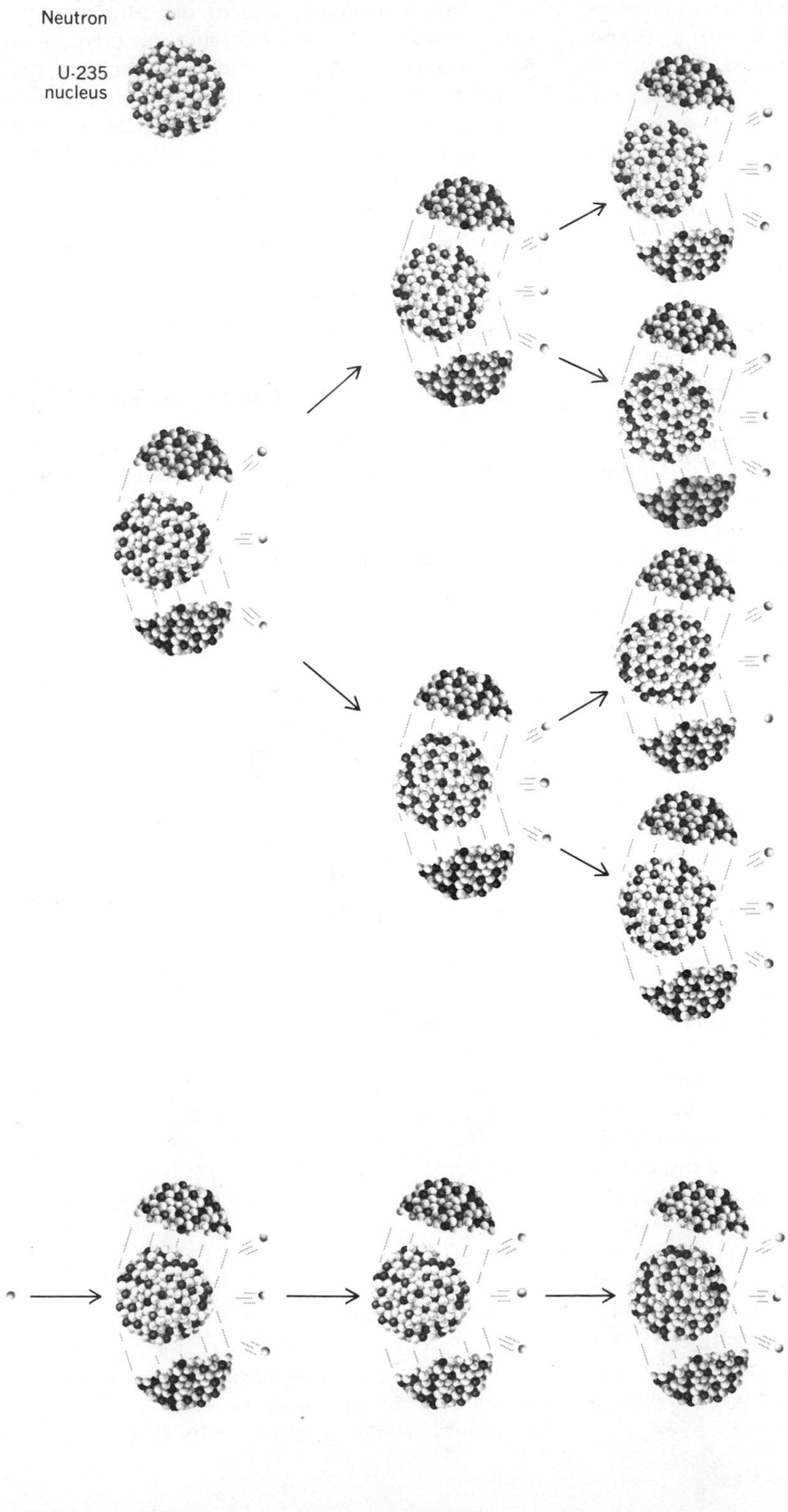

(*Top*) In an uncontrolled nuclear reaction, as in a nuclear bomb, the ever-growing chain reaction involves more and more atoms. (*Bottom*) In a controlled chain reaction the number of splitting atoms is maintained at a safe level (*see* text on p. 542).

formed into a large amount of energy. A new world of power was opening up for man, if he could learn to tap the energy of the millions of atoms that were available to him, if he could find effective "bullets" in sufficient quantity to split billions of atoms and cause them to release some of their energy.

An important clue came in the use of neutrons of the nucleus. As you recall from our discussion of the atomic architecture in Chapter 15A, the neutron is a particle of about the same weight as a proton but neutral as far as its electrical properties are concerned. It was soon discovered that the fact that the neutron was electrically neutral made it a most effective projectile in the arsenal of nuclear artillery.

Using the neutron on the heaviest of the natural elements, uranium, Hahn and Strassmann in 1939 found that they could induce uranium atoms to split into fragments, to undergo *fission,* producing simpler, lighter atoms such as those of barium and krypton.

True, this was no atom bomb. There was no explosion. Atom for atom, however, the energy released from the splitting atoms of uranium was far in excess of any reaction previously produced in a laboratory. This discovery of man-made nuclear fission opened up the possibility of tapping the energy stored in the nuclei of atoms as a source of large-scale power.

Before we go on with the fission story we must consider a characteristic of atoms that we have not yet mentioned. As found in nature uranium comes in several forms. Each of these types is called an *isotope.* The most common isotope is uranium 238, U-238. The number 238 is derived by adding the number of protons to the number of neutrons in the nucleus of this atom, thus obtaining what is called the *mass number.* (Because most of the weight of an atom is derived from its neutrons and protons the mass number is *approximately* equal to its *atomic weight.*)

Thus in U-238:

$$\begin{array}{r} 92 \text{ protons} \\ +\ 146 \text{ neutrons} \\ \hline 238 = \text{mass number} \end{array}$$

Uranium 235, one of the isotopes of uranium, like U-238, has 92 protons. It has only 143 neutrons, however, which gives it a mass number of 235. The chemical properties of an atom are determined by the number of protons and electrons, so U-238 and U-235 are chemically identical; such chemical twins are called isotopes. The differences in weight, however, are of extreme importance in the realm of inner nuclear happenings. Most of the atoms found in nature have these variant or isotopic forms.

Coming back to the uranium fission story scientists were curious about which type of uranium was splitting. They found that under the conditions of their experiments only the U-235 atoms were splitting. This isotope is relatively rare in natural ores; there is only one U-235 atom for every 140 U-238 atoms.

(*See* figure p. 539.)

Another fact of great importance was also discovered. When a neutron bombarded a U-235 atom, causing it to split, *other neutrons were shot out of the nucleus of the split atom* along with the fragments of fission. Various investigators estimated that, on the average, two or three neutrons were coming out of a single U-235 atom. A most important principle was thus established. If a neutron could cause a uranium atom to split, releasing a large amount of energy and, at the same time, a number of new neutrons, perhaps these secondary neutrons could repeat the process with other U-235 atoms. The possibility of a *chain reaction,* in which the splitting of one atom could trigger the splitting of all, stirred the wildest dreams of scientists.

NUCLEAR MACHINES AND NUCLEAR BOMBS

Between the laboratory discovery of the possibility of a chain reaction (1940) and the first successful bomb (1945) was a period in which this dream was made a reality. The first period of the hunt between 1940 and 1942 resulted in the making of a nuclear energy machine, a predecessor of the modern peacetime nuclear energy plant. From 1942 on, the problem for scientists working with the Army became the production of a nuclear bomb.

The Neutron Population

The successful building of an atomic machine depended on the answers to such questions as these:

Could a chain reaction really be kept going?
What would happen to the neutron population?
Could a chain reaction be controlled?

It will be helpful in considering these problems to think of a population of frogs in a pond. If the population is to remain steady every couple (a male and female), on the average, must be responsible in their lifetime for the production of enough offspring so that two of them will survive to reproduce ("zero population growth"). If less than two survive, the population will decrease. If more than two survive, the population will increase. In atomic energy the problem is the neutron population, for these are the bullets that split atoms. Let us consider a small number of U-235 atoms, 100, for example, that have just undergone fission in a mass of uranium containing both U-235 and U-238 atoms. Let us assume that each of these 100 atoms releases three neutrons. What will happen to these 300 atomic bullets? Some may escape to the air. Others may be captured by U-238 atoms, which do not help in the chain reaction because this form of uranium does not undergo fission when bombarded with neutrons. Some neutrons may strike impurities in the material, which does not result in the production of more neutrons. Some of these neutron bullets, however, will strike and split U-235 atoms, which themselves will produce three new neutrons each and thus continue the chain.

The important question in the chain reaction was this: How many of the neutron bullets produced would be effective in bombarding new U-235 atoms? If 99 or less of the 300 were effective in splitting new U-235 atoms the reaction would die down. It would not be a self-perpetuating chain. If 101 or more were effective then we would have an ever-growing chain reaction. Each round of nuclear fission would result in more and more atoms undergoing fission. The net result—an atomic bomb. If the reaction could be regulated so that just 100 neutron bullets were effective then we could have a controlled reaction. Nuclear energy could be tapped for peaceful uses (The term *atomic energy* is, strictly speaking, not accurate. The better term is *nuclear energy,* because the energy comes from the nucleus of the atom. Both of these terms are in common usage.)

(See figure p. 540.)

The Nuclear Age Begins

The first nuclear energy machine was built on a squash court underneath the stands of Stagg Field at the University of Chicago. This machine, called a nuclear *pile,* consisted of layers of uranium embedded in graphite. *Controls* made of strips of cadmium, which is a good neutron absorber or "robber," were inserted to regulate the reaction, to prevent the chain reaction from going too rapidly. The pile was built, layer upon layer, until a *critical size* was reached; that is, a size that contained the right amount of uranium for a controlled reaction. On December 2, 1942, the pile received its first big test. To operate the pile the cadmium strips were pulled out one by one. The intensity of neutrons increased rapidly as more and more U-235 atoms split, and then was maintained at a constant level. The machine worked! The nuclear age had begun!

More Fuel

In an atomic pile there is a mixture of U-235 atoms and U-238 atoms. The U-235 atoms split when bombarded with neutrons and in turn release more neutrons. The U-238 atoms, on the other hand, absorb the neutrons into their nuclei but do not fission. What does this increase in neutron count do to the U-238 atoms? Before answering, let us recall that, up to this point in history 92 elements or kinds of atoms were known to man. In 1940, in an experiment in which U-238 was bombarded with atomic particles, two new elements, number 93, now called neptunium, and number 94, now called plutonium, were produced. When the atomic pile was invented it was found that this transmutation of atoms went on there also. Plutonium was a by-product resulting from the capture by U-238 of a neutron. Plutonium became important to atomic scientists because, like U-235, it undergoes fission when it is bombarded with neutrons, releasing energy and more neutrons. Plutonium, then, could be used instead of the scarce U-235. A new source of atomic "fuel" thus became available.

(The word "fuel" when used in relation to atomic fission has an entirely different meaning from its use in relation to burning. In atomic (nuclear) fission the *nucleus* of the atom is split, releasing new particles and energy. In common burning, which is a *chemical* change, atoms of the fuel join oxygen atoms, releasing energy from the interchange and rearrangements of the *electrons* which whirl around the nucleus.)

The Nuclear Bomb

Could a nuclear bomb be produced? Could the chain reaction be stepped up so that all the atoms would undergo fission in 1 millionth of a second to produce a gargantuan explosion? Or would it fizzle out slowly? Work on these problems was going on in the greatest of secrecy on a mesa about 30 miles from Santa Fe, New Mexico, at Los Alamos.

The effectiveness of a bomb depends on the liberation of a large amount of energy in a very small amount of time. To obtain this result in a nuclear bomb, the chain reaction would have to produce an ever-increasing number of neutron "bullets" to hit their targets, the U-235 atoms. Experience with the pile and theoretical considerations showed that there was a size *below* which a mass of U-235 could not explode, because too many neutrons would escape from the surface of the mass and break the chain. On the other hand, if the bomb were *above* this *critical size* it would go off at the very moment of its manufacture. How could the problem be solved?

In principle it could be solved by separating the bomb into two or more masses *within its container* and then bringing the parts together at the moment that explosion was desired. This could happen after the bomb was launched. The explosion would take place as soon as the masses of U-235 were joined.

This was the theory, but would it work? The answer is given in the words of the War Department account of the first atomic-bomb test with which we opened this chapter.

ATOMS FOR POWER

(*See* p. 557.)

The constructive products of nuclear energy are of two kinds, both created by the controlled nuclear fission in an atomic pile. One is heat, the other is a wide variety of new radioactive substances called *radioisotopes.*

The Nuclear Plant

During the operation of a nuclear pile large amounts of energy in the form of heat are released by the splitting atoms. The great interest in atomic "fuel" is that it is such a compact source of heat. One pound of uranium has atomic energy equivalent to that obtained from the burning of 3 million pounds of coal. How do we harness this heat and put it to work? One way is to let it change water into steam and then use the steam to turn a turbine hooked up to an electric generator. Thus heat energy is converted to electrical energy. (*See* Chapter 19A for an explanation of electric generators.)

The Atomic Energy Commission and private industry are participating in the construction of different kinds of atomic power plants, which it is hoped will be competitive in cost with those run with the conventional fuels—coal, natural gas, and oil. The heart of the atomic plant is its *reactor,* which is a chain-reacting nuclear pile. One of the objectives in these projects is to maintain *neutron economy.* In any chain reaction one of the neutrons produced by a splitting atom is needed to split another atom. Any *extra* neutrons can be used to make *new* atomic fuel. Thus, as we found before, U-238 can be converted into fissionable plutonium. The reactor becomes not only a source of energy but a

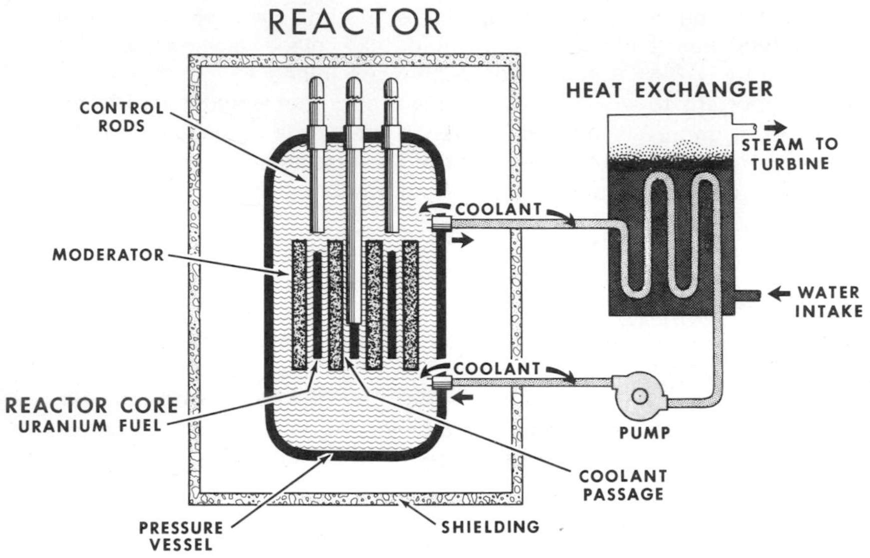

The heart of a nuclear power plant is the reactor in which the fissioning or splitting of the nuclei of atoms can be controlled and put to useful work. The coolant, heated to a high temperature by the splitting atoms, flows through a heat exchanger, where it turns water in a secondary system of pipes into steam. The steam is then piped to a turbine, which operates a generator of electricity.

breeder of new fuel! (This is the principle behind the *breeder reactor,* now being developed and tested.)

We therefore try to select an original fuel that will produce the best yield of available neutrons within the reactor. Uranium and thorium are two of the fuels being used.

Another point of interest is the efficiency with which the heat is converted into electricity. At present the transfer of heat is a two-step process. First a fluid, called a *coolant,* circulates through the reactor, is heated, and then flows out. Second, the coolant (now hot) heats water and converts it into steam, which turns the turbine of the electric generator. One problem under study is: What is the best coolant? In some of the reactors being tested water is the coolant; in others a liquid metal, such as sodium, is employed. In another power-reacting system, called the boiling-water system, no coolant is used. Here water is allowed to boil within the reactor, and the steam that is created is led directly to the turbogenerator, which in turn produces an electric current.

Also under investigation is the possibility of producing electricity directly from nuclear reactions in a nuclear plant. Should such a breakthrough occur, there would be no need for boilers, turbines, and generators.

Nuclear power plants are becoming a familiar sight on the American landscape. At the beginning of 1973, 29 plants were in operation and 55 were under construction. The Atomic Energy Commission estimates that by the year 2000 half the total electricity in the United States will be nuclear-generated. Nuclear power plants are in operation or are being constructed in Great Britain, France, and Russia, and in underdeveloped countries such as India, Argentina, and Brazil.

POLLUTION PROBLEMS

The problem of thermal pollution from the waste heat discharged by nuclear plants was discussed in Chapter 14A.

Another problem arises from the disposal of the high-level radioactive wastes of nuclear power plants. At present such wastes are initially stored in underground tanks. Tank storage, however, does not provide a long-term solution to the problem, since the tanks will eventually deteriorate. Final storage may be in such places as abandoned salt mines, which, it is hoped, will isolate these wastes permanently from man's environment. Concern has been expressed about the permanence of *any* site for high-level radioactive materials.

Of concern also is the potential hazard of radioactive pollutants escaping into the environment following damage to a nuclear plant from internal malfunctioning or from external catastrophes such as earthquakes.

The difficulties of finding suitable sites for nuclear plants is formidable, since no one wants such a facility near them. One proposal suggests the floating of nuclear plants in the ocean, 3 to 15 miles offshore, where there would be a constant supply of cool water needed for their operation. Still unknown, however, are the possible adverse effects of such a plant on the ocean environment.

Concern over radioactive pollution also arises from the increase in the number and capacity of plants now under construction and those planned for the future. Research is directed toward solving the environmental problems posed by the growth of the nuclear-energy industry.

ATOMS FOR TRANSPORTATION

In 1955 the *Nautilus,* the world's first nuclear submarine, was launched in Groton, Connecticut. The reactor of this submarine is surrounded by a lead shield to prevent the leakage of dangerous radiations. Water circulating through the reactor is piped to a heat exchanger. There, in turn, it heats other water, changing it into steam.

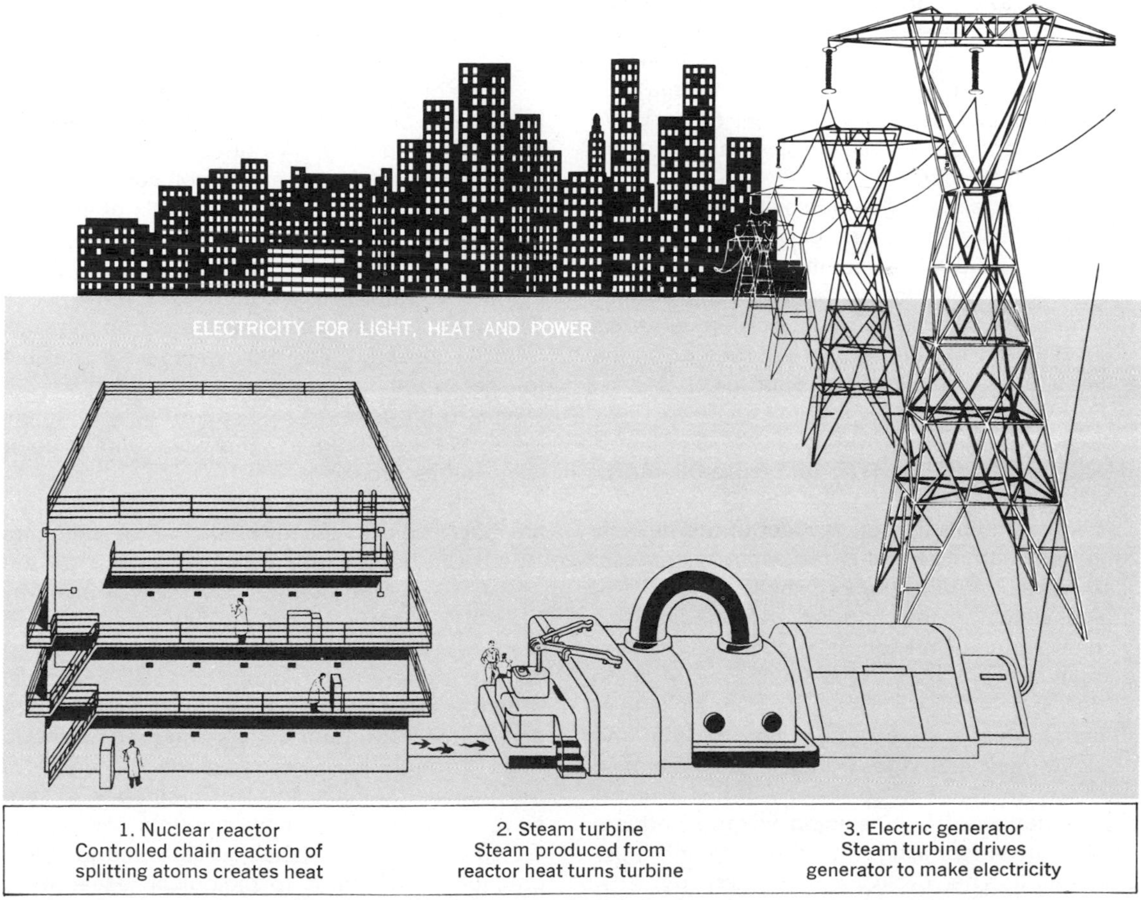
ELECTRICITY FOR LIGHT, HEAT AND POWER
1. Nuclear reactor
Controlled chain reaction of
splitting atoms creates heat
2. Steam turbine
Steam produced from
reactor heat turns turbine
3. Electric generator
Steam turbine drives
generator to make electricity

In a nuclear power reactor the heat produced by splitting atoms changes water to steam. The steam turns a turbine to drive a generator which produces electricity.

The steam strikes and moves the blades of the ship's turbine, which is connected to the propeller shaft.

Because reactors can run 1 year or more without requiring new uranium, the nuclear submarine can remain at sea almost indefinitely, cruising at speeds of nearly 30 knots for thousands of miles. Oxygen is not needed for atomic fuel, so the ship can complete missions without surfacing for air. In August 1958 the *Nautilus* completed its historic under-ice passage of the Arctic pack. Thus the nuclear reactor has made the true submarine a reality.

Since the launching of the *Nautilus* many other submarines propelled by nuclear reactors have been built. In 1962 the *Enterprise,* the first nuclear-powered aircraft carrier, was completed. The N.S. *Savannah,* the world's first nuclear-powered cargo-passenger ship, was launched in 1959 at Camden, New Jersey. The uranium fuel it carries could send her 14 times around the world without a stop, or power her for $3\frac{1}{2}$ years of operation. Other nuclear-powered craft are under construction.

Also under consideration by the government and by industry is the use of atomic energy for surface ships and for locomotive trains. Scientists believe that nuclear reactors will also play an important part in space exploration, either as a supplement to other power sources or as the basic source of power for propulsion.

RADIOISOTOPES IN THE SERVICE OF MAN

A most important by-product of the nuclear energy program are the *radioactive isotopes,* also called *radioisotopes,* those "twins" of atoms, which, once produced, have the ability to give off various kinds of radiation without further stimulation. Originally these isotopes were made only in special atom-smashing machines. One of these machines, called the cyclotron, is a kind of an atomic merry-go-round, in which atomic particles are made to go faster and faster under the influence of high electric voltage and are guided in a spiraling path by a giant electromagnet. The cyclotron, invented by E.O. Lawrence of California, produces high-speed protons that smash through their target material to force their way into the nuclei of atoms. Using the cyclotron, as well as other atom-smashing machines, scientists have produced hundreds of radioisotopes.

Since 1940 the nuclear pile has added considerably to the making of radioactive isotopes, sometimes called "tagged" atoms. In the pile, neutrons are the bullets that bombard the nuclei of atoms of various substances. The man-made isotopes produced in this way are then removed from the pile and placed in carefully shielded containers, ready for shipment to hospitals, to industrial laboratories, and to the many other users of these unique atoms, as we will discuss later in this chapter.

Tracers

One of the uses to which these tagged atoms have been put is that of serving as a tracer, a kind of atomic "spy." To understand the operation of a tracer recall the common school experiment in which a cut stalk of celery is placed in a glass of water to show the rise of water in the "pipelines" of the plant. The water is first colored with a dye, such as red ink. The progress of the water up the stalk is easily observed. The red dye makes it possible to see *where* the water goes, in *what part* it seems to be concentrated, and *how fast* it gets there. We are "tagging" the water with a color to reveal its presence.

(*See* pp. 298–9.)

Radioactive atoms give off radiations that are not visible to the eye but can be detected by use of instruments such as the *Geiger counter.* Because of this they can be traced as they move through the body of an animal or through the pipes of an oil refinery. The most complex chemical processes can be followed by substituting radioactive atoms for normal ones and then following them through invisible reactions by virtue of their telltale radioactivity. This method is so sensitive that incredibly small amounts can be detected and traced. It has already found many practical applications to biological research, in agriculture, industry, and the diagnosis and treat-

(*See* p. 553.)

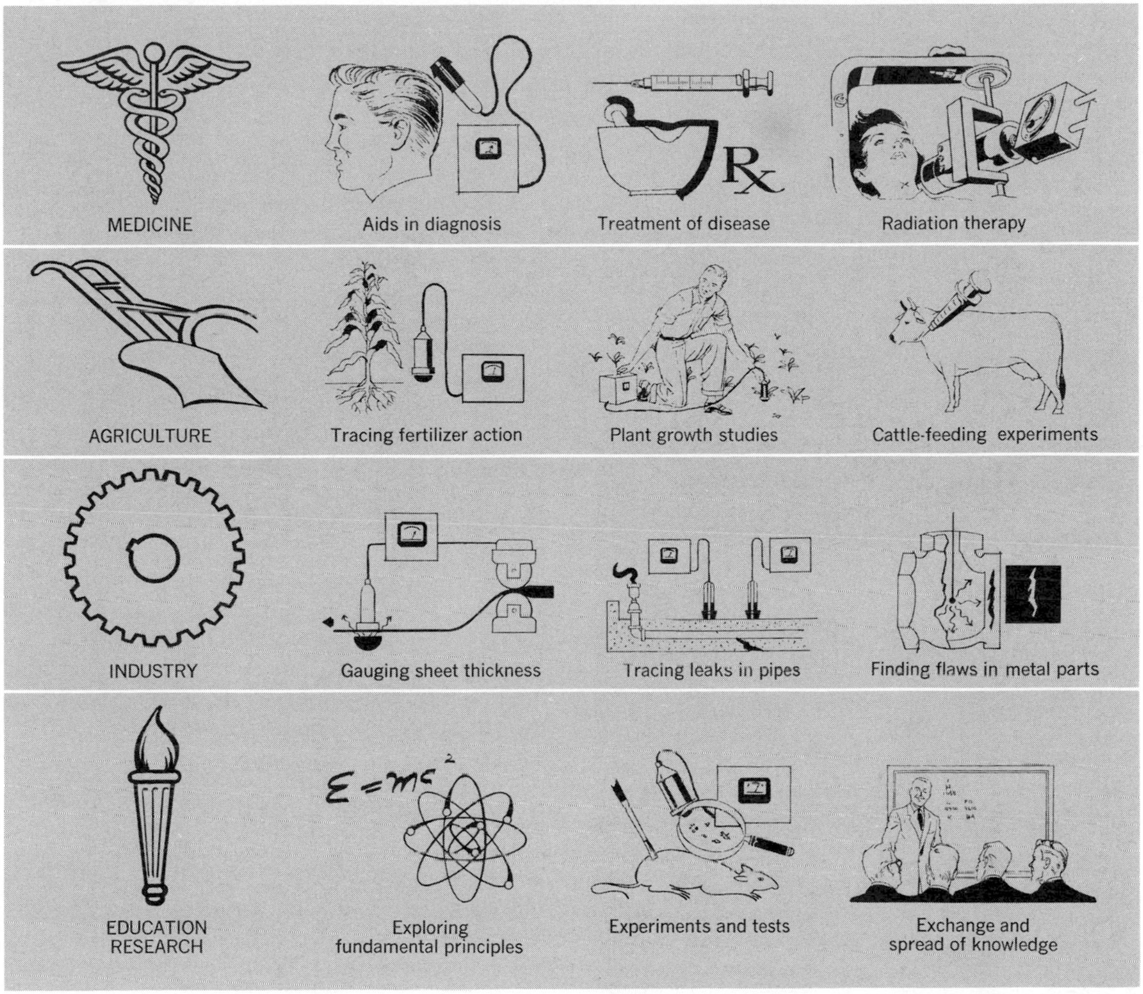

These sketches indicate some of the ways in which isotopes are being used today.

ment of disease. Let us look briefly at some of these.

Biological Research

The migration of mosquitoes from their home grounds was traced by breeding a batch in a pool containing radiophosphorus. The radiophosphorus was absorbed and retained in the bodies of the mosquitoes. Later, collections of mosquitoes made at a number of points and checked for radioactivity with a Geiger counter revealed their range and travel habits.

The effectiveness of a new intravenous diet of fat (one injected into the veins) was traced by injecting rats with fat containing tagged carbon atoms in its molecules. (In this, as in other tracer work with living things, the tracer corresponds in quality and in kind to the thing it traces. In the case of the fat just cited the tagged fat molecules are chemically identical with ordinary fat. As far as biological processes are concerned, the tagged atoms, and the molecules of which they are a part, do not behave differently from those normally present.) As the radioactive fat was burned, the rat exhaled radioactive carbon dioxide. The speed with which this "hot" carbon dioxide was breathed out reflected the speed with which the rat's body was using the fat.

Red blood cells have iron in them. Radioactive iron compounds injected into the bloodstream of a human being were eventually incorporated into the red cells. The rate of formation and breakdown of red blood cells was determined.

Photograph of a coleus leaf made at Brookhaven National Laboratory in Upton, New York, taken after radioactive phosphorus had been absorbed by the plant. Studies of this kind shed light on the concentration of phosphorus necessary to maintain a healthy plant under various conditions. (*Courtesy of Brookhaven National Laboratory.*)

The study of photosynthesis, the process by which plants make use of the sun's energy to combine atoms from carbon dioxide and water molecules to manufacture sugar, is being studied by using radioactive carbon dioxide gas as a tracer. An important discovery made with this tracer: The oxygen that becomes part of the sugar molecule ($C_6H_{12}O_6$) comes from the carbon dioxide (CO_2) and not from the water (H_2O).

Agriculture

Do fertilizers placed in the soil really reach their destination in plants for which they are intended? This is the type of question asked by agricultural scientists. The effectiveness of fertilizers can be evaluated by including radioactive forms of their atoms and then studying the radioactivity of the plants grown in soil containing this fertilizer. Thus radiophosphorus was placed in various fertilizers that employ phosphorus to find out how easily each gave up its phosphorus, how they reacted to various kinds of soils, and how best to apply the fertilizer to the soil.

Industry

Radioisotopes have already proved their value in industry, effecting savings of many millions of dollars a year. One use is the control of the thickness of sheet materials made of paper, plastic, rubber, textiles, and metals. In the machines through which these materials roll a radioactive "gun" is placed on one side of the material to be tested and a detector on the other side. The thicker the material, the less radiation gets through. The detector is hooked up to a recorder that signals any deviation from the desired thickness to the mechanism controlling it. This operation is done mechanically. Thus, radioisotopes serve as a sensitive gauge and as an automatic control.

Industry is finding many new uses for radioisotopes. These include the cold-temperature sterilization of foods; the location of leaks in water lines; the measurement of the wear of floor waxes, gears, and other materials.

Diagnosis of Disease

Radioactive iodine is used in the diagnosis of thyroid disorders. The thyroids are a pair of glands located on either side of the voice box. They pour a secretion into the blood, thyroxin, which regulates the body's metabolism. Thyroxin is manufactured by the thyroid gland from the iodine and other chemicals supplied to it by the blood. A patient with a suspected thyroid disorder drinks a glass of water containing radioactive iodine. The fate of the "tagged" atoms is followed with a Geiger counter. If very little iodine is taken up and used by the gland it may indicate that the gland is inactive. If there is a very rapid iodine intake, followed by an equally rapid discharge, the gland is probably overactive. Radioiodine is also used to detect thyroid cancers that may have spread from the thyroid gland to other parts of the body.

(*See* pp. 361–2.)

Radioactive phosphorus has been used in diagnosing brain tumors. This is possible because a brain tumor picks up phosphorus in greater quantity than does the surrounding normal tissue. The tumor cells do not distinguish between radioactive phosphorus and the ordinary kind. If a tumor is present more radiophosphorus will be present in the tumor than in other areas of the brain. The surgeon searches for the tumor with a sensitive Geiger counter 24 hours after the patient has received an injection of tagged phosphorus atoms.

Treatment of Disease

Becquerel, mentioned previously as the discoverer of natural radioactivity, also made the first observations of the effect of radiations on living tissues. After carrying around a tiny tube of radium salts in his vest pocket he noticed a severe external wound, resembling a deep burn, on his abdomen. Evidently radiations from the radium salts were destroying healthy tissue.

Scientists experimented with radium to determine whether it could destroy cancerous tissue. Many cures were effected. At first only those cancers close to the skin were treated effectively. Early malignancies of the breast and cancers of the womb, tongue, nose, and throat were checked. Later, internal growths in the stomach, liver, and intestines were controlled by radiation. In all of these the penetrating radiations disrupted the chemical makeup of the cancer cells and destroyed them.

Radium, however, showed no selectivity: Nearby healthy tissue was also destroyed. With the creation of a large number of artificially radioactive materials in nuclear piles a wide range of treatment became possible. A case in point was the use of radioactive iodine, previously mentioned as a tracer, for the treatment of cancerous thyroid glands. Taken in large doses radioiodine is concentrated in the thyroid. There it destroys cancerous tissue. Radiophosphorus is used to treat a blood disease in which the red blood cells multiply too rapidly.

ATOMIC DATING

In Chapter 6A we saw how the natural radioactivity of uranium atoms made them a useful "clock" for determining the age of rocks. The dating of the past in this way is based on the knowledge that the average rate of disintegration of uranium in rock is constant.

The regularity in the breakdown of a quantity of atoms applies to all radioactive materials. Scientists describe the rate of destruction of these atoms in the expression *half-life.* Let us see what half-life means.

Assume that a hospital acquires a supply of radium for use in cancer research and therapy. What will happen to this supply as the years pass, if none is given away or lost? The answer is that in 1,622 years, one-half of the original supply will have broken down.

What happens then? In the next 1,622 years one-half of the remainder breaks down again (leaving only one-quarter of the original supply). Every 1,622 years the supply of radium decreases by one-half. We say that the half-life of radium is 1,622 years.

Because uranium 238 has a long half-life, $4\frac{1}{2}$ billion years, it is useful in measuring long spans of time, such as the time since the formation of

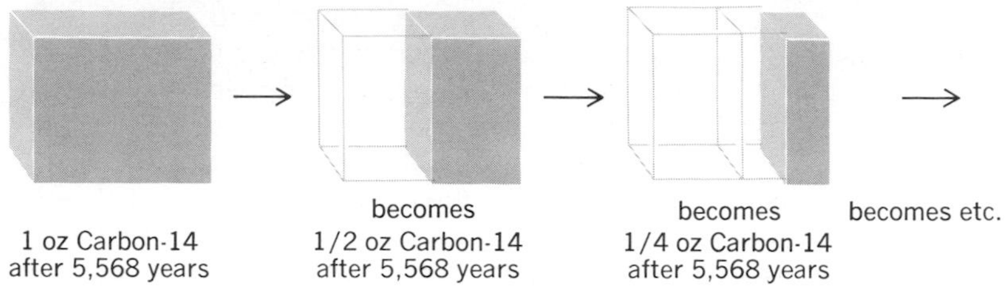

The regularity in the breakdown of a quantity of radioactive atoms provides scientists with a "clock" for dating ancient remains. The usefulness of a particular kind of atom, such as Carbon-14, for this purpose depends on its half-life, which, as shown here, is 5,568 years.

rocks billions of years old. But it is too crude a "clock" to measure the age of material formed more recently. In 1947 W.F. Libby found a way of dating materials formed during the last 70,000 years. This method is based on the decay of radioactive carbon, known as carbon 14 because its atomic weight is 14, in contrast to the common carbon 12.

Carbon 14 has a half-life of about 5,570 years. It is found in material of plant and animal origin, such as wood, marine shells, and charcoal. How does carbon 14 get into substances? It is believed that cosmic-ray particles from outer space produce neutrons which bombard the nitrogen atoms in the atmosphere. A neutron enters the nitrogen nucleus, knocks out a proton and changes it into carbon 14. (Consult the table on page 556 to see why the loss of a proton changes nitrogen into carbon.) The carbon 14 then combines with oxygen to form radioactive carbon dioxide, which plants and then animals incorporate in their tissue.

This happened in the past. It is also happening now. How can we make use of this information to determine the age of a bit of charcoal from the hearth of ancient man?

The concentration of carbon 14, as we have stated, decreases at the rate of one-half every 5,570 years. If the charcoal specimen we are studying contains one-half the concentration of carbon 14 of a plant living today its age is estimated to be 5,570 years.

With this new tool scientists are dating ancient animal remains, wood from Egyptian mummy coffins, soils, sands, sediments, and peat. Volcanic eruptions have been dated with radiocarbon. Radioactive elements other than carbon 14 are also being used to expand our collection of time clocks with which scientists are dating the past with greater accuracy.

THE HYDROGEN BOMB

The nuclear bomb and the nuclear pile derive their energy from the *splitting* of atoms from nuclear fission. The hydrogen bomb, with its far greater power, derives its energy from the *joining* of the nuclei of atoms. Essentially this process, called *fusion,* involves the forming of one atom of helium from four atoms of hydrogen.

In the already "old-fashioned" nuclear bomb *heavy* atoms, such as those of plutonium and uranium, are split into light ones; in the hydrogen bomb the *light* atoms of hydrogen combine to form heavier ones. (In hydrogen bombs isotopes of hydrogen, *deuterium,* and *tritium,* rather than common hydrogen, are used.)

Hydrogen fusion goes on in the sun and is the source of its heat and light. In the center of the sun fusion can go on because the temperature there of 20 million degrees centigrade is sufficient to cause the nuclei of light atoms to overcome the powerful forces of electrical repulsion they have for each other. Hydrogen fusion is one kind of *thermonuclear reaction,* so-called because nuclei of atoms combine at very high temperatures. The principal source of energy in stars stems from thermonuclear reactions. The most important of these changes is the conversion of hydrogen to helium as on the sun, our nearest star.

On earth we have been able to induce hydrogen fusion by first exploding a uranium fission bomb to produce temperatures as high as 50 million degrees centigrade.

In both fission and fusion energy is derived from the conversion of matter into energy in accordance with the formula $E = mc^2$. It is estimated that the sun loses some 4 million tons of its mass per second as hydrogen nuclei combine to form helium nuclei. In the fission of a uranium nucleus $\frac{1}{1000}$ of the mass is converted into energy. In the fusion of four hydrogen nuclei into helium $\frac{7}{1000}$ of the mass is so converted.

It has been estimated by scientists that an H-bomb could cause total destruction in an area with a radius of 4 miles in all directions from the point of detonation, covering an area of 50 square miles.

As in the atomic bomb the three agencies for inflicting damage are the blast wave, the heat flash, and the radioactivity resulting from the explosion. Estimates indicate that a single H-bomb could cause almost complete destruction of any city on the earth.

Ironically, the same hydrogen fusion that gives the sun energy to make life possible on the earth may, in the shape of man-made hydrogen bombs, be responsible for the extermination of that life.

But there is a bright side to the fusion picture! If fusion could be made to work at a steady and controllable rate, and if we could handle the enormous energy released, the world would have at its disposal a limitless source of power. Hundreds of scientists are now engaged in research which they hope will lead to controlled fusion.

NEW ATOMS

We have come a long way from the Greek idea of four basic elements—fire, water, air, and earth. We thought a few years ago, when we reached the number 92 we would have filled in all the atoms possible in the neatly arranged table of elements. But new places had to be found when man began to tinker with the nucleus of the atom, when scientists built heavier atoms in their nuclear machines. These new atoms are called the *transuranic elements* because they are heavier than uranium, the heaviest of the previously known elements. At this moment in our Atomic Age the total count stands at 105. We should say, however, that some of these newly created atoms exist naturally in tiny quantities for fleeting moments on the earth, and that possibly all of them existed in considerable amounts in early stages of the primordial creation of elements billions of years ago. But all these extra-heavy atoms are so unstable that they have disappeared; the few that may turn up now and then result from the bombardment of the earth by cosmic rays from outer space or from the natural radioactivity of uranium or radium.

The following are the new transuranic atoms:

Name	*Symbol*	*Number*	*Origin of Name*
Neptunium	Np	93	It follows next after uranium in the "atomic ladder," just as the planet Neptune follows Uranus in distance from the sun.
Plutonium	Pu	94	Named after Pluto, the planet beyond Neptune.
Americum	Am	95	Named for the Americas.
Curium	Cm	96	Named in honor of Marie and Pierre Curie.
Berkelium	Bk	97	Named in honor of the University of California at Berkeley for its role in the preparation of most of the new elements.
Californium	Cf	98	Named after the University of California.
Einsteinium	E	99	In honor of Albert Einstein.
Fermium	Fm	100	In honor of the "father of the Atomic Age"—Enrico Fermi.
Mendelevium	Mu	101	In honor of the Russian chemist, Dmitri Mendelev.
Nobelium	No	102	In honor of Alfred Bernhard Nobel.
Lawrencium	Lw	103	In honor of Ernest O. Lawrence.
Rutherfordium	Rf	104	In honor of Ernest Rutherford.
Hahnium	Ha	105	In honor of Otto Hahn.

Some of the important generalizations of this chapter are:

Atoms are divisible. They are composed of smaller particles that include electrons, protons, and neutrons.

Some atoms, such as those of radium and uranium, split spontaneously; they possess natural radioactivity.

The splitting, or fission, of the nucleus of an atom results in the formation of new kinds of atoms and the release of energy.

Matter can become energy; energy can become matter.

The destruction of a tiny amount of matter results in the liberation of an enormous amount of energy, as is indicated in the equation $E = mc^2$.

In the splitting of an atom some of its matter is converted to energy.

Neutrons are effective "bullets" for the splitting of atoms.

In a chain reaction each splitting atom releases energy, as well as neutrons for the splitting of more atoms.

The energy produced by nuclear reactors and nuclear bombs comes from a chain reaction of atoms undergoing fission.

There is concern about thermal and radioactive pollution from nuclear-energy plants.

Atoms can be made radioactive by bombardment with nuclear particles in the nuclear pile or in "atom smashers."

These atoms, called radioactive isotopes, are useful in the fields of medicine, agriculture, and industry.

Rocks and other ancient materials may be dated by determining the percentages of certain radioactive atoms remaining in them.

In the hydrogen bomb hydrogen atoms join to form helium atoms. This is called fusion, in contrast to fission that occurs in the nuclear bomb.

The energy of the stars is derived from atomic fusion.

In both fusion and fission matter is converted into energy.

Scientists have synthesized new atoms, heavier than uranium.

The energy of atoms has a potential for good or evil for mankind.

Discovering for Yourself

1. Find out about atomic particles other than the electrons, protons, and neutrons discussed in this chapter.
2. Observe with a magnifying glass in a darkened room the luminous dial of a clock or watch.
3. Keep a file of news clippings that explain the use of radioisotopes in medicine, agriculture, and industry.
4. Find out more about carbon 14 and about the peaceful use of atoms (*see* Bibliography).
5. Borrow a Geiger counter from a local high-school science department. Use it to detect radioactivity in a luminous watch dial and in some kinds of rocks.
6. Find out how the Curies discovered radium.
7. Find out about a community whose electricity is supplied through the use of nuclear energy.
8. Read to discover what new professions and other job opportunities have resulted because of our progress in the use of nuclear energy.

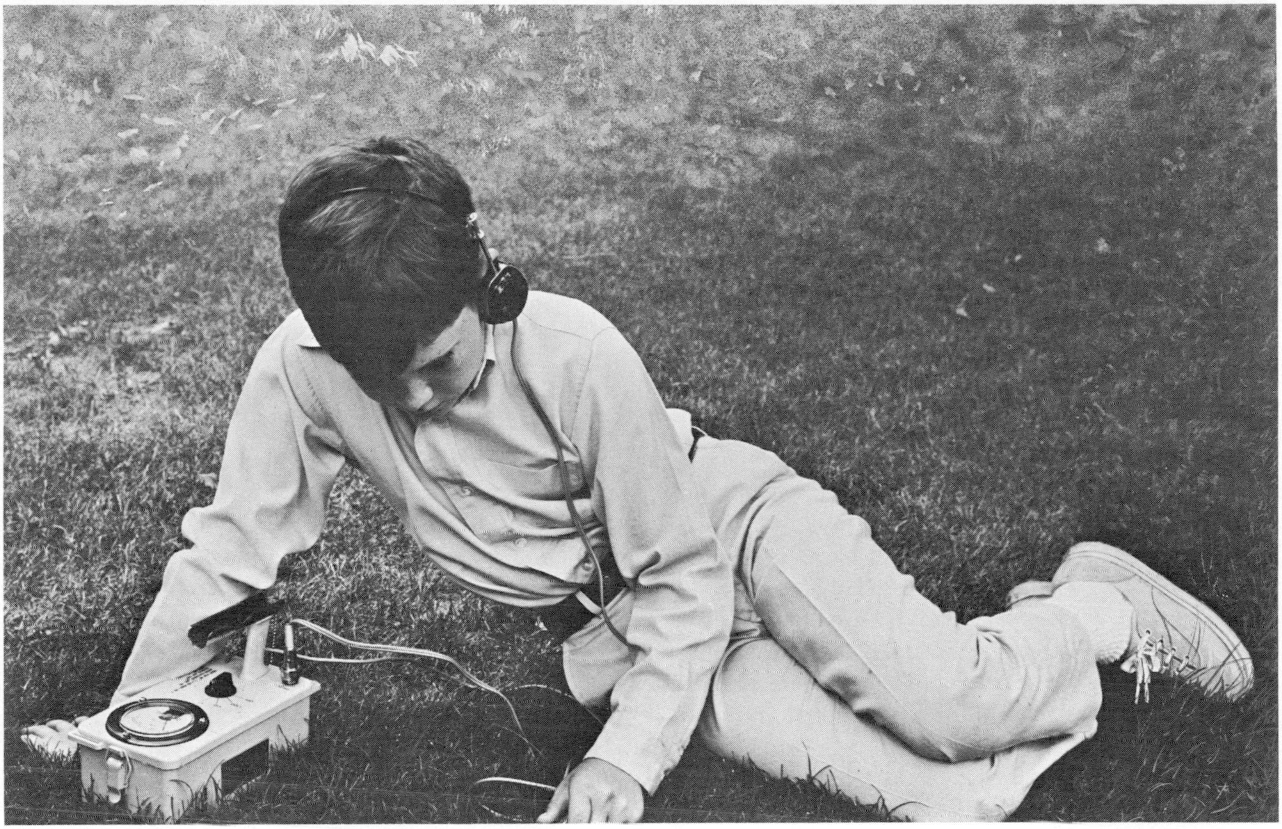

(Courtesy of John King.)

CHAPTER 17B TEACHING "NUCLEAR ENERGY AND ITS USES"

We are concerned with the energy that results when the nuclei of atoms are broken apart or put together, a source of energy that has become highly important in many ways. It can produce electric current; run the machinery that drives submarines and other ships; and is used in medicine, agriculture, and many other fields.

Chapters 15A and 15B provide some of the background material necessary for an understanding of nuclear energy and its uses. So does the material about electricity in Chapters 19A and 19B, and the discussion of transformation of energy from one form to another in several other chapters, as well as Chapters 14A and 14B, "Ecology and Survival."

Children become aware of nuclear energy in a number of ways. They hear about the controversy in the construction of a nuclear-energy plant for the production of electrical power in their area or state. Is there danger from radiation? Will waste heat kill fish in the rivers and other bodies of water used by the plant as a coolant? Should nations conduct nuclear-energy tests? Is nuclear energy useful for desalting water? How do radioisotopes save lives? How can nuclear "clocks" tell us about the age of the earth and its rocks? How can radioactive atoms help in agriculture? In industry? In space travel?

A discussion of the uses of nuclear energy may serve as a starting point for the study. Reading, discussion, and reporting are important; obviously few experiments are feasible at the elementary-school level.

Information about the nature of nuclear energy must naturally be kept simple. How far we go with explanations and discoveries depends on the interests and abilities of each group. Chapter 17A is to be used chiefly by the teacher who wants to become informed about this important aspect of science, rather than as a source of information that will be taught to pupils.

SOME BROAD CONCEPTS: "Nuclear Energy and Its Uses"

(*See also* Chs. 15A and B.)

All matter is made of atoms.
Atoms are made up of smaller particles such as electrons, protons, and neutrons.
Elements are different because their atoms are different.
The nucleus of an atom may be split to release energy.
The energy from atoms is an important source for man.
Radioactive atoms have many uses in health, agriculture, and industry.

FOR YOUNGER CHILDREN

Making use of the material suggested in Chapter 15B is probably as much as we can expect from young children with respect to such an abstract and complicated area of science.

FOR OLDER CHILDREN

What Are Atoms Like?

While the concept of the nature and structure of atoms is difficult for children to comprehend, the static electricity experiences may be helpful (the crackling sound heard when a rubber comb is drawn through hair, rubbed on a woolen coat sleeve, or when we stroke a cat's fur). If these activities are carried on in the dark, sparks can be detected. Recall that all matter is composed of molecules and that they in turn are composed of atoms. Atoms are composed of tiny particles—electrons (negative), protons (positive), and neutrons. The electrons whirl around a central part called the nucleus.

When a comb, for example, is rubbed on a woolen sleeve electrons from the sleeve are torn away and travel to the comb. This makes a negatively charged comb. This jumping of electrons produces a spark as in lightning. While these experiences do not help children to realize the extreme minuteness of the particles it helps them to know something of the nature of the atom's structure.

(*See* Ch. 19A.)

For further knowledge regarding the nature of atoms children will depend on reading (*see* Bibliography). They will read to find answers to such questions as: "What are atoms like?" "How do atoms differ from each other?" "How do scientists study atoms?" "What is the connection between atoms and elements?" "What is the difference between fission and fusion?" "What are the meanings of nucleus, electron, proton, and neutron?"

Illustrating the structure of atoms may be done by drawings using colored chalk or by making models to show the three dimensions with cardboard, wood, plastics, clay, wire, or other materials. Drawings in this book or in other sources (*see* Bibliography) will furnish the source. Scientific supply houses are also sources of such models. Parts of the atom—nucleus, proton, electron, and so on—may be indicated. Especially interested pupils will have original ideas for illustrating atomic structure. Remember that there is a great difference between making a model and understanding the real structure. Models only help in understanding the basic structure. The learning will be more effective when pupils explain their models, and as they do so indicate how atoms are different from each other as well as similar in some characteristics.

Flashes from self-splitting atoms[1] can be observed with a strong magnifying glass and a watch or a clock with a luminous dial, the kind that glows at night. Turn out the lights, wait 10 minutes for the eyes to become adjusted to the darkness, then note the soft glow from the dial. Now hold the magnifying glass near the eye and move the watch or clock until it is in sharp focus. Look steadily at the dial and, instead of a soft glow, there will be a shimmering sparkling light. A small amount of radioactive material was used on the clock hands and numbers of the watch. As the atoms of this material split small particles shoot out. A target for self-splitting atoms is provided in the form of a compound called zinc sulfide. The flashes are caused by atomic "bullets"—actually particles from radioactive atoms—hitting this chemical. Some

[1] *See* J. Schwartz: *Through the Magnifying Glass* (New York: McGraw-Hill, Co., 1954).

pupils will want to do more reading about radioactive materials and the life of radioactive elements (*see* Bibliography).

In learning about the nature of atoms, older children may prepare a chart, similar to the one here, to illustrate the makeup of some common atoms (elements).

Element	*Symbol*	*Electrons*	*Protons*	*Neutrons**
Hydrogen	H	1	1	0
Helium	He	2	2	2
Carbon	C	6	6	6
Nitrogen	N	7	7	7
Oxygen	O	8	8	8
Aluminum	Al	13	13	14
Iron	Fe	26	26	30
Nickel	Ni	28	28	31
Silver	Ag	47	47	61
Iodine	I	53	53	74
Gold	Au	79	79	118
Mercury	Hg	80	80	121
Uranium	U	92	92	146

* The number of neutrons of an element is not always the same. The numbers given here represent most of the atoms. For example, most oxygen atoms have 8 neutrons; but some have 8, 9, or 10. The different kinds of oxygen atoms are called isotopes of oxygen.

Information for the chart will come from reading in various sources. When the chart has been compiled, ask the children to study it to see what conclusions they can draw. "How are the atoms alike?" "How different?" They may observe:

1. In all atoms there are equal numbers of electrons and protons.
2. In some atoms the number of electrons, protons, and neutrons are the same; in many the number of neutrons is greater than either electrons or protons.
3. Atoms of heavier substances (gold) have more particles than lighter substances (aluminum).

Some pupils may wish to add other atoms (elements) to the list to check the validity of the preceding conclusions. Pupils may also wish to do some reading about the meaning of atomic weights.

How Can We Detect Radioactive Atoms?

If there is a Geiger counter available in the community (perhaps in a physics laboratory) pupils will profit by seeing it and testing materials with it. Luminous dials on clocks, some kinds of china (that contain uranium compounds), and small pieces of uranium ore will stimulate the counter. Interested pupils may make a report of radioactivity in their neighborhood by using a Geiger counter. Chemistry sets or mineral collections and other similar sources may have samples of rock that activate

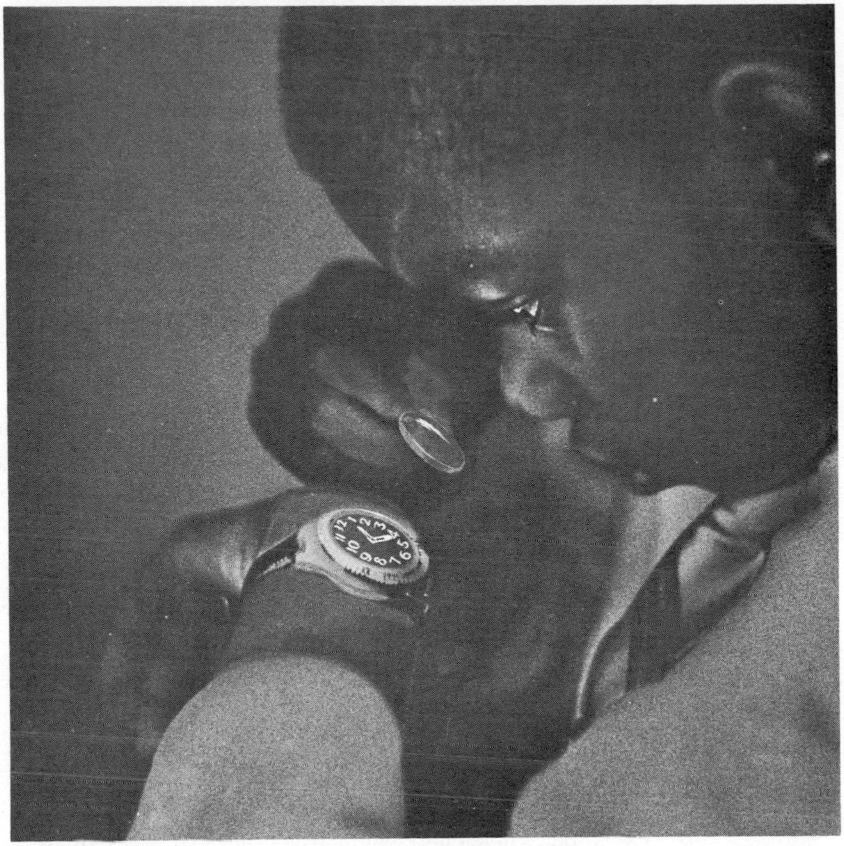

Radioactive atoms are splitting in the dial of this watch. As each atom splits, its products strike a substance which is thus made to glow. The shimmering spectacle is observed best with a strong lens in a darkened room. (*Courtesy of William Dippel.*)

the Geiger counter. Pupils can include such observations in their reports. Pupils will see that some radiation will pass through their hands and still cause the counter to react. Other methods of detecting and measuring radioactivity may be included in this "research," such as the use of sensitive photographic film and the electroscope.

How Is Atomic Energy Used?

There are many opportunities for interested individuals to report in class on the results of investigations on such subjects as the peacetime use of atomic energy, uses of nuclear energy in medicine, the atomic submarine, atoms and agriculture, people who have made important contributions to our knowledge of atoms, location of the sources of uranium, and the work of the Atomic Energy Commission.[2] These reports will of necessity be elementary. Several sources for such reports and discussions are listed in the Bibliography.

[2] M.O. Hyde and B.C. Hyde: *Atoms Today and Tomorrow* (New York: McGraw-Hill, Co., 1970).

OTHER PROBLEMS FOR OLDER CHILDREN

1. How do scientists study atoms?
2. What is the difference between fission and fusion?
3. How is carbon 14 used in dating ancient objects?
4. What are radioisotopes and how are they used?
5. What is the meaning of radioactivity?
6. What is atomic "farming"?
7. What is the meaning of atomic weight?

Resources to Investigate with Children

1. Atomic Energy Commission, Division of Technical Information Extension, P.O. Box 62, Oak Ridge, Tenn. 37831, for teaching materials.
2. Local scientist or physics department of high school or college for a Geiger counter for examination by pupils.
3. Magazines and daily newspapers for accounts of new uses for atomic energy and for other atomic-energy news events.
4. Industries that use atomic "tracers."
5. Atomic plants where electricity is being generated.
6. Local hospitals for use of radioactivity in tracers and treatment.

Preparing to Teach

1. Make some charts indicating the structures of atoms and construct a sample three-dimensional model of an atom to use as an aid to children when they are engaged in similar activities.
2. Keep a scrapbook of newspaper and magazine articles and pictures about nuclear energy. Classify them according to: (1.) what important science problems they are related to, (2.) what possible beneficial outcomes may result, (3.) where the discoveries were made. Use the book to give children an idea for making a similar one.

CHAPTER 18A

MACHINES AND HOW THEY WORK

(Courtesy of John King.)

MACHINES AT WORK

Machines do much of the work of the world. Walk down the street or drive through the country and you will see machines lifting, pushing, pulling, digging. Watch machines at work in the kitchen—scraping, chopping, beating, cracking, squeezing, prying, slicing. Visit a factory to see machines cutting, pounding, rolling, stamping, conveying, twisting. Watch children at play using machines for rolling, sliding, seesawing, whirling, flying, swinging.

EARLY MACHINES

We do not know definitely what machine was first used by man, but it may well have been a club. Primitive men in many places must have discovered its effectiveness as a weapon against wild animals. Even the simple club is a machine, because it made man's work easier by permitting him to apply a force to his advantage.

When man attached a pointed stone to a club to make it into a spear, or an edged stone to make it into an ax, he became more effective in coping with his environment and raising his standard of living. When he used a stout branch of a tree to pry up a heavy rock he was inventing a *lever,* a machine destined to find thousands of uses. From our study of the remains of stone-age man, we know that he used wood, bone, stone, or ivory to fashion tools such as axes, hammers, knives, spear points, arrow points, scrapers, drills, awls, saws, pins, and needles.

By the beginning of the Christian era the pulley, screw, and windlass had been invented. The wheel, which revolutionized transportation and without which our modern machinery would be impossible, had long been in use. We have evidence of the wheel's use from pictures and remains which show that chariots existed in Egypt and Babylonia several thousand years before the time of Christ. The American Indians did not use the wheel. (Although the wheel was a great mechanical invention it is not considered a machine when it turns around an axle of a wagon or chariot. We shall see later how the wheel can be part of a machine, in the sense that physicists define this word.)

SIMPLE MACHINES

The intricate mechanism of a watch, the complex construction of an automobile, and the elaborate machinery of a factory are all combinations of a few types of simple machines. These include the lever, the pulley, wheel and axle (including the gear), inclined plane, wedge, and the screw. These basic machines serve any of the three following purposes:

(*See* pp. 573–5.)

1. They increase speed. Example: an egg beater.
2. They increase force. Example: a car jack.
3. They change the direction of a force. Example: a single pulley.

Some machines serve two of the three purposes at the same time: While they are changing the direction of a force they either increase the speed or increase the force.

As you survey the many machines you encounter every day try to determine which of the three purposes they are accomplishing. Remember, however, that these *machines do not produce energy but make use of the energy supplied to them.*

THE LEVER

Children are amused when they are told that they can lift their teacher. The only material needed for a teacher-lifting machine is a block of wood and a plank about 6 feet long. The block is placed under the plank and near one of its ends. The teacher stands on the short end of the plank. The child is delighted to find that he can lift his teacher by pushing down on the other end. In using this device, which is a lever, the child is realizing one of the purposes of a machine, that of increasing force.

(*See* pp. 576–7.)

If the block is placed 1 foot away from the end where the teacher is standing the child (who will be 5 feet from the block) need exert a downward push of only 25 pounds to lift his 125-pound teacher. The effectiveness of the child's muscles is thus multiplied fivefold. The supporting block furnishes the pivot point, or *fulcrum,* for the lever. The child's part of the lever is five times as long as the teacher's, and his force is five times as effective.

Is this magic? It looks as if we are getting something for nothing—a 125-pound return for an investment of 25 pounds. This is true, but it is not the whole truth. If you watch the lever as it works you will notice that to lift the teacher 1 inch the child must push down on his end of the plank for a distance of 5 inches. In other words, the child's force must be exerted five times the distance that the *resistance* to this force (the teacher) moves.

In this illustration force is gained and distance is lost, but one thing is the same—*work.* The term work, as used by the physicist, means the use of *force through a distance.* The amount of work put in by the child is the mathematical product of the force (25 pounds) and the distance (5 inches). Compare this with the work put out in lifting the teacher (125 pounds $\times$ 1 inch) and you will see the result is the same.

The physicist sums this up by saying that the work put out equals the work put in. This ideal situation is true, however, only if losses due to friction are disregarded. (In the other machines discussed in this chapter frictional losses are similarly disregarded.) In the teacher-lifting machine the work put out is slightly less than the work put in due to the friction of the plank on the block as the plank moves.

Levers are in common use. In lifting a boulder a man is using the same principle as the child does in the teacher-lifting machine. Also, when a hammer is used to pull a nail its long handle makes it possible for the user to exert a strong pull. The hammer is a bent lever; the nail offers the resistance; the point of contact of hammer with wood is the fulcrum; and the pull of the hand holding the hammer serves as the force.

In other uses of the lever the fulcrum, or balancing point, is not always between the force exerted and the weight moved. In lifting a stump the fulcrum is near the end of the lever, where it is resting on the log. Here again, the man's advantage depends on the distance of his hand from the fulcrum as compared to the distance of the stump from the fulcrum. By using the lever the man's force is increased, but he must also exert his force through a greater distance.

In some cases we deliberately use a lever that gives us *less* force than we expend. One example is the use of a fishing pole. (Indoor fishermen may try this with a pencil instead of a pole.) Here the fulcrum is the butt end of the

Here levers are being used in two different ways to do work. How they are used depends partly on the amount of force required and partly on convenience.

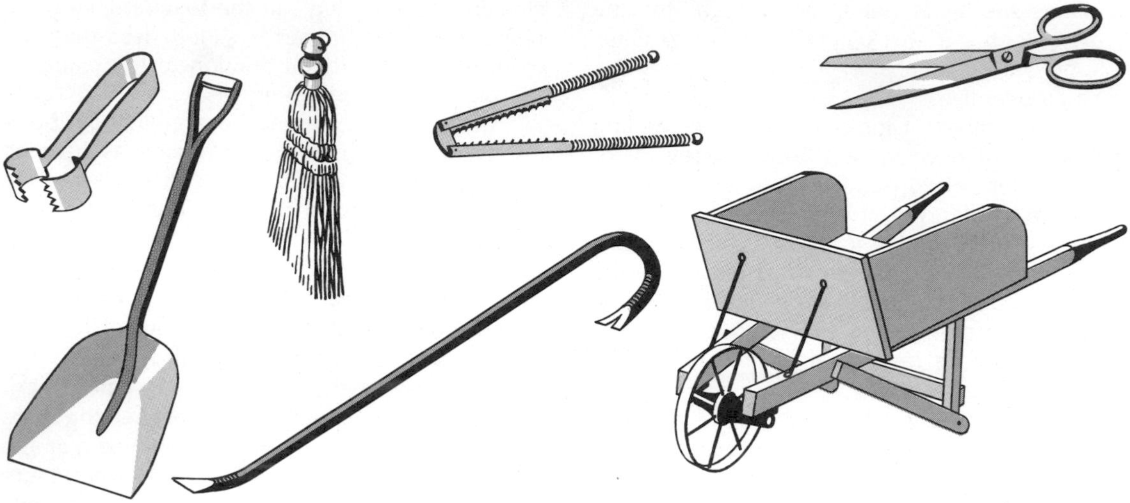

Can you explain how each of these machines helps make the job easier?

pole pressed against the fisherman's body. The force exerted is greater than the weight of the fish. However, in this case the gain is one of *speed*. The fish is jerked out of the water; it does not have a chance to escape from the fast-penetrating hook.

THE PULLEY

All of us have seen a flag raised to the top of a flagpole by the use of a pulley and a rope. This arrangement makes it possible to raise the flag without climbing the pole. A pulley used in this way is called a fixed or stationary pulley.

(*See* pp. 577–9.)

Fixed pulleys have many uses. They help to raise hay into barns, sails to the top of masts, and objects from the holds of ships to the wharves. They have many uses around factories, stores, and garages. Many windows are raised with the aid of fixed pulleys and sash weights. The weight is arranged so that it will almost lift the window by itself. Grasp the cord and lift up. You can feel the pull of the sash weight. One has to exert only a little force to lift a window that has been properly fitted with pulleys and weights.

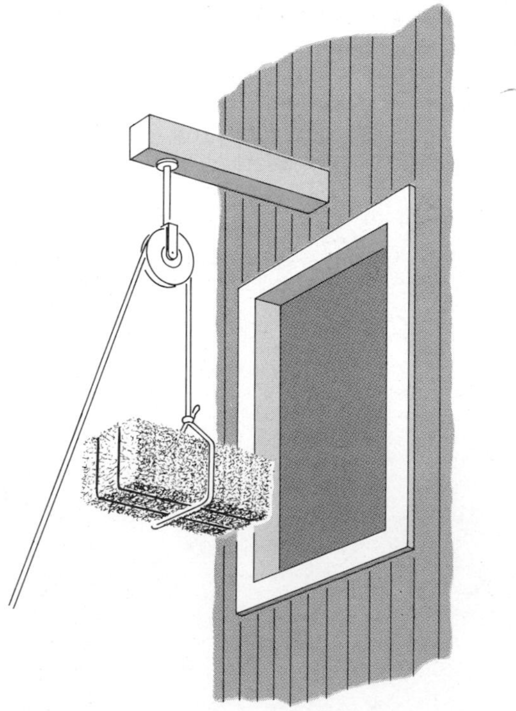

This single pulley does not multiply either force or speed but provides a convenient means of raising loads, flags, sails, and other items.

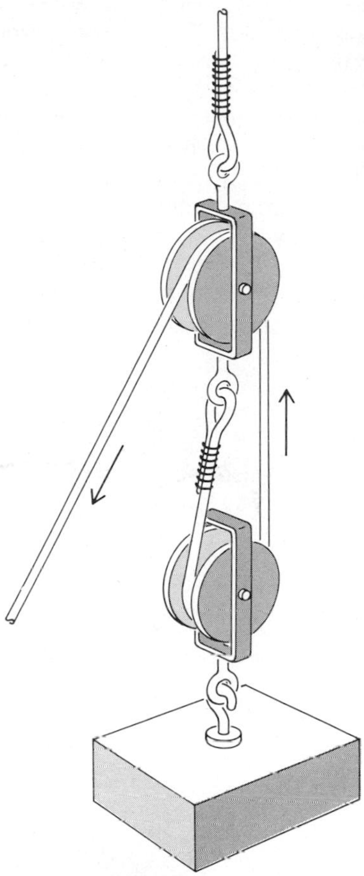

By use of this arrangement of pulleys force is gained at a sacrifice of distance. A man must pull the rope 2 feet to raise the weight 1 foot, but he can raise a weight with half the effort needed with a single pulley.

A fixed pulley does not increase the force but makes it more convenient to apply. With a fixed pulley as much force is required to pull down on the rope as to lift the weight without the use of the pulley. In fact, a little more force is needed, because we must overcome the friction between the rope and the pulley wheel. It is usually easier, however, to pull down than to lift up. One reason for this is that the *weight* of the person's body helps pull the rope. Note also that with a fixed pulley the distance moved by the rope being pulled is equal to the distance moved by the rope supporting the weight.

A combination of several pulleys, in which one or more actually move, is called a *compound pulley.* These magnify force. Using the pulley shown, a man can lift a 100-pound weight with a 50-pound pull if the loss due to friction is disregarded. You will recall that to gain force in the lever it was necessary to increase the distance through which the smaller force moved. The same is true here. The man must pull the rope down 2 feet to hoist the weight up 1 foot, but, as we have seen, he need pull with a force only one-half that of the weight.

Combinations of pulleys are often used in moving heavy objects. The more pulleys there are, the less force is required. Increasing the number of pulleys is, however, effective only up to a point. Beyond this point the additional friction and the resistance of the rope to being bent are greater than the advantage provided by the additional pulleys.

Each combination of pulleys is called a pulley block, and the arrangement of pulley blocks and their ropes is called a block and tackle. The block and tackle are in common use. Lifeboats are raised and lowered by them. Riggers hoist safes to the upper stories of buildings, and painters move their scaffolding with the block and tackle.

THE WHEEL AND AXLE

Every time you turn a doorknob you are using a machine called a *wheel and axle.* You will appreciate the value of this machine if you unscrew the knob and try to turn the axle with your fingers. Restored to its normal place on the axle the knob becomes a force-multiplying device. A little force applied on the rim of the wheel will cause a large force to be transmitted to the axle. The axle, in turn, turns the mechanism of the doorlock. The steering wheel of an automobile is another example of a wheel and axle.

(*See* pp. 579–80.)

A screw driver, when it is used for turning a screw, is a wheel and axle with the part gripped by the hand serving as the wheel and the steel shaft as the axle. Other devices employing the wheel and axle are the fishing reel and pencil sharpener, except that here the "wheel" has been reduced to one "spoke," or handle to which the force of the user is applied. A wrench, a brace and bit, a meat grinder, pepper mill, wall can opener—all illustrate the wheel and axle in use. In all, force is multiplied by applying it at a great distance from the turning axis or axle to overcome the great resistance at this point.

In the wheel and axle, as in the lever and in the pulley, force is gained but at the expense of distance. Consider the simple machine (called a windlass), shown on this page, for hoisting water from a well. Each time the handle (the wheel) makes one full turn the rope is wound one full turn around the axle. It is apparent that the distance traveled by the handle is greater than the distance traveled by the rope. Let us say that in this case it is five times as great. Then the effort needed to lift a 25-pound bucket of water will be only 5 pounds. The effort required is only $\frac{1}{5}$ that of the weight, but it must be applied for 5 times the distance.

Two sets of wheels and axles connected by a belt can also be used to *transmit* power. You may have seen such an arrangement in a shoe-repair shop. Here a continuous belt runs on two wheels. The lower wheel is turned by an electric motor. A belt transmits the motion to a wheel above, thereby turning the shaft to which the various buffing and sanding wheels are attached.

GEARS

Power can also be transmitted from one wheel to another by equipping the wheels with

All these machines make use of the wheel and axle. In all, force is multiplied by an investment of distance.

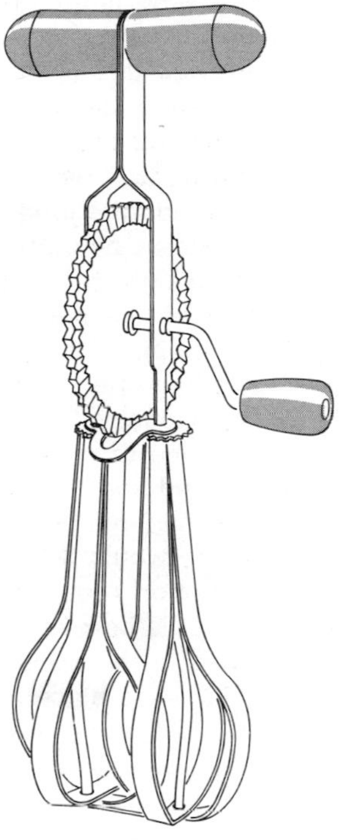

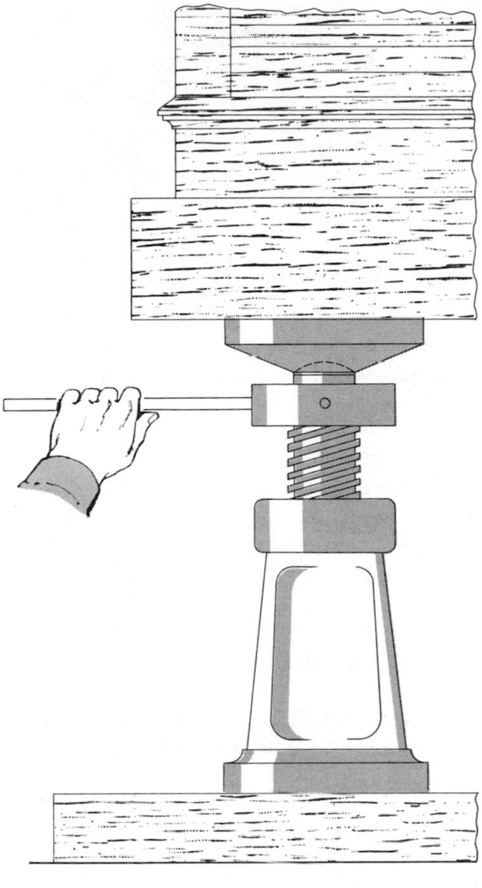

The gears in this egg beater increase speed and also change the direction of the force. The jackscrew increases force by multiplying the mechanical advantage of two machines, the screw and the wheel and axle (*see* page 567–8).

(*See* pp. 580–1)

intermeshing teeth. Such wheels are called gears, or gear wheels (which together with their mounting are variants of the wheel and axle). The purpose of gears, as of other machines, is to increase speed, increase force, or change the direction of a force.

A close look at an egg beater will help you understand gear wheels. An egg beater has a big wheel with a handle attached. Notice this large gear wheel and the two small gear wheels. Turn the handle and watch the wheels. You will see that the small ones turn faster. Watch carefully and you will see why. The teeth of the big wheel fit into the teeth of the much smaller wheels that turn the beater. Thus, the smaller wheels make many turns while the larger wheel makes one. You can check the effectiveness of your egg beater by marking a spot on the little one with a crayon and then counting the number of turns it makes for one turn of the large one. In one common type of egg beater the little wheel turns 5 times while the big wheel turns only once. Gears make it possible to operate the egg beater rapidly. The gears in this device also serve to change the *direction* of the force. Your hand revolves conveniently in a vertical plane; the egg beater blades swirl effectively in a horizontal plane.

Sometimes, as in a bicycle, the two gear wheels are connected by a chain. Notice that the front gear wheel, the one where the force is applied, is larger than the one on the rear wheel. If you turn a bicycle upside down and turn the

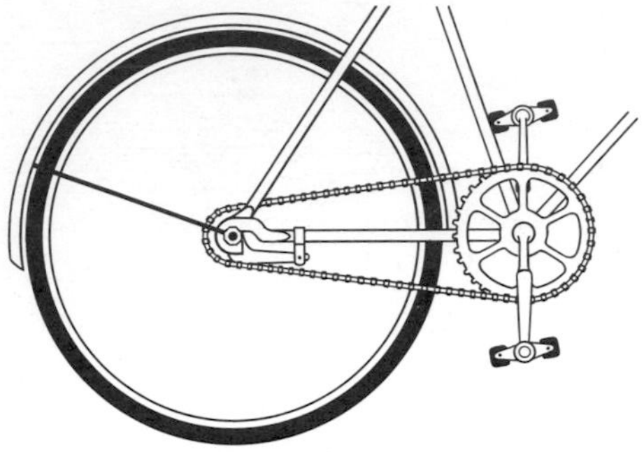

How many simple machines are involved in transmitting force from your foot to the wheel of your bicycle?

front gear wheel one complete turn you will find that the rear wheel makes several turns. Thus, one turn of your foot on the pedals gives you several turns of the bicycle wheel. Here again *speed* is gained by an investment of force.

THE INCLINED PLANE

If a man wants to raise a heavy barrel onto a truck he uses a board, resting one end against the truck floor and the other end on the ground. Then he rolls the barrel up the ramp he has made. He is using a machine called an *inclined plane,* which is simply a sloping surface. Why is the job easier this way? Is the man doing less work? Recalling the definition given before, of work as a force exerted through a distance, we would find that the same amount of work is needed to roll the barrel up the incline as to lift it straight up into the truck. Less force is used, but it has to be exerted for a longer distance. Essentially the job is easier, because at any one moment more of the weight is being supported by the plank and less by the man's muscles. The inclined plane of the plank thus serves to make the job a more gradual one.

(*See* pp. 581–2.)

Consider a specific example of this principle. Assume that the truck floor is 5 feet above the ground and that the plank is 15 feet long. Then the man must move the barrel three times as far as he would if he were lifting it straight up, but the effort required is only one-third as much.

It is believed that the huge blocks of stone used in the construction of the Egyptian pyramids were placed in position by being rolled up

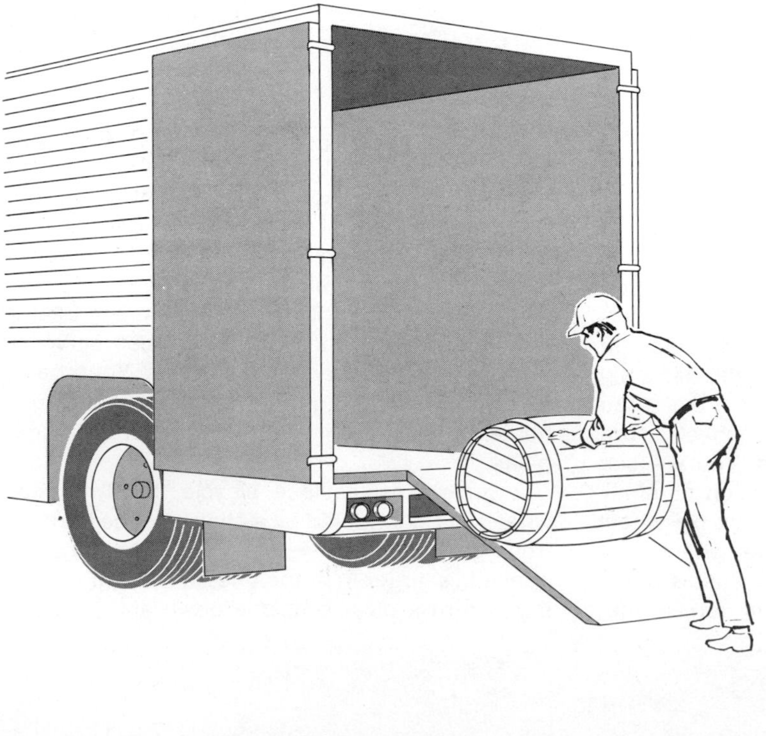

This ramp is a simple machine in which less force is needed to do the job—but at the expense of distance.

long, sloping hills of earth constructed especially for that purpose.

We encounter inclined planes frequently. Highways are carefully graded so that when we drive over them very steep hills are not encountered. The Guggenheim Museum in New York City has a continuous spiral ramp which makes the walk along its art-covered walls easier for viewers.

THE WEDGE

The wedge is a kind of inclined plane, but it is used in the opposite way a ramp or hill is. (*See* p. 582.) (A wedge is actually *two* inclined planes, fastened back to back.) On a ramp or hill objects are raised by rolling or sliding them up the incline. A wedge, on the other hand, moves objects by being forced under them or between them. The most common use of the wedge is in separating or splitting an object. An example of this is seen when the woodsman splits logs by driving an iron wedge into the wood with heavy blows of a sledge hammer. An ax is also a wedge, as is the chisel, knife, and even the common tack. With all of these, as

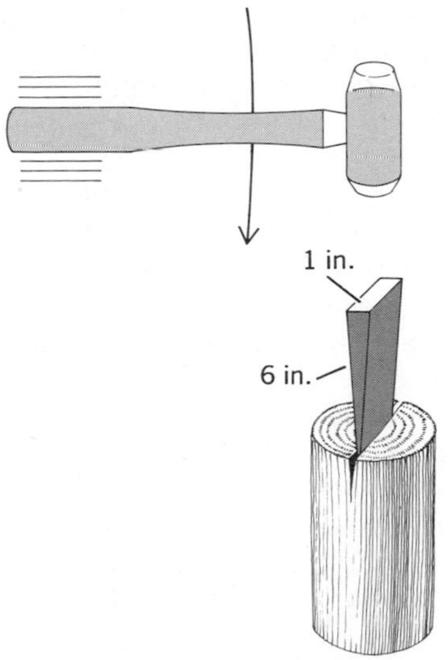

A wedge is a simple machine. Here, a 100-pound force is multiplied into a 600-pound force.

with the inclined plane, less force is needed because it is applied over a longer distance.

Consider, for example, the steel wedge that the woodsman drives into a log to split it. Assume that it is 1 inch thick at its outer end and 6 inches long. When the wedge has been driven in 6 inches the end of the log is split open 1 inch. The ratio 6:1 gives the theoretical advantage (the *mechanical advantage*) of this machine. For 600 pounds of force exerted on the log the woodsman must invest only 100 pounds of force. The actual advantage will be much less than this because of the loss due to friction.

THE SCREW

A screw is essentially a coiled inclined plane. You can prove this to yourself in the following (*See* p. 582.) way: Cut a rectangular piece of paper in half with a diagonal cut. The new edge made by the cut represents an inclined plane. Now roll the paper around a pencil, beginning with one of the arms of the right triangle and continuing down to a corner. The inclined plane is now a spiral around the pencil in the shape of a screw. On any screw this plane is called the screw's *thread.*

In actual use the screw is a combination of two simple machines: a wheel and axle *and* an inclined plane. An example of such a combination is a wrench turning a bolt. The wrench and the body of the bolt are the wheel and axle; the thread on the bolt is the inclined plane. The advantage of one machine is multiplied by the other, hence the combined advantage can be tremendous.

(*See* p. 565.) Consider the jackscrew. This machine is used to lift buildings when they are to be moved, or when the timbers that rest on the foundations are to be repaired. The jackscrew is essentially a *bolt* with a screw thread on it (to which a handle is attached), which fits into a *nut,* the base on which the jack stands. The handle serves as the wheel in the wheel and axle part of this machine. The weight to be lifted rests on the screw head. As the screw is turned, it *twists* out of the base and elevates the load resting on it. In a sense the load is riding up a hill—the spiral hill of the thread.

One complete turn of the screw may lift the weight only $\frac{1}{4}$ inch, but the mechanical advantage in force may be great. If the length of the jack handle is 21 inches, then in making one complete turn its outer end travels $2\pi \times 21$, or 132 inches—a circle of 11 feet. This confers an ideal mechanical advantage of $132:\frac{1}{4}$, or 528! A force of only 20 pounds could lift $\frac{1}{2}$ ton. The great multiplication of effort is paid for by having to turn the handle of the screw through a long distance to raise the weight only a little. Again the actual mechanical advantage is much less than the ideal mechanical advantage because of loss due to friction.

The great mechanical advantage of the screw makes it useful when a very heavy object is to be moved or lifted and only a small force is available. Some automobile jacks use a screw. Derailed locomotives are moved by jackscrews.

Many common devices around the house employ screws: adjustable piano stools, wood screws, food grinders, corkscrews.

FRICTION—LIABILITY OR NECESSITY

Friction occurs whenever two surfaces rub against each other. The work against friction (*See* p. 583.) generates heat, which you can detect if you rub the palms of your hands together. In most machines this heat represents wasted energy. In addition to being wasteful the heat that results from friction may cause serious damage. When the bearings or rolling parts of machines are not lubricated properly they may melt or "burn out."

What causes friction? A magnified view of the surface of an apparently smooth material would show that it possesses many irregularities, many jagged hills and valleys. According to classic theory friction is caused by the bumping and tearing of irregular surfaces as they slide over each other. More recent studies indicate that friction arises in part from the *attraction* of the molecules of the contacting surfaces. This is the same kind of attraction that makes water stick to your hands after washing; it is called *adhesion.*

Friction is reduced in machines by the use of wheels, bearings, and rollers, and by the application of lubricants. The ordinary wheels used on vehicles reduce friction, because they permit the surfaces involved to roll rather than to slide over each other. The friction of a wheel against its axle may be reduced by putting steel balls, called *bearings,* between the two. In this way the sliding friction of the hub of the wheel against the axle is replaced by rolling friction. You can see ball bearings if you take apart the wheel of a roller skate. When we put rollers under a heavy box or ball casters under furniture we are also substituting rolling for sliding.

Lubrication reduces friction, in part, because it fills in some of the irregularities of the surfaces and thus prevents their interlocking. When lubricants are used, the solid surfaces actually slide on the lubricant rather than on each other. Recent research in connection with the adhesion theory of friction, mentioned previously, indicates that the lubricant is effective because it increases the distances between the surfaces and therefore decreases the strength of the adhesive force.

A variety of lubricants—including oil, grease, soap, wax, and graphite—are used in gears and wheels. It is important to select the right lubricant for each particular use. Lubrication not only saves energy it also prevents unnecessary wear. This is well illustrated in the automobile. The entire mechanism must be constructed so that a sufficient amount of the lubricant will reach every moving part at all times.

Friction is not always a hindrance. We would not be able to walk without friction between our shoes and the ground, because our feet would slip backward. That is why walking on ice is difficult. Automobiles and trains would not be able to start without friction between the wheels and the surface beneath. Without friction the brakes in automobiles would be useless. Everyday activities would be impossible without friction. Doorknobs would slip through our hands without turning. Chalk would not write on chalkboards. The violinist's bow would slip silently across the strings.

We often increase friction intentionally. The baseball pitcher rubs resin on his hands to get a better grip on the ball, while the opposing batter rubs his hands in the dirt to get a better hold on the bat. When roads are icy we scatter sand over them and put chains on our tires.

DEVELOPING POWER

We have seen how machines multiply effort or speed or change the direction of a force. We have not considered the *source* of the force that is put into the machine. Let us turn now to those devices that develop power for man, making it possible to do a great deal of work in a short time.

As long as man used only his muscles his capacity for doing work was limited. To help his weak muscles man pressed into service such animals as the horse, ox, elephant, and camel. But the use of power on a large scale came only when man learned how to make engines to harness the movement of the wind and the rush of falling water, the heat from burning fuels and, recently, the enormous energy within the atom.

Currently scientists are experimenting with devices to capture the radiant energy of the sun. These are discussed in Chapters 14A and 16A.

A sail may be regarded as a machine which transfers energy from the wind to the boat. *(Courtesy of Monkmeyer.)*

Sailboats and Windmills

When primitive man hoisted an animal skin on a pole in his hollowed-out log canoe he was making use of the energy of the wind. Many kinds of sailboats have been built down through the centuries, but all of them are devices that capture some of the energy of the wind and use it to move the boat.

Windmill blades catch the wind, too, but are so designed as to convert its energy into a rotary motion. The energy thus trapped may be used to pump water, to grind grain, or to spin an electromagnet to generate electricity.

Water Wheels

The energy of falling water has been harnessed by water wheels. In the past, water wheels have furnished the power for crushing grain, for driving cloth-weaving looms, and for many other industrial purposes. Today, falling water's energy is converted into electricity. Special water wheels, called *turbines,* turn electromagnets that generate electricity. These hydroelectric generators, as they are called, are an important source of electrical energy in the United States, Canada, the U.S.S.R., and many other parts of the world.

(*See* Ch. 19A.)

Steam Engines

The invention of the steam engine was of major importance in the development of our industrial civilization. This engine uses the heat of burning fuel to change water into steam, and works on the simple principle that steam occupies much more space than the water it came from. One quart of water makes hundreds of quarts of steam. The energy of the expanding steam furnishes the power to run the engine.

In a steam locomotive water is heated in a boiler and converted into steam. Each puff of steam does its job of pushing a piston in a cylinder. The back-and-forth motion of the piston is conveyed by a connecting rod to the wheels, where it is changed to a circular motion.

A steam turbine achieves smoother operation than the piston type of engine. In the turbine many curved steel blades are set in a shaft in such a way as to receive the force of the steam. Most big ships are run by steam turbines. The spinning turbine turns a long rod, which is connected to the propeller that drives the ship. The steam turbine is also used, like the water turbine, as an engine for developing electrical power.

The burning of wood, coal, gas, and oil furnishes the energy for steam engines and steam turbines. Nuclear energy is now used to boil water into steam under great pressure. The energy of the steam spins turbines that turn the propellers in ships or make electricity in nuclear power plants.

(*See* Ch. 17A.)

Gasoline and Diesel Engines

We depend on the gasoline engine for motive power for automobiles and airplanes and for many other purposes. In the gasoline engine the power is derived from the rapid expansion of gases produced by the explosive burning of gasoline. This occurs inside each of the cylinders of the motor. A spark from a spark plug ignites the mixture of gasoline vapor and air. The explosion that results pushes the piston down with a force of several tons. This force is then converted by the crankshaft into a rotary motion and is transmitted to the driving wheels of the automobile or the propeller of the airplane.

The diesel engine, named after its inventor, Rudolph Diesel, also works by the energy of explosions. For fuel, it uses light oil instead of gasoline, which makes it more economical to run. Today, light, high-speed diesels are used more and more on trucks, buses, submarines, and locomotives. Diesels are also used to drive electric generators in places where it is sometimes convenient to have an independent or auxiliary source of electricity, as in hospitals, schools, department stores, and factories.

The jet engine and the rocket engine are discussed on pages 677–680.

Electric Generators and Motors

As we have seen in the preceding paragraphs the energy of wind, falling water, expanding steam, and exploding gasoline can be converted into useful motion. We shall see in Chapter 19A just how this motion is converted into electricity. We shall also see how electric motors convert electricity into motion.

Here are some of the important generalizations about machines:

Machines help in different ways. Some produce a gain in force, some in speed; some change the direction of a force.

Work is done when a force is exerted through a distance.

Disregarding the losses due to friction, the work put into a machine equals the work put out.

A gain in force in a machine is at the expense of speed; a gain in speed requires an investment of force.

Six simple types of machines include the lever, the pulley, the wheel and axle, the inclined plane, the wedge, and the screw.

Friction occurs when any two substances rub together.

All machines lose some of their efficiency because of friction.

Wheels, rollers, and ball bearings reduce friction by substituting rolling for sliding friction.

Lubrication reduces friction by filling in the irregularities of the contacting surfaces and by decreasing the attraction between them.

Friction can be an asset: It prevents slipping and makes possible thousands of everyday activities.

Man has invented engines to harness the energy of the wind, falling water, burning fuel, the sun, and the atom.

Discovering for Yourself

1. Observe the results of friction in your environment; indicate which examples are helpful, which harmful.
2. Observe a machine at work. Name the machine, describe its work, tell where the energy came from to operate it, tell what reduces its efficiency, and list any simple machines you are able to identify that are part of the machine you are observing.
3. Examine the machines in a kitchen. Classify them according to which of the simple machines they are.
4. Observe machines in your outdoor environment and keep a record of the inclined planes, levers, and pulleys that you see in use. In each case tell how the machine is helpful in gaining force or in some other way.
5. Observe an egg beater and a bicycle and compare their operations.
6. Watch a carpenter or a garage mechanic at work and describe and explain how simple machines help him to do work that he could not do without them.
7. Examine an antique machine and a modern one that were designed to do the same work. Compare their efficiency of operation.
8. Observe a building under construction. Describe the machinery being used, and compare this modern operation with one of a hundred years ago.

(Courtesy of Florida Department of Education.)

CHAPTER 18B

TEACHING "MACHINES AND HOW THEY WORK"

The material in this chapter lends itself to the development of the concept of *interaction*, the relationship among objects that do something to one another thereby bringing about a change. For example, study the picture on page 582. What happens when the child turns the large pulley wheel? It turns the small pulley wheel to which it is connected, but the smaller pulley wheel turns faster. Other illustrations in the chapter show similar interactions. The concept of interaction is important in science because it stresses: (1.) that changes occur because objects interact rather than because some mysterious "spirit" moves them, (2.) that these changes can be reproduced by others, if the conditions are the same, and consequently, (3.) that these changes are predictable.

Using and studying the simple machines in this chapter provide valuable inquiry experiences. They encourage *exploration, improvisation, experimentation* that can result in *discoveries* and lead to *applications* of science principles to everyday life. Look at the photograph that introduces the chapter. Since experience is said to be the best teacher get a tennis ball and a baseball and place them on an incline. "How are the balls alike?" "How are they different from each other?" Roll the balls down the incline and see what happens. Do this several times and observe carefully just as you would encourage children to do. What questions come out of this? If the two balls start at the same time from the top of the incline try to predict which one will reach the bottom first. Which ball will roll the farthest before stopping? (It may be necessary to shift the experiment to the classroom floor or the schoolyard to determine this. What would happen if you used a pingpong ball? A marble? If you let each ball hit a small box what would happen? If you wanted to roll the ball *up* the incline which would require a harder push? How could you make the balls roll more slowly down the incline? Faster? What does all of this have to do with skating or cycling on a hill? Skiing on a slope? Or carrying a load up a hill?

The approaches suggested in studying one machine—the inclined plane—can also be used for the others discussed in this chapter. If you have this experience yourself you see how important it is to begin by doing something, observing, raising questions, and then going on to further exploration.

SOME BROAD CONCEPTS: "Machines and How They Work"

Some machines produce a gain in force; some increase speed; some change the direction of a force.

Machines must have a source of energy to do work.

Machines are devices that transfer force.

Energy may come from muscles, electric current, or some kind of fuel.

Work is done whenever an effort overcomes a resistance and moves something.

The amount of work put into a machine equals the amount of work put out, disregarding friction. Machines do not save work.

The lever, the pulley, the wheel and axle, the inclined plane, the wedge, and the screw are types of simple machines.

All machines lose some of their efficiency due to friction.

There are several ways to reduce friction in machines.

FOR YOUNGER CHILDREN

Even very young children are interested in answers to "What makes it go?" and "How does it work?". Before they enter school their toys and the tools they use have introduced them to the world of wheels and gears. The following activities emphasize observations and experiences that have been carried on successfully with young children.

What Things Move on Wheels?[1]

Suggest that children watch at home, on the streets, at school, and elsewhere to find things that move on wheels. Ask them to observe how many wheels there are, look at them as they move, and try to tell what makes them move. After this make a short record of their observations. Use children's drawings or magazine pictures. After each picture place a number that tells how many wheels are used and, if possible, what made the wheels move (muscle, gasoline, and others). They may make use of toys with wheels in their observations and demonstrations by noticing how the wheels turn, how many there are, and so on.

How Do Things Move on Hills?

Refer to the inclined plane discussion in the introduction to this chapter. Help children recall their observations and experiences with hills—sliding downhill, riding roller coasters, and so on. Suggest that they try to build a hill using boards, bricks, and other materials. Groups of children can each make such a hill and then have the experience of rolling various sizes and shapes of balls, toy trucks, and other things down the hills they have made. For obvious reasons this is a good outdoor activity. Help the children compare the results of using steep hills and gently-sloping hills and of using different sized balls and other materials. They will observe that things roll down hill without a push, that round things roll more easily than square or flat things, and observe what happens when the objects reach a level surface. They may try rolling a round object *up* the hill and observe what happens.

What Kinds of Work Do Machines Do?

As children observe machines at home, at school, on a farm, in garages and filling stations, and elsewhere ask them to try to see what kinds of work machines do. A record of the observations may consist of: (1.) name of the machine, (2.) picture of the machine, (3.) where it was observed, (4.) kind of work it was doing (lifting, digging,

[1] J. Schwartz: *Go On Wheels* and *Uphill and Downhill* (New York: McGraw-Hill). *See also Science K–2* (Brooklyn, N.Y.: Board of Education of the City of New York, 1966). For subject matter information and many suggestions for helping young children make discoveries about machines.

and so on). The pictures may be children's drawings or from magazines. The record can then be used for discussion, and additions to it can be made from time to time. Children will become more observant of their surroundings and better able to describe and report their observations as a result of this experience.

How Can You Balance Your Seesaw Partner?

This experience constitutes a background for a later, more detailed study of levers and gives young children an opportunity to get the "feel" of the interaction of objects. Let them try out different combinations of children (both heavy and light), children of equal and unequal weights and see what happens as children shift positions nearer to and farther from the fulcrum. Suggest that they use the seesaw to try to tell which child is the heavier. They may choose partners to see which ones will balance. The activity begins with free play: "Let's see what happens if . . ." Then the group can discuss what they think they have observed. Finally they can gather around one seesaw to try out and demonstrate their ideas. They may be able to demonstrate how a heavier child can balance a lighter one, how two people can balance one, and so on.

After these experiences they can use blocks and other materials to make seesaws indoors to review the ideas they have learned. Use a variety of sizes and shapes of blocks, some equal, some unequal in weight. Suggest the use of other materials such as toys, stones, pails of soil. Some children will get the idea of using the seesaw as

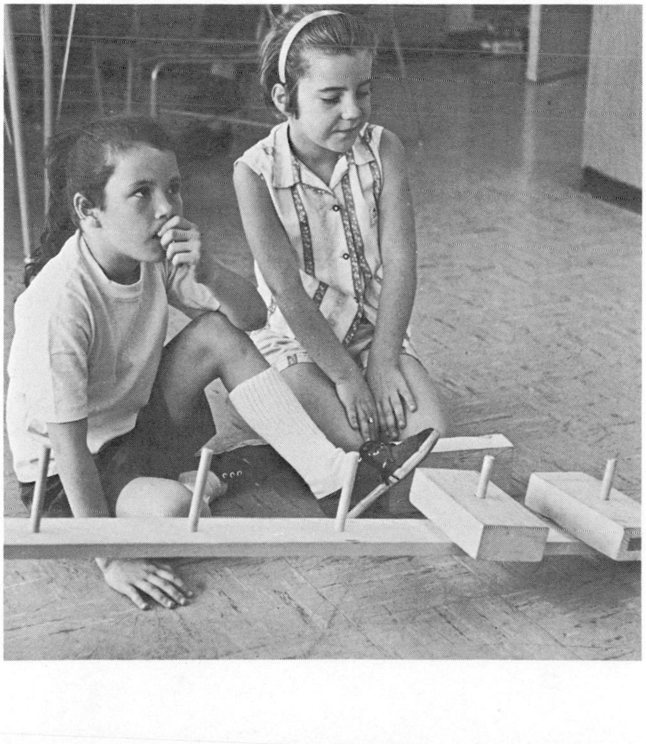

Two young pupils ponder the problems posed by balancing wooden blocks on a teeter-totter. The apparatus is carefully designed to engage children in activities which will lead to greater understanding of a specific science area. The large size of the apparatus appeals to the muscles as well as the minds of children. These pupils participated in a summer workshop (Elementary Science Study) held for the purpose of developing more effective teaching materials. (*Courtesy of the Elementary Science Study of Education Development Center, Inc.*)

a scale to determine relative weight. Others may suggest using a series of blocks of approximately the same weight as units of measure and draw such conclusions as: "The eraser weighs 2 blocks." "The toy truck weighs 6 blocks."

OTHER PROBLEMS FOR YOUNGER CHILDREN

1. What makes machines move?
2. How is friction helpful and harmful?
3. How do we use gears?
4. How do we use levers?
5. Where do we use pulleys?
6. How are machines used in the city? On a farm?
7. How do toys work?

FOR OLDER CHILDREN

How Do Levers Make Work Easier?

Direct experiences from which to make observations, hypotheses, inferences, predictions, and possible discoveries are important. Recall the description in Chapter 2 of the children using a board and brick as a lever arrangement to lift the teacher. A three-sided (triangular in cross section) length of wood, which can easily be made in a shop, works more smoothly than the brick. A large lever that pupils can work with is useful because pupils get the "feel" that the machine actually makes the work easier to do. In accordance with the directions already given, let them try to lift one another. Let pupils work in groups, and in the beginning do not give them any suggestions. After they have explored various possibilities urge them to exchange any ideas they may have observed. Which group has found the easiest way to lift a weight? Describe the way. Why do you think these conditions make lifting the weight easier?

Let a group demonstrate how placing the brick or piece of wood at various distances from the person being lifted shows that there is a relationship between the distance that the "push" moves and the ease with which the work is done. Urge pupils to try to determine whether there is a mathematical ratio between the "push" and the work done. Note that pupils may use the words force, fulcrum, and resistance as they discuss the lever, for they will soon come to realize what each is. It is important that such science vocabulary be introduced but not stressed to the point of getting in the way of interest, appreciation, and understanding. At the beginning they may substitute descriptive words such as teetering point, weight, pull, push, and so on for the technical ones.

The lever provides opportunity for the use of measurement to see the relationship between the distance that the forces moves (downward) to the distance the resistance moves (upward) (an example of interaction mentioned in the introduction). If the force moves four times as far as the resistance does, is it easier to move the resistance than it is if the force moves only twice as far? The relationships will be obvious if pupils actually measure the two distances. Try the experiment with the fulcrum placed so that the force moves 2 feet to raise the resistance 1 foot. Then move the fulcrum so that the relationship is 3:1, and so on. Pupils will soon feel the difference even though they may not have exact measures.

After using this lever pupils can go out and use a seesaw on the playground to see that if the force is far from the fulcrum (the teetering point) more weight can be lifted without increasing the force. They can try various positions and various numbers of pupils to check out the relationships between the force and the resistance. Again, measuring the distance that the force moves and comparing it with the distance that the resistance moves will help pupils to see why levers are useful. After pupils have had some experience with measuring they may be asked to estimate before measuring and computing.

After experimenting the pupils should try to bring useful levers to school and demonstrate how they work. For each lever they should try to measure to see how the force and the fulcrum position are related. Suggest that pupils answer such questions as: "Does the machine increase speed?" "Does it increase force?" "Does it change the direction of the force?" "What other advantages does it have?" They will see that not all levers gain force. It is important that the levers be demonstrated so that pupils will actually see how they operate. Examples are: (1.) A *claw hammer*—drive a nail into a board. Try to pull it out with your fingers. Then use the claw hammer. Observe how easily the nail comes out. Why? (2.) A *nut cracker* (two levers)—crack a nut with it. Observe the arrangement and see how far the force moves. (3.) A *can opener* (lever type)—make the observations suggested for other levers. (4.) A *pair of scissors* (also two levers). In all cases measuring the distance the force moves and, if possible, the distance the resistance moves is important.

How Do Pulleys Make Work Easier?

Direct experience using the flagpole is a convenient device to show pupils the principle of a fixed pulley. Urge observation and description of just what happens. "In what ways does the pulley help?" "How many are there?" "Is the pulley like the lever in any way?" They may observe the way in which the rope is placed through the pulley and see the advantage of a fixed pulley in getting the flag to the top of the pole. Help them to discover the relationship between the distance that the force (hand pulling rope) moves down and the distance that the resistance (the flag) moves up. Fixed pulleys do not save force. They are just convenient.

Pulleys can be purchased in many stores where toys are sold, in hardware stores, in marine supply stores, in variety stores; or they can be ordered from scientific supply houses. Pulley systems that actually help in lifting heavy things, as the lever lifted a pupil, are a great asset in helping pupils understand how pulleys operate.

First let pupils "mess around" with pulleys to make any observations possible. Then help them arrange pulleys as shown on p. 578. Let them operate the pulley systems to note the interactions and try to explain their observations. It is important for them

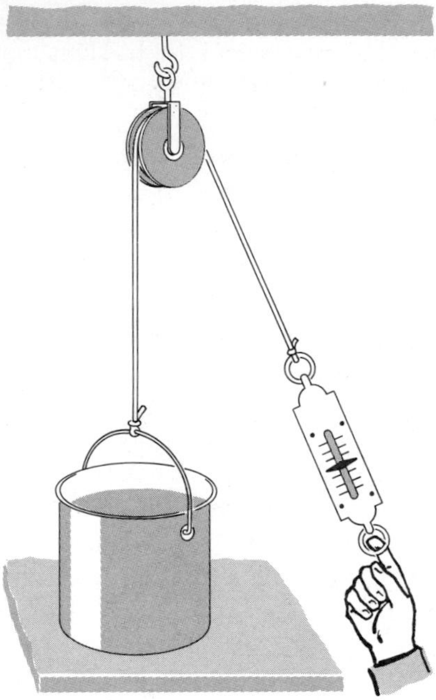

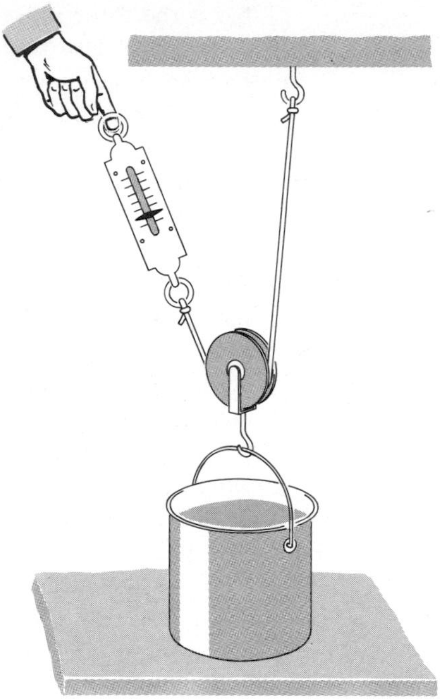

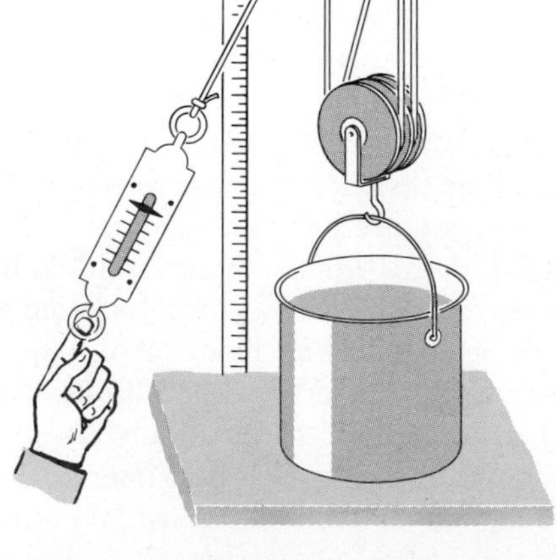

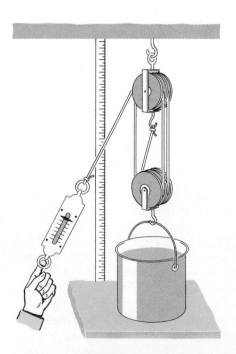

Using pulleys under different conditions and in various combinations along with the measuring device helps to make the scientific principles more easily understood. After such experiences children may observe the use of machines in their environment with greater understanding.

to see that in these pulley arrangements force is exchanged for distance; that is, much rope is pulled through the pulleys (distance) to make the weight easier to lift. Again they can observe to see the relationship between the distance that the force moves down and the distance that the resistance moves up.

Suggest to children: "You remember that in the case of the lever we measured with a ruler to see the relationship of force and resistance. Can you suggest some possible measurement we could make with pulley arrangements?" They can use a spring scale to show how the use of pulleys reduces the amount of force necessary to lift a weight. Again let them work in groups to use pulleys and the spring scale and try to make some inferences from their observations. If possible, use pulleys that can hold a heavy weight, such as a pail of sand or several books tied together. First use the spring scale to lift the weight directly. Note the reading of the scale. Now use a block of two pulleys at the top and two at the bottom and attach the spring scale to the rope that will be pulled. Lift the weight. Again read the scale. Use different weights. If possible, increase the number of pulleys on the block to three and four, and repeat in each case. Note the reading of the scale.

Pupils may observe pulley systems in garages, where one man easily lifts the whole front end of an automobile. In some schoolrooms fixed pulleys are used to raise the windows and window curtains. A weight concealed in the window frame helps to lift the window, and in some window frames the pulley can be observed at the top. Clotheslines often operate by means of pulleys. A bird-feeding station may be hauled away from the window on a pulley and line.

How Does a Wheel and Axle Make Work Easier?

It is easy to make a simple windlass that pupils can use in the classroom to lift things. The school custodian, a parent, or the shop teacher may be willing to work

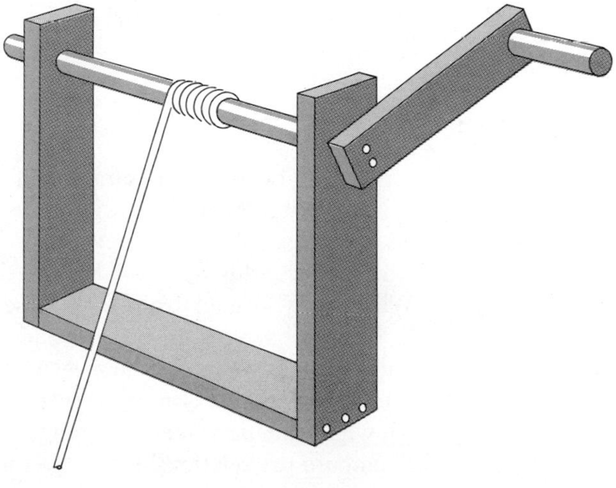

A handmade windlass, such as this, helps pupils to see the relationship between the distances traveled by the force and by the weight. Pupils can use their imaginations in thinking of various ways to use the machine.

with a committee of pupils in constructing it. It may be made of wood of any desired dimensions and operated from the side or corner of a desk. The one illustrated here is 18 inches long; the supports at the ends are 12 inches high. A broomstick serves as the axle and the handle is made of wood and nailed to the end of the broomstick. Strong twine is used as the "rope" to lift the weights.

Suggest that pupils use the apparatus to lift a pail of sand or some other heavy object and observe what happens. "Is it easier with the windlass?" "Why do you suppose this is true?" "Where is the force?" "The resistance?" "What relationship exists between them?" "Is it like any other simple machine?"

It may be necessary to explain how this is like the wheels they are accustomed to seeing (the handle is one spoke of the wheel). Pupils should see first that the handle is fastened to the axle and turns it. As they use the windlass they will see the relationship between the number of turns the handle makes (the distance the force travels) and the short distance the weight travels. Again this experience will be more meaningful if pupils can arrive at figures they can compare. The pupils will discover how to measure the distance that the force travels (the circumference of the circle made by the end of the handle) and compare it with the distance that the weight travels. They will then see that here, as in the case of other simple machines, force may be gained at a sacrifice of distance. Pupils should compare the handle of the windlass to the driving wheel of a car and see that it may be thought of as *one* spoke of an imaginary wheel that turns the axle. On this handmade piece of equipment the relationship is easy to see.

The pencil sharpener is another illustration of the wheel and axle. So is the doorknob of the classroom. A fifth-grade teacher once unscrewed the knob of her classroom door and asked some of her pupils to try to open the door. They could not. Then she put the knob on again and pupils saw how easy it was to open the door. To make clear the idea that the knob was a wheel and axle, the pupils pushed a nail through one of the holes into which the screws fit and used it to open the door. They could see that the nail constituted a spoke of a wheel. Pupils remembered this experience because they could see how the wheel and axle, a simple machine, made it easy for them to open the door.

How Do Gears Work?

The egg beater is an example of the wheel and axle that pupils can bring to school for observation. Arrange that pupils use egg beaters, observe the operation of the gears, and try to describe what they see. "What turns the big wheel?" "The small wheel?" "What relationship does one have to the other?" "What observations can you make?" "What can you infer from these observations?"

These observations will introduce the idea of gear wheels and make clear the relationship between the large gear wheel and the small one. Pupils can thus see an example of one wheel used to turn another. "How many times does the small wheel turn while the big wheel is turning only once?" Several egg beaters may be examined to compare the relationships of the turning of the large and small gears. Make a mark on one of the teeth of the small wheel so that you can tell when it has made one complete turn. Count the number of turns the small gear makes as the large one turns once. Ask the children to count the number of teeth of each of the gear wheels and see if they can figure out the relationship between the speed with which the two wheels turn. If the large wheel, for example, has six times as many teeth as the small gear, the small gear will make six turns for every turn of the large one. The different egg beaters may be compared by this count. This is a case where force is sacrificed to increase speed. In the egg beater pupils will see that gears also change the direction of the force.

Bicycles illustrate gear wheels and also the use of belts or chains to drive the wheels. They are easy to examine and should be brought into the classroom and demonstrated. It is easy to see how the pedal turns a wheel and how this motion is eventually transmitted to the rear wheel. Pupils can count the number of turns of the rear wheel for one turn of the pedals.

Pupils should be urged to find other machines in which belts of various kinds are used to make one wheel turn another. Shoe-repair shops, garages, and farms are good sources for examples.

How Does the Inclined Plane Make Work Easier?

Pupils can make a simple inclined plane with a board and some books and use a toy wagon to pull up a load. If they attach a spring scale to the wagon they can tell how much pull is needed. A rubber band may be substituted for a spring scale in this and in other experiences. The greater the stretch the more the pull. To determine the pull more accurately use a ruler to measure the stretched rubber band. This can be compared with how much force it takes to lift the load up the same distance without the use of the incline. The same procedure described in the section on pulleys can be used here to compare the distance that the force travels with the distance that the weight is lifted. When the inclined plane is used, the distance is greater but not as much force is needed. Suggest that pupils work out ways to change the slope of the plane and try to predict what difference the changes will make. If the slope is not very steep the distance is great, and the force may be less. If the slope is very steep the distance is less, but more force is needed. Estimating, measuring, and computing will help pupils to understand the "why" of various inclined planes.

An ideal situation for teaching the inclined plane results if the school custodian can help pupils to make one with boards somewhere in the building or on the school grounds. Use an empty barrel as the object to be lifted. In all probability pupils would have considerable difficulty in lifting the barrel 2 feet vertically, but with the boards utilized as an inclined plane they can easily lift the barrel 2 feet vertically by rolling it up the gentle slope. Experiences such as this not only help to bring about a real comprehension of the science principles involved but are also enjoyed by children.

Pupils can often find examples of inclined planes in the neighborhood. If bicycles are kept in the basement of the school, for example, an inclined plane is probably used to move them in and out. School supplies are often unloaded by the use of an inclined plane. Stores, factories, and many other places use them too. Pupils can observe the unloading of new automobiles at a nearby sales office and see how inclined planes are used.

How Does a Wedge Make Work Easier?

Again, the actual experience of using a simple machine and observing the effect is a reasonable way to begin: A small wedge can be driven into a piece of pine wood so that the wood will split. Suggest that children try different sizes and shapes of wedges to see how they push things apart. The wedge also changes the direction of the force. Short, thick wedges require more force to drive them than long, thin ones. Chisels, ice picks, axes, and knives are examples of wedges. If these tools are examined, pupils can see that they are actually inclined planes that wedge between things and push them apart.

How Does the Screw Make Work Easier?

Again the actual experience of using a simple machine and observing the effect is a reasonable way to begin. It is worth the trouble to bring an automobile jack (screw type) to school to see how it enables one person to lift an automobile. Jacks are made of more than one simple machine, but the lever operates the screw, and pupils can observe what happens as the screw makes many turns to lift only a short distance.

Pupils will find many examples of screws. The piano stool, for example, uses a screw, and they can see how it operates by watching it. The screw is an incline that winds around in a spiral. If they examine a large screw pupils can trace the spiral path of the grooves. Screws, like wedges and inclined planes, help us to gain force, but we sacrifice distance and speed.

What will happen to the small wheel when she turns the large one? What will happen to the large wheel if she turns the small one? Participating in the Science Curriculum Improvement Study (University of California), this pupil is observing evidence of interaction as she manipulates this simple apparatus. Many other examples of this principle of interaction are available in children's experiences: in the attraction and repulsion of magnets, in the sandpapering of wood, and so forth. The developers of SCIS believe that this approach will make children more conscious of the need for evidence before judging an event. (*Courtesy of the Science Curriculum Improvement Study.*)

How Does Friction Help and Hinder Us?

Use several sets of wooden blocks with flat surfaces. Suggest that children rub the surfaces together and report what happens. Rub them together briskly. Feel the surfaces. "How could you make the blocks move more easily?" Put drops of oil between them. Try it. "What happens?" Try soap, wax, vaseline, and other materials that the children suggest.

A simple device for measuring smoothness and roughness of surfaces can be made by using a flat block of wood with a rubber band fastened to one end of it with a screw eye. The stretch of the band shows how hard or easy it is to pull the block across a surface. With a ruler measure the stretch of the band as the block is pulled across the classroom floor, a cement sidewalk, a polished floor, a piece of glass, sandpaper, and other surfaces that children will want to try. Make a chart to show the stretches on different surfaces, so that it will be easy to compare them.

Urge pupils to observe the effects of friction on flat surfaces—their shoes on the floor, and so on. Suggest that the children lay the block on a roller skate and pull it with the rubber band. What conclusions can they draw now?

Reducing friction by the use of bearings is also easy to demonstrate. Roller skates, both those with bearings and those without, can be brought to school and compared. The wastebasket can be used to demonstrate how effective bearings are in reducing friction. Fill it with books and try to push it along the floor. Then set it on some marbles and try to push it along. Individual pupils can do this with piles of books to note the difference when marbles are used to reduce friction.

OTHER PROBLEMS FOR OLDER CHILDREN

1. How do garden tools help us?
2. What compound machines are used in our neighborhood?
3. What safety rules are important to use with machines?
4. What machines are used in house construction?
5. What machines are moved by wind, water, steam, and electricity?
6. How is the sun responsible for supplying various kinds of energy?

Resources to Investigate with Children

1. The kitchen at home (or at school) to observe how pulleys, levers, wheels, wedges, screws, and inclined planes are used.
2. Local buildings under construction to watch the use of machines.
3. Hardware store to observe kinds of machines for use in tool shops, garages, farms, buildings, and so on.
4. A garage to observe the use of pulleys for lifting motors, inclined planes, and many other machines at work.
5. A carpenter to explain proper use of tools and to show different kinds for different uses.

6. General merchandise catalogues for pictures of many different kinds of machines. Pictures show how complex machines are made from simple ones for the purpose of doing different types of work.
7. Toy stores to see machines used in various toys.
8. Dealers in agricultural implements to get a better understanding of machines used on the farm.
9. A manufacturing plant to see machines in operation.

Preparing to Teach

1. Plan a bulletin board that might be used as a summary of the study of simple machines. Also plan how to use it.
2. Plan a lesson designed to introduce the study of machines by raising searching questions. Indicate the grade, materials necessary, and the general procedure.
3. Make a list of materials you would need to teach a unit on machines. Classify the list according to: (1.) order from a supply house, (2.) find in the environment, (3.) to be furnished by the children.
4. Prepare an evaluation instrument that can be used to determine the extent to which pupils have attained objectives that you think are important in this unit.
5. Make a plan that might be utilized in order to help pupils answer the following: "How are machines used in our community?" Or "How would our way of living be different if we had no modern machines at our disposal?"

CHAPTER 19A

MAGNETISM AND ELECTRICITY

(Courtesy of Rapho-Guillumette, photo by Bruce Roberts.)

NIGHT WITHOUT LIGHT

We have come to take electricity for granted, but let it for some reason or other fail us and we suddenly become aware of its importance. The following excerpt from *Newsweek* recounts the events which followed a power failure that began on the evening of November 9, 1965:

The Longest Night

The northeastern U.S. is the Megalopolis—a vast intermeshing of cities, towns, suburbs, and exurbs. It is urban America of the mid-twentieth century brought to its fullest flower—and its fullest fragility. It is utterly dependent on turbine technology—a world that runs on electricity and on the faith that one has only to push a button, flick a switch or throw a lever to make electricity work. Electricity is its pulse, its power, its élan vital. And then one night last week the electricity stopped.

At 5:17 P.M. in Buffalo, 5:17 P.M. in Rochester, 5:18 in Boston, 5:28 in Albany, 5:24 to 5:28 in New York City, the clocks in the Megalopolis sputtered to a standstill. Lights blinked and dimmed and went out. Skyscrapers towered black against a cold November sky, mere artifacts lit only by the moon. Elevators hung immobile in their shafts. Subways ground dead in their tunnels. Streetcars froze in their tracks. Street lights and traffic signals went out—and with them the best-laid plans of the traffic engineers. Airports shut down. Mail stacked up in blacked-out post offices. Computers lost their memories. TV pictures darkened and died. Business stopped. Food started souring in refrigerators. Telephones functioned but dial tones turned to shrill whines under a record overload. Nothing else seemed to work except transistor radios. . . .

At its peak, the power failure was simply beyond human scale: it engulfed 80,000 square miles across parts of eight U.S. states and Canada's Ontario province—and left 30 million people in the dark.

MAGNETISM

Two Merging Streams

Historically, our knowledge of magnetism and our knowledge of electricity are two separate streams, originating in antiquity and merging near the beginning of the last century. In nature, magnetism and electricity are in fact intimately related, each one capable of producing the other. Almost all the devices referred to in the foregoing news story are indicative of how man, through his inventions, has made good use of this two-way relationship. Let us consider magnetism first. Later we shall investigate electricity and see how it is linked to magnetism.

The Magnet as an Iron Attractor and as a Compass

The phenomenon of magnetism has been known for centuries. The fact that certain kinds of iron or iron ore had the power to attract other bits of material containing iron must have been known in ancient Greece.

(*See* pp. 610–5.)

A second discovery made the magnet an important instrument in navigation. It was found that if a magnet were suspended so that it could turn freely it would swing into a north-south position. Thus the magnet becomes a compass. Some legends ascribe this knowledge to the ancient Chinese; presumably they used magnets as compasses more than 1,000 years ago. In the writings of Hebrews, Greeks, and Romans the magnet is often referred to as a "lodestone," meaning "leading stone" or "directing stone." Eventually a magnetized bit of iron was used in making a crude magnetic compass, but it is thought that this valuable instrument was not used much until the Middle Ages.

You can make a compass much like those used by early mariners by repeatedly stroking the

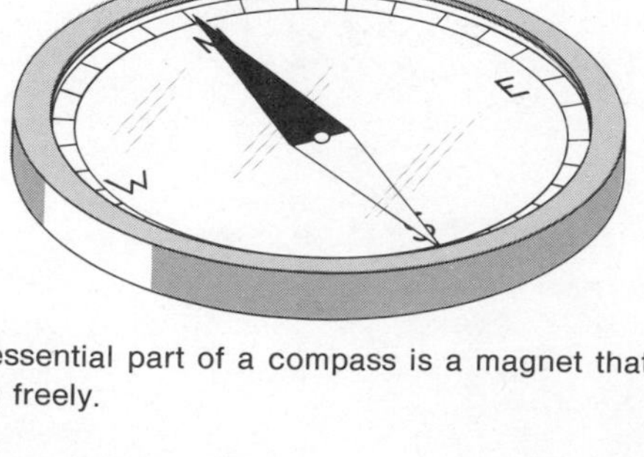

The essential part of a compass is a magnet that can swing freely.

length of a steel darning needle in one direction only with one end of a magnet and then laying the needle on a cork floating in water. The container for the water should not be made of iron. This kind of compass is essentially the kind used by Columbus in his voyage to America. Needles in Columbus' times were made of poor steel and did not retain magnetism very long. It was, therefore, necessary to remagnetize the needle every few days by rubbing it on a lodestone.

The discovery of the magnetic compass marked an important milestone in man's struggle to explore his planet. No longer did mariners have to govern their voyaging by the North Star or by landmarks along a coast. With the compass, directions could be determined accurately when clouds or storms hid the stars from view. This new invention made it possible for men to venture out into the great unknown—the oceans of the world.

In summary, the ancients knew three important facts about the lodestone:

1. It attracted and held bits of iron.
2. When freely suspended, it took a north-south position.
3. When pieces of steel were rubbed against it, the steel acquired the lodestone's power.

For centuries the practical uses of magnetism extended no further than the compass.

Natural Magnets

Natural magnets, or lodestones, are a kind of iron ore called magnetite (Fe_3O_4). Lodestones are usually irregular in shape; that is, they look like ordinary stones you might pick up anywhere. Like the artificial magnets with which you are probably more familiar, they attract iron. Small pieces of lodestone are inexpensive and are easily obtained from scientific supply companies. Small bits of iron (iron filings) or small carpet tacks will respond to the attraction of these stones. Like other magnets, lodestones have north and south poles (sometimes several sets of these), but it is necessary to do some experimenting to find them.

Artificial Magnets

The common artificial magnets found in schools are generally made in three shapes. Their shapes give them their names: horseshoe, bar, and U magnets. Except for their shapes they are the same, for horseshoe and U magnets are essentially bent bar magnets.

Artificial magnets are usually made of steel. In recent years more powerful magnets made of an alloy of iron, aluminum, nickel, copper, and cobalt, patented under the name Alnico, have found many practical uses. Magnets help close cabinet and refrigerator doors; they help us pick up pins and needles; they hold the lids of cans after the can opener has removed them; they keep papers on bulletin boards; they make cloth potholders stick to the sides of ovens; they hold kitchen knives on the wall; they are found in many toys. In all these gadgets either two magnets attract each other or a magnet attracts iron or steel.

Magnetic Attraction

If a magnet is laid flat in a dish of iron filings or small tacks and then lifted out, masses of filings or tacks cling to the ends of the magnet but very few near the middle. These ends, where the strength appears to be greatest, are called *poles*. All magnets, no matter what their shape, have poles. (In flat magnets, both rectangular and circular, used in many household devices and toys, each of the two flat surfaces is a pole.) Horseshoe and U magnets are given their partic-

Several forms of magnets: horseshoe, bar, natural lodestone, and U. Magnetism has been induced artifically in all but the lodestone.

ular shapes in order that both poles (where the magnetism is strongest) may be used together.

Most commonly we observe that magnets attract objects that contain iron; however, cobalt and nickel also respond well to a magnet's pull. Other substances respond to a magnet's influence, but it requires sensitive instruments to detect this.

Permanent and Temporary Magnets

Common magnets are often called *permanent magnets;* if kept properly they will retain their magnetism for a long time. To increase the life of bar magnets they should be stored in pairs, side by side, north pole next to south pole. Horseshoe and U magnets should have a "keeper," a piece of iron placed across their ends.

Some magnets are temporary in nature. Pick up an iron carpet tack with a magnet. To the end of this tack, bring another tack. You will find that the first tack picks up and holds the second. The second tack will hold a third. The length of the string of tacks you can make in this way will depend on the strength of the magnet, the weight of each tack, and the extent of your patience. If you now remove the magnet from tack number one, the others drop off rather quickly. Each tack was magnetized only temporarily. A steel sewing needle, on the other hand, will retain its magnetism for a much longer time, particularly if it is given its initial magnetism by stroking it with a magnet. Another kind of temporary magnet, and a very important one, is the *electromagnet.* This kind will be considered later in the chapter.

Magnetism Penetrates through Materials

Children soon discover for themselves, if they are allowed to experiment, that magnetism acts through many substances. If a magnet is brought toward tacks covered by a sheet of paper the tacks will cling to the underside of the paper. If tacks are placed in a drinking glass they can be manipulated from the outside by a magnet. Paper, glass, and wood—as well as air, water, copper, and many other substances—are "transparent" to magnetism. On the other hand, a magnet's ability to pick up and hold tacks is reduced if an iron object is interposed between the magnet and the tacks, because the iron retains some of the magnetic influence.

Attraction and Repulsion between Magnets

If a bar magnet or a magnetized steel needle is suspended in a horizontal position by a thread it will come to rest pointing north and south. The end of the magnet that points to the north is called the north pole of the magnet; the end pointing to the south, the south pole. A magnet thus suspended, as indicated previously, is essentially a compass.

If the north pole of another magnet is now brought close to the north pole of the suspended one the latter will swing sharply away. If the north pole is brought close to the *south* pole the attraction will pull the suspended magnet to the other one. In short, *like poles repel and unlike poles attract.* This is known as the *law of magnets.*

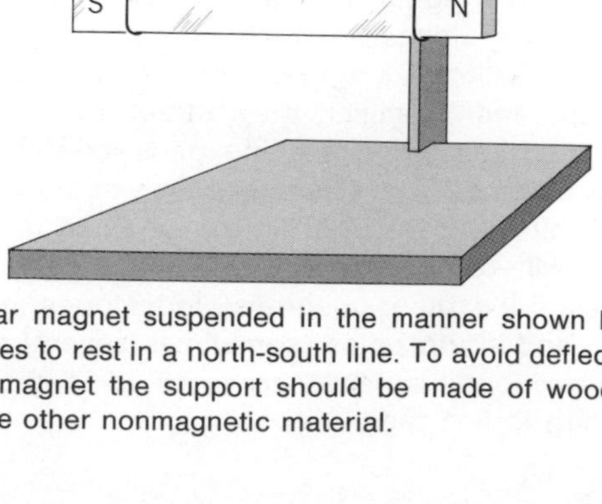

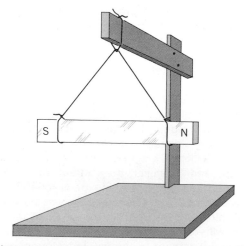

A bar magnet suspended in the manner shown here comes to rest in a north-south line. To avoid deflecting the magnet the support should be made of wood or some other nonmagnetic material.

Magnetic Fields

What is the nature of magnetic attraction? We do not know the full answer to this question, but we can trace the shape and direction and strength of the invisible *magnetic field* that exists around a magnet. This field can be explored with small bits of iron—iron filings. A bar magnet is placed on a table and covered with a sheet of paper. Iron filings are then sprinkled on the paper. A very interesting pattern develops as the iron filings come under the influence of the magnetic field. Each bit becomes a tiny temporary magnet and takes a position following the so-called lines of force that extend from the magnet.

(*See* p. 614.)

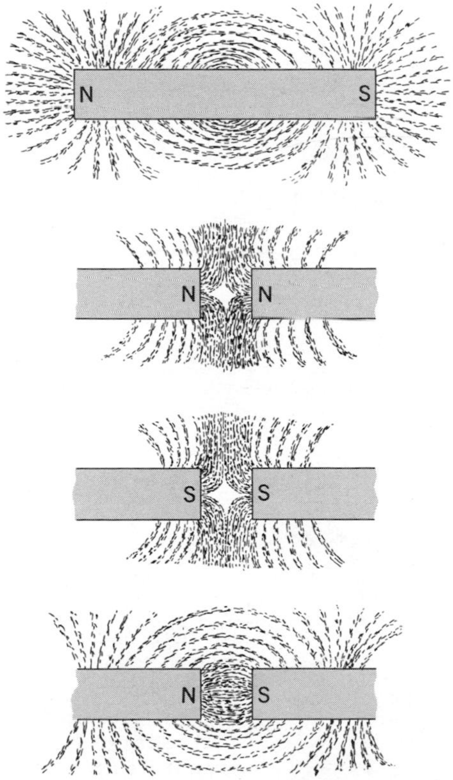

The magnetic field around a magnet can be explored with iron filings. The repulsion between similar magnetic poles and the attraction between opposite poles is revealed by these bits of iron.

Together, the filings form a map of the field. They reveal the presence of the invisible lines of force.

(*See* figure below.)

If like poles of two bar magnets are brought near each other under the paper and sprinkled with iron filings the repulsion of their lines of force is shown. Between two unlike poles the lines of force indicate mutual attraction.

The Earth as a Magnet

Why does a freely swinging magnet point in a north-south direction? The experiments in magnetic attraction and repulsion just described suggest the answer: The earth itself acts like a magnet. The earth's magnetic field exerts an influence on all man's compasses, causing them to line up in the direction of the field—in a generally north-south direction.

(*See* p. 615.)

The idea of the earth as a great magnet seems simple and logical today. Yet for hundreds of years speculation about magnetism had not suggested this notion to anyone. In 1600 William Gilbert, in his book *De Magnete,* proposed the concept of *terrestrial magnetism* to explain the behavior of compasses.

Practical mariners found that the compass needle does not point exactly toward the *geographic* north and south poles that mark the ends of the imaginary axis of the earth. Rather, it is attracted to the *magnetic* pole in each hemisphere. The magnetic pole of the Northern Hemisphere (the North Magnetic Pole) is located above Boothia Peninsula, nearly 1,200 miles from the geographic North Pole. Similarly, the magnetic pole in the Southern Hemisphere (the South Magnetic Pole) is located in Antarctica, some distance from the geographic pole. As a result, compass needles at most points of the earth point somewhat east or west of true north, as shown in the illustration. Navigators of ships and airplanes carry charts showing the angle difference (called *declination*) of a magnetic needle from true north for each point on the earth's globe. These charts are revised every few years, because the earth's magnetic poles shift slowly all the time (*see* figure p. 590).

The Wrong Name

Two facts presented in the preceding material may appear to be contradictory:

Fact 1 Opposite poles of magnets attract each other; like poles repel.
Fact 2 The north pole of a magnet, or compass, is attracted to and points toward the north magnetic pole of the earth.

Indeed, there is a contradiction here made by history not science. It is a contradiction in name only, not in principle. It occurred because the poles of compasses were named before the laws of attraction and repulsion were fully under-

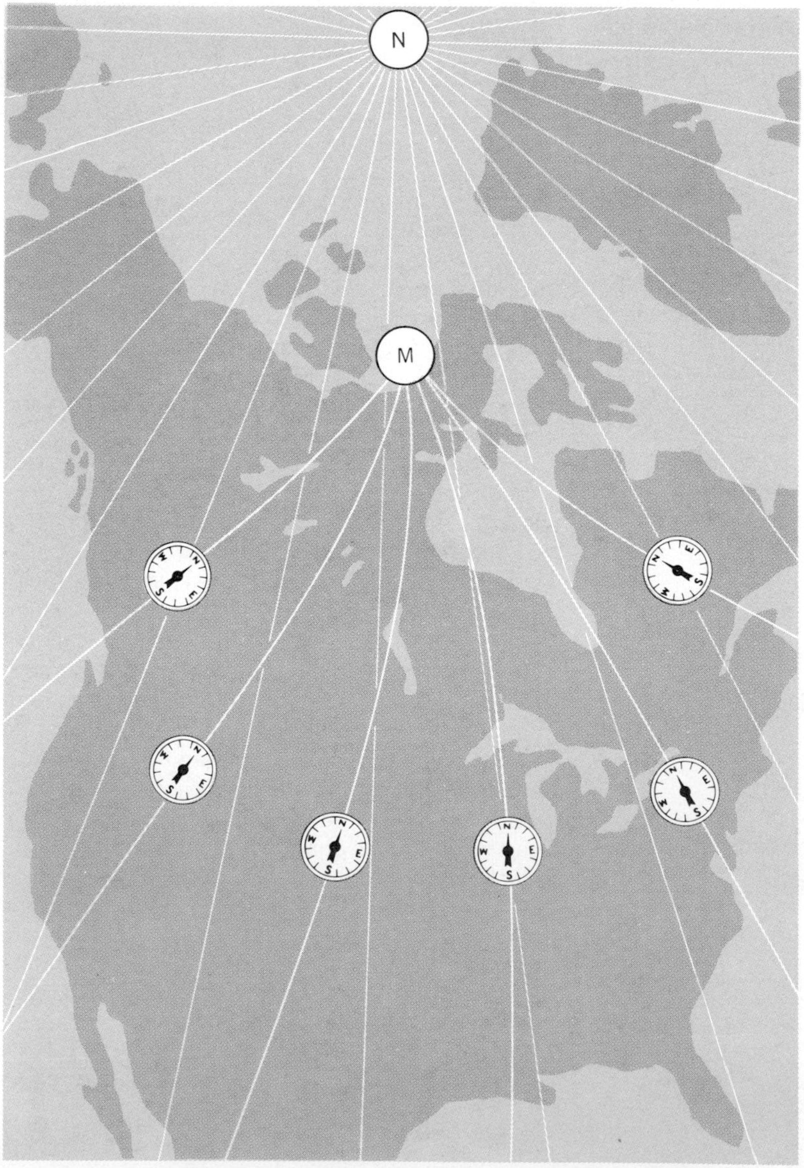

The north magnetic pole (M) is located at a distance from the true North Pole (N). As a result compass needles at most parts of the earth point somewhat east or west of true north. Navigators must compensate for this difference when they use the compass (*see* text p. 589).

stood. If we could alter the course of history we might want to call the end of the magnet that points to the north its south pole, and the one that points to the south its north pole. Then the principle of opposites attracting and the terminology used would agree. To change now, however, might cause endless confusion. Some texts compromise the issue by calling the north pole of the magnet the north-seeking pole and the south pole the south-seeking pole.

THE NATURE OF MAGNETISM

Magnetism, like many other everyday phenomena, presents many perplexing problems to scientists. And, as with many other phenomena, the atomic theory gives a plausible explanation. What, for example, is it that makes a substance magnetic? Scientists offer a tentative answer to this question. They point out that if you break a magnet in half, each half becomes a perfect magnet with new poles forming at the break. If you continue breaking these halves into quarters and so on, each new piece becomes a magnet with a north and south pole. This leads to the theory that magnetism resides in the smallest particles of the magnet, in its atoms. Indeed, there is ample evidence that *each atom of a magnetic substance is a tiny magnet—an atom magnet.*

(*See* pp. 484–5.)

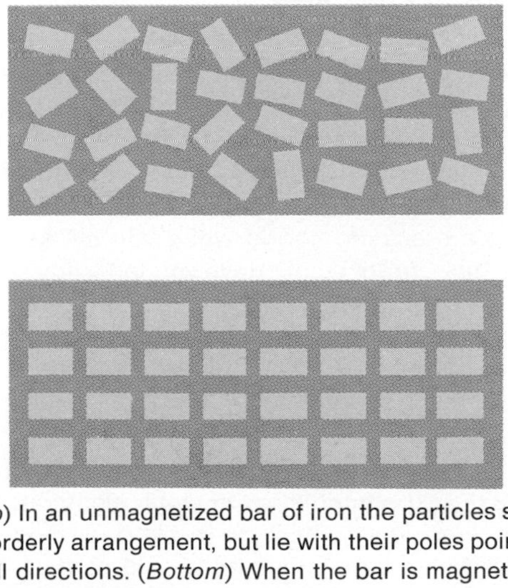

(*Top*) In an unmagnetized bar of iron the particles show no orderly arrangement, but lie with their poles pointing in all directions. (*Bottom*) When the bar is magnetized, the particles are arranged so that all like poles point in the same direction.

If magnetism is a characteristic that resides in atoms what is the difference between an unmagnetized bar of iron and a magnetized one? In an unmagnetized bar the atoms are arranged like a group of children who, after play, have flopped on the ground to rest. They face in all directions. In a magnetized bar the atoms are arranged like children seated in straight rows. In unmagnetized iron the atom magnets neutralize each other; in the magnetized iron the atom magnets add to each other to make the whole bar a magnet. Why does rubbing a steel needle with a magnet cause the needle to be magnetized? Under the close influence of the magnet each of the atom magnets in the steel needle is pulled into line.

Let us apply the atom-magnet theory to other everyday experiences with magnetism:

Why, for example, does frequent dropping (or hammering) of a magnet cause it to lose its magnetism? The answer: Because shaking up the atoms causes them to lose their common orientation and throws them into a random one.

Why does heating a magnet make it lose its magnetism? The answer: Heating makes the magnetic atoms move more vigorously, enough to disrupt their common alignment.

Why does an iron nail become magnetic if a magnet is brought near it without touching it? (This is called *magnetizing by induction.*) The answer: If, for example, the south pole of the magnet is brought near the nail, atoms in the nail are forced to line up according to the law of magnets with their north poles toward the south pole of the magnet—as long as the magnet is near the nail.

How does our theory explain why relatively pure iron (sometimes called soft iron) is a temporary magnet, whereas magnets made of steel do not lose their magnetism readily? The answer: Steel is essentially iron with a small carbon content—usually about 1 percent—and sometimes small amounts of other metals—such as tung-

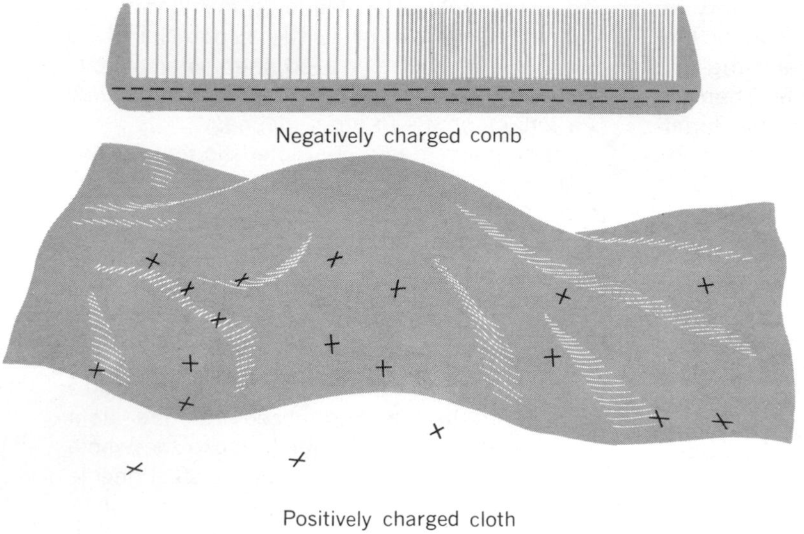

When a comb is rubbed on cloth the cloth loses electrons and the comb gains them. The comb acquires a negative charge of electricity, while the cloth acquires a positive charge.

sten, vanadium and so on—added to give it special physical and chemical properties. The carbon atoms seem to fit into the spaces between the iron atoms and limit their freedom to rotate or move. Thus, magnetizing a piece of soft iron does not require much energy, but once magnetized, the iron atoms can be readily disarranged. On the other hand, steel is more difficult to magnetize, but once the magnetic atoms are aligned, they resist being disarranged because the carbon atoms tucked into the spaces between them do not permit them to move about readily.

You may then ask *why* are some substances, such as those of iron, more easily magnetized than others? The answer is also found in the (*See* Ch. 15A.) atom. As we saw, electrons *revolve* around the nucleus of the atom. It has also been shown that each electron *rotates* on its own axis. (In this dual motion the electrons resemble the planets of the solar system.) The phenomenon of rotation, known as *electron spin,* causes each electron to behave like a small permanent magnet. It has also been found that each electron spins in one of two directions, which we might call clockwise or counterclockwise. In the atoms of most elements there are about as many electrons spinning in one direction as the other; this neutralizes their magnetic effect. In fewer elements—such as iron, nickel, and cobalt—there is a significant surplus of electrons spinning in one direction over that of the opposite. The unbalanced surplus (four in the case of iron) is responsible for the magnetic behavior of the atom as a whole.

STATIC ELECTRICITY

Electricity that accumulates and stays on a substance is customarily called *static electricity.* But we notice static electricity more when it is not static, when it jumps. Have you observed flashes of lightning in a thunderstorm? Have you heard a crackling sound when you stroked the (*See* p. 616.) fur of a cat? Have you felt a tiny shock after scuffing your feet on a rug and then touching a doorknob? In all these phenomena two things happened: (1) *Electricity accumulated,* and (2) *electricity jumped.* But this was not always known.

Thales, a Greek philosopher who lived about 600 B.C., experimented with static electricity. He discovered that when he rubbed a piece of amber with a woolen cloth it would pick up light objects, such as bits of straw, dried leaves, and cork. At the beginning of the seventeenth century William Gilbert, the discoverer of terrestrial

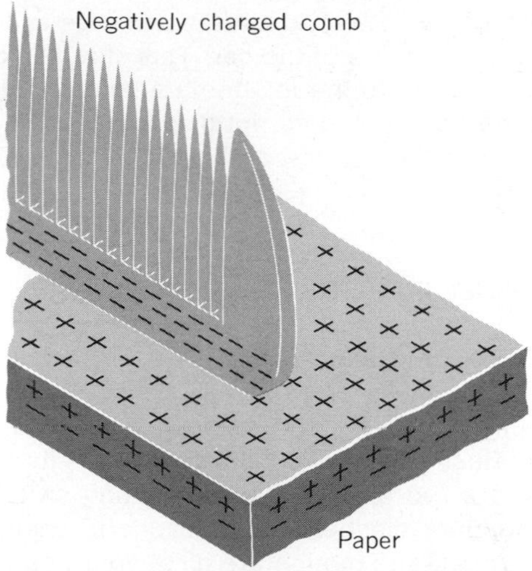

When a negatively charged comb is brought near a neutral piece of paper the electrons on the surface of the paper are repelled, leaving it with a positive charge.

magnetism, repeated some of Thales' experiments. He found that glass and sealing wax, as well as amber, would attract light objects when they were rubbed. Gilbert named this mysterious force electricity, after the word "electron," which means amber in Greek.

You can perform experiments similar to Gilbert's by rubbing a hard-rubber comb briskly on a woolen sweater or coat. Bits of paper will jump up to the comb and cling to it.

The study of static electricity was continued by many other scientists and led to many important discoveries. However, its fundamental cause was not determined until the nature and structure of the atom were known. As we learned in Chapter 15A the atoms of all matter are made of negatively charged electrons whirling around nuclei containing positively charged protons (as well as other particles). You recall that there are an equal number of electrons and protons in each atom; as a result, atoms are ordinarily electrically neutral.

Now consider what happens when a comb is rubbed on a piece of cloth. The rubbing of the two materials causes some electrons to be torn away from the cloth and to adhere to the comb. The atoms making up the comb seem to be "hungrier" for electrons than those of the cloth. They grab some electrons from the cloth. We say that the comb has acquired a *negative charge* of electricity. It now has more electrons than protons.

But what of the cloth? Some of its atoms are left with an electron deficit or, what amounts to the same thing, a proton surplus. We say that the cloth has acquired a *positive charge* of electricity. It now has more protons than electrons.

Electricity, then, is a phenomenon that stems from the electrical particles of which atoms are composed. Fundamentally, *matter itself is electrical.*

When we say that an electron has a negative charge of electricity and a proton a positive charge we are simply saying that there are two kinds of electric charges. We find that electrons repel each other and that protons repel each other, but that electrons and protons are attracted to each other.

Why does the charged comb, with its surplus of electrons, attract bits of paper that are electrically neutral? When the comb is brought *near* the paper two things happen:

1. The electrons in each of the atoms in the paper are repelled to the side away from the comb (because similar charges repel each other).
2. The surface layer near the comb now contains the positive side of the atoms in the paper, which causes it to be attracted to the negatively charged comb.

The comb acquires a negative charge when rubbed on wool. When, however, a glass rod is rubbed on a piece of silk the silken cloth picks up electrons, acquiring a negative charge, and leaves the glass rod with a positive charge.

Have you ever charged your hair by combing it? The comb removed electrons from your hairs and thus left them with a positive charge. Being similarly charged, each strand of hair repels its neighbor, and so the hair tends to stand on end.

Scuffing your shoes on a rug causes you to pick up electrons from it. These accumulate on the surface of your skin. You are a charged body! When you bring your finger to an object, such as a doorknob or a light switch, the electrons jump from you to that object. You are discharged!

Materials, then, become charged by grabbing or shedding electrons. Why not by grabbing or shedding protons? In atoms, as we have seen, electrons move in orbits around the nucleus. They are not held too tightly to the nucleus and may be removed easily, especially the outermost ones. Protons, on the other hand, are held by powerful forces within the nucleus. To move the positively charged protons it would be necessary to move the entire atom along with it. In solids such as the comb, glass, or silk that we have been considering, atoms are held in place and are not easily displaced by rubbing.

Lightning was discussed in Chapter 9A as a weather phenomenon. Further details are in order now, because lightning is a form of static electricity. In a cumulonimbus (thunderstorm) cloud the upper part becomes positively charged, while the lower part becomes negatively charged. As the cloud passes over the land it repels electrons near the ground (recall the comb-paper experiment) and causes the resulting positively charged particles to gather there. A series of streams of negative charged particles called *leaders* lash out from the cloud toward the ground but do not touch it. When a leader finally comes close enough to the ground the positively charged particles there jump the gap and travel upward toward the cloud on the path taken by the leader. This upward jump of charged particles, or *return stroke,* is the main lightning stroke. It may be succeeded by further downward and upward surges in the same path. All of this takes place in less than 1 second.

Lightning, evidently, is a composite affair, involving up and down flow of particles: negative ones toward the earth and positive ones to the cloud. The main flash—the one that is visible and produces the thunder—travels upward. Contrary to popular opinion lightning can strike more than once in the same place. The Empire State Building, the world's tallest building, is struck on the average of 48 times a year.

On highways you may have noticed flexible rods protruding upward from the road adjacent to toll booths. Do you know what they are for? While your car is traveling the rubbing of the wheel against the road causes a charge to build up on the outside of the car. This charge would be transferred to the toll-booth attendant, along with the coin, if it were not disposed of. Waving rods touch the car first and lead the charge into the ground.

CURRENT ELECTRICITY

Electron Traffic

Flick a wall switch—the room is flooded with light. Push the toaster handle down—its coils heat to a red glow. Move the starting switch of the vacuum cleaner—its motor starts spinning. Light, heat, and motion are all at your fingertips through the magic of electric current. You are the engineer. You control the flow of electricity in these and dozens of other devices that serve you daily. More precisely, you are a kind of traffic engineer; when you throw the switch you are completing a pathway over which electrons can flow.

For current electricity, as its name implies, is a flow—a flow of electrons, the particles that are part of the atoms of all matter. All matter contains electrons, so it is not necessary (or possible) to "make" electricity; all that is needed is something to push the electrons along. We shall see later how this is done with batteries and with generators.

The Electric Circuit

In understanding electron traffic it is helpful to know that *current electricity travels in a continuous path*—in an electric circuit. Every time you throw a switch to light a lamp or make a motor turn you are completing an electrical circuit; you are setting in place a bridge for electrons. Every time you snap a switch to "off" you are lifting the bridge out of the circuit.

(*See* pp. 612, 616–9.)

The electric cord that connects your table lamp to the wall socket contains *two* wires to make a circuit possible. At any one moment electrons are flowing into the lamp through one of these wires and out through the other. To complete your "view" of the circuit it would be necessary to go all the way back from the wall socket to the electric generator in the place where you live. When you flick the switch of your lamp you are starting a movement of electrons in a continuous circuit all the way from the generating station to your lamp and back to the generating station.

Highways for Electricity

The electron flow of an electric circuit takes place along a highway made of metal. Strip a (*See* p. 618.) lamp cord of its coverings and you find part of that highway in the twisted strands of copper wire. Examine the inside of an electric bulb and you will see the coiled filament made of the metal tungsten. From the powerhouse to the appliances in your home electrons are moving along metal paths. Materials that permit easy flow of electrons through them are called *conductors.* Silver, copper, gold, iron, nickel, aluminum, platinum, and lead are examples of metals that are good conductors of electricity. Carbon, although not a metal, is also a conductor of electricity.

Most nonmetals are poor conductors of electricity. Rubber is one of the poorest conductors. Cloth, leather, glass, porcelain, and many of the new plastics are poor conductors of electricity. All of these are termed *insulators,* which are used to keep electricity from going where it is *not* wanted. In a lamp circuit the plug is covered with rubber or some other nonmetallic material. The copper wires in the cord are covered with fabric and rubber or a plastic coating.

Electricians use rubber gloves so that they will not be shocked. Telephone and electric wires supported by poles are separated from the wooden crossarms by glass or porcelain insulators. The wood of the poles does not carry electricity when dry, but when wet can conduct electricity quite readily. Wires supported by steel towers require large insulators.

Pure water itself is not a good conductor of electricity, but almost any object becomes a good conductor when wet. Bathrooms become

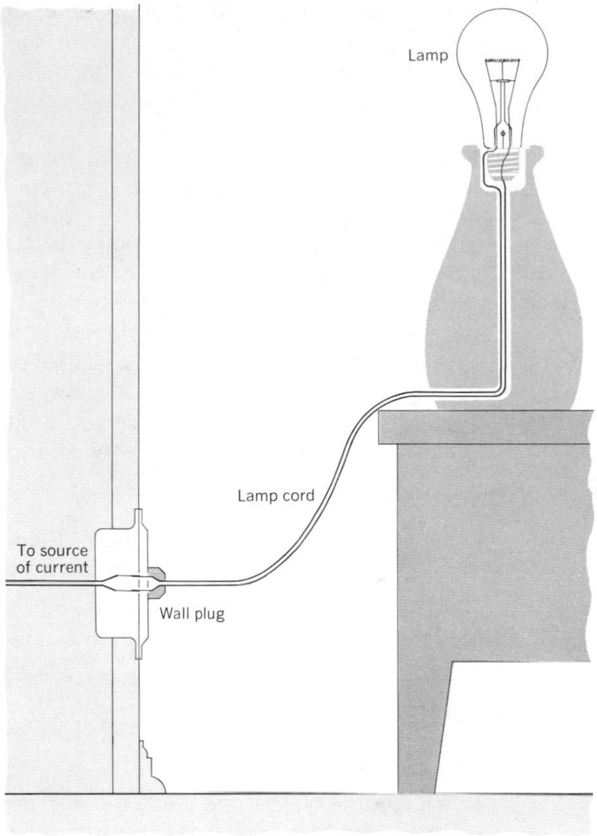

There is a continuous electric circuit between a lamp and the power station when the lamp is on.

electrocution chambers if individuals coming out of a tub or standing on a wet floor touch lamps or plug-in radios with poor insulation.

Resistance on the Electrical Highway

There is considerable difference in the ease with which electrons can travel through various conductors. Another way of putting this is to say that conductors vary in their opposition to the flow of electrons. The property of a substance that limits the flow of electrons through it is called its *resistance.* The resistance of any part of a circuit depends on:

1. *The nature of the material of which it is composed.* Copper offers about one-sixth the resistance that iron does. (Think of auto traffic on a smooth highway in comparison to that on a bumpy country road.)
2. *Its length.* A long wire offers more resistance than a short one. (Think of a long trip versus a short one.)
3. *Its thickness.* A thin wire offers more resistance than a fat one. (Compare a one-lane road with a three-lane highway.)
4. *Its temperature.* For most materials the higher the temperature, the more the resistance. (The automobile-highway analogy, an imperfect one at best, breaks down here, unless you wish to translate high temperature into very strong cross winds.)

As we shall see later in the section "Electricity for Light and Heat," we often deliberately place into the circuit parts that offer high resistance.

MEASURING ELECTRICITY

Certain units have been devised by scientists to measure electricity. We see these marked on many of the electrical appliances we use. Ampere, volt, ohm, watt, watt-hour are some of the common units we encounter.

An *ampere* is a measure of the rate of flow of electrons through a wire. A common 60-watt lamp requires about $\frac{1}{2}$ ampere. An electric flatiron takes about 4 or 5 amperes.

A *volt* can be thought of as a unit of electrical push behind each electron. A new dry cell has a push of about $1\frac{1}{2}$ volts; a storage battery in an auto, 12 volts; house circuits, 110 to 120 volts; long-distance electric wires, 200,000 volts or more.

An *ohm* is a unit of electrical resistance. It measures the resistance offered by any conductor to the flow of electrons. Copper is used in electric circuits because a wire made of this metal offers less resistance to the flow of electrons than a similar wire made of any other metal except silver.

The *watt* is a measure of electric *power,* which in turn is a product of the number of amperes (flow) and the number of volts (push). Thus, a lamp in your 120-volt house circuit through which $\frac{1}{2}$ ampere is flowing has a wattage equal to $\frac{1}{2} \times 120$, or 60 watts. Because the watt is a small unit, the *kilowatt,* equal to 1,000 watts, is often used.

The kilowatt-hour is the unit that measures the amount of electrical *work* done. The power company uses this unit in calculating your bill. Thus, in a 100-watt lamp used for 10 hours the work done is 1,000 watt-hours or 1 kilowatt-hour. If the cost of electricity is 5 cents per kilowatt-hour the cost for this will be 5 cents. Examine an electric bill and you will learn how many kilowatt-hours were used.

The names of all the units given here (and a number of others not mentioned) are derived from the names of scientists who made significant contributions to our understanding of electricity.

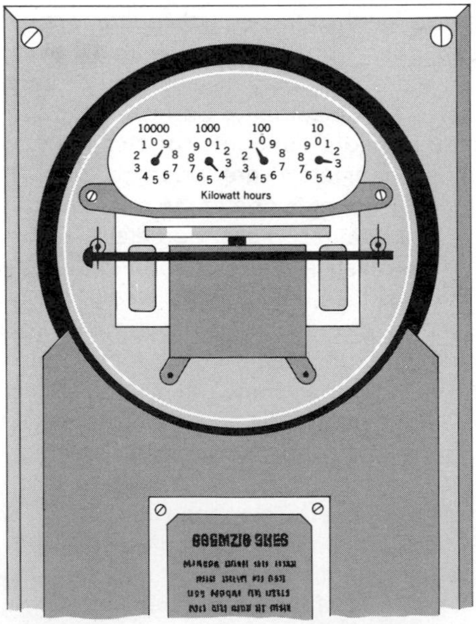

The electric meter, which is located in the basement or in the kitchen or on the outside wall of almost every house, is easy to read. The present reading on this one is 9,413 kilowatt hours. The amount used for any period is computed by subtracting the previous reading from this one.

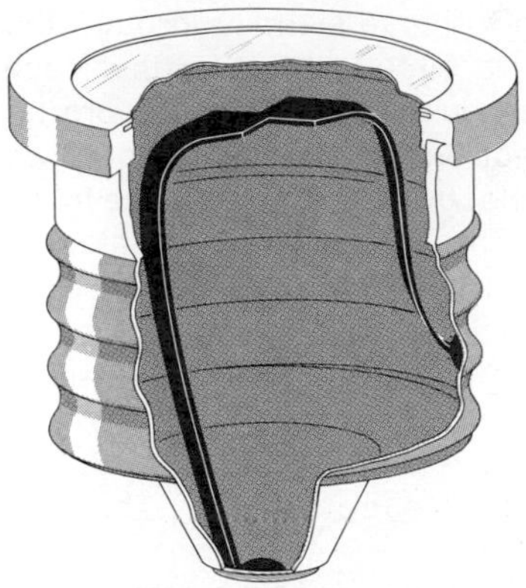

The fuse is the weakest link in the electric circuit. The heart of the fuse is a metal strip with a low melting point, shown here in black.

FUSES—THE WEAKEST LINK

When electrons flow through any conductor they cause the conductor to become heated. The amount of heat produced depends largely on the strength of the current and the resistance offered by the conductor. The heating effect of an electric current is due to the electrons jostling the atoms of the conductor, causing them to vibrate more vigorously. This vibration we have identified as heat.

(*See* pp. 618–9.)

If an electric wire is carrying too much current for its size (thickness) it will heat up considerably. If this happens in the wiring of a building it may set fire to some combustible material near it. To prevent this electric fuses are included in the wiring systems of buildings.

Examine an electric fuse of the screw-socket type. When this fuse is in place in a fuse box electricity flows through it; it is part of the electric circuit. The essential part of the fuse is a flat strip of metal with a low melting point. You can see this strip if you look through the window of the fuse. If you can manage to break the metal seal or the plastic window on a fuse and take it apart you will be able to inspect the fuse metal more carefully. Take it out of the container and apply a lighted match to its midpoint. The strip melts easily and falls apart. This is what is meant by the "blowing" of a fuse. Instead of a match the heat is provided by the surging of too many electrons through the fuse metal. The "blowing" of a fuse, then, is really the heating, melting, and breaking of the fuse metal.

(*See* p. 624.)

Fuses are described as the "weakest link in the electrical chain." They are made that way so that if there is any overloading of the circuit this link will break and thus cut off the flow of electricity. The heating that occurs when a fuse "blows" takes place within the safe confines of the fuse, so no damage is done. Excessive heating along the rest of the line and the danger of fire are averted. The destiny of a fuse is its destruction.

Fuses may "blow" for two reasons: overloading or short-circuiting. An electric iron plugged into a circuit already sustaining an electric broiler causes a large number of electrons to flow into that circuit from the supply that is always available from your electric company. The load may be too great for your electric wires to sustain, but before they can heat up sufficiently to cause damage the low-melting-point fuse metal melts and breaks the circuit. What should you do? The first thing to do is to unplug the appliance you plugged in just before the fuse "blew." Then go to the fuse box, equipped with a new fuse. You will probably see that one of the fuses looks different because of the break in the metal strip inside it. There may also be a deposit of vaporized fuse metal on its window. Unscrew this fuse and screw in the new one.

A short circuit may also cause a fuse to blow. If, for example, you have a long electric cord connecting your table lamp to a wall socket, and this cord is stepped on or frequently bruised by moving furniture over it, the insulation may be worn off at some point. The two bare wires then touch. A tremendous amount of current goes racing around this new and easy path. The electrons begin to heat up the wires in the circuit, but the fuse metal responds immediately by melting and breaking the circuit. What should be done? Again the offending appliance (or extension cord) should be unplugged and a new fuse installed. The worn cord should be replaced; further short circuits should be avoided by having an electrician install sufficient outlets so that long cords become unnecessary. Sometimes "shorts" develop inside electrical appliances. These should be repaired.

Extra fuse plugs should always be kept on hand. Some individuals "bothered" by fuses blowing frequently resort to dangerous alternatives. Instead of looking for the cause of the trouble they replace a burnt-out 15-ampere fuse with a 30-ampere fuse. They are thus substituting a less effective fuse for this particular circuit; the wires in the circuit, which are designed to carry only 15 amperes safely, may overheat dangerously before this fuse melts. These people are forgetting that a fuse is built not for strength but for weakness.

Another practice, even more dangerous, is the replacing of a burnt-out fuse with a penny. The penny, being made of metal, is a good conductor of electricity; in fact, too good. If the line is overloaded, or if there is a short circuit, the electric wiring system of the house is converted into a huge toaster, with the house getting the toasting.

In many homes *circuit breakers* are replacing fuses. As you might suspect from its name, a circuit breaker is a kind of switch. In one common type, an extra surge of electricity causes an electromagnet to attract an iron bar. The bar trips a latch that breaks the circuit. After the source of the trouble is eliminated, the circuit breaker is restored to its original position by hand. In another kind of circuit breaker a bimetallic (two metals) strip breaks the circuit when it is heated by the extra current.

(*See* pp. 600–2.)

GENERATING CURRENT ELECTRICITY

We found earlier in this chapter that we really do not manufacture electricity, that all matter has electrical particles in its atoms. Then why do we use a dry cell to ring a bell or a storage battery to start a car? Why do we plug a lamp into an outlet? Just what are we getting when we pay our electric bills?

Reduced to one word the answer is a push. We pay for the energy that is used to cause electrons to move steadily through the wires of the electric circuit. It is true that each atom in the copper wires of your lamp cord has a great many electrons in it. But it is only when some of these electrons are jarred loose from one atom and hop to the next one that we have an electric current. The process of electron passing may be initiated by the chemical action in a dry cell or battery. It may be the result of electromagnetic action in a generator. We shall study each of these sources presently. Both supply the energy for electron traffic. This is what we pay for.

How fast does electric current travel? Imagine a powerful generator of electricity in Chicago connected in a circuit to an electric lamp in San Francisco, which is about 1,860 miles away. Within $\frac{1}{100}$ second after closing the switch the lamp would flash on, because electricity travels at about the speed of light, which is 186,000 miles per second. However, *a particular electron* in such a circuit would take years to drift along the Chicago-San Francisco wire. To understand this seeming paradox think of a mile-long freight train starting up, with the engine in the rear *pushing* the whole train. Within a few seconds the first car is moving. But it might take 15 minutes for the engine car to cover the mile. This analogy suggests how the electric current can travel rapidly, although the individual electrons move very slowly.

Volta's Discovery

The chemical way of making electricity in cells and batteries is the older of the two methods used in making current electricity. An Italian scientist, Volta, discovered about 150 years ago that a chemical reaction could produce a continuous flow of electricity. He found, when he placed a strip of copper and a strip of zinc in an acid solution, and then connected the dry end of each of these metals with a wire, that electricity began to flow in the wire. He hazarded the brilliant guess that these metals were undergoing a chemical change in the solution, which produced an electrical force. Chemical sources of electricity dominated the field for 100 years

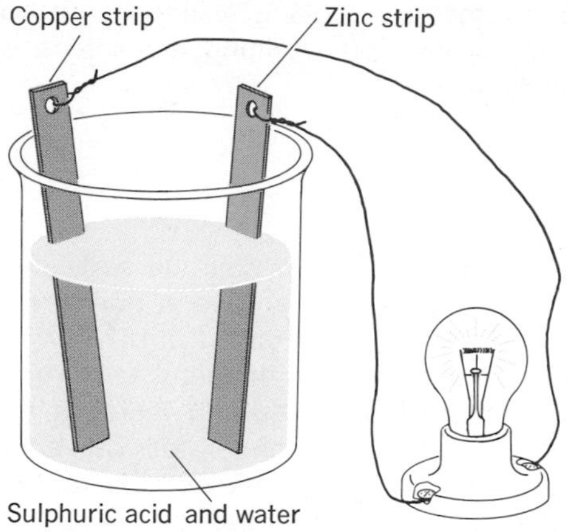

Chemical action in this simple wet cell produces a flow of electricity strong enough to light the small lamp.

after Volta's discovery. Our modern dry cells and batteries are based on Volta's work.

A full understanding of how the cell worked was only possible when the inner structure of the atom was known. We shall not describe the entire process involved, but will summarize the effect of the chemical activity occurring in a zinc-copper cell:

1. Extra electrons pile up on the zinc strip making it rich in electrons, or negative.
2. Electrons are lost from the copper strip making it "electron-hungry," or positive.
3. If a path, such as a wire, is provided outside the cell from the zinc to the copper plate, electrons will travel through the wire from the zinc to the copper.

Thus the chemical action in the cell is a kind of electron pump that produces an electric current.

The demonstration cell just described is called a "wet cell." The common "dry" cells used in flashlights and for portable radios are not really dry, for they would not work if they were. If you compare the dry cell with Volta's cell you will find that it has comparable but not identical parts. Zinc is still one of the metals used; in the dry cell it also serves as the container. Instead of copper a carbon rod is used; it stands vertically in the center of the cell. Instead of sulfuric acid in water a moist chemical paste of ammonium chloride fills most of the cell. As in the wet cell chemical action produces an electrical change. The zinc container accumulates electrons and becomes negative, while the carbon rod becomes positive. In the dry cell shown, two posts on top serve as a convenient place for attaching wires. This dry cell is commonly used to supply current for a bell or buzzer, and also for classroom experiments. It produces $1\frac{1}{2}$ volts, as do the small cells used in flashlights. (The size of the cell does not determine its voltage.) The dry cell is convenient to carry about because it is compact and because there is no liquid to spill.

Storage batteries (a battery contains two or more cells) have found an important use in automobiles. Contrary to popular opinion, storage batteries do not store electricity in the sense that a can stores fruit. When a battery is being charged by the generator of the car the electrical energy going into it produces a *chemical* change. Chemical energy is what is "stored." When the battery is used to turn the starter, operate the lights and heater, spark the gasoline-air mixture, or run the radio, it operates on the same principle as cells described previously. Chemical energy is converted into electrical energy.

The storage battery commonly used in automobiles has six cells arranged in series. Each cell produces 2 volts; the combined voltage is 12 volts.

Storage batteries are often installed in hospitals and other institutions as an auxiliary

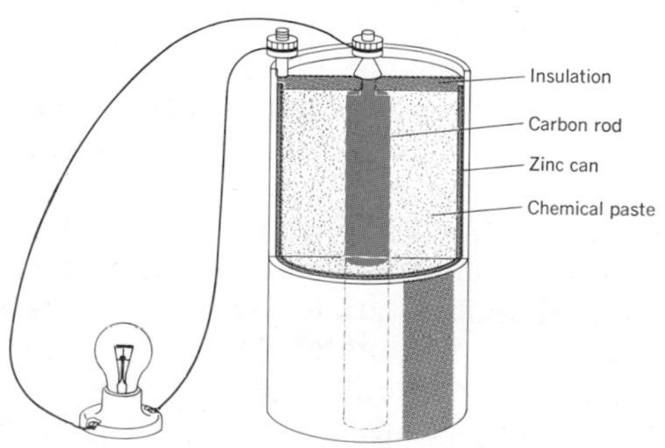

In a "dry" cell chemical changes produce an electrical current.

source of electricity, ready to supplant the regular supply in an emergency. They are also used in lighting buildings in country places not connected by electric lines to a central power station. These batteries are charged by a generator (to be discussed next) driven by a gasoline engine.

Generators

The English scientist, Sir Humphrey Davy, once said: "My greatest discovery was Michael Faraday." Michael Faraday began his scientific career as a bottle washer in Davy's laboratory, but soon took his place in the world of science. In his 50 years of research Faraday performed 16,000 experiments which he faithfully recorded in his scientific notebooks. One, a very simple one, was destined to make possible our modern electrical world, for Faraday discovered a new and simple way of making an electric current without using messy chemicals or clumsy batteries. In 1831 he found that under certain conditions *magnetism could produce electricity.* He discovered that when he moved a magnet near a coil of wire electricity flowed in the wire—although the wire was not connected to a battery. When he thrust the magnet into the coil electricity flowed one way through the wire. When the magnet stopped moving, the electricity stopped. When he pulled the magnet out electricity again flowed in the wire, but in the opposite direction. When he kept moving the magnet in and out a regular, but pulsating, current was produced. Faraday also found that moving the coil back and forth over the magnet had the same effect as moving the magnet in the coil.

Moving a magnet near a coil of wire or a coil near a magnet caused a movement of electrons in the coil. Note that only three things were needed: a magnet, a coil of wire, and motion. In the years that followed Faraday's classic discovery scientists found how to use the rush of falling water and the pressure of steam to provide the motion needed to turn huge coils of wire near huge magnets. Today, from hundreds of stations all over the country, power from water turbines or steam turbines is converted into electricity, which, a split second later, is turning a lathe in a nearby factory, cooking a dinner in a home, pumping water, and running a machine on a far-off farm.

AC and DC

The electron flow in a circuit connected to a dry cell or battery is always in one direction. This kind of current is called *direct current.* A generator can produce this kind too; however, 95 percent of the homes and factories in this country are supplied by generators with alternating current. In this type the electrons flow in one direction, come to a complete halt, and then go in the opposite direction. This change of direction occurs very rapidly, usually 120 times every second (60 cycles are thus completed in 1 second). That is why your electric light does not seem to blink.

Alternating current is preferred over direct current because it can be transmitted more economically from power stations to distant places. Alternating current can also be converted into direct current, where this is required for local use.

THE ELECTROMAGNET

Faraday and the American scientist Henry laid the basis for the making of enormous quan-

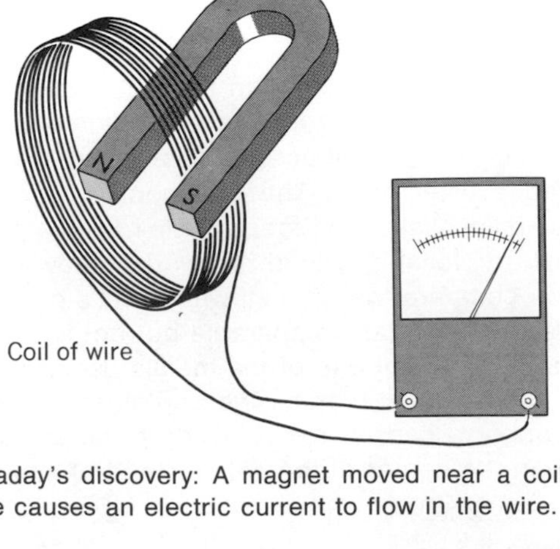

Faraday's discovery: A magnet moved near a coil of wire causes an electric current to flow in the wire.

(*See* pp. 619–21.)

tities of electricity by showing that *magnetism could be converted into electricity.* A few years before this Hans Christian Oersted, a Danish professor of physics, found that *electricity could be converted into magnetism.* While lecturing before a class Oersted accidentally pushed a compass under a wire connected to a battery. He noticed that instead of pointing north the magnet needle swung at right angles to the wire. This happened only when the current was on. Oersted was thus led to suspect that electricity had a magnetic influence, that a wire carrying electricity had a magnetic field around it. Such a wire might be regarded as an "electricity magnet" or, as we call it, an *electromagnet.*

It took another scientist named Sturgeon to show how to take advantage of Oersted's "magnetic" wire. He reasoned that if the magnetic field spread over a long wire could be concentrated, a very powerful magnet could be made. Care had to be taken, however, in the way in which the wire was lumped together. If in two adjacent parts of the wire the current were flow-

Faraday's discovery that magnetism can produce electricity led to the electric generator. In the TVA's Norris Dam the rush of falling water spins turbines which turn huge coils of wire near giant magnets. The powerhouse where this occurs is the rectangular concrete structure at the base of the dam on the right. (*Courtesy of the Tennessee Valley Authority.*)

ing in the opposite direction their fields would be neutralized. The only way in which one could wind a wire and have neighboring parts of the wire carry the current in the same direction would be to wind the wire into a coil or helix. Such a coil is called a *solenoid.*

You can demonstrate the principle of the electromagnet with a piece of insulated bell wire and a dry cell. Twist the wire into a coil by winding it around a cylindrical object, such as a pencil, for 40 or 50 turns. Remove the pencil, scrape both ends of the wire free of insulation and connect them to a dry cell. The coil will then attract and hold small bits of iron (iron filings). It will also cause a compass needle to be deflected from its original position. The coil behaves like a magnet as long as current is flowing through it. To make a much stronger electromagnet, wind the insulated wire around a large iron nail. This electromagnet will pick up heavy objects, such as steel scissors and knives.

The electromagnet has many advantages over permanent magnets. First, it can be made very strong. Its strength can be augmented by increasing the number of turns of wire in the coil or by increasing the amount of current. Perhaps you have seen huge electromagnets attached to cranes in junk yards picking up a load of scrap iron and dropping it into a truck.

A second advantage of the electromagnet is that it is a temporary magnet. That is why, in the lift magnet just described, it can pick up a load of metal and then drop it. When the current is on it is a magnet; when the current is off it is not.

THE TELEGRAPH

The fact that an electromagnet is a temporary magnet is the essential principle underlying the functioning of a telegraph. In 1831 Joseph Henry made an exciting demonstration in his class at Albany Academy. Winding many feet of wire around an iron bar he constructed a powerful electromagnet. He then strung a mile of wire leading from the electromagnet round and round the classroom, finally connecting its ends to a battery. Henry knew of Oersted's experiments. He knew that he could make an electromagnet acquire and then lose magnetism simply by completing and breaking the circuit. He reasoned that the switch with which he could do this might be a few feet, a few yards, perhaps a mile away from the electromagnet—if enough wire were provided.

(*See* pp. 621–2.)

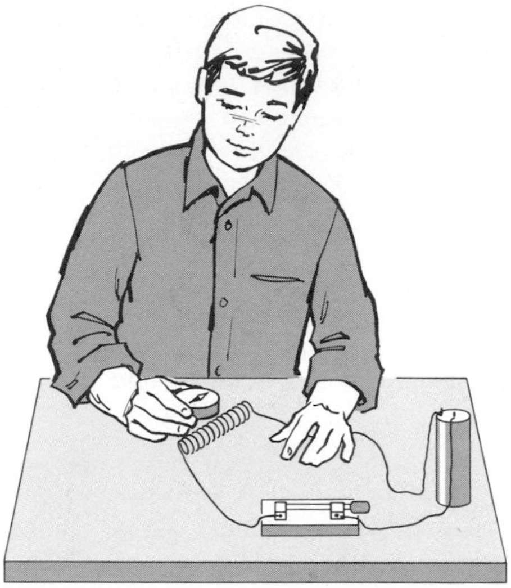

Oersted's discovery: An electric current flowing through a wire makes that wire behave like a magnet.

Near the electromagnet Henry placed a steel bar mounted on a pivot in such a way that when it moved, it would strike a bell. The students were thrilled when he threw the switch completing the mile-long circuit. The steel bar, now attracted by the electromagnet, swung around and struck the bell. The students sensed that a kind of message had been sent almost instantaneously over a 1-mile course.

Henry did not capitalize on his invention, but Morse did. Morse, an American painter, was intrigued with Henry's electromagnet, and he was determined to make it into a practicable telegraph. A person sending a message at one end of the line, he thought, could complete the circuit with a switch. A person at the other end, perhaps many miles away, would find that an electromagnet connected to this circuit was attracting an iron bar. When the sender broke the circuit the iron bar would no longer be attracted, and would, if connected to a spring, return to its original position. A quick on-off movement of the sending switch would make a quick click-clack of the receiving electromagnet and bar, a "dot." A slow on-off switch action would make a slow click-clack in the receiver, a "dash." A code of letters based on dots and dashes would make it possible to send messages instantaneously to individuals miles away.

With the help of other inventors Morse succeeded in making a practicable telegraph. In 1844 the famous message: "What hath God wrought!" flashed over the wires from Washington, D.C., to Baltimore.

The telegraph, like most inventions, represented the work of many men. Behind Morse stood a galaxy of scientists of whom a few are listed here.

Henry, whose work in 1831 we have just described.

Sturgeon, who in 1823 wound a single layer of wire on an iron core, thereby making the first electromagnet.

Oersted, who in 1819, as we have seen, discovered that an electric current had a magnetic effect.

Volta, who in 1800 established that the moist contact of dissimilar metals produced the electric current, and developed a reliable source of electricity in the battery that he invented.

Galvani, who in 1791 identified the circumstances leading to the production of current electricity when he found that two unlike metals applied to a frog's muscle made it twitch.

THE TELEPHONE

In the telegraph a spurt of electricity causes an electromagnet to attract an iron bar and make a click. In the telephone a spurt of electricity causes an electromagnet to attract an iron disc, which then emits speech. How is this accomplished?

The telephone is the product of two branches of science: sound and electricity. Sound will be considered in detail in Chapter 20A. For the moment it will help to know that

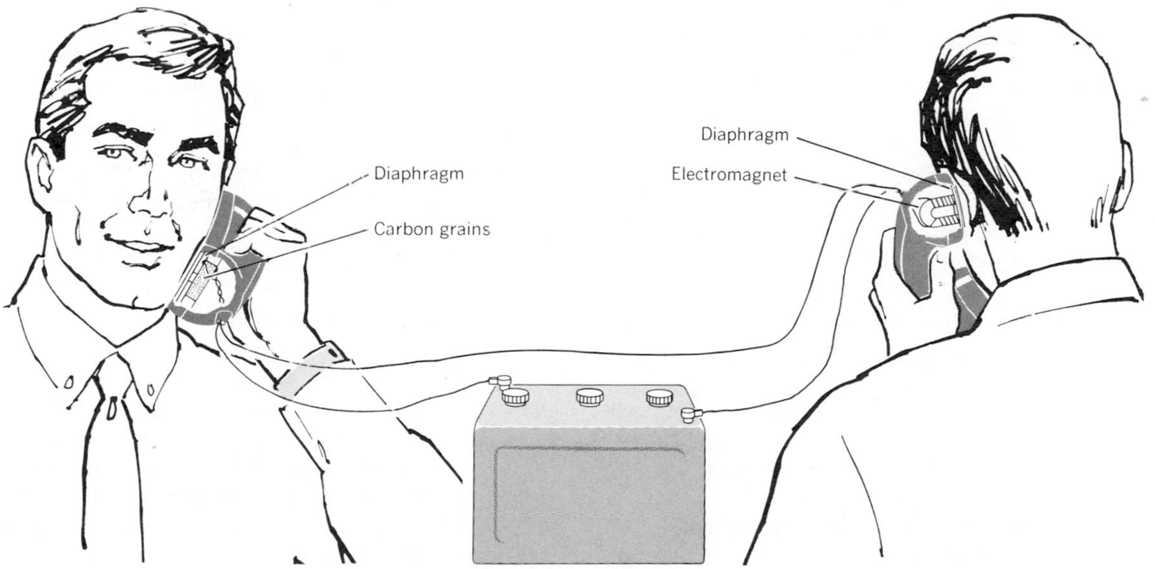

When you speak into the mouthpiece of a telephone you make the diaphragm there vibrate. This affects the electric current, which in turn causes the diaphragm in the receiver to vibrate and to duplicate the original sound (*see* text for details).

anything that makes sound—a drum, for example—does so by shaking rapidly, by vibrating. This vibration is transferred to the air and thence to our eardrums.

The telephone, invented in 1876 by Alexander Graham Bell, consists of two parts, a transmitter and a receiver. The transmitter into which you talk is part of an electric circuit that extends all the way to the receiver of the person at the other end of the line. The telephone exchange, besides connecting you to the person you are calling, provides the electricity needed for the circuit.

Inside the transmitter there is a little box filled with thousands of grains of black carbon. These grains are part of the electrical circuit: Electrons have to flow through them to complete the connection. When you speak, the vibration produced by your vocal cords causes the sides of the carbon box to move in and out. Each time the sides move in the carbon grains are squeezed together. Each time the sides move out the grains spread farther apart. This squeezing and unsqueezing does something to the flow of electricity (*see* figure p. 603).

When the carbon particles are squeezed together they are in close contact, making a broad, solid path for electricity. Electricity flows easily through them. When the pressure is released, the carbon particles spring apart and touch each other more lightly. Now the electrical path is thin and broken—resistance is increased—and the electricity flows weakly.

The effect of speaking, then, is to cause electricity to travel in irregular "spurts," now strongly, now weakly, through the circuit that connects the speaker to the listener. Note that the *sound vibration does not travel through the wires.* Instead, it causes electrons to move in varying amounts, instead of their usual steady stream. The sound vibration has been converted into a kind of fluctuating electrical impulse that is transmitted with lightning speed from speaker to listener.

The telephone receiver converts the electrical impulses back into sound vibrations. The essential parts of the receiver are an electromagnet and an iron disc. Let us see what the effect of a current varying in strength has on these essential parts. A strong flow of electricity makes the electromagnet stronger. It pulls harder on the disc. When the flow is weaker the disc moves back. In this way the fluctuating electrical circuit causes the disc, or *diaphragm,* to vibrate. The vibrating disc causes the air nearby to vibrate. The air vibrations strike the eardrum of the listener, and he hears a sound that is a duplication of the speaker's voice.

To summarize:

1. Sound vibrations cause fluctuations in an electric circuit in the transmitter of the telephone.
2. The fluctuating electrical impulses are transmitted along the line to the receiver.
3. In the receiver the electrical impulses, acting on an electromagnet, set the diaphragm in motion in a sequence of vibrations similar to those made on the diaphragm of the transmitter.

THE ELECTRIC MOTOR

In the telegraph and telephone an electromagnet attracts a piece of iron. In a motor there are two electromagnets, one of which drives the other.

We learned previously that an electromagnet has two distinct advantages over a permanent magnet:

1. It can be made very strong.
2. Its magnetism can be turned on and off.

To these we should now add a third virtue:

3. Its poles can be reversed.

You recall that a permanent magnet has a definite north and south pole. An electromagnet does, too, but the location of its poles depends on the direction in which the current is flowing. When the direction of the current is reversed (as it is when the connections of its wires to a dry cell are switched) the position of its poles is reversed: north to south and south to north.

You can detect the poles of an electromagnet by using an ordinary compass as the

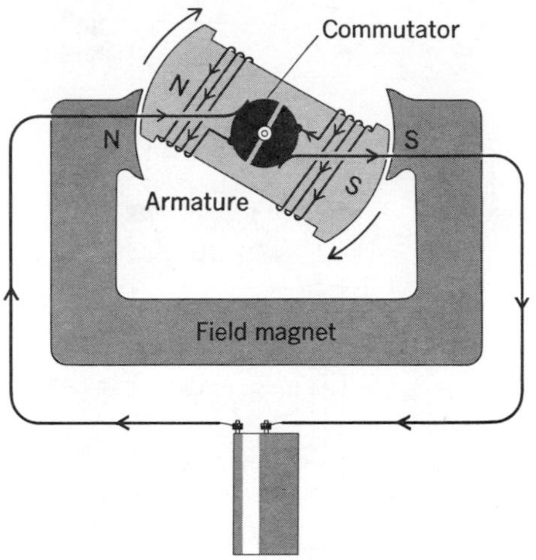

In a motor the poles of the field magnet attract the opposite poles of the armature, causing it to turn. The small arrows show the electron path.

"detector." Make an electromagnet by winding about two dozen turns of insulated bell wire in one direction around a large nail. Connect the ends of the wire to a dry cell. Bring a compass near one end of the electromagnet. Whatever the previous position of the needle it now points directly at the end of the electromagnet. Let us assume that the north end of the compass needle points toward the electromagnet. Then that end is the *south pole* of the electromagnet. Now move the compass to the other end of the electromagnet. The needle now swings around so that its south end points at the electromagnet. This identifies the *north pole* of the electromagnet. Disconnect the dry cell and reverse the wire connections. You will find, on testing with the compass, that the poles of the electromagnet have also been reversed.

One of the electromagnets in a motor is fixed in position. It is attached to the outer frame of the motor and is known as the *field magnet.* The other electromagnet is on the rotating shaft of the motor and is known as the *armature.* When the motor is plugged in current is furnished to the field magnets, producing north and south poles in them. Current is also furnished to the armature magnet, giving it north and south poles, too. The opposite poles of two electromagnets, like those of permanent magnets, attract each other. The armature magnet, being free to move, turns so that its north pole nears the south pole of the field magnet and its south pole nears the north pole. If nothing else happened, the motor would come to a complete standstill. However, just before the unlike poles reach each other the direction of the current is reversed in the armature electromagnet, thus reversing the position of its poles. North is now near north, south near south. These repel each other, so the motor keeps turning.

Just how is the direction of the current reversed in the armature? Recall the experiment with the electromagnet which demonstrated that switching the connections to the dry cell also reversed the poles of the electromagnet. In a motor the switching of connections is performed very smoothly with a device called a *commutator,* which is rigidly fixed to the armature and rotates with it.

Inspect the diagram to see how the commutator works. At the moment depicted, electrons are flowing from the outside (left) post of the dry cell to one side of the commutator, which is shown as a black circle in the center of the armature. Thence the electrons flow through the coiled wire of the armature back to the other half of the commutator, and then back to the dry cell. What do you think will happen when the armature makes a half turn? Do you see that the ends of the wires (actually the *brushes*) will touch opposite sides of the commutator? As a result the electrons will now flow in the opposite direction through the armature coil. When this occurs, the magnetic poles are also reversed: North becomes south and south becomes north.

The commutator, then, is the device that makes it possible to reverse the direction of the current and consequently the poles of the armature. The commutator, which is actually a split metal ring, acts as a switch to halt the flow of electrons in one direction and start them in the opposite direction at just the right instant.

The electric motor is the reverse of the electric generator. In the generator motion produces electricity; in the motor electricity produces motion.

ELECTRICITY FOR HEAT AND LIGHT

Two significant changes occur when electricity flows through a wire:

1. A magnetic field appears around the wire.
2. The wire becomes warm.

We have already discussed the first of these two effects. Let us now turn our attention to the heating effect of an electric current.

Many household appliances—such as electric toasters, percolators, irons, ranges, and heaters—change electrical energy into heat energy. Some of the energy of the moving electrons is turned into heat as the electrons are forced to move against the resistance offered by the wires of the appliance. This resistance is increased by making the wires thin or by using wires of some highly resistant material such as iron or nichrome (an alloy of nickel, chromium, and steel).

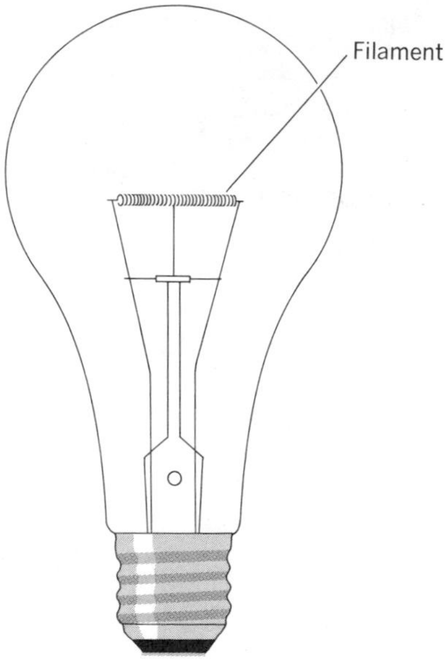

The electric bulb uses a very thin filament, which, because of its high resistance, becomes hot enough to glow brilliantly.

The common electric bulb uses a very thin filament, which because of its high resistance becomes hot enough to glow brilliantly, but, because it has a high melting point, does not melt.

The phenomenon of glowing when hot is called *incandescence.* Edison began his experiments leading to the invention of the electric lamp in 1877. Many scientists prior to this date had searched for a practical way of using electrical energy to produce light. It remained for Edison to show that a successful incandescent lamp has to have a hairlike filament to provide the necessary high resistance. The filament was enclosed in a sealed space devoid of oxygen so that it would not burn up. This was achieved by removing the air from the bulb and sealing it, thus creating a vacuum.

The first filament was a charred or carbonized piece of cotton thread. Later, after a long search, certain kinds of bamboo fibers, when charred, were found to produce a stronger filament. Carbon filaments were used in lamps for about 25 years. Eventually they were replaced by the more economical tungsten filament, which not only uses less electricity but also can be heated to higher temperatures without melting, thus yielding a whiter light. Another change, one that increased the life of bulbs, was the filling of the lamp with inactive gases, such as argon, that do not support burning. In these new lamps the evaporation of the filament was reduced; consequently, the lamps lasted longer.

The following generalizations are some of the more significant ones in the foregoing material:

Objects made of iron (and several other metals) are attracted by magnets.

When freely suspended, a magnet aligns itself in a north-south position. It becomes a compass.

Magnets are strongest at their poles.

Like poles of magnets repel, unlike poles attract each other.

The earth acts like a magnet.

The magnetism of a substance is due essentially to the magnetic properties of its atoms and to the arrangement of its atoms.

The magnetic behavior of an atom depends on the spin of its electrons.

A steel needle or rod can be magnetized by stroking it with a magnet.

Electricity stems from the electron and proton makeup of atoms.

Matter is essentially electrical in nature.

When two different surfaces are rubbed together and then separated, electrons may be torn away from one and deposited on the other. Both surfaces acquire a charge of static electricity.

The object that loses electrons acquires a positive charge; the one that gains electrons, a negative charge.

Like electrical charges repel; unlike electrical charges attract.

Lightning is an abrupt discharge of electricity through the air.

Current electricity is the flow of electrons in a circuit.

Electricity travels at about the speed of light.

A fuse is the weakest link in the electric circuit.

In cells and batteries chemical action starts electrons moving in one direction to make a current.

Moving a coil of wire near a magnet or a magnet near a coil of wire causes electrons to flow in the coil. This is the principle of the generator.

When electricity flows through a wire the wire becomes a magnet. This is the principle of the electromagnet, which is fundamental in the electric motor, the telegraph, the telephone, and many other devices.

Electrical energy can be converted into other forms of energy—into heat, light, sound, and mechanical energy.

Discovering for Yourself

1. Read an electric meter and explain how you did it.
2. Survey your environment to find unusual uses for permanent magnets.
3. Examine different kinds of worn-out electrical appliances. Write a list of the science principles that were used in constructing the appliances to make them efficient and useful.
4. Make a list of places in a house where accidents with electricity might occur, and suggest precautions that should be taken.
5. Find examples of static electricity in your environment. Keep a list of the places where you observed the phenomena and explain what conditions caused the charge to be generated.
6. Find out how tall buildings in your community are protected against lightning.
7. Locate the storage battery in a car. Find out its voltage, and why frequent addition of water is necessary. Find out what uses are made of the electricity that is generated.
8. Make a survey of electrical appliances in a house. Find out which ones use an electric motor, which use wires of high resistance.
9. Objects containing iron—such as radiators, railings, and others—often acquire magnetism from the earth's magnetic field. Use a compass to determine the north and south poles of these objects.
10. Saran Wrap is very good for demonstrating static electricity. Crease a piece 2

inches by 10 inches over a pencil, so that it forms an inverted V. Place your hand between the two "wings" thus formed. What happens? Why? Try placing various objects between the "wings" such as a pen rubbed on cloth, a piece of glass rubbed on silk, and so on. Are the wings attracted or repelled?

11. Buy a disassembled electric motor kit. Assemble the motor and explain how it works.
12. Take a flashlight apart and see if you can explain how it works. What is the path of the current? How does the switch make and break the circuit? Take out one of the dry cells and unscrew the bulb. Can you make the bulb light by using the cell? Look at the bulb with a magnifying glass. What is the path of electricity through the bulb?
13. "All matter is essentially electrical in nature." Find evidence for this statement in readings and in your environment.

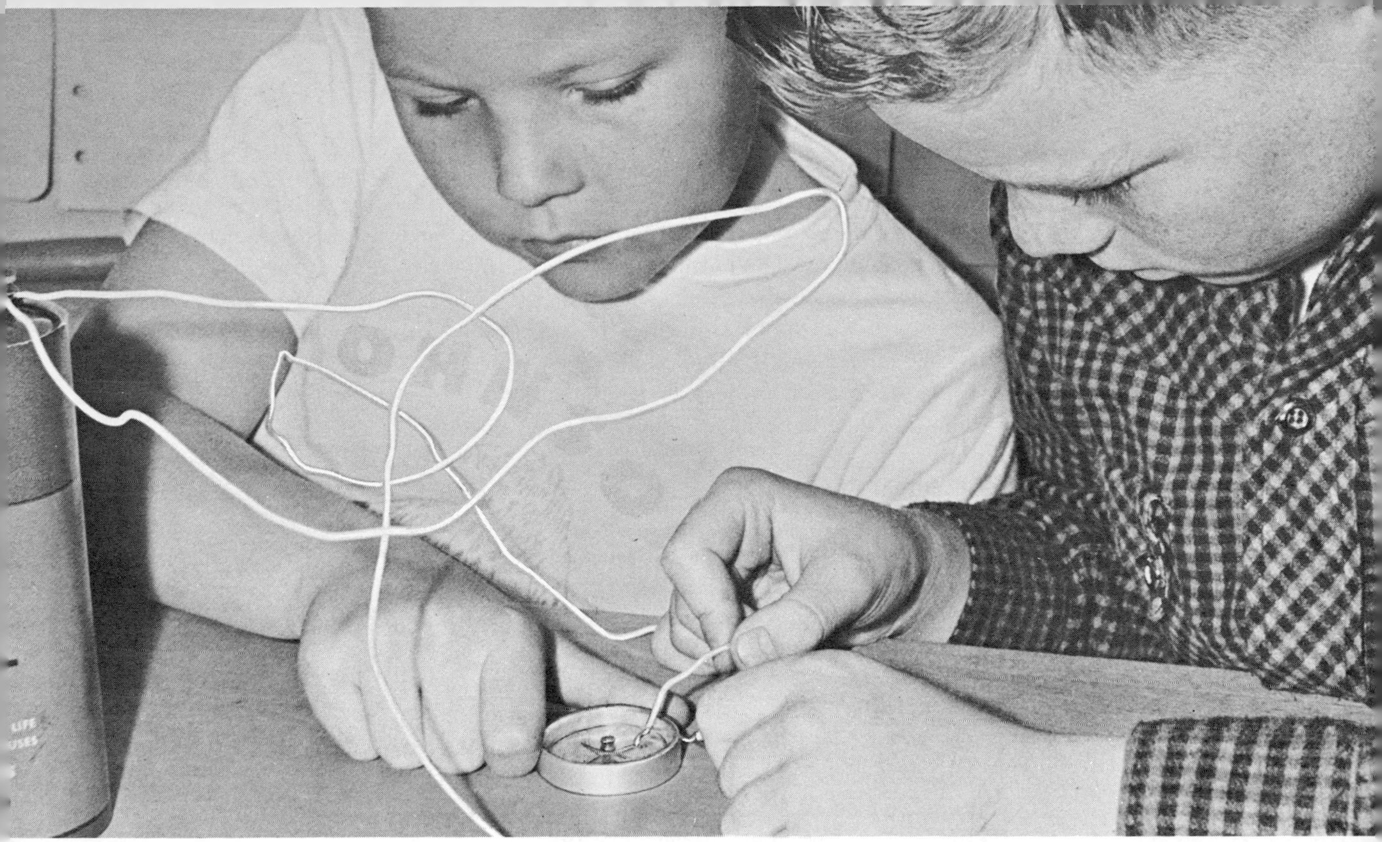

(Courtesy of Johnson Elementary School, Oklahoma City, Oklahoma.)

CHAPTER 19B TEACHING "MAGNETISM AND ELECTRICITY"

As in Chapter 18 the investigations here lend themselves to developing the concept of interaction. In the case of the magnet and paper clips the objects interact by moving together. Two magnets held with similar poles near each other interact by moving away from each other. The battery and bulb in an electric circuit interact: The bulb lights up; the battery expends electrical energy.

There are many opportunities for individual and small-group explorations—for observations, for formulating hypotheses and for testing them. There are unexpected occurrences—a magnet has lost its magnetism, a dry cell is "dead," a bulb is burned out, a compass needle behaves strangely, a connection is not tight. These are all opportunities for children to do some "real" investigation.

The natural tendency that children have to explore and manipulate comes into play; through a wide variety of activities and observations children raise very sensible and searching questions about magnetism and electricity, and can plan ways to answer them—a most desirable situation.

Note that you cannot get a shock from a dry cell. Their wires sometimes become heated, but there is no other danger.

SOME BROAD CONCEPTS: "Magnetism and Electricity"

Materials made of iron and a few other metals will be attracted by magnets.

Unlike poles of magnets attract, like poles repel.

A freely suspended bar magnet acts like a compass.

A steel needle can be magnetized by stroking it with a magnet.

An electric current will flow only through a closed circuit.

An electric circuit commonly consists of a source of electron "push," a conductor, and an appliance that uses the current.

Electrical energy may be transformed into other energy forms.

Electric current is controlled by switches, fuses, and insulating materials.

FOR YOUNGER CHILDREN

What Can a Magnet Do?[1]

Free play with magnets results in questions, some information, some speculation, some discussion, and some misinformation. In many classes children bring magnets of assorted shapes and sizes from home to add to the school supply. The more opportunity children have to work individually and independently with magnets and materials the better. Supply a box of assorted heavy and light things—some iron, some other metals, chalk, rubber, pieces of cardboard, wood, cloth, glass that children can test to see if magnetism will travel through them.

Provide an opportunity for children to discuss and report their observations. A list of these may be made. List correct as well as incorrect observations and then plan

[1] Refer to the lesson plan on magnets in Chapter 5.

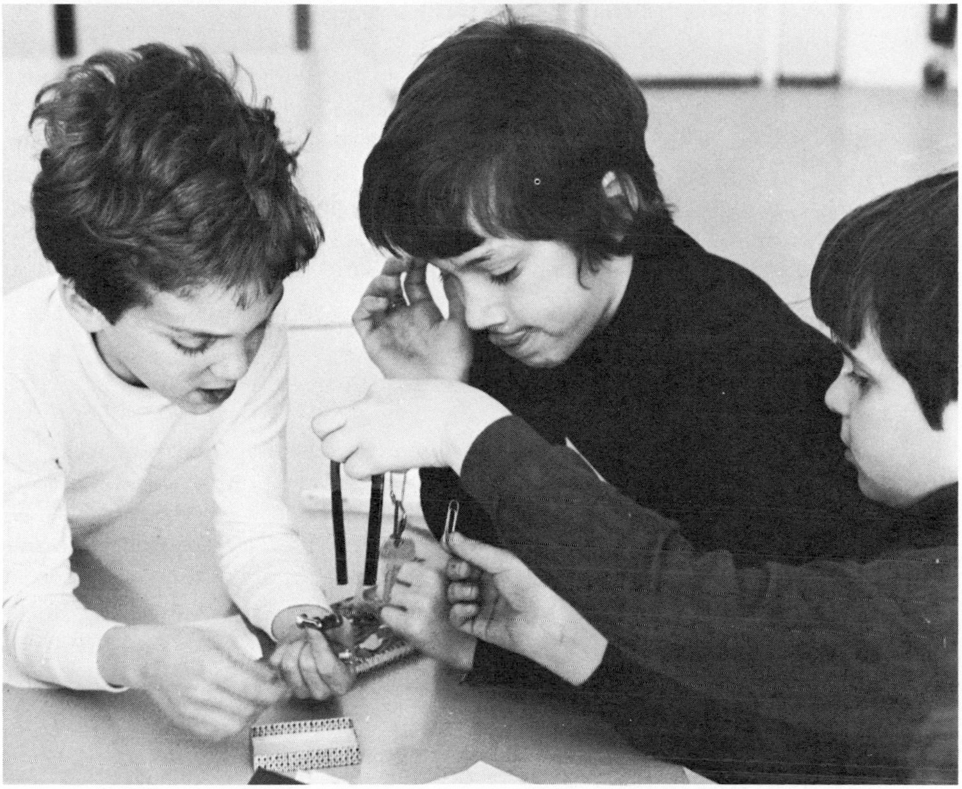

An opportunity to check your best guess. It will? It won't? From such experiences arise many other questions about the nature of magnets and magnetism. (*Courtesy of Phyllis Marcuccio.*)

ways of testing with the children. Children will, as a result of these and other related activities, be able to state and demonstrate such ideas as: Magnets attract some things and not others. Some magnets are stronger than others. Magnets are stronger at the ends. Magnetism can travel through some materials.

How Strong Is Your Magnet?

Testing to find out who has the strongest magnet helps children to become more exact in their observations and reporting. Supply each child or each small group of children with a magnet. How can we be sure whose magnet is strongest? Children may suggest using paper clips or some other iron objects as units of measure. Many children think that the largest magnets are strongest. Test this idea. They will soon discover that the ends are strongest. Children who have horseshoe magnets may demonstrate that when both poles are near each other the results are different than when they are at opposite ends, as in the case of bar magnets.

How Do Magnets Affect Other Magnets?

As children manipulate magnets they are almost sure to demonstrate that sometimes the poles of magnets pull each other, sometimes they push each other away. Cylindrical magnets demonstrate this idea graphically: One rolls the other when like poles are adjacent. Various toys are designed to make use of this law of magnets. Children discover that one magnet can push another. They may measure the distances through which the magnetism of various magnets operate by approaching a paperclip slowly with a magnet and then measuring the distance the clip "leaps" with a ruler.

What Does Electricity Do?

Encourage children to observe various things that electricity does over a period of several days at home, on the streets, in stores, at school, and elsewhere. Make a list of these things and use the list to develop vocabulary, as well as to help children develop an appreciation for the many uses of electricity. Encourage children to examine the list to see if they can work out a classification. There are several possibilities. A meaningful one is: (1.) Uses that give heat; (2.) those that give light; (3) those that make something move. The children may search in magazines and elsewhere for pictures that illustrate the list, and perhaps prepare charts according to their classification.

How Can We Connect a Dry Cell to a Bulb to Make It Light?

See the discussion suggested for older children later in this chapter and adapt it for use with younger children. Present them with a bulb, a dry cell, and some wires, and let them try individually or in small groups to light the bulb. A project of installing a small light in a playhouse in the classroom is an interesting motivation. As a result of having learned to light the bulb in the small circuit, pupils may be able to use what they have learned to make the more extensive installation, perhaps with the help of older children and the teacher.

Other Problems for Younger Children

1. How do we use magnets at home?
2. What is a natural magnet like?
3. How do magnetic games work?
4. What toys use electricity? What does the electricity do?
5. How can we make electricity by rubbing?
6. Where does our electricity come from?

FOR OLDER CHILDREN[2]

What Can We Discover by Experimenting with Permanent Magnets?

Pupils should be encouraged to manipulate magnets and make their own observations. Class experience with magnets may begin by letting pupils show the class any observations they have made. They should be encouraged to comment on their observations, to compare their experiences, and to raise questions. Encourage pupils to devise their own experiments and experiences to try to solve the problems; to propose hypotheses that they can try to test; to be as exact as possible; to formulate tentative answers; and to use several sizes, shapes, and kinds of magnets.

[2] *Investigating Magnetism and Electricity. Level 6* (Towson, Md.: Board of Education, Baltimore County, 1972). Detailed experiments, experiences, and specific suggestions for teaching.

Individual investigations with a sharing period provide opportunities for communicating and checking ideas. New problems are raised and new methods of investigating are devised. (*Courtesy of Phyllis Marcuccio.*)

What kind of things will a magnet attract?

How can we find out if some magnets are stronger than others? (By seeing how many paper clips the magnet can hold and by determining the number of pieces of paper through which the magnets can hold a paper clip.)

How can we tell where the strongest parts of the magnets are? (By observing how many paper clips or other iron objects are attracted at various places on a magnet.)

Through what kinds of things will magnetism travel?

(*See* p. 615.)

How can we make a steel needle into a magnet?

How can we make a simple compass with a bar magnet?

How can we tell whether a lodestone has poles? (Use a compass.)

How do the poles of magnets act toward each other?

These problems and others children may pose provide opportunities for children to work as individuals or in small groups, and for sharing their observations and findings. If possible, the activities should be unhurried and thus provide opportunities for children to progress at their own rates of speed. They should be encouraged to predict what may happen under different circumstances and to test these predictions.

Guide children not to generalize from one instance. For example, an experience with the use of *one* pin or nail is not sufficient evidence from which to conclude that "magnets attract all nails and pins." Children can discover that it is the material that an object is made of that is important, not the name of the object itself. Lifting a tin can with a magnet is no basis for saying that magnets attract tin. They do not, you know. Tin cans are made of steel and are merely covered with a very thin coating of tin; the magnetism travels *through* the tin and attracts the steel inside it, just as it travels *through* paper and attracts iron filings or tacks placed on it.

How Can We "See" Magnetism?

After children have experienced the push and pull of magnets under various circumstances they are curious about this invisible force. "Can you see it?" "Can you feel it?" Some children have seen "pictures" of magnetic fields like those on page 589. If possible, give each child or each small group of children a magnet, a small shaker of iron filings, and a piece of cardboard. Have them shake the filings onto the cardboard which is resting on a magnet. Let them compare their results. What can you discover by examining the results? (The force gets weaker as the distance from the magnet increases. Shows in what directions the force extends, and so on.)

(**Note:** *Children should be cautioned against rubbing their eyes when handling iron filings.*)

The activity is more meaningful when children understand that this is a way of "seeing" the invisible force of magnetism and not just a new way to play with a magnet. In effect the filings form a map of the invisible field of force surrounding the magnet. A piece of glass can be substituted for the paper.

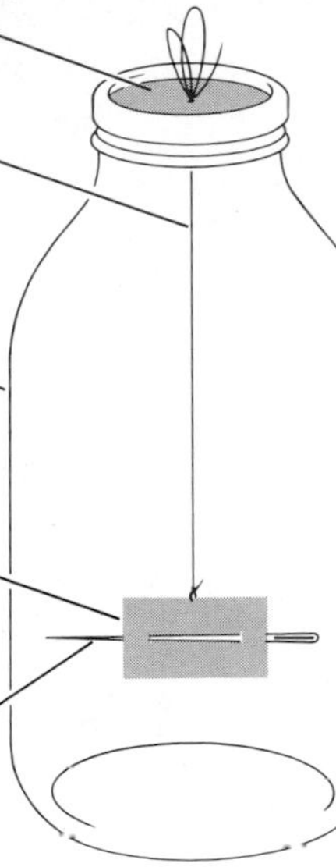

If a milk bottle is not available a jar may be substituted in making this simple compass. Two needles, magnetized in the same direction, may be used to make the compass work more effectively. Pupils should be encouraged to "invent" other variations.

How Can We Make and Use a Compass?

Give several bar magnets, some string, and some wooden supports to individuals or small groups of children, and suggest that they try to use the materials to find out which way is north. They will compare results and try to account for what happens. Refer to the lesson plan in Chapter 5 for suggestions for helping children make a compass using a flat cork, a magnet, a needle, and a saucer of water. The needle is magnetized by rubbing it (in one direction, not back and forth) on one of the poles of the magnet, and is then laid on the cork which is floating on the water. The needle will soon point north and south. Although the floating-needle compass is interesting historically (originally a lodestone, a natural magnet, was used in this manner) it is helpful to have a commercially-made compass for examination. As is the case of many of the other experiments in this chapter there are many opportunities to make this experiment more open-ended: "What will happen if you rub the needle back and forth?" "Is the pointed end of the needle always the north pole?" "Can you magnetize only *one* end of a needle?" "Can you demagnetize the needles?" "Can you use an unmagnetized needle as a compass?"

Compass study may include some of the following problems: "What are some of the different kinds of compasses in common use?" "How can we use a compass to tell the direction of the sun at different times of the day?" "How can you use a compass to tell where your house is from school, what direction your school faces, which way the wind blows, or to put directions on a map of the neighborhood?"

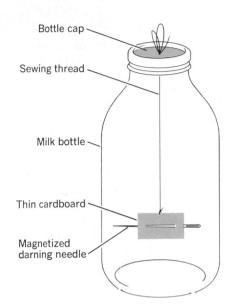

How Can We Make an Electric Charge?

Pupils can demonstrate a form of electricity by activities such as combing their hair, rubbing a rubber comb on a woolen sleeve, or holding tissue paper against the chalkboard and rubbing it rapidly with a silk cloth. Suggest that groups of children choose one of these demonstrations or similar ones to show their classmates; then observe the results and try to explain what they see. They may also do the demonstration illustrated here by using a piece of glass, two books, some tiny scraps of paper, and a piece of silk cloth. Lay the two books on the table about 4 inches apart. Sprinkle the scraps of paper on the table between the books. Lay the piece of glass over the books so that it covers the paper. Rub the glass vigorously with the silk cloth. The paper will jump up from the table to the glass. Experiment with books of various thickness to see how far the pieces will jump.

Some experiences with electricity are more effective if they take place in the dark, so that pupils can observe sparks. Pupils are then more likely to see the connection between static electricity and lightning.

Pupils will wonder about the connection between rubbing and static electricity. In the upper grades, discuss (or review) the structure of atoms. Every atom has electrons which whirl around a nucleus. When you run your comb through your hair you scrape electrons away from the hair and onto the comb, building up a greater charge of electrons. This charge is static electricity, although it is not static in the usual sense of the word. It can and does jump as observed in the sparks in some of the experiences and in the case of lightning.

Static electricity, then, results from the building up on a surface of particles from atoms. Looked at from another viewpoint static electricity reveals the electrical nature of all matter.

Static electricity experiments work better on dry days than on humid ones. Pupils will be interested in experimenting on different days to see that this is true. Some kinds of material, such as plastic wrap, show the effects of static electricity in almost any kind of weather.

How Can We Make an Electric Circuit?

Electrical circuits constitute an example of a system in which interaction of the parts is obvious; through experimentation and manipulation children can demonstrate

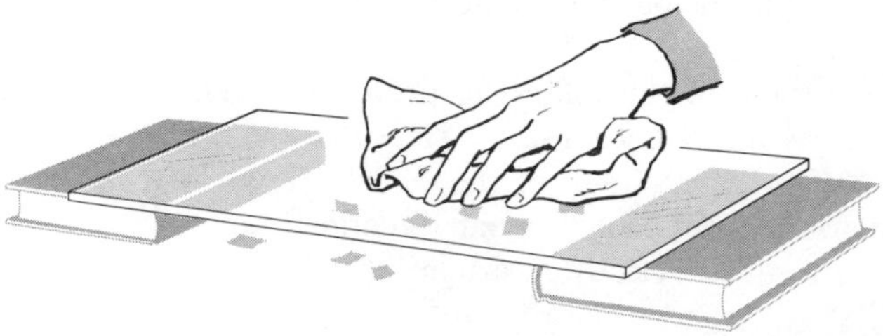

Rubbing a glass with a silk cloth is one way to demonstrate the phenomenon of static electricity.

these interactions. *Interactions in Electric Circuits*[3] is a sequence of experiences designed especially to help pupils see for themselves that change results from interaction of the members of a system (example: battery, conductor, light bulb). When the members of the system are properly arranged, the bulb glows indicating interaction.

The sequence of experiences begins with children finding out about circuits through the use of essential materials; then different materials are introduced in circuits; more dry cells are then added to circuits; next children study the effects of different strengths of batteries. Continued study introduces the idea of converting one form of energy (chemical energy in a battery) to another (heat and light energy).

The description presents the step-by-step procedures, and indicates the focus of emphasis as one leads to another. Material lists are included, as a practical help for the teacher. Although the guide suggests that the material is appropriate for grade 3 it may be adapted for use at other levels.

Another approach is found in *Batteries and Bulbs*,[4] where children begin by manipulating materials (flashlight batteries, small light bulbs, and wire) attempting to light the bulb. After children have had time to manipulate and experience some successes they attempt to draw some conclusions. They are urged to *describe* what happens and to *predict* what may happen. They construct their own rules, discuss them, evaluate and modify these descriptions. They then attempt some generalizing. The guide provides suggestions about procedures, lists materials needed, and includes suggestions to promote further related experiments.

Firsthand experiences by individual children, or at least in small groups, is essential. We suggest that each child or small group be given a dry cell, some wire, and a light bulb, with the suggestion that pupils attempt to light the bulb using the equipment. (It is perhaps better to furnish the pupils initially with wires having a few inches of insulation stripped from both ends of the wires.) A few pupils will probably be

[3] Conceptually Oriented Program in Elementary Science (COPES): *Teacher's Guide for Grade Three*, "Interactions in Electric Circuits" (New York: New York University, 1972).

[4] Elementary Science Study (ESS): "Batteries and Bulbs," *Teacher's Guide*, (Manchester, Mo.: Webster Division, McGraw-Hill Book Co., Inc.); and AAAS Xerox Edition: "Conductors and Nonconductors," *Science, A Process Approach* (Carlstadt, N.J.: Xerox Education Sciences). Includes material on thermal conductors. Stresses experimenting and formulating hypotheses.

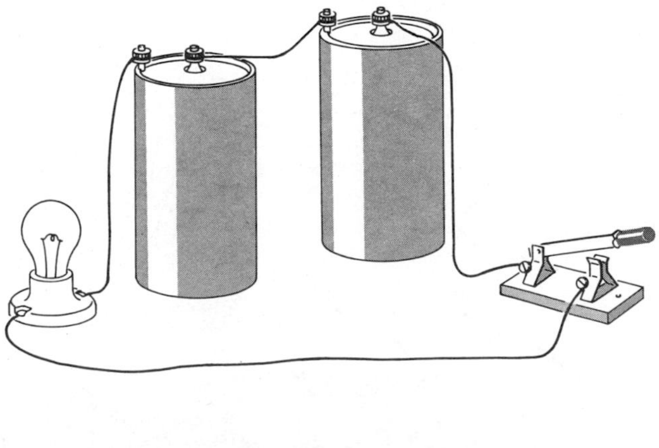

A knife switch is used between the dry cells and the lamp to make and break the circuit.

successful in a short time. Others will take longer. Do not hurry the manipulation; it may result in children "copying" from their neighbors instead of discovering for themselves.

Children may be urged to make simple line drawings[5] to show what they did, classifying them into "It Works"; "It Doesn't Work." Examination of the drawings and the material itself will form the basis for making inferences and for verification by comparing. From this simple circuit experience children will proceed to constructing circuits: using various switches, using more than one dry cell, lighting more than one bulb in the circuit, and connecting bulbs in series and parallel arrangements.

As children continue their experiences with circuits vocabulary develops—closed circuit, open circuit, conductors, and so on. Questions also arise that lead to further experiences. Examples: "Is copper wire the only material that will carry a current?" "How is a switch built to break a circuit?" "What happens when bare wires touch each other in a complete circuit?"

Children may be able to devise a circuit like the one pictured here; to test other materials to see if they, like copper, will conduct a current. They can test many materials—such as rubber, aluminum, iron, glass, cloth, and so on—by placing them in the circuit. They can then classify materials as conductors and insulators, and examine various circuits they have used to identify the conductors and insulators.

The pupils may discover what happens when bare wires touch by the following activities: Connect a dry cell to an electric bulb using copper wires that have had their insulation removed in several places. Ask pupils if they can put out the light without using the switch. Touch a bare spot on the wire to a bare spot on another. Touch (carefully) the wire in the circuit. It will be hot. When pupils use the short circuit they will note that when bare wires touch in a completed circuit heat is developed. An application of this idea is incorporated in the construction of fuses.

[5] Adapted from *Science Grade 5* (Brooklyn, N.Y.: Board of Education of the City of New York, 1966).

A simple piece of apparatus can be used to find out if materials are conductors or nonconductors of electricity. Materials to be tested can be laid across the two thumbtacks. The pupils will think of many materials to test.

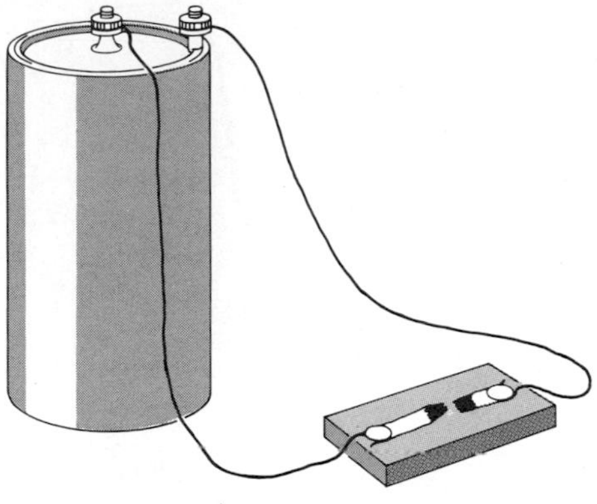

A piece of foil (from a chewing-gum wrapper or similar source) is used to illustrate how a fuse works. Pupils will learn that foil must be cut in a very narrow strip before electricity will melt it.

Pupils will devise variations of this experiment to show other ways of making short circuits. This experiment has application to the cause of fire in buildings and to the use of worn extension cords. Ask pupils to find them.

The drawing illustrates a simple demonstration showing how a fuse protects a house. Use a block of soft wood, two thumbtacks, a dry cell, some copper wire, and a narrow piece of metal foil or fuse wire (available from a supply house). Press the thumbtacks into the wood, and connect them with the *narrow* strip of foil, making sure that the foil makes a good connection with the tacks; then connect the wires to the cell. It is helpful to cut a notch on either side of the metal foil near the center to make a very narrow place in the foil. The foil melts. (If the demonstration does not work at first let pupils decide why. It may be because the foil strip is too wide or because the connections are not properly made. The problem solving involved in trying to decide why the demonstration does not work may be as important as understanding the demonstration itself.) Pupils should examine burned-out fuses to look at the fuse wire and note what has happened to it.

How Can We Make an Electromagnet?

Before beginning this activity pupils might review what they know about permanent magnets—they attract iron, have poles, are strongest at poles, like poles repel,

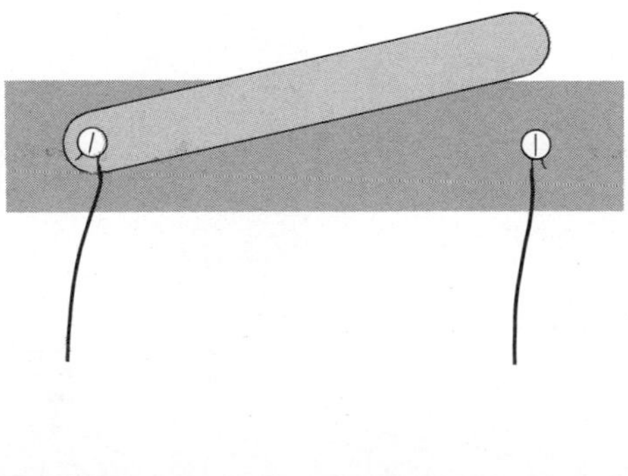

A simple switch. A homemade apparatus such as this sometimes teaches science principles better than any other materials.

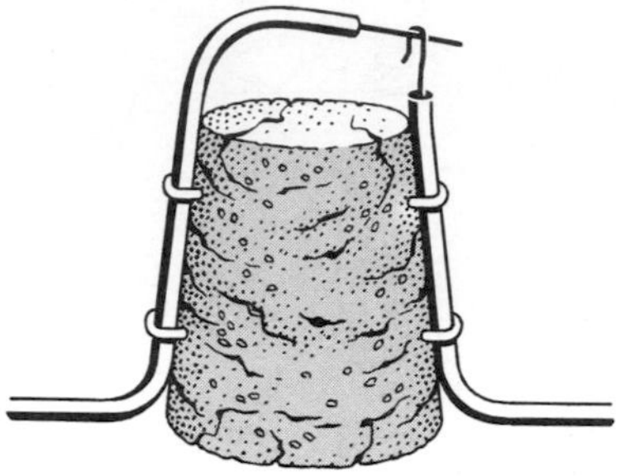

Pupils can think of variations of this cork switch by substituting different materials.

unlike poles attract, and so forth. These ideas will be used in comparing the permanent magnets they have used with the temporary magnet they will make.

Each child or small group of children should, if possible, be supplied with two dry cells, 2 or 3 feet of insulated wire, a large nail, a switch, and some iron thumbtacks. Suggest the problem: "Can you use these materials to make the nail into a magnet?" Let children try out their ideas using only one dry cell in the circuit.

Urge children to try their ideas. As a last resort give them some leads. This would be a good time to suggest that in order to conserve the source of energy they not leave the circuit closed for very long and not ever connect it directly across the terminals of the dry cell.

When several nails have been made into magnets ask: "Who do you think has the strongest magnet? How can we tell?" Test with the thumbtacks or paperclips by counting how many are held by the electromagnet. When the strongest magnet is discovered, ask if they can tell why this electromagnet is strongest? (More coils of wire.) "How can all of the magnets be made stronger?" Children make more turns of the wire.

Here is an opportunity for pupils to use mathematics in helping to discover relationships. Have them discover how many tacks (or paper clips) are picked up with 6 turns of wire, 12 turns, and so on, or with one dry cell.

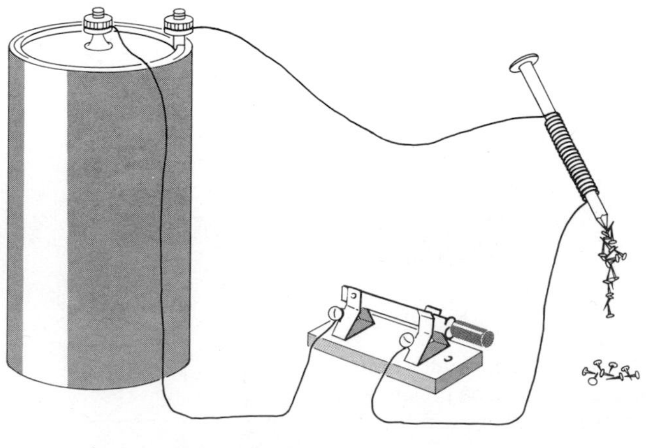

When electricity flows through it the electromagnet can pick up objects of iron. When the circuit is broken it drops them. An electromagnet is a temporary magnet; its strength can be changed and its poles reversed.

"In what other way can you think to make the electromagnet stronger?" (Use two cells.) Again test.

Now, using an electromagnet with only one cell and a switch, give compasses to the children and ask them to hold the compass near the electromagnet when the circuit is complete. "What can you discover?" (The magnet has poles.) "Can you tell by using the compass which pole is N and which S? How?" "How do you suppose you could change the poles of the magnet?" (Switch the connections to the dry cell.) Most children will need help here.

As children continue to use the electromagnets, such questions as the following may arise: "Can an electromagnet be made with uninsulated wire?" "Will a pencil work instead of a nail?" "Will a coil of wire work without any nail in it?" Children's questions will suggest other ideas to try.

(*See* Ch. 19A.)

Pupils can compare the electromagnets with the permanent magnets they have used. "How are they alike?" "How are they different from each other?"

After the electromagnet has been made and used, pupils can be asked to hunt for places where electromagnets are utilized at home, at school, and elsewhere. After the investigations the class can make a list. (It will include doorbells, electric motors, telegraph sets, and so on.)

How Does a Telegraph Work?

There are many ways to illustrate the principle of a telegraph key and sounder, from the simple one shown here to the more complicated ones found in almost any beginner's book on electricity. The key and sounder available from supply sources are much more easily understood after pupils comprehend the principle of this hand-made one. It shows that a telegraph set consists of an electromagnet, and a source of electricity, plus a circuit breaker separated by wires, as shown. The nail that is the core of the electromagnet is driven into a board so that it is held upright. Wire to make the electromagnet is wrapped around this nail. The electromagnet is connected to the dry cell and switch as in the drawing. The nail is held above the electromagnet loosely, so that when the switch is closed, the nail is pulled down (with a click) to the electromagnet. When the switch is opened again the nail pops up. This simple

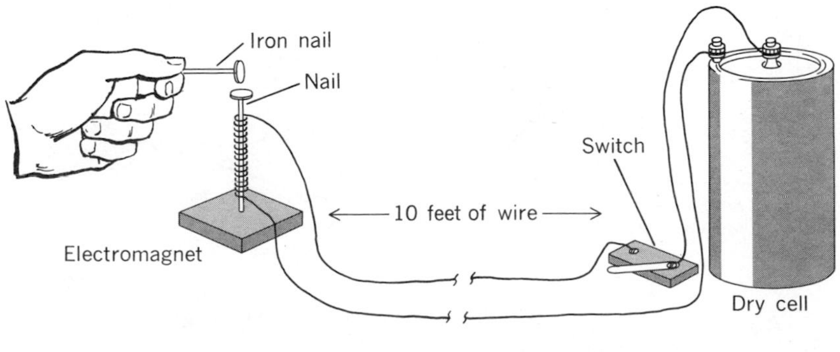

The principle of the telegraph is demonstrated in this simple circuit which can be constructed in a few minutes.

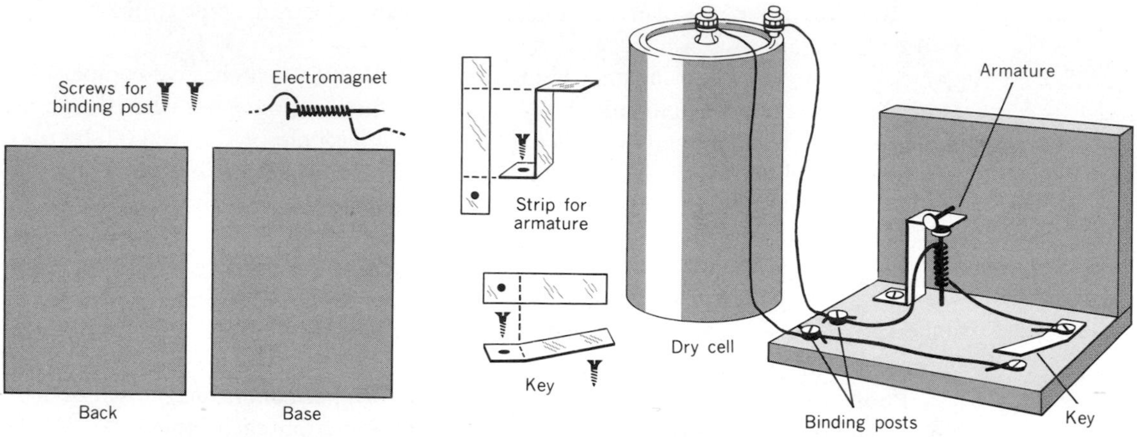

By using easily obtainable materials pupils can construct this key and sounder. A group of especially interested pupils may wish to do the construction and demonstrate the results to the class. Problems that arise through this experience are often real learning situations. (*From* Science and Children, *October 1966;* see *Bibliography, Magazines.*)

device provides opportunities for open-ended experimentation: "How long can we make the connecting wire and still have it work?" "Will a stronger electromagnet make any difference?"

How Can We Make Electricity?

Children can make a simple device which illustrates Faraday's discovery that magnetism can be converted into electricity. A bar magnet is thrust vigorously in and out of a coil of insulated wire. Start with 20 or 30 turns of wire. If the two ends of the coil are connected, electricity will flow in the wire. But how can you make sure? A simple meter (galvanometer) can be constructed as shown by wrapping a coil of wire around a compass. Connect the two ends of this coil to the two ends of the other coil. Now use the magnet as directed, and observe the compass needle. Here

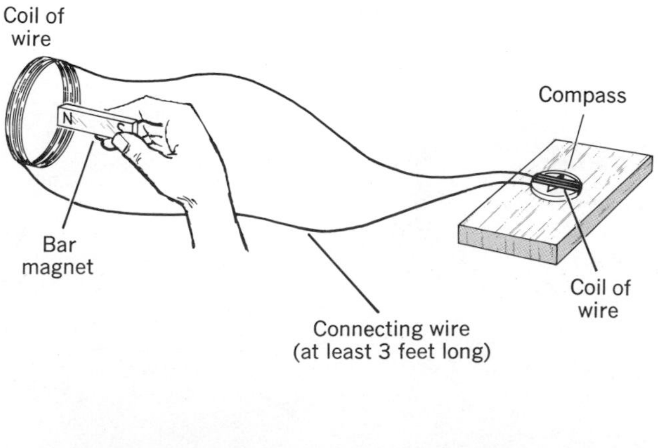

A magnet in motion produces electricity in a coil of wire. The deflection of a compass needle shows that an electric current is flowing.

we have an example of electricity being converted into magnetism (Oersted's discovery). In summary: (1.) In the "generator" the movement of the magnet in and out of the coil causes electricity to flow in the wire: magnetism → electricity; (2.) in the "meter" (coil of wire around a compass) electricity in the wire produces magnetism which deflects the needle: electricity → magnetism.
(**Note:** In huge generators the mechanical energy—motion—produced by flowing water or steam turns the magnets—electromagnets—near coils of wire and generates electricity in the same way.)

This is another example of open-ended possibilities: (1.) "What happens if there are more vigorous thrusts?" (2.) "More turns of wire in the generator?" (3.) "More turns of wire around the compass?"

What Are Some Safety Rules for Using Electricity?[6]

As children study electricity they may make their own safety rules from the knowledge they have gained. These rules can be checked against those given here, and any important ones that have been omitted can be added. Children should be encouraged to take this list home and to talk it over with their parents to decide which rules apply especially to their homes.

[6] W.L. Beauchamp, G.O. Blough, and M. Williams: *Discovering Our World*, Book 3 (Glenview, Ill.: Scott, Foresman and Company, 1957).

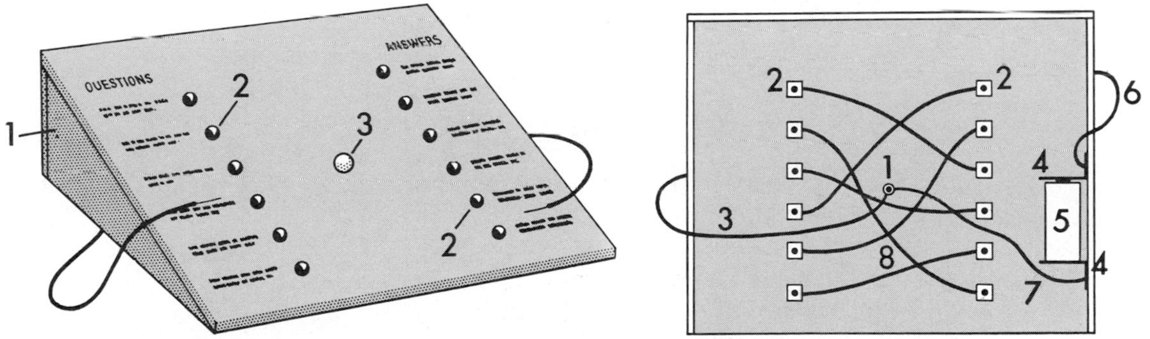

Front view (*left*): The questioner uses cards that have the questions on the left side and the answers on the right, but the answers do not correspond in sequence to the questions (1.) wedge-shaped side board; (2.) terminal made of stove bolt or copper fastener; (3.) flashlight bulb.
Rear view (*right*): Behind the board each "question" terminal is connected to an "answer" terminal. (1.) socket for flashlight bulb; (2.) ends of terminals; (3.) wire that reaches from flashlight bulb to front of board for contact with terminal; (4.) copper strips for holding flashlight battery; (5.) flashlight battery; (6.) wire that reaches from flashlight battery to front of board for contact with terminal; (7.) wire from battery to light bulb; (8.) wire connecting pairs of terminals.

The safe use of electricity is important to all of us, and these general rules, are stated simply and organized according to their applications. Rules such as these should not be merely memorized by children. As children study electricity they come to understand the reason for precautions, and consequently they see the sense of observing them. The rules apply to home, school, and any other place where electricity is used. (**Note:** *It is important to stress that children should not work with house current or replace fuses.*)

Safety Rules for Using Electric Appliances

1. Disconnect electrical appliances when they are not being used.
2. If there is a switch on an electrical appliance turn it off before you disconnect the appliance. Also be sure that the switch is turned off before you connect the appliance.
3. Never use an electrical appliance or an electric cord that you know is out of order.
4. Never try to experiment with an electrical appliance or an electric cord that is connected to the current in your home or at school.
5. Never touch an electrical appliance or cord or switch with wet hands. Also be sure not to touch them if any part of your body is touching a water pipe.

Safety Rules for Using Electric Wires

1. Never touch electric wires or use an electric cord on which the covering is worn.
2. Keep electric wires and cords from rubbing against things or becoming kinked. Rubbing may wear off the covering, and kinking may break it.
3. Stay away from broken wires that hang from poles or buildings.
4. Never climb a pole that supports electric wires.

Safety Rules for Using Fuses and Switches

1. Never try to repair a "burnt-out" fuse. Ask an adult to replace it with a new one.
2. When a fuse "burns out" always put in a new fuse that carries the same current. If the old fuse is labeled 15A the new fuse should be labeled 15A.
3. Never try to use a penny instead of a new fuse. The penny is made of copper. It will not melt until the copper wires do too. (*See* p. 619.)
4. Have a switch repaired at once if you get a shock when you use it to turn current on or off.

Safety Rules for Using Electric Heaters

1. Never use a knife, fork, or spoon to get bread out of an electric toaster while it is turned on. You may get a shock or a burn, or you may cause a short circuit.
2. Do not use a damp cloth to clean the outside of an electric heater while it is turned on. Disconnect the heater and wait until it cools.

3. Do not go away and leave an electric iron connected. It may cause a fire.
4. Do not hang wet clothes on an electric heater to dry. You may cause a short circuit or a fire.
5. Never touch an electric heater or any other electrical device while you are in a bathtub or while any part of your body is touching a water pipe, a faucet, or a radiator.
6. If you use an electric heating pad be sure that it has a waterproof cover. You may get a shock if perspiration soaks into it.

OTHER PROBLEMS FOR OLDER CHILDREN

1. What are the common sources of electricity?
2. How are houses wired for using electricity?
3. How does an electric motor work? (*See* p. 622.)
4. How can we make an electrical questioner? (*See* p. 623.)
5. How can we make a telegraph set? (*See* p. 621.)
6. How does a telephone work? (*See* p. 622.)
7. How do electrical appliances produce heat and light?

Resources to Investigate with Children

1. An electrical shop for odds and ends of wire, insulating materials, magnets, and other materials, as well as for information about electricity.
2. Ten-cent store for purchase of inexpensive electrical material for use in experiments.
3. A junk shop for metals to test as conductors, for magnets, and for other odds and ends.
4. The local power company for information about the source of electricity, its cost, and so on.
5. Western Union and the local telephone company for a visit to see how electricity is used in communication.
6. The school custodian to show pupils where electricity enters the school; the fuse box, the electric meter, the switches; how insulating materials are used for safety; to provide burned-out fuses; to read the electric meter; and for other similar purposes.
7. A local electric-appliance dealer for information on the various uses to which electricity is put in the community.
8. Children's homes for illustrations of ways in which electricity is used to do various kinds of work in the home.
9. The community for examples of the many kinds of work done by electricity in factories, homes, stores, in public buildings, on the streets, and so on.
10. Local hardware store or department store to see how many tools and appliances use magnetism and electricity.
11. Local radio or television station to see how programs are put on the air.

12. Local electricity-generating plants for information and for possible class visit to find out how electricity is produced and distributed.
13. Local electrical contractors for regulations related to electrical installations and uses of electricity.
14. Toy store for toys that use magnetism or electricity.
15. The local doctor for information on the uses of magnetism and electricity in the instruments that he has.
16. A street excavation to see how electric cables are connected to buildings.

Preparing to Teach

1. Make the electric questioner shown on page 623 and devise a lesson plan to show how and what you would expect children to learn from this construction.
2. Discover the following things about a specific house: Where does electricity enter? How many fuses are there? Which appliances use the most electricity? What is the source of the electrical supply? Prepare plans for a trip with an elementary-school group to make similar observations. Draw up a list of the observations you would plan for them to make.
3. Examine the activities, experiences, and experiments suggested in this chapter and plan how you would increase their "open endedness."
4. Survey the chapter and others in this section of the book to identify opportunities for the use of the metric system.
5. Make plans for an exhibit by the children of the various experiments and experiences in this chapter. Devise uses for this exhibit: (1.) To share the findings with another group that has not studied the material; (2.) to review the findings; (3.) as an exhibit in a display case in the school corridor. Suggest ways to help children improve their communication skills through this activity.
6. Survey sources of films and film strips that are available to supplement the materials in this chapter. Preview them and plan how they can be used with children.
7. Assemble the materials and perform the experiments in this chapter if you have not had previous experiences with them.

CHAPTER 20A

SOUND AND HOW WE USE IT

(*Courtesy of Monkmeyer*)

A WORLD OF SOUND

We live in a world of sound. Sounds excite, frighten, soothe, inform. Our language reflects our keen awareness of sound. In the country we mark the *hum* of mosquitoes, the *rustle* of leaves, the *lowing* of a cow, the *flutter* of wings, the *roar* of a waterfall. In the city we note the *blare* of automobile horns, the *rumbling* of trains, the *blast* of factory whistles, the *patter* of children's feet, the *cries* of street vendors. Each season, each mood of nature is announced by its own special sounds. Man also makes his contribution in the complex sound combinations he evokes from musical instruments—from violin strings, organ pipes, drumheads, and from his own vocal cords.

This chapter is the story of sounds. It is the story of how sounds are made, how sounds differ, how they travel, how they are detected, how sounds may be controlled.

WHAT CAUSES SOUND?

(*See* pp. 641–4.)

Pluck a stretched rubber band and listen to its sound. Look at it and observe the rapid back-and-forth motion—its vibrations. When the vibrations stop, the sounds stop.

Put your fingers on your throat and say "ah." Something inside is vibrating, something very much like the rubber bands. These vibrators are your vocal cords.

Place a thin plastic 12-inch ruler across the edge of a table so that about half of it protrudes. Hold it down firmly, with one hand placed just above the edge of the table. Slap it lightly with the other hand. Hear, feel, and see the vibrations.

Whenever a sound is produced, something is quivering, trembling, shaking back and forth—vibrating. That something may be a string, a membrane, a reed, a column of air. It may originate in an insect's wings, a ticking watch, an animal's throat, a tuba's horn, or a thunderbolt.

HOW IS SOUND CARRIED?

A tree crashes in a far-off forest. No human, no animal is present to hear the crash. Was a sound produced? The answer depends on our definition of sound. If sound is defined only as that which is heard, then no sound was produced. If sound is defined as a certain kind of vibration, then sound was produced, whether it reached the ears of a living thing or not.

(*See* p. 645.)

A tinkling bell starts a sound wave of condensation (air particles jammed together) and rarefaction (air particles spread apart). The wave moves away from the bell in all directions.

Sounds from crashing trees or vibrating violins or people's throats usually reach our ears through the air. Just how do sounds travel?

Consider a bell tinkling from the impact of its clapper. As the bell shakes, it imparts its rhythmic back-and-forth motion to the air particles—molecules—immediately around it. These molecules in turn pass the vibratory motion to the air molecules adjacent to them, and so on. In this way the vibration travels outward in all directions from its source. A small part of the air wave strikes a little membrane in your ear, your eardrum, and starts it trembling in the same way that the bell was trembling. A vibration originating in a bell has been transferred to air molecules and from air molecules to your eardrum. Later we shall see how we become *aware* of the sound.

Sound Waves

A *sound wave* set in motion by a bell has reached our ears. The only thing that has traveled is a vibratory motion; the sensation the sound evokes within us is quite another thing. A sound wave is often compared to what happens when a pebble is dropped into a quiet pond. A wave spreads outward until it strikes the edge of the pond.

So, when we say that sound is traveling through the air we really mean that a certain kind of wave is proceeding through the air. This may be compared to what happens when a policeman tries to hold back a curious crowd. As he pushes against the individuals near him they are forced back. In turn they force those behind them back, and so on over an ever-widening area. Each individual may have taken only one step backward, but the wave of "compression" has traveled many feet through the crowd.

In a sound wave the particles of air between the sounding object and your eardrum move back and forth only a tiny distance. Each impulse started by a vibrating object, such as a violin string, begins a wave in which air particles are successively jammed together and then spread apart. The part of the wave in which the particles are compressed together is called a *condensation;* and the part in which they are farthest apart is called a *rarefaction*.

A Medium for Sound

Astronauts on the moon had to communicate with each other by radio, for there is no air there. In a classic demonstration in physics the air is pumped out of a jar in which a ringing alarm clock is suspended. As the air is gradually exhausted from the jar, the sound gets fainter and fainter until it cannot be heard, although the clapper of the bell is seen moving. As air is admitted into the jar the alarm is heard again.

Gases such as air are not the only medium for the transmission of sound. When two stones are clapped together underwater, divers many feet away can hear the sound through the water. American Indians put their ears to the ground to hear the sound of far-off hoofbeats. The rumblings of a train many miles away can be detected by placing one's ear against the train rail. These illustrations show that sound travels well through liquids and solids.

THE SPEED OF SOUND

A flash of lightning is seen several seconds before the crash of thunder is heard, although both occur at the same time. The sound of a woodsman's ax reaches a distant observer's ears after he has seen the ax strike the wood. The white clouds puffing from a whistle of a far-off locomotive are seen before the shrill blast is heard.

(See p. 646.)

These and many other observations and experiments make it apparent that it takes time for sound to travel from the sounding object to our ears, certainly much more time than light takes to reach our eyes.

The speed of sound through air was determined by the Dutch scientists Moll and Van Beek in 1823. Two high hills 11 miles apart were used for this experiment. A cannon on one of the hills was fired. An observer on the other hill noted the flash of fire (the experiment was done at night to make it more visible) and then counted the number of seconds until he heard the report. The experiment was repeated a number of times. It was also checked by firing a cannon on the opposite hill, to cancel any error that might have been caused by the wind. From this experiment the average speed of sound was calculated to be about 1,100 feet per second. (In the experiments, it was assumed that light travels instantaneously. Actually, light travels at the rate of about 186,000 *miles* per second; this obviously would not affect the interpretation of the results of the experiment appreciably.)

Careful observations have shown that the speed of sound through air is 1,090 feet per second when the temperature is 32° F. (0° C.). Perhaps an easy way of remembering this is to consider that it takes sound about 5 seconds to travel 1 mile. In Chapter 9A this fact is used to provide a method for determining the distance of a lightning flash from an observer. At temperatures higher than 32° F. sound travels faster; and at lower temperatures it travels more slowly.

Sound travels more quickly through liquids and solids than through air. It travels about 4 times as fast through water, about 10 times as fast through pine wood, and about 17 times as fast through steel, as it does through air.

SOUND BOUNCES

Echoes

Have you ever heard your voice come back to you as an echo from a cliff, a building, or a hill? An echo is heard because sound bounces off these structures, just as a ball bounces off a wall. An echo also resembles the reflection of light from a mirror. An echo is a sound reflection.

Echoes are heard as separate sounds only if they reach the listener $\frac{1}{10}$ second or more after the original sound. It takes at least that time for the human ear to separate one sound from another. If you want to hear your echo you must stand at least 55 feet away from the reflecting wall. If you shout against a cliff 55 feet away the sound will travel 55 feet to the cliff and bounce 55 feet back to you, a total distance of 110 feet. Sound travels about 1,100 feet per second, so it can make this trip in $\frac{1}{10}$ second. The echo will reach your ear $\frac{1}{10}$ second after you hear your original voice. You will, therefore, just be able to distinguish it as an echo.

If, on the other hand, the reflecting wall is only 11 feet away, as it might be in your living room, the sound bounces back too fast, taking only $\frac{1}{50}$ second for the trip. In this case the sound reflection, known as a *reverberation,* only prolongs the original sound; it is not detected as an echo.

An echo may interfere seriously with hearing, particularly in a large gymnasium or in an auditorium. The echoes overlap the words of the speaker in such a way as to cause confusion. This difficulty may be overcome by using sound-deadening materials for the walls, ceilings, and floors. Soft materials—such as canvas, curtains, soft wallboards, and rugs—absorb sound waves and reflect little sound. Auditoriums often have soft wood walls for this reason. Restaurants, broadcasting and television studios, and rooms in schools and homes are also soundproofed to eliminate echoes and excessive reverberations of sound waves.

Concentrating Sound

Sound waves may be reflected from curved surfaces and concentrated in such a way as to increase audibility. Large auditoriums often have stages that are curved at the back like the reflector in an automobile headlight. Sound waves strike the curved surface and are reflected out into the auditorium.

Cheerleaders often use megaphones to shout directions to their "rooters." Megaphones, like band shells, permit sound to go out in only one direction. The energy is thus concentrated rather than dissipated over a wide space.

Before electronic hearing aids were common partially deaf people used ear trumpets, which are essentially megaphones used in reverse. The large end gathers more sound waves than the ear alone could catch. Your outer ear is a sound catcher, although you could hear very well without it. If you cup your ears you collect more sound waves and thus convey their energy to your eardrums.

The stethoscope is used by physicians to detect heart and other internal sounds that furnish clues to the condition of the body. The end of this instrument, which is placed against the patient, contains a diaphragm that is much larger than the human eardrum and consequently collects more sound energy. The tubing of the stethoscope channels the sound to the doctor's ears without much loss.

MEASURING DISTANCE BY SOUND

Echoes have been put to practical use by navigators for determining the depth of water under their ships. A vibrator attached underwater to the hull of the ship sends sound waves into the water. These hit the bottom and bounce back to the ship. The time between the emission of the sound and its reception as an echo is noted and the depth is calculated. If, for example, 1 second is required, the sound has traveled 4,500 feet. (The speed of sound in water is about four times its speed in air.) The bottom, therefore, is 2,250 feet down.

Sonar, a modern sounding device, gives both the direction of the returning waves and the time required for the round trip. In this way a detailed picture of the ocean depths is obtained. This picture may include underwater reefs, wrecks, mines, and even schools of fish.

Bats and Ultrasonic Sound

How can a bat fly through the total darkness of a cave avoiding all obstacles in its path? Before 1800 Lazzaro Spallanzani of Italy discovered that if the *ears* of a bat were covered, the bat would collide helplessly with large conspicuous

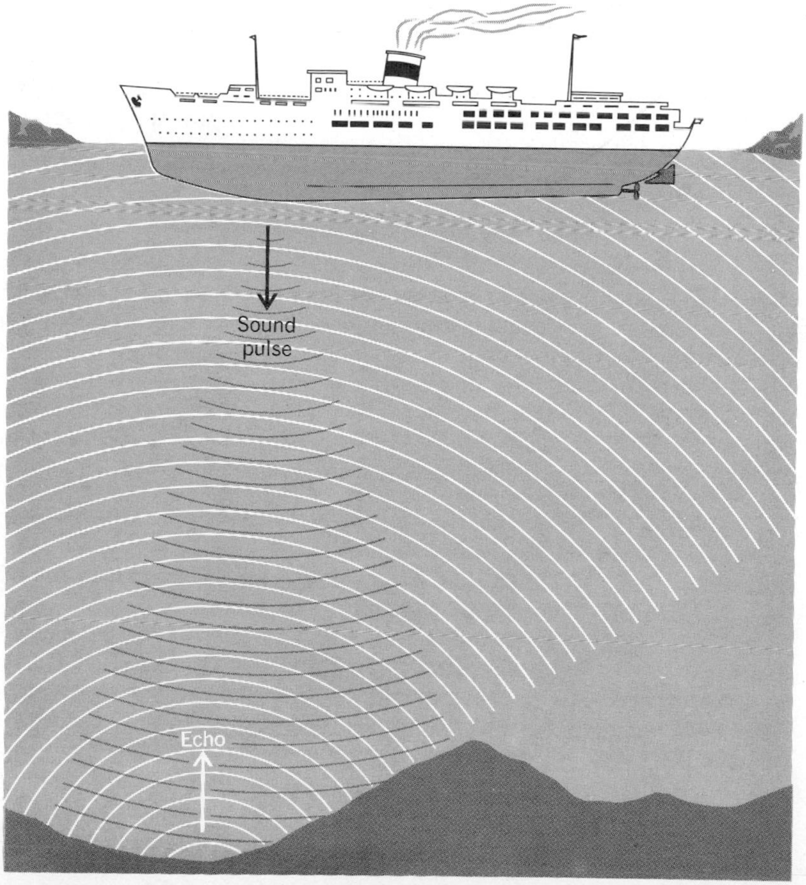

Sonar makes it possible for a ship to determine water depth to the ocean floor. The time elapsed between the sending of the sound from the sonar vibrator and its reception as an echo by the ship provides the information needed to determine the depth of the water.

objects. Thus, scientists were led to associate the agility of a bat in the dark to its hearing. But the almost silent flight of bats made them ask: Just what do they hear?

In 1920 an English physicist, H. Hartridge, suggested that bats might be hearing *ultrasonic* sounds. These are sounds that are too high-pitched for human ears to detect. Donald Griffin and Robert Calambo, American scientists, studied the problem intensively between 1938 and 1941. They found that the bats themselves emitted ultrasonic sounds from their mouths and that their ears were designed to receive them. They tested the skill of bats by having them fly through a darkened room divided in half by a row of wires hanging from the ceiling and spaced about a foot apart. The bats were successful in flying through the wires without touching them. Stopping the ears of the bat *or* covering their mouths with tape reduced their scores to the level of pure chance. In short, bats find their way around by sending sound waves out and by receiving echoes that tell them of nearby objects.

CHARACTERISTICS OF SOUND

How do we distinguish among the multiplicity of sounds that we hear when, for example, we listen to a full orchestra playing a symphony? There are three characteristics by which we identify sounds: loudness, pitch, and quality. All of these have to do with the nature of the vibrations that are producing the sound waves.

(*See* pp. 642, 646–7.)

We have compared a sound wave to a water wave. Let us identify some of the general characteristics of all regular waves. The distance between two adjacent wave crests is known as the *wavelength*. The number of waves that pass any point in a given period of time is known as the *frequency*. The height of a wave over the original undisturbed surface of the body of water is the *amplitude*. (When oceanographers refer to wave height, however, they measure the distance from trough, the lowest point, to crest, the highest point.)

Wavelength and frequency are related phenomena. If you drop one pebble in the middle of a pond every 10 seconds you will start a series of waves that will reach the shore 10 seconds apart. The frequency is 6 waves per minute. Let us assume that in this case the distance between each wave crest, the wavelength, is 12 feet. If you now drop a pebble in every 5 seconds, 1 wave will reach the shore every 5 seconds. The frequency then is 12 waves per minute. However, the distance between the wave crests, the wavelength, is shorter, only 6 feet in length. In other words, the greater the frequency, the shorter the wavelength. Or, in simple beachcomber language, the more waves, the less distance between them.

These characteristics of water waves apply to all regular waves—such as radio waves, light waves, and sound waves.

Loudness

It is obvious that when the tympanist strikes his drum hard a louder sound is produced than when he taps it gently. A powerful stroke causes the drumhead, and consequently the particles of air next to it, to move back and forth for a greater distance than does a gentle stroke. In terms of the sound wave the amplitude is greater. A powerful wave travels from the drum to you, making

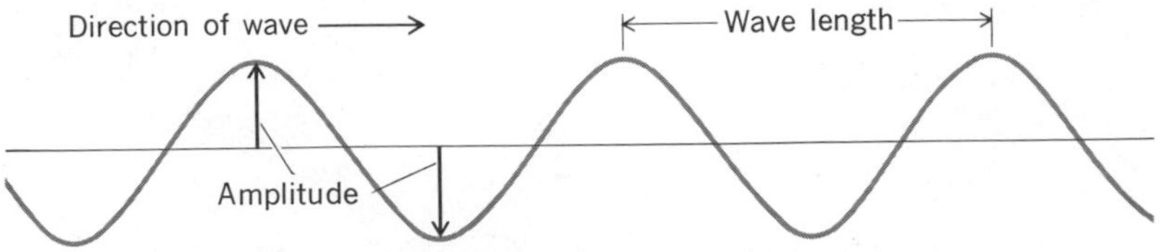

Representation of a sound wave. The amplitude, or height of the crests above or below the base line, determines the loudness of the sound. The wave length determines the pitch of the sound: the longer the wave length, the lower the pitch.

your eardrums vibrate back and forth vigorously. The loudness of the sound you hear depends, then, on how far the sound waves make your eardrums move in and out. In a literal sense the tympanist has "your ear."

Loudness depends also on the distance of the listener from the source of the sound. If sound waves were visible a sounding drum would be seen to be in the center of a series of concentric spheres, each sphere representing a compression of air particles. We recall that sound is a form of energy. The energy in this instance is first imparted to the drumhead by the tympanist, and then by the drumhead to the surrounding air. As the sound wave advances from sphere to sphere the energy is "spent" in setting more and more air particles in motion. The loudness or volume decreases with distance. In an auditorium this loss is partially compensated for by the reflection and concentration of sound by the sides, back, and top of the hall.

The crashing of cymbals starts a large wave moving across a concert hall. The strings of a piano, on the other hand, are not large enough to cause very much of a "splash" in the air. To make their sounds louder the strings are connected to a sounding board, which is set vibrating by the ends of the strings connected to it. Its broad area permits it to set a large amount of air into motion at any given moment. The same principle obtains in the violin, cello, and all other stringed instruments.

To demonstrate this principle rap the prongs of a fork against the heel of your shoe and listen for the sound. Do this again, but this time press the end of the handle against a wooden table. The sound is louder because the fork's vibration is transmitted to the table, which, in turn, causes a large amount of air surrounding it to begin vibrating.

The loudness of a sound may be measured by means of a sound-level meter. The unit for measuring sound is the *decibel* ("bel" from Alexander Graham Bell). The rustling leaves in a light breeze have a rating of about 10 decibels, sound within the average home about 20 decibels, a large railroad station about 55 decibels, a boiler factory 100 decibels. At 120 decibels sounds become physically painful. Continuous noise above 50 decibels is thought to be harmful to a person's emotional well-being. The problem of "noise pollution" in modern life is one that is compelling more and more attention.

Pitch

If sound is compared to an ocean wave, then loudness, as we have seen, is associated with the *height* or amplitude of the wave. Pitch, by the same analogy, is a characteristic determined by the frequency, the *number* of waves that pass a point in a given period of time. In the science of sound we say that pitch depends on the number of vibrations per second made by the vibrating body. By definition one vibration, sometimes called a *cycle,* includes both the backward and forward motion of the vibrating body.

(*See* pp. 642–5, 647.)

If you draw your fingernail over the back of a linen-covered book the nail will produce a sound because it is being vibrated by the many little ridges in the cloth. As you increase the speed with which you move your finger the pitch increases to higher and higher tones. The pitch of the note depends on the rapidity with which your nail is quivering; that is, the frequency of its vibration. Few vibrations per second produce a low tone; many vibrations per second a high tone.

The ear of a human being is able to pick up vibrations ranging from 16 to 20,000 vibrations per second (children exceed this upper limit), with the greatest sensitivity around 1,000 to 4,000 vibrations per second. Insects and other animals may detect sounds that humans cannot. Special dog whistles produce a high-pitched, *ultrasonic* sound that is audible to dogs but not to human beings.

There is quite a range of pitch represented in an orchestra. "A" above middle "C" of a piano should vibrate 440 times per second, if the piano is in tune. The scales used by musicians are based on this frequency. Some of the high piano strings vibrate 3,500 times per second. An organ can produce a frequency as low as 16 vibrations per second.

How are sounds of different pitch produced

in string instruments? If you look inside a piano you will see that three factors are responsible for the difference in pitch of the various strings: length, weight per unit of length (which depends on the thickness and the material used), and tightness. Low notes are produced by long, heavy, loose strings; high notes by short, light, more tightly stretched strings.

In general, a long string (or a heavy or loose one) vibrates slowly; consequently a low-pitched note is produced. A short string (or a light or more tightly stretched one) vibrates rapidly, producing a high-pitched sound.

In wind instruments the air in the instrument is made to vibrate by the player. Here the pitch is determined principally by the length of the column of air producing the sound. Different pitches are obtained by changing the length of the air column. Shorter air columns produce higher-pitched sounds; longer columns, lower-pitched sounds.

Quality

As we listen to a symphony orchestra we are aware not only of pitch and loudness but also of the quality of the sound of different instruments. The oboe sounds different from the clarinet; the bassoon different from the violin. How are differences in quality produced?

We recall that loudness depends on the strength and that pitch depends on the frequency of the sound wave. Quality depends on the "shape" imposed on the sound waves by the *overtones*. The production of overtones can be demonstrated by a simple experiment.

If you stretch a guitar string between two screws which are firmly set in a board, and pluck the string, it will vibrate throughout its entire length, producing a musical tone. This, the lowest tone that the string is capable of producing, is called its *fundamental*. If you now press down the middle of the string tightly with one finger and pluck either half-string, that part will vibrate to produce a tone one octave higher than when the whole string vibrates. This note is called the *first overtone*. Now, if you remove your finger quickly while half of the string is vibrating, the string will vibrate not only in half its length but also as a whole—*at the same time*. You then should hear two sounds—the note made by the string vibrating as a whole and the note made by the string vibrating in half its length.

If you now place your finger one third of the way from the end of the string (either end) and hold it down, plucking this third of the string will produce a note higher than the first overtone. This is the *second overtone*. Many other overtones are possible.

In the playing of musical instruments a large number of overtones are produced simultaneously with the fundamental tone. The number and intensity of the overtones are different in different instruments. Thus, "A flat" on a clarinet sounds different from "A flat" on a violin, because different overtones are produced. In singing or speaking some individuals are able to produce more overtones than others. They can do this in part because they are skilled in controlling their voices. The number of overtones given off by a violin and by other musical instruments depends on their construction, as well as on the skill of the musician.

The difference in character of two tones of the same pitch and loudness is due, then, to the difference in the relative prominence of the fundamental and the various overtones.

SYMPATHETIC VIBRATIONS

It is possible for one vibrating object to make another object vibrate without touching it. If you open a piano, press down on the loud pedal to remove the damper from the strings, and sing into the strings you will hear some of the strings sing back at you. Which strings? Those in tune with the pitch of your voice, with its fundamental tone and overtones. We call this a *sympathetic vibration*. If you sing at a different pitch different strings will sing back.

You probably have noticed that loose windows rattle and knives and forks chatter when certain notes are sounded on a piano or a radio. This happens because each sounding object has a natural frequency of vibration. If sound waves of that note strike it, it will respond sympathetically. Some singers are reputed to be able to shatter a fine crystal glass by singing loudly into it at its natural pitch.

Why does a sea shell held to the ear seem to have the "sound of the sea" in it? The air in the sea shell reinforces the slight sounds that are present in the environment by vibrating sympathetically with those in tune with it. The sound waves are bounced back and forth in such a manner that the reflections from the wall of the sea shell add up and strengthen the sound. These sounds are not the sounds of the sea unless you are listening to a sea shell on the seashore. This quality of responding sympathetically to certain sounds and reinforcing them is called *resonance*.

The human voice, produced by the vibration of the vocal cords, is reinforced by the sympathetic vibration of air in the throat, mouth, and nose, and is thus given its resonant quality.

MUSICAL INSTRUMENTS

For thousands of years people have invented and played musical instruments of various kinds. Drums, stringed instruments, and wind instruments have been found among the relics of very early man.

There are three general groups of musical instruments: the stringed instruments, such as violins, violas, bass violas, harps, and cellos; the percussion instruments, such as the drum and xylophone; and the wind instruments, such as the cornet, flute, and saxophone.

Stringed Instruments

In most stringed instruments the strings are usually held down by the fingers of the left hand and are plucked, strummed, or bowed with the right. Various tones can be obtained by varying the length of the strings. The harp is an exception to this. It has 46 separate strings because a change of length is not possible. However, the pedals on the harp can change the tension of the strings to make sharps and flats.

The wood and the air spaces in the body of a violin, along with the strings, are essential in producing a good tone. A good violin has the special virtue of vibrating faithfully with each string and with every pitch, even the high ones. A poor violin tends to "play favorites," amplifying some vibrations and neglecting others.

Percussion Instruments

Percussion instruments, such as the drum, depend on the vibration of a flexible head that is struck with sticks or with the hands. The head is stretched over a wooden or metal body. The vibrations of the head and body of the drum produce the sound. Pitch on some types of drums can be altered by stretching or loosening the skin. The kettledrum player loosens and tightens the head of the drum while playing.

Wind Instruments

In stringed instruments the musician causes strings to vibrate. The vibration is passed to the rest of the instrument, which causes the air to vibrate and produce the sound that reaches your ears. In wind instruments the player makes the air vibrate directly.

Blow across the tops of a series of bottles that have different amounts of water in them. Those with more *air* in them make a lower tone than those with little. The longer air column, like the longer string, produces the deeper tone.

In most wind instruments, from a piccolo to an organ, pitch is changed by changing the length of the column of air. In instruments such as the fife, flute, clarinet, saxophone, oboe, and bassoon the player lengthens the column of air by covering the holes in the instrument, and shortens it by uncovering the holes. He does this with his fingertips directly, or with the help of keys and pads.

In the trombone the lengthening and shortening of the air column is done by sliding a U-shaped tube in and out. In other brasses, such as the cornet, trumpet, tuba, and French horn, there are three curved tubes, each controlled by a key. As the key is pressed down the column of air that it controls is added to the total; when the key is released, the column is removed, or subtracted, from the total. By forming different combinations of these separate air tubes the musician is able to evoke the different notes needed.

In some wind instruments—for example, the cornet, tuba, trumpet, French horn, and trombone—the air is caused to vibrate by the vibration of the player's lips. In the clarinet, bassoon, saxophone, and oboe, on the other hand, wooden reeds are caused to vibrate by the blowing of the player. These, in turn, set air columns in the instrument vibrating.

The bugle has a fixed column of air. Tightening or relaxing the lips causes the rate of vibration to vary and thus produces different tones.

HOW WE SPEAK

Like all other sounds, speech is produced by vibrations. Stretched across the inside of the voice box, or *larynx,* are two folds of tissue called the *vocal cords*. It is the vocal cords that vibrate when we speak. The cords are elastic fibers that can be stretched and relaxed by the action of muscles in the voice box. You can illustrate the way that sound is produced by blowing upon the edges of a wide rubber band, stretched around two separated pencils so that the band's two segments are close together.

All the air that is breathed in and out passes through the voice box. Ordinarily, the vocal cords are relaxed on the two sides of the voice box. The air passes in and out between the vocal cords without producing sound. When you talk or sing, your brain sends messages along the nerves to the muscles controlling the vocal cords. The muscles pull the vocal cords together so that there is only a narrow slit between the cords, like that between the edges of the wide rubber band that you stretched. As the diaphragm and chest muscles force air out of the lungs the air makes the vocal cords vibrate. The pitch of the sound is controlled by making the vocal cords tighter or looser.

The natural range of pitch of the voice is determined largely by the length of the vocal cords. Women have higher-pitched voices than men because their vocal cords are shorter. Children's voices are higher than those of adults for the same reason.

The voice box is not the only part assisting in the making of speech. The lips, tongue, teeth, palate, and mouth help in the formation of spoken sounds. When we whisper, the sounds are produced by placing the mouth and tongue in the required positions without vibrating the vocal cords.

The quality of the human voice depends on the many spaces that resonate sympathetically with the vocal cords. These include the sinuses, the nasal cavities, the mouth, throat, windpipe, and lungs, as well as the voice box itself.

HOW WE HEAR

The ear is essentially a mechanism for the reception of sound waves and for the conversion of sound waves into nerve impulses. The ear consists of three parts: the outer ear, the middle ear, and the inner ear. The outer ear collects air vibrations; the middle ear amplifies them and passes them along to the inner ear; the inner ear changes the vibrations into nerve messages. The explanation that follows will be easier to understand if frequent reference is made to the illustration.

Outer Ear

The outer ear is composed of a shell of flexible cartilage and skin attached to the side of the head, leading to a canal that funnels inward. The outer ear acts on the principle of a hearing tube; that is, it collects and concentrates sound waves and conducts them, so that they strike against the eardrum. In man the value of this is slight—we could hear almost as well without the outer ears. In many animals, however, the external ear can be turned toward the source of the sound and

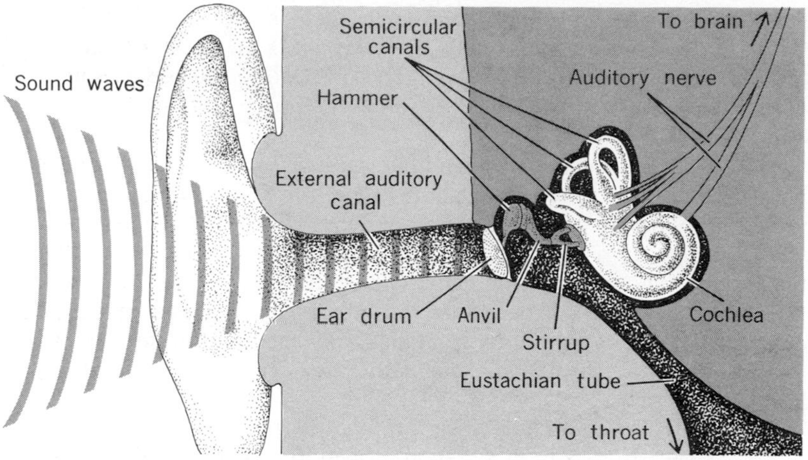

The delicate mechanism of the ear is shown here. Can you describe how the parts function in the process of hearing?

can play an important function in collecting sound waves.

The *eardrum* is set obliquely across the auditory canal, thereby providing a greater surface for receiving vibrations than if it were stretched squarely across it. It is a wonderfully designed membrane, with many delicate fibers running in concentric circles around it to make it elastic and springy, and with coarse fibers arranged like the ribs of an umbrella to give it strength.

Middle Ear

Within the middle ear is a chain of three little bones. The outer one, called the *hammer,* is attached to the eardrum. The hammer is connected by means of a joint to the bone called the *anvil*. This in turn is jointed to the *stirrup*. The foot plate of the stirrup rests against the *oval window* of the inner ear.

The three bones act as levers, magnifying about 22-fold the strength of the initial vibration received by the eardrum. This strengthened impulse is conveyed to the membrane covering the oval window.

Before ending our discussion of the middle ear we should mention the *Eustachian tube,* which connects the middle ear to the throat. The purpose of this tube is to permit the equalization of pressure on both sides of the eardrum. If, for example, you ascend in an elevator the pressure on the outside of the eardrum decreases with altitude. The air inside the middle ear tends to push the eardrum outward. However, some of the air escapes through the Eustachian tube into the throat, thereby equalizing the pressure on the eardrum. Chewing or swallowing helps clear the air pressure because it opens the end of the Eustachian tube near the throat. (This is why airline hostesses sometimes distribute gum when the pressure is being changed in the plane cabin.) When you descend in an elevator the pressure increases; the Eustachian tube permits air to flow from the throat *into* the middle ear.

Inner Ear

The inner ear is composed of the *cochlea* and the *semicircular canals*. Only the cochlea will be discussed here, because it is the auditory sense organ. (The canal apparatus is concerned with balance and with the sense of position. It is discussed in Chapter 12A.) The cochlea is a snail-shaped structure with $2\frac{1}{2}$ turns in it. It is filled with lymph, a fluid resembling blood except that it has no red blood cells in it. The sound waves from the eardrum are transmitted by the three bones in the middle ear to the fluid in the cochlea. Running through the cochlea is the important *basilar membrane,* upon which is a structure containing 24,000 *hair cells.* These cells are thought to be the true receptors of hearing.

Thousands of sensory nerve fibers are connected to the hair cells. These fibers join to form the auditory nerve, which leads from the cochlea to the brain. By a number of complex mechanisms, not fully understood, sound waves in the fluid of the cochlea are converted into electrical energy which triggers nerve impulses in the nerve fibers. These impulses travel along the auditory nerve to the brain, where they are perceived as sounds of varying pitch, loudness, and quality.

To sum up our discussion of how we hear: Sound waves pass from the eardrum to the three bones, then to the cochlea where they initiate nerve impulses, which are then transmitted to the brain.

In this chapter we have discussed the essential aspects of the phenomenon of sound. Here are some of the generalizations:

Sounds arise from vibrations.
Sound vibrations travel in a wave motion in all directions from their source.
Sound vibrations travel through gases, liquids, and solids.
Sound travels through the air at the rate of about 1,100 feet per second.
An echo is a reflected sound.
Porous, soft materials are good sound absorbers.
Waves, such as those of sound, are characterized by their wavelength, frequency, and amplitude.
Sounds are characterized by their loudness, pitch, and quality.
Loudness depends on the amplitude of the sound wave.
Pitch depends on the frequency, the number of vibrations per second.
Sounds cause our eardrums to vibrate.
The inner ear converts sound vibrations into nerve impulses.

Discovering for Yourself

1. Listen for sounds in your environment. Make a list of the things that make the sound. Explain what causes each sound to change in loudness and pitch.
2. Observe the inside of a piano to discover how sounds are made, how pitch is determined, how loudness is controlled, what the sounding board does, how the piano is tuned.
3. Devise some original experiments that show that some substances carry sound better than others.
4. Perform a demonstration that shows that sound travels more slowly than light.
5. Examine a variety of musical instruments to see how they make sounds and how pitch and loudness are controlled.
6. Examine a hearing aid to see how it works.
7. Collect some "sound-making" insects and try to see how they produce sounds.
8. Find out what a decibel is, and what ultrasonic and supersonic mean.
9. Find out what some cities and institutions do to reduce noise.
10. Try to obtain a model of the human ear and explain how it works.
11. Examine a phonograph record (78 rpm) with a 10-power magnifying glass. See if you can find the waves in the grooves that produce sound. Do the waves differ in length and height? How would such variations affect the sound?

12. Find out how fathometers and sonar are used to measure the depth of water.
13. Try to demonstrate and explain echoes.
14. Use a violin to demonstrate overtones. Also try to use a rope to illustrate them.
15. Make and use a megaphone. How does the megaphone affect sound? How can you prove this?
16. Make a survey of your community for sound pollution and try to find out what, if anything, is being done to reduce the noise level.

(*Courtesy of* Science and Children, *Abby Barry Bergman.*)

CHAPTER 20B
TEACHING "SOUND AND HOW WE USE IT"

Children are stimulated, mystified, informed, and delighted by many sound impressions. Capitalize on their fascination and experiences with musical instruments to teach them some of the important principles of sound—its production, nature, and its control. Children can make toy xylophones, for example, to illustrate principles of sound, and there are many simple experiments and experiences that they can either originate or take out of books. There are opportunities to observe and to use the senses for discovering that sound is associated with vibration.

SOME BROAD CONCEPTS: "Sound and How We Use It"

Sounds are caused by vibrations.
Sounds travel in all directions from their source.
Sounds travel through gases, liquids, and solids.
Some materials (soft, rough) absorb sounds.
Some materials reflect sound.
Sounds have loudness, pitch, and quality.
Sounds cause the eardrum to vibrate.

FOR YOUNGER CHILDREN

What Sounds Are around Us?

Listening is an obvious way to interest children in the sounds around them and make them aware of the number and variety of sounds in their environment. Start by sitting quietly and listening in the classroom. List the sounds heard and then take a walk through the school and outdoors to add to the list. Encourage children to add sounds they hear at home in various places indoors and out.

Encourage them to listen to animal sounds—insects, birds, and others. They may devise a game centered around listening to sounds made by the teacher or other children behind a screen and trying to guess what made the sound.

Let children try to describe the sounds they hear and tell how they are alike and different from each other. Classify the sounds as: (1.) high and low, (2.) loud and soft, (3.) pleasant and unpleasant. They may also classify sounds according to: (1.) those that warn us of danger (auto horns), (2.) those that give us pleasure (musical instruments), (3.) night sounds, and so on. Tap different objects in the schoolroom and listen to the sound. Listen to various toys that make sound (drums, whistles, and others.) Try to feel the vibrations.

Our main objective in the activities just described is to make children aware of the many sounds around them and to identify differences in these sounds.

How Do Musical Instruments Make Sounds?

Refer to the chart on page 647 and select the activities that are possible in your situation. They involve using the sense of touch and sight as well as hearing. Feel the various instruments as they make sounds. Use a magnifying glass to try to see strings that are making sound. Use the result to direct children's attention to: "What makes the sound?" "Can you describe what happens?" "How can you stop the sound?"

How Are Sounds Different from Each Other?

From the experiences children have had in listening to sounds, describing them, and learning what causes them they have come to realize that sounds differ in pitch, intensity, and quality. Let them try to make and identify high and low sounds, loud and soft sounds, and pleasant and unpleasant ones. Ask: "Can you tell why these sounds differ from each other?" Use the wooden chalk box pictured on page 644, some stringed instruments, or any other easily-observed sound maker that will demonstrate sound characteristics. Let the children use these things to make different sounds, and try to observe what happens when sounds are made. Not all young children will be able to associate the characteristics of sound with the vibrations that produce them.

Other Problems for Younger Children

1. What sounds do toys make and how are they different from each other?
2. How does the wind make different sounds?
3. How can we use bottles to make different sounds?
4. Will a meter (or yard) stick carry sound?
5. How can we make a tin-can telephone?
6. How do bells and horns make sounds?

FOR OLDER CHILDREN[1]

What Causes Sound?

Many experiences will help pupils to understand that sound is caused by vibration. One involves the use of a triangle, which may be obtained from a kindergarten. Strike the triangle to make it vibrate. Listen to the sound. Touch the triangle. What happens? Thrust the triangle into water after it has been struck. Describe what happens. The waves are caused by the vibrations. (Tuning forks may be used for this experience if they are available. They may be ordered from scientific supply houses. Some music teachers have small tuning forks.) Touching the vibrating triangle or tuning fork with the fingertips, what do you feel?

[1] Elementary Science Study (ESS): *"Whistles and Strings," Teacher's Guide.* (Manchester, Mo.: Webster Division, McGraw-Hill Book Co.). For grades 4–5. Directions for making and using sound producers; activities; equipment list.

Ask pupils to suggest other ways of showing that vibrations cause sound. Ask them to *compare* what they hear, to *predict* what will happen under different circumstances, and try to *make interpretations* of their experiences. Here are some possibilities: Stretch a rubber band; pluck it; listen to it; stop it from vibrating; listen again. This may also be done with a violin string.

Touch a piano or radio while it is playing to feel the vibration. Then stop the sound.

Hold the fingers against the throat while making a sound. Stop the sound and feel the throat.

After several such experiences pupils may *tentatively* conclude that "all sound is caused by vibration." This conclusion can then be checked by reading and investigating further.

After they have tried to decide in each case what vibrates to produce the sounds several pupils may, one at a time, make the sounds again, and the class can be asked to tell how these sounds differ from each other. Pupils will discover that sounds differ

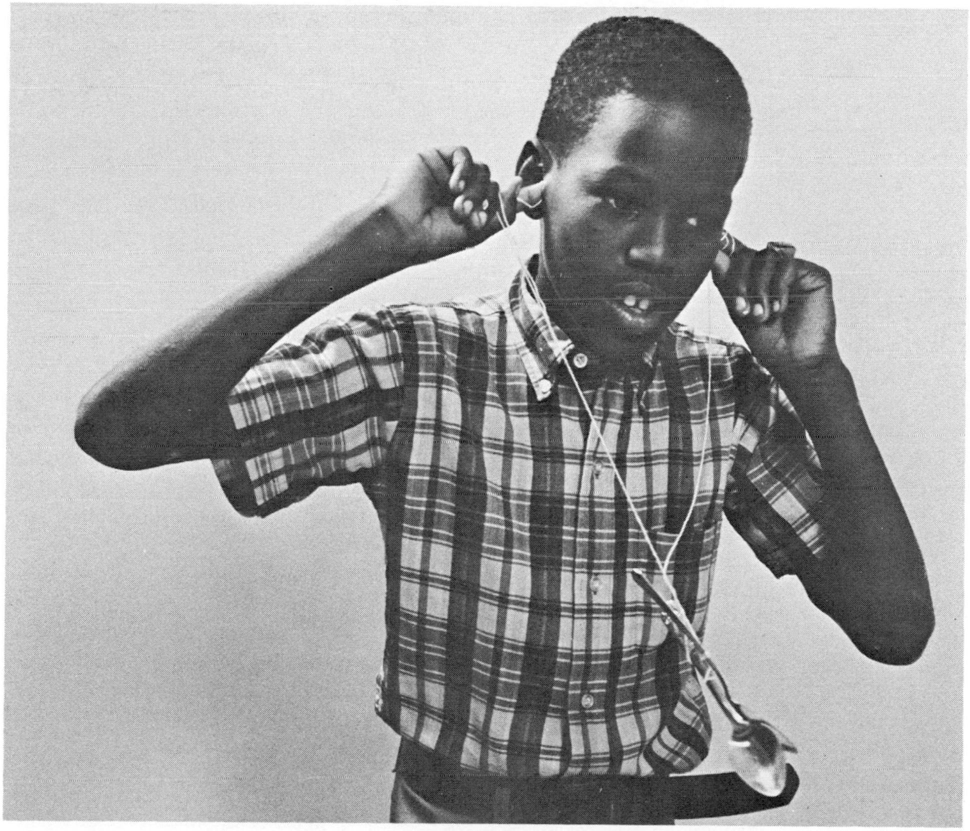

He hears beautiful chimes! Two spoons are tied together with a string about two feet long. One spoon is allowed to bang against the table. The ends of the string are held to the ears.

in loudness, pitch, and quality, although they will not necessarily state their observations in these terms. This will lead to the problem of why sounds differ from one another. Such an experience may be used to create interest and raise questions and problems.

How Can We Make High and Low Sounds?

An empty wooden chalk box or cigar box and some rubber bands can be used to make high and low sounds and to demonstrate how these are made.

Stretch a rubber band across the opening of the box and pluck it. (Thumbtacks can be placed at different distances down the sides of the box to hold the bands as they are stretched tighter.) Listen to the sound. Keep on tightening the rubber band and plucking it. Ask pupils to try to interpret. Now stretch a wide and a narrow rubber band across the box about equally tight. Pluck each and listen to the sound. Increase the tension of both and listen to each. Again urge pupils to interpret and to try to classify the sounds that are made (high, medium, low).

From these experiences pupils begin to realize that the more tightly the bands are stretched, the higher the pitch; and that thin bands produce a higher pitch than thick ones. If they watch the bands carefully they may be able to see that this difference is due to the speed of vibration. The use of a flexible ruler, as suggested on page 628, will also serve to show pupils the relationship between speed of vibration and pitch. Urge pupils to find other examples showing these ideas. The thick band and the loosely stretched ones vibrate so slowly that they can be seen moving back and forth, whereas in the thin and tightly stretched bands the vibrations are too fast to be seen. (*See also* the section on musical instruments page 647.)

Principles of sound can also be observed on a guitar. In many classes one or more of the pupils take music lessons, or at least have an instrument available. Let pupils predict (on the basis of what they have learned) how they think the instrument is built to: (1.) make sounds, (2.) make sounds of different pitch. Pupils notice the effect of stretching and loosening the strings; and they hear the difference between the sounds of thick strings and those of the thin ones. They can also see the effect of the length

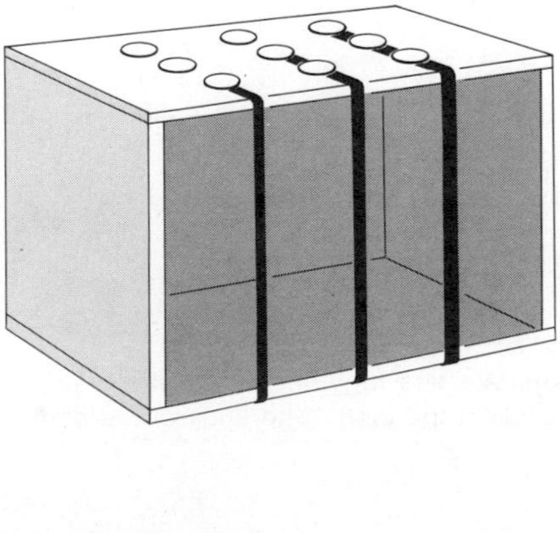

Rubber bands stretched across a chalk box, held in place with thumbtacks, illustrates the concept of pitch. Experiments may be performed with bands of various thicknesses and various tensions.

of the string on pitch. Pressing down on the string keeps part of it from vibrating. Consequently, they can see that the shorter the string the higher its pitch, and that long strings make sounds of lower pitch. Pupils can examine other stringed instruments (violin, viola, and others), and describe how they make sounds, predict from their observations what the differences in pitch will be between strings of different lengths and thickness, and interpret what they have observed.

How Does Sound Travel?

If there is a place in the school where iron pipes go from one floor to the next pupils can learn how sound travels through metal by noting that sound (made by tapping the pipe) will travel along the pipe from one floor to another.

There are many experiences that help children see that some things carry sound better than others. For example, if one child strikes a tuning fork at one end of a table and holds it in the air children at the other end of the table may not hear it. Ask: "Could we do something to make it possible to hear sound at this distance?" If the child sets the stem of the vibrating tuning fork on the table and the other children put their ears down to the table they can easily hear the sound. They can experiment to see which carries the sound of a tuning fork better, a yardstick or a necktie or another long piece of cloth. A long window pole may be used to demonstrate how solids carry sound by using the tuning fork—strike a tuning fork and then touch its base to one end of the pole while a student places his ear at the other. This can also be done by scratching one end of the pole with a fingernail and listening at the other. Many children may have had the experience of hearing sounds under water.

An interesting way to learn more about how sound travels is through a tin-can telephone.[2] This does not operate on the same principle as a real telephone, but it serves to show how vibrations from the human voice can be transmitted along a wire or string from one place to another.

To make the telephone, assemble two cans, two buttons, and several feet of wire or string. The cans should have one end removed neatly so that they will be safe to use. Punch a small hole in the center of the bottom of each can. Thread one end of the string through this hole to the inside of each can and tie it to the button. The telephone is used by two pupils standing far enough from each other to pull the string taut. One speaks into the can, holding it close around his mouth. The other holds the can to his ear. In answering, the process is reversed. Children may try different materials and variations of the cans to see if any of the variations make a difference (large or small cans, wire or string, and so on).

In summary: Various experiences and experiments should develop the concept that sound travels through air (you hear voices), through solids (tuning fork and table; string and "tin" can telephone), through liquids (under water in a swimming pool).

[2] G.O. Blough and M.H. Campbell: *Making and Using Classroom Science Materials in the Elementary School* (New York: Holt, Rinehart and Winston, Inc., 1954), pp. 159–162.

Does It Take Time for Sound to Travel?

Let a pupil carry a large drum or something else that will make a loud sound a block or so away from the rest of the class. When he strikes the drum with a broad gesture that can be seen at a distance, pupils will observe that they do not hear the sound until the drummer's arm is ready to strike the drum another time. They see the drummer because light travels from him to them. They hear the drum because sound travels from the drum to them. But the sound travels very slowly compared with the light. Pupils may recall that they have watched a man hammering on a roof in the distance and heard the sound when the hammer was already in the air ready to hit the nail again; or that they see lightning before they hear the thunder even though both occur simultaneously.

How Do Musical Instruments Make Sound?

Many pupils take music lessons. It is appropriate to apply the facts and principles they have learned in science to the instruments they play. Pupils who have had instruction from their music teachers about how the instrument produces sounds can demonstrate for the class.

What happens when you cover the openings? Through experiences with various musical instruments children are introduced to many of the important concepts of making and controlling sound. (*Courtesy of Abby Bergman.*)

As the musical instruments are demonstrated, pupils can observe and listen to discover what vibrates to make the sound, how the sounds are varied in pitch and loudness, and what influences the quality of the sound produced. For demonstration purposes pupils can play a scale.

Many pupils have never seen the inside of a piano. The boards are not difficult to remove and the strings and hammers are easy to observe. The three observations suggested in the preceding paragraph are appropriate for learning about the piano, as they are for the saxophone, cornet, violin, or any other instrument pupils are likely to bring in. A mouth organ is especially interesting to examine. If there is one available that is no longer usable the cover can be removed. Pupils can see the differences in the reeds.

If there is a music teacher in the school or in the community she will be able to contribute information that will not only help the pupils to understand the instruments but will enrich their study of sound.

The chart[3] summarizes activities and learnings related to musical instruments

[3]From *Science: Grades K–2* (Brooklyn, N.Y.: Board of Education of the City of New York).

ACTIVITIES AND LEARNINGS WITH MUSICAL INSTRUMENTS

	Drums	*Xylophone*	*Piano*	*Triangle*	*Cymbals*
What Children Do	Play on them with sticks or hands. Place small, tightly rolled up bits of paper on drumhead. Drum to see them dance. Hit drum gently; hit drum hard. Play on small and big drums.	Strike the bars with the sticks.	Notice how the sound is produced when a key is struck. Notice that the strings are of different length. Feel the piano while it is being played.	Strike the triangle. Listen to it. Strike it again. Touch it with the fingertips. Grasp the triangle firmly and strike it.	Strike the cymbals, listen. Strike the cymbals; touch the surface of one with the fingertips. Rub one of the cymbals gently with the fingers. Strike the cymbals; put your hand on one of them.
What Children Learn	Drums shake (vibrate) while they are played. A hard tap makes a louder sound than a gentle one.	The long bars make the low notes; the short bars make the high notes.	Felt-covered hammers strike the strings to make the sounds. Short strings make the high notes; long strings make the low notes. When the piano is played, we can feel a vibration.	The triangle makes a sound when we strike it. While it is sounding it quivers (vibrates). If it is held in the hand and struck a dull sound is produced.	Cymbals make sounds when they strike each other. While the cymbals are sounding, they shake. Rubbing a cymbal produces a muffled sound. Putting your hand on a sounding cymbal stops the sound.

commonly found in elementary schools. Children should be encouraged to prepare a chart of their own according to a plan they can devise.

OTHER PROBLEMS FOR OLDER CHILDREN

1. How are rooms made more soundproof?
2. How does a megaphone direct sound?
3. What are sympathetic vibrations?
4. How can flower-pot chimes, a xylophone, and a drinking glass scale be made?
5. How do we make sounds?
6. How do we hear sounds?
7. How are echoes made?
8. How does a phonograph record produce sound?
9. How does sonar work?
10. How do insects make sound?

Resources to Investigate with Children

1. The local motion-picture theater and other public buildings to see how soundproofing and other sound controls are accomplished.
2. The school and the custodian to learn about soundproofing in the school auditorium and elsewhere in the building.
3. Music teachers to show various musical instruments and explain how they produce and control sounds.
4. A music store to see and examine instruments and hear about how they produce and control sound.
5. A speech teacher to explain how we produce and control sound and how voices can be improved.
6. Builders' supply company to obtain samples of soundproofing materials.

Preparing to Teach

1. Assemble materials that children can use that will help them learn how sounds can be changed in pitch, loudness, and quality. Work out a plan for using these.
2. Devise a series of demonstrations children can do to show and explain what they have learned about sound.
3. Plan a series of drawings that could be duplicated and used by children to predict what would happen if the action were completed. For example: bell with hammer in position to strike, violin with fingers about to tighten a string.
4. Make a list of easily-obtainable materials that can be assembled to teach the ideas in this chapter.
5. Prepare a list of individual investigations that interested children might carry out and report on for their classmates.

CHAPTER 21A

LIGHT AND HOW WE USE IT

(Courtesy of Union Pacific Railroad.)

A WORLD OF LIGHT

A beam of light originating in the excited atoms of the sun starts on its way to the earth. Eight minutes and 93 million miles later it has reached the sidewalk outside your home. A child races through the steady stream of light, interrupts it momentarily, and causes a shadow to fall on the walk. Some of the light is reflected from the sunlight-bathed objects to your eyes, making it possible for you to see the scene outside your window.

Light is a messenger bringing us news of the universe. Light excites the most important sense, that of sight, initiating nerve impulses that our brain interprets as a distant star, a glorious sunset, a familiar face.

Light rules life. Plants and animals are governed by the rhythm of day and night. Sunlight provides the energy for the food-making process in green plants and consequently is essential for all life on our planet. The fossil fuels—coal, gas, and oil—have stored within them energy that winged down from the sun millions of years ago. The cycle is complete when the fuels are burned: The sun energy locked in their molecules is liberated as heat and light.

LIGHT TRAVELS

One of the most important discoveries made concerning light is that it travels, racing through space at the rate of about 186,000 miles per second. Nothing in our everyday experiences conveys this concept. When we pull up the shade of a darkened room the light seems to fill it instantaneously. Distances on earth are too short for the travel time of light to make much difference. It does have significance, however, for the viewing of heavenly bodies. If the sun were suddenly to stop shining we would continue to see it for about eight minutes, for, at the speed given above, it takes that time for light to travel from the sun to the earth. Moonlight (which is really reflected sunlight) takes about $1\frac{1}{3}$ seconds to travel the 238,000 miles from the moon to the earth. Other interesting implications of the traveling of light through space are discussed in Chapter 8A. We learned there that the distance covered by light in a year furnishes us with a yardstick, the light year, for measuring the universe.

WHAT IS LIGHT?

This question has been the subject of controversy for many centuries. Plato and other ancient philosophers believed that light was a kind of emanation *from* the eye that made objects visible. Sir Isaac Newton proposed the corpuscular theory of light in 1700. He believed that light was a stream of particles or corpuscles shot off by a luminous body. At about the same time Christian Huygens, a Dutchman, countered with the theory that light was a vibration, a wave that rippled through space. Each of these theories, those of Newton and Huygens, explains some phenomena satisfactorily but not others. Einstein theorized that a beam of light is a shower of small packets of energy, which he called photons. At present we can at least agree to define light as the kind of energy that causes us to see.

SHADOWS

Perhaps the simplest picture that nature paints of an object is its shadow. We notice (*See* p. 666.) shadows most in the early morning or late afternoon, when opaque objects, such as trees or people, cast elongated silhouettes. A moment's consideration will show that the object is not really "casting" anything, instead it is blocking the sunlight, which, streaming past its edges, traces the form of the object on sidewalk or lawn.

The earth, too, casts a shadow—into space. When the moon enters this cone-shaped shadow we have a lunar eclipse. When, on the other hand, the moon comes between the sun and the earth its smaller shadow sweeps across the earth, and we have a solar eclipse.

Not all substances are opaque to light. Glass and some plastics are transparent; they permit light from objects to pass through. Our ancestors used oiled paper in their windows to permit light to enter their houses. Substances, such as oiled paper or frosted glass, which allow some light to go through but through which objects cannot be clearly seen, are called *translucent.* In lighting our homes and schools we make use of various materials that transmit light differently.

SEEING THE THINGS AROUND US

A red rose in a glass vase is set on a white doily on a dark table—in a totally dark room. Your eyes are wide open, but you do not see any of these objects. Light a candle and they become visible. Why? Just how, for example, do you see the rose (*see* top p. 652)?

Light travels from the candle source to the petals and stem. Some of it is absorbed by the atoms of these plant structures, and some is reflected in various directions from the surface of the flower. Part of the reflected light enters your eye and causes an image to be formed in the back of the eye. This stimulates the nerve endings there to carry impulses to your brain, which interprets these impulses as a flower.

Although the flower reflects the candle *light* to your eye you do not see the candle flame as you would in a mirror. This is because the petals reflect light irregularly, in such a way as to reveal their own texture and shape rather than that of the candle. In other words it is the *effect* of the surface texture on light that makes the object visible. A perfectly smooth reflecting surface would not be visible; the source of light rather than the surface would be seen. It would be a mirror.

Even if you put an opaque screen between the candle and the flower you would still see the flower, because some of the candle light would be reflected from the walls and the ceiling to the vase. Light from the candle travels in all directions and is reflected in all directions.

The table appears darker to your eyes than the flower, the flower darker than the doily. Why? The atoms of the table surface *absorb* a good deal of the light (photons or waves) that strikes them, and convert it into heat. Very little is reflected to your eye. The red flower absorbs some light but reflects more than the dark table does. The white doily reflects the most light, absorbing very little. Thus, the variation in brightness of different surfaces under equal illumination is due to the different amounts of light energy soaked up and "bounced off" by their constituent atoms.

Why do the rose petals look red, the stem green? What makes an object have a color? To understand color we must know a little more about the nature of light itself. If a narrow beam of white light from the sun or from a lamp passes through a triangular glass prism a rainbow of colors appears on a screen or wall on the opposite side (*see* top p. 653). The white light fans out to form a spectrum of red, orange, yellow, green, blue, and violet, in that order, each color merging imperceptibly into the next. White light, then, consists of a mixture of many colors. Sir Isaac Newton showed this in a simple but ingenious experiment using two prisms. A beam of white light was directed at the first prism and emerged on the opposite side as a spectrum of colors. Newton then placed the second prism, upside down with respect to the first, in the path of these colored rays. The rays joined in the second prism to form a spot of white light on a screen (*see* bottom p. 653). White light can be separated into colors; these colors can combine to make white light. If, on the other hand, a narrow beam of green light were allowed to pass through a prism, it would emerge as green light.

The reason that we are discussing white light is that we live in a world that is bathed in it. The colors we see "in" objects (except for those that make their own light) are influenced by the fact that these objects are "painted" by a white light that is a combination of red, orange, yellow, green, blue, and violet.

To come back to the original question, why do the rose's petals appear red and its stem green? Bathed in white light the petals are receiving red, orange, yellow, green, blue, and violet rays. All of these are absorbed as energy into the atoms of the pigment of the petals *except the red ones.* This color is reflected; in your eye it stimulates certain nerve endings resulting in the sensation of red. In other words the color of an opaque object is determined by the kind of light it does *not* absorb, by the kind that bounces off it. *The red you see "in" the rose is the red*

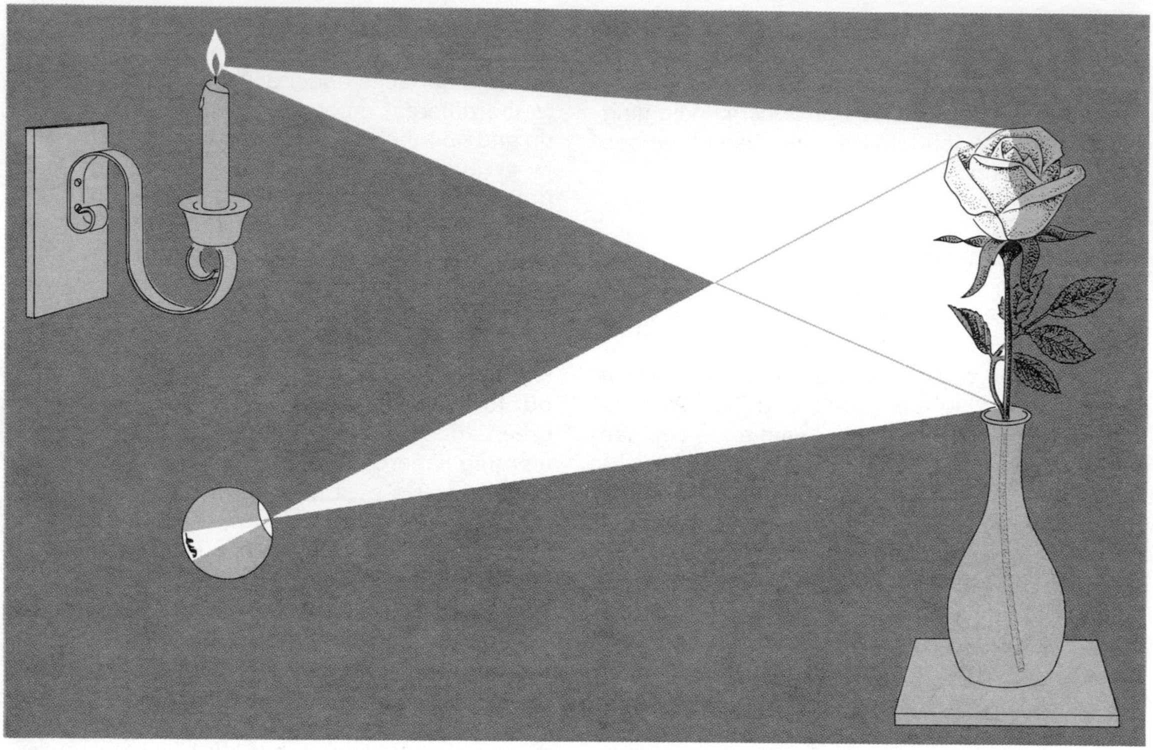

We see a rose because light travels to it and is reflected to our eyes (*see* text for further details).

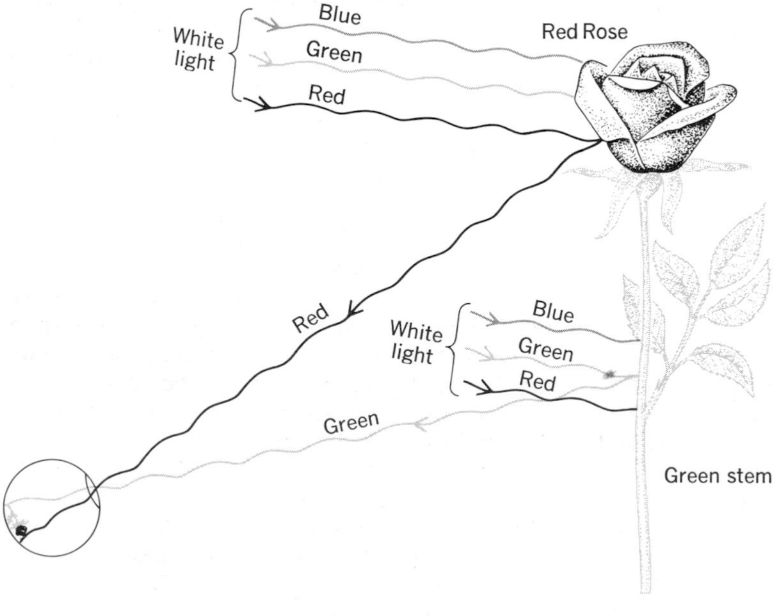

Roses are red because they absorb all the colors in white light except red. This color is reflected to your eye. Why is the stem green?

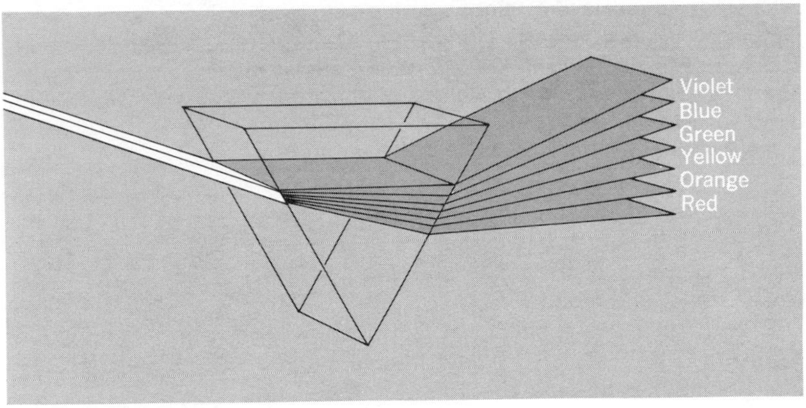

When a beam of white light is passed through one side of a triangular glass prism a rainbow of colors emerges from the other. White light is a mixture of many colors.

originally in the white light bathing the rose and then reflected from it. The green stem appears green because it absorbs most colors except those near the green part of the spectrum; it reflects green (*see* bottom p. 652).

A white flower reflects a large percentage of *all* the different colors in white light and so appears white. In nature there are very few objects that are pure red or blue or green. A red apple, for example, reflects more red than the other colors, but it also reflects a little blue and green.

RAINBOWS

White light, as we have learned, is a mixture of many colors. When white light, traveling through the air, passes obliquely through a substance of different density, like a glass prism or a body of water, the various colors separate to produce a spectrum. We see this in a classroom sometimes when sunlight passes through an aquarium.

Spectrum making on a large scale occurs

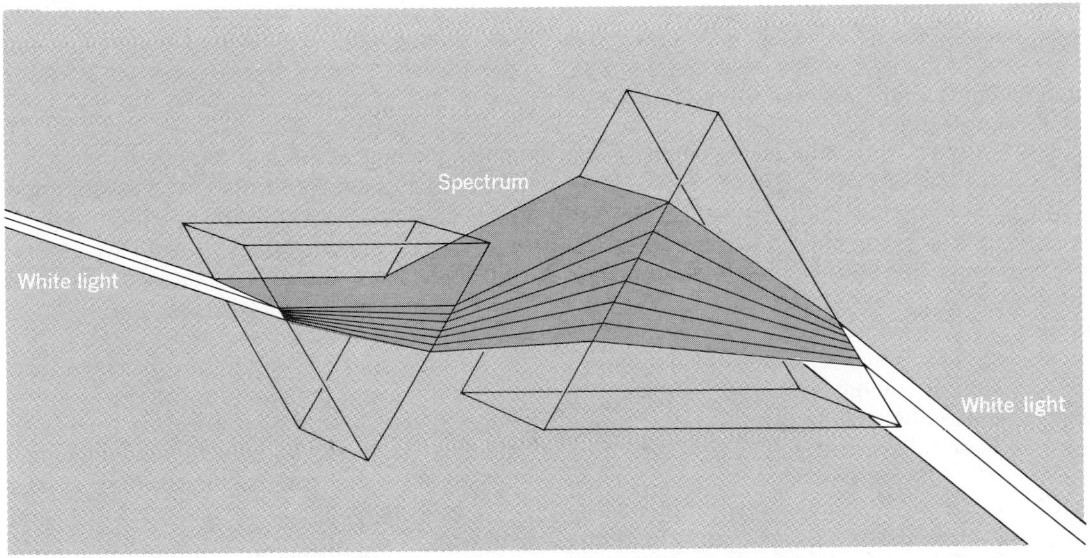

White light fans out to form a spectrum of colors; the colors rejoin to form white light.

when nature displays a rainbow in the sky. Here nature's "prisms" are thousands of water droplets left slowly settling in the sky after a shower. Each droplet fans out the white sunlight into a tiny spectrum, but the angle of vision of the viewer on the ground permits him to see only one of these colors in each of the bands that characterize a rainbow. From the highest part of the arch red is bent to the eye; then, in descending order, we can see the bands of orange, yellow, green, blue, and violet.

You can make a small but real rainbow by spraying a shower of droplets from a garden hose. Do this in the late afternoon when the sun is more than halfway down from overhead. Standing with your back to the sun, adjust the nozzle to the finest spray and direct it toward the east at a rather high angle. The rainbow will be more beautiful if the spray is directed toward a shaded or dark background. This homemade rainbow is produced in the same way as nature's larger ones.

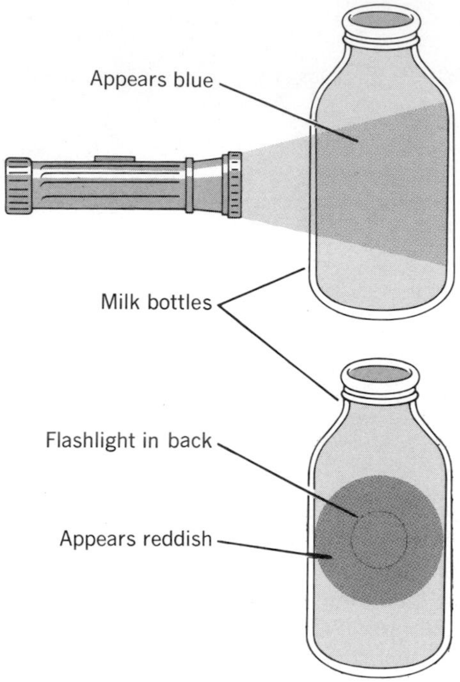

Demonstrating why the sky has color (*see* text for details).

WHY IS THE SKY BLUE?

The sky may also be red, orange, or other colors, gray or black. Before answering the question why the sky is blue it must be understood that the color we ascribe to the "sky" is an effect produced only in the lower part of the atmosphere—in the air up to 20 or 30 miles above the surface of the earth. This lower atmosphere, which is dense with air molecules and dust, has an interesting effect on sunlight.

Light coming from the sun is white, which as we have seen, is a mixture of all colors. When white sunlight bounces off the small particles of the atmosphere it is scattered in different directions. However, the blue light in the sunlight is scattered more than the red light. This blue light reaches our eyes from all parts of the sky, so that the sky appears blue. The sun itself appears yellow, which is a combination of the remaining colors in the sunlight; that is, those left after the blue has been subtracted.

A simple way of demonstrating atmospheric scattering of light is to stir a few drops of milk into a bottle of water. (The milk represents the air molecules and dust particles in the atmosphere.) Shine a flashlight against the side of the bottle. (The flashlight represents the sun.) The mixture will appear blue because the blue light has been scattered sidewise (to your eye) out of the flashlight beam by the milk particles. Now move the flashlight around to the back of the bottle so that you view its beam head on. (This is like looking at the sun directly.) The blue disappears and the light from the flashlight appears to be redder than normal. The blue has been scattered out of the beam and you are now viewing what is left—the reds and yellows which combine to give the effect of orange.

Sky color, then, is a characteristic of our lower atmosphere. As flights into space take us out of the lower atmosphere the sky around appears black at all times, because there are no atmospheric particles to scatter the sunlight. On the moon, which has no atmosphere at all, the sky is always black, even when the sun is shining.

MIRRORS

We noted previously that a perfectly smooth reflecting surface would not be visible, that the source of the light rather than the surface would be seen, that this kind of surface would be a mirror. How is an object seen "in" a mirror?

(See pp. 664–5, 667–8.)

Light, like a ball, bounces away from the objects it strikes. Consider a rose again, but this time see it "in" a mirror. How is this possible? Again we begin with light traveling from a source, such as a candle or perhaps the sun, and striking the flower. The light reflected from it on this occasion travels from its surface in many directions. Part of it strikes the walls of the room, part a mirror. In turn, the walls and the mirror reflect the light from the rose in all directions—part of it toward your eyes. Why, then, do you "see" a rose in the mirror and not on the wall?

A mirror produces an image because it bounces light in a way called *regular reflection.* Each individual ray from the flower is reflected from the flat, smooth, shiny surface of the mirror so that each point of the rose results in a corresponding point in its image. As a consequence a perfect image of the object is carried to the viewer's eye. When, however, rays of light are reflected from a relatively rough surface, such as the walls of the room, they bounce off in many directions. The light is scattered and so is the image. This is called *diffuse reflection.* This kind of reflection is useful; otherwise you would see your image on this page instead of the print.

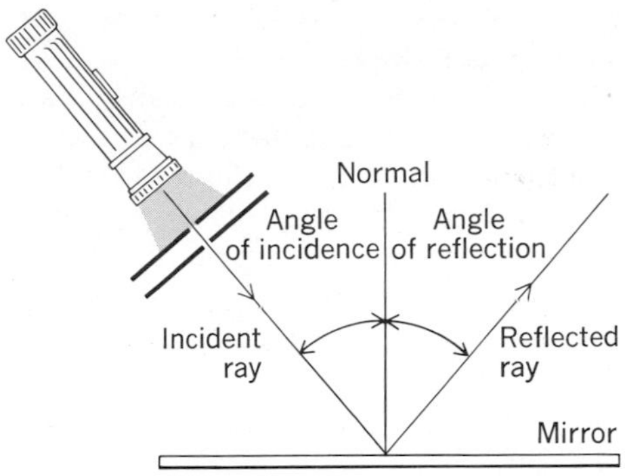

The law of reflection: The angle of incidence equals the angle of reflection.

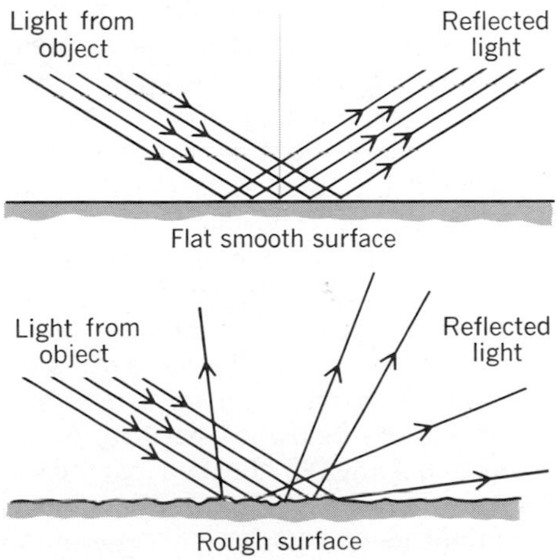

(*Top*) Regular reflection of light—as from a mirror. (*Bottom*) Diffuse reflection of light—as from a wall.

Let us examine the bouncing of light more carefully. Any billiard player knows that the angle at which a ball strikes the side of the table influences the angle at which it will rebound. In the absence of other factors (an irregularity in the table or a side spin imparted to the ball) the angle of strike with the table equals the angle of bounce. This is also true of a ray of light striking the surface of a mirror. However, the physicist erects an imaginary perpendicular to this surface (called the *normal*) at the point of contact and measures the angle between that perpendicular and the path of the incoming and departing light ray. The angle made with the incoming ray is called the *angle of incidence* and with the departing ray the *angle of reflection.* The angle of incidence equals the angle of reflection. This phenomenon is known as the *law of reflection.* This law explains the faithful point by point reproduction by a mirror of the original rose in the eyes of the viewer.

We commonly speak of looking *into* a mirror to see our reflection. Obviously, nothing occurs behind the mirror. It is true, however, that light coming from any point in front of a mirror, such as the light of a candle flame, appears to come from a point an equal distance behind the mirror. Although we speak of "mirror images" the image is actually formed in your eye from the light that the mirror has reflected to it.

Most mirrors are made of glass, the back being coated with a substance, such as silver, that will reflect light readily. Unbreakable mirrors are made of highly polished steel, although such mirrors do not reflect light as well as glass ones.

Convex mirrors, the kind that bulge out in front, produce small images of a large area. Because of this they are commonly used as rear-view mirrors on autos.

Concave mirrors are used in reflecting telescopes to gather light from a distant object, such as a star, and focus it so that it may be viewed. The telescope at Mount Palomar, as we have seen, has a concave mirror with a diameter of 200 inches—an area of about 220 square feet. Every bit of this enormous reflecting surface receives the essentially parallel rays from a single object, such as a star, and then reflects all of them so that they converge and meet in a single point in the tube of the telescope. Here it is reflected by a small plane mirror into an eyepiece, where it is viewed conveniently. Because stars are at great distances from the earth their images, even in the most powerful telescopes, are points of light—no details of the star itself can be seen. The significant advantage is that the light-gathering capacity of the huge concave mirror can make the stars appear a million times as bright. Very faint stars, which cannot be detected by the unaided eye, are thereby revealed. The sun, the moon, and the planets, however, *are* close enough to be magnified in such a telescope so that their details are revealed. Concave mirrors also are used in headlight reflectors of cars, in searchlight reflectors, and as shaving mirrors. The solar furnace, which can produce temperatures as high as 7000° F., is a large concave mirror that brings the rays of the sun to a focus.

Light is bent as it passes obliquely from one medium to another if the mediums differ in density. To the man on the bank the fish appears to be in the position of the unshaded fish. Actually, it is in the position of the shaded one.

LIGHT BENDS

If you have ever tried to catch a goldfish with your hands you know that the fish is not where it appears to be. Why is this so?

Light travels in straight lines, but its direction may be changed when it passes from a medium of one density to another. The fish fooled you because the rays of light reflected from it were bent as they passed from the water to the air. For the same reason a pencil or a spoon partially submerged in water looks crooked—so does the handle of a fishnet or the oar of a rowboat. Men spearing fish must aim below the spot where the fish appears or they will miss it. In all these examples we do not see light being bent; we see the effects of this bending.

The bending of light as it passes obliquely from one media to another is known as *refraction.* The apparent "twinkling" of stars (stars actually do not twinkle) is due to the bending of starlight as it passes through the various shifting layers of hot and cold air in the atmosphere.

The refraction of light by the earth's atmosphere makes it possible for us to see the sun when it is actually below the horizon. At sunrise and sunset the rays of the sun pass obliquely through the dense air of the lower atmosphere and are bent toward the earth. They no longer come in a straight line from the sun to the viewer. Thus, the rays are bent to our eyes, even though the sun is below the horizon. The effect of all this is to make the day longer than it would be if the earth had no atmosphere.

LENSES

The first lens used by man was the one that he has in his own eye. We have extended the use of this lens with the aid of many others. Lenses in eyeglasses correct the deficiencies in our eyes. Lenses in telescopes extend our view into space; lenses in microscopes permit us to penetrate into the mysteries of the minute; lenses in cameras help us make a record of the present for the future.

(*See* pp. 668–9.)

Lenses are useful because they are effective lightbenders: They are designed to refract light according to the purpose of the optical device they are used in.

There are two principal types of simple lenses. Those thicker in the middle than at the edges are called *convex lenses* or *converging lenses.* Those thinner in the middle than at the edges are called *concave lenses* or *diverging lenses.* As their names imply, a converging lens makes light passing through it converge or come together, whereas a diverging lens bends rays passing through it so that they diverge or spread apart.

Pictures from Lenses

A magnifying glass is a common example of a convex lens. A simple experiment that you can perform with such a lens will reveal what it does to light. First go to a room with a window brightly illuminated by light from the sky. Draw the blinds or shades on the *other* windows to darken them. Tack a sheet of white paper to a wall on the side of the room opposite the illuminated window. Hold the magnifying lens near the paper. Move the lens back and forth until you see a sharp image of the window on the paper. (At night you can get the same effect by using a bright lamp instead of a bright window.) Look at the image carefully and you will notice that it is upside down. The convex lens bends the light and causes it to form a small, inverted image of the window.

(*See* figure below.)

The Camera

If you could place a piece of unexposed photographic film on the wall instead of paper, and then develop it in the usual manner, you would find that you had made a negative of the image in the same way that a camera does. You have stripped the camera down to its two most basic essentials—lens and film. A *pinhole camera* even disposes of the lens, using instead a tiny hole to admit the light. A study of the diagram of this camera will show why cameras produce inverted images.

(*See* pp. 669–71.)

The common box camera is essentially a lighttight box with a lens in front, an opening for light, a shutter for allowing light to enter the opening for a fraction of a second, film, and a

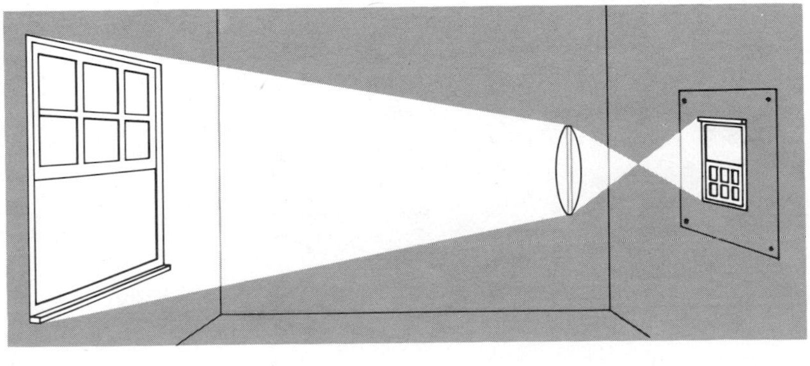

Your room can be a camera. All you need is a magnifying glass. How does the image compare with the original?

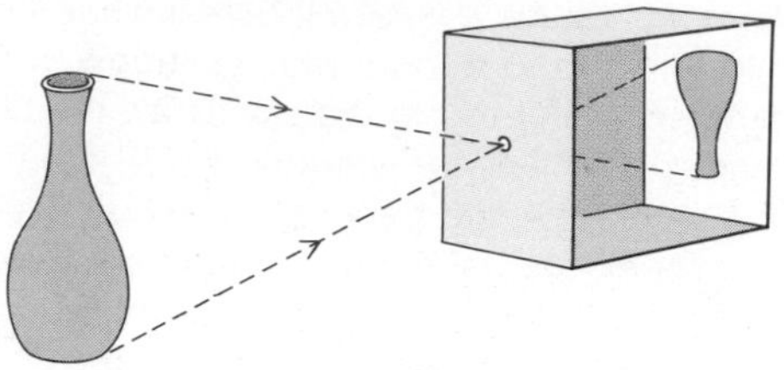

The camera in its simplest form is a lighttight box with a tiny pinhole at one end. This diagram shows how an inverted image is produced.

device in back for holding and turning the film. When the shutter is snapped open, light is admitted and passes through the lens, which focuses it on the film. There it produces a change in the silver salt that is embedded in a gelatin layer on the film. This change is made visible by development, which also serves to preserve the image on film. Since *light* actually causes *dark* grains of silver to be deposited on the film the developed film is a negative. White teeth are black in a negative, black hair is almost colorless because it reflects little light. In making a print light is made to shine through the negative to the photographic paper, which is also coated with a sensitive silver compound. Thus, a reversal of the image is effected, and a positive is produced.

In the previously described experiment with the magnifying glass focusing was done by moving the lens back and forth. In a box camera, and in other kinds of fixed-focus cameras, the only focusing that is done is accomplished by moving the entire camera; the lens is not moved in relation to the camera. Because of this the box camera is somewhat limited in its use; however, it can take satisfactory pictures of subjects that are from 6 feet away to as far as the eye can see. Cameras with focusing devices permit the lens to be moved back and forth to secure sharp focuses for each picture at varying distances. In cameras other than the simplest the amount of light admitted can be controlled in two ways: by varying the length of *time* the shutter is open and by regulating the *size* of the opening with a device called a diaphragm.

Motion Pictures

The process by which pictures are made to produce the illusion of motion may seem complicated but actually is quite simple. The principle is illustrated by a certain kind of picture book in which the pictures are printed close to the edge of the page. One holds the book's edge with the thumb, bends the pages, and then releases them rapidly one by one. If the pages slip by rapidly enough the illusion of motion is created.

Motion pictures are simply a series of still pictures projected on a screen in rapid succession. Each picture is motionless while it is being shown and is only slightly different from the one before it. Our eye receives each of these pictures and focuses it on its own "screen," the retina, in the back of the eyeball. The movie projector is constructed to make each image persist for $\frac{1}{24}$ second on the screen. The retina retains a picture for as long as $\frac{1}{15}$ second after it has disappeared. This phenomenon is known as *persistence of vision.* Because of the rapidity with which the pictures appear, the eye blends each image with the following one so that we get the impression of continuous, lifelike motion.

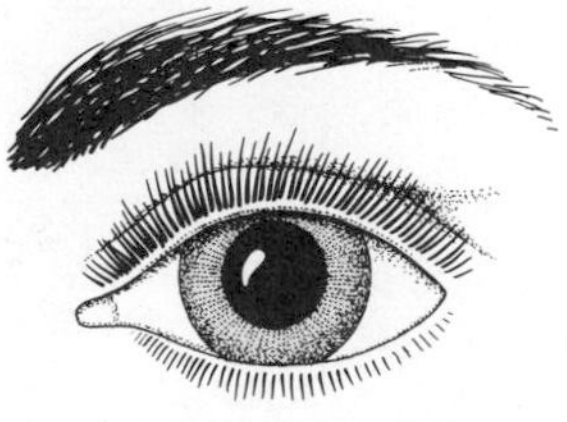

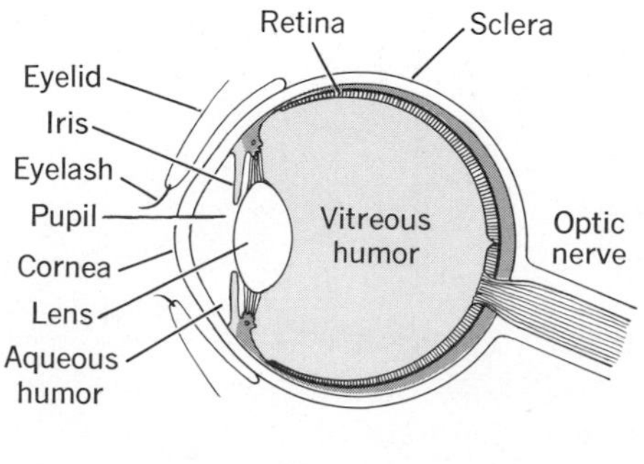

(*Left*) Front view of eye. (*Right*) Vertical section of eye. Which of the eye's structures can be seen in the front view (*see* the text for a description of how the eye functions).

THE EYE

The eye is often compared to a camera. The eye is a lighttight box, with dark pigment on the inside to prevent the bouncing around of light. It has a lens to focus light and a light-sensitive screen in the back on which an image is actually formed. It has an opening in front comparable to the opening of a camera; the size of this opening can be varied, as in a camera, to admit more or less light. It has a kind of shutter, the eyelid, that can exclude light (the eyelid also serves as a kind of windshield wiper to keep the eyes clean). The resemblance of eye and camera is even more detailed and striking than indicated by these items. We shall note some other similarities as we go along.

The Outer Eye

Observe your own eye in a mirror to find some of its external structures. It will be helpful if you refer to the diagram on page 658 as you make this study. You are looking at a portion of an almost spherical ball about 1 inch in diameter. You are looking right through a thin transparent membrane that guards the front of the eye, called the *conjunctiva*. This membrane is continuous with the inner surface of the eyelids. The conjunctiva is kept free of dust and is lubricated by the tears that are spread in a thin film every time you blink. After flowing over the surface of the eye the tears are drained by two tiny tubes, one in the inner corner of each eye, into the nose cavity. The continual washing and lubrication of the eyeball by tears prevents the delicate conjunctiva from becoming dry and inflamed. The tears also contain the substance *lysozyme,* which destroys bacteria.

Under the conjunctiva is the "white of the eye," the *sclera,* which is made of tough, fibrous tissue that extends around the entire eye to make up the "box" of this instrument. The sclera becomes transparent over the *iris* and *pupil,* forming the somewhat bulging *cornea.* The pupil is a hole in the iris through which light is admitted into the eye. It appears black because it is the opening into the dark cavity of the eyeball. The pupil is surrounded by the doughnut-shaped iris, which is the pigmented or colored portion of the eye. The iris is a muscle that controls the size of the pupil. You can see it at work if you sit for a few minutes in a dimly lighted room, with just enough light to see your iris and pupil in a mirror. When you switch on a nearby light the iris gets bigger and the pupil smaller. This reflex action of the iris automatically regulates the amount of light entering the eye. The need for such control becomes apparent when one realizes that the light from a sunny beach is thousands of times as strong as the light in a dim theater. In dim light the pupil opening is large to admit as much light as possible; in bright light it becomes small to reduce the amount of light. In a camera, too, a diaphragm is adjusted by the photographer to permit more or less light to enter the opening at its center.

The eyeball lies in a bony socket of the skull and is manipulated by the muscles that are attached to it. These muscles tilt the eyeball up and down, left and right, and in a rotary motion.

Inside the Eye

The internal structure of the eye can be understood with the aid of the diagram, which represents a vertical section of the eyeball from front to back. In this section we recognize some structures previously seen in the external view: the eyelids, cornea, iris, pupil, and sclera. In addition, we note two important structures—the *lens* and the *retina*—and two fluids—the *aqueous humor* and the *vitreous humor*. The aqueous humor is a watery fluid in front of the lens; the vitreous humor is a denser fluid behind the lens that fills most of the eyeball.

The Eye Makes a Picture

The lens of the eye acts like the lens of a camera: It gathers light, bends it, and forms a picture. The light rays are focused to make a sharp image on the light-sensitive retina in the back of the eye. As in the camera the image is an inverted one.

The lens of the human eye is not focused by moving it back and forth. Instead, focusing is accomplished by *changing the shape of the lens.* The eye lens is a transparent disc, convex on both sides and about $\frac{1}{3}$ inch in diameter. It is within the globe of the eye just behind the iris, and is made of a material whose shape can be altered by the action of muscles attached to it. When the lens is thin and flat it is adapted for focusing faraway objects. When it is fatter and rounder it is adapted for close vision.

The ability to adjust the lens shape is called *accommodation.* This works well in most young people. In older individuals the lens loses some of its elasticity, and eyeglasses are sometimes required to compensate for this.

The Screen of the Eye

The parallel between eye and camera holds for the light-sensitive retina, which is analogous to photographic film. In the retina there are two kinds of sensitive cells, the rods and cones. Cones are sensitive to light of different colors and are also used in bright light. Rods are sensitive to dim light; when stimulated, they produce sensations only of light intensity—of varying shades of gray. As you might expect, the retinas of some night animals contain only rods.

In light of intermediate strength both the rods and cones respond. As brightness increases, the cones take over entirely. This change corresponds to the photographer's use of "fast" or "slow" film in his camera.

The cones, then, are used in bright light and respond to varying colors in that light. How does the eye see color? It is thought that human color vision is dependent on the responses of three different kinds of cones, each with a different light-sensitive pigment. One type is sensitive to red light, one to green light, and one to blue-violet light. Color sensation is the sum of responses to impulses from all three types of cones. Thus, the human retina resembles not only black-and-white film but color film, which also contains three different chemicals sensitive to different colors. Colorblind individuals, apparently, lack either one or two sets of these cones.

Seeing with Our Brains

Impulses initiated by the 130 million light-sensitive cells in each retina are sent over nerve fibers to the brain. These are nerve impulses, not light waves. The brain interprets them according to the type of cell over which the impulse comes and the particular spot in the brain where the impulse is received. The brain produces some kind of a replica (not a picture) of the image on the retina.

What happens in the brain is fantastically complex; what one "sees" depends on many factors. An ink blot means different things to different people. Seeing is not simply a matter of the physics of light; it depends on the operation of the mind. The complex nature of vision was expressed well by Adelbert Ames, an expert in the field of visual perception: "What the eye sees is the mind's best guess as to what is out in front."

THE KEYBOARD OF LIGHT

Light is similar to sound in a number of ways. Both are messengers carrying information of the world about us to our senses. Both travel, although light travels almost 1 million times as fast as sound. Both apparently are wave phenomena; a wavelike disturbance proceeds in all directions from a source. In both the length of the wave (from "crest" to "crest") varies; in sound varying wavelengths produce sounds of different *pitch;* in light, different *colors.*

Color, then, is akin to pitch. Just as each note has a different wavelength so each color has its particular wavelength. The deepest red visible to the eye as a color has a wavelength of about 1/30,000 inch; the deepest violet at the other end of the spectrum has a wavelength of 1/60,000 inch.

We recall that some sound waves (the ultrasonic ones) cannot be detected by the human ear. This has its parallel in "invisible" light waves. Just beyond the violet is the invisible *ultraviolet,* with a shorter wavelength than violet. Ultraviolet radiation, found in sunlight, is important to life because it stimulates the production

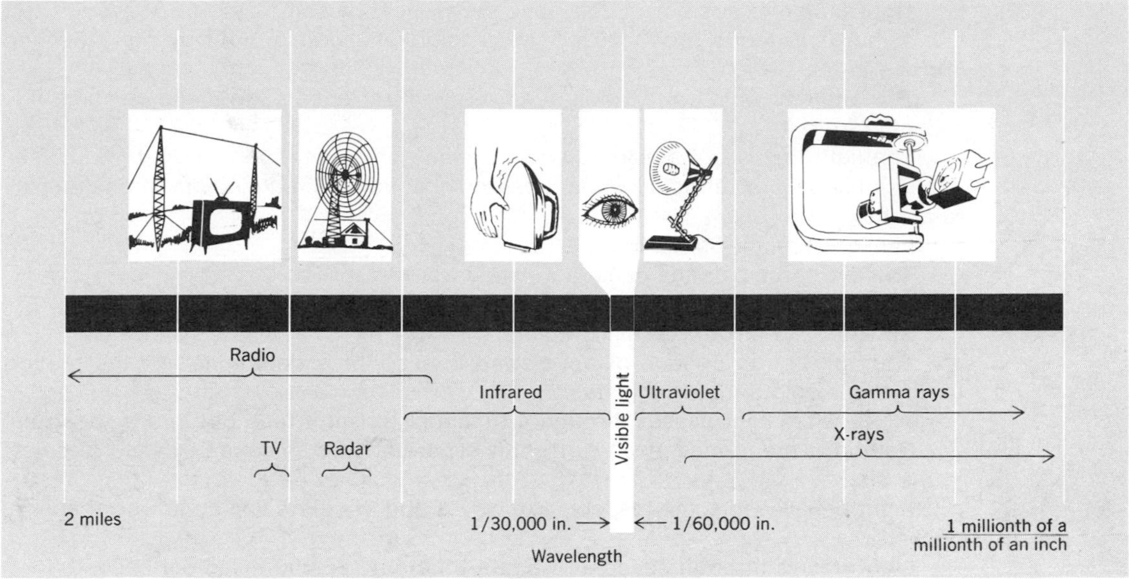

Visible light is a small part of the electromagnetic spectrum.

of vitamin D in organisms exposed to it. Ultraviolet radiation is also responsible for the sunburning and suntanning effects of exposure to sunlight. Although not detected by the eye ultraviolet does affect photographic film, and therefore the appearance of the developed image.

At the other end of the spectrum, just beyond the deepest red, is *infrared.* These waves, also occurring in sunlight, are extremely important, for they are the radiant heat waves that warm the earth. All warm bodies radiate infrared light. Infrared radiation affects special photographic film that is sensitive to this invisible color.

BEYOND THE REDS AND BLUES

Beyond the reds and blues there exists a larger spectrum of waves known as the *electromagnetic spectrum.* We can compare this spectrum to a supergrand piano containing not 7 octaves but 70. On the keyboard of this imagined piano, which is ten times as long as the conventional grand piano, visible light occupies only one octave, near the center.

As you run your eye over the keyboard you discover that this piano is capable of many effects: radio, television, radar, visible light, x-rays, and gamma rays. Note that as you move from radio waves at one end to gamma rays at the other the wavelength decreases progressively from about 2 miles to 1 millionth of 1 millionth of an inch.

Electromagnetic waves, first described in 1865 by James Maxwell, are another example of basic unity in nature. In Chapter 15A we found that all matter consists of the same fundamental particles—electrons, protons, neutrons, and others. The electromagnetic spectrum demonstrates that many forms of radiation consist of waves of the same fundamental nature, which travel at the same speed of 186,000 miles per second. Thus radio waves, light, and x-rays differ only in the lengths of their waves and in the frequency of their vibrations.

The following generalizations may be made from the material in this chapter:

We are able to see objects because they reflect or emit light to our eyes.

A mirror image is produced by the regular reflection of light by the reflecting surface to the viewer.

The angle at which a ray of light strikes a mirror equals the angle at which it is reflected from it.

The light that is not absorbed by an opaque object is reflected by it.

Light is bent or refracted when it passes obliquely from a medium of one density to another.

Lenses are light benders.

The eye resembles the camera in many ways.

The color of light is determined by its wavelength.

Sunlight is a mixture of many colors.

The color of an opaque object viewed in sunlight is determined by the portion of the sun's colors that it reflects.

When white light passes through a triangular prism it fans out into a spectrum.

Rainbows are formed when sunlight is separated into its colors by water droplets in the air.

Light behaves in some respects like waves and in others like a shower of energy packets.

Light travels through space at the rate of about 186,000 miles per second.

Visible light resembles other forms of radiation—such as radio waves, x-rays, and cosmic rays—in that all are produced by waves and all travel at the same speed.

Discovering for Yourself

1. Examine and use various kinds and shapes of lenses to see how they differ. Try to demonstrate the use of lenses in a microscope and in a telescope.
2. Experiment with sunlight (using lawn spray, prisms, and other pieces of glass; an aquarium; and so on) to break it into its component colors.
3. Look in your environment for examples of refraction, reflection, indirect lighting, direct lighting, glare, sodium lights, fluorescent lights.
4. Perform a carefully controlled experiment to prove that plants need light. Explain what you would expect children to learn from such an experiment.
5. Examine and use a light meter. Find out why it is useful.
6. Observe the use of photoelectric cells in your environment.
7. Use light to make a blueprint and explain what happens.
8. Examine a camera and a projection machine to see how they control and use light.
9. Experiment with production of shadows to see changes in size and sharpness.
10. Grow plants by using artificial light. Does the distance of the light from the plants make any difference? Can you use an ordinary reading-lamp bulb?
11. Make a color wheel and attach it to a motor, or find some other way to spin it. Experiment with various combinations of colors. Can you make white?
12. Examine a model of the eye and explain how the model might be used with children.
13. Some local astronomical societies help their members make telescopes. Investigate the possibilities of one of the members visiting your class and demonstrating the use of lenses.
14. Find out about those powerful sources of light called lasers.

(Courtesy of William Dippel.)

CHAPTER 21B TEACHING "LIGHT AND HOW WE USE IT"

Children note reflections, rainbows, colors, shadows, sunsets, and moonlight. They use cameras, magnifying glasses, and mirrors. They play shadow games; they mix colored paints. Problems for investigation come from observations and experiences such as these.

The study of light provides a simple direct consideration of *cause and effect.* We turn a mirror and the reflection moves. We move an object nearer a screen and its shadow changes in size. We move a lens closer to an object and its magnification changes. The sun moves low in the sky and shadows lengthen. A lamp is switched on and there is light.

SOME BROAD CONCEPTS: "Light and How We Use It"

We see things that reflect light or are themselves luminous.

Light is a form of energy.

Light travels from its source in all directions at about 186,300 miles per second.

Materials differ in the amounts of light they reflect, absorb, or allow to pass through them.

Lenses bend light rays.

White light is composed of the colors of the rainbow.

The color of an opaque object is determined by the portion of the sun's colors it reflects.

FOR YOUNGER CHILDREN

What Can We Do with a Magnifying Glass?

Frequent references have been made throughout this book to the use of the magnifying glass, because children enjoy using this important tool to explore and learn.[1] They have many ideas of their own about where and when to use it and they enjoy sharing their observations with each other. "Let's see what it looks like through the magnifying glass," can often be the first suggestion when gathering data by observations is indicated. If there is a science table, an aquarium, or a terrarium a magnifying glass will help to develop appreciations, as well as to explain and provide information. (*See also* Chapter 10B for other suggestions.)

What Can a Mirror Do?

In the primary grades the day-to-day experiences of children often provide exciting opportunities for learning and enjoying scientific happenings. The following experience is such an example. It arose accidentally. The teacher recognized the interest of the

[1] *See* J. Schwartz: *Through the Magnifying Glass* (1954) and *Magnify and Find Out Why* (1972) (New York: McGraw-Hill Inc.).

children and she acted as a guide in helping them explore and develop the situation; she helped them formulate and solve problems that involved: sensing the problem, making observations, attempting to see relationships, gathering data, applying these data, and eventually explaining the mystery. The experience is presented here as it was related by the teacher.[2] It illustrates what can happen when a teacher is interested, alert, and creative.

> In our kindergarten we had a problem of "What makes the lights on the ceiling of our room?" These lights were seen over a period of several months in a room where there is much sunlight. The following account describes briefly what took place:
>
> One day, hearing the children laugh, I looked up to see Donna making a reflection on the ceiling with the bottom of her tin lunch box. I asked Donna why she didn't use the top of her lunch box (which was painted dark red). She said it wouldn't work. I asked her to let me try it. I was sitting on the shady side of the room and it wouldn't work. I suggested to the children that they try to make a light on the ceiling with any kind of object. They tried paper, cardboard, a piece of wood, a towel, a pair of scissors, pocketbooks, and an aluminum pitcher.
>
> As we discussed our observations we agreed that to make a light on the ceiling two things were necessary—something *shiny* and *sunshine.* One child said one day: "I know what you call it. It is a reflection." After we got this far I produced about 12 or 15 small mirrors and let all the children make bright reflections.
>
> On another day there was a bright reflection in the shape of a ring on the ceiling. We called it the "doughnut" light. What made it? It must be something shiny in the sun. Children took turns trying to decide what it was. They examined everything on the sunny side of the room. One child decided that it was a 4-inch aluminum cap on the radiator. We covered the cap with cardboard and the reflection disappeared. When the cap was uncovered, the reflection reappeared. Many children covered it to see—so we were sure.
>
> On another day there were 6 or 8 pale balls of light on the ceiling. What made them? Here was the toughest problem we had struck. Again everything on the sunny side of the room was examined. All the vases and flowerpots were moved off the plant table. The problem remained unsolved for several weeks—just coming up now and then to pester us. On cloudy days there were no lights of any kind. On sunny days the pale balls were there. Upstairs in the hall, too, there were beautiful balls of light on the ceiling.
>
> Finally, one boy thought of climbing up on a chair and looking out in the yard. He discovered some pieces of broken glass outside and thought they might make the pale reflections. So he went out with a box and picked up the broken glass. Our pale balls of light were gone. But we made him go out and put the glass back! Upstairs, we climbed on chairs, and sure enough the lower roof was covered with many pieces of broken glass.
>
> On another day a large pale reflection danced all over the ceiling and then settled down to a small bright spot. After the same trial-and-error method of examination we found that it came from a cup of water on the plant table. When the water shook, the light danced; when the water was still, the light was still. One day, after a rain, we had pale dancing reflections and found clear puddles outside. The wind was ruffling the puddles.

[2] Anne W. Anderson, kindergarten teacher, Louisville Public Schools, Kentucky.

How Can We Make Colors?

(See Ch. 21A.)

As young children learn to identify and name colors they are often interested in finding colors in different places. Using a prism is fascinating to children. Encourage them to name the colors in the prism spectrum and note their sequence. An aquarium in the sunlight sometimes acts as a prism to produce a spectrum. Children may try to compare these colors with those of the prism. Lawn sprays may be arranged in the sunlight to produce a spectrum of colors. If the occasion arises, observing a rainbow phenomenon is an exciting experience not to be missed.

How Do Shadows Change?[3]

In addition to the experience with shadows described in Chapter 7B, which describes observing shadows out-of-doors, children can use a strong light, such as the bulb from a film-strip projector, to make observations and discoveries about the nature of light and shadows. First direct the light on a translucent screen or a white cotton sheet. Have children sit on the side of the screen opposite the light in a darkened room. Hold various objects between the light and the screen. Observe to see: (1.) "What happens when the object is moved closer to the screen?" (Shadow is smaller.) "Away from the screen?" (Shadow is larger.) (2.) "What happens when the object is turned?" (A ball looks the same; an object like a book changes.) Children will predict what will happen if the screen is moved or if the light is moved. Then try it. Have them try to identify "mystery" objects by their shadows on the screen.

Other Problems for Younger Children

1. What different things give us light?
2. How should we take care of our eyes?
3. How do you use your eyes to make discoveries?
4. What can you do with lenses?
5. What can you do with mirrors?

FOR OLDER CHILDREN

How Does Light Pass through Different Objects?

Use flashlights or some similar sources of light and supply each group of children with materials, such as pieces of clear glass, a mirror, frosted glass, paper, pieces of leather or rubber, aluminum foil, waxed paper. Begin by suggesting that children try to predict what will happen when the light is shone on each piece of material. Then

[3]Elementary Science Study (ESS): *"Light and Shadows, "Teacher's Guide,* Grades K–3. (Manchester, Mo.: Webster Division, McGraw-Hill Book Co.). Using common indoor and outdoor objects, children explore relationships in simple ways.

test the hypotheses, letting each group work independently. Finally, let them attempt a classification of materials according to objects: (1.) Through which all or almost all the light striking it can pass (transparent); (2.) through which only part of the light travels (translucent); and (3.) through which no light travels (opaque).

Follow this experience with a hunt to identify ways in which materials in the classification are used in their environment—lamp shades, package wrappers, medicine containers, and so on. As a lead into the next problem suggest that they compare the results of using a mirror with the other materials. How are they alike; how different?

What Do Mirrors Do to Light?

Try to provide each child or each small group of children with a small mirror, suggesting that they use the mirrors in any way they wish to collect ideas about how mirrors work (move the mirror in different positions—up, down, sideways, closer, farther away). Discuss their findings. Urge them to use the terms *object* for things they observe, and *image* for what they see in the mirror. Suggest that they use a mirror in the sunlight or in the path of a lighted flashlight. Caution them about reflecting strong sunlight into each other's eyes.

"What can you discover about the way a mirror reflects light?" With a flashlight and mirror children may be able to discover that the angle at which light strikes a mirror determines the angle at which it is reflected.

Another way of illustrating this idea is to use a large mirror in front of the classroom and ask selected pupils to tell which pupils they can see in the mirror and which ones they cannot see. Urge them to try to formulate a statement that will explain this idea. After some classroom experiences children can observe the uses of mirrors in stores and store windows, in automobiles, in elevators, in barber shops, and in dentists' offices, and discuss why the mirrors are shaped as they are and why they are placed as they are.

Suggest the children dust chalk from an eraser on half of the mirrors they are using. "Observe what happens." Try to explain it." (Smooth surfaces reflect more light than rough surfaces. The clean mirror reflects light in regular reflection. The dusty mirror scattered the light in a diffused reflection. The same idea may be illustrated by shining one shoe to make it a smooth surface and dusting chalk on the other one. Urge children to find other examples.

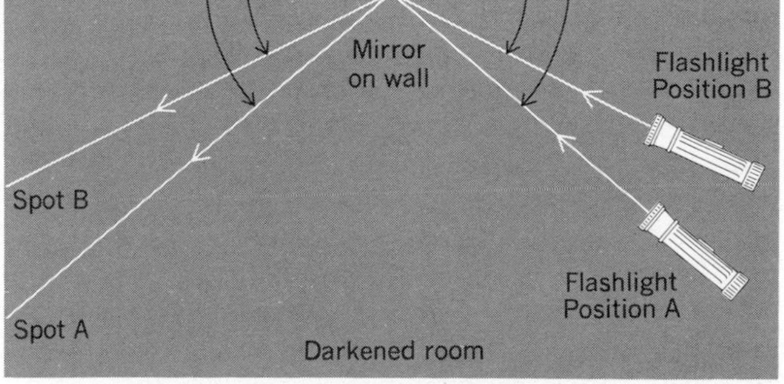

The angle of strike equals the angle of bounce.

Pupils may experiment with other materials (tin surfaces, glass, smooth paper, cloth, and so on) to see if they will reflect light, and try to explain what they observe. "What characteristic must a reflecting surface have?" "Do all materials reflect surfaces equally well?"

How Are Lenses Used?

The lens from a flashlight, a magnifying glass, lenses from a projector, from old discarded optical instruments, as well as an assortment of lenses purchased from a supply house and the eyeglasses of pupils in the class are all useful in the study of lenses.

Supply individuals or small groups of children with lenses of various shapes (convex, concave, different sizes, and so on). Suggest that children describe the shapes of the lenses and compare them with each other. Then ask the children to see what they can discover by using the lenses to look at print, at distant objects, and so forth. In a short time they may "invent" such devices as: a magnifying glass (one lens), a more powerful magnifying glass (two lenses next to each other), a telescope (one lens held at a distance from another), a burning glass (*see* safety precaution later).

Following their free experimentation and the reports of their findings, problems

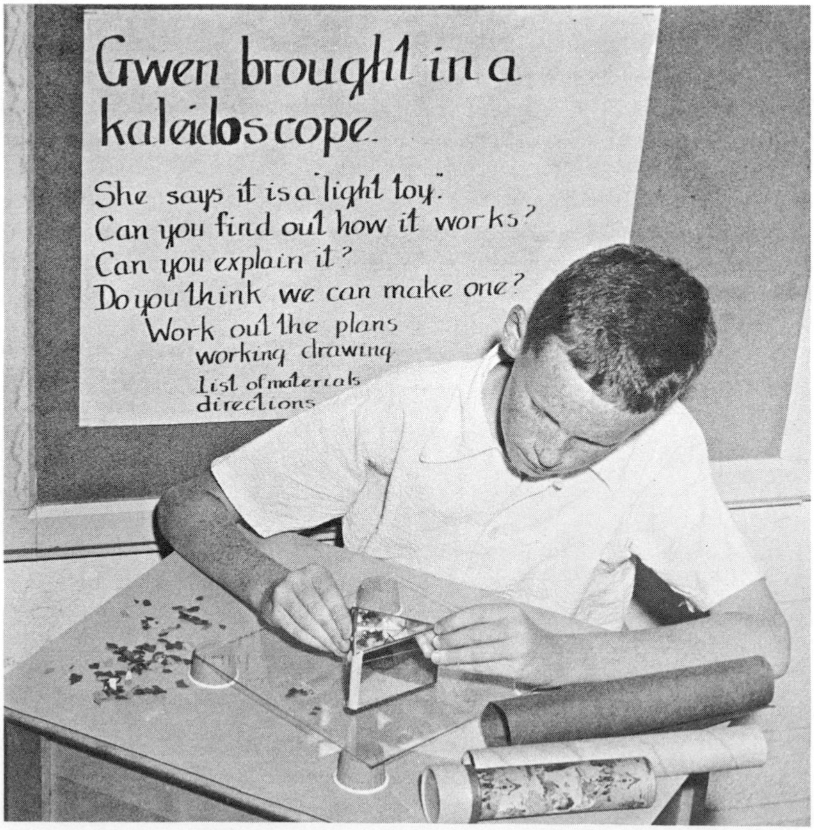

Examining the structure of the kaleidoscope will help pupils to understand the principles of the behavior of light and its reflections which are involved. New science problems will emerge as pupils make their own models of a kaleidoscope by taping together three pocket mirrors facing inward (as shown in the photograph) and by then dropping bits of colored paper into the triangle thus formed. *(Courtesy of Marjorie H. Campbell.)*

such as the following may be investigated: "How can you make an image with a lens?" Hold a large magnifying glass near a wall opposite a window. Move the glass nearer and farther from the wall. Watch until there is a sharp image of something near the window. This is called focusing. "How large is the image compared to the object?" "What position is it in?" (Upside down.)

Children may discuss: "What happens if we use two lenses?" They may attempt to demonstrate using the lenses they have on hand. (Convex lenses magnify. Concave lenses reduce.) Two convex lenses used together properly increase magnification as in a telescope. Pupils should certainly not be encouraged to wear one another's glasses, but looking through the various lenses to see how objects appear through them will help them to see how lenses differ.

A magnifying glass may be used in bright sunlight to focus light strong enough to burn paper. Exercise caution, for it is possible for pupils to burn themselves or one another by careless use of the glass. It is easy for pupils to see how moving the lens back and forth focuses the light and to see how the lens acts as a light "gatherer." It is interesting to note that the intense spot produced is an image of the sun. (***Note:*** *Children should realize that it is dangerous to look at the sun with any kind of lenses and that light from the sun should never be reflected into anyone's eyes.*)

How Does a Camera Work?

A general idea of how a camera operates may be demonstrated by darkening the classroom and asking children to turn their backs to a window which does not have its shade drawn. Suggest that they hold a sheet of white paper vertically with one hand and a convex lens in the other. Let them experiment to try to make a "picture" of the window on the paper by moving the lens back and forth. Ask them to describe the "picture." "Is it smaller or larger than the window?" "How else is it different from the window?" (Smaller, upside down.)

In almost any upper-elementary class there are pupils who have cameras. Urge children to bring their cameras, explain their operation in its simplest form, and then insert film and take pictures of the class. They can demonstrate loading the films, holding the camera, getting proper light, using the finder, and so on. They can also describe various cautions in the use of the camera to insure good results. In some instances it is even possible for them to explain how the film is developed. Pupils should understand where light enters the camera, where the lens is, what the shutter does, and how the picture is focused on the film. The demonstrator may also introduce pupils to the light meter and show how it behaves under various light intensities. The use of the camera can demonstrate many of the science principles involved in the study of light. If old cameras that are no longer used are available pupils can take them apart to see how a camera is made. Pupils may like to make a pinhole camera. Directions are given in books listed in the Bibliography.

Children should be encouraged to use their cameras to: illustrate a project, a trip, a study of the school environment, the progress of an experiment, or to prepare a photographic "essay."

How Are Blueprints Made?

Using light to make simple blueprints helps pupils to see how light can produce a chemical change on sensitive paper. Blueprint paper may be purchased at camera or art supply shops and in some drugstores, or from blueprint equipment companies (*see* the classified telephone directory). This paper changes color after a period of time, even in the dark, so it should be purchased fresh in small quantities. Small squares of glass will serve to hold the paper and the objects to be printed in place. Leaf blueprints, for example, are made by laying a leaf on the blueprint paper, covering it with a piece of glass, and holding it in bright sunlight for several seconds. Children will experiment to determine the best exposure time. After the blueprint is exposed, wash it in cold water. Dry it by spreading it on a newspaper. The leaf print will appear white, the remainder of the paper blue. Blueprint paper is covered with light-sensitive chemicals. These chemicals will dissolve in water. Wherever light strikes the paper the chemicals change. The new chemical that is produced is blue and does not dissolve in water. Sunlight strikes the paper and produces the new chemical in every place except under the leaf.

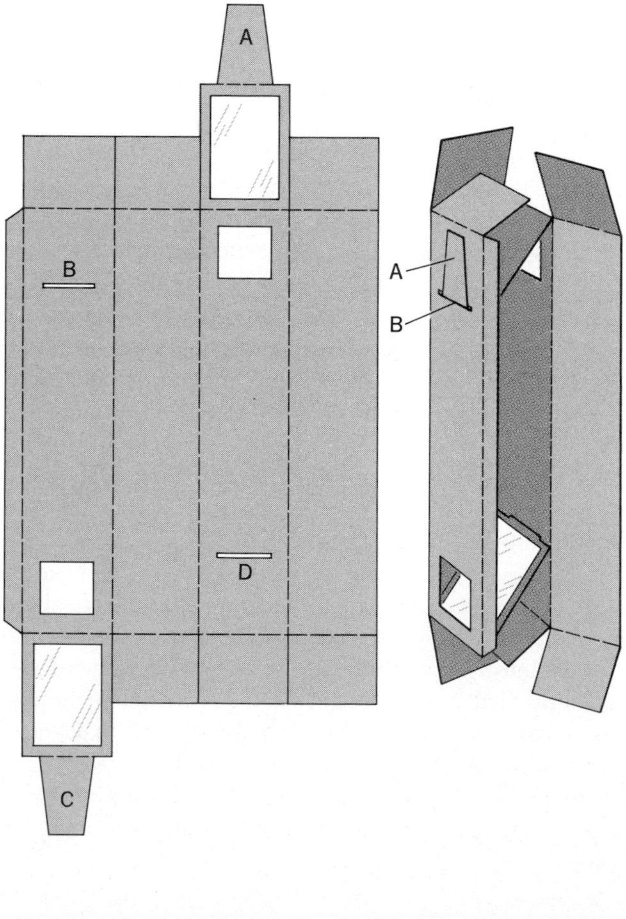

This pattern for a periscope can be cut out of heavy cardboard. Tabs A and C fit into slots B and D, but before the flaps are glued down make certain that the mirrors are at the proper angle. This can be determined by trying out the periscope before applying the glue.

A film negative (instead of a leaf) placed on top of blueprint paper and exposed as described previously, will help pupils understand how a print is made from a negative.

OTHER PROBLEMS FOR OLDER CHILDREN

(*See* p. 670.) 1. How can we make a periscope?
2. How do artificial lamps give light?
(*See* p. 668.) 3. How is a kaleidoscope built?
4. How do we see?
5. What are good lighting conditions for study?
6. What does a prism do to light?
7. How are motion pictures produced?

Resources to Investigate with Children

1. Local photographers, camera shops, camera clubs, and camera manufacturers for information about photography.
2. An optician for discarded lenses that may be used in performing simple experiments with light.
3. The power company or electrical institute to learn about the measurement of light, types of lighting, and the amount of light necessary for various activities.
4. Hardware and electrical supply stores to observe the various types of light fixtures and to learn how science principles are utilized in their construction and use.
5. The school building and the school custodian to learn how the school is lighted and, with the help of a light meter, to see how light is used for various purposes in school.
6. Children's homes to observe the different kinds of lighting fixtures and how they are related to light needs.
7. The National Society for the Prevention of Blindness, Inc., 79 Madison Ave., New York, N.Y. 10016 for *Catalogue of Publications and Films.*

Preparing to Teach

1. Assemble magazine pictures, photographs, and other illustrative material that may be used in teaching this unit. Plan how these may be used by children.
2. Examine books for children (*see* Bibliography and libraries) that are appropriate supplementary books, and annotate the list.
3. Select one or more items from the "Other Problems" and make a lesson plan to introduce questions and outline activities you would use with children.
4. List activities you would consider useful in stimulating interest in the topic of light.

CHAPTER 22A

FLIGHT AND SPACE TRAVEL

(Courtesy of U.S. Department of Transportation.)

THE AIR AGE OPENS

Over the desolate sands at Kitty Hawk, North Carolina, an odd machine made of wood, cloth, wire, and bicycle chains, and powered by a crude 12-horsepower engine, rose into the air for 12 seconds and flew a distance of 120 feet. Thus, on December 17, 1903, did Wilbur and Orville Wright make an ancient dream of man come true. This trip, the first heavier-than-air, powered flight, was the beginning of the air age. It marked the first time in history that a machine carrying a man had raised itself by its own power into the air in full flight, had flown without loss of speed, and had landed at a point as high as the place from which it had started.

For many centuries man had dreamed of flying like a bird. Leonardo da Vinci, the fifteenth-century painter and sculptor, was also an engineer and inventor who applied his genius to the problem of flight. Studying the flight of birds he designed several wing-flapping machines to help man soar in the air. He also suggested the use of rotating wings thus anticipating the modern helicopter. Da Vinci is credited with the invention of the "air screw" to pull a machine through the air, thus pointing the way to the modern propeller.

There is no evidence that any of Da Vinci's machines ever worked, or that his theories influenced the development of aviation. Indeed, it was not until 1930 that his full works were published. A man whose theories did influence aviation was Sir George Cayley, an English scientist. In 1809 he made a remarkably astute statement on the problem of flight. He said that flight would be possible if we could make a *surface* support a weight by the application of *power* to the *resistance of the air.* In this Cayley was giving proper recognition to:

1. *The supporting surface* (the wings of the modern plane).
2. *Power* (the motor and propeller—later the jet—that would pull or push the wings through the air).
3. *The air itself* (the "resistance of the air," as we shall see, provides the "lift" on the wing needed to overcome gravity).

WHAT MAKES AN AIRPLANE FLY?

Air is a real substance, just as real as liquid water or solid earth. A parachute falling through air descends slowly because its inside surface encounters and pushes against many air molecules. The crowded molecules, in turn, push back against the parachute retarding its downward drop. If the chute fails to open, however, it plummets to earth rapidly (*see* p. 704).

The "Kite Effect"

Because air is a substance it offers resistance to the movement of objects through it. At first this might seem to be only an obstacle to horizontal flight. But a simple experiment will reveal that this resistance can serve a helpful purpose too. Hold one end of a 9 x 12-inch sheet of paper, forefinger on top, supported by the thumb and second finger underneath. Hold it in a horizontal position, curved slightly so that it does not droop. Now tilt it at a slight angle, so that the opposite end of the paper is slightly higher than the end you are holding. Push the paper directly forward, but hold on to it. You find that the free, leading edge tilts up. Why? (*See* figure, p. 674.)

As the surface of the paper is pushed against the molecules that make up the air, it crowds them together. The crowded molecules, in turn, spring back and push against the paper. Part of this air resistance impedes the forward progress of the paper, but, because the crowded molecules beat against the paper in all directions, *part of the resistance serves to lift the paper,* tilting its free end up. With a little practice you can flick the paper or a piece of cardboard so that on leaving your hand the upward push serves to lift the entire sheet against the pull of gravity.

The sheet of paper that you have experimented with has some of the characteristics of an airplane wing. You have used it in a way that fulfills Cayley's requirements for heavier-than-air flight. You have applied power (the push of your hand) to the resistance of the air, and in that way you have achieved a small amount of "lift."

You have found that when a tilted surface

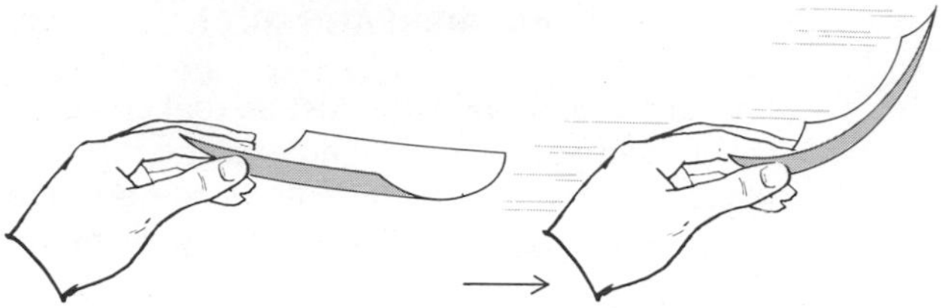

The "kite effect." When a surface is pushed against the air, the air pushes back. The text on pages 673–4 tells how this gives an airplane part of its lift.

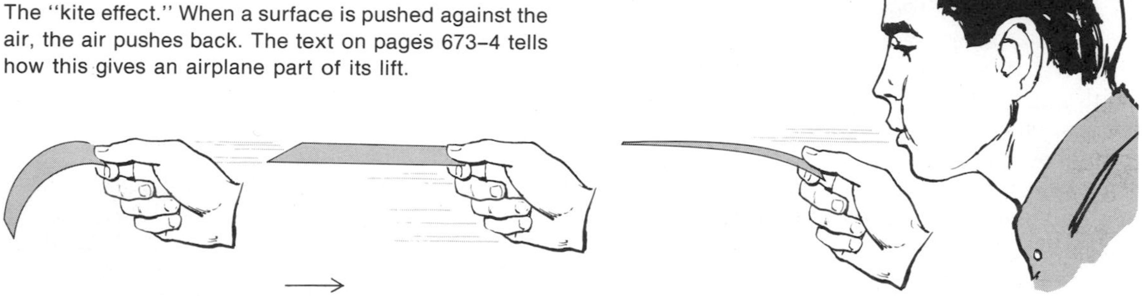

The "vacuum effect." The pressure on the upper surface is decreased. How does this effect help to lift an airplane?

is pushed against the air the air pushes back, partially slowing it down, partially lifting it up. A kite rises for the same reason, except that here the air (wind) moves against the surface to be lifted instead of the surface moving against the air.

The "Vacuum Effect"

Now take a look at a real airplane to find the flat, tilted surface that presses against the air. (*See* pp. 706–7.) You discover it in the wings, set at an angle so that their front edge, called the leading edge, is higher than their back edge, called the trailing edge. However, only the lower surface of the wings is flat; the upper surface is curved or arched. Why? To find the answer perform a second experiment with paper, this time with a strip about 2 inches wide and about 6 inches long. Hold it at one end between your thumb and forefinger, thumb on top (as shown), so that it falls in a curve not unlike that of the top of an airplane wing. Now *pull* the paper through the air. Its free end rises, as in the first experiment. You may argue with good reason that the lower surface is being pushed up, as in the previous experiment, by the impact of the air from underneath. This is true, but it is only part of the truth. To discover the role of the upper surface alone bring your fingers and the paper under your lips and blow over the *top* of it only. The paper rises again. Why?

We recall that air is a real substance made of bouncing molecules. We should also recall that because of the never-ceasing bouncing of these molecules, air, even when it is not moving as a mass (wind), exerts a push in all directions—up, down, sideways. At sea level this pressure amounts to about 15 pounds on every square inch of surface that the air impinges on. When an airplane is at rest on the ground on a windless day the pressure on top of the wing is counterbalanced by an equal pressure from the bottom. The net effect is zero. But when the wing begins to move forward through the air an interesting thing happens. The air flowing over the curved upper surface is forced to travel a greater distance and at a greater speed than the air on the lower surface. Rushing over the upper surface of the wing the air expends some of its energy in motion and consequently loses some of its pressure. Thus, the pressure on the upper surface becomes less (forming a partial vacuum) than the pressure on the lower surface. The higher pressure underneath lifts the wing, and therefore the plane, against the pull of gravity.

To summarize, two factors operate to give a moving wing its lift:

1. The impact of air against the lower surface of the wing (the "kite effect").
2. The decreased pressure on the upper surface of the wing (the "vacuum effect").

Of the two, the second contributes more to the total lift of a plane, accounting for about 80 percent of it.

The Propeller's Job

(*See* pp. 704, 706–7.) In your experiments the power to move the paper "wing" was supplied by your muscles. In the propeller plane the power is supplied by the engine. This power is conveyed by a shaft to the propeller.

Both the "kite effect" and the "vacuum effect" are involved in the operation of the propeller. Each propeller blade resembles a wing in its construction. As it is rotated, the action of its surfaces on the air gives it useful "lift," but in the direction in which the plane is moving. This propeller lift produces the forward thrust that drives the aircraft through the air at a speed necessary to give the wings their lift.

Contrary to the impression that some individuals have, the job of the propeller is *not* to blow a stream of air over the wings. Usually the propellers are placed so that this air stream or *wash,* as it is called, will not interfere with the normal flow of air over the wings. The job of the propeller is to pull the plane forward so that air will flow over the wings.

As an airplane races down the runway the propeller pulls it along the ground faster and faster until the impact of the air and the excess pressure on the under surface of the wings is sufficient to lift the plane into the air.

In jet planes no propellers are required; jet action, which will be explained later, thrusts the plane through the air.

HOW AN AIRPLANE IS CONTROLLED

Before heavier-than-air flight could be achieved, three problems had to be solved:

1. Efficient surfaces to support the weight had to be provided. We have seen how the arched wing solved this problem.
2. Adequate power without excessive weight had to be furnished. This had to wait on the development of light internal-combustion engines.
3. Stability and maneuverability in flight had to be attained.

We shall consider some aspects of the third problem now.

The Control Surfaces

Airplanes move in three-dimensional space. Reference to the diagram on page 676 will show three kinds of changes in position relative to this space. It might be helpful in understanding these to think of *yourself* as a plane, arms outstretched, flying through space like Superman. You might want to change your *pitch* so that the length of your body is tilted with respect to earth, pointing up or pointing down. The word pitch is also applied to a similar motion of a ship at sea. You might want to *yaw;* that is, alter the direction in which you are heading toward the left or toward the right. You might want to *roll* (or bank), so that one of your arms is higher than the other. Rolling is also a nautical term, well known to those who have suffered from seasickness.

The pilot is able to cause these changes in position by manipulating adjustable control surfaces that are hinged to the plane and can be turned like a door. When these surfaces are turned to "catch the breeze" they alter the position of the plane in the air.

Pitching is effected by moving the *elevator,* part of the tail of the plane. When the elevator is tilted up the plane's tail goes down and its nose up. When the elevator is down the opposite movement occurs.

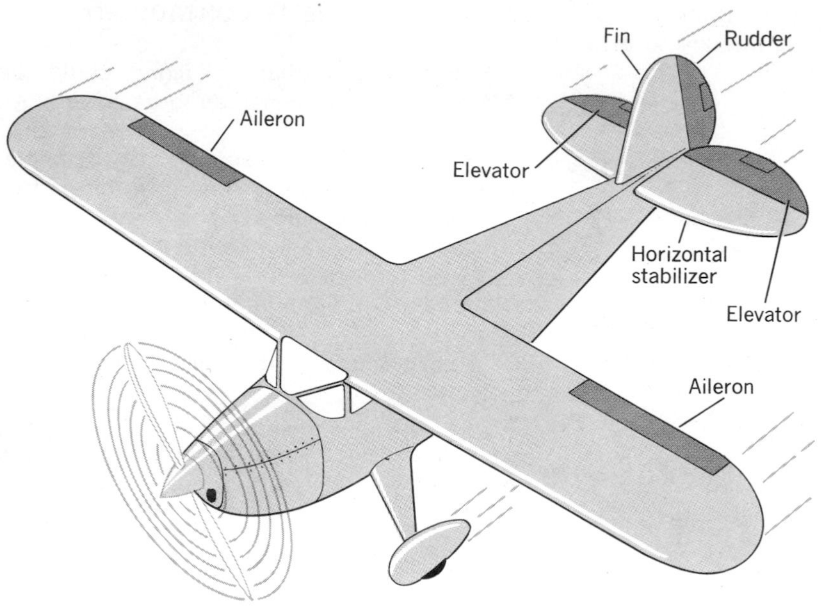

The control surfaces of a plane permit it to change its position in three ways. The text explains how the elevator, rudder, and ailerons are manipulated to control pitching, yawing, and rolling.

Yawing to the left or right is effected by moving the rudder, also part of the tail of the plane.

Rolling (banking) requires the operation of the two *ailerons,* which are hinged strips attached to the trailing edge of the plane's wings. The ailerons work in opposition to each other, so that when one is turned up the other automatically moves down.

One other control should be mentioned here—the engine *throttle,* which regulates the amount of forward *thrust* supplied by the propellers.

Having given the functions of the *movable* controls of a plane we must hasten to correct an impression that some may have about the function of the rudder. It is natural to assume that it serves exactly as a rudder does on a ship; that is, it is used in a similar way by a plane to execute right and left turns in the air. The rudder does help, as we shall see, but it is the ailerons and the wings that are the chief factors in turning. We quote from the *Flight Instruction Manual* of the United States Civil Air Authority in this regard:

> Turns are *not* made with the rudder. Turns are made in an airplane by tipping, or canting, the direction of the lift of the wings from vertical to one side or the other, causing this "lift" to pull the airplane in that direction as well as to overcome gravity. This is done by using the ailerons to roll the airplane toward the side to which it is desired to turn.[1]

The *Manual* goes on to say that the rudder is used while banking in a turn to correct the tendency of the plane to yaw toward the outside of the turn. In other words turning is done by tilting the plane so that part of the lift on the wings is used to pull the plane to the left or right. To try to turn by using the rudder alone is like trying to make a sharp turn in an auto while traveling rapidly on an icy road. The car may point in a new direction, but it continues skidding off in the original one.

In addition to the three angular motions of the plane—pitching, yawing, and rolling—there are the more obvious movements of the plane in space: its forward motion, which gets you

[1]U.S. Civil Air Authority: *Flight Instruction Manual,* Technical Manual 100 (April 1951), p. 43.

where you want to go; its sideways motion, caused by a wind across the direction of flight or by certain deliberate maneuvers; and the up and down movement in bumpy air, which sometimes makes you wish you had taken a train.

Built-in Stability

In addition to the elevator, rudder, and ailerons, all subject to the control of the pilot, the plane as a whole must possess inherent stability; that is, it must be designed to correct slight alterations in its position caused by upward, downward, and horizontal gusts of winds or by the plane's own movements. Flying would be impossible if the aviator had to adjust for each of these disturbances. To a great extent a plane must be able to take care of itself. In the tail of the plane a fixed vertical *fin* keeps the plane from yawing sideways. The horizontal stabilizer keeps the nose and tail from bobbing up and down. The wings prevent the tendency to roll. The placement of the wings at an upward-sloping angle (dihedral angle) to the body or *fuselage* of the plane increases the effectiveness of the wings as stabilizing surfaces.

JETS

The propeller, as we have seen, is a device that makes use of the air to pull the plane forward. Jet planes, however, generally have no propellers. How do jets work?

A simple experiment with a toy balloon illustrates the jet principle. If a balloon is inflated and then released, it zips around as the air escapes. We note that the balloon zips in the opposite direction from that of the escaping air. Why does the balloon behave in this way? (*See* p. 707.)

Jet action is an example of *Newton's third law of motion,* which states that for every action there is an equal and opposite reaction. When someone dives off your shoulders into water you feel a violent shove backward at the moment of diving. The jumping of the diver (action) resulted in your being pushed back (reaction).

In the balloon experiment the escaping air is comparable to the diver, and the balloon itself to the person supporting the diver. The air streaming out of the opening produces a kick backward or a *thrust* on the *inside* of the balloon in the opposite direction. Thrust, however, does not depend on the presence of air *outside* the balloon, for, as we shall see, jet action is possible, in fact more effective, in the vacuum of airless space.

There are a number of kinds of jet planes, but all work on the same principle. In all a large quantity of gas is produced by the rapid burning of fuel in a combustion chamber; the gas is blasted out of an opening in the rear end; and the reaction thrusts the plane forward—from the inside.

In the *turbojet,* the common engine of commercial planes, air is drawn into the front end of the engine. It passes into a rotating compressor where there are many rows of fanlike blades. These whirl the air, compress it, and hurl it back into the combustion chamber. Here it is mixed with kerosene, which is sprayed under high

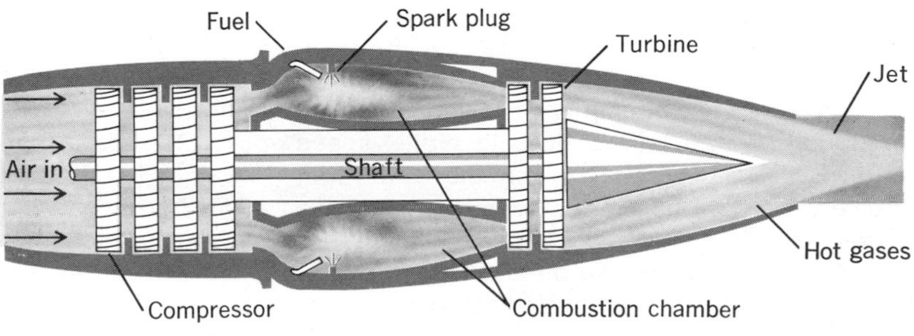

This turbojet illustrates some of the features common to all jets. The rapid burning of fuel in a combustion chamber causes a blast out of a rear opening. The reaction of the blast thrusts the plane forward.

pressure into the chamber. The fuel is ignited and a powerful explosion produces a large quantity of heated gas, which is squeezed into a tailpipe section and ejected with great speed, thrusting the plane forward. Before the expanding gases are allowed to escape they are directed onto the blades of a turbine rotor, which they cause to spin at great speed. The purpose of the turbine is to drive the compressor to which it is connected by a shaft.

In the *turbofan* engine, which resembles the turbojet, the turbines have the additional job of turning a set of huge, fanlike bladed wheels. These wheels pull in and push back additional air which flows *around* the engine and out through the tailpipe. This extra air supplements the gases generated in the combustion chamber. In this way thrust is increased without burning extra fuel.

In the *turboprop* the turbine also serves to turn a propeller. Both propeller action and jet action are used to move these planes, most of the thrust being supplied by the propeller.

The powerful jet engine made possible the construction of the "jumbo jets," a new generation of transports nearly double the size and capacity of their predecessors. In June 1968 the era of the jumbo jet began with the successful test flight of the Lockheed C-5 Galaxy, a giant U.S. military jet, in Marietta, Georgia. Seven months later the Boeing 747, the world's first commercial jumbo jet, made its maiden flight.

The 747 carries 375 passengers in contrast to the 199 passengers of the 707. But the next generation of jumbo jets, destined to carry 1,000 passengers, is now on the planning boards for the 1980s.

STOL

There are two directions in aviation development today. One has to do with higher-speed flight over long distances and the other with slower speeds and shorter hops. Consider the latter first.

Aircraft that can take off and land vertically or in very short distances are known as V/STOL (vertical/short takeoff and landing) aircraft. This term includes a variety of craft including autogyros, helicopters, and short takeoff and landing (STOL) aircraft.

One of our greatest transportation needs is for an effective short-distance travel service, for distances less than 500 miles. Envisioned is a plane which could carry 100 passengers or more, and could take off and land at an angle of $7\frac{1}{2}°$, about twice as steep as that of conventional planes. This capability would enable it to fly higher over nearby communities, thereby reducing the landing and takeoff noise. In addition, a quieter, less-polluting engine would be employed.

Because STOL aircraft can fly safely at lower speeds they can land in air fields only 2,000 feet long, compared with the 8,000 feet required by conventional aircraft. This would allow them to land at 90 percent of the nation's airports, instead of the 10 percent that are usable by present transports.

STOL aircraft are unique in that they can achieve high lift during takeoff and landing. They obtain this in part by extending large *flaps,* which increase the lifting surface of the wings. (These are also found on conventional planes, but are not as large.) In addition, part of the jet flow is directed *downward,* adding to the lift.

SUPERSONIC FLIGHT

As planes traveled faster and faster new obstacles to flight developed. When a plane moved at a speed of 750 miles per hour, approaching the speed of sound, a curious thing happened. The plane began to shake and bounce. Going still faster, at the very speed of sound, the shaking increased, becoming so violent that the wings were sometimes wrenched off the plane. At still greater speed the plane had smooth sailing again.

The plane had passed through an invisible wall in the air—the *sound barrier.* Just what is this barrier?

You recall from Chapter 20A that sound moves in a wave of compression; molecules of air are pushed closer together as the wave proceeds. This wave of compression advances at about 1,100 feet per second or about 760 miles per hour at sea level.

When a plane moves slower than the speed of sound (roughly 660 miles per hour at an altitude of 35,000 feet), the sound made by the plane speeds away from it. But when the speed of sound is reached, the plane keeps pace with its own sound waves. The compression waves cannot speed away from the plane. They pile up in front of the wings and body of the plane, forming a veritable wall called a *shock wave.*

Shock waves interfere with the smooth flow of air around the plane and cause irregularities in the forces that act on the plane.

When the plane succeeds in breaking through and flying at *supersonic speed*—that is, faster than the speed of sound—the sound waves no longer bother it, for they are left behind the plane.

Planes have been designed to move through the sound barrier without damage. A long, needlelike nose and thin, swept-back wings enable the plane to slip through the sound barrier smoothly. The *delta* or triangular wing is common in military craft designed for flight at supersonic speeds.

Work on the development of a commercial supersonic transport (SST) began in 1959 in the United States, and shortly after in the U.S.S.R. and in a joint project of Britain and France.

The United States SST was planned to have about $\frac{2}{3}$ the passenger capacity of the 747, but three times its speed. Traveling at about 1,750 miles per hour it would be able to fly from New York to Europe in only about $2\frac{1}{2}$ hours.

However, in 1970 the SST program in the United States came under fire in Congress. Ecologists contended that the SST constituted a danger to the earth's environment because it produced a sonic boom (discussed next); because of the increased noise in the immediate area of the plane on takeoff; the pollution of the upper atmosphere threatening the ozone blanket that shields the earth from ultraviolet radiation and disturbances which might influence the earth's weather. These arguments were contested by the proponents of the SST, but the ecologists won—at least for the time being. As a consequence the SST program was dropped here, but it has continued in France and the U.S.S.R., where test flights of faster-than-sound transports have been made.

Sonic Boom

A serious problem associated with supersonic flight is that of *sonic boom.* All aircraft, as they advance through the sky, compress the air ahead of them and start a pressure wave. At subsonic speeds (less than the speed of sound) the pressure disturbance moves out from the aircraft in all directions and is dissipated without disturbing those on the ground. But when the plane exceeds the speed of sound the pressure field is forced out behind the airplane. Here it is concentrated in two huge cones, one extending back from the nose, the other from the tail. High-intensity shock waves radiate out along these cones. When the bottom of the cones

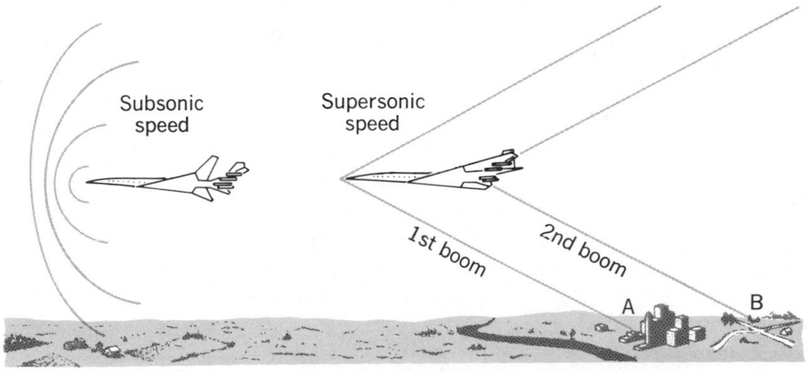

When an airplane exceeds the speed of sound it produces a sonic boom.

touch the ground their waves are heard as an explosive sound, sometimes single and sometimes double.

The cones and the associated booms would follow a supersonic plane throughout its entire flight path. If an SST flies across the country about 20 million Americans will be subjected to its continuous sonic boom, which would make it the most objectionable kind of sound pollution inflicted on our nation. Studies have indicated that the boom may cause some damage to homes and other structures, and is startling and annoying to people. One way of avoiding the problem is to limit the SST to ocean flights. Another is to have the SST fly at subsonic speeds over land.

THE ROCKET PLANE

Perhaps the ultimate stage in the flying machine is the rocket, which does not rely in any way on the air to sustain its motion. With the development of more and more powerful power systems the thrust provided by the rocket is sufficient to overcome the pull of gravity even without the "lift" provided by the wings of the conventional plane. When rocket planes leave the lower atmosphere and fly at heights of hundreds of miles or more the air is too "thin" for wings to be of any use anyway.

The rocket engine, unlike any of the others discussed so far, carries its own oxygen supply (or other chemicals which serve as oxidizers) for the burning of fuel and is therefore not limited to flight within the atmosphere. This, plus its enormous power-to-weight ratio, makes it the only known engine that can drive manned or unmanned vehicles into space.

Gunpowder, the traditional fuel used in older military rockets and in rockets used for firework displays, is not suitable for long-distance flights. Instead, new liquid and solid fuels are used. A rocket is propelled in the same way as a jet. The burning of fuel produces gases under high pressure which stream out of the nozzle. The jet action produced in this way creates the thrust that makes the rocket go.

On August 2, 1960, Robert M. White flew to an altitude of 136,500 feet—about 25 miles—in the X-15, a rocket-propelled plane. Since then speeds of more than 4,500 miles per hour and altitudes up to 67 miles have been reached in the X-15. This experimental plane was built to investigate the problems of reentry into the atmosphere from high altitudes while traveling at extremes of speed. Special design was required to make the X-15 maneuverable at high supersonic speed. The plane's structures also had to withstand the high temperatures created by air resistance as it plunged into the earth's atmosphere.

During its nine-year life span the X-15 produced an enormous amount of experimental and scientific data that led to rapid developments in aeronautics and astronautics. In the rocket plane we have a vehicle that operates in the atmosphere both as a rocket and as a plane, while outside the atmosphere it functions purely as a rocket. The rocket plane may well be an important component of future world transportation systems, providing high-speed, long-distance transportation.

The technologies of aeronautics and astronautics (*see* remainder of chapter) are being meshed to produce a new generation of space vehicles called *space shuttles* that would leave the earth as rockets and return as planes. The key feature of these vehicles is that, like airliners, they would be flown repeatedly between the earth and space and possibly in the future from point to point travel on earth. A fuller description of space shuttles is found on pages 696–699.

THE HEAT BARRIER

Another obstacle to rapid flight is the *heat barrier.* We get some notion of this barrier when we observe meteoroids enter our atmosphere. The friction between the meteroid, falling at the rate of 25,000 miles per hour, and the air causes it literally to "boil" away, leaving behind a trail of luminous gas; the phenomenon is popularly called a "shooting star." Similarly, when a plane flies through the atmosphere air friction heats the plane's metal skin; the faster the flight, the more intense the heat. Supersonic planes are affected by the heat barrier; their design and the materials used in their construction must be adapted for this condition. The heat generated is a menace also to the pilot, who would be roasted in his cockpit if it were not for refrigeration equipment installed in these planes. Solutions to some heat problems in relation to flight are discussed on pages 520–521.

ROCKETS AND SPACE FLIGHT[2]

The history of rockets is closely related to the history of space travel, because only with the rocket principle is space travel possible. The first recorded use of rockets occurred in 1232 A.D., when the Chinese repelled Mongols with "arrows of flying fire," which were actually incendiary firecrackers. Rockets were brought to Europe shortly after. In 1379 a crude rocket powered with gunpowder scored a lucky hit which destroyed a defending tower in the battle for Isle of Chiozza during the Venetian-Genovese War.

In the nineteenth century Sir William Congreve of Great Britain developed a rocket which was used extensively in the Napoleonic Wars. The "rockets' red glare" in the *Star-Spangled Banner* refers to the Congreve rocket missiles that the British fired against Fort McHenry during the battle for Baltimore in the War of 1812. A humanitarian use of the Congreve rocket was first patented in 1838. This was a device that

[2]In the material on space flight which follows, the authors have been guided by *Space: The New Frontier* and other publications of the National Aeronautics and Space Administration.

This is an illustration from Jules Verne's science-fiction novel, *From the Earth to the Moon,* published in 1865. The passengers in Verne's spacecraft are enjoying their first feeling of weightlessness. (*Courtesy of NASA.*)

carried a line from shore to a stranded vessel, enabling the distressed crew to be pulled to shore on a breeches buoy.

All rockets up to the twentieth century employed a solid fuel, such as gunpowder. In 1903 a Russian schoolteacher, Konstantin Ziolkovsky, proposed an interplanetary rocket in an article "Investigating Space with Rocket Devices." He urged that a spaceship be powered by a liquid-propelled engine supplied with liquid hydrogen and liquid oxygen. It is interesting to note Ziolkovsky's statement that "probably the first seeds of the idea were sown by that great, fantastic author, Jules Verne." Ziolkovsky's ideas remained unknown outside of Russia, and at that time the Russians gave them little attention.

Working separately, Herman Oberth, a Rumanian-German, and Robert H. Goddard, an American, laid the basis for modern rocketry. Oberth stimulated experimental rocket work in Germany with his book, *The Rocket into Interplanetary Space,* published in 1923.

Dr. Goddard, a professor at Clark University in Massachusetts, in 1919 sent to the Smithsonian Institution in Washington, D.C. a copy of a 69-page manuscript entitled "A Method of Reaching Extreme Altitudes." This paper attracted the attention of the press because of a brief comment on the possibility of shooting a rocket to the moon and exploding a load of powder on the surface. Shortly after, Goddard hypothesized that a liquid fuel would be superior to the powder pellets that he had been using to power his rockets. Between 1919 and 1926 Dr. Goddard worked to perfect his ideas. On March 16, 1926, a momentous day for rocket flight, the world's first liquid-fuel rocket was launched. Although it covered a distance of only 184 feet it proved that this kind of a rocket would work. Dr. Goddard continued his research in the more open spaces of the southwestern United States. In 1935 his rockets achieved altitudes of 7,500 feet and speeds of over 700 miles per hour.

Rockets played an important part in World War II. The V-2, a rocket-propelled missile, was fired at London and Antwerp. It has been estimated that had the Germans been given another six months of production time with the rocket, they could have turned the tide of the war.

On October 4, 1957, the first manmade satellite, Sputnik I, was rocketed into orbit by the Soviet Union. The Space Age opened. Less than four months later, on January 31, 1958, the United States launched its first satellite, Explorer I.

UP, UP, AND AWAY

Circling the earth today are many satellites (over 500 at the present writing) that, unlike the moon, were placed there by man. Included in the new array of manmade heavenly bodies are satellites for watching the weather picture, for surveying the earth's resources, for monitoring the earth's environment, for relaying telephone and television messages around the earth, for assisting air and sea craft in navigation, and for serving as astronomical observatories far above the dust and fog of our atmosphere-blanketed earth.

Spaceships have left the earth and visited the moon, Venus, and Mars. Some space vehicles now move in the vast regions of the solar system as tiny artificial planets of the sun. Others are penetrating the outer reaches of the solar system.

To place a satellite into orbit around the earth or to send a space ship to Venus, Mars, or the moon requires an understanding of gravity. At this point it might be well to reread the section, "Gravity and the Solar System," in Chapter 7A. Briefly, it was stated there that the strength of the gravitational force between two bodies depends (1.) on the amount of material in them (their masses) and (2.) the distance between them.

One implication of the laws of gravity of significance for space travel is that the attraction between two bodies—between the earth and an apple, for example—is a definite, measurable force. This fact removes gravity from the realm of the inexorable, the unconquerable. Gravity is something that can be contended with, can be opposed—although not yet abolished, science fiction claims notwithstanding.

The same apple that Newton is reputed to have observed falling from a tree can be made to travel away from the earth—if we engage a powerful "apple hurler" to pitch it outward with sufficient force. Later we shall examine the amount of force necessary for escape from the earth. For the moment let us consider one unique characteristic of gravity.

Assume that our imaginary earthbound "apple hurler" is allowed only one chance—one mighty heave—to send the apple on its way. Earth's gravity, however, tugs at the apple with unseen fingers every moment of its outward flight, slowing it down more and more. It looks like a losing battle, but that is not necessarily so, because the strength of gravity diminishes with distance. Although the apple is slowing down the pull on it by earth is getting weaker. What will happen to the apple? Will it be pulled back to earth? Will it go into orbit around the earth? Will it land on the moon, Venus, or Mars, or go into orbit around one of these bodies? Will it become an "apple planet" of the sun? The sections that follow will discuss the factors which control the destiny of objects hurled into space.

Getting into Orbit

What is necessary to make a satellite go into orbit around the earth? Conduct the following "thought experiment." (Incidentally, this is similar to one that Newton described.) Picture a cannon mounted on a huge tower which extends 200 miles above the surface of the earth. If a cannonball is allowed to roll out of the end of the barrel it will fall directly to the earth, landing somewhere near the base of the tower. If, however, the ball is fired with a small amount of powder in a direction parallel to the surface of the earth it will fall in an arc, striking the earth at some distance from the cannon tower. A larger charge will make it land at a point still farther away. As the launching speed of the cannonball is increased, its path carries it farther and farther around the earth. Finally a speed is reached that is sufficient to give it a circular path around the earth. The ball is in orbit.

Has gravity ceased to exert its influence on the cannonball? Not at all. An observer stationed in the cannon tower, watching the ball leaving the cannon, would see it falling constantly, but never striking the ground. At the speed at which it is traveling the curved surface of the earth "tips out" from under it. The ball remains the same distance from the ground and "falls around" the earth in a complete circle.

Let us carry the implications of this "thought experiment" to the launching of a satellite into orbit. First, there is no tower, so the satellite must be boosted up to the desired height by rockets with thrust sufficient to overcome the pull of gravity and the frictional resistance of the air. Second, at the point at which the satellite is placed into orbit it must be traveling at the right speed for that altitude (about 5 miles per second at a height of 200 miles) to counteract the force of gravity. Third, it must be traveling in a direction parallel to the earth's surface when the rockets burn out. An error of only 1°—upward or downward—may spell the difference between a successful orbit and one which brings the satellite so close to the earth that the resistance of the air will make it lose speed rapidly. Under such conditions it may not be able to complete a single orbit (*see* p. 708).

The earth itself is an example of a body moving rapidly enough (about 18 miles per second) in its orbit not to fall into the sun, but not so rapidly that it tears out of the solar system to wander in the Milky Way galaxy. Manmade satellites become less mysterious when we realize that they obey the same laws that govern all the planets in their orbits around the sun.

The Shape of an Orbit

Generally the path of most satellites resembles that of all the planets around the sun: They are ellipses. It is virtually impossible to put a satellite into a perfectly circular orbit around the earth; the orbit is usually ellipitical. The elliptical path of the Gemini-Titan IV, for example, brought this spaceship as far away as 179 miles from the earth and as near as 101 miles. When a satellite is at its greatest distance from the earth it is at its *apogee* (*apo,* from + *ge,* earth); when it is closest it is at *perigee* (*peri,* around, + *ge,* earth).

Staying in Motion

When people realize that once in orbit man-made satellites generally have no engines for propulsion (except for adjustments of position or special maneuvers), they ask: "What keeps a satellite moving?" This is a perfectly natural question, because our experiences on earth teach us that moving vehicles—cars, trains, boats—stop moving unless continuously propelled by some kind of engine. However, what is not always understood is that these moving objects are constantly opposing the force of friction that results from their contact with the ground, water, air, and so on. Without friction a moving car could coast along forever with the motor turned off. Newton expressed this idea in one of his laws when he stated that a body continues in uniform motion unless acted on by an unbalanced force.

At altitudes of 100 or more miles above the earth the effect of the atmosphere is negligible, so that there is practically nothing to slow down the speed of satellites. Some satellites have had a short life because they were launched into orbits that cut across the lower, denser portion of the earth's atmosphere. This may have occurred by design or by error. In either case friction with the air in these lower layers robs the satellite of the speed necessary to maintain it in orbit.

Speed and Orbital Distance

What speed is required to maintain satellites in orbit at various distances from the earth? Gravity decreases with distance, so the speed required decreases with distance from the earth. The table at the top of the next column shows the relationship of distance to velocity in orbit.

Height above Earth (miles)	*Velocity (feet per second)*	*Time for One Orbit*
0	25,900	84.5 minutes[a]
100	25,600	88 minutes
400	24,700	98 minutes
1,000	23,100	118 minutes
23,000	10,060	1 day
230,000	3,360	27 days

[a]Neglecting slowing caused by the earth's atmosphere.

This chart shows a number of other interesting relationships. At a distance of about 23,000 miles from the earth the orbital period is 1 day. Since the earth is spinning at the rate of 1 turn per day such a satellite would appear to stand still, provided it was placed in a circular orbit in the plane of the earth's equator moving in the same west-to-east direction as the earth. (A satellite's orbital plane may be imagined as a flat plate passing through the center of the earth. The plate's rim is the satellite's orbit.) Because both the satellite's revolution and the earth's rotation are completed once every 24 hours the satellite will remain in the same spot over the earth's equator at all times.

In August 1964 the communications satellite Syncom III was the first to be placed in such a stationary position. It achieved fame in the early days of communications satellite demonstrations because it transmitted live broadcasts of the 1964 Olympics from Japan over the Pacific to California. From here the telecast was sent over land lines throughout the United States. Three such stationary-type of satellites can provide a global communication network with uninterrupted 24-hour-a-day television and telephone service, because each satellite can "see" approximately one-third of the earth.

At a distance of 230,000 miles from the earth the period for one revolution is 27 days. There is such a satellite in existence—the moon itself!

Multistage Launching

Multistage rockets with 2, 3, 4, or more stages, mounted on top of each other in piggyback fashion, are often used for orbital or space flight. In succession each part of the vehicle separates from the space vehicle after it has burned its fuel, ultimately leaving only the payload—which may be a satellite orbiting the earth or a spaceship on its way to the moon, Venus, Mars, or elsewhere. What are the advantages of a multistage vehicle?

1. All the stages after the first stage have the speed of the prior stage imparted to them.
2. Dropping the stage after it has burned its fuel gives the succeeding stages less "dead weight" to carry as they push the vehicle into higher and higher speeds.

Thrust

The force produced by the huge rocket engines is measured in pounds of *thrust.* To boost a spacecraft into orbit from the ground requires a thrust greater than the total weight of the launch vehicle. Two factors determine the amount of thrust that a rocket can deliver: the rate at which the fuel is burned and the speed at which the resulting gases are exhausted from the jet.

To place an object in orbit around the earth requires that enough energy be imparted to: (1.) lift the object against the force of gravity to the desired height, and then to (2.) give it enough speed in its orbital path to counteract the force of gravity.

The atmosphere must also be taken into consideration in planning the trip from the moment of launch on the surface of the earth until the space vehicle is above the air. The vehicle must be streamlined so that air resistance is kept to a minimum. Speed in the lower atmosphere must not be too great, because friction increases with speed. Moreover, frictional heating results in temperatures that may adversely affect the material of the spacecraft.

A rocket rises slowly from its launching pad and gradually gains speed as it climbs. Thus it passes through the dense lower layers of the atmosphere with speeds at which friction heating does not constitute a serious problem. The rocket reaches full speed at heights where the air is too thin to cause any important resistance to flight.

Escaping from the Earth

A spacecraft sent to another planet or the moon must achieve *escape velocity;* that is, it must be able to coast away from the earth indefinitely with its engines turned off. This is done by accelerating the vehicle to a certain speed.

At or near the earth's surface escape velocity is slightly more than 7 miles per second, or about 25,000 miles per hour. If a space vehicle attains that speed, even if all its fuel is burned up it can escape from the earth.

The attainment of escape velocity does not mean that the spacecraft is free of the earth's gravitational influence, which extends to infinity. As it races into space the spacecraft is slowed by earth's gravity, but it will continue outwards until it becomes subject to the gravity of the moon or a planet or the sun. The classical saying "what goes up must come down" is no longer true.

At present multistage rockets are used to launch spacecraft into escape flights. Each rocket stage is fired in sequence at different altitudes until the escape velocity is achieved.

Escape velocity from any astronomical body depends on the strength of gravity on its *surface.* On Venus, whose mass and size is close to that of Earth, the escape velocity is 6.3 miles per second. On smaller Mars the escape velocity is only 3.1 miles per second. On the moon escape velocity is about 1.5 miles per second.

An Earth-Moon Trip

In a trip to the moon and back a spaceship is under the constant gravitational influence of both the earth and the moon. Consider some of the implications of this dual attraction:

1. As the ship coasts from the earth to the moon, earth's gravity slows it down from its initial speed of about 25,000 miles per hour to about only 2,000 miles per hour.
2. It reaches this slowest speed at a point about $\frac{9}{10}$ of the way to the moon. Here the gravitational pull of the earth and the moon are equal.
3. Entering the moon's sphere of gravitational

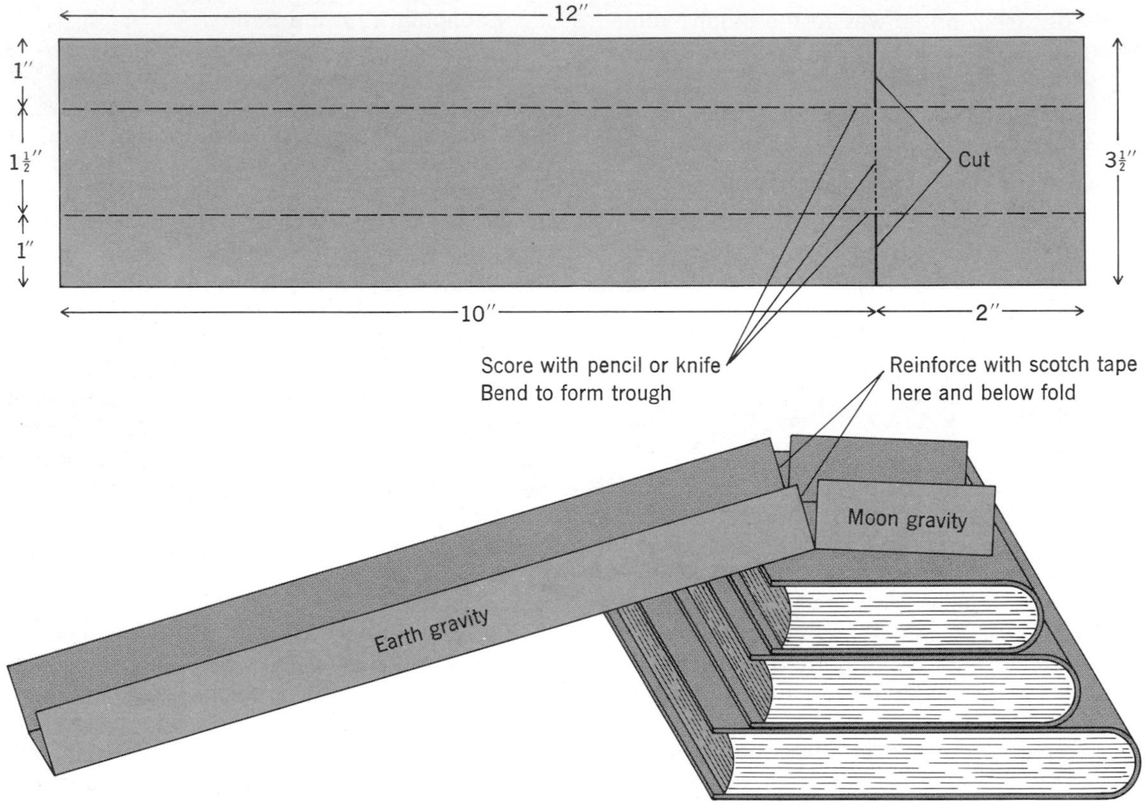

Making an Earth-Moon Launching Ramp:

1. Cut out a piece of cardboard 12 inches by $3\frac{1}{2}$ inches.
2. Rule two parallel lines down its length, each 1 inch from edge. Score each of the lines with a sharp knife or razor blade.
3. Rule a line across, 2 inches from one end. Score it and cut part of it as shown.
4. Fold on each long scored line to make a ramp with sides.
5. Bend the ramp on the short scored line to form a long and short "hill." Strengthen with Scotch tape under the peak of the "hill" and across the V-shaped opening formed by the bending.
6. Place the ramp on a flat surface. Elevate the short end by resting it on books.

influence the spaceship speeds up, reaching a speed of over 5,000 miles per hour.

4. Escaping from the moon requires approximately the same speed achieved in the closest approach of the coasting spaceship before braking by rocket action—over 5,000 miles per hour.

5. On the return trip the spaceship is first slowed down by the moon's pull. Reaching the sphere of earth's gravitational influence it speeds up, finally reaching 25,000 miles per hour.

Other details of an earth-moon trip will be found later in the description of the Apollo mission.

To demonstrate to yourself some features of

a round trip to the moon construct an earth-moon launching ramp. All the materials you need for this are the cardboard backing of a 9 x 12-inch pad, transparent tape, and a small sphere such as a ping-pong ball or a marble. Follow the instructions given with the figure on p. 686.

(See p. 709.)

To effect an earth-moon launch place the sphere (spaceship) at the foot of the long earth-moon ramp. Flick it with a finger. If it rolls back you have not given it enough finger thrust. (Your spaceship will not make it to the moon.) If the sphere flies across the room you have given it too much thrust. (Your spaceship will shoot past the moon and become a satellite of the sun.) If it just makes it to the top of the long hill and rolls down the short one you have made a successful launch.

Now try a moon-to-earth launch. Is as much finger thrust needed? Why? Play with your earth-moon ramp to see what other ideas are suggested by it. For example, does a heavier sphere (a marble instead of a ping-pong ball) require more thrust? If unhampered, will the sphere roll farther after completing an earth-moon trip than a moon-earth trip? What parallels do you see between your model and the five implications given in the foregoing text about earth-moon influence on space flights?

MAN INTO SPACE

When we place a man in a spaceship we are adding a complex and delicate structure to it. We can alter the nonliving mechanisms in a space vehicle to fit the conditions of space. But we have to take man more or less as he is—and alter the conditions to fit his needs. Man cannot be re-engineered (at least, not at present); he takes his way of living with him. He must breathe in about 150 gallons of oxygen in 1 day. His body temperature of 98.6° F. can be maintained only if the temperature around him is not too high or too low. Man's body is fitted to exist at or near sea-level pressure of about 15 pounds on every square inch of his body; if he is thrust unprotected into the zero pressure of space the internal pressure in his blood vessels and lungs would make him explode. To continue to function the body mechanism requires a constant supply of food and water. Wastes from his skin, kidneys, bowels, and lungs must be disposed of.

On earth man can survive the normal radiations from the sun and space that filter down through the atmosphere; in space, outside the atmosphere, he must be protected from powerful cosmic-ray particles and intense ultraviolet and other radiations. The rain of stones—meteoroids—that bombard Earth are burned up by friction with the atmosphere; in space these could be a hazard to the spaceship and the men in it. Man is a sensitive being accustomed to the rhythm of day and night, to working, moving, eating, to making changes in his earth environment. In space he faces the possible danger of fatigue because of the confinement of his "home" and his commitment to his major task there. Experiments on earth teach us that fatigue can result in a decline in power of perception, in indecision, and impaired judgment. On earth man moves in vehicles that accelerate him gently; in space vehicles he must endure for several minutes the strain of violent launch acceleration that multiplies his weight approximately 10 times. Deceleration on landing has the same effect. On earth man is subjected to the constant steady pull of earth's gravity; in a satellite or spaceship he enters the strange world of weightlessness.

In spite of these limitations man brings to a spaceship his intelligence, courage, determination, and creativity—characteristics that we have not yet been able to build into a machine. By adding man, we increase the chances of success of space missions because we add a being who can anticipate changes from the expected, who can detect incipient changes from the expected and alter plans, and who can respond to surprise. When the automatic control system for the Mercury spaceship's position in orbit became faulty Astronaut John Glenn took over and was able to control the capsule's movements by hand.

LIFE SUPPORT FOR MAN IN SPACE

How do we protect and support man in space? Although the precise methods will vary with the nature of the vehicle and the duration of the trip certain guiding principles can be stated.

Pressure

We must encase man in an airtight vehicle or space suit that protects him from the vacuum of outer space in which he travels. Pressure inside the cabin need not be as high as that on earth, which is 15 pounds per square inch. By reducing the pressure to about 5 to 7 pounds per square inch the weight of the air that the spaceship must carry is reduced. Moreover, the strain on the structure of the capsule—the tendency to burst open—is also reduced. (Reduction of air pressure in pressurized airplanes is done for the same reason.)

To protect an astronaut against the consequences of a possible break in the cabin wall he has available a close-fitting suit that automatically maintains the pressure needed around his body in case of an emergency.

Astronauts also don space suits when it is necessary for them to leave the cabin for a "space walk," or for the exploration of the surface of the airless moon. Under these circumstances the cabin is first completely depressurized—emptied of all air and reduced to zero pressure.

As we gain experience and develop more know how we will more and more provide "shirt-sleeve environments" for humans in space.

Oxygen

Oxygen must be carried along and delivered to the astronaut in regular and uniform concentration. There are several methods of supplying oxygen. One is to carry the total supply in containers either in gaseous or liquid state. A second method is to obtain oxygen from certain oxygen compounds. A third is to have green plants along, such as algae, to produce oxygen. A fourth method would be to split the oxygen away from the carbon dioxide breathed out by the astronaut and thereby reclaim it for use.

A major area of specific research is the kind of cabin atmosphere that should and can be provided for long space flights. Pure oxygen has been used successfully for the relatively short Gemini missions. However, laboratory studies indicate that lung damage can be caused by breathing pure oxygen for a long period. Studies are being made on the long-term effects of breathing pure oxygen and combinations of oxygen and such inactive gases as helium at different pressures.

The tragic fire that killed astronauts Grissom, White, and Chaffee while tests were being conducted in the Apollo spacecraft as it sat above its launching pad focused attention on the danger of using a pure oxygen atmosphere in a cabin. Oxygen supports combustion; anything flammable in the cabin burns in a flash if ignited.

Wastes

Waste gases, such as carbon dioxide and water vapor, must be removed from the cabin's atmosphere. Lithium hydroxide is a chemical that can remove carbon dioxide.

Water vapor exhaled into the atmosphere can be removed by condensation on a cold surface. The condensed water can then be reused as drinking water.

In addition to human wastes one must remove contaminants resulting from the operation of batteries, motors, and waste-removal systems, and from other parts of the total system.

Temperature

Research is being conducted in simulated space stations to determine the best methods for maintaining cabin air temperature and humidity for the comfort of the crew and for the proper functioning of equipment.

Acceleration

As a rocketship picks up speed on its way up, the astronaut feels heavier and heavier. This is similar to the experience we have momentarily when we are in an elevator that suddenly shoots upward. We feel ourselves pushed hard against the floor of the elevator. When a rocket ship accelerates, the astronaut also feels the extra push. The strength of this push is measured in "g's." The astronaut's weight on earth is, as we know, just the amount that the earth's gravity pulls on him. This amount is called "1 g." The "g" represents gravity's pull.

Shortly after a rocket leaves the launch pad it may have an upward thrust of about twice that of gravity's pull. The astronaut would then feel a 2-g push. A spring scale placed under a 150-pound astronaut at this time would indicate that he weighs 300 pounds. As the rocket picks up speed the astronaut may experience a push as high as 10 g's. You may imagine the weight of the body itself at such an acceleration by considering the difficulty in moving if 9 more persons of your weight lay on top of you.

Extra g's are also experienced when a spaceship slows down. This can be compared to the pressure against one's legs experienced when a downward moving elevator slows suddenly for a stop.

It is important to note that the increased g's result not from speed but from a *change* in speed. When we travel in jet airliners across the country at speeds of 400 miles per hour we often feel that we are motionless, unless we look at clouds and the landscape we pass.

As a spaceship leaving its launching pad picks up speed the blood in an astronaut's body would tend to pool in the lower part of his body—if he sat upright. His heart could not supply the force needed to carry blood to his brain, and he would lose consciousness. If, on the other hand, the astronaut lies on his back with his legs elevated the blood will not collect in the lower part of his body. In this position, also, the astronaut does not have to support the full weight of head, arms, and torso. The extra g's are distributed over the astronaut's back area.

Weightlessness

An astronaut in orbit around the earth is said to be in a state of weightlessness, also called zero g. For an understanding of weightlessness again enter the elevator in which you were a passenger in the discussion on acceleration. Imagine that you are standing on a weighing scale on the floor of the elevator. When the elevator is at rest the earth pulls you down with a force equal to your weight—let us say 130 pounds. The scale reacts by pushing you upward with an equal force. The dial consequently shows a reading of 130 pounds. It is the upward-supporting force of the scale (or any other platform that supports you) that gives you the sensation of having weight.

Assume now that the elevator is hoisted to the very top of the shaft and that someone cuts its cable. The scale is no longer supporting you because it is falling away from you as fast as you are falling toward it. Your *apparent* weight as shown on the scale is zero. If you release a book from your hand it appears to hover in the air. You and the objects in the elevator are weightless, not because gravity has been "turned off" but because you and all these objects are unsupported and are falling freely.

Objects inside an orbiting satellite are also weightless because they are falling freely. You will recall from the discussion on page 683 of the launching of the cannonball into orbit that it too falls freely. When a satellite is in circular orbit its orbital speed takes it away from the earth during each second just as far as gravity pulls it toward the earth. Although it stays the same distance from the earth it is constantly falling. The satellite, the astronauts, and all other objects in it are apparently weightless.

Thus it is shown that weightlessness is not produced by lack of gravity but by a particular kind of motion, which we might call *free motion.* (Customarily this is called *free fall,* but this term suggests falling down whereas in space a person or object can fall in any direction.) In traveling through space to the moon, or beyond, weightlessness occurs only when the spacecraft is coasting; that is, when the rocket engines are shut off and the spacecraft is subject only to the force of gravity.

John Glenn, weightless for 4 hours and 40 minutes in his history-making orbital flight of the Mercury, reported:

Objects within the cockpit can be parked in mid-air. For example, at one time during the flight, I was using a hand-held camera. Another system needed attention; so it seemed quite natural to let go of the camera, take care of the other chore in the spacecraft, then reach out, grasp the camera and go back about my business. [On eating, Glenn said] I had one tube of food that was squeezed into my mouth out of the tube. This presented no problem swallowing or getting it down at all.

I think the only restrictions of food would be that it not be particularly crumbly, like cookies, with a lot of little particles that might break off, because you wouldn't be able to get all these back unless you had a butterfly net of some kind.

Gemini IV astronaut White, the first American to walk in space outside his earth-orbiting spacecraft, reported that he could maneuver at will. "There was absolutely no sensation of falling. There was very little sensation of speed . . . You can't actually see the earth moving underneath you."

The astronauts all reported that the sensation of weightlessness is a pleasant one. There is no disorientation.

Weightlessness has not been a serious problem for astronauts thus far, but it has resulted in loss of muscle tone and loss of calcium from bones and in other effects on the cardiovascular system, body fluids, and endocrine and nervous systems. It is expected that we will know more about man's ability to endure weightlessness from tests to be conducted on manned space stations orbiting the earth for long periods.

(*See* pp. 697–8.)

Food

From what we have just quoted, it is apparent that it would not be comfortable for a weightless individual to eat the same way as he does on earth. The cereal on a spoon lifted to a spaceman's mouth would keep on traveling after

The Orbital Flight of Astronaut Glenn:

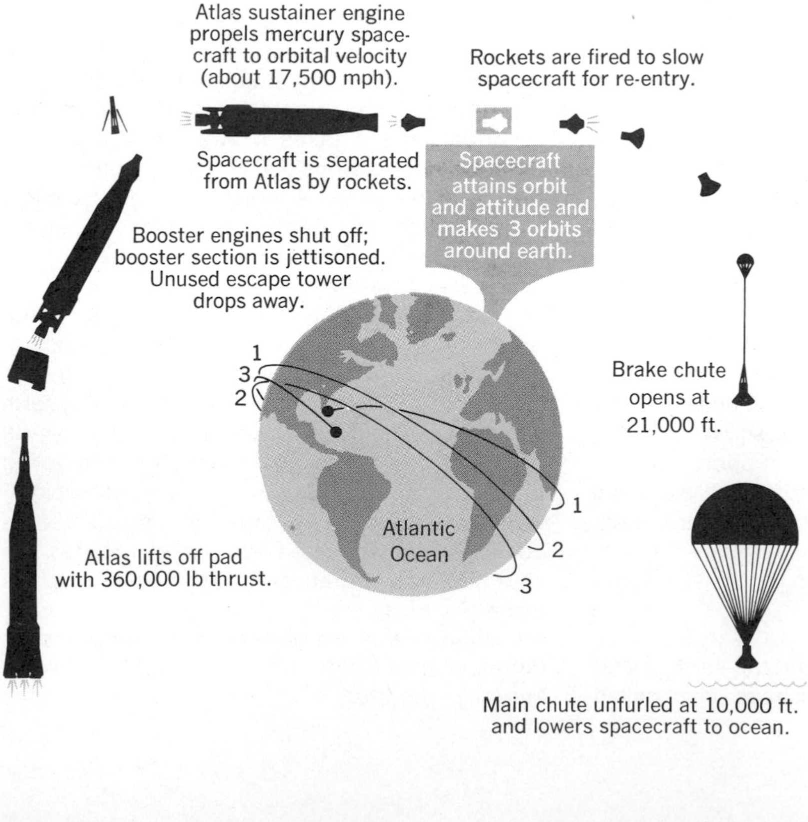
Atlas sustainer engine propels mercury spacecraft to orbital velocity (about 17,500 mph).
Rockets are fired to slow spacecraft for re-entry.
Spacecraft is separated from Atlas by rockets.
Spacecraft attains orbit and attitude and makes 3 orbits around earth.
Booster engines shut off; booster section is jettisoned. Unused escape tower drops away.
1
3
2
Brake chute opens at 21,000 ft.
Atlantic Ocean
1
2
3
Atlas lifts off pad with 360,000 lb thrust.
Main chute unfurled at 10,000 ft. and lowers spacecraft to ocean.

Lift off at Cape Kennedy: 9:47 A.M. EST February 20, 1962. Apogee (peak altitude): 141.2 nautical miles; perigee (low point in orbit): 86.84 nautical miles (about 160 and 100 miles, respectively, in statute miles). Touchdown, in the ocean southeast of Cape Kennedy, near Grand Turk: 2:43 P.M. EST. Total time, launch to touchdown: 4 hours, 56 minutes. Total time weightless: 4 hours, 38 minutes. Total miles flown: 81,000. Acceleration forces: During launch, 8 g, during re-entry, over 8 g.

the spoon had stopped and land on the roof of the spacecraft. Solid food will have to be placed directly into the mouth—by squeezing it from tubes. Liquids, such as water, cannot be poured into one's mouth because there is no gravity to cause it to leave the glass. Consequently, water is also packaged in squeeze tubes.

For long space trips of the future the total food required cannot be stowed and lifted from the earth. Some method of growing food must be provided. Algae, which can be grown in tanks, are often suggested. They reproduce rapidly, provide a high-protein food, and at the same time remove carbon dioxide from the cabin's atmosphere and supply necessary oxygen.

Water must be produced or reclaimed during flight. Water from the astronaut's urine, feces, breath, and sweat is one source. The wastes will be processed to reclaim water and chemicals that may be utilized to promote the growth of plants. Another possible source is the water formed by auxiliary rockets when hydrogen is burned (H_2 plus O yields H_2O).

THREE STEPS TO THE MOON

A major goal of the U.S. manned space flight program was to put men on the moon and to bring them safely back to earth. Step one was Project Mercury, in which astronauts first ventured into space and completed six flights ranging in length from 15 minutes to 34 hours. Step two was Project Gemini, which was concerned with further development of spacecraft and launch vehicles and preparation of astronauts for operations of ever-increasing complexity. Step three was reserved for Apollo; its climax was the lunar landing.

Mercury, Gemini, and Apollo were the three steps to the moon.

More importantly, they were steps in man's ability to operate in and use space. They have made it possible to explore another body of the solar system and to do important scientific research there. Our experience with these programs has led to our present understanding of the importance of having a flexible, economic space transportation system for our future work in space.

PROJECT MERCURY

Project Mercury paved the way for the moon goal by using one-man vehicles and proving that men could be sent into space and return safely to earth. Before manned flights began, Ham, the chimpanzee, successfully achieved a suborbital flight (less than a full orbit) in January 1961. In May of that year Alan B. Shepard made the first U.S. manned space flight. His suborbital flight of 19 minutes took his spacecraft 116 miles into space. Further milestones in Project Mercury included: the three-orbit flights of astronauts John H. Glenn, Jr., and M. Scott Carpenter in 1962, the six-orbit flight of Walter M. Schirra in 1963, and the 22-orbit mission of L. Gordon Cooper in 1963 (*see* figure p. 690).

Originally Project Mercury was assigned only two broad missions: (1.) to investigate man's ability to survive and perform in the space environment, and (2.) to develop the basic space technology and hardware for manned space flights to come. Beyond succeeding in these basic goals Mercury accomplished the following:

Explored the fundamentals of spacecraft re-entry—the return to earth.

Started a family of launch vehicles from existing rockets that led to new booster designs.

Set up an earth-girdling tracking system continuously reporting the location of spacecraft.

Trained a pool of astronauts for future space exploration.

Made scientific observations, including earth photography.

Project Mercury experiments also demonstrated that the high-gravity forces of launching and re-entry into the atmosphere, and weightlessness in orbit for as long as 34 hours, did not impair man's ability to control the spacecraft.

PROJECT GEMINI

Because it was flown by a crew of two astronauts the project was named Gemini, for the twin stars Castor and Pollux in the constellation Gemini. The 1965–1966 Gemini missions into space demonstrated that an astronaut can:

Maneuver the craft in space, changing its flight path, changing its orbital distance from the earth.

Leave the craft and do useful work in space.

Rendezvous: Find and move close to another object or craft in space.

Dock: Join and lock with another craft in space.

Function effectively during prolonged space flights of at least 2 weeks and return to earth in good physical condition.

Control the spacecraft during its descent from orbit and land it in a selected area on earth.

Perform scientific experiments in space.

Observe and photograph the earth from space.

Use earth photography for earth resource surveys.

All these Gemini accomplishments were essential for the big push to the moon.

Perhaps the most dramatic event in the Gemini series occurred on June 3, 1965, when astronaut Edward H. White II emerged from his craft and floated free in space for 22 minutes, tethered to his ship by a 25-foot "umbilical cord." The tether contained an oxygen hose and communication and electrical lines. It also contained a nylon safety line shorter than the other lines to avoid breaking any of these vital connections.

Astronaut White maneuvered himself in space by jet propulsion, firing a small jet of oxygen out of a hand-held gun in the opposite direction from which he wanted to move. As he floated in space above the bright blue earth White looked down more than 100 miles to see the maze of bays and waterways surrounding his own home near Texas.

PROJECT APOLLO

Apollo was the third step to the moon. Its goal was to land American explorers on the moon and bring them safely back to earth.

Three men served as the crew for Apollo, but only two landed on the lunar surface. The third kept the mother craft in orbit around the moon in readiness for the return of the two astronauts and for the journey back to earth.

To identify the achievements of but a few of the Apollo flights:

Apollo 8 was the first manned trip to the vicinity of the moon.

Apollo 11 involved the first landing of men on the moon.

Apollo 15 provided a superb example of how once a capability was developed, it could be used—in this case for science and exploration.

Apollo 17, the last of the manned lunar missions, placed a geologist on the moon, who collected new data about its history.

Although each of the Apollo voyages differed in detail the basic pattern of the moon flight was the same for all. To illustrate the Apollo flights we have selected that of Apollo 11, which was the first to place men on the moon.

The general plan of the voyage to the moon is shown in the illustration. The mission began with the launching of the Apollo-Saturn V vehicle on July 16, 1969. Apollo was the spacecraft; Saturn V the launch vehicle. On its launching pad at Cape Kennedy the 365-foot space vehicle stood as high as a 36-story skyscraper! Including its fuel, the entire vehicle weighed $6\frac{1}{2}$ million pounds. The crew was Neil Armstrong, Apollo 11 commander; Michael Collins, command module pilot; Edwin "Buzz" Aldrin, lunar module pilot.

The Launching Rocket

The Saturn V vehicle, 281 feet tall, was a three-stage rocket. The five jet engines of its first stage blasted into action at 9:32 A.M., lifting the spaceship with a thrust of over $7\frac{1}{2}$ million pounds. As the ship picked up speed a force of 4 g (4 times normal gravity) pushed the astronauts down on their couches.

Burning only for 2 minutes and 40 seconds, the engines rocketed the spaceship to an altitude of 41 miles and a speed of 6,150 miles per hour. Its engines then shut off, and the third stage was dropped into the Atlantic Ocean.

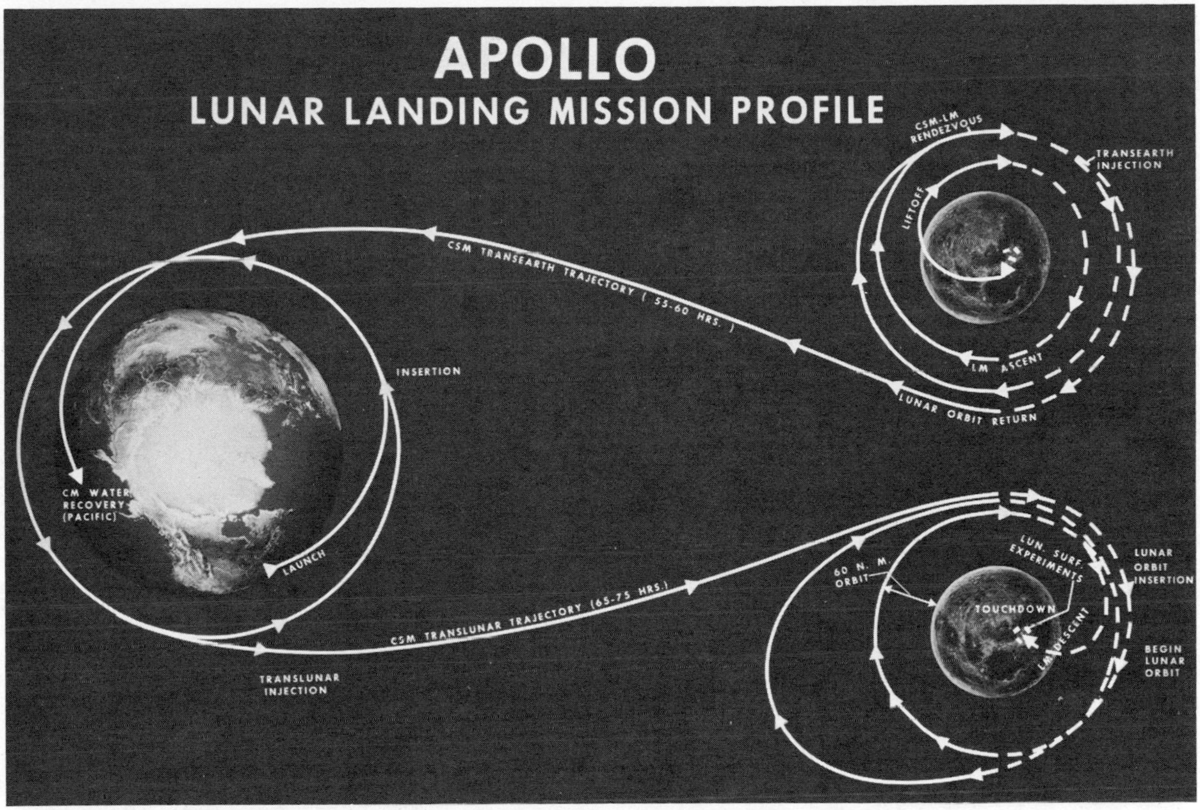

The flight plan of Apollo 11, destined to be the first to place men on the moon. As you read pages 692–696 on Project Apollo, refer to this plan. (*Courtesy of NASA.*)

Now the second stage fired, pushing the ship to an altitude of 115 miles and a speed of about 15,000 miles an hour. Having completed its assignment, stage IV was dropped toward the ocean.

The third stage now burned only enough of its fuel to boost the ship to a speed of 17,500 miles an hour, enough to place it in earth orbit at 117 miles altitude. It then stopped firing.

Apollo 11 made $1\frac{1}{2}$ earth orbits. The astronauts checked their systems while ground stations tracked the spacecraft, determined its orbital path, and prepared data for sending it on a lunar path.

Before the spaceship could start the long voyage to the moon, two primary requirements had to be met:

1. It had to be aimed in the right direction. This was not simply a matter of aiming at the moon, since the moon was a moving target. It had to be aimed at a point where the moon would be three days later, when Apollo would reach it.
2. It had to speed up to escape velocity of 24,500 miles per hour so that it could coast to the moon without the further use of rocket power.

The ground computers calculated the precise time and place in orbit to kick off. The stage III engines started up again, burned for 6 minutes and sent Apollo into its lunar path. This was now 2 hours and 44 minutes after liftoff.

Before continuing with the moon mission let us look at Apollo.

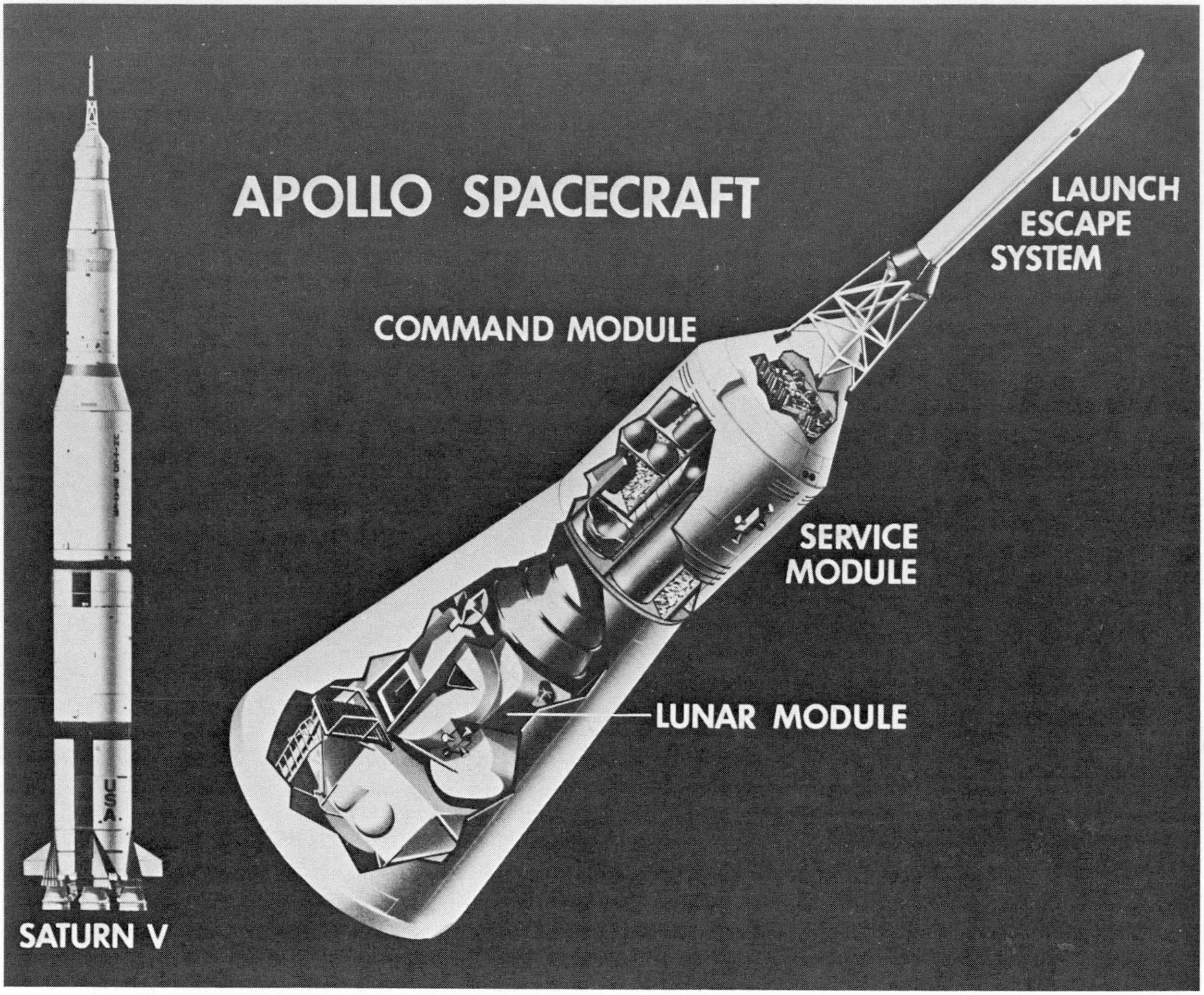

The Saturn V launching rocket and the Apollo spaceship (*see* text for details). (*Courtesy of NASA.*)

The Spaceship

The Apollo spacecraft consisted of three sections called modules. The *command module—Columbia* on this mission—was the only one that would return to the earth from the lunar mission. It contained the crew's living quarters and all the controls for various Apollo flight maneuvers. The command module was shaped very much like the original Mercury and Gemini spacecraft. One member of the three-man crew, Michael Collins, would remain on *Columbia* throughout the trip.

The *service module* was the primary propulsion system for the return from the moon and for course corrections during both the translunar and transearth trips. Its jets also slowed the spacecraft into its lunar orbit.

The *lunar module*—called *Eagle* on Apollo

11—would later be detached from the other two modules and descend to the moon. The lunar module was actually a two-stage vehicle. The bottom stage contained rocket engines which would slow it down for the moon landing to 3 miles an hour at a distance of 15 feet from the lunar surface. It was supported on the moon's surface by four strong legs. For the return trip this lower stage also served as the launch pad for the upper stage, which contained a cabin for the astronauts and the ascent engine. This rocket engine would propel the upper stage for its rendezvous and docking with the mother ship.

Earth to Moon

Return now to the moonbound Apollo spacecraft, leaving earth at a speed of about 7 miles a second. The next maneuver required that the three modules be rearranged so that the order would change from LM (lunar module)—SM (service module)—CM (command module) to LM—CM—SM. This made it possible for two of the astronauts to crawl directly from the CM to the SM. The switch completed, the third stage was jettisoned to fly into solar orbit, possibly to roam indefinitely in space.

Apollo 11 was now a three-module spacecraft. Flying for about two days it reached a point some 200,000 miles from earth, where its speed dropped to its minimum of about 2,000 miles an hour. It then entered the area where the moon's gravitational pull was stronger than that of earth. The spacecraft was now accelerated by lunar gravity.

Seventy-four hours after launch the spacecraft neared the moon at a speed of 5,700 miles per hour. The Apollo was turned so that the main engine nozzle of the SM pointed in the direction of flight. Its rockets burned for about 6 minutes, slowing the spaceship down to about 3,600 miles per hour. (When used in this way they are called retrorockets.) The spacecraft swung into a lunar orbit about 70 miles from the moon. Two of the astronauts, Armstrong and Aldrin, left the command module and crawled into the LM. Collins remained in the CM, which would continue in lunar orbit.

One-hundred hours—about 4 days—after earth liftoff the LM *Eagle* separated from the CM, *Columbia.* The moon is airless, so that parachutes could not be employed to slow the descent of *Eagle* to the lunar surface. Instead, retrorockets on the LM fired to make a safe and "soft" landing. Armstrong announced to Mission Control in Houston: "The *Eagle* has landed."

On the Moon

For several hours the astronauts remained in the LM, checking their life-support backpacks that would provide oxygen, pressure, and air-

Astronaut Edwin E. Aldrin, Jr., lunar module pilot for Apollo 11. Reflected in his shield is the photographer, Astronaut Neil A. Armstrong, and the lunar module. (*Courtesy of NASA.*)

conditioning on the moon. Before opening the hatch they had to depressurize the module to equal the zero pressure of the lunar vacuum.

On July 20, 1969, with the whole world waiting breathlessly, Neil Armstrong became the first human to set foot on the moon, uttering: "That's one small step for a man, one giant leap for mankind." Edward Aldrin joined him 19 minutes later.

In their brief 2½-hour visit the astronauts explored the moon's surface near the landing site; planted an American flag; took photographs; collected samples of moon rock; and walked, ran, and exercised in the moon's low-gravity environment. In addition they set up a group of experiments that would continue to radio information to earth on solar wind, meteoroid impacts, moonquakes, earth-moon distances, and moon size.

Back to Earth

On July 21, after completing their moon explorations, the astronauts climbed into the upper part of the LM, which blasted off with a thrust of 3,500 pounds for 7 minutes, lifting it to an altitude of 55 miles. It then docked with the orbiting mother ship—the CM and SM. After the astronauts crawled into the CM, the LM was jettisoned. The SM rocket engines ignited and built up to the lunar escape velocity of 5,700 miles per hour. The spacecraft was now on its way back to earth.

Lunar gravity slowed *Columbia* down for the next 18 hours, during which its speed dropped to 2,500 miles per hour. Then, entering the sphere where the earth's gravity dominated, the ship journeyed at ever-increasing speed until it reached the same velocity at which Apollo left the earth, about 25,000 miles per hour.

After using its jet propulsion power for final course corrections the SM was jettisoned, leaving the CM to use its own rocket thrusters to align *Columbia* for re-entry, blunt bottom first. Reaching the earth's atmosphere air resistance cut the velocity of *Columbia* to a safe point for the opening of the three giant parachutes and the subsequent safe splashdown in the Pacific Ocean.

From earth launch to earth splashdown the total moon trip took 195 hours, 19 minutes—or about 8 days.

SPACE SHUTTLE

(*See* figure p. 697.)

The next order of business in space transportation is the space shuttle, a vehicle that takes off like a rocket, orbits like a spacecraft, and returns like a jet airplane.

The space shuttle consists of two parts: an unmanned *booster* and a manned *orbiter.* At launching from earth the two vehicles stand vertically, with the orbiter attached piggyback to the booster. After the booster's rocket engines propel the orbiter to an altitude of 40 miles and a speed of about 8,000 miles an hour the two vehicles separate. The booster then plunges to earth where it is recovered, refurbished, and reused for future launchings.

With power from its own rockets the orbiter speeds up to 18,000 miles an hour and goes into orbit 100 to 700 miles from the earth's surface. After completing one of a number of possible missions the orbiter fires its rockets to slow it down and flies through the atmosphere to a selected airstrip on earth.

One of the important features of the space shuttle is its economy: It will be the first fully reusable space vehicle. With it, transportation costs to earth orbit will be reduced to about a tenth of present costs. The fact that it will land on a jet-sized airstrip on land, rather than at sea, precludes the need for a recovery force of ships, airplanes, helicopters, and frogmen.

Present preliminary plans call for an orbiter 120 feet long with a wing span of 75 feet. It will carry a two-man crew, and there will be room for two passengers in the main cabin. In addition, it can carry into earth orbit twelve passengers or spacecraft maintenance equipment. The interior of the space shuttle will be pressurized, enabling passengers and crew to ride in comfort without space suits. Takeoff and entry into the atmosphere will be relatively gentle, developing acceleration or deceleration forces on the occupants no higher than three times earth gravity.

While in orbit the pilots can open the doors

The space shuttle will be the first fully reusable space vehicle. It takes off like a rocket, flies in orbit like a spaceship, and lands on earth like an airplane. In this drawing of a proposed shuttle the orbiter with its crew rest piggyback on the booster (*see* text for further details). (*Courtesy of NASA.*)

to the bay and release unmanned satellites that can remain in orbit for years. Or the orbiter, which is capable of staying in orbit for a month, could conduct its own experiments. It might also be used to ferry scientists and repairmen to orbiting space stations—when these are built.

Among the space shuttle's other missions will be the retrieving of satellites for transport back to earth, the repair and maintenance of manned or unmanned spacecraft, the delivery of propellant fuels and space rescue—in the event of an emergency.

SPACE STATION

A manned station in permanent orbit around the earth, long a favorite of science-fiction writers, is now in process of becoming a reality. In 1971 the Soviets launched the first space station, *Salyut,* which was occupied briefly by three astronauts.

Skylab 1, America's first space station, was launched on May 14, 1973, orbiting the earth at a distance of some 270 miles. On May 25 three astronauts, flying an Apollo spacecraft, rendezvoused and docked with the workshop. They spent the next twenty-eight days in this hundred-ton vehicle, a record endurance run for man in a weightless environment (*see* figure p. 698).

It is too early at this writing to evaluate the harvest of data gathered by the first crew of Skylab 1. We do know that the astronauts were able to function well in space, working twelve or more hours a day, and taking long, unplanned space walks to make spaceship repairs. They took 30,000 photographs of the sun with Skylab's eight solar telescopes and 14,000 photographs of the earth. When developed and evaluated, these photographs of earth will show how effectively an orbiting spacecraft can be used as a platform for scientists "in residence" to study geology, agriculture, forestry, oceanography, and land use on the earth.

A second crew of three astronauts began a 59-day mission on July 28, 1973, to be followed by a third crew later in the year. They will carry out more than 50 experiments during the 8-month life of the workshop, including observations of the sun, the earth's atmosphere, and the earth's natural resources.

Later in this century a twelve-man and then a fifty- to one hundred-man space station is envisioned. The latter will serve as a permanent orbital departure point for lunar and planetary missions.

SPACE, SCIENCE AND TECHNOLOGY

Science principles developed over the centuries have guided the course of space explorations. Conversely, space techniques and structures developed in the space program have provided new tools for science and new processes, methods, and products for everyday living.

Space techniques have provided a new window on the stars and planets. The moon, Mars, and Venus all have been visited by spacecraft, which have yielded a tremendous amount of information about these bodies. Satellites have given us a better view of the earth. Photographs taken by TIROS, Nimbus, ESSA, Application Tech-

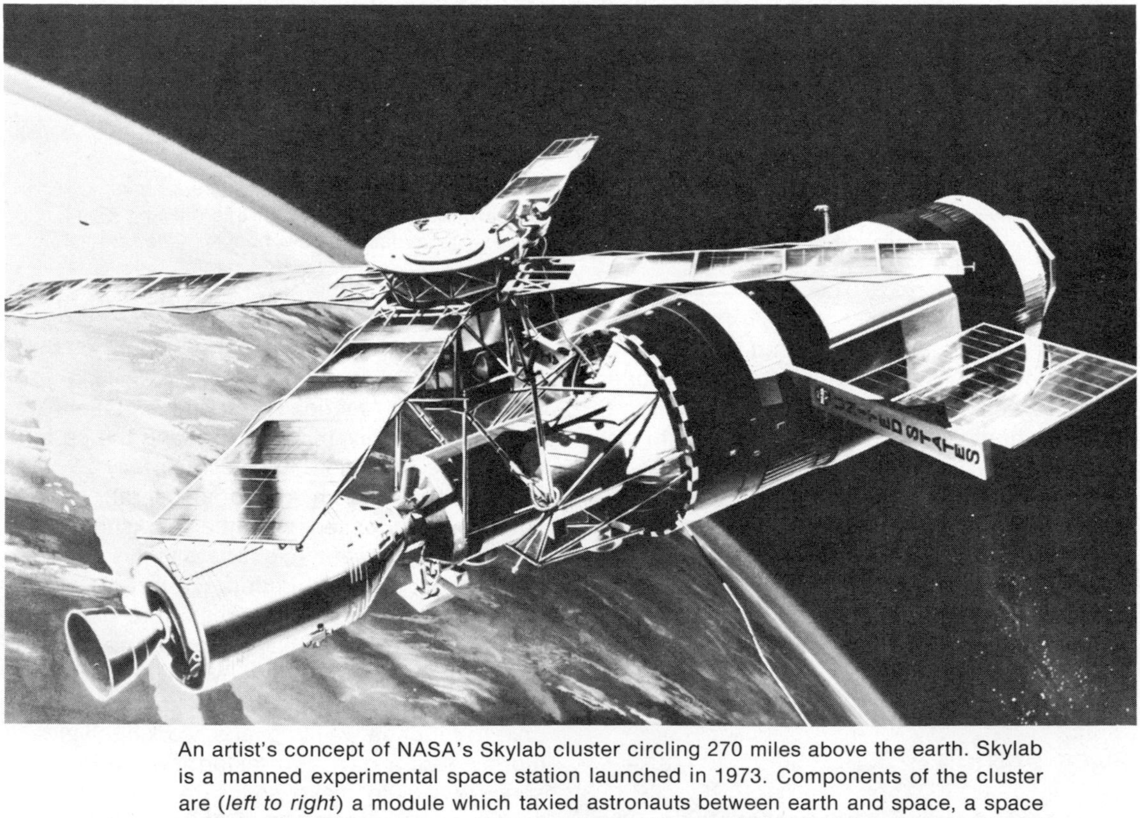

An artist's concept of NASA's Skylab cluster circling 270 miles above the earth. Skylab is a manned experimental space station launched in 1973. Components of the cluster are (*left to right*) a module which taxied astronauts between earth and space, a space dock, a telescope mount, an airlock, and a workshop. Skylab is 118 feet in length and is equipped with two sets of solar energy panels (*shown above*) to supply electrical power. (*Courtesy of NASA.*)

nology Satellites, Gemini, and Skylab 1 show what information can be obtained with observation of the earth from space.

A new era of earth study began on July 23, 1972, with the launching into earth orbit of the first of the Earth Resources Technology Satellites, known as ERTS-1. This earth-watching, 1-ton package of cameras and electronic scanners can perform such functions as measuring the world's wheat crop, detecting the spread of water pollution over entire oceans, mapping the movement of glaciers, and monitoring dozens of other phenomena on a scale never before possible. Information gathered will yield better understanding in such areas as agriculture, forestry, oceanography, geology, geography, ecology, and meteorology. Unlike previous space-science programs, all information gathered by ERTS-1 and its successors will be available to anyone everywhere. It is hoped that a truly global inventory of the storehouses and life-supporting systems of Spaceship Earth will come from this program.

Over 80 countries have now become involved in the space program, some of them quite extensively. Many countries carry out their own sounding rocket launchings. Dozens of countries use United States weather satellites for their own operational purposes. The communications satellite network spans the world. Tracking networks span the globe.

The exploration of outer space is no longer fantasy. Manmade satellites orbit around the earth performing a myriad of functions. Astronauts have orbited around the earth, "walked" in space, flown around and landed on the moon, and conducted scientific investigations in a space laboratory. Later will come space stations and flights to Mars. Still later may come flights beyond the solar system—perhaps to other worlds in space whirling around other stars.

The following are some of the important generalizations in this chapter:

The movement of the wings of a plane through the air provides the lift needed to offset the pull of gravity.

The lift on a wing moving through the air arises from (1.) the impact of air on its lower surface, and (2.) the decrease in pressure on its upper surface.

The propeller's or the jet's function is to provide the forward thrust necessary to move the plane through the air.

The position of a plane in the air may be altered by the movement of hinged surfaces—the elevator, rudder, and ailerons.

In jets, fuel is burned rapidly in a large chamber producing a large volume of gas. The gas streaming out of the opening of the jet produces a backward kick or thrust that moves the vehicle.

Jet action is an example of Newton's third law of motion, which states that for every action there is an equal and opposite reaction.

Rockets work on the jet principle; unlike jets, however, they carry their own oxygen supply and consequently can operate in airless space.

Rockets have made space travel possible.

To place a satellite into orbit it is necessary to contend with the resistance offered by the earth's atmosphere and with the pull of gravity.

If an object reaches a speed of about 5 miles per second or 18,000 miles per hour it can orbit the earth at an altitude of several hundred miles.

To stay in orbit a satellite must move fast enough to counterbalance the gravitational attraction of the earth.

Satellites maintain their speed in orbits high above the earth because there is no air there to slow them down.

The earth itself is a body in orbit around the sun, moving at the rate of about 18 miles per second.

The speed required to maintain a satellite in orbit decreases with distance from the earth.

Spaceships and manmade satellites in orbit around the earth move in elliptical paths. In this respect they resemble the moon's orbit around the earth and also the orbits of the planets around the sun.

If a space vehicle reaches the speed of about 7 miles per second or about 25,000 miles per hour it can escape from the earth.

The speed needed to escape from the earth does not depend on the mass of the escaping body: It is about 7 miles per second for all.

The velocity needed to escape from the moon is about $1\frac{1}{2}$ miles per second.

On its way to the moon a spaceship is slowed down by the pull of earth's gravity to about 2,000 miles per hour.

When a spaceship is about $\frac{9}{10}$ of the way from the earth to the moon the gravitational pull of the earth and the moon on it is equal.

To support the life of man in space we must cope with such factors as pressure, food and oxygen supply, suitable temperature, disposal of wastes, acceleration, radiation, and weightlessness.

When an astronaut is accelerated away from the earth or decelerated on re-entry he experiences extra weight or extra g's.

Weightlessness is experienced by astronauts in spaceships orbiting the earth or "coasting" through space. During weightlessness the apparent weight of an object is zero.

The next target in manned-space exploration is Mars.

Discovering for Yourself

1. Find out more about how progress in weather prediction has influenced aviation and how space launchings depend on weather forecasts.
2. Examine an airplane to see how the principles you have learned in this chapter are put into operation. Examine the wings, fuselage, tail, and other parts. Examine the instrument panel and find out what the pilot can tell by looking at the various indicators.
3. Visit a museum, if possible, to see various historic and modern aircraft.
4. Make a kite and fly it. Apply what you have learned to understanding how an airplane gets into the air.
5. Visit an airport for help in understanding the material in this chapter. Find out how weather forecasts relate to flight.
6. Assemble and try to fly a simple model airplane and use the experience to learn the parts of the aircraft.
7. Watch the takeoff and flight of a helicopter and an airplane and list the similarities and differences.
8. Search various newspapers and magazines for material with which to make a chronological list of space activities. Organize the material around such headings as: the moon, the planets, and so on.
9. Compare the source of thrust of a jet, an airplane, a helicopter, and a rocket.
10. Examine models of various rockets, satellites, or other space vehicles to see how they are shaped and constructed to perform their specific functions.

11. Swing a ball on a string on a vertical plane. Find out whether the length of the string, the weight of the ball, neither, or both affects the speed necessary to keep the ball "in orbit."
12. Various satellites are in orbit at different altitudes from the earth. Find out their purposes.
13. Project yourself twenty years into the future. How might supersonic airplane flights affect your way of living, vacationing? How might the environmental problems be solved? How may such flights affect other aspects of life—political, economic, and so on? How might the design of the city of the future be influenced?

(Courtesy of Port Authority of New York.)

CHAPTER 22B

TEACHING "FLIGHT AND SPACE TRAVEL"

Astronauts "take a walk" in space outside a spaceship, travel around the moon, land and ride on it, bring back materials from it, conduct experiments on it, and perform other feats that once were unbelievable. Satellites orbit the earth and send back all manner of information. The influence of gravity on rockets, satellites, and spaceships; weightlessness; and many other aspects of space exploration are in the everyday conversation of children. Scarcely a week passes without newspapers, magazines, television, and radio reporting new ventures or plans. Despite this, a visit to an airport, the sight of a jet plane, and even a look at small aircraft are still exciting experiences for most children.

No teacher can know all the answers about flight and space travel. It is not even necessary. A knowledge of the material in Chapter 22A is helpful for guiding learning activities. In addition to this the Bibliography suggests easily obtainable helpful resources. Chapters 7A, 8A, and 9A contain material related to this chapter.

SOME BROAD CONCEPTS: "Flight and Space Travel"

The movement of the wings of a plane through the air gives the lift needed to overcome the pull of gravity.

Propellors provide the thrust for some types of planes.

Jet engines propel some planes.

Some vehicles are propelled with rocket engines.

An object must reach a speed of 5 miles per second to orbit the earth.

To remain in orbit a satellite must move fast enough to counterbalance the earth's gravitational attraction.

Satellites maintain their speed high above the earth because there is no air to slow them down.

The speed required to keep a satellite in orbit decreases with the distance from the earth.

To escape from the earth a spaceship must go 7 miles a second.

On its way to the moon a spaceship is first slowed down by the pull of the earth's gravity. When it is about $\frac{9}{10}$ of the way to the moon it is speeded up by the pull of the moon's gravity.

FOR YOUNGER CHILDREN

What Happens at an Airport?

A visit to an airport is a memorable experience for many children especially if there is someone on hand to answer questions. Even if they are experienced travelers, and today many children are, they may not have had opportunities to observe and ask. If possible, arrange for children to go inside a large transport plane, see the instrument panel, talk with the pilot and a stewardess, find out about the cargoes carried by planes, observe the control tower, see different sizes and types of planes, and observe the general "goings on." Such a trip produces the best results if children have questions to ask and enough background to appreciate what they are seeing and hearing. For young children the trip should be relatively short and uncomplicated; for older children more detailed and comprehensive. In any case don't show them more than they care to see. Look in the "Yellow Pages" in your telephone directory for contacts in arranging trips, and see also the discussion of field trips in Chapter 3.

How Can We Make and Use a Glider?

Children can learn how the shape of a folded piece of paper can assist it to fly through the air by making paper gliders. Use $8\frac{1}{2}''$ x 11″ pieces of paper. Fold in half the long way and make a crease. Open the paper and fold both corners of one end to the crease. Close the paper on the crease then fold back the slanted ends to the edge of the paper. Outdoors or in a large room are good places to try the gliders and observe their flights; try to improve the flights by making changes in the size, shape, and other factors in the gliders. Let children measure and compare the distances and duration of various glider flights. Compare how the gliders operate indoors with how they behave outdoors on a windy day.

How Can We Make a Parachute?

In studying how things fall to the earth children may watch pieces of paper ($8\frac{1}{2}''$ x 11″) fall to the floor when they are dropped. They may try dropping the papers in different positions and from different heights and observe the falling time. They may make a crumpled wad of paper and compare the falling time, and discuss reasons for what they observe. Their discussion will begin to develop the idea that a flat piece of paper falls more slowly than a crumpled-up one because of the push of air. This activity may lead into the construction and use of small parachutes. Children will suggest various ways to make them. Use facial tissue and thread, or a handkerchief and string, for example. Suspend a toy figure, a small stone, or other object by the thread so that it hangs below the center of the open parachute. Fold the parachute

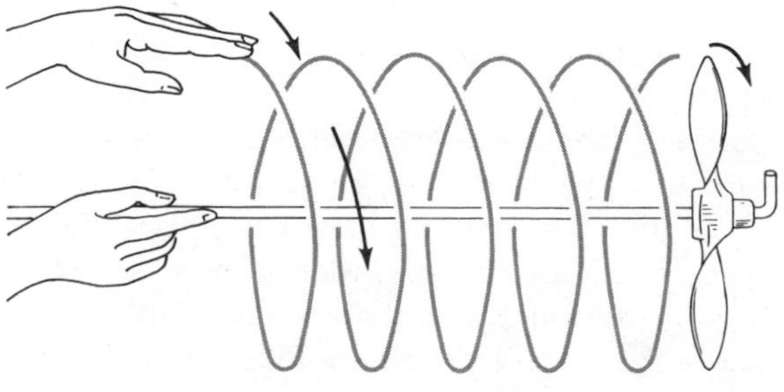

The toy plastic propeller is spun by striking it with the hand. As it spins, it advances along the piece of wire hanger, which is held horizontally. In this same way as the plane moves forward, its propeller pulls the airplane with it (*see* text pp. 706–7).

and the object into a compact mass and throw it up as far as possible and observe what happens. Children will try different materials, different lengths of string, weights of materials, and so on, and learn that parachutes fill with air when they fall and thus slow the fall of the objects. They can then attempt to apply this principle to the uses of real parachutes.

How Does Air Lift Things?

An interesting approach to solving this problem is to construct and fly kites, and try to find out: "How is the kite made so that it can be flown?" "How is it launched?" "Why does it sometimes fail to fly?" "What keeps it up?" "How can you make it go higher?"

Compare these observations with those made by using gliders and those made by using the materials pictured below and on page 705. Some of the experiences described in Chapter 9B may also be included.

Other Problems for Younger Children

1. How can we make a rocket blast off?
2. How is the earth like a space ship?[1]
3. What kinds of things do airplanes carry?
4. How are toy rockets built so that they can operate?
5. How are a variety of model planes alike?

[1] J. Schwartz: *The Earth is Your Spaceship* (New York: McGraw-Hill, Inc., 1963).

Another example of the use of simple handmade material. Here the "wind" is directed by means of a soda straw, and the "airplane wing" is made of paper and a strip of cardboard. Variations in shape and arrangement of the paper and force of the wind will help further understanding (*see* text p. 706). (*Courtesy of John King.*)

FOR OLDER CHILDREN

What Keeps an Airplane Up?

Pupils will perhaps need to review some of their experiments with air pressure, especially those which show that air pressure is exerted in an upward as well as downward direction. Holding a cardboard over a full glass of water and inverting the glass, for example, will help children see that air can press up.

To show the effect of an air current's passing over a surface let pupils hold strips of paper (2 inches wide and 4 or 5 inches long) so that they can blow a stream of air over the top. Until they begin to blow, the papers hang down. As soon as air is forced over the papers they stand out straight. Let pupils try this experience individually and then propose explanations for what happens. How does this help explain what happens to a plane? (*See* page 674.)

The paper-model airplanes (p. 705 and below) will also help pupils see more clearly how the parts of a plane respond to wind currents. An arrangement such as the one with the ruler and straw helps pupils understand how an airplane is lifted. The use of the rudder is illustrated by the paper "rudder"; and handmade gliders are also very useful in teaching the principles of flight. As children manipulate these materials urge them to observe and try to interpret what happens, and then apply their findings in solving the problem.

What is the function of the propeller in flight? Place a propeller from a model plane (it can be purchased from a hobby shop) on a stiff wire (coathanger wire will

The "rudder" may be made with folded file cards. Experimenting with various strengths and directions of air currents helps to demonstrate some of the effects of air on surfaces. (*Courtesy of John King.*)

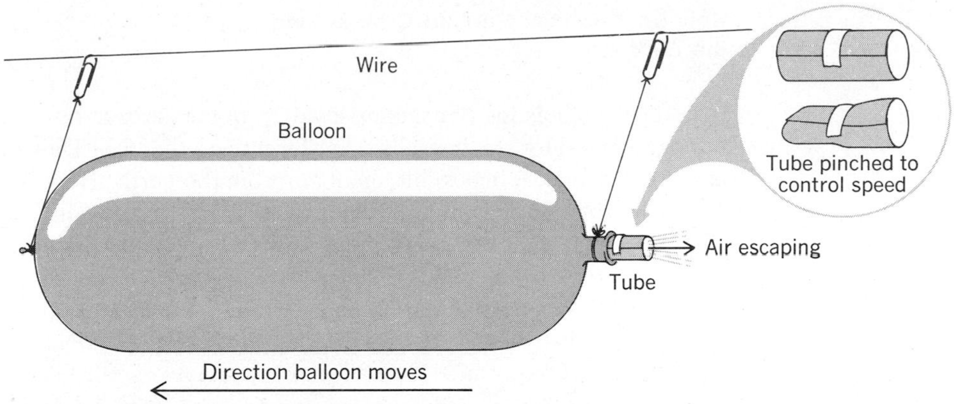

Some concepts about jet propulsion are more easily understood through the use of this apparatus (*see* text for explanation). Although this experiment may come under the category of fun it is an opportunity to see how pressure operates to provide a push forward, and how various factors may be regulated to control speed. (The books in the Bibliography describe other ways of arranging materials to illustrate these same principles.)

do). Strike the propeller sharply to make it spin and hold the wire horizontally—without a slant—so that gravity does not influence its motion. The children will observe that the propeller moves forward along the wire.

As a plane's propeller moves forward it pulls the airplane with it. This forward motion causes air to sweep over the wings and gives lift to the plane. (A common error is to think that the wind from propellers washing backward across the wings is responsible for lift. This is not true. Airplanes fly just as well when propellers are located behind the wings.)

How Does Jet Action Push a Plane?

As a preparation to an understanding of jet action let children blow up balloons and release them. What happens? How can you make the balloon move farther? In which direction (compared to the escaping air) do the balloons move? Why? How is this like a jet engine?

The jet-propelled balloon pictured here will help pupils understand the principle of jet propulsion. The "track" is made of wire stretched from one side of a room to the other. The balloon is held to the track by strings attached to paperclips. Inflate the balloon, and as the air escapes, the "jet" moves along the wire. Speed may be controlled by inserting a plug in the open end of the balloon which will regulate the amount of air that escapes. Make the plug of paper. Pupils can experiment with the size of the plug and get varying results.

How Do Satellites Get into Orbit around the Earth?

In addition to hoisting a spaceship away from the earth at faster and faster speeds, rocket engines used for earth satellites perform one other job. They direct the satellite into a *path* that makes it possible for it to orbit the earth. How is this done?

The following demonstration[2] requires only a string, a small weight (such as a wooden bead) attached to one end of the string with a paperclip attached to the other end, and a styrofoam ball—as shown in the illustration. The weight represents the satellite and the ball represents the earth. Hold the clip in one hand directly over the center of the ball so that the weight rests against the "equator" of the ball. The pencil is pushed partway into the ball and toward its center. The ball is positioned

[2] Adapted by permission from *Science Grade 6* (Brooklyn, N.Y.: Board of Education of the City of New York, 1972).

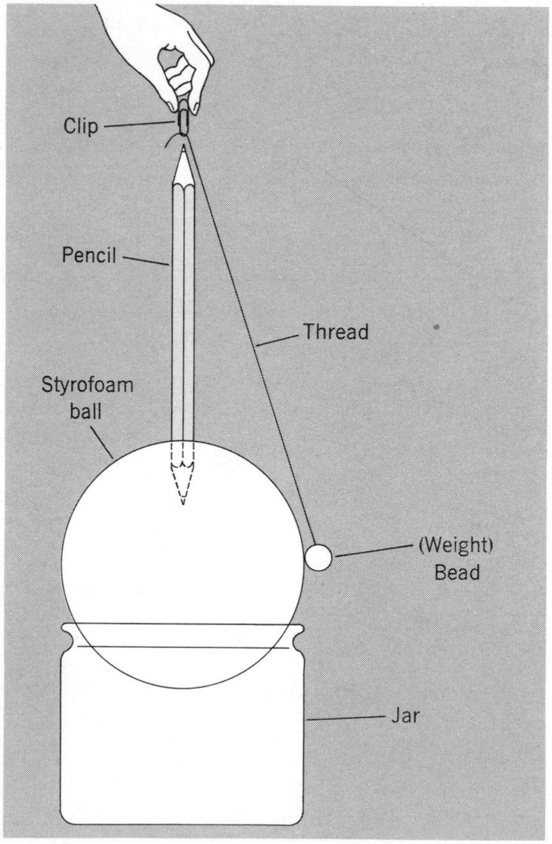

Model For Orbit Demonstration

(Adapted from *Science: Grade 6* by permission of the Board of Education of the City of New York.)

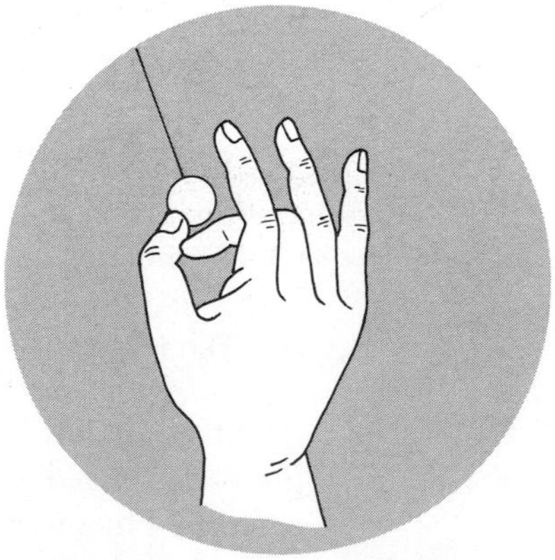

(fingers in position to snap ball)

(Adapted from *Science: Grade 6* by permission of the Board of Education of the City of New York.)

so that the pencil is vertical and points directly over the center of the ball. Ask pupils to try to launch the "satellite" into orbit around the earth by tapping it with a finger to move it from its resting position. They may tap it in any direction, but they must start from the resting position against the "earth." They are not allowed to maneuver it with the clip, which is held directly over the point of the pencil. They find that no matter what they do, the weight does not make a complete orbit. It always returns to the "earth." The best that it can do is return to the place from which it was launched.

Then how can it be launched into orbit? What must be done differently? Again no maneuvering with the clip is permitted; it must be held over the center of the ball and not moved. But pupils are allowed to *start* the satellite from wherever they please. They find that if they hold it away from the ball and push it parallel to its surface they can effect a successful launching of 2, 3, or more orbits. The position shown in the diagram is an effective one.

How hard do they have to push the weight to get it into orbit? If they give it a slight push it will not complete one orbit; it will fall back to "earth." If they snap it too hard it will go far out, but hit the "earth" again. A moderate push is most successful.

How Does Gravity Affect Space Flight?[3]

In preparation for solving this problem review the concepts of gravity in Chapter 7B. Children need to understand that the concept of gravity applies not only to the attraction that the earth has for bodies on it but also to attraction between heavenly bodies. All bodies in the universe attract each other. Their attraction depends on: (1.) the amount of material in them, and (2.) the distance between them (the attraction decreases as the distance increases).

The demonstration on page 686 serves to help pupils understand how spaceships escape from earth. Keep in mind that this is a demonstration—just as a ball and light are used to demonstrate moon phases, for example. The long trough *represents* the earth's gravity. The short trough *represents* the moon's gravity. The marble *represents* the spaceship.

If the marble is shot with the right force it will coast just past the dividing line and fall into the "moon." If too much force is used, the marble will skip over and beyond the "moon." If too little force is used, it will fall back to "earth."

Will it take as much force to launch a ball (spaceship) from the moon to the earth? No. Why? (Less of a hill; less gravity to overcome.)
(**Note:** This demonstration *should not* lead pupils to think that the earth's gravity *ends* and the moon's gravity *begins* at a given point. Both are present everywhere. The troughs merely show where the gravity of one is *stronger* than that of the other.)

[3] *Helping Children Learn Earth-Space Science*, "Satellite Orbits" by R.L. Bondurant and "The Orbit of a Satellite" by A.F. Eiss (Washington, D.C.: National Science Teacher's Association).

OTHER PROBLEMS FOR OLDER CHILDREN

1. What weather information is important to pilots?
2. How are satellites important to us?
3. What propellants are used in rockets?
4. What are some of the most difficult problems yet to be solved in space travel?
5. Why are rocket engines used in space travel?
6. What keeps a satellite in orbit?
7. What is it like on a space station?
8. What is a space shuttle?[4]
9. What is gravity like on the moon?
10. What is weightlessness?

Resources to Investigate with Children

1. Local airport to learn how airplanes fly and how they are controlled; to see types of aircraft, landing fields, and hangars; and to gain other information.
2. *Current Science*, a magazine for later elementary and junior high-school grades, for information about planes, air transportation, rockets, and satellites. (Order sample copy from American Education Publications, Education Center, Columbus, Ohio 43216).
3. Local airline ticket offices for maps, pamphlets, charts and other printed matter, and motion pictures about air transportation.
4. Pilots, to explain aviation matters and to answer questions about flying. Radio, for reports on "flying weather."
5. National Air and Space Museum, Smithsonian Institution, Washington, D.C. 20560, for pictures and information about historic flight craft.
6. Manufacturers of airplanes or airplane parts for materials and information about airplanes, parts, and instruments.
7. National Aerospace Education Association (formerly National Aviation Education Council), 806 Fifteenth St., N.W., Washington, D.C. 20005, for materials and information.
8. National Aeronautics and Space Administration Publications. Order from Superintendent of Documents, U.S. Government Printing Office, Washington, D.C. 20546. Very helpful materials. Ask for NASA Education Publications for August 1972.

Preparing to Teach

1. Keep a file of current news reports (clippings, pictures, and so on) that will help keep your background up-to-date. Plan ways to use this material in your classes.

[4] National Aeronautics and Space Administration: *Space Shuttle Emphasis for 1970's* and *Space Shuttle NASA Facts* (Washington, D.C.: Superintendent of Documents, U.S. Government Printing Office). Illustrated publications.

2. Write to NASA (item #8 in the "Resources to Investigate with Children" section of this chapter) for materials to read and assemble for use with children. Very helpful. Also write for *Space*, a free price list, No. 79A from the Superintendent of Documents, U.S. Government Printing Office, Washington, D.C. 20402, for complete information about government publications about space.
3. Watch the newspapers for announcements of the time and location of visible satellites. Try to observe these satellites for a number of evenings. Plan how you would use this activity with children.
4. Find out how the Jet Age is affecting your environment with respect to air pollution, noise, and city traffic. What problems may arise from supersonic jet flight? How may they be solved?

BIBLIOGRAPHY

PART I TEACHING ELEMENTARY SCIENCE

Professional Publications for Teachers

A Working Guide to the Elementary Science Study (Manchester, Mo.: Webster Publishing Division, McGraw-Hill, Inc., 1971), 126 pp. Complete description of the ESS program, with listing of materials available.

Anderson, Ronald, and others. *Developing Children's Thinking through Science* (Englewood Cliffs, N.J.: Prentice-Hall, Inc., 1970), 370 pp. A methods book.

Blackwood, Paul E. *Science Teaching in the Elementary Schools: A Survey of Practices* (Washington, D.C. 20402: U.S. Government Printing Office, 1965), 104 pp.

Blough, Glenn O., ed. *It's Time for Better Elementary School Science* (Washington, D.C.: National Science Teachers Association, National Education Association, 1958), 48 pp.

—— *You and Your Child and Science* (Washington, D.C.: National Education Association, 1963), 28 pp. For teachers and parents.

——, and Marjorie H. Campbell. *Making and Using Classroom Science Materials in the Elementary School* (New York: Holt, Rinehart and Winston, Inc., 1954), 229 pp. Directions for making and using materials and apparatus commonly needed in elementary schools.

Bruner, Jerome S. *The Process of Education* (New York: Random House, Inc., 1960), 97 pp. The paperback edition of a provocative book.

Carin, Arthur A., and Robert B. Sund. *Teaching Modern Science* (Columbus, Ohio: Charles E. Merrill Books, Inc., 1970), 625 pp. Methods of using the discovery approach.

Donaldson, George W., and Oswald Goering. *Perspectives on Outdoor Education* (Dubuque, Iowa: William C. Brown Company, Publishers, 1972), 233 pp. A collection of important articles on this subject.

The ESS Reader (Newton, Mass.: Education Development Center Inc., 1970), 236 pp. A collection of articles on science teaching.

Fifty-ninth Yearbook of the National Society for the Study of Education Part I. *Rethinking Science Education,* (Chicago, Ill.: University of Chicago Press, 1960), 338 pp.

Friedl, Alfred E. *Teaching Science to Children: The Inquiry Approach Applied* (New York: Random House, Inc., 1972), 377 pp. Suggestions for teaching science to children.

Gagné, Robert M. *The Conditions of Learning* (New York: Holt, Rinehart and Winston, Inc., 1965), 308 pp. A description and analysis of eight sets of conditions.

Gega, Peter C. *Science in Elementary Education* (New York: John Wiley & Sons, Inc., 1970), 631 pp. Methods and their applications in teaching science.

Goldberg, Lazer. *Children and Science* (New York: Charles Scribner's Sons, 1970), 146 pp. A guide for parents and teachers to a program of science based on children's curiosity.

Good, Donald G. *Science and Children Readings in Elementary Science Education* (Dubuque, Iowa: William C. Brown Company, Publishers, 1972), 422 pp. Collected readings.

Helping Children Learn Science (Washington, D.C.: National Science Teachers Association, National Education Association, 1966), 188 pp. A selection of articles reprinted from *Science and Children.*

Hone, Elizabeth B., and others. *A Sourcebook for Elementary Science* (New York: Harcourt, Brace Jovanovich, 1971), 475 pp. Techniques and procedures for teaching science.

Hurd, Paul DeHart, and James Joseph Gallager. *New Directions in Elementary Science Teaching* (Belmont, Calif.: Wadsworth Publishing Company, Inc., 1968), 166 pp. New experimental programs and other innovations.

Jacobson, Willard J. *The New Elementary School Science* (New York: Van Nostrand Reinhold Company, 1970), 579 pp. A methods book.

Karplus, Robert, and Herbert D. Thier. *A New Look at Elementary School Science* (Skokie, Ill.: Rand McNally & Company, 1969), 204 pp. Describes the Science Curriculum Improvement Study.

Kuslan, Louis I., and A. Harris Stone. *Teaching Children Science: An Inquiry Approach* (Belmont, Calif.: Wadsworth Publishing Company, Inc., 1972), 533 pp. Teaching suggestions, review of new curricula.

Lansdown, Brenda, and others. *Teaching Elementary Science through Investigation and Colloquium* (New York: Harcourt Brace Jovanovich, Inc., 1971), 433 pp. A science teaching methods book.

Lewis, June E., and Irene Potter. *The Teaching of Science in the Elementary School* (Englewood Cliffs, N.J.: Prentice-Hall, Inc., 1970), 574 pp. Teaching suggestions and subject matter.

Matthews, William H. III, comp. *Helping Children Learn Earth-Space Science* (Washington, D.C.: National Science Teachers Association, 1971), 255 pp. A collection of articles reprinted from *Science and Children.*

Piltz, Albert. *Science Equipment and Materials for the Elementary School,* U.S. Office of Education Bulletin No. 28 (Washington, D.C. 20402: U.S. Government Printing Office, 1961), 66 pp. Selecting and using scientific equipment.

——, and Robert Sund. *Creative Teaching of Science in the Elementary School* (Boston, Mass.: Allyn and Bacon, Inc., 1967), 217 pp. Methods of teaching.

Renner, John W., Don G. Stafford, and William B. Ragan. *Teaching Science in the Elementary School* (New York: Harper & Row, Publishers, 1973), 408 pp. Methods and approaches.

Sale, Larry L., and Ernest W. Lee. *Environmental Education in the Elementary School* (New York: Holt, Rinehart and Winston, Inc., 1972), 203 pp. A comprehensive treatment.

Schmidt, Victor E., and Verne Rockcastle. *Teaching Science with Everyday Things* (New York: McGraw-Hill, Inc., 1968), 167 pp. Experiments and experiences in many areas of science.

Selburg, Edith, and others. *Discovering Science in the Elementary School* (Reading, Mass.: Addison-Wesley Publishing Company, Inc., 1970), 495 pp. A methods book.

Sund, Robert B., and Rodger W. Bybee. *Becoming a Better Elementary Science Teacher* (Columbus, Ohio: Charles E. Merrill Books, Inc., 1973), 379 pp. Selected readings.

——, and others. *Elementary Science Discovery Lesson: The Earth Sciences; The Physical Sciences; The Biological Sciences* (Boston, Mass.: Allyn and Bacon Inc., 1970), 278 pp. Resource materials, activities.

Tannenbaum, Harold E., and A. Piltz. *Evaluation in Elementary School Science,* Office of Education Circular N 575 (Washington, D.C.: U.S. Government Printing Office, 1964).

Thier, Herbert D. *Teaching Elementary School Science* (Lexington, Mass.: D.C. Heath and Company, 1970), 273 pp. A methods book.

Triezenberg, Henry J., ed. *Individualized Science* (Washington, D.C.: National Science Teachers Association, 1972), 98 pp. A sampling of individualized science projects presently in existence. By various authors.

Victor, Edward. *Science for the Elementary School* (New York: The Macmillan Company, 1970), 785 pp. Methods and subject matter.

——, and Marjorie S. Lerner. *Readings in Science Education for the Elementary School* (New York: The Macmillan Company, 1971), 527 pp. An organized collection of readings from many sources.

Williams, David L., and Wayne L. Herman. *Current Research in Elementary School Science* (New York: The Macmillan Company, 1971), 436 pp. A compilation of current research.

General Subject-matter Background Books for Teachers*

Ashford, Theodore Askounes. *The Physical Sciences: From Atoms to Stars* (New York: Holt,

* *See also* listings for teachers in chapter items later in this bibliography.

Rinehart and Winston, Inc., 1967), 736 pp. An interdisciplinary treatment.

Asimov, Isaac. *Asimov's Guide to Science* (New York: Basic Books, Inc., 1972), 945 pp. Excellent, complete source of information.

BSCS. *Biological Science: An Inquiry into Life* (New York: Harcourt, Brace Jovanovich, 1963), 728 pp. The "yellow version" of high-school biology prepared by the Biological Sciences Curriculum Study.

—— *Biological Science: Molecules to Man* (Boston, Mass.: Houghton Mifflin Company, 1968), 840 pp. The "blue version" of high-school biology prepared by the Biological Sciences Curriculum Study.

—— *High School Biology* (Skokie, Ill.: Rand McNally & Company, 1963), 749 pp. The "green version" of high-school biology prepared by the Biological Sciences Curriculum Study.

Carter, Joseph, and others. *Physical Science: A Problem Solving Approach* (Boston, Mass.: Ginn & Company, 1971), 440 pp. General information.

Cotton, F. Albert, and Lawrence D. Lynch. *Chemistry* (Boston, Mass.: Houghton Mifflin Company, 1968), 660 pp. A high-school text.

Eisman, Louis, and Charles Tanzer. *Biology and Human Progress* (Englewood Cliffs, N.J.: Prentice-Hall, Inc., 1972), 530 pp. Good teacher background.

Fitzpatrick, Frederick L., and others. *Living Things* (New York: Holt, Rinehart and Winston, Inc., 1970), 468 pp. A general biology text.

Fuller, Harry J., and others. *The Plant World* (New York: Holt, Rinehart and Winston, Inc., 1972), 553 pp. A complete text.

Greenstone, Arthur W., Francis X. Sutman, and Leland G. Hollingsworth. *Concepts in Chemistry* (New York: Harcourt, Brace Jovanovich, 1966), 704 pp. A high-school text.

Heimler, Charles H., and J. David Lockard. *Focus on Life Science* (Columbus, Ohio: Charles E. Merrill Books, Inc., 1970), 561 pp. General treatment, good teacher background.

Inglis, Stuart J. *Planets, Stars and Galaxies* (New York: John Wiley & Sons, Inc., 1972), 482 pp. An introduction to astronomy.

Metcalfe, H. Clark, and others. *Modern Chemistry* (New York: Holt, Rinehart and Winston, Inc., 1966), 596 pp. A high-school text.

Namowitz, Samuel N., and Donald B. Stone. *Earth Science* (Princeton, N.J.: Van Nostrand Reinhold Company, 1965), 597 pp. A high-school text.

New York Times Almanac (New York: New York Times Company, published annually). A useful book of facts.

Ramsey, William, and Raymond A. Burckley. *Modern Earth Science* (New York: Holt, Rinehart and Winston, Inc., 1965), 664 pp. A high-school text.

Schwab, Joseph J., supervisor. *Biology Teachers' Handbook,* Biological Sciences Curriculum Study (New York: John Wiley & Sons, Inc., 1963), 585 pp.

Trump, Richard F., and David L. Fagle. *Design for Life* (New York: Holt, Rinehart and Winston, Inc., 1963), 664 pp. Modern approach to the study of living things.

U.S. Department of Agriculture, Yearbooks: *Soils and Man* (1938), *Climate and Man* (1941), *Grass* (1948), *Trees* (1949), *Insects* (1952), *Plant Diseases* (1953), *Water* (1955), *Soil* (1957), *Land* (1958), *Food* (1959), *A Place to Live* (1964), *Outdoors, U.S.A.* (1967), *A Good Life for More People: Landscape for Living* (1972) (Washington, D.C. 20402: U.S. Government Printing Office).

World Almanac (New York: Newspaper Enterprises Association, published annually). A useful book of facts.

Zumberge, James H., and Clemens A. Nelson. *Elements of Geology* (New York: John Wiley & Sons, Inc., 1972). 431 pp. A general reference.

Magazines for Science Teaching

American Forests (Washington, D.C.: American Forestry Association).

Appraisal: Children's Science Books (Cambridge, Mass. 02138: Harvard Graduate School, Longfellow Hall).

Audubon (Harrisburg, Pa.: National Audubon Society). Published bimonthly.

Curious Naturalist, The (South Lincoln, Mass.:

01773, Massachusetts Audubon Society). For children, nine issues a year.

Current Science and *My Weekly Reader* (Columbus, Ohio: American Education Press). Published weekly during school year.

Environmental Education (Madison, Wis. 53701: Dembar Educational Research Services, Inc., Box 1605). Published quarterly.

Journal of Research in Science Teaching (New York: John Wiley & Sons, Inc., National Association for Research in Science Teaching). Published quarterly.

Metropolitan Detroit Science Review (Detroit, Mich.: Metropolitan Detroit Science Club). Published quarterly.

National Geographic School Bulletin (Washington, D.C.: National Geographic Society). Published each week (October to May).

National Parks Magazine (Washington, D.C.: 1701 18th St. N.W. 20009, National Parks Association).

National Wildlife and *International Wildlife* (Washington, D.C.: National Wildlife Federation). Six bimonthly issues.

Natural History (New York: American Museum of Natural History). Published monthly (except July and August).

Ranger Rick's Nature Magazine (Washington, D.C.: National Wildlife Federation). Published eight times a year.

School Science and Mathematics (Indiana, Pa. 15701, P.O. Box 1614). Published monthly (except July, August, and September).

Science Activities. A Teachers Classroom Guide (Skokie, Ill.: 60076, Science Activities Publishing Co.). Monthly (except July and August).

Science and Children (Washington, D.C.: National Science Teachers Association). Published eight times a year.

Science Education (New York: John Wiley & Sons, Inc.). Published in February, March, April, October, and December.

Science News (Washington, D.C.: Science Service). Published weekly.

Science Teacher, The (Washington, D.C.: Journal of the National Science Teachers Association).

Science World (Englewood Cliffs, N.J.). A magazine for high-school science students; good teacher background.

Scientific American (New York). Published monthly. The advancing front of science, written by scientists.

Sky and Telescope (Cambridge, Mass.: Sky Publishing Corp.). An astronomy magazine, published monthly.

GENERAL BOOKS FOR CHILDREN*

Almy, Millie. *Logical Thinking in the Second Grade* (New York: Teachers College Press, Columbia University, 1971), 216 pp. A report for teachers.

Barr, George. *More Research Ideas for Young Scientists* (New York: McGraw-Hill, Inc., 1961), 158 pp. More ideas for discovery.

—— *Research Ideas for Young Scientists* (New York: McGraw-Hill, Inc., 1960), 158 pp. An excellent discovery book of experiences and experiments.

—— *Young Scientist Takes a Ride: Guide to Outdoor Observation from a Car Window* (New York: McGraw-Hill, Inc., 1960), 160 pp. Interpreting the scientific world from a car window is informative and interesting.

—— *Young Scientist Takes a Walk: Guide to Outdoor Observation* (New York: McGraw-Hill, Inc., 1959), 160 pp. Exciting suggestions for discovering science in the immediate environment.

Bendick, Jeanne. *Science Experiences: The Human Senses* (New York: Franklin Watts, Inc., 1968), 70 pp. Use of senses to discover.

Blough, Glenn O., ed. *Young People's Book of Science* (New York: McGraw-Hill, Inc., 1969), 446 pp. Interest-catching selections from many sources.

Brandwein, Paul F., and Hy Ruchlis. *Invitation to Investigate* (New York: Harcourt Brace Jovanovich, Inc., 1970), 160 pp. Develops skills in investigation.

Branley, Franklyn M. *Think Metric* (New York:

* *See* other sections of this Bibliography for specific related books.

Thomas Y. Crowell Company, 1973), 64 pp. An excellent introduction.

Busch, Phyllis. *Exploring as You Walk in the Meadow* (Philadelphia, Pa.: J.B. Lippincott Company, 1972), 40 pp. Suggestions about exploring and finding.

Cooper, Elizabeth K. *Science in Your Own Back Yard* (New York: Harcourt, Brace Jovanovich, 1960), 192 pp. Interesting, well-written information about common things, including living things, weather, soil.

Froman, Robert. *Wanted: Amateur Scientists* (New York: David McKay Company, Inc., 1963), 102 pp. What especially interested and talented pupils can do about science discoveries.

Lynn, Charles F. *Probability* (New York: Thomas Y. Crowell Company, 1972), 34 pp. Chances of success in predicting.

Milgrom, Harry. *Explorations in Science: A Book of Basic Experiments* (New York: E.P. Dutton & Co., Inc., 1961), 128 pp. Exciting experiences that help children understand their world.

—— *ABC Science Experiments* (New York: The Crowell-Collier Publishing Company, 1972), unpaged. Exploration for beginners.

Ruchlis, Hy. *Discovering Scientific Method: With Science Puzzle Pictures* (New York: Harper & Row, Publishers, 1963), 190 pp. An interesting approach to science through problems—not for beginners.

Schneider, Herman, and Nina Schneider. *Let's Find Out* (New York: Young Scott Publications, Inc., 1946), 39 pp. A science picture book with simple experiments.

—— *Let's Look Inside Your House* (New York: Young Scott Publications, Inc., 1948), 40 pp.

Schwartz, Julius. *It's Fun to Know Why: Experiments with Things around Us* (New York: McGraw-Hill, Inc., 1973), 156 pp. Experiments with iron, coal, paper, bread, and other common materials.

—— *Now I Know* (New York: McGraw-Hill, Inc., 1955), 32 pp. Finding the answers to puzzling aspects of the environment by experience and observation—for very young children.

—— *Magnify and Find Out Why* (New York: McGraw-Hill, Inc., 1972), 40 pp. Using the simple magnifying glass to make discoveries about crystals, plants, animals, and man-made things.

Books on Identification

General

Palmer, E. Laurence. *Field Book of Natural History* (New York: McGraw-Hill, Inc., 1949), 664 pp. Excellent, comprehensive, important for the elementary school library.

Animals

Bendick, Jeanne. *The First Book of Fishes* (New York: Franklin Watts, Inc., 1965), 72 pp.

Borror, Donald J., and Richard W. White. *A Field Guide to the Insects of America North of Mexico* (Boston, Mass.: Houghton Mifflin Company, 1970), 404 pp.

Brenner, Barbara. *Is It Bigger than a Sparrow?* (New York: Alfred A. Knopf, 1972), 38 pp.

Brevoort, Harry F., and Eleanor I. Fanning. *Insects from Close Up* (New York: Thomas Y. Crowell Company, 1965), 150 pp.

Burt, William H., and Richard P. Grossenheider. *A Field Guide to the Mammals* (Boston, Mass.: Houghton Mifflin Company, 1964), 284 pp.

Cavanna, Betty. *The First Book of Sea Shells* (New York: C.A. Watts & Co., Ltd., 1955), 38 pp.

Collins, Henry Hill. *Complete Field Guide to American Wildlife* (New York: Harper & Row, Publishers, 1959), 683 pp.

Conant, Roger. *Field Guide to Reptiles and Amphibians* (Boston, Mass.: Houghton Mifflin Company, 1958), 366 pp.

Cruickshank, Allan. *The Pocket Guide to Birds, Eastern and Central North America* (New York: Pocket Books, 1953), 216 pp.

Klots, Alexander B. *A Field Guide to Butterflies* (Boston, Mass.: Houghton Mifflin Company, 1951), 349 pp.

Lutz, F.E. *Field Book of Insects* (New York: G.P. Putnam's Sons, 1949), 510 pp.

Palmer, E. Laurence. *Palmer's Fieldbook of*

Mammals (New York: E.P. Dutton & Co., Inc., 1957), 321 pp.

Peterson, R.T. *A Field Guide to the Birds* (Boston, Mass.: Houghton Mifflin Company, 1947), 210 pp.

—— *Field Guide to Western Birds* (Boston, Mass.: Houghton Mifflin Company, 1961), 393 pp.

Pough, Richard A. *Audubon Bird Guide* (New York: Doubleday & Company, Inc., 1949), 312 pp.

—— *Audubon Western Bird Guide* (New York: Doubleday & Company, Inc., 1957), 316 pp.

Sanderson, Ivan T. *How to Know the American Mammals* (Boston, Mass.: Little, Brown & Company, 1951), 164 pp.

Swann, Lester A., and Charles S. Papp. *Common Insects of North America* (New York: Harper & Row, Publishers, 1972), 750 pp.

Wild Animals of North America (Washington, D.C.: National Geographic Society, 1960), 399 pp.

Zim, Herbert S., and others. *Golden Nature Guides: Insects, Birds, Mammals, Seashores, Reptiles and Amphibians, Fishes, Butterflies and Moths, Zoology* (New York: Simon and Schuster, Inc., 1949–1968), 160 pp.

Rocks, Minerals, and Stars

Joseph, M.J., and S.L. Lippincott. *Point to the Stars* (New York: McGraw-Hill, Inc., 1967), 96 pp.

Pearl, Richard M. *How to Know the Minerals and Rocks* (New York: McGraw-Hill, Inc., 1954), 380 pp.

Shuttlesworth, Dorothy. *First Guide to Rocks* (New York: Doubleday & Company, Inc., 1963), 30 pp.

Zim, Herbert S., and Robert H. Baker. *Stars* (New York: Simon and Schuster, Inc., 1957), 160 pp.

——, and E. K. Cooper. *Minerals: Their Identification, Uses, and How To Collect Them* (New York: Harcourt, Brace Jovanovich, 1943), 368 pp.

——, and Paul R. Shaffer. *Rocks and Minerals* (New York: Simon and Schuster, Inc., 1957), 160 pp.

Plants

Moldenke, Harold N. *American Wild Flowers* (Princeton, N.J.: Van Nostrand Reinhold Company, 1950), 453 pp.

Peterson, Roger Tory, and Margaret McKenny. *A Field Guide to Wild Flowers of Northeastern and Northcentral North America* (Boston, Mass.: Houghton Mifflin Company, 1968), 420 pp.

Rogers, Matilda. *The First Book of Tree Identification* (New York: Random House, Inc., 1951), 95 pp.

Stefferud, Alfred. *How to Know the Wild Flowers* (New York: Holt, Rinehart and Winston, Inc., 1950), 144 pp.

Zim, Herbert S., and Alexander C. Martin. *Trees* (New York: Simon and Schuster, Inc., 1956), 160 pp.

Bibliographies

Aerospace Bibliography, sixth edition, compiled for National Aeronautics and Space Administration by National Aerospace Education Association. (Washington D.C. U.S. Government Printing Office, 1972) 116 pp.

American Association for the Advancement of Science. *Science Books: A Quarterly Review* (Washington, D.C. 20005: 1515 Massachusetts Ave.).

Association for Childhood Education International. *Bibliography of Books for Children* and *Children's Books for $1.25 or Less* (Washington, D.C.). Revised frequently.

A Bibliography of Basic Books on Atomic Energy (Oak Ridge, Tenn.: USAEC Technical Information Center, P.O. Box 62).

Bibliography of Science Courses of Study and Textbooks for Grades K–12 (Washington, D.C.: National Science Teachers Association, 1201 16th St. N.W. 20036).

Carrajal and Nunzer. *Conservation Education—A Selected Bibliography* (Danville, Ill.: The Interstate Printers & Publishers, Inc., 1968). A publication of the Conservation Education Association.

Environmental Education for Everyone (Washington, D.C.: National Science Teachers Association, 1201 16th St. N.W. 20036, 1970). A bibliography of curriculum materials for environmental studies.

Growing Up with Science Books (New York: R.R. Bowker Company), 32 pp. Revised frequently.

Moore, John A. *Science for Society: A Bibliography* (Washington, D.C.: American Association for the Advancement of Science, 1971), 76 pp. A comprehensive list—science and technology in relation to man's problems.

National Council of Teachers of English. *Adventuring with Books: A Reading List for Elementary Grades* (Champaign, Ill.). Revised frequently.

Science Book List for Children (Washington, D.C.: American Association for the Advancement of Science, 1972), 253 pp.

PART II THE EARTH AND THE UNIVERSE

Chapter 6 The Earth and Its Surface

For Children

Adams, George F., and Jerome Wyckoff. *Landforms* (Racine, Wis.: Western Publishing Company, 1971), 160 pp., paper. A good general treatment.

Ames, Gerald, and Rose Wyler. *Planet Earth* (New York: Golden Press, Inc., 1963), 104 pp. Explorations and discoveries of scientists.

Arnov, Brnov Jr. *Homes Beneath the Sea: An Introduction to Ocean Ecology* (Boston, Mass.: Little, Brown & Company, 1969), 132 pp. Specific concepts of the marine ecology.

Bartlett, Margaret F. *Down the Mountain* (New York: Scott Publications, Inc., 1963), 63 pp. How soil is carried away and built up.

Bendick, Jeanne. *The Shape of the Earth* (Skokie, Ill.: Rand McNally & Company, 1965), 72 pp. Material about characteristics of the earth—not easily available elsewhere.

Bergaust, Eric, and William O. Foss. *Oceanographers in Action* (New York: G.P. Putnam's Sons, 1968), 96 pp. Pointed to career possibilities.

Branley, Franklyn M. *North, South, East and West* (New York: Thomas Y. Crowell Company, 1966), unpaged. Various ways to find directions.

—— *Gravity Is a Mystery* (New York: Thomas Y. Crowell Company, 1970), 64 pp. A beginner's book.

Carlisle, Norman. *Riches of the Sea: The New Science of Oceanology* (New York: Sterling Publishing Co., Inc., 1967), 128 pp. Treats many phases of ocean resources.

Carr, Albert B., and Robert S. Hopkins. *Islands of the Deep Sea* (New York: The John Day Company, Inc., 1967), 95 pp. Blends science, geography, and adventure in telling about oceanic islands.

Carson, Rachel. *The Sea around Us* (New York: Golden Press, Inc., 1958), 165 pp. This special edition for young readers has been adapted by Ann Terry White.

Coombs, Charles. *Deep Sea World: The Story of Oceanography* (New York: William Morrow & Company, Inc., 1966), 256 pp. Characteristics of the ocean, its life, and methods of study.

Fenton, Carroll Lane, and Mildred Adams Fenton. *The Land We Live On* (New York: Doubleday & Company, Inc., 1966). 96 pp. Describes the earth's surface and man's relationship to it.

Gallant, Roy A., and Christopher J. Schuberth. *Discovering Rocks and Minerals* (Garden City, N.Y.: Natural History Press, 1967), 125 pp. Where to find, how to study, and catalogue.

Galt, Tom. *Volcano* (New York: Charles Scribner's Sons, 1946), 102 pp. The story of the birth and growth of the Mexican volcano, Parícutin.

Goldin, Augusta. *The Bottom of the Sea* (New York: Thomas Y. Crowell Company, 1967), unpaged. Introduction to the nature of the bottom of the sea and what lives there—easy.

Keene, Melvin. *The Beginner's Story of Minerals and Rocks* (New York: Harper & Row, Publishers, 1966), 100 pp. Collecting, identifying, and studying rocks.

Ladyman, Phyllis. *Inside the Earth* (New York: William R. Scott, Inc., 1969), 32 pp. Geology: The forces that shape the earth.

Lauber, Patricia. *All about the Planet Earth* (New York: Random House, Inc., 1962), 138 pp. The earth's surface, the waters, the changes through the ages, and some of the methods of study.

—— *This Restless Earth* (New York: Random House, Inc., 1970), 129 pp. Earthquakes and volcanoes.

Matthews, William H. *The Earth's Crust #1* (New York: Franklin Watts, Inc., 1971), 92 pp. The earth's surface and changes.

—— *Soils* (New York: Franklin Watts, Inc., 1970), 72 pp. Formation, kind, importance.

May, Julian. *The Land Beneath the Sea* (New York: Holiday House, Inc., 1971), 40 pp. The ocean floor in detail.

Pearl, Richard M. *1001 Questions Answered about the Mineral Kingdom* (New York: Dodd, Mead & Company, Inc., 1959), 326 pp. A storehouse of information, useful for pupils and teachers.

Pine, Tillie S., and Joseph Levine. *Rocks and How We Use Them* (New York: McGraw-Hill, Inc., 1967), 48 pp. For beginners.

Ravielli, Anthony. *The World Is Round* (New York: The Viking Press, Inc., 1970), 48 pp. The earth's shape described for beginners.

Ruchlis, Hy. *Your Changing Earth* (Irvington-on-Hudson, N.Y.: Harvey House, 1963), 40 pp. The earth's origin and its changing forces through the ages.

Sanderson, Ivan T. *The Continent We Live On* (New York: Random House, Inc., 1962), 208 pp. Covers the geography, geology, and characteristic life of North America.

Sherman, Diane. *You and the Oceans* (Chicago, Ill.: Children's Press, 1965), 63 pp. Introduction to oceanography.

Simon, Seymour. *Science at Work* (New York: Franklin Watts, Inc., 1972), 87 pp. Experiments and experiences in oceanography.

Stephens, William M. *Science beneath the Sea* (New York: G.P. Putnam's Sons, 1966), 223 pp. The story of oceanography.

Stone, A. Harris, and Dale Ingmanson. *Rocks and Rills: A Look at Geology* (Englewood Cliffs, N.J.: Prentice-Hall, Inc., 1967), 70 pp. Changes in the earth's surface and a look at materials on the surface.

Tangborn, Wendel U. *Glaciers* (New York: Crowell-Collier and Macmillan, Inc., 1965), unpaged. What glaciers are; how they are formed; and why they move—easy.

Waters, John, and Barbara Waters. *Salt-water Aquariums* (New York: Holiday House, Inc., 1968), 176 pp. Detailed and illustrated, including some experiments.

Wyckoff, Jerome. *The Story of Geology* (New York: Golden Press, Inc., 1960), 177 pp. Our changing earth through the ages.

For Teachers

Berrill, Norman J. *Life of the Oceans* (New York: McGraw-Hill, Inc., 1966), 232 pp. Ecology of ocean life with information about some unusual animals.

Boyer, Robert E. *Geology: A Fact Book* (Northbrook, Ill.: Hubbard Press, 1972), 48 pp. General reference.

Dugan, James, and others. *World beneath the Sea* (Washington, D.C.: National Geographic Society, 1967), 204 pp. Excellent information and illustrations.

Earth Science Curriculum Project. *Investigating the Earth* (Boston, Mass.: Houghton Mifflin Company, 1967), 594 pp. Useful reference.

Engle, Leonard, and the Editors of *Life. The Sea* (Morristown, N.J.: Silver Burdett Company, 1967), 128 pp. General information.

Golden, Frederic. *The Moving Continents* (New York: Charles Scribner's Sons, 1972), 124 pp. General information about the origin of the continents.

Hubble, Lawrence. *The Earth* (Darien, Conn.: Teachers Publishing Corporation, 1964), 96 pp. One in a series produced with the National Science Teachers Association; information about geology, astronomy, and oceanography.

Maher, Kirtley F. *The Earth beneath Us* (New York: Random House, Inc., 1964), 320 pp. An unusual introduction to the science of geology.

Matthews, William H. *Introducing the Earth: Geology, Environment, and Man* (New York: Dodd, Mead & Company, Inc., 1972), 210 pp. General information.

Namowitz, Samuel N., and Donald B. Stone. *Earth Science* (Princeton, N.J.: Van Nostrand Reinhold Company, 1965), 597 pp. General comprehensive treatment.

Taber, Robert W. *1001 Questions and Answers about the Oceans and Oceanography* (New

York: Dodd, Mead & Company, Inc., 1972), 269 pp. A good informative reference.

Wyckoff, Jerome. *Rock, Time and Land Forms* (New York: Harper & Row, Publishers, 1966), 372 pp. The reasons behind the earth's changing landscapes.

Zumberge, James H., and Clemens A. Nelson. *Elements of Geology* (New York: John Wiley & Sons, Inc., 1972), 429 pp. A college text, combining physical and historical geology.

Chapters 7–8 Astronomy

***For Children*°**

Asimov, Isaac. *What Makes the Sun Shine?* (Boston, Mass.: Little, Brown & Company, 1971), 57 pp. Origins of the solar system.

Blough, Glenn O., and Ida B. DePencier. *How the Sun Helps Us* (New York: Harper & Row, Publishers, 1958), 36 pp. Easy.

Bonestell, Chesley. *The Solar System* (Chicago, Ill.: Children's Press, 1967), 60 pp. Information for especially-interested pupils and for teachers.

Branley, Franklyn M. *The Big Dipper* (New York: Thomas Y. Crowell Company, 1962), unpaged. Easy reading with large drawings.

—— *A Book of the Milky Way Galaxy for You* (New York: Thomas Y. Crowell Company, 1965), unpaged. Easy and informative.

—— *A Book of Planets for You* (New York: Thomas Y. Crowell Company, 1961), unpaged. Interesting information, easy.

—— *A Book of Satellites for You* (New York: Thomas Y. Crowell Company, 1971), unpaged. Easy.

—— *A Book of Stars for You* (New York: Thomas Y. Crowell Company, 1967), unpaged. Well-illustrated information for beginners.

—— *Man in Space to the Moon* (New York: Thomas Y. Crowell Company, 1970), 38 pp. Factual description of launching and landing of Apollo 11.

—— *Mars: Planet Number Four* (New York: Thomas Y. Crowell Company, 1968), 116 pp. Information about the "red planet"; discusses possibilities of life.

° For rocket and space travel books *see* Flight and Space Travel Bibliography, Chapter 22.

—— *The Moon, Earth's Natural Satellite,* revised (New York: Thomas Y. Crowell Company, 1972), 117 pp. Informative, well organized, interesting.

—— *The Nine Planets,* revised (New York: Thomas Y. Crowell Company, 1971), 86 pp. A guide to understanding the planets.

—— *The Sun: Our Nearest Star* (New York: Thomas Y. Crowell Company, 1961), 44 pp. The nature of the sun and our dependence on it. Easy.

Dietz, David. *Stars and the Universe* (New York: Random House, Inc., 1968), 135 pp. How research is carried out.

Gallant, Roy A. *Exploring the Planets* (New York: Doubleday & Company, Inc., 1967), 119 pp. History of astronomy and information about the planets.

—— *Exploring the Universe* (New York: Doubleday & Company, Inc., 1968), 64 pp. General information.

Heuer, Kenneth. *City of the Stargazers* (New York: Charles Scribner's Sons, 1972), 170 pp. Ancient astronomers; a blend of science, literature, history, and the arts.

Holmes, Edward. *Know About the World* (Racine, Wis.: Western Publishing Company, 1972), 76 pp. Origin of our solar system and evolution of life on it.

Hyde, Margaret O. *Exploring Earth and Space* (New York: McGraw-Hill, Inc., 1970), 174 pp. Describes research about the earth's surface and about space.

Irvins, Ann. *Stars and Constellations* (New York: Crowell-Collier and Macmillan, Inc., 1969), 28 pp. Stars and descriptions.

Joseph, Maron Joseph, and Sarah Lee Lippincott, *Point to the Stars* (New York: McGraw-Hill, Inc., 1967), 93 pp. Locating stars and constellations; maps and drawings.

Kettelkamp, Larry. *Investigating UFO's* (New York: William Morrow & Company, Inc., 1971), 96 pp. Information, not easily found elsewhere, about unidentified foreign objects.

Knight, David C. *Let's Find Out about Earth* (New York: Franklin Watts, Inc., 1968), 48 pp. Easy introduction to astronomy.

Pine, Tillie S., and Joseph Levine. *Gravity All*

Around (New York: McGraw-Hill, Inc., 1963), 48 pp. Easy reading.

Piper, Roger. *The Big Dish: The Fascinating Story of Radio Telescopes* (New York: Harcourt, Brace & World, Inc., 1963), 159 pp. How the telescope works, as well as some of the exciting discoveries made through its use.

Polgreen, John, and Cathleen Polgreen. *Sunlight and Shadows* (New York: Doubleday & Company, Inc., 1967), 57 pp. Shadows in relation to the sun and seasons.

Schloat, Warren. *Andy's Wonderful Telescope* (New York: Charles Scribner's Sons, 1958), 48 pp. The principles of the reflecting and refracting telescopes pictorially explained.

Schneider, Herman, and Nina Schneider. *How Big Is Big?* (New York: Scott Publications, Inc., 1950), 48 pp. Helps child understand how he fits into the scheme of the universe.

—— *You among the Stars* (New York: Scott Publications, Inc., 1967). A first book of astronomy, simplifying concepts.

Schwartz, Julius. *The Earth Is Your Spaceship* (New York: McGraw-Hill, Inc., 1963), 32 pp. Easy reading about the movements of the earth through space and their effects.

Simon, Tony. *The Moon Explorers* (New York: Four Winds Press, 1970), 128 pp. Story of the U.S. space programs; detailed.

Wetterer, Margaret K. *The Moons of Jupiter* (New York: Simon and Schuster, Inc., 1971), 96 pp. History of discovery and information about these bodies.

For Teachers

Abell, George. *Exploration of the Universe* (New York: Holt, Rinehart and Winston, Inc., 1969), 646 pp. A college text in astronomy.

Asimov, Isaac. *The Kingdom of the Sun* (New York: Abelard-Schuman Ltd., 1960), 151 pp. The methods of astronomy and their results.

Bergamini, David, and the Editors of *Life. The Universe* (New York: Time, Inc., Book Divison, 1968). Illustrated story of astronomy.

Huffer, Charles M., Frederick E. Trinklein, and Mark Bunge. *An Introduction to Astronomy* (New York: Holt, Rinehart and Winston, Inc., 1967), 381 pp. A college text.

Inglis, Stuart J. *Planets, Stars and Galaxies* (New York: John Wiley & Sons, Inc., 1972), 482 pp. General astronomy.

Jastrow, Robert, and Malcolm H. Thompson. *Astronomy: Fundamentals and Frontiers* (New York: John Wiley & Sons, Inc., 1972), 404 pp. General astronomy background.

Moore, Patrick. *Seeing Stars* (Skokie, Ill.: Rand McNally & Company, 1971), 47 pp. Easy reading for elementary teachers.

Pickering, James S. *Windows to Space* (Boston, Mass.: Little, Brown & Company, 1967), 218 pp. Astronomy for advanced students and teachers.

Skilling, W.T., and R.S. Richardson. *Sun, Moon and Stars* (New York: McGraw-Hill, Inc., 1964), 304 pp. Excellent information for the inexperienced teacher.

Chapter 9 The Air and the Weather

For Children

Bendick, Jeanne. *How to Make a Cloud* (New York: Parents' Magazine Press, 1971), 64 pp. Weather principles.

—— *Lightning* (Skokie, Ill.: Rand McNally & Company, 1961), 61 pp. Explanation of the phenomena and answers to questions.

—— *The Wind* (Skokie, Ill.: Rand McNally & Company, 1964), 80 pp. The nature and importance of wind.

Berger, Melvin. *The National Weather Service* (New York: The John Day Company, Inc., 1971), 124 pp. Services, techniques, instruments of the Weather Service.

Blough, Glenn O. *Not Only for Ducks* (New York: McGraw-Hill, Inc., 1954), 48 pp. The story of rain.

—— *Water Appears and Disappears* (New York: Harper & Row, Publishers, 1959), 36 pp. The story of evaporation and condensation, leading to an understanding of weather—easy.

Branley, Franklyn M. *Air Is All around You* (New York: Thomas Y. Crowell Company, 1962), unpaged. Easy.

—— *Flash, Crash, Rumble, and Roll* (New York: Thomas Y. Crowell Company, 1964), unpaged. How an electrical charge builds up in a thundercloud until it produces a lightning flash and thunder; reassuring instructions for safety during a storm.

—— *Rain and Hail* (New York: Thomas Y. Crowell Company, 1963), unpaged. Gives an explicit, simple explanation of what makes rain and hail.

—— *Snow Is Falling* (New York: Thomas Y. Crowell Company, 1963), unpaged. Simple text answers the questions about snow and snowflakes that children ask.

Buehr, Walter. *Storm Warnings: The Story of Hurricanes and Tornadoes* (New York: William Morrow & Company, Inc., 1972), 64 pp. Description and causes.

Kaufmann, John. *Winds and Weather* (New York: William Morrow & Company, Inc., 1971), 64 pp. Descriptions of kinds of weather.

Keen, Martin L. *Lightning and Thunder* (New York: Simon and Schuster, Inc., 1969), 94 pp. Superstitions, causes, safety rules.

Lehr, Paul E. *Storms* (New York: Golden Press, Inc., 1966), 58 pp. The origin and effects of storms; their forecasting and lore.

Milgrom, Harry. *Understanding Weather,* revised (New York: Crowell-Collier and Macmillan, 1970), 84 pp. With experiments.

Pine, Tillie, and Joseph Levine. *Air All Around* (New York: McGraw-Hill Inc., 1960), 48 pp. Properties of air and experiments to demonstrate them—easy

—— *Water All Around* (New York: McGraw-Hill, Inc., 1959), 48 pp. Experiments with evaporation and condensation and other properties of water—easy.

—— *Weather All Around* (New York: McGraw-Hill, Inc., 1966), 48 pp. Introduction to common phases of weather—easy.

Ross, Frank. *Storms and Man* (New York: Lothrop, Lee & Shepard, Co., 1971), 192 pp. Storms—their causes, effects, and control.

Rubin, Louis D. *Forecasting the Weather* (New York: Franklin Watts, Inc., 1970), 64 pp. Amateur forecasting.

Simon, Seymour. *Weather and Climate* (New York: Random House, Inc., 1969), 128 pp. Causes of weather and climate changes.

Spar, Jerome. *The Way of the Weather* (Mankato, Minn.: Creative Educational Society in cooperation with The American Museum of Natural History, 1967), 224 pp. Illustrated with many photographs and drawings; conveys feeling as well as the science of weather.

Stone, A. Harris, and Herbert Spiegel. *The Winds of Weather* (Englewood Cliffs, N.J.: Prentice-Hall, Inc., 1969), 64 pp. Experiments about winds and their causes.

For Teachers

Forrester, Frank. *1001 Questions Answered about the Weather* (New York: Dodd, Mead & Company, Inc., 1957), 419 pp. A mine of useful information.

Sutcliffe, R.C. *Weather and Climate* (New York: W.W. Norton & Company, Inc., 1966), 206 pp. Good science background for teachers.

Thompson, Philip D., Robert O'Brien, and the Editors of *Life. Weather.* (Morristown, N.J.: Silver Burdett Company, 1965), 200 pp. Picture and text story of the weather.

PART III LIVING THINGS

Chapter 10 The Nature and Variety of Life

For Children

Baker, Jeffrey J.W. *The Vital Process: Photosynthesis* (New York: Doubleday & Company, Inc., 1969), 64 pp. The story of food manufacture.

Bendick, Jeanne. *Living Things* (New York: Franklin Watts, Inc., 1969), 72 pp. Information about the nature of living things.

Blough, Glenn O. *After the Sun Goes Down* (New York: McGraw-Hill, Inc., 1956), 48 pp. The story of animals at night.

—— The Basic Science Education Series (New York: Harper & Row, Publishers, 1957–1959), 36 pp. *An Aquarium, The Insect Parade, The Pet Show, Useful Plants and Animals, Animals and Their Young, Animals that Live Together*—general information.

—— *Christmas Trees and How They Grow* (New York: McGraw-Hill, Inc., 1961), 48 pp. The story of the growth of a tree, tree nurseries, and conservation.

—— *Discovering Insects* (New York: McGraw-Hill, Inc., 1967), 48 pp. Learning about insects; suggested activities.

—— *Discovering Plants* (New York: McGraw-Hill,

Inc., 1966), 48 pp. Information about plants and how they grow.

—— *Not Only for Ducks* (New York: McGraw-Hill, Inc., 1954), 48 pp. How rain helps plants and other living things.

—— *Wait for the Sunshine* (New York: McGraw-Hill, Inc., 1954), 48 pp. Plants and the seasonal changes, with emphasis on food manufacture in plants.

—— *Who Lives in This House?* (New York: McGraw-Hill, Inc., 1957), 48 pp. Habits of animals that inhabit a deserted house.

—— *Who Lives in This Meadow?* (New York: McGraw-Hill, Inc., 1961), 48 pp. Animal life, its adaptation to environment, and interrelationship.

—— *Who Lives at the Seashore?* (New York: McGraw-Hill, Inc., 1962), 48 pp. Animal life along the shore and how to observe it.

——, and Marjorie Campbell. *When You Go to the Zoo* (New York: McGraw-Hill, Inc., 1955), 128 pp. Habits of zoo animals and details of how they are cared for.

Bridges, William. *Zoo Doctor* (New York: William Morrow & Company, Inc., 1957), 126 pp. An engaging account of how zoo animals are cared for, by the curator of publications of the Bronx Zoo.

—— *Zoo Expeditions* (New York: William Morrow & Company, Inc., 1954), 191 pp. Interesting and unusual information about the exciting business of collecting animals.

Buck, Margaret Waring. *How They Grow* (Nashville, Tenn.: Abington Press, 1972), 40 pp. Life cycles of 17 animals.

Butts, David P., and Addison E. Lee. *Watermelons* (Austin, Tex.: The Steck-Vaughn Company, 1968), 47 pp. With methods of discovery.

Cobb, Vicki. *Cells: The Basic Structure of Life* (New York: Franklin Watts, Inc., 1970), 70 pp. Functions, variety, and reproduction of cells.

Cole, Joanna. *Cockroaches* (New York: William Morrow & Company, Inc., 1971), 64 pp. General information.

Conklin, Gladys. *The Bug Club Book* (New York: Holiday House, Inc., 1966), 92 pp. Information about and suggestions for the study of insects.

Costello, David F. *The World of Ants* (Philadelphia, Penna.: J.B. Lippincott Company, 1968), 160 pp. Describes various kinds of ants.

Cooper, Elizabeth K. *Insects and Plants: The Amazing Partnership* (New York: Harcourt Brace Jovanovich, 1963), 142 pp. Details of the interrelationship of plants and insects.

—— *Science on the Shores and Banks* (New York: Harcourt Brace Jovanovich, 1960), 180 pp. Exploring the water's edge and discovering about the animals and plants that live there.

—— *Silkworms and Science* (New York: Harcourt Brace Jovanovich, 1961), 160 pp. The story of silk and the insects that make it.

Cooper, Margaret, and Linda Mantel. *The Balance of Living—Survival in the Animal World* (New York: Doubleday & Company, Inc., 1971), 126 pp. Habits and adaptations.

Cosgrove, Margaret. *Eggs—And What Happens Inside Them* (New York: Dodd, Mead & Company, Inc., 1966), 63 pp. Development of selected invertebrate and vertebrate animals; illustrated.

Darling, Lois, and Louis Darling. *A Place in the Sun* (New York: William Morrow & Company, Inc., 1968), 128 pp. The ecological relationships of living things.

Darling, Louis. *Chickens and How to Raise Them* (New York: William Morrow & Company, Inc., 1955), 63 pp. How eggs hatch and chickens grow.

Fenton, Carroll Lane, and Dorothy C. Pallas. *Birds and Their World* (New York: The John Day Company, Inc., 1954), 96 pp. Habits, adaptations, and other information.

Ford, Barbara. *Can Invertebrates Learn?* (New York: Julian Messner, 1972), 96 pp. Experimentation and observations.

Friendly, Natalie. *Miraculous Web* (Englewood Cliffs, N.J.: Prentice-Hall, Inc., 1968), 96 pp. Interdependence of living things.

George, Jean. *The Hole in the Tree* (New York: E.P. Dutton & Co., Inc., 1957), unpaged. Many creatures use the hole in the tree as it grows in size from a tiny place to a large one.

Guthrie, Esther L. *Home Book of Animal Care*

(New York: Harper & Row, Publishers, 1966), 302 pp. Much useful information about the care of animals in captivity.

Hammond, Winifred C. *The Riddle of Seeds* (New York: Coward-McCann, Inc., 1965), 63 pp. Nature, dissemination, and other interesting information.

Hoffman, Melita. *A Trip to the Pond: An Adventure in Nature* (New York: Doubleday & Company, Inc., 1966), unpaged. How to collect and study living things in a pond.

Hogner, Dorothy Childs. *Earthworms* (New York: Thomas Y. Crowell Company, 1953), 51 pp. Interesting information—easy.

—— *A Book of Snakes* (New York: Thomas Y. Crowell Company, 1966), 102 pp. Easy reading about the habits of common snakes.

Hoover, Helen. *Animals at My Doorstep* (New York: Parents' Magazine Press, 1966), 59 pp. Well-written and beautifully illustrated accounts of animals observed at close hand.

Hoyt, Murray. *The World of Bees* (New York: Coward-McCann, Inc., 1965), 254 pp. Comprehensive treatment.

Hutchins, Ross E. *Plants without Leaves: Lichens, Fungi, Mosses, Liverworts, Slime-Molds, Algae, Horsetails* (New York: Dodd, Mead & Company, Inc., 1966), 152 pp. Well-organized material not easily available elsewhere.

—— *The Carpenter Bee* (Reading, Mass.: Addison-Wesley Publishing Company, Inc., 1972), 62 pp. Life history and habits.

—— *This Is a Flower* (New York: Dodd, Mead & Company, Inc., 1963), 153 pp. Excellent photographs accompany comprehensive treatment of the flower.

Hyde, Margaret O. *Animals in Science: Saving Lives through Research* (New York: McGraw-Hill, Inc., 1962), 143 pp. A comprehensive picture of the usefulness of animals in medical discoveries.

Kohn, Bernice. *Fireflies* (Englewood Cliffs, N.J.: Prentice-Hall, Inc., 1966), 58 pp. Life history and description of research.

Lubell, Cecil, and Winifred Lubell. *In a Running Brook* (Skokie, Ill.: Rand McNally & Company, 1968), 64 pp. Living things that inhabit a brook.

Martin, Lynne. *The Giant Panda* (Reading, Mass.: Addison-Wesley Publishing Company, 1972), 72 pp. Facts about pandas in zoos, with photographs.

Rahn, Joan. *Seeing What Plants Do* (New York: Atheneum Publishers, 1972), 64 pp. Experiences and experiments to find out about plants.

Riedman, Sarah R. *Naming Living Things* (Skokie, Ill.: Rand McNally & Company, 1963), 124 pp. Information about classification not easily found elsewhere.

Russell, Solveig P. *Which Is Which?* (Englewood Cliffs, N.J.: Prentice-Hall, Inc., 1966), 32 pp. Explains differences between groups of animals—easy.

Schwartz, Julius. *Through the Magnifying Glass: Little Things that Make a Big Difference* (New York: McGraw-Hill, Inc., 1954), 144 pp. Flowers, roots, stems, and other common things examined under a magnifying glass.

—— *Magnify and Find Out Why* (New York: McGraw-Hill, Inc., 1972), 40 pp. Natural objects are explored with a magnifying glass. For young children.

Selsam, Millicent E. *Benny's Animals: How He Put Them in Order* (New York: Harper & Row, Publishers, 1966), 61 pp. Classification of animal life; not easily found elsewhere.

—— *Egg to Chick* (New York: Harper & Row, Publishers, 1970), 64 pp. Development in detail for young children.

—— *Plants that Move* (New York: William Morrow & Company, Inc., 1962), 127 pp. Includes experiments with leaves, flowers, and vines.

—— *Play with Seeds* (New York: William Morrow & Company, Inc., 1957), 93 pp. Experiences with and information about common seeds and how they are formed.

—— *How Animals Live Together* (New York: William Morrow & Company, Inc., 1963), 90 pp. Social life of animals interestingly presented.

Shuttleworth, Dorothy, and Suzan Swain. *All Kinds of Bees* (New York: Random House, Inc., 1967), 62 pp. Almost everything children want to know about bees.

—— *Gerbils and Other Small Pets* (New York: E.P. Dutton & Co., Inc., 1970), 126 pp. How to care for and study pets.

Shuttleworth, Floyd S., and Herbert S. Zim. *Non-flowering Plants* (New York: Golden Press, Inc., 1967), 160 pp. Helpfully illustrated information about plants without flowers.

Silverstein, Alvin, and Virginia Silverstein. *Cells: Building Blocks of Life* (Englewood Cliffs, N.J.: Prentice-Hall, Inc., 1969), 64 pp. General introduction to plant and animal cells.

Simon, Hilda. *Exploring the World of Social Insects* (New York: Vanguard Press, Inc., 1962), 114 pp. Excellent material, helpfully illustrated, clearly written.

—— *Wonders of the Butterfly World* (New York: Dodd, Mead & Company, Inc., 1963), 63 pp. Excellent material about the habits of common butterflies.

—— *Insect Masquerades* (New York: The Viking Press, Inc., 1968), 95 pp. With four-color paintings.

Simon, Seymour. *Animals in Field and Laboratory* (New York: McGraw-Hill, Inc., 1968), 160 pp. Science projects in animal behavior. With this aid children can experiment to discover many ideas about how common animals behave.

—— *Discovering what Gerbils Do* (New York: McGraw-Hill, Inc., 1971), 48 pp. General helpful information.

Stepp, Ann. *A Silkworm Is Born* (New York: Sterling Publishing Co., Inc., 1972), 96 pp. History, culture and life cycle.

Stone, A. Harris, and Irving Leskowitz. *Plants Are Like That* (Englewood Cliffs, N.J.: Prentice-Hall, Inc., 1968), 64 pp. Plant chemistry and behavior; experiments.

Tee-Van, Helen Damrosch. *Small Mammals Are Where You Find Them* (New York: Alfred A. Knopf, 1966), 148 pp. Small mammals and their habits are described and classified.

Vessel, Matthew F., and Herbert H. Wong. *Seashore Life of Our Pacific Coast* (Palo Alto, Calif.: Fearon, 1965), 60 pp. Useful in the study of shore life in any part of the United States.

Vevers, Gwynne. *Ants and Termites* (New York: McGraw-Hill, Inc., 1966), 32 pp. Large clear illustrations and easy reading.

Wheeler, Ruth Lellah. *The Story of Birds of North America* (New York: Harvey House, 1965), 128 pp. Adaptation to environment; conservation.

Weeks, Morris. *Inside the Zoo* (New York: Simon and Schuster, Inc., 1970), 96 pp. With special insight into what goes on in the zoo.

For Teachers

Allen, Arthur A. *Stalking Birds with Color Camera* (Washington, D.C.: National Geographic Society, 1963), 350 pp. Interesting details; excellent photographs.

Allen, Thomas B., ed. *The Marvels of Animal Behavior* (Washington, D.C.: National Geographic Society, 1972), 421 pp. A comprehensive, interesting treatment.

Audubon Nature Bulletins and Charts (New York: 950 Third Avenue, New York, N.Y. 10028). Write for description; very helpful material.

Barker, Will. *Familiar Animals of America* (New York: Harper & Row, Publishers, 1956), 300 pp. General information.

—— *Familiar Reptiles and Amphibians of America* (New York: Harper & Row, Publishers, 1964), 236 pp. General information.

Comstock, Anna B. *Handbook of Nature Study* (Ithaca, N.Y.: Comstock Publishing Associates, 1947), 942 pp. An old classic, but still invaluable as a source of information and concepts about common plants and animals.

Dubos, René. *The Unseen World* (New York: Oxford University Press, 1960), 110 pp. The relationship between microbes and other forms of life.

Galston, Arthur W. *The Life of the Green Plant* (Englewood Cliffs, N.J.: Prentice-Hall, Inc., 1961), 116 pp. The way a green plant functions.

Keeton, William T. *Biological Science* (New York: W.W. Norton & Company, Inc., 1972), 885 pp. Comprehensive information.

Mazzeo, Joseph A. *The Design of Life* (New York: Random House, Inc., 1967), 227 pp. The evolution of biological thought.

Milne, Lorus, and Margery Milne. *The Nature of Plants* (Philadelphia, Penna.: J.B. Lippincott Company, 1971), 224 pp. A good introduction to plant study.

Raskin, Edith. *The Pyramid of Living Things* (New York: McGraw-Hill, Inc., 1967), 102 pp. Interdependence of living things.

Schwartz, George, and Cornelius J. Troost. *Patterns of Life* (New York: American Book Company, 1972), 390 pp. A high-school biology text.

Stefferud, Alfred, and Arnold L. Nelson. *Birds in Our Lives* (Washington, D.C. 20402: U.S. Department of the Interior, U.S. Government Printing Office, 1967), 561 pp. Much interesting and useful information.

Wailes, James. *Living Things* (Darien, Conn.: Teachers Publishing Corporation, 1964), 96 pp. Information and activities (one in the series produced with the National Science Teachers Association).

Wetmore, Alexander, and others. *Water, Prey and Game Birds of North America* (Washington, D.C.: National Geographic Society, 1965), 463 pp. General information.

—— *Song and Garden Birds of North America* (Washington, D.C.: National Geographic Society, 1964) 400 pp. General information.

Wilson, Carl L., and others. *Botany* (New York: Holt, Rinehart and Winston, 1971), 752 pp. A college text.

Chapter 11 Living Things and the Seasons

For Children

Blough, Glenn O. *Bird Watchers and Bird Feeders* (New York: McGraw-Hill, Inc., 1963), 48 pp. Birds in winter.

—— *The Basic Science Education Series* (New York: Harper & Row, Publishers, 1958–1959), 36 pp. *Animals Round the Year, Birds in the Big Woods, Plants Round the Year.* General information.

—— *Soon after September* (New York: McGraw-Hill, 1959), 48 pp. Living things and the seasons.

Earle, Olive L. *Praying Mantis* (New York: William Morrow & Company, Inc., 1969), 48 pp. A good reference for children with questions.

George, Jean C. *Spring Comes to the Ocean* (New York: Thomas Y. Crowell Company, 1965), 109 pp. Changes that occur to animals that inhabit the seas.

Hussey, Lois J., and Catherine Pessino. *Collecting Cocoons* (New York: Thomas Y. Crowell Company, 1953), 70 pp. How to collect, care for, and identify cocoons; and how to raise the insects.

Hutchins, Ross E. *The Travels of Monarch X* (Skokie, Ill.: Rand McNally & Company, 1966), 64 pp. Describes methods of study of the monarch—easy.

Hyde, Margaret O. *Animal Clocks and Compasses* (New York: McGraw-Hill, Inc., 1960), 157 pp. Research into the habits of animals; suggested projects.

McClung, Robert M. *Moths and Butterflies and How They Live* (New York: William Morrow & Company, Inc., 1966), 64 pp. Easy but detailed information.

North, Sterling. *Hurry Spring!* (New York: E.P. Dutton & Co., Inc., 1966), 58 pp. Activities of spring; very well written.

Parker, Bertha M. *The Wonders of the Seasons* (New York: Golden Press, Inc., 1966), unpaged. Information and activities—easy.

Selsam, Millicent E. *How Animals Tell Time* (New York: William Morrow & Company, Inc., 1967), 94 pp. Material about rhythms in animal life not easily found elsewhere.

Shuttlesworth, Dorothy. *Animal Camouflage* (Garden City, N.Y.: Natural History Press, 1966), 63 pp. Coloration in a large variety of animals, and description of some experiments.

Sterling, Dorothy. *Fall Is Here* (Garden City, New York: Doubleday & Company, Inc., 1966), 96 pp. An excellent account of the changes in living things.

Stepp, Ann. *A Silkworm Is Born* (New York: Sterling Publishing Co., Inc., 1972), 96 pp. Help in raising insects.

Sullivan, Navin. *Animal Timekeepers* (Englewood Cliffs, N.J.: Prentice-Hall, Inc., 1966), 64 pp. Scientists explore how "inner clocks" affect the life and habits of animals.

Sutton, Myron, and Ann Sutton. *Animals on the Move* (Skokie, Ill.: Rand McNally & Company, 1965), 128 pp. The story of migration.

For Teachers

Barker, Will. *Winter Sleeping Wildlife* (New York: Harper & Row, Publishers, 1958), 136 pp. Detailed, interesting information.

Chapter 12 The Human Body and How It Works

For Children

Austrian, Geoffrey. *The Truth about Drugs* (New York: Doubleday & Company, Inc., 1971), 132 pp. Straightforward information.

Bendick, Jeanne. *The Human Senses* (New York: Franklin Watts, Inc., 1968), 70 pp. Exploring with the senses.

—— *What Made You You?* (New York: McGraw-Hill, Inc., 1971), 48 pp. A frank straightforward explanation.

Evans, Eva Knox. *The Beginning of Life* (New York: Crowell-Collier and Macmillan, Inc., 1969), 70 pp. Human reproduction.

Elgin, Kathleen, and John F. Osterritter. *The Ups and Downs of Drugs* (New York: Alfred A. Knopf, 1972), 64 pp. Simple, factual explanations.

Frankel, Edward. *DNA—Ladder of Life* (New York: McGraw-Hill, Inc., 1964), 126 pp. General information not easily found elsewhere.

Gordetsky, Charles W., and Samuel T. Christian. *What You Should Know about Drugs* (New York: Harcourt Brace Jovanovich, 1970), 122 pp. Valuable information.

Gruenberg, Sidonie. *The Wonderful Story of How You Were Born* (New York: Doubleday & Company, Inc., 1970), 38 pp. A straightforward account which may be read to young children or given to an older child to read for himself.

Hyde, Margaret C. *Medicine in Action* (New York: McGraw-Hill, Inc., 1956), 160 pp. Details of health practices, the duties of doctors, and research methods.

Kelly, Patricia M. *The Mighty Human Cell* (New York: The John Day Company, Inc., 1967), 127 pp. Most informative; answers the questions children ask.

Lauber, Patricia. *Your Body and How It Works* (New York: Random House, Inc., 1962), 77 pp. Illustrated text presenting details of anatomy and physiology.

Lerner, Marguerite R. *Who Do You Think You Are?: The Story of Heredity* (Englewood Cliffs, N.J.: Prentice-Hall, Inc., 1963), 61 pp. The story of heredity reduced to its simplest form; material not easily found elsewhere.

LeShan, Eda. *What Makes Me Feel This Way?* (New York: The Macmillan Company, 1972), 128 pp. To help children understand and deal with their feelings.

Levine, Milton, and Jean Seligman. *The Wonder of Life* (New York: Simon and Schuster, Inc., 1968), 116 pp. Written for preadolescent and adolescent children in a clear uncondescending manner.

Madison, Arnold. *Drugs and You* (New York: Julian Messner, 1971), 80 pp. General information.

May, Julian. *Do You Have Your Father's Nose?* (Mankato, Minn.: Creative Educational Society, 1970), 38 pp. How we inherit characteristics.

—— *A New Baby Comes* (Mankato, Minn.: Creative Educational Society, 1970), 40 pp. Development and birth of a baby.

Perry, John. *Our Wonderful Eyes* (New York: McGraw-Hill, Inc., 1954), 158 pp. Marvels of the eye and sight, with experiments to help understand.

Power, Jules. *How Life Begins* (New York: Simon and Schuster, Inc., 1965), 95 pp. Text, photographs, and drawings provide frank answers to children's questions and a biological basis for understanding the reproduction of life.

Schneider, Leo. *Microbes in Your Life* (New York: Harcourt Brace Jovanovich, Inc., 1966), 154 pp. An introduction to microbiology.

—— *You and Your Cells* (New York: Harcourt Brace Jovanovich, 1964), 156 pp. Introduction to cells and their nature.

Showers, Paul. *A Baby Starts to Grow* (New York: Thomas Y. Crowell Company, 1969), 33 pp. Describes gestation and birth.

Silverman, Alvin, and Virginia Silverman. *The Sense Organs—Our Link with the World* (Englewood Cliffs, N.J.: Prentice-Hall, Inc., 1971), 68 pp. General information.

Sullivan, Navin. *Controls in Your Body* (Philadelphia, Penna.: J.B. Lippincott Company, 1971), 64 pp. Explanations about the human body.

Tannenbaum, Beulah, and Myra Stillman. *Understanding Food* (New York: McGraw-Hill, Inc., 1962), 206 pp. The chemistry of nutrition.

Terry, L.L., and D. Horn. *To Smoke or Not to*

Smoke (New York: Lothrop, Lee & Shepard Co., 1969), 64 pp. The habit and how to cure it.

Weart, Edith L. *The Story of Your Brain and Nerves* (New York: Coward-McCann, Inc., 1961), 64 pp. How the nervous system works.

White, Anne Terry, and Gerald M. Lietz. *Man the Thinker* (Champaign, Ill.: Garrard Publishing Company, 1967), 80 pp. Material about how we think and act that is not found elsewhere.

For Teachers

Broderick, C.B., and Jessie Bernard, eds. *The Individual, Sex and Society* (Baltimore, Md.: Johns Hopkins Press, 1969). A handbook for teachers and counselors.

Child Study Association of America. *You, Your Child and Drugs* (New York: The Child Study Press, 9 East 89th St. 10028, 1971), 73 pp. Excellent information.

Children and Drugs (Washington, D.C.: Association for Childhood Education, 1972), 64 pp. A bulletin by several authorities, especially important for teachers.

Family Living Including Sex Education (New York 11201: Board of Education, 110 Livingston St., Brooklyn, 1967), 80 pp. Suggestions to teachers; bibliography.

Grams, Armin, *Sex Education: A Guide for Teachers and Parents* (New York: Interstate Printers and Publishers, 1969). Some selected school programs are described.

Hilu, Virginia, ed. *Sex Education and the Schools* (New York: Harper & Row, Publishers, 1966). Questions and discussions.

Julian, Cloyd J., and Elizabeth N. Jackson. *Modern Sex Education* (New York: Holt, Rinehart and Winston, Inc., 1967), 94 pp. Provides answers to questions high-school students ask; includes biological facts and discusses psychological problems of young people.

A Light on the Subject of Smoking and Why Nick the Cigarette Is Nobody's Friend (Washington, D.C. 20402: Superintendent of Documents, U.S. Government Printing Office, 1967).

Manley, Helen. *Family Life and Sex Education in the Elementary School* (Washington, D.C.: National Education Association, 1968).

McCulloch, Gordon. *Man and His Body: The Story of Physiology* (Garden City, N.Y.: Natural History Press, 1967), 156 pp. Informative; well-written; good illustrations including very helpful diagrams.

Chapter 13 The History of Life

For Children

Aliki, *Fossils Tell of Long Ago* (New York: Crowell-Collier and Macmillan, Inc., 1972), 34 pp. For young children.

Armour, Richard. *A Dozen Dinosaurs* (New York: McGraw-Hill, Inc., 1967), 32 pp. Information told in verse—easy.

Blough, Glenn O. *Discovering Dinosaurs* (New York: McGraw-Hill, Inc., 1960), 48 pp. Information and an account of how scientists work to make discoveries.

Cosgrove, Margaret. *Plants in Time* (New York: Dodd, Mead & Company, Inc., 1967), 63 pp. The evolution of plants; material not easily found elsewhere.

Craig, M. Jean. *Dinosaurs and More Dinosaurs* (New York: Four Winds Press, 1968), 96 pp. Good illustrations—easy.

Darling, Lois, and Louis Darling. *Before and After Dinosaurs* (New York: William Morrow & Company, Inc., 1959), 64 pp. A comprehensive study of the development and adaptation of these huge beasts.

Ensign, Georgianne. *The Hunt for the Mastodon* (New York: Franklin Watts, Inc., 1971), 80 pp. About the discovery in New Jersey and what followed.

Epstein, Sam, and Beryl Epstein. *Prehistoric Animals* (New York: Franklin Watts, Inc., 1956), 210 pp. History of the development of life on the earth and how such knowledge has developed.

Froman, Robert. *Billions of Years of You* (New York: Harcourt Brace Jovanovich, 1967), 62 pp. The development of life on the earth.

Green, Carla. *How Man Began* (New York: The Bobbs-Merrill Company, Inc., 1972), 80 pp. Clear discussion of the development of animals.

Holden, Raymond. *Famous Fossil Finds* (New York: Dodd, Mead & Company, Inc., 1966),

100 pp. Paleontologists at work and the importance of their discoveries.

Holsaert, Eunice, and Robert Gartland. *Dinosaurs* (New York: Holt, Rinehart and Winston, Inc., 1959), unpaged. A book to begin on.

Hussey, Lois J., and Catherine Pessino. *Collecting Small Fossils* (New York: Thomas Y. Crowell Company, 1970), 58 pp. For the beginner—how fossils were formed and may be collected.

Matthews, William H. III *Wonders of Fossils* (New York: Dodd, Mead & Company, Inc., 1968), 64 pp. Fossil "finds" and identification.

—— *Introducing the Earth* (New York: Dodd, Mead & Company Inc., 1972), 210 pp. Comprehensive, interesting.

Pringle, Laurence. *Dinosaurs and Their World* (New York: Harcourt Brace Jovanovich, 1968), 63 pp. Finding and studying fossils.

Rhodes, Frank H.T., and others. *Fossils* (New York: Golden Press, Inc., 1962), 160 pp. A guide to plant and animal fossils.

Ross, Wilda S. *What Did the Dinosaurs Eat?* (New York: Coward-McCann, Inc., 1972), 47 pp. Story of the "Age of Reptiles."

Shapp, Charles, and Martha Shapp. *Let's Find Out about Animals of Long Ago* (New York: Franklin Watts, Inc., 1968). A general treatment.

Swinton, William E. *Digging for Dinosaurs* (Garden City, N.Y.: Doubleday & Company, Inc., 1966), 33 pp. Easy, large pictures.

Whitaker, George O., and Joan Meyers. *Dinosaur Hunt* (New York: Harcourt Brace Jovanovich, 1965), 94 pp. The techniques of collecting and exhibiting fossils.

For Teachers

Colbert, Edwin H. *Dinosaurs* (New York: E.P. Dutton & Co., Inc., 1961), 300 pp. Discovery, study, and the resulting information.

Dott, Robert H., and Roger L. Batten. *Evolution of the Earth* (New York: McGraw-Hill, Inc., 1971), 649 pp. Historical geology with useful chapter on evolution and geologic times.

Fenton, Carroll L., and Mildred Fenton. *The Fossil Book* (New York: Doubleday & Company, Inc., 1958), 458 pp. An excellent background, with very helpful illustrations.

McAllister, A. Lee. *The History of Life* (Englewood Cliffs, N.J.: Prentice-Hall, Inc., 1968), 152 pp. Introduction to paleontology.

Moore, Ruth. *Man, Time, and Fossils* (New York: Alfred A. Knopf, 1961), 436 pp. The evolution of man.

Ranson, Jay Ellis. *Fossils in America* (New York: Harper & Row, Publishers, 1964), 402 pp. Nature, origin, identification, and classification—also guide to collecting sites in the United States.

Chapter 14 Ecology and Survival

For Children

Behnke, Frances. *The Changing World of Living Things* (New York: Holt, Rinehart and Winston, Inc., 1972), 170 pp. The interrelationships of living organisms.

Blough, Glenn O. *Lookout for the Forest* (New York: McGraw-Hill, Inc., 1954), 48 pp. A conservation story.

—— *The Tree on the Road to Turntown* (New York: McGraw-Hill, Inc., 1953), 48 pp. Conservation aspects of a tree's life.

—— *Useful Plants and Animals* (New York: Harper & Row, Publishers, 1959), 36 pp. How we use animals and plants in daily living—easy.

Buehr, Walter. *Water: Our Most Vital Need* (New York: W.W. Norton & Company, Inc., 1967), 102 pp. Sources, needs, cycle, and problems.

Busch, Phyllis S. *City Lots: Living Things in Vacant Spots* (Cleveland, Ohio: The World Publishing Co., 1970), 48 pp. Ecology of city environments.

—— *Exploring as You Walk in the City* (Philadelphia, Penna.: J.B. Lippincott Company, 1972), 40 pp. Observations in an urban environment.

Chester, Michael. *Let's Go to Stop Air Pollution* (New York: G.P. Putnam's Sons, 1968), 48 pp. Material not easily found elsewhere—easy.

Cunningham, Floyd F. *1001 Questions Answered about Water Resources* (New York: Dodd, Mead & Company, Inc., 1967), 258 pp. Information organized around answers to questions.

Darling, Lois, and Louis Darling. *A Place in the Sun* (New York: William Morrow & Company, Inc., 1968), 128 pp. The ecological relationships of living things.

Elliott, Sarah M. *Our Dirty Air* (New York: Julian Messner, 1971), 64 pp. Sources of pollution and suggested remedies.

Gallob, Edward. *City Leaves, City Trees* (New York: Charles Scribner's Sons, 1972), 64 pp. A beautiful book of information about city trees.

Gionnoni, Frances, and Seymour Reit. *Golden Book of Gardening: How to Plan, Plant, and Care for the Home Garden* (New York: Golden Press, Inc., 1962), 68 pp. Essential information about gardening.

Heady, Eleanor. *The Soil that Feeds Us* (New York: Parents' Magazine Press, 1972), 64 pp. Composition and importance of soil.

Helfman, Elizabeth. *Our Fragile Earth* (New York: Lothrop, Lee & Shepard Co., 1972), 160 pp. A conservation book.

Hoffman, Melita. *A Trip to the Pond* (Garden City, N.Y.: Doubleday & Company, Inc., 1966), 61 pp. Helps young explorers discover the variety of life in a small area of a pond. Includes a useful guide to capturing and caring for some pond animals.

Hungerford, Harold R. *Ecology: The Circle of Life* (Chicago, Ill.: Children's Press, 1971), 92 pp. Ecology for beginners.

Klein, Stanley. *A World in a Tree* (New York: Doubleday & Company, Inc., 1968), 64 pp. Insect, bird, and mammal life in, around, and under a tree during the year. Simple introduction to ecology.

Kohn, Bernice. *The Organic Living Book* (New York: The Viking Press, Inc., 1972), 91 pp. A guide for you and your environment.

Laycock, George. *Air Pollution* (New York: Grosset & Dunlop, Inc., 1972), 73 pp. Cause and effects of air pollution.

Marshall, James. *Going to Waste: Where Will All the Garbage Go?* (New York: Coward-McCann, and Geoghegan, Inc., 1972), 92 pp. The problems of waste disposal.

Mattison, Charles W., and Joseph Alvarez. *Man and His Resources in Today's World* (Mankato, Minn.: Creative Educational Society, 1967), 144 pp. Picture-text review of man's use and abuse of natural resources, with implications for urban conservation.

McCormick, Jack. *The Life of the Forest* (New York: McGraw-Hill, Inc., 1966), 232 pp. Animal and plant communities; photographs, some in color.

Millard, Reed. *Natural Resources: Will We Have Enough for Tomorrow's World?* (New York: Julian Messner, 1972), 189 pp. The state of the world's resources.

Milne, Lorus J., and Margery Milne. *Because of a Tree* (New York: Atheneum Publishers, 1963), 149 pp. Interdependence of living things and adaptation to environment.

Perera, Thomas B., and Wallace Orlowsky. *Who Will Clean the Air?* (New York: Coward-McCann and Geoghegan, Inc., 1971), 46 pp. For the youngest readers.

Perry, John. *Our Polluted World—Can Man Survive?* (New York: Franklin Watts, Inc., 1967), 213 pp. Pollution of our water and air—causes and consequences.

Pinney, Roy. *Vanishing Wildlife* (New York: Dodd, Mead & Company, Inc., 1963), 182 pp. A naturalist discusses conservation of wildlife, beginning with extinct species and highlighting the many conservation problems—excellent photographs.

Pringle, Laurence. *Pests and People: A Search for Sensible Pest Control* (New York: The Macmillan Company, 1972), 128 pp. Search for methods to deal with pest controls.

Schlichting, Harold E., and Mary Schlichting. *Ecology—The Study of Environment* (Austin, Texas: Steck-Vaughn Company, 1971), 48 pp. Introduction for the young reader.

Schwartz, Julius. *It's Fun to Know Why: Experiments with Things Around Us* (New York: McGraw-Hill, Inc., 1973), 156 pp. Simple experiments show how man obtains and uses natural products.

Simon, Seymour. *Science Projects in Pollution* (New York: Holiday House, Inc., 1972), 118 pp. Experimentation with common materials.

—— *Science in a Vacant Lot* (New York: The Viking Press, 1970), 64 pp. Exploring in an urban area.

Wright, Robert. *What Good Is a Weed? Ecology in Action* (New York: Lothrop, Lee & Shepard

Co., 1972), 128 pp. Weeds in relation to their environment.

For Teachers

Bates, Marston. *The Forest and the Sea* (New York: New American Library of World Literature, Inc., 1961), 216 pp. Paper.

Breeden, Robert L., ed. *As We Live and Breathe: The Challenge of Our Environment* (Washington, D.C.: National Geographic Society, 1971), 239 pp. Illustrated general information about air pollution.

Brennan, Matthew J., ed. *People and Their Environment: A Teacher's Curriculum Guide to Conservation Education* (Chicago, Ill.: J.G. Ferguson Publishing Co., 6 North Michigan Ave., 60602).

Brower, David, ed. *Wilderness* (San Francisco, Calif.: Sierra Club, 1961), 204 pp. America's outstanding leaders in conservation discuss what wilderness has meant to a nation's fabric, to its art, to its shape, and to its future.

Caldwell, Lynton K. *Environment: A Challenge to Modern Society* (New York: Doubleday & Company, Inc., 1971), 301 pp. Interactions of science, technology, and public policy.

Carson, Rachel. *Silent Spring* (New York: Fawcett World Library—Crest Books, 1962), 304 pp. The paperback reprint of this classic in conservation. *See* Chapter 14A.

Commoner, Barry. *The Closing Circle* (New York: Alfred A. Knopf, 1972), 326 pp. Nature, cause, and possible solutions of the "impending environmental disaster."

Environmental Education in the Elementary School. (Washington, D.C.: National Science Teachers Association, 1972), 44 pp. A selection of articles reprinted from *Science and Children.*

Fisher, James, and others. *Wildlife in Danger* (New York: The Viking Press, Inc., 1969), 366 pp. General reference.

Halacy, D.S. *Now or Never: The Fight against Pollution* (New York: Four Winds Press, 1971), 203 pp. General, excellent treatment.

Hoke, John. *Ecology: Man's Effect on His Environment and Its Mechanisms* (New York: Franklin Watts, Inc., 1971), 96 pp. Introduction to ecological concepts.

Hylander, Clarence J. *Wildlife Communities* (Boston, Mass.: Houghton Mifflin Company, 1966), 342 pp. Part I discusses the environmental factors affecting wildlife; Part II includes a study of the great environmental areas of North America.

Kaufman, Richard. *Gentle Wilderness* (San Francisco, Calif.: Sierra Club, 1964), 167 pp. With superb color photographs the author recaptures the feeling in naturalist Muir's *My First Summer in the Sierra;* a moving reminder that America cannot afford to lose any more of its "Gentle Wilderness."

Marzani, Carl. *The Wounded Earth* (Reading, Mass.: Addison-Wesley Publishing Company, Inc., 1972), 232 pp. For anyone interested in the environment.

Munzer, Martha E. *Planning Our Town* (New York: Alfred A. Knopf, 1964), 180 pp. Problems of planning towns in the future.

—— *Pockets of Hope: Studies of Land and People* (New York: Alfred A. Knopf, 1967). Studies of conservation problems in depressed areas.

Peterson, Roger Tory, and James Fisher. *Wild America* (Boston, Mass.: Houghton Mifflin Company, 1956), 425 pp. Two naturalists tour the United States and record their fascinating observations.

Petit, Sid S. *The Web of Nature* (Garden City, N.Y.: Doubleday & Company, Inc., 1960), 56 pp. Various ecological settings: marshes, prairies, forests, and others; need for conservation.

Platt, Rutherford. *The Great American Forest* (Englewood Cliffs, N.J.: Prentice-Hall, Inc., 1965), 269 pp. The drama of forests marching across continents in the past; the crucial importance of the forest today, and the tragedy of our vanishing wilderness.

Schultz, Beth, and Phyllis Marcuccio. *Investigations in Ecology* (Columbus, Ohio: Charles E. Merrill Books, Inc., 1972). Seventy cards with teachers guide that suggest activities, experiments, observations, and other very useful and practical helps.

Sears, Paul B. *The Living Landscape* (New York: Basic Books, Inc., 1966), 199 pp. Interrelationships of sciences and general conservation.

Shuttlesworth, Dorothy. *Natural Partnerships: The Story of Symbiosis* (New York: Doubleday & Company, Inc., 1969), 64 pp. A variety of examples are described.

Storer, John H. *The Web of Life* (New York: New American Library of World Literature, Inc., 1956), 128 pp. Excellent introduction to ecology—paper.

Udall, Stewart. *The Quiet Crisis* (New York: Holt, Rinehart and Winston, Inc., 1963), 209 pp. The race between education and erosion, between wisdom and waste (*see* Chapter 14A).

U.S. Department of Agriculture Yearbooks: *Soils and Man* (1938), *Grass* (1948), *Trees* (1949), *Insects* (1952), *Water* (1955), *Land* (1958), *A Place to Live,* (1964), *Outdoors USA* (1967), *Landscape for Living* (1972) (Washington, D.C. 20402: Superintendent of Documents, U.S. Government Printing Office).

Vickery, Tom R. *Man and His Environment: The Effects of Pollution on Man* (Syracuse, N.Y.: Syracuse University Press, 1972), 193 pp. A conference report.

Ward, Barbara, and René Dubos. *Only One Earth* (New York: W.W. Norton & Company, Inc., 1972), 225 pp. Important for every citizen.

Weaver, Elbert C., ed. *Scientific Experiments in Environmental Pollution* (New York: Holt, Rinehart and Winston, Inc., 1968), 40 pp. A laboratory manual of experiments and experiences (in cooperation with the Manufacturing Chemists' Association, Inc.).

Wilderness. The National Forests, America's Playgrounds (Washington, D.C. 20402: U.S. Department of Agriculture, U.S. Government Printing Office, 1968).

Additional Information Sources[*]

American Forest Institute, 1835 K St., N.W., Washington, D.C. 20006.

American Forestry Association, 919 17th St., N.W., Washington, D.C. 20006.

Audubon Society, 950 Third Avenue, New York, N.Y.

Conservation Foundation, 1717 Massachusetts Ave., N.W., Washington, D.C.

Defenders of Wildlife, 2000 N St., N.W., Washington, D.C. 20036.

Forest Service, U.S. Department of Agriculture, Washington, D.C.

Friends of the Earth, 30 East 42nd St., New York, N.Y. 10017.

National Park Service, U.S. Department of Interior, Washington, D.C.

National Wildlife Federation, 1412 16th St., N.W., Washington, D.C. 20036.

Sierra Club, 1050 Mills Tower, San Francisco, Calif. 94104.

Soil Conservation Service, U.S. Department of Agriculture, Washington, D.C.

Wilderness Society, 729 15th St., N.W., Washington, D.C. 20005.

Wildlife Management Institute, Bureau of Sport Fisheries and Wildlife, U.S. Department of Interior, Washington, D.C.

[*] Many bulletins and teaching aids are available from your state department of education or state conservation department at the state capital. Many states have the following resources: forestry agencies, park agencies, fish and wildlife agencies, soil conservation offices, and agencies that deal with minerals and waters. Be specific about your needs. If children write, send *only* one letter that has been carefully checked.

PART IV MATTER AND ENERGY

Chapter 15 Molecules, Atoms, and Chemical Change

For Children

Adler, Irving. *Atomic Energy* (New York: The John Day Company, Inc., 1971), 47 pp. The story of atomic energy and its uses.

Asimov, Isaac. *The Search for the Elements* (New York: Basic Books, Inc., 1962), 158 pp. Discovery and nature of the elements; a history of chemistry.

Freeman, Ira, and Mae Freeman. *The Story of Chemistry* (New York: Random House, Inc., 1962), 80 pp. For beginners.

Gallant, Roy A. *The ABC's of Chemistry* (New York: Doubleday & Company, Inc., 1963), 88 pp. Large book organized alphabetically to introduce young readers to the words and world of chemical change.

Greene, Carla. *Let's Meet the Chemist* (Irvington-on-Hudson, N.Y.: Harvey House, 1966),

48 pp. An introduction to chemistry through a look at the work of a chemist.

Hyde, Margaret O. *Molecules Today and Tomorrow* (New York: McGraw-Hill, Inc., 1963), 144 pp. General treatment.

——, and Bruce G. Hyde. *Atoms Today and Tomorrow* (New York: McGraw-Hill, Inc., 1970), 141 pp. General treatment.

Irwin, Keith G. *Chemistry First S-T-E-P-S* (New York: Franklin Watts, Inc., 1963), 49 pp. Chemistry applied to everyday phenomena.

Lefkowitz, R.L. *Matter All around You* (New York: Parents' Magazine Press, 1972), 64 pp. An introduction to matter and how it changes.

Poole, Lynn, and Gray Poole. *Carbon 14 and Other Science Methods that Date the Past* (New York: McGraw-Hill, Inc., 1961), 160 pp. The fascinating story of the methods of science that date the past; expertly told.

Sander, Lenore. *The Curious World of Crystals* (Englewood Cliffs, N.J.: Prentice-Hall, Inc., 1964), 64 pp. Everyday crystals, how to grow them, and study them.

Schwartz, Julius. *It's Fun to Know Why: Experiments with Things around Us* (New York: McGraw-Hill, Inc., 1973), 156 pp. Simple experiments that show how man obtains and uses salt, iron, coal, glass, paper, bread, wool, cement, rubber, soap, and plastics.

—— *Magnify and Find Out Why* (New York: McGraw-Hill, Inc., 1972), 40 pp. Easy experiments and observations to discover about common things.

Seaborg, Glenn T., and Evans G. Valens. *Elements of the Universe* (New York: E.P. Dutton & Co., Inc., 1958), 245 pp. Comprehensive treatment of the elements and how they behave—for upper grade pupils and the teacher.

Simon, Seymour. *Chemistry in the Kitchen* (New York: The Viking Press, Inc., 1971), 64 pp. More than fifty experiments that can be done at home.

For Teachers°

Barnaby, Frank. *Man and the Atom. The Uses of Nuclear Energy* (New York: Funk & Wagnalls Company, 1971), 216 pp. A useful reference.

Glasstone, Samuel. *Inner Space: The Structure of the Atom* (Oak Ridge, Tenn.: 37820 USAEC Technical Information Center, P.O. Box 62, 1972), 99 pp. General information. (Many other publications are available from this source. Several are free.)

Matter, Energy, and Change: Explorations in Chemistry for Elementary School Children (New York: Holt, Rinehart and Winston, Inc., 1960), 60 pp. Experiments and subject matter for teachers' background (prepared by the Manufacturing Chemists Association).

Trieger, Seymour. *Atoms and Molecules* (Darien, Conn.: Teachers Publishing Corporation, 1964), 96 pp. One in a series produced with the National Science Teachers Association; information and activities.

° *See also* suggested physics and chemistry texts listed in Part I of this Bibliography under "General Subject-matter Background Books for Teachers."

Chapter 16 Heat and How We Use It

For Children

Adler, Irving, and Ruth Adler. *Heat* (New York: The John Day Company, Inc., 1964), 48 pp. Nature of heat.

Branley, Franklyn. *Solar Energy* (New York: Thomas Y. Crowell Company, 1957), 117 pp. Explores possibilities of harnessing the sun's energy.

Pine, Tillie S., and Joseph Levine. *Heat All Around* (New York: McGraw-Hill, Inc., 1963), 46 pp. Easy.

Ruchlis, Hy. *The Wonder of Heat Energy* (New York: Harper & Row, Publishers, 1961), 186 pp. Story of the vital part heat plays in our world.

Simon, Seymour. *Hot and Cold* (New York: McGraw-Hill, Inc., 1972), 40 pp. Thermometers; experiments and observations.

Stone, A. Harris, and Bertram M. Siegel. *The Heat's On!* (Englewood Cliffs, N.J.: Prentice-Hall, Inc., 1970), 63 pp. General treatment with experiments.

Victor, Edward. *Heat* (Chicago, Ill.: Follett Publishing Co., 1967), 30 pp. An introduction to heat and temperature, with experiments and applications.

For Teachers

See suggested physics texts listed in Part I of this Bibliography under "General Subject-matter Background Books for Teachers."

Chapter 17 Nuclear Energy and Its Uses

For Children

Adler, Irving. *Atomic Energy* (New York: The John Day Company, Inc., 1971), 47 pp. Includes nuclear reactors.

——, and Ruth Adler. *Atoms and Molecules* (New York: The John Day Company, Inc., 1966), 48 pp. A good introduction to chemistry.

Bronowski, J., and Millicent E. Selsam. *Biography of an Atom* (New York: Harper & Row, Publishers, 1965), 43 pp. History of a carbon atom and the structure of atoms.

Kohn, Bernice. *The Peaceful Atom* (Englewood Cliffs, N.J.: Prentice-Hall, Inc., 1963), 66 pp. The story of the nature and use of atoms, with discussion of discoveries—easy reading.

McKowan, Robin. *The Fabulous Isotopes: What They Are and What They Do* (New York: Holiday House, Inc., 1962), 189 pp. Helpfully illustrated treatment that introduces nuclear science.

Potter, Robert D., and Robert C. Potter. *Young People's Book of Atomic Energy* (New York: Dodd, Mead & Company, Inc., 1967), 202 pp. For upper grades.

Radlauer, Edward, and Ruth S. Radlauer. *Atomic Power for People* (Chicago, Ill.: Melmont Publishers, 1960), 47 pp. Information not easily available elsewhere about the work of atomic power plants.

Schneider, Herman, and Nina Schneider. *How Big Is Big: From Stars to Atoms* (New York: Scott Publications, Inc., 1965), 48 pp. Relative sizes compared from a child's point of view.

Woodbury, David O. *The New World of the Atom* (New York: Dodd, Mead & Company, Inc., 1965), 80 pp. A brief survey.

For Teachers*

Anderson, William R., and Vernon Pizer. *The Useful Atom* (New York: Harcourt Brace Jovanovich, 1966), 191 pp. Present uses, some predictions and hazards.

Asimov, Isaac. *Inside the Atom* (New York: Abelard-Schuman Ltd., 1966), 223 pp. Information about atoms and the uses of atomic energy.

Frisch, O.R. *Working with Atoms* (New York: Basic Books, Inc., 1965), 96 pp. The story of nuclear fission.

Jaworski, Irene D., and Alexander Joseph. *Atomic Energy: The Story of Nuclear Science* (New York: Harcourt Brace Jovanovich, 1961), 218 pp. General treatment.

Levinger, Joseph S., and George Carr. *Secrets of the Nucleus* (New York: McGraw-Hill, Inc., 1967), 127 pp. One of the "Vistas of Science" books produced by the National Science Teachers Association—the structure and behavior of the nucleus of the atom.

Nehrich, Richard B. Jr., and others. *Atomic Light: Lasers—What They Are and How They Work* (New York: Sterling Publishing Co., Inc., 1968), 104 pp. Development, principles, operation, and uses.

Nuclear Terms—A Brief Glossary, 2nd ed. (U.S. Atomic Energy Commission, P.O. Box 62, Oak Ridge, Tenn., 1967), 80 pp.

Chapter 18 Machines and How They Work

For Children

Adler, Irving. *Energy* (New York: The John Day Company, Inc., 1970), 48 pp. The many forms and changes from one to another.

Bendick, Jeanne. *Why Things Work* (New York: Parents' Magazine Press, 1972), 64 pp.

* Write to Superintendent of Documents, U.S. Government Printing Office, Washington, D.C. 20402, for list of government publications on various phases of atomic energy; and to the United States Atomic Energy Commission, Technical Information Center, P.O. Box 62, Oak Ridge, Tenn. 37830, for list of pamphlets and other very helpful materials.

See suggested physics texts listed in Part I of this Bibliography under "General Subject-matter Background Books for Teachers."

Forms of energy and how they are used.

Blackwood, Paul E. *Push and Pull: The Story of Energy* (New York: McGraw-Hill, Inc., 1966), 192 pp. The origins and uses of energy.

Blough, Glenn O. *Doing Work* (New York: Harper & Row, Publishers, 1959), 36 pp. Easy story of simple machines and how they work.

Buehr, Walter. *The Story of the Wheel* (New York: G.P. Putnam's Sons, 1960), 47 pp. Changes in the world due to the development and use of the wheel.

Corbett, Scott. *What Makes a Car Go* (Boston, Mass.: Little, Brown & Company, 1962), 44 pp. Easy reading, helpful illustrations, information not easily available elsewhere.

Elting, Mary. *Trucks at Work* (Irvington-on-Hudson, N.Y.: Harvey House, 1962), 93 pp. Trucks of all kinds and how they are used.

Harrison, George R. *The First Book of Energy* (New York: Franklin Watts, Inc., 1965), 81 pp. A general introduction and treatment.

Hogben, Lancelot. *The Wonderful World of Energy* (New York: Garden City Books, 1957), 69 pp. Large book describing the history and uses of all kinds of energy.

Irving, Robert. *Energy and Power* (New York: Alfred A. Knopf, Inc., 1958), 140 pp. The history of energy and power, including atomic energy.

Hoke, John. *Solar Energy* (New York: Franklin Watts, Inc., 1968), 96 pp. Development and use of solar energy.

Miller, Lisa. *Levers* (New York: Coward-McCann, Inc., 1968), 41 pp. An easy introduction to levers and what they do.

Pine, Tillie S., and Joseph Levine. *Friction All Around* (New York: McGraw-Hill, Inc., 1960), 46 pp. Easy—explains friction and its importance.

—— *Simple Machines and How We Use Them* (New York: McGraw-Hill, Inc., 1965), 48 pp. Explanation for beginners.

Ross, Frank, Jr. *The World of Power and Energy* (New York: Lothrop, Lee & Shepard Co., 1967), 224 pp. Sources, uses, progress in using.

Saunders, F. Wenderoth. *Machines for You* (Boston, Mass.: Little, Brown & Company, 1967), 58 pp. Describes the uses and operation of heavy machines, which many children often see.

Schneider, Herman. *Everyday Machines and How They Work,* new ed. (New York: McGraw-Hill, Inc., 1950), 192 pp. Basic introduction; illustrated.

——, and Schneider, Nina. *Let's Look Inside Your House* (New York: Scott Publications, Inc., 1948), 40 pp. Experiences with water, heat, and electricity as they are used.

—— *Let's Look under the City* (New York: Scott Publications, Inc., 1954), 40 pp. How water, gas, electricity, and telephone calls come to the buildings in the city.

—— *More Power to You* (New York: Scott Publications, Inc., 1953), 119 pp. Development and use of power.

—— *Now Try This* (New York: Scott Publications, Inc., 1947), 40 pp. Experiments with friction, levers, and wheels.

Schwartz, Julius. *Go on Wheels* (New York: McGraw-Hill, Inc., 1966), 32 pp. Invites the young child to find out about wheels by looking at wheeled vehicles outdoors and by simple experiments.

—— *I Know a Magic House* (New York: McGraw-Hill, Inc., 1956), 32 pp. Explanations for everyday home happenings; for beginners.

Zaffo, George J. *The Giant Nursery Book of Things that Go* (Garden City, N.Y.: Doubleday & Company, Inc., 1959), 189 pp. For prekindergarten and kindergarten: fire engines, trains, boats, trucks, and airplanes.

For Teachers °

Cox, Louis. *Energy in Waves* (Darien, Conn.: Teachers Publishing Corporation, 1964), 96 pp. One in a series produced with the National Science Teachers Association; information and activities.

Dunn, Lois. *Motion* (Darien, Conn.: Teachers Publishing Corporation, 1964), 96 pp. One in a series produced with the National Science Teachers Association; information and activities.

° *See* suggested physics texts listed in Part I of this Bibliography under "General Subject-matter Background Books for Teachers."

Chapter 19 Magnetism and Electricity

For Children

Adler, Irving. *Electricity in Your Life* (New York: The John Day Company, Inc., 1965), 128 pp. The nature and uses of electricity—includes activities.

——, and Ruth Adler. *Magnets* (New York: The John Day Company, Inc., 1966), 48 pp. A clear explanation of why a magnet acts as it does.

Bendick, Jeanne. *Electronics for Young People,* 4th revision (New York: McGraw-Hill, Inc., 1972), 190 pp. General explanation.

Bendick, R., and J. Bendick. *Television Works Like This* (New York: McGraw-Hill, Inc., 1965), 96 pp. Illustrated behind-the-scenes story of telecasting.

Branley, Franklyn M., and Eleanor K. Vaughan. *Mickey's Magnet* (New York: Thomas Y. Crowell Company, 1956), unpaged. Discovering magnets by experimenting and observing—easy.

Freeman, Mae, and Ira Freeman. *The Story of Electricity* (New York: Random House, Inc., 1961), 79 pp. Introduction to electricity and some of its uses, from rubbed amber to the electron tube.

Knight, David C. *Let's Find Out about Magnets* (New York: Franklin Watts, Inc., 1967), 55 pp. Clearly written subject matter with activities—easy.

Lieberg, Owen S. *Wonders of Magnets and Magnetism* (New York: Dodd, Mead & Company, Inc., 1967), 64 pp. Discovery, uses, and general information.

Pine, Tillie S., and Joseph Levine. *Electricity and How We Use It* (New York: McGraw-Hill, Inc., 1962), 48 pp. Electrical circuits and how they are used—easy.

—— *Magnets and How to Use Them* (New York: McGraw-Hill, Inc., 1959), 48 pp. Simple experiences and information about magnets—easy.

Ruchlis, Hy. *The Wonder of Electricity* (New York: Harper & Row, Publishers, 1965), 218 pp. Detailed, broad in scope; a good resource.

Sacks, Raymond. *Magnets* (New York: Coward-McCann, Inc., 1967), 45 pp. Easy.

Schneider, Herman, and Nina Schneider. *Your Telephone and How It Works* (New York: McGraw-Hill, Inc., 1952), 96 pp. Information about how sound and electricity make the telephone work.

Schwartz, Julius. *I Know a Magic House* (New York: McGraw-Hill, Inc., 1956), 32 pp. First experiences with electrical devices and other "magic" in the house.

Seeman, Bernard. *The Story of Electricity and Magnetism* (New York: Harvey House, 1967), 123 pp. Contains experiments; shows relationship of electicity and magnetism—illustrated.

Sooten, Harry. *Experiments with Electric Currents* (New York: W.W. Norton & Company, Inc., 1969), 88 pp. The fundamentals of electricity.

—— *Experiments with Static Electricity* (New York: W.W. Norton & Company, Inc., 1969), 86 pp. Simple experiments.

Stone, A. Harris, and Bertram M. Siegel. *Turned on: A Look at Electricity* (Englewood Cliffs, N.J.: Prentice-Hall, Inc., 1970), 64 pp. Experiments, making equipment, and discoveries.

Yates, R.F. *Boy and a Battery* (New York: Harper & Row, Publishers, 1959), 120 pp. Using a battery to make and to experiment with electromagnets, current detectors, and fuses.

—— *Boys' Book of Magnetism* (New York: Harper & Row, Publishers, 1959), 166 pp. Games, experiments, and constructions with magnets and electromagnets.

*For Teachers**

Beiser, Germaine. *The Story of the Earth's Magnetic Field* (New York: E.P. Dutton & Co., Inc., 1964), 128 pp. The earth as a magnet.

Dunsheath, Percy. *Electricity: How It Works* (New York: Thomas Y. Crowell Company, 1960), 248 pp. Useful reference for teachers.

Morgan, Alfred. *The Boys' First Book of Radio and Electronics* (New York: Charles Scribner's Sons, 1954), 229 pp.

—— *The Boys' Third Book of Radio and Electronics* (New York: Charles Scribner's Sons,

**See* suggested physics texts listed in Part I of this Bibliography under "General Subject-matter Background Books for Teachers."

1962), 277 pp. For especially talented and interested children, as well as teachers.

Chapter 20 Sound and How We Use It

For Children

Berger, Melvin, and Frank Clark. *Science and Music from Tom-tom to Hi-fi* (New York: McGraw-Hill, Inc., 1961), 176 pp. How musical instruments produce sounds and how sounds are recorded.

Branley, Franklyn M. *High Sounds-Low Sounds* (New York: Thomas Y. Crowell Company, 1967), unpaged. The nature of sound with suggested activities.

Brown, Margaret Wise. *The Country Noisy Book* (New York: Harper & Row, Publishers, 1940), unpaged. The sounds that a dog named Muffin hears when he goes to the country for the first time—for prekindergarten.

Freeman, Ira M. *Sound and Ultrasonics* (New York: Random House, Inc., 1968), 137 pp. For more advanced children.

Irving, Robert. *Sound and Ultrasonics* (New York: Alfred A. Knopf, 1959), 146 pp. For beginners.

Kettlekamp, Larry. *Drums, Rattles, and Bells* (New York: William Morrow & Company, Inc., 1960), 48 pp. The story of sounds and how they are produced.

Knight, David C. *The First Book of Sound* (New York: Franklin Watts, Inc., 1960), 93 pp. Fundamental principles.

Pine, Tillie S., and Joseph Levine. *Sounds All Around* (New York: McGraw-Hill, Inc., 1958), 46 pp. Simple activities to teach basic principles—easy.

Showers, Paul. *How You Talk* (New York: Thomas Y. Crowell Company, 1967), unpaged. How the human voice is produced—easy.

For Teachers°

Cox, Louis T. *Energy in Waves* (Darien, Conn.: Teachers Publishing Corporation, 1964), 96 pp. One of the volumes in "Investigating Science with Children," produced by the National Science Teachers Association.

Neal, Charles, *Sound* (Chicago, Ill.: Follett Publishing Co., 1962), 32 pp. General treatment.

° *See* suggested physics texts listed in Part I of this Bibliography under "General Subject-matter Background Books for Teachers."

Chapter 21 Light and How We Use It

For Children

Adler, Irving. *Color in Your Life* (New York: The John Day Company, Inc., 1962), 127 pp. Color phenomena in everyday life explained.

——, and Ruth Adler *Shadows* (New York: The John Day Company, Inc., 1961), 48 pp. Formation and uses of shadows.

Alexenberg, Melvin L. *Light and Sight* (Englewood Cliffs, N.J.: Prentice-Hall, Inc., 1969), 48 pp. A treatment for beginners.

Campbell, Ann. *Let's Find Out about Color* (New York: Franklin Watts, Inc., 1966), 31 pp. Well-written and illustrated—easy.

Feravolo, Rocco V. *Junior Science Book of Light* (Champaign, Ill.: Garrard Publishing Company, 1961), 59 pp. For beginners.

Freeman, Ira M. *Light and Radiation* (New York: Random House, Inc., 1968), 125 pp. Well-written introductory material.

Harrison, George R. *First Book of Light* (New York: Franklin Watts, Inc., 1962), 85 pp. Experiments with home equipment help answer questions about light.

—— *Lasers* (New York: Franklin Watts, Inc., 1971), 92 pp. How, why, and the uses.

Hoke, John. *The First Book of Photography* (New York: Franklin Watts, Inc., 1964). The how and why of photography.

Neal, Charles D. *Exploring Light and Color* (Chicago, Ill.: Children's Press, 1964), 176 pp. Subject matter, experiences, and experiments.

Pine, Tillie S., and Joseph Levine. *Light All Around* (New York: McGraw-Hill, Inc., 1961), 48 pp. Easy-reading material about light and its nature; helpfully illustrated.

Polgreen, John, and Cathleen Polgreen. *Sunlight and Shadows* (Garden City, New York: Doubleday & Company, Inc., 1967), 57 pp. Changing shadows—easy.

deRegniers, Beatrice Schenk. *The Shadow Book* (New York: Harcourt Brace Jovanovich, 1960), unpaged. Photographs and rhythmic prose make this an appealing book for the very young.

Ruchlis, Hy. *The Wonder of Light: A Picture Story of How and Why We See* (New York: Harper & Row, Publishers, 1960), 148 pp. Light and its various phenomena explained, including more than a hundred diagrams and exciting photographs.

Scharff, Robert. *Rays and Radiation* (New York: G.P. Putnam's Sons, 1960), 72 pp. The nature of rays; helpfully illustrated.

Schwartz, Julius. *Now I Know* (New York: McGraw-Hill, Inc., 1955), 32 pp. Simple explanations of children's experiences with reflections, shadows, lightning, darkness.

—— *Through the Magnifying Glass* (New York: McGraw-Hill, Inc., 1954), 142 pp. Understanding and using a magnifying glass to see common things.

—— *Magnify and Find Out Why* (New York: McGraw-Hill, Inc., 1972), 40 pp. For younger children. Shows how the magnifying glass can be used as a tool of discovery to explain everyday phenomena.

Simon, Seymour. *Let's Try It Out—Light and Dark* (New York: McGraw-Hill, Inc., 1970), 48 pp. An introduction to light and optics.

Sootin, Harry. *Light Experiments* (New York: W.W. Norton & Company, Inc., 1963), 93 pp. Experiments help explain the principles of light.

Tannenbaum, Beulah, and Myra Stillman. *Understanding Light: The Science of Visible and Invisible Rays* (New York: McGraw-Hill, Inc., 1960), 138 pp. The story of light—artificial, natural, the eye, uses of light energy—with experiments.

For Teachers°

Asher, Harry. *Experiments in Seeing* (New York: Basic Books, Inc., 1961), 271 pp. Eye structure and how it works.

°*See* suggested physics texts listed in Part I of this Bibliography under "General Subject-matter Background Books for Teachers."

Hellman, Hal. *The Art and Science of Color* (New York: McGraw-Hill, Inc., 1967), 175 pp. A general comprehensive treatment.

Patrusky, Ben. *The Laser: Light that Never Was Before* (New York: Dodd, Mead & Company, Inc., 1966), 128 pp. An introduction and some detail about the development.

Weart, Spencer R. *Light—A Key to the Universe* (New York: Coward-McCann, Inc., 1968), 96 pp. The nature of light and a description of the important discoveries.

Chapter 22 Flight and Space Travel

For Children

Asimov, Isaac. *ABC of Space* (New York: Walker and Company, 1969), 48 pp. An alphabet of terms.

Bendick, Jeanne. *The First Book of Airplanes* (New York: Franklin Watts, Inc., 1958), 69 pp. Introductory information for young children; well illustrated.

—— *Space Travel,* rev. ed. (New York: Franklin Watts, Inc., 1969), 96 pp. About space, space travel, and rocket ships.

—— *Space and Time* (New York: Franklin Watts, Inc., 1968), 66 pp. Basic concepts.

Branley, Franklyn M. *Weight and Weightlessness* (New York: Thomas Y. Crowell Company, 1971), 34 pp. Easy reading explanation.

—— *A Book of Outer Space for You* (New York: Thomas Y. Crowell Company, 1970), 58 pp. Answers many questions about space travel.

—— *Man in Space on the Moon* (New York: Thomas Y. Crowell Company, 1970), 38 pp. Apollo 11 and the future.

—— *Rockets and Satellites* (New York: Thomas Y. Crowell Company, 1970), 34 pp. Space travel for beginners.

Becker, Thomas W. *Exploring Tomorrow in Space* (New York: Sterling Publishing Co., Inc., 1972), 160 pp. A detailed look at the space future.

Carlisle, Madelyn. *About Satellites* (Chicago, Ill.: Children's Press, 1971), 48 pp. History, function, and prediction.

Carlisle, Norman. *Satellites, Servants of Man* (Philadelphia, Penna.: J.B. Lippincott Company, 1971), 96 pp. A source book with spin-offs of the benefits.

Colby, C.B. *Space Age Spinoffs: Space Program Benefits for All Mankind* (New York: Coward-McCann and Geoghegan, Inc., 1972), 48 pp. Photographs and text about the benefits.

Corbett, Scott. *What Makes a Plane Fly?* (Boston, Mass.: Little, Brown & Company, 1967), 58 pp. Illustrated information about the structure and control of various planes.

Dwiggins, Don. *Into the Unknown: The Story of Space Shuttles and Space Stations* (San Carlos, Calif.: Golden Gates Junior Books, 1971), 80 pp. An imaginative journey into space.

Engle, Eloise. *Parachutes: How They Work* (New York: G.P. Putnam's Sons, 1972), 120 pp. History and evolution.

Freeman, Ira M. *The Look-it-up Book of Space* (New York: Random House, Inc., 1969), 130 pp. Dictionary, encyclopedia, bibliography.

Freeman, Mae. *When Air Moves* (New York: McGraw-Hill, Inc., 1968), 45 pp. Nature of air and explanation of flight and surface transportation using moving air.

—— *Space Base* (New York: Franklin Watts, Inc., 1972), 64 pp. An imaginary visit to a future orbiting space station.

Gottlieb, William P. *Aircraft and How They Work* (New York: Garden City Books, 1960), 50 pp. Practical experiments on flight and photographs and drawings.

Hyde, Margaret O. *Flight Today and Tomorrow* (New York: McGraw-Hill, Inc., 1970), 119 pp. Principles of flight and their applications, with discussion of future possibilities.

—— *Exploring Earth and Space* (New York: McGraw-Hill, Inc., 1970), 174 pp. Exploring inner and outer space.

Lukashok, Alvin. *Communications Satellites: How They Work* (New York: G.P. Putnam's Sons, 1967), 16 pp. The principles that underlie the operations.

May, Julian. *Rockets* (Chicago: Follett Publishing Co., 1967), 32 pp. A clear explanation of the nature and function.

McFarland, Kenton D. *Airplanes—How They Work* (New York: G.P. Putnam's Sons, 1966), 95 pp. An excellent treatment and good reference.

Milgrom, Harry. *First Experiments with Gravity* (New York: E.P. Dutton & Co., Inc., 1966), 56 pp. Gravity is explored by experiments with simple materials.

Moore, Patrick, and David Hardy. *Challenge of the Stars* (Skokie, Ill.: Rand McNally & Company, 1972), 62 pp. Man's progress into space.

Newell, Homer E. *Guide to Rockets and Missiles and Satellites* (New York: McGraw-Hill, Inc., 1961), 53 pp. Detailed descriptions of each of the space vehicles and weapons with excellent photographs.

—— *Space Book for Young People* (New York: McGraw-Hill, Inc., 1968), 171 pp. Facts about space, space travel, rockets, and satellites told by a NASA scientist. A useful guide to the earth and its place in the universe.

Pine, Tillie S., and Joseph Levine. *Gravity All Around* (New York: McGraw-Hill, Inc., 1962), 48 pp. What gravity is, how it helps us, its relation to space travel.

Rosenfeld, Sam. *Ask Me a Question about Rockets, Satellites, and Space Stations* (New York: Harvey House, 1971), 96 pp. Questions and answers on the subject.

Ross, Frank. *Model Satellites and Spacecraft: Their Stories and How to Make Them* (New York: Lothrop, Lee & Shepard Co., 1969), 160 pp. Twelve American satellites and how to model them.

Schwartz, Julius. *The Earth Is Your Spaceship* (New York: McGraw-Hill, Inc., 1963), 32 pp. Easy reading about the movements of the earth through space and their effects.

—— *Uphill and Downhill* (New York: McGraw-Hill, Inc., 1965), 32 pp. Experiences and experiments with gravity for the young child.

Shapp, Martha, and Charles Shapp. *Let's Find Out about Space Travel* (New York: Franklin Watts, Inc., 1971), 48 pp. Rocketry and space travel.

Simon, Seymour. *The Paper Airplane* (New York: The Viking Press, Inc., 1971), 48 pp. Adaptations of paper folding that help children learn science principles.

Zaffo, George J. *The Giant Book of Things in Space* (New York: Doubleday & Company, Inc., 1969), 154 pp. A picture book for young children.

For Teachers [°]

Abell, George. *Exploration of the Universe* (New York: Holt, Rinehart and Winston, Inc., 1964), 646 pp. Astronomy and space information.

Blashfield, Jean F., ed. *The Illustrated Encyclopedia of Aviation and Space* (Los Angeles: A.F.E. Press, 1971), 14 volumes. Reference for teachers and pupils.

Costa, Arthur. *Space* (Darien, Conn.: Teachers Publishing Corporation, 1964), 96 pp. One in a series produced with the National Science Teachers Association; information and activities.

Ruchlis, Hy. *Orbit* (New York: Harper & Row, Publishers, 1958), 147 pp. Force, motion, and gravity, and the relationship of these to space travel.

Shelton, William R. *Man's Conquest of Space* (Washington, D.C. 20036: National Geographic Society, 1972), 199 pp. Current information.

[°] Write to National Aeronautics and Space Administration, Washington, D.C. 20546, for list of educational publications. Very useful, and many are free. Also write to the National Air and Space Museum, Smithsonian Institution, Washington, D.C. 20560, for free material; and to the National Aerospace Education Association, 806 15th Street, N.W., Washington, D.C. 20005, for information.

See suggested physics text listed in Part I of this Bibliography under "General Subject-matter Background Books for Teachers."

INDEX